MW01070843

THESE ARE THE VOYAGES

ALSO BY MARC CUSHMAN

These Are the Voyages — TOS: Season One

These Are the Voyages — TOS: Season Three

I SPY: A History and Episode Guide of the Groundbreaking Television Series

THESE ARE THE VOYAGES
TOS: SEASON TWO

Marc Cushman

with Susan Osborn

foreword by Walter Koenig

Jacobs/Brown Press
San Diego, California

LIBRARY OF CONGRESS CATALOGUING-IN-PUBLICATION DATA
Cushman, Marc
These Are the Voyages – TOS: Season Two /
Marc Cushman, with Susan Osborn; with a foreword by Walter Koenig;
Edited by George A. Brozak and Mark Alfred,
with Thomas C. Tucker, Scott R. Brooks, and Judith Bleses
Publisher: Matthew Williams Brown

Includes bibliographical reference

ISBN 978-0-9892381-4-4
First edition hard cover, March 2014

Library of Congress Control Number: 2013940946
©2014 Marc Cushman. All rights reserved

This book is a work of journalism, protected under the First Amendment, and is not endorsed, sponsored, or affiliated with CBS Studios Inc. or the "Star Trek®" franchise. The *Star Trek®* trademarks, logos, and related names are owned by CBS Studios Inc. and are used under "fair use" guidelines.

No part of this book may be reproduced or transmitted in any form or by any means, electronic or mechanical, including photocopying or recording, or by any information storage and retrieval system, without permission in writing from the publisher.

Cover design: Susan Osborn, Leo Sopicki and Gerald Gurian
Interior Design: Gerald Gurian
Back photo of author: Mike Hayward Photography

Manufactured in the United States of America

Jacobs/Brown Press
An imprint of Jacobs/Brown Media Group, LLC
Los Angeles, California
www.JacobsBrownMediaGroup.com
www.thesearethevoyagesbooks.com

To Gene Roddenberry and Robert H. Justman
for their encouragement and invaluable help in providing the documents needed
for this telling of the *Star Trek* story.

To Dorothy C. Fontana, John D.F. Black, and Mary Black
for their extra efforts in supplying me with the information and further
connections to make much of what follows possible.

Acknowledgments

My appreciation to those who gave further encouragement and guidance and support:

For all her help going through the *Star Trek* show files at the UCLA Performing Arts Library (since absorbed into the UCLA Special Collections Library), my gratitude to Lauren Buisson.

For locating the Nielsen ratings for the original broadcasts of *ST:TOS*, I am indebted to Kate Barnett at Nielsen Media Services.

A special thank you to those who kindly granted interviews: Barbara Anderson, Jean Lisette Aroeste, Emily Banks, Hagan Beggs, John D.F. Black, Mary Black, Bill Blackburn, Antoinette Bower, Charlie Brill, Robert Brown, Judy Burns, Marvin Chomsky, Julie Cobb, Paul Comi, Joe D'Agosta, Leslie Dalton, Winston S. De Lugo, Elinor Donahue, Jack Donner, James Doohan, Doug Drexler, John M. Dwyer, Harlan Ellison, John Erman, Dorothy C. Fontana, Michael Forest, David Frankham, Ben Freiberger, Lisa Freiberger, Gerald Fried, David Gerrold, Patrick Horgan, Clint Howard, Bruce Hyde, Sherry Jackson, Lois Jewell, George Clayton Johnson, Robert H. Justman, Stephen Kandel, Sean Kenney, Walter Koenig, Nancy Kovack, Tanya Lemani, Trelaine Lewis, Gary Lockwood, Barbara "BarBra" Luna, Don Mankiewicz, Bruce Mars, Don Marshall, Tasha "Arlene" Martel, Richard Matheson, Vincent McEveety, Lee Meriwether, Lawrence Montaigne, Sean Morgan, Stewart Moss, Joyce Muskat, Julie Newmar, Leonard Nimoy, France Nuyen, William O'Connell, Garth Pillsbury, Leslie Parrish, Eddie Paskey, Roger Perry, Ande Richardson-Kindryd, Gene Roddenberry, Rod Roddenberry, Joseph Sargent, Ralph Senensky, Peter Sloman, Louise Sorel, Norman Spinrad, Malachi Throne, Bjo Trimble, Beverly Washburn, Andrea Weaver, John Wheeler, Grace Lee Whitney, William Windom, John Winston, William Wintersole, Morgan Woodward, and Celeste Yarnall.

Many of those who helped to make the original *Star Trek* are sadly no longer with us. In an effort to include their voices in this documentation, alongside the voices of those I was able to interview, I relied on hundreds of newspaper and magazine articles, as well as dozens of books. A full list of these sources can be found in the bibliography, but I wish to give special mention here to the following books and their authors:

Beam Me Up, Scotty by James Doohan with Peter David. *Beyond Uhura: Star Trek and Other Memories* by Nichelle Nichols. *The City on the Edge of Forever* by Harlan Ellison. *Eighty Odd Years in Hollywood* by John Meredyth Lucas. *From Sawdust to Stardust: The Biography of DeForest Kelley* by Terry Lee Rioux. *Gene Roddenberry: The Last Conversation* by Yvonne Fern. *Gene Roddenberry: The Myth and the Man Behind Star Trek* by Joel Engel. *Great Birds of the Galaxy* by Edward Gross and Mark A. Altman. *I Am Not Spock* and *I Am Spock* by Leonard Nimoy. *Inside Star Trek: The Real Story* by Herbert F. Solow and Robert H. Justman. *The Longest Trek: My Tour of the Galaxy* by Grace Lee Whitney with Jim Denney. *The Making of Star Trek* by Stephen E. Whitfield and Gene Roddenberry. *The Music of Star Trek,* by Jeff Bond. *On the Good Ship Enterprise: My 15 Years with Star Trek* by Bjo Trimble. *Science Fiction Television Series: Episode Guides, Histories, and Casts and Credits for 62 Prime-Time Shows, 1959-1989* by Mark Phillips and Frank Garcia. *Shatner: Where No*

Man ... by William Shatner, Sondra Marshak and Myrna Culbreath. *Starlog: Star Trek's Greatest Guest Stars*, edited by David McDonnell. *The Star Trek Compendium* by Allan Asherman. *Star Trek Creator* by David Alexander. *The Star Trek Interview Book* by Allan Asherman. *Star Trek Memories* by William Shatner with Chris Kreski. *To the Stars: The Autobiography of George Takei* by George Takei. *Trek Classics* by Edward Gross. *The Trouble with Tribbles* and the *The World of Star Trek* by David Gerrold.

For those who have either shared in the decades of work or have given their support and encouragement in other meaningful ways:

Mark Alfred, Barbara Asaro, Paul Barry, Judith Bleses, Scott Brooks, George A. Brozak, Dawn Cushman, Druanne Cushman, Steven Dai Watkins-Cushman, Kathleen Dougherty, Melody Fox, Karen Glass, Gerald Gurian, Gerald Hill, Andy and Sondra Johnson, William Krewson, Linda J. LaRosa, Bob Olsen, Mark Phillips, Patricia Satin-Jacobs, David Mark Peterson, Leo Sopicki, Paul Stuiber, Jeff Szalay, Kipp Teague, Thomas C. Tucker, Fred Walder, Eric Zabiegalski, and Michael Zabiegalski.

A final message of gratitude to those who rallied in the eleventh hour of Book 1 to make certain it could find its way to the fans of *Star Trek*:

Jef Allard, American Ninth Art Studios LLC, De Baisch, Toni Bates, Catherine Bell, John Bernardo, Jeffrey F. Bradander, Freda Callahan, John Campbell, Mark Chaet, Cliff Chandler, Brian Chapman, Benjamin Chee, Christian, Andrew Cohen, Ray Cole, Calo Corrao, Joe Corrao, Paul Covelli, Mark Craig, Kathleen Currence, Claude Demers, Cathy Evans, Paul and Joyce Flanzer, Ernest Frankel, Fuchsdh, Joseph Filice, Gene Gilbert, Aimee Gross, Jim Hartland, William H. Heard, Jr., Brenda F. Hemphill, David Hetherington, Daniel Hodges, Brad Hunziker, Anna Innocenti, Norman Jaffe, Caspar Jensen, Steve Kellener, Sandra Kerner, Robert Khoe, K.S. Langley, Ellen Levine, Debbi and Harvey Lazar, Steven Lord, Lochdur, Katia Destito Marburger, Marian, Ana Martinez, Daimos May, April Maybee, Terry Matsumoto, Maria McQuillen, Crystal Mechler, Sharad Mulchand, Sawn Oshima, Bob and Mitsue Peck, Eleni Prieto, J.R. Ralls, Bert Sackman, Stephen Sandoval, Marshall J. Simon, Ed and Nancy Soloski, Mariam True, Thomas C. Tucker, Franz Villa, Eileen White, and Hans de Wolf.

May you all live long and prosper.

TABLE OF CONTENTS

FOREWORD

"I'm not dot grin." (green). That's what Chekov said in "Catspaw," the first *Star Trek* episode in which the Russian appeared in 1967. The fact is he *was* that green and shared that particular disadvantage with the man who played him. I walked on to the *Star Trek* set that first day and thought: "This show will never last."

When I went in to audition for the role on the space series, casting director Joe D'Agosta tossed out the throwaway line "If you get the part it might recur." Right, and pigs fly battle cruisers. So, although I won the role I had little expectation that the job would be anything more than a one week diversion from my usual state of unemployment. I had no idea that the *diversion* would last forty-six years and counting.

"Who knew?" (Spoken aloud with an exaggerated shrug of the shoulders.)

I didn't, and thus the explanation for my callow sense of what the future might portend. The thing is, if that was my failure it was everyone else's failure too. Not Nostradamus, not the Mayans, not H.G. Wells could have predicted the course of things to come. After three years on network television, endless reruns, two years of *Star Trek* in animation, thousands of conventions the world over, twelve feature films and the spawning of four new *Star Trek* series with more than 730 episodes over the course of thirty-five television seasons. *Star Trek* is still going strong. Gene Roddenberry's original concept remains an indelible part of my memory, a constant presence in my life today and an inevitable influence on how the future arranges itself. I speak for a lot of fans who have paddled about with us from the beginning or caught the big wave along the way that I'm not alone in this canoe.

Good writers, good actors, good directors and producers, yes, all of that but one thing more. In the course of growing its popularity over four and a half decades *Star Trek*, the concept, has metamorphosed. It has gone from an idea to a self-perpetuating tangible entity of form and substance. Apart from its component parts it has developed its own identity. We need not think of a particular actor nor story nor philosophical posture for *Star Trek* to generate our enthusiasm and loyalty. It's there instantly. It's been a long time since Jackie Robinson was a Dodger, since Maurice "the Rocket" Richard skated for the Canadiens, since Kirkland and Baryshnikov danced with the American Ballet Theatre, but we still root for the teams and cheer the companies. It is inevitable that the names change but not our allegiance nor our pride. And that has become the banner of *Star Trek* as well. *Next Generation* came after *TOS* and was followed by *Deep Space Nine*, *Voyager* and *Enterprise*. Fresh faces succeed those who have already served. Uniforms are refashioned, ships are redesigned and time is reinvented. These differences notwithstanding, they all marched to the same brand and that brand is *Star Trek*.

Consider this brilliant analogy: You can have ham and cheese, lettuce and tomatoes, peanut butter and jelly, but if they come without rye, whole wheat, or pumpernickel, they become moldy in a jar or lie limply on a dinner plate. They don't become a *sandwich*. They need bread! Bread is the star! It has its own taste and texture. Its own tummy filling properties. It doesn't require vegetables, dairy, or porcine products to acknowledge and respect its worth and dignity.

And so, just as bread is the staff of life, so then is Star Trek *the stuff of dreams.*
(I knew I had a point in there somewhere.)

When I spoke to Marc Cushman about writing a foreword to the second book of his amazing, epic three-volume opus on the original *Star Trek* series, he suggested that I write my commentary with candor, intimacy, and personal interjection to most accurately report my close encounters of the second season. To do right by that instruction, however, I feel some digression might be in order. At least, to the extent that you get a sense of who I am and why I see things through these particular eyes.

You might have heard these stories before:

The time a teenager at O'Hare Airport in Chicago froze in his tracks in front of me and in total befuddlement screamed loud enough to stop hearts, "OH MY GOD, IT'S WALTER KLINGON!"

The time in Charlotte, North Carolina, when I was standing in the lobby of a hotel with fluted columns and Ionic capitals wearing my uniform from *Star Trek IV* through *VI* (never to be done again, by the way) awaiting a stretch limo to whisk me off to a ribbon cutting ceremony. A recently arrived guest, obviously mistaking my slick duds for those of a bellhop, (I can still see the dollar bill fisted in her right hand) asked me to help her with her bags.

Or the time in Honolulu while stepping over a brook by means of a very narrow bridge, I crossed paths with another tourist with nerves of Jell-O coming toward me. I'm sure her shaking was part of an irreversible disorder but by the time we were face to face it had graduated from tremors to a dance reminiscent of Chubby Checker's "Twist" from 1960. Fearing for her safety, I reached out my hand to steady her. One could say that she kissed my ring in gratitude. "Thank you, thank you…" she did say effusively, but the addendum sentence fragment "…Your Holiness" gave me considerable pause.

A Klingon, a Bellhop, and the Pope. True stories all. Is it any wonder that I felt a bit disoriented that whole second season of the show? The growing public popularity sprinkled with the acrimony of a few belligerent souls had me looking for solid ground among the ice floes.

So, to wrap it up, and put a period to the second season and what it meant to me: there I was, along with my cast mates, all targets of adulation wherever we appeared, but still sufficiently unknown by the uninitiated to be mistaken for the unworldly, religious figures and baggage handlers. On top of all that was the confusion of accepting so much love "out there" and then returning to the studio to play roles in *Star Trek* scripts that often seemed microscopic. That's what I meant when I said I was as "grin" (green) as the character I played. I had received an enormous break by being cast on such a show and I think I complained about it as much as I was grateful for it. I had no idea what I had fallen into. "Embrace it," I told myself. "Kick it down the road," I also told myself. My shrink thinks my description as to how I processed all this is excessive but honestly there were times when I envisioned my brain as a basket of snakes -- copperheads, water moccasins, pythons, cobras and rattlers -- all twisting around each other, getting knotted up, a lot of pushing and shoving, trying to make room for all the contradictory images and values I ascribed to myself. What did *Star Trek* tell me? Did I have a *lot* of talent, a *little* talent, *no* talent? If I had a lot of talent, shouldn't the Russian be a meatier player; if I had a little talent, why am I not dubbing voices in converted storage units for badly animated foreign films; if I had no talent, what the hell am I even doing on *Star Trek*?!

As confused as I was, I thought of quitting the series after the show's second season.

"Aye, aye sir." "Aye Aye, sir," "Aye, Aye sir." I mean, how many different ways is there to say that before the audience shuts its eyes, suspends consciousness, and begins snoring?

My wife, Judy, is more rational than I am. She pointed out the difference between reciting the sometimes anonymous "aye aye" stuff with waiting for my agent to call. My agent times his calls to the changing of the seasons. Let's see … that makes … one for Spring … one for Summer …!

The truth is there were also some memorable moments in Season Two episodes. "Trouble With Tribbles, "Who Mourns for Adonais," "I Mudd," "Mirror, Mirror," and "Deadly Years." Extremely well written, well performed stories that had every right to be seen and appreciated by millions of fans whose numbers would only grow with the passage of time. And considering the state of the "industry," which *always* has a work force thousands of times greater than employment opportunities, it would be madness to let it all dribble through my fingers over a bruised ego. So, the last word is, I feel lucky to have been aboard this "wessel."

However, there was not an abundance of faith for a third season pick-up amongst our crew. Those last days were pretty dour. We worked in near silence, each of us feeding off the others' discontent, waiting for the dreaded axe.

If I wasn't "dot grin" (green), neither should I have been that grim. All my hand wringing, all my self-doubts, all my Hamlet-inspired monologues were for nothing. There are well-charted trails and then there is destiny. What happened to me when I joined the gang of six was inevitable. There is no "To be or not to be." There is only the little spaceship that could … and did … and is still doing.

For me it all started in 1967 on a sound stage at Paramount Studios when we began shooting *Star Trek*'s second season.

As the song goes: "We've only just begun."

Walter Koenig
July 30, 2013

PREFACE

**Gene Roddenberry could never have known what an uphill battle *Star Trek*
would really be when he had this mountain built for the first pilot
(From the Matt Jefferies Collection; courtesy of Gerald Gurian)**

If this book were a television series, you would now hear a voice saying …
"Previously on *These Are the Voyages*" …

By 1964, Gene Roddenberry had earned the reputation of being a prolific and
imaginative writer, and a capable producer. He was also known for his shrewdness at self-
promotion and financial gain, as well as using the "casting couch" for affairs with aspiring
young actresses, Majel Barrett and Nichelle Nichols included. But what was quickly
becoming his Achilles heel was Roddenberry's tendency to ignore his superiors when he
disagreed with them.

While producing *The Lieutenant*, which was filmed in part at Camp Pendleton,
California, and made good use of Marine buildings, vehicles, uniforms, armaments, and
personnel, Roddenberry disregarded objections from both NBC and the Pentagon and filmed
an episode entitled "To Set It Right," a story about racial prejudice in the U.S. Military.
Roddenberry, who perceived himself to be a modern-day Jonathan Swift, a writer with a bold

cause, felt he was above the politics. The result: the Pentagon withdrew its support of *The Lieutenant* and, in an effort to repair the damage, NBC refused to air the offending episode. Believing in his greater right, Roddenberry chose to fight. He turned to the NAACP to pressure the network into letting America see the controversial episode. In the end, despite satisfactory ratings, NBC cancelled *The Lieutenant*. MGM, the financer of the series, wanted nothing more to do with Roddenberry … or his next series proposal -- *Star Trek*.

Lucille Ball did.

By 1964, Lucy was divorced from her Desilu Production partner, Desi Arnaz, and was looking for properties her studio could own. She enlisted Herb Solow, who had just been released from CBS. Solow was instrumental in helping Lucy acquire both *Star Trek* and *Mission: Impossible*. Prior to CBS, Solow had worked for NBC where he was still respected. Because of this, he convinced NBC, despite the network's misgivings over Rodenberry and Desilu's capability to realize such a demanding project, to order a *Star Trek* pilot … and, when it failed to sell, to then order a second pilot. It was a significant accomplishment considering that, after *The Lieutenant* fiasco, NBC wanted little to do with Gene Roddenberry. But the network's West Coast executives did trust Herb Solow. And they wanted to do business with Solow's new boss, the Golden Girl of CBS -- Lucille Ball.

Despite warnings from the Desilu Board of Directors that to take on both *Star Trek* and *Mission: Impossible* would surely ruin her studio, Lucy believed in her potential properties and took that gamble.

Stan Robertson was assigned by NBC to serve as Network Production Manager for *Star Trek*. His job: keep Roddenberry on a tight leash. The network didn't want any more firestorms like "To Set It Right." Through the course of Season One, Roddenberry's tendencies to buck authority had put strain on the relationship.

Robert H. Justman, who served as Associate Producer, had joined *Star Trek* at the outset. He was a brilliant nuts-and-bolts producer, the man responsible for seeing to all phases of the production, regardless of the seemingly impossible challenges the scripts presented. He also had a well-earned reputation for displaying his acid wit in his memos when critiquing those very scripts.

Another godsend for Gene Roddenberry and *Star Trek* was Gene L. Coon. He was hired to serve as the series' creative producer halfway through *Star Trek*'s first season, taking over for outgoing Associate Producer and Executive Script Consultant John D.F. Black. Black had become disenchanted with Roddenberry's propensity to severely alter scripts by renowned science fiction writers, such as Richard Matheson, George Clayton Johnson, Robert Bloch, Theodore Sturgeon, and Harlan Ellison. Roddenberry had even rewritten Black on his teleplay, "The Naked Time." All the haggling took a toll on both camps. After Black left and Coon was instated, Roddenberry withdrew to the safer position of Executive Producer where he could involve himself as much or as little as he liked. His contributions to the series, as a writer, and a rewriter, would decrease over time.

Star Trek, as Gene Coon would tell many, was the hardest show on television to write. Its characters were unique and the voices of those characters hard to mimic. Coon, like Roddenberry, and with the help of "D.C." Fontana (as her non-gender screen credit identified her), would rewrite most of the dialogue in nearly all of the scripts he would produce for the series. Regarding his good "right hand man" …

Dorothy C. Fontana had begun as Roddenberry's secretary. Her true calling, however, was screenwriting. It had been an uphill climb. TV action-adventure writing at this time was dominated by men, which is why Fontana went by "D.C." rather than Dorothy. She became *Star Trek*'s first female writer when Roddenberry gave her the script assignment for "Charlie X," and would become the series Script Consultant after being challenged to salvage "The Way of the Spores," a problematic script written by Jerry Sohl. She did, and it became the standout first season entry, "This Side of Paradise."

Star Trek was an immediate hit on NBC, but the network was reluctant to acknowledge this. By the end of the first season, Gene Roddenberry's approval rating with NBC was plummeting at warp speed, and, with the numerous headaches he had caused, some executives at NBC did not want to see *Star Trek* return for a second season. Executive feelings aside, the ratings reports included in Book 1 of *These Are the Voyages*, for every episode of the first season, dispel 45 years of folklore that *Star Trek* was a failure when first aired. To the contrary, it frequently won its time slot, and often was NBC's top-rated series of the night. Further, the memos and letters from 1966 and 1967 included in Book 1 dispel the folklore that the NBC brass didn't understand or like the series. What *was* clear, through testimonials of those who were there, and correspondences from that time, was how the relationship between Gene Roddenberry and NBC, having begun its downward spiral during the making of *The Lieutenant*, was continuing to nosedive. And, despite its popularity, *Star Trek* was on very shaky ground.

AUTHOR'S NOTE

In the pages that follow, many behind-the-scenes details about the inspiration and production of the *Star Trek* series and its individual episodes are shared with the public for the first time. This recounting is drawn from a variety of sources, including Desilu and Paramount archives (the *Star Trek* show files stored in the UCLA Performing Arts Special Collections), the ratings reports from A.C. Nielsen Media, the archived papers of many of the individuals involved, newspaper and magazine articles from the 1960s, personal interviews, and my own synthesis of bits of stories told by different people at different times, as published in a wide variety of outlets. Contextual information about the history and state of the television industry before and during the *Star Trek* era is drawn from public sources.

In regard to the ratings reports from A.C. Nielsen, the manner in which the information was presented varied as a result of source and date. Nielsen had multiple ways of gauging audience numbers, from its overnight 12-city Trendex reports, to the 27-city or 30-city reports that arrived a week later, to the national surveys which came a week after that and factored in rural areas, to periodic demographics reports. Some of these would estimate the audience numbers by ratings points, others by audience share, or by estimates of households watching, while others would cite two or more of these statistics. The complete significance of the Nielsen numbering systems from the 1960s may be difficult to interpret -- even for those whom this author spoke to who currently work at Nielsen Media Services. In order to determine the audience share for independent stations and give a full picture of the division of the ratings pie, I subtracted the share assigned by Nielsen to NBC, CBS, and ABC, thereby arriving at the percentage remaining for the independents. One thing is clear from all of these reports: which network programs for any given time slot came in at first, second, and third place. *Star Trek*'s placement, after more than four decades of misleading folklore, may surprise you.

The picture images presented on the front and back cover, and within this book, came from numerous sources, including vintage magazines; NBC publicity pictures for *Star Trek* from the 1960s; Lincoln Enterprises film trims (sold to the fans through Gene Roddenberry's mail order service in the late 1960s and early 1970s), and which were then restored by private collectors; and, for non-*Star Trek* images, numerous news and internet sources. In regard to the restored film trims, photo caption credits acknowledge the individual, group, or fan website which provided the image to this project or was involved in its restoration. On the few instances when two fan sites either claimed credit for the restoration or legal justification to contribute the image to this work, both sites have been listed.

1

A Second Season

**During a cast "table read" at the helm station, Nichelle Nichols strikes a sexy
pose for a behind-the-scenes photographer (Courtesy of Gerald Gurian)**

Webster's Dictionary says folklore is "an often unsupported notion, story, or saying
that is widely circulated." *Star Trek* has had more than its share.

Among other things, *Star Trek* folklore tells us the series failed in the ratings during
its NBC run in the 1960s. You'll read this in newspapers and magazines; on the internet; and
in perhaps every book that ever attempted to tell the story of the original *Star Trek*. The
experts behind all the misinformation provide no numbers to support their claims. They have
no documentation, only 45 years of ... well ... folklore.

In *These Are the Voyages – TOS: Season One*, the Nielsen ratings for all the episodes
from the 1966-67 television season were published for the first time. TvQ surveys were
reported, as well. The numbers plainly show that *Star Trek*'s first season was far from a
failure.

Star Trek had gotten off to a strong start with its premiere episode, "The Man Trap," winning its time period (according to an A.C. Nielsen's national survey) with 46.7% of the TVs in use across the United States. In fact, *Star Trek* was one of the Top 10-rated shows of the week.

The next episode to air, "Charlie X," tied with *My Three Sons* for the lead during the former's first half-hour, with 35.9% of the TV sets powered-up in America. According to the October 11, 1967 edition of *Daily Variety*, it came in No. 33 out of 90 primetime series, one notch above *The Ed Sullivan Show* on CBS, and out-performing other successful series, such as *Peyton Place*, *Batman*, *Hogan's Heroes*, and *Gunsmoke*, all having been assured long lives by their networks.

For Week Three, NBC ran the second pilot film and *Star Trek* again drew impressive numbers, clearly the ratings-winner from 8:30 to 9 p.m. For the second half-hour of "Where No Man Has Gone Before," factoring in a 1% margin of error, the race between the three networks was too close to call. For this episode, according to the October 3, 1966 edition of *Broadcasting* magazine, *Star Trek* came in No. 38 out of 90 primetime series, within one ratings' point of *Get Smart*, *Family Affair*, *The Beverly Hillbillies*, *Voyage to the Bottom of the Sea*, *I Dream of Jeannie*, and *The Man from U.N.C.L.E.*, and in a virtual tie with *Lost in Space*. All of these popular series had many more seasons ahead of them.

When Nielsen tallied surveys for the entire month of September, *Star Trek* placed at No. 31 of all the prime-timers.

As the sampling of ratings in the previous volume of *These Are the Voyages* reveals, *Star Trek* sporadically placed at No. 1 in its time slot and rarely dropped to No. 3. Most weeks, it drew very respectable numbers, commonly around 30% of the total viewing audience, with a strong 2nd place showing.

In early December 1966, right after A.C. Nielsen declared *Star Trek* the highest-rated color series from all three networks on Thursday nights, NBC's Mort Werner told *TV Guide* he thought "*Star Trek* could be in for a long run." A pick-up seemed assured. And why not? NBC, after all, was owned by RCA, the leading maker of color TV sets.

However, just one month later, on January 7, 1967, the same magazine reported *Star Trek* on a list of series that were "iffy" for renewal. And then NBC cut back the first season order ever-so-slightly, from 30 episodes to 29.

Jet magazine wrote on January 12, 1967:

> A group of top-notch science-fiction writers are urging science-fiction fans to join in a nationwide write-in campaign to save NBC-TV's *Star Trek* from an axing or from suffering a possible change in format due to a drop in Nielsen ratings.

The real numbers show, as they had so many times since the September premiere, that *Star Trek* was holding well against *Bewitched*, ABC's most popular series. It often beat *My Three Sons* on CBS, which placed at No. 15 out of all primetime series the previous year. But now, going head-to-head against *Star Trek*, it was shut out of the Top 30.

On October 31, 1966, *Broadcasting* magazine published results from a special study conducted by TvQ, a service of Home Testing Institute. In a nationwide survey, TvQ asked its participants to pick their favorite series. The results:

- In the 6-to-11-year-old demographic, *Star Trek* ranked No. 1.
- With teenagers aged 12-to-17, it ranked No. 3, just under *Time Tunnel* and *I*

Spy.

- 18-to-34 year-olds picked it as No. 5, under *I Spy* and three of the various networks' primetime movies.
- 35-to-49 year-olds placed it at No. 6, behind *Bonanza*, *Walt Disney*, and three nights of movies.
- The 50-plus crowd, thought to be the least likely to embrace a science-fiction series, nonetheless put *Star Trek* in the Top 10.
- When the survey asked participants to name their favorite *new* series, and then averaged together the answers from the various age groups, *Star Trek* was No. 1.
- Added together, out of all the 90 primetime shows, with all categories combined (new and old), *Star Trek* came in No. 2. It was bested only by *Bonanza*.

On November 14, 1966, Bruce Gordon, head of Desilu Sales, Inc. in Australia, wrote Gene Roddenberry:

Firstly, let me congratulate you on the tremendous success of *Star Trek*. I have just received a copy of the TvQ scores in which *Star Trek* comes out as the top show of the first five [series], and also the ratings on NBC have been excellent.

The ratings Gordon referred to, from A.C. Nielsen, tracking the first three months of the new season, showed *Star Trek* as NBC's Top-Rated Thursday series.

A further TvQ report, published in the December 5, 1966 issue of *Broadcasting*, and ranking favorites among viewers for the entire month of December, still placed *Star Trek* high.

- It was down one spot in the 6–11 year-old category, now at No. 2, bested by *Time Tunnel*, which had a 2% lead.
- For teenagers, ages 12–17, it was gaining, up to No. 2, also topped by *Time Tunnel*, with a 3% lead.
- 18-to-34-year-olds raised it a notch, to No. 5.
- Audience members 35 years old and over still placed the series among their Top 10 favorites, averaging at No. 5, tied with *Mission: Impossible*, the *NBC Saturday Night Movie* and *Family Affair*, and bested by *Bonanza*, *I Spy*, *Walt Disney*, and *Red Skelton*, respectively.
- Out of 90 prime-timers, based on all age groups, *Star Trek* placed No. 5.

Remarkably, it was at the time of this report that NBC indicated *Star Trek* as "iffy." If ratings weren't truly the issue, then what was behind NBC's hints of cancellation? Twenty years later, Roddenberry explained it, saying, "NBC was trying to reinvent itself for a younger audience. CBS had just taken *Lost in Space*; ABC had *Voyage to the Bottom of the Sea*, and NBC decided to try one, too. But science-fiction was not a good fit at NBC." (145-12)

Nor was Roddenberry.

In late November 1966, Roddenberry met with Harlan Ellison at Oblath's restaurant, a "luncheon joint" just off of the Desilu lot. The award-winning science-fiction writer was working on a *Star Trek* script at the time and recalled, "Gene had a drink in front of him. He looked at me and said, 'They're conspiring to cancel the show.' We were alone and Gene was

3

telling me that dark and inimical forces inside NBC were plotting the demise of the new space adventure series which I'd been devoted to. 'I need your help,' he said." (58-2)

"NBC was lying in wait for him," Ellison told this author, confirming the network's agenda to rid itself of anything to do with Roddenberry. "And when we started the letter writing campaign, they were astonished. They were amazed that they got thousands of letters. I knew how to pull the strings and I pulled every string I could." (58)

Ellison returned to Desilu, this time using studio space, stationery, and equipment to create and manage "The Committee." He enlisted the aid of seven of the biggest names in the world of speculative fiction -- Poul Anderson, Robert Bloch, Lester del Rey, Philip Jose Farmer, Frank Herbert, Richard Matheson, and Theodore Sturgeon -- and drafted a letter to spread the gospel about *Star Trek*. Working from membership lists of various science-fiction conventions, sci-fi fan clubs, and booksellers, Ellison and his cohorts sent out thousands of letters asking viewers to persuade NBC to keep *Star Trek* on the air. The Committee declared *Star Trek* to be written by "authentic science-fiction writers and made with enormous difficulty and pride," and said that the series was about "to suffer the Nielsen Roulette game."

The Committee's letter created a buzz in the science fiction community. For many, the news of poor ratings was a surprise. Terry Carr, Senior Editor of Ace Books, responding to the Committee on November 28, 1966, wrote:

> Odd to hear *Star Trek*'s in trouble. The early ratings I saw in *TV Guide* and elsewhere showed it in the Top Ten nationally.

With this first letter from The Committee, the negative and irreversible folklore about *Star Trek*'s place in the Nielsens began to spread. But, in those first few months of 1967, it served a purpose as protest letters from *Star Trek* fans poured in to the offices of NBC, the show's sponsors, newspapers, and TV magazines.

One letter published in *TV Guide* began:

> So NBC, with its infallible sixth sense, has decided that *Star Trek* [is] "iffy" for next season. That's not as "iffy" as my TV viewing is going to be in the fall if the only interesting [show] of this season [is] missing!

Another letter, signed "Trekker," read:

> This is an appeal to the public to stand behind the only intellectually stimulating program NBC has come up with in years. *Star Trek* at least rises above the typical "father is a slob, mother is a scatterbrain, and the children triumph" programs that fill the primetime every night.

Some were not satisfied with merely writing letters. KRON-TV, the NBC-owned station in Oakland, California, was subjected to a demonstration march from fans. Bjo Trimble, a science fiction enthusiast Gene Roddenberry had met at TriCon in 1966 when he screened "Where No Man Has Gone Before," and who would become a great friend to *Star Trek* over the next two years, was there. She remembered, "The very original march was when we [her husband John and children] were still up in Oakland. The Society for Creative Anachronism started the same year as *Star Trek* by a bunch of people in Berkeley who wanted to create medieval times. Most of us had some sort of costume, including a young man who made himself up as a Viking, with a horn helmet. We were sitting around talking and decided that it would be a fun thing to make an utterly harmless march on KRON and hand out things on *Star Trek*. Gene had already put out the 'I Grok Spock' bumper stickers, so we had things like that. We got there and KRON thought we were a riot and they locked the doors. They would come up, occasionally, and peer out the glass doors and see this crazy group of people with armor and skin costumes, which had to be pretty funny. There were maybe 15 of us, and all armed. I mean, some of these guys were carrying swords. They *were* medieval costumes, after all. I can't imagine what those poor people inside were thinking. Well, pretty soon the police arrived and talked to us. They saw that we were harmless and not a mob of any kind, so they just warned us about any overt action against KRON. We gave them some 'I Grok Spock' bumper stickers and they put them on their police cars. Months afterwards, we'd see police cars and they still had the bumper stickers. I guess someone high up at the department was a fan of the show." (177-8)

NBC continued to stubbornly classify *Star Trek* as "iffy," even as *Variety*, in its December 21 issue, reported how the series, along with *The Man from U.N.C.L.E.*, was helping to combat the competition of primetime movies. The trade said:

> Ratings show that both [series] are drawing plenty of young adults, the group most attracted to TV movies. Both shows are doing comparatively well against the first half hour of CBS' Thursday and Friday night pix.

On January 19, Roddenberry sent Mort Werner a letter, saying:

> I thought you would be interested in knowing that our *Star Trek* mail is suddenly showing a phenomenal increase. One example -- letters forwarded to us by *TV Guide* alone have jumped from the TV show average of 20 per week to 267 to *Star Trek* this week! Office mail is no longer delivered in a manila folder, but in cardboard cartons.

By early February, the cast had been released for summer hiatus with no word as to whether they were to return for a second season. Coon and Roddenberry, with Eddie Milkis and his team of editors and the various optical effects houses, still had post production to oversee, but this would only continue for another month. All others involved with the series, including Robert Justman and Dorothy Fontana, were sent home. It was an anxious time. Worse, it was a *waste* of time. If there was to be another season, stories needed to be developed, and scripts needed to be written. And both needed to happen soon.

Roddenberry went public with his discontent via Jack Hellman's column in the February 16, 1967 edition of *Daily Variety*. Hellman spoke first, writing:

> If *Star Trek* doesn't make the cut-off, as they say in golf -- and woe to those below its current Nielsen 19.6 [rating] not yet firmed for the next go-round -- it won't be because Gene Roddenberry, its exec producer, hasn't given it a seven-day week and a few nights to bring it off as the best researched show in television.

Roddenberry told Hellman:

> Turning out an hour show every week and maintaining a consistent quality is asking too much of a producer. A schedule of every other week would result in better shows because of time allowances. It would also be advantageous if the network would give us an earlier pick-up date so we can have [the scripting of] eight or 10 shows completed during the summer layoff. Buying properties for such a sci-fi series is not merely a matter of calling for scripts. We get our stories from so many different sources outside Hollywood that we must alert the writers that we'll be in the market for next season. But we're stymied and can't move when we should be reading scripts. (145-18)

Making statements to the press of this type did not help Roddenberry in his deteriorating relationship with NBC.

Certain higher-ups at the network were keeping mental lists of the growing strikes against him.

- The bad blood began when Roddenberry rallied civil rights groups to take action against NBC after the network refused to air "To Set It Right," an episode he produced for *The Lieutenant* which dealt with race hatred in the military. The network buckled after pressure came from the NAACP and reversed its decision, thereby televising the racially-charged episode. That broadcast lost them the endorsement of the Marines Corp., and the use of Camp Pendleton, California, as a filming location. And that contributed to the series being canceled.
- Roddenberry got a second chance, and a second series, with NBC, but irritated the network men with his extracurricular activates on the casting couch, and then again, by casting the unknown actress Majel Barrett, one of his lovers, as the female lead in the *Star Trek* pilot. The network asked that she be dropped from the cast. And then Roddenberry snuck her back, hidden under a blonde wig, as Nurse Christine Chapel. The network men were not fooled.
- As production of the first season progressed, Roddenberry became increasingly resistant to story and script changes requested by Stan Robertson, NBC's Production Manager assigned to *Star Trek*. Roddenberry went so far as to chew Robertson out for giving script notes directly to Dorothy Fontana for her teleplay, "Charlie X."
- And then there were those skimpy outfits Roddenberry encouraged costume designer Bill Theiss to put into *Star Trek*, including America's first look at the mini-skirt (standard attire aboard the Enterprise). NBC Broadcast Standards Department was forever fretting over the sexy female attire seen weekly on *Star Trek*.
- It got worse. Roddenberry encouraged his writers to develop stories which were overly provocative for NBC's taste, including the "hookers in space" of "Mudd's Women," and the story of a scientist (Dr. Roger Korby) who apparently was having sex with an android designed to look like a beautiful young woman. Worse still, a story where Captain Kirk's primal, dark side attempted rape on his female yeoman … "in living color … on NBC."
- Other stories dealt with drugs, or symptoms resembling the taking of drugs ("The Naked Time," "This Side of Paradise," and "Mudd's Women").
- Still, another story seemed to make commentary on U.S. foreign policy in Vietnam ("Errand of Mercy").
- Another intended to plant the first interracial kiss on American television (in "The Alternative Factor," until the network forced Gene Coon to write the taboo issue out).
- And, during all of this, and more, Roddenberry and his staff rarely brought an episode in on budget, or on schedule. *Star Trek* fell further and further behind and, finally, missed making a delivery date, forcing the network to air a repeat (of "What Are Little Girls Made Of?") during the first-run season,

thereby taking a beating in the ratings.

Despite all the strikes against Roddenberry at the network, he continued his campaign for renewal and sent a letter to NBC executive Herb Rosenthal, with a copy to Mort Werner, complaining:

> Members of my staff [are] threatening to quit rather than undergo [future] night and day schedules made necessary by further postponement. Writers we have trained and nurtured state they can wait for us no longer. I love you all but if *Star Trek* is going another season I must begin putting <u>at least</u> stories into work immediately. Herb, this is not something to negotiate. Take my word as a professional in my field that this is a cold fact coming out of time required to plan, design and execute *Star Trek* with the quality you want and which I demand. I am willing to invest my time and energies in getting these new stories underway. Desilu, already [into] deficit financing, is willing to invest further in staff salaries and facilities. What is our partner NBC investing? ... If it appears likely we may not or will not go another season, my hard work for this partnership demands you tell me now so that I may begin devoting my energies elsewhere.

Without official notification of a pick-up, the policies of The Writers Guild of America prohibited Roddenberry from assigning stories for development. He did, however, have a filing cabinet filled with unused stories and scripts. He was tempted to revisit some, just to have something on hand should the renewal come.

The two teleplays from Season One that had been rejected by NBC, and still being considered by Roddenberry -- because he resisted letting go of these -- were ST-3, "The Omega Glory," his post-nuclear war "parallel world" story where the Asian communists had won and the white-skinned Americans became savages, and ST-28, the notorious "Portrait in Black and White," his other parallel world tale where pre-Civil War era Blacks enslaved Whites. Roddenberry had written the first script; Barry Trivers the second, based on Roddenberry's story.

And then there were the handful of scripts started at the end of the first year, but held over.

ST-40, "Tomorrow the Universe," from December, 1966, was Paul Schneider's third full script for *Star Trek*, on the heels of "Balance of Terror" and "The Squire of Gothos." The subject dealt with a maverick member of the Federation who visited an Earth-like world, circa 1930, and manipulated its society with a philosophy founded on absolute obedience to authority -- Hitler and his Nazis. The late season assignment was given to Schneider in case the troublesome script for "The City on the Edge of Forever," by Harlan Ellison, didn't make it in front of the camera. It did, finally, and "Tomorrow the Universe" was put on hold.

ST-41, "Amok Time," arriving on December 12, 1966, was a late delivery from Theodore Sturgeon, based on an idea from Roddenberry. The premise involved Spock's return to Vulcan to participate in a mating ritual. Following the "Shore Leave" ordeal of slow writing, and worried that Sturgeon could not deliver a script in time, the story outline was paid for and then set aside.

ST-43, "Friday's Child," came in on January 11, 1967. With the ever reliable D.C. Fontana at the typewriter, this "don't-judge-a-woman-by-her-makeup" story was earmarked as production No. 30, the last of Season One. By the time the story outline was delivered, NBC had cut its order back to 29 episodes, delaying further development.

"That is the system that is American network television," Roddenberry complained to this author. "They wait until the last possible moment to make a commitment, then expect you to work 18 hour days to rush scripts into production. The people making these decisions have little knowledge as to what it takes to make a quality television series. They felt they were doing us a favor by saying, 'Okay, give us 16 episodes. Go. Do it now.' We'd work day and night, and weekends, and be expected to be grateful because NBC was doing us this favor -- giving *Star Trek* life for another 16 weeks on the air. And then it all stops and you wait to see if they are going to say 'Go. Do it now' again. This is how TV shows were made then, and really not much different now [1982]. And people wonder why every episode isn't a winner. They can't be. The networks make certain of it." (145)

Meanwhile, the fans continued to be vocal. *Star Trek* was now up to 4,600 letters a week, a staggering amount in 1967. Only *The Monkees* received more. And letters of protest poured into NBC every week concerning *Star Trek*'s possible cancellation. Of those, Roddenberry said, "A surprising number [were] from schoolteachers, professionals, and scientists." Most, however, came from the most desirable demographic to advertisers -- teenagers.

Among the letters arriving daily at NBC:

Dear Sir: Networks continually say they are looking for programs that are different from the others; ones that will attract the attention of the viewers. I, and the people who have signed the enclosed petition, feel that STAR TREK fills the requirements that networks feel they must set up to have a successful program. The signatures come mostly from the high school students attending El Rancho High School in Pico Rivera, California. (Signed) Debora S.

Dear Sir: We recently read that STAR TREK might go off the air, and we certainly don't want that to happen. We think it's a real tough show. We love the Captain and especially Mr. Spock. We think the episodes are very exciting and well done. We do hope that we can help save it. Please tell us if there is anything else we can do. Thank you. (70 signatures were included). Los Angeles, California.

Dear Sir: Our English class was divided into groups to decide on a good cause and try to help it. We are sixth graders interested in science and space. The whole class watches STAR TREK on Thursday nights. We want to ask you to keep it on next season. That is our good cause. (Signed) Mary H., Alan B., Michael J., Susan R. Pleasant View Elementary School, New Jersey.

Dear Sir: We of Hueytown High School have heard that you were taking off our favorite show, STAR TREK. We have signed this petition on behalf of STAR TREK (the only show that'll keep us home from a date). Our teachers teach Biology, English, Chemistry, American Democracy, and STAR TREK (every Friday morning). (Signed) Jennette H. Hueytown, Alabama.

For its February 20, 1967 issue, *Broadcasting* announced, "*Ironside* may replace *Star Trek* Thursday, 8:30-9:30." But no word as to whether the former would be moved ... or *re*moved.

And then NBC blinked ... just a little. The network agreed to put up $13,000 for story development. Roddenberry and Coon immediately took pitch meetings and rationed out the work.

Paul Schneider, Theodore Sturgeon, and Dorothy Fontana were sent back to the scripts each had started at the end of Season One. Robert Bloch returned for another job. Stephen Kandel was asked to do a Harry Mudd sequel. New blood was supplied by Jerome

Bixby, writer of nearly 50 sci-fi short stories, and Norman Spinrad, author of a pair of science-fiction novels. Also new to the show: Gilbert Ralston, who wrote the pilot episode for *The Wild, Wild West*; John Kneubuhl, another *The Wild, Wild West* scribe, and responsible for the creation of Dr. Miguelito Loveless; and Lewis Reed, the writer of 55 episodes of *Peter Gunn*.

In late February, *Broadcasting* magazine announced which NBC series were definitely being dropped. *Star Trek* was not on the list but, at the same time, it was still absent from the tentative fall schedule. At this point, there were only two primetime hours not yet spoken for -- Tuesday 7:30 to 8:30 p.m. and Friday 8:30 to 9:30.

Days later, on February 27, *Daily Variety* published NBC's rough primetime schedule for the fall. *Star Trek* was tentatively penciled in for Tuesdays, 7:30-8:30 p.m. There was a glimmer of hope.

On March 4, *Star Trek* had the cover of *TV Guide*. The episode aired that week ("The Devil in the Dark") won its time slot. But still no definite word from NBC.

On March 6, Ed Perlstein, Desilu's legal rep, sent a letter to Marty Beum, William Shatner's agent. Perlstein wrote that while *Star Trek* had yet to receive a pick-up, the studio was "expecting" a renewal to come and plans were being laid to resume production in late April. The big concern, and reason for the letter, was that Shatner was in Europe making a movie (*White Comanche*), as permitted by his contract after NBC had missed a deadline date for committing to a second season. With the clock ticking so loudly, Perlstein was hoping, should there be a launch, that Captain Kirk would make it back to the Enterprise.

Things can take forever in television. And things can change in a

First of three *TV Guide* **covers during** *Star Trek***'s NBC run**

minute. Later that same day, a Western Union telegram was hurriedly dispatched to Shatner at the Hotel Richmond, in Madrid, Spain. It read:

> Dear Bill -- good news -- official pick up <u>today</u> -- our five year mission continues 8:30 every Friday night -- best regards -- Gene Roddenberry.

Shatner, like Kirk, would stop at nothing to make it back to his ship.

Daily Variety ran the story the following day with its headline "NBC-TV Renewal for *Star Trek*," and reporting:

> [The] Thursday series had tentatively been moved to Tuesday, 7:30 p.m., for next season, but now is on the sked at 8:30 Fridays.

The article revealed that a new variety series with Jerry Lewis had been planned for the less desirable Friday night time-period, but last-minute shuffling now put it on Tuesday in the slot Gene Roddenberry would have given his eye teeth for.

Two nights later, on March 9, 1967, NBC cried "uncle" in public. During the end credits for *Star Trek* that night, with the premiere "The Devil in the Dark," a network announcer told viewers that the series would return in the fall. An on-air announcement of this type was unprecedented, but necessary. NBC wanted the letters to stop. The constant flow of mail, pleading for renewal, had been disrupting business.

A few days later, Gene Roddenberry got busy, making phone calls and writing letters to his key people in hopes of securing them for the new season. One, written on March 14, 1967, was to the man who had designed the Enterprise, as well as all the alien worlds it had so far visited. The note to Matt Jefferies read:

> Dear Matt: Just in case you hadn't heard, "STAR TREK" has been officially renewed by NBC. The slot appears to be 8:30 PM, Friday Nights. Please take this letter as a hearty congratulations for your part in winning the renewal, and also as a warm invitation from Gene Coon, Bob Justman, as well as myself, to rejoin the best Crew in Television when it begins production again. Hopefully, this past season was but the first of many more seasons to come for all of us. Affectionately, Gene Roddenberry.

Desilu celebrated the news on April 17, 1967 by buying a full-page ad in *Variety* and sharing some of the accolades that had been arriving in the mail from *Star Trek* fans. Among them, Ben Jason, Chairman, of the 1966 World Science Fiction Convention, congratulated Gene Roddenberry and *Star Trek* "For Distinguished Contributions to Science Fiction"; Alberta Moran, for Goddard Space Flight Center, Washington D.C., wrote to say *Star Trek* was an "unsurpassed production"; Richard Hoagland, Curator of Astronomy and Space Museum of Science, Springfield, Massachusetts, gave *Star Trek* an "A" for "Attainment"; Isaac Asimov called the series "the first good television science-fiction" and an "astonishing revelation"; Philip Cohn, Director of the Yale School in Miami, Florida, described the show as "stimulating, intriguing, well done!"; and Jack Hackley, Director of Aerospace Medicine at Brooks Air Force Base in Texas, said the show was "tremendous, thought-provoking, outstanding."

Just days earlier, on April 13, "Operation: Annihilate!," the final first-run episode of Season One, had aired. A week later, for the April 24, 1967 edition of *Daily Variety*, a list of the Top 40 primetime shows, according to A.C. Nielsen, was published. *Star Trek*, with "Operation: Annihilate!," checked in at No. 37 out of 90 prime-timers. Its Thursday night lead-in, *Daniel Boone*, renewed early by NBC with no fuss, hadn't made the Top 40 list.

Once the decision to renew was made, the network men quickly got off the fence and began praising *Star Trek*.

In August, 1967, NBC's promotional department sent out a pamphlet to its affiliates and sponsors called "*Star Trek* Mail Call." The network bragged that over 29,000 letters "of encouragement and support" had been received. The PR men wrote:

> These letters constitute an impressive tribute to the high degree of believability the series has attained. Of particular interest to prospective sponsors is the fact that an unusually large number were written by men and women associated with some technical phase of space exploration or aerodynamics. Others came from business and professional people, college professors and undergraduates,

housewives, high school teachers and students, and even grade school pupils. A number took the form of petitions.

One more letter of interest was soon posted. In the "letters" section of the May 27, 1967 issue of *TV Guide*, Paul L. Klein, NBC Vice President of Audience Measurement, wrote:

> *Star Trek* is the only science-fiction show on television with a scientific basis. I was instrumental in recommending *Star Trek* for the NBC schedule and have been one of the show's staunchest supporters during the agony of renewal time. Messrs. Roddenberry, Coon, and the whole *Star Trek* staff have deserved the public's approval, NBC's faith in them, and, as topping to the cake, were just recently honored by the National Space Club in Washington for their scientific validity.

Herb Schlosser, NBC Vice President of Programs at the time, said, "*Star Trek* was renewed because it was good and it was different. And we were proud to have it on NBC." (153a)

Schlosser took his praise one step further -- he went on record, saying he believed that a series with the ratings demographics *Star Trek* delivered *should* have been renewed, without hesitation, year in and year out.

Being proud of a series is one thing. Wanting to do business with a loose cannon like Gene Roddenberry was another matter entirely.

***

On March 16, a week after the series' official renewal, the pick-up specs arrived from Desilu Legal. The memo to the *Star Trek* staff said:

> Sixteen episodes firm, with NBC notification to us by October 16, 1967, as to whether or not they want us to proceed to produce a total of twenty-six films, subject to NBC's further right to increase the order for up to approximately thirty-two films.

Urgent phone calls went out. Don Ingalls, not held accountable for the fiasco involving "The Alternative Factor," and still friends with Roddenberry, was given a new assignment. Art Wallace, also close to "G.R.," and having pitched the "Space Moby Dick" concept a year earlier, finally got the chance to realize it on paper; it would become "Obsession" for the second season. Still on the lookout for new talent, pitch sessions were quickly arranged for John T. Dugan (a writer for the western *Laredo* and the WWII series *12 O'Clock High*), Margaret Armen (*The Rifleman* and *The Big Valley*), Max Ehrlich (*The Defenders* and *Assignment Foreign Legion*), David P. Harmon (*The Man Behind the Badge* and *Gilligan's Island*), Robert Sabaroff (*Bonanza* and *The Virginian*), Les and Tina Pine (*Mr. Lucky* and *Ben Casey*), and Daniel Aubrey (*Rat Patrol* and *Run for Your Life*). This time, unlike one year earlier, all the pros Roddenberry and producer Gene Coon met with were given assignments … although Aubrey and the Pines would not see their material produced.

"By the time we'd gotten into our second season, these guys were really cooking," Associate Producer Bob Justman proudly said of the two Genes. "Coon and Roddenberry would still get together and have preliminary writers' meetings, but because we'd been on the air for a while now, it was a much easier process. The prospective writers knew what the show was all about. They'd seen it on TV by now, or, if not, we could have them watch a couple of episodes.... Each writer would come in and throw story ideas at you. And, since our guidelines were by now so well defined, Roddenberry and Coon would sit there listening to these guys lob ideas, and they'd just go, 'No, no, no, yes, no, no.' If there was an idea that got a 'yes,' the two Genes would then sit with the writer, working with him to hammer out and shape the story. Once they'd done that, they'd say good-bye and the guy would go off and write us an outline." (94-4)

Next, Gene Coon took over, with the help of Script Editor Dorothy Fontana, working closely with the writers in an effort to bring every outline and each subsequent draft of a screenplay up to *Star Trek*'s high standards.

Justman said, "Coon, who was the fastest typewriter in the West, would do almost all of the rewriting and fixing." (94-4)

Star Trek's creator had not given up his control of the series. Justman said, "Once [Gene Coon] finished, the script would pass through Roddenberry's office, and he would usually just do a little cleaning up, a couple of minor changes here and there." (94-4)

Although the renewal had only been for 16 episodes, Roddenberry and Coon gave out 33 story assignments before the start of August 1967, a month shy of *Star Trek*'s second season premiere. Twenty-nine made it to screenplay. The goal was to have more scripts than needed so that any problematic ones, as the creative staff felt "Court Martial" and "The Alternative Factor" had been during the season before, could be reworked or even shelved rather than rushed into production.

"We had to plan for a full 26 episode season when it came to scripts," Justman explained. "In no way could we be caught short should NBC exercise its option [for a full year]." (94-8)

Not the producer NBC wanted to do business with
(Photo from Roddenberry.com)

But Justman knew *Star Trek* would have to be an indisputable hit in order for some individuals at the network to want to see that option for additional episodes exercised.

"Gene [Roddenberry] did not suffer fools gladly," he said. "And his opinions of the television networks were well-known. And well-known *by* the television networks." (94-1)

Some television producers play the networks' game; some try to get the networks to play theirs. The ones who fit into the latter category had better have a Top 20 hit or be prepared to lose their jobs ... or, if the series is inseparable with the creator/producer, then risk seeing their shows pulled from the schedule.

Among the producers of 1967 series that placed below *Star Trek* in the ratings who, despite the lower numbers, had job security, were John Mantley and Philip Leacock (*Gunsmoke*), Bruce Lansbury (*The Wild, Wild West*), Irwin Allen (*Lost in Space*), Fred Freiberger (*Iron Horse*), Jules V. Levy (*The Big Valley*), and Barney Rosenzweig (*Daniel Boone*). These producers, with their series, received their network pickups long before *Star Trek*, without a single protest letter being written. These producers did as their networks asked.

"Gene rebelled against certain types of authority," Justman said. "It was his nature to resist, even fight authority with reckless abandonment. He reveled in this. I can't say I recognized this tendency at the outset, but I understand it now. He'd had his fill of doctrinaire [network] thinking before we started the first season of *Star Trek*. NBC bought the series because of Herb Solow and, to a lesser degree, Lucille Ball. Not because of Gene Roddenberry." (94-1)

And Desilu's Herb Solow, as he himself later admitted, was no fan of Roddenberry. Nor was the old guard at the studio. Nor were certain powers-that-be at NBC.

"I could have been more of a company man," Roddenberry admitted in the late 1980s. "There are plenty of producers who do that. But look at what they produced. Here we are 20 years later with a second series, and five movies. Can you say that about *Lost in Space*? That show got a good time slot -- which we never had. But we're still here." (145)

***

Having survived Thursday nights from 8:30 to 9:30 p.m., against ABC's top series, *Bewitched*, and CBS's powerhouse *Thursday Night Movie*, was no cake walk. Yet *Star Trek* persevered. The new time slot, however, posed an even greater challenge.

It didn't take a programming genius to know that a series with a young adult audience would struggle on Fridays at 8:30 p.m. The high school and college student fan base were at football and basketball games, on dates, at the movies, or at parties -- anywhere but at home with mom and dad, sitting in front of their TV sets. So NBC did the smart thing, at first, and scheduled *Star Trek* for Tuesdays. The fall 1967

Nimoy and Shatner plug the "Change-in"
(Courtesy of Gerald Gurian)

13

competition on this night was of little consequence. ABC was replacing the five-year-old *Combat!* with *Garrison's Gorillas*, a show which would die after one season. CBS had *Daktari*, a moderate success in the middle of a three-year easy-ride. *Star Trek* was expected to win its new time slot. But then its new time slot was stolen away. Simply put: Jerry Lewis (who had first been offered Friday nights) was better liked at NBC than Gene Roddenberry.

The network tried to convince Roddenberry the new Friday night timeslot was a step up. NBC's warped reasoning was that by programming *Star Trek* on something other than a school night, the series would pick up the small fry -- kids who should be very responsive to a far-out space show and a guy with pointed ears. Better still, the network programmers were providing a "much stronger" lead-in than *Daniel Boone*, or so they said.

The TV incarnation of Tarzan had swung into America's living rooms the previous

Ron Ely and a chimp named Cheetah (NBC publicity photo)

season and performed moderately well. This was the second series for Ron Ely, last seen on a weekly basis in 1961, not in a loin cloth but in swim trunks, for *The Aquanauts* (AKA *Malibu Run*), about a salvage diver looking for treasure and adventure at the floor of the ocean. It only lasted 18 episodes. Now, with *Star Trek* following, NBC claimed to expect that *Tarzan* would achieve greater success.

In reality, *Tarzan*'s novelty had already waned during the summer repeat season, competing poorly against CBS's sci-fi/western/spy show, *The Wild, Wild West*.

The back-end support offered by NBC was dismal. At 9:30 p.m., the network programmed the new sitcom, *Accidental Family*. Following his first series -- the short-lived *My Mother the Car* -- Jerry Van Dyke was cast as a widowed nightclub

Jerry Van Dyke and Lois Nettleton in *Accidental Family* (NBC publicity photo)

Ralph Taeger as *Hondo* (ABC publicity photo)

**Jim Nabors and Frank Sutton in *Gomer Pyle, U.S.M.C.*
(CBS publicity photo)**

comedian who buys a farm to serve as a safe place to raise his son. Lois Nettleton served as baby-sitter (for the son) and love interest (for Jerry). Next, at 10 p.m., was *The Bell Telephone Hour*, a television showcase for prestigious adult music (meaning, nothing that was in the pop charts or aimed at a youthful audience). Once a hit, when it started in the late 1950s, *The Bell Telephone Hour*, with its mix of classical, show tunes, jazz, and swing era music, was already on its last legs.

The competition on ABC was a new TV version of a 1953 John Wayne western, *Hondo*. Ralph Taeger, who had already starred in two short-lived series (*Klondike* and *Acapulco*, both on NBC and both co-starring James Coburn), took the lead as Hondo Lane, a former confederate officer who journeyed west following the Civil War and took an Indian bride. After seeing his wife killed in a massacre of Indians by the U.S. cavalry, Hondo, accompanied only by his dog, Sam, continued traveling the West, seeking ways to prevent further violence between the Army and the Indians. ABC believed Taeger was a star-in-the-making, and that the pro-Indian, anti-violence theme of the series would appeal to teens and young adults of the late 1960s. A western, regardless of its liberal theme, would appeal to the older crowd, and, by adding a dog to the cast, the kids might watch, too.

The competition on CBS was stronger. At 8:30 p.m. was *Gomer Pyle, U.S.M.C.* The sitcom that spun out of *The Andy Griffith Show* had been a Top 10 hit for all of its previous three seasons, and still gaining in popularity. It was especially popular with pre-teens, and their folks, and the folks' folks, making it perfect for the "family hour." *TV Guide*'s resident critic Cleveland Amory even liked Gomer, telling us:

> Well, sir, if you can stand another barmy army show -- this one about a cute boot in the Hollywood Horse Marines -- you too are going to have fun. For Gomer, who in Sergeant Carter's opinion is a goof-off, a gold-brick and a pea-brained knucklehead -- is not only as fine a broad comedian as your screen has mustered up this season; he is also, beyond a doubt, the gravest threat to our national defenses since the British burned Washington.

At 9 p.m. was the popular *CBS Friday Night Movie*. The opener for the new season was guaranteed to crush its competition -- *The Great Escape*, with Steve McQueen and James Garner leading an all-star cast.

There is a well-known adage in television that says network men never forget who causes them trouble … or embarrassment. Gene Roddenberry and NBC equated to a bad marriage. And, when marriages go bad, the children suffer the most. *Star Trek* was Roddenberry's child. And it was about to suffer.

The NBC programmers in Canada were wiser. In the frostier regions of North America, *Star Trek* would be scheduled on Wednesday nights, not Fridays.

Despite the disappointing timeslot in the U.S., Herb Solow, for an interview published in the March 28, 1967 edition of *Daily Variety*, and trying for a positive spin, hinted that *Star Trek* could possibly succeed because of its uniqueness. He told *Variety*'s Dave Kaufman:

> I don't see any show coming next fall that has a new film form. You've got the same westerns, adventures, and comedies. No one is experimenting with a new form -- good, bad or indifferent. I don't see anything on the schedules that's creative. Next season will be a season of sameness. The networks want to play it safe.

Solow believed his studio's *Mission: Impossible* to be "the most stylized show on the air," attributing it to originality in scripts, casting methods, use of "inserts," plus a built-in premise of suspense. He said:

> In the past, there have been concrete examples of ingenuity. *The Monkees*, whether you like it or not, is experimental. The same was true of *Batman* and *Star Trek*. It took a lot of guts to do these shows a little differently. (161-7)

Solow was putting on a brave face. There was no one in Hollywood who believed the move to Friday nights would be advantageous for *Star Trek*, not even the NBC programmers.

***

With the new season came a new budget -- a smaller one. It was now down from $195,000 per episode to $187,500. So far, only four episodes had been made for less than the first season cap of $195,000: "The Man Trap," "The Naked Time," "Charlie X," and "Tomorrow Is Yesterday." Only four out of 29. The new streamlined budget seemed impossible.

Regardless, Desilu had little choice but to slash costs. With *Star Trek* and *Mission:*

Impossible both going into a second season, and a third studio-owned hour, *Mannix*, premiering on CBS, the question remained whether a small outfit like Lucille Ball's TV company -- which was built on relatively inexpensive sitcoms filmed live before a studio audience -- could afford to be so gutsy.

Mission: Impossible, although with a smaller audience share than *Star Trek*, had brought home numerous Emmy awards. And its network had no issues with creator/producer Bruce Geller. In time, the series would probably pay for itself. *Star Trek*, it was felt, was a different story. The network's hesitation to renew was a clear signal to the studio heads that the series might not make it into syndicated reruns.

"Back then, the thinking was you needed 150 or so episodes to have a strong syndication package," said John D.F. Black, *Star Trek*'s first season associate producer. "We made 26 to 30 episodes a season in those days. So the plan was to keep Kirk and his crew out there for five years. That's why it was a five-year mission. And that's the only reason." (17)

So far, with the NBC pickup, *Star Trek* was only guaranteed one-and-a-half seasons. In the meantime, with the production of each new episode, Desilu went further into the red.

A headline in the March 29, 1967 edition of *Variety* announced, "Desilu's Budget Soars to Record $21-Mil for '67-'68." The previous year's budget was $15,000,000, and that was already breaking the bank. Now, the old guard's prediction that the studio might go bust was coming true.

And then the "For Sale" sign went up. Lucy needed to find a buyer ... or close shop within a year.

**The studio that Lucy and Desi built ... up for sale ...
because of *Mission: Impossible* and *Star Trek* (file photo)**

With all this drama outside the soundstages, *Star Trek*'s second season -- what many believe to be the original series' high watermark -- was set to begin.

2

Casting Off, Season Two

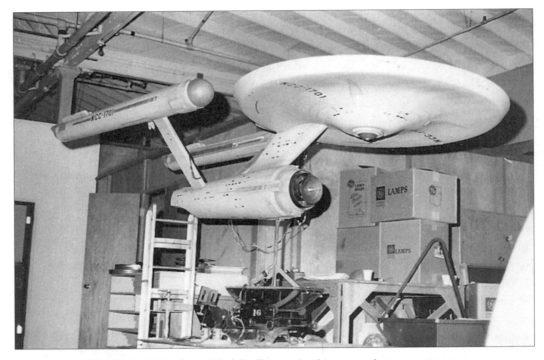

**The 11-foot, 2-inch model of the Enterprise, in storage, between seasons
(Courtesy of Bob Olsen)**

Star Trek finally had its network pick-up, albeit with a reduced budget and diminished status in the NBC schedule. One battle won, many more yet to fight.

During Season One, the 11-foot, 2-inch Enterprise model had been filmed by only two effects houses -- The Howard Anderson Company (who were the first to work on *Star Trek*) and Linwood Dunn's Film Effects of Hollywood. The latter was brought in when Anderson fell behind, nearly causing *Star Trek* to miss air dates, including the very first -- the NBC series premiere. As Anderson struggled to complete the photographic effects for "The Corbomite Maneuver," the episode that was intended to launch the series but ended up being ninth to air, the large model of the Enterprise was loaded on a flatbed truck and moved across the Desilu lot to a stage belonging to Film Effects of Hollywood. Beginning with "Balance of Terror," Lin Dunn's company became the primary supplier of the Enterprise shots. Helping out, providing other types of optical effects, were two additional post houses -- Westheimer Effects and Cinema Research.

This was meant to remain the formula for Season Two -- four competitors working toward a common goal. The plan was short-lived.

On April 4, 1967, Gene Roddenberry and Robert Justman met with Don Weed from Film Effects of Hollywood. Later, Justman wrote Roddenberry:

> On April 4th when we had a meeting with the fellows from Lin Dunn's outfit, we insisted at the time that they please get down to work and turn us out the 19

shots that we had ordered composited on the Enterprise. There was to be no need for any further delay and the shots could be done well, because of the fact that they [Film Effects] were no longer under pressure in turning out individual shows for us.

Two weeks later, Justman wrote to Roddenberry:

Today is Wednesday, April 19, 1967. Eddie Milkis [*Star Trek* post production supervisor] and I have just returned from the cutting room where we ran two composited blue backing shots of the U.S.S. Enterprise. Don Weed from Lin Dunn's outfit had told us that he had composited four shots, but only sent two over because the other two weren't any good and he wanted to re-do them.... We ran both shots in the cutting room with [*Star Trek* film editor] John Hanley. One shot was the Enterprise entering frame from Camera Left and proceeding across Frame and exiting out Camera Right. Photography on the Enterprise was fine, but there were no moving stars in the shot, so the Enterprise appeared to move through Frame very slowly. This shot will [only] be usable after it has been printed down a bit and some blue added so that the ship does not flare. We have asked for this shot to be composited also with moving stars, so that we get an impression of much greater speed. Hopefully, the printing down of the shot will also have the effect of eliminating the Matte area, which is apparent around the Miniature.

The difficult and time-consuming process of filming the Enterprise
(Courtesy of Gerald Gurian)

Even with all these problems, this shot was the best of the two -- and these two were the only ones delivered so far of the 19 shots ordered. Justman, having been down this dark road before with the Anderson Company during Season One, continued:

Now, let's get on to the other shot we saw tonight. This was a shot of the Enterprise entering from behind Camera Left and heading away from camera at a fairly good clip. There were no moving stars in this shot. The Enterprise was too light in color. It jiggled like crazy after it had entered and continued its erratic movement until it stopped in the B.G. [background] and just hung there for a while. When questioned about this shot on the phone this evening, Don Weed said "Well, the fault lies in the original material"! This was said to Eddie Milkis, as if <u>we</u> had furnished the original material and he [Weed] just went ahead and composited it because that's what he had to work with. Nothing was mentioned about the fact that he shot the original material for us. Certainly something should have been said when the original Blue Backing shot was selected as to whether it would composite correctly or not. Additionally, it struck him as a rather novel idea that there should be moving stars in the shot. Evidently, all the experience that Don Weed has accumulated during the past season has been phasered out of existence. If this is the case, he hasn't learned a thing and neither has anyone else over at Film Effects of Hollywood.

Justman paused from his dictating long enough for his secretary to leave a large gap on the page while transcribing. One could imagine the heavy sigh, before he continued:

Filming the 11-foot, 2-inch Enterprise against a blue screen
(Courtesy of Gerald Gurian)

At the present time I am quite morose. I can see many thousands and thousands of dollars going down the drain -- in addition to many days and nights of sweat and toil and strain and heartache. I am in hopes that the balance of the 19 shots will be useable. Certainly 50% of what we saw tonight is unusable. I will have to wait until I have seen more material before I go ahead and do anything. However, if what I have seen and heard tonight is any indication, we would be completely incompetent as film makers and creators if we continued our association with Film Effects of Hollywood.

Justman dictated a note the next day, saying:

Today is Thursday, April 20, 1967. Eddie Milkis has left town today for a short vacation. He tried for part of the morning to attempt to reach Don Weed on the phone to continue following up on our shots to be composited. Being unable to contact Don Weed or anyone else at Film Effects of Hollywood, he called [*Star Trek* editor] Don Rode, who then proceeded to attempt to reach Don Weed. Rode was unsuccessful for most of the day…. I, myself, was finally able to reach Don Weed late in the afternoon…. [Rode] was then able to talk to Weed and they set up a meeting for Friday morning at 9:30.

The next day, Justman was back on his dictation machine, saying:

Today is Friday, April 21, 1967. Don Weed did not show up for his 9:30 appointment with Don Rode. However, Gene Roddenberry showed up on time for his 10:30 appointment with Don Rode. I have just spoken to Don Rode and it is now 2:00 p.m. To this hour, we have not heard from Mr. Weed and I have asked Rode to call Don Weed and find out what gives.

A few hours later, Justman picked up his Dictaphone and said:

It is now 5:00 p.m. Don Rode just called me. He was finally able to reach Don Weed. They now have an appointment to meet at 9:00 a.m. this coming Monday, April 24, 1967. Stay tuned in.

After the weekend, Justman reported:

Today is Monday, April 24, 1967. Don Weed showed up about 10:00 a.m. and we ran six more of the 19 shots that he is compositing for us…. We saw 5 of various Enterprise Fly Bys. One of the shots had some jiggle motions in it, which we shall have to cut away from, and one of the shots had a speed-up and slow-down as the ship headed left to right and exited frame. The one in which the ship exited frame can be fixed by judicious snipping of frames on its slow movement sections. None of the shots that he delivered to us had any moving stars…. One of the shots has a problem with stars bleeding through the body of the ship…. The one thing missing in the left to right Fly Bys that you will note is that the model was originally photographed and was panned in and out of frame, instead of being dollied in and out of frame [as Anderson Company had done]. This means there is no changing perspective and we have a slight loss in believability due to the fact that aside from the flashing lights there is no discernible movement within the model itself. When Anderson photographed the model, he dollied past it so that there was a change on the perspective between the two power pods and various other structural members of the model. This gave it an illusion of life, in that further away portions of the model moved past us more slowly than the foreground portions of the model. One added thought. Don Weed was going to have an estimate on how much the Opticals were going to cost on "Catspaw" [the first episode to film for the second season] by the end of last week. He took the script with him the early part of last week and was going to get a budget up on it. We haven't heard anything yet.

One final note from Justman on the subject, handwritten and not dated, read:

Discussed it all in person with Gene who agreed we should drop Lin Dunn's optical house (Hollywood Film Effects) and do business elsewhere with other optical houses that could deliver what we needed on a timely basis and a price that we could afford.

Film Effects of Hollywood, responsible for the Enterprise shots seen in "Balance of Terror," and the Galileo shuttlecraft in "The Galileo Seven," abruptly exited the picture. New on the screen, working in conjunction with Anderson, Westheimer, and Cinema Research, were Effects Unlimited and Van der Veer Photo Effects. It now took five post effects houses to keep up with the needs of this one series.

***

The problems continued.

Leonard Nimoy, who received more mail and media attention than anyone else in the cast, wanted a raise. Nimoy knew his popularity was a double-edged sword and wanted to be properly compensated. As the public's love for Spock grew, the danger of being forever typecast as the guy with the ears increased.

DeForest Kelley once remarked, "Aw, this show -- a whole day shooting with Nimoy... a fine actor, but those damned ears! I don't care what I do, it's like working with a dog -- *those ears*... You could kill yourself but those ears will take the scene." (98-1)

"Leonard had two major concerns," Bob Justman said. "First, that the show wouldn't be picked up, and second, that, if we *were* picked up, he'd have another agonizing year of putting on and taking off his -- by then -- world-famous ears." (94-8)

Nimoy's salary and freedom were controlled by his *Star Trek* contract. However, Alex Brewis, Nimoy's agent, believed a contract was not binding if the conditions under which it had been written no longer existed. Nimoy was originally hired to play a secondary character to William Shatner's lead. It could now be argued -- and it was -- that Mr. Spock brought as much to *Star Trek* as did Captain Kirk.

The arguments between producer and actor are never limited to merely money. Nimoy also felt he, not only Roddenberry or Coon, should have a say when it came to his character.

Nimoy prepares to walk
(Courtesy of Gerald Gurian)

Roddenberry was livid over Nimoy's "demand" regarding the creative property of Mr. Spock. Desilu was more concerned with an increase to the budget.

Nimoy was making $1,125 per episode [$7,900 in 2013], a respectable paycheck by 1967 standards but nowhere near a number considered to be "star level." He wanted his agent to renegotiate for $3,000 per episode, all the while happy to settle for $2,500 -- just over twice what he was currently making. Brewis, more certain of Nimoy's value to the series, demanded $9,000. It was a staggering jump.

"The ramifications were huge," said Desilu head Herb Solow. "The extra money demanded by Nimoy was bad enough. The problem was that if he got an increase, all the other contract actors would be standing in line for theirs." (161-3)

The studio, of course, refused. A minor verbal counter-offer was made, accompanied by subtle threats of suspension and legal action. Nimoy's camp responded: "No raise, no deal."

Producer Gene Coon, returning from a short vacation, found a letter from Roddenberry dated April 1, 1967. It began:

> Sorry to have to greet you back with this news, but our contract negotiations with Leonard Nimoy and his representatives seem stalemated. There is a possibility that we might have to start our second year of *Star Trek*, or even continue the show, without Mister Spock.... Since we find it impossible to bargain with him, since they refuse to accept our best offers, or even discuss them reasonably, we've had no option but to inform Nimoy and his agents that he is "picked up" on the original contract and ordered to report for work per our schedule. He counters that he will refuse to work -- at which time we have no choice but to suspend him and take legal action.... Frankly, Nimoy and his representatives are very near trying to blackmail us into submission by holding "Mister Spock" as hostage. In their enthusiasm over a first-year success, over considerable mail volume and public adulation, they are kidding themselves into believing a very successful and much-wanted actor named Nimoy joined us and did it all. And that our posture should be totally that of humble gratitude. I won't play that game, nor will Desilu.... Accordingly, I've been working with [casting director] Joe D'Agosta on creating a new Vulcan Science Officer who can go to work on our first show.

It was no April Fools' joke. Two days earlier on March 30, Joe D'Agosta had prepared a list of actors who could join the cast as the new resident Vulcan. Mark Lenard, the Romulan commander in "Balance of Terror," was at the top. Another being seriously considered was Lawrence Montaigne, who had appeared as Decius, the defiant Romulan officer in that same episode. Also on the short list: David Carradine, later of *Kung Fu* fame.

Montaigne, who had more youth appeal than Mark Lenard, and came closer to Nimoy's looks and physicality than David Carradine, was selected. The studio took out an option, guaranteeing the actor a part in at least one upcoming episode in exchange for him keeping his schedule open for the possibility of recurring work.

Solow was very direct with the message he delivered to Alex Brewis. Nimoy must report back to work with the contract he currently had or face termination and a lawsuit. Further, should

And the ears go to … Lawrence Montaigne (from Maartenbouw.blogspot.com)

Nimoy think Desilu was bluffing, the studio already had someone to take his place. Solow told Brewis, "It's not important who plays the role; any good actor can do that. It's the pointed ears that count; they're the star." (161-3)

On April 6, an incensed Leonard Nimoy fired off a letter of his own to Desilu legal rep Ed Perlstein. In part, he wrote:

> [Under] the terms and conditions as stated in the contract and as subsequently amended in your verbal offer, I do not feel I can perform the services you call

23

for.... Since the studio has chosen to take a "freeze" attitude, I am prepared to deal with whatever "consequences may arise from my action.".... I feel in all fairness that you are entitled to as much advance notice of my intentions as possible.

And then a third party got involved. Herb Solow revealed, "NBC, the original campaigner against the Spock character and the pointed ears, hearing through Leonard's agent that he might walk off the show, was furious." (161-3)

The network had been monitoring the influx of fan mail and understood the importance of Nimoy to *Star Trek*. Solow was told to keep Spock on the Enterprise. There would be no further discussion.

Nimoy won the battle by getting the raise he originally had in mind, not the outrageous one his agent had asked for. He would now be paid $2,500 per episode, with a raise of $500 per episode for each year to follow, plus payment of

Nimoy and Roddenberry in happier times, during filming of "The Cage" (Courtesy of Gerald Gurian)

residuals increased through the fifth repeat. In addition, Nimoy would receive $100 per episode for expenses. He also received a more lucrative merchandising deal. To Roddenberry's chagrin, there was one last concession -- Nimoy was guaranteed a right to give input on the scripts.

Roddenberry continued to fight'... on a different battlefield. In a letter to Marion Dern, at *TV Week*, he wrote:

> [Without] taking away from my dear friend, Leonard Nimoy... it is Shatner's extraordinary dramatic ability and talent which often sets up the scene and gives Leonard a solid foundation and contrast which makes Mr. Spock come alive. Bill was trained in the old Canadian Shakespeare school with all its discipline and both his work and professional attitudes reflect this rich background.

Taking issue with Charles Witbeck over an article he had written giving Nimoy and Spock credit for saving *Star Trek* from oblivion on Thursday nights, Roddenberry responded with a letter printed in the *Los Angeles Herald-Examiner*, saying:

> Mr. Spock did not "save *Star Trek* from oblivion." We agree that Leonard Nimoy has done an excellent job in portraying the character, but in all fairness, [I] must point out that Mr. Spock was conceived at the same time as the rest of the format and is being played today almost exactly as conceived over five years ago. We believed Spock would "catch on" and are delighted to have this belief and plan proved right.... Again, we in the *Star Trek* office are all fans of Leonard Nimoy also. He is an excellent and hard-working actor and his talents have brought many interesting dimensions to the role. His ability helped us stay on the air but to credit him with a "save" overlooks the contributions of Bill Shatner and the other extraordinary talented actors on the show, the fine writers we had,

the excellent directors, the whole *Star Trek* production "family."

In a letter to Isaac Asimov, Roddenberry expressed concerns that his choice for the star of *Star Trek* was being eclipsed by a character (and an actor) who was supposed to be a second banana. He wrote that it was Shatner's "fine handling of a most difficult role that permits Spock and the others to come off as well as they do."

Asimov wrote back:

Everybody in the show knows exactly how important and how good Mr. Shatner is, and so do all the actors, including even <u>Mr. Shatner</u>. Still, when the fan letters go to Mr. Nimoy and articles like mine ["Mr. Spock Is Dreamy" for *TV Guide*] concentrate on him, one can't help feeling unappreciated. Andy Griffith had to face it when Don Knotts got the Emmys [five wins for each of the five years he was a regular on *The Andy Griffith Show*], and Sid Caesar when Carl Reiner got them [four nominations, two wins, besting Caesar on his own show], and so on.... The problem, then, is how to convince the world, and Mr. Shatner, that Mr. Shatner is the lead. It seems to me that the only thing one can do is lead from strength. Mr. Shatner is a versatile and talented actor and perhaps this should be made plain by giving him a chance at a variety of roles. In other words, an effort should be made to work up story plots in which Mr. Shatner has an opportunity to put on disguises or take over roles of unusual nature. A bravura display of his versatility would be impressive indeed and would probably make the whole deal more fun for Mr. Shatner.

Roddenberry appreciated Asimov's suggestions. Before the second season was over, Kirk would dress up as a World War II Nazi, be garbed as a Roman slave, and as a warring tribesman on a primitive planet. He'd be consumed with guilt and vengeance as he chased a vampire-like cloud-monster, then battle in hand-to-hand mortal combat with a fellow starship captain. Story concepts dealing with Kirk growing old, Kirk being inhabited by a godlike alien, and Kirk's mind and body being taken over by a vengeful woman, were put into development. And the lighter side of Kirk, and Shatner, would come across in a pair of comical episodes.

The final consensus, however, was, "if you can't beat 'em, join 'em." Kirk and Spock would be a team. After conferences with Gene Coon,

Team work – a perfect combination
(NBC publicity photo; Courtesy of Gerald Gurian)

Roddenberry sent a final letter to Asimov on the subject, writing:

Shatner will come off ahead by showing he is fond of the teenage idol; Spock will do well by displaying great loyalty to his Captain. In a way it will give us one lead, the team.

***

In another attempt to keep Leonard Nimoy from getting too much credit, a change was made to the opening title sequence. Gene Roddenberry's name now came before Nimoy's. "*Star Trek* ... created by Gene Roddenberry ... starring William Shatner ... and Leonard Nimoy as Mr. Spock." And the creator's name would return at the end of the episode, as Executive Producer.

Herb Solow said, "I again marveled at [Gene's] seemingly unending drive to fashion himself the single master, the absolute proprietor of *Star Trek*." (161-3)

Roddenberry later said, "It was done that way with many shows from that period. Still is. *The Fugitive* was a Quinn Martin Production -- stated in the opening titles, not only with a separate [title] card but with Bill Conrad's voiceover. All QM shows opened that way. Irwin Allen took acknowledgement in the opening titles of his shows. The main title sequence of *Star Trek* was designed that way at the start of the first year, but, after two episodes ["The Man Trap" and "Charlie X"] I took my name off. Having that credit seemed to bother certain people. With the second year, I had it put back in. And it still bothered certain people. Perhaps my name shouldn't have been in the titles at all -- front or closing. Just Desilu and NBC. They would have still found something to complain about." (145)

There was another change in the credits -- but this one, involving DeForest Kelley -- didn't seem to upset anyone.

Robert Justman was the instigator of the change. He later said, "It became apparent to me as well as to Gene very early on that the character of McCoy was going to be a 'linchpin' -- a 'fulcrum' upon which one side was balanced with the other. De was very effective in this role, and I was very aware of this." (94-1)

On December 1, 1966, Justman wrote Roddenberry, stating his desire to provide Kelley with better compensation, including a more visible credit, "because of the performance he gives us" and because Kelley was "one helluva nice guy." Justman added, "He has been more than the kindly ship's doctor to all of us."

Justman followed up on April 6, 1967, writing:

> [I] have had our contractual obligations researched by the Legal Department and can discover no objection to giving DeForest Kelley [starring] credit on our new Main Title. In addition, I have checked with Stan Robertson and he assures me that NBC welcomes the idea, as they think very highly of DeForest Kelley and the character he has helped create.

Shortly after the premiere of Season Two, Kelley told a tabloid writer, "Being a star is nice. It's as if everything that you know deep down inside of yourself you have, has been officially noticed and rewarded. Well, I wasn't a star when the show went on the air. But the fans looked and they liked what they saw. They began writing letters. Mail poured in and the bosses were, frankly, surprised. I guess that's when they began to think that maybe Kelley was star material after all." (98-13)

Kelley's agent found a way to get his client compensation beyond co-star billing. *Star Trek* quietly raised the good doctor's salary from $850 to $1,250 per episode. In 2013 dollars, this would be $8,700, or a yearly income of $226,200 (based on 26 episodes), plus residuals -- small potatoes for the type of money TV stars make in this day and age, but not bad for a man who shared a two-bedroom house with his wife and had a small dog (but no kids). Kelley's new good fortune meant that he could repair and refurbish the San Fernando Valley house.

"I guess I finally realized the popularity of *Star Trek* and the success of my role when people began stopping me on the street to comment on the show," Kelley said in the November 1967 issue of *TV Star Parade*. "This tremendous interest is something I hadn't been accustomed to…. I'd been fighting the heroes a long time, making a good living playing heavies. Then this series came along. It kind of shook me. It changed my image. I'm not a heavy any longer. And I'm working every day with the same people. It's interesting. A whole new thing happened to me when our space ship blasted off." (98-11)

For a tabloid interview in 1967, he said, "The greatest luxury I've allowed myself is an electric garage door opener. That gives me the greatest kick."

Now that the garage was easier to get into, he purchased another "kick" -- a new Thunderbird.

And now *Star Trek* had three stars
(NBC publicity photo courtesy of Gerald Gurian)

Nimoy and his Buick
(Courtesy of Gerald Gurian)

Nimoy used his raise in salary to replace his battered old car with a new Buick.

Then, one day, Kelley backed his new Thunderbird into Nimoy's new Buick. Fortunately, both could now afford auto insurance.

George Takei was given a raise, as well, now up to $800 per episode, with a guarantee of seven out of the first sixteen. And, again, residuals.

James Doohan remained at $850 per segment, with a guarantee of seven, although everyone knew he would appear in more.

Nichelle Nichols was not as quick to reenlist. She had envisioned a much bigger part for herself in *Star Trek*. There was no question she had been given a few good moments, including showing off her singing voice in two episodes. And there were other perks. Nichols, as Uhura, appeared on the giant-sized cover of the January 1967 issue of *Ebony* magazine, heralded as "the first Negro astronaut, a triumph of modern-day TV over modern-day NASA."

Despite this, Nichols felt the character of Uhura had been underappreciated. In an article for the July 15, 1967 issue of *TV Guide*, entitled "Let Me Off at the Next Planet," she complained, "My problem is being a *black* woman on top of being a woman." Elsewhere in the article, she said, "The producers admit being very foolish and very lax in the way they've used me -- or *not* used me."

In her book, *Beyond Uhura*, Nichols told how she was denied respect. Case in point: She recalled discovering that someone in the Desilu mailroom had stopped the delivery of the bulk of her mail. Two workers from the department confided to the actress that most of her mail was being held back and told her,

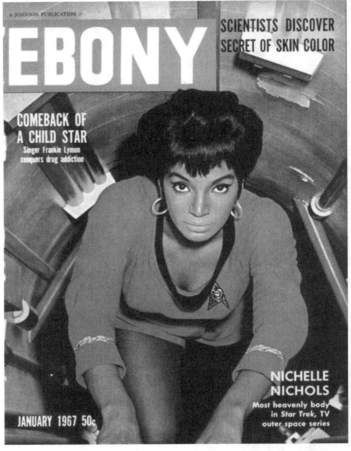

Ebony **magazine puts a spotlight on the first black woman in space (January 1967 issue)**

"Yours is the only fan mail that matches Shatner and Nimoy's."

"Days later I saw for myself the boxes and bags of mail from all over the country, from adults and children, all colors, all races," wrote Nichols for her memoir. "To say I was stunned does not even begin to convey how I felt. It was 'just' fan mail, but to those who had ensured that I worked without a contract, who seemed at every turn to remind me that I was dispensable, this was the ultimate humiliation." (127-2)

Before writing her own book, Nichols told an interviewer, "The thing in 1966 was that everyone was scared to death of having a Black *and* a woman in an equal role. *They* had just gotten through having a battle with Gene Roddenberry over Majel Barrett in a strong female role, and they were scared to death of the South, and the whole thing." (127-8)

It could be argued that Nichols was stereotyping NBC the same way she felt NBC was stereotyping her. Would network affiliates really boycott *Star Trek* if Uhura was given a few more lines of dialogue? All but a small handful were already airing the racially mixed *I Spy* each week, which presented a Black in a lead role, equal in all ways, including the amount of dialogue he spoke, to his white counterpart.

Herb Solow stated, "To set the record straight, once and for all, no one at NBC ever commented negatively to me about Nichelle because of her race, or approached me or any other Desilu executive to hint, instruct, or demand that Nichelle Nichols be fired.... It must be understood that NBC executives Mort Werner, Grant Tinker, Herb Schlosser, and Jerry Stanley were unanimous in their desire to feature and protect all minorities, including women, in the product that they broadcast to the American audience." (161-3)

The fact remained, Uhura was doing less on the Enterprise. The writers, now led by Gene Coon, were having trouble keeping the communications officer plugged into stories that seemed to call more for Kirk, Spock, and McCoy. In the first drafts of the scripts, which Roddenberry always made a point of showing to Nichols, Uhura had more to say and do. Very little of this ever seemed to make it into the finished episodes.

Nichols recalled, "When they began cutting [my lines], virtually down to 'Hailing frequencies open,' from really fine, substantial parts, I just couldn't take it." (127-8)

At the end of the first season, Nichols went to Roddenberry and announced she was quitting *Star Trek*. Unlike Nimoy, with no contract to say otherwise, she was free to abandon ship.

Nichols recalled, "That weekend, I went to what I remember as a NAACP fundraiser, though it could have been something else. Whatever it was, I was in Beverly Hills; I was being seated at the dais as other notables were coming to join us at this event. One of the organizers of the event came over to me and said, 'Miss Nichols, I hate to bother you just as you're sitting down to dinner but there's someone here who wants very much to meet you and he said to tell you that he is your biggest fan.' I said, 'Oh, certainly.' I stood up and turned around and who comes walking over toward me from about 10 or 15 feet, smiling that rare smile of his, is Dr. Martin Luther King.... And he walks up to me and says, 'Yes, Miss Nichols, I am your greatest fan.'

"You know I can talk, but all my mouth could do was open and close, open and close; I was so stunned. Dr. King starts to tell me about how *Star Trek* is the only show that he and his wife, Coretta, allowed their little children to stay up and watch. And he goes on about what the show means and my role in it and how I've created this character with dignity and knowledge. Finally, I said, 'Thank you so much, Dr. King. I'm really going to miss my co-stars.' Dr. King looked at me and the smile went off his face and he said, 'What are you talking about?' I told him. He said, 'You cannot,' and, so help me, this man practically repeated verbatim what Gene said. He said, 'Don't you see what this man is doing who has written this? This is the future. He has established us as we should be seen. Three hundred years from now we are here.... When we see you, we see ourselves, and we see ourselves as intelligent and beautiful and proud.' He goes on and I'm looking at him and my knees are buckling. I said, 'I ..., I ...," and he said, 'You turn on your television and the news comes on and you see us marching and peaceful, you see the peaceful civil disobedience, and you see the dogs and see the fire hoses [being used by the police], and we all know they cannot destroy us because we are there in the 23rd century.' That's all it took. I went back on Monday morning and told Gene what had happened. He sat there behind that desk and a tear came down his face, and he looked up at me. I said, 'Gene, if you want me to stay, I will stay. There's nothing I can do but stay.' ... He opened his drawer, took out my resignation and handed it to me. He had torn it to pieces. He handed me 100 pieces and said, 'Welcome back.'" (127-11)

This time Nichols got a contract -- a guarantee of nine episodes of the first sixteen, at $650 each ($4,550 per episode in 2013), plus residuals. *Daily Variety*, a bit late getting the news ("Friday's Child," the third episode filmed for Season Two, had just wrapped), made the announcement on May 31, 1967, with Dave Kaufman writing:

> Leonard Nimoy and Nichelle Nichols, regulars of *Star Trek*, have resolved their
> salary demands with Desilu, re-signed for next term.

On June 14, 1967, *Variety*, published the article "Negro Employment in Network TV
Extends to Seven Nights Next Fall." Murray Horowitz wrote:

> In the 1967-1968 season, there will be at least one network show every night of
> the week that will regularly utilize Negro performers.

Saturday would be the new
night for *Hogan's Heroes*, with Ivan
Dixon in the cast; Sunday had Greg
Morris in *Mission: Impossible*;
Monday had Gerald Edwards in the
new series *Cowboy in Africa* and, as
Horowitz called him, "the Jackie
Robinson of TV," Bill Cosby in *I
Spy*, starting its third season;
Tuesdays had Robert Hooks in the
freshman *N.Y.P.D.* and Hari Rhodes
in the sophomore *Daktari*;
Wednesday had Louis Armstrong on
Kraft Music Hall; Thursday had Don
Marshall in *Ironside*, taking over *Star
Trek*'s old time slot; and on Fridays,
"Nichelle Nichols returns to her role
as the communications officer aboard
the Enterprise in *Star Trek*."

Horowitz continued:

First series to cast a White and a Black with equal
status, the award-winning *I Spy*
(*TV Guide*, March 25, 1966)

> In addition to a growing
> consciousness of the real
> world within the medium,
> there have been other factors
> contributing to the wider use
> of Negro performers in TV.
> One is the success of the *I Spy*
> series. It has not only won Cosby an Emmy, but next season he will have his
> own special.... Another sign of the changing times is that series producers are
> becoming more worldly. They recognize, for example, that the Russians too are
> involved in space exploration. Ergo, an actor portraying a Russian will become
> part of the crew in *Star Trek* next season.

***

It had been in the works for a while. As early as September 22, 1966, just weeks after
the premiere of *The Monkees*, Roddenberry sent a memo to casting director Joe D'Agosta,
saying:

Davy Jones of The Monkees, the prototype for Pavel Chekov (NBC publicity photo, 1966)

Keeping our teenage audience in mind, also keeping aware of current trends, let's watch for a young irreverent, English-accent "Beatle" type to try on the show, possibly with an eye to him recurring. Like the smallish fellow [Davy Jones] who looks to be so hot on *The Monkees*. Personally I find this type spirited and refreshing and I think our episode[s] could use that kind of "lift."

And then the irreverent, English accent "Beatle" type became an irreverent Russian accent "Beatle" type. Although no one was able to confirm the story, Roddenberry told how an article in *Pravda*, the official newspaper of the Communist party, criticized *Star Trek* as being "typically capitalistic." Allegedly, *Pravda*'s main complaint was that on this ship with a crew supposedly representing all the countries of Earth, there were no Russians. Helping to add validity to the story (which many people over the years have dismissed as a publicity stunt) is an October 10, 1967 letter Roddenberry sent to Mikhail V. Zimyanin, Editor of *Pravda*, Central Committee of the Communist Party of the Soviet Union, Moscow, Russia. Roddenberry informed Zimyanin that he had learned of the article concerning *Star Trek* and that the series now had a Russian serving on board the Enterprise. His

With the addition of a Russian accent, Walter Koenig wasn't just monkeying around (NBC publicity photo, courtesy of Gerald Gurian)

name: Pavel Andreievich Chekov. There is no evidence that Zimyanin ever responded.

"The Chekov thing was a major error on our part," Roddenberry said in 1968. "And I'm still embarrassed that we didn't include a Russian right from the beginning. However, now it's Russia's turn to be embarrassed." (145-4)

"Embarrassed" because Roddenberry knew Gene Coon intended to have some fun with the proud new character at the expense of his homeland.

In the June 21, 1967 issue of *Daily Variety*, Roddenberry, explaining why *Star Trek* would now feature a "young Russian beatnik spaceman," said, "I don't want any more bad notices in *Pravda* -- I have enough in Hollywood."

As for the casting of Chekov, director Joseph Pevney made a suggestion. He had worked with a young actor named Walter Koenig on an episode of *Alfred Hitchcock Presents* and felt Koenig would make "an interesting Russian-type fellow." (141-2)

The episode of Hitchcock, "Memo from Purgatory," had been written by *Star Trek* veteran and now opponent, Harlan Ellison. Koenig recalled, "I was opposite James Caan. James was the good guy and I was the bad guy. Joe kept saying, 'You're going to be a star.' Well, James Caan became a star. I finished the show and went home to my usual life. But Joe really came through by getting me onto *Star Trek*." (102)

Roddenberry had a vague recollection of Koenig, who had appeared in an episode of *The Lieutenant*. Also in the cast, *Star Trek* veterans Gary Lockwood and Paul Comi. The director, later to give direction to Koenig on *Star Trek*, had been Vincent McEveety.

Hollywood was a smaller town then. Koenig had already taken direction from John Meredyth Lucas on *Ben Casey*, and would again, on *Star Trek*. He had appeared in an episode of *Mr. Novak*, "With a Hammer in His Hand, Lord, Lord!," which was written by former *Star Trek* associate producer John D.F. Black. This episode won Black the Writers Guild Award and then got him his job on *Star Trek*. In two other *Mr. Novak* episodes, Koenig worked with former *Star Trek* director Michael O'Herlihy ("Tomorrow Is Yesterday"). Future *Star Trek* director Murray Golden directed Koenig in an episode of the World War II espionage series, *Jericho*. And Koenig had a prominent role as a villain in an *I Spy*, being filmed at Desilu during *Star Trek*'s first season. All signs seemed to be pointing toward *Star Trek* ... a show Koenig had never even seen.

Gene Coon, however, had another actor in mind, although the production records for *Star Trek* do not specify who. What is known is that Coon's choice was invited in for a reading. Koenig was, too.

"We both read, and afterward I didn't even get to go home," Koenig reminisced. "I just sat around for forty minutes, and then Bill Theiss came in and said, 'Follow me.' He then took me to wardrobe where he got out one of those cloth measuring tapes and he started measuring me from my crotch to my cuff. I said, 'What are you doing?' And he said, 'I've got to make you a uniform. You just got hired.' I swear, that's how I found out I had the part. No congratulations, no ceremony, just this guy with a tape measure between my legs. It certainly did not hint at the significance *Star Trek* would ultimately have in my life." (102-8)

Koenig was told this job would be a "one-shot deal," a single assignment for the episode "Catspaw." And, for that, he was given a Beatles wig to wear. Two weeks later he was back, for "Friday's Child," then, several days later, for "Who Mourns for Adonais?," and, several days after that, for "Amok Time."

Koenig's involvement was both sudden and immense, and that displeased George Takei.

At the end of the first season, Takei had approached Roddenberry and Coon, explaining why Sulu should be given a bigger place on the series. He appreciated the stand-out parts he had in a number of episodes but, like Nichelle Nichols, believed his character had been underused. He hoped there would be more to do in the new season. Takei left the producer's offices assured that there would certainly be more business for Sulu in the future. However, when Takei returned from the summer break, he discovered that the story points and lines of dialogue normally assigned to Sulu were now being shared with his new partner at the helm, Chekov.

For his memoir, Takei wrote, "The spirited lobbying I had mounted to enhance Sulu's role had all been for naught. I had gained nothing but a new competitor.... I was prepared to dislike this interloper, this thief of my effort. All right, I'll admit it -- I hated him! Sight unseen, I churned with venom for this Walter Koenig! This Walter sailed into our second season on the wings of fate, wearing that silly Prince Valiant wig, and plucked off the fruits that rightfully belonged to me." (171-4)

Adding insult to injury, Takei was asked to share his dressing room with Koenig. And because of this, he remembered the veins in his scalp swelling up.

Interviewed for this book, Koenig said, "George writes that he felt threatened by my presence; that he hated me. But I didn't see that. And I'm a pretty sensitive guy. I can sense when somebody is unhappy with me. I never had the feeling. But then again, he is so stoic. When I read his book, that he felt that way, I was really surprised. I was shocked. He had turned it off so well." (102)

Koenig didn't notice it because the bitterness was short-lived. Takei met Koenig and was convinced he was obsessing over how terrible he believed he looked in that wig.

"I feel ridiculous with this on," Takei recalled him complaining. "I feel like a walking joke." (171-4)

Koenig remembers it differently and said, "I wasn't as uncomfortable with it as I've been made out to be. My hair had started to thin and I sort of liked the fact that I had a full head of hair. It was just that it was far more youthful that I was."

Koenig was 30. Chekov was 22.

But Takei thought the wig looked silly and therefore, he was sure, Walter must have felt the same way. And, because of this, something odd happened. Takei admitted, "Even in my hatred, I couldn't help but feel a bit sorry for Walter. He looked so pathetic. All the bile that churned inside me began to dissolve at the sight of another actor reduced to public humiliation every time he stepped in front of the camera." (171-4)

Suddenly Takei had a reason to bond with Koenig. They could sit side by side at the helm and suffer the slings and arrows expected of supporting players. And they would become friends.

***

There was someone new on the set also. Charles Washburn, one of the first African-Americans to enter the Directors Guild of America's apprentice training program, was added to the crew as Assistant Director. A small part of Washburn's daily routine was to check in Shatner, Nimoy, and Nichols, who arrived for a 6:30 a.m. makeup call. Nichols needed her eye makeup, Nimoy his ears, and Shatner his hairpiece. Kelley, Doohan, Takei, and Koenig arrived at 7:15. They required less work. Washburn would also take the breakfast orders.

On set, among other things, the new A.D. was in charge of the turbolift doors.

"I manned the button for the doors to swoosh open," Washburn said. "No matter how [Shatner] pivoted, hesitated, or changed, I would key the man on the doors just right." (180-2)

Al, the man on the doors, an old-timer described as "well past his game and worn out," was wedged into a tiny, hot space. Sometimes Al got sleepy as cast and crew went through setups and shots and retakes.

"I didn't know this," Washburn said, "but the guys did." (180-2)

The "guys" included William Shatner, who often made the Christmas party blooper reel, bouncing off the doors with amused surprise.

And then someone in the crew would yell, "Check the light!" The light, triggered by Washburn's button, told the old fellow in the dark space to pull open the turbolift doors. Everyone knew the light was working fine. But the light was always blamed to spare the dignity and, more importantly, preserve the job of Al, the turbolift door man. "Check the light" was crew lingo for "Wake up, Al." (180-2)

Charles Washburn with Nichelle Nichols (Courtesy of Gerald Gurian)

With Al awake, Walter Koenig wearing his wig, Nimoy and Nichols back in the fold, Kelley assured co-starring status, and Shatner having jetted back from Spain just in the nick of time, the first episode of *Star Trek*'s second season was ready to begin principal photography. The script which offered generous portions of both tricks and treats was appropriately called "Catspaw."

Episode 30: CATSPAW

Written by Robert Bloch
(with D.C. Fontana, uncredited)
Directed by Joseph Pevney

From *TV Guide*, October 21, 1967 issue:

> "Cats-Paw [sic]." Castles, dungeons, witches and black cats pervade this episode as Kirk seeks a rational explanation of -- and escape from -- the alien forces that have lured him to Pyris VII. It's a dark, forbidding planet devoid of life, at least as earthlings know it. Script by Robert Bloch.

Antoinette Bower with William Shatner in NBC publicity photo (Courtesy of Antoinette Bower)

Sylvia and Korob are visitors to this dead world, an advance probe from a colonizing race looking to push out into the galaxy. Taking human form, Sylvia now has a growing desire to experience and enjoy pleasures of the flesh. And she wants Kirk.

"Catspaw," designed to be a Halloween show, examined the hidden torture chamber known as the subconscious mind. McCoy says it: "Illusions and reality. Sometimes I wonder if we'll ever know the difference."

The stronger theme comes courtesy of Gene Roddenberry and his final rewrite. It explores how human sensation -- emotional as well as physical -- can block out all reason and must be managed and even fought. Hedonism combined with perverse curiosity, or sociopathic behavior, as we are shown here, will inevitably lead to one's downfall.

SOUND BITES

- *The Witches:* "Remember the curse! Wind shall rise! And fogs descend! So leave here, all, or meet your end!" *Kirk:* "Spock … comment?" *Spock:* "Very bad poetry, Captain."
- *Kirk:* "If we weren't missing two officers, and a third one dead, I'd say someone was playing an elaborate trick-or-treat joke on us." *Spock:* "Trick or treat, Captain?" *Kirk:*

"Yes, Mr. Spock. You'd be a natural. I'll explain it to you one day."

- *Sylvia:* "You like to think of yourselves as complex creatures, but you are flawed. One gains admittance to your minds through many levels, for you have too many to keep track of yourselves. There are unguarded entrances to any human mind, Captain."

ASSESSMENT

"Catspaw" is an entertaining episode, if one is satisfied with a spook-house ride and not looking for much logic or reason. The silliness begins in the Teaser, after crewman Jackson returns to the ship, dead, with a voice emitting from his corpse, threatening "a curse." Despite this warning, and with no security guards to accompany them, Kirk, Spock, and McCoy beam to the planet. This hardly seems like a sensible command decision on Kirk's part. With Scott and Sulu having beamed down earlier and now missing, the Enterprise is without its top officers.

More suspension of reality comes before the end of Act I as Kirk, Spock, and McCoy fall ten feet onto a hard stone floor, where they lie unconscious, but without having suffered broken bones, cuts, or concussions. Robert Justman took note of this during the script writing process, telling Gene Coon:

> Everyone revives in the dungeon pit. Doc announces that no bones are broken
> and, looking down, discovers that his phaser is gone. Luckily, these captors have
> left them with their <u>genitals intact</u>. (RJ30-1)

Coon ignored Justman's sarcasm. The scene stayed as written.

Perhaps "Catspaw" should be viewed as a guilty pleasure. It *is* entertaining. And, for its time and budget, well-made. The direction, photography, music, set design, and casting are all effective. The writing, from a perspective of pure entertainment, is not without its cleverness. And not completely mindless. There are, after all, those underlying themes.

"Catspaw" was scheduled to air four nights before Halloween, in a new time slot with a much younger audience. This, then, was a Trick-Or-Treat ... and *Star Trek* for the kids.

THE STORY BEHIND THE STORY

Script Timeline
Robert Bloch's contract based on pitch, ST #51: March 6, 1967.
Bloch's story outline: March 9, 1967.
Bloch's revised story outline, gratis: March 14, 1967.
Bloch's 1ˢᵗ Draft teleplay: March 29, 1967.
Bloch's 2ⁿᵈ Draft (Mimeo Department "Yellow Cover 1ˢᵗ Draft"): April 14, 1967.
D. C. Fontana's rewrite (Final Draft teleplay): April 24, 1967.
Gene Roddenberry's script polish (Revised Final Draft): April 27, 1967.
Additional page revisions by Gene Coon: May 4, 5 & 10, 1967.

Robert Bloch's script for "What Are Little Girls Made Of?" had to be heavily-rewritten by Gene Roddenberry. If not for Bloch's high esteem among fans of science fiction and horror, he might never have been invited back.

Bloch's next story idea, "Sleeping Beauty," treaded on territory explored in "Space Seed" and was passed over. In its place, Roddenberry and Coon suggested he do what he did best -- the macabre.

"They wanted a Halloween story," Bloch told *Starlog* magazine in 1986. "I wanted to do something that would involve changes in appearances. So, I decided that instead of having the usual Jekyll-and-Hyde transformation, I'll have a female who was capable of chameleon-like adaptations. And the rest just fell into place." (18-4)

Dorothy Fontana, offering insight as to how the story meetings were going for the second season, recalled, "We all sat in on the script pitches. It was Roddenberry who usually would say 'yes,' because he was usually there. But, if he wasn't there and Gene Coon said 'yes,' I don't think that it was ever thrown out. Roddenberry knew that Coon had good sense of what would work on the show. But Roddenberry made himself available for these pitches." (64-1)

As he had done with "Little Girls," Bloch borrowed elements from one of his own short stories, this time "Broomstick Ride," first published in December 1957. For that tale, an Earth ship arrives to explore a planet called Pyris, where the captain and his crew encounter what seem to be witches and warlocks. The witches can read minds and, because of the images they see in the subconscious mind of the Earthmen, believe the humans present a danger. To defend themselves, the leader of the witches conjures up a miniature of the Earth ship and throws it onto the hot coals of a brazier. This causes the real space ship to explode.

For "Catspaw," Bloch kept the name Pyris, the witches, the mind reading, the misunderstanding concerning the subconscious, and the creation of a miniature space ship to be subjected to intense heat.

As for the episode's title, according to Webster, "Catspaw" means "a dupe" or "a person used by another to do dangerous, distasteful or unlawful work" ... as Scott, Sulu, and McCoy do, under the mental influence of Sylvia.

Bloch did a free polish of his March 9 outline, delivering a new story draft on March 14. Robert Justman was not pleased ... not so much in the writing -- he had yet to comment on that -- but in the genre. Not knowing whether Roddenberry or Coon, or both, had approved the story, he wrote to Roddenberry, with "cc" to Gene Coon and Dorothy Fontana:

> Although I find many problems within this Story Outline, I feel that they're all exceeded in importance by one enormous error. It has always been our intention that the *Star Trek* series be an "action-adventure" show. This story departs radically from that direction in that we have here a "supernatural-fantasy." ... Should both NBC and you surprise me and decide that this would be an eminently suitable project for *Star Trek* this season, then I am prepared to give you specific criticism on the various aspects contained within the Treatment. (RJ30-1)

Coon didn't want to wait for Justman's specific criticism and sent the treatment to NBC. Stan Robertson, the network production manager assigned to *Star Trek*, was not overjoyed. He wrote Coon:

> This story outline is approved provided that all of the "magic" elements are deleted and that, in their places, the writer substitutes those incidents and ingredients which are more in keeping with our action-adventure format. (SR30)

Robertson insisted that Bloch resolve the story in a manner which would not ...

... leave the viewer with the feeling, implied or otherwise, that the basis for what has transpired during our drama has been magical, mystical, or any form of the occult. (SR30)

Robertson also felt the material portrayed too many dark themes. He told Coon:

I would suggest that you consult very closely with our Broadcast Standards Department concerning those scenes such as that at the end of the Teaser in which [the script reads] "face of dead man, his pale flesh shrivels and blackens before their eyes." This, as I know you realize, could, if not handled properly, shock and offend the viewer. (SR30)

Robert Justman agreed about not wanting to see the corpse change color and decompose, and, now that he knew the story was to be further developed, wrote to Coon:

I say forget it. Let's not have any shriveling up and turning black of corpses, unless, of course, you wish to win the 1967 "throw-up" award. (RJ30-2)

Robert Bloch took the notes into consideration and delivered his teleplay on March 29. A pleased Roddenberry wrote to Coon:

Bob seems to be most anxious to work with us this year and seems more pliable and anxious to please than last year. (GR30-1)

But there were things that could not be allowed to happen in *Star Trek* ... like the killing off of a regular character. In this early draft of the script, it wasn't a crewman named Jackson who beams into the transporter room and drops dead. It was Sulu. Of this, Justman told Coon:

Kirk makes a statement that Sulu is dead, but that Jackson and Saunders may still be alive down on the planet. Are we going to bury Sulu? Is this the end of Sulu in the *Star Trek* series? If it isn't, don't you think that we ought to show the audience that Sulu is really alive at the end of our Fourth Act? If there is no way to bring Sulu back to life, then I would suggest using somebody else to get killed in the beginning of our story. (RJ30-2)

Justman also counted too many challenging sets, including the exterior and interior of a castle, with corridors, dungeons, and a "Great Hall." Of this, he told Coon:

The "Great Hall," as established in Scene 47, is not likely to be as great as we would like. (RJ30-3)

Beyond the sets, Justman saw red regarding the various animals, one creeping, others flying, and the animal tricks thereby needed. He wrote:

At the bottom of Page 17, the cat pushes the Castle door open and enters. If the Castle door is as massive as we have been led to believe, that little creature is a mighty strong pussycat.... I've never yet seen a cat that moves from place to place by going exactly "sideways." Of course, with what the cat has to do in this story, it probably would very well be a sideways style, dancing cat.... Please, let's have business with that pussycat only when absolutely necessary. We could spend many days just trying to get what is necessary out of the cat as it is.... If you know anyone who has a couple of swarms of trained bats available for hire, please let me know so that we can tie them up [in casting] for this show. (RJ30-2)

38

Then there was Bloch's tendency to recycle ideas, even if those ideas did not come from one of his own earlier stories. Besides making reference to "the Old Ones," as he had in "What Are Little Girls Made Of?," he also borrowed from Roddenberry and the first *Star Trek* pilot. Justman pointed out:

Sylvia's dialogue in scenes 106 and 109 is so reminiscent of Vina's dialogue in scenes 66B of "The Menagerie" that it is startling. (RJ30-2)

Bloch was allowed to keep the reference to "The Old Ones," but the dialogue in scenes 106 and 109 had to go. His 2nd Draft teleplay was delivered on April 14.

Dorothy Fontana, lobbying for more business for the series' regulars, wrote Coon:

Would like to suggest that instead of Jackson and Saunders, who we don't know from Adam, the members of the landing party left under Sylvia's control be Sulu and Scott.... That way, we make use of regulars who are perfectly good actors.... Also, because Sulu and Scott are so terribly important to us, it gives Kirk even stronger, more personal motivations for getting his men back. (DC30-2)

The one problem this created, as pointed out earlier, was that Kirk puts all the ship's high ranking officers in jeopardy.

The tinkering continued. Justman told Coon:

Why do Kirk, Spock and Doc McCoy so contently approach the heavily-laden table in order to partake of food and drink? Does Korob have them under some terrible spell? Are Jackson and Saunders in the room with them pointing guns at them to make them do whatever Korob wants him to do? Or didn't we leave Jackson and Saunders back out in the Corridor as our trio entered the Great Hall? Why does Kirk do whatever Korob wants him to do? I raised this question before, after reading the first draft of this teleplay. Evidently the question is unanswerable. I hope it isn't unanswerable because Bill Shatner is going to want to know the answer to the question. So is the audience.... The dialogue evolves fond memories of the various horror movies and Abbott and Costello features that I used to see as a kid. (RJ30-2)

Roddenberry agreed, saying:

The dialogue is full of clichés, such as, "Aha, I see I must now persuade you." Too often it is "radio dialogue" which tells us what we are seeing, and generally suffers from a question / answer pacing. The result is neither our own characters nor the villains sound very interesting.... Bob [Bloch] has not succeeded completely in meeting our need that there be a firm and logical scientific basis through the story. Our people should say from the very first that there is a scientific explanation and be actively seeking that explanation all through the story. They should be speculating as to who and what Korob and Sylvia are and should, as the story progresses, begin to make some shrewd guesses. (GR30-2)

Dictating a memo to Coon while he read the script, Justman also found issues with the story's logic, saying:

Well, Korob comes in and frees our humans. And they believe what he tells them and I consider this very gullible.... I am really beginning to feel that this whole story is a big fake. (RJ30-2)

39

Fontana saw fake, too, and told Coon:

Korob's sudden about-face seems unmotivated. Might it not be better if he never wanted to do any of this anyway, but is controlled by Sylvia? In helping our heroes, he is also trying to free himself, but is killed for his effort. (DC30-1)

Roddenberry agreed, writing:

I see absolutely no indication that there is any tension or disagreement between the two which will later lead to each trying to double-cross the other.... Do they have a basic disagreement whether it is moral or even remunerative to invade Earth's galaxy? ... Our audience will buy almost any answer as long as it makes sense and is consistent throughout this script. (GR30-2)

Fontana wrote to Coon:

There are still holes in this piece, Gene, and lack of action, although we do have magic stunts to keep things alive. Suggest we get together with the Great Bird [Roddenberry] and figure out what this story is all about. I get a distinct feeling that the characters are aimless and have no really great reason for doing what they're doing. And I can't find a theme in it. Illusion versus reality and the difference between the two? The merits of one against the other? What? (DCF30-2)

Roddenberry was formulating a new theme for the story, as he pointed out to Coon:

Page 44, Kirk begins to use his masculine charms on Sylvia. Good, at least he is trying <u>something</u>. It could be even logical, i.e., if she has taken on a perfect female human form, perhaps one of the costs of this is inheriting all the female emotions and illogic which go with it. Kirk might indeed try to use this to his advantage. (GR30-2)

These comments, plus some rewriting from the staff, led to a pair of interesting scenes between Korob and Sylvia, creating conflict between the two, but also establishing the story's new theme in examining how pleasure can lead to moral corruption.

In one, Sylvia caresses her own form, and says, "We have none of this... and I like it... to feel, to touch... to understand the idea of luxury. I like it, Korob... and I don't intend to leave it."

Korob reminds her, "We have a duty to the Old Ones."

Sylvia fires back, "What do they know of sensations! This is a new world!"

Korob scolds, "You are cruel. You torture our specimens."

She smugly responds, "That, too, is a sensation. I find it stimulating.... I will squash you, Korob. And that, too, would be an interesting sensation."

The question was who would contribute these yet-to-be-written lines of dialogue? Bloch had not been making the changes already requested. Justman pointed this out, telling Coon:

I am still unable to locate a swarm of trained bats for Scene 28. How about a slightly tattered parakeet? (RJ30-2)

Roddenberry had an answer, writing to Coon:

40

We have here a good action-adventure script, but insofar as having the final level of quality we want in *Star Trek*, it is only slightly improved from the first [draft]. I see little point in sending it back to Bloch for polish and suggest the time it would require with him could be better spent by you or Dorothy putting it into shooting shape. (GR30-2)

Coon handed it off to Story Consultant Dorothy Fontana. She later said, "I didn't do too much to change the characters and certainly not the surprise at the end -- that these little things weren't actually the powerful creatures that we thought they were. But there was a lot of dialogue rewriting." (64-3)

Many of the things Fontana scaled down, or completely removed, involved the cat. Bloch had Kirk, Spock and McCoy first meet the animal outside the castle, as the little rascal pushes the giant door open. Fontana solved a potential production problem by having the door open on its own. Bloch had Sylvia, while in the form of the giant black cat, claw Korob down with a huge paw. Fontana changed this and had Korob retreat behind the heavy dungeon door, which is then knocked down, landing on Korob and pinning him to the floor. And then she tossed out the swarm of bats.

As for the additions, it was in Fontana's draft where the small metallic model of the Enterprise was encased into a clear glass block, thus putting a force-field around the real Enterprise and preventing any further rescue attempts.

The changes Fontana made, in fact, were enough for her name to be added to the title page of the script, right under that of Robert Bloch. But she balked, saying, "I insisted my name be taken *off*, because I didn't feel I had done that much. As I recall, it was Gene Coon who put my name on the script. And I said, '*Don't!*'" (64-1)

Roddenberry got the script next and made cuts of his own, including, unfortunately, a scene that opened Act I in sickbay.

In this deleted scene, McCoy reports to Kirk regarding Jackson's death and says, "There's no sign of an injury; none. No organic damage, internal or external."

Kirk asks, "Then why is Jackson dead?"

McCoy answers, "He froze to death."

Spock counters, "That doesn't seem reasonable, Doctor. The climate on Pyris VII approximates that of Earth's central Western hemisphere during the summer solstice."

McCoy says, "I know that, Spock. But reasonable or unreasonable, Jackson froze to death. He was literally dead on his feet when he materialized in the Transporter Room."

Kirk ponders this, saying, "He was about to speak.... <u>Someone</u> spoke. There seems to be a good deal more to the planet than our sensors have been able to detect! With Scott and Sulu virtually marooned down there…"

Kirk is interrupted by a call from the bridge. Uhura tells him that the sensors no longer register Scott or Sulu and, in fact, indicate no life on the surface at all. Kirk then makes the decision to beam down.

As rewritten, all of this was replaced by a Captain's log voiceover, with Kirk telling us, "I am beaming down to the planet's surface to find my two missing crewmen … and discover what killed Jackson."

Roddenberry also added more sizzle to the hedonistic Sylvia.

It was Coon, during the last of his script polishing, who added the delightful line where Kirk tells Spock he would be a natural for Halloween.

Pre-Production
April 24-28 and May 1, 1967 (6 prep days).

Joseph Pevney was hired to direct. A new Second Season deal had been drafted -- he and Marc Daniels, with only a few exceptions, would alternate as *Star Trek*'s resident directors.

All the primary characters were present for the first voyage of the new season, and Walter Koenig was introduced as Ensign Chekov.

Pevney, who had previously directed Koenig in an episode of *Alfred Hitchcock Presents*, said, "I thought he would be an interesting Russian-type fellow… so I brought him in, and he had a new career. He looks so great. He's got a great face. He has some kind of an interesting accent, but it sure ain't Russian. In any event, who cares?" (141-2)

Antoinette Bower, 35, having a field day as the lustful, sensuous, power-mad Sylvia, was no stranger to TV. She often appeared as strong-willed females and had recently played one on Gene Coon's last series -- *The Wild, Wild West*.

Women's Costumer Andrea Weaver, beginning a two-year stay on *Star Trek* with this episode, as well as Costume Designer Bill Theiss, recalled one of the outfits worn by Antoinette Bower as their favorite from the series. Weaver, only 20 when she joined *Star Trek*, said, "The fabric had little metallic dots in it which reflected the light, so it looked as if it had lights in it. Another one of the advantages of having Bill was his selection of fabrics, because he could create a new look for the lead girl every

Antoinette Bower poses for NBC publicity photo
(Courtesy of Antoinette Bower)

seven days by picking out unique materials. It was the '60s, so all that stuff was available, which isn't available anymore -- all those unusual kind of fabrics." (180a)

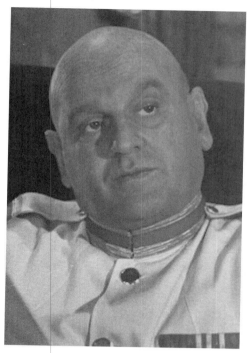

Theodore Marcues, in a 1966 episode of *The Wild, Wild West*

Theodore Marcuse, perfect as Korob, was 47. His menacing looks kept him active in television for 16 years. Typecast as villains and megalomaniacs, he had recently played the commandant of Devil's Island, *twice* during the same year -- 1966 -- for *The Wild, Wild West* and *Time Tunnel*. Marcuse was killed in an automobile accident on November 29, 1967, just one month after "Catspaw" first aired. His final role, another turn on *The Wild, Wild West*, aired a few months later.

Jay "Jimmy" Jones made his first of many appearances on *Star Trek*, even though his character, Crewman Jackson, dies. The fall Jones takes from the transporter platform hints that he was also a stuntman.

"In the first episode I did, 'Catspaw,' I was dead the minute you saw me," Jones said. "They needed an actor who could do his own falls…. My father thought the series was great, but I didn't like science fiction. It wasn't until the

reruns that I realized what a terrific show it was. When I got my 'Catspaw' script, my only line was, 'One to beam up.' I had no idea what that meant. The next day, a neighborhood kid went by on a bicycle. I asked him, 'Do you watch *Star Trek*?' He said, 'Yeah!' I asked, 'Do you know what beam up means?' This kid explained it all to me." (93b)

The next *Star Trek* job for Jones (beyond doubling for James Doohan in "Who Mourns for Adonais?") was just a few weeks away, as Ensign Mallory in "The Apple." He would be "beamed" in that one, as well. He would die there, too.

Jones said, "Gene Roddenberry took a liking to me and the word came down I was to get as much work as I could handle." (93b)

**Walter Koenig and Michael Barrier
(Unaired film trim courtesy of Gerald Gurian)**

43

Michael Barrier was back for the third time as Lt. DeSalle. His other episodes were "The Squire of Gothos" and "This Side of Paradise." This was Barrier's last episode, despite an understanding with Gene Coon that he would continue as a recurring character (see "Production Diary, Day 1, Tuesday").

John Winston, for his fourth of eleven appearances on the series, is seen as Lt. Kyle, the Transporter Chief.

Of the regulars, William Shatner never looked better. After a few months off from *Star Trek*'s grueling schedule, he had slimmed down considerably.

Should you wonder what it cost to build a castle on a soundstage in 1967, the budget, for the construction alone, was set at $9,375. However, since the work was done on a Saturday and Sunday, time-and-a-half pay was required for the union workers. The final cost was $13,416. This did not include set dressing ... merely the building of the interior of a castle. In 2013, that final price tag equates to over $94,000.

Production Diary
Filmed May 2, 3, 4, 5, 8, 9, 10 & 11 (2 day), 1967.
(Planned as 6 day production, running one and a half days over; total cost $217,285)

Filming of the second season began Tuesday, May 2, 1967. Monday had been the Memorial Day holiday in the U.S. ... and was also the day Elvis Presley, at 32, wed 21-year-old Priscilla Beaulieu at the Aladdin Hotel in Las Vegas. Anyone watching TV that night was probably tuned to CBS with their top-rated comedy block of *Gilligan's Island*, *The Lucy Show*, *The Andy Griffith Show*, and *Family Affair*. NBC hoped they were watching *The Monkees*, but, now that the repeat season had begun, Gilligan and the other castaways had the Pre-Fab Four beat. It was a different story in the record stores. *More of the Monkees* was the top-selling album, while Frank Sinatra and daughter Nancy had the song getting the most spins on radio stations – a song called, oddly enough, "Something Stupid." *Thoroughly Modern Millie*, starring Julie Andrews with Mary Tyler Moore, was No. 1 in the movie houses. And the *Star Trek* company returned to Desilu Gower Stage 9 for sequences on the ship's bridge set.

The mood was generally good; all were happy to be back making more *Star Trek*s. The excellent episode "The Naked Time" had repeated the previous Thursday on NBC and, earlier that day, the Emmy nominations were announced. *Star Trek* was up for numerous awards, most notably Best Dramatic Series. As covered in *These Are the Voyages – TOS: Season One*, this had never happened before with a science fiction series.

Despite the good news and exuberant feelings, the seeds of discontent were planted at this time -- one concerning Shatner and Nimoy, the other having to do with Nimoy and the front office.

Days before "Catspaw" commenced production, the latest issue of *TV Guide* featured the "Mr. Spock Is Dreamy" article by Isaac Asimov, making much ado over Nimoy's character and not a word about Shatner's. The media attention had clearly shifted. And now there was buzz concerning Nimoy's upcoming record album release (*Mr. Spock's Music from Outer Space*, scheduled for June), along with scuttlebutt about his contract disputes with Roddenberry and Desilu and the doubling of his salary. With the morning issue of *Daily*

Variety came the news that Nimoy had just been nominated for an Emmy, as Best Supporting Actor, while the series' lead had been ignored by the Academy. William Shatner had good reason to feel his position on the series was being challenged. His instincts as an actor, and a star, would have him fight to secure his personal status and Kirk's dominance in the scripts. Nimoy would feel compelled to compete and fight for his and Spock's place.

Much had changed between Nimoy and the series' writers/producers as well. Despite his recent victory in the contract dispute, or perhaps because of it, Nimoy suspected there was an inclination in the writers' room to diminish Spock's importance in the series. In fact, on this day of filming, with the company's move from the bridge to transporter room set, Spock somehow got lost along the way. And this created a continuity mistake in the episode's Teaser. Jackson is beaming up from the planet; Scott and Sulu are still down there, missing. Kirk and Spock hurry from the bridge on their way to the transporter room. The action in the script reads, "Kirk and Spock practically run for the elevator." Yet, for the next scene, just a few lines away on the same page in the script, the action merely states, "The doors of the Transporter Room snap open and Kirk strides in."

Nimoy later complained that the writers were so focused on Kirk, and so much less on Spock, that some scenes in scripts established both characters entering a room, where Kirk would then do all the talking, Spock would react by arching an eyebrow and, after this, Kirk would leave -- *alone*. The writers, Nimoy said, had forgotten that Spock was even there. It seemed an outrageous accusation. Yet the script for "Catspaw" supports Nimoy's memory and validates his hurt feelings. Coon, Roddenberry, and Fontana, all having a hand in these rewrites, not only dropped the character while en route to the transporter room but failed to catch the mistake. Director Joseph Pevney failed to catch it, too. In defense of the aforementioned writers, producers, and director, Nimoy was given the script ahead of time and, as a provision of his new contract, allowed to give notes. He apparently failed to catch the omission, too … until after the episode was filmed and it was too late to be rectified.

Day 1, Tuesday, was spent on the bridge set. Koenig, enjoying the congenial production crew and fellow performers,

Day 1: The first day back, minus Shatner and Nimoy. DeSalle (Michael Barrier) with Nichelle Nichols (Courtesy of Gerald Gurian)

45

said, "Most of the stuff I had to do was on the bridge. I didn't have a great deal of interaction with the regular cast because they were down on the planet." (102-9)

This day marked the addition of something new to the *Star Trek* bible. We get our first mention of the "credit," the currency used in these galactic times. Lt. DeSalle says it when talking about the chances of penetrating the force field surrounding the Enterprise. His line, "Maybe we *can't* break it, but I'll bet you credits to Navy beans we can put a dent in it." Substitute the word "dollars" for "credits" and you arrive at the old adage coined by early 20th century U.S. sailors, whereby the person making the wager is so confident of winning that he'll gamble valuable dollars against undesirable military grub.

Writer David Gerrold gets credit for coming up with the "credit." It was in his first story outline of Gerrold's "The Trouble with Tribbles" (called "The Fuzzies"), from February, delivered to the *Star Trek* offices in March, and read by Coon while the producer was doing his polish on "Catspaw."

As for DeSalle, he wears a red top instead of the gold/green seen during the first season. Kirk's Captain's log entry establishes that he is now Assistant Chief Engineer, indicating a promotion from helmsman. There was a reason Gene Coon went out of his way to put this line into the script and, accordingly, changed DeSalle's uniform color. With Scott now the third highest ranking officer on the Enterprise -- promoted to Lt. Commander in the series' bible for this new season and being the one to command the bridge in the absence of Kirk and Spock -- Coon decided there was a need for someone to be running engineering on such occasions. DeSalle was given the job and actor Michael Barrier, as reported on this day in the same issue of *Daily Variety* which carried the Emmy nominations, was "signed" for a recurring role. Within weeks, however, as more new scripts came in, it was discovered that

when Scott was left in command, the scripted action always played between the bridge and whatever was happening with Kirk and Spock on the planet ... with no side-trips to engineering needed. DeSalle's promotion did the opposite of what was intended and Barrier abruptly departed the series.

Day 2: Bill McGovern quickly slates the shot as Shatner takes a blast of dirt kicked up by gigantic fans, while Kelley and Nimoy shield their eyes, waiting for the call for "Action!" (Courtesy of Gerald Gurian)

Day 2, Wednesday. Work began on Stage 10 and the exterior surface of Pyris VII, with a camera tie-down for the materialization effect of

46

Kirk, Spock, and McCoy, followed by their encounter with the images of witches reciting "bad poetry," the wind storm, then the sudden appearance of a castle.

The lighting and photography are exceptional throughout this episode, including here, with use of blue gels, smoke machines, and something else -- a new innovation from cinematographer Jerry Finnerman. He later recalled, "Gene said, 'I don't accept all your suggestions, but I think the ones we do -- most of them -- are just great; you are really helping the show.' Like, I had them sprinkle gold and silver flakes over the sand, so, when you put a backlight on it, it would shimmer. And on the rocks, I had them put a lot of sheen, so, when we lit the rocks with a backlight, or a cross-light, they would glimmer. So, I got bolder and bolder." (63-3)

The glimmer is here, in the rocks, showing through the blue-tinged mist. Just turn the brightness level on your TV down until the Star Fleet uniform pants are solid black and you will get an approximation of how *Star Trek* looked in the 1960s. This was before Paramount chose to "improve" its look through video enhancement by changing the contrast levels, resulting in an overly-bright picture, losing much of Jerry Finnerman's richly-textured cinematic quality.

As for the mist flowing over the rocks and around Kirk,

Day 2: McGovern slating the witches (Courtesy of Fred Walder) … and a castle (Courtesy of Gerald Gurian)

47

Spock, and McCoy's feet, Jim Rugg said, "We had a combination of effects. Some of it was steam and some of it was dry ice in hot water which would roll out and cover the floor like ground fog." (147)

All the striking scenes featuring the exterior surface of Pyris VII were shot this day.

Day 3, Thursday. On another part of the Stage 10, Matt Jefferies built an elevated section of the interior of the castle corridor. These scenes were meant to be shot the previous day, but were barely begun. Pevney was falling behind and, as Robert Justman had predicted, much of the blame was put on the black cat.

Even movie cats do not always hiss on cue, nor can they be counted on to run down a corridor in a specific manner just because the camera happens to be rolling. Work continued, slowly, advancing to the point where Kirk, Spock, and McCoy fall through the floor and are then seen lying one level below, out cold, amidst rubble. A later scene where Kirk and Spock climb up from the dungeon through the jagged hole in the floor was also secured.

Filming wrapped early enough for anyone interested to get home and watch "Mudd's Women" repeating on NBC.

Day 4, Friday. Production resumed on a new and temporary location for *Star Trek*, Desilu-Gower Stage 8, for the other perspective of the jagged hole in the corridor floor (previously seen in the ceiling of the dungeon). The corridor outside the dungeon door was filmed here, as well. Then back into the dungeon proper, for the sequences featuring Kirk, Spock, and McCoy shackled to the

Day 4: Filming on Stage 8 for the scenes in the dungeon (Courtesy of Gerald Gurian)

walls and confronted by the zombie-like Scott and Sulu.

In a rare moment on the series, James Doohan reveals that he is missing a finger. When Doohan served in World War II, he was wounded, hit in the chest, leg and right hand (losing his middle finger) by friendly machine gun fire. He recovered from his wounds, but minus the finger. Doohan knew instinctively how to hide the missing digit from the camera and almost succeeds in doing so here, even with his hand prominently raised, as Scotty holds a phaser on Kirk, Spock, and McCoy.

Day 5, Monday. A full half-day behind, Pevney got the last of his shots in the dungeon, with McCoy now being one of the zombies. Next: "The Great Hall," also located on

Stage 8. A detailed metallic miniature of the Enterprise was created by David "Bud" Morton for this episode and used in the filming on this day. There was only one. It was first filmed for the scene where Sylvia dangles it over a candle flame.

Day 6, Tuesday. The entire day was spent filming more scenes set in the Great Hall. The small metal miniature of the Enterprise was seen again, this time encased in a block of Lucite. This miniature was later donated to the Smithsonian National Air and Space Museum by Matt Jefferies, still and forever preserved in that Lucite block.

Day 6. An unaired wide angle shot showing Kirk and Spock sitting before a feast befitting a king (above). In the broadcast version, we only saw close angles; and Antoinette Bower (below)
(Film trim from the Matt Jefferies Collection; courtesy of Gerald Gurian)

Something else that was nice to look at: the villainous Sylvia and the array of sexy outfits she models while attempting to seduce Kirk. Robert Justman had some very definite ideas about the casting of this role when, discussing the script weeks earlier, he wrote to Coon:

> When Sylvia changes her appearance on Page 43, we are going to have to be quite certain that the audience understands that it is

still she and that they can see some definite change. A change in the color of her hair won't affect the people who will watch our show in black and white. We shall have to swap wigs on her, and change her clothes. And, if we are lucky enough to cast a woman with a plenty good build, we should be able to take advantage of her construction in this sequence. Let us reveal some flesh. (RJ30-2)

Production crew member measures the distance from camera to Shatner and Bower for the purpose of selecting a lens (Courtesy of Antoinette Bower)

Day 7, Wednesday. The last of the Great Hall scenes were captured during the morning hours of this unplanned day of production. Everything shot here and now had been meant to happen on the previous day. In the afternoon, also on Stage 8, the miniatures of the dungeon corridors were filmed, as the black cat scurried past, and the blue screen sequences of the cat needed for the matte shots (where it towers over Korob) were taken.

Day 8, Thursday, May 11. Another half day was needed to finish the problematic episode. The cat was not cooperative and many takes were made, and much film exposed, to get the needed prancing and hissing.

Douglas Grindstaff, *Star Trek*'s sound effects man, needing recordings of the cat for the soundtrack, recalled, "I wanted it hissing. I got the trainer [and] we brought in a dog, and shoved the dog at the cat to get him to hiss. The cat put his paws right through the trainer's boots, and right into his skin. He had to pet the cat to get it to release its grip." (76-1)

Pevney, usually good at staying on schedule, as proven with "Arena," fell behind and the filming of "Catspaw" stretched out to seven and a half days. Blamed for many of the delays was that damned cat. The average episode of the series required 36,000 feet of exposed film. With all the specialty shots, including those animal shots, *and retakes of those animal shots*, this first attempt at a reduced budget ate up 45,650 feet, and this too pushed the final cost higher than anyone dreamed it would go.

Post-Production
Available for editing: May 12, 1967.
Rough Cut: May 21. Final Cut: June 6. Music Score recorded on June 21.

Bruce Schoengarth and Edit Team 2 got the first episode of the new season. Schoengarth did the cutting on eight episodes during the first year, starting with "Mudd's

Women" and including classics such as "The Naked Time," "The Squire of Gothos," and "Tomorrow Is Yesterday."

Roddenberry had sent Schoengarth a letter on March 14, 1967, saying:

Dear Bruce: Just in case you hadn't heard, *Star Trek* has been officially renewed for next season by NBC. The slot appears to be 8:30 PM, Friday Nights. Please take this letter as a hearty congratulations for your part in winning the renewal, and also as a warm invitation from Gene Coon, Bob Justman, as well as myself, to rejoin the best Crew in Television when it begins production again. Hopefully, this past season was but the first of many more seasons to come for all of us. Affectionately, Gene Roddenberry.

It was the same letter that Matt Jefferies received from Roddenberry. And the same letter that many on the crew received … with only the name at the top changed.

Shatner with film editor Bruce Schoengarth (orionpressfanzines.com)

The opening title sequence got a makeover, again.

Alexander Courage, who composed the music, recorded it first, as heard in the first nine episodes aired by NBC in 1966. He used an electronic violin to play the melody. Gene Roddenberry didn't care for the sound (which was also prominent in the score for "The Man Trap," also by Courage, and which Roddenberry said was "grating"). Fred Steiner was asked to record a new version of the opening theme, as heard through the remainder of Season One -- action/adventure style, led by a brass arrangement. But now Courage got his theme song back. He said, "I had Loulie Jean Norman, who came in to do the voice, and that was mixed with a muted trumpet and a flute, a vibraphone and an organ. So it was a tremendous mixture of things, and I didn't want any one of them to be predominant. But Gene Roddenberry wanted to hear a lady's voice coming out, you see. So, in dubbing, it came out that you hear Loulie Jean." (37-4)

Roddenberry said, "[Courage] added the human voice, which I thought was brilliant. If anything said 'human,' this said it. This was Circe and Ulysses -- very Earth. The same thing could have been done, I suppose, on any number of electronic devices, but it needed the human touch, the little human imperfection that we have in our voices, that no instrument can quite give us yet." (145-25)

The opening title sequence was now much more invigorating, with added reverb on William Shatner's spoken intro, a new peppier recording of the Alexander Courage theme music, and the Enterprise speeding past camera with a dramatic "whoosh."

Music Editor Robert Raff recalled, "The opening visuals of the ship zipping by in the main credits were originally silent. There were no sound effects; it felt empty. So Gene [Roddenberry] asked the sound effects guys to put in some rocket ship noise. They did, and he wasn't happy with it. The sound didn't quite make it, so he turned to me and asked, 'What can you do?' I said, 'I don't know. Give me a day.' What I ultimately ended up doing was taking an effect called a cymbal shimmer, where a musician will hit the cymbal very softly with a mallet, and it will go 'Ddddjjjjj ...' Laying the cymbal shimmer against the visual image didn't sound unique -- you could realize what it was, and I knew Gene wouldn't buy that. So I took a cymbal shimmer hit, where the musician had struck and then rolled off to diminuendo, and I ran it backwards in the recording room. Then I shaved the impact off, so ultimately we got that 'ffffffssssshhhwwwwt' noise that you hear on the screen now when the little ships run by. In hindsight it looks very easy, but it was an experiment and I was very nervous about it. I didn't know what Gene would say." (143a)

Roddenberry loved it. So would the audience.

Gerald Fried, having impressed Robert Justman greatly with his score for "Shore Leave," received the first music assignment of the new season. Justman had been pushing both Roddenberry and Coon to have Fried return. In a memo dated February 17, 1967, Justman told Roddenberry:

> After seeing and hearing how well Mr. Fried's music works for us, I wish to make the strong recommendation that we have a meeting with Mr. Fried with respect to securing his services to score *Star Trek* next Season... should we be renewed. I cannot say enough about the quality of this man's work. He has enhanced the value of every *Star Trek* show that his music has been used in.

Fried had only scored "Shore Leave," but various pieces of the score had been tracked into other episodes throughout the remainder of the first season to great success.

Like Fried's previous score, the mood in "Catspaw" is often playful. In an interview for this book, Fried recalled, "I remember I used a lot of clarinets because, to me, a cat's paw -- a cat's tread -- is a very clarinety sound." (69-5)

Also in the score: arrangements that are jazzy, then eerie, then melodramatic. It all works, creating a sound in "Catspaw" that is the cat's meow.

Of *Star Trek*, Fried said, "They took it more seriously, and the stories had more substance. There was a quality that I have not experienced too much in movies and television.... They were doing something special and wonderful. So it really wasn't just another TV show.... That kind of infected us, and it was exciting to work on." (69-3)

Fried's energized arrangements set the tempo for much of the music associated with the series' second season. The fanfare heard in accompaniment of the Enterprise, in particular, like the overall feel for Season Two, is bold, jubilant, and invigorating.

Westheimer Company provided the photographic effects and, in this magic show, there were many. The cost: $14,150 (over $99,000 in 2013).

Of the end result for all the hard work from those involved, writer Robert Bloch said, "I do have some quibbles about the way in which things were done. It wasn't their fault, but they just didn't have the budget. 'Catspaw' cried out for the use of opticals in post-production effects. Shooting a cat's face in tight close-up is not exactly any substitute for having a giant cat. Running down a few feet of cardboard corridors isn't the same thing as having your characters trapped in a labyrinth of frightening proportions!" (18-4)

William Shatner concurred, saying, "Unfortunately, due to the usual budgetary restraints, we couldn't afford the necessary optical effects that would have made the [giant] cat seem more realistic and scary. And the heavy black strings used to guide the puppets of alien Sylvia and alien Korob are distinctly noticeable." (156-2)

Indeed, dark colored thread is visible when used to make the alien puppet creatures move. As the creatures die, the strings go lax. This is noticeable now -- not so noticeable in 1967, when television sets were smaller and not in High Definition.

As for Bloch's complaint about the cat running down cardboard corridors, you watch and decide. In this writer's opinion, the matching of the miniature corridors and the full-sized ones seems quite creditable. The trick is effective.

However, budget-wise, the new season was getting off to an alarming start. The studio-mandated per-episode allowance was down to $185,000. The total cost of "Catspaw" was $217,285. This equates to more than $1.5 million in 2013. And this was more than any studio was willing to spend for a TV show in 1967. It was certainly more than Desilu could afford.

One of many shots needing optical effects.
For this, Shatner smashed the glass ball on the end of the wand against the table.
Westheimer then took this section of film and added in the flash of an explosion
(Film trim from Matt Jefferies collection; courtesy of Gerald Gurian)

53

$1.5 million may seem to be a very good budget. In 2013, however, studios spend between $2 and $3 million for an episode of a one-hour drama, the sliding scale depending on the studio, its deal with the network, the genre, and the cast. Taking this into consideration, the *Star Trek* company was being asked to do an awful lot with terribly little. One episode was in the can and *Star Trek* already had a second season deficit of $28,260. This would have to be made up … or else.

Release / Reaction
Premiere air date: 10/27/67. NBC rebroadcast: 5/24/67.

"Catspaw" aired four days before Halloween, 1967. Talking to this author, Dorothy Fontana said, "That was planned all along to be like a Halloween show. When Bob [Bloch] pitched it, we said, 'That's got to be the Halloween show for sure!' I liked it. I thought it was pretty good." (64-3)

Syndicated review, from *TV Key Previews* (October 27, 1967, *The News Journal*, Ohio), read:

> Today's top TV shows are previewed and selected by Steven H. Scheuer and his *TV Key* staff of experts who watch the screenings, attend the rehearsals and analyze the scripts in New York and Hollywood.... "Catspaw." This is a good show for Halloween. On a strange planet, the Enterprise encounters a weird alien pair (played by Antoinette Bower and Theodore Marcuse) who seems to deal in illusions and haunted houses, but are more concerned with controlling the invaders. The character of the girl called Sylvia should particularly appeal to male viewers who would like their girl friends to look a bit different on each date.

TV SCOUT column by Joan Crosby (May 24, 1968 *The Pittsburgh Press*, Pennsylvania; repeat broadcast), read:

> This is a scary show, set on a dying planet with most of its people gone. There are plenty of dungeons, witch types, and other horror show props, including guest star Antoinette Bower, who is very effective as the planet's leader. She is determined to save her race and is equally determined that Captain Kirk should help her.

RATINGS / Nielsen National report for Friday, October 27, 1967:

8:30 to 9 p.m.:		**Audience share:**	**Households:**
NBC:	*Star Trek*	27.6%	11,870,000
ABC:	*Hondo*	25.5%	10,700,000
CBS:	***Gomer Pyle, U.S.M.C.***	**41.8%**	**14,670,000**
Independent stations:		5.1%	**No data**

9 to 9:30 pm:		**Audience share:**	**Households:**
NBC:	*Star Trek*	27.8%	No data
ABC:	*Hondo*	26.9%	No data
CBS:	***Friday Night Movie***	**32.1%**	**No data**
Independent stations:		13.2%	No data

54

"Catspaw" was great fun for the kids on a Friday night just before Halloween. But so was *Gomer Pyle*, and the latter, one of the top-rated shows on TV, easily won its time slot from 8:30 to 9 p.m. This would be the case throughout *Star Trek*'s second season. *Hondo*, ABC's new one-hour western, came in third, also a common occurrence during this year. *Star Trek* almost always fitted in the middle. The movie at 9 p.m. was the 1963 adventure film *Rampage*, starring Robert Mitchum as a man's man on an African safari.

NBC provided little back-end support to *Star Trek* and gave many in the viewing audience a good reason to join Mr. Mitchum in Africa. Back in the days before VCRs and, later, DVRs, you either watched it or you missed it. If you were the head of a family that was spending an evening together around the TV – and most American homes had only one television set at this time -- and you chose *Star Trek*, then you would have to join the movie on CBS already in progress or go to ABC for the start of *The Guns of Will Sonnett*, and be asked to believe that 74-year-old Walter Brennan could be the fastest gun in the West, or stick with NBC. And not many wanted to stick with NBC. According to A.C. Nielsen, out of the 11,870,000 households that tuned in for "Catspaw," only 7,170,000 stayed for what immediately followed -- the unpopular Jerry Van Dyke sitcom, *Accidental Family*. And only 5,880,000 of them stayed for the 10 p.m. show -- the NBC news special "Justice for All," taking a hard look at how most people in America could not afford lawyers. Things were going exactly as the industry experts -- sans NBC execs -- had predicted.

RCA color TV ad featuring *Star Trek*, October 1967

***

The week that "Catspaw" first aired, NBC's parent company, RCA, began running ads in numerous national periodicals using images from *Star Trek* to help promote its new line of color TV sets. *Star Trek* was NBC's most colorful show. It was a match made in an ad man's heaven.

From the Mailbag

Fan letter received shortly before the premiere of the second season:

> Dear Mr. Roddenberry... Your TV show *Star Trek* is great! I know other adjectives but they are over used. I hope you will be able to continue *Star Trek* indefinitely. This show is on our *must watch* list and I even work our social engagements so that I am home on Thursday evenings.... Please continue the intelligent and technical style of this show. It is my pleasure to watch. Thank you.@ Michael U. (Old Westbury, N.Y., July 23, 1967).

The response:

> Dear Mr. U.: Thank you so much for your praise, it means a good deal to us. After all, you, the audience, is what keeps us going. We too hope *Star Trek* will be on the air indefinitely and letters like yours will keep us there. Please note that you will have to start changing social engagements on Friday evenings starting in September, same time and same network, just a different day. Hope you'll stay with us. Sincerely yours, Gene Roddenberry, Executive Producer, *Star Trek*.

A note from an industry insider:

> Dear Gene... I felt compelled to write you this fan letter to tell you how much I've enjoyed *Star Trek*.... I am quite happy you're moving to a new time slot next season. It will ease my conscience about watching *Star Trek* instead of *Bewitched*.... Best wishes for continued success, Regards Dick (Michaels), Screen Gems, Associate Producer, *Bewitched*.

And the response:

> Dear Dick, thank you for your letter. Not only was it good to hear from you but sentiments were most flattering.... Since I'm a *Bewitched* fan, the move to Friday night is enjoyable to me also.... Best to everyone there. Sincerely, Gene Roddenberry.

Letter from Roddenberry to a fan, dated April 7, 1967:

> Dear Mr. Knapp: I was flattered to learn of your interest in the hand phaser used in *Star Trek*. It is difficult to imagine how weapons in the future will be made and used. It is gratifying that this one prop has been believable and interesting to you.... Due to the prohibitive cost of the manufacturing of these guns for actual film use, it is impossible for me to send you one. However, facsimiles of these guns and other *Star Trek* props will be merchandized in the near future so that you will be able to buy them at your local department or toy store for a nominal sum.... Sincerely, Gene Roddenberry, Executive Producer, *Star Trek*.

Memories

Antoinette Bower said, "We spent a lot of time trying to seduce the real cat into coming through the tunnel... and it was a fun job mainly because of the lovely cast -- who obviously had no idea that *Star Trek* would become the huge cult thing it still is." (19a)

4

Episode 31: METAMORPHOSIS
Written by Gene Coon.
Directed by Ralph Senensky.

From *TV Guide*, CLOSE-UP listing, July 13, 1968 issue:

CLOSE-UP

STAR TREK
8:30 ④ ⑳

COLOR The officers of the Enterprise take part in a strange drama born of an alien's love for a human being.

Kirk, Spock and Dr. McCoy are transporting a critically ill woman back to the starship when a shimmering, multicolored cloud draws their shuttlecraft to a remote planetoid.

The sole human inhabitant is Ephram Cochran, who explains that the cloud, which he calls the Companion, saved his life 150 years ago, granted him immortality, and has provided for him ever since. One more fact is chillingly clear: The Companion has kidnaped the officers to provide Cochran with human companions—forever.

This episode won an Emmy nomination for special effects. Script by producer Gene L. Coon. Kirk: William Shatner. Spock: Leonard Nimoy. Dr. McCoy: DeForest Kelley.

Guest Cast

Ephram Cochran ....Glenn Corbett
Nancy Hedford ....Elinor Donahue

William Shatner and Leonard Nimoy

A love story -- pure but not at all simple. The theme and agenda: to expose and then dispel racial prejudice. This is another *Star Trek* that, at first, appears to be a Man-against-Beast tale, but, as we discover, is all about a man pitted against himself. Zefram Cochrane (the correct spelling), an ambitious man who lived for science and then traveled into space to die alone, must overcome his own rigid thinking and prejudice if he is to finally experience true love.

SOUND BITES

- *Cochrane:* "All the comforts of home. I could even offer you a hot bath." *Nancy Hedford:* "How perceptive of you to notice that I needed one."
- *Kirk:* "Zefram Cochrane died a hundred and fifty years ago!" *Spock:* "True, his body was never found …" *Cochrane:* "You're looking at it, Mr. Spock."
- *McCoy:* "Why, a blind man could see it with a cane; you're not a pet, you're not a specimen kept in a cage -- you're a *lover*." *Kirk:* "Isn't it evident? Everything she does is for you -- provides for you; feeds you; clothes you; brings you companions when you're lonely." *Cochrane:* "Is this what the future holds? Men with no notion of decency or

morality? Well, I may be a 150 years out of style, but I'm not going to be the fodder for any inhuman monster." *Spock:* "Fascinating -- a totally parochial attitude."

ASSESSMENT

"Metamorphosis" is not driven by action or accented with humor and, therefore, may not jump to mind for many fans compiling a Top 10 list of favorite *Star Trek* episodes. Yet all the elements -- purposeful writing, sensitive acting, inspired direction, stylistic camera work, lighting and set design -- combine in tasteful harmony. This gentle, heartwarming tale is certainly among the series' best.

During Season One, Gene Coon, under pressure from NBC, had a hand in writing the heart out of "The Alternative Factor," a script gutted by the removal of an interracial love story. The architects of *Star Trek*, with that episode, and by showcasing a sexual attraction between a white man and a black woman, had forgotten the first rule in imitating the works of Jonathan Swift -- to comment on the hot issues of the day by staging them in a time and place, and in a way, which was alien to conventional man's thinking. Only then could taboo subjects be broached. Now, six months older and wiser, Coon took a page from Swift for this approach to a truly mixed romance.

Through the course of the story, we meet three unforgettable characters: the lonely Zefram Cochrane; the "unloved" Nancy Hedford; and The Companion, a diaphanous cloud that encircles and protects Cochrane. The surprise is that The Companion is female and it loves the man. All three characters affect Kirk, Spock, and McCoy profoundly. This delicate story, about unselfish and pure love, will touch your heart.

THE STORY BEHIND THE STORY

Script Timeline
Gene Coon's story outline, ST #59: April 7, 1967.
Coon's 1ˢᵗ Draft teleplay: April 14, 1967.
Coon's 2ⁿᵈ Draft (Mimeo Department "Yellow Cover 1ˢᵗ Draft"): April 19, 1967.
Coon's Final Draft teleplay: April 21, 1967.
Coon's Revised Final Draft teleplay: May 3, 1967.
Additional page revisions by Coon: May 8, 12, 13 & 17.

"Metamorphosis" was Gene Coon's fourth original screenplay for *Star Trek*. As with the others, "Arena," "The Devil in the Dark," and "Errand of Mercy," there is a strong message, fused with a powerful and imaginative science fiction story. In the previous episodes, the theme had to do with man overcoming racism. That theme is present here too, but this time Coon delivers his statement with a sentimental touch.

"It was really a lovely story and a very touching one," said Dorothy Fontana. "I think Gene did it with great deftness and delicacy." (64-11)

Coon finished his story outline on April 7, 1967, nearly a month before production was due to resume on the series for its second season. A few days later, Robert Justman wrote to Coon:

> I have read "Metamorphosis" and I like it very much. Naturally, it is not an action piece, but if you can think of anything to get some action into it, it wouldn't hurt. It wouldn't help, but it wouldn't hurt. (RJ31)

Stan Robertson at NBC also liked "Metamorphosis," telling Coon:

> This is a fine storyline which has the potential of being developed into a very

successful screenplay for our series. (SR31-1)

But, as Justman predicted, Robertson was concerned over the lack of physical excitement in the story. And the network man had another concern, which he discussed with Coon one day earlier on the telephone. He now wrote:

> As we agreed, rather than becoming involved in what could be a touchy moral argument and a question of religious ethics, you will <u>not</u> have the Companion take over the body of Nancy after the latter's death. Instead, prior to Nancy's death, while she is still ill, you will have the Companion "merge" with Nancy and become part of her and the life she will lead with Cochrane. (SR31-1)

This change, Robertson believed, would prevent offending certain religious groups.

Coon dashed off a 1st Draft script, dated April 14, 1967. Addressing Robertson's concerns about a need for more action, he had The Companion deliver an electrical shock to Scotty outside the shuttlecraft (later to be changed to Mr. Spock). Also, when Kirk, Spock and, for this version, Scotty, attempt to "short out" the creature, she retaliates and attacks, subjecting them to near suffocation.

The universal translator finally makes an appearance in *Star Trek*. The device had always been planned. Roddenberry, Justman, and Coon were well aware of how reality was suspended whenever aliens spoke English. But, for the benefit of the TV audience, for the sake of telling a story simply, and to the liking of NBC and its advertisers, aliens, such as those seen in "The Return of the Archons" and "A Taste of Armageddon," spoke as contemporary Americans would. In The Companion's case, with a creature lacking vocal cords, the translator seemed a suitable solution. Coon even had a theory as to how it could work. Explaining the device to Cochrane, Kirk says, "There are certain universal ideas and concepts common to all intelligent life. This device instantaneously compares the frequency of brain wave patterns, selects those ideas and concepts it recognizes, and provides the necessary grammar."

Pete Sloman, at De Forest Research, argued against Coon using the device. In an interview for this book, Sloman said, "They tried a lot harder at *Star Trek* than they did at *Lost in Space* and some of those other shows to get the science right. But if there was ever a conflict between drama and science, drama won. And I understand why it has to be that way, because you're not getting an audience of particle physicists. You're getting an audience of 'everybody out there,' and *they* have to understand what's going on. And even in good science fiction, you have to do science that later turns out to be wrong. But there were some times when they just had to have a particular thing happening. My biggest gripe about any science fiction gadget on the entire show was the universal translator. It's impossible. There is no way to explain it unless the device itself is telepathic. It just cannot work." (158a)

But Coon could not have told his story without it. Sloman added, "Gene Coon gave me a statement which epitomized what I personally found annoying about science fiction on television, including *Star Trek*. But I understood why he did it. I'd called him up and said, 'Gene, we're two hundred and thirty years, or whatever it is, in the future at this point. Don't you think the metric system may have taken over by then? But you're still using pounds.' And he said, 'Pete, we don't want it to be authentic. We want it to *sound* authentic.' That's it. And, despite that, I met a lot of scientists and engineers who loved the show, even though they knew it was wrong." (158a)

After getting feedback from his colleagues, and ignoring some from De Forest Research, Coon revised his script with a 2nd Draft, dated a mere five days after his 1st Draft, and a Final Draft coming just two days after that.

Fontana read the latest version and told her boss:

> May I suggest Jim Doohan's going to get very sick of being zotzed? This is the third property we have with this incident in it, albeit it is the first we will shoot. The other two are, of course, "The Changeling" and "Who Mourns for Adonais?" If we can't change this, let's consider changing that point in the other stories. (DC31)

Coon liked how Scotty got "zotzed" in the other two stories so he made a change here, having Spock take the voltage instead. He went one step further and took Scotty out of the shuttlecraft and off the planetoid altogether, putting him back on the Enterprise, commanding the bridge in Kirk's absence.

Other changes:

- The shuttlecraft, which had been called the Edison, was now the Galileo, allowing for recycled footage to be used from "The Galileo Seven."
- Commissioner Hedford, in previous drafts, didn't become sick until after the shuttlecraft was forced down on the planetoid. Now, creating a much more effective ticking clock, her illness serves as a catalyst for the story -- the reason the shuttlecraft is racing to reach the Enterprise in the first place.
- Cochrane is played cooler. In previous drafts, when learning about The Companion's gender and her love of him, he had reacted far more dramatically, even melodramatically. He flew into a rage, threw rocks, and even attacked The Companion with a club. This tantrum had ended Act III. The merging of Nancy Hedford and The Companion didn't happen until nearly the end of the story. Now, it is the merging of these two which ends Act III -- a far more sensitive handling of the story. This sensitivity extends into the new Act IV, as Cochrane struggles with his prejudice and comes to terms with his own feelings and his love for this alien.

As it had happened with "The Devil in the Dark" and "Errand of Mercy," no one else on staff, other than giving feedback, was involved in the writing of the script. Fontana said, "Gene was producing, so nobody really touched the script. Gene Roddenberry had a say, but whatever changes they decided to do, he [Coon] did them himself." (64-3)

As things turned out, NBC should have been happy. Throughout the first season, Stan Robertson had been asking for different types of action/adventure stories -- planet shows, atypical shows, important shows, shows with name guest stars, and shows that began with something/anything other than a shot of the Enterprise in space. He got all of these with "Metamorphosis." Of the latter request, the Enterprise isn't seen until 27 minutes into the episode, the only time the ship is absent for this long in the series. But Robertson was not entirely pleased (see "Release / Reaction").

Pre-Production
May 2-5 and May 8-10, 1967 (7 days prep).

Ralph Senensky, having directed the excellent "This Side of Paradise" in Season One, returned for his second *Star Trek* assignment. Regarding the script for "Metamorphosis," he said, "It was written by the incomparable Gene Coon and was spooky and eerie and had a potent message. I was really anxious to make this voyage." (155-5)

Regarding Stan Robertson's desire for "name" guest stars, now he would get two.

Glenn Corbett, cast as Zefram Cochrane, was 37. He gained stardom when hired to replace George Maharis on the popular CBS series, *Route 66*. As Lincoln "Linc" Case, Corbett sat in the passenger seat of a Corvette next to Martin Milner during the series' final year-and-a-half. Ralph Senensky knew Corbett from that series, having directed a couple of episodes. *Route 66* was actually Corbett's second series -- he was the lead in a short-lived NBC sitcom *It's a Man's World*, from 1962-63. His third series, which ran for one season, a year before this episode of *Star Trek*, had Corbett saddling up as part of an ensemble cast in the hour-long western, *The Road West*.

Director Ralph Senensky (Courtesy of Ralph Senensky)

"I had no trouble getting actors interested," casting director Joe D'Agosta said. "*Star Trek* offered them interesting roles. But our casting budgets were low, with a $2,500 top -- *one* $2,500 top, not two. So I'd try making the two or three picture deal and put them in a *Mission: Impossible* or a *Mannix*. It worked sometimes, but not with all actors. So I'd have to beg the production manager to pull money out of the sets so that I could afford to hire certain actors, or I'd have nothing left for 10 or 20 smaller parts I had to fill." (43-4)

Fortunately, this episode didn't have those 10 or 20 smaller parts, so D'Agosta was able to

Martin Milner and Glenn Corbett, Filming *Route 66*

budget $2,500 each for two top guest stars. It was the casting of the second star, to play Assistant Federation Commissioner Nancy Hedford, that would raise a few eyebrows.

Elinor Donahue was 30 and best known for playing extremely likable and youthful characters on TV sitcoms. She was only 17 when she first played Betty Anderson in 1954 on TV's *Father Knows Best*. That job lasted five years and 192 episodes. Next, she moved to *The Andy Griffith Show*, as Ellie Walker, the girlfriend of Sheriff Andy Taylor, during 1960 and 1961. A third sitcom, *Many Happy Returns*, which ran from 1965 through 1966, had her playing the daughter of series lead John McGiver. Choosing Donahue for the role of a dying and bitter woman was a stunt referred to in the entertainment business as "casting against type."

When the idea of hiring Donahue for "Metamorphosis" came up during a meeting between Gene Coon, Ralph Senensky, and Joe D'Agosta, it was decided to bring forward *Star Trek*'s big gun to sell the idea to

Jane Wyatt and Elinor Donahue, of *Father Knows Best*, on the cover of *TV Guide*, January 1960

the actress. Donahue was married to Harry Ackerman, former Vice-President of CBS and, at this time, Head of Production for Screen Gems, the No. 1 supplier of situation comedies to the three networks. Roddenberry had worked for Screen Gems, making pilot films in the late 1950s and early 1960s. So, instead of casting director D'Agosta, he would be the messenger.

Donahue said, "Mr. Roddenberry called and asked if I would be interested in doing a role in *Star Trek*, and he explained to me what it was because I wasn't familiar with the show. He described the character to me and I said, 'That would be fun.' I was pretty much retired then, because I was having babies. It seemed like every year I'd do just one fun 'something,' and *Star Trek* was the one for that year. And it *was* fun. I'd never played two characters at once [Commissioner Hedford and The Companion], and it was probably the first time I had the opportunity to play someone who was a little brusque and uptight, and angry, as Commissioner Hedford was." (50)

Casting against type is a gamble that fails nearly as often as it succeeds, which is why the *Star Trek* staff felt it would take a small miracle, or a phone call from Roddenberry, bypassing Donahue's agent, to overcome any resistance.

When Donahue received the script, she knew she had made the right decision. She later said, "The script was just beautiful. Wonderful statements being made." (50)

Production Diary
Filmed May 11 (2 day), 12, 15, 16, 17, 18 & 19 (2 day), 1967.
(6 day production; total cost: $198,493)

The week "Metamorphosis" began filming, the United States bombed the North Vietnam capitol of Hanoi. The top movie in America was an Italian import -- the spaghetti

Kelley purposely blows a line to get a reaction out of Shatner.
Note Nimoy, to the right, losing it (Courtesy of Gerald Gurian)

western *For a Few Dollars More*, starring Clint Eastwood. The title song to the movie *The Happening*, performed by the Supremes, was the most-played record on U.S. radio stations. Runner up: "Sweet Soul Music" by Arthur Conley. The top-selling album in stores was still *More of the Monkees*, keeping *The Mamas and the Papas Deliver* and *The Best of the Lovin' Spoonful* out of the No. 1 spot on *Billboard*. The most popular Wednesday night TV series, playing as the *Star Trek* cast studied their scripts for the next day, included the CBS comedy block of *Green Acres*, *The Beverly Hillbillies,* and *Gomer Pyle, U.S.M.C.* (the latter of which *Star Trek* would be going up against in the fall when it too would move to Friday nights). *I Spy* was NBC's best bet of the night, and was given a CLOSE-UP listing in *TV Guide* for "Sophia," an episode filmed in Italy. Jack Webb and Harry Morgan had the cover of *TV Guide*, and an article about *Dragnet 1967* (which followed *Star Trek* on NBC each Thursday night). The magazine cost 15 cents. A quarter would buy you a gallon of gas. A loaf of Wonder Bread was double that amount.

Filming began after the wrap of "Catspaw" and a lunch break, on Thursday, May 11, 1967, on Stage 10. First up: all the scenes outside the shuttlecraft, including meeting Cochrane, the scene where Spock is attacked and given an electrical shock by The Companion and, later, McCoy coming to Spock's aid.

Nearly the entire episode was shot on Stage 10 -- *Star Trek*'s planet stage, which also housed the shuttlecraft. After the wide open spaces Ralph Senensky had enjoyed with "This Side of Paradise," he now had to rely on his own inventiveness and that of cinematographer

Jerry Finnerman to overcome the confinement of the stage. Note the camera views of Glenn Corbett through a hole in a rock formation as he approaches the shuttlecraft. This clever shot was necessary to conceal the limitations of the stage walls.

Matt Jefferies said, "False perspective was used to create an illusion of distance.... To achieve the effect of distance, you've also got to have something up close as a comparison. You get something that will cut your shot, that's close to the camera, then you've magnified the distance to the far end." (91-11)

There was a reason why that "something up close as a comparison" was a hole in a rock formation. Senensky said, "Otherwise we were shooting off the set. The set was just not high enough. It was the only way, and that was Jerry Finnerman's contribution. I was still learning about cameras and the nine millimeter [lens] was a new weapon." (155-3)

The nine millimeter, also known as the wide angle lens, made a small area look much larger. But when shooting on Stage 10, every solution brought about new problems. Senensky explained, "It's very interesting that [the editors] don't stay on that shot too long, when he runs toward camera, because it would have looked like he had on those magic boots with which you can take a step and every step is a mile. He covers that huge distance in about five strides." (155-3)

"The other thing [when getting a false perspective] is they had to keep the camera at normal eyeball height," Matt Jefferies added. Referring to one experience on *Star Trek*, perhaps not this one, Jefferies said, "I went up there one day and they had the camera on a cart on top of a six-foot platform. I said, 'Fellas, we're not going to get any distance. You've turned the set into a little sand pit.' They said, 'No, it's going to be fine.' I said, 'OK, I'm going to stand here until you move the camera. You can either pick me up and move me, or call Justman or Roddenberry.' They finally moved it. Otherwise the whole idea of perspective was just gone. You can make that 150, 170 feet look like 10 miles shooting long, but unless you're shooting a point of view of somebody up on a rock, you've got no reason to be high up." (91-11)

After production wrapped for the day, the Hugo award-nominated episode "The Corbomite Maneuver" had its second airing on NBC.

Day 2, Friday, May 12 -- the first full day of production. The company moved to Stage 9 but, for the first half of the day, shot something other than the Enterprise sets. Only the bridge was needed for this episode, so other ship sets were collapsed to make room for the interior of the shuttlecraft, moved here from Stage 10, which then allowed for a larger area of that stage to be used for the planetoid sets. The interior shuttlecraft scenes were filmed on this morning, comprising the show's Teaser and first moments of Act 1.

After the lunch break, Shatner, Nimoy, Kelley, and Donahue were dismissed and series regulars James Doohan, George Takei, Nichelle Nichols, Eddie Paskey, and Bill Blackburn, along with several extras, manned the bridge. This was the first episode of the series where Kirk is never seen on the Enterprise.

Days 3 and 4, Monday and Tuesday. The majority of the scenes inside Cochrane's house were filmed.

Elinor Donahue quickly learned that doing anything for the first time could be immensely challenging. Concerning her character, she said, "The opening scenes, where she was tough and liberated, were very hard for me." (50-3)

Day 4, filming The Companion's attack on Kirk and Spock
(Courtesy of Gerald Gurian)

Particularly hard on these days were the scenes in which her character has an emotional breakdown. The actress had played emotionally-charged scenes before, as a sometimes desperately emotional teenager on *Father Knows Best*, and began to approach her performance here in the same way. She later admitted, "I remember we were doing the crying scene and I had really worked myself into a dither so I could *really* cry. Shatner whispered in my ear and said, 'You know, you don't have to put yourself through all of this. You can just act a little bit; you don't really have to cry.' And he was absolutely right. You don't have to get yourself all in a froth. On stage, perhaps you need to cry those tears, but on television, where they are doing many different angles,

Day 5. One half-day behind, trying to finish in Cochrane's house
(Courtesy of Gerald Gurian)

you've got to keep it going for a really long time. Once you've stepped in those waters, so to speak, you're in it up to your hips." (50)

Day 5, Wednesday. Senensky was running late. The morning hours were spent finishing the scenes inside Cochrane's house which had been planned for the day before. Throughout the afternoon, the scenes outside Cochrane's house were filmed.

Regarding the scene where Kirk speaks to The Companion, Donahue recalled, "They made sure that I knew my voice was *not* going to be that of the entity. But something which was truly fun was I got to do the dialogue with Mr. Shatner while they were filming his scene where he was talking to it. I stood on a ladder so he could look up at me and I did the dialogue with him. I had learned a long time ago from Robert Young and Jane Wyatt to stay on set for that. They were there all the time to do the 'off camera dialogue' with us. They were very specific about that. They never walked away. So they taught me." (50)

Among the fine performances, including those of Glenn Corbett and Elinor Donahue, that of William Shatner must also be cited. Watch as he pleads his case with The Companion, expressing his beliefs concerning human needs and the love between a man and a woman. The excellent wording came from Gene Coon. The delivery is pure Shatner. Ralph Senensky remembered, "Bill Shatner was a fine actor. The day that he did the scene where he talked to The Companion with the translator, and, after the take, Gene Coon, in the screening room said, 'That's why we pay him the big money.'" (155-6)

Matt Jefferies sketch of Cochrane's hut
(Matt Jefferies Collection; courtesy of Gerald Gurian)

Day 5. Cochrane summons The Companion
(Unaired film trim courtesy of Gerald Gurian)

"No one could have done Kirk the way Bill did," said George Takei. "His energy, his vitality, his passion, and his supreme self-confidence -- that's Bill, and that's Captain Kirk." (171-3)

Of the structure, designer Matt Jefferies said, "The idea was based on a 1927 or '28 filling station in Burbank. I found it in the AAA magazine. I liked those crazy outriggers on it. I wanted something that was different, and we got away with this because we didn't have an entrance or an exit to put up with. It was a terrible cheat, but it worked." (91-11)

Elinor Donahue had stepped into a strange new world. The set designs and lighting techniques certainly contributed to putting her on unfamiliar ground, but her greatest memories came from interacting with the *Star Trek* regulars. She said, "All the actors were absolutely terrific toward me. Leonard was a little on the distant side, but I think that was more the character he was playing and him trying to stay in that frame of mind. So he wasn't real friendly, but the crew -- Doc and all those others -- they were just darling -- except for Mr. Shatner. He was a little off with me from the get-go. It felt as though he was looking down at me, as if I wasn't quite up to snuff. And maybe I wasn't. I don't think personally that I was the world's greatest actress. But they wanted me and there I was." (50)

Shatner had been a serious actor of the stage, and the star of a somber and message-heavy series called *For the People*, and Elinor Donahue was, simply put, from the world of sitcoms. "Metamorphosis" was an excellent script filled with subtle themes that Shatner had fair reason to believe Donahue would not be able to achieve.

Donahue remembered, "At the table reading, I didn't pronounce Glenn Corbett's character's name correctly and Shatner got very upset about that. Finally, the director said, 'Will you just knock it off! Leave the young lady alone. Just leave her be.' He really told Shatner off. And he did stop after that." (50)

Glenn Corbett between takes (Courtesy of Kipp Teague)

Day 6, Thursday, May 18, 1967. Cochrane's house was removed and the area around it redressed to represent the opposite direction, looking away from the house -- the scenes where Cochrane communes with The Companion.

The planet area, built into only one corner of Stage 10, proved sufficient when only a few scenes from an episode were being shot. But "Metamorphosis" required over 50 minutes of edited film, and 50 pages of story, to be covered against that one corner. And Senensky had to shoot everything in only one direction -- toward the same two stage walls.

"They had to move everything in and out,@ he said. "One day they would set up the shuttlecraft in that direction. Then they had the house in that direction, and I had to shoot all of that. When they did the reverse -- the shooting away from the house -- they had to take the house out and redress the set. In the scene where Kirk and Spock stand and watch Cochrane having his meeting with The Companion, it's all the same site." (155-3)

Matt Jefferies said, "There would be four different set-ups around the edge of that stage gunning into that corner. They would shoot the first one, then move to the next one, and then the next one. Then we'd begin to shift the first one around, change it a little bit and we could bring them right back to it again. That was one reason, especially with the planet set, I spent damn near all of my time on the stage because we couldn't pre-program this stuff; we just had to do it by eyeball and shift it around." (91-11)

Even with the limitations of filming on a cramped soundstage, "Metamorphosis" benefits from the indoor surroundings. The mood of this episode is enhanced through the beautiful lighting, with hues of purple and orange splashed on the panoramic background.

Senensky fondly recalled, "That purple sky is miraculous, and the clouds. Jerry [Finnerman] was a master. And you don't find that today. Because, back then, the art of cinematography wasn't written down in books; it was taught from master to master." (155-6)

Finnerman said, "It was just a matter of reading.... I'd read the script and then come to the conclusion of whether it was a love story or if it was a story about evil, and then I'd go from there. I'd pick my colors; I'd never ask the producers, and they gave me omnipotence to do anything I wanted." (63-3)

Senensky added, "Jerry Finnerman also contributed another effect to the set. He thought our sky should have clouds, so when we were ready to film, the doors to the soundstage were closed, the fans were turned off, every person was instructed to stand perfectly still, there could be NO movement. The special effects people then came in with their bee smokers and wafted smoke up above the trees. Presto -- we had clouds. It's a beautiful effect that added to the reality." (155-5)

After the beautiful effect, and the wrap for the day, at 8:30 p.m., the Hugo award-winning episode "The Menagerie, Part 1" had its NBC encore airing.

Day 7, Friday, May 19. A final half-day of shooting (for a total of six, since the production began at the halfway mark on its first day) finished with the scene on the knoll where Cochrane talks with the merged entity which is now Hedford *and* The Companion.

Donahue, at the time, still fighting the acting habits which traced back to *Father Knows Best*, recalled, "I think the thing that made it quite so good was the cinematographer -- Jerry Finnerman. As I was coming out of makeup and hair touchups, he started to walk alongside of me and he said, 'I want to tell you something, I've lit you perfectly. You put your head in this spot when you sit down there, and don't move your head. You have this tendency to bob your head around' -- which I do – and he said, 'If you move one inch, I'll break your arm.' He said it in that kind of 'nice guy way'; kidding, but at the same time serious -- I could *not* move." (50)

The acting tip came while shooting the climactic moment in the episode where the human and The Companion had merged. Donahue recalled, "When I commenced to do the speech, I realized in not moving, I was feeling more. My bad habit of the past was, instead of letting the emotion coming out, I would try to show the emotion and I'd move around too much. But this time I just sat there, and it just happened. And I think we did it in one take. Now I could be mistaken, but I remember them doing a print of the first take and then moving in for a close up, and we did maybe one or two of those. There was a camera glitch or I flubbed a line or something, so we did a couple of those, but it didn't take very long to do my direction, then we did the over shoulder toward Glenn. It was interesting when I saw it, because I learned a valuable lesson, which I would always try to use down the road when I was doing anything similar to that, where I had to make a speech, and that was that it was really, really important to keep still. I was very grateful to him." (50)

Ralph Senensky said, "I thought Elinor Donahue did a fine job. I think the last scene she does with Glenn, she was just lovely in it." (155-6)

Elinor Donahue remembered the mood on the set as being "lovely, very warm and comfortable." She said, "Shatner got nicer, and I actually got invited to the infamous barbeque where he would have barbeque lunch. It was him, Doc, and Spock. They had like a man's man get-together -- a special private lunch out behind the soundstage. I don't know who he was who prepared the food -- somebody's helper or a wardrobe guy, or something, and he had this hibachi and they would fix lunch on this hibachi, and I got invited to go. A big honor." (50)

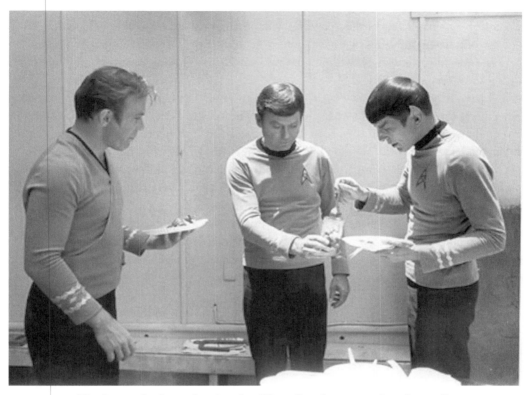

The famous barbeque lunches that Elinor Donahue remembered so well
(Courtesy of Gerald Gurian)

Senensky was taken by both of his guest stars, saying, "I'd worked with Glenn on *Route 66*. I'd directed him in the two-part episode which introduced his character, and he was good in that, but he's better on *Star Trek*. Looking back at the show now, I can see that he was a better actor than I realized at the time that we were doing it. At that time, I knew he was good. But now I look at it and I can see that it was better than good. He had a nice personality and was very professional." (155-6)

Donahue said of Corbett, "He was extremely nice. We enjoyed doing our scenes together; he was wonderful. The scene that we did where I was leaning up against the tree was probably one of the most memorable ones that I did with him." (50)

Senensky finished on schedule, at 1 p.m. on the seventh day. After the lunch break, Joseph Pevney took over the company for a move to Stage 9 and commencement of production on "Friday's Child."

Post-Production
Available for editing: May 12, 1967. Rough Cut: May 31. Final Cut: June 8.
Music Score recorded on June 28, 1967.

The final role cast in "Metamorphosis" came after principal photography ended. That part went to Elizabeth Rogers, who provided the voice of The Companion. The 33-year-old had been playing minor parts for producer Irwin Allen on his various series, as well as numerous voiceover jobs.

69

Elizabeth Rogers said, "As I recall, Majel Barrett was supposed to do the voice but was unavailable. I was a last-minute replacement." (145c)

Ralph Senensky said, "I remember the voice of The Companion, which was originally very metallic and seemed unreal, with no emotion and no feeling, which didn't work. I worked with an actress who had done voiceovers and what we found was a cadence where she would speak slowly, with not too much inflection. I think it works and I love the way the show came out." (155-2)

Rogers returned to *Star Trek*, to be seen on camera, as Lt. Palmer, Uhura's infrequent replacement, for "The Doomsday Machine" and "The Way to Eden."

James Ballas and Editing Team #3 had their hands full with this job. Coon's script ran long and a great deal of snipping had to be done. Most of the trims helped. There were lines of dialogue, especially regarding Commissioner Hedford's illness and her displeasure over being taken away from her diplomatic assignment, which were redundant. With all her complaining, if not for some of the cuts, the character would have come off less likable. But one section of cut dialogue resulted in losing useful information concerning the origin of The Companion and why the entity could not leave the planetoid for more than "a tiny march of days." In the script, but not on the screen, Spock tells Kirk, "There is no doubt that this planetoid, indeed, this entire asteroid belt, are what remains of a planet, probably one with a highly advanced civilization."

Cochrane adds, "Spock could be right. I've found some artifacts. I couldn't identify their purpose, but they were definitely manufactured by an intelligence."

Spock continues, "One can deduce that the creature outside, Mr. Cochrane's Companion, may possibly be the last survivor of this long dead culture."

The Westheimer Company created The Companion. The shots of the shuttlecraft were reused from "The Galileo Seven," with Westheimer adding in the alien entity and new star backgrounds. Richard Edlund was the actual designer of The Companion. A decade after this, he would win an Oscar for his work on *Star Wars*.

Also effective, the colors selected for the planetoid as seen from space, matching the beautiful hues already established by Jerry Finnerman on Stage 10. Joe Westheimer and his team did more than match the color of Finnerman's skies; they also paid close attention to a scarf Ralph Senensky had Elinor Donahue hold up and gaze through.

Senensky recalled, "I needed something to get into the scene between Cochrane and Nancy. I decided I would have this cloud, recently turned into a human, look and marvel at the scarf Nancy had in her possession. I admit, not knowing at the time what The Companion was going to look like, that I had no further motivation in my choice of this action. That the vision of him through the scarf was as she was used to seeing him when she was a cloud at that point had no significance to me. As it turned out, it was an added unforeseen bonus." (155-5)

It is likely that Richard Edlund, after viewing the footage of Glenn Corbett as shot through the scarf, used this as his inspiration for the colors seen in The Companion. Senensky wasn't so sure, saying, "One day, walking back to the office after a screening of the completed film, Gene Coon said to me he was just amazed; how did I know to have the scarf and The Companion look alike? And I had to admit it was just one of those freak wonderful accidents that can happen. Now, from the vantage point of 43 years later, I can wonder when did the lab start working on the effect for The Companion. We didn't shoot the Cochrane-Nancy scene until the final day; in fact, I think it was the last scene to be filmed. Did the lab start work on The Companion before or after that sequence was in the can? Did they see that scene before or after? … But who cares! It worked!" (155-5)

Regarding the scarf held by Elinor Donahue, director Ralph Senensky said, "As it turned out, it was an added unforeseen bonus."
(CBS Studios, Inc.)

There was one more magic element to be added to "Metamorphosis" -- the music.

George Duning began his association with *Star Trek* with the scoring of this episode. Justman hired Duning on the strength of his numerous romantic film scores, including 1957's *Picnic* and 1953's *From Here to Eternity*. Duning received two of his five Oscar nominations for those films.

Duning said, "I was still working at Columbia Pictures as a contract composer, and Robert Justman had become one of my fans through my motion picture scores. He called and asked whether they could borrow me occasionally to do *Star Trek*s, which were also a lot of fun." (55-2)

Justman said, "George Duning was a particular favorite of mine. I had heard his music and I was knowledgeable enough about music to know that when you wanted something emotional, you couldn't do any better than George Duning. He was most surprising to me because he was so down to earth and so kind, and so ready and willing to do whatever was asked of him. He did an exquisite job on 'Metamorphosis.'" (94-9)

Interviewed by Allan Asherman, Duning said, "I would run the picture, say, nine o'clock in the morning, we'd have one screening and then they'd turn it over to me and my music editor. We'd stop the picture, he would start timing the cues on his moviola in his cutting room and I would go to my office and start working out the ideas for the music. By the end of the day I was already getting timing cues so that I could start writing the actual cues. That's the way it is in television. Never enough time, really." (55-2)

Despite keeping the production down to six days (spread over seven, with midday start and wrap times), "Metamorphosis" ended up costing $198,493 (just under $1.4 million in 2013). The studio mandated budget of $185,000 per episode was looking to be unrealistic.

With the first two episodes of the new season having gone over budget, *Star Trek* now had a deficit of $45,708. Desilu was expecting some future episodes to cost less to compensate for this overspending.

Release / Reaction
Premiere air date: 11/10/67. NBC rebroadcast: 7/19/68.

NBC did not want the atypical "Metamorphosis" to be programmed too early into the new season, in a time slot the network expected would be more kid-friendly. On June 21, 1967, Stanley Robertson wrote to Gene Roddenberry:

> Our feeling's that neither "Metamorphosis" nor "Catspaw" should be scheduled as one of the four or five programs to begin our 1967-68 season. As you recall, after viewing both rough cuts, we felt that while both were acceptable episodes, they were not truly representative of the excitement and the wide audience appeal we feel our series will have this year.

"Catspaw" had always been intended to air the week of Halloween (as the seventh episode of Season Two). "Metamorphosis," per NBC's wishes, was delayed and slated to be the ninth episode to beam across America and Canada.

TV Key Previews, a syndicated newspaper column by Steven H. Scheuer, from the November 10, 1967 issue of *The News Journal*, Ohio, said:

> "Metamorphosis." An off-beat love story. Pulled off course, our heroes land on an asteroid inhabited by a once famous space explorer, presumed dead for about a century. As the story unfolds, they learn not only what has kept the man alive for all these years but why. It's a tale that is very unusual, even for this series. Glenn Corbett and Elinor Donahue join the regulars tonight.

TV SCOUT, a syndicated newspaper column by Joan Crosby (taken from the November 10, 1967 issue of *The Pulaski Southwest Times*, Virginia), was not impressed. Crosby said:

> Credit *Star Trek* with some good imaginative stories -- and then duck when this far-out story launches your way tonight. Are you ready for a love affair between a man and a cloud? No, it is not the man who loves the cloud, it is the cloud that loves the man, holding him in its (or her) jealous arms. It takes Captain Kirk to convince the cloud (honest!) to let him go. Or something.

Elinor Donahue recalled, "I remember watching it at home. And I am quite often nervous about watching something I'm in because there is nothing you can do about it once it's out there. But I was very pleased with it; very happy." (50)

Sadly, the overall audience was not that large, at least according to A.C. Nielsen.

RATINGS / Nielsen National report for Friday, November 10, 1967:

8:30 to 9 pm, with 58.9% of U.S. TVs in use.	**Share:**	**Households:**
NBC: *Star Trek* (first half)	21.4%	9,180,000
ABC: *Hondo* (first half)	26.0%	10,700,000
CBS: **Gomer Pyle, U.S.M.C.**	**42.4%**	**15,340,000**
Local independent stations:	10.2%	-

9 to 9:30 pm, with 58.6% of U.S. TVs in use.	**Share:**	**Households:**
NBC: *Star Trek* (second half)	20.4%	No data
ABC: *Man in a Suitcase (second half)*	26.5%	No data
CBS: **Friday Night Movie**	**38.4%**	**No data**
Local independent stations:	14.7%	No data

The movie on CBS was 1963's *Palm Springs Weekend*, billed as "a teen-age comedy sprinkled with songs." It starred Troy Donahue, Connie Stevens, Ty Hardin, Stefanie Powers, and Robert Conrad. The teens had a dilemma this night and *Star Trek*, with an episode that, as indicated by the coming attraction trailer as well as TV listings, had little action, lost out. It hit bottom, its lowest rating for the Second Season.

The back-end support from NBC was lethal. *Star Trek*'s 20.4% audience share, was nonetheless strong compared to what happened on the network immediately following "Metamorphosis." *Accidental Family* only managed a 12.9% audience share, and then the numbers dropped again to a 10.3% share for the 10 p.m. "special," *Just a Year to Go*.

***

"Metamorphosis" received an Emmy nomination for its photographic effects. In the May 16, 1968 issue of *Variety*, Roddenberry ran a full page open letter of congratulations to Joseph Westheimer, reading:

> Dear Jo: Because of the unique requisites of our series, we of *Star Trek* have long been aware of the major contribution of Special Photographic Effects to our industry. Your nomination by the Television Academy doubly pleased us -- because of our long association with you, and because our episode, "Metamorphosis," was singled out to share this honor with you. Warmest regards, Gene Roddenberry, Executive Producer, *Star Trek*.

For the repeat airing of "Metamorphosis," *TV Guide* provided its "spotlight" half-page CLOSE-UP listing -- the sixth time this had been done for *Star Trek*. The result was a strong second place in the Nielsens, but there was still no beating *Gomer Pyle*, especially with Gomer on the cover of *TV Guide* that week.

RATINGS / Nielsen National report for Friday, July 19, 1968:

8:30 to 9 p.m.:		Share:	Households watching:
NBC:	*Star Trek* (first half)	24.6%	8,460,000
ABC:	*Man in a Suitcase* (first half)	15.5%	5,430,000
CBS:	***Gomer Pyle, U.S.M.C.***	**45.7%**	**12,040,000**
Independent stations:		14.2%	**No data**

9 to 9:30 p.m.:		Share:	Households watching:
NBC:	*Star Trek* (second half)	25.2%	No data
ABC:	*Man in a Suitcase (second half)*	16.4%	No data
CBS:	***Friday Night Movie***	**36.0%**	**No data**
Independent stations:		22.4%	No data

The movie on CBS was a repeat of 1961's *Portrait of a Mobster*, starring Vic Morrow and Leslie Parrish, and directed by *Star Trek*'s own Joseph Pevney. ABC's new contender by this point in the season, *Man in a Suitcase*, starred Richard Bradford as a former U.S. intelligence agent working as a private detective and traveling the world ... living out of his suitcase.

Star Trek held a strong second position for its entire hour and remained NBC's top-rated Friday night show. The back-end support from the network helped account for the ratings success of an otherwise obscure B-film on CBS. Of *Star Trek*'s 8,460,000 homes,

73

only 3,420,000 stayed for the network's 9:30 offering -- "McCarthy for President." The number dropped further at 10 p.m., for the NBC News special "What's Happening in America?" The question should have been, "What's happening with NBC?"

***

The critics and writers for *Cinefantastique*, in an issue of the magazine devoted to *Star Trek*, picked "Metamorphosis" as being among the Top 10 episodes from the original series.

DeForest Kelley also considered this as one of his favorites.

Radio Talk Show psychologist Dr. Laura Schlessinger, a fan of *Star Trek*, said, "The [episode] that resonates in my mind the most is the one where they have the female scientist on board.... The scene that was so remarkable to me was when she was going to die and the [Companion] goes into her body, and initially she says, 'Wow, look at the senses, you can see and touch. This is wonderful to be human.' And suddenly she realizes the isolation. I have used this in lectures when I was talking about how we really become intimate when we're isolated packets of thoughts and flesh and experiences, and how do we bridge that when we cannot really connect? That was what I would use as an example -- an alien creature finding out what it's like to be in our body -- to enjoy the realm of the senses and then realize the ultimate isolation." (153)

From the Mailbag (You Can't Please Everyone)

Fan letter from late November 1967:

> At this writing, there have been ten episodes of the new season. I grant you that #5 ("The Apple") didn't trek very well. The immediate-previous episode, Jerome Bixby's "Mirror, Mirror" was absolutely tops. The worst one to date is a staff job credited to producer Gene Coon. His "Metamorphosis" made idiots out of all of the cast, violating practically all the characterizations. At Westcon >67 I took Harlan Ellison's denunciation of Gene L. Coon as "Mister Mediocrity" with a grain of salt, having read a book by Coon [*The Short End*] which was not exactly bland or predictable. But Coon's *Star Trek* episode was the sheerest chunk of soap opera ever foisted on that program; it just plain STUNK. Buz (Seattle, Washington).

Memories

In absolute disagreement with "Buz," D.C. Fontana rejoiced, "'Metamorphosis,' to me, was a very affecting and touching script. I loved it." (64-1)

Elinor Donahue said she was "very, very pleased" and, perhaps more importantly, in memory of her late husband, she said, "It was Harry Ackerman's most favorite thing that I ever did." (50-2)

Harry Ackerman told this author, "No one who ever saw *Father Knows Best* can forget Elinor and her character from that series, and she has given many delightful performances over the years, but that *Star Trek* touched my heart. I was very proud of her when I saw it." (1aa)

Ralph Senensky said, "That was my favorite. That show just rolled off like clockwork. It was just such a joy to do, and I was very into it. 'Metamorphosis' struck me as the most poetic and imaginative show that I did." (155-6)

5

Episode 32: FRIDAY'S CHILD

Written by D.C. Fontana
(with Gene Roddenberry, uncredited)
Directed by Joseph Pevney

William Shatner and Julie Newmar in NBC publicity photo
(Courtesy of Gerald Gurian)

From NBC press release, issued November 19, 1967:

Dispatched to the mineral-rich planet Capella to negotiate a mining treaty, Captain Kirk and a landing party are imprisoned when they intervene in a scheduled execution, in "Friday's Child," on NBC Television Network's colorcast of *Star Trek* Friday, Dec. 1. Julie Newmar guest stars…. Eleen (Miss Newmar), the widow of assassinated ruler Akaar (Ben Gage), faces execution to prevent her unborn child from becoming legal heir to the country's ruling power. Kirk (William Shatner), Spock (Leonard Nimoy) and McCoy (DeForest Kelley) realize they have violated a tribal law by their intervention and face death as a consequence unless they get help from the hovering Enterprise. Too late, they discover they are cut off from the ship and have been left stranded.

Maab, the new tribal leader -- known as "High Teer" -- and his supporters among this seven-foot tall warrior race, favor doing business with the Klingons, represented by Kras. Condemned to death, Kirk, Spock, McCoy, and Eleen, who is close to giving birth, flee for their lives, seeking refuge in the mountains. Meanwhile, the Enterprise, with Mr. Scott in command, has been lured away by a Klingon vessel.

The theme of this story is one of personal sacrifice and the true meaning of courage.

SOUND BITES

- *McCoy*: "Say to yourself, 'The child is mine, the child is mine, it is *mine*.'" *Eleen*: "Yes ... it is yours ... it is *yours*."
- *Scott*: "There's an old, old saying on Earth, Mr. Sulu. 'Fool me once, shame on you. Fool me twice, shame on *me*.'" *Chekov*: "I know that saying. It was invented in Russia."
- *Spock:* "Oochy-woochy coochy-coo?" *Kirk:* "An obscure Earth dialect, Mister Spock. Oochy-woochy coochy-coo. If you're curious, consult linguistics."
- *Spock:* "The child was named Leonard James Akaar?!" *McCoy:* "Has a nice ring to it, don't you think, *James*?" *Kirk:* "Yes, I think it's a name destined to go down in galactic history, *Leonard*. What do you think, Spock?" *Spock:* "I think you're both going to be insufferably pleased with yourselves for at least a month ... *sir*."

ASSESSMENT

"Friday's Child" is everything NBC was asking for: fast-paced action/adventure with a story that unfolds primarily on a planet, filmed at outdoor locations, with a top-name guest star.

The script and Joseph Pevney's direction have great energy and wit. The rapid transposing of action on the planet and on the Enterprise, along with numerous well-placed moments of humor, keep everything moving at a brisk clip and provide for an entertaining tale. The casting is also effective. Julie Newmar, in particular, is delightful as the unhappily pregnant Eleen.

The theme -- the one Roddenberry inserted into the script with his rewrite -- of personal sacrifice and the true meaning of courage, has Kirk and company instinctively putting their lives on the line for Eleen and her unborn child. Eleen, at first, has no appreciation or even understanding of their actions. In the end, she learns from their examples and offers her life for theirs and for the child she didn't think she wanted. Even more poignant, Maab, the new leader of the fearless Capellans, also learns about true courage ... and sacrifice. As do we.

THE STORY BEHIND THE STORY

Script Timeline
D.C. Fontana's story outline, ST #43: January 11, 1967.
Fontana's 1st Draft teleplay: March 17, 1967.
Fontana's 2nd Draft teleplay: April 19, 1967.
Fontana's script polish (Mimeo Department "Yellow Cover 1st Draft"): April 20, 1967.
Gene Coon's script polish (Final Draft teleplay): Early May 1967.
Gene Roddenberry's rewrite (Revised Final Draft teleplay): May 11, 1967.
Additional page revisions by Coon: May 18, 1967.

Dorothy Fontana, having delighted *Star Trek*'s producers and the network with her scripts for "Charlie X," "Tomorrow Is Yesterday," and "This Side of Paradise," described her latest writing assignment as "basically an adventure," but admitted that, "In a way it was sort of a women's lib story. But I didn't mean it that way." (64-13)

What drew Fontana to the this story was her hunch that it could be interesting to watch a pair of pawns become the most powerful players in the game, especially if one of the pawns were a woman in a very male dominated society ... and the other was her unborn baby.

Fontana wanted the primary female character to be the polar opposite of how women were routinely portrayed on television at this time. Eleen was both cunning and deceitful in her efforts to prosper in a ruthlessly male dominated society. And the last thing she wanted was to care for another.

"My feeling was that not all women are mommies," Fontana said in an interview for this book. "Some women do not like their children; some women do not want to have their children; some women abuse their children, and that was a very real fact for me. I knew that, and I wanted to subtly bring it out, not that you can beat up a kid on screen, obviously, but she [Eleen] was willing to sacrifice the child for her own life. She was a selfish woman." (964-1)

In this way, Fontana was following Roddenberry's lead, using *Star Trek* to tell stories and making commentary that could not be done on other types of shows. Fontana also enjoyed creating the brutal tribal culture, saying, "I really had a good time with that -- the symbolism with birds; the fact that [these people] were all very tall. I was borrowing a little bit from Arabic tribes, but I also was borrowing from the monarchies of Europe where they were so regal all the time. I wanted to have that feeling, of people who were very noble in their bearing and very regal in their look, but were kind of primitive." (64-2)

The story outline, from January 11, 1967, was written during the tail end of production of the first season. This was earmarked as that season's episode 30, until NBC cut the order back to 29.

Robert Justman, always a fan of Fontana's work, was quick to respond, writing to Gene Coon:

This outline is plenty nice…. [But] how come everybody speaks English down on this planet? (RJ32-1)

Nearly every episode produced so far during that first season could explain away the convenience of English-speaking people by parallel world stories (as in "Miri"), or alternate universe stories ("The Alternative Factor"), or aliens so superior that they could easily comprehend the language ("The Corbomite Maneuver," "Shore Leave," "The Squire of Gothos," "Arena," and "Errand of Mercy"), or that a translation device was being used (as with the Gorn in "Arena" and The Companion from "Metamorphosis"). None of that would work here. But to tell a story like this, the two sides were going to have to talk. And NBC was not going to go for subtitles.

Stan Robertson at the network didn't have a problem with aliens speaking English. His attention was elsewhere. In his memo to Coon, he wrote:

An excellent action-adventure story which, in the hands of D.C. Fontana, who I believe has written some of our more superior *Star Trek* episodes, should become an excellent screenplay. I am pleased to see that we have another story primarily away from our starship and one which obviously will be filmed on location. (SR32)

Other elements of the story did not appeal to Robertson. He told Coon:

My major concern is that, in this present form, this story is much, much too violent. We both know that we can do good television action-adventure without the number of killings and acts of physical conflict which are contained in this outline. (SR32)

NBC Broadcast Standards and Practices agreed -- naturally. The censors told Coon:

The amount of violence indicated seems somewhat excessive and should be minimized. (NBC-BS32-1)

Fontana's story was both violent and dark. Her script, delivered March 17 (after NBC authorized a modest amount of story development money for a possible second season), reduced the body count, although only slightly. With this intentionally unpleasant tale, *Star Trek*'s only female writer was showing off her versatility.

Roddenberry was not bowled-over this time by Fontana's work and sent a somewhat critical three-page memo to Coon, saying:

Not that "Friday's Child" is a disaster... there is a story line here; lots of potential... but it's going to take some imagination and hard work to realize it fully. (GR32-1)

One thing Roddenberry wanted changed was the way the Capellans spoke. Justman had been fishing for an explanation as to why they would communicate in English. Roddenberry would be happy if they just spoke their English differently than we spoke ours. As written, he felt it was "a bit too colloquial." One example he cited was how Akaar tells Kirk, "We are not an industrial people, Captain." Roddenberry suggested the line instead read, "We are herdsmen. To dig into the ground for metals is a thing strange to us."

Roddenberry got his way. In the next draft, the aliens spoke English like Native American Indians in one of his TV western scripts of the 1950s.

Roddenberry also asked that the Federation's interest not be limited to "mining rights." In future drafts, Kirk offers to share knowledge, medicines, and other things to help advance the Capellans. Further, Roddenberry felt there needed to be more risk for Kirk and the landing party. It was his idea that the Enterprise would be lured away by a distress signal, leaving Kirk, Spock, and McCoy to fend for themselves. This constituted a substantial change to the plot. He was nonetheless confident in Fontana's abilities, telling Coon:

I know Dorothy will come through for us in her usual fine style. (GR32-2)

Justman, having complained about the natives speaking English, otherwise took odds with Roddenberry's request for numerous story changes, writing to Coon:

I think this is a very good first draft and really doesn't need too extensive of a rewrite. (RJ32-2)

Of course, even when Justman liked something, he felt he could still like it better. His five pages of notes suggested, among other things, that the script was "too talky" and that the physical aspects would be difficult to do on budget and in keeping with the mandated six-day production schedule.

When Fontana's 2nd Draft script hit, on April 19, Justman wrote Coon:

A much better version of the screenplay. More excitement, more action, more better! So let's get on with it. (RJ32-3)

"Let's get on with it" didn't mean it was ready to film, merely ready to go through another draft. Justman's biggest worry at this point had to do with the character, or lack of decent character, in the mother of Friday's child. Eleen was becoming less and less appealing in his eyes, prompting him to write:

I must say at this time that I dislike Eleen as a person immensely. Our audience is going to dislike her immensely also and wonder why our heroes keep on lugging her along with them, when it is apparent that there will be no gratitude returned for what they do. I think perhaps we are making a mistake in having her portrayed as a rat-fink. I think we want to empathize with her -- not hate her. Also, at the end of the script we find out that Eleen was motivated by the fact that she had been having an affair with some other fellow. How come she let him touch her when she was married to Akaar? Somewhere there is an inconsistency in her thinking, which doesn't please me. (RJ32-2)

In Fontana's version of the story, the unfaithful and conniving Eleen hates her baby so intensely that, after escaping from Kirk, McCoy, and Spock, she brings the newborn to Maab. She is willing to let him kill the baby in exchange for permitting her to live. Kirk and company are captured while attempting to rescue the infant. In the end, Eleen actually outfoxes herself and is executed for committing adultery.

The story was different in many other ways than that which was eventually aired on NBC.

- Chekov does not appear in the script. His lines are spoken by a crewman named Frost.
- There are no Klingons on the planet, therefore no Klingon named Kras (the clear antagonist in the final version). In fact, other than for the subplot where the Enterprise is lured away from the planet by a distress signal and then challenged by a Klingon ship -- which Fontana added at Roddenberry's request -- the Klingons are discussed but not seen.
- McCoy never previously visited the planet.
- There is no "young and inexperienced" Security Guard who draws his phaser in the Teaser and, as a result, gets killed.
- Akaar has a teenage son from one of his other wives, who is next in line to be "High Chief of the Ten Tribes."
- Maab is Akaar's brother and is completely ruthless. Besides killing his older brother, Maab has Akaar's teenage son murdered, and then he sets out to kill the unborn child that Eleen carries.
- At the end of the story, Maab is executed for treason when it is learned he had been secretly negotiating with the Klingons.
- As for Eleen's baby, he is left to be raised by his grandfather -- Eleen's father -- until old enough to rule the tribes.
- The only light moment comes with the Tag scene, with the baby being named Leonard James Akaar and Spock's observation that McCoy (Leonard) and Kirk (James) were bound to be insufferably pleased with themselves for at least a month.

Gene Coon did a polish on the script at the start of May, attempting to soften some of the harsher aspects with the insertion of more humor. But Coon's Final Draft script missed the mark in Roddenberry's opinion, so he did a substantial rewrite, dated May 11.

Among the changes made by Roddenberry was the removal of Eleen's negative characteristics, including her having cheated on her husband and wanting to kill the baby. She was still difficult with Kirk, McCoy, and Spock -- there would be no story if she weren't -- but she behaves this way because of her beliefs, not because of greed and lust.

Among the additions by Roddenberry:

- Kras the Klingon was now in the story.
- McCoy was now established as the know-it-all expert on the Capellan culture due to a two-month stay on the planet a few years earlier.

- The death of security guard Grant when he draws his phaser on Kras (providing a dramatic ending for the Teaser, but having Kirk appear unwise in choosing to take this greenhorn to the planet).
- The addition of Chekov. Roddenberry had been responsible for the introduction of the character in "Catspaw." It was his idea to bring him back now.
- A more positive theme. Beside the change in Eleen's character, with the selfless act of courage and sacrifice on her part in the final moments of the story, Maab was now a much more honorable man. Instead of being killed for treason, as Fontana had it, Maab takes responsibility for his bad judgment and sacrifices his own life for the good of the others. Each character in the story now had his or her courage tested (including Scott on the Enterprise) and each, with the exception of Kras, the story's villain, proves themselves to be brave and willing to make sacrifices for that which they believe to be right.

Fontana knew the rules of the TV game. As story editor, she was doing her share of rewriting on scripts by others. She also appreciated positive themes and certainly had written her share. But some of the changes Roddenberry made upset her. She said, "I didn't like the tack it took on the woman, played by Julie Newmar. I wanted her to be pretty ruthless. I wanted her to be, at the end, willing to sell her child for her own life -- *just sacrifice the kid* -- because you didn't see that kind of woman on television. And Gene wanted the traditional woman-has-baby, loves-baby, automatic, no question about it, will do anything for child. All the trappings were still there, the basic adventure of the story was there, and the culture of the episode stayed pretty much the same. The only thing I didn't have was that they couldn't touch her. Gene put that in. It was taboo to touch her, which, of course, precipitated the scene later on between her and McCoy where she slugs him and he slaps her right back. That was Gene's, too. I freely admit that. But I didn't like that script as much after it was changed." (64-1)

Roddenberry, defending his rewriting of a staff member to this author (in the 1980s), said, "One thing I am pleased with about *Star Trek*, and offer no apology for, is the positive themes present in many of our shows. You look at the fans 20 years later and you see, by and large, very positive-thinking individuals. That's what you find at the conventions. They come from all walks of life, but they share those ideals. It is clear there *was* an influence. Television, if used properly, is a wonderful tool for not only education, but examples of humanitarian values. Literature has always been a teacher, and a means of conveying lessons in character. And that was *Star Trek*, by design. Dorothy's story for that one ['Friday's Child'] attempted to teach the importance of good character and good conduct by showing the negative results of bad characters and bad conduct. And that is certainly one road to take in telling a morality play. I preferred, for *Star Trek*, and with that story in particular, to take a different road in communicating that message. Now, no writer likes being rewritten. But I stand behind the choices made on that one. I think that show works." (145)

The day after Roddenberry's rewrite was distributed to the staff, Fontana wrote to Gene Coon requesting that her pseudonym, Michael Richards, be used as the screen credit. She later said, "'I threatened to take my name off of it and Gene persuaded me not to." (64-1)

Despite Fontana's displeasure, others embraced the changes. Justman was one, and told Coon:

I like what has been done so far with the character of Eleen, but I do wish we could go just a little bit further and see her make a more definite change from her original attitude of hostility toward one of understanding and appreciation. (RJ32-3)

It was one sentence among six pages of dense notes. One beef Justman had, concerning the idiocy of the red-shirted security guard who is quick to go for his phaser in the Teaser and thusly dies, read:

> Grant shows a lamentable lack of discipline by immediately going for his phaser weapon when he sees Kras, the Klingon, in evidence among the party which greets them on the surface of the planet. Since we are not at war with the Klingon Empire in this show, Grant deserves getting chopped down for what he attempted to do. Captain Kirk should also draw a rebuke from Starfleet Command for such a lamentable lack of discipline on the part of one of his crew members. (RJ32-3)

Coon wanted a strong cliffhanger for the end of the Teaser and ignored Justman's valid point. Justman had more success in swaying Coon when he suggested involving Chekov further by including him in the script's Teaser. Having just seen footage from "Catspaw," Justman agreed with Roddenberry that this young Russian in the Beatles wig had added greatly to that episode, and therefore wanted to elevate the new character's importance. Chekov was given no lines for the briefing room scene but, by being present, early attention is put on the conspicuous character, as well as ushering in his first scene with series regulars Kirk, Spock, and McCoy. In another part of the script, Coon instigated a soon-to-be recurring Chekov gag. After Scott remarks, "Fool me once, shame on you; fool me twice, shame on me," Chekov boasts that he knows the saying -- it is an old Russian expression.

Giving Justman the "little bit further" change he wanted to see in Eleen, from hostile to appreciative, Coon added more moments of humor between her and "MAC-COY," such as when she tells the doctor, to Spock and Kirk's astonishment, "bring *our* child here," and the very cute "Oochy-woochy coochy-coo" business at the story's end.

Pre-Production
May 12 and May 15-18, 1967 (5 days prep).

Joseph Pevney was back in the director's chair for the second time in the new season (following "Catspaw"). His first task, work with casting director Joe D'Agosta, as well as Gene Roddenberry and Gene Coon in selecting the guest players, and one of them had to be a star.

Julie Newmar, as Eleen, was a hot property on television and clearly deserving of the title of "guest star." The 5'11" beauty got her big break when cast as one of the brides in the 1954 MGM musical *Seven Brides for Seven Brothers*, then as Stupefyin' Jones in 1959's *Li'l Abner*. That same year, Newmar went to Broadway and won a Tony Award for her performance in *The Marriage-Go-Round*. In 1965, she got her own TV series, opposite Bob Cummings, as the sexy robot in *My Living Doll*. That role put her on the cover of *TV Guide*. During 1966 and 1967, Newmar gained further national fame as Catwoman on the immensely popular *Batman*.

James Doohan said, "An offbeat piece of casting it was to have Julie Newmar as Eleen, a nine-months-pregnant woman. Julie has always been aggressively proud of her figure." (52-1)

**Julie Newmar as Catwoman on *Batman*
(ABC publicity photo)**

Newmar's explanation to this author: "I did it because they asked me and there was an aura of sincerity to them. And to the character. I'm not a *Star Trek* fan. I'm a ballet dancer; I'm in the arts; my world and interests are quite different than that of science fiction. But I know when I read something if it is worthwhile, and I know that in the first few pages. Good writing, that's what saves a show. The heart of any show is the writing. We had it with *Batman*. And you've got it with *Star Trek*." (126-3)

Tige Andrews was cast to play Kras, the Klingon heavy. Prior to this, he was a regular on two popular series -- as one of Sgt. Bilko's misfits, on *The Phil Silvers Show*, and the cigar-puffing Johnny Russo, on *The Detectives*.

Joseph Pevney said, "Tige was a very close friend of Shatner's. That's how he got the role. He came from Canada, that's where Shatner knew him from, so when the time came to cast the role in 'Friday's Child,' he [Shatner] asked me to 'read' Tige and see what I thought of him. And I liked his look, he had a great look, and he worked out fine, I thought." (141-2)

"I had enjoyed *Star Trek* before doing 'Friday's Child,'" Andrews said. "When the producers offered me the role of Kras, I was very pleased to do it.... This was the first time that I had been given the opportunity to wear a costume in a film role, and I was very much into the role. I particularly remember feeling more like 'someone else' during the filmmaking. It was a fun

Clarence Williams III, Michael Cole, Peggy Lipton, and Tige Andrews of *The Mod Squad* (ABC publicity photo)

part." (3)

Andrews was 47, and one year away from his third and most memorable series role, playing Captain Adam Greer on *The Mod Squad*.

Very nearly every tall actor and stuntman in Hollywood was called in to work for "Friday's Child."

Michael Dante was Maab. At 36, and standing 6'2", Dante had worked mostly in westerns, as cavalrymen, cowboys, outlaws, and Indians. He had second billing as Red Hawk in *Apache Rifles*, under Audie Murphy, and, during the time this *Star Trek* was filmed, he had third billing as Sitting Bull in the ABC series *The Legend of Custer*.

Recalling the events that brought him to *Star Trek*, Dante said, "I was contacted and summoned to Gene Roddenberry's office and he and I were the only two there. There was no one else -- not Joe D'Agosta or Robert Justman; no Gene Coon, just Roddenberry. I was flabbergasted because it had never happened to me before like that. There was

Michael Dante in the 1967 ABC series, *The Legend of Custer* **(Courtesy of Michael Dante)**

always a casting person in the room, or a director, or someone else to give the approval, but never a private meeting with the boss man -- the executive in charge and the inventor of the show." (45-1)

Dante was unaware that Roddenberry was good friends with Samuel Peeples, the creator and head writer on *Custer*. Or that Peeples had written the *Star Trek* pilot film, "Where No Man Has Gone Before" and had even turned down the invitation from Roddenberry to be the producer (the job that then went to Gene Coon instead). And this afforded Dante a private audience with "the boss man."

Roddenberry said, "My way of casting is different. Actors come prepared to answer the questions they are typically asked at casting calls. Suddenly, with me, they find themselves discussing topsoil and a whole range of subjects that have nothing to do with being cast. The reason for this questioning is that I am interested in getting a feel for them as people. The way I cast is to try to learn who this actor, this person, really is. I try to find out if they fit in with my idea of the character." (145-23)

Dante told this author, "So Roddenberry said, 'I saw you on a show a couple of nights ago and I thought you were great. You've done a lot of westerns, so I know you'll understand what we're doing -- it's like a western in the sky. It's good guy, bad guy, no grays; we know in the end who is the culprit. You're perfect for this role. And Julie Newmar will be cast in the piece. I want you to take this script and read it. Let me know what you think. If you like it, it's yours.' That was it; the grand treatment. So I went home and read it. The script had comedy, it had action, and it had drama. That's what I liked about it, and I thought it was different from most of the scripts [written for television] because it had all three of those elements, which was rare and certainly not easy to pull off. Action and drama can easily mix, but not always comedy. And it was my first science fiction job, so when I read it I was excited about it, because of being a sci-fi as well as having the action. And, of course, the opportunity to work with Julie appealed to me, too. So I called my agent and said, 'Yeah, I love it; I want to do it.'" (45-1)

Dante dialed into Roddenberry's theme for the revamped story and said, "Maab wasn't a villain; he had this very strong concept of what his laws were. He was willing to die to preserve his people, which he did, and that's a very powerful character from which to draw upon. Everything he did he was willing to back up with his life." (45)

Cal Bolder played Keel, Maab's right-hand tribesman. He was also 36, and had served as a California Highway Patrolman. After making an impression on a Hollywood agent he pulled over for speeding, Bolder, who stood 6'4", quit law enforcement for a brief career in TV at playing big lugs, cowboys, and bad guys.

Ben Gage, 52 and standing 6'6", played Akaar, the High Teer. With a splendid baritone singing voice, Gage began in show business as a big band vocalist, then, for the movies, dubbing in the singing voices for, among others, Victor Mature, George Montgomery, and Dana Andrews. Big Ben Gage also did a dead-on impression of Big Jim Arness, *Gunsmoke*'s Marshall Matt Dillon. He showcased that impersonation, as Sherriff Mort Dooly, in the comical "Gun-Shy," one of the most infamous episodes of *Maverick*.

This episode marked Walter Koenig's (and Ensign Chekov's) second appearance in *Star Trek*.

Production Diary
Filmed May 19 (half- day), 22, 23, 24, 25, 26 & 29, 1967.
(Planned as a 6 day production, running 2 day over; total cost: $211,880)

Friday, May 19, 1967. The U.S. continued to bomb Hanoi, North Vietnam. England, the U.S., and the U.S.S.R. ratified a treaty banning nuclear arms in outer space. "Groovin'" by the Young Rascals was getting more spins on radio stations than any other song. The Monkees were still at the top of the album charts with their second LP album (*More of the Monkees*), featuring the hit single, "I'm a Believer." The biggest film in the movie houses was a documentary on Bob Dylan called *Don't Look Back*. Mom and dad were pleased to see a coming attraction trailer for *The War Wagon*, starring John Wayne, due to open in a week. You could see either for a dollar-fifty. Elizabeth Montgomery, of *Bewitched*, had the cover of *TV Guide*. Johnny Carson had the cover of *Time*. And *Newsweek* picked Ronald Reagan for its cover. "The Menagerie, Part 1" had its encore airing on NBC the night before. Following it, right after *Dragnet 1967*, was *The Dean Martin Show*, and these three series combined together to make NBC the ratings champ from 9 to 11 p.m.

Day 1. The morning had been spent on Stage 10 as director Ralph Senensky completed "Metamorphosis," needing only guest performers Glenn Corbett and Elinor Donahue. After the lunch break, Joseph Pevney took over the company, and the series regulars filmed the first scene to be seen in "Friday's Child," staged in the briefing room.

Work on the ship's bridge followed with the last scene in the episode, the only one on the bridge to feature Kirk, Spock, and McCoy.

Day 2, Monday. Work continued on Stage 9. Since only two Enterprise sets were needed for this episode, other ship sets were collapsed, allowing space for the small cave set

and the immediate rocky area outside the mouth of the cave. The morning was spent filming with Shatner, Nimoy, Kelley and, for her first work on the episode, guest star Julie Newmar. Here, Eleen gives birth, experiences her big "character turn," knocks McCoy out, and flees so that she can give her life to save her baby and the Enterprise men. This scene wasn't just about the birth of a baby, but the birth of the story's unlikely hero.

Day 2: The mouth of a cave that was built onto Stage 9 (Both photos courtesy of Gerald Gurian)

Newmar remembered what motivated her performance, saying, "It's two words: reaching deeper. For me, when watching other actors, it's 'Can you move me; move me to change my mind; move me to open my heart; move me to cry those tears that I couldn't allow myself to do in my own life?' It isn't up to me to know the great wonder of all things, all the themes that may be hidden in the story, but I have to know more about that character than the writer or the director or anyone else on Earth. If I do that, and if that truth is complete and allowed to be seen, not cut the wrong way, or directed against the themes, then what I do works for the whole." (126-3)

After the filming of the scene where McCoy is knocked out with a well-placed rock, the on-location actors were dismissed for the day. Lunch was called and then the company made the move back to the bridge set to film the sequences with Scotty in charge.

James Doohan was now being prominently showcased as the series' unofficial fourth lead. Interviewed for a 1968 fanzine, Doohan said, "It took a long time to build up the character. They really didn't care about him in the first year. They knew the ship had to have an engineer, because ships don't just run by themselves. But if you just say, 'Gee, my engines aren't running' or 'I'll fix it right away, sir,' it's a one-dimensional character, nothing human. The second season they started to get more in [for Scotty]." (52-8)

"Friday's Child" provided Scotty with his fourth turn -- the second in a row -- at running the bridge during Kirk's absence. Doohan said, "I thought I ran the ship beautifully, to tell the truth. It was a nice change of pace, although I think Scotty's best place was in the engine room." (52-1)

The choreographed movements here, with and around Scotty, were designed to conceal the missing finger from Doohan's right hand. Note how, on the rare occasions when Scotty sits in the Captain's chair, Doohan's right hand is either placed on his lap and held by his left hand, or tucked out of sight behind the armrest. When Scotty is in movement, the right hand hangs below the camera framing or is positioned behind his back. The one time the hand with the missing finger might have been prominently visible, as

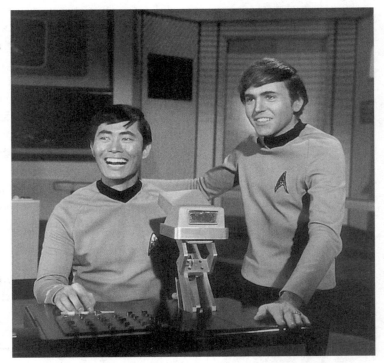

George Takei and Walter Koenig and Sulu's viewscope -- the latest gadget designed by Matt Jefferies and realized by Jim Rugg (Courtesy of Gerald Gurian)

Scotty signs a command report, Doohan waits until a female Yeoman crosses between him and the camera before raising his hand. He signs the report and then lowers his right arm as she again crosses. By the time she clears camera, Doohan's hand is again below that of the camera framing.

Day 3, Tuesday. The final bridge scenes were filmed with Mr. Scott commanding Uhura, Sulu, and Chekov. Something new at the helm: Sulu's view scope, which rises up out of the console. The impressive gadget was as state-of-the-art as 1967 gizmos got.

Walter Koenig, for his memoir *Warped Factors*, recalled, "The cast was uncommonly friendly. James Doohan (Scotty), Nichelle Nichols (Uhura), and DeForest Kelley (Dr. McCoy) made me feel instantly welcome. It is a tribute to them, I think, that I wasn't made aware of the concerns they had regarding their own status on the series. I was never treated as an interloper or as a threat to their portion of the pie." (102-13)

Day 4, Wednesday. The company spent the first of two days at Vasquez Rocks, filming all the sequences as Kirk, Spock, McCoy, and Eleen flee Maab and those loyal to him through the rugged terrain.

**Day 4: Bill McGovern slating a shot at Vasquez Rocks
(color image available at startrekhistory.com and
startrekpropauthority.com)**

With the company for the first time, Michael Dante said, "In this society, superiority over the other tribes was essential. That was at the heart of this character. And the costume they gave me helped in that regard. When I put on that costume, it was tight fitting and had the cape, and that gave me a stature of being even taller. It was a grandiose bigger-than-life attitude that came upon me the minute I put on that costume, because wardrobe is so important. And they had a bunch of body builders in the cast -- big, huge guys. So we were something to behold." (45-1)

Normally the month of May is a safe time to journey into the desert for a day of production but, during this time in 1967, Southern California was experiencing a heat wave.

**Day 4: Michael Dante being outfitted under heavy robes
in the sweltering heat at Vasquez Rocks
(Courtesy of Gerald Gurian)**

"Man, it was hot," Michael Dante said during an interview for *Starlog*. As Maab, Dante's costume was better suited for winter. "I remember that Julie [Newmar] and director Joe Pevney had a difference of opinion. This discrepancy got a little heated between them, and 'heated' was uncalled for! It was about 110 degrees where we were working, and Julie had certain things that she wanted to define about her character's motivation and movements. Joe finally said, 'Motivation, schmotivation! I want you to move over here!' ... I said to Julie, 'Hey, it's hot out here; let's get going. Let's do it and get on to the next scene, because I'm gonna roast under this costume! Have a little sympathy!' ... She looked at me, smiled, and her sense of humor took over. That was the end of it. It was nothing tragic, but it *was* terribly hot. We had to drink a lot of water to avoid dehydration." (45)

Day 4. "Those rocks were made of styrofoam and papier-mache," said Michael Dante (Courtesy of Gerald Gurian)

Newmar said, "It wasn't much fun; having the pillow strapped to me, sticking out of my front; and that stiff kind of dialogue these people spoke; and the dusty, dry, hot environment that we worked in. I'd been on the stage, and a member of the Actors' Studio with Marlon Brando and all those great artists, and TV's a different dog. It speaks all about haste. I always had the ability to go between the three art forms of stage and film and TV, but each one has demands and kind of abuses you in its own way. But you get through it." (126-3)

Day 5: Bill McGovern slating a shot including Dante, Newmar, and Andrews (Courtesy of Gerald Gurian)

Pevney saved the avalanche scene for the end of the day. Dante said, "These rocks were made of styrofoam and papier-mache, and it was kind of comical. We had a rehearsal and I wasn't quite under the rock ledge. When the rocks rolled down, one of the prop men didn't get one in place and it clobbered me. In reality, it would have crushed every bone in my body. Joe Pevney got a kick out of that." (45)

Regarding his coworkers and the drive back to Desilu, Dante said, "Shatner was very professional. I thought he did a good job; believable. And he was cordial. We had a few laughs and, other than the heat, enjoyed the shoot. And, of course, Julie can be very fey -- which means she's a little way-out there; a little different. We had a nice chat when we rode back in the bus. The studio had provided the bus to take us out to Vasquez Rocks and back to Hollywood where our cars were parked. We had a great time on that ride. Julie was a character; she has a strange sense of humor." (45-1)

Day 5, Thursday, May 25. Pevney filmed the after-effects of the avalanche followed by the climactic confrontation between the Capellans, Kras, and the Enterprise men. And then the cavalry came over the hill, in the form of Scott and the security team.

The inhospitable conditions of the location filming continued. Dante said, "It was even hotter the second day -- 117 degrees out there. I lost seven pounds that one day alone. We couldn't drink the water fast enough. It was so hot, because we were boxed in. My outfit [had] no outlet. There was no air. It was all tight, around my face, no air getting in to the costume whatever. It was just totally sealed from top to bottom. All I kept thinking about was 'Let's get this done and get the hell out of here. Let's just do it in one take. Please, everybody, just get it done.' The cameras were getting overheated, too -- they had to ice the cameras! They put a blanket on top of the camera and then put an ice pack on top of the blanket so the equipment wouldn't clam up. Everybody was not moving around in their normal gait. Whatever assignment they had, whether behind the camera or in front of the camera, they were moving just a little slower. The less movement we had, the better we all were. They had a couple of those large umbrellas -- like beach umbrellas -- for us to sit under, to get a little shade. It wasn't so bad on the top of the hill, but down below, with the confines of those rocks, it was like a vacuum. There was no circulation; no wind, no breeze to come through, it was like we were walled into a hot box. So by the second day of that, everyone was feeling pretty worn out." (45-1)

After wrap, the crew made the two-hour drive back to Desilu, and then each person's individual drive home before the NBC 8:30 p.m. encore broadcast of "The Menagerie, Part 2."

Day 6, Friday. The company was back at Desilu Stage 10 for "Ext. Encampment," "Ext. Tent," "Ext. Bush Area Behind Tent" and, lastly, "Int. Kirk's Tent."

Newmar, now doing the scenes which would introduce her character, having had to trade in her Catwoman costume for the robes of the uncomfortably pregnant wife of a Teer, said, "It was good for the actor in me, because

Day 6, back at Desilu, Stage 10
(Unaired film trim courtesy of Gerald Gurian)

an actor always wants to stretch -- *and they stretched me!*" (126-3)

89

Michael Dante said, "The interior of the stage -- the area outside of the tent -- was absolutely fantastic. The sets were most impressive for a series from that era -- the lighting and the set decorating. It was remarkably inventive and colorful." (45-1)

Day7, Monday, May 29. More difficult filming in the tents on Stage 10, with the last of the sequences in "Kirk's Tent" followed by "Int. Akaar's Tent." Jerry Finnerman learned a bitter lesson about trying to light enclosed tents. While not entirely bad, these sequences were perhaps the least visually impressive of any in a *Star Trek* episode, resulting in a mandate in the writers' room -- no more tent scenes -- *ever* (see The Story Behind the Story of "A Private Little War").

All problems aside, Joseph Pevney continued to amaze and delight his producers. This ambitious production, with location filming, explosions, landslides, sweltering heat, and numerous hard-to-light tent sequences, wrapped only one-half day over schedule.

Post-Production
Available for editing: May 31, 1967. Rough Cut: June 15. Final Cut: June 28.
Music Score recorded on July 7.

Fabien Tordjmann was back as head of the third editing team for their first job of the new season. He said, "We had about three weeks, usually alternating three episodes -- one editor would pick up a show that would shoot for six days, sometimes seven but usually six, and then he'd start putting it together while the second one was shooting. By the time the third one was shooting, we should have been through with the first one. But, of course, it took some time. It was often delayed, because it takes longer to edit than to shoot, and so by the end of the season it was pretty tight." (176)

Gerald Fried, with his second assignment of the season, turned in a score that is one of the most invigorating in any *Star Trek* episode. For this, Fried wrote the series' first "Klingon theme," introduced when the doomed Enterprise Security Guard spots a Klingon among the tribesmen. There are also quaint melodies and arrangements designed to hint at tribal culture, and light musical stings to accompany the episode's moments of humor. But the main accent is on adventure. The distinctive eruptions of music, laid over the fight sequences, went on to be used often in other episodes. The Enterprise has new signature music, as well, which plays as the ship orbits Capella IV, then races through space.

Van der Veer Photo Effects created the optical photography, including phaser shots, men disintegrating, and the transporter effect. Not quite state-of-the-art was the Klingon ship that blocks the Enterprise's path. A better one was on the way (see "Elaan of Troyius").

At a total cost of $211,880 (which equates to roughly $1.5 million in 2013), "Friday's Child" was $31,880 over budget. Three episodes were now completed, and Season Two had a $76,588 deficit.

Release / Reaction
Only NBC airing: 12/1/67.

Steven H. Scheuer reviewed the episode for his syndicated column, *TV Key Previews*. Among newspapers across the country to carry the review was *The News Journal*, out of Mansfield, Ohio, on December 1, 1967. Scheuer wrote:

> "Friday's Child." A good adventure tale tonight. Trying to obtain mining rights from a planet inhabited by primitive tribes, our heroes find themselves in direct competition with the Klingons -- an unscrupulous rival of the Earth federation to

which the Enterprise belongs. The fighting here is with boomerangs and bows and arrows, but the day is saved by Dr. McCoy's skill in psychiatry and obstetrics.

Judy Crosby reviewed the episode for her syndicated column, *TV SCOUT*. Among the papers which ran her notice on December 1 was the *Pittsburgh Press*, in Pennsylvania. Crosby said:

> Julie Newmar stars in this exciting episode which might have been stretched into a two-parter. Captain Kirk and a landing party arrive on a strange planet to negotiate a mining contract. They find the inhabitants to be a giant race who put little value on human life and instead put a greater stress on violence and the success of politicians and of the powerful. The landing party is shocked to witness the preparation for an execution. The victim is the widow of an assassinated ruler and she must die because she is pregnant and her child could be legal heir to the throne. Of course, Captain Kirk and company rescue her but they are soon captured themselves by the giant people.

Michael Dante was watching the night "Friday's Child" had its network airing. He said, "I thought the comedy between the doctor and Julie was well played. It is surprising that they found the time to show it and develop it within the confines of an hour show, minus the commercials. So you have maybe 50 minutes to get all of that in. It was a lot of story for 50 minutes. That's what I thought when I saw it for the first time, how surprising it was that they were able to squeeze in everything that they wrote and that we filmed without chopping and editing it to death, and that they could make their point and, at the same time, give it the three dimensions of action, drama, and comedy, rather than a one dimensional piece like most TV. And to do it so well that all three elements could be appreciated!" (45-1)

RATINGS / Nielsen National report for Friday, December 1, 1967:

8:30 to 9 p.m., 57.5% of U.S. TVs in use.	Share:	Households:
NBC: *Star Trek* (first half)	26.6%	10,860,000
ABC: *Hondo* (first half)	22.5%	10,020,000
CBS: ***Gomer Pyle, U.S.M.C.***	**43.4%**	**15,680,000**
Local independent stations:	7.5%	No data

9 to 9:30 p.m., 59.5% of U.S. TVs in use.	Share:	Households:
NBC: *Star Trek* (second half)	26.7%	No data
ABC: *Hondo* (second half)	24.2%	No data
CBS: ***Friday Night Movie***	**37.0%**	**No data**
Local independent stations:	12.1 %	No data

The movie on CBS was the sexy 1962 comedy *The Horizontal Lieutenant*, starring Jim Hutton and Paula Prentiss. *Star Trek* came in second for its entire hour.

Four of *Star Trek*'s second season episodes were not given repeat showings on NBC. Surprisingly, the entertaining "Friday's Child" was one.

***

James Blish adapted Dorothy Fontana's script into short story form for the Bantam paperback *Star Trek 3*, published in April, 1969. Gene Roddenberry's rewrite was nowhere in sight and the story ends as Fontana had wished, with the death of Eleen, paying the price for her treachery.

From the Mail Bag

Dear Sir: All our teachers like STAR TREK because they think it might encourage our minds. Also, they think it's very interesting. We all like the characters (especially Mr. Spock and the doctor) and what they do. Bonnie H. (5th Grade), Anaheim CA.

Memories

Dorothy Fontana lamented, "I've never really cared much for that episode, because I couldn't get the message I wanted across on it -- that not all women are mommies, not all *mothers* are mommies. I felt [Gene] changed the whole attitude. In changing that central character, he changed the story." (64-1)

Joseph Pevney saw nothing wrong in the rewriting of "Friday's Child." He said, "That was a funny show; a *great* show." (141-2)

Julie Newmar, responding in 2010 to a question as to whether "Friday's Child" holds up, "despite the foam rocks, those crazy costumes, and primitive effects," said, "But it's always in the story, isn't it? It's the involvement that people have in the story, in the characters, whether they love or hate the characters. And that's there.... I was very amazed with Bill Shatner's performance. He is the superstar he deserves to be. And, oddly enough, I was very surprised at my own performance. I liked it." (126-2)

Tige Andrews said, "I'm part of the majority. I have seen much of *Star Trek* because I enjoyed it. It was a well-written series, with good production values. I'm a fan." (3)

Michael Dante said, "The fans truly love the characters [of *Star Trek*]. I had fans saying, 'We really hated to see Maab die. We hoped you would come back or be a running character.' The fans are wonderful, and they're in a class by themselves." (45)

6

Episode 33: WHO MOURNS FOR ADONAIS?
Teleplay by Gilbert A. Ralston and Gene L. Coon
(with D.C. Fontana, uncredited)
Story by Gilbert A. Ralston (premise by Gene Roddenberry, uncredited)
Directed by Marc Daniels

**Production Day 6. Michael Forest and Leslie Parrish, with costumes
that were held in place by glue
(Photo courtesy of Gerald Gurian)**

From *TV Guide*, Sept. 16, 1967:

Mortals battle an immortal when the spaceship Enterprise is seized by the Greek god Apollo. Kirk turns to science for a means to overcome Apollo's mythological powers.

The alien super-being, having once visited Earth and believed to be a god, longs for the days of old. He is demanding that the crew of the Enterprise remain on his lonely world of Pollux IV as his worshipers, and he has selected Lt. Carolyn Palamas, the ship's Archeology & Anthropology Officer, as his mate.

The hook: the "ancient astronaut" theory comes to *Star Trek* as mythology mixes with science fiction. The theme: the sadness of lost celebrity. Apollo tells us, "The Earth changed. Your fathers changed. They turned away … until we were only memories…. A god cannot survive as a memory."

SOUND BITES

- *Apollo:* "Captain Kirk, I invite you and your officers to join me. But do not bring that one. The one with the pointed ears. He is much like Pan. And Pan always bored me."

- *Apollo:* "I am Apollo." *Chekov:* "And I am the Czar of all the Russias!" *Kirk:* "Mr. Chekov." *Chekov*: "I'm sorry, sir; I never met a god before." *Kirk:* "And you haven't yet."

- *Kirk:* "Apollo ... you'll find we don't bow down to every creature who has a bag of tricks." *Apollo:* "Agamemnon was one such as you, and Hercules; proud and arrogant. They defied me -- until they felt my wrath." *Scott:* "I would like to point out that we are quite capable of some 'wrath' ourselves."

- *Apollo:* "Zeus … Hermes … Hera … Aphrodite … you were right. Athena … you were right. The time is past. There is no room for gods. My old friends, forgive me.… Take me."

ASSESSMENT

"Who Mourns For Adonais," suggesting that the ancient gods of Earth were space travelers, was daring for U.S. television in 1967. Even more risqué, the hot topic of an alien/god wanting to mate with a human, and then ravishing her with a wind storm driven by his fury.

But there are problems. Kirk and Spock are separated for most of the story, and this rarely worked for *Star Trek*; nearly half of the episode takes place on a single set; at times the story stagnates; and the small cast is used in a redundant fashion. More than once we see Scotty recklessly rushing forward, foolishly daring to take on a super-being like Apollo, only to be put in his place by lightning bolts and back-handed electrically-charged swats. And this brings up another problem: Scotty is out of character. Yes, he's infatuated by Carolyn Palamas, and that can explain -- even excuse -- some of his act-first-think-later antics, but nowhere in sight is the calm, seasoned officer whom we have often seen running the bridge during Kirk's absence. Gene Coon, as a writer, had a tendency to over-use exclamation marks in his dialogue, and Marc Daniels, as a director, was inclined to let his cast play their parts BIG. As a result, James Doohan, for the first time in the series, over acts. And, for the second time (following "Errand of Mercy"), Kirk comes off overly macho, and overly anxious to sacrifice his life. This is a caricature of a hero, not a real flesh-and-blood ship's captain.

Regarding the plotting, some of the tricks here have been used before -- a female crew member falls in love with a charismatic stranger, against Kirk's advice, and struggles to decide where her loyalty lies ("Space Seed"); a powerful alien detains Kirk and company, who becomes vulnerable when they discover he is channeling his energy through an object open to their attack ("The Squire of Gothos"); and Kirk plays out a dangerous theory that his adversary is over-taxing himself and might be defeated by a mass rebellion ("Charlie X"). In addition, also from "Charlie X," Apollo's exit from the story is reminiscent of Charlie Evans's dramatic send-off.

And yet "Who Mourns for Adonais?" is a popular episode, one which many fans name as among their favorites. "Adonais" makes up for its shortcomings with a thought-provoking premise, passionate writing, some heartfelt performances, and never-before-seen images, such as a giant hand in space grabbing hold of the Enterprise and nearly crushing its hull. The story's ending, both dramatic and tragic, as a distraught Apollo casts himself to the wind, is impossible to forget. Michael Forest's stirring performance, aided by Fred Steiner's poignant score, serves as a fitting set-up to Kirk's final commentary: "Would it have hurt us, I wonder, just to have gathered a few laurel leaves?"

THE STORY BEHIND THE STORY

Script Timeline
Gene Roddenberry's concept, "Olympus Revisited": December 5, 1966.
Gilbert Ralston's contract: February 20, 1967.
Ralston's story outline, ST #50, "Last of the Gods": March 8, 1967.
Ralston's 1st Draft teleplay, now "Who Mourns for Adonais?": April 7, 1967.
Ralston's 2nd Draft teleplay: April 19, 1967.
Gene Coon's polish (Mimeo Department "Yellow Cover 1st Draft"):
May 8, 1967.
Coon's second script polish (Final Draft teleplay): May 15, 1967.
D.C. Fontana's rewrite (Revised Final Draft teleplay): May 26, 1967.
Gene Roddenberry script polish (2nd Revised Final Draft teleplay):
May 29, 1967.
Additional page revisions by Gene Coon: May 31 and June 1, 1967.

"Who Mourns for Adonais?" began with a different title. Gene Roddenberry came up with the concept in early December 1966, calling it "Olympus Revisited." In late February of 1967, after *Star Trek* received an allowance from NBC for further story development, the premise was assigned to freelance writer Gilbert Ralston, who worked from his home in Nevada.

Ralston was a former newspaper man from Ireland. For television, he had written episodes for *The Naked City*, *Ben Casey*, *I Spy*, and *The Big Valley*. He helped create *The Wild, Wild West*, being the writer of that series pilot episode. On the big screen, Ralston wrote the screenplay for the 1971 film *Willard*. He received an Edgar nomination for that work and followed it with a sequel, about a rat named *Ben*. Past and future triumphs aside, "Who Mourns for Adonais?" was Ralston's only script for *Star Trek*.

Ralston seemed a good choice to further develop "Olympus Revisited." He said, "Immodestly, I'm an expert in Grecian history, and I got interested in some of the characters tucked away in my various textbooks. Using Apollo just seemed like a good idea. And Gene Coon liked it very much." (144-2)

Ralston turned in his story outline, "Last of the Gods," on March 8. In this version of the story, and all versions of the script to follow but the very last, Lt. Palamas becomes pregnant by Apollo.

Robert Justman, if nothing else, liked the premise, and wrote to Gene Coon:

I am very pleased with this property and think that it would make a very interesting and cerebral story for us. I feel that we have a real change of pace for *Star Trek*. (RJ33-1)

Roddenberry, however, was concerned that Ralston was writing science-fantasy, or science-mythology, and not action-adventure science fiction. He requested a meeting and Ralston flew out from Nevada. After discussing the story and its various plot turns with Ralston, Roddenberry left a memo for Coon, telling him:

Our main problem with this outline seemed to be that it edged into fantasy now and then. My meeting with Gil consisted mainly of finding a firm inner logic for the story, which emphasized that these "Gods" are merely unusual life forms. (GR33-1)

Jean Messerschmidt, at NBC Broadcast Standards, wasn't bothered by the fantasy, but the controversy. She requested that "the religious aspects be treated with dignity and good taste" and that "Carolyn's pregnancy not be treated lightly or as commendable." (NBC-BS33)

Stan Robertson had concerns, too. Since Coon was on holiday, the NBC Production Manager wrote to Roddenberry, saying:

> I believe we have the making here of either one of the most provocative and exciting *Star Trek* episodes we have considered to date, or one which could do irreparable harm to our series. I believe that we become involved in the very touchy area of "audience believability and acceptability" -- which is of critical importance to the success of our series -- when we delve into stories surrounding mythology or fictionalized characters from the lengthy history of world literature. How will our viewers accept or not accept the fact that our heroes have ventured into "another galaxy" in which Apollo does exist? We have all prided ourselves on the fact that *Star Trek* is a series which is believable -- that in 200 years or so the voyages of the Enterprise could actually take place.... We know that we feel as strongly as you do that we do not want these creative points to carry us over into the harmful domain of fantasy which, as conceived and developed, you know better than I, *Star Trek* isn't. Will this story carry us across that point? (SR33)

One of the "creative points" Robertson fretted over was the giant hand in space. He argued:

> Such devices remind me of *Lost in Space* and *Voyage to the Bottom of the Sea*. In short, that which is not based on the believable. (SR33)

After returning from his vacation, Gene Coon addressed Robertson's notes, instructing Gilbert Ralston to include information in the script telling that the hand was not a human appendage, nor a projection, but a field of energy. As for meeting Apollo in another galaxy, Coon, like Roddenberry, believed the story was relevant.

To honor Stan Robertson's concerns however, more explanations were added, including Kirk's line, "Say five thousand years ago a highly sophisticated group of space travelers landed on Earth ... around the Mediterranean."

McCoy concurs, "Yes, to the simple shepherds and tribesmen of early Greece, creatures like that would be gods."

Kirk concludes, "Especially if they had the power to alter their forms at will and command great energy. In fact, they couldn't have been taken for anything else."

Ralston's 1st Draft script arrived from Nevada on April 7, 1967. Creating some confusion, the writer had opted for a new title, "Who Mourns for Adonais?," one that requires some explaining:

Adonais was an elegy written by English poet Percy Bysshe Shelley in 1821 after the death of fellow poet John Keats. Line 415 reads, "Who mourns for Adonais?" The Hebrew word "adonai" translates to "god." Adonis was the name of the Greek god of beauty. Shelley combined the word "adonai" with the name "Adonis" to come up with "Adonais."

Regarding the script, Coon confided in his staff that he was disappointed. So was Robert Justman, who wrote Coon:

> You were right. This script does not bear out the promise contained within its opening pages. It starts out quite excitingly and then falls apart in no time at all.... The opening gimmick of an enormous hand stopping the Enterprise and holding it immobile in space is a strong, <u>strong</u> gimmick. But that's it in the area of gimmicks. And about the only progress I can say that we have made between

his story outline and first draft screenplay is that there is a certain amount of useable structure. But there are some bones missing in the skeleton and these need to be inserted before we can put some weight on the creation. (RJ33-2)

Much of Justman's criticism centered on the story's characters. He lectured:

One of the major hang-ups I find in many of the stories that we have to go through is that people seem unreal. This usually occurs when the people say or do the things that the writer wants to have them say and do, because by doing that they will not slow down the story or get in the way of the mechanics of it. But this usually ends up as a hindrance to the property. Human beings should say and do things because… they are the human things to say and do. In this respect, I think you will have to agree with me that the word "motivation" is as important in the writing of a show as it is in the acting of the show.… When these properties are not inherent in the character as written, the character is not well rounded or believable, or interesting, or even actable. Therefore, I find humanity lacking in all the characters as written in this particular script. I find Godliness lacking in the character of Apollo as written in this script. (RJ33-2)

And then there were the usual monetary concerns, amplified by about 10. Justman wrote:

That's an interesting trick that Mr. Apollo does -- I mean, growing in size until he is enormous. The last time I saw that was in *Aladdin and His Magic Lamp*. This trick is not impossible to do, but is going to be very time consuming and inordinately expensive for a television show.… Apollo shoots blasts out of his finger; our people shoot lots of phaser blasts back at him in the Temple; the ship is shooting phaser blasts down at the Temple; the Temple is starting to fade and shimmer; a tree goes up in flames, pillars crumble and fall, the Temple starts to come apart; Apollo runs right into the middle of the Temple Optical and tries to prevent the pillars from crumbling and the Temple from fading and disappearing, as our people continue to fire; Apollo starts to grow and expand in size… and I turn in my resignation and go off to the South Seas… and Gulf-Western finds out about the cost of this show and reneges on the whole Studio purchase. (RJ33-2)

Gulf-Western Corporation, which had just acquired Paramount Pictures, was negotiating to purchase cash-poor Desilu. Expensive episodes like "Who Mourns for Adonais?" were not going to help close the deal.

Dorothy Fontana needed a four-page memo to express her disappointment. Among the sore points she listed for Coon:

Pages 19-20 -- I don't believe or like Scott on these two pages. He's acting like a stubborn pig-head in the face of demonstrated fact -- whatever Apollo is, it is apparent he's real.… [Later] Scott behaves like a berserk Tarzan… totally out of character with the sound, sensible man we've known.… [Later] Scotty is a bit naïve… with such comments to Carolyn as "I don't know what's happened to you," and "I never thought you'd be a traitor." (DC33)

Coon, a staunch believer that emotion on the small screen should be played big, ignored many of Fontana's warnings concerning Scott. He did, however, pay attention to her other concerns, such as:

Suggest we define and redraw the relationship between Scott and Carolyn, Carolyn's previous involvement with Holloway, and her new involvement -- perhaps against her will -- with Apollo. (DC33)

Sam Holloway, in this version of the story, was a crew member whom Carolyn

Palamas had fallen in love with, who then died. Then Scott became interested. Carolyn, on the rebound, seemed interested, too, until she met Apollo. Like love itself, the story got very confusing.

Fontana's memo continued:

> Carolyn says she loves Apollo. This is a big, big switch from 24 hours ago. I feel we must portray Apollo's more than human attraction -- show Carolyn being wooed -- unable to help herself. Otherwise she is just a shallow, fickle broad.... She comes off rather badly, I think, and I suggest a re-examination of her character and relationships. (DC33)

Fontana's memo would win her a crack at rewriting the script herself ... but not just yet.

Coon topped Justman's and Fontana's memos when he sent Ralston an 18-page letter, filled with highly-critical notes. Among his concerns were instances where the script had too little action, the *Star Trek* characters were *out* of character and, worse, the potential drama just fell flat. Coon wrote:

> Let's speak generally for just a moment, Gil.... Basically, I feel that the character development not only in our personnel of the sky, but, more importantly, the character of Apollo, have not been developed to full realistic extent. Adonais, or Apollo, after all, is a God, or at least he was so considered at one time during Earth history. I believe he should act like a God. He should talk like a God; and yet he comes across here rather mortal. (GC33-2)

Coon told Ralston to drop the opening scene where the crew holds a funeral for Holloway, whom they were then going to jettison into space. He also wanted any references to a back-story involving a past romance between the deceased crewman and Carolyn stricken, telling Ralston that the "relationship between Sam and Carolyn is unworkable for us." Carolyn, for the most part, was unworkable, too. Coon added that she came off as "very shallow and very quick to change her mind, and rather unlikeable." (GC33-2)

As with many first drafts, Coon found that Kirk was not coming across in a proactive manner. To rectify this, he suggested Kirk order Carolyn to "lead Apollo on." And finally, to avoid further 10-page memos from Robert Justman, Coon asked Ralston to simplify the ending and minimize the firefight.

Ralston revised his script, addressing some of Coon's notes, ignoring others. He trimmed expenses from the climactic optical-driven fight between Apollo and Kirk and the Enterprise, somewhat. He made Kirk more proactive, somewhat. He made Apollo more godlike, somewhat. He did *not* get rid of the burial in space of Sam Holloway but, in an act of defiance, merely changed the name of the crew member in the casket from Holloway to a different Sam – this one named Atkins. And he did *not* remove references to a past relationship between Sam and Carolyn.

Coon, then, rolled up his sleeves and did a rewrite of his own. Curiously, after asking for the removal of the funeral, and the plot contrivances that came with it, Coon left the burial in space and the past romance in his first rewrite -- the May 8 Yellow Cover 1st Draft. The reason for this was the very nature of a Yellow Cover 1st Draft teleplay -- to retain as much of the work from the original writer as possible before sending it to the network for approval, or the spending of more money on further rewrites.

Much of the awkward dialogue from Ralston's two drafts remained.

In the Teaser, when Kirk, McCoy, and Spock notice Scott's infatuation with Carolyn, Kirk remarks, "Would you believe this thistle-hearted Hibernian is showing signs of the grand passion?"

McCoy, speaking the one line to make it into the shooting script, says, "Even from here I can tell his pulse rate is up."

In a line soon to be deleted from the script, Spock adds, "I find it rather disappointing. I would expect Mr. Scott to share his meals with a reactor or a generator, but not a woman."

Justman, never a fan of the potentially expensive burial in space bit, or Carolyn showing an interest in Scotty merely because she was on the rebound, wrote to Coon:

> No sooner have we pulled the chain and flushed the body of Sam Atkins into space, than [Scott] starts making up to Carolyn, who, as we discover, had a bit of a thing going with the aforesaid Mr. Atkins. (RJ33-3)

Justman's greatest concern remained the script's structure. He told Coon:

> I find that this script is weak in one particular way. It does not seem to me that it builds correctly in a dramatic sense. Our antagonists and protagonists exist parallel to each other, but in reality never do seem to come head-to-head or nose-to-nose in a constantly building dramatic conflict. There are certainly occasional outbursts of energy, but they seem to be individualistic physical acts which are dropped or scattered fortuitously here and there, in order to spark an otherwise noticeable lack of action happening in this story. (RJ33-3)

Justman was also concerned about the story's ending, where it is learned that Carolyn Palamas is "with child" … or, more so, "with god-child." He told Coon:

> I have just read the Tag Scene on board the Bridge of the Enterprise. I imagine that you have had anguished phone calls from various persons at the National Broadcasting Company who have been able to recover from their fainting spells after reading this sequence. (RJ33-3)

Roddenberry wrote to Coon the same day. He said:

> I think the rewrite helped this script enormously. But I do think it needs some further work…. Perhaps part of what we miss in this early part of the meeting with Apollo is definite individual attitude by various landing party members. Let's have one, say Chekov, totally unable to accept any possibility there is such a thing as a "god." Let's have Spock fascinated by what is to him, simply and logically, a highly advanced life form. Let's have Kirk, as always, very concerned about his vessel. This is an ideal script to focus audience interest in Kirk and his enormous problems of a ship Commander. We can do Bill [Shatner] a lot of good in this show by showing his cleverness, his strength, his ability to extract and correlate all the various abilities, specialties, and strengths of his people. Let's let him be angry at the proper times. Let's let him be impatient when they don't come through for him. Let's let him force them when necessary, trick them when necessary, pat them on the back when necessary. In short, let's let Kirk be a leader. If we can solve this problem, Bill will get his Emmy Nomination next year and, more importantly, we may avoid huge problems which could plague us in the future. (GR33-2)

The "huge problems," of course, had to do with Leonard Nimoy just receiving an Emmy nomination and Shatner being passed over. Shatner's approach to playing Kirk in the first season was, for the most part, restrained. Now, with the changes about to be made to the script in which Kirk is determined to take a lightning bolt in his chest so that the others can have a chance to jump Apollo, plus Shatner's decision to play it big, there would be no talk of an Emmy. And if imitation *is* indeed the sincerest form of flattery, William Shatner would be flattered for years to come.

Coon made these changes with his May 15 rewrite -- the Final Draft script. Kirk was not only written to be more proactive, but Spock was left behind … to command the Enterprise. In previous drafts, Sulu had been in acting command. Now Sulu's lines were reassigned to Spock and, on the planet, many of Spock's lines were given to Chekov.

For one scene in the previous draft, when Kirk decides it is time to have a talk with Carolyn about her feelings toward Apollo, Spock had offered to assist. It was a good set up that fell flat when Kirk says, "Mr. Spock… You are a man of many talents and skills, but what you know about love I could put under the eyelid of a gnat and not make it blink."

The rewrite brought about an improvement. For the new draft, Chekov says, "Perhaps if I assisted." Kirk gives him a look and asks, "How old are you?" Chekov answers, "Why, twenty-two, sir." Kirk considers this for a half second, before saying, "Then I'd better handle it."

More lines reassigned to Chekov which were originally intended for Spock involve the mystery of Apollo's energy source and how he channels it through his body. Chekov says what Spock had to say in the previous draft, that, "Some creatures can generate and control energy with no harm to themselves -- the electric eel on Earth, the giant dry-worm of Antos IV, the fluffy…" McCoy interrupts him, saying, "Not the whole encyclopedia, Chekov." Chekov defends himself, saying, "The Captain requires complete information."

A new line now, adding an in-joke to the dialogue switching, has McCoy saying to Kirk, "Spock's contaminating this boy, Jim."

Little moments like these actually improved the script. Others, dealing with Apollo and Carolyn, brought about more improvements.

Dorothy Fontana said, "I think Gene Coon basically enhanced the relationship, the fact that the god wanted this woman to not only be his consort, but the foremost among his worshipers. And then the antagonistic relationship between Kirk and Apollo. Kirk wasn't going to fall on his knees and worship a god. No way. Again, it was a matter of character development." (64-19)

Helping us to accept and even like the character of Carolyn Palamas, a scene was added where Kirk orders her to spurn Apollo. And this brought about a memorable exchange of dialogue. Trying to deny her broken heart, Carolyn says, "I must say, Apollo, the way you ape human behavior is remarkable…. I've never encountered any… specimen like you before." Apollo is stunned. He tells her that he believes she loves him. She hurts him further, saying, "Be logical…. I'm a scientist…. I'm not some simple shepherdess you can awe. I could no more love you than I could love a new species of bacteria."

Fontana, regarding her turn at rewriting the script -- the Revised Final Draft, dated May 26 -- later said, "Sometimes it wasn't so much a problem of making it work, but making it work in terms of the production. I remember lots of cutting and pasting and moving stuff around on pages, and cleaning up dialogue. Marc Daniels was the director, and Marc wanted things changed, in terms of the scene order, and Gene [Coon] was already on another script, and he said, 'You do it.' He was a very generous man in that way. He'd say, 'I wrote that, but I have another one to fix up, so you do it, it's okay with me.'" (64-1)

Much of Fontana's work was to keep the episode from becoming visually stagnant. She explained, "We were working on a very tight set. It was a big, brilliant set -- it was just beautiful -- but we had to get off that set with the script so that we could show more aspects -- move the characters around, get different looks than just that one set." (64-14)

Gene Roddenberry gave the script a quick polish of his own -- the 2nd Revised Final Draft, from May 29 -- and it was here that Kirk became not just antagonistic toward Apollo but perhaps to the point of foolhardiness.

On May 31, the morning the cameras were set to roll, Gene Coon went through the script and gave it what he thought would be a final touch-up. The next day, on June 1, as production entered its second day, Coon was called upon to do some further editing. There was nothing left to add, only something to take away, per the insistence of the NBC censors -- that controversial "Tag scene" (see "Production Diary," Day 2).

Even with the cut, everyone involved in the writing process -- Ralston, Coon, Fontana, Roddenberry, and Justman, too -- believed they had come up with something special. Dorothy Fontana shared the credit for the episode's success with two others, both having joined the project after the writing process had concluded. She said, "That script ultimately worked very well, I think, because of the actor you got and the actress you got -- Leslie Parrish and Michael Forest." (64-1)

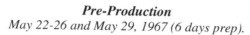

Pre-Production
May 22-26 and May 29, 1967 (6 days prep).

Director Marc Daniels

Marc Daniels was back in the director's chair for the first time in Season Two. Dorothy Fontana said, "Marc was a very efficient director. He got the job done on time and on budget. And he had a good story sense. I know because I worked with him on the rewrite of 'Who Mourns for Adonais?' We were trying to figure out the best use of the set, and improving the character -- the character of the god. Adonais had been rather stiff, starchy. We needed him to be a god who had emotions; a god who was going to fall in love with this girl. But, also, he wanted minions; he wanted people to idolize him. He wanted to be worshipped as a god. That's very human, actually, when you think about it. You want people to like you on a human level. If you are a god, you want people to worship you. So, we had to inject a lot of that. And Marc was very helpful." (64-3)

A great lesson was learned during the previous year -- only a few directors were able to stay within the six-day schedule and still deliver the quality the producers wanted. Two men in particular had proven their abilities here -- Daniels being one; Joseph Pevney the other. Bob Justman said, "I decided to mainly use only two directors for the second season. It would be more efficient to have successful *Star Trek* veterans alternating episodes rather than run the risk of breaking in directors new to the show." (94-8)

Daniels' new contract called for him to alternate with Pevney. Ralph Senensky would fill in when one of the others was ill or otherwise unavailable.

101

The casting of Apollo was a challenge. The script described him as "looking impossibly handsome and imposing," as well as tall and muscular. The manner in which he was written also seemed to require an actor trained in Shakespeare, for Apollo was very much like a tragic Shakespearean character with many long, highly dramatic passages of dialogue.

Robert Justman had written Gene Coon about this, saying:

> If at all possible in casting the part of Apollo, we should attempt to serve the talents of a very handsome actor who has been well scholared in classical Stagecraft -- in fact, an Englishman or Irishman might be the way to go. Another direction might be to cast someone with the talents of Mark Lennard [sic]. He would have the presence and the ability to deliver all of Apollo's beautiful speeches. (RJ33-4)

Michael Forest remembered, "Someone at *Star Trek* called Craig Noel, the head of the Old Globe Theater in San Diego, and described the character. They wanted to know if there was an actor there who could fill this bill. He told them about me. And it was interesting, because I went in, I believe, three times to interview. They wanted a British actor

Leonard Nimoy with Michael Forest in *Deathwatch*
(1966, Altura Films International)

to begin with and, as a matter of fact, asked me to do it with a British accent. They felt that the British idiom would be better sounding in terms of language. And I said, 'I don't think it would be wise for me to try to do that for this particular role but I can give you a kind of mid-Atlantic theater speech.' They told me to read it again. I did, then I was asked back to read it that way again for someone else. It seemed to me they really weren't sure what they wanted. But, eventually, I was cast." (65)

Michael Forest was 37. The former amateur boxer was 6'3" and had been a leading man for director Roger Corman in numerous films, as well as a frequent player on TV. Among his television credits: multiple appearances on westerns such as *Cheyenne*, *Laramie*, and *Gunsmoke*. In the sci-fi genre, he had prominent roles on *The Outer Limits*, *The Twilight Zone*, and *One Step Beyond*. Forest knew Leonard Nimoy and appeared with him in the critically acclaimed 1966 film *Deathwatch*.

Between TV, film, and stage work, Forest was a busy actor, but he wanted the role of Apollo badly enough to endure three separate auditions. He admitted, "When I read for it, I thought, 'This is a pretty good script,' compared, particularly, to what I had been doing up to that point on television and in films. I had studied Shakespeare for years, worked at the Shakespeare festival in San Diego, and done Shakespeare throughout the country, so when I saw this role, I thought, 'This is the kind of thing that is closest to my heart.' I could see the dimensions of this character -- a character bigger than life; a major kind of force, and the script had that kind of tragic ending to it that was like Shakespeare. The character had layers, he had dimension, whereas much of the television serials at that time were so shallowly written that there was very little you could do as an actor. You're doing the best you can, of course, but you're limited by the material. Not with this." (65)

Leslie Parrish, a former model turned actress, was cast to play Lt. Carolyn Palamas. By this time, Parrish was a familiar face on television. Thanks to casting director Joe D'Agosta, she had worked for Roddenberry on *The Lieutenant* and, just prior to arriving here, appeared in two episodes of *The Wild, Wild West*, one in which she played a green-skinned space traveler. For her work on the big screen, with 1963's *For Love or Money*, Parrish was nominated for a Golden Globe award as "Most Promising Female Newcomer," even though she had appeared in many popular movies prior to this, including *The Manchurian Candidate* in 1962. Her first starring role on the big screen, in fact, was in 1959, as Daisy Mae, for *Li'l Abner*. At this time in 1967, she was 32 and splitting her time between acting and organizing rallies against the Vietnam war.

Leslie Parrish, actress, model, classical pianist
(Courtesy of Leslie Parrish)

"I wasn't as busy acting as I had been before because of the time I was putting into the anti-war cause," Parrish said. "But I had done shows with Gene [Roddenberry] before, so maybe he thought of me and asked for me. I just went in for a meeting with Gene, and Joe, and Marc Daniels, and that was that." (134a)

John Winston, as Lt. Kyle, got sprung from the transporter room and assigned to the bridge, taking Spock's place at the science station.

Eddie Paskey, as Lt. Leslie, took Chekov's place, as navigator.

Production Diary
Filmed May 31, June 1, 2, 5, 6, 7 & 8, 1967
(Planned as 6 day production, running one day over; total cost: $203,623.)

Filming began on the last day of May 1967, immediately following the Memorial Day holiday (falling on Tuesday in those days, not Mondays). *More of the Monkees* was still America's best-selling record album, now in its sixteenth week at the top. On the *Billboard* singles charts, Aretha Franklin moved to No. 1 with "Respect," nudging out "Groovin'" by the Young Rascals. CBS was the top-rated network from the night before with *Daktari* and *The Red Skelton Hour*. Red's guests were Ozzie and Harriet Nelson and singer Barbara McNair. In the movie houses, and selling the most tickets (at $1.25 each), was *The War*

103

Wagon, starring John Wayne and Kirk Douglas.

Ken Berry, Forrest Tucker, and Larry Storch of *F Troop* had the cover of *TV Guide*. Inside, two separate letters regarding *Star Trek*. Paul L. Klein, Vice President NBC, Audience Measurement, rapped the editor's knuckles for an article that ran in a previous issue which stated that *Star Trek*, like all TV science fiction, lacked "scientific validity." He wrote, in part:

Contrary to being without "scientific validity" *Star Trek* is the only science fiction show on television with a scientific basis. It is fiction though and it is television, and it does allow the viewer to participate. In fact, it allows the viewer to go beyond even the scope of the writer.

Leslie Parrish backstage with DeForest Kelley
(Courtesy of Gerald Gurian)

Another letter was intended to rap the knuckles of resident critic Cleveland Amory for giving Star Trek a mixed review. It told him:

Dear Mr. Amory: Don't feel bad. In the next few days you're going to get 5,227 letters of protest about your review of *Star Trek*, mentioning your "total inanity" and "bad puns." Now there are only 5,226 to go.

Amory had since reassessed *Star Trek* and decided that he liked the series after all.

Day 1, Wednesday. The start of filming for "Who Mourns for Adonais?" was typical of every episode of *Star Trek*. Fred Phillips and his makeup department had a 6:15 a.m. call time. Both Leonard Nimoy and William Shatner arrived at 6:30; Leonard for his ear job, Shatner for his hair. And Nichelle Nichols was there at 6:30, as well, for her hair and

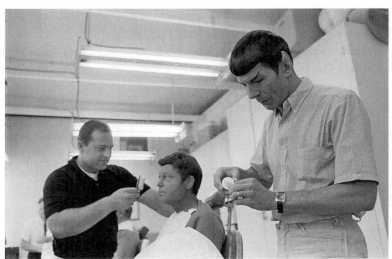

6:30 to 8 a.m., Monday through Friday
(Courtesy of Gerald Gurian)

makeup. The second assistant director (2nd A.D.) was there to take breakfast orders. The remaining male players were given an extra half-hour to get to the studio. The camera and lighting crew arrived at 7 a.m. to begin preparing the set. Also reporting to work at 7 a.m. were the property man, sound men, costumers, assistant director, and director Marc Daniels. The sound mixer and camera operator were given a little more time to wake up. Their call time was 7:30 a.m.

The entire day was spent on the Stage 9 bridge set. Jerry Finnerman was out sick this first day and replaced by Arch Dalzell. The 45-year-old cinematographer was the D.P. for the1960 cult film *Little Shop of Horrors*, as well as the television shows *The Rebel*, *Mister Ed*, and *The Addams Family*. The title song for *The Addams Family* may have told us they're "creepy" and they're "spooky," but the scenes Dalzell lit and shot on the bridge were not quite as shadowy as those done by Finnerman. In the Teaser, note the elevator doors behind Kirk as one example. They are lit both bright and flat, instead of with textured shadow patterns at the top, as Finnerman always did.

Leslie Parrish was noticing the lighting, but more so the blinking ones coming from the bridge computers. She said, "That bridge set was pretty awesome. I loved the computers. We didn't have them then for personal use. But when they came out, I was one of the first to get one. The future has always been much more real to me than the present. So when I walked into *Star Trek*, I felt I was at home. I thought, this is the way it ought to be. Not just with the computers, but with the people -- the way they were portrayed, in a time when it didn't matter what race you were or where you were from. The ideals and values were marvelous. It had Gene [Roddenberry] all over it -- *his* values. I just loved him. I felt a kindred soul with him." (134a)

Day 2, Thursday, June 1. The Beatles released *Sgt. Pepper's Lonely Hearts Club Band*. To no one's surprise, it was awarded a Gold Record certificate before it even got into the stores. Meanwhile, another full day was spent on the bridge of the Enterprise. Finnerman had returned, bringing his cinematic dark tones and shadows back to the show.

One bridge sequence planned for this day was not filmed -- the episode's "tag scene." Writer Gilbert Ralston had been daring in that he ended the story with the discovery that Carolyn Palamas, after her time alone with Apollo on the planet, was now pregnant. The creative staff loved this idea and kept it in the script. NBC's Jean Messerschmidt was trying to be cooperative with the *Star Trek* producers; she knew how vital the plot point was. But, as production neared, word of the controversial subject matter began to spread to other departments beyond that of Broadcast Standards.

"The network absolutely would not allow that," Dorothy Fontana said. "Oh my God, intercourse outside marriage! Usually we could sneak by a lot of stuff, [but] it was ultimately stricken." (64-1)

The twist ending, which would have made "Adonais" one of *Star Trek*'s most talked about episodes for decades, was in every draft of the script, including the 2nd Revised Final Draft, from May 29, 1967. Two days later, as the scene was about to go before the cameras, revised script pages were delivered to cast and crew. The controversial ending had been removed.

The scene, tragically lost, had Spock and Kirk in conference at the command chair. McCoy enters from behind them, looking somewhat bemused. Kirk says, "Yes, Bones?"

McCoy begins, "I'm used to interesting problems ... but I've just been confronted with a brand new one. Carolyn Palamas became slightly ill at breakfast this morning.... I just finished examining her. She's pregnant."

Kirk and Spock react in surprise. McCoy says, "You heard me."

"Apollo?" Kirk asks.

"Apollo -- positively," McCoy answers. "Now I'll give you an interesting question to chew on. What will the child be? Man ... or god?"

Even Spock is at a loss for words. Kirk stares back at McCoy, awestruck, as we FADE OUT.

With one less scene to shoot, the company broke early and cast and crew were sent home in time to relax in front of the TVs for the NBC repeat broadcast of the *Star Trek* episode "Charlie X."

Day 3, Friday, June 2, 1967. The company worked on Desilu Stage 10, and the impressive temple set. The original plan was to shoot this on the backlot but, due to all the various effects required, including a violent rain storm, Robert Justman was opposed to the notion. He wrote Gene Coon:

> These sequences will have to be set up on a sound stage. As presently written,
> with the light changes and the wind and the lightning and the opticals, we have
> absolutely no control unless it is done inside. Incidentally, why does it have to
> start raining? The answer is that it does not have to start raining. (RJ33-2)

The rain was cancelled, saving both time and money. And then set designer Matt Jefferies built as much of Mount Olympus onto Stage 10 as *Star Trek*'s budget could provide for.

Michael Forest recalled, "When I saw the temple, I thought, 'Hey, it's pretty impressive.' I remember sitting up there on that throne while they were lighting me, thinking, 'Well, this is kind of interesting,' because, in terms of the actor approaching a role, you begin to feel like that person you're portraying. You're affected by the physical surroundings -- in this case, the throne and the columns." (65)

The scenes planned for this third day of production were the landing party's encounter with Apollo, them reacting to him growing taller for the first time, Apollo changing Carolyn's uniform for an ancient Greek-era gown, and Scotty getting slapped away when he charges the angry "god." But Marc Daniels, *Star Trek*'s fastest director, with a well-earned reputation for staying on schedule and covering an average of ten script pages each day, was falling behind. Filming the scenes where Apollo grows to the size of a giant, dwarfing the Enterprise party, and requiring crane shots as well as numerous other camera tricks, was taking longer than anticipated. The slap that would send Scotty flying through the air had to be put off until the next day.

Day 4, Monday, June 5. There were some long faces on set this day. The Emmy awards took place over the weekend. *Star Trek*, nominated for more Emmys than any other science fiction series in the history of television, including Best Drama Series and Best Supporting Actor (Nimoy), came away empty-handed. You couldn't sense any disappointment from the cast by watching the scenes shot on this day. When the camera was rolling, the series regulars put aside their disenchantment and rose to the challenge.

Jay Jones, doubling for James Doohan, finally received the slap from Apollo. Jones said, "Apollo back-flips me over a table, but I hit the corner, so they chained it down and I did it again. This time I caught the table's edge in the kidneys. By the end of the day, I was pretty sore. Then they wanted to do the wire gag known as a neckbreaker. You wear a vest under your clothes, and it's attached to a pulley. Three 200-pound guys [holding the other end of the cable], jump off a six-foot ladder and it takes up the slack. It jerked me across the stage. We thought it would take me 10 to 12 feet and it took me 18. I flew right over Shatner's head. My head snapped against the [concrete] floor, and I went through the wall, although that was cut

**Day 4. The slap from a god that sent stunt-double Jay Jones to the hospital
(Courtesy of Gerald Gurian)**

from the print. I was out cold. They rushed me to the hospital with a concussion." (93b)

There was further drama on the set this day. Michael Forest recalled, "When we were shooting that, that was the week of the Six Day War in Israel [June 5-10, 1967]. Everybody had their little portable radios tucked to their ear listening to what was going on. The whole week we were filming, that war was happening." (65)

**Day 5. Filming on Stage 10 for the Temple set. Pictured left to right:
Michael Forest, Bill McGovern with clapboard, Walter Koenig,
DeForest Kelley, William Shatner, and James Doohan
(Courtesy of Gerald Gurian)**

Director Daniels finished a full half-day behind.

Day 5, Tuesday, June 6. After watching the "dailies" of the footage taken the previous day, it was decided the stunt where Jay Jones flew backwards had to be done again. Jones, however, due to his injury, was unable to work. James Doohan was insistent he could do the stunt.

"I had to

talk them into letting me do the fly-back," Doohan said. "I had a harness on under my red shirt. They pulled me back when [Apollo] zapped me. I practically flew backwards, and if there hadn't been other stunt guys there to catch me, I might've gone through a back wall." (52-1)

After reviewing the two versions of the stunt, it was decided to use the one featuring Jones, after all.

Day 6, Wednesday, June 7. Work continued on Stage 10. More dialogue was covered between Kirk and his landing team and Apollo. And then came the dramatic climactic scene where the temple is struck by phaser fire and a distraught Apollo aims energy bolts toward the sky and the orbiting Enterprise.

The numerous

Day 6. Leslie Parrish said, "In our last scene together -- Michael and me – we were crying…. We were *really* crying."
(Unaired film trim courtesy of Gerald Gurian)

camera tie-down shots, as animated lightning bolts (to be added during post production) were taken, but turned out to be time consuming. Daniels was three-quarters of a day behind when the camera stopped rolling, well into time-and-a-half overtime pay.

Day 7, Thursday, June 8 -- an unplanned day of production. The temple set on Stage 10 had been given a makeover during the night by Matt Jefferies and his team. It was now a charred ruin. Apollo's farewell speech was filmed with him "spreading himself to the wind" and vanishing, as Carolyn Palamas weeps.

"The sadness of these characters; it was vivid," Leslie Parrish said. "The feelings that we had were so honest and that intense. I never considered myself a method actor but, when I got something like this, I just poured my heart and soul into it. For an actress, it was a beautiful, beautiful opportunity. But the tragedy of it really struck me. And I felt that they loved each other. And the decision of what we [the Enterprise crew] decided to do in the end was the right one, but just agonizing. It was painful to me. In our last scene together -- Michael and me -- we were crying. I was crying because of what I had done to him. And he was crying because it *was* being done to him. And after, we were *really* crying." (134a)

When the lunch break came, the regular cast members were dismissed; only Forest and Parrish were needed for the remaining scenes. Daniels continued on a different part of Stage 10 for the scenes where Apollo and Carolyn talk privately in the garden area. The production schedule identified the final of these sequences as "Rape of the Wind."

Leslie Parrish's gown was the subject of great concern during the entire shoot, but especially on this day. James Doohan fondly recalled, "She was absolutely lovely, and I can tell you that a lot of sticky glue went into keeping her costume together." (52-1)

"A breathtakingly beautiful girl in one of my favorite scripts," said costume designer

William Theiss. "I felt this design, while Greek in feeling, was a completely fresh idea, i.e., the front of the dress was held up by the weight of the train which fell over the shoulder to the floor." (172-4)

Parrish said, "I especially loved Bill Theiss for that crazy gown. What happened is he threw a bolt of cloth over me -- this beautiful cloth -- and just pinned it at my waist and said, 'There, that's your costume.' The weight of it held it over my shoulder." (134a)

Leslie Parrish, wardrobe test
(Courtesy of Gerald Gurian)

"Ahh, the gown," said Dorothy Fontana. "The Theiss theory of titillation was that you could show a lot of basically non-sexual flesh, like the back, the side of the leg, bare arms, bare shoulders, skimpy in those areas, and people would be waiting for the dress to fall. But, of course, Bill made sure the outfit never did fall ... well, sort of. The weight of the cape over her one shoulder kind of held the front of the dress up -- so that was okay if she was just moving easily -- but when she had to be throwing herself on the ground, rolling around, she had to be glued into that thing." (64-2)

Walter Koenig said, "What made the episode for me was Leslie Parrish. I was on the set with her and she was glued into that costume, *literally*. And my tongue was hanging out, to have someone that close, and that beautiful, with that skin and that body. My God, just striking. I was praying that that gown would get caught on something and come right off. But no!" (102)

Costumer Andrea Weaver said, "It's true. Leslie Parrish's costume was glued on to her. Now we use a material which has two-sided Scotch tape; very strong Scotch tape, but then we didn't have that; all we had was glue. So the clothes that needed to be attached were glued on. And after three or four days that can get hard on the skin." (180a)

Parrish said, "There was one little section, yes, they had to glue it to me every day. And it was a different piece of skin every day -- and every day they'd rip it off and there went my skin and, finally, I didn't have much skin to glue it to. It was really painful." (134a)

Regarding "The Rape of the Wind," Parrish added, "That was a really, really violent scene -- it was hard to do. The fan [they used] was a monster. They don't even call it a fan. They have another name for it. It was like ten feet [round]. It was huge. And I think there were three of them. I mean, I was taking a pounding. It was hard to stay together -- that gown just didn't want to stay on. At that point, it was too much to ask of a gown like that." (134a)

Fontana added, "Jean Messerschmidt, who was our Broadcast Standards person, would usually nearly have a heart attack every time she'd see a Bill Theiss gown, or a costume that *almost* made it at covering the girl." (64-1)

Roddenberry said, "How much skin [we were] permitted to show used to be almost a matter of geometry and measurement. I remember doing shows that showed the inside of a woman's leg. Those shows were turned down because, for some reason, the inside of the leg was considered vulgar." (145-23)

Michael Forest said, "In those days you had to be careful -- the censors were very strict; you couldn't do certain things. In fact, you won't believe this, but I had to take the hair off my chest, because, evidently, gods do not have hair on their chests. I've never seen a real god. Have you? I don't know what they have. But, apparently, it's not hair." (65)

Forest was not aware that starship captains had no hair on their bodies, either. Shatner had first been subjected to the razor, per Roddenberry's instructions, for "The Corbomite Maneuver" in 1966.

At the end of the day, Forest, cleanly shaved, was the only cast member needed. The blue screen shots were taken where Apollo, as a giant, looks down on the landing party personnel, and his disembodied head talks from space, and his disembodied hand grabs the Enterprise.

Day 7. Michael Forest standing on a pedestal before a blue screen, enabling him to look down at where the tiny Earthlings would be (Photo courtesy of Gerald Gurian)

Forest said, "I hadn't done anything with those type of effects. Most of the stuff I was doing at that time was a lot of cops and robbers, cowboy stuff and mystery stuff. This really was special. But one of the things that was difficult was when they put me up against the blue screen. I was supposed to become taller. I guess I was up on some kind of a pedestal. But I had never been up against a blue screen like that one and I didn't know quite what to do. They said, 'Just stand there and look down,' and I thought, 'Well, okay, they obviously know more about technical aspects of this than I do, and I can trust them.' But it was funny doing that; not knowing how it was going to come together." (65)

Marc Daniels finally wrapped, one day behind schedule and deep into union overtime.

Leslie Parrish said, "The six-day schedules were difficult. We did work late. I remember the last scene we shot was like at ten or eleven at night. But nobody cared. Everybody was so into it. It was joyous doing that. There were some sets [on other shows] where it was more like work. But I loved going there." (134a)

Marc Daniels said, "Six days is not very much time to do an hour show. You could barely get it done if everything went right. Well, if one element goes sour, where are you? It's just incredible and impossible, and the miracle is that anything comes out that's worthwhile at all." (44-3)

This one, however, had taken seven days.

Forest, who had worked six of those seven days, recalled the *Star Trek* set as being a friendly one. Marc Daniels was "likable and professional," as were his fellow actors.

Leslie Parrish concurred, saying, "Marc Daniels was a gentle director. I think he was a compassionate director. He spoke to you softly. He made his contributions that way." (134a)

Of Parrish, Michael Forest said, "Leslie was a delightful person to work with; no problems; never any difficulties; we would just discuss what we were going to do and we would do it. She was excellent and very personable. William was a bit of a problem, however. You never saw me standing with him; we were always in different shots. We would be talking to one another, but we wouldn't be on camera at the same time. I'm sure that's what he stipulated -- because I was so much taller." (65)

Time plays tricks on one's memory. Some things did go sour. And it was actually six days ... plus one.

Post-Production
Available for editing: June 9, 1967. Rough Cut: June 23. Final Cut: June 29.

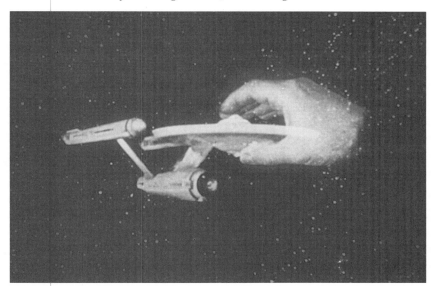

Music Score recorded on July 12.

Bruce Schoengarth took on his second assignment of the new season, heading up Edit Team 2. He had already cut the standout episodes "Mudd's Women," "The Naked Time," "The Squire of Gothos," and "Tomorrow Is Yesterday."

A sight never before seen on TV – and a state-of-the-art photo effect for 1967 (Courtesy of Gerald Gurian)

The camera footage was delivered to him on June 9, 1967. He finished his rough cut, under the supervision of Marc Daniels, on June 23. The final edit, under the supervision of Bob Justman, with notes from the two Genes -- Coon and Roddenberry -- was completed on June 29. Clever cutting helps make all the tricks in this episode work, such as Apollo growing and Scotty getting electrified.

Effects Unlimited provided for the photographic effects elements. Their collaboration with director, editor, and *Star Trek*'s special effects man, Jim Rugg, is the reason for the success of the shot where Apollo grows to giant proportions. The result is a combination of optical effects, clever camera angles, and inventive editing. Another innovative effect was the attention-grabbing image of the giant hand in space, grasping the Enterprise. This was a stunning visual for 1967 television.

Fred Steiner, Robert Justman's favorite *Star Trek* composer, returned to the recording studio for the first of four Second Season episodes. Already to his credit: "The Corbomite Maneuver," "Mudd's Women," and "Charlie X." His work here -- a partial score, recorded July 12, 1967, blended with tracks from previous episodes -- is quite effective.

"It's my favorite score and I think it's one of the best episodes of *Star Trek*," Steiner said. "It has a little bit of everything and there are some moments that I'm very fond of, particularly where I develop Captain Kirk's theme with a duet for the French horn." (168)

The fourth episode of the season was the fourth episode to go over-budget. "Who Mourns for Adonais?" came in at $203,623, which equates to more than $1.4 million in 2013 currency. And this went over the mandated Desilu per-episode allowance by $23,623.

Season Two's deficit was now up to $100,211 (nearly three-quarters of a million dollars in 2013). The red ink was about to turn a brighter red with the next episode to film -- "Amok Time."

Release / Reaction
Premiere air date: 9/22/67. NBC repeat broadcast: 5/10/68.

As with most episodes of *Star Trek* (except for those which were late in their delivery to NBC), a screening was held for the press in hopes of generating positive notices.

Steven H. Scheuer reviewed the episode for his syndicated column, *TV Key Previews*. Among numerous newspapers across the country, the review was carried by *The News Journal*, of Wilmington, Ohio, on September 22, 1967:

> "Who Mourns for Adonais?" This one offers a fanciful explanation for the existence for Gods of Greek mythology and the reason for the end of their reign on Earth. Captain Kirk and his crew find themselves at the mercy of a mysterious force in space that assumes a human form that is larger than life. He insists on being worshipped as the Greek god Apollo. How he demonstrates the love of a God, the wrath of a God and the disappearance of a God will keep fans tuned in to their set.

Judy Crosby reviewed the episode for her syndicated column, *TV SCOUT*. Among the papers which ran her notice on September 22, was the *Monessen Valley*

BETTER LOOK AT THE BEST

TARZAN
7:30 IN COLOR Can the king of the jungle save Jai's elephant when the animal is called a killer?

ACCIDENTAL FAMILY
9:30 NEW SHOW IN COLOR Jerry finds himself in danger of losing custody of his son. Jerry Van Dyke and Lois Nettleton.

STAR TREK
8:30 NEW DAY IN COLOR A mysterious being tries to subject Capt. Kirk to his power. William Shatner, Leonard Nimoy star.

TONIGHT ON
NBC 4

THE BELL HOUR
10:00 IN COLOR "Many Faces of Romeo and Juliet" has excerpts from four versions of the classic story. An all-star cast.

112

Independent, in Pennsylvania.

> The old and the new come together neatly in a good *Star Trek* episode that takes the starship Enterprise to Mt. Olympus, where ship and crew become the guests of the Greek God Apollo. Actually, they are more captives than guests as the imposing Grecian deity tells them that he has long been expecting their arrival and wants them to settle down on his planet as "permanent residents."

Most newspapers, however, did not have a TV critic to assess and even explain the storylines of the shows. Instead, they depended on whatever promotional material was sent out from the studio or network.

Roddenberry was miffed that the Desilu department in charge of promotion had dropped the ball with an episode he felt such pride over. After reading descriptions of the episode in the *Los Angeles Times* and *Los Angeles Herald-Examiner*, he fired off a letter to Howard McClay, head of the studio's PR Department, writing:

> I am frustrated and disappointed. I am referring to *Star Trek* "This Week's Story" paragraphs which appear in *TV Times* and *TV Weekly*…. I assume these represent syndicated items which go all over the country. I was shocked a week ago at the descriptions of our premiere show, "Amok Time," reading something like, "<u>Mr. Spock has a strange malady and is forced to fight Captain Kirk.</u>" I could not believe my eyes. Here we had a show chosen over many others because of its enormous promotional value… because it would show Mr. Spock's millions of fans a look at his home planet, plus the double whammy of the fact that Mr. Spock was going there in the episode to marry and mate. Can you top that? Yes, the second week's description did! With the fight with other networks… and all of our hard work riding on attracting audiences during these early weeks, I read a description of our second show in the *L.A. Times* and the *L.A. Herald-Examiner Magazines* which I simply cannot believe. In the *TV Times* we see: "The leader of a Greek-like community, which is slowly becoming extinct, threatens the Enterprise crew unless they join his colony." And in the *Herald-Examiner TV Weekly*: "Leader (Michael Forest) of a Greek-like community threatens the Enterprise crew unless they join his colony, which is slowly becoming extinct." … First, this asinine description is totally untrue. The episode "Who Mourns for Adonais?" is the story of a huge and strange creature <u>who claims to be Apollo, last of the Greek Gods! This is a creature which reaches up from its planet and with its hand grabs the huge U.S.S. Enterprise in flight</u>. It is also the story of the madness of this creature in demanding that it be worshipped. It is many other exciting things and any one of them is a hundred times more exciting than the description given. … We must know, Howard, what the upcoming story line descriptions are <u>and something must be done about them now before we lose anymore audience because of them</u>. Millions of people judge what show they are going to watch by these descriptions…. This is damned serious and damned important. (GR33-3)

The culprit was not Desilu after all, but NBC. The synopsis describing the plot of the episode that irked Roddenberry so can be traced back to the first paragraph of the NBC press release for "Who Mourns for Adonais?" Issued August 28, 1967, the press release said:

> The leader of a strange and slowly dying community patterned after the civilization of ancient Greece demands the Enterprise crew join his colony as permanent residents, in "Who Mourns for Adonais?" on the NBC Television Network's colorcast of *Star Trek* Friday, Sept. 22…. Capt. Kirk (William Shatner) rejects the request of the Greek-like god who calls himself Apollo (guest star Michael Forest), despite threats of violence against him, Mr. Spock (Leonard Nimoy) and the rest of his crew. Unfortunately, Apollo gets the upper hand by turning his attentions to lovely scientist Carolyn Bassett [sic] (guest star

Leslie Parrish), who is romantically involved with him despite Kirk's admonitions.

"Who Mourns for Adonais?" did respectable business when it premiered on September 22, 1967, as the second episode to be aired in the new season.

RATINGS / Nielsen National report for Friday, September 22, 1967:

8:30 to 9 p.m.: 56.1% of U.S. TVs in use.	**Share:**	**Households:**
NBC: *Star Trek* (first half)	25.5%	10,920,000
ABC: *Hondo* (first half)	22.5%	9,800,000
CBS: **Gomer Pyle, U.S.M.C.**	**46.7%**	**16,460,000**
Local independent stations:	5.3%	

9 to 9:30 p.m.: 57.7% of U.S. TVs in use.	**Share:**	**Households:**
NBC: *Star Trek* (second half)	26.7%	No data
ABC: *Hondo* (second half)	22.9%	No data
CBS: **Friday Night Movie**	**38.2%**	**No data**
Local independent stations:	12.2%	No data

The movie on CBS was the television premiere of a big-screen hit, the 1962 John Ford western, *The Man Who Shot Liberty Valance*, starring John Wayne, Jimmy Stewart, Vera Miles, and Lee Marvin. CBS sprung for an ad in *TV Guide* and elsewhere. NBC spent nothing to promote *Star Trek*.

"NBC didn't go out of its way to promote many shows in the mid-to-late1960s," Dorothy Fontana explained. "It wasn't the same as it is today, with promo after promo in every commercial break." (64-4a)

Regardless, *Star Trek*, again, was a second-place entry. There is no shame in these numbers, especially taking into account the competition and NBC's lack of support. Nielsen estimates that there was an average of two people watching in every household. That gave *Star Trek* an estimated national audience of nearly 22 million people. And *Star Trek* was still the top-rated NBC Friday night show. The network's numbers tumbled once *Star Trek* left the airwaves and millions of viewers tuned away from NBC to avoid the sitcom *Accidental Family*, down from 10,920,000 households to 7,390,000, and *The Bell Telephone Hour*, with stars of the theater, opera, ballet, and musical stage in interpretations of the ancient love story of *Romeo and Juliet*, which lowered the households tuning in to 5,770,000. The other two networks, meanwhile, saw their ratings rise all the way to 11 p.m.

***

Many of those who worked on the series were proud of "Who Mourns for Adonais?"

Director Marc Daniels picked it as his favorite *Star Trek*, because of the subject matter and that "it all came together so well."

Costumer Bill Theiss referred to it as one of his "favorite scripts."

Composer Fred Steiner said, "I think it's one of the best episodes of *Star Trek*."

And the fans liked it, too. One such fan, actor Jason Alexander, who later played George on *Seinfeld*, told *TV Guide* (Vol. 44, No. 34) that this was his favorite episode from the original series, calling it "thought-provoking, beautiful, and very sad."

Walter Koenig added, "After Harlan Ellison's 'The City on the Edge of Forever,'

'Who Mourns for Adonais?' was the second-most emotionally evocative show, I believe, that we did on *Star Trek*." (102-13)

Vic Mignogne, writer, director, producer, and star (he plays Kirk) of *Star Trek Continues*, was so taken by "Who Mourns for Adonais?" that he made a sequel. Mignogne said, "What intrigued me so much about 'WMFA' was that Apollo just faded away, broken and in despair. Where'd he go? We didn't know -- presumably to join the other gods. So when my dear friend Barbara Luna [Marlena from "Mirror, Mirror"] told me that Mike Forest wanted to do something *Trek* related, I imagined an Apollo redemption story. Mike loved the idea and came out of retirement to reprise the Greek god in the *Star Trek Continues* premiere episode, "Pilgrim Of Eternity" [the title taken from a line in the same poem as 'Who Mourns for Adonais']. Mike's performance was brilliant, and the great privilege to act with him was more than I ever imagined when I watched the original episode as an 11 year-old boy."

Memories

Gilbert Ralston didn't mind being pressured to make the script for this episode better. To the contrary, he said, "I liked *Star Trek* because of Gene and some of the people who originally worked on it. Their conception was highly intellectual and very sophisticated, and it was fun to write because they were very demanding in so far as literary quality was concerned. Shows like that were always a pleasure." (144-2)

As for Leslie Parrish, the woman who played Lt. Commander Montgomery Scott's love interest, James Doohan said, "I met her on the show and dated her a couple times. There was just something about her. She was a charming dinner companion, absolutely gorgeous, but she knew how to break down and be a good talker. There were no airs to her at all." (52-1)

Leslie Parrish said, "The cast was absolutely great. James Doohan was a darling, darling man; such a sweetheart. You couldn't know him and not love him." (134a)

Parrish holds other fond memories of her experience on *Star Trek*. She is also proud of the results of that work, saying, "Whenever I watch it, I go right back to the whole thing again and cry my way through it. I relive it. My impression of it is that it's one piece of work that I'm very proud of. Of all the work I did, this is outstanding, because it is rooted in something in which I believe so deeply." (134a)

Walter Koenig said, "I think Michael Forest is a terrific actor. He was actually perfect in that role -- great presence, and great resonance, too. So you believe the god-like figure. But what made it for me was the vulnerability of that character. Even though he's this massive man that is used to giving orders, he is tragically needy." (102)

Michael Forest told this author, in 2011, "People will look at me, then look away, then look at me again before coming over and asking, 'Excuse me, did you ever do an episode of *Star Trek*.' And I'll say, 'Well, yes, I did.' And, one time, in Europe, after I said that, this one lady looked so startled, and she said, 'You're Apollo!' And I said, 'Yes, that was the name of the character, so I guess I am.' And she looked like she was going to faint. It's amazing -- the irony of it -- but that show has given me more mileage than any other show that I ever did. And I did some pretty good films over the years, here and in Europe. But people ask what I'm most recognized for, and I say, 'It has to be the *Star Trek*.'" (65)

7

Episode 34: AMOK TIME

Written by Theodore Sturgeon
(with Gene Roddenberry, Gene Coon, and D.C. Fontana, uncredited)
Directed by Joseph Pevney

Arlene Martel and Leonard Nimoy, NBC publicity photo
(Courtesy of Gerald Gurian)

NBC press release:

MR. SPOCK'S STRANGE MALADY ON PLANET VULCAN FORCES HIM INTO COMBAT WITH CAPTAIN KIRK ON FIRST *STAR TREK* OF 1967-68. The strange illness of Mr. Spock and a bizarre Vulcan custom presided over by T'Pau (guest star Celia Lovsky) force Captain James Kirk and Mr. Spock into a deadly combat against each other, in "Amok Time," starting the second season of *Star Trek* Friday, Sept. 15 on the NBC Television Network. The series stars William Shatner as Captain Kirk, Leonard Nimoy as Mr. Spock and DeForest Kelley as Dr. McCoy.... Capt. Kirk grants his seriously stricken executive officer aboard the United Space Ship Enterprise permission to return to his native planet of Vulcan, where Spock reveals an ancient practice compelling him to marry or face death.... Also starring in this episode are Arlene Martel as T'Pring and Lawrence Montaigne as Stonn.

From *TV Guide*, September 9, 1967:

"Amok Time." The Enterprise begins a second year in space with a visit to Mr. Spock's native planet. Obeying an ancient Vulcan marriage rite, the science officer engages in mortal combat with his fiancée's chosen champion -- Captain Kirk. Script by Theodore Sturgeon.

Spock's logic has been ripped from him by the *pon farr* -- "the time of the mating; the blood fever." T'Pring, his selected consort by arrangement of their parents when both were young, has spurned Spock and uses Kirk in her plan to be free of the half-Vulcan. Kirk believes he is doing Spock a service in protecting him from the bigger, stronger Stonn, the one T'Pring truly wants. But Kirk is being set up, as is Spock … as are we.

"Amok Time" tricks us into understanding ourselves, as we watch the most logical being of all crumble. The daring theme: how sexual urges and the necessity to procreate overcome reason. Is this Man-against-Man as the climactic fight to the death between Kirk and Spock might have us believe? Think again. Spock is always a prime example of Man-against-Himself.

SOUND BITES

- *Kirk:* "You have been called the best First Officer in the Fleet. That is an enormous asset to me. If I'm to lose that First Officer, I want to know why." *Spock:* "It has to do with … biology…. Vulcan biology." *Kirk*: "You mean, the biology of Vulcans? Biology as in reproduction? Nothing to be embarrassed about, Spock. It even happens to the birds and bees." *Spock:* "The birds and the bees are not Vulcans. If they were … if any creature were as proudly logical as we … and had their logic ripped from them … as this time does to us…. There are precedents in nature, Captain…. On your Earth, the salmon. They must return to that one stream of their birth ... to spawn … or die in trying..." *Kirk:* "But you're not a fish, Mr. Spock." *Spock:* "No. Nor am I a man. I'm a Vulcan."

- *Spock:* "Stonn, she is yours. After a time, you may find 'having' is not so pleasing a thing after all as 'wanting.' It is not logical, but it is often true."

- *T'Pau:* "Live long and prosper, Spock." *Spock:* "I shall do neither. I have killed my captain... and my friend."

ASSESSMENT

Gene Roddenberry, TV's Jonathan Swift, was at it again. He was the one who came up with the concept for this episode.

We understand how the sex drive and the need to procreate can influence and make or break one's life. But in 1967, sexual hormones and mating urges were never discussed on television during the family hours. When Spock said that he was not a "man" but an alien, a creature to be compared to a salmon, *Star Trek* once again found a way to sneak past the censors.

"Amok Time" is filled with many firsts -- the first trip to Vulcan, the first Vulcan hand salute, the first reference to "Live long and prosper," and the first time Mr. Spock, under his own will, expressed emotion … when learning that Kirk was not dead. It was the second time Kirk and Spock fought (see "This Side of Paradise") and the third time a regular cast member was killed, then resurrected (see "Charlie X" and "Shore Leave").

"Amok Time" is stark and startling more than 45 years after it first aired. The writing is tight and concise. For its time, the production is impeccable. The performances are uniformly superb. Even as the cameras were rolling, everyone suspected this would be the season opener, so extra care was taken to get everything just right. And everything was.

117

THE STORY BEHIND THE STORY

Script Timeline
Gene Roddenberry concept: December 5, 1966.
Theodore Sturgeon's pitch notes, "Spock Blows Top": December 6, 1966.
Sturgeon's story outline, ST #41, "Amok Time": December 12, 1966.
Sturgeon's 1st Draft teleplay: March 29, 1967.
Sturgeon's 2nd Draft teleplay: May 5, 1967.
D.C. Fontana's rewrite (Mimeo Department "Yellow Cover 1st Draft"):
Mid May 1967.
Gene Coon's script polish (Final Draft teleplay): May 31, 1967.
Gene Roddenberry's script polish (Revised Final Draft teleplay): June 1, 1967.
Gene Coon's second script polish (2nd Revised Final Draft teleplay):
June 5, 1967.
Additional revised script pages by Coon: June 7 & 8, 1967.

Gene Roddenberry, brainstorming with Gene Coon, hatched the idea for "Amok Time." The premise was then handed to sci-fi novelist Theodore Sturgeon, coming off his first *Star Trek* writing job -- "Shore Leave." This second assignment for Sturgeon was meant to be part of the first season, among the last episodes produced.

On December 15, 1966, of Sturgeon's story treatment, NBC's Stan Robertson wrote:

> This is a superior outline and one which should add more to the in-depth
> audience appeal for Mr. Spock. (SR34)

Robertson immediately saw the potential in this story to be among the best in the series and, from a broadcasting point of view, the most important. And that demanded it be given special attention.

In Sturgeon's outline, Spock is observed acting strangely by many in the crew, far more than in the filmed version. Robertson was instrumental in changing this, telling Coon:

> I think we should minimize any attempts on the author's part of having Spock
> running around the ship and being engaged in various little cameos with the
> other members of the crew, to point out that there is something amiss with him.
> We have done this several times in other stories with Spock and various other
> members of our permanent crew [Kirk in "The Enemy Within," Spock in
> "Operation: Annihilate!" and everyone in "The Naked Time" and "This Side of
> Paradise"]. The point is that we can show Spock's condition by briefly playing it
> off McCoy and Kirk, who are more involved with him than others. (SR34)

In Sturgeon's first take on the story, Kirk was skeptical over the news from McCoy that Spock's condition was serious to the point of life or death. Robertson wrote:

> I think Kirk's reaction to being told that he must get Spock to the planet Vulcan
> as soon as possible or Spock will die is not keeping with the warm
> characterization of our starship captain. We realize that he must consider what is
> best for the entire spaceship, but he, more than anyone aboard, knows Spock and
> is closer to him, so it seems his reactions would be a little different than outlined
> here. (SR34)

Wanting to see more of Vulcan than the outline depicted, and more Vulcans than just the one girl Spock was to marry, Robertson warned:

> The planet Vulcan, and those who inhabit it, have been built as such a mystery
> throughout our series that unless we establish more of the planet than is outlined
> here, and unless we show some other Vulcans other than the girl, we will indeed

be "cheating" our viewers. (SR34)

The monarch T'Pau would be added, as would Stonn and numerous others in the marriage procession.

Robertson felt Kirk needed a better reason to fight Spock than the original treatment indicated, where he only engaged in the combat because he was chosen and the Vulcan law demanded his involvement. Robertson suggested that Kirk proceed "perhaps with the idea that it would save Spock's life."

Added into the script, Kirk's line to McCoy, "You said this fight might save his life. So I'll give it to him. What's a black eye against that? Besides, that's T'Pau of Vulcan over there. All Vulcan in one package. Do you think I can back out in front of <u>her</u>?"

Robertson also wanted better clarification as to why Spock would die if not returned to Vulcan, and this led to the chilling comparison to salmon swimming up stream.

With these notes in hand, Sturgeon was sent home to write the script.

Dorothy Fontana said, "'Amok Time' took a lot of time to get out of Ted Sturgeon, who wasn't really used to television pace. He was used to writing his short stories and his novels at his own speed." (64-1)

It was now clear that this was going to be a Second Season episode. Regardless, three months after Sturgeon had started the script, Roddenberry sent word to the writer's agent:

> We must get our first draft from Ted Sturgeon soon or regretfully cut him off and assign the project to another writer. Where is he, how is he, <u>what is he doing</u>? (GR34-1)

Sturgeon relented and sent in what he had on paper ... so far. Robert Justman was quick to respond, writing to Roddenberry:

> I have read the first two acts of "Amok Time" as submitted by Ted Sturgeon on March 29, 1967. I find it hard to receive only two acts of this epic. Is it because we will receive the next two acts <u>next season</u>?! (RJ34-1)

Pete Sloman of De Forest Research, who read all the *Star Trek* scripts, along with Joan Pierce, for technical accuracy, was accustomed to the hurry-up-and-wait drill whenever Theodore Sturgeon was put on assignment. He said, "Sturgeon was very famous for turning in scripts anywhere between two days and two weeks <u>after</u> the shoot date, because he just couldn't get it done in time." (158a)

And this meant that "shoot dates" had to constantly be pushed back. It had happened with "Shore Leave." It was happening now with "Amok Time." It would happen again with further story and script assignments given to Sturgeon -- stories and scripts that would never find their way in front of the camera due to the writer's tardiness.

More pressure was put on Sturgeon. The balance of the script was delivered a few days later.

Robert Justman and Dorothy Fontana each had much to say about the 1st Draft script which, coming from Ted Sturgeon, as with "Shore Leave," was an imaginative but loosely structured tale.

In a seven-page memo to Roddenberry, Justman said:

> Naturally, I am very pleased by the concept of this script. So, therefore, enough of praise and let me get on with the areas I would like to have fixed.... At times in the story we tend to get very cute and precious. We should not get so cute and precious that people start laughing at us rather than with us. (RJ34-1)

119

Roddenberry, a firm believer in keeping *Star Trek* serious and as far away as possible from the campiness of *Lost in Space*, agreed. Surgeon was instructed to be less cute and less precious.

Fontana, with her four-page memo to Roddenberry, took issue with a character Sturgeon had invented -- Maggie, a young female crew member smitten with Mr. Spock. D.C. wrote:

> We should eliminate the whole Maggie-in-love bit. If you really insist on having some female sick at heart over Spock's "marriage," why not pick up the "Naked Time" relationship of Christine Chapel in love with Spock? Christine, at least, is a mature woman we have met before and know -- not some drippy-eyed kid we don't care about. Needless to say, any replacement of Maggie by Christine would also require a different approach to the character and her feelings for Spock on a much more adult level. (DC34)

Maggie was taken out, Christine Chapel was put in.

Regarding further changes, Justman was the instigator of a couple of excellent scenes. He told Roddenberry:

> I think one of the weaknesses of this script is that we do a lot of talking about how Mr. Spock is suffering, but we are never alone with him to actually see him attempting to control himself. (RJ34-1)

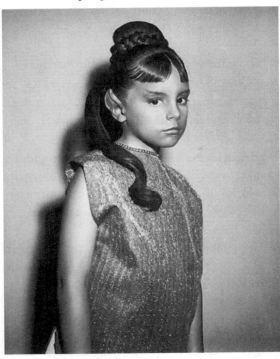

Mary Rice as young T'Pring
(Courtesy of Gerald Gurian)

The scenes eventually to be added included a tormented Spock staring hypnotically at his computer monitor, studying the picture of a female Vulcan child (T'Pring, age 7) and, later, smashing that same monitor with his fist when Uhura calls from the bridge.

Regarding the arrival of the marriage party on Vulcan, Fontana wrote:

> We are cheating the audience when we indicate a Vulcan flying machine by sound alone. I do not suggest we make a Vulcan flying machine. I suggest we have T'Pring arrive on foot or by travois or dogsled or howdah or anything but a flying machine we can't show our audience. (DC34)

Justman echoed this, writing:

> I suggest that the welcoming committee should arrive by some other means. Would you believe walking? (RJ34-1)

Roddenberry and Coon opted for a sedan carried by a couple of muscular Vulcan males.

Neither Justman nor Fontana thought much of Sturgeon's invention of a Vulcan language, or the many instances of its use, including numerous pages of Vulcans talking to Vulcans *in* Vulcan. Fontana begged Roddenberry:

<u>PLEASE</u> eliminate all the Vulcan dialogue and keep it in English. Saves translation and it will keep everyone informed of which player is where. Also, I anticipate the biggest laugh of the year in Scene 58 when T'Pring utters some kind of large Vulcan pronouncement and Spock stares back at her, saying, "T'Pring! Klart!" (DC34)

Justman referred to Sturgeon Vulcan-speak as "mumble-jumbo" and told Roddenberry:

I think for the purpose of our viewing audience, all conversations should be in English. However, we can space the Vulcans' speeches with various esoteric words from time to time -- which should add sufficient flavor. By the way, I liked the language that our lady from New Orleans invented in the [script] "Shun-Daki." It sounded and read like a real language, as opposed to the words contained within this script. (RJ34-1)

The lady from New Orleans was Darlene Hartman, who had submitted unsolicited stories, and even a full spec script, to *Star Trek*. Roddenberry and Coon had taken a liking to Hartman, who would one day blossom into a successful and well regarded science fiction author, and they would soon put her on assignment for the script "Shol" (to be discussed later).

Gene Coon's secretary, Ande Richardson-Kindryd, said, "Kellam de Forest was a lovely man and he was really good, but Peter Sloman and Joan Pierce were the reader and the second reader on the *Star Trek* scripts. I think Peter created the Vulcan language after the writers first played around with it. I remember him going crazy one day because the syntax wasn't correct. I said, 'Peter, you're creating a language; only you will know if that is the correct verb or not.' They were the brightest people. Joan's specialty was England; anything British; anything to do with royalty. And Peter had his specialties -- language, regional dialect, slang, as well as anything to do with science fiction. Everyone had an area so that if a script came in, you had a second read for someone who had the experience. They had a lot of books, I'll tell you. They had books everywhere! And they were always on the phones calling somebody. That's how you did it before everyone had a computer on their desk -- a computer like Spock had. Those were still just ideas on *Star Trek*." (144a)

Pete Sloman said, "They did try on *Star Trek*. And they got many things right. But one of their problems was their TV writers didn't understand science fiction, and their science fiction writers didn't understand TV. And that's why you had wonderful scripts from people like Theodore Sturgeon and Jerry Bixby and Harlan Ellison which would have to go through so many changes. And then you had an occasional TV writer who just didn't understand the concept of what science fiction was all about. It was a very tight and very narrow sort of walkway that Roddenberry and all these other people were on. So the scientific accuracy of *Star Trek* could have been a lot better. But it could have been so much worse, that I give them an absolute A+ for effort." (158a)

As for Spock's competitor for the hand of T'Pring, later to be named Stonn, Sturgeon had come up with a name that amused Justman, who wrote Roddenberry:

I think the writer has made a Freudian slip in naming Spock's rival. Spor is an interesting name. It has a certain built-in connotation. How about re-naming him Sperm? (RJ34-1)

And then there was an unintentionally funny sequence as T'Pring spins around, again and again, before pointing out her challenger to Spock's marriage rights. Justman wrote:

We are missing a good bit when Spock's lady friend chooses his opponent. First of all, she should hesitate and lead the audience to believe that she is going to select that great big Mr. Spor to fight with Mr. Spock. And then, at the last minute, she should turn and indicate Captain Kirk. After all, if you're going to set up the character of Spor, we ought to do something with it -- at least we ought to do something more than we presently have in this version of the script. And, anyhow, I fall down and laugh every time we spin Spock's girl friend around like a "gyroscope." (RJ34-1)

Fontana was falling down, too, but not necessarily laughing. She said:

Can we have another way for T'Pring to pick her champion rather than spinning around like a dervish and stopping to point at Kirk? (DC34)

Regarding Sturgeon's wish that there be a viewing audience to witness the fight, Justman wrote:

Why raise the point of the whole world watching this mortal combat if we never show the whole world watching this mortal combat? Why don't we just not refer to it and stay out of trouble? This will also save our establishing a certain similarity between this show and the script that John Kneubuhl is writing ["Bread and Circuses," which, among other things, lampooned network television]. (RJ34-1)

Fontana responded similarly, writing:

There are references here and earlier to "a whole world watching." Is this on *Candid Camera*? I don't know if we would like a whole world which intrudes on what is basically a personal ceremony. Do they also watch the "spawning"? I'll bet they don't have NBC Broadcast Standards to contend with. (DC34)

The reference was removed.

Regarding the climactic fight scene, Fontana wrote:

Leonard [Nimoy] will kill himself if he must do Scene 62 in which he behaves like a snorting bull. I strongly recommend an examination of the dialogue and characters here. (DC34)

In his memo, Justman said:

Spock starts acting like King Kong. I believe that this is the wrong way for Mr. Spock to behave.... I think that we should still attempt to play the fact he is barely keeping himself under control -- but he shouldn't snort and beat himself on the chest and exclaim loudly, "Kikki-nee klart!" (RJ34-1)

The snorting and beating was replaced with:

Spock looks toward Kirk and there is absolutely no sign of recognition in his eyes. He scowls.

The "Kikki-nee klart" was replaced by something less likely to prompt snickers -- "Klee-fah!"

The staff notes were on Roddenberry's desk. Now, what to say to Sturgeon? The last time Roddenberry sent rewrite instructions to Theodore Sturgeon, regarding the 1st Draft of "Shore Leave," Sturgeon responded with a letter filled with hurt and anger. So Roddenberry chose a different tack this time. He gave the task to Coon.

Gene Coon's letter to Sturgeon was somewhat short, for Coon, that is. It ran eight pages. Coon opened gently, writing:

First of all, Ted, let me say that we are all generally pleased with the first draft of "Amok Time," although, of course, a certain amount of polishing and so on will be necessary. (GC34-2)

"A certain amount of polishing" translated to "a great deal of rewriting." Coon's memo continued:

We have to learn why Spock will die if he doesn't get to Vulcan in eight days. What kills him? Swollen gonads?… [And] since we have established that Spock either gets to Vulcan within eight days or dies, why doesn't he do so when he doesn't get married or laid? We must establish a sound explanation and have it explained or a lot of people will be unhappy with us.… I have met with some resentment on the name "Spor" from Bob Justman. He thinks it might be slightly… suggestive.… I know, Ted, you have gone to a great deal of trouble to invent the Vulcan language, but people just don't dig invented languages… and actors never seem to be able to sell them.… If the entire world is watching their ceremony, we get the feeling it is much like when a young couple gets married on Earth today, then the groom takes the bride to bed on *The Tonight Show*.… I would much prefer not to see Spock do a bad imitation of King Kong by striking himself on the chest and snorting.… We play Spock as being unemotional when he sincerely thinks that he has killed his captain. For heaven's sake, at this point let him register some honest surprise, some reaction, some overt human emotion. And let him not be ashamed of it! (GC34-2)

Among the many critiques, Coon did as D.C. Fontana had hoped and told Sturgeon to replace the far-too-young and far-too-annoying lovesick crew girl Maggie with the older, more palatable, lovesick Nurse Chapel.

Theodore Sturgeon did not respond with an angry letter but, after two weeks of silence, by sending in his 2nd Draft teleplay.

Roddenberry told Coon that he liked the script, "generally," saying:

Ted's writing has a vitality which is good for the show. He is beginning to understand our format and our characters and should do increasingly better scripts provided we see he is always launched off with a good, sound story. It seems to me the more action and jeopardies [sic] in the story, the less inclined he will be to make the script talky. (GR34-3)

But Roddenberry also had issues. He took notice that Spock was now more often talked about than seen, and told Coon:

If he wrote the scenes with Spock in them, Ted would be forced to feel along with Spock and that would hurt and it is much less painful to keep it at a distance, talk about it rather than feel it. Sure, it hurts to be a Vulcan coming into heat. But the writer has to feel that hurt in order to write it -- and the audience is going to have to feel it or we won't have a teleplay which takes advantage of everything inherent in the story. (GR34-3)

Finally, after eight pages of concerns and complaints, Roddenberry warned Coon:

This is a critical script for *Star Trek*! There should be no doubt in anyone's mind that the Spock characterization has caught the public's fancy. Carelessness now may see that character and characterization irreparably damaged. This must be one of our best and most carefully thought out scripts of the year. If there is any doubt about this, I would much rather see this episode shot a month or two from now, replaced with something less important which we can quickly hammer into shape. Let's not rush this one! (GR34-3)

The script was not sent back to Theodore Sturgeon for further work but, instead, handed off to Dorothy Fontana. Her rewrite -- the Yellow Cover 1ˢᵗ Draft -- was the first version to be distributed to the cast.

Fontana later said, "Mostly, again, it was pulling together things that were not *Star Trek* and making them *Star Trek*. There were some glitches, like the first scene, as I wrote it, you see Nurse Chapel going into Spock's quarters and she has the soup, and then she comes out screaming and the soup comes flying out after her. The way Ted originally wrote that scene was that Chapel comes to Kirk and says, in a sense, 'You should see what just happened; what Spock did.' You can't do that. You have to show it. You can't say, 'You should have seen it.' Yes, you *should* have seen it. It was things like that. And then, with the so-called love story -- the bride and the man she really wants -- I put in the fact that she was very calculating, saying, 'You'll be gone. I'll still be here, and Stonn will be here.' Like the Julie Newmar character [in "Friday's Child"], but Gene didn't allow it there. So I brought some of that into this one.... [And] the characters needed to be more clearly defined and motivated and -- since I had become the resident "Vulcan expert" -- I got that task.... But delving into the Vulcan culture that nobody had ever seen before -- the ceremony, the formality, this woman who was head of the council, T'Pau -- that was all basically Sturgeon. But we made it more *Star Trek*." (64-3)

Pleased with Fontana's rewrite, Leonard Nimoy wrote to Roddenberry:

> Have just finished reading "Amok Time" and am very, very happy with it. I think that the story very successfully involves all our central characters in strong and meaningful relationships. There's a strong line of suspense and emotional contact throughout the script. (LN34)

But Nimoy didn't appreciate Spock showing an "emotional experience with Kirk" at the conclusion of the story, especially since it was to be played in front of McCoy and Nurse Chapel. Recalling his suggestion for "The Naked Time," he wrote:

> I think that Spock would go off and do that by himself. (LN34)

In that earlier episode, Nimoy's recommendation was dead-on, leading to the excellent scene in which Spock had his breakdown alone in the briefing room. Here, however, the writers -- Sturgeon and Fontana -- had the better idea. Audience reaction regarding the highly emotional scene has long since proved them right.

Nimoy concluded:

> All in all, a very gratifying script to read and am looking forward with great pleasure to shooting it. (LN34)

Robert Justman and director Joseph Pevney felt there was still more work to do. Justman wrote Coon:

> The teleplay swings along like Gangbusters for the first three acts, but I am sad to state that in my opinion it falls down badly in the last act. I feel I have to agree with Joe Pevney that the Fourth Act needs straightening out to a great extent.... I say "krykah" to Act IV. (RJ34-4)

Later the spelling would be changed to "kroykah."

Gene Coon had his turn with the script and, especially, Act IV. His version was the Final Draft, dated May 31.

Gene Roddenberry left his imprint on the script, as well, for a Revised Final Draft, dated June 1. Coon got it back for a 2ⁿᵈ Revised Final Draft from June 5, plus two additional sets of page revisions from June 7 and 8. Finally, all were satisfied. They had to be --

production was to begin the next day.

"Amok Time" was pushed back several weeks to be the fifth episode filmed for the new season. The "less important" script Roddenberry spoke of, to be "quickly hammered into shape" and hurried into production, was "Catspaw." Three more followed -- "Metamorphosis," "Friday's Child," and "Who Mourns for Adonais?" -- allowing "Amok Time" more time for the script to be finessed and the planet Vulcan to be imagined and realized.

Shortly after Sturgeon's 1st Draft script arrived, Roddenberry wrote to Coon:

Spock's planet must be somehow different than ours.... [A] hot and arid place with slightly less atmosphere and slightly more mass and gravity.... Fortunately for us, arid locations are quite easy to come by in Southern California -- although we may want to go to a further exterior than something like "Vasquez Rocks," and actually go for something like the sand dune location out of Palm Springs or Mohave. (GR34-2)

Justman disagreed. He argued that they could not mix scenes shot outdoors with others shot on a stage, even with the use of rear-projection process shots, and keep Vulcan looking truly un-Earth-like. He told Coon:

We can create any color sky we wish on Stage 10. If we do use "process" [combining dialogue filmed on the soundstage with exterior shots taken in the desert], we are trapped into going for blue sky.... Let's instead try to get some sort of forced perspective on Stage 10 and take advantage of the elements that we have there to work with. (RJ34-4)

"'Amok Time' was a little difficult to do," admitted Dorothy Fontana. "In terms of production, how the heck were we going to do this? *Where* were we going to do this? We finally ended up doing it on the stage, because no location that they looked at was really right. You couldn't dress it up enough to make it look exotic enough, so we decided, 'Okay, we've got to do this on the stage.'" (64-1)

Set Designer Matt Jefferies, in a 1968 interview for *Inside Star Trek*, issue 12, said, "'Amok Time' was rough just to get the feeling and everything in it... considering what we knew or thought we knew about the Vulcans at that time.... Because of the uniqueness of the show, I couldn't send to a prop house and get what I needed. We had to build almost every prop used on the series. There aren't many prop houses that stock items such as Vulcan wind chimes."

Before Jefferies could make the props or design the set, he had to visualize everything. The man who drew the blueprints for the Enterprise now had to conceive an entire world and its people.

"People familiar with the series know Spock as a logical, stoic individual," Jefferies said. "Since he is only half Vulcan, the inhabitants of his home planet would be even more so. Therefore, we not only had the three dimensions of the set to take into consideration, but a philosophy as well. *The set had to reflect the people.* What we came up with is actually quite simple in appearance but straightforward. It looked like something carved from the rim of an extinct volcano. As Spock himself might say, 'It's extremely logical.'" (91-10)

The script guided Jefferies. The description there:

125

A fairly level arena area. Rocks around the edges give a half-natural, half-artifact aspect, as if the wind and rain had carved something like a Stonehenge, or reduced Stonehenge to something like this.

In "Amok Time," before we ever see Vulcan, we get a sense of Vulcan, with a visit to Spock's quarters. We had gotten a glimpse of Spock's shipboard living space in "The Menagerie," but now the entire cabin would be seen. Of this, Roddenberry wrote Jefferies:

> Spock's quarters may be used to suggest many things about the planet we do not have an opportunity to show. Also, the dressing, lighting, art, and other aspects of Spock's quarters are extremely important to maintaining the level of audience interest in this character. (GR34-4)

Jefferies envisioned Spock's quarters as giving evidence of the hidden side of this Vulcan's personality, the polar opposite of Spock's well-maintained cool.

Arlene Martel with Nimoy in NBC publicity photo (Courtesy of Gerald Gurian)

During all of the final writing and designing, Joseph Pevney was hired to direct. This was already his third episode for the new season (following "Catspaw" and "Friday's Child"). He continued to work full time at *Star Trek*, directing every other episode and spending the time in between giving feedback on the scripts, sets, props, costumes, and editing. He also had a big say in the casting.

Arlene "Tasha" Martel was 31 when hired to play Spock's intended bride, T'Pring. She had been on *The Outer Limits, The Twilight Zone, The Wild, Wild West* and, in a recurring guest role as Tiger, in *Hogan's Heroes*. Her first encounter with *Star Trek* happened two years earlier when she tried out for the role of Dr. Elizabeth Dehner in "Where No Man Has Gone Before."

"I read for the pilot, for the part that Sally Kellerman ended up doing," Martel said. "But I couldn't possibly do something that would require wearing full contact lenses. My eyes are really sensitive. Even when I see someone else put them in, I have to look away." (116)

Pevney first saw Martel several weeks before the casting sessions for "Amok Time." Martel recalled, "They brought me in for 'Catspaw.' And, after I did the read, they were buzzing amongst themselves. I heard the words 'Save her,' but I didn't hear what they were thinking of saving me for. I was disappointed, because this was a good part, this alien woman [Sylvia]. But then I thought, 'Well, maybe they are men of their word; maybe they are indeed saving me for something better. And, with all due respect to 'Catspaw,' this was the one that became a classic; a *favorite* favorite." (116)

Lawrence Montaigne had been seen previously as a Romulan in "Balance of Terror." And he only took that role to work with Mark Lenard. His role in "Amok Time," as Spock's rival, Stonn, was a sort of consolation prize -- except at the time Montaigne didn't see it as such. He had, after all, been told just a few months earlier that he would likely be a series regular, since it was looking like negotiations between Desilu and Nimoy would fail.

"They called my agent and were drawing up contracts," Montaigne remembered. "And I had spoken to Robert Justman, and Bob told me I couldn't play Spock but they were going to create another role … to take over as the Vulcan on the ship. And, since I had to stay available, there was a contingency clause -- if Leonard does a 180 [and returns to the series], I'd get offered another part. Meanwhile I kept calling my agent and saying, 'You know, I'm not working.' And he

Director John Sturges, with Charles Bronson, John Leyton, James Coburn, and Lawrence Montaigne, on the set of *The Great Escape* (lawrencemontaigne.com)

said, 'Listen, don't be greedy, you've got this series. This is written in stone; you're in, boy.' And, of course, it didn't turn out. But they called and said, 'Would I do another role?'-- which was Stonn. When I saw the script I had a heart attack. I had five lines! I didn't really want to do it. I turned the part down." (119a)

For Montaigne, small roles of this type represented a step backward. During the last few years, he had been featured in the all-star WWII epic *The Great Escape*, as Haynes, in charge of "diversions," and worked with William Shatner in "Cold Hands, Warm Heart" in *The Outer Limits*. In 1967 alone, Montaigne appeared in more than a dozen primetime series,

Celia Lovski, with Shatner, for NBC publicity photo
(Courtesy of Gerald Gurian)

including two episodes each for *Dr. Kildare, Time Tunnel, Felony Squad, The Invaders, The Man from U.N.C.L.E.* and, as the Joker's right hand man, Mr. Glee, *Batman*. Now, after refusing work for over a month, he was offered what he felt to be a bit part. Montaigne said, "And then Roddenberry called me at home and he started talking about how important this role was and this and that and the other thing, and then he said something to the effect of, 'If you want to work at Paramount again you've got to do this.' It wasn't those exact words but that's what he was intimating. And so that was how I got in on 'Amok Time' … and the rest is history." (119a)

Celia Lovsky, at 70, portrayed the legendary Vulcan T'Pau. She began as a stage and film performer in Germany, but fled when Hitler took control. In the 1930s and 1940s, she was married to Peter Lorre. She returned to acting after divorcing, this time in Hollywood, appearing in more than 40 films and over 200 television programs, including the 1958 movie *Twilight of the Gods*, directed by Joseph Pevney.

Majel Barrett made her first appearance of the second season here. *Star Trek* fan Bjo Trimble was a frequent visitor to the set and recalled, "We were aware, even at that time, that, yes, Gene had women in his life besides his wife. And that was so Hollywood that I think we didn't pay that much attention. I mean, that seemed like the nature of everyone we knew in Hollywood. But, first and foremost, he had kind of a long-standing relationship with Majel. And every time he'd walk on the set, Majel, even though she was a good actress, was easy to read. Those big eyes just revealed whatever she was thinking. And if she didn't hide herself in the character, of whatever else she was playing, she'd look at Gene and her eyes would go soft. I mean, I'm a woman, hello! I'd look at her and I'd look at Gene, and Gene would be very, suddenly, not looking at her. Or, if he did, it would be a quick little glance and that would be all. And that was

**Bjo Trimble observed that Barrett's face would always brighten when around Roddenberry, betraying her feelings for him
(Courtesy of Gerald Gurian)**

almost a tip-off right there. But Gene, honestly, just liked women. A woman would walk by in her little short skirt -- all the extras -- and he'd give them a big smile." (177-8)

Expecting that "Amok Time" would be the season opener, an extra day was planned for the production -- for a total of seven.

Production Diary
Filmed June 9, 12, 13, 14, 15, 16 & 19, 1967.
(Planned as 7 day production; total cost: $200,906)

Filming began on Friday, June 9, 1967. This was the week that the Six Day War between Israel and Egypt was raging in the Middle East, and Israeli forces mistakenly attacked the U.S.S. Liberty in the Mediterranean, killing 34 U.S. crewmen. In the entertainment world, The Monkees' appearance at the Hollywood Bowl was big news. *More of the Monkees* was still the top-selling album in America. But Aretha Franklin had the song getting the most radio play, with "Respect."

The night before, as Shatner, Nimoy and the rest of the cast studied their scripts, Dean Martin welcomed guests Buddy Greco, Bob Newhart, and the McGuire Sisters on his NBC TV variety show. Ninety minutes earlier, the network repeated the other *Star Trek* episode written by Theodore Sturgeon, "Shore Leave," and *TV Guide* picked it as the show to watch that night with its coveted CLOSE-UP listing. *Star Trek* ranked as NBC's top-rated show for the night, attracting 31.4% of the viewing audience with an estimated 10,980,000 households, according to A.C. Nielsen. ABC came in second, with that network's No. 1 rated series, *Bewitched*, being watched in 8,730,000 households. *My Three Sons* on CBS attracted 8,180,000. At 9 p.m., *Star Trek*'s lead increased further, to a 32.7% of the active TV sets in America, leaving 29% for ABC's *That Girl* and 23.3% for the *CBS Thursday Night Movie*, with *Damn the Defiant!*, starring Alec Guinness.

Shatner poses for NBC publicity photo
(Courtesy of Gerald Gurian)

For Day 1, work commenced on Stage 9 with the teaser and the first part of Act I in the ship's corridor, followed by Spock's quarters. The rest of the scenes there, between Kirk and Spock as the latter is ordered to speak of things no Vulcan has ever told a human before, and the scene between Chapel and Spock, were tackled next. Present this day: William Shatner, Leonard Nimoy, DeForest Kelley, and Majel Barrett.

The cast members were excited over the excellent material. William Shatner said, "There was such a feeling of 'What a joy, what a kick.' It was so well written. They [Roddenberry, Coon, Fontana, Sturgeon] were writing things that hadn't been done on television before." (156-4)

Over the weekend, Israeli forces captured the Wailing Wall in East Jerusalem, and also took Jericho and Bethlehem. And then the Six Day War was suddenly over.

Day 2, Monday, June 12. More work on Stage 9 with the scene between Kirk and Spock in the turbo-lift elevator, Spock making his agonizing walk from there to sickbay, the physical exam by McCoy, then the meeting between Kirk and McCoy afterwards in the latter's office. Also, Kirk's side of the subspace radio conversation with Admiral Komack. The last bit of business to be filmed was the episode's Tag scene, as Spock joyfully discovers he has not killed his captain and friend.

At the end of the day, after the regular players were excused, Byron Morrow dropped by to provide his side of the subspace radio conversation with Kirk, in a corner of McCoy's office dressed to pass for that of Admiral Komack.

Day 3, Tuesday. Only William Shatner was needed in the early morning for the brief scene in Kirk's quarters where the Captain lies on his bed, deeply troubled, then calls the bridge to discover Spock has ordered a course change to Vulcan. Next came all the episode's bridge scenes, featuring the only work in "Amok Time" by Nichelle Nichols, George Takei, and the new kid on the block, Walter Koenig. This was Chekov's fourth *Star Trek* and the last to feature him wearing the black 1965-era Beatles wig.

Koenig said, "I had not been offered a contract for the series and so I had no guarantee I'd be working from show to show, but each new week would come and there would be another script to learn. I loved the surprise of discovering each time that I'd be in yet another episode." (102-13)

Day 4, Wednesday. As it was for Leonard Nimoy, Arlene Martel had an early call time, well before the sun had risen, allowing her to be transformed into a Vulcan.

"It was very exciting," Martel said of her two-hour session in makeup. "I always looked different than the girl next door, anyway, but this was the first time I'd been given prosthetics. I

A member of the production crew smoothes out the dirt to hide footprints before filming the beam-down sequence (Courtesy of Gerald Gurian)

remember how painstakingly involved [Fred Phillips] was. I told him, 'I'm very sensitive about anyone doing my eye makeup,' and he said, 'Don't worry; don't give it a thought. I'll respect your sensitivity about your eyes.' And he was so careful. And it was so wonderful how he made me look. He really loved women and making them up to look their very best. And I thought I looked gorgeous with pointed ears. How's that for ego? But, with the makeup he did, I looked stunningly gorgeous." (116)

Martel was not as pleased with the alien gown Bill Theiss put her in, saying, "My costume actually made me bleed! It was made of metallic wire and, at the end of each day I was bloody right underneath my rib cage. Bill Theiss could have easily put something in to make it more comfortable, I'm sure. He was a very sweet man. He wasn't sadistic. But I didn't speak up; I was feeling too timid being there; too happy to have this particular acting job. But I wasn't happy to have that costume. The design, which I understood, was very geometric. I had a really good body, which they concealed totally, and I thought it looked like a maternity dress! I thought, 'Maybe they see the character as trying to conceal that she is pregnant.' So that's what I gave myself, that idea about her." (116)

This was the first of four days of filming on Stage 10 and the impressive set built by Matt Jefferies of the ancient ruins on the planet Vulcan. For the inhospitably hot and arid world, Jerry Finnerman chose a red sky.

Martel vividly recalled, "The set was just staggering. That was my first impressive set, other than on *The Outer Limits* ["Demon with a Glass Hand"], which was really massive, too. The sky was wonderful, that angry, passionate color. I believed [Jerry Finnerman] achieved his desire to make the show look like a film, totally. He was a master at what he did." (116)

Nimoy and Shatner look toward director Joseph Pevney, while Martel, Lovsky, and Montaigne seem to look toward Shatner for their direction (Courtesy of Gerald Gurian)

Filming began with Kirk, Spock, and McCoy's arrival on Vulcan, followed by the march of the marriage procession, including T'Pau, T'Pring, and Stonn.

Martel said, "Not only was the set terrific, for those days, but the things that shook, and the weapons, and the whole pageantry of their entrance into the scene. That was very gripping to me. The whole ritual was so compelling and exciting. And the story had such substance. I was just caught up in the fervor of it; what it was about -- being true to your nature; being true to your impulses; and I was very in tune with that concept. I mean, it was the '60s and there was all this freedom suddenly happening; *sexual freedom*. And the

Bill Montgomery slates a shot on Stage 10
(Courtesy of William Krewson and Gerald Gurian)

script was kind of honoring T'Pring as a woman, I think. She wasn't taught our cultural thing of, you know, you do as you're told. She was very respectful of who *she* was. I thought that she was very logical, and intellectually centered rather than emotionally controlled. And she knew what would be best for her, things I have not known for me. I've made impulsive, emotional decisions; just the opposite of that character -- that's what I am." (116)

And now Martel was being asked to play her opposite. Recalling her first attempt at realizing the cool and calculating T'Pring, she said, AWhatever I was doing was still too emotional, because the director, Joe Pevney, kept leaning over and saying 'Give me less; give me less.' Usually a director says, 'Give me more!' But he said, 'Give me less,' and I gave him

131

less. He said, 'No, I want even less than that.' And I said, 'Well, if I give you any less, I'll be doing nothing!' He said, 'That's just what I want you to do!' So that's what I did. I was just *there*, and I responded, but I didn't respond as Arlene would respond; I responded as T'Pring would. Arlene was 'act first and think later.' T'Pring was 'think first and then act upon what

you know.'" (116)

Lawrence Montaigne was finding the experience less intriguing than Martel. He said, "Roddenberry and I had had a big falling out, because when I went in to do the wardrobe on 'Amok Time,' they wanted me to shave my chest and I went berserk and called my agent. My agent came down, they went into conference and

Kelley watches as Nimoy demonstrates his concept for the Vulcan hand salute (Courtesy of Gerald Gurian)

then Gene finally let me wear that sort of turtleneck black gizmo underneath the coat. But after that, I was on his shit list. He would come down on the set and he wouldn't even acknowledge me." (119a)

Joseph Pevney, picturing the conversation he had with Nimoy about the Vulcan salute, recalled, "I said to him, 'We've got to get something special in the greeting, like a handshake or a hello.'" (149-5)

An example of the hijinks on the set during the filming of "Amok Time" (Courtesy of Gerald Gurian)

Interviewed in 1968 on the *Star Trek* set, Nimoy said, "I decided that the Vulcans were a 'hand-oriented' people. They touch index fingers to greet each other with a gesture like this … [holding up his hand in a double-fingered version of Churchill's victory sign] … and they have a greeting which says, 'Live long and live prosperous.' Now I haven't been able to work those kind of ideas into every script, but this is the kind of thing I'm working for." (128-17)

Of the salute, Pevney said, "It worked magnificently." (149-5)

Nimoy remembered, "[Joseph Pevney] was intrigued, liked the idea and he went to Celia Lovsky [T'Pau], explained to her what we would do. The problem was that Celia couldn't do it. We figured out a way through a simple camera trick to get it done. The camera moved in close on her and, below the camera frame, she got her right hand in the proper position. When the time came, she was ready [and] got that hand up there and the Vulcan hand salute was born. When you see the episode again, watch carefully and you'll notice that her hands are below the frame-line and then the hand pops up." (128-14)

Day 5, Thursday. A second day on the Vulcan set, covering the remainder of the pre-fight dialogue.

Shatner and Nimoy do the close-ups (above), while stunt men perform in the wider angles (below) (Courtesy of Gerald Gurian)

Arlene Martel recalled, "Bill Shatner certainly didn't help my concentration. He kept trying to break me up, saying very risqué things that were a play upon the Vulcan words, like 'pon farr.' He had his own take on that, and the other Vulcan terminology, all sexual innuendos. And he *is* funny! And so there's all this giggling. I pleaded with him, 'You're going to get me fired.' Finally, the director came over and said, 'Do I have to separate you two?' He spoke to us like we were kids misbehaving in school. And I thought, 'Oh God, here it comes, they're going to fire me.' Bill made it very difficult -- both fun and difficult. Leonard, on the other hand, was very remote, as was his character. He and I had worked together on a show before, called *The Rebel*, with Nick Adams. He played my brother-in-law, and we were mountain people who talked with a drawl. It was a totally different character. And we had fun with that. So I understood he was just staying in

133

character, as Spock. He didn't make an apology, he would just go off by himself; knowing how to protect himself that way. And I respect that, an actor honoring their work and doing whatever they have to. But I didn't know how to keep from reacting to Bill Shatner. And Joe Pevney was very irritated with me." (116)

Lawrence Montaigne, who knew Nimoy from years before, remembered a curious prank. He said, "I was all dressed in my costume, with my ears, the whole nine yards, and they called lunch. So, I went with some of the other actors to the commissary. As we sat down, a tour bus pulled up outside and they unloaded all these tourists. They came into the commissary and they immediately made a beeline to my table. 'Mr. Nimoy, Mr. Nimoy, can we have your autograph?' I'm sitting there going, 'Oh my God.' I didn't want to embarrass anybody, so I signed Leonard's name. Well, after lunch, we head back to the set and Leonard's sitting off somewhere in his little chair, sequestered by himself, meditating. I walked over and I said, 'Leonard, you won't believe, the funniest thing happened.' He looked up and grunted, and I told him how I was sitting in the commissary and all these tourists came in and mistook me for him and wanted *his* autograph. And I said that I told them, 'Go fuck yourselves!' *He was mortified!* It was a stoned-faced Nimoy. It was priceless." (119a)

After all the giggling, and all the reprimanding by Pevney, the cast was dismissed for the day. This night, at 8:30 p.m., "The Devil in the Dark" had its NBC repeat airing.

Day 6, Friday, June 16, and Day 7, Monday, June 19, 1967. These two days were also spent on the temple set on Stage 10, leading up to the fight-to-the-death between Kirk and Spock.

Pevney said, "The fight was absolutely excellent, and one of the most exciting we ever did. What made it dramatically interesting was that it took place between Kirk and Spock." (141-3)

Of the dialogue that followed, Nimoy said, "I was thrilled. I was really touched by the storyline, and by the dramatic power of the scene which immediately follows the fight wherein Spock appears to have killed Captain Kirk. Later, as we shot this scene, and T'Pau says to Spock, 'Live long and prosper,' I was almost overcome by the emotion of the scene. Spock was to reply to T'Pau, 'I shall do neither, I have killed my captain and my friend,' but I could barely choke out those moving words." (128-13)

Post-Production
Available for editing: June 20, 1967. Rough Cut: June 28, 1967.
Final Cut: July 7, 1967. Music Score recorded on July 19, 1967.

James B. Ballas and Editing Team 1 had their work cut out for them. "Amok Time" had an overabundance of material. And this meant some scripted dialogue had to be left on the cutting room floor. One of these trims included what would have been a lively exchange between McCoy and the dignified and authoritarian T'Pau. In the episode, T'Pau asks McCoy, "And thee is called?" He responds, "Leonard McCoy, ma'am." In the script, but not in the episode, T'Pau, not sure if she heard correctly, asks, "Coy?" He politely corrects her, "<u>Mc</u>Coy, ma'am." She scolds him, "<u>Coy</u>. We do not employ titles!"

Concerning another cut, Theodore Sturgeon recalled, "They ran the episode through in the screening room and I was waiting for a certain line of Spock's that I had written … 'You can have her. After a time, however, you may find that having is not so pleasing a thing as wanting.' I'm immensely proud of that line, and it was also crucial to the entire plot of that *Star Trek* episode.… *It was gone.* Now, usually, I'm a very quiet and unaggressive person. I don't like to make trouble. But this time, I just flipped out. I went roaring down to Bob

134

Justman's office... and I just raised hell. After a little while he gradually began to understand what I was saying and he jumped up and said, 'Come with me.' He went right down to the [editing] room where they were cutting my episode. After some judicious trimming on the editor's part, that line was reinserted." (169b)

The Westheimer Company provided the optical effects, which included our first look at the red planet Vulcan from space.

Composer Gerald Fried contributed some of the most memorable music in the series. The Enterprise's fanfare, as heard at the start of Act I, is epic. "Spock's Theme" is also striking, conveying the complexity and the darkness of the character. Fried explained, "I was kind of pleased coming up with that one. Here was Spock trying so hard to be human and enjoy some of the perks of humanity, and he was unable to do so. And I said, what could express that in music? Well, a lyrical line to a bass guitar. By definition, he has to clunk it out. So I gave him that lyrical line, and the characteristic of the bass guitar made it sound like he was struggling." (65-5)

The man playing those clunky notes was the great jazz guitarist Barney Kessel.

"The Vulcan March" is introduced when Spock confides in Kirk about the mating ritual of his race, then, with more musical emphasis, as the Vulcan marriage party makes their dramatic entrance and, finally, with quicker tempo still, during the fight sequence between Spock and Kirk.

Fried recalled, "I wrote the most [unwelcoming] processional music I could think of.... A lot of percussion... and a lot of rigid themes, like a fanfare theme. And I wanted to make it as formal and scary as I could think to make it." (69-4)

This piece of music would be used often throughout the second season. It is, perhaps, the most recognized piece of soundtrack music from any television series and has been mimicked in many other TV shows and movies over the decades.

The final price tag of $200,906 was $20,906 more than Desilu wanted "Amok Time" to cost. These numbers in 2013 would top $1.4 million, at nearly $150 grand above the provided allowance.

The Second Season deficit had increased again, now at $121,117.

Release / Reaction
Premiere air date: 9/15/67. NBC repeat broadcast: 4/26/68.

The buzz about a Spock sex story had begun as early as June 28, 1967, when Dave Kaufman wrote in his *Daily Variety* column:

Maybe they should call it *Sex Trek* instead of *Star Trek*. Leonard Nimoy, who plays an emotionless alien in the Desilu series, will have it better this year.

Roddenberry told Kaufman, "We are creating a mating drive that makes him go to his own planet every seven years, to look for a woman, or he dies. We have kept it reasonably within TV continuity."

"Continuity" at this time, in regards to television, meant very little or no sex. "Amok Time" was pushing the limits.

A few weeks before "Amok Time" aired on NBC, it had a sneak preview at the 25th World Science Fiction Convention -- also known as NyCon 3 -- on Labor Day weekend, at the Statler-Hilton Hotel in New York. Attendance was 1,500 fans. The screening received a standing ovation. Later, during the weekend event, "The Menagerie, Parts 1 & 2" won the grand prize -- the coveted Hugo award, as Best Science Fiction Presentation of 1966. Also nominated: the motion pictures *Fahrenheit 451* and *Fantastic Voyage*, and two additional *Star Trek* episodes -- "The Corbomite Maneuver" and "The Naked Time."

Roddenberry, Coon, and Justman, as well as the programmers at NBC, liked "Amok Time" enough to use it to open *Star Trek*'s sophomore season. It was a clear signal to the viewing audience that, just because the series was now a Friday night show, it was not dumbing itself down for the kids. This was adult material.

NBC actually spent a little money promoting *Star Trek*, along with all their series, for the fall kickoff week. In a half-page ad for *Tarzan* and *Star Trek* in *TV Guide* (and numerous other newspapers across the country), the network promotion people wrote: "The awesome reaches of space hold new peril and unimaginable wonders for Kirk, Mr. Spock and Space Ship Enterprise."

NBC publicity photo promoting the episode's duel hooks: Spock fighting Kirk, and the appearance of a Vulcan Woman (Courtesy of Gerald Gurian)

7:30 **TARZAN** The Jungle Lord
IN COLOR and his animal allies roar into action as wild and free as their homeland. Big adventure actually filmed in the jungle!

8:30 **STAR TREK** The awesome
NEW DAY reaches of space hold new peril
IN COLOR and unimaginable wonders for Kirk, Mr. Spock and SpaceShip Enterprise.

NBC WEEK

136

Steven H. Scheuer reviewed the episode for his syndicated column, *TV Key Previews*. Among numerous newspapers across the country, the review was carried by *The Galveston Daily News*, out of Galveston, Texas, on September 15, 1967:

"Amok Time." This is a good show for regular fans. This intelligent science fiction series should win even more fans as it begins its second year in its new Friday night time slot. It starts off with an interesting episode centered around the pointy-eared Mr. Spock, the Enterprise's unemotional first officer who has to return to his home planet to marry the doll selected for him once he gets the mating urge. Because of a strange Vulcan custom, he is forced into a duel to the death with Captain Kirk during the visit. This is an absorbing tale through-out, helped by effective performances by regulars William Shatner, Leonard Nimoy and De Forest Kelly.

Judy Crosby discussed the episode for her syndicated column, *TV SCOUT*. Among the papers which ran her review on April 28, 1968 (for the NBC repeat of "Amok Time"), was the *The Pittsburgh Press*, serving Pittsburgh, Pennsylvania:

Star Trek has some very imaginative writers, including the one who decided tonight to make Mr.Spock the center of a sex scandal. The usually unemotional Vulcan has an unusual biological makeup where his nervous system erupts into "reproductive periods," so much so that he threatens to kill unless he is returned to his native planet. All of that happens at the beginning of the show, causing Captain Kirk to acquiesce and take Spock home. What happens there is even stranger. Arlene Martel guest stars as the lovely Vulcan who is betrothed to Mr. Spock.

Arlene Martel was watching *Star Trek* on the night "Amok Time" first aired. She said, "It bowled me over. I thought it was outstanding. I forget who I was watching it with, but they said, 'Wow, they've got to bring you back! What a character!" (116)

RATINGS / Nielsen 12-City Trendex report for Friday, Sept. 15, 1967:

8:30 to 9 p.m.:   **Audience share:**

NBC:	*Star Trek* (first half)	23.7%
ABC:	*Hondo* (first half)	17.8%
CBS:	**Gomer Pyle, U.S.M.C.**	**45.3%**
Local independent stations:		13.2%

9 to 9:30 p.m.:

NBC:	*Star Trek* (second half)	21.3%
ABC:	*Hondo* (second half)	14.6%
CBS:	**Friday Night Movie**	**48.7%**
Local independent stations:		15.4%

The movie on CBS was the television premiere of *The Great Escape*, the 1963 all-star World War II epic with Steve McQueen, James Garner, Richard Attenborough, James Coburn, Charles Bronson, and David McCallum. The first half had aired the previous night on *The CBS Thursday Night Movie* to phenomenal ratings and expectations were that even more people would tune in for the action-packed finale, including McQueen's famous motorcycle jump over rolls of barbed wire.

There was certainly no question that *The Great Escape* and *Gomer Pyle, U.S.M.C.*, the previous season's 10th most popular series, would dominate. And they did. *The Great*

Escape, was No. 1 and No. 2 in the weekly Nielsens. *Gomer Pyle* came in at No. 5.

As for *Star Trek*'s backend support from NBC, to help battle the CBS movie, few were interested in the new Jerry Van Dyke sitcom *Accidental Family*. *Star Trek*'s 21.3% of the TV sets running in America dropped to 15.8% for *Family*, then dropped again to 10.1% for an NBC news special at 10 p.m. concerning recent rioting in American cities.

Ironically, the biggest winner this night was Lawrence Montaigne. He was, after all, in the cast of both *The Great Escape* and *Star Trek*.

***

"Amok Time" was one of four Season Two episodes nominated for a Hugo award in 1968.

Trek: The Magazine for Star Trek Fans, #7, ran a poll in 1977 to determine the first series' most popular episodes among fans. "Amok Time" came in second, bested only by "The City on the Edge of Forever."

Entertainment Weekly chose this as the 5th best *Trek* of all, calling it a "don't miss episode."

Star Trek 101, published in 2008 by Pocket Books, included "Amok Time" in its list of "Ten Essential Episodes."

Director Joseph Pevney named "Amok Time" as one of his favorites.

Leonard Nimoy ranked this "powerful and meaningful" episode among his half-dozen favorites. In the late 1990s, for an interview with the Sci-fi Channel, Nimoy said, "To this day, images from that show crop up around the world. Spock doing [the Vulcan hand salute] and 'live long and prosper'. I [recently] saw a very large billboard in Hollywood for an auto lube company that said, '*Lube* long and prosper' -- and you get it, you know what the origin is."

From the Mailbag

Before the airing:

> Dear Sirs, it has been reported that you are looking for a Vulcanian girl for *Star Trek*. Sirs, too many Vulcanians spoil the program! Please leave Spock as the only Vulcanian, because, even though Spock has no emotions, you never know with a Vulcanian girl around. So don't get one, because I'm afraid I agree with all my friends -- if we can't have our Spock to ourselves, we'll turn the channel. Selfish but true. Ellen D. (Garnerville, New York).

Because there were so many concerned female fans writing in about this, Roddenberry prepared an official reply from the top:

> On behalf of the *Star Trek* organization, we thank you for your letter and your concern for Mr. Spock. There are no plans for Mr. Spock to permanently have a Vulcan girl at his side. We do however plan to visit the planet Vulcan next year. We hope that you and your friends will continue to watch *Star Trek* and find enjoyment in it. Yours Truly, Gene Roddenberry, Executive Producer.

After the broadcast:

> Dear Mr. Roddenberry: First, a word of thanks for *Star Trek*. I think you've done a fine job with the show. I'm told that you have something less than unlimited facilities at your command, so you should be doubly commended....

The Sturgeon show last week was a fine start to what I hope will be a very successful season. Edward L. Ferman, editor, *The Magazine of Fantasy and Science Fiction.*

Dear Mr. Roddenberry, I viewed your first *Star Trek* show [of the season] -- so did my teenagers, because Friday night football starts next week. Yer kidding! "Amok Time" explains that the <u>intelligent</u> Mr. Spock responds to an once-in-a-lifetime instinct to go upstream the way the salmon go upstream, overcome by nausea and ready to fight at the drop of an alka-seltzer! Fizzzzz (le)!... If Shatner and Kelley had not played with roguish, twinkling eyes, we viewers would have bitten our tongues in cheeks, too. Your first effort to turn the Vulcanian on may well turn him off for good. Yer not only kiddin' but yer killin' his cool! As a space trio, Kelley, Nimoy and Shatner are topnotch! <u>But</u> you need writers with as much empathy for the men in space as for the men on horseback in the Wild West! Mrs. Martha T. (Livonia, Michigan).

Dear Mr. Roddenberry and Mr. Nimoy, I'm glad NBC changed *Star Trek* to Friday night because now I can stay up and watch. It is true I may go out on Friday, but I wouldn't miss *Star Trek* for anything. My sister also likes *Star Trek*. She thinks it's the <u>best show in the universe</u>.... The show I liked the best was the first one of the second season, a trip to the Vulcan planet. I was rooting for Mr. Spock the whole time, but don't get me wrong, I like the Captain, too, although I like Mr. Spock better. I have many reasons for liking Mr. Spock, a few of which are: he's funny when he doesn't mean to be, he's cute, he knows everything about everything and over explains them, he's starting to display emotion, and he's altogether cool! Leanna W. (age 11, Santa Monica, California).

Dear Joe [Pevney] ... Your creative direction of "Amok Time," which opened *Star Trek*'s 1967-68 season, deserves the highest praise. I wanted you to know from the personal perspective that I am most grateful, and, from a professional perspective, I can only give unreserved praise for the job you did. Thank you very much. Gene [Roddenberry]. (September 18, 1967)

Memories

Theodore Sturgeon recalled, "One reason *Star Trek* worked is that it was a writer-oriented show. I was all over that lot. Wherever I wanted to go, I was free to go. I studied the actors. I wrote Kirk just exactly the way Bill spoke."

Arlene "Tasha" Martel said, "Ted Sturgeon was there while we were making 'Amok Time.' And he came over and introduced himself, and said, 'You are my creation. I created you!' I said, 'No, you didn't. You just wrote about me. I created me. God created me.' He liked that answer. Our friendship was sparked by that. He was very affectionate toward me, but respectful and kind. He had wonderful humor, and wonderful intellect, and wonderful heart. And this began a friendship that would still be continuing today if he was here. I believe it still is continuing, even though he's not here. He wasn't one to hide his feelings. He was a nudist. So, he wasn't one to hide his body, either. More power to him. He was one of the original originals." (116)

Leonard Nimoy said, "An excellent script. Very poetic, dramatic, intense -- and important for Spock and for the Vulcans, because it was the first time we were going to go to Vulcan and see other Vulcans. I felt it immediately…. And there was that wonderful payoff where I believed I had killed Kirk. Great moment." (128-7)

8

Episode 35: THE DOOMSDAY MACHINE

Written by Norman Spinrad
(with Gene L. Coon, uncredited)
Directed by Marc Daniels

From NBC press release, issued on September 22, 1967:

A strange device that is programmed to destroy every planet in the galaxy also threatens the Enterprise, in "The Doomsday Machine," on NBC Television Network's *Star Trek* colorcast of Friday, Oct. 20. Captain Kirk (William Shatner) and some of his crew find the

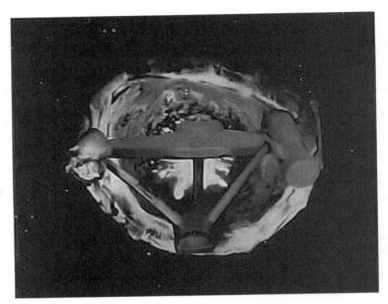

An epic battle in space, by 1967 standards
(Unaired film trim courtesy of Gerald Gurian)

wreckage of another star ship, the Constellation. The only survivor is its dazed commodore, Matt Decker (guest star William Windom), who reveals that the alien machine attacked his ship. Decker and Dr. McCoy (DeForest Kelley) are beamed back to the Enterprise, where Mr. Spock (Leonard Nimoy) has been left in command. Kirk and Scott (James Doohan) remain aboard the Constellation to attempt repairs. Decker, crazed with grief over the loss of his crew, takes over command of the Enterprise and orders an attack upon the destructive machine.

The hook: *Moby Dick* meets *Dr. Strangelove*... in outer space. As in *Moby Dick*, it is a study of obsession and revenge. Like *Strangelove*, there is a lesson to be learned when fearful people put their trust in weapons of mass destruction.

SOUND BITES

- *Decker:* "They say there's no devil, Jim, but there is. Right out of hell; I saw it!"
- *Kirk:* "Matt, what happened to your crew?" *Decker:* "I had to beam them down.... We were dead -- no power, our phasers useless. I stayed behind. The captain... last man aboard the ship; that's what you're supposed to do, isn't it? And then it hit again, and the transporter went out. They were down there... on the third planet." *Kirk:* "There is no third planet." *Decker:* "Don't you think I know that? There was, but not anymore! They called me; they begged me for help -- four hundred of them! I couldn't ... I couldn't ..."
- *Kirk:* "Know what a 'Doomsday Machine' is, Bones?... A weapon ... built

primarily as a bluff. It's never meant to be used. So strong it would destroy both sides in a war. Something like the old H-bomb was supposed to be…. A 'Doomsday Machine' that somebody used in a war uncounted years ago. None of them are left, but their machine is still destroying."

ASSESSMENT

The Cold War was in its second decade. In 1964, Stanley Kubrick used that dangerous game of bluff, with both the East and the West aiming H-bombs at one another in an effort to *not* start a war, as the basis for the film *Dr. Strangelove (or How I Learned to Stop Worrying and Love the Bomb)*. But Kubrick did not have NBC's censors to contend with. A controversial story of this type could not be produced for television in this era … unless it was disguised.

"The Doomsday Machine" is an epic adventure, depicting a life or death battle raging across a pulverized solar system. Commodore Decker is *Moby Dick*'s Captain Ahab. He's lost his ship and has the blood of 400 crew members on his hands. Decker's only chance to live with himself is to destroy the thing that brought him such profound anguish. At risk, the blood of 400 more -- Kirk's crew. Guilt makes Decker blind to this, as he says, "I've been prepared for death since I … killed my crew…. A commander is responsible for the lives of his crew -- and for their deaths. I should've died with them."

After a nuclear bomb is used to neutralize the "Planet Killer," Kirk says, "Ironic, in a way. Back in the 20th century, the H-bomb was the ultimate weapon -- *their* doomsday machine -- and we used something like it to destroy another doomsday machine. Probably the first time such a weapon was used for constructive purposes."

"The Doomsday Machine" sent a warning across America, in the guise of entertainment for kids.

THE STORY BEHIND THE STORY

Script Timeline
Norman Spinrad's story treatment, "The Planet Eater": February 5, 1967.
Spinrad's contract, ST #46, "The Planet Eater": February 21, 1967.
Spinrad's story outline: March 2, 1967.
Spinrad's revised outline, gratis: March 6, 1967.
Spinrad's 1st Draft teleplay: April 5, 1967.
Spinrad's 2nd Draft teleplay, now "The Doomsday Machine": May 8, 1967.
Gene Coon's script polish (Mimeo Department's "Yellow Cover 1st Draft"):
May 10, 1967.
Coon's second script polish (Final Draft teleplay): Late May 1967.
Coon's third script polish (Revised Final Draft teleplay): Early June 1967.
Coon's fourth script polish (2nd Revised Final Draft teleplay): June 14, 1967.
Additional page revisions by Coon: June 15 & 19, 1967.

Writer Norman Spinrad had published two novels -- *The Solarians* and *Agent of Chaos*, and had a third, *The Men in the Jungle*, due soon -- all prior to working for *Star Trek*. He had seen both *Star Trek* pilots at WorldCon, where he also met Gene Roddenberry. In early 1967, he wrote a review in *Cinema* magazine on the upcoming film *2001: A Space Odyssey* and mentioned *Star Trek* favorably.

Spinrad said, "Gene attended a science fiction convention showing his first pilot, which was very good. And also the second one he did. So, when I wrote the thing about *2001*, which I was involved with in various ways, and I thought what Gene did was better than what Kubrick did, that's how I ended up being asked to come in and pitch something." (165-1)

Roddenberry's note to Spinrad, from January 17, 1967, read in part:

> I professionally enjoyed your article in *Cinema* about science fiction and personally and emotionally enjoyed your kind reference to *Star Trek*.... When will you get time to discuss the possibilities of doing a *Star Trek* script for us? Or, if nothing else, let me give you a cup of coffee on the *Star Trek* stage. (GR35-1)

Spinrad said, "I don't know if I was a feather in his cap or we were a feather in each other's cap, but he did want to get some people with some science fiction credibility to write. He had George Clayton Johnson, Harlan Ellison, Ted Sturgeon, Bob Bloch, and Richard Matheson. Perhaps that's why he wanted me." (165-1)

Spinrad took Roddenberry up on his offer -- not for a cup of coffee but for a writing assignment. Upon receiving Roddenberry's letter on January 20, Spinrad immediately wrote back, suggesting:

> Enterprise comes upon a relic of a mysterious long-vanished alien race, noted for their advanced technology and macabre, unpleasant humor. The device is a semi-sentient computer which is able to take from the minds of Spock, Kirk, and possibly a "menace character." Their subconscious image of the ideal woman [is turned into] flesh. It is a kind of hideous alien joke. (NS35)

In Spinrad's story, all three men would invent females so utterly appealing and seemingly perfect that these women would prove irresistible. But the "menace character" Spinrad suggested was a psychotic former governor and, due to his mental illness, it is believed that one of the women could also possess a "corrupt mind" -- but which? Kirk, having completely fallen for one of the women, fights to keep his mind clear and make a decision. Will he pull the plug on the computer in order to kill the evil woman, even though this will take away the two who are programmed only to please?

Three days after Spinrad wrote his letter, and suggested his story idea, Roddenberry shared the concept with Dorothy Fontana. She recommended "passing," telling her boss:

> The three irresistible women, we've done in "Mudd's Women." The women being creations of men's minds, we've done in "The Menagerie," and "Man Trap," and, to some extent, in "Shore Leave." The paranoid ex-governor in the brig, we've done to some extent in "Dagger of the Mind." The fact the governor's woman is a kind of "sinister wonder woman," product of his mind, we've done to some extent in "What Are Little Girls Made Of?" The two love stories for Kirk and Spock -- "The City on the Edge of Forever" and "This Side of Paradise." And somehow the idea of our Captain and First Officer in love with extensions of their own minds seems very egotistical on their part. If we want to give Spinrad a crack at *Star Trek*, we need a better theme and premise. (DC35-1)

Spinrad said, "So [Roddenberry] called me back and I went in there and he said 'Look, we're running out of money; can you come up with something that we can shoot on standing sets?' I was, like, 25 years old and hadn't written for television, but understood what he meant, because I was a friend of Harlan Ellison and I watched what he was doing with various things and I realized that he was writing stuff that would cause the national debt to shoot up. I had written a novelette that never sold, which had to do with a spaceship and was basically the story of 'The Doomsday Machine,' just with a different captain. And so I talked to Gene about that, something they could shoot redressing the sets of the Enterprise." (165-1)

Spinrad sent Roddenberry a rough treatment for "The Planet Eater" on February 5, 1967, giving him a free look at the fantastic story of a mysterious thing that wanders into a solar system patrolled by the Federation, which not only eats planets but severely damages one starship before turning on the Enterprise.

Roddenberry and Gene Coon liked what they saw -- or, at least, liked it enough to justify putting an up-and-coming science fiction author on assignment. And, because Norman Spinrad was not a member of the Writers Guild, *Star Trek* was getting a deal -- a savings of $500. Spinrad's contract, dated February 21, 1967, was for $4,000, if the writer went full term from outline to teleplay to revised teleplay. WGA members were guaranteed $4,500.

"The Planet Eater" was the first writing assignment to be given out after NBC advanced story development money for a possible second season, even though the network had yet to officially renew the series. Three other stories, left over from the end of Season One -- Theodore Sturgeon's "Amok Time," D.C. Fontana's "Friday's Child," and Paul Schneider's "Tomorrow the Universe" -- were already in development.

The revised story treatment for "The Planet Eater," the first to be paid for, was dated March 2.

Dorothy Fontana recalled, "It was an interesting kind of concept. It was one we hadn't actually talked about. In other words, we hadn't had a show like this. Norman Spinrad was an established science fiction writer. And Gene liked it." (64-3)

Robert Justman, however, was not amused by the idea of a galaxy-hopping creature that gorges itself on planets. His sarcasm-laced memo to Gene Coon said:

I honestly submit that this would be a swell 7:30-type show.... But I honestly feel that we cannot afford to make it. I suggest we employ a story cutoff. (RJ35-1)

The "7:30-type show" Justman was referring to was *Lost in Space*. But even Irwin Allen, saving money by recycling monsters and sci-fi props between his three series, *Voyage to the Bottom of the Sea*, *Time Tunnel*, and *Lost in Space*, couldn't have afforded to take on a whale of a tale like this.

NBC had not yet seen the story outline, but Coon told Stan Robertson about it over the phone. Stinging a bit from Justman's reaction, Coon dropped Roddenberry a note, saying:

Stan Robertson seems enthusiastic about "The Planet Eater." Does this counterbalance Bob Justman? (GC35-1)

Robertson was not really enthusiastic about the story but the idea of a high-profile guest star. Coon had told the NBC exec that Robert Ryan had expressed interest in doing a *Star Trek* and the role of Matt Decker in "The Planet Eater" would make a nice fit.

Spinrad was asked to revise his story outline, *gratis*, and further develop the character of Decker so that the role would be suitable for a name actor. Spinrad said, "If you're going to steal, then steal from the best -- and the whole concept of it was really *Moby Dick*, in a way. So Decker was supposed to be Ahab. And Gregory Peck played Ahab in the movie, and you can see similarities between Peck and Ryan, in their look and acting styles. So I wrote for Robert Ryan -- I could see in my head that Decker was Robert Ryan." (165-1)

Spinrad finished his 2nd Revised Story Outline on March 6, which Gene Coon then sent to NBC.

Stan Robertson was worried. With Coon out of the office and on vacation, he wrote Roddenberry:

Can one accept the fact that there is a "creature" beyond our galaxy that is so immense and huge that it can eat entire planets? We must tread cautiously. We have prided ourselves, all of us on both sides of the creative structure of *Star Trek*, that our program is a much superior product to all of our competitors in this area of television entertainment. One of their constant devices is such a gimmick as contained in this outline. By stooping to their level, I think that we will not only lose the sophisticated and loyal audience our mail seems to indicate we have, but will, I believe, act as a limiting force on the larger share of audience we hope to reach in the upcoming season. (SR35-1)

Roddenberry broke protocol, as he had a few times in the past with other celebrated writers, and sent Robertson's memo to Spinrad, allowing him to see the opposition his story was up against. Then the two talked. In a memo left for Gene Coon upon his return to work, Roddenberry shared:

"The Planet Eater" lacks clean line scientific extrapolation and believability. [I] discussed this with [Norman] and think we have some meeting of the minds on what the story needs. (GR35-2)

When the 1st Draft script arrived on April 5, Fontana and Justman joined forces to register their complaints. In her memo to Gene Coon, Fontana's main gripe was how the planet-eating creature had "no more intelligence than an animal." She didn't feel a creature without intellect, no matter how hungry, could prove much of an adversary for the cunning Kirk and brainy Spock. She told Coon:

There is a lot of talk in this one -- something which may be helped by editing and polishing. The opticals and miniature work ought to drive us to the poorhouse. On second thought, at what they will probably cost, we will have to WALK to the poorhouse. (DC35-1)

Justman was far more critical. His 12-page memo to Coon stated:

My feelings about this property are completely unchanged from our previous discussions when it was in outline form only. As your Associate Producer, and, even more so, as your friend, I earnestly entreat you to junk this screenplay and pay off the writer. (RJ35-2)

Justman's primary concern remained budget and, in this regard, he likened "The Planet Eater" to *Star Trek*'s most expensive episode thus far -- "The City on the Edge of Forever." He told Coon:

Not only is this an abortion, it is a most expensive abortion. At least in the case of "The City on the Edge of Forever," it was always evident that Harlan's writing had style and more than a touch of genius. In addition, Harlan's screenplay was suffused with mystery and romance. The only mystery I can find with "The Planet Eater" is the mystery of how we allowed ourselves to go to screenplay and not cut it off at story. (RJ35-2)

Coon wrote a long letter to Spinrad -- *19 pages long*. He began, "Generally speaking, this is a most commendable first effort for *Star Trek*." One area of contention: "The dialogue is tremendously overwritten.@ (GC35-2)

Spinrad, experienced at writing novels, was getting a crash course regarding the differences between a written literary format and a TV format. He later said, "I went over to Harlan Ellison's house and said, 'Harlan, I've never written a script; show me a script so I can see what it looks like. And, in those days, they didn't have 'Final Draft' or any of these script writing programs. I didn't even have a computer. I wrote it on a typewriter. Everybody did.

You had to set the tabs on the typewriter. The idea of doing that now is just really weird. But that's all we had. And then Harlan showed me something that was very interesting -- he picked up a script and just thumbed through it and he said, 'You can tell if this is good or bad by how big the dialogue sections are. If they're too big, no good.' Which is quite true. You're not doing Shakespeare in soliloquies for five minutes." (165-1)

The rest of the lessons were coming from Gene Coon, including a very relevant one concerning the visuals. He told Spinrad not to have the Enterprise's boarding party beam onto the bridge of the Constellation, as the script currently had it. He wrote:

> There will be great audience confusion in cutting back and forth from the bridge of the Enterprise to the bridge of the Constellation. This can be solved by playing the Constellation scenes from the Auxiliary Control room, not the bridge. (GC35-2)

The two starships would be of identical design. Coon therefore created a formula for Spinrad to follow. The only bridge to be seen would be that of the Enterprise. The only Auxiliary Control room and engineering deck to be seen would be on the Constellation. He continued:

> By playing all the Constellation sequences in a confined area -- Auxiliary Control, Engineering, etc. -- all of which are close together, we could get away from the awkward problem of how do we get around on an automated ship in which the power is dead. Elevators don't run, doors don't slide open, and so on. (GC35-2)

Further, it was Coon's idea that the doors on the Constellation would be frozen in the half-open position, allowing the boarding party to squeeze through. He also had many ideas concerning the overall story, including:

> I believe the Eater should not be a living creature. I think the Eater was constructed in some other galaxy, uncounted millions of years ago, by a super race, and the purpose of the Eater is to mine. (GC35-2)

Since the Eater was now a mechanical device and not a being, Coon suggested a change in the title to "The Doomsday Machine."

Norman Spinrad made the requested changes and sent in his 2nd Draft. Surprisingly, after being so bothered by the caliber of the writing in the story outline and the first draft teleplay, Robert Justman was suddenly especially complimentary toward Spinrad. The reason: the novice TV writer had called on Justman more than once in an effort to be educated as to what should and should not be done in regard to screen writing. That extra effort had earned him the respect of *Star Trek*'s hard-working, and often highly critical, associate producer. Justman now told Coon:

> The writer has enormously improved the dialogue in this rewrite, as compared with the previous version. Not only are the speeches shorter -- more concise and to the point -- they are also pithier and, therefore, more believable.... Norman Spinrad is really going to come on in this business, if this latest version is any indication. It is apparent that he is a talented writer and if he can learn to operate within the artificial limitations of commercial television, why then he should go on to become an enormous success. Also, although I may find it exasperating when debating with him, he does not give in easily and fights to the death for what he believes in. And this is a trait in which I believe very strongly. One should only give up as little as one absolutely has to give up in the creative process. (RJ35-3)

145

Justman had been won over by the writer, but not so in regards to certain aspects of the script. His 10-page memo continued:

> The sheer weight and number of special footages needed for this show as presently written indicates to me that this show will exceed in Optical costs as did other episodes, such as "Balance of Terror," "The Corbomite Maneuver" and "The City on the Edge of Forever." I realize that the writer has in numerous instances indicated that certain shots are to be re-used again and again throughout the script and I think that is sporting of him to do that and decent of him to understand my concerns.... [But] my instincts tell me we are perpetuating a felony by attempting to produce a show such as this with the amount of money we have available to us for an individual *Star Trek* episode. (RJ35-3)

Monetary concerns notwithstanding, Justman told Coon he still had trouble swallowing the idea "that a machine of this sort could destroy a whole galaxy and then start eating up solar systems within our own galaxy." (RJ35-3)

And he didn't care for the title change, saying:

> I should like to state that I prefer the original title of "The Planet Eater." It's a much zappier title for a story like this.... And I feel we should save a title like "The Doomsday Machine" for a story <u>about</u> a doomsday machine. (RJ35-3)

Justman's memo gave Coon an idea -- the machine wasn't built to mine, but to destroy. And, with this, a giant step in the right direction was taken. Coon asked Spinrad for a free polish on the script, which would be designated as the May 10th "Yellow Cover 1st Draft" script, adding in the doomsday angle.

Spinrad later said, "The title itself comes from a concept by Herman Kahn, a political military guru -- the idea being that a doomsday machine is something that assures mutual destruction. If you've got a doomsday machine, nobody's going to attack you because they'll destroy themselves, too. And you're not going to attack anyone else with it because you'll also destroy yourself." (165-1)

Herman Kahn was an employee of The RAND Corporation and had published *On Thermonuclear War* in 1960. In his book, Kahn argued that it was vital to convince the Soviets that the United States had a *second strike* capability. This would leave no doubt in the minds of the Communist leaders that even a perfectly coordinated, massive attack against the U.S. would guarantee a measure of retaliation that would leave them devastated as well. But Kahn didn't believe this should be a bluff. He was an advocate in having a very real Doomsday Machine. Stanley Kubrick later acknowledged that Kahn was one of the models for the character of Dr. Strangelove. While making that movie, Kubrick immersed himself in Kahn's book. He also visited Kahn at The RAND Corporation and, in the film, had Dr. Strangelove refer to a report on the Doomsday Machine as coming from "The BLAND Corporation."

Spinrad said, "The title was a good title -- whoever changed it -- because the whole of the thing came directly from Herman Kahn's concept, and my reaction to that, imagining how a thing built by one civilization at war with another lasted beyond the civilization that created it. I didn't invent the concept, exactly. I did a first draft, then a second, then a bit of polishing, and that was about it. I never knew there was any resistance to the script because I was working with Gene [Coon] and he never said anything like that to me." (165-1)

Coon sent the Yellow Cover draft to NBC, De Forest Research, the Desilu/*Star Trek* department heads, as well as to the cast and Gene Roddenberry. This draft was actually the first that Roddenberry would see.

Roddenberry responded quickly, sending Coon a 12-page memo, beginning:

Spinrad has done a good job on this first *Star Trek* script, and I think he might well become one of our series regulars. I hope so. (GR35-4)

Among his suggestions for changes, Roddenberry wrote:

[When] beaming Kirk back… let's consider the possibility of the transporter <u>not</u> being fixed yet. We can have quite a bit going for us if Scotty is working frantically to get it fixed by the time Kirk gets the other ship into the mouth of The Thing. (GR35-4)

Gene Coon listened to everyone's complaints and suggestions, then did a rewrite of his own, the Final Draft in late May. Roddenberry's idea for jeopardy on top of jeopardy, and a louder ticking clock, was added. Also put into the script: dialogue clarifying that "The Thing" from another galaxy was built as a futuristic version of an H-bomb, and, at this time, Matt Decker was given a more fitting end. In previous drafts, he had lived, only to tell Kirk that he was aware of his mistakes. It was Coon's idea to have the self-tortured character die by piloting a shuttlecraft into the mouth of the machine, and to make his sacrifice have meaning by clueing Kirk in on a way to destroy the planet eater. With these changes, the script found its magic.

Stan Robertson agreed, finding "The Doomsday Machine" to be "a very exciting teleplay," but he wanted the pacing sped up. He felt this type of story should move at a breakneck speed from the very start of the Teaser. Coon would accelerate the pacing with the next draft.

Justman, of course, had notes, too. He told Coon:

In Scene 40, Kirk suggests that if the creature gets too close to the Enterprise, they should use warp drive to get out of its way. Who is to know how close is close? Does anyone yet have an idea of the creature's power or range to use its power?... In Scene 41 ½ on Page 19, Kirk asks if the creature has made any hostile moves yet. I guess it's a matter of semantics. If a creature like that was chasing me, I'd consider it to be a hostile move without anything further being done by the creature. (RJ35-4)

Coon prepared a Revised Final Draft, dated June 14, and further page revisions coming in on the 15th and 19th.

Even with all the rewriting by Coon, one problem remained -- there were still those photographic effects that scared Robert Justman to death. How could a show with the budget of *Star Trek* afford to create a Doomsday Machine, as well as a derelict starship, and stage a space fight? The answer, or, at least, half of it, came from a very unexpected source.

Pre-Production
June 9, 12-16 & 19, 1967 (7 days prep).

Five months before this episode was filmed, AMT manufactured the first Enterprise model kits. One of those kits found its way into this production. The U.S.S. Constellation was actually a $3 plastic model, blackened and punctured, with the rear end of the warp engine nacelles burned until the plastic melted.

Now the only problem was how to show the giant Planet Eater, and to show it pull the Enterprise into its maw. Again, AMT came to the rescue. A second $3 plastic kit provided an Enterprise small enough to allow the miniature of the Planet Eater to remain just that -- a miniature, several feet long. The machine was actually a large airport windsock dipped into Plaster of Paris.

Even with these cost-cutting innovations, the photographic effects bill would still be substantially higher than the norm. Even cheap space props take time to film. To compensate for this, "The Doomsday Machine" had to be filmed in less time than any previous episode. And that meant this assignment would be given to *Star Trek*'s fastest director.

Marc Daniels took on his second directing assignment of the new season with the offer of a bonus. As had happened with Joseph Pevney during the filming of "Arena," Daniels was promised an extra $500 if he could stay on schedule (a price which would equate to roughly $3,500 in 2013). This time, however, the schedule only allowed for five days of filming instead of the standard six (or the more-often-than-not six and a half to seven days that most episodes took). With more script pages devoted to descriptions of photographic effects than any previous teleplay, and only six sets called for, all on Stage 9, Daniels believed he could make that $500 bonus. But the necessary pushing of the cast and crew resulted in resentment and moodiness on the set (see Production Diary).

The big guest star Gene Coon had hoped for -- Robert Ryan -- was unavailable during the days slated for production. Joe D'Agosta scrambled to find a worthy replacement. Daniels recommended an actor he had enjoyed working with in the past. Based on the outcome, *Star Trek* may have actually traded up.

William Windom and Inger Stevens, of
The Farmer's Daughter, **share the cover of the**
May 2, 1963 issue of *TV Guide*

William Windom, at 43, was a star on TV. He had started on stage, and was even William Shatner's understudy for *The World of Suzie Wong* on Broadway. In the movies, Windom played prominent character parts, such as the prosecutor fighting Gregory Peck in *To Kill a Mocking Bird*. On TV, he had already made 150 of what would one day be more than 400 appearances, including his three-year stint as Inger Stevens' co-star on *The Farmer's Daughter*. That series ended one year before Windom's appearance here.

Windom later said, "I don't know why I got it. Probably because the director had seen me before and liked it and decided he wanted to use me. I used to be known as 'Willie the Weeper' because I could cry on command. Whenever they had a guy breaking down, they'd think of me. But I hadn't seen the show when I came in to do that one. I do remember when I got the script that it seemed like imaginative stuff. I didn't put that all together with being *Moby Dick* or whatever they were trying to do. I didn't see that much depth in it. All I could see was the science fiction part, and the Willie the Weeper part." (187)

148

Marc Daniels said, "William Windom is a terrific actor. When you get an actor like that, you don't get a [phony] 'performance' out of him. Maybe you need to steer him in some direction if he's going wrong, but the chances are that he does it himself." (44-3)

Norman Spinrad said, "The character of Decker changed with William Windom, because he was a different sort of actor; played it in a different kind of way. That was a little disappointing in a way -- not that he did a bad job, but it was conceived a little bit differently. If they're telling you they have an actor in mind, you're sort of taking that into account and molding your character based on what you think that actor can do. And, in the case of 'Doomsday Machine,' Robert Ryan wanted to do one. You'd be surprised how many people of note in feature films really wanted to do a *Star Trek*. Robert Ryan and even Milton Berle -- who was a good actor, who could also be a serious actor. There were a lot of people like that who really wanted to do it, and so they would try to get a script to somebody like that. So that was all in my head when I wrote it. The thing got modified because it ended up being, for whatever reason, William Windom instead of Ryan." (165-1)

Also in the cast was Elizabeth Rogers, as Lt. Palmer, sitting in for Uhura. Nichelle Nichol's character was included in every draft of the script except for a last-minute rewrite the day before filming commenced when she became unavailable.

Rogers said, "I got the part when Uhura [Nichelle Nichols] had a singing engagement. I was used as an instant 'threat' replacement." (145b)

Rogers had provided the voice of The Companion in "Metamorphosis." The "instant threat" worked. Nichols kept herself available to *Star Trek* and Rogers was not called on again ... until "The Way to Eden" in Season Three.

The three crewmen who beam to the Constellation with Kirk, Spock, and Scott were named after the series' three assistant directors -- Rusty Meek, Elliot Schick, and Charles Washburn.

Richard Compton, as Washburn, worked as a bit actor in the late 1960s and early 1970s before becoming a writer, director, and producer. His behind-the-camera TV credits include work on the 1990s sci-fi series *Sliders* and *Babylon 5*. He also directed for *Star Trek: The Next Generation* and *The X-Files*. And he directed William Shatner again, in *T.J. Hooker*.

John Copage played Elliot. He had already appeared on *The Man from U.N.C.L.E.* and *Bewitched*.

Tim Burns was Russ. His acting jobs included *The Wild, Wild West* and *The Invaders*.

Production Diary
Filmed June 20, 21, 22, 23 & 26, 1967.
(5 day production; cost $176,336.)

Filming began Tuesday, June 20, 1967. On this day, Muhammad Ali was convicted of refusing induction into the armed forces. After three years of fighting, U.S. casualties in Vietnam were approaching the 20,000 mark. And Paul McCartney admitted on TV that he took LSD.

Pop culture was experiencing a renaissance. James Bond was back, and back on top in the movie houses, with *You Only Live Twice*. *Get Smart*, spoofing spies like Bond, was a hit on TV, and Don Adams and Barbara Feldon had the cover of *TV Guide*. The Monkees still had the top spot on Billboard's album charts, this time with their third offering, *Headquarters*. Remarkably, *Headquarters* replaced *More of the Monkees* after 18 weeks at the top, which, in turn, dethroned their first long player -- *The Monkees* -- which sat at the

149

summit for 13 weeks. Vying for the top spot, *Sounds Like* by Herb Alpert and the Tijuana Brass. About to take both down a notch, The Beatles with their masterpiece *Sgt. Pepper's Lonely Hearts Club Band*. Mitch Ryder and the Detroit Wheels had an album out called *Sock it to Me* (*Laugh In* would get the phrase from them), and a member of the *Star Trek* cast was doing well for himself in the LP charts with *Leonard Nimoy Presents Mr. Spock's Music from Outer Space*.

Production on "The Doomsday Machine" began on Stage 9 with the bridge set. It was the first of two and a half days spent there. Filmed this day: the Teaser and the first part of Act I, prior to Kirk leaving the ship, and the tag scene, after his return.

Seen for the first time here: Kirk's wraparound tunic. The reason for the new uniform-top traces back to a memo Roddenberry sent to Coon, stating:

> Perhaps we should re-evaluate our decision not to give Kirk an individualistic change of uniform. In view of our attempt to keep him strong in the lead of our show, we should dress him up a bit more; make him stand out. (GR35-3)

It was one more way Roddenberry was trying to put attention on Shatner and just a bit less on Nimoy, who had recently caused such trouble for the producer.

Another first is seen when Kirk, while in conversation with Spock, walks past the main viewing screen on the bridge. The move was much more complex for this era than one might think. With Shatner passing between camera and the view screen, the usual matte shot (inserting one image into another) could not be used. And, without the benefit of CGI (Computer Generated Images, still decades away), the only solution for accomplishing this effect was to utilize rear screen projection, requiring a fair amount of time and care for a director trying to shoot an entire episode in only five days.

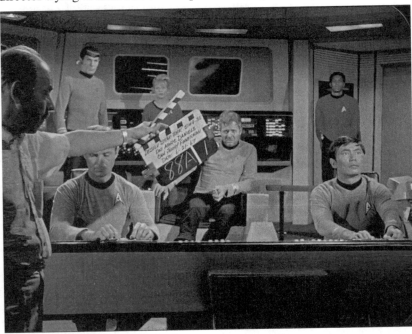

Day 2, Wednesday. Again, a full day on the bridge, now without Kirk, as Spock and Matt Decker fight for control of the Enterprise. Another fight was going on behind the scenes. William Shatner was not needed this day for filming and Spock was being featured as much in the script as Kirk. With all the media attention on

Day 2. Left to right, Bill McGovern, Leonard Nimoy, Bill Blackburn, Elizabeth Rogers, William Windom, unknown extra, and George Takei (Courtesy of Gerald Gurian)

Spock, along with the new contract, pay raise, and Emmy nod for Nimoy, Shatner decided it was time to take a stand.

Norman Spinrad recalled, "Shatner was nuts at this time. You often have the case where the character takes over the actor. But in Shatner's case, the actor was taking over the character; because he was so into being the star and there was no way that he was going to let Nimoy steal scenes. Leonard wasn't trying to do this, but Shatner apparently had this thing where his contract called for him to have more lines of dialogue than anyone else. And he actually sat there with a blue pencil taking Spock lines out of the script. I watched him do this. There was one scene that I wrote where they were talking on the communicator, and it was Kirk to Spock, then Spock to Kirk, then Kirk, then Spock. And Shatner actually took out Spock's reaction line because it gave Spock one too many lines. Marc Daniels went through five takes but it didn't work. And I really wasn't supposed to do it, but I couldn't stand it anymore, so I pulled Marc over and said, 'This isn't working; you need another line in there.' And he told me we couldn't have it in there because Shatner was counting the lines, so Spock couldn't talk. And I said, 'Well can't Leonard just grunt?' I mean, Shatner was really going there. Yeah, he was separated from a lot of action, but it's a good thing he wasn't up against Robert Ryan. I'd seen Shatner in a lot of things before there was a *Star Trek* and he was a good serious actor, but this thing really screwed up his head. Later on he really recovered from that, and I admire Bill Shatner these days. And you can laugh about this stuff now. But, at that time, he was very serious about it." (165-1)

Shatner – protecting his status and counting lines
(Courtesy of Gerald Gurian)

Bjo Trimble, often a visitor on the set, recalled, "I do know there was tension, because Shatner was stealing lines. He was saying, 'Kirk should say this.' So the lower echelon of actors resented it. He apparently didn't try this with DeForest Kelley. It seemed they were on more affable terms than he and Leonard Nimoy. But Shatner was going through his divorce at this time -- and it was a bad divorce." (177-8)

William Windom was also on set this day. He said, "'The Doomsday Machine' was *my* show, no doubt about it. Convincing Shatner and Nimoy of that was not easy. They were being very protective of their roles, and I remember that they were feuding. I didn't have anyone to laugh about it with because everyone there took it all so seriously -- but I thought it was funny. I've seen it on other shows, of course. That happens a lot -- counting lines in scripts, and whose chair is bigger and closer to the set, and 'Where's my parking place?' All that crap. I felt like telling them to get over it. But William Shatner, in his defense, had a buzzing in his head [tinnitus, caused from an explosion during the filming of 'Arena']. At the time, he had a noise in his head that nearly drove him nuts. Medically, they couldn't fix it; it just went on and on. It was a handicap to him, and I'm sure it made him nervous. And that can account for some of it." (187)

A buzzing in the head, a bad divorce, a co-star with an Emmy nomination and a hit record, and story structure which kept Captain Kirk out of many dramatic moments, added up to be a big conflict for Shatner. But it wasn't the only source of tension on the set. Marc Daniels was pushing the cast and crew to do something they had never accomplished before -- shoot 50 minutes of network entertainment in five days.

Jerry Finnerman said, "[Marc Daniels] was a little grumpy and he pushed me a lot; he pushed me more than any other director that I've worked with. And we clashed. Yeah, we clashed. But I think the Director of Photography should take just as long to light a scene as a director takes to rehearse it…. I had a contract; there's not much they're going to do to me… but it was unpleasant." (63-3)

For the scene filmed this day where Matt Decker sits in Kirk's command chair and compulsively fiddles with a handful of cassette cartridges, William Windom admitted he was paying homage to Humphrey Bogart. He recalled, "*The Caine Mutiny* stuff, with the tape cartridges or whatever they were in my hand, I just dreamt that up without being told. So I had fun with that. I thought it was worthwhile to show us something of that character -- him trying to maintain his dignity, and his authority, but with guarded expressions. So I needed something for the audience to see that could convey that not all was as right as he wanted the others to believe. And I was thinking *The Caine Mutiny*. I like stuff like that. But just for that piece of business. As for the rest of what I was doing, we're all products of what we've done; what we've gone through. So it came from somewhere. You don't have a lot of time in TV to think about it. You just pull up what you think will work." (187)

Day 3, Thursday, June 22. A final half-day of filming on the bridge without Shatner. After the lunch break, Commodore Decker and security man Montgomery fought in the corridor, followed by a move to the transporter room for Kirk's dramatic return to the Enterprise. After this, with the series regulars released,

Day 3: John Winston as Lt. Kyle and, behind clapper, Roger Holloway as Lt. Lemli (Courtesy of Gerald Gurian)

William Windom and the production unit remained for an early evening move to Stage 10 to the shuttle craft where Decker faces his death. Windom had to react to what Decker was seeing, and no one at this point had any idea what the Doomsday Machine would look like.

Windom remembered, "I'll tell you how we got the big blowup scene. By then I'd gotten to know the director pretty well. And we got along fine. I liked him; he liked me. And I didn't know he'd done so many of them until much later. But he had done quite a few. And I was amazed at how bright he was to talk to. And then the time came to do the scene and he handed me the script and there were no lines -- just me looking at camera and getting ready to die. So he said, 'I don't know what to do with this, William. I'm going out to have a smoke. You and the cameraman work it out.' Now, if it was a stage piece -- like I started off doing back in New York -- you really have to know what you want to do. You're responsible for what the audience in the theater leaves with. But the cutter is responsible in the movies and on TV. They can cut this up any way they want. So I just tore into it and pulled up everything I could think of to do, knowing they'd use what they liked and throw away what they didn't." (187)

After Windom went bananas, "The Squire of Gothos" had its repeat broadcast on NBC at 8:30 p.m.

Day 4. William Windom getting into character
(Courtesy of Gerald Gurian)

Day 4, Friday. Work continued on Stage 9, now dressed to appear as the battered Constellation. The entire day was spent on one set -- the Auxiliary Control room. First up were scenes of Kirk and McCoy discovering a delirious Commodore Decker and learning of the space devil that destroyed his ship and killed his crew. After McCoy and Decker depart to beam back to the Enterprise, Daniels called for a lunch break. William Windom and DeForest Kelley were excused for the day, then the rest of the Auxiliary Control scenes featuring Kirk with Scott and Washburn were filmed.

Day 5, Monday. More filming in Auxiliary Control, this time with only Shatner. Watching Kirk struggle at the controls of the derelict Constellation in an effort to stay in the fight serves as an ironic visual metaphor for Shatner's equally diligent effort to keep his character in the story and maintain his status in the series above that of Nimoy.

153

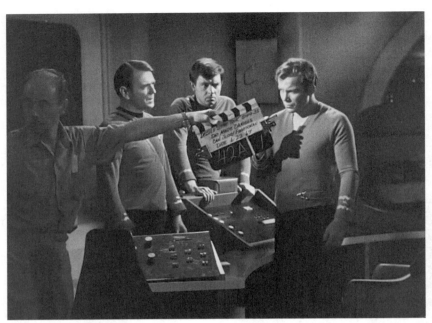

Bill McGovern slating James Doohan, Richard Compton, and William Shatner (Courtesy of Gerald Gurian)

David Gerrold, on set researching for his own script "The Trouble with Tribbles," recalled, "They were about to shoot the scene where Kirk witnesses Decker's death [on the viewing screen]. Marc Daniels… suggested that Kirk show his grief and pain by lowering his face. At the same time, Jerry Finnerman… was making adjustments on a key light -- much of *Star Trek*'s mood was set by his creative use of colors and shadows…. Shatner was sitting behind a control console while Daniels and Finnerman discussed the best way to throw a shadow across him. Abruptly Shatner suggested that the light be only across his eyes, so that when he lowered his head, his face would go into shadow, thus heightening the effect of his grief. Daniels and Finnerman exchanged a glance…. They tried it and it worked…. A little thing? Perhaps. But it proved to me that William Shatner was a professional's professional. His first concern was the story and the show." (73-6)

After the lunch break, DeForest Kelley, James Doohan, Richard Compton, John Copage, and Tim Burns joined Shatner for the scenes in the trashed corridors of the Constellation. Shatner and Kelley were then dismissed, as Doohan, Compton, Copage, and Burns stayed to film the sequences in the damaged engineering section.

One brief scene Daniels did not direct was of Scotty being tossed around engineering as the Constellation lurches from one speed to another. This was recycled from "Tomorrow Is Yesterday." Daniels had not provided sufficient footage for this portion of the episode. With only five days to shoot, he could not be faulted.

James Doohan was the last cast member needed, during the late afternoon and early evening, for the sequences in and about the Jefferies Tube. Doohan shared, "The Jefferies tube was not the most comfortable of sets to work in. It was a tube with a hole in the top, and the tube was set at an angle of fifteen degrees from the perpendicular." (52-1)

Some improvising was done on set by Doohan, with a bit of "G-rated" cursing. He said, "When Scotty goes leaping up the Jefferies tube to try to fix the malfunctioning transporter, he mutters a curse. People ask me what I was saying, and I hate to disappoint them, but it was just something along the lines of 'Bragus blath' -- a made-up Scottish curse. I knew Scotty had to express his impatience somehow, and that seemed the best way to do it." (52-1)

And that was a wrap. Daniels had done the near-impossible by finishing in only five days. But he had much experience at this. Several years earlier, he was quoted by *Variety* as saying, "An hour show is a frightening thing in a way because every little thing depends on someone else. By careful planning, however, you can prepare these things so that the 50 or 60 people involved have a chance to do their jobs correctly. They all know their jobs very well and they are all anxious to make things work. The cameramen... are vastly ingenious and skillful. I very soon found that they can do anything at all and that there are practically no limitations to what you can plan for the telling of your story." (44-5)

The producers were thrilled by Daniels' amazing feat. Jerry Finnerman, the head of the camera crew, was not. He said, "I remember we really got humping, and Marc says, 'I promised them... we have to do this show in five days.' So, we did the show in five days and, you know, they gave him a $500 bonus. Nobody thanked me; I never saw any of that money." (63-3)

Walter Koenig concurred, saying, "Marc was the opposite of Joe Pevney, who was a delight to work for. Marc never smiled. I figured he was just unhappy, or hated me. Now that may not be who he was; but that was the character I created in my mind." (102)

Most, however, found Daniels to be pleasant and calm. Perhaps it was the strain of a five-day rush job; perhaps opposing personalities. TV and movies work best when filled with conflict. And it has always involved a great deal of conflict in making TV and movies.

On his way out the door, William Windom said, "Everyone there took what they were doing so seriously. I like to poke fun at science fiction, or anything else, for that matter. But they were just enraptured with these cardboard control panels and the lights that went on and off. It was like kids being taken to the zoo. On one hand, it was ludicrous. On the other hand, it wasn't any worse than a lot of television we had in those days. I was glad for the job. I like working. And I worked a lot. But it's a lot of crap." (187)

Post-Production
Available for editing: June 27, 1967. Rough Cut: July 6. Final Cut: August 8, 1967.
Music Score recorded on August 30.

**A composite shot of image of the 11-foot, 2-inch model with AMT
Enterprise model, burned and painted to appear as the Constellation
(Unaired film trim courtesy of Kipp Teague and Gerald Gurian)**

Donald R. Rode, the man responsible for assembling *Star Trek*'s coming-attraction trailers, was chosen to lead a fourth editing team to ensure the episode delivery schedule to NBC did not get interrupted as it had during the first season. With this job, Rode received his first screen credit on a television program.

No *Star Trek* episode before this had such rapid cutting throughout, and cutting which was so dependent on optical effects. And that meant Rode, in respect to the opticals, was cutting blind. When the photographic effects were finally delivered, some timed out too short to fill the spaces he had provided. So Rode reused a second or two here and a second or two there to make shots of the Planet Eater last as long as needed.

"The Doomsday Machine" showcased Rode's abilities. For this episode, he received his first of four Emmy nominations.

Cinema Research Corporation, the fifth optical house to work on the series, had their hands full -- especially since the company was new to this type of work. Their optical experience included a pair of 1965 films, *The Beach Girls and the Monster* and *The Wizard of Mars*. In some shots of the Planet Eater, parts of the cone-shaped machine are semi-transparent, allowing stars to show through. There was a reason for this. Film footage of the Planet Eater model was laid over footage of a star field. The brighter image won out.

Norman Spinrad was unimpressed by the windsock dipped in Plaster of Paris. He complained, "The whole idea when we started this was it was half-machine and half-being. So, when I finished the first draft of the script, Gene [Roddenberry] asked me to draw the thing -- not that I'm that good of an artist -- but I did, and what I drew was sort of half-alive and half-machine. When I saw the rough cut of what they shot, I said, 'Gene, that thing looks like a windsock that's been dipped in cement.' And he said, 'Yeah, well, actually, it is a windsock that was dipped in cement.'" (165-4)

In 1967, the difference between what an author of books might imagine and what could actually be realized on TV was vast. For that era and that medium, a battle in space between two starships and a Doomsday Machine was epic.

Composer Sol Kaplan added the last element of brilliance: a score that later influenced music in motion pictures such as *Jaws* and *Star Wars*. Kaplan had previously composed the music for "The Enemy Within." This was his second and final assignment for *Star Trek*. Although some of Kaplan's motifs are used to the point of redundancy, such as the Enterprise fly-by theme during the Teaser, the music throughout is sweeping, exciting, and memorable. Kaplan broke the components of the story down, with their visual elements, and assigned each a specific theme. The Enterprise in space has one, as does the Doomsday Machine, Decker, the transporter unit, and the climactic countdown.

"To score any film well is a great challenge," said Kaplan. "For *Star Trek*, in addition to creating the 'right' musical motifs and moods, a composer would have to create musical 'sounds,' yet always make the audience believe that what they were seeing and hearing could be happening for real.... The score must fuse with all other creative and cinematic elements to make the film an artistic entity." (95a)

Even with the numerous photographic effects needed, "The Doomsday Machine," with a total cost of $176,336, came in $8,664 *under* budget -- the first episode of the Second Season to not exceed the money allocated by the studio. In 2013's dollars, the cost of this episode equates to just over $1.2 million, which was a bargain, especially considering that in 2013 a one-hour sci-fi drama is budgeted for more than double this amount.

The Second Season deficit dropped $11,453 to $112,453. Roddenberry, Coon, and Justman needed to find more bargains like "The Doomsday Machine."

The week AThe Doomsday Machine@ first aired on NBC, *Star Trek* had a two-page color spread in *TV Guide*, promoting the upcoming episode "I, Mudd," showing the various sets of twins which had been collected for the filming.

RATINGS / Nielsen 12-City Trendex report for Friday, October 20, 1967:

8:30 to 9 pm: 54.5% of U.S. TVs in use. Audience share: **Households:**

NBC:	*Star Trek* (first half)	25.1%	10,020,000
ABC:	*Hondo* (first half)	23.8%	10,020,000 [sic]
CBS:	***Gomer Pyle, U.S.M.C.***	**44.9%**	**15,740,000**
Local independent stations:		6.2%	No data

9 to 9:30 pm: 54.8% of U.S. TVs in use. Audience share: **Households:**

NBC:	*Star Trek* (second half)	26.1%	No data
ABC:	*Hondo* (second half)	24.3%	No data
CBS:	***Friday Night Movie***	**37.0%**	**No data**
Local independent stations:		12.6%	No data

The Friday Night Movie was the 1963 comedy *Love Is a Ball*, starring Glenn Ford and Hope Lange. CBS bought ad space in *TV Guide* and newspaper TV magazines. NBC played the miser and hoarded its promotional money. Regardless, *Star Trek* landed the No. 2 spot for its entire hour, besting *Hondo* on ABC in audience share (25.1% to 23.8% from 8:30 to 9 p.m., and 26.1% to 24.3% from 9 to 9:30 p.m.), and was NBC's top-rated Friday night show. According to Nielsen, *Tarzan* began the night for the network with 9,740,000 households. *Star Trek* grew this number to 10,020,000. *Accidental Family* dropped the ball, and the audience, to 5,320,000 households. The 10 p.m. NBC special "Canada Faces the Future" lowered the take to 4,090,000.

***

"The Doomsday Machine" was one of five episodes from 1967 to be nominated for a Hugo Award.

Entertainment Weekly picked this as the fourth best *Star Trek* ever.

After writing "The Doomsday Machine," his first venture into television, Spinrad tried again with another script for the series -- "He Walked Among Us." It was not produced (more on this later).

Director Marc Daniels tried his hand at writing for *Star Trek*, too, with a story outline turned in during the third season, called "The Beast" (an assignment that would be cut-off by producer Fred Freiberger). But Daniels, the director, wanted to write for *Star Trek*, and he liked the premise for "The Doomsday Machine" so much that he borrowed many elements from the story for "One of Our Planets Is Missing," a script he wrote for a 1973 episode of *Star Trek: The Animated Series*.

David "The Trouble with Tribbles" Gerrold declared, "'The Doomsday Machine,' a modern-dress retelling of Ahab and the whale, was one of *Star Trek*'s best episodes (in my humble opinion)." (73-6)

Memories

Nearly four decades after the fact, Norman Spinrad said, "I had a different vision in my mind of what the Doomsday Machine would look like, and so did Gene. It was just a matter of running out of budget. As far as the story went, I wasn't displeased with the way the thing came out.... Overall, I wasn't unhappy with it at all." (165-3)

When asked what his favorite *Star Trek* was, James Doohan answered, "The Doomsday Machine."

He said, "For one thing, it had William Windom in it. Very good actor. And it was a very strong role -- a very self-tortured character. Very driven. And a strong statement about nuclear weapons. And the effects were extremely good; that was an epic story for television in that time. It wasn't a standout role for Scotty, but it was okay, and I was pleased. I saw it not long ago and I still find it to be very exciting television." (52)

William Windom said, "I watched it when it aired. I looked at it and quickly looked away. My kids looked at it closer. I felt they did what they [the makers of *Star Trek*] could with what they had to work with. But I don't watch *Star Trek* very often, no. It has an appeal to a great deal of people, and I'm trying to respect that, and that's what I'm trying to buy into. So I do, but I don't have to participate in it myself. I hope you don't make me look too sarcastic and smart assed. But I am sarcastic and smart assed, so do whatever you want." (187)

(Author's note: Having interviewed William Windom, he was sarcastic and smart assed... and absolutely delightful. May he rest in peace.)

Episode 36: WOLF IN THE FOLD

Written by Robert Bloch
(with Gene Coon and Gene Roddenberry, uncredited)
Directed by Joseph Pevney

William Shatner and Tania Lemani in NBC publicity photo
(Courtesy of Gerald Gurian)

From NBC press release, issued November 27, 1967:

Captain Kirk (William Shatner) risks the lives of his entire personnel when he transfers a murder investigation to the Enterprise in "Wolf in the Fold" on NBC Television Network's *Star Trek* colorcast Friday, Dec. 22.… Kirk, Mr. Spock (Leonard Nimoy) and Dr. McCoy (DeForest Kelley) take Scotty (James Doohan) to pleasure planet Argelius II to help him recover from an injury. A beautiful dancer, Kara (Tania Lemani), is knifed to death while with Scotty and evidence points to him. During the investigation, two more women are murdered and Scotty again is suspected. The inquiry is bogged down by Hengist (guest star John Fiedler), the Argelian administrator, until Kirk insists it be moved to the Enterprise. Then evidence begins to point to a Jack the Ripper-type. Charles Macauley portrays Jaris, ruler of Argelius and Pilar Seurat, his wife Sybo, a seeress.

An incident in Mister Scott's recent past seems to suggest a motive. The head injury he suffered and is still recovering from was the result of an accident caused by a woman -- an explosion on the Enterprise which not only endangered Scott and his engineering crew but his precious engines. Even Kirk begins to doubt Scott's innocence.

The hook was irresistible: *Jack the Ripper* in outer-space. More than just reinventing the story of a notorious serial killer, the concept is expanded to suggest that certain living things depend on human emotions such as fear to sustain themselves.

SOUND BITES

- *Scott:* "I heard the poor lady scream.... I went toward her. But there was something in my way.... Cold it was. Like a stinking draft out of a slaughterhouse."

- *McCoy:* "But ... a being which feeds on death?" *Spock:* "In the strict scientific sense, doctor, we all feed on death. Even vegetarians."

- *Kirk:* "That thing can control all the operations of this ship ... including the life support systems." *Morla:* "You mean ... it could kill us?" *Spock:* "Indeed, I suspect it will try. But not immediately.... We know it feeds on fear and terror. It now possesses an unparalleled opportunity to glut itself. There are nearly 440 humans aboard this ship. But death is not enough for it. It will surely attempt to breed fear and terror before it kills, to make the most of this chance."

в *Kirk:* "That was due to happen next ... life support malfunction." *The Entity, over intercom:* "Captain Kirk!... You and all aboard your ship are about to die." *Sulu:* "This is the first time I've heard a *malfunction* threaten us."

в *Kirk:* "Bones, what's your sedative situation?" *McCoy:* "I've got some stuff that would tranquilize an active volcano."

в *The Entity:* "You will all die horribly -- in searing pain.... I may cut off your oxygen and suffocate you. I may crush you all with increased atmospheric pressure; heighten the temperature until the blood bubbles in your veins." *Sulu:* "Whoever he is, he sure talks gloomy.... With an armful of this stuff, I wouldn't be afraid of a supernova."

ASSESSMENT

"Wolf in the Fold" is entertaining, although it has an atypical story arc -- hedonistic sexploitation gives way to gothic horror, then murder mystery, complete with candlelight séance and screams in the dark, followed by courtroom drama, a sci-fi funhouse romp and, finally, broad comedy. Mr. Spock is quite absent from the first half of the episode where the pacing seems slow due to a pair of unusually long exposition scenes, each lasting several minutes. But the story picks up as it evolves and shifts from one genre to the next. In fact, at times it picks up too much.

Some of the fear and terror injected into the script is hard to fully appreciate, with overlapping action, dialogue and sound effects. It's easy to miss some attempts at taking life, such as the turbo-lift doors nearly cutting Spock in two, or the verbal threats "Jack" announces over the ship's address system. Still, this episode has plenty of highlights, such as the scene where Kirk carries the drugged and groggy "Jack" (the always enjoyable John Fiedler) over his shoulder as the murderous entity giggles drunkenly, "Kill, kill, kill you all."

Like "Catspaw," also by Robert Bloch, "Wolf in the Fold" is a guilty pleasure.

THE STORY BEHIND THE STORY

Script Timeline
Robert Bloch's story outline, ST #62: April 20, 1967.
Gene Coon's revised story outline: April 21, 1967.
Bloch's 1st Draft teleplay: May 15, 1967.
Bloch's 2nd Draft teleplay: June 1, 1967.
Staff's script polish (Mimeo Department "Yellow Cover 1st Draft"): Early June 1967.
Gene Coon's rewrite (Final Draft teleplay): Mid June 1967.
Gene Roddenberry's rewrite (Revised Final Draft teleplay): June 21, 1967.
Additional page revisions by Coon: June 22, 23, 26 & 27, 1967.

With "Wolf in the Fold," horror genre writer Robert Bloch, following "What Are Little Girls Made Of?" and "Catspaw," turned in his third script for *Star Trek*. The title is explained in a line of dialogue by Spock. He says, "I point out that an entity which feeds on fear and terror would find a perfect hunting ground on Argelius; a planet without violence, where the inhabitants are as peaceful as sheep; where the entity would be as a hungry wolf … in that fold."

When putting together elements for this latest script, Bloch did as he had with his other *Star Trek* assignments and borrowed from his stockpile of short stories. This time, he took from "Yours Truly, Jack the Ripper," first published in *Weird Tales* in 1943.

"That was *their* idea," Bloch said, referring to *Star Trek*'s two Genes. "They wanted me to do a Jack the Ripper story in the future. So I said, 'All right, let's put him into a computer or something instead of having him skulking around with a knife on shipboard.'" (18-4)

In Bloch's original outline, Sulu, not Scott, is accused of murdering a woman on Argelius II, and the action quickly moves from planet to the starship, where the helmsman is put on trial. At this point, much earlier than in the final version, the "Ripper" takes over the computer and, thereby, the ship. Also different, the events surrounding this take-over are more horrific than what was filmed and aired on NBC, with additional attempts by "Jack," using the mechanics of the starship, to frighten, maim, and kill crew members.

Based on his regard for James Doohan's acting, it was Associate Producer Robert Justman's idea to change the accused from Sulu to Scotty, for a "better chance at dramatics." Justman's memo to Coon continued:

> I like the idea of starting off a show down on a planet somewhere. Please let me cast the part of Kara, the entertainer who "dances to the music of the flute." For a murder mystery, I find that there are too many suspects and too many speaking parts. I feel we should trim down…. I suggest that Sulu/Scott have recovered consciousness in the alley, to discover that someone had placed the knife in his hand. I find it hard to believe that an innocent bystander always picks up the murder weapon and gets caught with it in his grimy hand. (RJ36)

In this early version, McCoy is not only absent at the nightclub on Argelius, he is very nearly missing throughout, prompting Justman, still pushing for Scott to replace Sulu in the story, to tell Coon:

> Has it occurred to you that Dr. McCoy is missing from the story? Don't you feel that he ought to be with us in <u>every show</u>? Therefore, I have an idea. We are blowing some very good dramatic values if we discover that Sulu/Scott is innocent after all at the end of Act 1. Let's have Kirk arrive on the scene to find Sulu/Scott unconscious and a medical Orderly dead and murdered by stabbing. And then let's have Dr. McCoy revive [Sulu/Scott] from his state of unconsciousness to say that it must have been Sulu/Scott who committed this fresh murder, because nobody else was around at the time. Incidentally, the medical Orderly who is killed must be a female if we are to maintain the "Jack the Ripper" idea in this story. Unless I am highly mistaken, Jack the Ripper only preyed on female prostitutes. (RJ36)

And then, of course, there were budget concerns. In just one example of this, Justman wrote:

> On Page 2, let's go directly to the interior of the Home of Jaris and Juliette. Since it is night, there would be no need to establish the exterior of this "classic, almost Grecian-Temple structure set in a peacefully beautiful park." Besides, we

couldn't afford it! (RJ36-1)

Justman ended his memo to Coon with: "I hate and detest and don't believe Act IV." (RJ36)

Act IV involved a lengthy battle of wills between Kirk and the ship's computer, with the captain using logic to defeat the Entity, as he had done with Landru -- the computer -- in "The Return of the Archons." As in that episode, which Robert Bloch had an opportunity to watch, the computer shorts out. Worse, Bloch had the onboard computer explode, resulting in a great deal of damage to the ship.

Coon didn't ask Bloch for a rewrite. To save time, he made a few changes himself.

In Coon's April 21 Revised Story Outline, there was still too little of McCoy, still Sulu as the accused murderer, and the Enterprise computer still went ka-blooey.

Looking for a way to get McCoy into the story sooner, Script Consultant Dorothy Fontana suggested to Coon that the doctor be there from the start, accompanying the others to the nightclub. Beyond this, her main opposition concerned Bloch's idea to have the thrust of the story to be the Entity's taking over the ship's computer -- an event which would last for half the episode. Fontana wanted that cut back. And she didn't like the ending, prompting her to write:

> Do we have to do the old "feed-the-computer-logic-make-it-drop-dead-give-up-or-anything-else-we-must-have-to-do-to-resolve-the-story" bit? We've really done it to death and it ought to be allowed to rest in peace. (DC36-1)

Already having been used in "The Return of the Archons," the "bit" was also present in the story outlines for "The Changeling" and "I, Mudd," both turned in one month before "Wolf in the Fold."

Two days after Fontana gave her notes, NBC's Stan Robertson wrote to Coon, saying:

> The crux of how successful this most intriguing storyline is as a screenplay is how simplified and believable the writer can convert the quasi-scientific philosophy of the existence of a Jack the Ripper in the era of our series. (SR36)

Robertson agreed with Justman on two important points:

> We must play this story as a mystery, involving our crewman from the Enterprise in it as a prime suspect until as late as possible, possibly until the Tag of the third act... [and] it would seem more feasible from a practical standpoint to utilize Mr. Scott as our suspect rather than Sulu, since not only is the former a more proficient actor but a person in our series who I believe has not been given the exposure in our stories that his prominence on the crew denotes. (SR36)

Scotty was in. Sulu, to George Takei's chagrin, was out, although Takei was nonetheless given some delightful business to do, including a chance to act very stoned.

Pleased by this change was the episode's director, Joseph Pevney. He said, "Jimmy Doohan was very easy to work with. A good, solid performer, always anxious to do a good job, and always knew his words, inside and out; an angel as far as directors are concerned." (141-2)

Doohan, of course, was happy over the change, saying, "I got to do some acting. Here was Scotty being threatened, having to protect himself, but he didn't know how. I thought, 'Thank God, they're doing something with me.'" (52-1)

On May 18, Robert Bloch delivered his 1st Draft screenplay. Dorothy Fontana was appalled. She wrote Coon:

I will not comment on the quality of the dialogue. Sufficient to say… "Oi." … There is definitely not enough Spock. We don't dig deeply enough into Scotty…. All we see from Scott is hostility. That we don't need; we need a man crying out that he is innocent in the face of all the facts against him…. Jaris [the head of the local government] has no character. No one has any character. (DC36-2)

After five pages of such criticism, D.C. signed her memo "Jackie the Ripper." Roddenberry was more harsh. He wrote Coon:

There's no doubt an occasional murder-mystery on *Star Trek* gives us a change of pace. However… this will require a detailed and deep rewrite and I strongly recommend that we get a memo to Bloch on record, listing where he is off on question of format, continuing characters, and logic. Further, it is important that the writer understand that WGA [Writers Guild of America] contracts require such a rewrite at our discretion if he is to be paid his full fee. There seemed to be some doubt about this once in the past [on "What Are Little Girls Made Of?"]. (GR36-1)

Translation: Robert Bloch owed *Star Trek* a Revised 1st Draft script for the money already advanced him.

Among some of Roddenberry's specific complaints, as with Fontana, was the depiction of Scotty. His memo to Coon continued:

Scotty comes off as a most disagreeable character. Much better if he were horrified at the possibility that he may have committed the crime, anxious to help determine the facts even if it means his career and freedom. (GR36-1)

The rest of the characters struck Roddenberry as shallow. He told Coon:

None of our running characters, including Kirk, show the depth of conflicting emotions. They must feel doubt as it becomes more and more apparent that Scotty has committed murder. (GR36-1)

Roddenberry found Act I to be "generally slow." He wrote:

The rambling dialogue and lack of activity comes out of the fact we have no genuine conflict here…. [This script] is now in danger of coming off as another -- and even slower -- "Conscience of the King." Perhaps by finding a firm, logical and consistent back-story and set of rules for the society on this planet, we might come up with some answers which would lend "sf" [sci-fi] color and excitement…. Why not use the fact we have two highly different cultures?… There may be something in this to create some conflict…. With a growing interest today in the "hip" culture of non-violence, love and permissiveness, why not adapt these characteristics for this planet? There is fun in that, excitement, contrast, and interesting conflict coming out of the ways of that culture and the ways of our *Star Trek* people. (GR36-1)

Roddenberry had tried to develop a couple of *Star Trek* sex stories for Season One but, other than "Mudd's Women," none had worked out. He did sneak some naughtiness into his rewrite of Bloch's "What Are Little Girls Made Of?" with the android Andrea programmed to please a man in all ways, and, for this new season's first episode, it was Roddenberry's idea to make the theme in "Catspaw" have to do with lust and an alien's first experience at pleasures of the flesh. "Wolf in the Fold" offered the opportunity for some playful sexiness, too.

And with this, it was decided not to "cut-off" "Wolf in the Fold" at first draft. Bloch would get to write that freebie Revised 1st Draft.

Gene Coon's letter to Bloch began:

Dear Bob, brace yourself. As usual, when I sit down to dictate a memo, I get pretty verbose. I undoubtedly will not make this an exception. (GC36)

What followed were 16 pages of single-spaced notes dissecting every nuance of the script. Among other things, Coon wanted a change made in the way Kirk battled and defeated the Entity in the computer. Instead of using logic against it, which Fontana had lobbied against, Coon suggested Kirk pose a question -- asking the computer to calculate the value of pi to the last place. Another change was to *not* have the computer blow up, but instead have the Entity flee the machinery so it could be captured, sedated, and beamed into space. Coon also wanted significant changes made in the depiction of Scotty. He wrote:

I am a little worried about the words you have given Engineer Scott. He is quite aggressive, quite belligerent and, despite his injury, this is hardly the Scott we have come to know and love. He could be a bit touchy, unquestionably. However, I do not believe he would be quite as belligerent, aggressive, and, quite frankly, as obnoxious as you have made him. I don't really like Scott very much throughout this script. (GC36)

Bloch made these changes without protest and turned in his rewrite on June 1, which was then distributed to the creative staff.

Fontana wrote Coon:

There is still a great deal of clarification to be done, and some restructuring, as well as a total dialogue polish.... Mister Spock must be used more, and I feel Kirk would employ Spock's natural Sherlock Holmes talents earlier in this script. (DC36-3)

Justman echoed these feelings in his latest memo. But neither he nor Fontana knew of Coon's need to minimize the use of Spock in this episode. A week earlier, the Emmy nominations had been announced, with Nimoy receiving acknowledgment ... and Shatner ignored. That same week, there was an article in *TV Guide* raving over Spock ... again with Shatner/Kirk ignored. And Coon had just circulated the mimeographed 1st Draft script for "The Doomsday Machine" to the cast. Spock not only had much more business than Kirk, he had much more *interesting* business. William Shatner, *Star Trek*'s top-billed star, had reason to not be happy.

"Doomsday" needed some rewriting, but the structure and what worked best for that story did not provide much opportunity to take from Spock and give to Kirk. "Wolf in the Fold" was Coon's opportunity to shift balance the other way and he hoped to prevent further ill feelings on the set. Not only did Coon appear determined to keep Spock out of the first half of the show, he chose to speed through the rewriting process and scheduled "Wolf" to immediately follow "The Doomsday Machine" on the production roster. This would give assurance to Shatner that the creative staff, unlike the studio's promotional department, hadn't turned their backs on him. The structure for this script also served NBC's Stan Robertson, who had been asking for more planet-based stories and more focus on the differences between the societies which lived on these worlds and our own. Coon's mind was made up -- Spock and the Enterprise would have to wait until the start of Act III.

It was now time for the staff to take over. The Yellow Cover 1st Draft came in early June. It was one of those, as Dorothy Fontana described it, "clean it up, make them sound like our people, but don't mess with the structure" jobs. Coon was resisting allowing any significant changes to be made, doing what he believed would best appease Shatner and

Robertson. With less than two weeks before the start of production, Roddenberry checked in, writing Coon:

> This script, more than any other in work, needs bold and creative thinking. It's going to be a hard fight to get all the excitement we want into this story. (GR36-2)

Even though Coon had taken care to keep Kirk in more of the story than Spock, among the problem areas Roddenberry identified in his eight-page memo was the need for *more* Kirk. Being in a script and *doing* something in a script are two different things. Emphasis on Kirk's conflict needed further amplification, including his wanting to help his engineer while having to maintain peaceful relations with the leaders of Argelius; this coupled with the doubt Kirk feels when the man he has been fighting for appears to have killed one of the Captain's own female crewmembers, as well as the planet-leader's wife. And Kirk had to appear more threatened by the danger to his ship once Jack the Ripper moved into its computers.

Roddenberry also wanted more science fiction, and more clarification and consistency regarding "the place, the people, their customs." (GR36-1)

One way to accomplish this, to Roddenberry's thinking, was to add in more sex. Not shy about such things with Coon, he confided:

> Let's establish that the nature of this place keeps women eternally young, beautiful, and remarkably busty. Perhaps hormones work better here. At any rate, let's cast and clothe in that direction with a vengeance. This place is remarkably peaceful because the women are beautiful and they screw a lot. Isn't that logical? Or, if we can't be logical, let's at least be provocative. (GR36-1)

Coon's revised script was the Final Draft from mid June. Among the changes: more of Kirk *doing*, not just *being*, and more emphasis on the culture and the laws of Argelius II. Coon's description of the café in the episode's Teaser went as follows:

> Most of the men, except for our people, have at least one beautiful, exotic woman with them -- and the women are all lush, scantily clad, and most, most friendly. We should get the impression that this would be a perfectly splendid place for a man -- especially a space man who had been out there somewhere for a long time -- to visit.

And Coon added more science fiction, mixed in with the macabre, mystery, and terror. Kirk and Spock both argue that humans and humanoids make up only a small percentage of known life forms; the possibility of entities capable of deriving sustenance from other creatures' emotions; how creatures of this type would likely exist without form and could be practically immortal; about the Drella of Alpha Carina 5 and the Mellitus cloud creatures of Alpha Majoris One. It was now sci-fi-y enough for the character of Hengist to rise up during the trial and angrily cry out, "This is fantastic!"

One idea that was too fantastic for NBC concerned the drinks served to Kirk, McCoy, and Scott while visiting the café. David Gerrold, working at *Star Trek* on his own script "The Trouble with Tribbles," remembered hearing Gene Coon on the phone arguing with Stan Robertson. Gerrold said, "In the Teaser of that show, Robert Bloch had postulated a nine-layered drink; each layer of liquid caused the imbiber to experience a different emotion. Kirk, Spock [sic], Scotty, and McCoy were sitting in a pub on Argelius II and drinking these concoctions -- and experiencing grief, joy, rage, love, envy, unhappiness, etc., in unison.... The network thought this bore an uncomfortable resemblance to a psychedelic drug or narcotic. NBC's Broadcast Standards said so. Gene Coon told them they were 'full of horseshit.' I'm sure he felt better for it -- but the drink was excised from the script." (73-6)

Fontana continued to be concerned that Spock was very nearly absent from the first half of the story, and told Coon so in a memo. By this time, Justman had stopped arguing on this issue and, in his latest memo to Coon, clearly held little regard for the story being told. He wrote:

> I suppose it is necessary to have a séance in the show.... [But] for the benefit of the viewers who have to see our show in black and white, I suggest that someone announce out loud the various color changes that occur during the séance sequence. For instance, McCoy could say, 'Gee whiz! That weird red light has just changed to green, Captain Kirk!' Someone else could take the change from green to white.... I found another point to disagree with Dorothy about. Let's not give Spock any more to do in the first two acts. Let's save him for the last half of the show. In fact, Leonard Nimoy would probably prefer not to be in this show at all. (RJ36-2)

Once Coon finished with his draft, Roddenberry did a polish of his own -- the Revised Final Draft from June 21.

"Of course I kept a close eye on the scripts," Roddenberry told this author. "You can see that in the memos. I wasn't rewriting everything as in the first year. Gene Coon was handling most of that by the second season. And we made sure he had good support [with Dorothy Fontana] -- someone he could hand work off to. But, because of the system set up by the networks, having you wait until the last possible moment to find out if you have been picked up, then you have to develop 16 or more stories simultaneously, I sometimes would take on the final rewrite of a script to free Gene and Dorothy to stay busy on others that were coming in. Don Ingalls' Vietnam war parallel ["A Private Little War"] was one. And Bob Bloch's script. You can check the dates on those. Sometimes we were still rewriting as they were being filmed." (145)

"I was a little surprised when I saw it on the screen," Bloch said of the finished episode. "I was never told who had a hand in making the changes and revisions but I rather suspect it was 'D.C.,' because I think most of 'em were pretty good." (18-1)

Not D.C. this time; this one came from G.R. and G.C.

Despite being pleased with his bigger role, James Doohan had mixed feelings about the ending. He found the Tag scene -- an attempt at humor by Gene Coon -- to be unforgivably illogical. Kirk tries to talk Spock into beaming down to the planet with him "to check out a place where the women are sooo ...," a line Kirk never finishes because network standards would not allow us to hear the particulars. Doohan considered it "interesting" that Kirk would consider leaving the ship in the care of "430 drunk drivers!" (52-1)

Pre-Production
June 20-23 & 26, 1967 (5 days prep).

Joseph Pevney had only five days to prepare this episode, since Daniels' episode -- "The Doomsday Machine" -- was shooting in five days rather than six. Casting had to be done quickly.

John Fiedler was 41 when he played Mr. Hengist. Because of Fiedler's unique looks and, more so, his unique voice, he worked often in television and in films. He was Cadet Alfie Higgins on the 1950s TV series *Tom Corbett, Space Cadet*. He visited *The Twilight Zone* and *Get Smart*, and was one of the jurors in *12 Angry Men* -- all prominent roles. In a few years he would be one of Felix and Oscar's regular poker buddies in *The Odd Couple* movie and series, and then spend several years on the psychologist's couch on *The Bob Newhart Show*. He would also provide the voice of Piglet in *Winnie the Pooh* cartoons from 1968 until his death in 2005.

Joe Pevney called Fiedler one of his favorite actors, saying, "He doesn't look like an actor, doesn't sound like an actor, *and* he's an excellent actor. In 'Wolf in the Fold' he was very interesting, and quite good." (141-2)

Fiedler once remarked, "People will come up and say, 'Gosh, I thought it was you. Then I heard your voice, and I *knew*.' Nine times out of ten, they don't know the name." (61-2)

Fiedler's casting as Hengist was perfect. With that face, and that voice, few watching would suspect Hengist of being Jack the Ripper.

Charles Macaulay, seen here as Prefect Jaris, had appeared in *Star Trek* once before, looking quite different as Landru, in "The Return of the Archons." He was 39.

Pilar Seurat, playing Sybo, with a knife in her back, was 29. She was a former dancer who ventured into television in the late 1950s, working often whenever a pretty Asian face was needed, including prominent roles on *Hawaiian Eye*, *Adventures in Paradise*, and *I Spy*. Joe D'Agosta had cast her previously in *The Lieutenant*.

Charles Dierkop, as Morla, the jealous boyfriend of Victim #1, and the story's red herring, was 30. He was one year away from saddling up in *Butch Cassidy and the Sundance Kid*, as a character named Flat Nose Curry, followed by countless TV appearances, including 91 episodes of *Police Woman*, as Det. Pete Royster.

John Fiedler as Mr. Hengist
(Unaired film trim courtesy of Gerald Gurian)

Charles Macaulay (above) in his previous *Star Trek* appearance, as Landru, and (below), here, as Prefect Jaris

John Winston, playing Lt. Kyle, the transporter room chief, got to have a bit of fun in the Tag scene, happily sedated. Winston, who started out on *Star Trek* as a bit player but had extensive experience on the stage, was being given more prominent roles with each appearance. He said, "*Star Trek* was almost a mixture of comedy and melodrama. It was Shatner, because he was so clever with it all, which gave it credibility. He was the star. He was the sun, and the rest of the cast, being the rest of the planets, circulated around him." (189a)

Tania Lemani (AKA Tanya Lemani, AKA Tanya George) was the first victim. She worked both on and off screen as an exotic dancer and played a Persian slave girl in the unsold pilot *Alexander the Great*, which aired in 1968, three years after being filmed. Alexander himself was played by the star that all the planets were circling -- William Shatner.

Lemani recalled, "When I walked onto the set on *Alexander the Great*, I saw him, and he had this little skirt on and he had the cutest legs, and I thought, 'Oh my God, who is that Greek god?' And they said, 'That's William Shatner.' And I go, 'Oh my God.' I was, like, 16 years old. And, as we were filming, he kept looking and smiling, and finally came up to me and whispered to me with his very, very, very sexy voice, and saying that he wants to take me out.

Don Adams and Tania Lemani in *Get Smart!*
(NBC publicity photo)

He wants to see me. And I'm looking at him and thinking, 'Well, yeah, I want to go out with him.' My heart was pounding and I was getting nervous. But I said, 'Oh, I'm sorry, I'd love that, but you're married.' And he said, 'Well, what's that got to do with anything?' You know how he is -- a big Romeo. And I said, 'Well, I just don't go out with married men.'" (72)

Two-and-a-half years after that meeting, Lemani, at the ripe old age of 19, had already appeared in several TV shows, including *The Man from U.N.C.L.E.*, *McHale's Navy*, *I Dream of Jeannie*, and *Get Smart*.

"They wanted someone who had acting experience, and dancing," she said. "So I auditioned. Roddenberry was there, and Gene Coon, and the casting person was there [Joe D'Agosta], and Joe Pevney, the director. And Gene [Roddenberry] was a lovely, lovely man. He was very warm, very personable. He smiled and he talked to you as if you were his relative. He made you feel comfortable." (72)

Lemani had never seen *Star Trek*. She explained, "At that time, I was working at a restaurant at night in the Greek Village, dancing, and, during the days I would go on interviews for work in TV or films. So that's why I didn't get a chance to see the show. But, when I read the script, I didn't have a problem imagining what it would be like. I thought it was very clever. What kept that show good was the scripts." (72)

Day 1, filming the trial on Stage 9
(Unaired film trim courtesy of Gerald Gurian)

Day 2: Bill McGovern slates the brief fight sequence climaxing the trial
(Courtesy of Gerald Gurian)

Filming began Tuesday, June 27, 1967. This was the week 200 people were arrested during a race riot in Buffalo, New York. And Major Robert Lawrence, Jr. became the first black astronaut. Sadly, he would never make it into space. He would die later in the year in a plane crash. Also in the news: Keith Richards of the Rolling Stones was sentenced to one year in prison on drug charges. And actress Jayne Mansfield was killed in a car crash. She was 34.

It was the Summer of Love. The hippie movement had taken to the streets of San Francisco. The Association hit No. 1 on the pop singles charts with "Windy," and would stay there for four weeks. The Beatles took over the No. 1 album position from The Monkees, for the first of 15 weeks, with *Sgt. Pepper's Lonely Hearts Club Band*. You could take home a copy for $5.98. *The Dirty Dozen* was tops at the box office.

Day 1 began on the briefing room set for the trial scene that dominated Act III, where Scott is proven innocent and the true identity of the killer is learned.

A curious shot involved James Doohan's hand... or what the viewer would assume was the hand of James Doohan. During the trial, the script called for Scotty's right hand to be flat on a lit sensor pad -- a futuristic lie detector. Doohan said, "Director Joe Pevney had no desire to risk throwing a viewer mentally out of the scene with a startling, 'Hey, look, Scotty's missing a finger!' I, as always, preferred to keep it out of the limelight. So we had a stunt hand step in for Scotty." (52-1)

Eddie Paskey said, "I was Jimmy's hand double. He was missing a finger and anytime he would run the controls on the transporter room or something like that, those were my hands." (135-2)

Day 2, Wednesday. A second full day in the briefing room, where Hengist is revealed to be the entity known as Jack the Ripper. Stuntman Paul Baxley, "doubling" for John Fiedler, bore little resemblance to the actor. During the fight scene between Hengist and Kirk, it is clear that Fiedler had been replaced by Baxley. But keep your eye on William Shatner, who proves to be quite daring and fast on his feet. As Hengist kicks Kirk in the chest, Shatner, doing his own stunts, slams against the wall, then bounces off, lunging back toward Baxley and sending the stuntman in the bald cap to the floor with a quick right hook.

Day 3, Thursday, June 29. The company spent the first of three days on Stage 10, beginning with the interior of the main room of the Jaris' house. The bulk of Act I was filmed, as Scotty was interrogated further by Hengist, with Jaris present, and Yeoman Tankris beaming down.

"Miri" was repeated on NBC this night.

Day 4, with Charles Dierkop, Joseph Bernard, John Fiedler, William Shatner, Charles Macaulay, DeForest Kelley, and Pilar Seurat (Unaired film trim, courtesy of Gerald Gurian)

Day 4, Friday. The morning was spent finishing in the main room of the Jaris' house, with the séance.

Joseph Pevney, a daring director, had Jerry Finnerman, a daring cinematographer, mount a lightweight Arriflex camera high in the rafters of Stage 10, aimed straight down on the circular table for the séance scene. A shot of this type is time consuming. And so was the dolly shot that followed, making a circular journey on a track panning from face to face of those gathered round that table. With a six-day shooting schedule, Pevney and Finnerman were risking overtime with these elaborate setups.

After the lunch break, filming continued in the underground room of the Jaris' house where Scotty was discovered again holding a knife, and with another dead woman at his feet -- Lt. Tankris. Mid-afternoon, still on Stage 10, the company moved to the interior café set, filming the scene that opened Act I where Scotty was first interrogated by Hengist.

Day 5, Monday. The morning was spent filming the episode's Teaser, featuring Kirk, McCoy, and Scott being entertained by the Argelian dancer.

Roddenberry got into the act in helping to choose the outfits worn by the various beautiful and voluptuous women in the café. His memo on the titillating subject told Bill Theiss:

> Suggest we consider clothing all females in the script in some particular striking shade of crimson or red. The costumes can differ if we want, but this is the female color on this planet. (GR36-3)

Joseph Pevney also vested himself in the process of choosing the right look for the women on a world that prided itself on being hedonistic. Tania Lemani said, "The first thing that I had to do was go there for makeup -- for four days in a row. They were experimenting with different makeup on me. The first time they took hours and hours of putting different colored feathers on my eyebrows, my eyelashes, my toes, my ears. And feathers were coming from all over, and I kept sneezing. I couldn't see where I was going. So, each time they would do all that and take me to Joseph Pevney and he'd look and he'd say, 'Less, less,' and this went on for *four* days. I didn't care, because they were paying me. And, finally he says, 'Don't use anything! I want to see your pretty face.' And that's how it happened. No feathers or nothing, just regular face." (72)

Lemani's fifth day at the studio was her first day on set. She remembered, "The stage was big, and it was a very nice set, with a little stage for me to dance. Of course, we rehearsed a few times, and they had other people sit in for the main actors, and then the actors came in and we had another run through. That's when I was introduced to all of the guys. And I looked at Shatner and I think I said, 'Oh, do you remember me from *Alexander the Great*?' And he said, 'Of course I remember you.' And, of course, he was flirting." (72)

Day 5. Lemani said of Shatner, "And, of course, he was flirting." (Courtesy of Gerald Gurian)

Lemani, with an eye-opening close-up, kicked off "Wolf in the Fold." There was no Enterprise flyby, no Captain's log, just a sudden fade up to those exotic eyes Joseph Pevney fussed over so. With the crash of a cymbal, followed by Alexander Courage's Orion Slave Girl Theme from "The Cage," Lemani wiggled and jiggled in an outfit that was quite revealing -- a bit too much so for NBC's taste.

"In those days, you were *not* supposed to show your belly button on TV," Lemani said. "And they would glue things into your belly button. It was some kind of a flower. But it would pop out. So that would slow things down, stop and go, more than normal. And they had to do that a few times, because it wouldn't stick there." (72)

It was known before the film was sent to editing that this episode would begin with a close-up on the exotic female dancer, well into her provocative performance. Credit Stan Robertson of NBC. He had been very clear about his disfavor of Teasers always beginning with a shot of the Enterprise. Only "The Conscience of the King," "Tomorrow Is Yesterday," and "The Devil in the Dark" had started differently. By this point, the seventh episode of the new season, his request became an order and "Wolf in the Fold" was the first of several scripts to have the standard *Star Trek* opening written out and replaced with immediate action on the surface of a planet.

Besides keeping the series from losing its luster through "sameness," Robertson's reason for insisting on the change was to better hook the younger audience NBC expected to tune in on a Friday night. Gene Coon, not buying for one minute that 10-year-olds would have a problem seeing each episode open with a spaceship, chose to thumb his nose at the network by opening with this very adult-oriented close-up of a sexy and scantily-clothed woman in a club for hedonistic grownups.

Lemani remembered, "Joe Pevney was very creative. What impressed me about him was, when they did my close-up, he was talking to me, and he told me, 'Imagine this and imagine that, and look right into the camera and imagine that you're going into Scotty's mind. And he was saying several things like that. And then when the close-up came, he wanted to light it up a certain way. He took his time. And when they showed it in the dailies, people who were watching literally let out a gasp, because it was on the big screen, and such a *big* close up, and it was so striking." (72)

During the afternoon hours of Day 5, and still on Stage 10, the portion of the Teaser outside the café was filmed in the fog-covered street, and then leading to the alleyway where Scotty is seen with the first victim.

Regarding the time she spent playing a corpse, Lemani said, "There was no stunt double. That was me lying there, breathing in all that artificial fog. They used that stuff a lot in those days and, of course, you would choke on it a bit. I had to come up for fresh air a few times, or ask for water just to get the taste of that fog out of my mouth. I'd take a deep breath and hold it for as long as I could. You could breathe it, but it was not pleasant." (72)

Day 6: Ending on a high … with the bridge crew sedated and elated
(Courtesy of Gerald Gurian)

Cast and crew took Tuesday off. It was the 4th of July.

Day 6, Wednesday. Back on Stage 9 now, filming resumed with the bridge scenes, followed by the sequences in the ship's corridor (the delightful scene where Kirk carries a giggling Hengist slung over his shoulder), then on to the elevator scene where the Entity tries to chop Spock in two

172

by slamming the doors on him. Pevney was racing to finish and not go into a seventh day, and, in his rush, botched this scene up. The one and only camera angle he got of Spock entering the elevator and the doors whooshing toward him was obscured. The script told us, "Kirk enters first, Spock immediately after, but the doors start to slam shut before Spock is all the way in. Kirk sees this and yells 'Spock!' He grabs Spock and yanks him forward into the elevator as the doors clang shut. Spock turns and regards the door with interest. He says, 'Fascinating. Apparently our friend learns very quickly.' Kirk says, 'Too quickly.'"

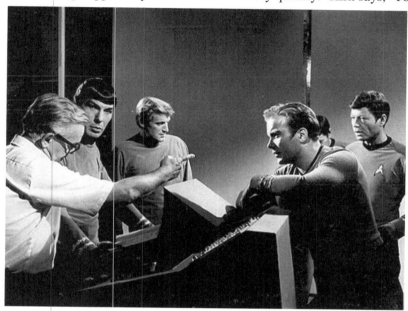

**Joseph Pevney gives direction on the transporter room set
(Courtesy of Gerald Gurian)**

The lines are there, as is the action. But, with no clear view of what is happening, the impact of the moment is lost.

And, finally, onto the transporter room, where Hengist is beamed into space.

With a script tailored to showcase Kirk over Spock, some saw an improvement in Shatner's mood during the filming of "Wolf in the Fold."

Others did not. Tania Lemani, on set for one day, but in the makeup room and the screening room on three other days, saw a happy company and was particular impressed by Shatner, who she said made her visit to *Star Trek* great fun. John Fiedler, present for all six days of filming, saw things differently, saying that Shatner was bossy and generally unpleasant. The recollections of most involved with *Star Trek* tell us that throughout the production of the series the mood on the set was exceptionally good and that the so-called "Shatner/Nimoy feud" was short-lived. Many remarked that cast and crew seemed like a family. But families do fight.

Post-Production
*Available for editing: July 7, 1967. Rough Cut: July 21. Final Cut: July 27.
Musical Score: tracked music.*

Bruce Schoengarth and Edit Team 2 did the cutting, their third assignment of the season, following "Catspaw" and "Who Mourns for Adonais."

Van der Veer Photo Effects handled the optical work, including the colorful swirling images on the ship's view screens when "Jack" invades the computers. Roddenberry had suggested to Coon to aim this episode at the growing "hippie" culture in America, with its depiction of a society built on free love. A psychedelic light show couldn't hurt. And it didn't. By 1967 standards, it was an impressive eyeful.

Composer Gerald Fried was given credit for music in this tracked episode. Much of what is heard came from his original scores for "Catspaw," "Friday's Child," and "Amok Time."

"As a composer, it's disturbing to hear music I wrote for one scene appear somewhere else," Fried said. "I suppose if I were a producer with a budget staring me in the face, I would probably do the same. I can't say I like it, but I have no control over it." (69-2)

"Wolf in the Fold" came in $9,718 over budget. The total cost of $189,718 equates to a little over $1.3 million in 2013, about half of what would be spent on an episode of a one-hour series of the same time. The Second Season deficit increased to $122,171 (just under $900,000 in 2013).

Release / Reaction
Only NBC airing: 12/22/67.

Steven H. Scheuer reviewed the episode for his syndicated column, *TV Key Previews*. Among numerous newspapers across the country, the review was carried by the Wilmington, Ohio *New Journal*, on December 22, 1967:

> "Wolf in the Fold." Among the shows worth watching tonight is *Star Trek*. It has a good celestial ghost story, which starts with a murder investigation on a distant planet, but then ends as a real weird tale. Scott is suspected of being the murderer, only before the case can be solved, two other violent deaths occur. And guess who did it? Jack the Ripper.

Tania Lemani took the night off from dancing when "Wolf in the Fold" had its only NBC airing.

"I saw it when it played and I loved it," she said. "It turned out to be better than the script. The writing helped make that show, but, of course, so did the actors. I thought that all the actors played off of each other beautifully. And I think that's what made that show great -- the actors *and* the stories." (72)

Star Trek's competition, besides *Gomer Pyle* and *Hondo* at 8:30, was the movie on CBS at 9 p.m. -- the 1962 Cold War drama *Escape from East Berlin*, starring Don Murray, and based on a true story of a family tunneling under the Berlin Wall to free themselves from Communism.

"Wolf in the Fold" is the only first run episode of the original *Star Trek* for which a ratings report could not be located.

***

This episode had everything Stan Robertson relentlessly asked for: a Teaser that did not begin with the standard shot of the Enterprise in space, a plotline unlike any other, taking place on an alien world with customs of a society foreign to our own, and a story utilizing Mr. Scott. And yet, despite following Robertson's guidelines, "Wolf in the Fold" was buried in the schedule, airing less than a week before Christmas. And there was no network repeat.

"That rarely had anything to do with the network," Robert Justman revealed. "The decision regarding which episodes to repeat was primarily mine. I picked the ones I liked. Now, of course I liked them all. But I did not like them all equally." (94-1)

As for its writer, Robert Bloch dropped by later in the season to discuss another script assignment, but chose to pass on any further work. He explained, "I didn't care for what was happening to *Star Trek* towards the end of the second season. I said to myself, 'This isn't going to be anything that I'm likely to be interested in.' The original concept had become so eviscerated that I would just rather stay away. Not that I'm a purist, but when a show reaches that point, that's trouble.... Life is too short." (18-4)

Bloch was referring to the change in command in the *Star Trek* offices. But that's another story ... still to come.

Memories

Samuel Peeples said, "I've always been a 'Jack the Ripper' buff, so Bob's version of a science fiction Jack the Ripper has always amused me, and I enjoy it very much." (136-3)

John Fiedler, Jack the Ripper himself, said, "*Star Trek* is the thing more people stop and ask me about than anything else I've ever done, because it plays all the time.... I think about those old episodes -- and I *have* watched them lately -- and they didn't have the technical stuff that came along later.... So what they did instead was rely on good stories.... The one I was in was a good story, with very few trick effects." (61)

Tania Lemani, in a conversation with this author 43 years after "Wolf in the Fold" first aired, said, "Those scripts were clever. When *Star Trek* became so popular, I understood why. Because when you look at every episode, the stories were so good. And so uplifting, really. They all had such great, uplifting messages. And I think that's what people related to. And they still do. And that's what makes this show as popular as it is. Right now, I go and sign autographs, and these little kids come up to my table. *Little kids!* And they even know the title. They say, "Ah, I've seen 'Wolf in the Fold.' I'm so in awe by it all. I think it's wonderful." (72)

10

- *Enter John Meredyth Lucas* -

Mother Bess Meredyth, son John, and step-dad, famed-director Michael Curtiz (www.eightyoddyears.com)

The man who would eventually become *Star Trek*'s third primary writer/producer, after first apprenticing with three story assignments, began his association with the series here.

John Meredyth Lucas was 48 and the product of a show business family. His father was silent film actor, writer, and director Wilfred Lucas, and his mother, Bess Meredyth, was both an actress and writer. After Wilfred Lucas died, Bess married Academy Award winning director Michael Curtiz (*Casablanca*), who adopted young John and helped get him his show business start. In time, Lucas would certainly prove he had talent, but his story is otherwise a classic example of how in Hollywood it's not so much what you know but *who* you know. And, of course, it doesn't hurt to be in the right place at precisely the right moment.

Lucas recalled, "When college worked no better than all other educational schemes, discussions were held to determine what was to become of me. Mike [Curtiz] solved the problem by securing me employment as an apprentice script clerk at Warner Brothers." (110-6)

A script clerk, or "script continuity" person, must use a stopwatch to time the length of every camera "take," then make notes into the script describing the wardrobe worn by each person in the scene, how their hair was styled, and their positions -- standing, sitting, arms folded, holding a drink, etc. -- at the time of speaking a line of dialogue so that all of the various camera angles and takes would match.

On one occasion, when a continuity error was made and an actor had been filmed wearing the wrong wardrobe, Lucas broke protocol and frantically rewrote some lines of dialogue in the script to explain the change in clothing. When he brought the problem to the attention of the director, he was prepared to lose his job. The director threw the expected fit, but then, as he looked at the proposed changes to the script, calmed down and said, "Yeah, that could work." Shortly thereafter, Lucas was hired at $50 a week as a "junior writer." After several scripts had been written, but none produced, Lucas left Warner Brothers and accepted a job at Twentieth Century Fox as an assistant director. He later admitted, "Mike had, of course, spoken to [studio head] Darryl Zanuck." (110-6)

From here, Lucas eventually was elevated to dialogue director. In that day, many film directors, having come to Hollywood from Europe during the silent movie era, were not fluent in English. Mike Curtiz, who had immigrated from Hungary, was one such director. The job for a dialogue director, then, was to rehearse the cast and help convey the instructions from the man sitting in the director's chair who was so difficult to understand. Lucas, having years of experience training his ear for a Hungarian accent, and choppy, incomplete English wording, was an ideal translator for Curtiz.

From script clerk, to junior writer, to assistant director, to dialogue director, Lucas was learning the business from the near-bottom up.

A big break for Lucas came through his friendship with Hal Wallis, who had produced many of Michael Curtiz's films for Warner Brothers, including *Casablanca*, *Captain Blood*, and *The Adventures of Robin Hood*. Lucas not only knew Wallis (who was a friend of the family) but spent many evenings at the producer's home where there was a projection room. Here, the two entertained themselves watching movies and discussing their merits. Wallis felt Lucas had a keen sense of story and invited him to try his hand at writing a film noir screenplay for a movie to star Charlton Heston. *Dark City* was released by Paramount to positive notices and good business in 1950. Also featured in the cast was a young Jack Webb, who, along with his partner, writer James Moser, would use the script as a template for a radio series they went on to create, called *Dragnet*.

Wallis kept Lucas busy, writing an Alan Ladd western, 1951's *Red Mountain*, followed by 1952's *Peking Express*, starring Joseph Cotten. Lucas could have continued as a screenwriter of B-pictures at Paramount, but the pay there was even worse than it had been at Warner Brothers, and the contract the studio offered for a second year of service was for the same dismal money as the previous year. Lucas chose to bid Hal Wallis farewell, then packed up his typewriter and moved over to Columbia to write a sequel to a movie his step-father had directed (*Captain Blood*), to be released in 1952 as *Captain Pirate*.

Work soon followed at Universal, including writing *Tumbleweed*, a western for Audie Murphy. While there, the studio provided Lucas with a bungalow to work from. One bungalow over was Jack Webb's former partner, writer/producer James Moser, who had just finished a movie for the studio and was now preparing to start work on a TV series he created -- *Medic*, starring Richard Boone. As payback for borrowing from *Dark City* for *Dragnet*, Moser invited Lucas to write for *Medic*. Having an interest in medicine, and having no further interest in B-pictures, Lucas quickly accepted the offer. He later recalled, "After writing several scripts, when I felt I had made myself, if not irreplaceable to *Medic*, at least desirable, I told Jim Moser I wanted to direct my next script. The idea was not greeted with whole-hearted joy but was finally agreed to." (110-6)

When *Medic* folded, Lucas returned to Columbia Pictures. During his previous tenure there, he made valuable friends and now, with some directing credits to his name, he was able to go to work for the studio's newly-formed television arm, Screen Gems, as both a writer and director.

Lucas first learned of Gene Roddenberry when both worked on a Screen Gems syndicated television series *Whiplash*, which starred Peter Graves, later of *Mission: Impossible*. Roddenberry did several scripts, as did Lucas, who also worked on the half-hour western as associate producer and frequent director. The series was filmed in Australia, which required Lucas to move his family and spend the better part of a year overseas. The hard work and the responsibility that went with it gave Lucas increased status upon his return to the States.

After arriving back in Hollywood, Disney offered Lucas work as both a writer and director on TV's *Zorro*. Lucas also found work in both fields on the prestigious *Alfred Hitchcock Presents*. And a second turn as a producer was about to fall into his lap. One night, Lucas attended a cocktail party where he ran into his old agent, Wilton Schiller. Schiller had since left the literary agency to become a television producer. His current series was the medical drama *Ben Casey*, which had been created by Jim Moser (Lucas' boss from *Medic*). Before the party ended, Lucas had another job.

Lucas recalled, "[Taking *Ben Casey*] was not a hard decision, given my interest in medicine. I did several scripts and then began to direct some. When the executive producer, Matt Rapf, left to take over another show Moser had created, Wilton became executive and asked me to step in as producer. I did. I also managed to still do some writing and directing. … When *Ben Casey* went off the air, Wilton took over as producer of the long running *The Fugitive* series with David Janssen. I came in as co-producer. After a while of that, I started directing episodes…. When *The Fugitive* went off the air, Wilton took over as producer of *Mannix*, which starred Mike Connors, one of the nicest actors I have ever worked with. I came in to write some scripts, then Wilton convinced the executive producer, Bruce Geller, to have me direct." (110-6)

Lucas made a good impression on Geller with his first assignment and was signed to a multi-episode contract. And this, once again, put him in the right place at precisely the right time … this time to help Gene Coon exit *Star Trek*.

The parking space assigned to Lucas at Desilu was outside of the *Star Trek* offices. Because Gene Coon was a heavy smoker, he often kept the window to his bottom floor office open. Coon would pause from doing yet another rewrite to chat with Lucas as the latter came and went from his car. Lucas said, "One night, when I had left the set, [Gene] leaned out the window and asked if I would write a script for him." (110-6)

The contract with *Mission: Impossible* was for directing only, which freed Lucas to try his hand at something he had always wanted to do -- write science fiction.

11

Episode 37: THE CHANGELING

Written by John Meredyth Lucas
(with D.C. Fontana, uncredited)
Directed by Marc Daniels

From NBC press release:

Following a series of space attacks, the Enterprise captures its adversary, a cylinder containing a voice which announces itself as Nomad, in "The Changeling" on NBC Television Network's colorcast of *Star Trek* this evening at 8:30 p.m. Mr. Spock (Leonard Nimoy), after correlating all information, determines that Nomad is the space probe launched from Earth in the year 2002. The cylinder reveals that it was sent to probe for biological impurities and destroy all that is not perfect. When Nomad kills Scott (James Doohan), then brings him back to life, and erases the memory of Lt. Uhura (Nichelle Nichols), Captain Kirk (William Shatner) devises a plan to destroy the cylinder.

One of two NBC publicity pictures promoting "The Changeling." See the second under "Release / Reaction" (Courtesy of Gerald Gurian)

Nomad was indeed originally launched from Earth, but with a mission to seek out new life forms, not destroy those lacking perfection. After a collision in space with Tan-Ru, "the other," an alien automated probe with its own programmed mission of collecting and "sterilizing" soil samples, the two computerized devices combined into one, with a new mission. Nomad now is intolerant of error, and determined to return to Earth with the mission to sterilize the imperfect biological units who "infest" the planet. But Nomad has made an error of its own -- it has mistaken Captain Kirk for Jackson Roykirk, its long dead creator.

The retooled *Frankenstein* theme is at play here: a creation of man goes wrong when it gains a will of its own ... and a mission. But the tried-and-true theme goes deeper. All people, to some extent, seek perfection. Without the ability to understand this, one will always be disappointed. Perfection, as it relates to man, cannot truly exist.

SOUND BITES

- *Nomad, regarding McCoy:* "This is one of your units, Creator?" *Kirk:* "Yes, he is." *Nomad:* "It functions irrationally."

- *Nomad, about Uhura:* "That unit is defective. It's thinking was chaotic. Absorbing it unsettled me." *Spock:* "That 'unit' is a woman." *Nomad:* "A mass of conflicting impulses."

- *Spock, after Kirk defeats Nomad:* "Congratulations, Captain; a dazzling display of logic." *Kirk:* "Didn't think I had it in me, did you?" *Spock:* "No, sir."

- *Kirk:* "It thought I was its mother, didn't it? You think I'm completely without feelings, Mr. Spock? You saw what it did for Scotty. What a doctor it would have made. My son, the doctor."

ASSESSMENT

"The Changeling" is well made, and popular among fans of the series. It does, however, borrow from previous *Star Trek* episodes.

- This is the second time the Enterprise encounters a star system where all intelligent life has perished. "The Doomsday Machine" did it first.
- This is the second time we see a pair of Enterprise security officers unable to control someone or something they are asked to keep an eye on, and who are then zapped away. We saw it first in "Charlie X."
- This is the second time *Star Trek* paid homage to *Frankenstein*. It was done before in "What Are Little Girls Made Of?"
- This was the second time Kirk uses logic to defeat a computer. He did it to Landru, in "The Return of the Archons."
- This is the second time we see Kirk rid himself of a problematic intruder by beaming it out into space. He did this trick before in "Wolf in the Fold."
- This is the third time Spock administers the Vulcan mind meld in an attempt to communicate with an alien or unlock repressed memories in another being. The first time was "Dagger of the Mind." The second was "The Devil in the Dark."
- This is the second time we see Scotty react hastily and leap before he thinks. He did it in "Who Mourns for Adonais?" and was nearly killed.
- And, with that, there is another recycled idea, this time borrowing from "Shore Leave" and "Amok Time." In the first, McCoy died. In the second, Kirk died. Now it's Scotty's turn.

Gene Coon, quick on the typewriter, was equally quick to re-use plot devices, whether writing a script of his own or guiding and rewriting one from someone else. He believed all was fair in love and writing, as long as the end product entertained and enlightened. The critics did not always agree.

For "In Flight," a 1957 episode of *Suspicion*, the critic for *Daily Variety* said Coon's script was "beset with clichés and stereotyped characterizations." For the season premiere of *Cimarron City*, one of the series Coon helped develop during his tenure at Universal, *Daily Variety* said, "Big production (and they have it) can't overcome the creative shortcomings, particularly a cliché plot.... Jules Bricken's direction was obviously hampered by Gene L. Coon's old-hat story." *Daily Variety* called "The Tallest Marine," a segment of *General*

Electric Theatre, "a cliché-filled story," saying that the performances and direction were "okay within the limitations of Gene Coon's familiar script."

Looking over the reviews from Coon's career, as both a writer and producer, he was often criticized for not always connecting the dots in a storyline. One example, for a movie called *The Girl in the Kremlin*, the critic for *Weekly Variety* wrote:

> The screenplay written by Gene L. Coon ... is more often than not illogical, with the hokum laid on thick. No trouble is taken to explain many of the situations and in such far-fetched surroundings the players can't be very convincing.

There are certainly a few giant holes in logic during the entertaining and enlightening tale of "The Changeling." The energy bolts launched by Nomad at the Enterprise, we are told, are the equivalent of 90 photon torpedoes. Yes, 90! It is surprising that the shields can withstand even one of these blasts, let alone four. Later, we are told Uhura's mind is wiped clean but that she can be re-educated from kindergarten to advanced college level in a matter of a week or two! And then there is Nomad's bag of magic tricks -- like raising the dead and absorbing the energy of photon torpedoes. Nothing is explained. We are asked to accept all of this without question.

As a writer or a producer, Coon delivered some of *Star Trek*'s most entertaining and meaningful stories. On the other side of the coin, many of the episodes he presided over were the ones which leaned most toward formula, as well as suspension of belief.

All nitpicking aside, "The Changeling" is a certainly a clever and enjoyable trek.

THE STORY BEHIND THE STORY

Script Timeline

John Meredyth Lucas' contract, ST #5, "The Changeling": March 13, 1967.
Lucas' story outline: March 15, 1967.
Lucas' revised story outline, gratis: March 16, 1967.
Lucas' 1ˢᵗ Draft teleplay: April 7, 1967.
Lucas' 2ⁿᵈ Draft teleplay: delivered end of April, 1967.
Mimeo Department "Yellow Cover 1ˢᵗ Draft" teleplay: May 1, 1967.
D.C. Fontana's rewrite (Final Draft teleplay): May 29, 1967.
Gene Coon's rewrite (Revised Final Draft teleplay): June 29, 1967.
Additional page revisions by Coon: June 30 and July 5 & 11, 1967.

Lucas had been a science fiction buff since he was a boy when, one summer, he stayed with his Aunt Vi. He recalled, "A drugstore two blocks from Auntie Vi's house, where I used to walk to get ice cream cones, had a large magazine rack. One day I finished my cone quickly and started to browse through the magazines. I found *Science Wonder Stories*. I read the first one sitting on the floor of the drug store, [then] ran back to Aunt Vi's to get the extra money to buy the magazine. From that moment on, I was hooked. I read every issue of *Science Wonder Stories*, *Amazing Stories*, then *Science Fantasy*. I looked forward to the time when the extra thick *Amazing Stories Quarterly* came out." (110-6)

Regarding his inspiration for "The Changeling," Lucas said, "I had always been fascinated by the concept of the machine as God. That was really the spark for it; the selling point.... It was simply a fascinating concept that a machine could, in a very real sense, come to life. In the story it was accidental, but it became a very real, judgmental being -- and a threat." (110-3)

181

Another spark may have come to Lucas in January 1965 from the last first-run episode of *The Outer Limits*. Being a fan of science fiction, Lucas would certainly have enjoyed "The Probe," involving an alien automated craft which lands in the oceans of Earth after encountering one of our deep space exploratory devices, and nearly kills all it encounters because of its programming to sterilize. The similarities began and ended there and were so otherwise unrecognizable that even the diligent Robert Justman -- who worked on *The Outer Limits* -- did not make reference to this while reading the various story outlines and teleplays for "The Changeling."

Gene Coon was also intrigued by machine-as-God concepts, and bought more than one for the second season (see "The Apple"). The machine-is-a-god story in "The Changeling" was even more engaging for Coon, and later for Roddenberry, because it was topical. NASA had been sending unmanned space probes in search of scientific data and new life since the late 1950s. In 1960, Pioneer 5 was the first successful "interplanetary space investigations" launch. Voyager, still a decade away from launch, but planned as the first space probe to leave this solar system and head into deep space, was already on the drawing board. Voyager was even mentioned in Lucas's story and script (but not in the staff rewrite). The delicious hook: What if one of these probes in the near future were to encounter the alien life and information it sought -- life and information that would come back to haunt the probe's creators?

As for the title, a changeling, in European folklore, is the offspring of a fairy, troll or elf, secretly left in the place of a kidnapped human child. Changelings could be identified by their malicious temper and other unpleasant traits.

Coon wrote to Roddenberry days after his meeting with Lucas, saying:

> I have assigned a story to John Meredyth Lucas, called "The Changeling." It is an interesting concept dealing with the discovery of what might be called Mariner 210 -- a highly sophisticated robot space probe launched several hundred years ago, with the capability of reprogramming itself and developing a most formidable threat to all life. You might well consider the possibility of using John to direct his own story. He has been directing many for Quinn Martin and I understand they are very pleased. (GC37-1)

Coon then left for a two week vacation. Roddenberry was manning the fort when Lucas delivered his outline on March 15. Lucas did a quick rewrite the following day based on verbal notes from Roddenberry, which was then distributed to the staff for feedback. Robert Justman responded first, writing Roddenberry:

> I find many pages of philosophical rationalizations and discussions. It reminds me of the weather. Everybody talks about it, but nobody does anything about it. <u>We need action, emotional conflict, drama and crises.</u> We are lacking these things so far and I am now on page 23. (RJ37-1)

By the time Justman got to page 28, the last page in Lucas' outline, he had dictated enough notes to fill five single-spaced pages of his own. All negative.

Roddenberry was less critical. He left a note on Coon's desk the day the latter returned from vacation, saying:

> So far I've rather liked working with this man and have, as in the case of Gil Ralston ("Who Mourns for Adonais?"), high hopes for further scripts. (GR37-1)

In the story, the robot ship "Mariner" had been designed to think for itself since it would travel out of communication range from its creator on Earth. But Mariner suffered serious damage and its programming became corrupted after colliding with a meteoroid. Unlike in later drafts, Mariner did not meet and merge with an alien probe called "The Other." Instead, it made repairs on its own. Because of its corrupted thinking (described by Lucas as "brain damage"), Mariner, instead of merely seeking out life, began seeking out perfect life.

Creating a back-story which would account for Mariner's skewed thinking, Lucas explained, "Built in a Clean Room, with every precaution taken to protect it from dirt and bacterial life forms, it has, in its damaged wanderings, translated that into a directive to destroy all organic life forms." (110-6)

During the attack on the Enterprise, Kirk orders Sulu to maneuver behind a lifeless planet for safety. Instead of sending out a radio signal to communicate with the unknown assailant, Kirk releases a "hydrogen cloud" into space so a giant image of his face can be projected onto it, allowing him to be seen as well as heard (through some unspecified frequency) -- one more reason why Mariner mistakes him for its maker. Another significant difference, here, is that Mariner is not small in size; it cannot be brought onto the Enterprise. Therefore, Mariner sends out an exploratory portion of itself -- a probe's probe -- to be beamed aboard. Once there, Kirk escorts this subpart of Mariner to the bridge (instead of it finding its way there on its own, as in the filmed episode). The crew member whose brain is drained by the probe is not Uhura, nor a regular, but is Yeoman Barbara Watson, who attracts Mariner's attention with her whistling. And Scott is not killed as a result of trying to protect the whistling Yeoman but, rather, in a completely different scene, where he is zapped to death when, out of curiosity, he touches the probe. There is no Vulcan mind-link in this version of the story. And Kirk does not use logic to defeat Mariner but, instead, flash feeds it the Enterprise computer files containing the complete maddening history of Earth, including its varied works of literature, poetry, and music. This drives Mariner -- the mother ship, as well as its mini-probe -- out of its mechanical mind and it blows apart in space.

Coon asked for a revised draft of the treatment, the final weighing in at 29 pages, a hefty number for a story outline to be sent to the network.

NBC production manager Stan Robertson generally liked the story. After analyzing fan mail, he and his colleagues believed storylines which "establish a greater link between our heroes floating out in space and the Earth of their era" would benefit the series. He wrote:

I strongly believe that this particular storyline would lend itself perfectly to our desires to improve *Star Trek* in [that] area. (SR37)

Robertson suggested the situation involving the female crew member who has her brain emptied out needed to be resolved. He wrote:

We aren't sure if she'll recover or if she'll remain a "vegetable" for the rest of her life. (SR37)

Robertson, perhaps in a mind-link with Justman, continued:

This outline is theoretically exciting but in actuality, as it appears on paper, there seems to be a great deal of discussion back and forth, theorizing and moralizing on the point of our crew members. While I think these points are important to

183

the body of our story, they appear to be carried to such an extreme that we may possibly lose the visual excitement we must have in each of our episodes if we are going to attain the mass audience we are all seeking. (SR37)

The network's Broadcast Standards' department had an opinion, too, writing:

Care should be taken that the references to Kirk as "The Creator" or "a god" are in the terms of the Mariner's understanding so the viewer will not misinterpret such references as being to the Deity. (NBC-BS-37)

Like Mariner in his story, Lucas was flash-fed all the information and told to proceed to script. He wrote fast, generating 60 pages in only three days, finishing on April 7. Roddenberry commented first, writing Coon:

Rather than having Altair [the new name for Mariner] or its parent body "out there somewhere," why not have this small probe-vessel [be] all there is to it, incredibly miniaturized and incredibly powerful. If we handle it this way, we will at least be meeting our antagonist, [and] can create some "personality" for it -- not a far off thing -- and when we destroy it, we'll be destroying a present and visible antagonist. (GR37-2)

This constituted a major improvement in the material. Roddenberry's notes continued:

It's not a bad first draft for a first time writer on *Star Trek*. But we should now, if we intend to use him again, sit down and straighten out a few areas of logic, believability, scientific extrapolation, action-adventure, and so on. (GR37-2)

Justman read the memo from Roddenberry, and then sent one of his own to Coon -- a humdinger, seven pages in length. He said:

I think Gene has been too kind. This is a bad first draft for a first-time writer on *Star Trek*.... I found myself so overwhelmed by this teleplay that I was unable to come to grips with it professionally.... We are deficient in the area of story, logic, believability, dialogue, characterizations, and so on, and so on, and so on, and so on. Good luck! (RJ37-2)

Story Consultant Dorothy Fontana wrote Coon:

This script, in general, is much too slowly paced. Everyone talks -- no one takes action. I recommend deep cuts in dialogue and revamp of the action structure.... DO NOT WAIT TO DO THE RESTRUCTURING. AFTER THE SECOND DRAFT IS IN WE ARE FORCED TO DO IT IF THE AUTHOR HAS NOT. (DCF37-1)

Fontana had good reason for capitalizing every word in those last two sentences. Two months earlier she had been given the task of doing a major restructuring of "Operation: Annihilate!" after Stephen Carabatsos had already finished three drafts of the script, each approved by Coon. Two months before that, she did a major restructuring of "The Way of the Spores," transforming it into "This Side of Paradise," and, again, this was done after the original writer, Jerry Sohl, turned in three drafts of his script, again approved by Coon.

Justman had more to say about the first draft, telling Coon:

Since I don't believe that this hunk of machinery could have evolved from something much simpler, then it naturally follows that I don't believe it could have the capability within it that the writer has put into it. This means that I am striking at the heart of this story. At least, I think I'm striking at the heart of this story. I'm still not sure what the story is all about. (RJ37-2)

Regarding one scene in particular, Justman's sarcasm betrayed his disdain for the material. Speaking of the scene where Yeoman Barbara Watson is "whistling" and, thereby, gets her brain drained by Altair, Justman told Coon:

It seems to be an accepted fact that most beautiful young actresses cannot whistle well. Therefore, it is going to be difficult to cast the part of Barbara. However, Wally Cox is at present unemployed and is available for dramatic roles. And I happen to know for a fact that Wally Cox is possibly the best whistler in the State of California. Would you consider casting Wally Cox in the part of the Yeoman? If not, do you think that Wally would look well in a long wig and falsies? In any event, let's have the Yeoman whistle the *Star Trek* theme. (RJ37-2)

Justman's teasing continued, with:

I have a secret way to handle this small spaceship so that it moves with our people and yet at the same time we do not see any wires. You must have this script rewritten before I will tell you my secret. I don't want to blow a good secret on a bad script. (RJ37-2)

Coon, writing to Lucas, whom he liked, said:

John, this is a splendid first draft, unquestionably one of the better ones from a writer who has not done a script for us before. (GC37-2)

However, included with the compliment were 15 single-spaced pages of critical notes. Coon wrote:

Generally speaking, the overall problem is that we do not have enough specific threat or action once the Altair [probe] is aboard our ship to maintain the two or two and a half or three acts which are under discussion. (GC37-2)

Coon told Lucas that Scotty's death and Barbara's brain draining were not enough. He wanted to add another threat, suggesting that Altair improve the Enterprise engines, resulting in a near explosion. He also suggested Altair kill other crewmen. Both ideas made it into the episode.

Coon continued:

Both Roddenberry and myself feel that the small cylinder we bring aboard is indeed the main Altair, it is not a probe sent out from the main ship, but it *is* the main ship, incredibly miniaturized and sophisticated and having evolved far beyond its original crudities. By doing so we will be able to personalize the threat, we'll be able to see it right there, realize that this is the source of all the danger and we will also, by doing so, be able to cut out some dialogue toward the end of the script which really is not too important. (GC37-2)

Two weeks later, at the end of April, Lucas sent in his 2nd Draft teleplay (which was then sent to the Mimeo Department and reformatted to be the "Yellow Cover 1st Draft," dated May 1, 1967). There was only one Altair now, and it was small enough to beam aboard. It had a personality, and an ego, very much as portrayed in the episode. Chekov is in this version of the script, and highly visible throughout (although he didn't make it into the filmed episode). And Lucas captured the flavor of the series well. For the most part, dialogue for the series' regulars, perhaps with exception of the young Russian Ensign, sounded correct. But, despite sounding like the *Star Trek* characters, their thinking and actions were off-kilter.

For this draft, the last to be worked on by Lucas, Altair doesn't fire four energy bolts at the Enterprise, as we would later see, but subjects the ship to continuous unrelenting bombardment, lasting an entire Act. When Kirk's image is projected onto the hydrogen cloud, it is so he can ask for terms of surrender. This is the Act I break on page 16. Altair does not beam aboard until page 25. The time in between is filled with attempts to communicate and come to terms for the surrender. It is a slow ride.

Once on the ship, Kirk, as in the previous draft and story outline, takes the deadly machine directly to the bridge. And this seems blatantly foolish. We are now on page 27. Almost immediately, in an attempt to send a signal to Earth, where it hopes to return, Altair blows a hole in the hull, causing sudden atmospheric changes, alarm bells to sound, and a rush by crew members to make emergency repairs. While this could have been exciting, it creates a situation where Kirk appears even more foolish, since, on page 31, he leaves Altair on the bridge while he goes to the briefing room to discuss the situation with his officers. On page 35, while Kirk is still away, Altair, back on the bridge, kills Scotty, and this ends Act II.

When we return, Kirk is called to the bridge and races from the briefing room. Remember this -- you will be feeling déjà vu over it later.

When Kirk, McCoy, and Spock step onto the bridge, they discover Scotty's "brain case is smashed like an eggshell." After Altair repairs the "Scott unit" in sickbay, Kirk tells this dangerous machine to go back to the bridge and wait. Is he kidding?! Apparently not. He then returns to the briefing room to continue the conversation with Spock and McCoy over what to do next. Incredibly, they hope Kirk will not try to destroy the machine. McCoy marvels over its medical abilities. Spock marvels over a machine capable of such inventive thinking. Scotty, after being told his head "looked like a squashed watermelon," marvels over the engineering that must go into the making of a machine such as this.

And now for déjà vu, part 1. Kirk is called to the bridge again for another emergency. This time, because Altair has drained the brain of Yeoman Watson. Again, he and his officers rush from the briefing room to the bridge. Act III ends as they come to realize Altair intends to return to Earth and "sterilize" all imperfect life forms.

Amazingly, in Act IV, Kirk's officers still carry on the debate as to whether Altair should be destroyed. Kirk berates them, saying (and not sounding at all like Kirk), "My entire staff is falling flat on their faces.... You're like savages bowing down before idols. You worship the machine for its flawless logic and technology. Mr. Scott for its power. Dr. McCoy for its ability to heal. You're all forgetting the fact that it's incompatible with biological life because you all want something from it." Again, Kirk adjourns to discuss the situation further in the briefing room while, again, leaving Altair on the bridge. And, again, he receives an emergency call to return to the bridge.

Déjà vu, part 2. Again, Kirk races from the briefing room, heading topside. This time, Altair is modifying the engines and the ship is traveling too fast, which could result in its destruction. Kirk fights his last fight with Altair here. He admits that *he* is a biological unit and that he created Altair, so therefore Altair cannot be perfect. This only makes Altair want to know more about Man and his Earth. Instead of debating it further and using logic to defeat his enemy, Kirk grants Altair its wish and tells Spock to flash feed it all the poetry and broken-hearted love songs and TV and movies and pulp fiction and romance novels from all time. And, as Altair takes in all of this, it goes mad. The ending is the same as aired -- the machine is beamed into space and blows itself to smithereens.

Coon was somehow satisfied enough to skip past the usual script polish made at this stage and, instead, bound Lucas's 2nd Draft in yellow covers and then distributed this to the staff. But, breaking with procedure, Coon did not share the draft with the network or the cast.

Roddenberry, while still impressed by Lucas, wrote Coon, "I think this is a highly interesting story." But *Star Trek* story's had to be more than merely interesting. Roddenberry added:

> It is slow in parts, it does not yet extract the full potential of the situation, but seems to me certainly a better than average start by a first writer on the show. (GR37-3)

Because Altair was the story's antagonist -- its villain -- Roddenberry believed it needed better explanation and motivation. It had to become multi-dimensional. He told Coon that this machine, just like a flesh-and-blood bad guy, needed a back-story fleshing out "its programming; its ability to refuel; how it does all it does." He suggested:

> The only possible answer to the above seems to me it has somehow in some far place "crossed itself" with another machine or intelligence.... Could it have been another space vehicle, lost by another even greater civilization? Perhaps Roykirk's basic genius was in the fact that he had been able to build into his machine <u>intelligence</u>! The other vehicle, although containing abilities and technologies vastly greater than ours is still essentially a machine and thus our Earth vehicle was the dominant one in their "meeting." (GR37-3)

Again, Roddenberry had made a substantial contribution to the material. He had other ideas, and told Coon:

> The danger of Altair to the Enterprise needs to be developed further. Same comment for its eventual danger to Earth and human-populated systems. Same comment that I had last year for "Charlie X" -- i.e. Altair should be now gradually making a "Hell ship" out of the Enterprise. (GR37-3)

Another significant contribution had Roddenberry writing:

> Can we use Nurse Chapel instead of Barbara in the whistling sequence? Would prefer a continuing character here if we can find a way to avoid her brain being washed clear of all "intelligence." (GR37-3)

Coon and Fontana preferred to make it Uhura. This allowed Nichelle Nichols her third chance to sing on the series (a new rendition of William Hatch and Gene Coon's "Beyond Antares," last heard in "The Conscience of the King"). It also inspired the delightful scene where Christine Chapel helps Uhura learn to read again.

Although these moments with Uhura are entertaining, they do bring about a suspension of belief and, therefore, perhaps weren't such a good idea, after all. Even fellow *Star Trek* writer David Gerrold questioned the sense of this plot point, commenting, "Uhura having her mind wiped clean served no useful purpose except to demonstrate the menace of the Changeling. As a result, the terribly loose end forces her to relearn everything. But, fortunately, she did so within a week and was back at her post in time for the next episode." (73-8)

Roddenberry closed his seven-page memo, writing:

Although my comments have been quite detailed on this and I have been very critical on small things, I think it is a good script, will be an even better one soon, and could make one of our best episodes. (GR37-3)

Robert Justman, playing devil's advocate, wrote Coon:

This memo goes to you and a copy goes to Mr. Roddenberry. No one else is going to get a copy of this memo. As you will recall, when I first read the Xerox version of this script [the writer's first draft], I wrote you an immensely long and carping diatribe against it. I have just finished reading the yellow cover mimeo version of this story.... I have also read Mr. Roddenberry's memo to you on this same script, which he dictated on 5-8-67. I agree with everything Mr. Roddenberry has written, with the exception of two points.... My memo is going to be the shortest of all because it would take several 45-minute tapes for me to get down everything I object to in this teleplay. Therefore, I shall hit only certain major items. The two areas in which I disagree with Mr. Roddenberry are as follows. Gene makes the statement that this is "a better than average first start by a first writer on this show." I disagree very strongly. I feel that there was a very good idea originally contained in this teleplay, which has not been handled well at all. I think this script is atrocious. It is slow, boring, unbelievable, replete with papier mache characterizations and illogical actions. The other area in which I feel Mr. Roddenberry is mistaken is when he says it's obvious the writer has "studied his *Star Trek* Guide considerably." It is not evident to me at all. If he has studied it considerably, he hasn't absorbed very much. And, in fact, Gene gives the lie to his own statement by thereupon turning out page after page of objections to things that had been written, which are obviously at odds with the *Star Trek* Guide. Knowing the Great Bird [Roddenberry] as well as I do, I can only assume that the reason why he said the two things in his memo that I object to is because he probably expected that the writer of this teleplay would be reading his memo and, Gene, as always, doesn't want to hurt anyone. I am in hopes that the writer will never read this memo of mine or my previous memo on the Xerox version, as I am certain that they are quite devastating. (RJ37-3)

It was not standard practice for memos written by the staff to be shared with the series' freelance writers. But this writer -- John Meredyth Lucas -- was suspected of being a friend of Gene Coon's. Roddenberry had therefore been extremely kind in his critique. Justman, however, had just been Justman -- harshly frank, with an acid wit, and, more often than not, was absolutely right.

Justman continued:

Incidentally, there seems to be no correlation between the beginning of this story and what finally develops out of the beginning of this story. The attack from the unknown assailant, or assailants, in outer space and its relationship to the small device that we finally bring on board the Enterprise is extremely tenuous. I still feel as if we had started to tell one story and then changed our mind and ended up telling another story. The original idea, however, of a machine which is, in effect, a thinking machine and all-powerful and completely logical and totally impregnable is, I think, a very good idea. I do wish we had a screenplay on that subject for all of us to read and prepare. (RJ37-3)

Dorothy Fontana, also highly critical, but with a bit more tact, wrote Coon:

This script still seems to me like a great deal of talk and very little action.... I never believed that cloud and Kirk's projection and I still don't believe it. If Altair cannot be reached on any radio frequency, why should it respond to an image projection and voice transmission on some unspecified frequency?... We can make a substantial cut here, taking out a lot of talk AND a difficult optical -- and I think we should consider it.... As I said, I think this whole piece needs much cutting and insertion of action for whole talk sequences. Flip you for it? dcf.

No flip of the coin was needed. Fontana was given the rewrite. Her version -- the Final Draft -- was finished on May 29. Uhura was now the brain-drain victim. Altair was now Nomad. Pacing was faster. And the characterizations were correct.

This was the first version of the script to be shown to the cast. For his memoirs, James Doohan recalled, "So there I was, reading the script, and I get to the end of the second act. It's always important that a second act break be as strong as possible, because that's the half-hour mark and you want to make sure you hold on to the viewers into the next half hour. Well, they'd picked a doozy of an act ender this time. Dr. McCoy looks up from the red-shirted individual. He's just given one of his customary detailed examinations, which consists of checking for a pulse and that's pretty much it. What chilled my blood was that the person wearing the red shirt this time was Scotty, apparently having been killed after a futile attempt to pull Uhura from Nomad's clutches.

"Now, I had been signed for six more episodes. Nonetheless, that was a real heart-stopper. Why hadn't anyone said anything to me? Were they planning to? Were they going to call my agent? Slowly I turned the page to the top of act three, in hopes that Scotty would suddenly sit up, blinking and saying, 'You're a little premature this time, Doctor.' But no, Scotty was still dead. Kirk is upset. Things weren't looking good. And then I got to the part where Nomad's asking Kirk whether repairs should be [made to] 'the unit Scott.' I heard a hoarse sound and realized that it was my breath finally being released. I wasn't dead. I was a plot twist." (52-1)

Robert Justman was ecstatic over Fontana's rewrite. His next memo to Coon read:

I believe screen credit as indicated on the title page of this script and the cover is incorrect. Shouldn't it be "Teleplay by John Meredyth Lucas *and* D.C. Fontana, story by John Meredyth Lucas"? This is a very good rewrite by D.C. Fontana, as usual. (RJ37-4)

In comparing the various drafts of the scripts, it's fair to say that at least 50% of the dialogue in the filmed version of this episode came from Fontana. But, as with "Catspaw," D.C. refused acknowledgement. When asked about turning down a screen credit on "The Changeling," she said, "Generally speaking, [a] dialogue rewrite was a given on a lot of freelance scripts, and not just on *Star Trek*. The simple explanation is, we were on the show all the time, we saw the dailies, rough cuts and final cuts, and we simply had more of an 'ear' for our characters than outside writers. Generally speaking, that kind of revision did not impact the original writer's credit." (64-4a)

Gene Coon took no credit either for the changes he made with his June 29 Revised Final Draft, as well as the three sets of page revisions, dated June 30, July 5 and, after filming had begun, July 11.

June 27-30 and July 3 and July 5, 1967 (6 days).

As early as April 17, Justman, unhappy with the written material thus far, did not want to also be unhappy with the crucial prop needed to realize the menace in this episode. He wrote to Coon:

> We had better be very clever and have Mr. Jefferies design a spaceship that can be built out of Styrofoam, so that it will not have too much weight and so that we will be able to use very thin threads to suspend the ship with. The thicker the threads, the easier it is to see them and the more difficult it is for us to conceal them. (RJ37-2)

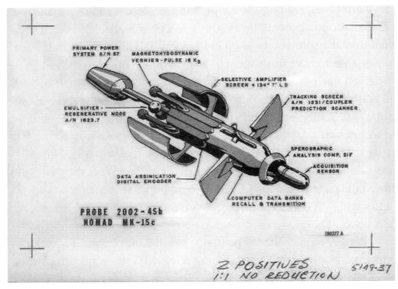

Roddenberry disagreed about the Styrofoam. In a memo from May 8, he suggested to Coon that Altair would have to be "mostly supported from underneath so that it should look heavy, complex, capable of doing everything we say it does." He continued:

Matt Jefferies sketch of Nomad – before merging with "The Other"
(Courtesy of Gerald Gurian)

> It is <u>most</u> <u>important</u> that we build an excellent and totally believable "Altair." This is our guest role! I know that it will cost something and take a little time to have it glide around the vessel and do the various things it does, but I think you will agree with me that to do any less would be as bad as trusting an "extra" in a guest star role. (GR37-3)

By June 1, Justman was finally happy with the script -- as rewritten by Fontana, with Altair now named Nomad. Justman anxiously wrote Gene Coon:

> If we could get the "Nomad" built and functioning in time, this script could very well follow "Amok Time" on our shooting schedule. (RJ37-4)

It would take longer.

Nomad -- both the original design, as launched from Earth, and the one that merged with an alien probe -- was the creation of Matt Jefferies. The building of the ego-driven machine, however, fell into the lap of special effects wizard Jim Rugg. The trick in having Nomad move, as Justman suggested, was to keep it light enough to be supported by thin and virtually invisible wires. And yet, as Roddenberry suggested, it had to *look* heavy enough to appear formidable and believable. This would require support from a dolly below. The answer was to have more than one Nomad.

Director Marc Daniels said, "'The Changeling' was another one that required a great deal of ingenuity. We had to have *three* different Nomads mounted in three different ways -- one on a wire, to hover in a room; one on a dolly, to be moved through corridors and onto the bridge; and one on the floor. You just couldn't take one on a wire through the door, hence the dolly system. But, if you wanted to see Nomad in all its authority, you would put it on a wire." (44-2)

Vic Perrin, the Control Voice from *The Outer Limits*, was selected to speak for Nomad. This was the second time Perrin was heard in *Star Trek*. He also voiced the Metron, in "Arena."

"I was on the set for that one," Perrin said of "The Changeling." "Normally, you would do the voice afterwards, but the robot had flashing lights that had to be synchronized to my voice." (138)

Blaisdell Makee played Lt. Singh. In "Space Seed," he had been Lt. Spinelli. The native Hawaiian worked for 12 years in television, mostly as South Seas islanders in series such as *Hawaiian Eye*, or American Indians and Mexican banditos in numerous westerns.

Also on camera was director Marc Daniels, who posed to have his picture taken, as Jackson Roykirk. For the portrait, he wore Scotty's red dress uniform top.

Production Diary
Filmed July 6, 7, 10, 11, 12, 13 & 14 (2 day), 1967.
(Planned as 6 day production, running 2 day over; total cost $174,700.)

Irving Feinberg (on left), and Jim Rugg with one of three variations of this episode's "guest star" (Courtesy of Gerald Gurian)

Filming began Thursday, July 6, 1967. *The Dirty Dozen* was king at the box office, with the James Bond movie, *You Only Live Twice*, holding at second place. Among the top books on *The New York Times* Best Sellers' List: *The Eighth Day*, by Thornton Wilder,

191

Washington D.C., by Gore Vidal, and *Rosemary's Baby*, by Ira Levin. "Windy," by The Association, was still getting the most spins on AM radio stations across America. "Little Bit O'Soul," by The Music Explosion, was in second place. The top album in record stores, for now and months to come, was *Sgt. Pepper's Lonely Hearts Club Band* by the Beatles. Chet Huntley and David Brinkley, the faces of NBC nightly news, had the cover of *TV Guide*. Johnny Carson had the cover of *Look*. The cover story for *Time* magazine this week: "The Hippies: Philosophy of a Subculture." This was "The Summer of Love," after all.

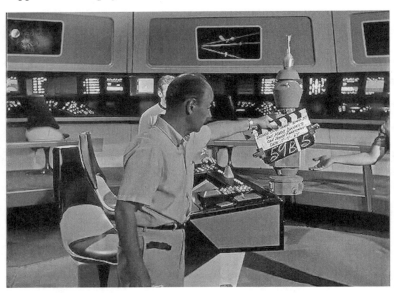

Bill McGovern slating a shot for Day 2 on the bridge, and Nomad with DeForest Kelley, in an unaired film trim (Courtesy of Gerald Gurian)

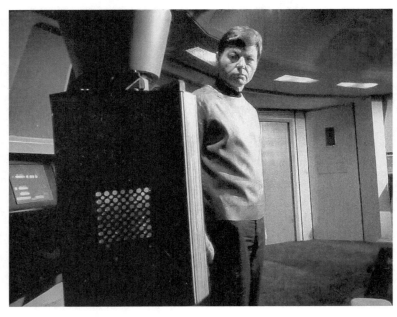

The entire episode, a bottle show, would be filmed on stage 9. First up: the bridge scenes, starting with the Teaser, followed by the sequences needed for the majority of Act I. Eddie Paskey sat at the helm's navigational station for this episode instead of his usual engineering post on the bridge. And he wore gold instead of red. This was done so he would match the standard stock footage shot of the main viewing screen, which also revealed the shoulder of the navigator.

After production ended this day, "Arena" was repeated on NBC.

Day 2, Friday. Another full day on the bridge. Daniels tackled the scene where Uhura gets her brain wiped clean and Scotty is killed. Stunt performer Jay Jones, having returned after the flip he took for Scotty in "Who Mourns for Adonais?" (which landed him in

192

the hospital), did another flip for Scotty here -- this time without injury.

"Gene Roddenberry took a liking to me and the word came down I was to get as much work as I could handle," Jones said. "I started doubling for James Doohan, and later for Leonard Nimoy… I'd dream up stunts and work with the directors and cameramen on how we could use them in scenes. I've been on some shows where the directors are trying to get you killed. I've done other shows where the directors really care about your safety. On *Star Trek*, the same stunt guys were called back regularly. It was a great group of people." (93b)

Day 3, Monday. The two scenes in the transporter room were filmed, with Nomad's arrival and departure. The scenes in Auxiliary Control were also successfully captured.

Day 4, Tuesday. The engineering room was filmed, as well as all sequences in the ship's corridors, including camera tie-down shots for the disintegration of the second pair of security men (second to die; first to be filmed).

Day 4. Bill McGovern slating a pair of shots in engineering (Courtesy of Gerald Gurian)

Day 5, Wednesday. The scenes in sickbay were shot -- Scotty brought back to life by Nomad, and Chapel teaching Uhura from a first-grade reader.

Day 6, Thursday, July 13. Spock's mind link with Nomad in the brig was filmed, followed by the tie-down shots as Nomad penetrates the brig's electrical barrier and disintegrating the two security men in the corridor outside. The final scheduled scene, in the briefing room, was begun, but left unfinished.

"Tomorrow Is

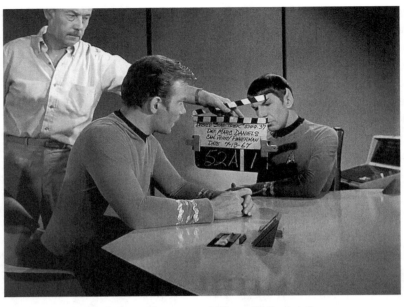

Day 7: McGovern, Shatner, and Nimoy in the briefing room
(Courtesy of Gerald Gurian)

Yesterday" repeated this night on NBC.

Day 7, Friday. Daniels used his first couple of hours of the morning to complete the unfinished briefing room scene from Thursday. And, with his final call for "cut," completed filming "The Changeling" one-quarter of a day behind. At mid-morning, the company moved into the ship's corridor, as the director's chair was surrendered to Joseph Pevney for the start of filming on "The Apple."

Day 8, Friday, July 21. Some re-takes were needed, requiring Pevney to pause from shooting "The Apple" and get some additional coverage for "The Changeling." With these shots, the filming of the entire episode had taken a total of six and a half days, spanning eight. Though slightly over-schedule, this was nonetheless an amazing feat, considering the time required to manipulate three different full-size Nomad models through the ship, and numerous tie-down shots needed for optical effects.

Post-Production
Available for editing on July 17, 1967. Rough Cut: July 25. Final Cut: August 1, 1967.
Music Score: tracked.

Fabien Tordjmann and Edit Team 3 had their second assignment of the season, following "Friday's Child."

The Westheimer Company provided the excellent optical effects. The energy bolts fired from Nomad are impressive for 1967, as is the optical effect draining Uhura's mind, the zapping of Scotty, Nomad's breaching of the force field surrounding the brig, the phaser beams fired and the disintegration of crewmen in red shirts, as well as the explosion in space when Nomad meets his dramatic end. Two transporter effects were also included with this job. *Star Trek* got a great deal, with a total cost of $6,123.72. The special effects budget, which included the building of three different Nomads, was $9,500. The Enterprise flybys and the firing of the photon torpedoes were stock shots.

Composer Fred Steiner was credited for the music in this episode even though it was all tracked. Most of the cues came from Steiner's previous scores, including "The Corbomite Maneuver" and "Who Mourns for Adonais?" Also included, not from Steiner's pen, was William Hatch and Gene Coon's original song "Beyond Antares."

Even with the extra half-day of production, the cost of building the various Nomads, and the money needed for all those optical effects, "The Changeling" came in under budget. There was no need for new sets or guest stars, helping to keep costs down. The total price: $174,700, which equates to a little more than $1.2 million in 2013. The savings of $5,300, below the studio allowance, reduced the season deficit to $116,871.

Release / Reaction

Premiere air date: 9/29/67. NBC repeat broadcast: 5/17/68.

A second NBC publicity photo used in promoting this episode (Courtesy of Gerald Gurian)

Steven H. Scheuer reviewed the episode for his syndicated column, *TV Key Previews*. Among numerous newspapers across the country to carry the review on September 29, 1967 was *The News Journal*, out of Mansfield, Ohio:

"The Changeling." There is a killer machine behind a series of space attacks tonight on *Star Trek* and serious science fiction fans may find this super-sophisticated tale of interest. Captain Kirk is not only faced with a mysterious machine that kills but he finds his imagination and logic strained to the absolute limit of his ability. What he has to combat is the force of a thinking machine called Nomad, a probe that was sent out on a peaceful space mission by a scientist in the year 2002 and believed destroyed. Instead, it merged with a destructive alien probe and kills anything that is imperfect. This human imperfection is both the key and instrument of Captain Kirk's very interesting solution.

Judy Crosby reviewed the episode for her syndicated column, *TV SCOUT*. Among the papers which ran her notice on September 29, 1967, was *The Morning Herald*, in Lexington, Kentucky:

The Enterprise crew encounters a surprising adversary -- launched from Earth in the year 2002. It is a computer on a biological probe which has been programmed to destroy not only impurities but anything that is not perfect. And this is one killer that you can't talk out of its mission. The premise here is better than the presentation.

195

RATINGS / Nielsen National report for Friday, September 29, 1967:

8:30 to 9 pm, 56.1% of U.S. TVs in use.	Share:	Households:
NBC: *Star Trek* (first half)	25.9%	11,370,000
ABC: *Hondo* (first half)	25.9%	11,540,000
CBS: **Gomer Pyle, U.S.M.C.**	**45.0%**	**16,130,000**
Local independent stations:	6.2%	**No data**

9 to 9:30 pm, 60.4% of U.S. TVs in use.	Share:	Households:
NBC: *Star Trek* (second half)	25.3%	No data
ABC: *Hondo* (second half)	26.0%	No data
CBS: **Friday Night Movie**	**37.8%**	**No data**
Local independent stations:	12.6%	No data

The race between *Star Trek* and *Hondo* was almost too close to call, with A.C. Nielsen showing the two series tied between 8:30 and 9 p.m., then having the ABC western nudge ahead by less than a single ratings point for the second half-hour. CBS was the clear winner with *Gomer Pyle*, followed by the television premiere of Alfred Hitchcock's classic *North by Northwest*, starring Cary Grant. The No. 1 network bought ad space in *TV Guide* and other television periodicals and newspapers for the movie, as ABC did for *Hondo*. NBC didn't spend a dime. And the network gave *Star Trek* little programming support. *Star Trek*'s 11,370,000 households dropped to 4,590,000 after the show left the air, making room for coverage of a speech by President Lyndon B. Johnson from 9:30 to 10:00, and a well-meaning but underachieving NBC news special, "Our Endangered Wildlife," from 10 to 11 p.m.

The Trendex report from this night, counting noses in New York, Los Angeles, and 10 other large cities, give *Star Trek* a strong second place showing.

Averaged rating for 8:30 to 9:30 pm:	Rating:
NBC: *Star Trek*	16.9
ABC: *Hondo*	11.2
CBS: **Gomer Pyle, U.S.M.C. / Friday Night Movie**	**22.5**

***

Cinefantastique magazine picked "The Changeling" as one of the original series' 10 best.

"The Changeling" must have been a favorite of Gene Roddenberry's, too. He would borrow from this idea for his 1974 TV movie and pilot film, *The Questor Tapes*, co-written with Gene L. Coon. The story featured a robot with damaged memory circuits, searching for its creator. And then, again, more heavily, for 1979's *Star Trek: The Motion Picture*. The plot for the first *Trek* big-screener dealt with a probe from Earth which had been altered and was now returning home in search of its creator. In this, as in "The Changeling," only the Enterprise stands between the god-like machine and total destruction of Mother Earth.

"If anything, it's a little hard to sustain that plot for a full movie," John Meredyth Lucas said. Fully aware of the act of near-plagiarism, he added, "The plot, of course, I recognized." (110-3)

From the Mailbag

Written to John Reynolds, President of Desilu Studios, on October 6, 1967, the week after "The Changeling" first aired and ratings reports were released:

> Dear John: I discussed with (Herb) Schlosser, and he will take back to Mort Werner and (Don) Durgin, the fact that we are displeased with the lineup on NBC on Friday nights, that in the face of this terrible lineup *Star Trek* remains the top-rated show for NBC but could do much better if it had better lead-in and lead-out shows. Gene Roddenberry.

Memories

Nichelle Nichols said, "It was one of my favorite stories. I like the warmth between myself and Majel rrett. It was beautiful." (127-3)

Dorothy Fontana said, "You know, we loved Nomad. Loved Nomad!" (64-3)

12

Episode 38: THE APPLE

Teleplay by Max Ehrlich and Gene L. Coon.
Story by Max Ehrlich.
Directed by Joseph Pevney.

Shatner and Keith Andes in NBC publicity photo
(Courtesy of Gerald Gurian)

From *TV Guide*'s October 7, 1967 issue:

"The Apple." Kirk finds himself in a situation disturbingly parallel to the snake's in the Garden of Eden. To save his starship from destruction by a powerful god-machine, Kirk must destroy a paradise that the machine provides for its subject.

Vaal, the worshipped one of Gamma Trianguli VI, has control over more things than the subservient natives. It also monitors and maintains the planet's idyllic environment, and has an arsenal of natural weapons at its disposal. When the Enterprise crew intrudes, Vaal attacks with killer plants, deadly storm clouds with lightning bolts, and rainbow-colored rocks which are highly combustible and serve as land mines. Even the Enterprise is in danger, as an energy force grabs the ship and pulls it into the atmosphere.

The heavily disguised theme was a chancy subject for 1967 U.S. television -- to be free, we must question authority figures, including those in the form of gods.

SOUND BITES

- *Kirk:* "Mr. Chekov, Yeoman Landon, I know you find each other fascinating, but we did not come here to carry out a field experiment in human biology."

- *Spock:* "Doctor McCoy's potion is acting like all of his potions -- turning my stomach."

- *Kirk, after the death of one of his men:* "Garden of Eden … with land mines."

- *Akuta:* "You are welcome in the place of Vaal." *Chekov:* "Now we're welcome. Awhile ago this whole planet was trying to kill us. It doesn't make sense." *McCoy:* "Nothing does down here."

- *Spock:* "The good Doctor seems concerned that the Vaalians attain true human stature. I submit that there is no cause for worry. They have taken the first step. They have learned to kill."

- *Kirk:* "It's no trick to put fruit on trees ... and you might even enjoy it. You'll build for yourselves, think for yourselves, work for yourselves ... and what you create is *yours*. That's what we call freedom."

ASSESSMENT

"The Apple" has many clever ideas. Comparing Kirk to Satan is certainly one. And, for 1967, those optical effects -- the lightning storm lashing out at red-shirted crew members, and the phaser-driven firefight against a godhead Vaal -- were impressive works. Jim Rugg, *Trek*'s special effects guru, earned his pay, setting off explosive charges on a soundstage, rigging a Vaal-controlled plant that shoots poisonous barbs, and choreographing Spock to be thrown backwards by an invisible force-field.

Matching the special effects was the wacky, tacky set with rich green coloring everywhere and the contrasting orange sky behind it all … and a serpent's head of stone, with flashing eyes, in the middle of a jungle. Something this visually jarring was never to be duplicated.

There was also a sly message targeting a new type of workplace in America where every day more and more people were being hired as data keypunch operators, *feeding* information into the computers and machines that we were becoming dependent upon. Disturbed, McCoy comments, "It's obscene! Humanoids living only so they can service a hunk of tin!"

These attributes aside, "The Apple" barely succeeds in doing more than providing escapism. With all its grand intent, thundering effects, and high body count, the episode stumbles over a flawed premise and a theme which feels redundant within the greater scheme of the series.

At the core of this apple is a retelling of "The Return of the Archons." Even the script structure contains recognizable plot points: ship under attack while orbiting planet and unable to rescue landing party; Kirk and party treated as infection; computer in control of human-like population; Kirk must save himself in order to save his ship. We saw the formula to some degree in "A Taste of Armageddon," "Catspaw," and "Who Mourns for Adonais?" Even the big finale to "The Apple," with the Enterprise phaser beams knocking out the planet's power source, seems recycled from "Adonais." But the biggest stumbling block is that the natives speak English, even though this is their first contact with people from Earth.

Star Trek often bent rules with aliens speaking as if they studied Earth linguistics, but rarely completely broke the rules. The tribesmen in "Friday's Child" spoke English but they at least had past contact with Earth, as had the Romulans in "Balance of Terror," the Klingons in "Errand of Mercy," Landru and his people in "The Return of the Archons," the people of Eminiar VII in "A Taste of Armageddon," and Apollo in "Who Mourns for Adonais?" However, for the first time in the series, "The Apple" demands a complete suspension of disbelief in this area. Taking this suspension a step further, are we to assume Vaal taught its worshippers the English language but chose to withhold words such as "children" and "love"? Akuta, speaking like a white guy playing an Indian in a bad 1950s TV western, tells Kirk, "Your words are strange." Apparently, since Kirk is able to communicate with him, they are not strange enough.

Watching "The Apple," in some ways, is like sitting through an episode of *Gilligan's Island*. Don't think too hard, just sit right back and enjoy the tale.

THE STORY BEHIND THE STORY

Script Timeline

Max Ehrlich's story outline, ST #60, "The Apple": April 10, 1967.
Ehrlich's revised outline: May 2 & 4, 1967.
Ehrlich's 1st Draft teleplay: May 29, 1967.
Ehrlich's Rev. 1st Draft teleplay: June 20, 1967.
Gene Coon's polish (Mimeo Department "Yellow Cover 1st Draft"): June 28, 1967.
Coon's second rewrite (Final Draft teleplay): Early July 1967.
Coon's third rewrite (Rev. Final Draft teleplay): Early July 1967.
Coon's fourth rewrite (2nd Rev. Final Draft teleplay): July 12, 1967.
Additional page revisions by Coon: July 13 & 19, 1967.

Screenwriter Max Ehrlich was 57. He began as a newspaper writer, and then hit the airwaves where he was immensely successful at writing radio drama in the 1940s and early 1950s, including scripts for hit series, such as *The Big Story* and *The Shadow*. He also wrote for print, with *The Big Eye*, a popular science fiction novel published in 1949, and followed with 13 more books, including the sci-fi mystery *The Reincarnation of Peter Proud*. On television, in the science fiction genre, he provided several scripts for *Tales of Tomorrow*, including an adaption of Jules Verne's *20,000 Leagues Under the Sea*. He also wrote a *Voyage to the Bottom of the Sea* (with guest performer George Takei). Outside of sci-fi, and on series for which Ehrlich provided numerous scripts, he wrote action-adventure (*Assignment: Foreign Legion*), mystery-thrillers (*Suspense*), courtroom drama (*The Defenders*) and law and order (*Tallahassee 7000*). He even wrote an episode of *The Wild, Wild West* and contributed one script to William Shatner's short-lived series, *For the People*. And Ehrlich had experience at working on staff, as Script Editor for the 1959-60 series, *No Hiding Place*.

The TV critics often gushed over Erhlich's writing. It was Erhlich's script "Nightfall" that was used to launch the series *Sure as Fate* in 1950. *Variety* said:

> Preem [premiere episode of] *Fate* program was a tough gangster story in the Dashiell Hammett / Raymond Chandler idiom… excellent pace… some of the slickest dialog yet seen on video.

The same critic found Ehrlich's writing for *Treasury Men in Action* to be "tight and forceful." For the first of a two-part 1957 episode on *Studio One*, "Mutiny on the Shark," a different *Variety* critic wrote:

Ehrlich turned in a masterful first part -- he set the stage, developed his conflicts and ended in a moment of strain and suspense.

For another episode of the prestigious anthology series, the TV critic for *Daily Variety* said:

Max Erhlich's teleplay, "Balance of Terror," was a spine-tingling cloak-and-dagger drama, presented in the best tradition of these spy stories.

Ehrlich was everything *Star Trek* sought: a successful science fiction novelist with substantial experience in television, who had been championed by the critics. Gene Coon very much wanted to like the material Ehrlich brought in. His colleagues were not as impressed.

Ehrlich's story outline for "The Apple" was dated April 10, 1967. Dorothy Fontana wrote to Coon:

We have in this piece the exact, but totally unexciting duplicate, of "Return of the Archons" .... Nowhere in this piece is there an indication of how Vaal was built, how "he" took over the minds of these people, etc. At least in "Archons," a creation and purpose was given to the computer. (DCF38-1)

Coon wanted to leave some questions unanswered. Vaal may have been a machine, but who was to say the maker of that machine was not something on par with a god? This machine, after all, could control plants and clouds, and throw lightning bolts from the sky. It took care of people who lived in the garden, keeping them free from worry and disease. In return, they worshipped the machine. Yet Vaal is the villain and, in a sense, a character standing in for Satan is cast as the hero. Coon liked the irony. And the naughtiness. Fontana didn't. She told Coon:

I do firmly believe we require a massive rewrite of this story. In fact, forget this entirely and get the writer to work on a genuine original or else cut it off <u>now</u>. (DCF38-1)

Robert Justman's memo to Coon was less critical -- at least, at the outset. He wrote:

There is a very interesting premise contained within this outline.... If we can sufficiently disguise the resemblances [to "Return of the Archons"] and get some other kinds of shtick to occur, stuff some action into it early, and make sure that we have lots of dusky maidens running around in mini-sarongs, we might have a chance at making a go of this project. Otherwise, we might take Mr. Spock's suggestion that is given on Page 1 of the outline, in which he says that perhaps it is better to move on and forget the whole thing. (RJ38-1)

Roddenberry's message to Coon:

I'm afraid this is another one of those lightweight outlines which barely contains enough urgency, jeopardy or story for a <u>half</u>-hour script. (GR38)

Coon, the diplomat, wrote Ehrlich:

Max, we seem to have a few problems with your story outline. (GC38-1)

Coon was well-known for sticking with a script because he fell in love with a single story element or some intellectual or literary concept within. He told Ehrlich:

In several areas it is too similar to stories we have done before. However, this

201

can be corrected reasonably easily, and still maintain the same basic story, which I want very much to do.... We have here, on this planet, a form of symbiosis. The machine, in all ways, cares for these people and these people in turn care for the machine. They perform certain functions without which the machine would die. Any machine un-lubricated, un-set, un-governed, un-tended, will eventually die. However, I do not believe these primitive people should be automatons. This is one of the areas in which we are too close to one of our previous shows. They are simply humanity "before the fall." Innocent, pleasure-loving, naive, very primitive. Nothing evil. Nor do they move around like zombies. They are primitive people who essentially are at a cultural dead-end.... That is most important. (GC38-1)

This was the idea which had gotten under Coon's skin. Referencing the tragic end to "Who Mourns for Adonais?," he told Ehrlich:

Gods must be worshiped or they die.... In this case, worship is symbolized by the service the primitive natives perform, when they oil it and so on. If the Enterprise people manage somehow to keep the primitives from rendering their necessary services to the machine, the machine will cease to function. It will die.... I would like strongly to urge you to be perfectly clear in the Tag that we have simply played out the "Garden of Eden" allegory with the great machine in the role of God and Satan being played by Kirk. (GC38-1)

But for every story element which intrigued Coon, there was an equal point other members of the creative staff disliked.

Of Ehrlich's revised outline from May 2, Roddenberry wrote:

The villagers are like Polynesians. Why not stay on Earth and do a Polynesian story? We've got to challenge our writers into inventiveness. The way many of these stories are going, it is going to appear by mid-season that the galaxy is populated almost exclusively by very Earth-like humanoid bipeds, and that we have been lying to the audience all along about the galaxy being a place of strange, exciting, and unearthly things. (GR38-2)

Roddenberry was not only taking issue with Max Ehrlich but with Gene Coon. A good portion of his memo was referring to the letter Coon had written to Ehrlich, with Roddenberry continuing:

Neglect kills gods. Fine. A good point; interesting. But lack of oiling doesn't. If our theme is "What really is a god?" then let's challenge the writer to develop that theme into a meaningful story. At the end of the story, what have we gained? We have gotten back to the Enterprise. Is that all? At the risk of being cruel, I think we must ask the writer, "Was this trip really necessary?" (GR38-2)

Later that day, Stan Robertson, on behalf of the network, gave Coon permission to develop "The Apple" into a screenplay -- with three conditions. It had to be made less similar to "The Return of the Archons"; it had to be "more believable"; and Coon was told to "toughen up an otherwise soft story." (SR38)

After mulling over the memos from Roddenberry and Robertson, Coon wrote another long letter to Ehrlich. He suggested the action Vaal takes against Kirk and his people be more aggressive, utilizing this planet's ability to repel and even kill. Gamma Trianguli VI needed to declare war on Kirk's landing party, the way the human body declares war on an invading virus. He suggested replacing the "rain storms" Ehrlich described with strong winds, thunderbolts and lightning. He also instructed Ehrlich to make the natives less human by giving them "horns" or an *un*human-like skin coloring. And he stated that having the natives oil the machine was not enough in itself. There had to be something more -- "a certain kind of fuel" which the villagers could dig up and bring to the machine, something like coal, yet far more volatile.

On May 29, Ehrlich's 1st Draft script arrived. Two days later, Coon received a memo from Dorothy Fontana. She was bothered that the story which, in her mind, was still too similar to "The Return of the Archons," was now also similar to "Who Mourns for Adonais?" Beyond this concern, she wrote:

> All the action in this piece is not only contrived, but it is either totally impossible or incredibly expensive for us to do.... Story structure is bad. We are up to the end of Act II before we even see Vaal, our "heavy." There is no decisive action on the part of our principals. We lose the ship for long periods of time, but nothing is happening up there anyway. There is no sense of jeopardy or urgency about our people's predicament. And the resolution is far too easy and contrived.... Recommend total rewrite and restructure. (DCF38-2)

The feedback from Roddenberry, Justman, and NBC was also anything but encouraging.

Coon wrote a long letter to Ehrlich. It began:

> Dear Max, I would be less than honest with you if I did not start out by saying we have ourselves a mess of a problem with this First Draft. (GC38-3)

Among other things, Coon suggested the head tribesman, Akuta, have antennae implanted in his head, allowing communication with Vaal. Also, the Enterprise needed to be under attack, drawing the ship into the atmosphere and, more importantly, into the story. And this change would up the ante for Kirk, while adding greater urgency. Then there was the depiction of the series' regulars -- all wrong. Coon told Ehrlich:

> Max, I don't know if I ever gave you several copies of *Star Trek* scripts to read. I must say that you have substantially missed the characterizations and, indeed, missed the spirit of the dialogue of our people. (GC38-3)

In his densely-typed 21-page letter, Coon gave Ehrlich a crash course in *Star Trek*. He lectured:

> Incidentally, this isn't a landing party from Earth. We are not from Earth. Our home port may be Earth, and, in fact, the Enterprise was built in San Francisco [before being assembled in space], but we do not come from Earth. We are from the United Federation of Planets. I would examine very closely also everything we say to Akuta and these primitives. We have established in earlier shows that sometimes it is very damaging to a primitive civilization to understand that we come from a vast Federation of highly advanced beings, who in every way are thousands of years ahead of them. This can be extremely damaging. We must be very vague about where we come from and what we are doing. What we simply tell them is that we are friends and would like to help them.... As I told you at the very beginning, you will never write a more difficult show in your life than *Star Trek*. It is immensely difficult to write. Every point has to be logically perfect. (GC38-3)

Ehrlich's Revised 1st Draft fell short of the logical perfection Coon sought. It fell even shorter by Justman's measuring. His memo to Coon began:

I have just finished reading "The Apple." <u>Please rewrite</u>! (RJ38-2)

At this stage, Vaal, as he had been all along, was inside a large building which Kirk and company were unable to enter. Justman commented:

We cannot afford a building such as is described in this script.... Incidentally, it's going to be very interesting to find out about the audience reaction to the fact that Captain Kirk attempts to talk to a building numerous times within this script. I don't care how "burnished" a building may appear in the noonday sun, no amount of talk is ever going to convince the viewer that the building is going to say something in return.... In the meantime, I'm still waiting for Adam and Eve to show up. I'm also waiting for a snake to show up. By this time I'd even settle for John Huston [played in and directed the 1966 film *The Bible: In the Beginning*] to show up.... Well, on Page 47, Captain Kirk finally takes action. The script characterizes him as "pacing around angrily." ... He wants to destroy the building. However, now we have a new adversary. Mr. Spock tries to argue with him and tell him that he shouldn't do this. (RJ38-2)

Justman took particular issue with the antennae Coon asked Ehrlich to add into the script. He wrote:

Maybe we can get Ray Walston to play the part of Akuta. Please refer to Page 48. Notice that the "tiny electrodes behind his ear" vibrates. Did the author ever write the *My Favorite Martian* show?... Well, here we are on Page 49, and Captain Kirk and Dr. McCoy are deciding that they are going to tell the people on this planet how to live. There is something about the dialogue on this page that sounds as if it had been written by the C.I.A.... Please look at the middle of Page 50. There is a SHOT OF VAAL. The script indicated that Vaal is listening. How do you show a building listening?... I am rapidly coming to the conclusion that writing for television is the equivalent of grand larceny in any other business! (RJ38-3)

Coon decided not to ask for another script draft. He paid Ehrlich off and rewrote the teleplay himself.

Fontana, usually a fan of Coon's clever and heartfelt writing, delivered a slap to her boss's face concerning the June 28 "Yellow Cover 1st Draft." Her 8-page memo, in part, read:

You know my strong feelings about this particular script. I think it would be a big detriment to us to even think of shooting it in its present shape. It is, flatly, a monumental bore. (DCF38-3)

Robert Justman told Coon that he had "cleaned it up enormously," but Justman still felt there was much work ahead with the script ... work that would have to be done quickly, with filming scheduled to begin in just three weeks. His memo added:

I hesitate suggesting to you that we scrap this script, since we have put in so much time on it already and since we do not have a plethora of other scripts to back us up. (RJ38-3)

Knowing there was no turning back on this creative property, Justman told Coon:

Instead of constructing a building named Vaal, with its accompanying matte painting routine, why don't we construct a Tahitian-type idol named Vaal? We might, perhaps, pattern the design of this idol on the statues which have been found on Easter Island. (RJ38-3)

Justman envisioned the frightening idol standing 15 feet high with a mouth large enough for the village inhabitants to step into while feeding fissionable rocks to the machine god. It was also Justman's idea to replace the scene where a tree falls on one of Kirk's security men with something more science-fictiony: a plant that could project "barbed, deadly-looking lances." He also suggested changing "laser-type balls from the sky" to something more godlike, such as lightning bolts. And Justman suggested Vaal's eyes light up each time these lethal acts take place.

Gene Coon was soon at his typewriter, incorporating Justman's ideas into the teleplay. His Final Draft script was distributed to the department heads one week later, with less than two weeks left before the start of production. With this script, Matt Jefferies could get started designing the world of Vaal, which

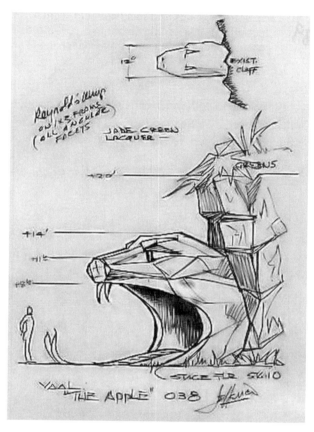

Matt Jefferies' design drawing for Vall
(Courtesy of Gerald Gurian)

included Vaal itself. There was a blueprint now, mapping out the various explosions, optical effects, killer plants, Tahitian huts, and the giant serpent's head of rock which was needed. With this, it was decided the production would be better served if filmed within the controllable environment of Sound Stage 10.

De Forest Research was now invited to furnish Coon with its notes and, typical of that company's assistants, Joan Pearce and Peter Sloman, every element of the script was scrutinized to a standard that few TV shows of the era were held to. In regard to the name of the planet, Delta Milo Six, Joan Pearce (after consulting to science fiction buff Sloman) wrote Coon:

> There is no constellation "Milo." If there were, the proper form for this name would be Delta Militis Six. For actual constellation and planet, suggest: "Gamma Trianguli Six."

In the script, after examining a chunk of rock that would soon explode, Spock says, "Light in weight, like pumice. Same … pitchblende, hornblende, quartz … fragile, no cleavage…" And, of this, Pearce said:

205

This description of the rock is scientifically unacceptable. The proper name for pitchblende is uraninite. It is extremely heavy. Hornblende is also very heavy and has excellent cleavage. Quartz is fairly heavy. Since Spock can break the rock in his hands, the sample would seem to have good cleavage to make this possible. For scientific credibility, suggest: delete "light in weight, like pumice"; change pitchblende to uraninite and change "no cleavage" to "good cleavage."

Clearly, less scientific sci-fi series, such as *Lost in Space*, did not consult De Forest Research.

While the other departments kicked into high gear, Coon turned out a Revised Final Draft, followed by a Second Revised Final Draft one week after that on July 12, just two days before production was to begin.

Pre-Production
June 27-30 and July 3 & 5, 1967 (6 days prep)

Joseph Pevney, *Star Trek*'s best action director, was given the chore. Working with Jim Rugg, he had already directed explosions for "Arena" and "Friday's Child." "The Apple" explosions would be a snap … or would they (see Production Diary)?

**Keith Andes and Marilyn Monroe in *Clash by Night*
(1952, RKO Radio Pictures)**

Keith Andes, as the copper-skinned, bleached-haired Akuta, was 47. Since the age of 12, he had been performing on radio. In the early 1950s, Andes was billed as a leading man in smaller Hollywood films, including the role as Johann Strauss in 1955's *The Great Waltz*, and in the arms of Marilyn Monroe, in *Clash by Night*. On television, he worked regularly throughout the 1960s and 1970s, including stints on *The Outer Limits* (with James Doohan) and, just before coming here, a three-episode story arc as an American agent gone bad on *I Spy*. Andes also starred in his own series, *This Man Dawson*.

Celeste Yarnall, as Yeoman Martha Landon, was 23. At 19, with over two million votes cast, she was chosen as the final "Miss Rheingold," ending a 20-year tradition. She represented the New York-based beer company in TV and magazine ads and at the 1964 World's Fair (Emily Banks, from "Shore Leave," had been the previous year's winner). Yarnall immediately found work on TV, in *My Three Sons*, *The Wild, Wild West*, and *The Man from U.N.C.L.E.*, among others, and had just returned from Spain where she

**Celeste Yarnall, with "The King," in *Live a Little, Love a Little*
(MGM, 1968)**

was the title character in the feature film *Eve*, co-starring Robert Walker, Jr. (Charlie Evans in "Charlie X"). From here, she went on to appear with Elvis Presley in 1968's *Live a Little, Love a Little*. With that movie and the release of *Eve*, she was voted the Foreign Press' Most Photogenic Beauty of the Year at the Cannes Film Festival. Simultaneously, she was named Most Promising New Star of 1968 by the National Association of Theater Owners.

Yarnall recalled, "When my agent suggested doing a guest star role on *Star Trek*, I was told that Joe [D'Agosta] was looking for something really exciting for me, and that Gene Roddenberry was one of the ones who really wanted me to do the show. When I came in to learn about this role, it was discussed, 'Well, do we want to save Celeste for something more exotic; for something where we can really costume her up?' And they asked, 'Celeste, do you want this or do you want to wait for something else?' Well, in television, you always worry about the ax falling on a series, so you take the work when you can get it. The 'something bigger' may never come. And working with an actor of the quality of Bill Shatner was appealing. I mean, he was in the Dostoevsky story, *The Brothers Karamazov*. He is a *very good actor*. And, in the script, I get to carry a weapon; I'm in the fight scene; I'm the romantic interest of Chekov; and I'm the sex education teacher of that planet! So I said, 'Of course, I want to do it.'" (196-3)

David Soul, painted copper, playing Makora, was 23. One year after this, he gained fame alongside fellow *Star Trek* guest players Robert Brown and Mark

**David Soul (on the right), with Bobby Sherman and
former *Trek* guest star, Robert Brown, in
Here Come the Brides (ABC publicity photo)**

207

Lenard, and teen heartthrob Bobby Sherman, in *Here Come the Brides*. His big success, as Hutch on *Starsky and Hutch*, was still eight years away.

After a three-episode layoff, Chekov is back, sans the Beatles wig. His own hair was now long enough, allowing him to pass for a Davy Jones wannabe. Yarnall said, "I had been warned about Walter having to wear this wig, but it looked like it was his hair to me. But I had been properly prepared for it." (193-3)

John Winston returned as Lt. Kyle, this time assigned to the helm.

"I was getting lead roles in small stage productions during this time. That satisfied the actor in me. *Star Trek* paid the bills. And because I gave them what they wanted, which was to show up on time, know my line or two, hit my marks, and not create problems, they kept bringing me back and giving me a bit more to do with each appearance." (189a)

Shari Nims played Sayana, the native girl who has a romantic scene with David Soul. She had just appeared in an Elvis Presley movie, *Easy Come, Easy Go*, and an episode of *The Wild, Wild West*.

Mal Friedman was the first red-shirt to go. He played Hendorff and was killed by flower power -- a flower with the power to shoot deadly thorns. He was making the rounds in TV at this time, playing minor yet necessary characters. He told writer Mark Phillips, "[I was] an aspiring actor whose day job consisted of my own business of cleaning floors and carpets of private residences. One of my customers was the wife of Gene Coon. They were both very nice and I enjoyed plenty of warm and interesting conversations. I believe,

Candid shot of Shari Nims with Shatner (Courtesy of Gerald Gurian)

largely at her bidding, they came to see a children's theater production of *Around the World in 80 Days*, in which I played Passepartout. On the basis of that, Gene introduced me to *Star Trek*'s casting director and arranged that I be given the part. It was obvious the role wouldn't require a Lawrence Olivier to render a fair interpretation of it, but I was nonetheless appreciative of the opportunity." (69a)

And then Friedman read the script. He said, "I hadn't been a real Trekker, but occasionally I watched the program and enjoyed the episodes. However, while I recognized that stark realism was not a central element to the series, it seemed to me that 'The Apple' truly strained one's capacity to suspend disbelief.... A group of shapely, platinum-blonde white people being liberated from the thrall of some mysterious computer-like entity in the bowels of a cave whose mouth is in the shape of an oversized defanged lizard, from which

208

mix derives some kind of moral about virtues of self-sufficiency? Forgive me if I sound like a snob, but I really found that premise, even with liberal allowance for artistic license, a bit much to swallow." (69a)

**Bill Blackburn under heavy makeup
(Courtesy of Bill Blackburn)**

Dick Dial was Kaplan, the second red-shirt to die -- from a lightning bolt. He worked on numerous *Star Trek*s as a stunt man. On *Sea Hunt*, he had been Lloyd Bridges' stunt double in 154 episodes. He was currently working as Peter Graves' stunt double on the Desilu lot, for 88 episodes of *Mission: Impossible*.

Jay Jones was the third red-shirt to die. He played Ensign Mallory, the guy blown up by a highly combustible rock. He had also played Jackson, the red-shirt who dropped dead off the transporter platform in the Teaser for "Catspaw." He often did stunts, usually standing in for James Doohan. "The Apple" marked Jones' second trip to the hospital for *Star Trek* (see below) -- "Who Mourns for Adonais?" being the other.

Jerry Daniels was the fourth crewman in red to die. He played Marple, who gets his skull cracked by a club-wielding villager. He worked with Celeste Yarnall again, for the 1971 horror film *The Velvet Vampire*.

Bill Blackburn, who so often appeared as a member of the Enterprise crew, switched sides and joined the People of Vaal, one of those who would try to kill Kirk and his landing party.

Production Diary
Filmed July 14 (2 day), 17, 18, 19, 20, 21 & 24, 1967.
(Planned as 6 day production, finishing three-quarters of a day over; total cost $205,980.)

Production began mid-morning Friday, July 14. It was on this day that the United States launched Surveyor 4 to the Moon. It was meant to land there, but exploded during the attempt. Social unrest was also exploding, and doing so all across America. Twenty-seven died in a race riot in Newark, New Jersey. In the next few days, there would be more rioting in Illinois, North Carolina, and Tennessee. And a prison riot in Florida resulted in the death of 37.

A different type of riot happened at a rock concert in Forest Hills, New York, where teenage girls kept chanting "We want Davy! We want Davy!," marring a performance by Jimi Hendrix, who, remarkably, had been booked to open for The Monkees.

The Summer of Love was in full-swing. *The Big Mouth*, starring Jerry Lewis, was champ at the movie houses. *The Dirty Dozen* dropped to second position. "Lucy in the Sky with Diamonds," "With a Little Help from My Friends," and "She's Leaving Home" were all over the radio. And that meant The Beatle's pop masterpiece, *Sgt. Pepper's Lonely Hearts Club Band*, was still the top-selling album in America. The melodic tones of Scott McKenzie's voice was pouring from transistor radios across the country, too, telling anyone thinking of coming to San Francisco to wear flowers in their hair. And Desilu's boss woman, and *Star Trek* backer, Lucille Ball, had the cover of *TV Guide*.

Meanwhile, at Desilu studios, once Marc Daniels finished "The Changeling," Joseph Pevney spent the remainder of the day on Stage 9, beginning with the delightful Tag scene in the ship's corridors, then moved on to film the bridge sequences.

Celeste Yarnall was needed in the wardrobe room this day for her fitting. She remembered, "When they first put the yeoman's dress on me, it didn't fit, and I said, 'I'd like it shorter.' I'd just come back from Europe, and I told them, 'You know, the girls are really wearing their mini-skirts short in London right now.' So, Bill Theiss said, 'Let's re-cut this for her.' And another lady said, 'Well, don't you think *she's* ever going to come back and want that dress?' And he said, 'Oh, no, *she's* never coming back.' Well, you know who *she* was; whose dress they were talking about? Grace Lee Whitney won't like hearing this, but they re-cut and shortened Yeoman Rand's dress for me." (196-3)

Star Trek **writer David Gerrold, visiting the set, said,**
"As far as the eye could see, green, green and more green"
(Photo courtesy of Fred Walder)

Day 2, Monday. Stage 10 became the planet of Gamma Trianguli VI. Set decorator Joseph Stone turned the soundstage into a lush jungle. He had five Emmy nominations awaiting him, and one win. None were for *Star Trek*.

David Gerrold, splitting his time between writing the upcoming "The Trouble with Tribbles" and visiting the set, soaking up all he could about *Star Trek*, remembered, "The set for this episode [required] an orange sky and a green jungle -- not just a little jungle either. The jungle filled the soundstage; more than filled it -- overflowed in every direction. Far off on the horizon, tall palms were waving in the wind, dark clouds scudded the sky. As far as the eye could see, green, green and more green. As far as the second season was concerned, the budget for greenery had been *blown*." (73-6)

Those greens alone took $5,040 away from the budget. That would be more than $35,000 in 2013. And that was to rent, not to buy.

Celeste Yarnall remembered her first day on Stage 10 vividly, saying, "The stage was big; it was a really good size set. The rocks were all papier-mache, of course. But, when that set was lit, what you saw on the screen was what I saw standing there -- amazing colors. It was so beautiful to the eye; to the brain; it was so rich." (196-3)

The production schedule identified this first area as "Ext. Jungle." Pevney filmed the episode's Teaser and first half of Act 1, including the death of Hendorff from the thorn-spewing plant.

"The special FX were accomplished very simply," said Mal Friedman, who played Hendorff. "They stopped camera, put a circular-shaped Styrofoam pad under my tunic, stuck in the thorns, put me back into position, [and] started rolling. Add a puff of smoke and *voila*, there I was with thorns in my shirt." (69a)

Shatner, in good spirits before the explosion which further damaged his hearing (Courtesy of Gerald Gurian)

After shooting the scene where Spock, standing next to Kirk and McCoy, tosses away a rainbow-colored rock, the production abruptly stopped. DeForest Kelley recalled, "There was a big explosion that blew up in front of us, and the special effects man had placed TNT into it. That's what it sounded like. It was a terrible explosion, and the three of us absolutely went deaf with it." (98-1)

The moment was captured on film. Watch when the rock Spock discards explodes. Shatner puts his hand to his ear as the concussion hits and the three stars nearly fall over. Ever the professionals, they remained in character for the couple seconds needed to complete the shot, despite the shock and the stabbing pain in their ears.

"The explosions were immense," said Celeste Yarnall. "They didn't give us cotton for our ears. I don't remember anyone yelling 'Fire in the hole!' I just remember stuff going off around us. And, being on a soundstage, there was a lot of reverberation. It was horrific. It really was. I remember a lot of yelling about '*This is way too much!*'" (196-3)

Kelley said, "We went to a Hollywood doctor's office and it was a pretty big shock when the three of us [in costume] walked in!" (98-1)

Less funny was the aftereffects. Two decades later, Kelley admitted, "I have a constant reminder of that show; a constant ringing in my ear.@ (98-1)

Yarnall acknowledged that Kelley was not alone, saying, "That's when Bill Shatner had his ears damaged, and they've rung ever since. He got tinnitus from that." (196-3)

Shatner actually got tinnitus from an explosion during the production of "Arena." The condition was now worsened, substantially.

Day 3, Tuesday. Pevney continued shooting the Jungle Area, finishing Act I and

211

nearly all the scenes from Act II scripted for this setting. The action included Spock getting shot with thorns, the landing party discovering they could not beam up, and the death of the second red-shirt (Kaplan) who was struck by lightning and went up in a puff of smoke. With all the special effects and the injuries, Pevney was one-half day behind.

Day 4, Wednesday. Pevney finished with the "Ext. Jungle" set. A short move put them into the "Clearing" where he quickly captured all the sequences needed from this area, including the death of the third red-shirt, Mallory, by one of those land-mine rocks. This resulted in another casualty among the cast.

"I had to lobby director Joe Pevney for that scene," recalled Jay Jones, who played Mallory. "He was a dear man and refused to let me do it. He felt it was too dangerous. I held out. I said, 'I don't want to do this stunt the Mickey Mouse way.' He finally said okay. Well, I was wrong. I got hurt.

"There was a 'jumper trampoline' buried in the ground. When I hit the trampoline, the explosion was supposed to go off. Well, the timing had to be perfect, and it wasn't. The special effects guy was a hundredth of a second too late. I was directly over it when the blast hit. In the episode, you can see me literally blown toward the camera. The force hit me in the stomach, burned my side, blew the skin off my rib cage and impacted all of this dirt into my sinuses. I couldn't open my eyes or breathe. They rushed me to the hospital emergency room.

"They had filmed the explosion from another angle as well, and it was incredible. I looked like a human fireball. It wasn't used because NBC felt it was too violent." (93b)

The company kept working. Next up, the crew's encounter with Akuta, then a move to the interior "Guest Hut" for various scenes from Acts III and IV.

Representatives from NBC Standards and Practices were on set, watching like hawks. Gene Coon had snuck some sex talk into the script. It was something no one on family-hour network entertainment shows talked about in 1967. But Kirk talks about it in that hut. He wonders what would happen if one of the Feeders of Vaal were to die in an accident; how would they go about creating a replacement? Yeoman Landers is put in the hot seat, asked to speculate. Looking flustered, she says, "But these people … if they don't know how … what I mean is … if they don't seem to have any natural … I mean … How is it done?" Spock says, "It is reasonable to assume that they would receive the necessary instructions." McCoy interjects, "From a machine? That I'd like to see!"

Broadcast Standards wanted to see, too, and see that the naughty business was handled discreetly.

Yarnall said, "They were really concerned. They didn't want it thought that I was spending too much time in this hut with these four or five men. It was explained to them by the producers that this is the 23rd Century; that men and women are equal; there's no reason for concern. But it didn't matter. This *isn't* the 23rd Century. *This is 1967.* And this is American TV. So they had some changes made, and some good moments were left on the cutting room floor." (196-3)

Even with the dreaded network censors on his set slowing things down, Pevney held at one-half day behind.

Day 5, Thursday. Pevney filmed all the Ext. Village sequences as seen in Acts III and IV, constituting the first time all the villagers were seen together. Makeup artists Fred Phillips and his team had their hands full. All of the "Feeders of Vaal" wore body makeup to color their skin copper.

Day 5, Exterior Village set (Courtesy of Gerald Gurian)

Yarnall said, "I remembered how they said they wanted to save me for something more exotic. I was thinking about that when I saw those other poor girls, itching in the grass skirts and all that body makeup, and those wigs, so miserable and uncomfortable. And David Soul -- he was pretty itchy, too, painted copper with the body makeup. They'd have to go to lunch in all that, walking into the commissary. And I remember thinking, 'Thank God I can just wear this cute little mini!'" (196-3)

Next up: the fight. Yarnall said, "None of us were singled out as not being capable. I participated in a fight scene. It was very good for the liberated spirit of today's woman because, I think, we were treated as equals. The show was progressive that way." (196-2)

The female Yeoman survived the fight. Marple, the last of the red-shirts did not. And, with this, "The Apple" marked the highest body count of Enterprise men-in-red to date.

**Shatner and Kelley, running lines while on Stage 10
(Courtesy of Gerald Gurian)**

Later in the day, Pevney filmed "Ext. Flowery Area" for the little bit of romance between Chekov and Yeoman Landon. Celeste Yarnall recalled, "Walter was very nice. But I had a particular problem at the time. Something had happened when I was in Europe; I used a cosmetic on my nails that had

213

**Celeste Yarnall hiding the nails on one hand
(Unaired film trim courtesy of Gerald Gurian)**

caused a serious nail infection. And when I got back to the States, it got worse and worse, and, right before the filming, I'd gone to a dermatologist and he literally drilled my nails from the nail bed out! So in every shot, you'll see me hiding one hand -- I believe the right -- because I had no nails, and I wasn't allowed to cover it up because there was a tincture that had been painted on my nails to try to kill this infection. So you'll see me folding my arms a lot. Now, when I'd guest star on a show, the first person besides the director I like to make friends with is the Director of Photography, which in this case was Jerry Finnerman, a wonderful man. I told him about my problem and asked if there was any way he could be sure to photograph me so that the hand with no nails would stay hidden. And he said, 'Don't worry, just concentrate on your performance, I'll make sure we never see it.' Now, it comes time to do the kiss with Walter. And I need to keep that hand down. So I have to lean in a certain way. But he's trying to lean in a different way. [Laughs] Typical man, trying to lead." (102-13)

Koenig recalled, "I was feeling rather flattered by the aggressive way she grabbed hold of me until I realized that she was positioning my body so that it is her face that dominates the camera frame. I guess that's what you call the tricks of the trade." (102-13)

Yarnall added, "I didn't know at the time that he hadn't been told about my hand and the reason why we were positioned as we were. So he's wanting me to turn a certain way,

Day 5 brought a challenge for the makeup department -- 10 copper-skinned natives; and filming Vaal on Day 7 as Bill McGovern slates a shot (Courtesy of Gerald Gurian)

214

but I couldn't, and this meant his head was blocking mine from the camera. And I'm trying to go against this, and he's trying even harder to get me to do it his way." (196-3)

Things went smoother next as Makora (David Soul) and Sayana (Shari Nims) mimicked the kiss they just witnessed. Later, for this same camera set-up, Pevney filmed Akuta showing the other Men of Vaal how to kill. Prop master Irving Feinberg needed a few plump melons for this.

"I went to the Farmers' Market and bought seven beautiful and expensive Persian melons," Feinberg recalled in a 1968 interview for fanzine *Inside Star Trek*, issue #4. "The proprietor proudly informed me that their flavor was as great as their price. I left him in a state of shock when I told him that I wasn't going to eat them, I was going to smash them. When I returned to the studio, I had these melons painted to change their outer appearance. In order to change their inner appearance, I injected a vegetable dye into their interiors with a hypodermic needle. This made them look properly disgusting when they were smashed."

Keith Andes about to smash open one of Irving Feinberg's special Farmers' Market melons (above); and Day 7 (below), filming Vaal (Courtesy of Gerald Gurian)

"He was funny, that prop man," said Yarnall. "He was so protective of those props. I remember when I would take a break and sit down in a chair off set, he'd run over and want his phaser back. He wasn't going to lose sight of it. It was like he only had one of them." (196-3)

David Gerrold echoed Yarnall's words, recalling, "I got my hands slapped by Prop Man Irving Feinberger [sic] for touching a hand phaser." (73-6)

Feinberg collected his props as Pevney finished filming, three-quarters of a day behind.

Day 6, Friday. More of the Village set was shot and Pevney was still behind. Not helping matters, he also had to shoot pick-up scenes for "The Changeling" on this day.

Day 7, Monday, July 24. All scenes involving the godhead Vaal were shot, ending with Kirk telling the out of work Feeders of Vaal that they were free to find their own way in life … including finding out about sex. Pevney needed the entire day, wrapping the episode in six and three-quarters days.

Post-Production
Available for editing on July 25, 1967. Rough Cut: August 3. Final Cut: August 8.
Music Score: tracked.

James Ballas and Edit Team 1 had their third assignment of the season, following "Metamorphosis" and "Amok Time."

With this episode, Music Editor Jim Henrikson offered a good example of his talents, since all cues were from the music library. It was Henrikson's job to know every piece of music available to the series, and choose which would work best. The soundtrack to "The Apple" shows how music from various episodes could be combined to create an exciting and thoroughly effective new score.

The Westheimer Company provided the photo effects, including red stormy clouds, lightning strikes, an exceptionally-long materializer effect as the landing party tries and fails to beam up, Spock's encounter with the force field, and phaser beams raining down on Vaal. The shot of the Enterprise firing its phasers was lifted from "Who Mourns for Adonais?," but the recycling did little to help keep costs down. All those lightning bolts and phaser beams ran the optical effects bill up to $35,160. The total hit, from start to finish, was $205,590. In 2013, this comes to nearly $1.5 million.

With "The Apple" pricing out at $20,590 over the studio's per-episode allowance, the Second Season deficit grew to $137,441 … or nearly one million in 2013's deflated dollars. Desilu was bleeding out.

Release / Reaction
Premiere air date: 10/13/67. NBC repeat broadcast: 7/12/68.

Steven H. Scheuer reviewed the episode for his syndicated column, *TV Key Previews*. Among numerous newspapers across the country to carry the review on October 13, 1967 was *The News Journal*, out of Mansfield, Ohio. Scheuer wrote:

> "The Apple." A good science fiction yarn. The Enterprise investigates a strange planet inhabited by ageless yet seemingly harmless humanoids who serve a mysterious god. This is the kind of story this series handles quite well and even though the plot and solution seem far-out, the script is intelligently written, well played and oddly enough, believable. Keith Andes guest stars.

Judy Crosby reviewed the episode for her syndicated column, *TV SCOUT*. Among the papers which ran her notice on October 13, 1967, was *The Monessen Valley*, in Monessen, Pennsylvania. Crosby said:

The attractiveness of *Star Trek* has been the believability of its far-out science fiction. It slips a little tonight in this regard, where the Enterprise sets down in a paradise. The god providing this "paradise" for his emotionless people is actually a machine. Soon after the arrival of the space travelers, the humanoids begin to show signs of being human and Captain Kirk and his party are ordered destroyed. Keys to the plot are the paradise itself and the god's voice, that of guest star Keith Andes.

While "The Apple" was not considered a favorite by very many *Star Trek* fans, or some of the creative staff, one person was so bothered by what he saw, he actually became ill. Jay Jones, who went to the hospital after the explosion that killed his character, Mallory, said, "Dad was a huge *Star Trek* fan, and [when watching] he could tell that stunt went terribly wrong. [And he] had been a stuntman all of his life. When he saw that stunt on TV, he knew I really ate it. He literally got sick to his stomach." (93a + 93b)

RATINGS / Nielsen National report for Friday, October 13, 1967:

8:30 to 9 pm, 55.7% of U.S. TVs in use.	**Share:**	**Households:**
NBC: *Star Trek* (first half)	24.7%	10,140,000
ABC: *Hondo* (first half)	23.3%	9,910,000
CBS: ***Gomer Pyle, U.S.M.C.***	45.2%	15,620,000
Local independent stations:	6.8%	No data

9 to 9:30 pm, 58.1% of U.S. TVs in use.	**Share:**	**Households:**
NBC: *Star Trek* (second half)	24.4%	No data
ABC: *Hondo* (second half)	23.7%	No data
CBS: ***Friday Night Movie***	**40.0%**	**No data**
Local independent stations:	11.9%	No data

The movie on CBS was 1963's *Spencer's Mountain*, starring Henry Fonda and Maureen O'Hara. Star Trek placed second for its entire hour.

How easily *Star Trek* beat its rival on ABC depended on where one lived. The National survey is above. The 12-city Trendex report (a faster survey focusing on larger cities only) is below. Shows such as *Gomer Pyle* and *Hondo* had rural appeal, while *Star Trek*, according to A.C. Nielsen, had city appeal.

Averaged rating for 8:30 to 9:30 pm (Trendex report):	**Rating:**
NBC: *Star Trek*	12.6
ABC: *Hondo*	9.3
CBS: ***Gomer Pyle, U.S.M.C.* / *Friday Night Movie***	24.4

From the Mailbag

Letter from Irving Feinberg to a fan who had written in:

Dear Mr. K: I was flattered to learn of your interest in the hand phaser used in *Star Trek*. It is difficult to imagine how weapons in the future will be made and used. It is gratifying that this one prop has been believable and interesting to

217

you…. Due to the prohibitive cost of the manufacturing of these guns for actual film use, it is impossible for me to send you one. However, facsimiles of these guns and other *Star Trek* props will be merchandised in the near future so that you will be able to buy them at your local department or toy store for a nominal sum…. Thank you for your interest in *Star Trek* and, I hope, that during our new season, we will continue to provide you with a look at our distant future which is both entertaining and believable. Irving A. Feinberg, Property Master, *Star Trek*.

Memories

Dorothy Fontana said, "There are some scripts I'm not too enamored of -- one being 'The Apple,' which we made work, but it was not a good show. Other people loved that show. Okay, well, your tastes are different than mine, then. That's all." (64-1)

Celeste Yarnall was one of those who loved "The Apple" and finds its theme to be relevant to this day. As for the production, she said, "I did feel like an outsider that first day. I was intimidated. The cast was like a big family. They had this tremendous camaraderie. But after a day of filming, I felt very much at home. William Shatner was terrific to work with. He's an incredible actor and a lovely human being. And being beamed up was great fun!" (196-1)

Mal Friedman, regarding his death scene, as Hendorff, told writer Mark Philips in 2001, "[W]hen people find out I played him, that's when I've seen the power of the *Star Trek* mystique. I've felt a certain reverence and even awe given to me from young people. The mere fact that I was part of it is enough for them." (69a)

13

- Enter Jerome Bixby -

Bixby's screenplay for *It! The Terror from Beyond Space* played like an episode from *Star Trek* (MGM, 1958)

The writers who contributed the most material to *Star Trek* were Gene Roddenberry, Gene Coon, and Dorothy Fontana. No one else came close. Coon had 13 screen credits on the series. Roddenberry took 12. Fontana had 10. And all three did substantial rewriting on many other scripts which would have justified them taking further credit on the screen had they wished. The fourth most prolific writer was John Meredyth Lucas, with four produced scripts, two additional assignments which did not make it before the camera, and numerous uncredited rewrites of scripts by others. And then there was Jerome Bixby, the fifth most produced writer at the original series.

Of the events that landed Bixby his first script assignment for *Star Trek*, the renowned science fiction writer said, "They didn't approach me, *I* approached *them*." (16-2)

Bixby, at 43, had dabbled in television, writing several episodes of the 1960 series *Man into Space*, but was best known as a prolific writer of sci-fi short stories. One such story, "It's a Good Life," was adapted by Rod Serling for *The Twilight Zone*. The famous horror tale starred a seven-year-old pre-*Lost in Space* Billy Mumy as a monstrous boy who sends people he doesn't like into "the corn field." On the big screen, Bixby wrote *Curse of the Faceless Man*, *The Lost Missile*, and the cult classic *It! The Terror from Beyond Space*, which two different writers tried to adapt into a *Star Trek* property ("Alien Spirit," by Norman Katkov, written on assignment as ST #15, in 1966, and "Sisters in Space," by Robert Sheckley, also on assignment in 1966, this one as ST #25).

In 1966, Bixby provided the story for the epic big screen sci-fi film, *Fantastic Voyage*. While that movie was filming, he amused himself by writing a spec script for a new series he fancied called *Star Trek*. The title was "Mother Tiger."

Otto Klement, Bixby's agent, submitted the screenplay to Desilu on November 15, 1966 with a humble note, reading:

> I don't know what led him into the speculative venture of writing a complete original screenplay usable only for one program. He told me that he loves the program and had a lot of fun writing it.

Klement knew it was very unlikely that *Star Trek* would buy an unsolicited screenplay. Television doesn't work that way. Ideas are pitched, outlines written and, if approved by the network, a script assignment is given out, with the producers and network providing notes throughout the process.

On December 6, 1966, Roddenberry wrote to Gene Coon:

> Like this effort very much indeed! Skillfully done and with a flair for a *Star Trek*, which is unique among our first drafts.

Coon wrote to Klement, informing him that *Star Trek* had all its scripts for the first season and that the series had yet to be picked up for a second year. Nonetheless, he said, "We *are* interested in Bixby." Two months later, Coon summoned Bixby as a writer for the new season, but he did not want "Mother Tiger."

Bixby's spec script had the Enterprise encountering a "sleeper ship," an idea already used in "Space Seed." If purchased, this part of the story would have to be changed. Besides this, the primary premise involved finding an alien baby in suspended animation who, when revived, evolves at an accelerated rate, growing into a beautiful woman, the sole survivor of her kind. And she is about to procreate. This idea, concerning an alien who is the mother for the next generation of her race, made the story too similar to "The Devil in the Dark." Curiously, Gene Coon's story outline for "Devil" was dated November 29, 1966, two weeks *after* "Mother Tiger" was submitted.

"I always found that rather a curious coincidence," Bixby said. (16-2)

There were no hard feelings. All Bixby wanted was a chance to write for his favorite television series. That opportunity came in February, 1967.

14

Episode 39: MIRROR, MIRROR
Written by Jerome Bixby
(with Gene Roddenberry, Gene L. Coon, and D.C. Fontana, uncredited)
Directed by Marc Daniels

Spock with a goatee! ... for an episode set to film during the famed Summer of Love --
a network ad man's dream come true
(Unaired film trim courtesy of Gerald Gurian)

From an NBC press release:

Captain Kirk (William Shatner) and part of his crew are turned into evil
counterparts of themselves when an ion storm sweeps them into another
universe in "Mirror, Mirror" on NBC Television Network's *Star Trek*
colorcast.... While on the planet Halkan negotiating for high-powered crystals,
the storm strikes and sweeps Kirk and crew members to an identical Enterprise.
There they encounter a hostile counterpart of Spock (Leonard Nimoy) and a
scheming Sulu (George Takei). Kirk learns that he is romantically linked with
Marlena (guest star Barbara Luna), who soon discovers that he is not the evil
"Kirk" and tries to help him and his crew escape.

Complicating the matter, "The Empire" -- this dimension's savage counterpart to
Kirk's Federation -- has ordered Kirk to destroy the peaceful Halkans, who refuse to be
intimidated over supplying dilithium crystals. If Kirk fails to obey, he will be killed and the
next in line for the captaincy will order the attack. The barbaric crew of this Enterprise
advance in rank by assassinating their superiors.

The help provided by Marlena, who holds the rank of "captain's woman," is her knowledge of the secret weapon that *her* Kirk used to become captain and to stay alive -- an alien device called the Tantulus Field, which can monitor the movements of his enemies and kill instantly from afar.

The theme behind all this fun is spoken by Kirk. He asks the Mirror Spock, "When change is predictable; inevitable; beneficial; doesn't logic demand that you aid it?!" Mirror Spock responds, "One man cannot summon the future." Kirk sells the idea, saying, "But one man *can* change the present.... What about it, Spock? In every revolution there's one man with a vision."

As it often did, in the guise of sheer entertainment, *Star Trek* told its young audience to go boldly where they had never gone before ... and to make a difference.

SOUND BITES

- *Mirror Spock:* "Terror must be maintained or the Empire is doomed. It is the logic of history." *Kirk*: "Conquest is easy. Control is not."

- *Mirror Spock, to Mirror Sulu:* "I do not want to command the Enterprise. But, if it should befall me, I suggest that you remember that my operatives would avenge my death ... and some of them are Vulcans."

- *Mirror Kirk to Spock:* "Has the whole galaxy gone crazy?! What kind of uniform is this?! Where's your beard?! What's going on?! Where's my personal guard?!... Spock! What is it you want? Power?" *Spock, in awe of a truly primal human:* "Fascinating."

ASSESSMENT

"Mirror, Mirror" is imaginative and unexpected. The biggest surprise is that this far-out concept, which is built like a house of cards, is not only accessible but seems to work on all levels. Writing, directing, acting, costuming, and music all come together to make a near-perfect episode.

The theme of this story rings clear -- a government which oppresses its people, destroying trust and patriotism, cannot survive. It may take centuries, but governments of this type will eventually topple. The comparisons from 1967 are easy to spot. The good Federation is the United States. The evil Empire is one-part the Soviet Union, one-part any military dictatorship, and there were many coming into power and making the news as this script was being written. In Africa there were ten alone, and several more in Latin and South America. On April 21, 1967, as the story outline for "Mirror, Mirror" was expanded into a teleplay, a military "junta" seized power in Greece, resulting in what the press called "The Regime of the Colonels," as one military officer seemingly replaced another in a real-life game of King of the Hill.

There is one flaw in "Mirror, Mirror" -- the story's lack of logic. If the crew of the I.S.S. Enterprise are darker versions -- or opposites -- of those on the good ship Enterprise, then why are the Halkans peace-loving and meek in both universes? And does it stand to reason that every member of the Enterprise's crew -- the people Kirk normally interacts with -- would have an alternate self on the I.S.S. Enterprise, having survived the barbarism of their place and time? And would the same four -- Kirk, McCoy, Scott, and Uhura -- be beaming up in two different universes at the same instant? It was a rare occurrence that Scott and Uhura were members of a landing party, let alone in two universes, simultaneously. This is pure fantasy. But it doesn't matter. "Mirror, Mirror" is wonderful escapism and its accolades were well established in 1968 when the Hugo awards took notice.

THE STORY BEHIND THE STORY

Script Timeline

Gene Roddenberry's story synopsis, "The Mirror": March 11, 1964.
Jerome Bixby's contract: February 22, 1967.
Bixby's story outline, ST #47: February 27, 1967.
Bixby's revised outline, gratis: March 2, 1967.
Gene Roddenberry's rewrite of story outline: April 1, 1967.
Bixby's 1ˢᵗ Draft teleplay: May 26, 1967.
Bixby's 2ⁿᵈ Draft teleplay: June 1967.
D.C. Fontana's polish (Mimeo Department "Yellow Cover 1ˢᵗ Draft"): July 1967.
Gene Coon's script polish (Final Draft teleplay): July 17, 1967.
Additional staff page revisions: July 18, 19, 20 & 24, 1967.

After turning down "Mother Tiger," Gene Roddenberry and producer Gene Coon invited Jerome Bixby to pitch some new ideas. The one that clicked was a reworking of a short story he had published in 1952 called "One Way Street." Bixby later said, "I thought of a parallel universe for *Star Trek*, a very savage counterpart, virtually a pirate ship, into which I could transpose a landing party." (16-2)

The memory plays tricks. Bixby's original take on "Mirror, Mirror" did not offer "a very savage counterpart" or "a pirate ship" or even a "landing party being transposed." Bixby's original Mirror Enterprise had only subtle differences from the one Kirk came from. It was manned by a good and decent crew, and Kirk traveled to it alone, with no landing party in tow. Bixby's story did present a parallel universe, but this was something not new to *Star Trek*. Roddenberry had touched on this in his 1964 series proposal, with the synopsis for "The Mirror." There were no pirates in Roddenberry's version, only a duplicate Enterprise, much like in Bixby's. Harlan Ellison had included the idea of a savage alternate universe, with a pirate Enterprise, as a sub-plot for his original take on "The City on the Edge of Forever." And, of course, there was that other parallel universe story, the one that was actually filmed but no one on staff liked -- "The Alternative Factor."

Bixby's approach, although completely different than he remembered and from what was eventually produced, nonetheless intrigued Coon and Roddenberry, and they sent the writer home to work out the specifics. His 19-page story outline arrived on February 27, 1967.

Associate Producer Robert Justman wrote to Coon:

This is a very interesting conception, albeit carrying a resemblance to a disastrous effort entitled "The Alternative Factor," which I am sure you will recall. (RJ39)

Coon had been the guiding force for the "disastrous effort." But the similarities ended with that comparison. "Mirror, Mirror" was nothing like "The Alternative Factor."

Justman, in his 5-page memo, continued:

223

I predict that there is going to be a bit of soul-searching and hearts-skipping-a-beat-type conferences in attempting to whip the far-out-Science-Fiction-type aspects of this story into suitable television dramatic fare.... On Page 3 we have reference to an alien creature which is supposedly a pet. Please delete this reference, if you have any feelings for me at all.... On Page 14, Mister Kirk, bounder that he is, embraces his new-found wife and kisses her madly. And if you ever had your madly kissed, you know what I'm talking about. But, seriously folks, don't you think that this is rather unsporting of our Captain? Kissing a girl who is married to another fellow in another dimension?... Near the bottom of Page 17 is it absolutely necessary that Captain Kirk faint? If he does have to faint, I would suggest that he do so after reading the budget on this show. Then he would have proper motivation. (RJ39-1)

Coon had Bixby revamp his outline, *gratis*. The version he turned in on March 2, 1967, as with the previous one, was light years away from what eventually went before the camera. In this tale, Kirk is beaming up from the planet Rigel IV when the Enterprise is struck by a violent "warpstorm." The transporter room Kirk materializes in is only slightly changed from the one he expected. There to greet him are Spock, Scotty, and McCoy. It is McCoy who has a beard, not Spock. Before Kirk can speak, Spock tells him how "the war is going badly." Kirk, needing time to think, goes to his quarters, which he sees has a noticeable feminine touch. He wonders if he is dreaming all of this and tries to clear his mind with a shower. When he emerges from the shower, "nude," he is greeted by Anna, his wife in this parallel universe. And so ends the Teaser.

In Act I, Kirk, using the computers, discovers that this Federation is at war with a race called the Tharn who have recently conducted surprise attacks. He has many questions and the computer becomes suspicious, refusing to answer further without a security code. Kirk has the right code -- one thing from his universe that seems to be unaltered here -- but he now knows that this Enterprise and its computer do not function the same as in his universe.

Kirk is called to the bridge to receive a subspace call from Admiral McNulty informing him that the Federation is losing its war with the Tharn and therefore must surrender. Kirk is ordered to rendezvous with elements of the Tharn fleet and turn over the Enterprise to their leader, who will then lead the ship to the nearest Starbase. Meanwhile, the crew is becoming suspicious of their captain. He doesn't know certain details about them, about the ship, or about the universe they live in. And Kirk is having dizzy spells. The bearded McCoy wants to examine him, but Kirk stalls.

The Tharn rendezvous takes place. Kirk notices their ships do not have shields to withstand a phaser blast. He is confused how they could have beaten the Federation. He tells Spock that a phaser barrage could destroy any number of enemy ships. Spock replies, "Phaser, Captain? What's a phaser?"

In Act II, the Enterprise leads ten Tharn vessels to Starbase One. During this time, Kirk tries to come up with a way to create a phaser weapon. Anna, knowing her husband's kiss and that this is not her man, puts a knife to Kirk's throat, accusing him of being an imposter, *a Tharn spy*. Spock conducts a Vulcan mind probe on Kirk and discovers that he is from a parallel Enterprise and of no danger to them. He may even be able to help. Efforts are stepped-up to develop a phaser, which is used to defeat the Tharn.

Kirk holds himself together until the danger to the Mirror Enterprise has passed, then collapses. Mirror Spock and Mirror Scott know they must find a way to get him home. By recreating the conditions which affected the transporter during the warpstorm, they are able to beam Kirk back to his own Enterprise. Once there, a pretty nurse tends to Kirk in sickbay. She is Anna. Kirk smiles and says, "I wondered if we'd meet in this universe."

Script Consultant Dorothy Fontana didn't hate it. But the story worried her. She wrote Coon:

> Page 4 -- we have the beginning of symptoms of weakness and dizziness affecting Kirk. Suggest we not have this, if possible, as we did the same thing in "Enemy Within," along with the transporter malfunction bit. (DC39-1)

This plot point would be removed.

Fontana also felt better explanation was needed to demonstrate Kirk going from one universe to the other. She wrote:

> Since later on in the piece Bixby puts forth a supposition that Kirk is a foreign body in this universe, a disrupting factor, perhaps we could do something optically or photographically to indicate that. (DC39-1)

Flipping the Enterprise while in orbit was the answer.

Other comments by Fontana which would help to shape the story:

> On Page 3, it seems a bit presumptuous of the computer to start questioning Kirk. After all, a computer is programmed to give information, not question the operator. (And if this world has a computer advanced enough to reason and ask questions, how come they haven't developed the phaser?) Suggest the computer on war-time security would simply cease to give information if Kirk were asking the wrong kind of questions. The same resolution can be effected.... Page 13... My reaction to the fact that Spock and Scotty rigged a synthetic warpstorm is: oh? And the fact that they have programmed the Transporter to reproduce such conditions elicits the following: oh! Suuuuurreee they did, Harry. Now then, why do Spock and Scott reappear with him? Which ones are they? Where is the other Kirk? How does he get back? Aren't they all surprised to have Kirk (original) come back from where he wasn't? Won't he have to tell them where he was before they all flip out trying to figure how he's in two places at once? How do they send back the parallel world Kirk? And stuff like that. (DC39-1)

And "stuff like that" was bound to blow NBC's transistors. Robert Justman concurred. His memo to Roddenberry stated:

> I am in receipt of a copy of a memo written on a Story Treatment entitled "Mirror, Mirror." I would like to compliment the writer of this memo, one D.C. Fontana, who shall henceforth walk in beauty like the night. Most every point made by said D.C. Fontana is meritorious and correct and reflects much of what I feel about the above mentioned story. No doubt in future, D.C. Fontana shall become acerbic enough to merit my complete approval. No doubt a continued association under my tutelage will do much to increase the acidity content of D.C. Fontana's critiques.

Before further work on "Mirror, Mirror" could take place, Stan Robertson, speaking for NBC, rejected the story outline. His letter to the two Genes stated:

> It's highly confusing and, as written, does not contain the substantial structure to show enough promise to be developed into a successful *Star Trek* screenplay. Even though the basic idea of the story is a very intriguing one, I would suggest that in your conversations with the writer, you emphasize the point that, in our

opinion, he has failed to include several of the important ingredients which have been among the outstanding features of our series. This would be believability, credibility and visual excitement.... In summary, Gene, let me tell you that I feel that in talks with the writer of the above storyline and all those who will be writing for us this year, your feelings on what the foundation of all *Star Trek* stories must contain should be made very clear. What I refer to is your point that our episodes must have an action-adventure premise as opposed to philosophical motivation. The latter point can be "laid in" as you state, if first we have the former. (SR39-1)

Gene Coon was hip-deep in rewrites, including trying to make "The Apple" work, so Roddenberry rewrote the outline, sending it to Coon on April Fools' Day with a note, saying:

This is my rewrite of Bixby's rather complex "Mirror, Mirror." Frankly, I did this in one two-hour session with the microphone and, having not had time to read or analyze it, need your corrections and comments as soon as possible so that we can mimeo it, send it to NBC and get a copy to Bixby, so he can start on the first draft of the teleplay. (GR39-1)

Roddenberry hadn't merely simplified the descriptions and found a way to make a parallel universe comprehensible; he had completely reinvented the story, with a nod toward his own creation, "The Mirror." Roddenberry kept the germ of the idea from Bixby, and one name, that of the Tharn -- but not as the name of a race, now only as a person. Tharn became the "spokesman for the alien race" -- the Halkans.

Of his rewrite, Roddenberry told Coon:

Each system in each universe has its own system of checks and balances, which result in approximately the same thing. This is, in fact, close to our basic theme -- i.e., there are countries ruled by fascism or military juntas, which exist and evolve just as efficiently as other countries, which are ruled democratically. The main difference is not in how things evolve -- the real difference is that, in one, life is valueless, full of fear and terror, and never exploits the full potential of most of the citizens, whereas, in the other country, emphasis is on the pleasant life, security, the worth of the individual. (GR39-1)

Coon tidied up Roddenberry's outline and sent it off to the network. Stan Robertson, unaware that Roddenberry had done the writing, still credited Jerome Bixby. His letter, sent to Roddenberry, began:

This storyline in its present form is far superior to the original submission, primarily due to the writer having eliminated those elements which were confusing and difficult to follow. I think that all of us associated with *Star Trek* will profit from the fruits of your discussions with the writer of this story, which resulted in a rather drab and weak storyline being beefed up into an exciting and suspenseful one which has great promise as a screenplay. (SR39-2)

Robertson reversed his previous decision, now accepting the story for further development. But the approval did not come without a knuckle-rapping. He told Roddenberry:

As we begin a new season, you might want again to remind your writers, directors, and the other members of your creative team that the visual element we are looking for in *Star Trek* does not mean "to add violence," nor does the high dramatic quality we wish carry the connotation of inserting implied sex or

226

the types of costuming and dialogue which would offend our viewers. (SR39-2)

"Mirror, Mirror" was the most daring and *risqué* concept yet attempted, with plenty of violence and oodles of sex. But it also gave the network many things Stan Robertson had insisted on: a story that begins on a planet, not on the Enterprise, as well as a premise, story structure, and a look unlike anything *Star Trek* had done before. No one could accuse this fantastic tale of treading anywhere near "sameness."

Bixby, following Roddenberry's blueprint, turned in his 1st Draft teleplay on May 26. Three days later, Roddenberry sent a memo to Coon, writing:

> You are quite right, an excellent script from Jerome Bixby, who shows every sign of being an excellent *Star Trek* writer. (GR39-2)

There were, of course, problems. It took Roddenberry eight pages to list them all. He continued:

> The script needs considerable straight-lining. Desperately needed are scenes where we, in effect, sit down and say, "This is where we are; this is what we've seen; what does it add up to?" As it now stands, we have an excellent story which our audience will not be able to follow and which requires considerable re-reading, even by ourselves, to understand what is going on. It is going to have to be laid out much more clearly and explicitly. Part of this is Bixby getting into too many subjects which could easily be avoided. For example, on Page 11, Kirk says, "We've got two theories: massive change in our normal setting, or we're someplace else." I had to read this several times to understand what he meant. Later on, Kirk gets into whether our civilization is an empire or a federation, the nature of the society on the planet below, and so on. In this and in other places he is considering too many things and too much detail all at the same time. We've got to decide what is essential.... Seems to me, Gene, quite a few of Bixby's scenes move to a climactic moment and continue on and on and on long after we should leave that scene and keep the story progressing. I won't mention specifics here, I'm sure you will see the places this happens. Not that it is as simple as cutting the take off a scene but rather Bixby's scenes do not build steadily ascending into a climax. (GR39-2)

It was Roddenberry's idea to better utilize the regular supporting cast. He told Coon:

> Let's consider if we actually need Security Officer Hudson. Could Sulu possibly do what this role does?... We don't make much use of him. Is it possible to give Larson's [another Security Officer] business to him? If we end our show on the Bridge of our real Enterprise instead of Sickbay, we would have an interesting moment when Uhura rejoins the Bridge complement and gives the innocent Sulu a nasty look.

Coon implemented the change, having Sulu play the ruthless scar-faced security officer. And the new drafts of the script would also have the tag scene staged on the bridge. But the fun bit of action and reaction between Uhura and the "innocent" Sulu as suggested by Roddenberry was not realized. Other suggestions made by Roddenberry at this stage in the script's development were ignored by Coon, despite the fact that Roddenberry, in a sense, outranked him. Among the ideas from Roddenberry's memo that fell on deaf ears:

> Costume costs can also be reduced by holding generally to the Enterprise wardrobe even on the "other" Enterprise. No really good reason why they can't stay somewhat the same and it would avoid the sticky question of Kirk and the

Landing Party beaming aboard this strange ship in a costume different from the one the others wear.... Suggest we lose the salute method of arms across the chest. We used it for an alien race in "Balance of Terror" and will also use something of the same sort in Kneubuhl's "Bread & Circuses" script. Let's find another kind of salute that does the same for us.... COMPUTER VOICE. Let's keep it female. In this manner it relates to the computer voice we have heard on our own ship, stays recognizable as the computer. If we put a male voice in, it opens up the questions of whether or not the computer works the same, whether or not this is Hudson or someone who is disguising himself as the computer, etc. Even as a female voice it can still be played cold and harsh.... MARLENA. Again, re-reading the script, I still feel we should have met her earlier. We seem to throw away the fact that she is the wife of Kirk. Or at least we don't seem to make enough of it. In later scenes with her, is it possible to suggest that even the Kirk of this other world has some redeeming qualities? We suggest that Spock is such a wonderful thing that he is something of the same in two worlds, but we do not do as much for our series lead actor. A script would not be hurt at all if we begin to see from what she says that even this strange Kirk of this other world had had some doubts about the logic and decency of the kind of life they lead. Perhaps it had not progressed very far but I would tend to like our real Kirk better if I thought that his duplicate had been in progress, even in the early stages, of beginning to doubt the system in this parallel universe. (GR39-2)

Well aware of how long a letter from Gene Coon could run, Roddenberry closed:

.... Let's encourage him [Bixby]. Make him feel a part of the group. And, in this regard, I think it is important this first time that we not daze and crush him with one of our 20-page memos. This means a little extra work to you in consolidating what you will undoubtedly receive from me and the others. (GR39-2)

Coon kept his letters to Bixby on the shorter side -- short for Gene Coon, anyway. And Bixby, thrilled to be writing for his favorite TV show, was happy to make the changes, for a 2nd Draft, in June.

Dorothy Fontana got her turn with the script, creating the Mimeo Department 1st Draft in early July. And she steamed-up the role for Uhura with much of the teasing of Sulu on the bridge.

"In any show I wrote, or rewrote, I was always trying to get something more for the women," Fontana said. "More for Nichelle, more for Majel, more for anybody that we had as a female guest lead. A lot of times the stuff for Nichelle and Majel got cut out, which I hated. But I was not the final arbitrator on those." (64-3)

NBC Broadcast Standards (B.S. Department) had words of caution regarding the latest draft. Many words. The producers were told, in part:

Page 5: Caution on showing the results of the Agonizer here and on Page 6 and the Agony Booth on Page 28 & 29 so they are not unnecessarily shocking or alarming to the viewer.... Page 12: Chekov's attention to Uhura here and on Page 48 should be staged so that no impropriety is suggested.... Page 33: Caution on the embrace between Kirk and Marlena here and in the scene starting on Page 44 and, as usual, avoid the open mouth kiss. The negligee noted on Page 44 must be kept within the bounds of accepted television standards.... Page 34: Please delete the word "damned" in Marlena's line, "To every woman in the damned universe..." Changing the line to read "To every woman in the universe of the damned…" would be acceptable.

"Damned universe," in the mind of the network censor, was a verbal attack against the universe. It suggested shaking a fist at the sky and yelling, "Damn you," and "damn" or "damned" could not be used in this context on television in the 1950s and 1960s. "In the universe of the damned," however, implied that this universe was a place where those who have been damned by society or government or God must live. That use of "damn" was allowed. This was how it was in the United States regarding what could and could not be beamed out over the public airwaves in 1967.

Coon polished the script, creating a Final Draft on July 17, with page revisions on July 18, 19, 20 and, just one day before filming began, the 24th. By the time those last pages were in, Fontana and Coon, with input from Roddenberry, had provided close to half the dialogue. But Bixby was still the preeminent writer, and received all the credit.

Pre-Production
July 17-21 and July 24, 1967 (six prep days).

Marc Daniels returned for his fourth directing job of the second season. For more than two months, Daniels and Joseph Pevney had alternated episodes. While one was busy filming, the other prepped for his upcoming episode while, at the same time, supervising the editing of his previous one.

Barbara "BarBra" Luna was 27 when she signed aboard the Enterprise as Marlena, the captain's woman. She had been on the stage in New York as a child and, having blossomed into an alluring woman, was already a prolific actress in television and films, with multiple turns on *Zorro*, *Hawaiian Eye*, and *The F.B.I.* She had also played opposite Desi Arnaz in "So Tender, So Profane," an episode of *Desilu Playhouse*, as his wayward Cuban sister.

Luna said, "I had done so many roles as *the* Señorita, *the* Japanese girl, *the* Chinese girl, and *the* Hawaiian gal, that when I left New York, everyone told me I'd be typecast when I got to Hollywood.' So I thought, 'Oh my God, I'm going to be

**Barbara Luna and Fabian, in *Five Weeks in a Balloon*
(1962, Irwin Allen Productions)**

typed!' But it was the sci-fi world where I *wasn't* hired just for my ethnicity. In fact, when I read the script for 'Mirror, Mirror' and saw the part they had written for Marlena, I remember thinking, 'Wow, why did they ask *me* to do this?' There was nothing ethnic about it; there was no accent; she was just a female, and I thought that was so very interesting that they

229

chose someone of my type to play her. It was very exciting that Gene Roddenberry had created a show that had those kind of roles -- not only were we *not* hired based on our ethnicity, but the roles were powerful. I mean, in 1967, for a woman to have that kind of power, as with Marlena, where with just one little push of the button she could kill." (111-3)

In the sci-fi genre, Luna had appeared on *The Outer Limits*, *The Wild, Wild West*, and *The Invaders*. Joe D'Agosta liked Luna enough to also cast her in two *Mission: Impossible* episodes. Luna would work with William Shatner again in an episode of his 1980s series *T.J. Hooker*.

"It's amazing, this one TV show is my most famous credit," Luna said three decades later. "I've worked with Jimmy Stewart, Henry Fonda, and Yul Brynner, but people care more about *Star Trek*!" (111-2)

Vic Perrin, 51, and on his third *Star Trek*, finally got to show his face. He is Tharn, the Halkan Leader. Perrin had already supplied the voice for the Metron in "Arena" and Nomad in "The Changeling." A sought-after actor during the Golden Era of radio drama, Perrin was also well-regarded within the television industry as the Control Voice introducing each episode of *The Outer Limits*. As an actor, Perrin was well-liked by Jack Webb and appeared in 24 episodes of *Dragnet*, including several color episodes being produced at this time. In science fiction, Perrin played a Martian in "People Are Alike All Over," an episode of *The Twilight Zone*, with *Star Trek* guest star Susan Oliver (Vina from "The Cage").

"I was on camera for only one *Star Trek* episode, yet I think almost as many people recognize me from 'Mirror, Mirror' as they do from *The Outer Limits*' sound," Perrin said. "I have been recognized as Tharn on an international basis, ranging from London, Munich, Tokyo, and Singapore." (138)

John Winston, returning as Lt. Kyle, is given one of his better acting roles in the series, screaming and writhing, the victim of Mirror Spock's agonizer.

Pete Kellett played Farrell, Kirk's henchman. He was a stuntman/actor and appeared often on television, including multiple turns on *Gunsmoke*. Returning to *Star Trek*, he would be seen briefly as a Klingon in "Day of the Dove" and a Morg guard in "Spock's Brain."

Garth Pillsbury was Chekov's henchman, who then turns on him to work for top dog Kirk. He'd return to *Star Trek* as the Troglyte Prisoner leaping from the city suspended in the sky, in "The Cloud Minders." Of his first *Trek*, Pillsbury said, "My agent called and said, 'I have a small part for you in a show called *Star Trek* and we've set up an appointment for you to read for it. And keep in mind that this guy's kind of a smart ass guy.' So I walked into the casting director's office and there were four or five people at this table, and I kind of acted a little like a wise guy. And a couple people thanked me profusely as I was going out, and I thought, 'Well this is fantastic, I'm sure I'm going to get this part.' A week went by and I called my agent and said, 'Phil, what happened to the *Star Trek* thing? I thought I did very well.' He said, 'Yeah, everybody liked you except for the director, who thought you were a wise guy.' So now another four or five days go by and I get a call from my agent and he says, 'Garth, you've got the part. Of all the people that read, you did the best, so they decided to go with you anyway, even though the director still thinks you're a wise guy.'" (143a)

Regarding his sixth appearance in the series, and his second in a row since growing his hair long enough to appear sans the Beatles wig, Walter Koenig said, "During that first year, I had no contract. But, for some reason, they would bring us the next week's script while we were shooting the current episode. I'd look to see if Chekov was still there. And, more often than not, he *was* there. This was all during the spring and summer as we were shooting these episodes. None had aired, so there was no reaction yet from the fans, and my psychological disposition is to just assume the worst. I never really allowed myself to think that I was going to be a recurring character until they told me I was a recurring character. So it was exciting to see my name in the next script to film, and they were certainly giving me some good roles in those first several episodes." (102)

Production Diary
Filmed July 25, 26, 27, 28, 31 and August 1 & 2, 1967, plus August 11 (2 day).
(Planned as 6 day production, running 1 2 days over; total cost: $188,530.)

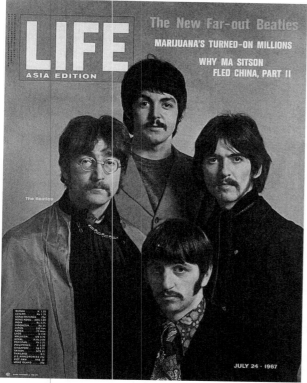

"Mirror, Mirror" filmed during the Summer of Love, while The Beatles (seen here on the July 24 cover of *Life* magazine) were at the forefront of pop culture.

Filming began Tuesday, July 25, 1967. "Light My Fire" by The Doors was the most-played song on the radio; *Sgt. Pepper's Lonely Hearts Club Band* the best-selling album in the stores. *The Dirty Dozen* was again the top box office movie in the U.S., after being displaced for one week by *The Big Mouth*, starring Jerry Lewis. You could see either for $1.50 … less if a matinee. A can of Shasta Cola during the movie cost a dime. A Snickers bar was a nickel. For the teenagers trying to look cool, a pack of cigarettes cost 27 cents in the stores -- 35 cents from a machine. And you could still smoke in the movie houses. Prices were good, but wages were not. Minimum wage was $1.65. The average doctor cleared about $50,000 a year. Shatner, one of the top-paid stars in TV, was only making a bit more than double that amount. "The New Far-Out Beatles" had the cover of *Life* magazine, showing off their new *Sgt. Pepper* period threads. And Michael Landon, Dan Blocker, and Lorne Green, in their *Bonanza* duds, had the cover of *TV Guide*.

Joseph Pevney was a half-day late finishing "The Apple" when he handed the production company over to Marc Daniels. Work began at the end of the story -- on the "normal" bridge with the tag scene where Kirk, back on *his* Enterprise, meets the Marlena of his universe. Also filmed, the bridge sequences from the Teaser, where Spock responds to Kirk's communication from the planet.

Remembering her first day on set, Barbara Luna said, "It was just another TV job …

231

except that you walk in and you see this guy with funny ears, and a very interesting cast, and the sets … and effects. But we certainly didn't know what this was going to turn out to be." (111-3)

Next up: the normal ship's brig and corridor area, where Spock imprisons Kirk's counterpart, as well as those of McCoy, Scott, and Uhura. A move to the normal transporter room came next, as Kirk and his landing party, still in regular uniforms, are beamed back to *their* Enterprise. Daniels completed all of this in only half a day, finishing on schedule. What he didn't get to, what had been planned for this day but then pushed back due to "The Apple" running late, were the remaining scenes from the Teaser.

Day 2, Wednesday. The schedule had been revised overnight. Scenes in the transporter room and sickbay were supposed to be filmed, but now the company played catch-up, starting the day on Stage 10 and the Halkan planet set. Thanks to Jerry Finnerman, many of the skies on the alien worlds were sheer pop art. This one is a sheer pop masterpiece. But masterpieces take time. The new schedule dictated that the company was to finish filming here by the lunch break. It was, after all, only a couple of pages of dialogue. But Finnerman's "lighting gag" -- simulating lightning flashes against violet skies -- took longer than anticipated. By the time the scene was completed and the company made the one-hour move back to Stage 9, and the sickbay set was lit, it was too late to keep the cast members any longer. Daniels, the director who rarely ran late, was three-quarters of a day behind.

Day 3, Thursday, July 27. Scenes in "mirror" sickbay of the I.S.S. Enterprise were filmed.

Costume designer Bill Theiss raised eyebrows with Nichelle Nichols and Barbara Luna's bad-girl uniforms. The gold sashes worn by each man on the I.S.S. Enterprise and the different insignias, as well as Kirk's sleeveless top,

Day 3. Filming on the sickbay set (Courtesy of Gerald Gurian)

are quite memorable. It was here that the red-shirted security men began wearing a black waistband. The purpose was to differentiate them from others who wore red shirts, such as technical and engineering officers. This look carried over to the good ship Enterprise for future episodes.

The only noticeable flaw in "Mirror, Mirror," as often happened on a Marc Daniels set, is the staging of the fight scene. Many shots were framed too close and held too long. Anyone with good vision or a TV screen bigger than 13 inches could tell that stunt "doubles"

232

were being used. Daniels had done it this way in "Court Martial" and "Space Seed."

Nimoy said, "The studios simply do not want actors doing those things when there's a possibility for them to be hurt because, if they're hurt, it shuts down production. They would much rather -- although it seems like a crude way to put it -- [that] it be a stuntman, because the production won't get shut down. And, of course, a stuntman gets well paid for doing that. That's his business. He knows how to do it. If he gets hurt that's part of his profession." (128-25)

Daniels said, "Nichelle Nichols was furious because I used a stuntwoman in the fight. She said, 'I want to do that; that woman doesn't look anything like me!' I said, 'You've got to be out of your mind. This is a complicated stunt. You could get badly hurt unless you know what you're doing, and the production couldn't afford to have you knocked out.'" (44-3)

The stunt wasn't actually that complicated, Daniels was being over-cautious. And this was one more reason why he was a very much in-demand director in television. He usually stayed on schedule, usually brought shows in on budget, and no series' regulars ever got hurt.

The afternoon hours were spent in the "mirror transporter room" for the landing party's entrance and exit from the parallel universe. Come quitting time, there were still numerous camera set-ups left to be filmed. Cast and crew were sent home, with production still three-quarters of a day behind.

On this night, NBC repeated "The Return of the Archons."

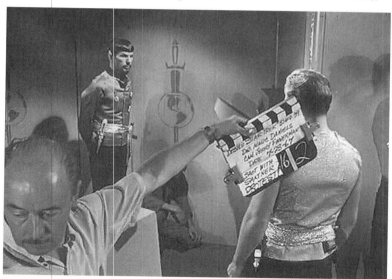

Continuing to remake the shooting schedule -- with a shot taken on Day 4 which had been planned for Day 3 (Courtesy of Gerald Gurian)

Day 4, Friday. Work resumed in the transporter room, before a hasty move to Kirk's quarters. The schedule was about to be changed again -- this time due to illness. Barbara Luna recalled, "When you're working in television, there is no such thing as calling up and saying, 'I am sick; I can't come in.' But, when I woke up that morning, I was so ill that my temperature was about 103 and I had no voice. So, when I got to the studio, they looked at me and said, 'Oh my goodness, she is so contagious.' And, of course, what we had left was the kissing scene with Shatner and the dialogue between us in his cabin. So, the doctor said, 'If she just *looks* at anybody, they're going to get it -- she is *that* contagious. You will have nobody left in the cast; you'll have nothing to film. Send her home!' Which is what they did. I felt so badly, because I had never,

233

never, ever missed work. But I felt so sick that it seemed like a whole month before I could come back, even though it may have only been a couple weeks." (111-3)

Filming continued minus Luna with the only scene on this set not to involve her -- a four-page dialogue sequence between Kirk, McCoy, and Scott, and the computer with a dispassionate male voice (in spite of the objection raised in one of Roddenberry's earlier memos about this). In the late afternoon, Daniels took Kirk's single shots for the other scenes in this room, the ones which would be completed later with Luna. The cast was excused early as the schedule was made

Day 4. A scene featuring the almost-too-sexy-for-primetime designs of Bill Theiss … and Barbara Luna showing signs of her flu bug (Courtesy of Gerald Gurian)

over again and the company moved camera and lights to engineering, where production would resume on Monday.

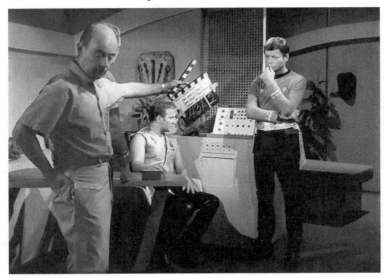

Day 4. Bill McGovern slates a shot in Kirk's cabin (Courtesy of Gerald Gurian)

Day 5, Monday. Scenes in the "Mirror engineering area" were shot, but from a perspective not seen before in the series. The Emergency Manual Monitor -- a part of engineering -- was a new set, built on stilts and positioned to overlook the engineering room. It effectively opened up the main room by increasing its apparent depth. The set would be used again in future episodes.

After the lunch break, Pevney began shooting on the I.S.S. Enterprise bridge.

Day 6, Tuesday. The scenes on the bridge were completed, including the memorable encounter between Uhura and the sinister Sulu where she flirts with him, then slaps his face and pulls a knife. This was one of Nichelle Nichols' most memorable moments in the series. Her look, in her bad-girl parallel universe uniform, is stunning. This may also be George Takei's finest hour on *Star Trek*. The evil Sulu is delicious. Takei said, "The alternative universe image of Sulu as a dark villain in 'Mirror, Mirror' showed something interesting about his human side. And, in 'Naked Time,' he was crazed. Ironically, we only get a chance to see Sulu when he is *not* Sulu." (171-7)

Shot at the end of the day were the sequences in the corridors and the Jefferies Tube with Scott and, standing below him, McCoy, who was now a reluctant assistant engineer.

Day 7, Wednesday, August 2. Scenes in the elevator and the corridor outside were filmed, including the fight between Kirk and the evil Chekov and his henchmen.

Garth Pillsbury, who began by following orders from Chekov, then switched to Kirk's side, said, "I'd never been on a set like that before and it did impress me. I thought, 'Wow, what an incredible job they did making this look real from the camera's point of view.'" (143a)

The scene begins with Kirk exiting the elevator and getting smacked in the face. Pillsbury was the one cast to give the hit to the face. He recalled, "I said, 'Okay, I'll do that.' And Shatner says, 'Oh no, no, you won't. I'm going to get a stunt man to do that.' So they had a stunt man step in. But that was me taking the fall when Kirk did the punching. And you wanted to see me punched. That's why my agent said the character was kind of a wise guy; his look is telling us that he's thinking, 'Man, I just did you a favor'; like he's just begging for it. And Kirk decks him. But Shatner didn't hit me. People can't tell from the angle of the camera, with his hand moving so fast. But he knew how *not* to hit me. He just didn't trust me to be as careful, and you can't blame him. He gets a broken nose and they're done for the day. I get a broken nose and the director yells 'cut' and they move on to the next scene. So everything went just fine. And then Marc Daniels yelled 'cut,' I was out of there for a year until 'The Cloud Minders.' Marc Daniels didn't have much to say to me. I did my lines, I got decked and I left." (143a)

Regardless, Daniels took great care with the direction and many fine touches are present. Note how the shot which opens this scene begins with instant action, when Kirk exits the elevator and is smacked in the face. Other examples of Daniels' sense of detail include the relaxed posture of the security men on the bridge whenever Kirk is not present, and how they snap to attention when he is. These men were not even mentioned in the script. Also, from the scene being filmed this day, it was Daniels' idea to assign a Vulcan henchman (played by Russ Peek) to Spock when he confronts Kirk in the corridor. Kirk's henchman was in the script; Spock's was not.

For this scene, while pinned in the agony booth, Walter Koenig was called on to scream. This was his first scream in *Star Trek*. There would be more. "You scream once, you're a screamer ever after," Koenig bemoaned. (102-11)

The brief scene in Spock's quarters, requiring only Nimoy, ended principal filming. But the episode was unfinished and would remain so until Barbara Luna was well.

Day 8, Friday, August 11. Nine days had passed since Marc Daniels finished "Mirror, Mirror." "The Deadly Years" wrapped at noon on this day and, after the lunch break, Daniels got the company back from Joseph Pevney to finish the scene which had been started on July 28. Barbara Luna was looking lovely as ever, although a few pounds lighter.

Day 8. Barbara Luna, back after nearly two weeks, with a new costume designed to conceal her weight loss (Unaired film trim courtesy of Gerald Gurian)

Luna recalled, "That outfit I wore didn't fit after I'd fallen ill -- after missing those couple of weeks. I've always been tiny but, I guess, in those two weeks, because I was just so ill, that I must have lost a little bit of weight, because when I went back into the cabin to shoot that scene, and I'm in the doorway, whatever I was wearing, my original costume, was just hanging on me. I said, 'No, no, no, no, not good.' Roddenberry came in and said, 'Put her in something else.' And Bill Theiss, being the genius he was, put me in a bikini, and he brought in more material, and, right there on the set, I mean literally, he just draped that material on me. And I'm standing in the doorway and you could see right through it. I almost looked nude. And, for that time, this was very daring." (111-3)

As for that kiss which was nearly two weeks in coming, the second and much more passionate kiss between Kirk and Marlena in the episode, Luna said, "I enjoyed 'the kissing scene.' Bill is a good kisser." (111-2)

During the filming of this episode, cinematographer Jerry Finnerman lowered the shipboard lighting levels more than usual for the I.S.S. Enterprise. To simulate how this looked when originally broadcast, before remastering, sneak the brightness level down on your TV until the dark pants are absolutely black. Then you may see why Finnerman received a Producers Guild Award honoring his contribution to cinematography, for his work on the original *Star Trek*.

It was more than just the level of the lighting, however, but also the texture and colors chosen, as demonstrated in the scene that was filmed the final add-on day. Finnerman said, "I got a little braver and I thought, 'What if I add a little color to the sets?... I remember it was in Bill Shatner's cabin... it was a love scene.... I built the lamps and I put nice, beautiful magenta on, and I warmed them up [with] different colors along the walls where I cut the light off.... So, I decided I'd add a little color for backlight to accentuate the walls, and put some color in [the lady's] hair, and Bill's hair." (63-3)

Suddenly, the interior of the Enterprise looked better than ever. Everyone at *Star Trek* agreed. NBC felt differently.

Finnerman said, "We shot the scene and, the next day, I get a call from Gene and he says, 'The head of NBC is coming over to talk to us; he doesn't like the way you're shooting the show with colors.' ... And [the NBC man is] criticizing everything I do. And he said... 'No colors on the walls, no colors on the people, it won't transmit good; it doesn't look

236

good,' and he said, 'And another thing is you're getting too artsy with your lighting.' I said, 'What do you mean?" He says, 'Well, you go in there and you shadow Bill Shatner, you know, put a 'cutter' on him [shadowing all his face except for a slice across his eyes], or you got slices on the wall.' He said, 'Take the light and light fully, because color takes care of itself.' That was the old opinion -- *color takes care of itself.* Well, that insulted me. I said, 'Let me tell you something, look at Harry Stradling's work [*The Picture of Dorian Gray*]; look at Ernie Haller's work [*Gone With the Wind* and "Where No Man Has Gone Before"]; look at [Leon] Shamroy [*Cleopatra*] or Charlie Lang [*Sabrina*], they don't light with a full light and light the whole set. I'm telling *this* story; I have to accentuate it with dimension; you can't do it when everything is lit.' Well, he started to go on and Gene Roddenberry -- thank God I had good producers who backed me and liked me -- he said, 'Look, Ed, we don't know exactly what Jerry is doing, but we like what we see and we're not going to change the style.' So, that was it, he left, [but] he wasn't too happy. And I continued my style, which was the style of Harry Stradling. And it's an interesting style." (63-3)

Post-Production

Available for editing on August 14, 1967. Rough Cut: August 22. Final Cut: August 24.
Music Score recorded on September 8, 1967.

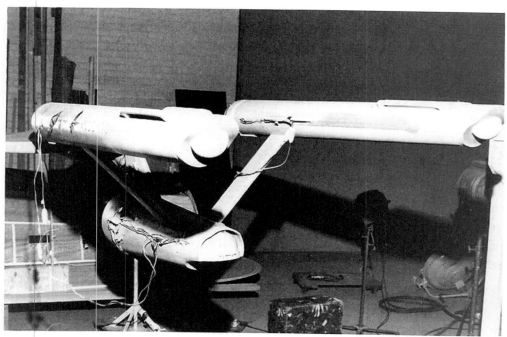

The reason the 11-foot, 2-inch Enterprise model was only shot from the starboard side.
The port side had openings for the electrical cables which powered the interior lights
(Courtesy of Bob Olsen)

Bruce Schoengarth, working with Editing Team 2, delivered his 12th episode, including classics such as "The Naked Time," "The Squire of Gothos," and "Who Mourns for Adonais?" Schoengarth enhanced Marc Daniels' idea for jumping from scene to scene with great vitality in the cutting.

237

Van der Veer Photo Effects created a unique transporter effect, as used by the Mirror Enterprise. A similar process would be used by the Klingons in "Day of the Dove" and by those beaming to the sky city in "The Cloud Minders."

The Mirror Enterprise is seen orbiting the planet from left to right in the Teaser, revealing the ship's port side. This is actually the 11-foot, 2-inch model with points on the nacelles, as it appeared in 1964 while being filmed for the first pilot. The newer version of the model could only be shot from the starboard side, due to holes cut into the port side to allow for access to the internal lights. Also, for

From Van der Veer Photo Effects: composite shot, combining footage taken on the Stage 10 planet set with a camera tie-down shot from the Stage 9 bridge set (Courtesy of Gerald Gurian)

this one brief shot, the planet is red. Throughout the rest of the episode, the planet is purple with some spots of red, matching the color of Jerry Finnerman's sky on Stage 10.

Composer Fred Steiner recorded a new score for this unusual episode, including the lush, sensuous theme to introduce the "captain's woman." A reworking of his "Balance of Terror" Romulan motif became the theme for the twisted Mirror Universe.

For an episode with so many visual pluses, "Mirror, Mirror," at a cost of $188,530, only ran $8,530 above the studio mandated per-episode allowance. The deficit on cash-poor Desilu was now up to $145,971 … more than a cool million in 2013.

Release / Reaction
Premiere air date: 10/6/67. NBC repeat broadcast: 4/12/68.

Steven H. Scheuer reviewed the episode for his syndicated column, *TV Key Previews*. Among the numerous newspapers across the country to carry the review was Lima, Ohio's *Lima News*, on October 6, 1967:

> "Mirror, Mirror." Fans of this series will probably be intrigued by this complicated space tale. All of the favorites of the *Star Trek* crew are suddenly transposed into savage doubles of themselves, wreaking incomprehensible damage to the important diplomatic project that the space ship had been negotiating. The details of the plot are not nearly as interesting as the character changes and subsequent conflicts between Mr. Spock and Captain Kirk.

Judy Crosby reviewed the episode for her syndicated column, *TV SCOUT*. Among the papers which ran her notice on October 13, 1967, was *The Edwardsville Intelligencer*, in Edwardsville, Illinois:

"Mirror, Mirror." *Star Trek* has the look of *Voyage to the Bottom of the Sea* tonight, where every few weeks that submarine crew finds themselves fighting their duplicates. Here, it is a massive ion storm that is credited with transforming similar starship characters from a different universe. Mr. Spock is sadistically malevolent with his mustache and beard, dealing out punishment with a devil's joy. Captain Kirk, who has not been transformed, discovers that his Kirk counter-part is dealing in genocide, among other things, and that these creatures in his spaceship have a unique system of progression, through assassination.

RATINGS / Nielsen National report for Friday, October 6, 1967:

8:30 to 9 pm, 56.5% of U.S. TVs in use.	Share:	Households:
NBC: *Star Trek* (first half)	23.6%	9,740,000
ABC: *Hondo* (first half)	24.5%	10,580,000
CBS: **Gomer Pyle, U.S.M.C.**	**44.7%**	**15,900,000**
Local independent stations:	7.2%	No data

9 to 9:30 pm, 58.3% of U.S. TVs in use.	Share:	Households:
NBC: *Star Trek* (second half)	23.2%	No data
ABC: *Hondo* (second half)	24.8%	No data
CBS: **Friday Night Movie**	**41.0%**	**No data**
Local independent stations:	11.0 %	No data

The movie on CBS was *Viva Las Vegas*, starring Elvis Presley. On this night, with the younger viewers wanting to see the King, *Star Trek* fell to No. 3.

Again, the numbers leaned in a different direction when only metropolitan areas were polled. The national report had *Hondo* with a 1% audience share above that of *Star Trek*. The 12-city Trendex report showed the opposite, this time with *Star Trek* taking a similar lead over *Hondo*.

Averaged rating for 8:30 to 9:30 pm:	Trendex rating:
NBC: *Star Trek*	14.2
ABC: *Hondo*	13.6
CBS: **Gomer Pyle, U.S.M.C. / Friday Night Movie**	21.2

All of the inspired work on "Mirror, Mirror" came together to create an episode worthy of a nomination for a Hugo award -- one of five *Star Trek* nominations for 1967, with the winner to be selected at the awards show on Labor Day weekend, 1968.

Nichelle Nichols named "Mirror, Mirror" as one of her favorite *Star Trek* episodes. She said, "I loved any of the episodes in which the various characters were able to interact with one another and advance the storyline at the same time. We *were* the first ensemble cast." (127-3)

William Shatner considered this to be among *Star Trek*'s "very finest." (156-8)

Trek magazine took a poll in the mid-1970s. Its readers picked their favorite episodes. "Mirror, Mirror" came in No. 10.

Entertainment Weekly's editors picked "Mirror, Mirror" as the third best episode

239

from the original series, writing, "Worth repeat viewings, if only to see Spock's goatee."

Star Trek 101, a reference work published by Pocket books in 2008, placed "Mirror, Mirror" among the original series' ten best.

From the Mailbag

Received shortly after the first broadcast of "Mirror, Mirror":

> Dear Mr. Theiss, I have intended to write this letter ever since Sherry Jackson, the comely android, "turned on" Capt. Kirk in her kangaroo-pouch jump suit (suppose a cigarette ash had slithered down into wide open places ... what then???). Or perhaps it went a little further back when Susan Oliver tried to belly-dance her way into Capt. Pike's heart (even all *those* wide open spaces didn't cow our dauntless hero).... So far this season there have been only a few episodes and I see you're falling back into your *wild* and wooly ways. Leslie Parrish's costume in "Who Mourns for Adonais?," though quite revealing, might be excused as being reminiscent of the beautiful and inspiring ancient mythologies. Incidentally, what held that costume in place -- tape or determination -- or both? But I honestly thought the costume (or lack thereof) worn by "the Captain's woman" in "Mirror, Mirror" was crass, vulgar, tawdry, and altogether unnecessary. We got the point from the text. You needn't have drawn pictures. When the semi-nude mistress made her appearance, my husband and I decided our children should retire. They may have missed the implications on the dialogue, but they could hardly miss the outfit she *didn't* wear.... If *Star Trek* was a second-rate, unimaginative vehicle, peopled by second-rate, untalented thespians, it may have need of the bizarre costumes heretofore mentioned -- if only to bolster lagging ratings. But such is definitely not the case. *Star Trek* is, without a doubt, one of the best series ever produced, thanks to Gene Roddenberry. The story-line is without parallel and completely authentic (my scientist husband keeps close tabs), and it boasts not one, but several actors so dimensional in their portrayals, any one of who could singly carry a series, at least in my opinion.... It falls upon your able shoulders to provide us with a futuristic wardrobe which should be "way out" but *not* "way off." Mrs. Connie K. (Ellicott City, Maryland).

The response:

> Dear Mrs. K.,... Thank you for your letter regarding the costumes. We agree with you regarding Bill Theiss's imaginative creative ability. On the other hand, you should be aware that he must necessarily design costumes in keeping with the producer's instructions and the content of the script. The female buccaneer's costume was dictated by the thematic content of that particular script, and was certainly not designed in any way to promote "tawdry semi-nudity." It is inevitable that different people have different ideas and attitudes toward what is in good taste. I have children too and would put nothing on the screen I thought was wrong for them to see. No doubt if our positions were reversed, you would occasionally do things which I might object to. But as long as either of us are sincere and honest with himself or herself, then it is an honest difference of opinion and we can both live with it. Sincerely, Gene Roddenberry, Executive Producer, *Star Trek*.

Memories

Vic Perrin reflected, "At that time, there was a congeniality among the people doing series television. You felt you were part of the family even though you were only in for a day or so. You had that feeling on *Star Trek*, of being wanted, accepted.... The memories I have working on that show are all pleasant ones. You were made to feel welcome and important to the scene's success." (138)

Barbara Luna said, "I've had five-year-olds come up to me -- and I mean recently [2011] -- and say, 'Marlena! Marlena!' I mean, for being in just one episode, I've had five action figures [made out of me]. I think that's history making. I just don't get it. I understand the popularity of the show; and I understand that 'Mirror Mirror' is one of the more popular segments, but I watched the show recently and I come into it 20 minutes after it starts, so I don't understand why I get the compliments that I do. I just don't quite understand why that performance stands apart from any other shows that I did, like a role on *The Big Valley*, which I liked, and *Hawaii Five-O*, which was just great. I'm told how 'Mirror, Mirror' is popular with the fans but, comparatively speaking, I don't quite see it. I know that 'Trouble with Tribbles' is right up there, and I understand why. And 'Amok Time.' And I happen to like the one with Joan Collins ['The City on the Edge of Forever']. I love that. So, comparatively speaking, I don't quite get it that 'Mirror, Mirror' is as popular as it is. I can only suspect that, well, maybe because Leonard Nimoy wore a beard. [laughing] And he looked great!" (111-1)

Dorothy Fontana had no problem getting it. She said, "A great concept. We hadn't done anything like that. It was a fun show to do." (64-3)

15

Episode 40: THE DEADLY YEARS

Written by David P. Harmon
(with Gene L. Coon, uncredited)
Directed by Joseph Pevney

Promotional photo, with an aged DeForest Kelley and William Shatner (Courtesy of Gerald Gurian)

From NBC press release, issued November 13, 1967:

Captain Kirk (William Shatner) loses command of the Enterprise when he takes a landing party to a planet to check the progress of a scientific experiment and exposes all of them to a disease, in "The Deadly Years" on NBC Television Network's *Star Trek* colorcast Friday, Dec. 8.... There are only three survivors of the scientific group, all under 30, and they die almost immediately from rapidly advancing old age and senility. Kirk, Spock (Leonard Nimoy), Scott (James Doohan), Dr. McCoy (DeForest Kelley) and Dr. [sic] Galway (Beverly Washburn) become infected and only Ensign Chekov (Walter Koenig) seems immune. They return to the Enterprise to develop a cure. Kirk, due to his sudden senility, is replaced by Captain [sic] Stocker (guest-star Charles Drake), a passenger who nearly loses the ship. Sarah Marshall portrays Janet Wallace.

Wallace is a former flame of Kirk's and traveling to Starbase 10 with Stocker. After Stocker pressures Spock into conducting a ship's hearing to evaluate Kirk's competence, then relieves the Captain, he orders the Enterprise to proceed to Starbase, via a shortcut across hostile Romulan space.

Advancing old age is the monster here and proved to be a truly frightening one in the eyes of the youth-obsessed audience that dominated America in the 1960s … and have since moved into their middle or senior years. Going one step further, it is an examination of the tragic aspects of aging, the loss of status and forced retirement, using Kirk as the primary

242

subject as he is reduced to a mere shadow of his former self … and losing his one true love, the Enterprise.

SOUND BITES

- *Spock*: "Doctor, the ship's temperature is increasingly uncomfortable for me. I have adjusted the environment in my quarters to 125 degrees, which is at least tolerable." *McCoy*: "Well, I can see I won't be making any house calls on you!" *Spock*: "I was wondering if there was something which could lower my sensitivity to cold." *McCoy:* "I'm not a magician, Spock, just an old country doctor." *Spock*: "Yes, I always suspected."

- *Chekov*: "Give us some more blood, Chekov. The needle won't hurt, Chekov. Take off your shirt, Chekov. Roll over, Chekov. Breathe deeply, Chekov. Blood samples, Chekov; marrow samples, Chekov; skin samples, Chekov! If, *if* I live long enough, I'm going to run out of samples!" *Sulu*: "You'll live." *Chekov*: "Oh, yes. I'll live. But I will not enjoy it."

ASSESSMENT

As with "Mirror, Mirror," it shouldn't have worked. "The Deadly Years" is one of *Star Trek*'s more fantastic and unbelievable episodes. Even if we accept the concept of the "physical degeneration" that resembles accelerated aging to the degree of 30 years to the day, the idea that an injection of an adrenalin derivative could rejuvenate members of the crew in a matter of minutes and have them return to the same exact age, physical state, *and haircut*, as before being afflicted, seems absurd. Yet the magic that was *Star Trek* insured this far-fetched concept translated into an hour of entertaining and even compelling television.

THE STORY BEHIND THE STORY

Script Timeline

David P. Harmon's story outline, ST #70, "Hold Back Tomorrow": May 1967.
Harmon's revised story outline, gratis, now "The Deadly Years": June 5, 1967.
Harmon's 1ˢᵗ Draft teleplay: June 19, 1967.
Harmon's 2ⁿᵈ Draft teleplay: July 3, 1967.
Gene Coon's script polish (Mimeo Department "Yellow Cover 1ˢᵗ Draft"): Mid July 1967.
Coon's rewrite (Final Draft teleplay): July 27, 1967.
Additional page revisions by Gene Coon: July 31 & August 2 & 3, 1967.

David P. Harmon, 48, wrote three scripts for *Star Trek* (including one for the 1970s animated series). His television career began in 1953, scripting numerous cop shows and westerns. For the big screen he wrote several small budget movies which went on to achieve semi-cult status. The psychological-western *Johnny Concho*, starring Frank Sinatra, borrowed from *High Noon* with its theme of one man standing alone against tyranny. For Roger Corman, Harmon wrote 1957's *Rock All Night*, about a hangout for teenagers taken over by a pair of escaped killers who hold the teens captive. *The Shadow in the Window* flipped the scenario, having a band of teenagers, led by a psychotic (John Drew Barrymore), take over an isolated farmhouse, killing the owner and holding hostage a woman and her young son (played by a pre-*Leave it to Beaver* Jerry Mathers). *The Last of the Fast Guns* has been called a "film noir, thriller western." *Reprisal!* was a western that made a bold statement about prejudice against Native Americans. And then there was 1962's *Wonderful World of the Brothers Grimm*, the grand George Pal "road show" picture, with a running time of over two hours, not counting the overture and intermission. Back on television, Harmon was especially liked and worked often on *The Detectives*, starring Robert Taylor, *The Aquanauts*, featuring underwater adventures with Ron Ely (later to become TV's Tarzan), and *Man with a Camera*, Charles Bronson's series about a former war photographer turned freelancer. Harmon also wrote comedy, including several episodes of *Gilligan's Island*, as well as serving as script consultant on that series for its third season. And he mixed science fiction with comedy in the short-lived *It's About Time*.

Harmon got to know Gene Roddenberry and Gene Coon when he served on the Writers Guild Board of Directors. One day while on the Desilu lot for a meeting, Harmon popped in to say "hello" to Coon. Someone else popped in to say "hi" a few minutes later -- Jack Arnold, who had directed a pair of screenplays Coon had written (*No Name on the Bullet*, starring Audie Murphy, and *Man in the Shadow*, starring Jeff Chandler and Orson Welles). It was reunion time; Arnold knew Harmon, too, since both had worked together at *Gilligan's Island*.

Harmon explained. "[Jack] mentioned to Coon that I had done some shows for him, and he suggested I do a script for *Star Trek*. Naturally, this put Gene and me both on the spot, but [Gene] agreed that it would be a good idea." (79-2)

Harmon was invited to come back when he had a story idea to discuss. Of the genesis for "The Deadly Years," he said, "I was inspired to write the script by examining the American syndrome versus the Oriental reverence of old age. The concept of youth and beauty is such a shallow one, simply because it doesn't last very long. That's the inch of truth I was looking for. How important is it in the overall scheme of things in a person's life, if at all? But we make it important." (79-2)

Harmon's May 1967 treatment was called "Hold Back Tomorrow."

Dorothy Fontana sent a memo to Coon, recommending the title be changed since John T. Dugan's "Return to Tomorrow" was already on the production slate. She also suggested McCoy be included in the landing party and he too be affected by premature aging. At this stage, the story had only Kirk, Spock, Scotty, and Uhura subjected to the strange phenomenon.

Fontana also requested Nurse Chapel be added to the cast, since so much of the story revolved around sickbay.

Roddenberry sent Coon his reaction to Harmon's outline two days later, writing:

> Perhaps there is a story in this, but the writer does not seem to have found it. As it now stands, it would make a slow, talky script. First of all, there is little legitimate conflict between the characters involved. Essentially it is a story of men against "something," not men against men, or man against himself. Not that we need a villain, but if we don't have one then certainly our people must fight at least the villainy within themselves. Here, they fight neither. (GR40)

Indeed, there was a complete lack of conflict between the characters, except that Commodore Cooke (later to be named Stocker) wanted to take command of the Enterprise from the aging Kirk. But his character was murky. It is not even explained why he was on board the ship. And the hearing to determine if Kirk is fit for command was run by Cooke alone. Not drawing Spock into the power play was a lost opportunity for conflict between him and Kirk.

Roddenberry had other concerns, telling Coon:

> It seems unbelievable that Kirk and the others would age so far in about 72 hours. A story like this should -- with dissolves and voiceovers -- stretch out for

several weeks.... The disease is never explained. As always on *Star Trek*, our minimum need is something that can be made to sound possible. Neither does the "cure" sound possible. (GR40)

Roddenberry was also protective of Uhura, and Nichelle Nichols' image. Nichols would have been displeased to know a great acting part was snatched away from her by a former lover who did not wish to see her as anything other than young and beautiful. Roddenberry told Coon:

Recommend that if we do this story -- rather, if we find a way of doing it -- that we do not have Uhura grow old. (GR40)

Harmon was asked to revise his outline, *gratis*. The title was changed to "The Deadly Years." Cooke was now being ferried to Starbase 10 where he was eager to assume his command post. McCoy was among the afflicted. Uhura was not. Lt. Galway was added to take Uhura's place and be the female in the group who was ravaged by sudden age. The disease was explained, somewhat, as caused by a form of radiation. The aging period was stretched by a few days. The Man against Man element (Kirk versus Cooke) was sharpened, and a dose of Man against Himself was added (Kirk's denial over no longer being fit to command). And Nurse Chapel was now included in the sickbay scenes.

This draft was sent to NBC. Overall, Stan Robertson was happy, especially with how the Teaser began on the surface of a planet instead of the Enterprise. He wrote Coon:

Let me reiterate my feelings of how pleased we are to see a storyline with an opening which is different from what had become our almost "standard" beginning. (SR40)

But Robertson had misgivings. He told Coon:

The major concern we have is that it appears to us that the writer has paralyzed beyond dramatic necessity and subsequent viewer interest a point which was made and made very excitingly in our Teaser and in Act 1. That is, the factor of the mystery ailment which has suddenly struck down some of the most important members of our crew at an astonishingly fast rate. It would seem that after having established that fact, in order to strengthen our story, we would want to compound the pressures with which our heroes are faced by laying in earlier the added jeopardy of the Romulan attack. Our point is that we all know that Kirk and his people will survive the mystery ailment, and, after we have been initially confronted with it, our next question is how will they? (SR40)

Coon ignored Stan Robertson's suggestion. Many at *Star Trek* were coming to believe that the network production manager was unable to comprehend how story outlines only appear to lack excitement because the things that create excitement -- the execution of the story, through character conflicts prompted by dialogue -- had yet to be inserted. Roddenberry would later write a scolding letter to Robertson, saying:

We welcome comment but no one here is going to sit quietly when we receive letters which seem to suggest that on the slender basis of a story outline you can guess all our plans and conversations about the story and can make the final omniscient decision that it will or will not translate into a good or varied script. (94-8)

Coon trusted, or gambled, that Robertson would see the true potential of the story's dramatic elements once the scenes were fleshed out in a teleplay.

Harmon's 1st Draft script was completed on June 19.

Fontana wrote Coon:

This story has excellent potential, but… I find a great many things wrong with this draft, <u>including the plot</u>. (DC40-3)

Some of the great many things wrong, as indicated in Fontana's seven-page memo, included:

> McCoy -- we all know -- is some ten years older than Kirk. Why is he not aging more than Kirk? Scott is also older -- comparable to Doc. He should logically be aging more than Kirk…. Believe Spock, due to his much longer lifespan, would be less affected or more slowly affected -- but he too should begin to show some signs of aging…. I suppose we need Cooke, but the situation is too much like that of Decker in "Doomsday Machine." I would almost rather lose [the] Cooke angle of the story and build up Janet's part. (DC40-3)

In "The Doomsday Machine," Commodore Decker takes command of the Enterprise away from Spock during Kirk's absence. Here, in this draft, Commodore Cooke, by conducting the competency hearing, wrests command away from both Spock and Kirk.

Fontana continued, gunning for Cooke, telling Coon:

> Page 8 – Cooke's statement that his records show differently… that none of the research team had reached thirty… is thickheaded. But since he makes this kind of statement throughout the show, I probably shouldn't quibble…. Cooke makes a bonehead remark when he says he's sure the Romulans, when they understand the emergency, will honor it…. Cooke, as stupid as he seems to be, would know about the Romulan's invisibility shields. (DC40-3)

Fontana was not any more pleased with the character of Janet, a scientist traveling aboard the Enterprise, who previously had been a lover of Kirk's. Fontana wrote:

> It seems pretty bitchy of Janet to tell Kirk there was only one problem between them … her husband. With him gone there is no reason why they can't pick up exactly where they left off. It suggests an illicit romance, and colors her as a tramp…. Page 67 -- Kirk apologizes for having "forced himself on Janet." With one kiss? What kind of Boy Scout is he? Besides, she was asking for more than that, and he wouldn't give it. Janet is quite right when she says he didn't do anything wrong. I think we can amend that speech so she can say "You didn't do anything <u>at all</u>." … Please rewrite Kirk's line "Can I offer you a cup of coffee? Or something?" Please do not have them exiting into Kirk's quarters. Can we please get rid of Janet? (DC40-3)

Justman also noticed the Tag scene where Kirk offers Janet "a cup of coffee or something," then escorts her from the corridor into his cabin, with the door sliding shut behind them and picture fading down. His comment to Coon:

> As far as I'm concerned, this show ends at the bottom of Page 72. The scene in the Hallway between Kirk and Janet, which follows, I feel should be eliminated. I feel this very strongly. I think NBC will agree with me, but not for any dramatic reasons. (RJ40-2)

Fontana was looking for ways to get more to do for the supporting regular cast members. She told Coon:

> Page 23 -- Ensign Chekov is twenty-two [not 19 as Harmon wrote]. Also, I count three scenes and about ten lines for him in all. If we are going to use him, we must use him well and fully…. Pages 28-29 -- Instead of Yeoman Atkins with the report business, why don't we use Uhura? She could make some kind of routine report to him… and then have him ask for it again. This way we would save a bit player and also use one of our regulars more…. Pages 39-40 --

[During the hearing] it should be Uhura and not Yeoman Atkins who answers questions about the report. This can be combined with the testimony on the following page about the Code Two and Code Three error.... Page 59 -- It is noted that Christine has been moving in and out of Sickbay for the past three acts, "like the unobtrusive nurse she is." I remind you we pay a great deal of money for her to act unobtrusive in three acts. If she's going to be there, she should be doing things. Can we get rid of the stupid dame Janet and use Christine more? (DC40-3)

Justman commented:

For Christ's sake! I just looked carefully at Page 59 and discovered that Nurse Christine Chapel has been moving "in and out of Sickbay for the past three acts, like the unobtrusive nurse that she is." I suggest that we eliminate this reference. Otherwise, you're liable to discover that I am going to move out of *Star Trek* like the unobtrusive Associate Producer that I am. And I may not return. Ever! $333 a day is not unobtrusive, insofar as I am concerned. (RJ40-2)

To keep his associate producer from moving out of the building, and to appease Ms. Fontana, Coon gave Nurse Chapel a few obligatory lines of sickbay-type dialogue.

Fontana's notes continued:

Kirk doesn't do much except stand around. He should refuse to give up command no matter what, until -- in a very stormy and emotional scene -- Spock is forced to relieve him of command.... [And] Kirk's speeches are formal to the point of boredom. He also has a tendency to make hero statements, such as, "It's a calculated risk a Starship commander often has to take." In the immortal words of R. H. Justman ... ech!" (DC40-3)

Justman passed along the remainder of his immortal words with fewer instances of "ech" than normal. He told Coon:

You may be surprised to discover that I consider this a very fine first draft screenplay. Very unusual for a first time writer on our series to come up with something this close to a shootable version. Granted, the script is over-long and our characters quite often say the wrong things at the wrong times, but the script is the sort of script that we attempt to get and it is replete with excitement and suspense. (RJ40-2)

Regardless, Justman came up with 11 pages of problems. He told Coon:

I am rather distressed by the fact that we intimate that Captain Kirk was playing hanky-panky with Janet while her husband was still alive. I would much prefer to set up a situation whereby Kirk and Janet couldn't make it with each other because each one was extremely intent upon following a most difficult and demanding career. (RJ40-2)

This was done, and served the story well. It was established that the husband came along *after* Janet and Kirk parted company due to conflicting career goals. It was Coon's idea that the husband was older, providing the interesting situation where, after Kirk begins to age, Janet is more attracted to him.

Referring to a game of bluff Kirk plays with the Romulans, Justman added:

I like the "Corbomite Maneuver" play. However, we will need a line of explanation for the benefit of new viewers. (RG40-2)

Coon disagreed that explanation was needed. He felt the reactions of the bridge crew members would signal to viewers that this was a familiar part of Kirk's bag of tricks, even if they had not seen "The Corbomite Maneuver."

Justman continued:

> Do we need Cooke at all in this story? Is he not rather extraneous when compared with the major threads of this story?... I don't feel that he hurts the story at all, but I do feel that his areas within the screenplay at the present time do need careful examination. (JG40-2)

Careful examination determined that Commodore Cooke *was* needed. In fact, *more* Cooke was needed. And by suggestion of De Forest Research, a name change was needed too, to keep the audience from being bumped out of the story as their minds wandered, recalling the exploits of the famed British explorer Captain Cook.

Finally, Justman had thoughts regarding the aging process of the inflicted crew members and shared with Coon:

> Incidentally, I feel that we are going to have to set up a definite number of makeup changes for each one of our characters in this show. And we cannot have too many of them, because we will never have enough time to shoot the show if we are continually fooling around with the aging process. Therefore, with respect to Captain Kirk, I suggest about four different changes. The first change would be Kirk in normal 34-year-old state. His second change would be the same makeup, but he would move more slowly and indicate a certain lack of quick reflex action. His gait would be slower and he might limp just a trifle. He would be slightly stooped or hunched over as he moved. There would be definite indication of weariness and other physical attributes which Bill Shatner could so well provide. His third change would be a definite makeup change in which he would appear to be approximately 55 to 60 years old. There would be lines and wrinkles on his face. His hair would be graying. There would be a very definite slowing down of his movements and his limp would be much more pronounced. Aches and pains would be apparent in the way he moved. Naturally, his speech would slow down appreciably at times and his voice would have a weakness which would become very apparent to the audience. Also, the pitch of his voice would have a tendency to vary. Weariness would be very evident. His fourth makeup change would be the change which shows the most difference. Here we would have a need for facial appliances. There would be heavy wrinkles and creases. There would be dark shadows under his eyes and his hair would be white at the temple only. He would be jowly and his gait would have slowed to a shuffle. He would be very erratic in his speech, in that at times he would be speaking rather quickly and then suddenly hesitate and slow down appreciably. The pitch of his voice would alter frequently and his projection would not be very strong at all. His eyes would be watery. His uniform would fit badly in the respect that it would seem over-large on him. This is very important and would help Bill enormously in his characterization. By the time he reaches this last change, his tunic should be over-large and the sleeves should be too long. Also, he would hold onto objects in order to maintain his balance at times. All in all, I think Bill could have a ball with this concept and I am certain that our regulars could also. (JG40-2)

Harmon's 2nd Draft was dated July 3. Justman had seven pages of notes. His memo told Coon:

> I get the feeling from reading Chekov's dialogue that he has been written as a Polack-Bohunk [someone ridiculed for their Polish or East European descent], rather than a quite bright, Russian intellectual.... I am disturbed by the fact that I feel we have had a better scene in the previous version. I am referring to the sequence between Kirk and McCoy when the doctor discovers that Kirk has

been afflicted with arthritis. I think that the scene played much better and the dialogue was much more believable for him to detect the signs of encroaching old age and to make the logical deduction that perhaps everybody who transported down with him and Kirk to the planet may have been affected in an examination. I like the idea of him calling Scotty to come up for an examination. I like the idea of him bringing up the fact that even he is starting to look older. (RJ40-3)

But Coon liked the idea of the shock of seeing Scotty walk into sickbay out of the blue with grey hair and a face creased with lines. For the most part, the scene stayed as written.

Justman had more. He told Coon:

I do feel that we have gotten some of our people much too old much too soon in this story. After all, this is only the beginning of Act III. If we have Arlene past seventy already and Scotty also over seventy, and have McCoy about sixty and Kirk not quite as old as McCoy, then where the hell do we go from here? Are we going to end up with our people over one hundred years old apiece? I suggest that you refer back to my well-thought-out analysis in my previous memo.

Justman was satisfied with the changes made to give Cooke/Stocker a stronger presence. And he liked the name change, too. He told Coon:

This Briefing Room Scene in Act III is a highly dramatic and exciting scene. It is therefore, as we should all realize, not necessary to have action in order to have interest. Please remind me of this the next time I complain about an Act being uninteresting or dull. All we need to do is have some exciting dramatic conflicts and everything falls right into line…. I consider the character of Stocker much improved in this rewrite. However, I do wish he wouldn't cop out too much in his last scene. (RJ40-2)

Coon, in one of many changes made to the script for the Yellow Cover 1st Draft, got rid of the copout and, instead, had Stocker graciously tell Kirk that he was now aware of exactly what a starship could do … with the right man at the helm.

And now, with the right man having been at the typewriter keys, the script was sent off to the network and the cast.

Leonard Nimoy responded with a note to Roddenberry, writing:

I would like to refer you to the fact that in the past we have established that Vulcan life span is approximately three times that of humans. That being the case, Spock being on the high side of 50 (page 23) leaves some question as to whether that age is meaningful, perhaps the best thing to do is to drop the Vulcan age entirely, or be much more specific about it and actually point up the fact that Spock may be again to the point of 100 years or more, which would bring him more in line with some of the aging processes that are taking place with the other people. (LN40)

Roddenberry agreed and had Coon change the line from McCoy to say, "You are perfectly healthy, for a normal Vulcan on the high side of 100!"

Nimoy's memo continued:

I believe we're missing a very valuable opportunity in having [only] Captain [sic] Stocker interrogate Kirk and the other witnesses at Kirk's hearing. This could in effect be a very powerful dramatic scene between Kirk and Spock, since it is strongly established that Spock does not want the hearing to take place at all, and we'd have some excellent drama to play with that sub-text working. Spock is forced not only to attend, but to actually prosecute. (LN40)

Roddenberry talked it over with Coon. Nimoy had given them an excellent idea. Fontana had made a suggestion along this line earlier, but without the element that made it possible, that Spock would be following Starfleet regulations and pushed into doing so by Stocker. Coon rewrote the script again, creating the July 27 Final Draft. Spock was now reluctantly running the hearing and personally questioning each witness, at great embarrassment to Kirk. This prompted the excellent scene in Kirk's quarters where Spock brings the bad news, and his Captain throws him out, saying, "You disloyal, traitorous … You stabbed me in the back the first chance you had.… Get out of here! I don't ever want to have to look at you again."

Nimoy's comments also prompted the memorable moment in sickbay, and the stinging line from Kirk to Spock, "What are you doing here? … Maybe you'd like to relieve Dr. McCoy!"

Coon polished the material further, with page revisions dated July 31, August 2, and August 3. Filming began the same day as the final script changes, which deleted what could have made for an entertaining sequence, seeing Kirk rejuvenate. Of this, Justman had written Coon:

> I like the idea of having Captain Kirk get younger as he makes his way toward the Bridge. However, when he enters the Bridge on Page 68, he still should not be his old youthful self. He should still move a little stiffly and a little slowly. His voice should be slightly cracked. (RJ40-2)

Until the last draft, this is how the script played. When the makeup schedule was being prepared for what was planned as a standard six-day production, the ramifications of this process became clear. It would push filming into a seventh day. Coon therefore struck the sequence from the script, replacing it with a scene in sickbay, with a shot of Kirk's lower torso and legs as he contorts on a bed, and Janet Wallace telling McCoy, "The aging process has stopped. He's becoming stronger."

As it turned out, the six days would go to seven anyway (see Production Diary).

Pre-Production
July 25-28 and 31 & August 1 and 2, 1967 (7 days prep).

Still alternating episodes with Marc Daniels, it was now Joseph Pevney's turn to direct. "The Deadly Years" was his eleventh assignment for the series.

Charles Drake, hired to play Commodore Stocker, was 49. He had enjoyed a long career in film and television beginning in 1939, primarily in key supporting roles. He was

Charles Drake, with Lex Barker and Merle Oberon during filming of *The Price of Fear* (Universal International Pictures, 1956)

the young, sympathetic Dr. Sanderson in *Harvey*, the hero from *You Never Can Tell*, Shelley Winters' cowardly boyfriend in *Winchester '73*, and he had a brush with science fiction in 1953's *It Came from Outer Space*.

Sarah Marshall, as Dr. Janet Wallace, was 34. She was nominated for a Tony award in 1960 and, in television, had prominent guest roles on *The Twilight Zone*, *I Spy*, and *The Wild, Wild West*. She had also worked with Shatner twice before, on stage in *The World of Suzie Wong*, and in an episode of *The Nurses*.

Marshall was excited to be cast. She said, "I was just like a fan. I couldn't wait to meet Leonard Nimoy, and see how the sliding doors worked." (114)

Days before Marshall was able to meet Al, the sliding door man, she met Bill Theiss.

"I remember the costume fittings

Sarah Marshall and Peter Graves in *The Alfred Hitchcock Hour* (Revue Studios, 1963)

were much more extensive than normal," she said. "Normally you go on these shows and somebody would have a line of dresses and you'd get fitted for them. But for *Star Trek*, they made them from scratch because they had to be futuristic. I remember that dress to this day, the feel of it and everything. It was wonderful." (114)

Dorothy McGuire and Beverly Washburn in *Old Yeller* (Walt Disney Productions, 1957)

Beverly Washburn, as Arlene Galway, the only non-regular to grow old, was only 23. She had been appearing regularly on television since 1950, starting when she was only six, and was a regular on *The New Loretta Young Show*, playing one of the star's seven children. She was also featured prominently in the film *Old Yeller*.

"I wasn't really all that familiar with *Star Trek*," Washburn later admitted. "So I had no idea at the time that this was going to go on to be such a phenomenon later, *like all over the world*. I have to admit I hadn't even seen it. I had to go in and read for the role, and they kind of explained it to me." (179a)

Carolyn Nelson, the blonde yeoman who is forced to offer testimony against Kirk, would soon become the wife of director Joseph Sargent ("The Corbomite

251

Maneuver") and appeared in many of his films, including *The Taking of Pelham One Two Three.*

For this episode, Majel Barrett did double-duty. She appeared as Nurse Christine Chapel, for the fifth time in the series, and also provided the voice of the Enterprise's computer.

And then the real work began.

Production Diary
Filmed August 3, 4, 7, 8, 9, 10 & 11 (2 day), 1967.
(Planned as 6 day production, running 2 day over; budget raised to $186,230).

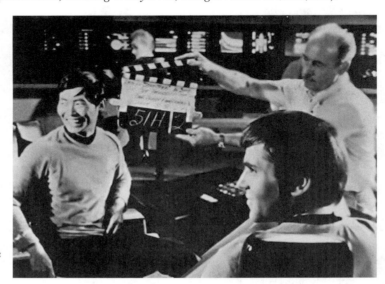

Day 2. A lighter moment on the bridge set
(Courtesy of Gerald Gurian)

Filming commenced on Thursday, August 3, 1967. This was the week the U.S. launched Lunar Orbiter 5 to the Moon (without warp drive, the journey took three days). Here on Earth, 45,000 more U.S. troops were sent to Vietnam. Many of them had been drafted. Mick Jagger and Keith Richards of the Rolling Stones were released from prison after serving 30 days of a one-year sentence for drug possession. 70,934 spectators attended the Chicago All-Star Football Game to see quarterback Bart Starr and the Green Bay Packers defeat the All Stars 37 to zero. The Packers had won the first Super Bowl earlier in the year. "Light My Fire" by the Doors was still the No. 1 song on American radio. That would soon change. The Beatles had just released "All You Need Is Love." The new song would become the anthem for the Summer of Love. The top-selling album, of course, was *Sgt. Pepper's Lonely Hearts Club Band.* Underneath it: The Monkees' *Headquarters* and Jefferson Airplane with *Surrealistic Pillow. In the Heat of the Night* with Sidney Poitier and Rod Steiger was new in the movie houses and already the box office champ.

On the night of the first day of production for "The Deadly Years," NBC was repeating the *Star Trek* episode "Balance of Terror," which *TV Guide* gave its CLOSE-UP listing to as the show to watch. As it happened often during *Star Trek*'s first season, the series won its time slot and proved to be NBC's highest-rated Thursday night show. On this night, *Star Trek* pulled in 32% of the TV sets running in America, with an estimated 10,650,000 households. *Bewitched*, on ABC, came in second, with 29.7% and roughly 8,620,000 households. On CBS, *My Three Sons* settled for third place, with 24.7% and 7,300,000 households. At 9 p.m., *Star Trek* was still in the lead, with 31.6% of the viewing audience. The CBS movie had 31.6% and *That Girl*, on ABC, brought in 27.5%.

The camera first rolled on the Stage 10 planet set, for the Teaser with Kirk, Spock,

McCoy, Scotty, Chekov, and Galway -- all at their normal ages.

Beverly Washburn recalled, "I had talked to some people about it, saying I was going to be on the show, and they said, 'Oh, that's a great show.' And I was so happy to hear this, and to be a part of it. I hadn't really done anything quite like that." (179a)

After lunch, and a company move to Stage 9, the numerous Act I sickbay scenes were filmed. Washburn said, "It was a warm and welcoming set, and they made me feel very much at ease and calm. But it was a very loose set, too. As an actor, you try to come prepared and know your lines, and I had done that. But everybody just kind of joked around and had fun. And that may have thrown me off a little. I had this one scene, where I was starting not to feel well because I'm starting to age, and I came into the sickbay and I had the line that was something like, 'I don't understand it, I'm just not feeling well.' And so when I came in, I got totally wiped out and I said, 'I feel like hell, I can't remember my next line!' And everybody just cracked up. They didn't get upset or annoyed or anything. It was just hilarious. But I had no idea they would put that on the year-end blooper reel and all these years later it's still being shown at the conventions. It was fun, and it was a great cast." (179a)

Day 2. On Friday, the bridge scenes from Acts I and IV were filmed, which featured normal Kirk and, for the latter, an aged Spock. Also shot were bridge sequences from Acts III and IV, with Stocker in command.

Day 3, Monday. First up was the scene with normal Kirk and Dr. Wallace in the ship's corridor. As this was filmed, Fred Phillips and his staff aged Kelley, Doohan, and Washburn. During the lunch

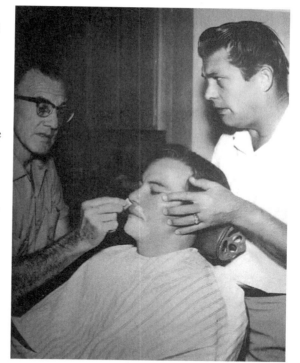

Three stages of Shatner's makeup (this page and next) (Courtesy of Gerald Gurian)

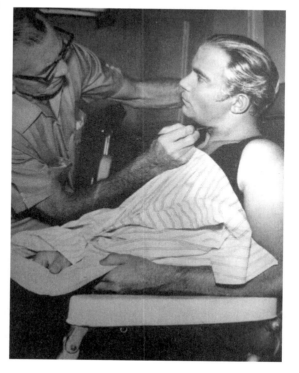

break, as the company moved to sickbay, Shatner went through the aging process. Once he was ready, work continued in the examination room.

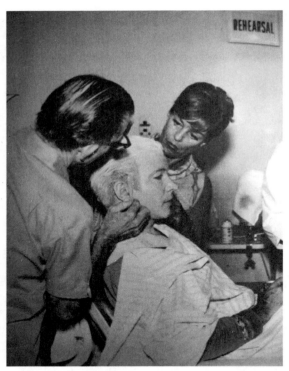

REHEARSAL

**Shatner's final phase of makeup
(Courtesy of Gerald Gurian)**

Beverly Washburn remembered, "When I auditioned, I remember one of the questions they asked me was if I was claustrophobic, because what they had to do was make a plaster cast of my face and I had to breathe through a straw for four hours while the cast was drying. Then they took off the plaster cast, from which they made a rubber mask. When I went in to makeup, they'd put this rubber mask on my face and then they would apply all the wrinkles and everything. Fortunately, I was not claustrophobic. But it was pretty tedious, because I was in makeup four-and-a-half hours. There were quite a few people working on us all at once. It was a big makeup room and we were like on an assembly line -- like busy little bees -- trying to get this done. And having it taken off was also a major procedure because you had all this spirit gum that sticks to your skin that had to be pulled off gently because it would rip your skin or hurt you. So it was quite an ordeal." (179a)

Day 4, Tuesday. Fit to be tied, Pevney was falling behind and still on the sickbay set, filming a scene planned for the day before, where elderly Kirk and McCoy catch the ancient Lt. Galway as she dies.

Washburn said, "Unfortunately, I died, *and I wasn't even wearing red*. The fans know what that means because, typically, if you're wearing red on that show you know you're going to die. And I was wearing blue, so that became a running joke with everyone. And I fell into William Shatner's arms. I always say, 'Well, at least I got to die in Captain's Kirk's arms -- so it wasn't a total loss.'" (179a)

Filming did not begin at the normal start time of 8 a.m. Pevney fumed, "Two or three hours later I would get my first take. It was just ridiculous. It was just a gimmick on the show. Who in the hell cared if the wig wasn't precisely wrinkled in the right place? Nobody's going to know. But the actors no longer cared about schedules." (141-3)

After the lunch break and a move to the bridge, sequences with the older Kirk were filmed. As the company moved to the briefing room, Shatner had his old-age makeup stripped away for the scene involving normal Kirk, Spock, and McCoy, with Stocker and Wallace. After Pevney filmed the wide establishing shots, he went in for Shatner's close-ups. Then Shatner was rushed back to makeup to be transformed to age 65 to 70. While this was happening, Pevney covered the other players' single shots for the briefing room, then quickly made a company move to Kirk's quarters where Old Kirk is informed that he has lost command. Time was not on Old Kirk's side.

Shatner complained, "I spent three hours in the makeup chair one afternoon, just getting made up, and finally, I was ready about five-thirty or six o'clock. I came out on the set after having spent three hours with this painful -- and boring -- process of application, and they said, 'Okay, you're ready? Well, we have to quit. We have to cut at six-twelve.' And I said, 'You can't. I just spent three hours getting made up.' And they brought the producer down -- Gene Coon -- and he tried to go longer, but it was the policy of the studio to quit at six-twelve. So with great reluctance, they quit for the day -- and I ripped off three hours of work without ever once having stepped before the cameras." (156-9)

Shatner's angry old man bit, which director Pevney thought "was not very good," and chatting with the crew on the ship's corridor set (Courtesy of Gerald Gurian)

Shatner actually began ripping it off in front of the camera. In a film clip that would be featured in the *Star Trek* company Christmas party blooper reel, Shatner said to the camera, "Bob Justman, I'm going home now … after spending three hours putting this [expletive deleted] makeup back on. And it's your fault!"

Day 5, Wednesday. This was the most challenging day. The series' regulars had a 4 a.m. call time for a day's work that would last more than 14 hours. Kirk, Spock, McCoy, and Scott, all very old, were needed on camera at the same time. Fred Phillips was given help. With three additional teams, he spent two to six hours each on the aging cast members.

DeForest Kelley said, "I only worked half days on that show because I was in makeup the other half. I'd sit in the chair for a while, then I'd take a break, go to the john, come back and they'd work some more. It was a tremendous makeup effort. There were three makeup men working on me all the time, on my hands and on my face. Leonard was lucky on that show. He was blessed by the fact that Vulcans don't age as fast as humans." (98-8)

Traditionally, female cast members always have an earlier call time than the men, so Sarah Marshall was surprised on her first day to find the series' regulars -- all men -- had beaten her to the makeup chairs. "Pre-dawn!" she exclaimed.

255

"I mean... they had to be there at 4 [a.m.] for the whole episode because they were aging. I rolled in at 7:30 and they'd been sitting there sweltering in those rubber masks for hours. That was the best part. Normally the women have to be there an hour-and-a-half earlier and then people like Bill Shatner sail in and gets his makeup on in fifteen minutes. To have the tables turned was absolutely wonderful!" (114)

Day 5: The trial in the briefing room (above; courtesy of Fred Walder); Kelley getting touched up on set (below; courtesy of Gerald Gurian)

The first scene scheduled was the one missed the previous day, in Kirk's Quarters, with Old Kirk, Old Spock, and Dr. Wallace.

As Robert Justman had suggested, William Shatner wore a bigger uniform top to create the illusion that, as he ages, Kirk's body mass was shrinking.

Next up on this day, the "Trial" in the briefing room. Old Kirk and Old Spock were now joined by Old McCoy and Old Scott. This scene was expected to take a full day, yet it didn't get underway until after the lunch break. They would return the next day to finish it, with another 4 a.m. makeup call.

Day 6, Thursday, August 10. Again, a busy day for the makeup men and four principal cast members. Kirk was made to look 65 and, later, for his fourth stage, to 85. McCoy and Scott were made to appear their oldest, as well. Spock remained at Stage 2.

Filmed this day, the final part of the trial, followed by scenes with an aged Kirk and Spock in the ship's corridor, then a move to the sickbay exam room for the most elderly stage we would see any of the actors. Work started here, but was not completed.

Joseph Pevney recalled, "The big problems [with filming 'The Deadly Years'] were with the egos of the actors, as I remember. Very difficult.... DeForest was very upset, because he had the feeling that this show was *his*, that he was the chief character in the show, and I was spending more time with Bill than I was spending with him." (141-2)

Kelley had thought long and hard about how he was to approach the role. He said, "I began to fall back. I had that in mind from the beginning, that the older he became, the more he would fall back into what he really had a feeling in his heart for. Fortunately, it worked very well." (98-2)

But, according to Pevney, Kelley felt Shatner was copying him. The director said, "We had quite a thing on the stage after the makeup was applied, when he said, 'Bill can't do that, that should be me.' I tried to explain to him the situation. He was playing this old man, and doing it quite well, incidentally, and Bill, I think, was maybe copying some of the things DeForest did to give him an aged look, because Bill was not very good as the old man." (141-3)

Later that night, NBC repeated "This Side of Paradise," again highlighted by *TV Guide* with America's top selling magazine's CLOSE-UP listing. For the second week in a row, *Star Trek* won its time slot, with 9,610,000 households compared to the 8,510,000 tuned in for *Bewitched* on ABC and the 8,340,000 for *My Three Sons* on CBS.

Day 7, Friday, August 11. The production was extended into the first half of a seventh day. For the last scene in sickbay, Shatner, Nimoy, Kelley, and Doohan had to go through the grueling makeup process one more time. At the lunch break, Nimoy, Kelley, and Doohan

James Doohan posing on the engineering set (above) (Courtesy of Kipp Teague) and, for Day 7, Shatner and Kelley at their oldest ages on the sickbay set (below) (Courtesy of Gerald Gurian)

were dismissed. Pevney checked out, too. Shatner had his old age makeup stripped away for his love scenes with the now healthy Barbara Luna, finishing "Mirror, Mirror" under the direction of Marc Daniels.

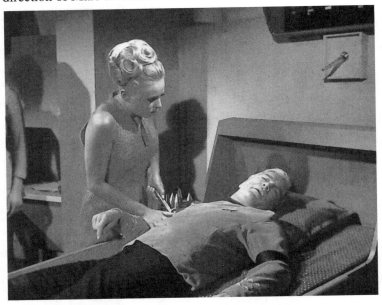

Day 7: Filming in sickbay with Sarah Marshall and William Shatner
(Unaired film trim courtesy of Gerald Gurian)

"The Deadly Years" was a remarkably ambitious TV production for 1967. The producers must have been half-mad to consider taking it on. They were very nearly completely mad by the time it was over.

There were some mistakes, of course. McCoy's hair gets longer as he ages, but retracts to its normal length when he turns 46 again. Kirk's hair thins during his middle-aged years but, once he becomes elderly, thickens. These minor quibbles aside, Fred Phillips deserves recognition for going where no makeup artist had gone before in television.

As for those ages, Kirk is said to be 34. Shatner, at the time this episode was filmed, was actually two years older. Nimoy was also 36. Kelley and Doohan were both 47. To become Old Scotty, James Doohan remembered being in makeup for roughly three hours a day. It was a lot of work for little notice. He said, "They didn't give me any lines during most of the sequences, which is why I sat there looking forlorn and deflated." (52-1)

Post-Production
Available for editing: August 14, 1967. Rough Cut: August 23. Final Cut: September 9.
Music score: tracked.

There were other reasons for the slow downs. Pevney complained, "As you get older, you slow down your speech pattern, and the footage must have dragged on forever. Nobody figured that a page count to time the script is no longer correct when people are older, because they have to stutter and all that business. All of a sudden, toward the second or third day of the show, we began to realize we were going to be way over length. I don't know who did the editing on that show, but it was quite obvious that we'd be overlong." (141-2)

Donald R. Rode, with Editing Team 4, who had edited a season's worth of coming attraction trailers for *Star Trek*, was given the task of fitting all the stammering into 51 minutes. Rode trimmed wherever possible, and some portions of the filmed script were left on the cutting room floor. These cuts included a pair of scenes between Kirk and Dr. Wallace which would have more fully explained their past relationship.

The Westheimer Company got off easy. Other than the transporter shimmer that opens the Teaser, and selected matte shots, such as inserting a shot of outer space into the viewing screen, no optical effects were needed. Footage of the Romulan ship was lifted from "Balance of Terror." The shots of the Enterprise taking hits from an energy weapon were

258

from "Errand of Mercy," while various flybys and planet orbiting shots were from other past episodes.

Composers Sol Kaplan and Fred Steiner shared the music credit, with most of this score coming from earlier episodes. Kaplan's "The Doomsday Machine" music is sprinkled throughout, and Steiner's "Marlena's Theme" from "Mirror, Mirror" works nicely when Kirk, young or old, interacts with Janet Wallace.

"The Deadly Years" topped out at $186, 230. This raised the season-to-date deficit to $152,101.

Release / Reaction:
Premiere air date: 12/8/67. NBC repeat broadcast: 8/16/68.

Steven H. Scheuer reviewed the episode for his syndicated column, *TV Key Previews*. Among numerous newspapers across the country to carry the review was the Mansfield, Ohio *News Journal*, on December 8, 1967. Scheuer wrote:

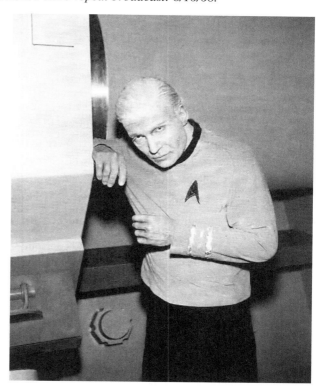

> "Deadly Years." Another imaginative tale that is well worth watching tonight. It involves a strange visit to a planet which injects all who land on it with a galloping case of old age and death. Everyone that is except for one person. Although Captain Kirk, Mr. Spock and McCoy are all smitten with an advanced state of old age and infirmities, it is Chekov, who also landed on the planet, who escapes. The enigma of Chekov's continuing good health and youth finally lead to a discovery of a cure but not before a number of people have died of hoary old age and the Captain himself is removed from command. An intriguing episode.

**Publicity photo of Shatner at his oldest
(Courtesy of Gerald Gurian)**

Judy Crosby reviewed the episode for her syndicated column, *TV SCOUT*. Among the papers which ran her notice on December 8, 1967 was *The Evening News*, serving Daytona Beach, Florida. Crosby wrote:

> A good imaginative script that is never over-played or over-costumed, as it might have been and this makes *Star Trek* a good bet tonight. It concerns a planet that has a strange ability to increase the aging process greatly. In fact, everyone on an Enterprise landing party, except Chekov, finds themselves rapidly approaching senility. And as he returns to the spaceship Captain Kirk find himself one of the victims. His judgment becomes so rattled that he is relieved of command by a passenger on the spaceship while the additional crew

strives to find a cure as the Enterprise reels through space. Charles Drake guest stars.

RATINGS / Nielsen National report for Friday, December 8, 1967:

8:30 to 9 p.m., 61.1% U.S. TVs in use.	Share:	Households watching:
NBC: *Star Trek* (first half)	28.6%	12,770,000
ABC: *Hondo* (first half)	21.8%	9,800,000
CBS: **Gomer Pyle, U.S.M.C.**	**43.6%**	**16,180,000**
Independent stations:	6.0%	No data

9 to 9:30 p.m., 61.8 U.S. TVs in use.	Share:	Household Watching:
NBC: *Star Trek* (second half)	28.1%	No data
ABC: *Hondo* (second half)	23.6%	No data
CBS: **Friday Night Movie**	**36.8%**	**No data**
Independent stations:	11.5%	No data

The movie on CBS was the 1965 Elvis Presley vehicle *Tickle Me*. *Star Trek* did respectable business for NBC, with its nationwide Nielsen showing of 28.6% of U.S. TVs running at 8:30 p.m. The big city numbers were more impressive, with a 19.4 rating and a 29% share of the TV audience in a survey targeting New York City and Los Angeles.

From the Mailbag

Received the week following the premiere broadcast:

> Dear Mr. Roddenberry ... Last night's episode (aging quickly) was pretty good. Aside from the continuing criticism about the important officers beaming down all the time, the only quibble I have is minor -- the story dragged a bit during the scenes when Kirk was relieved of command. I sensed padding.... I dug the detail of having Kirk and the others wear shirts a size too large for them during the extreme aging -- a neat, realistic touch.... But if Spock was so damned cold why didn't he simply wear more clothes?... The episode previous to this one was a bummer -- the Spartan tribe sword-and-adventure thing ["Friday's Child."]. Basically it wasn't science-fiction, simply adapted Marco Polo material. Richard G. (Venice, California).

Memories

Sarah Marshall said, "The stories were just fantastic. It's like we take them for granted now. But you only have to see some other science fiction and then only one of *Star Trek*'s episodes to realize that those [other] films were dreadful. They promised all of these wonderful twists and turns and never delivered, and *Star Trek* always delivered. I thought they were fabulous stories... I thought ['The Deadly Years'] was a very well written episode and it was a joy to see it." (114)

Beverly Washburn said, "It was a fun role. I got along with everybody. And William Shatner was quite the cut-up. He was making a lot of jokes about how he was getting old. And he never came on to me because, well, look at me in that episode! But he kind of had a reputation for coming on to actresses. So it was kind of funny when he was getting older because he would make jokes, like, he'd get a cane and come up to the young extras on the show and be kidding around -- and he was quite funny. And they were all very nice and pleasant. I remember DeForest Kelley was very soft-spoken and warm. And Leonard Nimoy was nice, but quiet and more serious; not as much of a character as William Shatner." (179a)

Publicity photo for an episode the producers and the studio hoped would win Kelley an Emmy nomination (Courtesy of Gerald Gurian)

Magazine writer Seli Groves, researching a story for *TV Picture Life*, was visiting the set shortly after "The Deadly Years" filmed. For her article, she reported how a member of the crew spoke of DeForest Kelley, saying, "He's really great. You know, there's talk of him being nominated for an Emmy next time around. He's just finished a segment where he ages to a ninety-year-old man. When he walked off the set, a burst of applause from the other actors and the crew broke out. He didn't go to the screening room later but I did and the audience there also applauded his work. If you ask me, it's about time Hollywood took notice of DeForest Kelley and made him a star."

Kelley later said, "There was a great disturbance at the studio at the time, because they felt I should have been nominated for that show, but I was not. They were very upset about it." (98-2)

But there was satisfaction for Kelley, even though snubbed by the Emmys. In a different interview, he said, "The really big kick I got out of doing that show was the effect my makeup had on my wife, Carolyn. When she saw me as a ninety-year-old man, she almost fainted!" (98-13)

16

Enter David Gerrold

Star Trek had yet to buy an unsolicited story or script … until episode 42 … which, in turn, led to a second assignment for the young writer -- helping out with episode 41.

David Gerrold, 23, was a fan of science fiction. He said, "In those days, there wasn't a lot of science fiction... there were like maybe 90 science fiction writers in 1967. There were maybe 300 to 500 science fiction books. So the really dedicated fan could have read every major science fiction book. And I started when I was nine. By the time I was 20, I had read everything published since 1930." (73-1)

Gerrold had recently graduated from USC, where he studied film. He had also just sold his first script, for an animated educational film called *A Positive Look at Negative Numbers*. And that got him an agent.

David Gerrold (photo: Dik Daniels)

On September 8, 1966, Gerrold was watching the premiere of *Star Trek*. He remembered, "I looked at the 'salt vampire' episode and I said, 'They're going to screw it up.' That was my immediate reaction, full of arrogance. 'Look, the guy with pointed ears, no emotions, there's no drama there, they've got to get rid of him. They're going to do Monster of the Week, and they really need to do real science fiction.'" (73-1)

Despite his criticism, Gerrold was impressed enough by *Star Trek* to try writing a story treatment. Three days later, he finished an epic 60-page tale, called "Tomorrow Is Yesterday." This was different than the episode of the same title soon to be written by D.C. Fontana. In Gerrold's story, the Enterprise discovers a giant "generation ship" called the Voyager, which is on a collision course with a populated planet. Voyager had been launched from Earth more than a century before. After a mutiny and the passage of so many years, the people on Voyager have come to believe their enclosed world is the totality of existence. As a result of the mutiny, the populace are divided into two warring camps. Kirk must reestablish amity; convince them their "world" is in danger, then change the ship's course.

It some ways, the third season episode "For the World Is Hollow and I Have Touched the Sky" seems patterned after Gerrold's story.

Gerrold's agent submitted "Tomorrow Is Yesterday" to *Star Trek*. On October 3, Gene Coon wrote back:

> Mr. Gerrold's outline was by no means inadequate. It is, as a matter of fact, <u>very</u> adequate. Unquestionably your young man can write. He has a good imagination

and a good sense of structure. Unfortunately, his ideas of what is possible in television are somewhat grandiose. This is a fault which is found in the majority of vastly more experienced writers, so don't say I am picking on Mr. Gerrold. I am not. I am impressed by him.... Because I am so impressed, I would be delighted to meet with him and tell him more of our specific needs.

Gerrold said, "Either Gene L. Coon was an enormously generous man or a very desperate producer. I just think he was an enormously generous man. He loved encouraging new talent." (73-1)

While a few more scripts were needed to finish up the first season, Coon was not about to gamble on an untested writer. Instead, he assigned himself three -- "Arena," "Errand of Mercy," and "The Devil in the Dark" -- and gave out four additional assignments (Steven Carabatsos on "Operation: Annihilate!," Paul Schneider on "Tomorrow the Universe," Theodore Sturgeon on "Amok Time," and Dorothy Fontana on "Friday's Child"). Only the three by Coon and the Carabatsos script assignment made it into the first season. Two of the others were held over for the second year. Schneider's script was jettisoned. Regardless, Coon spent time with Gerrold, praising him for the quality of his story outline and educating him on the limitations of television production and the needs of a series such as *Star Trek*. Gerrold remembered Coon telling him, "We have a problem finding good stories because science fiction writers don't know scripts and script writers don't know science fiction. So, if you can do both, let us see some stuff from you. Submit stuff for next season." (73-1)

The stage was set for one of *Star Trek*'s most popular episodes (see "The Trouble with Tribbles"). That first job at *Star Trek* for Gerrold immediately brought about a second -- a bit of script doctoring on the episode scheduled to shoot right before his.

17

Episode 41: I, MUDD

Written by Stephen Kandel
(with Gene Roddenberry, David Gerrold, D.C. Fontana, and Gene L. Coon, uncredited)
(story elements by Gene Roddenberry and Gene Coon, uncredited)
Directed by Marc Daniels

From NBC press release, October 13, 1967:

> The Enterprise crew finds itself at the mercy of an Earthling who rules a colony of female androids, in "I, Mudd" on NBC Television Network's *Star Trek* colorcast of Friday, Nov. 3…. Roger C. Carmel (a co-star of NBC-TV's *The Mothers-in-Law*) guest-stars as Harry Mudd, reprising the character he portrayed in "Mudd's Women," one of last season's *Star Trek* episodes. Mudd has created several hundred sets of girl androids, with each set bearing the same names and looks. He becomes bored and wants to leave but the androids have

NBC promoting double the pleasure, double the fun
(Courtesy of Gerald Gurian)

undertaken the project of studying humans and refuse his request. Mudd offers them a starship captain in exchange for himself and orders his chief coordinator, Norman (guest-star Richard Tatro), to bring the Enterprise crew to him. Capt. Kirk (William Shatner) then sets out to find a flaw in the patterned behavior of the androids. Rhea [sic] and Alice [sic] Andrece co-star as twin Alice Androids. Kay Elliot is featured as Mudd's wife, Stella.

The message of "I, Mudd," which takes second to the comedy antics, is that humans will stagnate and die without the necessary struggles to strive forward. And one other thing: All people have a little madness in them.

SOUND BITES

- *Mudd:* "Do you know what the penalty for fraud is on Deneb Five?" *Spock:* "The guilty party has his choice: death by electrocution, death by gas, death by phaser, death by hanging ..." *Mudd, interrupting:* "The key word in your entire peroration was ... d-d-death."

- *Spock:* "You went to substantial risk and effort to bring a starship here. Logically, you must have a compelling motive." *Mudd:* "Spock, you're going to love it here. They all talk just like you do."

- *Mudd:* "Behind every great man there is a woman, urging him on. And so it was with my Stella. She urged me into outer space. Not that she meant to, but with her continual, eternal, confounded nagging.... Well, I think of her constantly. And every time I do, I go further out into space."

- *Kirk:* "Harry is a liar. Whatever he tells you is a lie. Understand, Norman? Whatever he tells you is a lie." *Mudd:* "Listen carefully, Norman, I am lying." *Norman:* "You say you are lying. But if everything you say is a lie, then you are telling the truth. But you cannot tell the truth, because everything you say is a lie. But if you lie, you tell the truth... but you cannot, for you lie. Illogical.... Please explain. You are humans. Only humans can explain their behavior." *Kirk, mocking Norman:* "I am not programmed to respond in that area."

ASSESSMENT

This is *Star Trek*'s campiest episode. It was also the first all-out comedy. Is "I, Mudd" good? The answer depends on one's tastes. Most love it.

The Teaser, the longest and most action-packed of any in the series, starts the episode off with a bang. Act I remains nearly as intriguing. Then we are led to the throne room, and the return of Harry Mudd. After this, the episode makes an abrupt turn and it is hard to take anything seriously. Regardless, there are interesting twists in the story and wit in the writing, directing, and acting.

"I, Mudd," in theme and with the set design of the underground chambers is reminiscent of "What Are Little Girls Made Of?" Roddenberry even snuck in the idea about a human male being pleased by a beautiful female android. The naughtiness is less subtle here. Much had changed between 1966 and 1967 regarding what could be said or suggested on prime time TV. One example is when Chekov is in the company of two alluring Alice models. Alice 322 asks, "You desire something, Lord?" Chekov eyes them, and says, "You're Alice ...?" One says, "I am Alice 118." The other says, "I am Alice 322." Chekov says, "Oh. Well, it doesn't make much difference. You're both lovely.... What a shame you're not real." Both answer, in unison, "We are, Lord." Chekov says, "I mean, real girls." Alice 118 says, "We are programmed to function as human females, Lord." Chekov, surprised, asks, "Harry Mudd programmed you?" They both answer, "Yes, Lord." Chekov asks, "That unprincipled, evil-minded, lecherous kulak Harry Mudd programmed you?" They say, "Yes, Lord." Chekov smiles ... and says, "This place is even better than Leningrad."

Another replay taking place here is that this is the third time Kirk talks a computer to death. In the past, logic was the weapon. This time, illogic.

Those two slight comparisons aside, this episode is like no other. In 1967, with all its wannabe Doublemint twins and trick shots to duplicate the duplicates even further, "I, Mudd" was a marvel. Today, it is a curious delight.

THE STORY BEHIND THE STORY

Script Timeline

Gene Roddenberry's story idea, "Reason," from series proposal: March 11, 1964.
Roddenberry's story concept, with Gene Coon "I, Mudd": December 5, 1966.
Stephen Kandel's deal memo, ST #54: March 20, 1967.
Kandel's story outline: March 23, 1967.
Kandel's revised outline, gratis: April 20, 1967.
Kandel's 1ˢᵗ Draft teleplay: May 31, 1967.
Kandel's 2ⁿᵈ Draft teleplay: June 25, 1967 (rec'd June 30).
Roddenberry's polish (Mimeo Department "Yellow Cover 1ˢᵗ Draft"): July 21, 1967.
David Gerrold's rewrite (Final Draft teleplay): Late July, 1967.
D.C. Fontana's rewrite (Rev. Final Draft teleplay): August 4, 1967.
Gene Coon's page revisions: August 7 & 8, 1967.

The premise for the new Mudd story had been around for a while. As part of his 1964 series proposal, Gene Roddenberry included a springboard for a Man against Machine tale, called "Reason." His title referenced a short story by Isaac Asimov, also with the title "Reason" and first published in 1941. Asimov's story pitted robots with highly-advanced reasoning abilities against the humans who created them. The robots had decided the humans were too short-lived to be of much value. Roddenberry's "Reason" told how the U.S.S. Yorktown encounters a planet in the "Isaac IV group" (the name being a nod toward Isaac Asimov) where all intelligent organic life has perished, leaving a perfectly functioning robot society. Roddenberry's robots, like Asimov's, acquired the ability to think, and to therefore *think* they could reason, and thereby *reason* that they could and should make decisions for themselves.

In December 1966, Roddenberry, brainstorming with Gene Coon, took the idea in a new direction, asking what would happen if Harry Mudd, on the loose again, came across this mechanical society? The two Genes settled on the title "I, Mudd," which pays homage to a pair of literary properties: Asimov's 1950 science fiction anthology, *I, Robot*, which included the author's version of "Reason," and Robert Graves' 1934 novel, *I, Claudius*, where Claudius reluctantly becomes Emperor but wishes he could escape the role.

Roger C. Carmel said, "'Mudd's Women' was a pretty big success and they got a lot of positive reaction from it. So they wrote one especially for me the next season." (29-4)

Scheduling the writing and production was tricky. Stephen Kandel, who had created the character of Harry Mudd, was now a staff writer and associate producer on ABC's *Iron Horse*, which he co-created with *Star Trek* veteran director James Goldstone. And Roger C. Carmel, the actor who played Harcourt Fenton Mudd, had been cast in *The Mothers-in-Law*, an NBC situation comedy produced by Desi Arnaz. A sequel to "Mudd's Women" was dependent on Kandel and Carmel's availability. Because of this, "I, Mudd" was put into development early, and classified as a "rush."

Kandel turned in his outline on March 23, 1967. It barely resembled the "I, Mudd" we would come to know. In this version, a strange mix of V.I.P. passengers were traveling aboard the Enterprise. One was Idris Vane, a woman so taken with her own looks that she was tempted to trade her mortal flesh-and-blood body for that of an android -- an artificial body fashioned in her image and incapable of aging. Also on board was her traveling companion, Brother Mercy, a depraved preacher, and several robots, all identical in appearance, all called Norman. As they had done with Idris, and with the help of Brother Mercy, the robots attempted to entice the crew into wanting to live among a world of robots programmed only for their pleasure. Meanwhile, the Enterprise journeyed to the robots' place of origin, which Kirk had orders to investigate. And this would bring about the unexpected reunion with Harry Mudd, the mastermind behind all the mechanical scheming.

Roddenberry, thrilled to receive the story only three days after assigning it and eager to get a jump on the scriptwriting process, sent a letter to Kandel, telling him:

Delighted to get the outline last Friday and would like you to get into First Draft immediately. (GR41-1)

Despite being "delighted," Roddenberry included three pages of notes, explaining to Kandel:

As a captain of a Starship assigned patrol of an entire sector of our galaxy, Kirk is a "Captain Horatio Hornblower" of the space age, with enormous problems on his mind, involving the whole Earth Federation and its many colonies, its diplomatic problems with other races. Items of this size, and Kirk's general demeanor, attitude, and personal dignity, must believably reflect the enormity of his responsibilities and the personal disciplines he has to acquire. (GR41-1)

This made it clear that, even with a potentially amusing episode, Roddenberry nonetheless expected his *Star Trek* to remain thought-provoking and primarily serious. And Kirk would always be carrying a great burden on his shoulders. In other words, he wanted "I, Mudd" to play like "Mudd's Women."

Later in the story, as crew members are duplicated as robots, we get two Kirks. Of this, Roddenberry wrote:

We've done duplicates of Kirk twice during the first year and have agreed with NBC we will hold back on this for a while. However, we've never done a duplication of Spock. Does this offer any ideas to you? (GR41-1)

Also problematic: Harry Mudd was overshadowed by other characters, such as Idris Vane, Brother Mercy, and all the Normans. And Mudd's entrance was late -- more than halfway through the story.

With these problems, Roddenberry had jumped the gun by telling Kandel to begin writing the script. Furthermore, NBC had yet to approve the outline. And Gene Coon, on vacation, had not even read it.

The following day, Bob Justman wrote to Roddenberry:

We have got to have more Harry Mudd and less of the other characters in this story…. If this is to be a return engagement between Captain Kirk and Harry Mudd, then I think we are complicating it with the addition of extraneous other characters, such as Idris Vane and possibly Brother Mercy. (RJ41-1)

Justman did, however, like the idea that there would be multiple Normans.

Of Brother Mercy or, more so, the idea of mocking Bible-thumping preacher types, Stephen Kandel later said, "It was guaranteed to offend almost everyone. I talked to Gene and we had a lot of fun with it. He loved the idea, but he said, 'We're going to have a nightmare with the network about this.' And I said, 'That's the whole fun of it.'" (95-1)

Three days after Justman voiced his concerns, NBC's Stan Robertson contacted Roddenberry. The network wanted Brother Mercy taken out of the story. Robertson wrote:

We both know that it is very difficult to portray a character on television who borders on being a religious fanatic without offending a great mass of our audience, or so emasculating the character that you totally destroy him as a believable human being. (SR41)

Robertson also agreed with Justman on a fundamental point, saying:

The outline, as written, is a little too complex and should be simplified. In its most elementary form, this should be simply a story of our heroes versus Mudd. The other characters should merely be for the purpose of acting as "tools" in this struggle. (SR41)

Like Justman, Robertson was bothered that there was too little Mudd in this Mudd story. Further, he was concerned that, when the character finally made his entrance, no explanation was given as to what we should expect from him or how Kirk even knew him. Of this, Robertson wrote:

We cannot assume that all of the viewers who will be watching this forthcoming episode will have seen our earlier show. Therefore, it would seem that early in our story, as soon as possible, we would want to "marry" that which was the past with that which is the present in the mind of the viewer, as far as the colorfulness of Mudd is concerned. (SR41)

This suggestion led to the banter between Kirk, Spock, and Mudd, at the start of Act II in the filmed episode. It is a recap for the benefit of Mr. Chekov, who is new to the ship and missed the previous encounter with Mudd. More so, it is a recap for the viewing audience. But this was one of the smaller changes to be made.

Gene Coon returned from his vacation on April 1 and found a memo from Roddenberry. It read:

Steve [Kandel] has a problem of turning his stories constantly in the direction of "space pirate" type science-fiction; characters and stories which would work better on *Lost in Space*. (GR41-2)

The buck had been passed. Coon read the outline, as well as the story notes from Roddenberry, and notes from Justman, and notes from Stan Robertson. And then advised Kandel to stop writing the script and revise the outline instead … for no additional pay.

Kandel, busy rewriting *Iron Horse* scripts, put his *Star Trek* assignment off, not delivering his revised story outline until April 20th. Brother Mercy was out. Idris Vane remained. To Kandel's thinking, she was a necessary "tool." She was the one with the robots, and the robots were the reason the Enterprise was being sent on this mission of discovery. They were the bait.

Justman read the retooled outline, then dictated a memo to Coon, saying:

I don't believe the character of Idris Vane. It's hard to accept a rational human being deciding to betray her confreres in order to get a "permanently beautiful robot-manufactured body" and then, to compound this, she does a complete turnaround and betrays her new Robot allies in order to help Captain Kirk later. (RJ41-2)

Kandel was asked to make more changes, and to make more sense of Idris Vane, as he proceeded to teleplay. His 1st Draft script arrived May 31.

Justman, in a massive 14-page memo, wrote Coon:

Steve Kandel has come up with a piece that is highly entertaining at times, but, at the same time, illogical and inordinately expensive to produce. This should in no way be a surprise to us, because this is exactly the sort of property he delivered to us with "Mudd's Women." There is, I grant you, a certain amount of humor contained within the story and, as usual, Steve Kandel is quite good with humor. (RJ41-3)

Justman, with his own brand of humor, added:

It is very kind of the writer to specify four beautiful robot women. Would you believe two, or at the most, three beautiful robot women? Also, why should they wear "simple white shifts" [a loose fitting dress that hangs down from the shoulders] when we could attire them rather scantily and win some new viewers for the show? (RJ41-3)

Justman's summation:

Too big, too expensive, too many sets, too many parts. (RJ41-3)

Story Editor Dorothy Fontana wrote Coon:

The biggest problem I find in this script is that it is 90 percent talk and no action, no major jeopardy to our people. There is little definitive action on Kirk's part -- or on anyone else's. The character of Idris and Mudd are very shallow. Idris, in particular, contributes very little to any aspect of the show. (DC41-1)

Fontana had another beef. Kandel had called for a scene involving every single man and woman on the Enterprise to be seen all together on the android planet in a sort of spa resort, tended to and tempted by the androids. Kandel clearly did not know how many men and women this involved. D.C. did, and she told Coon:

Under no circumstances will we ever see the entire crew of the Enterprise together. Even Kirk does not know what the entire crew of the Enterprise looks like all together. (DC41-1)

One day later, a memo from Gene Roddenberry arrived. It began, "The script is full of bright, inventive things and situations." And then G.R. listed the bright, inventive things which could *not* be done -- six densely-typed pages worth. He wrote:

Many of my concerns in this draft revolve around Steve's apparent unfamiliarity of our format. I would really feel much more secure when he goes into his next draft to know that he has re-read the *Star Trek Guide* and perhaps accepted our invitation to come in and see a couple of episodes. He's been very busy on his own show the past year and I suspect he has seen no more *Star Trek* episodes than you and I have of other shows around town.... I don't know if I can put my finger exactly on what bothers me, but the sum of it still seems to come off a bit "Buck Rogerish." The speeches written for the characters seem to indicate these characters know they are in a science-fiction piece and are playing the "wonder of it all" rather than being real people in a real situation.... Let's suggest the female androids have more potential than simply looking like girls. This is a grownup show.... On Page 54, the robots deciding humans are illogical, deciding to spread their durability and logic over the galaxy, is the first time the script begins to pick up interest for me. If this had happened at the beginning of Act Two, Mudd luring our space ship here to get out from under this monstrous situation he has created, then I think we might have a fairly interesting story, assuming we had other action-adventure elements to it. The above is also a possibility for a theme, which the whole script sorely lacks. Are robots better? Maybe they are -- a powerful theme should always be capable of arguments on both sides. If we go this direction, we will have found ourselves a wonderful new "enemy," a new threat to the Federation group -- indestructible, super-efficient, super-logical androids. A race of them which, with our starship, might well win. (GR41-3)

As Roddenberry continued to list his concerns, his mood, which began on a somewhat pleasant note, soured. He told Coon:

> Mudd comes off as a nothing in this script -- one of the large groups of people who stand around asking and answering questions, helping the writer fill up the pages with exposition. I'm sorry, Gene, as I go over this script again, I get more and more bitter. No conflict, no characterizations, no building jeopardy. Only at the very end do we begin to get into anything approaching an exciting story. I think the first thing we have got to do, Gene, is to sit Steve Kandel down and flatly and plainly tell him that he has dogged it. He's using science fiction as an excuse to avoid thinking out a story, to avoid all the tried and true rules of character, action, mounting jeopardy, etc. He's also neatly avoided any semblance at all to a central theme.... He is a bright and inventive writer. I heard it said that he is a good writer. I think we have got to challenge him to prove it. And I think the best way to do it is not by a memo -- that can come later -- but by a head to head meeting in which we back him into a corner. (GR41-3)

Coon didn't want a head-to-head meeting in which he would back a pro like Stephen Kandel into a corner. Instead, the following day, he wrote to Kandel. His sweet-and-sour 14-page letter began:

> You have given us a script full of bright inventive things, and a great deal of interesting and exciting humor. At the same time, there are certain elements of the script which do not work for us. (GC41-2)

Some of the elements had to do with pleasing the network. Coon wrote:

> Please do not specify anywhere in the script that the robots regard Norman as their god. Their emperor, their ruler, their king, their chief, whatever you wish, but not god. There is an NBC block on that. (GC41-2)

Other elements had to do with continuity.

> We have established well, in earlier scripts, that under no circumstances is the crew to obey an order from the Captain, or anyone else, saying that all hands shall beam down. As a matter of fact, this is an impossibility. At least one person would have to remain on the Enterprise to run the transporter. Any order coming from the ground would have to specify that a skeleton crew be left on duty. (GC41-2)

Other elements in Coon's critique had to do with cost.

> You give us a full shot of the crew of the Enterprise. WOW! (GC41-2)

Others had to do with selling out -- something TV producers, sadly, have to be willing to do. Coon told Kandel:

> It comes to my attention that our cigarette sponsors may possibly take great exception to Harry Mudd coming up with two cigars. In addition to which, we firmly hope, believe and pray -- and I light another cigarette as I say this -- that in three hundred years from now, the filthy, dirty, delightful habit of smoking will be a thing of the distant, historic past. (GC41-2)

Ironically, Coon would die in seven years, at age 49, of lung cancer. For now, he closed:

> Despite the flaws, it is a great pleasure to read a script written by a man who obviously knows how to put words together. It is stamped with a very high class professionalism, and is a joy to read. Now, let's just get it in shape in which it will be a joy to act, photograph, cut, dub, and, eventually, hopefully, release.

(GC41-2)

Kandel fulfilled his contract with a 2nd Draft teleplay on June 30. Of this, Fontana wrote Coon:

> Steve has changed this somewhat, but there are still holes in the story and flaws in the characters. A number of key people come up very, very flat. (DC41-2)

Fontana, like Justman, wanted to lose the character of Idris Vane and suggested utilizing "one of our regular women" to sell the point that a human might be tempted to trade a body that ages for a body that does not. She wrote:

> I think it is more important for us to focus on our principals and Harry Mudd, plus the androids. These people are our story and Idris Vane is so much dead weight. We could always use Uhura in this scene. She might have a disinterested curiosity in the mechanical bodies, [and] the others might be holding such a possibility out to her in order to try to "corrupt" her. Let's not use Idris. (DC41-2)

As for the other regulars, D.C. told Coon:

> I have a feeling throughout that Kirk does not do enough. Both he and Mudd come off very flat. Kirk should be moving, doing, at least protesting more. Spock is not used to good enough advantage, either. He is the computer expert. Essentially speaking, robots are computer based. Surely we can come up with some good suggestions and business and not be standing around all the time. (DC41-2)

Fontana ended her fault-finding memo:

> I know -- good luck in all my future endeavors. dcf. (DC41-2)

Justman was less critical, something which could throw the entire staff into a state of confusion. He told Coon:

> No doubt I continually end up surprising you with my reaction to various scripts. Well, here comes another surprise. I like Steve Kandel's script very much! I dislike many, many things contained within it, but there is nothing we cannot fix.... I find my imagination stimulated by the property and I think it can be one of the most entertaining *Star Trek*s we have ever attempted. I would suggest we throw Dorothy Fontana on the re-write as soon as possible. In this way, we might be able to produce the show while Roger C. Carmel is still available to us. (RJ41-4)

It was Justman's idea to make the female androids identical twins. He continued:

> I shall now bring up a suggestion which I consider to be absolutely brilliant! Instead of having Alice and Barbara in the Throne Room, I suggest that we have the part of Alice played by twins and name them Alice I and Alice II. We can introduce Barbara a little later on in the story and I think that we can have a great deal of fun and create a great deal of interest if we attempt this routine.... I know that there are several sets of very good-looking girl twins in town who can act sufficiently well for our purposes. I think by casting twins, we can more easily sell the fact that these Androids are really Androids and not human beings. You will note the script [still] describes the girls as wearing "simple white shifts." This, I hope, is liable to end up as the most incorrect description we have ever had on *Star Trek*. Their outfits must be zingers! I want every curve to be visible to our viewers. They don't necessarily have to be naked, but I do think that [a] body stocking will work, if we can cast the right girls. (RJ41-4)

Justman would get his twins -- and body stockings. The script, however, still had a long way to go.

"I, Mudd" had begun with Roddenberry and now Roddenberry wanted to try finishing it, especially since Justman had pointed out all the naughty possibilities. His polish was the Yellow Cover 1st Draft, dated July 21. Among Roddenberry's changes, one humorous moment not included in the yet-to-come shooting script, where an examination reveals Norman to be a machine, and Scotty expresses an urge to take him apart, and then quickly adds that it is "nothing personal." Norman, of course, understands.

The first two Acts were fun, but the problem remained that Harry Mudd still did not appear until halfway into the story, on page 32.

Gene Coon was busy rewriting many other scripts. Dorothy Fontana, as well, was doing other rewrites. After Roddenberry turned in his rewrite, he left the office to work on assignment preparing a teleplay for a Robin Hood TV movie that was never to be made. Coon then thought of David Gerrold.

Gerrold, fresh off his first *Star Trek* writing assignment, "The Trouble with Tribbles" [the next episode to be produced], had made an impression on Coon. He had also saved *Star Trek* money. Gerrold said, "They only paid me $3,000 for 'Tribbles,' which was bottom of the scale." (73-1)

Because fledgling television writer David Gerrold was not yet a member of the Writers Guild of America, he was not entitled to the full union rate of $4,500. Coon, however, felt Gerrold had earned the right to receive the same pay as other writers on the show -- other writers who had performed less impressively. The question was how to get that extra $1,500 into Gerrold's pocket without upsetting the Desilu bean counters.

Gerrold said, "[Gene] calls me into his office and hands me the script and says, 'What we want to do is get down to the planet in the first Act ... not at the end of thirty minutes, but at the end of fifteen.'" (73-1)

Everyone knew the story didn't kick in until Kirk and company were reunited with Harry Mudd, but no one had a solution.

"On that particular night," Gerrold remembered, "they had just rerun an episode ['A Taste of Armageddon'], where somebody flips open Kirk's communicator, imitates his voice and orders Scotty to beam the entire crew down. And, of course, Scotty doesn't believe it. So, Gene L. Coon says to me, 'How are we going to get the entire crew down on the planet?' Now, I didn't know they'd been fighting with this problem for two weeks. I said, 'Well, you can't have Norman, the android, imitate Kirk's voice, because, on the episode that was just telecast last night, Scotty didn't believe it. So, Scotty's not going to get any stupider. These androids have already demonstrated in the Teaser that they're much stronger than human beings. So they can just grab the crew and beam them down ... and you actually don't even have to show it. You just have one android walk in and report to Norman and say that they have just completed beaming down the crew of the Enterprise.' And this look comes over Gene Coon's face ... 'You just solved in one line of dialogue what we have been arguing about for two weeks in the office. I want you to do the rewrite on the script. Have the whole crew down on the planet as fast as possible, then we want to do all this illogical stuff.'" (73-1)

The "illogical stuff" was the crux of the episode's comedy, as Kirk and his crew create confusion in the androids by behaving erratically.

"A Taste of Armageddon" repeated on NBC on July 20. Gerrold turned in his undated rewrite roughly one week later. Harry Mudd now appeared on page 17.

Gerrold's other contribution was the idea of expanding on Justman's suggestion to have real-life twins appear as the androids, multiplied through various camera angles and editing room trickery. He later said, "So we had 500 identical androids of beautiful girls. Gene says, 'Why did you do that?' And I said, 'Because I thought it was funny.' He goes, 'Okay.' Of course, it made for the gag with Stella." (73-1)

Stella, the unpleasant android made in the likeness of the unpleasant wife that Mudd had abandoned, was already in the script. But it was Gerrold's idea that the story should end, to the horror of Harry Mudd, with Stella having been duplicated hundreds of times over.

While working on the rewrite, Gerrold spent time on the *Star Trek* set, soaking up as much as he could about what was and was not possible in production.

"Marc Daniels was the generous type," said Gerrold. "He took time to explain things to me. And he was a legend. I mean, the guy invented the three camera sitcom. He did all the *Lucy*s. It was a privilege to be in the same room with him. The joke is, I didn't know who Marc Daniels was the whole time I was working on *Star Trek*, except that he was an old-time director with a lot of credentials ... and everybody respected and loved him ... and he was a great guy. And, maybe a year or two after *Trek*, I'm watching an old *I Love Lucy* episode and the credit comes on – 'Marc Daniels.' And, 'Oh shit, am I stupid.' It hadn't hit me. I mean, I knew the name, but I hadn't made the connection." (73-1)

Coon, pleased by Gerrold's rewrite, designated it as a "Final Draft," then handed the script over to Dorothy Fontana for a good cleaning. Her rewrite -- the Revised Final Draft -- came in on August 8. She had taken Kandel's writing, Roddenberry's writing, and Gerrold's writing, and blended them together into something that was now cohesive and felt like *Star Trek*, even though this atypical episode was, in a way, very much unlike *Star Trek*.

Coon contributed page revisions of his own, dated August 7 and 8, making it five writers who had their fingers in the stew known as "I, Mudd." Filming would start six days later. And Joe D'Agosta had plenty to do in finding himself some twins.

Pre-Production
August 3 & 4 and 7 – 11, 1967 (7 days prep).

Roger C. Carmel on *The Man from U.N.C.L.E.*
(MGM TV 1965)

Marc Daniels returned for his tenth directing assignment on the series and his first and only *Star Trek* comedy.

It was already known Roger C. Carmel would reprise the role of Harry Mudd. Stephen Kandel said, "Roger C. Carmel was wonderful as Harry. He inhabited the character and expanded it. He developed the character physically as an actor." (95-2)

Working often in television since the late

1950s, Carmel had become a prominent guest star in the last few years, thanks to standout roles on hit series such as *I Spy*, *Batman*, and *The Man from U.N.C.L.E.* And now he was busier than ever, and unavailable throughout June, July, and early August, filming the first 16 episodes of *The Mothers-in-Law*. After that, the series went on a two-month production hiatus. Therefore, "I, Mudd" was slated to film between middle and late August, allowing time for pick-up shots, should any be needed.

Richard Tatro, 28, was hired to play Norman, the head android. His performance is right on the mark -- humorless, yet, even as he commandeers the Enterprise, somehow non-confrontational. The unusual speech pattern of separating each word with the slightest pause contributed to making this a challenging performance, but added greatly to its success. Tatro had been in television and films since 1961, usually with small roles. He had been featured in three 1966 episodes of

**James Hurst and Richard Tatro in *Branded*
(www.riflemanconners.com)**

Branded, as Lt. Douglas Briggs, and received fair supporting roles in mid 1960s B-films such as *Sins in the Suburbs*, *Warm Nights and Hot Pleasures*, and *Pandora and the Magic Box*. A popular series like *Star Trek* should have represented a turn in Tatro's career, but this is his last known filmed performance of any consequence.

Walter Koenig was given another good role, with George Takei no doubt envious. The producers believed Chekov, with his youthful innocence, offered more comedic possibilities on Mudd's world than Sulu. Also, having Chekov among those seen on the planet opened a door for Kirk to give us a recap concerning Harry Mudd.

In the days before the Internet, the most challenging aspect of the casting was Mudd's mechanical women.

"I remember trying to find out where to find twins," Joe D'Agosta said. "I called SAG for twins and they were of no help. I did everything I knew how to do, with my resources being very limited, mainly because of my own lack of knowledge on how to seek out some of this stuff. I didn't even know there were twin societies. And I just happened to be driving down Hollywood Boulevard and there were a couple of twins walking along. They were good looking, sexy looking, as I recall, even a little on the 'experienced side,' if you know what I mean. So I pulled my car over and said, 'Excuse me, do you want to be on TV?' It sounded like a line, made all the worse because I didn't even have a business card to give them. We didn't carry them in those days. So I just wrote my number down. But they called. I wasn't searching, I just happened to be driving by and there they were. I brought them in and they read terribly. They had no experience at *this*, and Bob Justman objected to the hiring of them. And I said, 'Bob, they're pretty. Bob, they're *twins*!' So he stopped objecting. They were fine." (43-4)

D'Agosta could not recall if these twins were cast as the Maizie series or the Barbara series. Either way, they were seen but not heard. All dialogue was given to the Alice series.

Alyce and Rhae Andrece appear as the beautiful Alices. After the first 10 minutes of the episode, there is barely a shot where one or both are not seen or heard. Alyce Andrece was given a screen credit as playing Alice #1 through #250, with sister Rhae playing Alice #251 through #500. This was not actually the case, but production records indicate, when on camera together, Alyce was assigned a lower number than that of Rhae. This was done to help director, crew, and cast know at a glance which Andrece they were talking to.

Right before filming "I, Mudd," in June 1967, the Andrece sisters appeared in ads for *Gunn*, the feature film based on the *Peter Gunn* TV series. They were not in the movie, just a tool for catching people's attention for the 30 second

Publicity shot featuring Alyce and Rhae Andrece (Courtesy of Gerald Gurian)

promo spots. After this, they appeared in a 1968 episode of *Batman*, a 1969 episode of *Bonanza*, and a 1970 exploitation film called *Hell's Bloody Devils*. They were also singers and recorded two albums with their group The Sound of Feeling, where jazz met folk and both met the Summer of Love.

Tom and Ted LeGarde played the Herman series. Despite having some of their more prominent scenes left on the cutting room floor and being kept mostly in the background, they were well-known entertainers in country music, having released several singles and albums

Stella (played by Kay Elliot)

beginning in the late 1950s, along with frequent TV appearances. They even hosted their own TV series in Los Angeles, *The LeGarde Twins Show*, on KTLA-5 from 1957 to 1958.

Tamara and Starr Wilson appeared as the Maizie series, while Maureen and Colleen Thornton appeared as the Barbara series.

Last but certainly not least …

Kay Elliot played Stella Mudd … and all of her frightening duplicates. Elliot, the face and voice that drove Harry Mudd into outer space, was 38 and had just begun a 13 year stay in television, almost always in unflattering roles. Among these: she played Aunt Hagatha, the witch in a couple episodes of *Bewitched*, and was featured alongside two other *Star Trek* guest players (Paul Carr of "Where No Man Has Gone Before" and John Crawford of "The Galileo Seven") in 1973's *The Severed Arm*. And Joe D'Agosta also cast Elliot in a 1968 episode of *Here's Lucy* ("Lucy and Eva Gabor").

Production Diary
Filmed August 14, 15, 16, 17, 18, 21 & 22, 1967.
(Planned as 7 day production; budget set at $182,431).

The week "I, Mudd" began production, *Born Losers* (the first of the Billy Jack movie series, starring Tom Laughlin) and *Bonnie and Clyde* (with Warren Beatty and Faye Dunaway) were battling for top spot at the box office. On radio stations, the two most popular songs were "Light My Fire," by The Doors, and "All You Need Is Love," by The Beatles. Each would take a turn at No. 1. In the record stores, The Beatles and The Monkees were competing for top record album honors, with *Sgt. Pepper's Lonely Hearts Club Band* and *Headquarters*, respectively. Mike Douglas, host of a popular daytime talk show, had the cover of *TV Guide*. You could read all about him for only 15 cents.

The consensus was that "I, Mudd," with all the trick photography that was needed, would take longer to film than the usual *Star Trek*, so an extra day was allocated. A seven-day shooting schedule was a luxury for Marc Daniels, but he would need every minute.

Filming began Monday, August 14, 1967, on Stage 9, for the Enterprise sets. William Shatner had the day off. Nimoy and Kelley were present for their brief encounter with Norman in the corridor. James Doohan was needed for his physical confrontation with Norman in engineering. Also shot was Norman in "Emergency Manual Control," the upper deck of engineering.

Day 2, Tuesday. The company was now on Stage 10, for "Int. Anteroom" and the start of filming in the "Int. Throne Room." Roger C. Carmel and the numerous sets of twins began working this day.

Carmel said, "It was such a joy returning. You would have thought I was a regular member of the cast; that we had done a dozen episodes together. They couldn't have been friendlier." (29)

A triple split-screen, requiring a single strip of film to be run through the camera three times -- an amazing feat for 1967 TV (CBS Studios, Inc.)

Marc Daniels said, "Probably the biggest problem had completely to do with all the twins we had to present. It required a lot of trick photography, and it was necessary for us to be absolutely precise or else the story wouldn't have worked." (44-2)

The process was more difficult than one might suspect, looking back from the vantage point of today -- a time filled with computer-generated animation and post production effects. In 1967, in an effort to avoid expensive matte shots, the split-screen effect was created in-camera by covering a portion of the lens and running the same section of film through a second time or, in one case here, a third time (when Mudd introduces the Alice series and is surrounded by six of them).

Regarding the process, Carmel said. "It was real hit and miss. They'd have the twins stand on one side of me and, to take the shot, cover one side of the lens with some black material so that only half of the film running through the camera was exposed. Then they'd have the girls go to the other side of me, move the black cloth to cover the opposite side of the lens and run the same strip of film through again. Now the full strip of film had been exposed and two girls became four. But they wouldn't know until the next day if it had worked. The director and the fellow in charge of the camera crew would watch the dailies, then let us know if we had to do a portion of a scene again. As I recall it, they got it right almost every time." (29)

This was the first day to feature the pair of twins whom casting director Joe D'Agosta had spotted on Hollywood Boulevard. Walter Koenig related the story: "There was much snickering among members of the crew on the second day of the shoot and I found myself eavesdropping. The fashion of the day was miniskirts, and Joe's discoveries were apparently doing far more than their part in wearing revealing attires. This was determined in the cafeteria by the best boy, two grips, and a gaffer, who simultaneously choked on their hard-boiled eggs when the girls, in their civilian garb, bent over to get a better look at the salad bar. Neither was wearing underwear." (102-13)

Day 3, Wednesday. Work continued in the throne room. The wardrobe department made sure the set of twins who were a bit on the "experienced side" were now wearing underwear. And Jerry Finnerman was having a wonderful time painting the walls with his lighting gels, and his favorite hues -- various shades of purple, including magenta.

Carmel said, "Remarkable what he [Finnerman] could do with a white wall. I'd played a villain on *Batman* [Colonel Gumm], so had worked on some wild looking sets, but that fellow knew his way around a box of colored gels." (29)

The scene that finally got Walter Koenig a smile out of director Marc Daniels (CBS Studios, Inc.)

Walter Koenig, for his memoir, wrote, "I did several shows with Marc [Daniels] before I ever saw him smile. That precedent-setting occasion was during a scene I was doing for the episode 'I, Mudd'… in which Chekov sits on a throne between two voluptuous androids and says, 'This place is even better than Leningrad.' Up until then I assumed that, in his eyes, everything I had done [had] sucked." (102-13)

Day 4, Thursday, August 17. More filming in the throne room, this time for the episode's Tag scene. All the twins were needed with Mudd and the Enterprise officers for this scene as well as a photo shoot conducted by *TV Guide*.

Daniels continued to direct under the watchful eye of the *TV Guide* photographer, and took great care to pose the lovely Andrece

**Portrait for *TV Guide* article, shot on Day 4 of production
(Courtesy of Gerald Gurian)**

sisters in very nearly every shot taken on Mudd's planet, sometimes using split screen or body doubles to create the impression that there were a multitude of any one particular alluring model.

Also shot this day, Mudd being surrounded by three nagging Stellas, putting a big burden on the shoulders of cinematographer Jerry Finnerman. Again, this required a double split screen. The cameraman was working blind. Until the film was processed, there was no way to know if the effect had worked. But it did work, beautifully.

Star Trek was not on NBC this Thursday night, being pre-empted by a music special, "An Evening at Tanglewood," wherein The Boston Pops Symphony Orchestra performed well-known motion picture themes.

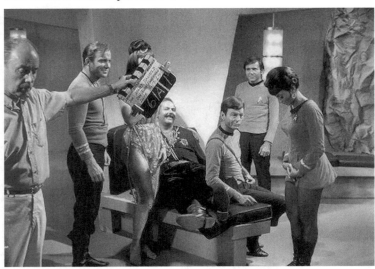

Day 5, Friday. Work continued on Stage 10, now in the "Interior Lounge" for numerous sequences including one complex scene which was left out of the completed episode. Production photographs have survived, as did the shooting script which describes the action during which Enterprise crew members are pampered by the devoted androids. One Enterprise crewman lays on a chaise

**Day 5: Bill Montgomery slates a scene in the "Interior Lounge" set
(Courtesy of Gerald Gurian)**

lounge, being fed grapes by Alice #73. Another is served wine by a different shapely android, while a crew woman gets a back massage from a muscular male android. Alice #500 entertains more crew members with a stringed instrument. Meanwhile, a crewman is offered a plate of interesting looking food by a smiling member of the Barbara series (#321), as Maizie #88, Trudy #313, and Annabelle #007, along with male androids #27 and #444 (the LeGarde twins), tend to various Enterprise crew members. This was what was left of the part of Kandel's script in which we were to see the entire crew of the Enterprise. It was pruned back for filming, but nonetheless ended up being extravagant and expensive to stage. And then it was left unused during editing (see "Post Production").

**Deleted scene from the "Int. Lounge" set
(Courtesy of Gerald Gurian)**

While the cast ate lunch, the company moved to Stage 9 where many Enterprise sets had been collapsed to make room for a new set, "Int. Control Room," which involved Spock, Norman, and one of the Alice models.

Day 6, Monday. More work on Stage 9 and the control room set. The absurd moments from Act IV were filmed, as Shatner, Nimoy, Kelley, Doohan, Nichols, Koenig, and Carmel acted illogically, causing the Andrece sisters and Richard Tatro to short-out. Perhaps encouraged by a former *I Love Lucy* director, cast members appeared to be serving just a bit too much ham with their cheese.

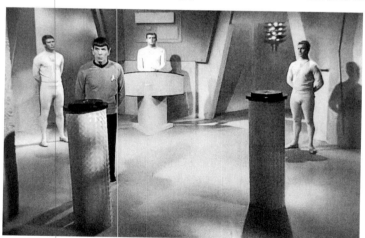

**Deleted scene from the "Int. Control Room"
(Courtesy of Gerald Gurian)**

(102)

Walter Koenig said, "I wasn't worried about whether it was too comical or not. I just assumed that there would be an occasional episode like this. I remember it was fun to do, but I don't remember being shocked or surprised. I didn't worry that it was taking the show in a different direction as others might have. I was too close to it. I couldn't see the forest through the trees."

Roger C. Carmel said, "It was a lot of fun! Bill Shatner, that very dignified captain, is really at heart a very crazy kind of comic.... On *Star Trek*, he had to be the responsible leader, so he didn't have much of a chance to let out on screen that comic devil inside him. He sure did let it out on the *Star Trek* set though! We had a hell of a good time!" (29-2)

279

After the lunch break, the company moved into another new set on Stage 9 -- "Int. Workshop." This was the area on Mudd's planet where androids were created. Uhura appeared to be dazzled by the process. And that was all we would see. The bulk of the material would never see a TV screen.

Day 7, Tuesday. No twins were needed. Remaining on Stage 9, Norman attacked and knocked out the helm

Blooper featuring hijinks on the set during Day 6 of production (Unaired film trim courtesy of Gerald Gurian)

operator in Auxiliary Control. The rest of the day was spent filming the remainder of the episode's Teaser and portions of Act I on the bridge set.

Post-Production
Available for editing: August 23, 1967. Rough Cut: August 31.
Final Cut: September 8. Music Score recorded September 22.

James D. Ballas and his assistant, comprising the two-man Film Editing Team 1, had already cut seven episodes of *Star Trek*, including "This Side of Paradise," "Space Seed," "Amok Time," "Metamorphosis," and "The City on the Edge of Forever." With all the split screen work, the complex camera angles creating the multiple Alice units, and a script that was over 70 pages long, there was an overabundance of material and a challenging job ahead of the two-man unit. The reason for the longer-than-normal length to the script was because, at the same time this one had been receiving its final polishing, the teleplay for "The Trouble with Tribbles" was going through the same process. A memo from Justman to Coon, concerning the latter, stated:

> [T]he pace of this show should be rather rapid. I don't envision our pages averaging anything more than 45 seconds a page, due to the type of show it is. This sort of show, with strong comedic overtones, must necessarily move very rapidly. Therefore, I feel that we will need at least 66 full pages to enable us to get anything approaching sufficient footage. (73-6)

To Justman's thinking, it is always better to run long than short. Long can be cut down. Short is just short. Unfortunately, sometimes that which is cut out is something we would have liked to have seen.

Van der Veer Photo Effects was responsible for the optical work, although all the shots of the Enterprise were recycled from other episodes.

Composer Samuel Matlovsky, who provided music for TV's *Flipper*, was hired by Robert Justman to write a partial score for "I, Mudd." Tracked music was used for the Teaser and most of Act I, but once the surreal world of Harry Mudd's android planet becomes the setting, something stranger and lighter in nature was needed. *Star Trek* had done nothing like this before. In the producer's opinion, what Matlovsky came up with did not quite fit the bill, either.

Roddenberry, in a memo to Wilbur Hatch, wrote:

Recently on the *Star Trek* episode "I, Mudd," we were shaken up to find that the composer disregarded many of Robert Justman's and Gene Coon's instructions and brought in music which really was not in keeping with the format established for our show. As it happened, our first indication of this was when Gene Coon visited the scoring stage and heard the music being played. By that time, as you know, it is too late to do much about it. (GR41-4)

But there was time to do something about Matlovsky. He was not asked to return.

Release / Reaction
Premiere air date: 11/3/67. NBC repeat broadcast: 4/5/68.

"I, Mudd" had a hell of a gimmick, prompting *TV Guide* to run a two-page color spread two weeks before the episode first aired on NBC. The title of the article: "4 X 4 Twins ' 2000 Androids."

Steven H. Scheuer reviewed the episode for his syndicated column, *TV Key Previews*. Among numerous newspapers across the country, the review was carried by the Mansfield, Ohio *News Journal*, on November 3, 1967. Scheuer wrote:

"I, Mudd." An amusing science fiction fantasy takes over *Star Trek* tonight. A human outlaw, Harry Mudd, well known as a thief and a no-gooder by Captain Kirk, finds himself in a unique position of being king to a planet of androids. Since the androids are programmed only to serve a human master, Mr. Mudd gives them orders to bring Kirk and his Enterprise crew to

Shatner-sandwich. The star happily posing with the statuesque Andrece twins (Courtsy of Gerald Gurian)

the planet, where they will stay forever. The result is a knotty problem for Captain Kirk.

Judy Crosby reviewed the episode for her syndicated column, *TV SCOUT*. Among the papers which ran her comments on November 3, 1967, was *The Pittsburgh Press*, in Pittsburgh, Pennsylvania:

Roger C. Carmel, who has gained more fame with his role of Roger in the new *Mothers-In-Law* series than as Harry Mudd on *Star Trek*, is back in that role tonight with a good story. It's about a band of female androids and Mudd is their

281

captive leader, but he's bored and he bargains with this unusual group of twins to permit his departure. In return, he will provide them with a starship captain (guess who?).

After all the promoting, A.C. Nielsen gauged the size of the viewing audience.

RATINGS / Nielsen National report for Friday, November 3, 1967:

8:30 to 9 p.m., 57.6% of U.S. TVs in use.	**Share:**	**Households:**
NBC: *Star Trek* (first half)	25.0%	11,090,000
ABC: *Hondo* (first half)	20.9%	8,570,000
CBS: *Gomer Pyle, U.S.M.C.*	**49.5%**	**17,300,000**
Local independent stations:	4.6%	-

9 to 9:30 p.m., 59.8% of U.S. TVs in use.	**Audience share:**
NBC: *Star Trek* (second half)	24.0%
ABC: *Hondo* (second half)	19.8%
CBS: *Friday Night Movie*	**44.7%**
Local independent stations:	11.0 %

A second Nielsen survey, this one concentrating on 12 key metropolitan areas, also had *Star Trek* in second place, well above the third place entry on ABC.

Trendex 12-city phone survey:	**Average rating, full hour:**
NBC: *Star Trek*	15.2
ABC: *Hondo*	8.0
CBS: *Gomer Pyle / Friday Night Movie*	**25.9**

The movie on CBS was the 1963 John Wayne western *McLintock!*, with Maureen O'Hara. *Star Trek*, in an episode with so many female doubles, had nearly double the audience as the competition on ABC and made a respectable showing against the powerful CBS lineup. According to the Trendex report, *Star Trek* was again NBC's top-rated Friday night show. *Tarzan*'s Nielsen rating of 13.8 was raised to 15.2 by *Trek*, even with no back-end support to sustain an audience against the balance of the CBS movie and the premiere of ABC's new lawyer drama, *Judd for the Defense*. NBC's help on this night, besides the sitcom *Accidental Family*, was the *Bell Telephone Hour*, presenting "Benjamin Britten and his Aldeburgh Festival," about the classical music conductor's recent event in England. It would have been swell fare for PBS.

The big question, with the return of Harry Mudd and all the sexiness, including the gorgeous Andrece twins multiplied by a couple of hundred, was: would NBC promote this episode? The answer: of course not. The network instead paid to buy a half-page ad in *TV Guide* and the television sections of countless newspapers across the country to promote how "[Benjamin] Britten is seen conducting and taking a few moments out to discuss the creative process and the demands made upon [classical music] artists by the public."

***

William Shatner was fond of this episode, as well as others being made at this time. Regarding this period in the series' production, he commented, "The characters seemed really alive, and our stories were sharp, exciting, intelligent, and frequently quite funny." (156-8)

Star Trek intended to do more Mudd episodes. Stephen Kandel said, "I did a number of Harry Mudd stories that never got made. The first, 'Deep Mudd,' picked up where 'I, Mudd' left off. The robots had collected the remnants of a lost, highly-advanced culture and Mudd found a suit which was, in effect, armor which adapted to its flesh-and-blood inhabitant and gave him extraordinary military prowess. What Mudd did was use the suit to escape and then the suit began modifying Mudd into a kind of an interstellar pirate. And the question was: whether Mudd, the lighthearted con man, would become real mean or would he be able to escape from the suit that gave him superhuman powers but took his soul as a payment. He had to con the suit, which was a computer-operated creature in its own right." (95-1)

Money issues, and Gene Roddenberry's desire to stay clear of pirate stories, kept this idea from advancing further.

"They told me during the third season that they were going to write another one for me in the next season," said Roger C. Carmel, "But, of course, there never was a next season." (29-2)

Carmel would act with William Shatner again, in an early 1970's episode of *Ironside*. And he did play Harry Mudd once more, although in voice only. "Mudd's Passion," scripted by Kandel, was aired on NBC in 1973 as an episode of *Star Trek: The Animated Series*.

Carmel said, "When I did the shows, I never thought it would evolve into this. I don't think any of us thought of it in terms of the immortality it seems to have achieved." (29-4)

Memories

Leonard Nimoy said, "Roger Carmel…. He's a marvelous actor and he had a tremendous impact on the audience." (128-25)

Walter Koenig said, "I really liked the man. He was terrific. He had that wonderful ability to be totally free in the work. He didn't care if it was silly, or whatever it might have been, he just was free to do whatever was asked of him and have a good time doing it. He was just a delight. Everybody liked him." (102)

"I get a lot of recognition from the *Star Trek* shows I did," Carmel said 20 years after filming the second Mudd episode. "People stop me on the street and want to say hello to ol' Harry…. How can you say anything bad about somebody who comes up and tells you they love you? They're very nice and very polite and enormously varied. All different types, from school kids, to older people, to rock-and-rollers, to conservative types. It's amazing!" (95-2)

In another interview, with this author, he said, "People in the industry knew me as Roger C. Carmel. Friends call me "Roger C." But everyone else calls me Harry Mudd. I'll be in a restaurant or walking down the street and I'll see the look on their face, then the smile, then they'll come over and put their hand out and say, 'Harry Mudd!' Not, 'Didn't you play Harry Mudd?' But they say it like I'm this old friend they once knew but haven't seen in a while. Perhaps I should change my name to Harcourt Fenton Mudd. Great name, isn't it?" (29)

18

Episode 42: THE TROUBLE WITH TRIBBLES

Written by David Gerrold
(with Gene L. Coon, uncredited)
Directed by Joseph Pevney

The iconic avalanche of tribbles
(Unaired film trim courtesy of Gerald Gurian)

From an NBC press release:

Millions of parasites swarm over the Enterprise and help Captain Kirk (William Shatner) defeat a hostile empire, in "The Trouble with Tribbles" on NBC Television Network's *Star Trek* colorcast.... Guest stars are William Schallert as Nilz Baris, Federation under-secretary of agricultural affairs; William Campbell as Koloth, a Klingon captain; Stanley Adams as Cyrano Jones, and Whit Bissell as Mr. Lurry, space station manager.... The Enterprise receives a distress call from space station K-7. Mr. Lurry introduces Kirk to Baris, who is out from Earth to plant grain on the planet Sherman. Lurry fears that the hostile planet, Klingon [sic], plans to steal the grain. Jones gives Lt. Uhura (Nichelle Nichols) one of the parasites called tribbles, to keep as a pet. More of the tribbles appear and multiply. When some of them die from eating the grain, Mr. Spock (Leonard Nimoy) and Dr. McCoy (DeForest Kelley) discover a spy among Baris's agricultural team.

Again, NBC was giving away the whole plot, with its press release to newspapers across the nation. *TV Guide* put it more simply, and better, and without spoiling the ending, for its December 29, 1967 issue:

Captain Kirk, assigned to protect a vital grain shipment at a space station, finds that he has troubles with tribbles. That's right, tribbles: balls of purring fluff that live on grain -- and are incredibly prolific.

Writer David Gerrold described his story as "Man against Klingon; Man against Man; and Man against Nature" … in the form of the tribbles. (73-6)

The theme? Dorothy Fontana summed it up, saying, "David wanted to, basically, tell a story about how things that look soft and cuddly and non-dangerous, can sometimes be the most dangerous thing you encounter." (64-2)

And perhaps the most dangerous thing to any species is overpopulation. This topic would be examined in great detail one year after this, in the 1968 book *The Population Bomb*, by Professor Paul Ehrlich. *Star Trek* would tackle this issue again in 1968, although in a much less subtle fashion than "Tribbles," in "The Mark of Gideon."

SOUND BITES

- *Baris:* "Captain Kirk, I consider your security measures a disgrace! In my opinion, you have taken this entire very important project far too lightly." *Kirk:* "On the contrary, sir, I consider this project to be very important. It is *you* I take lightly."

- *Korax:* "There is one Earthman who doesn't remind me of a Regulan Blood Worm – that's Kirk. A Regulan Bloodworm is soft and shapeless, but Kirk isn't soft. Kirk may be a swaggering, overbearing tin-plated dictator with delusions of godhood, but he's not soft."

- *McCoy:* "I can tell you this much -- almost fifty percent of the creature's metabolism is geared to reproduction. Do you know what you get if you feed a tribble too much?" *Kirk:* "A fat tribble?" *McCoy:* "No. You get a whole bunch of hungry little tribbles."

- *McCoy:* "The nearest thing that I can figure is that they're born pregnant."

ASSESSMENT

"The Tribbles with Tribbles" is one of *Star Trek*'s most beloved episodes. Although it's meant to induce laughter, all the elements needed for a successful dramatic story are present. At jeopardy is the starvation of an entire world, the balance of power between good guys and bad, and an Enterprise invasion by an alien life form with a proclivity to breed. Not to mention, Kirk has a headache.

In this tale, espionage, territorial disputes, bureaucratic ego, and tribbles all combine to create a story that is hard to categorize but impossible not to enjoy. Some may prefer *Star Trek* to be a more serious affair, but who could resist falling in love with a tribble?

THE STORY BEHIND THE STORY

Script Timeline

David Gerrold's "spec" treatment, "The Fuzzies": February 1967.
Gerrold's story outline, "A Fuzzy Thing Happened to Me," still on spec: June 13, 1967.
Gerrold's revised story outline, still on spec: June 17, 1967 (received June 23).
Gerrold's revised story outline, now on assignment, ST #72, received June 26, 1967.
Gerrold's 1st Draft teleplay, "The Trouble with Tribbles": June 30, 1967.
Gerrold's 2nd Draft teleplay: July 19, 1967.
Gene Coon's polish (Mimeo Department "Yellow Cover 1st Draft"): July 21, 1967.
Gerrold's script polish / edit, gratis (Final Draft teleplay): July 25, 1967.
Coon's further script polish / edit (Revised Final Draft teleplay): August 1, 1967.
Additional page revisions by Coon: August 15, 16, 18 & 21, 1967.

After producer Gene Coon invited David Gerrold to think about some story ideas that could be done within *Star Trek*'s restrictive budget [see Chapter 16], the aspiring writer told his mentor that he was toying with a story dealing with prolific fuzzy creatures. He remembered Coon saying, "Sounds cute, but it would probably cost too much. We'd have to build the creatures. No, think of something else." (73-6)

In March of 1967, after *Star Trek* had received its pick up, Gerrold submitted three story outlines: "The Protracted Man," "Bandi," and, despite Coon's polite turndown, "The Fuzzies."

Gerrold said, "Any other writer would have said, 'Oh, well, that's a dead end,' [but] I'm going to write it as an outline and show them how it can be done." (73-1)

In "The Fuzzies," at the recommendation of Gerrold's agent, the setting was not a space station but a small colony on an undeveloped planet known as the "Trading Post." The characters later to be developed as Nilz Baris and Arne Darvin were here, but with different names and job titles. Damon Jones, later to be Baris, assisted by his twitchy assistant (think Arne Darvin) had purchased a large quantity of grain, stored in warehouses at the trading post. He was planning to ship the crop to the planet Barth. The Barth Corporation, which owned 40% of that planet's usable land, didn't want Jones' grain. They had grain of their own, which the corporation was making a nice profit from, and therefore made an official protest to the Federation that the grain Jones wanted to send to Barth would "destroy the ecological balance" of the planet. In other words, they didn't want competition. Jones feared the Barth Corporation would sabotage his crop. The Federation, on the side of free enterprise, sent Kirk with orders to safeguard the grain until it could be shipped to Barth.

Once there, Kirk authorized shore leave for his crew. Yeoman Janice Rand, among the first to beam down, met Cyrano Smith, a colorful planet "locator" who was in the business of selling large corporations the rights to the worlds he found. He was also dealing in "fuzzies," small colorful balls of fluff that varied from tennis ball-size to volley ball-size. They had no legs, no eyes, just small soft mouths. When stroked, they throbbed and purred. They moved by pulsing and flexing their bodies, or rolling, depending on how far and how fast they wanted to go, and had only two senses -- a heat detection sense and a food detection sense. Smith was selling his fuzzies to local store keepers who, in turn, were selling them to those visiting the trading post … visitors like Janice Rand. She took her fuzzy back to the Enterprise.

Almost immediately, the fuzzies began breeding at an alarming rate, both on the planet and on the ship. McCoy dissected one and discovered they were "asexual," reproducing at will -- a will that grew as they ate. And they managed to get into everything. The ship's cook complained that fuzzies had even gotten into his flour stores. When Kirk and Spock looked into the Enterprise's huge flour bin they saw no flour, only a "seething mass of fuzzies." The grain bins at the "trading post" were also emptied of grain but filled with fuzzies.

Next, the Enterprise engaged in pursuit of Cyrano Smith, who fled in his small scout ship. Smith was apprehended and returned to the planet on charges of "tampering with interstellar shipments." However, they soon discovered that the fuzzies who ate the grain were dead -- all 1,771,561 of them (according to Spock's calculation). Tests revealed a virus in the grain, which, when consumed, prevented the consumers from taking in enough nutrition to survive. The fuzzies starved in a warehouse filled with food.

Smith recognized Jones' assistant as being an employee of the Barth Corporation. It was then discovered that the assistant infected the grain, and he was taken into custody. As for Smith, Kirk chose a punishment to fit the crime. Smith would stay at the trading post until he got rid of every last fuzzy.

Although different than the classic episode, the germ of the idea behind "The Trouble with Tribbles," as well as some of the structuring, was present. Some of the characters and plot turns were already in place, as well.

Gerrold didn't hear back from Coon's office until June, at which time he was called in for a meeting. Gerrold remembered Coon saying, "I'm not buying your story yet, David. I'm only interested in it. You haven't written the kind of outline that I'll buy; that's what we're going to talk about." (36c)

Janice Rand, of course, had to go. And Coon didn't want any references to corporations. His hand-scribbled note on Gerrold's story treatment said, "Big business angle out. One planet against another." (36b)

Gerrold was invited to try again with the understanding he was *not* being put on assignment to write anything, only that whatever he wrote would be read.

Days later, on June 13, Gerrold turned in his second try, now with the stranger title of "A Fuzzy Thing Happened to Me." The Interstellar Trading Post had a name: Topsy, and Gerrold offered the idea that it could remain a frontier town, for cost purposes, or be changed to a space station. There was more urgency in the beginning, with the Enterprise receiving a distress call from the trading post. Once there, a new character is introduced, Mayor Lurry, owner of Topsy. The character of Damon Jones had now been renamed Nilz Baris. Despite the name change, the character was the same -- a farmer-turned-businessmen who recently imported a new type of grain, and fears his competitors are out to sabotage his crop. The grain is now identified as triticale (tri-tih-cay-lee), a hybrid of wheat and rye. Baris' twitchy assistant has a name in this new draft: Arne Darvin. Rand was out and Uhura, with Sulu, was among those who embarked on the shore leave, encountering Jay Damon Cyrano (same character as Cyrano Smith in previous version). Uhura was given a fuzzy and returned to the Enterprise with it. New to the story: Baris becoming distressed when a private ship of his biggest competitor, Joseph Mackie, arrives, and Kirk confronting Mackie, who was described as "a pure villain-type." Kirk liked him even less than Baris and posted guards around the warehouses containing the grain.

Meanwhile, as in the previous draft, the fuzzies were multiplying. New here: A fight breaking out in a bar at the trading post between Kirk's men, including Scotty, and crewmen from Mackie's "yacht." The fight started when one of Mackie's men made derogatory remarks about Kirk's abilities as captain.

From here, the story evolved much the same as it had previously.

Coon sent the outline to Script Consultant Dorothy Fontana for her evaluation. She responded:

> I agree wholeheartedly that this story is one we should purchase. It needs more action, especially on Kirk's part, but it is overall different, thoroughly plausible, shootable and, most importantly, has the elements of fun grounded in serious problems for our principals that made "Shore Leave" so well received.... Even though we are actually overbought, I would recommend purchase of the story only, with another writer to be assigned teleplay. I would even prefer to see this story done in lieu of a couple of the ones we now have on assignment because of its difference and charm. It is, in my opinion, a story we cannot afford to lose this season. (DC42-1)

Forty years later, in conversation with this author, an amused Fontana recalled, "David still quotes it, that I wrote, 'This is a very nice story; I think we should assign it to a seasoned writer.' But Gene Coon said, 'I like this story and I'm going to let the kid do it.'" (64-2)

Gerrold was called in for another meeting. Coon reiterated that the plot point of small business against big business had to go. His note to Gerrold: "Must be a force hostile to well being of Federation in this area." (36b)

Having seen "Errand of Mercy" a few months earlier, Gerrold asked if he could use

287

the Klingons as the hostile force. Coon, the creator of the Klingons, liked the idea. Changing Mackie's yacht for a Klingon battle cruiser gave the story the danger element it lacked.

De Forest Research informed Coon that Gerrold had not invented the name "triticale," but it was a true hybrid, developed in Canada. Coon told Gerrold, "Then let us invent a vastly superior improvement." (36c)

The solution: "quadro-triticale."

Gerrold's third attempt, with a new title, the June 17 outline of "A Fuzzy Thing Happened," provided a suitable blueprint for the classic episode to come. Like quadro-triticale, Gerrold's 24-page treatment was a hybrid in its own right -- part outline, part teleplay. Gerrold intentionally wrote certain sections of his outline in screenplay form in order to demonstrate to Coon that he could structure scenes and write dialogue suited for *Star Trek*. By this time, he was confident Coon would buy the story; he wanted a chance at writing the teleplay, as well.

Many scenes that made it into the finalized episode are present. The fight in the "local bar and grill" (it had yet to be determined if Topsy was a planet settlement or a space station) was now between the Earthmen and the Klingons. Scotty throws the first punch because the Klingons have insulted the Enterprise, calling it "a sagging old rust bucket." The delightful scene where Kirk disciplines his men, then speaks to Scotty and discovers it was he who started the fight, is also here, although shorter and not as realized as in the episode. And, while opening a door to the storage compartments, a great mass of fuzzies tumble out, burying Kirk. Also, for the Tag scene, Scotty admits to Kirk that he transported all the fuzzies from the Enterprise to the Klingon ship.

Coon sent the outline to Fontana. Her response:

> This is still a delightful story, but I feel it needs some straight-lining, delineation of purpose and character.... We should lay in a definite attitude for Kirk. I suggest he is not happy with this particular role of policeman ... He doesn't care for watching over a pile of wheat.... The fuzzies need to grow more and more a nuisance. At some point, possibly in the third act -- late -- or fourth act, I think the fuzzies must also become a menace to the ship -- not just getting into the grain barrel in the galley, but spreading into the engine mechanisms or clogging the life support ventilation system.... I would not like to have the fuzzy purr. It should have some other sort of sound to indicate it is pleased -- something strange but nice -- maybe almost a bird song or trill -- but something not normally associated with a furry animal. (DC42-2)

Fontana closed her five-page memo, writing:

> Now, having read and memo'd this 24-page story outline, I find in my "in" basket a new version of the story that runs 31 pages. I will dutifully read that version and report verbally ... if you please. (DC42-2)

Gerrold was a fast writer. And a hungry writer. This was now his fourth draft of the story, *gratis*. He later revealed, "Finally, Gene Coon bought my outline. He had been about to hand it back to me for one more rewrite, just on the last two pages, then changed his mind." (73-6)

Coon's words, via Gerrold: "Hell, I'll buy it now and you can bring in the two pages tomorrow." (36c)

Having paid Gerrold $650, Coon could submit the story to NBC for its approval. Even though Fontana's ideas had yet to be included, Stan Robertson was jubilant, and wrote Coon:

Excellent story! The writer has shown great imagination and grasp of our series. The touches of humor, with the underlying and very evident threat of jeopardy, are superbly played against one another. If the screenplay is as successful as the story outline, this should be one of the most visually exciting and provocative *Star Trek*'s ever put on film. (SR42)

Gerrold recalled, "Gene L. Coon said, 'We're not going to assign this to a writer for two weeks. So, if you brought in a script version before that time, we'd of course be willing to read it.'" (73-1)

Gerrold didn't feel Coon was being unfair. According to him, "It was necessary. It would have been unfair if he had tried to do it to me a *second* time -- because if he was buying a second script from me, that meant he knew I could deliver a finished product and was asking to see one 'on spec.' Only so long as I was *unproven* would I be required to prove myself this way -- and that meant only *once*." (73-6)

Two weeks was -- and still is -- the normal amount of time given to a writer for a first draft script. Coon wanted to see if Gerrold could write like a pro, at the speed of a pro. Gerrold was faster. He delivered his script on June 30, in just three days. It was 61 pages long, a good length for a first draft.

Coon called Gerrold in for a story conference. He had scribbled notes across every page of the script, including:

Let's establish better that the quadro-triticale is of extreme importance to the Federation.... Make Kirk stronger, more in control.... Flesh out considerably.... Explanations! Reasoning! Decisions! (36b)

Coon gave Gerrold a six-page memo from Justman, prompting Gerrold to later say, "[Justman] presented one of the friendliest demeanors on the lot -- but don't let his looks fool you. Beneath that warm furry exterior, there lurked the heart of a miser. You would have thought he was spending his *own* money. And vicious? Well, no -- not really. But anyone who would send a six-page, single-spaced, one-thousand-words-to-the-page memo to a new writer, listing in glaring detail all the faults in his first rough draft script, is the kind of man who would sacrifice naked girl scouts, cookie packages still clutched in their hands, before a giant statue of Mammon, the god of money, while cackling gleefully and muttering arcane verses from the *Wall Street Journal*." (73-6)

Among all the glaring details of all the faults in Gerrold's first rough draft script, Justman wrote:

I dislike the Teaser very, very much. I consider it quite bad.... Set construction costs for this show are liable to be very, very high due to construction of Trading Post sets.... The Main Promenade of the Trading Post, as indicated on Page 12, is a swell thing, but who can afford it?... Cyrano is a very interesting character and could stand some more development. In many ways he reminds me of Harry Mudd. Does he remind you of Harry Mudd? (RJ42)

The feedback wasn't all critical. Gerrold had wanted to set his story on board a space station but was told this was too expensive. Justman, the miser, gave Gerrold a present, writing:

I like the idea of having this Trading Post within the confines of a Space Station. We could probably get a Miniature Space Station built and photographed and we would have something for ourselves for future shows. (RJ42)

Regarding Dougherty, a young crewman seen in the Teaser and then again during the fight with the Klingons, it was Justman's idea to change this to Chekov, creating yet another plum role for the series' newest regular.

And then there were the Fuzzies. Justman's memo continued:

> We should do some further investigation with regard to the Fuzzies and what they are to look like. I think it is important not only to develop the Fuzzy which is visually interesting and which we can also make for peanuts, but it should be something that we would have a great interest in marketing as a promotional device. (RJ42)

Coon had notes, too. He liked the scene where Kirk finds out Scotty threw the first punch, but Gerrold had neglected to milk it enough. Coon wrote:

> Get some fun out of this. Like every man's entitled to his own opinion, joke being he didn't get mad when Kirk was insulted, but he flipped when the ship was. (36d)

And Coon was still unhappy with the climax, that Darvin was revealed as a spy because Cyrano recognized him. His note to Gerrold:

> Let us somehow determine that Darvin is a Klingon agent. This will mean making something more of him … somehow get the goods on Darvin. (73-6)

Gerrold later said, "Almost at the last moment I realized, 'I know what this script needs, it needs a connection between Klingons and tribbles. That's how we figure out who the Klingon spy is, because the tribbles don't like the Klingons and Klingons don't like the tribbles.' It just came to me on the spur of the moment that I hadn't tied these two separate stories together." (73-1)

Another change that was needed was for Gerrold to come up with a different name for the Fuzzies. De Forest Research notified Coon that science fiction author H. Beam Piper had written a book called *Little Fuzzy* about the discovery of fur covered creatures called "Fuzzies." Although the 1962 book had nothing to do with purring balls that multiply at an alarming rate, Desilu Legal rightfully wanted the name changed.

Gerrold compiled a list of cute sounding names, including shaggies, gollies, goonies, roonies, willies, puffies, poofies, tippies, tribbies, triblets, and tribbles. Of these, he was bothered least by tribbles, and the name gave him an idea for a new title -- "You Think You've Got Tribbles?"

Coon hated it -- the title, not the name – and asked Gerrold not to use it. Gerrold thought, "Why call the creatures tribbles if you don't take advantage of at least one good pun?" (73-6)

A better pun was around the corner.

There was one more hurdle to cross. De Forest Research also discovered that Gerrold's script shared one similarity with a 1952 book by Robert A. Heinlein called *The Rolling Stones*. The story took place on Mars and featured a fuzzy little creature being raised as a pet by an Earth boy growing up there. The small animal was called a Flat Cat. It produced a soothing vibration when petted … and it was born pregnant.

"I thought David Gerrold's 'Trouble with Tribbles' was loads of fun," Pete Sloman of De Forest Research said. "We did, as you know if you read the notes on that, check with Heinlein about that. Joan [Pearce] said she talked to Heinlein and he said he had no monopoly on cute, fuzzy critters." (158a)

It was Joan Pearce's job, however, to report the similarity to Gene Coon. Ande Richardson-Kindryd, Coon's secretary, said, "Gene loved writers. That's why he would mentor young writers, like David Gerrold and Russell Bates [who would go on to co-write the script for the 1974 episode 'How Sharper Than a Serpent's Tooth' for *Star Trek: The Animated Series*]. For Gerrold, Gene called Heinlein personally and asked him to please let this go. We knew about it when De Forest Research caught it. Joan caught it and something had to be done. So Gene got on the phone immediately to Heinlein and was begging, 'Please let us do this script. He's a young writer; he didn't intend to rip you off.' Gene really went to bat for David Gerrold, or that script would have never gone." (144a)

Gene Roddenberry claimed to be the one who talked to Heinlein, and that Heinlein agreed to let it go, saying that both Gerrold and himself "owed something to Ellis Parker Butler," author of a 1905 short story called "Pigs Is Pigs."

Pigs … Flat Cats … Tribbles. Parce … Coon … Roddenberry. It seems Robert A. Heinlein's phone was ringing quite a bit that day.

Coon bought Gerrold's script, gave him more notes, then advised him to proceed to 2nd Draft. Gerrold later expressed, "Just as the premise went through two versions, and the outline through three, so would the script go through a series of metamorphoses and changes. Each time, it would get a little bit closer to what we wanted it to be. Like a sculptor who carves away everything that doesn't look like an elephant, we would trim away everything that didn't look like *Star Trek*…. Gene Coon never once told me what I had to do -- instead, he kept telling me what I *couldn't* do, and it was up to me to come up with something that fit. 'We need something here,' he would say. And I would start spewing ideas at him until he heard one he liked." (73-6)

Three weeks later, on July 19, Gerrold's 2nd Draft appeared. At 71 pages, it had evolved from corporate treachery to a story of espionage and the perfect vehicle to comment on the Cold War between Russia and America. Although a serious theme, the tone would be anything but.

"We didn't set out for it to be a comedy," said Gerrold. "As the script went through a number of drafts, we started putting in more and more jokes. Everybody was saying, 'Let's have fun.'" (73-1)

Gene Roddenberry, as Gerrold remembered, was not present when "Tribbles" was evolving from a light drama with elements of humor to an all-out comedy. He said, "Roddenberry was out of town ... which, I think, was one of the reasons 'Tribbles' turned out so good. He's a meddler ... he couldn't let a script go across his desk without changing it. Now, a lot of what he did was good, but he's not what you would call a funny guy. He's not a man with a sense of humor. If he'd been there, 'Tribbles' would not have been funny. There would have been that heavy seriousness about it. And the whole point of the episode is that it's charming and funny. Roddenberry could never have been lightweight, charming, fluffy, or funny." (73-1)

The decision to push the comedy was Gene Coon's. Gerrold said, "More than anything else, I needed guidance -- personal tutelage, if you will. And Gene Coon worked closer with me on 'The Trouble with Tribbles' than most collaborators would have. If it were up to me, Gene Coon would be entitled to half the credit for the episode." (73-6)

The Yellow Cover 1st Draft script came on July 21, just two days after Gerrold's 2nd Draft. Some minor polishing had taken place, but no cutting … yet. And there was much that needed to come out. The script, once typed by the Mimeo Department in the format used for TV scripts, was revealed as being bloated to the staggering page count of 80. The tab margins and spacing Gerrold used while typing allowed more words on each page than the manner in which the Mimeo Department did. And more words equates to more screen time.

Gerrold later marveled, "At a rate of one page per minute -- and allowing for commercials -- we had enough story to tell *Star Trek*'s first ninety-minute episode." (73-6)

Gerrold was in the office the morning the script came back from the mimeo department. Coon hadn't yet arrived, so Gerrold took a copy of the giant script to the soundstage where he sat and slashed while the company filmed "The Apple." He recalled, "After lunch I was called in to Gene Coon's office. He fixed me with his most penetrating, severe producer's stare. 'David,' he said, holding up a yellow covered copy of 'The Trouble with Tribbles.' 'Your script is too long. It's going to have to be cut.' 'I know,' I said, handing him one of my copies. 'Here are my cuts.'" (73-6)

Gerrold remembered Coon seeming "flustered." It was not the place of the freelance writer to decide where the cuts should be made; this was the job of the producer. But Coon, weary from all the work, accepted Gerrold's marked up copy of the script. He then did some marking of his own. The result was a much thinner Final Draft, dated July 25.

Coon oversaw additional page revisions, from August 15, 16, 18, and 21. The last set of pages cleared Coon's typewriter only two days before the start of production.

"This was not to say that Gene Coon was rewriting my work heavily," Gerrold later said. "Rather he was *un*writing. Or maybe the proper word is editing. Actually, there is no word to describe exactly what Gene Coon was doing -- but to my mind the situation came as close to being the ideal writer-producer relationship as I have ever experienced." (73-6)

Examination of the various script drafts supports this. Although he has often stated that Coon should have shared the teleplay credit, Gerrold, with "The Trouble with Tribbles," may have been one of the least rewritten freelance writers to have worked for *Star Trek*.

Pre-Production
August 14–18 and August 21 & 23, 1967 (6 days prep).

Joseph Pevney returned to direct and, like Daniels with "I, Mudd," was surprised when handed the script. There is a lightness to the writing not present in any other *Star Trek* script, a sense of humor that is not just entertaining to read but helpful to director and actors.

For example, for the character of Koloth, Gerrold wrote into his script:

> Koloth is the Klingon commander and like the last Klingon commander that we saw, he is an evil-looking S.O.B. One has only to look at Koloth to know that he hates dogs and children and is generally up to no good.

Descriptions in the script, such as these, made casting an easier process.

For the Klingon commander, Coon wanted to bring back John Colicos -- Kor from "Errand of Mercy." He felt a recurring adversary for Kirk would be good for the series. But Colicos was unavailable to take the job,

William Campbell one year earlier, as the Squire of Gothos (NBC publicity photo, courtesy Gerald Gurian)

so Coon called another actor he was fond of, and who had worked well in *Star Trek* before.

William Campbell, who was Trelane in "The Squire of Gothos," said, "When I walked into the meeting, they asked me what my conception of Captain Koloth was…. [I told them] 'Let me put it this way: I would never let anyone else hurt Kirk because *I've* got to hurt him -- in fact, I'll never kill him because I want to make the suffering long.' They said, 'That's exactly what we want.'" (27-5)

Campbell, 43 at this time, worked steadily in TV and films, usually as 1950s and 1960s contemporary punks or thugs, or villains in America's Old West. Campbell had prominent billing in big screen hits like *Escape from Fort Bravo*, *Man Without a Star*, *Backlash*, and the Elvis Presley vehicle, *Love Me Tender*. Coon knew Campbell from an episode of *The Wild, Wild West*, where he again played a bad guy, and Coon served as producer.

Campbell returned as Captain Koloth in "Blood Oath," an episode of *Star Trek: Deep Space 9*.

Stanley Adams, as Cyrano Jones, was 52, and in the middle of a quarter-century acting career with 200 roles in movies and on television. He appeared often on *Wagon Train* and *Gunsmoke*. He would return to *Star Trek*, not as an actor, but as a writer, for the episode "The Mark of Gideon."

Joseph Pevney said, "Stanley Adams was a good comic. And, you know, they didn't see him in that role at all. They said, 'Oh my God, no, you're kidding, Joe …' Stanley was funny; God, he was funny in that show. A wonderful, broad, heavy humor. Wonderful!" (141-2)

Stanley Adams as Captain Courageous (on right), for a pair of 1967 episodes of *Batman* (ABC publicity photo)

David Gerrold helped plant an idea into the minds of Joseph Pevney, Gene Coon, and Joe D'Agosta regarding the casting of Arne Darvin, the assistant to Nilz Baris. In the script, Gerrold wrote how an irked Kirk tells Baris, "You issued a priority one distress call because of a warehouse of wheat?!!," and Darvin injects himself into the conversation, correcting Kirk by saying, "Quadro-Triticale." Gerrold then typed: "Kirk starts to look at Darvin, but he is not worth it."

Charlie Brill, the evil Arne Darvin, was a young man with a long acting pedigree. He said, "I've been in this thing since I was seven years old. I did Broadway. I did *Peter Pan* with Jean Arthur and Boris Karloff in 1950. I did a lot of dramatic live television in the 1950s as a child actor." (21-1)

And then the child actor grew up to be a standup comedian with his wife and comedy partner, Mitzi McCall. McCall & Brill had the dubious distinction of following The Beatles when the curiosity from England first appeared on *The Ed Sullivan Show* on February 9, 1964. It was the most-watched show on television up to that time with an audience of 70 million, but very few were paying attention to McCall & Brill. Sullivan had The Beatles open the show and then brought them back for a second set, with Brill & McCall, and a handful of other acts that the teenagers in the audience had little interest in, sandwiched in between. Brill called it "the night of terror" and said, "A million pre-teenage kids screaming all during our act and Mitzi and I were standing next to each other and couldn't hear what the other was saying. And that was messing up our timing. And we thought that the people at home couldn't hear. So we spoke *louder*!" (21-1)

**Comedy team Charlie Brill and Mitzi McCall
(Casting photo)**

And that made the kids scream louder. "We want the Beatles!"

There's an old adage -- in Hollywood it's not what you know but *who* you know. Brill, who didn't know what *Star Trek* was, nonetheless had the inside track. He said, "Mitzi and I were Ann-Margret's opening act for years, and then Mitzi became pregnant so we couldn't do the nightclub act anymore. Leonard Nimoy, who was a friend, said, 'Why don't you come down and do my show? I'll introduce you to the people you need to meet.' And I said, 'What show?' And he said, 'I'm on a show called *Star Trek*. Meet me tomorrow morning at Paramount. I'll leave you a walk-in, then ask for me and I'll introduce you around.' So I went down to Paramount and he had left me a pass and I asked for him and they brought me onto the set. He said, 'Come on with me,' and he brought me into a big, *big* office. And the man behind the desk looked at me and said, 'Arne Darvin!'

And I said, 'Arne Darvin? What is that; like a Jewish holiday?' And Leonard said about me, 'Yeah, that's our Arne Darvin.' And then the guy behind the desk said, 'Okay, thanks for coming down.' So I walked out of the office and I said to Leonard, 'That went nowhere.' And he said, 'You just got a job, you schmuck.' And I said, 'On what?!' He said, 'On *Star Trek*! You're in the script after the next one!'" (21-1)

Brill would reprise the role of Arne Darvin more than three decades later for "Trials and Tribble-ations," an episode of *Star Trek: Deep Space 9*.

William Schallert, cast as the uptight Nilz Baris, had just finished three seasons playing Martin Lane, the dad on *The Patty Duke Show*. He was 45, and at this time, had an infrequent recurring role as Admiral Harold Harmon Hargrade, the founder of C.O.N.T.R.O.L., on *Get Smart*.

William Schallert, TV dad on *The Patty Duke Show* (ABC publicity photo, 1963–1966)

Whit Bissell, as Lt. Gen. Kirk, on *Time Tunnel* (ABC publicity photo, 1966-67)

Ed Reimers was the "You're in good hands with Allstate" guy, from the 1960s

Whit Bissell was 59 when he played Mr. Lurry, the manager of Deep Space Station K-7. One year earlier, he was a regular on Irwin Allen's *Time Tunnel*, as Army Lt. Gen. Kirk (no relation).

Paul Baxley, as Ensign Freeman, was 43. He served in Hollywood as a stuntman and stunt coordinator, and occasional actor (usually when stunts were required) for over four decades. During his career, he doubled for Marlon Brando and Darren McGavin. Baxley also doubled for William Shatner on a couple occasions when Shatner's regular stuntman, Dick Dial, was not available. Among his 13 *Star Trek* appearances, Baxley "doubled" poorly for John Fiedler in "Wolf in the Fold," played the Black Knight in "Shore Leave," and one of the natives in "The Apple." He returned to appear as an Enterprise crewman again, reassigned to Security, for "And the Children Shall Lead" and "Assignment: Earth."

Michael Pataki played Korax, the troublemaking Klingon who starts the barroom brawl. He was 29, had been on television since 1958, and had just begun a three-year recurring role on *The Flying Nun*, as Roberto. He would work with Shatner again in 1982 for an episode of *T.J. Hooker*, and then back to *Star Trek* for "Too Short a Season," an episode of *Next Generation*.

Ed Reimers, who played Admiral Fitzpatrick, was spokesman for Allstate Insurance in the 1960s. In the ad, he held his hands out, palms up, and said, "You're in good hands with Allstate." And then a small dollhouse would appear in his cupped hands. When shooting his scene for this episode, as he talks via video screen to Captain Kirk, Reimers caught a tribble tossed his way by someone off camera, then placed it into his cupped hands and said, "Oh, and, Captain, you're in good hands with tribbles." The gag made it into the blooper reel at the end of the season and was screened often at *Star Trek* conventions over the decades.

George Takei was originally planned to be a big part of "The Trouble with Tribbles," with Sulu handling much of the dialogue later reassigned to Chekov. But Takei had received an offer to appear in John Wayne's Vietnam action movie *The Green Berets*, which was set to film at this time. Without knowing that *Star Trek* would rerun well into the new millennium and *The Green Berets* would have a short shelf life, Takei asked for time off. This was granted, with his leave of absence from *Star Trek* commencing on August 22, 1967, the day before "The Trouble with Tribbles" began filming, and scheduled to continue through October 4, five days before episode 16 would commence principal photography. His absence would actually go on for a much longer period. More about that later as the *Star Trek* company waits, and then waits some more, for the return of Lt. Sulu.

As for the primary guest stars, the tribbles: Wah Chang designed the fuzzy creatures. Hundreds were sewn. Some staffers remember they were made from carpet, others from fur. Whatever the material, the task of making them come alive was given to Irving Feinberg and Jim Rugg.

"Believe me, I had tribble trouble," Feinberg said in 1968. "I had about one thousand tribbles made in four different sizes and four different colors. Some of them were fitted with balloons which could be inflated to make the tribbles pulsate. Others contained motors which moved them about." (58a)

For the larger tribbles, Feinberg used battery-operated toy dogs. He cut the heads off the dogs, then covered them in fur.

More inventive cost-cutting: The Enterprise miniature used in the shots with Space Station K-7 was actually one of the plastic model kits by AMT.

Production Diary
Filmed August 23, 24, 25, 28, 29 & 30, 1967.
(6 day production; budget set at 184,994)

Day 1: Filming in McCoy's medical lab -- the slate says 8-22-67; Bob Justman's production records say 8-23-67 -- bet on Justman (Courtesy of Gerald Gurian)

Production began Wednesday, August 23, 1967, the same day a major air battle took place in the skies over North Vietnam between the Vietnam People's Air Force and the United States Air Force. And it was on this day that The Beatles traveled to Wales to begin studying Transcendental Meditation under the Maharishi Mahesh Yogi. They could afford the trip. Their *Sgt. Pepper's Lonely Hearts Club Band* record was in its eighth week (out of fourteen) as the top-selling album in U.S. record stores. And their "All You Need Is Love" single was the most-played song on the nation's radio stations. David Janssen and Barry Morse had the cover of *TV Guide*, putting a spotlight on the final episode of *The Fugitive*, as, after four years on the run, Dr. Richard Kimble catches up with the one-armed man. The finale would become the highest-rated television show to this date, beating the record previously held by *The Ed Sullivan Show* for its February 9, 1964 program -- the one that introduced America to The Beatles (and featured Charlie Brill and Mitzi McCall).

Roddenberry was back in town and, reportedly, not happy with what he was seeing. Also less than thrilled about the shift *Star Trek* was making into comedy with this episode, and "I, Mudd," were Leonard Nimoy and Robert Justman. Others -- Gene Coon and Dorothy Fontana, as well as Shatner, Doohan, Nichols, and Koenig, were delighted to see boundaries being pushed. Joseph Pevney was also enthusiastic. And why not? He had, after all, directed episodes of *The Munsters*. Pevney even fought for the chance to push the envelope on "Tribbles," getting the most out of the comedy sequences.

"I fell in love with that show," Pevney said. "I really enjoyed doing it, and I enjoyed working with Leonard and Shatner to make them think in terms of typically farce comedy. The show was successful, and I was happy about that. I was proven right, that you *can* do comedy if you don't kid the script, and if you don't kid *Star Trek*. If you stay in character, you can have wonderful fun with *Star Trek*, and the kinds of things you can do with it are endless -- if you don't lose the whole flavor of Enterprise discipline." (141-2)

According to Gerrold, Pevney was very serious about his comedy. The writer said, "Joe Pevney was a nice guy, but focused on the job. I talked to him one time and he just kind of ignored me -- was too busy -- he never even turned to me and said, 'Nice script, David.' Whereas Marc Daniels, when he heard I was working on a script, said, 'Do a good job.' I got encouragement. Nothing against Joe, I think Joe's a terrific director. I thought he did a great job on 'Tribbles.' I just never got into a relationship with him, whether it was because I was coming across like a fanboy or whether he was too busy. You know, it could have been me as much as him." (73-1)

The first day of production dealt with the scenes on the bridge, without tribbles and then filled to the brim with them, including a tribble that was the equivalent to a whoopee cushion on Kirk's chair. Then the company moved into the ship's corridors, followed by McCoy's lab and office where the doctor and Mr. Spock discuss the merits or lack thereof concerning tribbles. And Kirk has a headache.

Bob Justman's production reports state that the medical lab scene was shot on August 23, 1967. The clapboard, held by Bill McGovern as the camera began rolling says August 22. But "I, Mudd" was still filming under the guidance of Marc Daniels on August 22. A possible explanation: as production crews rush through filming, the white tape placed on a clapboard with the date written across it is sometimes accidentally left on from the day before … and it could be several camera "takes" before anyone notices. On a hectic TV production schedule, anything can happen … and quite often does.

New on the set was John Dwyer, who had taken over as the series set decorator.

Dwyer recalled, "I had gotten the show because Joe Stone, who had been doing it as the set decorator, was a buddy of mine, and he told them, 'You need John Dwyer on this,' which was flattering. So I came in and met Matt [Jefferies] and we hit it off pretty good. And I guess the decorators from before I came in weren't necessarily the ones that everyone wanted to do the show. I think I just hit it off with them. And it's a mindset. It's like some people did westerns well. I did science fiction well." (57-4)

Carl Biddiscombe was the series' first set decorator, leaving half way through the first season and being replaced by Melvin March. Joseph Stone, the third to go through the revolving door, replaced March at the start of the second season. With Dwyer, *Star Trek* finally found the right man for the job -- the man who would stay for the remainder of the series … and even won *Star Trek* an Emmy nomination for his contributions.

Dwyer had reported to work one week earlier to watch and learn, and begin prepping his first episode. He said, "I came in four days before they started filming the 'Tribbles' episode, during 'I, Mudd.' Joe [Stone] didn't like *Star Trek*. He didn't have a touch for science fiction. I love to design stuff, and most decorators don't. So Joe wanted to do something else. And that's fine, because, for me, it was fun.… Carl didn't enjoy the show, either. Neither one of them had a good time because they didn't really understand what we were doing. Science fiction is an art form, but it's also telling a story, and it's a time period." (57-4)

Dwyer was allowed to pick his own crew. He said, "Mike May was my main assistant. I didn't want anybody left over from Joe's crew -- they weren't my type of people, they really weren't into doing the science fiction. So Mike was my lead man, and he and I did most of the stuff, with an additional occasional person." (57-4)

As for his first episode, Dwyer said, "It was a good one to start with, because most of it was shot on the ship, or the space station, which was the same basic look as the ship. I didn't have to stick my neck out too far. And that was good, because, in television, the first show is, in a sense, your trial period and, if you didn't get through it, then you were gone." (57-4)

Dwyer also came in during the filming of two back-to-back comedies, making his introduction to *Star Trek* even more positive. He said, "The No. 1 thing about *Star Trek*, and I'm sure everyone has said this, is family. Everyone pulled together. No 2 was you could come in and just do things without a lot of people jumping on you. There was a lot of freedom; they encouraged inventive thinking. And I loved 'The Trouble with Tribbles.' I thought it was wonderful -- because it was a comedy, of course. And what was interesting about that was, normally, I don't spend forever on the set, but that wasn't always the case here. My work on the set is usually done ahead of time, and the director comes in to say this was great and go on to the next one. So I don't usually get to see it filmed. But occasionally I'll sneak back to see what's going on. And I had to do that with that one. And that's what started it off for me, with everyone having a good time." (57-4)

Day 2, Thursday, August 24. The briefing room scenes were filmed, including Teaser, Act 1 and Act 3 sequences. Then, onto the transporter room. Then, "Int. Admiral Komack's Office" [later changed to Admiral Fitzpatrick], which utilized one wall of the transporter room for background.

"Work was getting done at a very steady pace," said David Gerrold. "It wasn't a boring set to be on. [Jerry] Finnerman would go off and he would have the next shot set up. He had a big enough lighting crew so the director could say, 'This is what I want after this.' So, while he's shooting this, the lighting crew is doing the next set. The director and the cast are going 'bing, bang, bing,' with a little bit of rehearsal. It was a very fast set. And I love that." (73-1)

Day 3, Friday. The delightful recreation room scenes were filmed as, first, Uhura gives away tribbles and Scotty reads technical manuals, then tribbles get into Kirk's chicken sandwich and coffee!

A rare occurrence took place this day: James Doohan allowed himself to be photographed with his right hand fully displayed to the camera -- the hand missing the middle finger at the knuckle. He had little choice, since Scotty was to rush into the recreation room with both hands and arms filled with tribbles. The scene played fast and no one could have noticed the missing digit at the time. Only decades later, with DVD slow motion scanning and digital screen capturing, has the brief appearance of Doohan's right hand been exposed.

Day 3. Note Scotty's right hand (to your left), and the missing middle finger (CBS Studios, Inc.)

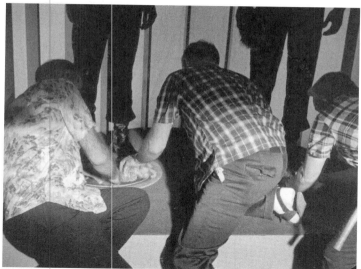

Day 3. Production crew members place tribbles at the feet of Kirk and Spock for the camera tie-down shot where they beam from the tribble infested Enterprise back to the space station (Courtesy of Gerald Gurian)

At midday, the company moved to Stage 10 for the first scenes in Mr. Lurry's office on the space station.

Charlie Brill said, "I hadn't seen the show; I didn't know anything about it. But I went onto the set and I saw the guys in wardrobe, so I knew it was a sci-fi thing. But that's all I knew about it. And then I found out it was like a popular show. I loved the costumes they were wearing and I laughed at Leonard's ears. I pointed at them and laughed. He was okay with it; he's among the nicest people on Earth. I liked Bill Schallert. We got along famously. And I hated the haircut they gave me. They cut my sideburns off and my hair was combed forward, like a little boy. I couldn't wait for it to grow back." (21-1)

Brill was in many of the scenes filmed this day and the next. He recalled, "Everybody was quite serious about their jobs. And everybody had a tribble. All the actresses had tribbles. They kept petting them; they loved them! Everyone but me! So I had nothing to hold; nothing to do with my hands when they were filming me. If you look at both scenes where I'm with the Enterprise people, my arms are folded. Because those costumes didn't have any pockets! So my arms would have just been hanging at my sides. So I folded them. I wish I could say I did that as an acting technique to portray arrogance. You can make believe I did. But the truth is, I just didn't know what to do with my hands. No pockets!" (21-1)

Concerning the star of *Star Trek*, Brill said, "I loved what he [Shatner] did in that episode. He plays comedy great. Leonard, of course, was brilliant. And there were laughs on that set. A lot of shows are too serious when they're being made. But not that one. We had a lot of fun." (21-1)

Day 4, Monday. Work continued in Lurry's office. Then, onto the "Storage corridor" for a scene that had the production crew in stitches.

Joe Pevney, the man supposedly in charge, said, "Bill is a delicious comedian. He loves doing comedy.... My only problem was making sure that they never went overboard." (141-2)

Al Francis, the camera operator, said, "Bill Shatner and some of the others were clowning around on the set. Joe was having a little problem with that, and he really barked at them. He told them that they were going to have to settle down, and he didn't want any more noise on the set. I was looking through the camera at the time, and I could see Shatner's eyes go over to him; here's a guy who really means business, and he'd

Day 5. Bill McGovern slates a shot to be taken on the space station trading bar (Courtesy of Gerald Gurian)

better be quiet. I burst out laughing. Joe said that of all the people to start laughing when he'd gotten everything under control, it would be me. And, I'll tell you, it was hilarious, because then everybody just broke up." (66-1)

Charlie Brill added, "When the tribbles come out of the door and fall all over Kirk, we were hysterical. And one landed on his head. They did it in one perfect take." (21-1)

It was a perfect moment, and a perfectly-exasperated reaction from William Shatner, preserved on film.

Day 6: Irving Feinberg's tribbles gathered in one place at one time (Unaired film trim courtesy of Gerald Gurian)

Day 5. Tuesday. Some pick-up shots were taken in the storage corridor before the company moved onto the space station bar set for the scenes where Chekov and Uhura are first shown a tribble by Cyrano Jones.

Day 6. Wednesday, August 30. It is an old Hollywood tradition to shoot the fight scenes last, just in case one of the performers gets a black eye. On this day, still on the bar set, the brawl between "Earthers" and Klingons was filmed.

James Doohan insisted on doing many of his own stunts and Pevney, unlike fellow *Trek* director Marc Daniels, was agreeable. You will have to look hard to find Jay Jones briefly doubling for Doohan.

"I did about 95 percent of my own stunts in the big fight scene," Doohan said. "About five percent, they used a stuntman, where some flying through the air was involved. It took about two hours to film the whole fight, once everything was lit. It was still a lot of fun to do. My stuntman, Jay Jones, said to me, when I had done all this stuff, 'If I ever become famous, would you be *my* stunt man?'" (52-1)

Under Joseph Pevney's skillful direction, "Tribbles" eased along, on budget and within its six-day shooting schedule.

Looking back at the experience, Charlie Brill said, "When Mitzi and I were on *The Ed Sullivan Show* with the Beatles, John Lennon was in the guests' room with me and he was doing these doodles -- drawing little cartoons on napkins. And he gave them to me. And I left them there. And then I was on the 'Tribbles' and everyone was taking tribbles home with them. But not me. So I missed out on some John Lennon doodles and some original tribbles. If Renoir had done a painting of me, I would have left that behind, too!" (21-1)

Post-Production
Available for editing: August 30, 1967. Rough Cut: Sept. 13. Final Cut: Sept. 15, 1967. Music Score recorded on October 5, 1967.

The AMT model of the Enterprise orbits Deep Space Station K-7, the latter acquired from Douglas Aircraft
(CBS Studios, Inc.)

Bruce Schoengarth and Edit Team 2 pulled it all together. The sound editor was Douglas Grindstaff. While Roddenberry may not have been pleased with the overt comedic approach taken during the final scripting and production of "Tribbles," he nonetheless was very involved in the creation of the episode's soundtrack. Grindstaff recalled, "He would call me up and tell me a script was being written, or stop by with a prop -- for instance, a tribble. He showed it to me, and we talked about how we should go sound wise with it. It had to make a very pleasing sound, it had to rear up when somebody approached and it didn't like him. There had to be a sound for one individual tribble, another for several tribbles, then a few more, then more than that, and eventually the sound had to fill the whole ship. I found a dove 'coo,' I flipped the track over and shaved off part of it with a razor blade. I then made a loop out of it, put it on a variable speed machine and changed the pitch of it to different frequencies.... I then went to a screech owl for the sound of the tribble rearing up, took the

301

screech and played with it and got variations of it. Then I took a bunch of balloon sounds, where you'd get a balloon and rub it, and we mixed that with other squeaky sounds that we had in the library, playing with all these at variable speeds, mixing them and making new sounds out of them, and putting them all together until we came up with the various composite sounds used throughout the whole show." (76-2)

The Howard Anderson Company provided the optical effects, which included an AMT model of the Enterprise orbiting Deep Space Station K-7. As for the space station, model builder Richard Datin said, "What Roddenberry had done was acquire a model of sorts from Douglas Aircraft of a space station and then I utilized that and modified it for that episode. At Howard Anderson's, during filming, I sat under it and rotated it and turned lights on and off. Then I was matted out of the shot." (46)

Composer Jerry Fielding scored his first of two episodes for *Star Trek*. He was chosen due to his background in comedy, having written music for *Bewitched*, *McHale's Navy*, and *Hogan's Heroes*. He also wrote the theme music for the latter. His work on action-adventure shows included *Star Trek*'s lead-in on NBC, *Tarzan*.

Fielding would be called back by Justman to score another off-beat *Trek*: the surrealistic "Spectre of the Gun." After that, he hit the big time, on the big screen, in 1969's *The Wild Bunch*, for which he received an Oscar nomination. Two other Oscar nods: *Straw Dogs* and *The Outlaw Josey Wales*. The directors of those two movies, Sam Peckinpah and Clint Eastwood, respectively, hired Fielding often. Other scores included those for Peckinpah's *Junior Bonner*, starring Steve McQueen, and a pair of Eastwood films -- *The Gauntlet* and *The Enforcer*.

Release / Reaction
Premiere air date: 12/29/67. NBC repeat broadcast: 6/21/68.

Steven H. Scheuer reviewed the episode for his syndicated column, *TV Key Previews*. Among newspapers across America to carry the review on June 21, 1968 (when "Tribbles" repeated on NBC) was *The Daily Star*, in Oneonta, New York. Scheuer said:

> An entertaining and amusing story about the rabbits of the future called tribbles. When merely one of these cuddly, loveable animals is taken aboard the Enterprise, its reproduction rate floods the starship with tribbles. However, they do save the day for Earth and foil a Klingon plot in this light-hearted, change-of-pace story.

Judy Crosby also reviewed the episode on June 21, 1968, for her syndicated column, *TV SCOUT*. Among the papers running the review was *The Edwardsville Intelligencer*, in Edwardsville, Illinois. Crosby told us:

> This series does not often get involved with comedy situations but when it does, it does it right, as in "The Trouble with Tribbles." Tribbles are tiny, fluffy, purring parasites with a fantastic ability for reproduction. It is this proliferation that provides the funny moments after Lt. Uhura is given one of the puff balls as a pet and she takes it back aboard the Enterprise. It also provides the means by which Captain Kirk uncovers a murderous agent in their midst. William Schallert is the guest star.

Charlie Bill and Mitzi McCall were watching the night "Tribbles" aired on NBC. He recalled, "We liked it; we laughed; we thought it was great. I hated my performance, of course, but everyone else was good. Yeah, we loved it." (21-1)

RATINGS / Nielsen National report for Friday, December 29, 1967:

8:30 to 9 p.m., 59.4% U.S. TVs in use.	Share:	Households:
NBC: *Star Trek*	26.9%	11,480,000
ABC: *Hondo*	26.0%	11,140,000
CBS: **Gomer Pyle, U.S.M.C.**	**44.1%**	**15,960,000**
Independent stations:	3.0%	-

9 to 9:30 p.m., 58.4 U.S. TVs in use.	Share:	Households:
NBC: *Star Trek*	28.4%	No data
ABC: *Hondo*	28.6%	No data
CBS: **Friday Night Movie**	**31.2%**	**No data**
Independent stations:	11.8%	No data

Star Trek was second place winner at 8:30 against the last episode of *Hondo*, but only slightly. Once 9 p.m. came around, it was a much closer horse race ... for everyone. The movie on CBS was 1961's *Portrait of a Mobster*, starring Leonard Nimoy's good buddy, Vic Morrow, a big draw on TV at the time due to his popularity on *Combat!* The movie won, with *Star Trek* and *Hondo* close behind. The latter two were at a virtual tie.

Star Trek was almost always NBC's highest-rated series on Fridays. *Tarzan*, the 7:30 to 8:30 show, handed-off 11,310,000 households to *Star Trek*, which increased them, only slightly on this night, to 11,480,000. Nearly half changed channels at 9:30, avoiding the struggling sitcom *Accidental Family* and dropping NBC's audience to 5,940,000, then another drop, to 4,870, for *The Bell Telephone Hour* featuring a tribute to classical music with 91-year-old Pablo Casals at Vermont's Marlboro Festival.

NBC, or perhaps it was Bell Telephone, sprung for a half-page ad in *TV Guide* and other news publications, for the 10 p.m. show. As usual, no promotion money was spent on *Star Trek*, but nonetheless it was still the network's peak show for the night.

It was another close race when "Tribbles" repeated in the summer. The CBS movie, 1964's suspenseful *Topkapi*, which won Peter Ustinov an Oscar and co-starred Maximilian Schell and Melina Mercouri, only managed to attract 27.0% of the TV audience, while *Star Trek* placed second with 26.3% and *Man in a Suitcase*, an ABC detective show, pulled in 25.4%. The remaining 21.3% went to the independent stations. And *Star Trek* was still NBC's top-performing Friday night show.

***

"Tribbles" was nominated for a Hugo Award in 1968.

The second book ever written about the making of the original *Star Trek* (the first being 1968's *The Making of Star Trek*) was devoted to this episode. David Gerrold published *The Trouble with Tribbles: The Birth, Sale and Final Production of One Episode* in 1973.

Cinefantastique magazine named "Tribbles" as one of the 10 best from the original series.

"Tribbles" was voted the single best episode of the original series by viewers of Sci-Fi Channel's *Star Trek* 40th Anniversary Celebration.

Star Trek 101, published in 2008, put this on a list of the 10 best from the original series.

Nichelle Nichols liked it, too. She named this as one of her favorites.

And then there were the sequels ... "More Tribbles, More Troubles," in 1973, for *Star Trek: The Animated Series*, written by Gerrold and featuring the voices of the series regulars as well as guest player Stanley Adams, and "Trials and Tribble-ations" in 1996, for *Star Trek: Deep Space 9*, with Charlie Brill returning to play an older Arne Darvin.

"Tribbles" has stood the test of time. Regardless, the different opinions between the two Genes about what *Star Trek* should be were about to come to an impasse.

From the Mail Bag

Sent the day "The Trouble with Tribbles" first aired on NBC, addressed to Mr. Charles Revson, President, Revlon, New York.

> Dear Mr. Revson: It has recently come to my attention that there is a very good chance that *Star Trek* will not be renewed by NBC for the coming year. This is indeed very sad news to all of us in the science-fiction field, from the fans and the readers to the professional writers and editors. Because the program is of such high quality -- this year has been just superb, and every week the program gets better, in all aspects -- the audience for serious science fiction has increased tremendously. Since you are one of *Star Trek*'s sponsors, I thought to register my support, enthusiasm, and affection for the program with you. I have dropped similar letters to the powers that be at NBC, for whatever good that will do. My hope is that your continued support of *Star Trek* will help rescue the Enterprise from network oblivion. Happy holidays! Cordially, Judy-Lynn Benjamin, Associate Editor, *Galaxy* Magazine.

Sent after the broadcast:

> To Whom It May Concern ... Why have most Klingons been dark-skinned with forked eyebrows, but the Klingons in "The Trouble with Tribbles" had light skin and ordinary eyebrows? Tim C.

The response:

> Because there are different races of Klingons, just as there are different races of Earthmen. Also, because, when Fred Phillips looked up information on Klingons for "The Trouble with Tribbles," the photos he found were poorly lit and gave the appearance of light skin and ordinary eyebrows. Since then, he has followed the "Errand of Mercy" style of Klingon. Ruth Berman, for *Star Trek*.

Memories

William Shatner said, "'The Trouble with Tribbles' was so much fun that the trouble *we* had with tribbles was keeping a straight face." (156-2)

James Doohan said, "This episode probably did the most since 'Wolf in the Fold' to establish Scotty's character and dynamics. That was a lot of fun. I loved the scene where Kirk is trying to figure out if Scotty started the fight over love of his captain and it turns out that the far more important insult involved the ship. *How dare they!* ... All in all, David Gerrold wrote a very solid script." (52-1)

Dorothy Fontana said, "Whenever I am asked what *Star Trek* episodes are my favorites, I always reply 'The City on the Edge of Forever' and 'The Trouble with Tribbles.' Both stories are unique in that they show sides of Captain James T. Kirk that were seldom displayed on the show -- a sense of humor and a fine appreciation for the ridiculous ['Tribbles'] and a genuine growth of love and poignant loss ['City']."

Walter Koenig said, "Very funny. I thought Bill was terrific. He played it perfectly. He really showed that he has a delightful sense of humor. And he could be very attractive that way. I remember his consternation of these things, these tribbles, and how they affected the rest of us. Yeah, it was a lot of fun." (102)

This was Joseph Pevney's absolute favorite, but the director remembered that not all were happy over the good fun. He said, "We had done some comic sequences in *Star Trek*, but this was the first out-and-out comedy we had done on the series, and Roddenberry was not in favor of it too much. He didn't cotton to the idea of making fun on this show." (141-2)

Samuel Peeples, who helped develop *Star Trek* with his teleplay for "Where No Man Has Gone Before," said, "I thought that the one with the fuzzy little creatures wasn't my idea of what the show should be. It was awfully cute and awfully nice, but it covered an area that I felt was unnecessary for that particular type of series." (136-3)

Leonard Nimoy also didn't appreciate "Tribbles" at the time of its production. He felt it was "frivolous." (128-3)

Jerry Finnerman was not a big fan of "Tribbles," either. Even 35 years after the accolades had been flooding in, he said, "Ah, it was campy. You know, everybody talks about that show, but it was just campy. That's all I can say. A Christmas show; for Christmastime. That's all." (63-3)

Robert Justman said, "I felt it went too far, comedically, and it worried me about believability. I felt it was just a little too character-ish. It worried me right up to the time that the show aired and we got a response, and it seemed that everybody liked it.@ (94-12)

William Campbell said, "After 'The Trouble with Tribbles' was aired, I felt 'Wow,' because I got such a response from playing the Klingon. Even the neighborhood kids teased my wife about being 'Mrs. Klingon.' People were writing to me about the eyebrows and the costume, and the way I played the part. And I thought to myself... this Captain of the Klingons will be a good adversary.... They respect each other's abilities, even though they're still adversaries." (27-7)

Coon had told Campbell that Koloth would become a recurring character. But the idea was discarded after Coon left the series.

"I think Roddenberry zigged when he should have zagged," Campbell said. "He never should have allowed the Kirk and Koloth thing to die."

Charlie Brill, from the vantage point of 2013, said, "I'm amazed at the loyalty of the fans. When I go to the conventions, I'm amazed that they know everything I said; they know everything I did; they know all about me. And I'm flattered. It's an annuity for the rest of my life. It was by the grace of God and by the grace of Leonard Nimoy that the whole thing happened." (21-1)

19

Labor Day Break, 1967

By the time the *Star Trek* company suspended production for the industry-wide two-week Labor Day holiday, much had changed at Desilu.

Desi Arnaz's idea -- which Lucille Ball tried to carry on in his absence -- had been a good one. Studios make money by renting out their facilities, but real profits, and growth, come from owning the series. What had been a formula for success with *I Love Lucy* and *The Untouchables* was now the formula for failure with *Star Trek*, *Mission: Impossible*, and, ultimately, Desilu.

At a glance, Desilu looked good. It claimed to have the largest and most complete film studio devoted to television in the world. There were three

Lucy and Desi, the birth of a dream
(franklymydear-blog.blogspot.com)

facilities -- two in Hollywood and one in Culver City, the latter including the Desilu 40 Acres backlot, with *Andy Griffith*'s Mayberry, *Gomer Pyle*'s Camp Henderson, and *Hogan's Heroes*' Stalag 13. The company showed earnings of $19,000,000 in 1966, more than half coming from the rental of stages, equipment, props, and back lots, to series owned by others. Danny Thomas and Sheldon Leonard were the best customers at Desilu, who, along with *The Andy Griffith Show* and *Gomer Pyle, U.S.M.C.*, rented space for *That Girl*, *Accidental Family*, *The Guns of Will Sonnett*, *The Danny Thomas Hour*, *I Spy*, and *Good Morning, World*. Also, Desilu tenants in 1967 were series producer Don Fedderson, with *Family Affair* and *My Three Sons*, Bing Crosby Productions, with *Hogan's Heroes*, and the former president of the studio, Desi Arnaz, with his new venture, *The Mothers-in-Law*. Other revenue sources came from syndication of older studio-owned series, such as *The Untouchables*. But, even with $19 million in earnings, the cost of running the studio was greater, primarily because of the current studio-owned properties, M*ission: Impossible* and *Star Trek*. Only *The Lucy Show*, in its sixth season, was turning a profit.

And then CBS ordered a fourth studio-owned series from Desilu -- the hour-long detective show, *Mannix*.

As *Star Trek* ventured into its second year, the burden of producing three hour-long weekly series proved to be too great for a studio lacking deep pockets. Desilu had lost the battle.

Desilu's neighbor, Paramount Pictures, and Gulf + Western, its cash-rich parent corporation, were looking to expand. Paramount had no television properties (studio-owned series), or a relationship with any of the networks. So, even with its money woes, Desilu was an attractive acquisition.

Danny Thomas, whose T & L Productions rented space at Desilu, was also interested in acquiring the studio. But Gulf + Western offered a better deal.

Negotiations between the two studios were well-underway in early February 1967. By mid month, Lucy's lawyer, Milton "Mickey" Rudin, was making progress with G + W board chairman Charles G. Bluhdorn. Lucy, however, was resistant. During a key make-it-or-break-it moment, she slipped away for an appearance on *The Jackie Gleason Show*, in Miami. When Lucy refused to take her attorney's phone calls, Rudin flew to Florida where he found her hiding out in a Miami hotel.

"Everybody had heard about the merger," Lucy later said. "I couldn't make up my mind. [Mickey] had to have an answer, he said. Twenty-four hours or we blow the deal. Well, we went over the whole thing again, and I started to cry. 'I need an hour,' I told him. 'I just gotta have an hour.'" (9-1)

Charles G. Bluhdorn, and Lucy, cutting the ribbon that ended a dream, July 26, 1967

Lucy finally agreed to call Bluhdorn. "I talked to him. And do you know what he said? He said, 'Miss Ball, one of the things I am prepared to like about you is that you care.' I cried again. Then I said 'yes.'" (9-1)

Gulf + Western Industries absorbed Desilu Studios in a $17,000,000 stock-exchange deal. G + W combined Paramount's holdings with Desilu's three-studio, 62-acre property. In return, Lucy's 60 percent of controlling interest in Desilu stock was traded for $10.2 million in Gulf + Western stock. Hollywood's first woman studio mogul stepped down from her throne.

Besides giving up Desilu, *Star Trek*, *Mission: Impossible*, and *Mannix*, Lucy made arrangements to end *The Lucy Show*. The series was a hit. It was the second-highest rated show on TV, just under *The Andy Griffith Show*, and just above *Gomer Pyle*. All were filmed at Desilu. But Lucy still owned her series and she wasn't about to hand it over to Gulf + Western. Instead, she would sell it into syndication and then, for the 1968-69 television season, launch a new series called *Here's Lucy*. Paramount could own that show, and CBS would happily place it into Lucy's long-standing Monday night slot.

On July 26, 1967, as the *Star Trek* cast and crew were busy filming scenes for "Mirror, Mirror," Lucy -- with Charles Bluhdorn at her side -- cut a ribbon where a wall had once stood between Paramount and Desilu. She told the visiting press, "Mr. Bluhdorn is interested in keeping the lots alive, not inactive, and that is what I want. It's a natural marriage, and I was happy to make it."

When asked if Desilu and Paramount would co-produce television and motion-picture properties, Bluhdorn promised, "We'll cooperate in everything."

As *Star Trek* moved toward completing its preliminary second season order of 16 episodes, and continued to carry the brand of Desilu, Lucy remained a figurehead at the studio. But Lucy's industry savvy told her that this would be a temporary situation. In an interview with Hollywood columnist Rex Reed, she said, "I never wanted to be an executive, but when my marriage to Desi broke up after 19 years, I couldn't just walk away from my obligations and say forget it. We were an institution. So I took on all the responsibilities. Now I've just sold the whole damn thing to a bigger corporation, and pretty soon they'll take my name off the door ... and I'll be free."

Lucy had put on a brave face for the press. And the makers of *Star Trek* would soon learn that they had lost their staunchest supporter.

***

Initially, Gene Roddenberry and Robert Justman felt the Desilu takeover by Paramount would be to their advantage. Paramount had storage houses, filled with more props and set pieces, more specialty shops, more stages, more outdoor sets, more personnel, more of everything a producer might need to improve the look of his show. But bigger companies come with bigger problems -- more red tape, more micromanaging, and more inclination toward corporate thinking.

On August 10, 1967, as the standoff nature of the bigger studio was becoming evident, Roddenberry wrote to Herb Solow:

> Dear Herb: Since the first signs [that] Paramount and Desilu would merge, we on STAR TREK have been interested in how the additional facilities could be used to improve both our product and our efficiency. As I mentioned to [*The Lucy Show* producer] Leo Pepin today, we have several times asked questions about what might be available there in the way of standing sets, specialized stages, specialized optical equipment, wigs, costumes, backdrops, and so on. In items where we can make guesses, such as wigs or costumes, we have already made some inquiries. In other areas, we have to depend upon those at Paramount to make suggestions to us. I've yet to receive any such calls or suggestions or even questions about our needs and problems other than through the excellent Mr. Pepin, who I can hardly expect to be immediately and totally filled in on Paramount facilities. Are any of the production people over there aware that we

are anxious to cooperate for our mutual benefit?

Mutual benefit, however, requires mutual goals. And Roddenberry's agenda was very different from the studio's. He wanted to produce quality television. Gulf + Western wanted to turn a profit. Roddenberry and Robert Justman quickly learned that the corporate bean counters were worse than anything *Star Trek* had experienced under the management of cash-poor Desilu.

Roddenberry wrote to Justman on September 21:

> As I understand the new Paramount-Desilu television methods, it will be our responsibility to turn out STAR TREK scripts which in the final shooting version will budget out at $180,000 or $182,500, depending on the final figure determined between John Reynolds and myself. Thus, somewhere between the first draft of the teleplay and the final shooting script we must make revisions which satisfy both our series needs and at the same time gives us an episode which budgets out properly and can be shot in six ten-hour working days.

So far in the second season, only two episodes had been made for these amounts (or less): "The Doomsday Machine," which had been filmed in five days (allowing more money to be spent on the photographic effects), and "The Changeling," which also had been a "bottle show," requiring no new sets and no guest stars, only a large prop named Nomad. The new budget seemed more impossible than the limiting budgets that had come before. Even if Roddenberry and Justman could fashion scripts to be shot in six days, those days, according to Paramount, would have to be shorter.

A 10-hour workday on a television production (which does not include time in makeup), provides precious little time to achieve all that must be done. Set preparation takes time, lighting takes time, camera blocking takes time, rehearsing takes time. And even when the camera would begin rolling shortly after 8 a.m., Paramount mandated that the set be wrapped by 6:30 p.m.

Nimoy, a new breed of minstrel

Producing a series should get easier with each new season. The costumes are made, the established sets built, the format locked in, the characters explored, the production crew primed, and a string of writers and directors who have displayed a knack for the series now assembled. *Star Trek*'s hardest days, however, were still to come.

***

With *Mr. Spock's Music from Outer Space* a best seller, and the single, "A Visit to a Sad

309

Planet," on the charts, Dot Records sent Nimoy back to the recording studio to cut a follow-up single.

"The Ballad of Bilbo Baggins," from Nimoy's second album, and written by producer Charles Green, was an insipid comedy song with a lyric that had something to do with J.R.R. Tolkien's *The Hobbit*. However, the song gained notoriety with Nimoy's appearance on the July 28, 1967 episode of *Malibu U*, a short-lived variety television series hosted by Ricky Nelson. Nimoy, sans the pointed ears, lip-synched the song in a campy music video, accompanied by a group of color-coordinated young women, singing and dancing on a beach, and all wearing plastic elf ears.

The "Bilbo Baggins" single, snuck out in September, failed to chart. Forty years later, thanks to the Internet and that outrageous campy performance, it has become Nimoy's best-known recording.

"Cotton Candy," a pop ballad written by Cliff Ralke, a member of the *Star Trek* camera crew, was given the B-side.

***

The creative staff at *Star Trek* was not pleased with Bantam's first paperback, from January 1967, which translated the teleplays they had worked so hard on into short story form. Nimoy was actually the first to complain (on February 7, just weeks after the release of the first collection), when he forwarded a letter from a fan to Gene Roddenberry. The January 25 letter from J. Mallory, of Seattle, Washington, read:

First Bantam *Star Trek* paperback, with cover art by James Bama

> Dear Mr. Nimoy: Is there anything you can do about subsequent editions of the paperback *Star Trek*, adapted by James Blish? I have never before been so disappointed in a product of a recognized science fiction writer. Aside from depicting the Terrenes on the Enterprise as a bunch of bigoted nincompoops, Mr. Blish completely depersonalized Mr. Spock and pretty well clouded his image by using unsuitable descriptive words when his evidently miniscule vocabulary failed to provide more fitting ones. In addition, he completely edited out the portions of each script which I, at least, think have been the highlights of the series; for example, in "The Naked Time," the scene in which Mr. Spock realizes that he

310

has become infected with the inhibition-suppressing disease, locks himself in a conference room while trying to get control of himself, and ends up clouting Captain Kirk across the room.

Blish, for that first volume, had only included the portions of the stories that could be told from Captain Kirk's point of view, the series' chosen protagonist. He had also been largely ignoring the character of McCoy.

On August 22, after reading the manuscript for the second Bantam paperback, Dorothy Fontana wrote Roddenberry:

> Because this is an adaptation of my script "Tomorrow Is Yesterday," perhaps I am more touchy on it than on others. But, Mr. Blish has left out an important moving point of this particular story -- that Captain Christopher has to be returned to Earth because his son has not been born yet. The ending of "Tomorrow Is Yesterday" is most unsatisfying. The story simply stops -- unresolved. We end on the note of "we'll try the slingshot effect and maybe it'll get us back to where we started from and maybe we'll return Christopher to Earth." There is none of the drama of the actual doing, returning Chris and finally reaching "home" themselves that wraps the story. I take strong objection to this and urgently request that you read it to see if you agree.... The ending of the "Court Martial" story is singularly flat and dull. Please read and consider. He has taken out the physical confrontation of Kirk and Finney which topped the whole story. What is the use of having an antagonist who is never, ever seen throughout?... "Operation: Annihilate!" -- this is the big blunder. Whoever provided Blish with the script did not give him a shooting script with all changes. He must have received a "gray cover" which was almost totally rewritten by the time we got it to shooting stage. As a result, this adapted story is not only not what we put on the air, but it's pretty bad. Well, at least it lacks all the personal elements and urgency we placed in the story -- the fact that the three people we find on the planet in the radio station are Kirk's brother Sam, his sister-in-law Aurelan, and nephew Peter; that both the brother and sister-in-law die, etc. I feel strongly this should be revamped to conform with what we did air.... Incidentally, I also recommend you read the story because to me the ending is again totally unsatisfying. It just stops.... I don't care if it does take a page or two more -- a story teller tells the whole story or he's a lousy story teller. After all, it's what we get paid for. Why should Blish be any different?

On August 24, Roddenberry sent notes from his production staff on Blish's second manuscript to Desilu's Ed Perlstein. He also included a copy of the *Star Trek* Writers' Guide. Roddenberry wrote:

> It is important to us that *Star Trek* books reflect certain things well established in the series.... I am sure that Mr. Blish, as a professional writer himself, would want it no other way.

Later that day, Perlstein wrote to Arlene Donovan, Senior Editor for Bantam Books in New York, passing along the staff notes, the Writers' Guide, and a further request, writing:

> I would like to indicate that we would like a little more recitation on Dr. McCoy, as DeForest Kelley, who plays Dr. McCoy, is being received exceptionally well and is being treated very strongly and as one of the important performers in the series.

On top of all their other duties concerning the writing and production and delivery of a weekly TV series, the *Star Trek* creative staff had now become book editors.

***

Late August / Early September 1967. Between the productions of "The Trouble with Tribbles" and "Bread and Circuses," the *Star Trek* stages went dark for two weeks, allowing Gene Roddenberry and key cast members to make the rounds, giving interviews and personal appearances. Shatner and Nimoy even visited with Barbara Walters -- in their *Star Trek* uniforms – live, on the *Today* show.

August 14, 1967. Gene Roddenberry was among those to be presented with the first NAACP Image Awards at the Beverly Hilton Hotel in Beverly Hills. The National Association for the Advancement of Colored People honored Roddenberry for *Star Trek*, Leonard Kaufman for *Daktari*, Edward H. Feldman for *Hogan's Heroes*, Sheldon Leonard for *I Spy*, and Bruce Geller for *Mission: Impossible*, among others, for "their efforts to portray Negroes in a better light."

August 30, 1967. *Daily Variety* ran the

Another weekend, another parade for Mr. Spock. With or without the pointed ears, Leonard Nimoy was in constant demand (www.beyondspock.com)

Star Trek fans included NASA scientists and technicians, during the launch of Mariner 5 in October 1967 (trekcore.com and startrekpropauthority.com)

headline, "With *Trek* on Hiatus, Stars on the Promo Prowl." The primary targets, according to the article, were key "Nielsen cities." Shatner would visit Portland, Milwaukee, Cincinnati, Miami, New York, and Indianapolis. DeForest Kelley would hit Dallas, Fort Worth, and Atlanta. Roddenberry would fly to Washington and New York.

Nimoy was in great demand and kept especially busy. He received offers daily to make personal appearances at fairs, car dealerships, and anywhere an increase in attendance could spur sales. In one offer alone, a Connecticut amusement park was willing to pay him $2,000 for a few hours of his time, and pointed ears were optional.

Between celebrity appearances, serving as the grand marshal in a parade, and dropping in on various TV shows to perform his new single, Leonard Nimoy was also keeping company with scientists. In a letter to Roddenberry, he wrote:

Dear Gene: I would like to outline some of the thoughts that are still fresh in my mind resulting from a very exciting trip to Washington, where, as you know, I represented STAR TREK as a guest of honor for the National Space Club.... The trip broke down into two major areas: One was a very extensive tour through the Goddard Space Flight Center; second was the Goddard memorial dinner, which was attended by 1500 members of the National Space Club, and at which the principal speaker was Vice President Humphrey.... I must start by telling you that I felt somewhat ill at ease. As an actor in a TV drama, dealing with people who are involved in the reality of the space program, I had no way of knowing what the scientific community attitude towards our show would be. I was met at the airport by Mrs. Alberta Moran, who is the Executive Secretary to Dr. Clark, head of the Center, and was driven to the Sheraton Plaza Hotel, where even while checking in I was besieged by fans with questions about the show, and specifically its future life on NBC.... The next morning my wife and I were driven to Goddard Center, and upon arriving discovered that a major part of the population, secretaries and scientists alike, having learned that we were coming, were waiting to greet us at the front door. This was the first real taste that I had of the NASA attitude towards STAR TREK.... I do not overstate the fact when I tell you that the interest in the show is so intense, that it would almost seem they feel we are a dramatization of the future of their space program, and they have completely taken us to heart -- particularly since you and the rest of the production staff of STAR TREK have taken such great pains in the area of scientific detail on our show. They are, in fact, proud of the show as though in some way it represents them.... The trip through Goddard was very exciting, and I found them constantly pointing out equipment and procedural activities as they are specifically related to equipment and procedures on our show. In the communication room for example, comments were made such as "this is the equivalent of the communications panel on the bridge on your ship".... At the reception prior to the dinner, I was introduced to [astronaut] John Glenn and the other men who were to sit on the dais at the dinner. They were all most cordial, many of them wanting autographs and pictures for themselves and their children.... During this time I encountered representatives of various important engineering, scientific, and electronic firms, who were in Washington specifically for this dinner, and who are providing in some way, materials or information for the space program. They were most interested in the show as a vehicle through which they might promote their theories in order to popularize them and thereby gain acceptance at the real scientific level. Ion propulsion for the Enterprise, for example, was one of the theories most strongly put forth.... In general, there is a very strong interest in the scientific possibility as expressed by

313

science fiction writers and STAR TREK since these ideas stimulate the thinking of the more pragmatic scientists whose job it then becomes to implement these theories…. In short, it was an exciting privilege to be able to represent the show in that environment.

James Doohan on a tour of a space facility with pilot Bruce Peterson (NASA Dryden Flight Research Center Photo Collection, 1967)

Meanwhile, the promotion push continued.

August 31, 1967. Roddenberry was present as *Star Trek* was honored at the Smithsonian National Air & Space Museum in Washington, D.C. The second pilot film was put on exhibit, where it remains to this day, with more than a few differences from the broadcast version.

September 1, 1967. Shatner's first stop, as *Variety* had reported, was Portland, Oregon for an appearance on NBC affiliate KGW-TV and local newspaper interviews.

September 2, 1967. Shatner traveled to Salem, Oregon, appearing at the Oregon State Fair, then off to Seattle, Washington, for another TV interview, this one for NBC's KING-TV, and another local newspaper Q & A.

On the same day Shatner visited Salem, Oregon, there was a sneak peak of *Star Trek*'s second season in New York City, at NYCon3, for the 25th World Science Fiction Convention. Fans of the genre came together for a celebration, the Hugo Awards, and the first public screening of "Amok Time."

The true potential of the merchandising of *Star Trek* became evident at the convention. Prior to the gathering, the AMT model kit of the Enterprise had been doing staggering business and was well on its way to moving over one million kits by Christmas. And Leonard Nimoy's Dot Records album, *Mr. Spock's Music From Outer Space*, was also a major success. Both items were selling briskly on the convention floor but, more significantly, this was when Roddenberry discovered that the discards of *Star Trek* could have great monetary value.

A major event at the convention was a benefit auction, proceeds of which were to bring Japanese science fiction fan Takumi Shibano to the United States. Bjo and John Trimble, heads of the auction committee, asked Roddenberry to donate *Star Trek* memorabilia for the event. Among items sent in: scripts, sketches by Matt Jefferies, a green velour female's tunic, Kirk's torn shirt from "Amok Time," several retired pairs of Spock ears, a copy of Roddenberry's original series proposal for *Star Trek*, and a copy of the writers' bible. There was also a box filled with small balls of fur, labeled "tribbles" -- although no one at this time knew what a tribble was. The donated items became the second biggest draw at the convention, bested only by the Hugo Awards. Within two and a half hours, the $5000 needed to bring Shibano to America was raised.

"[That] was when *Star Trek* fandom first came together and became a force in and of itself," said John Trimble. "People who met each other at the convention went off and started producing fanzines and formed clubs." (177a)

Roddenberry was well aware of the offers Nimoy received and the sales of model kits. Now, with the success of the *Star Trek* auction at NYCon3, he saw the potential in a new business. The launch of Lincoln Enterprises (AKA *Star Trek* Enterprises) was just a few months away.

As for the 1966 Hugo Awards program, the nominating committee admittedly did not hold a high opinion of TV science fiction. At this point, only *The Twilight Zone* had been acknowledged with a single Hugo, and the very rules set by the committee diminished a television show's chances for victory. Only the episodes aired prior to January 1, 1967 -- half of *Star Trek*'s freshman season -- could be considered. And those episodes would need to stand on their own like a movie, not be considered part of a greater whole.

In an effort to better the odds, Roddenberry wrote a letter on November 4, 1966 to Andrew Porter, secretary of NYCon3. He argued that it was a mistake to nominate science fiction series based on single episodes. To Roddenberry, this was akin to judging a novel by a single chapter.

Getting nowhere with Porter, Roddenberry tried again, on November 17, with a letter to the convention's co-chair, Ted White. Using a different tack, Roddenberry argued that it was unfair to pit a 50-minute TV episode shot on a tight budget against a big-screen feature film with a large budget and less time restraints.

Ignored once again, Roddenberry wrote a third letter. Again, the recipient was Ted White.

On May 5, 1967, nearly six months later, White sent a stinging response, writing:

I'm sure it must be disappointing to you to find that you are in competition with *Fantastic Voyage* and *Fahrenheit 451* for the Hugo Award this year, but, unfortunately, the Hugo Awards are not geared for your exclusive set of interests, nor will they be.... There is no question in my mind that if we allowed *Star Trek* to be voted as a series, it would easily win the Drama Hugo. Indeed, if *Star Trek* were not on the air, it might even be that *Time Tunnel* could win on that basis.

White accused Roddenberry of "shamefully" exploiting the previous year's convention by screening "Where No Man Has Gone Before" to thunderous applause. He now warned: "The dignity of the convention was compromised last year. It will not be this year."

And then a final slap in the face. White suggested that Roddenberry wished "full credit for not only the conception of the series as a whole, but for each episode, as well," and added, "Perhaps I am uninformed on the subject, but that strikes me as presumptuous."

Someone had clearly poisoned the waters at NYCon3 for Gene Roddenberry. The toastmaster for the convention that year, by the way, was Harlan Ellison.

"We were a fairly well knit band," Ellison said. "Dick Matheson, Charles Beaumont, and Bradbury, and Asimov -- we knew each other for years, and we liked each other as people and respected each other as talent. And so when Roddenberry tried to stick his nose in, and tried to get somebody on his side, it fell very flat." (58)

Regardless, when the nominations came in, four episodes of *Star Trek* had won consideration: Jerry Sohl's "The Corbomite Maneuver," John D.F. Black's "The Naked Time," and Roddenberry's "The Menagerie, Part 1 and Part 2." This was impressive, especially considering that no episodes of *Voyage to the Bottom of the Sea* were nominated, nor were any from *Lost in Space, The Time Tunnel*, or *It's About Time*. The formidable competition, as White had stated, were those two major motion pictures: *Fantastic Voyage* and *Fahrenheit 451*

After Ted White's letter, Roddenberry gave up all hope of bringing home the grand prize. Worse, fearing an ambush, he decided to not attend NYCon3. Instead, on June 19, 1967, he sent a letter to his new friend Isaac Asimov, explaining why he would sit the convention out. The word "humiliation" was prominently used.

Roddenberry said, "I'm surprised that anyone who reaches my age is totally sane, because life is often a process of being knocked down and stomped on and laughed at and rejected. I don't recall not being rejected." (145-23)

"Gene was a very insecure man, even though he had been a Marine [sic] and he had been a cop," Harlan Ellison said in an interview for this book. "When you become an icon, most people forget that you're made of human clay. Gene more than most of us. He had flaws that ran deep and wide. And he allowed them to get in the way of his judgment and of his interaction with others." (58)

Those at the very top of the awards program did indeed disrespect Gene Roddenberry. But they couldn't control the judges. "The Menagerie," with Part 1 and Part 2 combined, won the Hugo Award for Best Filmed Science Fiction of 1966. *Star Trek* prevailed. But not without one last snub. Roddenberry was not notified of his victory. He received the belated good news from Asimov. The grand winner in Hugo's only non-literary category was left to make his own inquiry as to how to go about picking up his award.

September 4, 1967. The "Shatner Talks *Trek* Tour" continued. Next stop, Milwaukee, Wisconsin, for two televised live appearances -- first on *The Coffee Break Show*, followed by *The Noon Show*, both on NBC station WTMJ-TV.

September 5, 1967. Shatner was now in Cincinnati, Ohio, chatting it up on the *50/50 Club* for NBC's WLW-TV. He stuck around and did it all again for the same station's *The Afternoon Show*.

September 6, 1967. Shatner was in Miami, Florida, seen on NBC affiliate WCK-TV.

September 7, 1967. Shatner landed in New York to appear on the network flagship station WNBC-TV.

September 9, 1967. Shatner was now in Indianapolis, visiting *The Jim Gerard Show* on WFMB-TV.

September 10, 1967. Shatner wrapped his promotional tour in Philadelphia, appearing on *The Mike Douglas Show* at KYW-TV, shown live in that market and syndicated across the country on a tape delay.

On September 18, after returning to Los Angeles, Shatner wrote to Roddenberry, saying:

> I can't stress enough how impressed I was by the trip, and how much we accomplished in appearances at the individual stations. Without exception, the station promotional people were delighted to have us in their cities and expressed the hope that it wouldn't be too long between visits. They assured us, and we were convinced, that appearances in their cities mean as much as two or three points in the ratings.

***

On September 1, 1967, *Star Trek*'s first fanzine was published by Sherna Comerford of Newark, New Jersey, and Devra Michele Langsam, of Brooklyn, New York. Comerford, 25, was a research assistant in psychobiology at the Rutgers Institute of Animal Behavior. Langsam, 24, was a children's librarian for the Brooklyn Public Library. Their fanzine, *Spockanalia*, issue #1, was circulated on the convention floor of NYCon3. It contained a letter from Leonard Nimoy, wishing the young women luck.

The editors wrote:

> In June, we learned from *Star Trek*'s Associate Producer, Robert H. Justman, that the tentatively scheduled season opener (September 15th) will take place, in part, on the planet Vulcan. We have since learned that the show, "Amok Time," was written by no less an author than Theodore Sturgeon. In the course of the program, Spock will meet his assigned wife, for the purpose of satisfying the Vulcan mating drive. Vulcans -- or, at least, Vulcan males -- must experience sex every seven years, or die.... We have been told that the story is handled with the same care and skill that made *Star Trek* our favorite program in its first season. Look out, September 15th -- here we come!

Comerford and Langsam understood that the pen is mightier than the sword, writing elsewhere in the fanzine:

> We are eternally grateful to the people who pick up the check for our favorite program. However, it has come to our attention that small but important segments of action are cut from the broadcast received in some cities, especially those in the parts of the country that get their master broadcast from New York City. The time gained is used for additional commercials. The most blatant example discovered thus far is in "Dagger of the Mind." Only a fraction of the audience saw the approximately thirty seconds that showed Spock become entrapped in Van Jager's [sic] mind, to such a degree that Dr. McCoy was forced to tear him free physically.... This scene was not vital to the action of the plot, but it was quite important in the development of the characters of Spock and McCoy. It also was an extremely dramatic moment.... If you would like to protest this commercial padding, write to WNBC-TV, 30 Rockefeller Place, New York.

Another announcement in the premiere issue:

317

According to Bjo Trimble, *Star Trek* still has renewal problems. If we want the show to continue (<u>if</u> we want ...!), we must continue the campaign. Letters should be addressed to: Mort Werner [address included]. Write soon and often. Good <u>continuing</u> public response is a <u>sine qua non</u> for any TV series, especially one in prime-time. If we appear to lose interest, so will NBC.

***

The Trimbles had met Roddenberry a year earlier in 1966, during the Labor Day holiday at Tricon (the 24th World Science Fiction Convention). He invited them to call the next time they were in Los Angeles. While traveling from their home in Oakland to L.A., they decided to take Roddenberry up on his invitation, never thinking he would actually respond. Bjo Trimble said, "But he came onto the phone immediately, saying, 'Hi. How are you; *where* are you?' We said we were in the San Fernando Valley. He said, 'Well, we can have a late lunch. Come on in to Desilu. I'll leave a pass at the gate.' And we

John and Bjo Trimble at FUN-CON, 1968
(Los Angeles Science Fantasy Society)

thought, 'Wow,' but said, 'Well, yeah, sure.' We went in and he took us to lunch and was very affable; very kind. We were later told by some people that the predictions in Hollywood were bad for the show because it didn't follow any of the outline for other shows, and, since it was so new and so weird, they predicted that it would fail. And so Gene was so thrilled to have people like it. In fact, he let fans come visit the set, until he found out their insurance wouldn't cover it. But he did take us to lunch; we talked about the show and he was so thrilled that his creation was responded to by the fans. We talked for quite a while, and then he took us to the set. We were impressed by the workmanship and by the enthusiasm, from both the workers and the actors. So Gene said -- and he meant it -- 'Next time you're down, give us a call and you can come visit the set again.' And we thought that was kind of fun. And we did. We had a friend who could babysit the kids and it was really kind of a nice little mini-vacation when we came down." (177-8)

During the second season, the Trimbles moved closer to *Star Trek*. Bjo Trimble said, "John got transferred down here, and shortly after that, his employer said, 'Well, we're going to have to let you go,' as companies seem to often do after they cause all this upheaval by moving the whole family. Both of us were speed typists, so we got a job with a script typing service. In those days, they didn't do anything in-house at the studios and they sent the scripts out. And there were only three of these services, I believe, and all had to be close to the studios. The one where we worked was the closest to Paramount and Desilu, so we got a lot of scripts from them -- the Marlo Thomas Show [*That Girl*] and things like that. And *Star Trek* scripts kept coming across the desk. And they'd bring them over to us and say, 'You're the science fiction fans; you may even understand this gobbledygook.' So we began to get more and more acquainted with *Star Trek*. Then John talked them into letting us make the deliveries, so they would let him deliver the scripts over to the studio. And John, at that point, got to talk to Gene a lot." (177-8)

Entrenched in the awareness of *Star Trek*, the Trimbles, in time, would make their presence known when once again NBC threatened cancellation. For now, however, their days were spent typing *Star Trek* scripts. Bjo said, "Those scripts were far better written than any we were seeing for other shows. Gene had this idea of going one step farther than what was going on at the other shows, with their producers, that you couldn't turn a western into a science fiction show just by having a rocket instead of a horse; a space gun instead of a six-shooter. And he would hire real science fiction writers. And that suddenly raised the quality of *Star Trek* to another whole sphere." (177-8)

20

A Tale of Two Genes: Roddenberry versus Coon

Some described Gene L. Coon as a rough and tumble guy; a former newspaper man; former Marine; distant or tough. Others saw him as a humanitarian; a romanticist; a writer, who was sympathetic and caring of others, especially other writers. The lengthy memos he wrote while at *Star Trek* indicate the latter assessment of his character. His scripts indicate it, as well. He was, after all, the man who wrote "Metamorphosis," an unusual and epic love story.

Ande Richardson-Kindryd, Coon's secretary at *Star Trek*, said about her boss, "Gene was always a writer. That's what he loved. And that was a gift he gave me, because the scripts would always hit my desk first and he'd say, 'Okay, tell me about it. Tell me the story.' And we'd talk about it." (144a)

Gene L. Coon poses with his secretary Ande Richardson-Kindryd, with NBC's Stan Robertson in background (Courtesy of Ande Richardson-Kindryd)

Coon also had a knack for comedy writing, which means an ability to see the funny side of life. And that, too, affected the mood around the *Star Trek* offices. Of this, Richardson-Kindryd said, "Because of Gene's sardonic sense of humor, I used to answer the phone in a low, sultry voice and say, 'Coon's coon, can I help you?' You could do that there. Gene Coon allowed you to be who you were and have a sense of humor about things. And Gene was always encouraging me not to take crap, so I took off the straight-haired wig I wore, which my mother had always wanted me to wear and which most black women wore at the time when working in offices, and I was really feeling *me*, and no one was going to be able to mess with me about that. There I was with my Afro haircut, and I'd pick up the phone and I'd say, 'This is Coon's coon.' And if whoever was on the other end sounded shocked or said, 'Oh, uh, is this Mr. Coon's office?,' I'd change my voice back to a professional demeanor and quickly say, 'I'm sorry. Yes, this is Mr. Coon's office. Can I help you?' But, by then, I was able to say to myself, 'I am who I am, and I don't care what names you put on me.' And I thank Gene for that." (144a)

Coon provided Richardson-Kindryd with both emotional and financial support. She said, "They didn't pay secretaries much then, and I was a single mom, so we had a strict budget. But Gene always got me the most he could. He'd have me put down some overtime each week on my time sheet so I would make a little more." (144a)

During his tenure at *Star Trek*, the writer of "Metamorphosis" became a character in an unusual and epic love story himself. Its roots went back to the close of World War II. At that time, when he was discharged from the Marines, Coon took advantage of the G.I. Bill and enrolled in Columbia School of Broadcasting. The class consisted of eight former Marines and two young women. Coon soon developed a fondness for one of the girls, Jackie Owings, and she seemed to return the feelings, although she was engaged to be married.

Richardson said, "Jackie was one of the two girls. Joy, who Gene would eventually marry, was the other. But Jackie was the one he fell for. I think she was 19 at that time. But, because she was engaged, and because Gene was such an honorable person, he couldn't just come out and say to her what he felt. He was really a super-straight person in that sense. His values and his ethics were impeccable. I never saw anything different. And so he didn't say anything to Jackie." (144a)

Coon did write to Jackie, professing his love for her, but ethics stopped him from sending that letter. In time, Jackie misinterpreted Coon's lack of action for disinterest and stayed committed to the man she had agreed to marry, even though she had doubts about the union.

Richardson-Kindryd said, "So they all went off to work for different radio stations, except for Joy, who was still there. And Gene had taken a notice. It was never a passionate love. It was just that she was there." (144a)

A devastated Coon, on the rebound, began dating Joy Hankins. Within a year, they were married. Ten years later, Coon had become terribly unhappy in his marriage.

"She didn't love him as much as he'd hoped," James Doohan recalled. "Gene said that's what broke his heart." (52-1)

Nichelle Nichols witnessed the incompatibility first hand at an awards dinner where she was seated near the two Genes and their wives. For *Beyond Uhura*, she wrote, "I had the bad luck to witness the two soon-to-be ex-wives insulting their respective husbands for all the world -- and their husbands -- to hear. Everyone at the table was obviously uncomfortable witnessing the wives' withering putdowns while Gene and Gene sat silently, smoking their cigarettes, staring off into the distance. Then the two Genes quietly and politely excused themselves from the table and did not return until the very end of the evening."

As fate would have it, a short time later, Coon had a reunion with his first crush. Jackie was now divorced and, as Ande Richardson-Kindryd recalled, had turned to modeling under the name Jackie Mitchell. One day, while driving to the studio, Coon spotted a giant image of Jackie looking down at him from a billboard on Sunset Boulevard. When he arrived at work, he began sifting through casting photos.

Richardson-Kindryd said, "Gene was looking through a casting booklet one day, and he said, 'Ande, see if you can get this woman to come over for an interview and don't mention my name.' And he told me to find out if she was the former Jackie Owings. So I called the agent and he confirmed that her maiden name was Owings. She wasn't really an actor; she was a model and preferred the runway where she had contact with the audience. But I invited her over for a casting meeting, anyway, even thought there really wasn't any casting in mind for her. She came in and Gene was so excited. Well, they went into his office and they didn't come out for hours. And when they did, Gene was a totally different man. And this was about a week before he broke up with Joy." (144a)

Jackie, going under the name of Jacqueline Fernandez when interviewed for *Great Birds of the Galaxy*, said, "I remember clearly that the first thing I asked him was, 'Are you happy?' and he just broke down and cried. It was overwhelming. We made a lunch date for the next day. I had never stopped loving Gene. You don't get over a first love. You move forward, but it remains a treasure in your heart. We got together the next day, and the feelings between us were still strong and I said to him, 'I never want you to leave again.' ... After lunch, we talked some more in the car and Gene told me that he'd become so unhappy in his marriage that he'd recently bought himself a gun, planning to kill himself. That would have been his way out. So when he found me again, he just threw all caution to the wind and, by six o'clock, we'd decided to get married."

Gene Coon's friend, William Campbell (who played Trelane in "The Squire of Gothos" and Koloth in "The Trouble with Tribbles"), recalled that Coon broke the news to Roddenberry before even telling his own wife. It was at a party. Roddenberry mentioned to Coon that Joy seemed in "really fine spirits." Coon responded, "Well, yes, but I don't know how she's going to react after tonight.... I'm leaving her tomorrow." (27-6)

According to Campbell, Coon couldn't bring himself to give his wife the bad news. But Joy sensed something was wrong and asked her husband if his quiet behavior of late had anything to do with her. Coon told her everything. They cried together through the night and, in the morning, Coon put his papers into a briefcase and left.

Richardson-Kindryd said, "I screwed up, because Gene asked me to send Joy some roses, and I thought roses were boring, so I sent her flowers, and it turned out they were the flowers that he and Joy had during a very romantic period in Hawaii. It brought up past memories of a time that was gone. It really hurt Joy. It just broke her heart. And I always felt horrible. She was a nice lady." (144a)

"Actually, he felt so incredibly guilty about leaving Joy that he just left her with everything," Jackie Fernandez said. "Absolutely everything." (60)

Ande Richardson-Kindryd confirmed this, saying, "That's when he was really stressed -- that period, because he had Jackie, and he was still looking after Joy. He had the new house to pay for, and the old house to pay for, and the dogs he left behind, which he loved, so, of course, he had to get new dogs. And he didn't want Jackie to work, so he got her a Mercedes immediately, and took good care of Jackie. And, Joy, too. But Joy got *everything*. He would even still have her send the vet bills for the dogs." (144a)

Amidst all this change in Gene Coon's personal life, there was great change churning in his professional life, too.

***

The two Genes had much in common. Both had a passion for writing and a flare for writing *Star Trek*. They were stimulated by intellectual concepts and were prolific and ambitious. Together, they anguished over the relentless battles between series producer and those they answered to at the studio and the network. And the two were also romantics at heart, although they exhibited it differently. Gene Coon sought to find love in the arms of one woman, while Roddenberry was willing -- if not happy -- to share with many. There were other differences.

Gene Roddenberry aspired to be famous, and perceived by his peers and the public as the Jonathan Swift of his time -- an influential writer of stories about social stigmas, prejudice, sex, politics, and religion. Gene Coon, while often making a profound point in his stories and teleplays, was happy to merely entertain. He was not driven to be revered as a creator of message-heavy drama, like Roddenberry. And he was not about to risk his career over a single TV show. Roddenberry was.

"I've never been afraid of a fight," Roddenberry said. "When you're the producer of

**Roddenberry craved literary prestige
(photo from Roddenberry.com)**

a television series, there isn't a day when you're not fighting someone -- the studio men, the network men, the advertising men, even your own men. I came in prepared for that. The problem I had was I couldn't stand [guard on] every watch. I needed help. But no other producer was going to fight as hard as I would." (145)

There was never any question that Gene Roddenberry appreciated Gene Coon immensely. Roddenberry recognized Coon's writing talents and willingness to work tirelessly, as he himself and Robert Justman had for so long. But there were, nonetheless, fundamental differences between the two Genes regarding the tone and direction of *Star Trek*. Roddenberry disliked redundancy. He had complained to Coon about story elements in the past which resembled those in others, such as a female crewmember falling for an Enterprise visitor, then turning against captain and ship to stand by her new man. It happened in both the early scripts for "The Alternative Factor" and "Space Seed," under Coon's supervision, contributing to the failure of the former when the plot point was eliminated.

On June 19, 1967, Dorothy Fontana wrote to Roddenberry, with cc to Coon, saying:

I have noticed an alarming amount of similarities in the stories we have purchased and have in work, and I suggest examination of them before we come down to shooting scripts. "The Apple" and the proposed Darlene Hartman story ["Shol"] are very close in their lush Polynesian type backgrounds and a simple people serving an all-powerful god. "Friday's Child" and "A Private Little War" are so close to each other in story that I don't even like to think about it. "The Doomsday Machine" and "Obsession" both have starship Captains with a revenge motive who are intent upon destroying an alien creature or machine. We have to deal with God in actuality or in reference in "The Apple," "Who Mourns for Adonais?," "The Changeling," and [Paul Schneider's] "He Walked Among Us." Our people are captured by aliens and have mates forced upon them in "Gamesters of Pentathlon"[later to be named "The Gamesters of Triskelion"] and "By Any Other Name." We have to do with disembodied brains in "Gamesters of Pentathlon" and "Return to Tomorrow." In "Amok Time" and "Bread and Circuses," Kirk and Spock are pitted against each other in mortal combat. In "Amok Time," Spock "kills" Kirk. In "Bread and Circuses," Kirk "kills" Spock. "Gamesters of Pentathlon" also has physical combat as a main story point.

Roddenberry responded the next day, writing to Fontana, also with cc to Coon:

I was pleased to get your memo regarding the similarities in various stories we have in work because I have been concerned about the same thing.

Gene Coon, demonstrated by his work on *Star Trek*, clearly believed that if something worked once, let it work again. Roddenberry's memo made a clear demonstration of its own -- that the recycling of ideas must stop and Fontana was now the watchdog. He wrote:

> The most practical answers, since they are in work, is the one you suggest -- careful inspection and remedial surgery while they are in outline and first draft. For this, Gene Coon will be depending very much on you. Both of us have been extremely pleased with your memos and the story sense displayed, as well as the creative suggestions.

In many of the instances Fontana listed, changes were made, with the earlier script or story outline usually winning out over the latter one to arrive at the production offices.

- The Hartman script was shelved, eliminating the possibility of comparisons between it and "The Apple."
- "A Private Little War" was modified to be less like "Friday's Child," which was further along in development.
- "By Any Other Name," lagging behind "Gamesters of Pentathlon," forfeited the idea of using crew members as breeding stock.
- The disembodied brains in "Return to Tomorrow" were changed to illuminating spheres, again yielding to "Gamesters," a story that was advancing more confidently toward production.
- McCoy took Kirk's place in fighting Spock to the death in "Bread and Circuses," so that Spock and Kirk could have at it in "Amok Time," slated to film first.
- Spock would not "die" in "Bread and Circuses," so that Kirk *could* in "Amok Time"… and then die again, in "Return to Tomorrow," and Scott could die in "The Changeling."
- And "He Walks Among Us," bogged down and delayed through a series of unsuccessful rewrites, was shelved, leaving the path clear for the other three scripts it resembled to divvy up the god themes.

But there was a bigger difference between the two Genes than opposite opinions on the repeating of plot gimmicks. In the weeks leading up to the convention and the second season premiere, Roddenberry had been distracted from *Star Trek*, busy writing a television pilot based on Robin Hood. When he embarked on this project, the scripts for "I, Mudd" and "The Trouble with Tribbles" were being finalized and, while certainly light in tone, "Tribbles" was not yet a comedy, "Mudd" not yet a farce. By the time Roddenberry finished his Robin Hood script, on August 25, 1967, and returned to *Star Trek* on August 28, "I, Mudd" had completed filming and "The Trouble with Tribbles" was already three days into production. Both episodes, through a series of rewrites during Roddenberry's absence, had advanced from semi-comical to all-out comedies.

Roddenberry arrived on set in time to witness hundreds of tribbles being dumped onto Captain Kirk's head. Laughter rang out all over Desilu Stage 10. The crew and much of the cast were having a ball. Roddenberry fell silent. The next day, after the filming of the campy space station bar fight, he headed to the screening room to look at the footage from "I, Mudd." It was funny stuff, but the series' creator wasn't laughing. And then he read the latest draft of the next script to be filmed. In Roddenberry's words, "Bread and Circuses," his idea for a parallel world story with a serious message about slavery, had turned into something more resembling "a comic opera [in] 1967 Rome."

Coon, who had cut his teeth in comedy with pilot scripts for *McHale's Navy* and *The Munsters* was, in Roddenberry's mind, proving to be a questionable babysitter for *Star Trek*. And Coon appeared to have seduced Shatner, Doohan, Nichols, Koenig, Fontana, Daniels, and Pevney into enthusiastically following his lead into what some might consider *Lost in Space* territory. Only Justman, Nimoy and, from afar, Samuel Peeples, seemed concerned over the shift in tone.

Joseph Pevney, who directed "The Trouble with Tribbles," said, "Roddenberry was not in favor of it too much. He didn't cotton to the idea of making fun on this show." (141-2)

"Coon and Roddenberry had something of a falling out," said an anonymous *Star Trek* insider, as quoted by Edward Gross in *Great Birds of the Galaxy*. "Nobody's really talked about it, because the details weren't very well known, [but] apparently they had a disagreement about the direction of the show or what Coon was doing with the show. I suspect part of it was that Coon was letting the show get too funny. Although the audience responded very well to the humor in *Star Trek*, Roddenberry had gone off on an extended vacation [sic] and Coon, during that vacation, bought a lot of scripts and pushed a lot of things through production, and the show worked very efficiently without Roddenberry there. Roddenberry came back and found that a lot of changes had been made.... So they had a falling out."

"I was always determined not to let *Star Trek* cross over into *Lost in Space* territory," Roddenberry said. "I was never opposed to humor in *Star Trek*, but I did make a conscious effort to draw the line at camp." (145)

Humor, of course, is subjective. What one person finds to be funny can often be something another sees as objectionable.

"Gene L. Coon's characters joked with one another," David Gerrold said. "Roddenberry always took the show too seriously and everybody preached. I think Roddenberry wanted to be a preacher. [He] said, 'In the future our people work together,' but what he would write would be sermons. In Gene L. Coon's scripts, people interacted with each other in a whole different way and didn't preach." (73-4)

Taking the counterpoint, Gene Roddenberry's son Rod said, "David Gerrold is certainly entitled to his opinion. And my dad wasn't perfect. But, I think that there isn't too much depth in that episode ['The Trouble with Tribbles']. And it doesn't really elevate *Star Trek* to where it is today. So I'm glad my dad was preachy." (145a)

After lengthy behind-closed-door discussions between the two Genes, Coon decided he wanted out. The creative differences contributed greatly to his rash decision, but there were other factors at play. Coon's true calling was writing. He didn't mind producing and, in fact, would produce again, but a series such as *Star Trek*, due to its unique premise and highly distinctive characters, required extensive reworking of other writers' scripts, which caused hurt feelings. And this, in addition to fights over creative direction with Roddenberry, and the critical nature of the memos from Justman, Fontana, Robertson, and even Joan Pearce at De Forest Research, was wearing Coon down.

"When I came along, he was tired," said Jackie Fernandez. "I think it was a combination of everything and he was just ready to quit." (60)

"The problem is that we wore him out," said Justman. "[And this] is why he ultimately left in the middle of the second season." (94-7)

"He was happy on *Star Trek* for quite a while," said Doris Halsey, who managed Coon with her late husband Reece Halsey. "Then both personal and professional things started weighing on him. [And] he was having personal problems with Shatner and Nimoy.

325

He had a very low respect for actors, except his friends." (77)

Unlike most series, *Star Trek* had a pair of extremely ambitious and talented stars who were competing with one another, one of which was actually counting who had the most lines in the scripts, and both of which were making numerous suggestions for story and script changes.

"That wasn't a problem for me," said John D.F. Black, the man who sat in the producer's chair before Gene Coon. "Bill and Leonard wanted different things. Leonard wanted to be accepted as a serious actor. Bill wanted to be a star. As Leonard's popularity grew, I can see that Bill would worry about who had more lines. Of course he would. Captain Kirk was the series' lead, and the series' lead *has* to have more to do. And that means more to say. Leonard didn't worry about that. He was more concerned with *what* we had him saying, not how much he said. I understood that. I started as an actor, so I knew the difference between the two (Shatner and Nimoy]. I knew they were qualified to play those parts. They were good at it. They were perfect. But I don't think Gene Coon respected them. He wasn't an actor and didn't understand the concerns of actors. An actor has to have an axe to grind in his own way. An actor has a role and he wants it to be as good as it can be in that context. But Gene Coon didn't get it. So he was at odds with it." (17)

Mary Black, who worked as John D.F.'s assistant, said, "The one thing I specifically remember during the transition week [as Gene Coon was taking over from Black at *Star Trek*], it was clear he didn't have very high regard for us. I was bringing something into Gene Roddenberry's office and Gene Coon had a temporary desk in the outer office, where Dorothy was, while waiting to move into John's office. I gave Gene Coon a smile and a nod -- one of those 'hello' glances -- and the look on his face was amazing. John and I have always felt that if you dislike someone, you don't have to show it. But Gene Coon did show it. So, I would think it was possible if Gene Coon did not like a particular actor, he would not bother to hide it." (17a)

"I can certainly understand the difficulties he experienced in working with G.R.," John D.F. said. "But any upset he felt over his dealings with the writers or the actors was his own doing. I never had trouble with the writers or the actors. There was no reason to have trouble. But G.R. did. And Gene Coon apparently did." (17)

Regarding the day Coon made his decision, Glen Larson, his friend and future colleague, at *It Takes a Thief*, said, "Gene had two scripts on his desk in front of him which he had to rewrite. He suddenly put his pencil down and finally said, 'This is it,' and he got up and walked out. It had been an around the clock, very draining experience." (106)

Ande Richardson-Kindryd said, "The creative differences, and the humor element Gene was putting in the show, could have been part of the problem that led to him leaving. He wasn't talking so much about that. He was offered another job and he took it. A lot less hassle. Because, by that time, the Great Bird [Roddenberry] was just sort of slipping in and out of the back door, and he was there and then he wasn't there, and then he was, and then he wasn't. And a lot of that was just pressure on Gene [Coon]. And every script that came through, he twiddled with it to make it more *Star Trek*. It hurt him terribly when he would get some of the letters from some of the writers. And that's not because he was overly sensitive. This was a guy who was a combat reporter, and who covered the atomic testing in Nevada, which was probably one reason why he died so young [at 49]. Who knows? But the pressure was there. And the personality clashes were there. And Gene just decided he'd had enough." (144a)

John Meredyth Lucas, the writer of "The Changeling" and the unproduced *Star Trek* story outline "The Lost Star," remembered, "While I was still directing at *Mannix*, I wrote another script for *Star Trek* ("Patterns of Force"), finding time at night and between takes. Then Gene Coon called me on the set and asked me to stop by his office when I finished." (110-6)

Lucas stopped by Coon's office, expecting to discuss his latest writing assignment. Instead, he recalled Coon saying, "Why the hell don't you take over? You produced *The Fugitive* and *Ben Casey* and that shit." (110-4)

Lucas later said, "And I of course jumped at the chance, because I've always loved science fiction. I asked Coon why he was leaving, but he never really explained it." (110-4)

Coon believed his exit from the show could be expedited if he was able to offer Roddenberry a worthy successor.

"At first, Gene Roddenberry wouldn't let him leave because he had a contract," said Glen Larson. "The only way they'd let Gene out [was] if he continued to write for the show." (106)

Lucas was invited to Roddenberry's home that Sunday. He said, "I met his wife

John Meredyth Lucas
(memoryalpha.com)

Eileen and his children. We got on well, exchanged our mutual love for science fiction, [then] I left. Gene Roddenberry stopped me the next day on the lot and said, 'My wife says she bets you're the one.' That was flattering but hardly a firm offer. The following day I got a telegram from Gene officially offering me the job."

The one thing blocking the way was the contract Lucas had signed to continue as a regular director on *Mannix*. He went to see the friend who had gotten him that job, *Mannix* first season producer Wilton Schiller. Lucas said, "I talked to Wilton, who saw the advantage to me and knew where my heart was. He was willing to give me my release but his boss, [Executive Producer] Bruce Geller, was not forgiving."

Lucas got his release from *Mannix*, but he would never work on one of Bruce Geller's shows again.

John Meredyth Lucas signed a contract with Desilu on August 30, 1967.

Daily Variety broke the news the next day with the front page headline "Gene Coon Quits; Lucas Reins *Star Trek*." The trade paper reported Coon "asked for his release, on grounds he wants a long vacation from television and wants to work on a theatrical screenplay."

Days after his release, and weeks before he would actually leave the *Star Trek* offices, Coon made arrangements to go to work for Universal, where he had helped develop *McHale's Navy* and other series in the early 1960s. As *Daily Variety* reported, his first job, once he cleared *Star Trek*, was to write a feature film script for his new employers -- the western *Journey to Shiloh*, based on a novel by Will Henry (aka Henry Allen), and starring James Caan. After that he would be put back to work as a writer/producer in television, with

327

Glen Larson as his associate producer, on *It Takes a Thief*, slated for a midseason premiere on ABC in early 1968.

Perpetuating the "official story" 30 years after the fact, Robert Justman went on record in his book with Herb Solow (*Star Trek: The Inside Story*), saying, "I wrote my last memo to Gene Coon on September 5, 1967, one day after the Labor Day holiday. He left the show that week, exhausted; he had come close to a complete nervous breakdown." (94-8)

Ande Richardson-Kindryd disputes Justman's claim that Coon was having anything close to a breakdown. And while it is true that Justman began addressing his memos to Roddenberry and Lucas after September 5, with "cc" to Coon, it is also true that Coon was still the series producer, and held that position for another month. There was a different reason for Justman's memos not going to Coon.

To Justman's thinking, Coon was abandoning *Star Trek*. Further, he was turning over his job -- as top producer -- to someone who barely knew the show and, as Justman would write in numerous memos, was not proving to be a good *Star Trek* writer. Worse, Coon had not even considered offering the job to Justman, which would have advanced the talented and hardworking associate producer to being the series' primary producer.

Richardson-Kindryd said, "Bob wanted to be the producer and he kept seeing new producers coming in all the time and he wasn't the producer yet, so I can imagine he didn't like that a lot." (144a)

Contrary to Justman's statement in his book with Herb Solow that Coon left the series within a week after September 5, Coon was obliged to finish producing NBC's initial order of the second season -- those first 16 episodes. Thirteen were in the can and Episode 14 ("Bread and Circuses") was scheduled to begin filming the following week when the key cast members returned from their promotional tour. "Journey to Babel" and "A Private Little War" were slated to follow. Only after that would Lucas be in charge, provided there was anything left to be in charge of.

The new season, with *Star Trek* about to premiere in its horrific Friday night time slot, was still 10 days away. "Amok Time" would kick things off on September 15. NBC's decision to order additional episodes wouldn't come until at least two weeks after that, when the ratings for "Amok Time" and "Who Mourns for Adonais," the next episode to air, could be examined. Regardless, scripts needed to be ready for production should that renewal come. Lucas inherited the job, and a pile of scripts, some of which had already been rewritten by Coon. From these, he was to select some of the less demanding ones, polish the scripts further and prepare them for filming. And, for another month, anyway, Coon would be there to give guidance, notes, and apologies for the ones that were not in very good shape.

21

Episode 43: BREAD AND CIRCUSES

Written by Gene L. Coon and Gene Roddenberry
(with some plot and character development by John Kneubuhl, uncredited)
Directed by Ralph Senensky

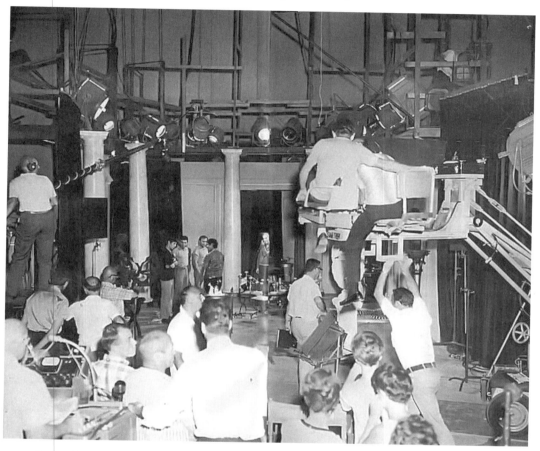

Guest player Lois Jewell (Drusilla) said, "It was a very big crew. And there was a lot going on. Sometimes people just wanted to be on the set. They knew somebody who knew somebody, so there would be visitors there, too." (Photo courtesy of Gerald Gurian)

From NBC press release, issued February 20, 1968:

Captain Kirk (William Shatner) and his officers, searching for survivors of a lost ship, become prisoners of the despotic ruler of a planet with 1960s technology and Roman Empire customs, in "Bread and Circuses" on NBC Television Network's *Star Trek* colorcast of Friday, March 15…. Despite protective efforts by Septimus (Ian Wolfe), peaceful leader of the slaves, and Flavius (Rhodes Reason), champion gladiator, Kirk, Spock (Leonard Nimoy) and McCoy (DeForest Kelley) are captured by Claudius Marcus (Logan Ramsey), who keeps the populace in line by staging TV spectacles of gladiator competitions. Kirk meets Merik (guest-star William Smithers), commander of the lost ship, who sacrificed his crew to save his own life. Kirk is offered the same terms and slave Drusilla (Lois Jewell) as an added inducement.

The world is strangely similar to Earth in size, atmosphere, culture, and language. And in faith. While Rome is the prime power, the rebel slaves have turned away from the empire to become followers of what the Romans believe to be a religious cult -- "The Children of the Son."

The theme is one of spiritual awakening, and predestined fate, bundled-up in a satire of network television.

SOUND BITES

- *Spock:* "Fascinating how close this atmosphere is to your twentieth century. Moderately industrialized pollution, containing substantial amounts of carbon monoxide and partially consumed hydrocarbons ..." *McCoy, interrupting:* "The word was 'smog.'" *Spock:* "I had no idea you were that much a historian, Doctor." *McCoy:* "I'm not. I wanted to stop you before we got the whole lecture on the subject."

- *Spock:* "Were I able to show emotion, Doctor, your new infatuation with that term would begin to annoy me." *McCoy:* "What term? 'Logic?' Medical men are trained in logic, Mr. Spock." *Spock:* "I had no idea they were trained, Doctor. From watching you I assumed it was trial and error." *Flavius:* "Are they enemies, Captain?" *Kirk:* "I'm not sure that they're sure."

ASSESSMENT

"Bread and Circuses" is action, adventure, drama, comedy, and science fiction, all woven together with an intriguing high-concept premise.

This was the second time the Enterprise encountered a parallel Earth world. "Miri" was first. The modern day Jonathan Swift technique for making comment on contemporary issues Roddenberry so embraced was less subtle here than in most episodes. But, in this instance, being part-satire, the lack of subtleties works. The target was 1967 network TV. In other words -- NBC.

The jabs: the televised gladiatorial events include fake applause and catcalls, making mockery of the laugh track utilized by all television comedies of the time; dialogue like "You bring this station's ratings down, Flavius, and we'll do a special on you!"; "We've pre-empted fifteen minutes on the early show for you, *in full color*!"; and Kirk, having been informed he will be executed live on TV, is told, "You may not understand, since you are centuries beyond anything as crude as television." His reply, "I've heard it was ... similar."

Satire well in place, this episode also includes moments of intense drama, rich in conflict. The heavier-than-usual McCoy-Spock confrontation in the jail cell, where McCoy nails Spock on his fear of showing emotion and the true reason for it, is stirring. McCoy says, "Now I know why you're not afraid to die, Spock -- you're more afraid of living. Each day you stay alive is just one more day you might slip, and let your human half peek out. That's it, isn't it? Insecurity. Why, you wouldn't know what to do with a genuine, warm, decent feeling." Spock considers McCoy's words, then levels his antagonistic colleague with a challenging look of his own -- something that smacks of emotion ... and he merely says, "Oh, really, doctor?"

Ralph Senensky's direction is inspiring. When Spock applies his famous neck pinch to a Roman policemen in the jail cell, the man's head jerks toward camera, eyes bulging from sockets. The visual is so effective that there was no need for the familiar "FSNP" music cue to accompany it. Elsewhere, when Septimus says to Kirk, "May the blessing of the Son be upon you," Senensky cuts to a shot of the sun blazing in the sky, then has the camera pan down to reveal Kirk and company hiking across the landscape. This was a sleight-of-hand trick. The director explained, "My concern was that the whole thing about the 'Son,' which they talked about from early on, might not be a mystery when we got to the end. We didn't want to tip that we were doing a Christ story from the word go. That took some doing." (155-4)

The quality of the direction and the action choices is apparent throughout -- but this is not to say the episode is perfect. Any time we see Kirk, Spock, and McCoy beam down *alone* to a hostile planet, the unbelievability-meter spikes off the chart. And, as anyone could guess, they fall prey to the natives and are prevented from returning to their ship, as they were in "The Return of the Archons," "A Taste of Armageddon," "Errand of Mercy," "Catspaw," "Friday's Child," and "The Apple" -- all Gene Coon-produced episodes. The novelty and excitement of this plot contrivance was wearing thin. Also, a few passages in the script dealing with the brotherhood of man, and the coming of Christ, seem overly sentimental and somewhat preachy, courtesy of Mr. Roddenberry's rewrite. But Roddenberry's passion for the material, and its message, more than made up for a few stilted lines.

"Bread and Circuses" is well worth repeated viewing.

THE STORY BEHIND THE STORY

Script Timeline
John Kneubuhl's contract, ST #48: February 22, 1967.
Kneubuhl's treatment, from Roddenberry and Coon's idea,
"Bread and Circuses":
March 5, 1967.
Kneubuhl's revised treatment, gratis: March 17, 1967.
Kneubuhl's 1st Draft teleplay, now "The Last Martyr": April 12, 1967.
Kneubuhl's 2nd Draft teleplay: late April, 1967.
Kneubuhl's script polish, gratis (Mimeo Department "Yellow Cover 1st Draft"),
changed back to "Bread and Circuses": May 2, 1967.
Gene Coon's 1st Draft teleplay: July 21, 1967.
Coon's 2nd Draft teleplay (Final Draft): August 9, 1967.
Coon's 3rd draft teleplay (Revised Final Draft): August 15, 1967.
Additional page revisions by Coon: August 24 and September 5, 1967.
Gene Roddenberry's rewrite (2nd Revised Final Draft): September 11, 1967.
Roddenberry's script polish (3rd Revised Final Draft): September 12, 1967.
Additional page revisions by Roddenberry: September 13, 14 & 20, 1967.

Writer John Kneubuhl, the first to work on the script, was 47. He was a native of American Samoa, a group of islands in the South Pacific. Dorothy Fontana said, "John was a Samoan prince. No kidding. And he was an Olympic swimmer, twenty years before." (64-1)

Kneubuhl's family relocated to Hawaii, where he was raised and schooled, before achieving higher education at Yale. He returned to Hawaii in the mid-1940s and became well-known as a local playwright, with stage productions that focused on the Samoan and Hawaiian cultures.

In the early 1950s, Kneubuhl relocated to Los Angeles to pursue a career as a television writer. One of the first series to give him regular employment was *Medic*, starring Richard Boone. Gene Coon and John Meredyth Lucas also worked there as writers, with Lucas doing double-duty as a director. In 1958, Kneubuhl made it onto the big screen -- or, at least, the big drive-in screen -- as both writer and producer of a low budget horror film called *The Screaming Skull*. He wrote more chilling kiddie fare with 1965's *Two on a Guillotine*. But TV was primarily where the former prince-turned-Yale-man-and-playwright toiled. Prior to *Star Trek*, Kneubuhl wrote five episodes of *Thriller*, two for *The Invaders*, and seven for *The Wild, Wild West*, where he created the character of the evil dwarf Dr. Miguelito Loveless. Kneubuhl was also a well-liked and frequent contributor to *Adventures in Paradise*, *Wagon Train*, and *The Fugitive*.

Gene Roddenberry and series producer Gene Coon came up with the concept for "Bread and Circuses." Kneubuhl took it on with great enthusiasm, starting with the title. The term "bread and circuses" traces to ancient Rome. It refers to the Emperor distributing loafs of bread at the coliseum and providing gladiatorial entertainment to pacify the unemployed masses.

Kneubuhl turned in his treatment on March 5, 1967. Roddenberry wrote back:

> Dear John: The format which has worked most successfully for STAR TREK requires, we find, more jeopardy than is presently in "Bread and Circuses." We found that translating SF to a visual medium requires an immediate line of jeopardy which is <u>very apparent to the audience.</u> For example, on Page 3 Kirk gets captured and will hang in twelve hours unless something happens and the Enterprise has been fooled into thinking he is enjoying a quiet vacation with a girl. Not that I am recommending that specifically for your script. But in the case of your story, our jeopardy line is hurt badly by the fact Spock and the Enterprise (capable of wiping out the entire planet) is aware they are captives and theoretically could beam down at any moment and save them all. (GR43-1)

Structure problems, aside, Roddenberry was intrigued by the concept of a modern day society (circa: Earth 1967), which participated in slave trading. Of this, he said:

> Since in ancient Rome the slave system had an economic reality and logic, we will have to find some reality and logic for that system here. Obviously if we are in a 20th century level civilization which employs combustion engine and etc., slavery would have to have some other function than horsepower. Perhaps they enable our "Romans" to lead lives of uncomplicated luxury by taking a great number of decisions and modern complexities out of their homes. (Incidentally, that's not a bad idea, I could use a couple of slaves myself. Or on second thought, considering what we pay for our housekeeper, maybe I've got one. What a terrible thought, i.e., that I have a slave and instead of feeding her I give her money to go out and feed herself, and probably not as well as I'd feed and clothe her if she lived more closely with the family. Yes, a terrible thought. I really feel guilty.) (GR43-1)

Roddenberry put his guilt aside and returned to the matter at hand, a story outline which was not up to *Star Trek* standard. His letter ended:

> I think you can do better if I push you around a bit and smile quiet little smiles at you while you are -- equally elegant -- trying to defend your premise. (GR43-1)

Roddenberry wasn't buying Kneubuhl's depiction of the slaves, which the former didn't feel had evolved to any degree from the slaves of ancient Rome. There was also too much running around in the city, too much information given away in the story too quickly, and not enough jeopardy. Roddenberry also felt the outline was confusing to read and would not please the network. He asked for a free rewrite.

Kneubuhl sent in his revised treatment on March 17, along with a note to Roddenberry, saying:

> My own outline is far more detailed than this, but this is as brief as I could get it for NBC purposes. I'm not a very good premise writer, I'm afraid. Never was. As you suggested, I'm into a trial stab at teleplay, and am deep into it. It's fun and it moves like lightning. The quality of slow, mounting surprise as to where the guys are -- a quality which does not come across in this summary -- works fine. Thanks for the drink and the fine company the other day. John. (JK43)

Of Kneubuhl's March 17 outline, Associate Producer Robert Justman wrote to Roddenberry:

> I like the idea of a story in which we happen upon a civilization as new as today, but with the trappings and traditions of Ancient Rome. I like the idea of Kirk and Spock being forced to face each other in mortal combat in order to save the lives of their shipmates. However, after reading this treatment, I feel there are tangential story lines which we don't need and also feel that we do not build and resolve our conflicts correctly. (RJ43-1)

The idea of Kirk and Spock facing off in the arena was later dropped when a similar scene showed up in the script for "Amok Time." There were other ideas in Kneubuhl's story that Justman was not pleased about. His memo continued:

> I think the chase between our Landing Party and the wolves pursuing them is interesting, but not germane to our story. I would rather have them pursued by some human antagonists, who are much easier to give direction to and who are much more cunning than wolves. I might believe killer dogs, controlled by Squads of Roman Soldiers out to find the intruders.... If you wish to retain the "wolf," let's just use a large, fierce German Shepherd. We have had sad experience in the past dressing dogs with various types of accessories. The dogs usually end up looking like dogs with various types of accessories strapped on to them. (RJ43-1)

Justman got his German Shepherds, controlled by Roman soldiers.

In Kneubuhl's treatment, the survivor from the Federation ship, living among the Romans, was a Vulcan named Jeroth. Justman pointed out it would be impossible for Jeroth to fit in, even if he always wore a helmet, due to his yellowish complexion and arched eyebrows. His memo continued:

> I personally would rather save the idea of having Spock nose-to-nose with another Vulcan for some other show. We have had this idea in mind for some

333

time and I feel that we ought to make the most ingenious use of this idea when it suits our purpose. I don't think our purposes are best served by using this idea in this particular story. The big gimmick in this show is that Kirk and Spock must fight each other. Let's at least consider saving combat between Spock and another Vulcan for another show in which that will be the central Theme. (RJ43-1)

On March 23, 1967, Stan Robertson at NBC wrote Roddenberry:

Very exciting storyline, Gene, which has many plus items in its favor. Interesting idea that we are faced with a 1967 "updating" of what Rome might have been like if that civilization had lasted through the ages. (SR43-1)

What Stan Robertson didn't like was how the story began, like so many others, on the Enterprise. He told Roddenberry:

You will begin putting into works, or will change stories already in works, so that we have a mixture of programs in which some will begin on the Enterprise and other on planets. As of this date, we have not received any submissions which fall into the latter category. (SR43-1)

Robertson was also concerned that too many of *Star Trek*'s treks were taking the NBC audience into the past rather than the future. From Season One, the plot device of visiting Earth's past, or a planet resembling Earth in an earlier time, was presented in "Miri," "Tomorrow Is Yesterday," "and "The City on the Edge of Forever." It was also attempted in the unproduced scripts, "Portrait in Black and White," "Tomorrow the Universe," and an early version of "The Omega Glory." And now Robertson was seeing a few new stories being developed along this line. He wrote:

This should be our final story of the forthcoming Season in which we update, or attempt to go back and examine a society, system, or civilization of the past. While this is not exactly a *Time Tunnel* type gimmick, I strongly believe that while such stories may be intriguing to write, and do contain a certain amount of visual excitement, they can become "tired" and, carried to any further extreme, such stories could give *Star Trek* a feeling of duplication or similarity. We both know that we can find the type of action-adventure stories we are looking for without overdoing what I think is an "easy way out" to create excitement and appeal. (SR43-1)

Despite these instructions from the network, it wouldn't be the last "easy way out" for the season. Still to come: Earth parallel worlds in "A Private Little War," "A Piece of the Action," "Patterns of Force," "The Omega Glory," and Earth itself, circa 1968, in "Assignment: Earth."

Kneubuhl was given the green light to go to screenplay. When that script arrived, on April 14 (dated April 12), it had a new title -- "The Last Martyr."

For this draft, the character of Proconsul Marcellus (later renamed to Claudius Marcus) is far more vicious and emotionally unstable than the character portrayed in the filmed episode. And he pretends not to be the top of the government, creating a not-too-believable illusion that the true leader is Merik, the Federation ship captain who lives amongst the Romans. Further, Marcellus leads his people to believe that Merik is a god.

Script Consultant Dorothy Fontana wrote Coon later that day:

I feel John can punch this up a great deal. It drifts now -- and I miss character conflict. Kirk does not do a great deal.... I believe Marcellus may be the key here. Since it is indicated he is a little off-center -- holding some of the madness of the Caesars -- why not play this more? Kirk can run head-on into this man.... When Kirk tries to cross him to get to Merik, Marcellus goes into a rage. Or maybe a quiet rage with a later neatly planned attempt on Kirk's life. Whatever is decided, I strongly suggest the character conflict come down to Marcellus and Kirk slamming heads.... Please consider changing the title back to "Bread and Circuses." I like it much better than "The Last Martyr." (DC43-1)

Justman wrote to Coon:

This is one of the better first drafts by a first time writer on our series. Granted that there are some things that are not correct, but John has been plenty right about most everything.... It is quite evident that John Kneubuhl is a skilled dramatist and I would like to recommend giving him another assignment as soon as we can. (JR43-2)

On April 17, Roddenberry wrote to Coon:

Kneubuhl is a good writer, no doubt of that, but some very major parts of this are missing [the] target by a mile. It comes off as a comic opera [of] 1967 Rome and not as a real living Civilization with believable people who would believably be in the position they hold.... If we've got a Roman emperor involved with a television station and the games they have there, then it's got to be made as believable as if the President of the United States was so involved. (GR43-2)

Kneubuhl's 2nd Draft script arrived in late April. It was sent to the Mimeo Department for reformatting (the May 2 "Yellow Cover 1st Draft"). The title was still "The Last Martyr." Roddenberry wrote to Coon on May 9, saying:

I think this script needs much more comment on the strange parallels.... We can't allow ourselves to get so blasé about our *Star Trek* space travel that our characters seem to be saying "ho hum, another Earth parallel, complete with humanoid bipeds almost exactly like ourselves." Understood, of course, that we don't want to weigh our stories down with philosophical dissertation. But there must be a middle road.... Incidentally, I don't agree with Bob's comments about a "Roman Life" magazine being too expensive for us to do. It is this type of detail which can make our stories feel real. Would suggest we get a cost estimate on things like this before we turn them down. (GR43-3)

The cost estimate checked out okay (see "Pre-Production").

Concerning Kneubuhl's second draft script, Stan Robertson wrote Coon:

One of the things this script lacks, we believe, is an exciting enough Teaser to whet the appetites of the viewers, to "hook" them on to watching the remainder of the episode.... We realize that the character, Merik, is later proven not to be a "god" in this re-creation of Roman culture, but our initial reaction, and we're afraid will be that of the viewers, was that we had another story in which we had an Earthman ruling an alien society [as in the unproduced "He Walked Among Us," by Norman Spinrad]. Since, in outline and script form, we have utilized this device on one or two other occasions in material for the coming season, we

335

would urge you to dispense with this in the future. I'm sure you understand as readily as we do how, even though the plot lines are not the same, the fact that in the mind of the viewers we are retelling an old story. (SR43-2)

Robertson, as the voice of NBC, was a fair watchdog for consistency problems and story holes. He told Coon:

A plot flaw seems to make itself evident in Act III. In this act, Kirk talks at great length about Captain Merik. However, we have not established until this point if Kirk had known him or knew about him prior to this present encounter. It would seem that when we first are aware of the fact that it is Merik down on the planet, Kirk would at that point display some manner of prior association. (SR43-2)

It was Fontana's idea to add a stronger hook to the Teaser, suggesting Uhura tune into a live television broadcast from the planet showing the barbaric arena games.

Coon, Roddenberry, and Justman had more ideas requiring further changes. John Kneubuhl was asked to provide a Revised 2nd Draft, *gratis*. Citing personal and health problems as the reason, he declined, and then abandoned the project.

The screenplay Kneubuhl left behind told the same story as the filmed version, but was handled in a much different way. In the Teaser, the Enterprise encounters a "pod," which Kirk orders beamed aboard. It contains a "message tape cartridge" and portions of a captain's log, and this reveals the pod is from the Intrepid, a Federation vessel commanded by Captain Andrew Merik, reported missing five years earlier. A voice from the ship's log, fragmented and interrupted by static, reveals, "On Captain Merik's orders … every day now, for the last three days … until there are only six of us left on board … Captain Merik has just ordered the rest of us to beam down … we cannot disobey a direct order … but something is …" The message then fades into static.

Kirk beams down with McCoy and Sulu. Spock, suffering from a badly inflamed appendix, waits behind on the ship, scheduled for surgery upon McCoy's return. The landing party materializes in a cemetery at night where Roman soldiers chase after runaway slaves (including Flavius). They are captured but, when the soldiers radio in by "walkie-talkie," instructions are returned to treat Kirk and his men as "honored guests." The Enterprise men are taken into the city where they first meet Marcellus, whom we are told is the aide to the proconsul, and then the proconsul himself -- *Captain Merik*. Marcellus is overly protective of Merik, going as far as to answer questions directed at the former captain by Kirk. The official story, seeming a bit rehearsed, is that the Intrepid crew died of a plague, with only Merik surviving. The marooned captain was nursed back to health by the Romans, then invited to become proconsul because Marcellus respected Merik for his leadership qualities and technical abilities.

Meanwhile, Spock beams down with two security men in search of Kirk, but is immediately captured by Roman soldiers who were expecting a search party to arrive from the Enterprise and had lain in waiting. Back in the city, Kirk is taken to witness "classical games" being staged for broadcast over live television. Marcellus explains the reason for the games, telling Kirk, "In an orderly society one needs to find outlets for people's animal nature. Without those outlets, who knows what animality might break out in homes, in towns, and in the city streets, against all law and order?"

Marcellus, who appears to be the true leader of the Romans despite claiming not to be, wants Kirk to order the remaining members of his crew to beam down. Kirk, of course, refuses, prompting Marcellus to dispatch Kirk to the televised games, pitted in combat against Spock in a duel to the death. To insure the two men fight, and that one kills the other, McCoy, Sulu, and the two security men are forced to kneel down with swords placed against the back of their necks. If Marcellus doesn't see blood spilled within two minutes, he'll have McCoy, Sulu, and the security men beheaded.

Kirk and Spock have no choice but to fight. During the combat, Spock tells Kirk to plunge a sword into his left chest where the human heart would be. In a Vulcan, this is actually where the appendix is found. Spock promises he can survive for a few hours after being inflicted with such a wound. Kirk reluctantly stabs his friend. Spock, appearing close to death, is carried away. But Marcellus refuses to allow McCoy to tend to Spock until Kirk relents and orders the remainder of his crew down. Merik, whom we now know is merely a pawn, pleads with Kirk not to give in to Marcellus. He confesses that he only ordered his own men down after being tortured. The greatest torture, however, was being forced to watch as his men died in the arena games. Merik now longs for death. Marcellus sadistically obliges, killing Merik. Kirk moves quickly and gets the upper hand on Marcellus, retrieving a phaser and pointing it at the ruler's head. Marcellus reveals himself a coward and begs for his life. This helps Kirk to incite the slaves to riot and take control.

With Kneubuhl now out of the picture, Gene Coon wrote the next few drafts of the script. He restructured the story and jettisoned much of what the freelancer had written, adding in nearly all new dialogue, including snippets of lighter moments. His second pass through the script, listed as the Final Draft, from August 9, 1967, carried the shared credit "teleplay by John Kneubuhl and Gene L. Coon; story by John Kneubuhl."

Robert Justman told Coon:

I understand what you are attempting to do near the top of Page 13. This is something we've discussed previously. However, I feel that we are establishing a dangerous precedent for our show if we can prove that our landing party can be under constant scanning procedure at all times if they are down on the surface of a planet. Perhaps we could establish the fact that Scott can determine what sort of a place they are in, so long as their communicator is activated. Anyhow, let's discuss this a little further in person…. There is a puzzling point made in scene 30 on Page 28. And that is that Captain Merik evidently beamed back up to his ship and sent his whole crew down prior to setting up "self-destruct mechanisms." If he was able to go back up to his ship, how come he just didn't skedaddle out of there and escape from the clutches of our evil [Claudius] Marcus? Somehow something has to been lost in translation. I think we are going to have to establish the fact that Merik followed this previously-mentioned procedure because Marcus had a number of his crew already in his clutches and, therefore, was able to exert leverage upon Merik as a result of this fact…. I think we ought to make up our minds as to whether we want Mr. Chekov in this show or not. At times we establish him on the Bridge and at times he has nothing to do or say. Insofar as I can determine, he is not integral to this present version…. Perhaps we might be able to get a little more mileage out of the Drusilla character. Perhaps Marcus might attempt to subvert our headstrong Captain by having her exert her feminine wiles upon him. (RJ43-3)

Coon addressed Justman's notes, and added in the sizzle with Drusilla, in a draft dated September 5.

Coon then was rewritten by Roddenberry, who was back in the *Star Trek* offices after being on assignment writing a never-to-be-produced Robin Hood screenplay. Roddenberry was determined to give the script a more serious tone, and also to lose what little remained of Kneubuhl's writing. He handed his revised draft to director Ralph Senensky on the morning of September 11, at 6 a.m., after staying up all night in an effort to steer the material back toward the flavor of what *Star Trek* had once been -- serious science fiction. Even with the changes, Coon's influences were felt, especially in the scenes filmed early in the production. The outdoor sequences at Bronson Canyon came first, on September 12. Much of the Spock-McCoy feud, and the humor that normally accompanied it, was present. Roddenberry sent fresh pages to the set later that day, to be shot the following morning. On Wednesday, September 13, the company finished location filming and moved to "Paramount Test Stage" where the jail cell set had been built. Some McCoy/Spock sparring was present here, as well, but less so than in the version written by Coon. More rewrite pages followed, always one day ahead of the production. Gene Coon's imprint faded with each new set of revisions.

In a letter to friend and science fiction writer John Campbell, Roddenberry said of his rewrite:

> My idea, which I hoped to dramatize, was that economic fetters are much more efficient and more easily manipulated than iron chains. By showing a parallel planet in which Rome did not fall and still had the institution of slavery, I had planned to dramatize the thought that slavery fell simply because it was an expensive and inefficient way of keeping people in bondage. (GR43-4)

Lip-service was certainly given to some of these ideas, in snatches of dialogue found in "Bread and Circuses," but the main thrust of the story aimed elsewhere with a statement about Christianity ... and a satire on broadcast TV.

In a September 15 memo from NBC, Roddenberry was told to remove the line from the script where the Games Announcer says, "In living color." That line, more than any other, was too close for comfort for the network whose announcer introduced its prime time shows by saying "The following program is brought to you in living color ... on NBC."

The line was reworked to merely say, "In color." As for some of the other changes the network requested, Roddenberry wrote to Ralph Senensky on the set, saying:

> They ask that -- and I laughed at this -- that the Master of the Games enunciate "skewer [them]" ... [to prevent the line from sounding like "screw them"] ... And Claudius' speech in which he admits he gave Kirk some last hours as a man [with Drusilla] be said straight and with no suggestion of a leer of any kind. (GR43-6)

Next came the latest report from De Forest Research. Again, the scrutiny that *Star Trek* put itself through to insure scientific accuracy (or, at least, probability) was unparalleled. Concerning a line of dialogue in the script where Kirk is told: "Captain, no sign of bodies whatsoever," and Kirk replies: "Then whatever destroyed it, the crew managed to beam down somewhere," Joan Pearce wrote:

> There is no basis for this assumption. The crew could have been entirely

338

annihilated in the blast, and if any bodies had remained, they could have been deformed by explosive decompression, or could have drifted away from the wreckage. Suggest delete "whatsoever" and add "[the crew] <u>might</u> have managed."

Considering the line, "Only one sixteenth parsec away, Captain; we should be there in seconds," Pearce said:

This is equivalent to the driver of an automobile traveling at 60 mph, saying, "Only a few feet away. We should be there in seconds." Suggest the Enterprise will be traveling at low sub-light speed (e.g. 5000 km./sec.) and the system be 100,000 km. away.

In the script, Spock says, "Six million who died in your First World War, the eleven million in the Second, the thirty-seven million in your Third..." Pearce, without the benefit of a computer and the Internet, set the producers right, telling them:

In WWI there were 8.5 million deaths; in WWII 30,538,000. 37 million for WWIII seems conservative; suggest 260 million.

Regarding the line of dialogue, "He commands not just a... spaceship, Pro-consul... a starship," Pearce, after checking with her second reader, Peter Sloman, wrote:

Technically, a spaceship is any vessel which can travel in space. A starship is any spaceship capable of interstellar flight, which would include both the Beagle and the Enterprise. Suggest "Not just a starship,... Pro-consul... a starcruiser."

Another line of dialogue said, "Complete Earth parallel; the language here is English!" Pearce, speaking on behalf of Peter Sloman, complained:

English is not the only Earth language today. But if an Earth language has been developed, why not Latin, to correspond with the Roman civilization? Might beg further explanation.... That there would be a city called Rome is equally as unlikely as the evolution of Earth's languages. Suggest delete "Roman".... An exact parallel to Earth could develop only if climate, weather, land masses and conditions, populations, ecology, natural catastrophes, flora and fauna -- everything -- were the same. Otherwise, there <u>must</u> be slight variances, and in a world as different as this planet is, granted the development of a slave-based aristocratic culture like that of ancient Rome, still the English language and the name Rome, as well as Latinized names, is scientifically almost impossible, and begs any kind of explanation.

Curiously, many of the notes in this report were ignored.

Pete Sloman of De Forest Research later said, "You have to take some of *Star Trek* more as parable than as works of drama. Roddenberry had ideas he wanted to get across. And science fiction is very good for getting interesting ideas across because it makes you think about familiar things in strange ways and vice versa. That was something he was very much interested in, so a lot of the times they would sacrifice accuracy. You had the same problem with Vulcan. How did this planet get the name of a Roman god. Now, it was explained that supposedly there was influence on our ancient Earth cultures by the Vulcans because they were the ones who later gave us the starship -- the warp drive and all of that. But you just had, at one point, to decide, 'Okay, this is going to be bad science; this is going to be impossible,

339

but we are basically doing what is akin to fantasy and, to make the stories work, we have to change things. And I'd grumble and throw things. But I understood what they were doing." (158a)

While much of Coon's humor remained, by the time Roddenberry finished tinkering with the script, even as the episode was filming, enough had been changed to warrant a shared credit -- between Roddenberry and Coon. Kneubuhl's name was nowhere in sight.

When the smoke cleared and the production wrapped, Roddenberry asked Coon to contact the Writers Guild on behalf of the producers. Coon wrote Mary Dorfman at the WGA on September 19, telling her that he and Roddenberry "developed the story idea," then "called in" John Kneubuhl and "gave him the story," which, "while not completely developed, was considerably developed." (GC43)

Coon acknowledged that Kneubuhl added some ideas of his own into his treatment, which, after being approved by NBC, progressed to first and second draft screenplays, but then said:

> One day John called and told me that he simply could not finish the screenplay and requested that he be withdrawn from the project.... This was granted. At this time, I went back to the original story, the one by Roddenberry and me, and wrote a brand new First Draft, with different structure, dialogue, character development, and so on. (GC43)

Coon told Dorfman that Roddenberry handled the final rewriting:

> Despite the fact that John Kneubuhl withdrew from the project, he did indeed receive full pay as per contract, even though he did not in the strictest sense fulfill the terms of his contract. (GC43)

Coon reminded Dorfman that the last time a *Star Trek* script went before the Arbitration Board (with "Space Seed"), the Board misunderstood the intent of the producers and improperly arbitrated between Roddenberry and Coon, giving credit to Coon but denying Roddenberry his just due. Coon now insisted that he and Roddenberry should jointly share the credit and that Kneubuhl's name be withheld. He told Dorfman:

> Strictly speaking, I do not see why arbitration is called for, since "Bread and Circuses" is a completely original story with the producers of the program to begin with, and the final product was completely written -- not rewritten, but written -- by the two producers of the show. Roddenberry and I are certainly not competing [with one another] for credit.... We are not asking for arbitration between Gene Roddenberry and Gene Coon.... We have made equal contributions to the script, and since we are both production executives, and since we do not, unlike many writers, regard each other as enemies, we hope for a calm, rational, and sensible adjudication of the issue. (GC43)

After arbitration, it was determined Roddenberry and Coon would indeed share the "written by" credit. Surprisingly, considering the story originated with the producers, the Guild determined John Kneubuhl would receive a "story by" credit. Of this, Kneubuhl declined.

Later, on October 2, Roddenberry wrote to Adeline Reilly, a Desilu legal rep, stating that he did 75% of the writing on "Bread and Circuses," and that the script was based on his original idea, not one that came jointly from him and Coon. (GR43-7)

Director Ralph Senensky remembered both Genes rewriting "Bread and Circuses" even as the cameras rolled. Robert Justman's production records from this time, however, indicate that the work was one-sided, stating, "G.R. rewrote the script as it was being filmed." All the memos that were sent to the set, along with fresh script pages, came from Roddenberry.

Pre-Production
September 5-8 and September 11, 1967 (5 prep days).

This was Ralph Senensky's third *Star Trek*, following his excellent directorial work on "This Side of Paradise" and "Metamorphosis." As always, first order of business was to cast, a process which was rarely done more than a week before the start of production.

Ian Wolfe, 71 at this time, was

Ian Wolfe as Septimus (CBS Studios, Inc.)

Senensky's choice for the elderly and wise Septimus, leader of the slave rebellion. Wolfe made over 300 appearances before the camera between 1934 and 1990. One of his first and, in Wolfe's opinion, most important, was as Maggs, in the 1935 original version of *Mutiny on the Bounty*. Senensky said, "There are times when I wonder if any movie back in the thirties and forties was made without Ian in the cast." (155-5)

William Smithers (above, in unaired film trim; courtesy Gerald Gurian) and Logan Ramsey in "The Falcon," on *Mission: Impossible* (www.aveleyman.com)

This was the first of two guest appearances in *Star Trek* for Wolfe -- the other being as the librarian in Season Three's "All Our Yesterdays."

William Smithers, the cowardly and traitorous Captain Merik, AKA Merikus, was 40. He played hundreds of roles on TV and in the movies between 1952 and 1994. Among his list of credits, over 50 turns on *Dallas*, as Jeremy Wendell.

Logan Ramsey, seen here as Claudius Marcus, the Roman leader, was 46. His career spanned 1948 through 1999, racking up over 100 appearances before the camera, including an episode with William Shatner in the latter's short-lived series, *For the People*. He was also cast by *Star Trek*/Desilu casting director Joe D'Agosta in four episodes of *Mission: Impossible* when Leonard Nimoy was a regular.

Rhodes Reason, the muscular Flavius Maximus, was 37. The 6'2" actor had his own series in the late 1950s, called *White Hunter*. He was also a regular (as Sheriff Will Mayberry) in the 1961-62 series, *Bus Stop*. Joe D'Agosta saved Desilu money, booking Reason for a three-shows-for-the-price-of-two deal (including 1967 episodes of *Mission: Impossible* and *The Lucy Show*). Reason was so accommodating that D'Agosta brought him back for five segments of *Here's Lucy*.

Rhodes Reason as the title character in *White Hunter* (ITC, 1957-59)

Lois Jewell played Drusilla. She was a very familiar face, and body, on TV and in print, even though she had few credits on network TV shows. Jewell said, "I modeled all over the world and, because I was with Eileen Ford Modeling Agency in New York, I worked there a lot, as well. I did a lot of cosmetic print work and a lot of cosmetic commercials. I was the 'Albolene [makeup] Girl,' representing a cream to take off makeup, which they even used at the studios. I made about 80 TV commercials, such as Avis Rent A Car, and a lot of cigarette commercials -- Kent, Camel, Pall Mall -- even though I never smoked in my life!" (92a)

Regarding her casting in "Bread and Circuses," Jewell said, "I was sent out by an agent to see someone at *Star Trek*. I don't remember who I met with, but it wasn't Gene Roddenberry. I never even met him. I got the part right away, though. I just went once to see them and my agent called me later and said, 'You're on!'" (92a)

Jack Perkins played the Master of Games. The actor/stuntman was 45 and specialized in playing drunks, stumbling and slurring his way through episodes of *The Munsters*, *Adam 12*, *All in the Family*, *The Odd Couple*, *Happy Days*, and *CHiPs*.

William Bramley, the Head Roman

Lois Jewell wearing another of Bill Theiss' risqué outfits (CBS Studios, Inc.)

Policemen, was 39. Just as Perkins was hired to play inebriated individuals, Bramley was often cast as cops. His most famous cop role: Officer Krupke, from *West Side Story*. They even sang a song about his character, appropriately titled, "Gee, Officer Krupke."

Shatner posing with Gene Winfield's "Reactor"
(Both photos this page: courtesy of Gerald Gurian)

Bartell LaRue, a well-employed voiceover performer from this time, made one of two appearances in front of the camera on *Star Trek*, seen here as the ringside announcer. The other appearance was for the upcoming "Patterns of Force." Before this, he was the voice of the Guardian of Forever in "The City on the Edge of Forever." Some say he even provided the voice for Trelane's father in "The Squire of Gothos." Production records indicate it was Doohan. Doohan said so, too. (52 & 52-1)

Sulu is still absent from the bridge, as George Takei remained on loan to John Wayne and *The Green Berets*. Bill Blackburn sat in.

A pair of props made especially for this episode were in the form of magazines from the modern day Rome.

The futurist car seen briefly in the news footage report was designed by Gene Winfield, who had built the shuttlecraft.

"I had designed and built an all-aluminum show car called 'The Reactor,'" Winfield said. "This went around the country in auto shows to show the kind of custom work I could do. It was later used on *Bewitched* and an episode of *Star Trek*." (188)

Winfield's "Reactor," after receiving a makeover to change its look, also turned up in *Batman*, as the Catwoman's car.

THE GALLIAN

THE NEW HEAVYWEIGHT CHAMPION

4024

One of two magazine "props" created for the episode
(Courtesy of Bob Olsen)

Filmed September 12, 13, 14, 15, 18, 19 & 20, 1967.
(Planned as 6 day production, running one day over; cost $192,330)

Tuesday, September 12, 1967. The Beatles still had the top-selling record album in America with *Sgt. Pepper's Lonely Hearts Club Band*, now in its twelfth week at the summit. The Doors' self-titled debut was the second biggest seller, as the Monkees third album, *Headquarters*, dropped to No. 3. The most-played song on U.S. radio stations was "Ode to Billy Joe," by Bobbie Gentry, stopping Dianna Ross and The Supremes from getting to the top with "Reflections." Warren Beatty's *Bonnie and Clyde* continued to lead the pack at the box office. NASA's Surveyor 5 made the first chemical analysis of lunar material. And filming began on "Bread and Circuses" for the first of two days at Bronson Canyon.

Shatner checking out Gene Winfield's "Reactor"
(Courtesy of Gerald Gurian)

Star Trek and Ralph Senensky had visited this location before, filming sequences of "This Side of Paradise." On this day, and the next, they filmed the Landing Party's arrival, then Kirk, Spock, and McCoy being captured by Flavius, and then captured again by the Roman police. Also on the schedule: filming in the caves, most prominently in the one which had recently been used as the entrance to the Batcave on *Batman*. The interior cave dialogue sequences for this episode were filmed here, not on a soundstage. Senensky said, "Again Jerry Finnerman has to be commended.... When

Kelley and Nimoy in one of the more poignant McCoy/Spock scenes (Courtesy of Gerald Gurian)

filming an interior away from the studio, everything had to be lit from the floor. There wasn't the advantage of lighting from above. Filming within the confines of the cave just added to the difficulty. But Jerry still managed to do more than just get it photographed. In the cave, as in his work back at the studio, there was an artist at work." (155-5)

Ian Wolfe recalled how, during the sequence in the cave, his part was made substantially smaller as a result of William Shatner. He said, "I heard Bill talking to the director. Bill had quite a bit of say-so. He felt that the scene with me, in the cave, was all wrong. And, you know, he was right! I agreed with him. I didn't say, 'Oh, damn.' I thought every word he said was right. So, they cut most of that scene out." (190)

At the studio, Stage 10 was used for most of this episode, with jail sets, the Emperor's apartment and the television studio where the life and death gladiator games are played. One outdoor sequence was needed for the episode's Teaser, when the bridge crew watches a televised news broadcast showing Roman police manhandling slaves. This shot -- the only one to feature "The Reactor" (or the "Jupiter 8," as established in the episode) -- was taken outside Stage 10 on the Gower Street lot.

DeForest Kelley in the dungeon set illustrates Jerry Finnerman's ability to "paint with light." (Courtesy of Gerald Gurian)

For the scenes filmed in the cell block -- including interior jail cell and corridor outside the bars – Senensky had to cover 10 pages. There are three different sequences which take place here. Senensky said, "Television scenes at this time rarely ran longer than three minutes. The [jail] scene was more than twice that … and it was not a scene that allowed for any movement once the five people entered and were seated. Plus which, any movement would have required additional camera setups and time to light them. The scene was a lot of talk. It was on days like this that I was grateful and appreciative of the five talented actors who comprised the cast [Shatner, Nimoy, Kelley, Rhodes Reason, all in the cell, and William Bramley, the head policeman at the door of the cell]. Bill Shatner, Leonard Nimoy and DeForest Kelley, after a long 12-hour day [which included time in makeup] … would then go home with the requirement to work on the scenes for the following day's work. To do it at all was an accomplishment. To do it with such skill -- I bow my head in admiration." (155-5)

While filming the scenes on the jail set, as Captain Kirk prepared to shoot the lock off the door to the cell, giant Ted Cassidy appeared out of nowhere, dressed as "Injun Joe" from *The New Adventures of Huckleberry Finn*. He swooped in, picked up and carried off William Shatner, who, in the arms of Cassidy, called back to his colleagues, "Hey, I don't know about you, but this is not the way it should work!"

Senensky said, "Everybody except Bill knew that Ted was going to come in, pick him up, and carry him off. We staged that, and it survives until this day [on a well-circulated *Star Trek* blooper reel]." (155-3)

Cassidy added, "The production company that made *Star Trek* is the kind of production company that likes to have fun. Almost every show, they would engineer some kind of outtake. I mean, it wouldn't happen naturally. They would figure out what to do to make a funny piece of film for Christmas, you know, for the [blooper reel]. There was nobody on the production end who was really nervous as they usually are on all the shows. This was a very fun, *fun* kind of thing to do. I do remember *Star Trek* with fondness." (31)

Senensky was mostly frustrated by the more restrictive second season budget while shooting the arena scenes. He belabored, "The

Shatner's first try at firing the machine gun
(Courtesy of Gerald Gurian)

sequence in the arena is that part of our story most harmed by the time restrictions imposed by the new management [Paramount]. It was literally put together on the run…. The satiric look at live television was there, [but] the spectacle of the Roman arena was less than it should

have been. There was so much more that could have been done that would have been exciting and entertaining, but it needed time to stage and rehearse, with care taken to avoid injury to the actors involved. It should have been the breathtaking set piece of the production. But those wolfhounds in the black suits were nipping at our heels." (155-5)

One of the arena scenes Ralph Senensky wished he had more time to film
(Courtesy of Gerald Gurian)

Behind-the-scenes photos revealed that the cast enjoyed this trek (above); and Day 7, September 20, 1967 (below) (Courtesy of Gerald Gurian)

Regardless of the nipping, director and crew fell behind. This ambitious episode, with location filming, a larger than usual cast, and numerous action sequences involving stunts, could not have been filmed in six days, with each day ending at 6:18 p.m. This time, it took a full seven.

Day 7. Production of "Journey to Babel" had to be pushed back, allowing Senensky and company to film the scenes in the "Proconsul's Apartment."

Lois Jewell, working only one day in front of the camera, said, "I remember the costume and I remember the fitting for that costume, as well. I guess it was very risqué in those days. There was no back to it at all. And you could not see the belly-button. That wasn't allowed on television at that time. They used double-edged tape to keep me all tucked in…. I had to go in for costume fittings and all that stuff, and then they took me onto the set and we did a walk-through, and then they filmed the three scenes I was in. In those days, they didn't give them a lot of time to make these hour-long shows." (92a)

As for her love scene with Kirk, Jewell said, "William Shatner was polite and he was a professional; he was a wonderful person to work with. He made it easy for me." (92a)

It had been a stressful seven days. Despite the anxiety over running late, the direction, lighting, and performances remained excellent.

Post-Production
Available for editing: September 21, 1967. Rough Cut: October 3. Final Cut: October 9.
Music Score: tracked.

Fabien Tordjmann and Edit Team 3 did the cutting, including, when Ian Wolfe wishes Kirk and company to be blessed by the "Son," the nice sleight-of-hand trick of cutting from them to a shot of the sun blazing in the sky. That suggestion came from Ralph Senensky.

347

Many others came from Gene Roddenberry, who was again very present in the production offices and the editing rooms.

"Roddenberry was fine," Tordjmann said. "He was very picky, and sometimes we'd chafe under that because we'd have to deliver a film, but on the other hand we'd recognize that he was right in there trying to do the thing that would correspond more to the new way that this show was being done. It was not like *Lost in Space*, with just gimmicks. And, above all, I think all of us were concerned about human beings, following Gene's lead. He has been proven right. The human element is often lost nowadays." (176)

Van der Veer Photo Effects provided the optical effects, with new shots of the Enterprise being handled by Film Effects of Hollywood, uncredited. The sequences showing the Enterprise orbiting the planet are more spectacular than in the past, with the planet bigger in scope.

This was only one of two episodes in the series to delay the show title and writers and director credits at the top of Act I until after the start of some physical action. The reason for this had nothing to do with style, but lack of coverage. Robert Justman, anticipating a problem, wrote to Gene Coon while the script was still being written:

> I don't feel we need the [Captain's log] Narration for the head end of Act I. If we do, we're gonna have to come up with some sort of business to cover the amount of footage needed to handle the episode title, writer's credits and director's credits. Fact is, we ought to always indicate to the director that these requirements are standard and necessary at the beginning of Act I. I have run into a couple of instances this season where we have had a fair amount of trouble finding enough room for those credits, due to the fact that the director did not allow for them in his handling of the scenes or due to the fact that we did not arrange for some sort of script action to cover this need. (RJ43-3)

The business they came up with was the materialization effect, and Kirk, Spock, and McCoy, finding themselves on the top of a hill.

Release / Reaction
Only NBC air date: 3/15/68.

Steven H. Scheuer reviewed the episode for *TV Key Previews*. Among newspapers across America to carry the review on March 15, 1968 was *The Charleston Gazette*, serving Charleston, West Virginia. Scheuer said:

> An interesting supposition provides the basis for this episode. The Enterprise comes across an Earth-like planet where the Roman Empire never fell, where its civilization approximates that of our 20th century. Although this allegory does not completely come to grips with its ambitious idea, the scenes showing commercial telecasts of the gladiatorial match are hilarious.

Judy Crosby also reviewed the episode on March 15, 1968, for her syndicated column, *TV SCOUT*. Among the papers running the review was *The Radford News Journal*, in Radford, Virginia. Crosby wrote:

> *Star Trek* has been vaulting between outer-space imagination and back-tracking through history ["A Piece of the Action," and "Patterns of Force" having aired

first], which is what it does tonight. This is a Roman orgy of sorts, with the Enterprise depositing its crew on a planet that has reached the level of the Roman Empire at its height, where the starship officers are forced into televised gladiatorial combat. This one is loaded with all of the elements of a movie spectacle, including slave girls (Lois Jewell), gladiators (Rhodes Reason plays the champ) and the despot, played by Logan Ramsey, who keep the masses happy by staging these bloody spectacles. Of course, he intends to star Captain Kirk and Mr. Spock in one of these battles.

Mock up magazine ad for the magazine created for this episode (Courtesy of Bob Olsen)

Lois Jewell remembered watching "Bread and Circuses" when it had its NBC airing. She said, "My husband and I watched it on a friend's TV, which was a lot bigger than ours, and in color. And everybody was impressed. I especially was pleased. I enjoyed that story. It really had a lot going on in it, with worshiping the sun, and then it turned out to be the Son of God. Other shows at that time really weren't telling those kind of stories or making any kind of statements. It was really an outstanding series." (92a)

RATINGS / Nielsen National report for Friday, March 15, 1968:

8:30 to 9 p.m., 57.9% U.S. TVs in use.

		Share:	Households watching:
NBC:	*Star Trek*	**37.2%**	**16,130,000**
ABC:	"The Actor"	9.3%	5,150,000
CBS:	*Great Gold Rush*	32.9%	13,050,000
Local independent stations:		20.6%	No Data

9 to 9:30 p.m., 58.4% U.S. TVs in use.

		Share:	Households watching:
NBC:	*Star Trek*	**37.5%**	**No Data**
ABC:	"The Actor"	8.4%	No Data
CBS:	*Friday Night Movie*	33.3%	No Data
Local independent stations:		20.8%	No Data

349

This episode, which spoofed network television, obviously displeased NBC. "Bread and Circuses" was pushed back from the 43rd filmed to the 54th aired and was not given a repeat broadcast. And whether by coincidence or design, "Bread and Circuses" originally aired on March 15, 1968, AKA the Ides of March, the day Julius Caesar was assassinated in 44 BC.

NBC should have been more appreciative. Not only was *Star Trek* the network's top-rated Friday night show, but "Bread and Circuses" won its time slot -- big. In fact, this was the highest rated second season episode. There was a reason -- CBS bumped its massive hit *Gomer Pyle* at the last minute for a 30-minute news special called "The Gold Rush '68," making much ado about nothing -- the supposed "gold crises of 1968" which was touched off by a short-term speculation on the rise in the price of gold. ABC also alienated its regular audience, serving up a one-hour documentary filmed in the London theater district, called "The Actor," examining what it is to be a thespian.

The CBS movie at 9 p.m. was a repeat of *McLintock*, a Western starring John Wayne and Maureen O'Hara. On this night, *Star Trek* beat the Duke hands down.

Memories

Ralph Senensky said, "I was unhappy with that episode.... because of the arena stuff, which was rushed. That was the first show I was given to do under the new regime.... The takeover by Paramount of Desilu Studios affected me, with the tightening of the budgets and the shorter schedules, and I'm sure that must have affected the cast. There were just bad vibes at that time. I work fast, I was not a slow director, but I was at ease when I worked. And, all of a sudden, this was a time when I was tense. I didn't feel as secure in my feelings about what I was doing as a director. Despite this, the part I liked about that episode was how it mocked network TV. That almost made it worthwhile." (155-6)

22

Episode 44: JOURNEY TO BABEL

Written by D.C. Fontana
Directed by Joseph Pevney

Mark Lenard, Leonard Nimoy, and Jane Wyatt in NBC publicity photo (Courtesy of Bob Olsen)

NBC press release, issued October 19, 1967:

Jane Wyatt guest-stars as Mr. Spock's Earthling mother in "Journey to Babel," a drama in which murder and pursuit by an alien vessel plague the Enterprise as it transports ambassadors to a vital council meeting, on NBC Television Network's *Star Trek* colorcast Friday, Nov. 17.... The delegation includes Mr. Spock's (Leonard Nimoy) mother, Amanda (Miss Wyatt), and his Vulcan father, Sarek (guest star Mark Lenard). Tellarite ambassador Gav is murdered and Sarek is the prime suspect. When he suffers a heart attack, Dr. McCoy (DeForest Kelley) determines that only a transfusion from Spock can save him. Meanwhile, Captain Kirk (William Shatner) is attacked and wounded. Spock, despite Amanda's pleas, refuses to aid his father and insists on taking over for Kirk.

Sarek and his son haven't spoken in years, as a result of Spock's decision to join Starfleet. Meanwhile, it is learned that Kirk's attacker, an Orion spy disguised as an Andorian dignitary, and the spaceship shadowing the Enterprise, are on a suicide mission, determined to sabotage the diplomatic gathering at all costs.

This is a story of stubbornness, sacrifice ... and love.

SOUND BITES

- *Amanda:* "It hasn't been easy for Spock -- neither Vulcan nor human." *Kirk:* "I gather Spock disagreed with his father over his choice of a career." *Amanda:* "My husband has nothing against Starfleet. But Vulcans believe peace should not depend on force. Sarek wanted Spock to follow his teaching as Sarek followed the teaching of his father." *Kirk:* "And they're both stubborn." *Amanda:* "A human trait, Captain?"

- Amanda, to Spock and Sarek: "Logic! Logic! I'm sick to death of logic! Do you want to know how I feel about your logic?" *Spock, to his father:* "Emotional, isn't she?" *Sarek, to his son:* "She has always been that way." *Spock:* "Indeed -- why did you marry her?" *Sarek:* "At the time, it seemed the logical thing to do."

- McCoy, To a bedridden Spock: "Shut up!" *McCoy, to a bedridden Kirk as he starts to protest:* "Shh, shh!" *McCoy, to himself after Spock and Kirk become silent:* "Well, what do you know? I finally got the last word!"

ASSESSMENT

"Journey to Babel" offers a look at the generation gap, a hot topic in the 1960s, as well as examining the complexities of relationships within the family. The theme is one of personal sacrifice.

- Sarek wanted Spock to sacrifice his personal agenda to honor the traditions of their culture and family.
- Amanda has certainly sacrificed much of who she once was to live as the wife of a Vulcan.
- Spock is willing to make a great sacrifice too -- he will let his father die in order to stay true to his oath to Starfleet and safeguard the ship and its passengers.
- Once relieved of this duty and burden, Spock will make an abrupt turn and risk his life to save his father.
- Against doctor's wishes, Kirk is willing to sacrifice his well-being to get back to the bridge so that Spock can tend to his family duty.
- And the Orions are willing to sacrifice their lives – and hundreds of other lives -- for what they believe.

Some of these sacrifices are motivated by love, some by tradition, some by blind obedience.

It is fitting, and a clever addition to an already well-constructed script, that the story within the story has to do with an interplanetary conference which may ensure peace ... or make it impossible. Ambassadors from the Federation's different worlds struggle to find common ground for decisions, as do Spock and his father. One plot line parallels the other as this taut and passionate story unfolds.

"Journey to Babel" is one of *Star Trek*'s best.

THE STORY BEHIND THE STORY

Script Timeline
D.C. Fontana's story outline, ST #65: June 23, 1967.
Fontana's 1ˢᵗ Draft script: August 8, 1967.
Fontana's 2ⁿᵈ Draft script (Mimeo Department "Yellow Cover 1ˢᵗ Draft"):
August 22, 1967.
Gene Coon's script polish (Final Draft): Late August 1967.
Coon's additional script polish (Revised Final Draft): August 31, 1967.
Gene Roddenberry's script polish (2ⁿᵈ Revised Final Draft): Sept. 19, 1967.
Further staff script polishing: September 20, 21, 26 & 27.

During *Star Trek*'s first season, a story was developed entitled "Journey to

Relocite," where the Enterprise is used to transport the ruler of one planet to make peace with the people of another. This was the setup for a story of barbarism, lust, and seduction. It was later discarded. But the title, and this vague setup, may have served as one of a few different story springboards for Dorothy Fontana and her fifth script for *Star Trek*. The one springboard that Fontana recalls came from a standout first season episode. Fontana said, "There's a line thrown in 'The Naked Time' [written by John D.F. Black, with additional writing by Gene Roddenberry] about how Spock never told his mother he loved her, and then, in 'This Side of Paradise,' I allude to the fact that his mother was a teacher and his father was an Ambassador. That sort of ran around the back of my mind for a little while, and I thought, 'These are two interesting characters, let's learn a little more about them.' When I proposed the story to Gene Roddenberry, he said, 'Go, run, jump,' and I came back with 'Journey to Babel,' which pretty much was done as written." (64-1)

Fontana went, ran, jumped, and did not stop at merely bringing Spock together with his parents, but she also looked for a story rich in drama and conflict that would justify the reunion. As the title indicates, "Journey to Babel" is a story about communication -- between husband and wife, father and son, and delegates of different races from different worlds.

The episode title is a reference to the eleventh chapter of Genesis in the Bible's Old Testament. As told there, all of mankind spoke one language until their pride led them to build a great tower to consolidate their power. God reacted to this achievement by "confusing" the languages of man, so that everyone no longer spoke the same. The story served as an explanation for the many languages and cultures throughout the ancient world.

When D.C. Fontana chose "Journey to Babel" as her title, she was signifying that her story was a real "Journey to Confusion" for not only Kirk and his crew, and Spock and his parents, but for the battling delegates as well.

"It was really a story about communication, and why people stop communicating, and why they begin again," said Fontana. "What kind of love moves that? Why would this woman want this man? Why would this man want this woman? Why are Spock and Sarek not talking? What was the riff? And this was, of course, when 'generation gap' was the big buzzword, and I just went with it. It was basically a love story, not between the man and the woman but between the father and his son, and how it had to be resolved without ever admitting, of course, that Vulcans are capable of that emotion. And then you threw in the adventure, and you threw in the intrigue, and do all the stuff to dress it up, but that story is really about love." (64-1)

NBC's Stan Robertson both liked and feared the idea of "Journey to Babel." On July 7, 1967, he wrote to Gene Coon:

> We believe that this particular storyline has the potential of holding a most unique position in the total scope of our series. It can either be developed into one of the most interesting, effective, and audience appealing shows we have ever done or it can be one which will do immeasurable harm.... All of us associated with *Star Trek* are naturally aware of the viewers' interest in Mr. Spock and all things which pertain to him and his Vulcan background.... Spock has emerged as one of those truly phenomenal characters which television produces all too rarely.... With the above in mind, when we delve visually and dramatically into the side of Spock's life, which we have verbally alluded to, it is obvious that we must be particularly careful that we do not destroy all of the mystery, the allure, the glamour, and the uniqueness which the audience associates with the character. (SR44)

Robertson insisted that, if Coon were to green-light this script assignment, the story and all its details must be "technically accurate." To illustrate his reservations he offered an example of what could go wrong. As the story outline was presently written, Sarek's heart attack had him clutch his chest. Of this, Robertson wrote:

> All of us dedicated *Star Trek* fans know that Vulcans don't have their hearts in their chests. As we know, our viewers will be quick to spot inaccuracies such as this. (SR44)

Robertson closed by saying he was happy Fontana and not someone else was handling the script.

Fontana turned in her 1st Draft teleplay on August 8. The story began on the planet Vulcan, not the Enterprise.

Robert Justman wrote to Gene Coon:

> This will be a fine, exciting shipboard tale.... [But] we are in the county poorhouse with regards to cast and extras. These cast people and extras carry with them the requirements of wardrobing and makeup and also being paid. It is becoming a well-known fact here at *Star Trek* that our ability to pay hard cash dollars has no relationship to the increasing popularity of our program. No doubt by the time we reach our fifth year on the air, our show will consist of one long sequence in which Kirk, Spock and McCoy discuss what has just happened to them on the ship in a 62-page Briefing Room scene.... Since this is a shipboard show, and since we are going to be heavy in the area of cast, extras, wardrobing, makeup and Optical Effects and Miniatures -- let's play the content of the Teaser on board the Enterprise [instead of on Vulcan].... To make up for all of the savings of money and to give you a thrill, no doubt NBC will say to us, "Gee whiz! Fellas, why don't you open this show on a planet?" You will therefore be able to say to NBC, "Go shove the planet up your ...!" This will give you immense satisfaction. (RJ44-1)

Justman had 10 more pages of notes, including:

> I don't think that Kirk ought to be cut on the face and arm by the Andorian. I think a body wound would be more like it. This would enable us to sell a loss of blood and a possible infection a little easier. It will also save an enormous makeup problem with regard to a cut and the healing process concerned with it. (RJ44-1)

Kirk's face and arm wounds were changed to a stab near his heart in Fontana's 2nd Draft from August 22. And the trip to Vulcan was replaced with a trip to the transporter room, where Sarek and his party of four beam up.

Years later, Fontana said, "They put some money into that, to the tune of the costumes, the makeup, masks ... the food spread out that was dyed all different colors ... and so on. You always did trade-offs in that sense. If you went on location, you had to give away your costume and makeup. If you stayed on the ship you could do more.@ (64-2)

In his next memo to Gene Coon, concerning Fontana's rewrite, Justman asked that a dinner scene be changed to a cocktail party. He wrote:

> My reasons for this change are clever. We can save a complete redress on a set and also get a less static scene if we do not place scenes 11 through 13 in a "Dining Room." A Dining Room would also call for our construction of a new table and also serving people, which does bother me to some extent. We can get the same sequence and a lot better looking sequence by playing it in the Recreation Room where everybody is having cocktails after dinner. Therefore, no one really needs to be seated. We can get some movement from various Extras and Principals contained within this room and we get a fluid scene, as

opposed to a static one. (RJ44-2)

It was also decided to *not* beam up Sarek and four others from Vulcan. To save money, they would arrive by shuttlecraft instead. The shots of the shuttle, like so much else, were re-used from previous episodes. To illustrate just how costly the transporter effect was, the building of the hangar deck set on Stage 10 was less expensive than having a group of people beam on board. The actual cost of each transporter effect -- one person only, either materializing or dematerializing -- was $810 (about $5,700 in 2013). Multiply that by the number of characters beaming up, or beaming down, and multiply it again by how many times people were described as beaming up or down, and *Star Trek* had a budget that was rapidly dematerializing.

In an effort to bring the spending under control, Roddenberry sent a memo to his post production supervisor Eddie Milkis on September 18, writing:

> As we expected… we are limiting ourselves to one or the other end of the transporter effect. Either we see a landing party leave the ship or we cut straight to the planet surface and see them arriving. But this does create a problem since, hopefully, *Star Trek* will continue with audience growth. What of those people who have never seen both ends and really will not understand how the transporter works?… Suggest a careful examination of those shows still being edited with some analysis whether or not we can use stock footage from last year… [or shots which show] limited angle on dematerialization in transporter room that includes only Kirk and Spock or possibly McCoy too.

This problem, for "Journey to Babel" anyway, was eliminated with the move to the shuttle hangar, but this memo gives insight as to why in many of the future episodes (especially in the third season) it was only Kirk, Spock, and McCoy who beamed down. Fewer optical effects; fewer extras.

Coon made the necessary changes to the script in late August, before giving up his post as series producer. In early and mid-September, additional page revisions were turned in, courtesy of Gene Roddenberry. Fontana said, "Most of the time, we staffers did rewrites or revisions of our own rewrites. However, occasionally, one of us would rewrite the other, to get a fresh point of view on the script." (64-4a)

Of the changes, she said, "One scene was added where Amanda talks to Kirk about Sarek's relationship with his son. It seemed to me that that would have been inappropriate, and that she would not have blurted out all of this to Kirk. I did not have anything to do with that scene, and I think Gene Roddenberry rewrote it." (64-22)

Pre-Production
September 12-15 and September 18-20, 1967 (7 days prep).

Director Joseph Pevney found 13 to be a lucky number. This, his 13th directorial episode for the series, would become a classic. And he would deliver it on schedule and within budget.

Mark Lenard made his first appearance here as Sarek. He was paying an alien 102 years old, which was soon established as late middle age for a Vulcan. In human years, the actor was 37. Lenard had already impressed the series' producers by his portrayal of the Romulan commander in "Balance of Terror." He looked good in those ears and managed, with restrained emotion, to become a character of wisdom, dignity and compassion. This put him at the top of the list to play Spock's father.

Lenard, as Sarek, would return six more times. Three of the six were on the small screen -- the 1973 animated series' episode "Yesteryear," also written by Fontana, then in "Sarek," on *Star Trek: The Next Generation*, and once more for that series, in "Unification." On the big screen, Lenard played Sarek in *Star Trek III: The Search for Spock*, *Star Trek IV: The Voyage Home*, and *Star Trek VI: The Undiscovered Country*. He also played a Klingon in *Star Trek: The Motion Picture*, thus making him the first triple-threat *Trek* alien.

Mark Lenard as Sarek
(Unaired film trim courtesy of Gerald Gurian)

Robert Young with Wyatt, Emmy Award winners for
Father Knows Best
(Academy of Television Arts and Sciences)

Jane Wyatt, as Spock's mother, was already a favorite TV mom, thanks to the sitcom *Father Knows Best*. But Wyatt was famous prior to her work in television. She achieved star status in 1937 when cast opposite Ronald Coleman in *Lost Horizon*. After enjoying a successful film career throughout the 1940s, including being cast opposite Dana Andrews in *Boomerang* and Randolph Scott in *Canadian Pacific* (both 1947), Wyatt moved to television to co-star in *Father Knows Best* from 1954 through 1960. There, she won three Emmy Awards for playing Margaret Anderson, the mother who knew even better than her husband.

Wyatt told *Starlog*, in 1990, "My agent called up and said, 'Do you want to be on *Star Trek*?,' and I said, 'What is it?' ... I had a look [at the show], and they sent a script, and I thought it would be fun."

Wyatt returned to the role of Amanda, wife of Sarek, for the big screen treatment of *Star Trek IV: The Voyage Home*.

This episode introduces the blue-skinned Andorians and the pig-nosed Tellarites. Along with Humans and Vulcans, they are among the members of the United Federation of Planets.

Reggie Nalder played Shras, the elder Andorian ambassador. He was 60. With severe burn scars on the lower half of his face, Nalder was usually cast in villainous roles. In

Alfred Hitchcock's second version of *The Man Who Knew Too Much*, from 1956, Nalder played Rien, the assassin. He was the cold Russian operative in *The Manchurian Candidate*, and he was also prominently featured as the horrific vampire Barlow in the 1979 mini-series *Salem's Lot*.

William O'Connell played Thelev, the Orion spy disguised as an Andorian. Beginning in 1959, he appeared often on television. You can see him without the blue makeup, as Dr. Winterich, in "The Night of the

Reggie Nalder in *The Man Who Knew Too Much* (Paramount Pictures, 1956)

Pistoleros," an episode of *The Wild, Wild West*, and, courtesy of casting director Joe D'Agosta, in a 1967 episode of *The Lucy Show*, followed by 1968 episodes of *Mannix* and *Mission: Impossible*.

John Wheeler played Gav, the Tellarite ambassador with a pig-nose. He'd been active in front of the camera since 1960. He said, "I did quite a bit of live TV in New York, and commercials as well as stage work. I'd been in *Sweet Charity*, directed by Bob Fosse." (180b)

William O'Connell in 1968 episode of *Mannix* (www.aveleyman.com)

With Broadway stage work on his resume, Wheeler moved with his wife to Los Angeles, expecting bigger and better things. And then his agent got him a meeting at *Star Trek*. He recalled, "I went in to see Gene Roddenberry. I hadn't seen the show; didn't know much about it. He gave me some pages to read and he said, 'I want you to use your voice differently; try to make your voice lower.' So I made it low as I could. And then I went home and my agent called and said, 'You got the job.' It was my first job in Hollywood. I was

John Wheeler as Gav (CBS Studios, Inc.)

going to work three days and they were going to pay me $600, and I said, 'God, I've been working for $200 a week on Broadway, so this is terrific.' But I had no idea that I was going to be in that costume with all the makeup covering my face. A week or so later I was told I had to come in and go to the makeup department at Desilu and they put a plaster mask all over my head and left me two little straws to breathe through. They said, 'We hope you're not claustrophobic.' I said, 'Hell no, I'll do anything for work.' And that's when I found out that, for my first TV job on the West Coast, I'd be hidden behind a mask!" (180b)

Billy Curtis, one of the two copper-skinned aliens of small stature, was 58. Among his roles: the Munchkin Mayor in *The Wizard of Oz*, and one of the guys who crawled out from the center of the Earth in *Superman and the Mole Men*. His longest running job was as Mayor McCheese for McDonald's fast food restaurants.

William Blackburn continued to sit at the helm for Sulu, as George Takei worked alongside John Wayne in *The Green Berets*. Blackburn appeared in 59 episodes of the original *Star Trek*.

Russ Meek, who played the Vulcan aide to Spock's counterpart in "Mirror, Mirror," is seen here as one of Sarek's Vulcan aides. He had also played the Vulcan "Executioner" in "Amok Time."

Production Diary
Filmed September 21, 22, 25, 26, 27, 28, 1967.
(6 day production; budget set at $171,439).

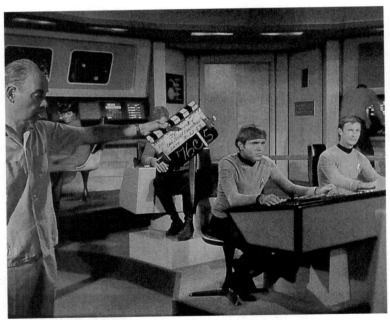

Day 2. Bill McGovern slates a shot on the bridge.
Note Kirk, in command chair, in his injured posture.
At the helm, Walter Koenig and Bill Blackburn
(Courtesy William Krewson and Gerald Gurian)

Thursday, September 21, 1967. The new fall television season had arrived. The night before, NBC had the top show from 7:30 to 8:30 p.m. with the first hour of *The Virginian*, until viewers switched channels to make CBS king at 8:30 with *The Beverly Hillbillies* and, at 9 p.m., *Green Acres*. Box office champ *Bonnie and Clyde*, starring Warren Beatty and Faye Dunaway, still had them lining up at the movie houses. "The Letter" by the Box Tops was the song being played the most on U.S. Top 40 radio stations. And *Sgt. Pepper's Lonely Hearts Club Band*, by The Beatles, was still flying off the shelves in record stores. The Doors' debut album, featuring "Light My Fire," was a close second. Julie Andrews had the cover of *Look* magazine. The Beatles had *Time* magazine's cover. And the Monkees were on the cover of *TV Guide*.

Day 1, Thursday. Filming of "Journey to Babel" began on Stage 9 for scenes in Kirk's quarters and then on to the bridge, where Pevney shot all the scenes needed for the show's Teaser, Act I, Act II, and Act III.

Day 2, Friday. The first half of the day was spent finishing up on the bridge, with the sequences from Act IV, and the climax as an injured Kirk takes command from Spock. After the lunch break, the company resumed work in the ship's corridors for the scene where Kirk is attacked by Thelev, and the discovery of the Tellarite ambassador's body dangling upside-down at the end of a Jefferies tube.

John Wheeler, having his death scene this day, hanging upside down, said, "It was hotter than hell in that costume, I'll tell you that. I thought I was going to melt. But they gave me lots of water. They treated me wonderfully. For that scene, where I'm dead, they put a rope around my ankles and hung me by the feet. I had three fingers on each hand and they wanted to make sure everyone saw that … just in case no one recognized me from my pig face. So that's why I was hanging with my arms out like that." (180b)

On this night, NBC premiered "Who Mourns for Adonais?" It placed second in the Nielsens, with 10,920,000 households tuning in across America, a million more than *Hondo*, the competition on ABC. *Star Trek* was also NBC's top-rated show of the night.

Day 3, Monday. Further work in the ship's corridors, this time for the scenes requiring an assortment of aliens. This was the day the makeup department had to jump into high-gear, with the afternoon spent in the recreation room, featuring all the alien ambassadors. It was the single largest assembly of alien creatures in television and film history ... until *Star Wars*.

"That was a good show in certain areas," Joseph Pevney

Day 3: Jane Wyatt, DeForest Kelley, Mark Lenard, William Shatner, and Reggie Nalder (Unaired film trim courtesy of Gerald Gurian)

said. "I thought the greatest contributor to it was the makeup artist. He did a fabulous job of bringing alien humanoids on board. *Star Wars*? The entire sequence in the bar looks like it came from this episode." (141-3)

"I literally arrived at 5:30 or a quarter of six in the morning," said William O'Connell. "I was told makeup would take a little time, and they put on, like, a matte finish for an actor, and then the hair, the antennae, and so on and so forth. It took, I think, almost two hours. So it was laborious. But I didn't mind." (130)

John Wheeler had it worse as his facial features were buried under a mask with a pig snout. He remembered, "It took them five hours every morning to get me in that shape, with the applications and everything they put on. I had two guys working on me. The hair that I had on my face, they laid that on individually, pretty much hair by hair. And then they put a wig on me. Every morning I was sitting there with Spock and he was getting his ears put on and I was getting my face put on. The only thing I think they do better nowadays is they tie in

359

the eyes a little better, so it doesn't look like you're looking out through two holes." (180b)

Regarding the out-of-this-world assembly of aliens and famous TV faces, Wheeler said, "I had just done two years [sic] on the stage with Robert Preston in *We Take the Town*, and Mark Lenard was in that show with me. So I knew Mark and recognized him immediately, even with that haircut, the eyebrows, and pointed ears. And the director on that was Joseph Pevney. I had worked with his wife Mitzi at the Brussels fair in 1958, where we did *Wonderful Town* there. So, when I came to the set, there they were, and it was like old home week. But it was really bizarre, the whole thing. And in the middle of it, Jane Wyatt,

who of course I recognized from her dramatic films and *Father Knows Best*. Very elegant, classy lady, and surrounded by all of us. Yes, really bizarre." (180b)

Wheeler said, "They worked pretty fast. I tried to do everything in one take. And that's the way it was for many of them. But there was one thing that my being new to Hollywood and film resulted in. It is in one shot of me sitting at a table in a corner and

Day 4. Shatner and Wyatt in engineering, from an unaired film trim (above; courtesy Gerald Gurian), and backstage photo of a little girl named Trelaine, visiting the set (below; courtesy of Trelaine Lewis)

looking at Shatner and those guys. I'm holding a drink in one hand and, when they cut away from me and then seconds later come back, it's in another hand. It really shocked me when I saw it later." (180b)

Day 4, Tuesday, began on Stage 10 for the hangar deck scene, followed by a move to Stage 9 for scenes in engineering and then Sarek's guest quarters.

A guest on the stage this day was nine-year-old Trelaine Lewis.

A friend of her mother's was also a friend of Cliff Ralke, a member of the camera crew. Because Trelaine was a fan of *Star Trek*, the family friend arranged through Ralke for mother and daughter to visit the set.

Trelaine said. "I can still visualize the big door that opened into the stage and that, right when you walked in, the crew had this large bucket of Tootsie-rolls and stuff. That was kind of cool for a kid to see. And I remember being really fascinated by how old the actual stage was, with all the pulleys and little cubbyholes. I was just sort of wandering around and looking at everything. I actually wasn't that interested in what they were filming because it was a very incidental scene." (108a)

Regarding the cast, Trelaine said, "I met Nimoy, and I don't know if he was in character or not, but he was very tall, and very quiet, and very intimidating. It wasn't the makeup that made him seem intimidating to me; there was just something about his manner and that was very quiet. He smiled in the picture that was taken of me with him and Shatner, but, otherwise, he was very serious." (108a)

Of guest star Jane Wyatt, Trelaine said, "I had no clue who she was whatsoever. My mom was impressed by her and said to me, 'My God, we're going to meet so'n'so.'" We were taken over to where she was sitting in a chair, and she turned and she was so gracious, like, 'Oh, hello, fans.' But I had no freakin' clue. I just looked at her and went, "Uh ... hi.' She was sort of this grand dame. And I was looking toward my mom for clues. My mom tried to explain to me who she was, but I didn't watch *Father Knows Best*. I wasn't into family dramas. At that point, I was watching *Gilligan's Island* and *Patty Duke*, and those kind of shows." (108a)

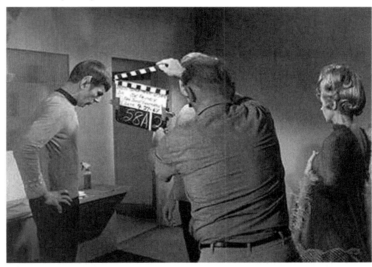

Day 5: Sickbay scene with Nimoy, Kelley (hidden by Bill McGovern), and Wyatt (above); and Mark Lenard with Majel Barrett (below) (Courtesy of Gerald Gurian)

Making a better impression on the nine-year old was Shatner. She said, "I have to tell you that Shatner was really cool. On the set, he paid total attention to me. He was so, *so* nice. The thing I remember the most is we were on the engineering set and there were these round pod things that were part of the set. They were like blow-up balls that you get at Toys R Us. And they bounced. And Shatner was bouncing these balls over to me, to the point where we kept screwing up the shot. The director had to say, 'Okay, stop it now,' and just sort of give Shatner 'the look.' And I remember Shatner rolling his eyes and looking at me, like, 'Oh oh.' And then he'd push the ball at me again and laugh. It was almost like he was a little kid. He was just a really nice guy." (108a)

Day 5, Wednesday, was spent filming sickbay and the exam room. Pevney was staying on schedule.

Frequent visitors to the set during the second season were John and Bjo Trimble. Bjo said, "Joseph Pevney was very efficient. He was unhurried but he still got things done when he wanted to get them done. We were off to the side and able to watch him work, and how people reacted to him. And when he offered a piece of advice, like how he wanted something done, even Shatner and Nimoy listened to him. And Nimoy didn't always listen to direction. Each director who came in had their own ideas as to how Spock should act, so neither Nimoy nor Shatner took well to direction or criticism. But Pevney managed to do it so it never seemed like direction or criticism; just a friendly suggestion." (177-8)

Or, as Trelaine Lewis recalled, Pevney would give one of them "the look."

Day 6, Thursday, brought more work in the exam room, back into sickbay, then finally Spock's quarters.

Beyond the makeup and colored food, "Babel" boasted some excellent performances. Leonard Nimoy said, "Mark [Lenard] had a real sense of dignity and authority that the character needed, and Jane [Wyatt] was very human, which was exactly what that character needed. They

Day 6, the operation scene is filmed in sickbay
(Courtesy of Gerald Gurian)

were terrific together. And they asked me if I had any suggestions about the Vulcans, about the Vulcan ideas, and I said, 'It seems to me that I've come around to think that the Vulcans are in some ways hand oriented people -- it has a lot to do with the hands.' I said, 'Maybe you and Jane could find a way to demonstrate that when you walk together ... and, instead of holding hands, they'd touch fingers -- which I thought was a wonderful touch." (128-7)

Mark Lenard said, "Sarek, like many people of strength and societal importance, believes in the superiority of the Vulcan way. They have struggled and tortured themselves and worked to create what they think is the perfect society. If not perfect, at least more in keeping with the way they feel the creatures in this galaxy should live. And the fact that Sarek's son, Spock, whom he nurtured and taught, the one who expresses the best that is the Vulcan society, should go off and share all this knowledge with others, hurt him deeply."

(107-3)

Jane Wyatt said, "I went there thinking, 'Well, we'll all have a good laugh over this.' But not at all. Everybody in makeup, having their ears put on and everything else, were *so* serious. That's what made it so good -- they were dead serious." (194)

Post-Production

Available for editing: September 29, 1967. Rough Cut: October 10;
Final Cut: October 13, 1967. Music Score: tracked.

James D. Ballas and Edit Team 1 handled the cutting with an emphasis on action cuts, jumping from one scene to another already in progress, such as the fight between Kirk and Thelev. In the script, and as filmed, Kirk is walking down the corridor near his quarters when Thelev jumps him. In the edited episode, Ballas cuts to the fight in progress, adding an accelerated pace to the episode.

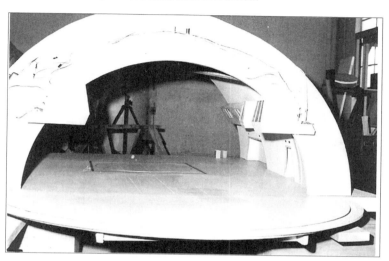

Two different views of the shuttle bay miniature, spanning ten by six feet, and standing six feet high (Courtesy of Bob Olsen)

The Westheimer Company handled the optical effects, which were limited to the Orion ship, seen on the bridge's viewing screen, and a matte shot of Uhura, on a monitor in engineering. All other opticals were recycled from past episodes, which explains why we see two different colors firing from the Enterprise's phasers, one blue, one purple.

The shots featuring the shuttlecraft docking with the Enterprise had been filmed for the first season episode, "The Galileo Seven." The miniature of the shuttle bay had been designed by Matt Jefferies and constructed by Richard Datin. It was over ten feet long, more than six feet wide, and six feet tall. The price, one year earlier: $2,100.

"Journey to Babel" was a rush job. It was the 15th episode produced for the second season, but the producers and NBC were so pleased with it that "Babel" was 10th to air. To meet the air date of the coming attraction trailer, one week before the episode itself, a different optical house had to be called in, which is why the effect in the trailer for the Orion

363

ship speeding past the Enterprise is different than what appears in the actual episode.

John Meredyth Lucas received his first *Star Trek* producing credit with this episode. It was a mistake; Gene Coon was the actual producer. However, by the time the production had ended and credits were added, Coon had left *Star Trek*. The name of Lucas, Coon's replacement, was inserted by the post-production crew because of this staffing change. The error has never been corrected.

Release / Reaction
Premiere air date: 11/17/67. NBC repeat broadcast: 7/5/68.

Does Mother Know Best on 'Star Trek'?

IN A RARE TV appearance, Jane Wyatt (who starred in the old "Father Knows Best" series) plays Amanda, the earthling mother of Mr. Spock (Leonard Nimoy) on NBC's "Star Trek" Friday night. In the episode, "Journey to Babel," murder and pursuit by an alien vessel plague the Enterprise, and Mr. Spock refuses to help his stricken Vulcan father despite the pleas of his mother because he feels his first duty is to the starship and his captain.

The Boston Sunday Herald **TV magazine**
(Sunday Herald Traveler), **November 12, 1967**

Steven H. Scheuer reviewed the episode for *TV Key Previews*. Among newspapers across America to carry Scheuer's syndicated column on November 17, 1967 was the *Kokomo Tribune*, serving Kokomo, Indiana. Scheuer said:

Fans of the Vulcan Spock won't want to miss this one. The Enterprise is host to a delegation of dignitaries from various planets, all aboard to attend an important council meeting. Spock's parents -- his human mother and estranged Vulcan father -- are among the most select guests. While murderous shenanigans and insidious plots pop up in this story with startling regularity, the real interest here revolves around Spock's unusual parentage.

Judy Crosby also reviewed the episode on November 17, 1967, for her syndicated column, *TV SCOUT*. Among the papers running the review was *The St. Petersburg Times*, in St. Petersburg, Florida. Crosby wrote:

The fans of *Star Trek*'s weird, wise and unworldly Dr. [sic] Spock are in for a first-rate episode tonight as the story closely examines his unusual breeding and his relationship with his mother, an Earthling, and his father, a Vulcan. Jane Wyatt makes a rare TV appearance as his mother, with Mark Lenard as Ambassador Sarek, his father. The story takes place on a space journey that is besieged with emergencies, including a murder. Spock's father is accused, which gives the story the necessary excuse for digging into the unusual father-son connection. There is also a very unique sequence aboard the Enterprise featuring several outer space types, which gives the makeup and costume people a big challenge.

The first nose-counting survey taken by A.C. Nielsen was by making random phone calls in a dozen metropolitan areas, including New York and Los Angeles.

RATINGS / Nielsen 12-city "overnight" Trendex survey.

Averaged rating for 8:30 to 9:30 p.m.:	**Average Rating:**
NBC: *Star Trek*	13.4
ABC: *Hondo*	11.5
CBS: **Gomer Pyle, U.S.M.C. / Friday Night Movie**	**18.5**

The movie this night was the 1963 comedy *Call Me Bwana*, starring Bob Hope. CBS promoted with ads in television magazines, entertainment sections of newspapers and *TV Guide*. NBC did nothing to help *Star Trek*. In the cities, *Star Trek* was the second place entry. By the time the rural areas were added in, for the National Report, *Hondo* slipped in front for No. 2 bragging rights.

RATINGS / Nielsen National report for Friday, November 17, 1967.

8:30 to 9 p.m., 55.6% U.S. TVs in use.	**Share:**	**Households watching:**
NBC: *Star Trek* (first half)	23.3%	9,070,000
ABC: *Hondo* (first half)	25.0%	9,800,000
CBS: **Gomer Pyle, U.S.M.C.**	**42.9%**	**14,730,000**
Local independent stations:	8.8%	No data

9 to 9:30 p.m., 58.4% U.S. TVs in use.	**Share:**	**Households watching:**
NBC: *Star Trek* (second half)	22.6%	No data
ABC: *Hondo* (second half)	25.4%	No data
CBS: **Friday Night Movie**	**37.5%**	**No data**
Local independent stations:	14.5%	No data

According to the July 27, 1968 issue of *TV Guide*, Home Testing Institute (TvQ), one of the three ratings services at this time (A.C. Nielsen and Arbitron being the others), used the month of November 1967 (which "Journey to Babel" just closed) to conduct an extensive survey to find out *who* was watching what. For the age group of 12 to 17, *Star Trek* was the fourth most watched series on television, just under *The Guns of Will Sonnett*, *The Second Hundred Years,* and *The Monkees*, respectively.

***

We learn of Spock's childhood pet, a "sehlat," in this episode. In D.C. Fontana's sequel, the 1973 episode of *Star Trek: The Animated Series* episode, "Yesteryear," we meet that pet, named I-Chaya.

Nimoy listed "Journey to Babel" as one of his favorites.

A *Star Trek* fanzine poll from the mid-1970s chose this as the third most-liked episode, right under "The City on the Edge of Forever" and "Amok Time," and immediately above "The Menagerie" and "The Trouble with Tribbles."

Science fiction genre magazine *Cinefantastique* selected this as one of the series' 10 best.

Entertainment Weekly, in its tribute issue to *Star Trek*, placed "Babel" at No. 10.

From the Mailbag

To Sherna Comerford and Devra Langsam, co-editors of *Spockanalia*:

About the Vulcan heart... I have consistently placed it on the right hand side of the body, in the area of the lower rib cage. That way, it would still be protected by bone as it is in the human, but might perhaps have a little more room since we have always tried to say the Vulcan heart is a larger organ and stronger than the normal human's. In "Journey to Babel," McCoy should rightfully have been operating from the right-hand side of Sarek... but the director chose to shoot from that direction so McCoy had to be on the other side." Dorothy Fontana, December 8, 1967.

Joseph Pevney made the decision to go against the script and Dorothy Fontana's wishes due to what he believed to be the best positioning for the lights and camera, with time allowances taken into consideration.

Memories

Dorothy Fontana said, "'Journey to Babel' was one of my favorite shows. It was a real love story, me and that script. I thought I had a pretty good lock on Spock." (64-1)

David Gerrold said, "Two of *Star Trek*'s very best episodes were 'Amok Time' and 'Journey to Babel' ... both of these episodes were true dramas. All of the conflicts and relationships were honest." (73-7)

John Wheeler said, "*Star Trek* was so far ahead of its time. And, at that time, the world wasn't ready for anything like that and it just grabbed hold of people. And it's been an amazing run." (180b)

William O'Connell said, "When I stepped onto the sets of *Star Trek*, I had a very hyper-critical eye. I wasn't impressed. After I saw the segment, my attitude changed and I valued the series. Thelev was absolutely committed to his cause of disrupting the conference. When he was caught, I tried to project his vulnerability. His mission of destruction ended with him taking the slow-acting poison. It was a nicely balanced episode." (130-1)

Jane Wyatt said, "Oh, it was great fun ... Shatner was really entertaining. I had great fun with him on the set. My 'son,' he was more dour... at that time, he didn't really talk much.... Mark Lenard was very good -- [and] so good looking when he gets his *Star Trek* clothes on, and his ears are so good! And I think my 'son' is better-looking with his ears, too. I think *all* men ought to wear pointed ears. They're very becoming, aren't they?" (194)

Mark Lenard shared, "I was in New York and I went into a theater and somebody came up to me and said, 'I have seen your segment of *Star Trek* 39 times.' I said, 'Oh, an infrequent viewer, huh?'"

23

Episode 45: A PRIVATE LITTLE WAR

Written by Gene Roddenberry
(story by Don Ingalls, using the pseudonym of Jud Crucis)
Directed by Marc Daniels

Even with a monster in the episode, NBC chose to promote the sex appeal, with Shatner and Kovack in publicity photo (Courtesy of Bob Olsen)

From NBC press release, issued January 3, 1968:

An inhabitant of the imperialistic planet Klingon is sent to execute the takeover of peaceful, primitive Neural, forcing Captain Kirk (William Shatner) to wage "A Private Little War" on NBC Television Network's *Star Trek* colorcast of Friday, Feb. 2.... Kirk and his officers beam down on Neural for a routine meeting, only to find that Klingon's Krell (Ned Romero) already has stirred up trouble between the Plains people, under the leadership of Tyree (Michael Witney) and the Hill people, under the leadership of Apella (Arthur Bernard). Tyree's wife, Nona (guest-star Nancy Kovack), wants her husband to make use of Kirk's super weapons so that she can become queen. The resulting war brings about a costly peace.

The stakes increase with each perilous step Kirk takes. Spock is wounded by a warring tribesman's flintlock rifle. As the First Officer fights for his life back on the Enterprise, Kirk falls victim to the poisonous fangs of an apelike creature known as the "mugato." The only chance of saving the Captain's life is to surrender him into the care of a local witch-doctor, an alluring and ambitious woman who wishes to use Kirk and his technology to gain power for her and her man, Kirk's old friend and "blood-brother," Tyree.

The theme is still debated today. Do superpowers have the right and the wisdom to choose sides and supply arms in civil disputes?

SOUND BITES

- *Kirk:* "There came a time when our weapons grew faster than our wisdom, and we almost destroyed ourselves. We learned from this to make a rule during all our travels never to cause the same to happen to other worlds."

- *McCoy:* "Well, Jim, here's another morsel of agony for you: since Tyree won't fight, he will be one of the first to die."

- *Kirk:* "Spock, ask Scotty how long would it take him to reproduce 100 flintlocks." *Scott, cutting in:* "I didn't get that exactly, Captain. A hundred what?" *Kirk:* "A hundred … serpents. Serpents for the Garden of Eden. We're very tired, Mr. Spock. Beam us up home."

ASSESSMENT

The Vietnam War was raging in Asia and a division of political and personal philosophies was splitting American public opinion down the middle. Network television, especially prime time entertainment shows, stayed carefully neutral. This *Star Trek* episode is believed to be the first entertainment show to make commentary on American foreign policy as it pertained to Vietnam and the heated debates over that undeclared war. And this makes "A Private Little War" notable, and historic.

Subtlety, however, was not Gene Roddenberry's style. He has Kirk ask McCoy: "Remember the 20th Century bush wars on the Asian continent, two giant powers involved, much like the Klingons and ourselves? Neither felt they could pull out …"

"I remember," McCoy interrupts. "It went on bloody year after bloody year!"

"What would you have suggested, that one side arms its friends with an overpowering weapon," Kirk counters. "Mankind would never have lived to travel space if they had. Bones, we can't take this planet back to where it was! The only solution is what happened then … a balance of power."

"And if the Klingons give them even more," McCoy challenges.

"We give this side exactly that much more," Kirk says. "The trickiest, most difficult, dirtiest game of them all. But the only one that preserves both sides."

Roddenberry wanted to be sure that everyone watching got the point … and the reference. Detractors cite "A Private Little War" as preachy. Supporters call it honest and direct. Just as Vietnam had split America into two distinct camps, this episode created a division of its own.

There is another division. Separating Kirk and Spock was rarely a good idea, and this episode suffers from the lack of connection between the two prime characters. In Ingalls' original story outline, a security man was shot by the Hill People, not Spock. The Vulcan was present when Kirk was attacked by the mugato (called gumato in the original script). It was Spock, not McCoy, who killed it, and he used a spear, not a phaser. But Roddenberry felt the story lacked personal jeopardy. He decided Spock should take a bullet, as well as making Kirk a blood-brother with Tyree. The choices were questionable.

There are other questionable plot devices. The action is relentless and character elements are thin. Case in point, we are told that Kirk and Tyree are blood-brothers and best of friends, but little of what we see conveys how such a bond was formed. Much of the script goes this way. We are told things and are expected to accept them without explanation or substance.

The episode's strength lies in the Vietnam parallel. The comparisons were obvious to adults, teens, and even children, and "A Private Little War" became a topic of conversation for years to come.

THE STORY BEHIND THE STORY

Script Timeline

Don Ingalls' story outline, ST-49, "Ty-Ree's Woman": April 30, 1967.
Ingalls' new story outline, gratis, now "A Private Little War": June 1, 1967.
Ingalls' revised story outline, gratis: June 5, 1967.
Ingalls' 2nd revised story outline, gratis: June 10, 1967.
Ingalls' 1st Draft teleplay: August 7, 1967 (delivered on Aug 12).
Ingalls' 2nd Draft (Mimeo Dept. "Yellow Cover 1st Draft"): August 30, 1967.
Gene Coon's script polish (Final Draft teleplay): Early September 1967.
Gene Roddenberry's rewrite (Revised Final Draft teleplay): Sept. 20, 1967.
Roddenberry's script polish (2nd Revised Final Draft): Sept. 25, 1967.
Additional page revisions by Roddenberry: September 26, 27 & 28, 1967.

Following the horrific rewriting of his first *Star Trek* script, "The Alternative Factor," reluctantly gutted by Gene Coon due to censorship and casting issues, Don Ingalls believed he had suffered again with Gene Roddenberry's rewrite on "A Private Little War." Ingalls remained friends with Roddenberry, but was so disturbed over the handling of the script that he removed his name from the episode. The story credit reads Jud Crucis. This was Ingalls' way of getting in the last word. A rumor quickly spread that the pseudonym stood for "Jesus Crucified."

This story had been under the microscope since Roddenberry assigned it to Ingalls. On April 1, 1967, Roddenberry wrote to Gene Coon:

> Had a meeting with Don and discussed some ideas which seemed to catch his imagination. But this one seems to be going very slow. It's possible we should ask for an early meeting with Don and see what he's up to and where he is on it. (GR45-1)

At this point, ST-49 was merely called "Untitled." After the meeting between Roddenberry, Coon and Ingalls, there were still differences of opinion, but they at least had a title ... and a premise.

In "Ty-Ree's Woman," Ingall's first try at the story outline, the planet was called Neural (think "Neutral"). The people were Neuralese. The Klingons in this story represented the Communist influence in the cold wars of 1967 Earth. The Federation took the role of the United States. The message was clear and so were Kirk's limited powers. At one point, comparing himself to his Klingon counterpart, Kirk tells McCoy, "I'm like him, Bones. I obey orders and I hope my way is right.... This 'little' war has been fought a million times before in a million different places and it will be fought a million more times ... and there isn't a damn thing you or I can do about it ... but in *this* little war it happens that my orders are to help these people and keep the other side from winning ... and that's what I intend to do."

Also, at this point, the name was Ty-Ree, later to be simplified to Tyree. On May 8, Roddenberry wrote to Coon:

> I'm much afraid of going into script with this outline. If we do, we are going to have something of the same problem we had on "Friday's Child," i.e., a lack of

urgency and jeopardies involving our main characters, a lack of unified dramatic build, a lack of firm science-fiction elements. Am sure the script can be made to work with Don's inventiveness and talent, but we must challenge him to find these elements before he goes any further.... Would Don do this same story on a *Virginian* or *Gunsmoke*? I think if he takes a long hard look at it he'll decide he wouldn't. Look at it as a fight between two Indian tribes, one of which has been armed with fire arms. What would be the Virginian's reason for being there and getting personally involved? Same question for Matt Dillon [of *Gunsmoke*]. More important, what is the theme? Don writes best when he has a meaningful, powerful theme. What is he saying here -- don't screw up simple societies?... The things at stake in Viet Nam [sic] are much more important and powerful than a charitable attitude toward simple people in the world. (GR45-2)

Robert Justman had other concerns. He wrote to Coon on May 26:

I find certain areas in this treatment are reminiscent of other shows including one of which GR wrote ["The Omega Glory"], but we have not yet produced because of various physical factors. (RJ45-1)

Other things were just too unbelievable for Justman, including Coon's determination to bring back Klingon commander Kor from "Errand of Mercy," whom the producer had also tried to get into "The Trouble with Tribbles." Coon wanted Kirk to have a recurring adversary. Justman didn't, and told Coon:

Kirk gets close enough to the headquarters to recognize Kor.... Here we are in the outer reaches of our galaxy and who should Captain Kirk run into but good old Kor -- an adversary that he has encountered before and with whom he has been unable to get very far [away from]. Just think of it -- billions of stars and millions of Class M-type planets and who should he run into but a fella he has had trouble with before. No wonder Kor doesn't recognize him at first. The coincidence is so astounding that he must feel certain that it couldn't possibly have happened. (RJ45-1)

Justman also felt Ingalls' plotting lacked explanation, and told Coon:

Why have the Klingons introduced rifles to this civilization instead of their own particular weapons, which we have previously established in another show? I think I know why, but perhaps we ought to spell it out, so that the audience understands that the Klingons still wish to retain absolute control and don't want this civilization to get too advanced, or to be difficult to handle eventually. (RJ45-1)

Also nervous over the projected cost, Justman ended with a threat:

If you go to screenplay with this story in its present form, I swear I'll start to write longer and longer memos. (RJ45-1)

Not wanting "longer and longer memos" from Justman, Coon chose to have Ingalls restructure his story in a revised outline, *gratis*, which was then revised again for no pay.

Of the third attempt at an outline, Dorothy Fontana wrote to Coon, on June 8, saying:

This story is much improved. However ... I wish this story did not bear such a strong resemblance to "Friday's Child." Is there any point to bringing in the Romulans rather than the Klingons? Is there any point to making the Neuralese less Arabic and perhaps more Mongolian or Apache Indian or something? (DCF45-1)

Coon followed Fontana's suggestion regarding the description of the Neuralese. But he was set on the idea of making the Klingons recurring villains ... even if Justman had talked him out of using Commander Kor.

At this point in the story, it was Kirk, not Spock, who was wounded in the Teaser. Of this, Justman told Coon:

> Let's have a Security Man or some nondescript fellow get killed or wounded by the pursuers. Let's not have Kirk get wounded at all, as we are going to have difficulty believing that Nona can cure Kirk of a bullet wound by using homeopathic medicine later on in the story. Instead, we should have Captain Kirk wounded by the Creature he encounters with the others as we proceed along into Act I. (RJ24-2)

It was decided that Spock would take the bullet. And, going with Justman's suggestion, Kirk would fall victim to the animal's poisonous fangs and need saving by Nona. Roddenberry wrote to Coon the following day:

> I think it is a good, highly professional outline. Again, I'm struck by the possibility that, properly handled, Don Ingalls could become a principal and highly useful *Star Trek* writer. (GR45-3)

Roddenberry suggested:

> I think it is terribly important that the Klingons are operating in complete secrecy. It is vital to this story, to the whole logic of it that the Klingons attempt to preserve the illusion that all this is "normal" planet development; that the people with their guns developed gun powder themselves. Thus, if Earth people interfere, the Klingons can argue that it is Earth people who are upsetting the delicate balance of a world here.... In other words, the situation is even closer to the Viet Nam situation. North Viet Nam tries to preserve the illusion, or at least tried to preserve it for some time, that they were not sending men and materials to South Viet Nam. And that way they insisted it was the United States which was the meddler and the aggressor. (GR45-3)

Roddenberry didn't feel Ingalls was utilizing the Jonathan Swift aspects of *Star Trek* enough, and told Coon:

> Don has done a good Viet Nam parallel in this but somehow I sense something is missing. Perhaps it is not carrying the parallel all the way -- i.e. in the Viet Nam situation if either side makes a mistake there will be a worldwide holocaust. So the stakes are terribly great. In this story, not to be unkind, the stakes seem merely that Earth or the Klingon Empire will prove the other side is "cheating" and there will be angry words but it will end there. (GR45-3)

Ingalls was asked to revise his outline again -- a fourth draft -- and this work too was done *gratis*. Finally, Ingalls was instructed to proceed to teleplay.

When that script arrived, on August 11, Justman wrote Coon:

> Why is Kirk so autocratic with McCoy and Spock? Why does he insist so strongly upon following orders? I realize that you are attempting to draw ... a parallel between this story and the Vietnam situation with respect to escalation and balance of power, but I don't think that we are doing our moral position in Vietnam any appreciable good at all -- but we are certainly causing our Captain to behave like a schmuck! (RJ45-3)

Coon wrote Ingalls:

> I would like a little more rationality from Kirk besides simply saying he has to do this because he is ordered. After all, in the current situation in Vietnam we are in an intolerable situation. We are doing that which we are forced to do and we can find no other way to do it.... A point we should bring out is that, despite

our good intentions, quite technically we are meddling, even though we are forced into it by prior Klingon meddling. What we don't want to happen is for our meddling to become common knowledge. Granted, we are forced into it, but it is still a violation of the treaty. Captain Kirk and his men, in this particular show, are put rather in the situation of the current day CIA which has secret instructions to go in and overthrow a government. This is not necessarily a moral or a decent thing to do, but it is something that must be done.... If we are to honor our commitments, we must counterbalance the Klingons. If we do not play it this way and it is admittedly the hard way, the Klingons will take over and threaten the Federation, even as the situation is in Vietnam, which is, as I remember, if Vietnam falls all Southeast Asia falls. Please let us have Kirk give a logical presentation of his own and the Federation's dilemma. Yes it is evil, but we have never been able to figure out another alternative. (GC45)

Justman had other concerns, and wrote Coon:

This can make an interesting *Star Trek*, but much surgery is going to have to be performed. There are too many strong similarities to "Friday's Child" ... For instance, we again have the strong-willed Wife of a Tribal Chief as a lead character. We again have our people hiding out in the mountains from pursuers. We again have the nose-to-nose confrontation between Captain Kirk and his Klingon adversary.... [And] we have a striking resemblance to what we have just shown on "The Apple." I refer to the South Sea Island Jungle Village, as described herein. Why do we have to have a village at all? Why can't this be a campsite and really have more primitive looking people with furs and animal pelts for clothing? (RJ45-3)

That same day, Fontana wrote to Coon:

I have a lot of bones to pick with this script that, aside from the heavy-handed [writing], is visually reminiscent of "The Apple" ... Please let us not have tents. I was informed in fluent profanity about all the difficulties encountered trying to shoot the insides of tents on "Friday's Child." (DCF45-2)

Justman had one last concern -- that Nona could hold her own in a physical confrontation with Kirk. He wrote, "Bill Shatner won't like the scene description about Nona being nearly as strong as he is." (RJ45-2)

Before the next draft, it would be decided that Nona, with her seductive ways and by rubbing the leaf of a mysterious plant on the skin of her intended victim, could leave a man confused and disoriented, as well as submissive.

On August 21, Coon conveyed many of the staff's concerns to Ingalls, along with one of his own. He wrote:

There is a touchy area in almost all the scenes between Ty-Ree and Nona. We seem to get the impression that Ty-Ree is impotent in regarding his wife. Granted, he has a lot on his mind, but I'm sure you and I have a lot on our minds, but we manage to get in our screwing with our lawful wedded spouses from time-to-time.... The impression throughout this script is that Ty-Ree just isn't making it with her. Certainly Nona can't complain that she isn't getting enough attention, but please let's not get in the implications of sexual impotence as far as Ty-Ree is concerned.... I also believe strongly that we should have a scene in which we see Nona's ambitions; in which we see that she is an incipient Lady MacBeth. This scene should have Nona try to spur Ty-Ree to fight, to conquer, to take over everything, to become unquestioned ruler of not only his own people, but the hill people who drove them away from their homes. Nona wants to be a queen. Let us establish it. (GC45)

Coon continued to work closely with Ingalls to raise the bar on "A Private Little War." From late August 1967, with Ingalls' 2nd Draft teleplay, Justman told Coon, "This script reads better now than it did before. And for that, I thank you." (RJ45-4)

With the "thank you" out of the way, Justman got down to business, writing:

> While it is dramatic, I feel that the ending of this script is wrong for *Star Trek*. It offers the viewers no hope that things will ever be better for Mankind. It tells the viewers that we are going to be making the same mistakes hundreds of years from now as we are making today and as we have made in the past. It will show them that we can never learn and that power begets injustice. I, personally, don't believe that we help our show either. This is about as downbeat a note as we could strike to end a segment of this series. One of the most important things we have attempted to say in this series is that there is hope for mankind and that things will be better for humanity in the future. We must not let Captain Kirk say, "There just isn't one damn thing you or I can do about it!" Kirk must hold out hope and the promise of better things to come -- let this show end that way! (RJ45-4)

Coon disagreed. He didn't want to end this particular episode on a happy note, feeling the statement was more poignant with a somber ending.

Coon's subsequent script polish, the Final Draft, came in early September.

With Coon's sudden resignation in mid-September -- although he would remain in the office, tutoring his replacement (John Meredyth Lucas) and rewriting the upcoming "A Piece of the Action" -- the teleplay for "A Private Little War" was handed off to Roddenberry.

Roddenberry's first work on the script, the Revised Final Draft, cleared his typewriter on September 20. Ingalls said, "Mine was more of an adventure in a vacuum. Gene's was more a political statement. His story was more tilted to parallel Vietnam than I did." (89)

Credit Gene Roddenberry, then, in spite of heavy-handed writing and preaching, for the most important aspect of "A Private Little War" -- a strong statement.

John Meredyth Lucas, pleased to see "A Private Little War" on the production schedule, said, "I was intrigued by the opportunity to say *anything*. We were doing anti-Vietnam War shows long before it was popular with many people, including the network, not realizing what we were saying." (110-3)

NBC's Broadcast Standards and Practices saw what was going on, with some of Roddenberry's dialogue ruffling the peacock's feathers. A September 25th letter from the B.S. Department told Lucas that they would not air the dialogue which at that point closed the script, where McCoy says to Kirk, "You got what you wanted," and a bitter Kirk retorts, "Yes, I did. A war that might go on for 40 years. Thousands dead. Development frozen. Yes. I might even get a medal."

Lines like these were changed by Roddenberry, with revisions dated September 26, 27, and 28, ending just one day before the start of filming. Kirk tells Scotty to make 100 flintlocks to be sent down to the planet, then corrects himself, and sadly says, "100 serpents." With this, Kirk leaves the order hanging in limbo. We would never know if the delivery was made. Kirk says that he and McCoy are tired and asks to be beamed home.

By the time all the rewriting had finished, there was too little left of Ingalls' script for him to get the "teleplay by" credit. Roddenberry would get that. Ingalls was assigned the "story by" credit, as determined by the Arbitration Board for the Writers Guild. Ingalls' reaction, both to the rewriting and the WGA decision, was to give instructions for his name to be removed and a pseudonym to be used for the screen credit -- Jud Crucis. Ingalls said it really didn't mean "Jesus crucified," as rumors had it, but "judicious crucis," which, as he explained it, described "a form of combat in which two kings would send out their two Paladins to battle each other, rather than two armies. Whoever won the fight, won the war." (89)

The two kings in Ingalls' mind were he and Roddenberry. And Roddenberry won.

Pre-Production
September 21-22 and September 25-28 (6 days prep).

Director Marc Daniels said, "I remember that episode provided a problem in terms of wardrobe. The people on this planet were supposed to be dressed in prehistoric clothing, and we discovered that costuming them would cost a fortune. Bill Theiss, who was always adept at handling such crises, bought a bunch of cheap sheepskin jackets, cut off the sleeves and turned them inside out. We were always trying to work around things like that because of budgetary limitations." (44-4)

Michael Witney, one of the actors in a sheepskin jacket, played Tyree, leader of the Hill People. He was 36 and had been on TV since the early 1960s. He had been a regular in

**Michael Witney with Sally Field in *The Way West*
(United Artists, 1967)**

the 1963-64 series *The Travels of Jaimie McPheeters*, with a young Kurt Russell as the title character, and also featuring Charles Bronson among the regulars, and Meg Wyllie (The Keeper in "The Cage"). Don Ingalls was one of the producers.

During the time when this *Star Trek* was made, Witney was featured prominently in the big screen hit, *The Way West*, with Sally Field, and starring Kirk Douglas, Robert Mitchum, and Richard Widmark. Witney had plum roles just around the corner in the films *Darling Lili* (in 1970, under Julie Andrews and Rock Hudson), *Doc* (in 1971, as Ike Clanton), and then took the lead in *Head On* (1971). He met his wife-to-be while appearing on her short-lived mid 1970s sitcom. The actress and sitcom were named the same: *Twiggy*. He and Twiggy also starred together in the 1974 film, *W.*

Nancy Kovack, as Nona, was a familiar face and figure on television from this era. She was 32. By the time she was 20, Kovack held eight beauty contest titles. She began work on television as the "Vanna White" of her time, on the early 1960s game show *Number Please*, a predecessor to *Wheel of Fortune*. Her film career included *The Great Sioux Massacre*, as Libbie Custer, *Jason and the Argonauts*, as Medea, and the Three Stooges' last film, *The Outlaws Is Coming*, as Annie Oakley. Kovack was in such demand that, in the two years leading up to her appearance in this *Star Trek*, she appeared in five films (including *The Silencers*, starring Dean Martin as Matt Helm), and nine guest star roles on TV, including *The Man from U.N.C.L.E.*, *The Invaders*, *I Spy*, *The F.B.I.*, and two turns on *Batman* (as Queenie). Gene Coon was impressed by Kovack and took her along for two

**Nancy Kovack in NBC publicity photo
(Courtesy of Bob Olsen)**

appearances on his next series, *It Takes a Thief*. Shortly after, Kovack appeared in *Mannix*, for which she received an Emmy nomination.

**Booker Bradshaw as Dr. M'Benga
(CBS Studios, Inc.)**

Booker Bradshaw played Dr. M'Benga, standing in for McCoy in sickbay. Bradshaw was only 27 but his scholarly demeanor made him a popular choice when a black actor was needed to be a doctor. During the same year, Bradshaw portrayed another doctor, on *Tarzan*. He was M'Benga here, B'Dula there.

Bradshaw remembered, "I was hired by Gene Roddenberry for *Star Trek* because I was, quote-unquote, 'The most intelligent black actor in the country.' They said, 'We want to represent Blacks as having a brain, so we'll make him a doctor' ... [but] I didn't want to play a doctor.... I come from a family of doctors, and that year I played one in *five* TV shows, including *Tarzan* and *The Girl from U.N.C.L.E.* If I had wanted to be a doctor, I would have gone to medical school." (20)

Bradshaw, again as Dr. M'Benga, returned to *Star Trek* for "That Which

Survives."

Ned Romero played the villainous Klingon, Krell. He was 41 and had been working often in television, usually in westerns, playing Amercian Indians and Mexican cowboys and banditos. Within one year in either direction of this production, he was Wild Bear in the telefilm *Winchester 73*, Charlie Blackfoot in the Clint Eastwood western, *Hang 'Em High*, and, on television, Running Feet on *Custer*, White Wolf on *Bonanza*, Tza-Wuda on *The Virginian*, and Chief Running-in-a-Circle on *Death Valley Days*. It suited Romero fine. He was part Chitimacha Indian.

Romero had been a semi-regular in TV's version of *Shane*, in 1966, and was a regular on Burt Reynolds' 1970-71 series, *Dan August*, in 26 episodes as Sgt. Joe Rivera. In 1975, he starred as Chief Joseph, the lead in *I Will Fight No More Forever*, a well-received movie about the plight of the American Indian. Romero would return to the universe of *Star Trek* for "Journey's End," a 1994 episode of *Star Trek: The Next Generation*, and "The Fight," in 1999, for *Star Trek: Voyager*.

Ned Romero in the lead role from
I Will Fight No More Forever
(1975, David Wolper Productions)

Janos Prohaska as the mugato
(Unaired film trim courtesy of Gerald Gurian)

Janos Prohaska, 48, designed, fabricated, and wore the ape-like suit of the mugato. Prohaska was last seen sidling around on Stage 10 as the Horta from "The Devil in the Dark." Playing apes and bears, however, was his main source of income. He appeared as an ape in three episodes of *Gilligan's Island*, he was Bobo the Gorilla in two episodes of *Land of the Giants*, and Darwin the Monkey in "The Sixth Finger," for *The Outer Limits*. His most frequent job was as Cookie Bear on *The Andy Williams Show*.

Prohaska made his apes and bears and unearthly creatures in the garage of his rather modest home in Santa Monica. He said, "From the whole block, the children in my neighborhood know when I have finished a monster. I do not know how they know when I have finished a new one, but they know.... Most of the time I do not want to be frightening....

376

I'd rather do something funny, not killing."

Majel Barrett returned as Nurse Chapel, thanks to Roddenberry's rewrite, and is given the best role of the four supporting regulars. Her scenes with Spock are enjoyable and memorable.

Production Diary
Filmed September 29, October 2, 3, 4, 5, and 6, 1967.
(6 day production; budget set at $179,427).

Day 1. Filming on Stage 9; Scene 30, Take 2
(Courtesy of Gerald Gurian)

Filming began on Friday, September 29, 1967. *Bonnie and Clyde* continued to reign at the movie houses, as did *Sgt. Pepper* in the record stores. And "The Letter," by The Box Tops, was still the most-played song on Top 40 stations across America. Sally Field, in her costume from *The Flying Nun*, had the cover of *TV Guide*. Henry Fonda chatted with Johnny Carson the night before on *The Tonight Show*. And *Star Trek* began shooting the last episode for its initial second season order from NBC, the sixteenth episode of the year and the last to credit Gene Coon as producer.

For Day 1, filming took place on the bridge, followed by the transporter room, the medical exam room, and then sickbay. It was a lot to fit into one day, and the production was running late by the time the final shots in sickbay were being taken. Booker Bradshaw, playing Dr. M'Benga, recalled, "That line where Dr. McCoy says, 'Thank God his heart's where his liver is, or he'd be dead by now,' took fifty takes. We couldn't get through that line without laughing, and when we finally stopped laughing, the cameraman laughed and jiggled the camera on the 50th take. We had to do the scene again." (20)

All the hijinks resulted in the Friday afternoon sequences running into early evening. Leonard Nimoy, who had little to do other than lie on a table, was becoming impatient. According to Bradshaw, the Texas State Fair offered Nimoy "a fortune" to fly in and appear as Spock for "ten minutes." Before starting the final scene of the day, where Dr. M'Benga was to repeatedly slap Spock in an effort to bring him out of a self-induced coma, Nimoy explained to Bradshaw that as soon as the scene was filmed he was going to ride his bicycle to a waiting helicopter, get on a jet and fly to Texas. Bradshaw remembered Nimoy saying, 'Okay, look, we all laughed over the heart-and-liver thing, but we're *not* going to laugh over this scene.... When you slap me, make sure that it's realistic. Don't do a stage slap. I want you to really hit me. I want to do this scene only once!'" (20)

When the director called for action, Bradshaw rushed into sickbay where Spock, still in a coma, was speaking, giving instructions to Nurse Chapel to strike him. Bradshaw stepped between Barrett and Nimoy and raised his hand. He later said, "I've never slapped anyone as hard as I hit him, and his [pointed] ears flew off. There was mass hysteria on the set. People were rolling on the floor, the cameraman was in convulsions.... Well, Leonard was pissed off. He's chasing me around the set, saying, 'I'm gonna kill you!' And I'm yelling, 'Please! I did what you told me to do!' [And] the director's saying, 'What's going on here? Don't you understand a stage slap, Bradshaw?' ... I say, 'Look, all I wanted to be was a classical actor. I don't need this. I'm going home!' Leonard says, 'In a pig's ass you are. Do a stage slap this time.'" (20)

Nimoy went back into makeup and Bradshaw was given a second shot at the slap.

All was well that ended well ... almost. Nimoy, in a hurry to leave for Texas, began looking for his bicycle. But it was missing. The lighting crew, acting on instructions from Shatner, had hoisted the bike into the rafters.

Bradshaw remembered the normally unemotional Mr. Spock yelling, "That's not funny! I want that bicycle down right *now*!" (20)

Nimoy said, "(Bill Shatner) enjoys practical joking. I guess the bicycle stories by now are legendary. He insisted on hiding my bicycle, time after time after time. I guess there's something funny about audiences picturing Leonard Nimoy, as Spock, riding a bicycle in the first place. And I guess it's funny that Leonard Nimoy, as Spock, is looking for his bicycle because Bill Shatner has hidden it somewhere. People love that story." (128-9)

While Nimoy flew to Texas, most of the cast and crew stayed home to watch the premiere of "The Changeling" on NBC at 8:30 p.m.

Day 2, Monday, October 2. After Nimoy returned from the Texas State Fair, the company traveled to Bell Ranch, separating the San Fernando Valley (in Los Angeles County) from Simi Valley (in Ventura County) for three days of location work. On this day, the scenes filmed were described on the production schedule as taking place in or around "Ext. Forest," "Ext. Planet Clearing," and "Ext. Ambush Trail." Among the action filmed were all the scenes in the Teaser, as

Day 2: Shatner waits while a scene not involving him is filmed with a lightweight Arriflex camera, being held by crewman to the right (Courtesy of Gerald Gurian)

Kirk, Spock, and McCoy first beam down and Spock gets shot.

On location during these days was Charles Washburn, in his first year working for *Star Trek* as an assistant director, with *Star Trek* being the first series to hire a Black to work in that position. Washburn said, "I had interviewed to be an A.D. at an NBC affiliate, because some production friends told me they wanted to hire a Black for the control room. But they never called me back. Months later I wrote to my friend asking who got the job and he said, 'Charlie, they didn't hire anyone. They never intended to. They just wanted to be able tell people they were looking for a Negro.'"

Day 2. Nimoy and Shatner with Assistant Director Charles Washburn (above) and talking with director Marc Daniels (below) as a camera crane shot is prepared (Courtesy of Gerald Gurian)

It was a different situation at NBC Burbank, where Stan Robertson was promoted to be the first black network production manager, and at *Star Trek*, where Ande Richardson-Kindryd served as Gene Coon's secretary and, one year later, Charlie Washburn worked under the various visiting directors. Washburn was immediately embraced by the company, and soon was given an affectionate nickname. He said, "The crew and casting director on the lot called me 'Charlie Star Trek'…. Working closely with all the extras was a big part of the job, even to the point of knowing who would be getting a 'bump' or 'double whammy,' which is what we called an added amount of time to an extra's base pay rate if he or she was given some pertinent story business."

And this was certainly the case with all the extras working on "A Private Little War," as each played members of the two warring camps.

Star Trek was a series that was filled with firsts, so Washburn was more than merely the first black A.D. in Hollywood. He said, "I'm proud to say I was the first A.D. to be goosed by an electrician on *Star Trek* when I was up on the rigging one day putting together the call sheet. After it happened, [gaffer] George Merhoff smiled and said: 'Hey, Charlie. Now you're part of the group.'" (180-5)

Another first: This was Marc Daniels' first time shooting on location for the series. The result of his work is energized and professional.

Daniels said, "The rocks out there are incredible -- those stratified rocks that I tried to put into the picture... those big pieces of geological strata you find in Box Canyon." (44-3)

While Daniels was admiring the rocks and the natural light, he failed to notice the buildings in Los Angeles County's San Fernando Valley. Toward the end of the episode, when Nona struggles with the Villagers, those buildings can be seen briefly in the background.

Day 2: "Actor down" -- the scene where Spock gets shot (Courtesy of Gerald Gurian)

Daniels also failed to notice that William Shatner was playing his part a bit over the top. The director, with a sitcom background, was not good at pulling in the reins on an actor playing his role too big, especially when that actor was the star of the series.

Day 2. Shatner and Nimoy react to a preview issue of *Mad* magazine, including a parody of *Star Trek* (Courtesy of Gerald Gurian)

Nancy Kovack didn't mind Shatner reaching a bit for the stars. She said, "I thought William Shatner was very underrated. He was wonderful; very professional, and a lot of fun. He could be played with. And he really had a lot of technique. I was always envious of people who had worked long enough to develop multiple techniques, and he had, and still has, and I love to watch that applied. So it was really fascinating to me as an actor to watch him work, while I was there and again on the screen. I'd say, 'Oh, there he goes again.' He uses all these little techniques, and they are very subtle. Only he knows. Well, maybe a few other people know. But he's really terrific." (103a)

Costumer Andrea Weaver cited this episode as being difficult from a wardrobe perspective, with the numerous fur costumes, including the one designed for the mugato. "Gene Roddenberry was very particular about matching," she recalled. "The costumes were usually sewn on because he didn't want to see zippers or hooks. So the costume was sewn on the actor, then taken off, then sewn on again, more than a few times a day. It had to look exactly the same in every shot. And Mr. Roddenberry didn't allow any weak links. But Gene was not difficult to work for; he just wanted to know that you cared. The bar was high and he didn't put up with anybody who didn't want to do it the way he wanted it done." (180a)

While on location that first day, a copy of the December issue of *MAD* magazine was delivered for the cast and crew to get a sneak peak of the parody, "Star Blecch." The December issue was actually released in early November, and the preview copy was ready a month before, allowing Shatner and Nimoy to pose with it for a promotional picture.

Day 3 (above), as Bill McGovern slates the attack of the mugato; Day 4 (below), filming at Tyree's camp (Courtesy of Gerald Gurian)

Day 3, Tuesday. Production moved on to the "Attack Site" where Kirk falls victim to the mugato. Later, the scene where Kirk comes upon Nona bathing in a stream under a waterfall was filmed, as both are attacked by the mate of the mugato.

Regarding the shots of Nona bathing in the stream, to which NBC would later loudly object (see "Post Production"), Nancy Kovack said, "I didn't do that scene. They only saw my character from the back. Well, it was somebody else with a great back because I don't remember ever doing that." (103a)

Day 4, Wednesday. This was the last day to be spent at Bell Ranch, with more filming in and around Tyree's camp. Also shot, the climactic battle where Nona is killed.

Kovack said, "I had to get up at 3:45 in the morning to wash my hair, set my hair in rollers -- you know, this wasn't big star time -- and arrive on the set an hour later at 6 a.m. And I was there on the dot, so by the time 8 or 9 p.m. comes up, I'm exhausted. But I have to learn the lines for the next day and go to bed by 11 p.m. to get up at 3:45 a.m. again. So there's not much left to concentrate on outside of what you have to do on the set. And you *have* to be alert on the set." (103a)

Day 5. A full day on a cave set built on Stage 10. (Unaired film trim courtesy of Gerald Gurian)

Day 5, Thursday. The company was back at Desilu, filming on Stage 10 for the scenes inside the cave.

Set Designer Matt Jefferies said, "Some of the caverns were done with Reynolds [aluminum] Wrap. As soon as were through with it, it was so damn fragile that we'd ashcan it. Reynolds Wrap was a marvelous material. The painter used to tease me; he'd say, 'Here comes Matt -- give him a spray gun.' What I did was, I said everything that shoots in that direction and up, we'll do in green lacquer, and everything going the other way and down, we'll do in blue lacquer so the metallic comes through it. As they'd move around the wall we would change color." (91-11)

Day 6, Friday, October 6. Production this day took place on the Paramount lot in an area called "Paramount B Tank." This was a large concrete enclosure that could be filled with thousands of gallons of water to form what could pass for the surface of a lake or even a section of ocean (with proper lighting and camera angling). But at this time, in the fall of 1967, it was dry and there was a Middle Eastern type village built inside.

Set Decorator John Dwyer said, "They'd drain all the water out of it and they'd build a set into it. And that one was there for something else that was being shot. And we had to strike when the iron was hot, and take advantage of existing sets like that." (57-4)

Also built into the tank was the "Int. Workshop" set, where the villagers pretend to be manufacturing flintlock rifles. This was the only day Ned Romero was needed, for the part of Krell, the Klingon.

"Mirror, Mirror," the fourth episode of the second season to air on NBC, would have its premiere broadcast at 8:30 p.m.

Of the six day schedule, Nancy Kovack said, "It was a lot of dialogue to do each day, yes, and they did throw it at us and did change it quickly. But if one is immersed in working daily, that person has a capacity to absorb immediately whatever's on the page. I used to be able to look at five pages, like Shatner did, and after only a few minutes I'd know it all. I don't know how I did that back then, and I did it every day, and I could do it so simply. But you have to be in the groove to do that. It's a sort of mental discipline." (103a)

Marc Daniels was in the groove, as well. Remarkably, he did indeed finish this action-packed episode within the designated six days. The studio was happy. NBC was not.

Post-Production

Available for editing: October 9, 1967. Rough Cut: October 17, 1967.
Final Cut: October 20, 1967. Music Score: tracked.

On November 2, 1967, Stan Robertson at the network wrote to producer John Meredyth Lucas:

> The rough cut, viewed by us on Tuesday afternoon, was, in the form which screened, unacceptable.... We realize, John, that the episode in question was not produced by you, but, as a guideline for the future, we must reiterate our position that the costuming, the implied sex, and the forms of violence as we discussed, are totally unacceptable to NBC for airing over our facilities.

Among the trims were camera shots of Nona's fur-skinned outfit, which didn't always sufficiently cover up Nancy Kovack's busty figure; the implied sexual relationship between Tyree and Nona, which Gene Coon wanted added to the script; the sequence where Nona is bathing in a pond; the attack of the mugato; the graphic killing of Nona, and the brutal fight between Tyree, Kirk, and the Villagers.

Once the trims were made, NBC agreed to air the episode, and air it more than once. "A Private Little War" was now everything Stan Robertson and the network were looking for -- action/adventure, with a purpose, staged away from the Enterprise, and actually filmed on location. And it even had a monster.

Robert Justman said, "'A Private Little War' was eventually approved by [Broadcast Standards] and was first broadcast on February 2, 1968. Surprisingly, Stan Robertson never seemed to realize that the story was supposed to be an allegory about the growing 'police action' in Vietnam. In fact, no one at NBC made the connection and took us to task. But the audience did; we got letters; lots of letters." (94-8)

Series Script Consultant Dorothy Fontana said, "We could say, in essence, [whispering] 'Vietnam' ... because we were telling a science fiction story. 'Gee, that didn't apply to Vietnam, did it?' We got away with a lot of political comment on *Star Trek* because it was science fiction." (64-2)

In the end titles of the episode, Janos Prohaska is credited with playing the "gumato." This was actually the mugato. In the script it was called a "gumato," which is why it is listed that way in the credits. But DeForest Kelley had trouble pronouncing the name, so it was changed during filming.

Also in those end titles, as Gene Coon's credit appears, we see the Enterprise orbiting a different planet than before. The continents and oceans we had previously seen are missing and the planet is now smaller, darker, and presented in various shades of blue. The reason for the switch: the company that prepared the titles for *Star Trek* had made a mistake. Gene L. Coon was supposed to receive the producer's credit here, as well as on "Journey to Babel," but the title card read John Meredyth Lucas instead. When "Journey to Babel" was aired on November 11, 1967, someone noticed that Lucas was listed as the producer. Roddenberry was notified of the mistake and discovered the same error with "A Private Little War." Before shipping the latter episode to NBC, the end title card from "Catspaw" crediting Gene Coon, was spliced in, replacing John Meredyth Lucas's name.

This was the final producing credit Coon would receive on the series, even though his stamp was on many episodes to come. He had taken the pitches, given out the assignments, read the outlines and scripts, and provided page after page of meticulous notes on each before stepping down and turning his office over to Lucas. Up next for Coon, work at

383

Universal, starting with a screenplay (*Journey to Shiloh*), then serving as writer/producer for *It Takes a Thief*. Among the jobs to follow, writing a script for producer Robert Justman on *Then Came Bronson*, and collaborating with Gene Roddenberry on the TV-movie and "back-door pilot," *The Questor Tapes*, which would be aired after Coon's death in 1974. Coon died on July 8, 1973, of lung cancer. He was 49.

Van der Veer Effects handled the opticals, including the beams from numerous hand phasers, the disintegration of two mugato creatures, the red hot glowing boulders in a cave, and a few transporter effects. It all made for an expensive animation bill. To compensate, all shots of the Enterprise were recycled from previous episodes. Shots of the ship orbiting the planet were taken from "Bread and Circuses" ... except for that last one, which was lifted from "Catspaw."

Gerald Fried got the music credit. Most of the cues came from his scores for "Catspaw," "Amok Time," and "Friday's Child." A bit of Sol Kaplan's "Doomsday Machine" music was thrown in for good measure. There was one piece of new music from Fried. As Kirk tells Scott to "beam us home," the music is somber and poignant. It is also unique to the series and is not heard in any other episode.

Writer Don Ingalls did not ask for further *Star Trek* assignments, and no further ones were offered. But he did work again with William Shatner, as the last producer on *T.J. Hooker*.

Release / Reaction
Premiere air date: 2/2/68. NBC repeat broadcast: 8/23/68.

Nancy Kovack in publicity photo (Courtesy of Bob Olsen)

Hal Humphrey, the entertainment correspondent for *The Los Angeles Times*, for an article published while this episode was in development, wrote:

Because *Star Trek* takes place in the 21st Century [sic], Roddenberry finds it easier to take on subject matter which, if it were pinned on contemporary characters and situations, would probably be tossed out by the network as too controversial. For example, war between the planets on *Star Trek* can be condemned. Here on Earth in 1967, TV would rather not make a comment on war.

On the night that "A Private Little War" had its premiere on NBC, a teenager named Doug Drexler was watching ... or trying to. He recalled, "In the second season, we were picking up the transmission over antennas that were on your roof and looked like fish bones spread out. And the images weren't that great. And I remember one night, it was 'A Private

Little War,' and I thought, 'Oh my God, this is such a good episode,' and then all of a sudden in the middle of it I get this interference and sound that goes through the whole thing, like 'Baum, Ber, Baum. Buss, Baum, Ba.' I'm going nuts because, you know, back then, you don't have video tape, you don't have DVD, so if you missed it, that's it, you've missed it … unless it got re-runned, if you were lucky. And I realized it was a ham radio operator who lived in the neighborhood and apparently was going to transmit every Friday night at that time of night. I literally went out and hunted down the house where the ham radio antenna was and knocked on the guy's door. He must have thought I was crazy, but he stopped transmitting on that night. He didn't have to do that, but that shows how crazy I was. I was a child possessed to find out who this guy was. He wasn't highly-communicative. He was kind of blank-faced while I was explaining to him why he had to stop, because I think he thought I was out of my mind. He was an older guy. I guess he was probably in his mid-sixties. And he smiled and he said, 'Okay, I can do that.' And that was the end of it. He didn't talk to me anymore about it or anything like that. He just listened carefully and agreed. And he never did it again. But it's hard for me to describe the desperation I felt when the TV started flinching." (52a)

Drexler would later have a hand in the "Save Star Trek" campaigns of 1968 and 1969, and then go on to work in the post production department for *Star Trek*, on many of the later series and films, as an illustrator, a scenic artist, a digital modeler, and technical advisor. He would win an Emmy for his work as a member of the visual effects team on *Battlestar Galactica* in 2007 and again in 2008, and an Oscar for his work as a makeup artist on *Dick Tracy*. He credits his career in television and motion pictures to watching *Star Trek* in the late 1960s.

RATINGS / A.C. Nielsen National report for Friday, February 2, 1968:

8:30 to 9 p.m., 61.7% U.S. TVs in use.	Share:	Households watching:
NBC: *Star Trek*	27.3%	12,320,000
ABC: *Operation: Entertainment*	25.6%	12,250,000
CBS: **Gomer Pyle, U.S.M.C.**	**41.6%**	**15,900,000**
Independent stations:	5.5%	No data

9 to 9:30 p.m., 62.4 U.S. TVs in use.	Share:	Households watching:
NBC: *Star Trek*	28.3%	No data
ABC: *Operation: Entertainment*	27.2%	No data
CBS: **Friday Night Movie**	**30.2%**	**No data**
Independent stations:	14.3%	No data

Star Trek, still NBC's top-rated show on Friday, placed second for its entire hour. In third position, ABC's new competitor, *Operation: Entertainment*, an "entertain-the-troops" variety show making the rounds to various military bases. On this night, comedian Dick Shawn hosted from a base in San Diego, with special guests the McGuire Sisters. The movie on CBS was a second airing of 1960's *The Apartment*, starring Jack Lemmon, Shirley MacLaine, and Fred MacMurray. *Star Trek* was behind by less than a mere 2% of the TV sets in use from 9 to 9:30 p.m.

Sent to the co-editors of fanzine *Spockanalia* shortly after the filming of "A Private Little War":

> Dear Sherna and Devra... Thank you very much for your most interesting fanzine. The contributions were bright, witty and informative.... I am pleased that Spock's friends also care about McCoy.... Regarding your questions of how I feel about space medicine and having a non-human aboard the Enterprise -- space medicine I can take, even though computers have removed a great deal of mental challenge and true personal discovery.... As for Spock -- what the blazes do I know about Vulcans? I reach for his heart and come up with his liver -- his blood is green as well as an indelible stain. I recently brought aboard a young Dr. M'Benga -- who interned in a Vulcan hospital -- to get Spock off my back. I can't be bothered with rubbing my nerves raw about a physical jigsaw, I have enough problems without taking on all of Spock's peculiarities, mental or physical. He is capable of undoing every single thing I have learned in all of my years of medical training -- and I don't intend to let him do it. I have warned Captain Kirk that one more Vulcan aboard our ship -- just one more -- and I will resign from the service.... I hope this letter will clarify my position and feelings regarding space medicine and Spock's place in space with me. Most sincerely, Dr. McCoy (DeForest Kelley) October 30, 1967.

Sent to *Spockanalia* a month later:

> Dear Devra and Sherna... I have read with interest Dr. McCoy's comments on Space Medicine and particularly his complaints about having to treat a Vulcan.... If you can imagine what it would be like to have a toothache treated by a screaming witch-doctor, shaking ancient instruments and yelling unintelligible incantations, you have some idea of what a Vulcan experiences when treated by the ship's surgeon.... Live long and prosper, Mr. Spock (Leonard Nimoy). December 28, 1967.

Memories

Marc Daniels said, "I like the science fiction aspects of *Star Trek*, but I also like the fact that in the first two seasons there was some genuine dramatic appeal and social feeling about them, and they weren't gimmicky in terms of just being space operas. 'A Private Little War' is an example." (44-4)

Walter Koenig added, "Once in a while when we did an episode that had sociopolitical implications, then I felt very proud that we were dealing with a subject of that type. But there was one episode that confounded me because it seemed to be taking the position that was contrary to the general position of the show. And that had to do with the balance of power. And I thought that isn't the philosophical concepts that are consistent with *Star Trek*. That can only generate thinking leaning toward anger and fear and, inevitably, war. The thinking behind it, the way I read it, was almost fascist. That was a dangerous premise to beam across the country under the guise of entertainment. So I was surprised." (102)

Dorothy Fontana said, "It was a whole question of war balance. Because, on this planet, there was a restricted war with low-cal weapons, if you will, escalated by the Klingons. Well, God save our guys, so right away, you increase the state of art on your side. And then they go up a notch. And then *you* go up a notch. But, after a while, you have to take responsibility for this, and that's what 'A Private Little War' was all about. I thought the message was very good. The show wasn't great, but it was pretty good." (64-1)

24

Mid Season, 1967

Who's the boss?
New producer John Meredyth Lucas
with the man in charge
(Courtesy of Gerald Gurian)

Ande Richardson, Gene Coon's secretary was now working for John Meredyth Lucas. She said, "Gene told me that he was going to Universal and he would get me a job just as soon as he could. But they had a feudal system there and they didn't allow people to bring anyone with them. So, I stayed and worked for John Meredyth Lucas and then Fred Freiberger [the third season producer]. Lucas was very good. He came from old Hollywood and he cared. He was sensitive. Also, he was a director, so he had that creative eye for it. And I thought he did pretty well. But he didn't have the level of humor that Gene had. Lucas didn't have it and Freiberger certainly didn't have it. The rapport between us wasn't all that wonderful. We both did our jobs. Lucas was a nice person; he was a thoughtful person, but it wasn't the close relationship I had with Gene Coon, that's all." (144a)

After the deal was made for Lucas to replace Coon as producer of *Star Trek*, Gene Roddenberry suggested he come along to a filming location in the Hollywood Hills. Cast and crew had returned from a two week hiatus and were busy shooting scenes for "Bread and Circuses." Lucas recalled, "Roddenberry drove me up to introduce me as the new producer. When I got out of his car, many of the crew, people I had worked with on other films, came to speak to me. It was reunion time. Roddenberry was impressed. Then William Shatner came around the corner of a camera truck, took one look in our direction, turned on his heels and left. I was stunned. I had never met the guy, what the hell could he have against me? ... Gene said nothing but, next day I found out it was Gene that Shatner was mad at." (110-6)

Shatner had an axe to grind with Roddenberry over the news that Coon would be departing. Gene Coon may not have enjoyed dealing with actors, including Shatner and Nimoy, but William Shatner thought the world of Coon. He enjoyed the elements of humor which had found their way into many of the scripts and liked doing an occasional all-out comedy, such as "I, Mudd" and "The Trouble with Tribbles." Shatner was very pleased with the current direction of the series, feeling it had risen to its highest level and he credited much of this to Coon. And now Roddenberry, who hadn't been around in the last month while focusing on a script for a Robin Hood TV pilot instead of *Star Trek* was, in a sense, taking the fun away.

Lucas tried not to take it personally, even though Shatner's attitude, and that of some of the others, made it clear that they were not happy to see him taking over as show runner.

There were other problems. Lucas said, "The second shock came when I, and all other producers on the lot, were called into the executive offices of the studio and informed that, due to a high level corporate takeover, we were now part of Leisure Time Division of Gulf + Western Industries. I suddenly felt like Charlie Chaplin on the production line in *Modern Times*. From a command position on the sort of show I had always wanted, in which I felt pride, I was reduced to a cog in the wheel of a vast industry machine." (110-6)

Lucas was told that the Desilu brand would stay on the last three episodes being produced by Coon. After that, if there was a pickup up by NBC, the Paramount logo would be the one placed at the end of the credits. The penny-pinching, however, had already begun.

***

While it was clear that William Shatner was not happy with Roddenberry, Lucas soon learned that the supporting cast was certainly not happy with Shatner.

Nichelle Nichols blamed Roddenberry and Coon, saying that a lack of strong leadership had provided William Shatner with an opportunity to take more control. For her book *Beyond Uhura* she wrote, "Without anyone's consent, Bill Shatner stepped into the role, bossing around and intimidating the directors and guest stars, cutting other actors' lines and scenes, and generally taking enough control to disrupt the sense of family we had during the first season."

Shatner rebutted: "I felt very strongly about every area of the show. If I could see a point in the story line that could be improved, I would not hesitate, but

A publicity photo that betrayed the growing tension between Nichols and Shatner during the second season (Courtesy of Gerald Gurian)

leap eagerly into the fray and said, 'Here's what I think' ... There were times when I suggested dialogue or script changes or ways to play a scene.... There were many times when the point was taken and used, and there were other times when they said, 'We can't do that.' And I accepted that." (156-9)

George Takei remembered how Dorothy Fontana would occasionally give the cast members an advance peek at the early drafts of scripts. He, James Doohan, and Nichelle Nichols would see scenes and sections of dialogue written to emphasize the characters they played. But those scenes and lines would soon vanish.

Takei said, "[W]hen the final shooting script was delivered, the eagerly awaited scene or line would now be in someone else's mouth, and invariably, it was Bill's.... There would always be reasonable justification for the change. And reasonable arguments could be made to counter them. But Bill was the star. That was

Walter Koenig and George Takei, feeling there were fewer lines in the scripts for them because of Shatner (Courtesy of Gerald Gurian)

the one inarguable fact. Even if an idea had originated with one of us, if Bill wanted it, he got it. Even if I tried to ad lib an entirely appropriate 'Aye, sir' to a command, he would nix it, claiming it would take away from the rhythm of the scene. This despite the fact that some of us had precious little to do in so many of the scripts. But Bill seemed totally immune to the sensitivities of the efforts of those he worked with." (171-4)

Walter Koenig said, "This thing with changing the dialogue became a sore point of contention with all the supporting actors. It's one thing to go into an episode and you see the pages for that day and you have one, two or three lines. You assume that everyone in the producer's office has passed on the scenes for that day and decided that this is how they should be. We accepted that we were the supporting cast and we would be under-represented. But you have your lines and know where you're supposed to be and then on the set things change so the attention can be refocused completely on the lead, you see what little you had now being taken away. The line we had now becomes another line for Shatner. The focus is completely on this side of the set and they aren't going to record you. You haven't only lost a line or two, but you now don't even remain in the shot! You would think he had enough already. So that's what made us furious. That's when we all looked at one another and rolled our eyes. We knew it was coming." (102)

Writer Harlan Ellison said, "It all boiled down to him not liking that Leonard had more and better lines than he did. He would count lines of dialogue, *literally*. He sat on the sofa in my living room and did the same thing. And he would always give you some hyperbolic rationalization why Leonard should not have three lines on a page where he only has one. And it never made any sense at all, but you got the sense after a very short time that either you made the changes or he would go back and rat you out, which is what he did with Roddenberry. He went to Roddenberry and said, 'Well, it's an uneven script and I'm not getting my due and you'd better get in there and do some rewriting.' Because up until that time, Roddenberry loved the script. He had no problems with it. Roddenberry chose Shatner over Nimoy, always. He didn't know where the gold laid in that show." (58)

Nichols complained, "One day, just as we were setting up to shoot a scene in which Uhura had an important part, Bill refused to do it. 'Somehow, it's not just right!,' he kept saying. And, as he, the director, and some other production people went off to discuss it, I became perplexed. This wasn't the first time this had happened, but since, in this case, Uhura's lines concerned her communications experience, I didn't see how they could be cut. We went on to shoot another scene while they rewrote the 'offending' segment to Bill's satisfaction. Later, when I scanned the revised script, my lines had been cut down to 'I have Starfleet Command, sir,' before he and Spock took over. 'Just a minute,' I said. 'What is this about?' Caught totally off-guard, Bill stammered, 'Uh, Nichelle, baby, it's nothing personal. This is for the good of the scene. There's no reason for you to say this.' ... I was furious, but I was not alone. The entire cast knew how I felt, because Bill was doing it increasingly often, and to them, too." (127-2)

Shatner responded, "In truth, in most situations like the one she described, Nichelle's lines probably *were* unnecessary in terms of our story line, and they *were* most likely tacked onto our script in an effort to get Uhura involved in the episode. However, while they may not have been vital to our plot, they were indeed vitally important to our show in that they showcased a regular cast member, and, of course, to Nichelle, whose role was at stake. This is a perspective that blindly eluded me on the set, and with that in mind, I must admit that Nichelle's criticism is probably valid." (156-8)

Koenig added, "This is the amazing thing -- I didn't realize that the others felt the way I did. Other than a few looks of that type, we never discussed it. No one wanted to stand up to him because he was the big cheese. They wouldn't make these shows if he wasn't there. And I think we all felt, without ever verbalizing it, that if we protested, he would tell the producers, 'I don't want this person in the show.' And who are they going to go with? Plus the fact that we were so conditioned into believing that we were excess baggage. We were really insignificant to the story, regardless of that the fans were very enthusiastic. We really thought that we were insignificant. No one ever came to us and asked us our opinion on anything. They always went to Bill and Leonard. And all the important conversations regarding the story started with them and ended with them. So I feel pretty confident that we all felt the same, that if we stood up, we'd face the possibility of being dropped from the show. Shatner never said that. He never even implied it. It's just that the power that he had was very apparent." (102)

Shatner was not the only one nixing Doohan's, Koenig's, Takei's, and Nichols' chances to have a bigger role in various episodes. Dorothy Fontana decided that it should be Spock, not Sulu, who found romance in "This Side of Paradise." Stan Robertson and Robert Justman requested that Scott, not Sulu, be the murder suspect in "Wolf in the Fold." Justman often had to make the hard recommendation to remove Scott, Sulu, Uhura, or Chekov from a particular episode due to budgetary concerns. Also, there were three stars listed in the opening credits now. According to Deforest Kelley, he and Nimoy often worked in conjunction with Shatner when reassigning lines of dialogue.

Kelley said, "If he disagreed with how a director was setting up a scene, Bill would say how he felt it should be done. And, as the star, Bill often got his way. Bill would say, 'I think we ought to do so and so, I think this ought to be your line, De, and not mine.' And Leonard and I would do the same. We'd give each other lines. Actors don't like to give lines away. But we did. We did it for the show. But that's what *made* the show." (98-4)

Regardless, Shatner was the star of the show. He was the most vocal, the most powerful, and the most rewarded. And so he was the most blamed.

John Crawford, who played High Commissioner Ferris in "The Galileo Seven," said, "I was very unhappy with *Star Trek*. William Shatner was having an ego problem and, every time I walked on to the set, I could just see it. I was not allowed to move around the set during the entire scene. He kept saying, 'No! No! No! No! This is the bridge of the ship and we can't be moving around.' Well, that's a lot of bullshit." (41)

Sean Kenney, who appeared in four first season episodes (as the crippled Captain Pike in "The Menagerie, Parts 1 and 2" and as Lt. DePaul (in "Arena" and "A Taste of Armageddon") shared, "I soon realized that, yes, Bill Shatner was not well liked and in fact was disliked. But, then again, he was the Captain of the ship and he took his role seriously, on and off the set." (100-3)

Leslie Parrish, guest star in "Who Mourns for Adonais?," said, "William Shatner was a very professional actor; a wonderful actor. But he was kind of strange." (134a)

Yvonne Craig, who appeared in "Whom Gods Destroy," complained that Shatner was "maddeningly narcissistic," and said, "He not only moved me around physically in the scene for the benefit of his profile, but suggested line reading so that he could respond in a way that he predetermined.... I was astonished that the director allowed this to go on, but he had allowed himself to be subordinate to the whims of the series' obvious 'Star.'" (39-3)

Sherri Jackson, who did a love scene with Shatner in the first season episode, "What Are Little Girls Made Of?," said, "I was a little nervous working with Shatner because I had heard that he was a New York actor from the theater, and I don't usually like actors like that, because often they don't translate well to the small screen. They do all this theatrical stuff. And, after being on the theater in New York, they become sort of pompous, like they think Hollywood TV is just a joke and that the theater is where the real acting is done. And Shatner did strike me as being very cocky. I'm not saying that he was unpleasant with me. In fact, he kind of flirted with me. But I don't think the people on the show were crazy about him. They respected him, but liking him is different." (90-1)

Lezlie Dalton, who was a member of Dean Martin's Golddiggers, and appeared in "By Any Other Name," said, "I found William Shatner to be like a high school kid. Kind of strutty and full of himself. He wasn't rude; he wasn't abusive in any way, but he was just kind of boyish; very boyish." (43a)

Bobby Clark, one of the men who played the Gorn in "Arena," as well as doing stunts on numerous other episodes of *Star Trek*, said, "Shatner's always good to work with. But I'm not a bonafide actor; I'm a stuntman. So I'm doing physical stuff with him; not lines of dialogue. I give him credit -- the man worked hard. But, over time, unless he was wanting to work with people, he started treating them like shit." (31e)

Hagan Beggs, who appeared in three first season episodes as Lt. Hansen, said of Shatner, "He didn't seem to get involved with us too much. I thought Shatner sort of did his work and then disappeared back into his dressing room. He wasn't interested in any other sort of social stuff really. At the time, I felt, 'Well, no wonder, he has a shitload of stuff to learn.

He has to stay focused.' But, in my opinion, he was separate from the rest of the cast, who were more inclined to sort of stick around a bit or chit chat. He didn't. As soon as his scene was over, he'd go, 'Thank you,' and he'd head right to his dressing room. I know that Jimmy Doohan didn't seem to get along with him too well. I don't know what they had going, but Jimmy a few times would say, 'Ah, that fucking Shatner. Jesus Christ.' It was sort of normal kvetching. I never paid too much attention. But I could see that Jimmy was at odds with Shatner a little bit." (12-1)

John Fiedler, who played the incarnation of Jack the Ripper in "Wolf in the Fold," said of Shatner, "He's impossible!... He was terrible to me, [and] to everybody else, too. And during the episode I was on, Gene Roddenberry called him into his office, and they laid him out on the carpet. Didn't do any good." (61)

Fiedler went on to say, "One of my friends is Jimmy Doohan... we used to be roommates in New York. And he hated [Shatner]... like most of the regulars. They can't stand him. He's impossible.... He was rude [and] he told everybody what to do." (61)

People usually find what they are looking for in a person. Good or bad.

Tania Lemani, the exotic dancer from "Wolf in the Fold," saw a very different William Shatner than John Fielder did, even though both were in the same episode. She said, "I had a wonderful time with him. I hear from people all the time, 'Oh, he's terrible,' or 'I hear he's horrible' ... but I didn't see that side of him. He was fun-loving and light." (72)

DeForest Kelley said, "I don't think I've ever seen an actor with that kind of discipline. And I've worked with a lot of actors. I've seen him on rare occasions get into trouble in a scene -- under really terrible circumstances -- late at night, time pressures; he had mounds of dialogue, and such difficult dialogue. Rarely did he get in trouble, but, when he did, I've seen him stand there and laugh at himself -- really get hysterical -- but keep going and keep going and coming back to it until he would finally get it. Great discipline. Phenomenal. I admire him because he could laugh at himself." (98-4)

Women's Costumer Andrea Weaver said, "I was 20 so, in terms of a personal friendship, I was closer to George and Walter, just because of their ages. But everybody was wonderful, the cliché of a family, working together. I was on the set every day and there was no star attitude that I ever saw." (180a)

Pamelyn Ferdin, one of the child actors from "And the Children Shall Lead," who had a crush on Shatner, admitted, "I was his shadow. When he would sit in the makeup chair, I would sit by him and talk to him the whole time. He was very nice to me. I'm sure he knew. To appease me, on the last day of shooting, he asked me to marry him. He gave me this cigar band for a ring. It was so sweet. I told him I would marry him on the day I got out of high school." (59)

Brian Tochi, another of the children from that episode, said, "I remember William Shatner being so nice. I heard stories otherwise throughout the years, but he was so terrific to us." (175)

Trelaine Lewis, a nine-year-old girl visiting the set during the production of "Journey to Babel," said, "I have to tell you that Shatner was really cool. On the set, he paid total attention to me. He was so, *so* nice." (108a)

Barbara Luna, guest star in "Mirror, Mirror," said, "When the camera wasn't running, William Shatner could just say 'hello' to me and I'd fall over laughing. I think he is just one of the funniest men ever." (111-3)

Celeste Yarnall, who appeared in "The Apple," said Shatner was a "charming, wonderful person." (196-3)

Lois Jewell, who had a kissing scene with Shatner in "Bread and Circuses," said, "William Shatner was polite and he was a professional; he was a wonderful person to work with. He made it easy for me." (92a)

Louise Sorel, who kissed Shatner in "Requiem for Methuselah," said, "I just loved working with him, because he's so damn funny." (163-3)

Nancy Kovack, who did some kissing with Shatner in "A Private Little War," said, "He was wonderful; very professional and a lot of fun." (103a)

Michael Dante, who played Maab in "Friday's Child," said, "He was very professional. And he was cordial. We had a few laughs and enjoyed the shoot." (45-1)

Stewart Moss, who appeared in a pair of episodes ("The Naked Time" and "By Any Other Name"), said, "I really enjoyed Shatner. My own personal relationship with the guy on set was terrific. His self-deprecating humor was marvelous because, obviously, the man has an ego." (122-3)

Morgan Woodward, guest star in two episodes ("Dagger of the Mind" and "The Omega Glory"), said, "Shatner has a great sense of humor and he likes a good joke. He was always telling jokes. It was always a pleasure to be around him." (192-3)

Eddie Paskey, who appeared in 59 episodes of *Star Trek* and also served as Shatner's lighting stand-in, said, "Bill is a nice guy. You hear so many reports, that he was an egomaniac and he was this and he was that. I'm sorry folks, that's not the way he came across to me nor is that the way he came across on the set. He was willing to help, he was willing to bend. I just loved Bill." (135-2)

Julie Cobb, who appeared in "By Any Other Name," said, "Shatner was wonderful. He was very serious about the work, but otherwise funny, and sweet and caring. Very nice." (32-1)

Lee Meriwether, a former Miss America and guest star in "That Which Survives," said, "Bill was fun; I loved working with him. I knew he was a character from almost the minute I met him. I thought 'Here's a guy with a great sense of humor.'" (118-3)

Vincent McEveety, director of six episodes of *Star Trek*, said, "I just think Bill's very enjoyable to work with and I liked him a lot…. And he's a gentleman; a total professional, there's no question about it. I never had any problem about that at all." (117-4)

Barbara Anderson, Lenore Karidian from "The Conscience of the King," said, "Bill Shatner was really great and made it fun. He had great humor, but he was very serious at that particular time, as well. I would suspect he knew that something might happen with his career because of that show." (1)

Malachi Throne, who played Commodore Mendez in "The Menagerie, Part 1 and 2," said, "Bill was fun. But he was also forthright and adamant about everything, because that was his character." (173)

Bruce Mars, Finnegan from "Shore Leave," who spent an entire day brawling with Shatner, said, "Shatner was very nice to me, asking me what I was doing and what I wanted to do [in the fight scene]. You never really know what to expect -- incredible arrogance or whatever -- but I remember thinking, 'This guy's a really good guy.' And he made sure I had a couple good scenes during the fight. He'd say, 'Let's do this and let's do that' and 'Ah no, the camera should be here not there,' and he would go talk to [director] Bob Sparr about it. So he got me some good moments and I have nothing to say but good things about him." (113a)

Emily Banks, playing Yeoman Barrows, also in "Shore Leave," said, "Bill's a lovely man; very talented; very calm.... We had a good time." (9a)

Robert Brown, who was cast after the start of production in "The Alternative Factor," to replace John Drew Barrymore as Lazarus, said, "I was living a nightmare because I was playing catch-up. I was being pushed and chased every day.... And all this rushing created an uncomfortable feeling. Not from Shatner. He couldn't have been better.... Shatner and I got along really well." (24-1)

Walter Koenig, despite resenting Shatner's tendency to commandeer other actor's lines, said, "Bill Shatner was obviously the leader of the troop, and his mood established what the emotional tone on the set would be. He brought to his work a contagious ebullience and a sense of fun. There were a lot of laughs on the show. If he hadn't been there, there would have been far fewer." (102-13)

DeForest Kelley added, "There is a lot of Kirk in Bill. Bill is a man of tremendous energy [and] intellect. He's a very bright guy. He would have been a leader in anything. He has a great sense of character interpretation [and] script interpretation. And he has that deep concern about the people on his ship, and a great deal of deep concern about the show and the people on the show.... Bill is the driving force, the energy that is so necessary to *Star Trek*. No one could ever take his place." (98-4)

Leonard Nimoy often said very nearly the same thing.

***

Celebrity gossip magazine, circa 1967

Then there was the infamous Shatner/Nimoy feud.

It was only logical that it should happen. Or, at least, be reported. Feuds always make good copy.

For the December 1967 issue of *Photoplay*, a feature article offered a scoop on "Outer Space's Inside Battle." The subhead asked, "Is the infinite realm of *Star Trek* big enough to handle both William Shatner and Leonard Nimoy?" Trying to find an answer, Rhonda Green wrote:

When *Star Trek* premiered via the home screen last TV season, it was a welcome offering -- the public took a fancy to the way-out series about life among the planets. It was to be a glimpse into the future and the ratings proved the program was to have its own successful future. The star of the series,

William Shatner, quickly became one of the viewers' favorites. And during the run of the series, the fans at home also began to rally around the show's co-star, Leonard Nimoy. By the end of last season, the series boasted two stars -- equally popular with the TV audience.... At this point one thing is certain -- Bill and Len are back for another season of *Star Trek*ing. And one more thing is certain -- there is no getting around that big black monster -- publicity. The public has already demanded to know more about these two stars and the press is busy supplying the stories. Include in that group the gossips and rumor mongers.... The number one rumor making the rounds these days is one concerning the private war that Bill and Len are waging -- that success has made them the worst of enemies.

John D.F. Black, *Star Trek* associate producer, script consultant, and writer, from Season One, said, "I never believed it. It wasn't happening when I was there. And I don't believe it happened after I left. Bill and Leonard wanted two different things. Bill first and foremost wanted to be a star. Leonard wanted to be regarded as a great actor. They were two very different men with two different agendas. And that worked for *Star Trek*. And that worked for them." (17)

In a 1967 issue of *TV Radio Show*, for an article called "The Truth Behind the *Star Trek* Feud!," we were told:

No battle lines have yet been drawn on the *Star Trek* set, but the situation is best described by the comment of an actor who worked on the show recently. "You soon find out," he said, "that Nimoy is the star, but Shatner is the boss." The oddest aspect of the relationship, however, is that neither Shatner nor Nimoy want a feud, yet the circumstances of the series, the differences of their personal histories and their professional attitudes are ingredients that make the situation ripe for conflict between them. One *Star Trek* co-worker explains it this way: "It's a feud only because there isn't another word for it. What's happened is that Bill and Leonard have been shoved into a strange contest by a caprice of the public." ... What [happened] is probably one of the strangest twists in TV history.... Early this year... Nimoy's mail began to increase. In six weeks it doubled to hundreds of letters weekly, then to thousands. He is now one of the most popular stars on television. Changes between Nimoy and Shatner are hard to point out. They do not, of course, argue and quarrel, in the accepted sense of an open feud. But significant, perhaps, is that in some dozen stories read by this writer about Nimoy and Shatner, neither is once quoted mentioning the other. "The touchy part about this feud, if you want to call it that," says a member of the cast, "is that Leonard made no attempt whatsoever to outdo Bill. Len simply performed with high competence." Those close to him interpret Leonard's reaction as very much in character. He is a real professional, to whom the job is more important than anything else; a man who enjoys his new-found stardom, but still considers himself an "actor," not a "star" .... Some insiders believe that Shatner's alleged long history of professional frustration and the grueling work schedule he keeps was the reason for his recent separation from his wife, Gloria. Columns were buzzing with gossip after Bill moved out and for a time the 11-year marriage seemed ready to founder on the rocks. Bill stayed away for a month and then reconciled with Gloria. They are now back together. The separation did one thing for Shatner. It got his name in print.... For a time he was getting more coverage than Nimoy. But Nimoy is again in the forefront. His mail, instead of leveling off, has now gotten so heavy that he has hired a secretary to cope with the flood of letters.... As stated earlier, there are no sharp signs of the feud, but there is the fear that it may soon become more obvious. Tension on the *Star Trek* set is, at times, overpowering. "The electricity over there," says one visitor "is so heavy you could charge a battery with it. I got the impression that Shatner and Nimoy's co-workers are almost afraid to say anything for fear of setting off a bolt of lightning."

At the height of the "reporting," Shatner's publicist, Frank Liberman, wrote to Roddenberry:

> I'm sure you're aware of the fact that Bill Shatner has always said only complimentary things about Leonard Nimoy and his fellow cast members. Needless to say, he will continue this policy -- not only for his own good but for that of the series.... Nevertheless, there has been some innuendo around town.... The innuendo I referred to... comes from various gossip columnists and fan magazine editors who are looking for angles and are sometimes creating trouble on their own. This sort of thing went on with Robert Vaughn and David McCallum and I guess it will always happen when two men are involved in a series.

Nimoy said, "The whole feud thing, I think, was amplified out of proportion by the fan magazines who needed something exciting to write about. And it's much more exciting to write about arguments on a set than to simply report that all is peace and quiet and that the show is being done professionally." (128-15)

Shatner added, "There was never any feud. There were, on occasions, mostly between Leonard and I, a difference of opinion and sometimes, in a moment of pique, one or the other of us would get angry. You've got to realize that for three years, all of us -- but particularly, Leonard and I -- were thrown into each other's company for twelve hours or more a day. And here were two people who had never met before. We never asked to be married to each other, but we were, in effect, married. We were more constant companions than [with our] wives. And, if you use that as a basis for judging the relationship, we had a far happier marriage than most marriages are. We got along famously." (156-9)

Bobby Clark said, "Shatner and Nimoy are great friends. When they're together, they're great. They get along fine. But Nimoy prefers to be over here if Shatner is over there. He's not going to compete with Shatner. No interest in doing that." (31e)

Herb Solow offered his perspective, saying, "All actors have egos. If they didn't have egos, then they wouldn't be actors.... So, when you have a series with more than one actor, you have the usual problems. I must say that the actors' egos on *Star Trek* were not as bad as they were with the actors on other series with which I've been involved. The difference on *Star Trek* was that one man, William Shatner, was hired and contracted as the star of the show. The writers wrote for him as the star. The billing said that he was the star.... The second group, Jimmy Doohan, Nichelle Nichols, George Takei... were upset at times over the fact that, as Leonard and Bill both became more important in each episode, some of them had to lose lines or scenes.... I can say that's the way it was and it's an industry thing that's not going to change. It's that way on just about any show." (161-5)

Grace Lee Whitney said, "Sure, Bill and Leonard had a few words. Bill and I had words. George and Bill had words. Jimmy and Bill had words. Everybody had words with Bill. But the show would never have flown without Bill. It was a very tough job for him. He worked very hard. Bill was the star, we all knew it." (183-6)

David Gerrold said of the supporting players, "Shatner saved their jobs. If it hadn't been for Shatner, the show would have gone down the tubes.... Here's a guy who's the star of the show, who gets more interviews, photo requests, everything requests, more demands on his time, plus he's in more shots than anybody else, and the rest of the cast is saying, 'Well, isn't he being an arrogant prick?' No, he's not an arrogant prick, he's being a workaholic, doing the best to keep that damn show alive. And they can't see it. And, I feel, instead of writing tell-all books about what a terrible person he was on the set -- which I never saw, I only saw a hard working, brilliant, incredibly committed man -- they should have all been grateful for the boost to their careers that they got from *Star Trek* that they couldn't have gotten any other way, and to be part of something legendary. That's big." (73-1)

Nimoy said, "The chemistry on that show between the actors was pretty remarkable, and I think quite rare for a television series." (Photo courtesy Gerald Gurian)

There would soon be a semblance of peace on the set. As Lucas spent more time on the stage, as well as in the *Star Trek* offices where he was being groomed to step in for Gene Coon should the NBC renewal come through, the cast began to warm up to him. He said, "I went on the set, never bringing up the problem, listened to complaints the actors had about their parts and each other and acted as though there was nothing wrong. Gradually the tension eased and we had a happy company again -- save for the negative occasional friction encountered when dealing with any actors." (110-6)

Leonard Nimoy gets the last word on the subject. He said, "They're a terrific bunch of people. We were very lucky. The chemistry on that show between the actors was pretty remarkable, and I think quite rare for a television series." (128-25)

***

Then, there was "the midsection at mid-season. Some referred to it as the "Battle of the Bulge." Others, "the expansion of a character." It was all about William Shatner's weight.

It had been a minor problem during the first season. Shatner showed up for work on "The Corbomite Maneuver" as he had for the pilot film, trim and fit. But as the grueling shooting schedule progressed, week after week, his weight increased. He didn't have as much time for exercise ... or sensible meals. He ate on the run, mostly whatever the studio commissary was cooking up for breakfast and lunch and then, exhausted at the end of the day, home for a late dinner, time to read the script pages for the next day's shooting, and off to bed. Weekends were for the kids -- his three daughters -- and all else that needed to be done, including promoting *Star Trek*. And, again, meals were consumed mostly on the run.

Sherri Jackson said, "I usually keep my mouth shut, but when I want to make a comment, I'm usually very truthful. I don't sugarcoat it. And so I talked to Shatner about his costume. I was actually trying to help him, and I said, 'You know, first of all, those pants are way too short. You should make them longer so it will make you look taller. I also told him that his shirt was too short in the front, and it made it look like his belly was bigger. He just laughed it off." (90-1)

The midsection at mid-season
(CBS Studios, Inc.)

Gene Roddenberry, however, was not laughing. In a letter, dated March 23, 1967, he praised his star on the performance from "The City on the Edge of Forever." The compliment, although deservingly sincere, was meant to soften Shatner up. And then Roddenberry got to the point. He wrote:

> You were so good [in "City"] that the audience may miss the fact that you have been in these last episodes of the year showing your weight a little too much. We find ourselves having to stay away from Longer Shots whenever possible, as the simple plain lines of our basic costume renders most unflattering any extra poundage around the waist. I get concerned about this, Bill, since we are playing to an audience that is most weight conscious today -- and also very youth conscious. The whole nation has gone that direction, and poundage adds years photographically.

The ploy was a success. When the cast returned to Desilu studios on May 2, 1967 for "Catspaw," the first episode of Season Two, Shatner's cheek bones dominated his tight, sculptured face. His weight was lower than ever before.

Within two months, the battle of the bulge resumed.

As the film cutters began to leave more and more exposed footage on the editing room floor, Bill Theiss came up with a new shirt that everyone hoped might disguise the growing problem.

Dorothy Fontana said, "The shirt that Bill Theiss devised, the wrap-around, worked best when [Bill Shatner] was gaining weight. It tended to conceal, whereas, with the regular shirt, you could see the bulges." (64-2)

The solution proved to be a short-lived one. Once a few more pounds were added, and with the way the wrap-around tunic clung snugly to Shatner's abdomen, a new problem surfaced.

Robert Justman said, "Bill wore lifts to help him attain his advertised height of 5'11". And the heels threw his posture awry, pushing out his stomach and making him look swaybacked." (94-8)

The wraparound tunic disappeared after the filming of "The Immunity Syndrome." Shatner was back to wearing his standard uniform top ... which now appeared to be a size smaller. Shatner was no longer laughing it off.

Justman said, "Bill Shatner stopped me in the middle of the studio street. This was the first time he'd ever complained to me about anything, and he

Eating on the run ... and the wraparound tunic, which Dorothy Fontana said "tended to conceal" the bulges (Photo from *TV Star Parade*, December 1967. Courtesy Gerald Gurian)

was furious. 'Look at this goddamn uniform, Bob!' The bottom of the velour tunic was headed north and barely concealed his stomach. He tugged to pull the fabric down over the top of his uniform trousers, which headed south. 'The goddamn material shrinks more every time it's cleaned. The women are the ones who are supposed to have bare midriffs on this show, not me!'" (94-8)

Fontana added, "There were unflattering references to Captain Fatty. But the man really could not help it. It was not his fault. With that work grind we had, it was tough on him. And we asked for multiple shirts but, still, you were constantly cleaning them. By the time you got to the end of the season, the shirts shrunk up quite a bit so you were seeing a little tummy bulge underneath, too." (64-2)

Costumer Andrea Weaver said, "The standard in the industry is that clothes go out overnight for cleaning. And those uniforms were made out of stretch velour, which didn't work out very well. Bill Shatner had three or four shirts, but the problem was which of them would be the best that day, the one that has the least shrinkage. And it wasn't just shrinkage. The fabric didn't hold its shape. It was very challenging." (180a)

Private conversations between Roddenberry, Justman, and post-production supervisor Eddie Milkis even went so far as to bring up an idea of collecting unflattering film clips of Shatner and sending them to the actor. But this didn't have to happen. Shatner himself was a very self-motivated individual.

Shatner said, "I'd gradually, well, deteriorated to the point where the first shows came on, the first thirteen, and I would see [in comparison] how much weight I had gained [since the start of the season]. Then I'd go on a crash diet -- and I'd lose weight by the end of the season.... I'd start off slim, and get to my fat period, and then taper off again. And the knowledgeable people who watched the show have written me or told me in person that

they'd made bets as to what time of the season a particular show was shot, based on the fact of how much weight I had gained." (156-9)

He also returned to his exercise regimen. Charlie Brill, who played Arne Darvin, the Klingon spy in "The Trouble with Tribbles," said, "All I remember about William Shatner was that he was doing pushups every minute. He was completely committed to that show. A very talented man. And always doing pushups." (21-1)

Fighting the battle of the bulge (Courtesy of Minka)

***

Working on *Star Trek* was a 12-plus-hour day for the creative staff, the production

Filming Season One's "The Corbomite Maneuver"
(Courtesy of Gerald Gurian)

team, and the cast. And this would continue five days a week for eight or more months at a time. What enabled everyone involved to keep working, and to continue doing their best, was their love for the project, and the humor they shared. William Shatner was often at the center. He was the instigator in most of the onslaught of bad puns, and the relentless practical jokes played on co-workers. And also the laughing fits before the camera. But DeForest Kelley got in his fair share of mischief making, and, often, the goal was to get Leonard Nimoy to drop

out of the Spock character and crack a smile. Even the behind-the-scenes personnel would contribute to the silliness. The stories have been told elsewhere. But a picture is worth a thousand words … and laughs. Here are some:

Nimoy and Kelley in a laughing fit during filming of Season One's
"The Conscience of the King (above), and the three leads using their phasers --
or communicators -- as if they were doing a commercial for electric shavers
(below), while on location for "Operation: Annihilate!"
(Courtesy of Gerald Gurian)

**Shatner and Sherry Jackson celebrate the end of Season One's
"What Are Little Girls Made Of?" (above), and Takei and Shatner
(below) blow a scene from "Tomorrow Is Yesterday"
(Courtesy of Gerald Gurian)**

Leonard Nimoy's son Adam, in Vulcan ears, is sent onto the bridge during
filming to surprise -- and get a smile out of – his dad (above), and Shatner
breaks up James Doohan (below) in Season One's "The Naked Time"
(Courtesy of Gerald Gurian)

Kelley blows a line to get a reaction out of Shatner … and, as a bonus,
a good laugh from Nimoy (above), and Shatner gets fresh with Nimoy (below)
during the filming of "The Immunity Syndrome"
(Courtesy of Gerald Gurian)

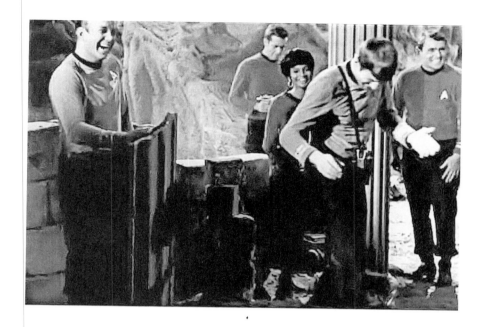

Levity while making "The City on the Edge of Forever"
(above), and Shatner and Nimoy having a ball (below)
during the filming of "Patterns of Force"
(Courtesy of Gerald Gurian)

Shatner loses it during the making of "Mirror, Mirror" (above),
and Shatner even gets smiles out of the three androids
while filming "I, Mudd" (below)
(Courtesy of Gerald Gurian)

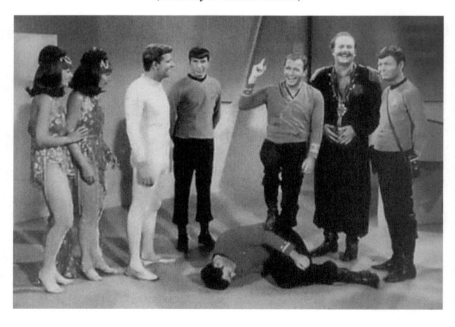

In an effort to loosen Bruce Hyde up, director Marc Daniels rings his neck during filming of "The Naked Time" (above; courtesy of Bruce Hyde), and Kelley and Shatner break up during production of "Amok Time" (below) (Courtesy of Gerald Gurian)

Shatner (hidden by clapboard) has Kelley (sitting on left) and Nimoy in stitches,
but no reaction from the ever sour-faced camera slate guy,
Bill McGovern (above), and proving that not everything about
Season Three's "The Empath" was darkly serious (below)
(Courtesy of Gerald Gurian)

While filming Season Three's "Spectre of the Gun," Kelley has Shatner
laughing to the point of tears (above), and Shatner finally gets a smile out of Bill
McGovern (below), while filming "Wink of an Eye" with Kathie Brown
(Courtesy of Gerald Gurian)

In the last days of September 1967, as the *Star Trek* company began filming "Journey to Babel," no one knew whether this would be their second-to-last trek (with "A Private Little War" to follow and possibly end it all). NBC had no answer for Roddenberry and Lucas. The ratings had yet to be analyzed for the new season. Of course, to anyone who was privy to the various A.C. Nielsen audience surveys -- and, back in 1967, unlike today, those statistics were closely guarded -- *Star Trek* had already proven itself.

During the summer of 1967, as *Star Trek* reran the best of its first season, the series made the Nielsen Top Ten list for the most popular shows among teenagers. It came in at Number 9. As for general nose counting, *Star Trek* placed well among Nielsen surveys, as well. On many nights it won its time slot. Yet the network decided to exile the series to Friday nights.

NBC claimed that the move would benefit the show. The official attitude was best summed up by a letter to Gene Roddenberry from NBC executive Dan Durgin, dated March 16, 1967. It read:

> Congratulations on *Star Trek*. I think it will do even better with the strong *Tarzan* lead-in and on Friday night when the same number of adults will be available to it, but substantially more young people. The competition of *Gomer* should be less formidable than the present competition of *Bewitched* because, as you know, *Gomer*'s big appeal is rural and *Star Trek*'s big appeal, like *Bewitched*, is in the big cities.

Cast and crew, as well as many TV insiders, knew better than NBC ... or, at least, better than NBC claimed to know.

One such insider was Hal Humphrey, the entertainment correspondent for *The Los Angeles Times*. *Star Trek* was given the cover story for the newspaper's August 13, 1967 TV magazine. For the article called "*Star Trek*'s Upward Flight," Humphrey wrote:

> Except for *The Monkees*, the greatest mail puller among TV series the past season was NBC's *Star Trek*. According to executive producer Gene Roddenberry, *Star Trek*'s weekly mail averages 4,000 pieces. "And lots of it is highly literate mail," says Roddenberry proudly. "Letters from graduate students at Harvard and from Astro physicists have come to my desk. *Star Trek* has become an 'in' show, which makes us very happy.... We're up for an award this year from the world Science Fiction Association when it holds its convention. The only other two nominees are movies.... And the Smithsonian Institute has asked for our pilot film for its archives.... We were making out fine where we were, but now we may lose many of the young people who've been watching, because Friday is the night they like to go out," reports Roddenberry. "I have no idea why NBC changed nights."

Humphrey added:

> This next season Roddenberry plans more exploratory type stories which he hopes will have even greater appeal to young adults. Whether his Friday night viewers on NBC, many of whom will have just finished watching *Tarzan*, are going to appreciate his efforts is no doubt one of the things disturbing Roddenberry about the move this year.

Several weeks later, as "Bread and Circuses" was being filmed, the ratings for the first episodes to air for the second season were tallied. The results had been anxiously anticipated. Regardless of the expected dip in the ratings, *Star Trek*, as it had been on Thursdays in the fall of 1966, was again the highest-rated program for NBC on the night that it aired. The network soon knew that *Star Trek* could be counted on to beat *Hondo*, the competition on ABC, but it was clearly no match for the big guns at CBS. Or was it?

The demographics reveal that *Star Trek* was a Top Ten series in the Nielsens with the 12-to-17 crowd, besting even *Gomer Pyle*. And in some markets, mostly big cities, the numbers were better. In October 1967, *The Santa Monica Outlook*, a local Los Angeles-based newspaper, conducted a television ratings survey of its own, polling 10,000 people. *Star Trek* came in No. 1 with young adults between the ages of 20 and 30 and, again, at No. 1 with both men and women between 30 and 40. Overall, counting the combined TV audience for an entire week, regardless of age or sex, *The Outlook* found *Star Trek* to be the fifth most watched weekly show on television in the Los Angeles area.

But, for the first few weeks of this new season, on a national level, while just counting noses and not factoring in the audience demographics, A.C. Nielsen drew a bleaker picture. While *Star Trek* won its time slot with its season premiere of "Amok Time" in the metropolitan markets, this episode that everyone on the series was so proud of slipped down to third place once Nielsen's national survey was completed. There was no fighting the season kick-off of *Gomer Pyle* and the television premiere of *The Great Escape* on CBS, but NBC had even lost out to ABC -- albeit only slightly. The premiere of *Hondo* finished sixth-tenths of a ratings' point ahead of *Star Trek*. Roddenberry, his staff, and the series' cast and crew were crushed.

With the second episode to air, "Who Mourns For Adonais?," the Nielsens were up more than three ratings points, closing the gap between NBC and CBS. *Star Trek* was now in second place, five-and-a-half ratings' points above *Hondo*.

September 26, 1967, half way through the filming of "Journey to Babel," NBC finally orders more episodes ... a pickup of only two
(Courtesy of Fred Walder and startrekalchemy.blogspot.com)

Although not willing to make a full season commitment, NBC did at least place an order for a pair of interim episodes, allowing *Star Trek* to remain in production for another few weeks. This news came half way into the filming of "Journey to Babel" on September 26.

Two scripts which had been somewhat developed by Gene Coon, "Obsession" and "Gamesters of Triskelion," were put through a rapid series of rewrites by Gene Roddenberry and John Meredyth Lucas. Remarkably, the company would not miss a single day of production.

25

Episode 46: OBSESSION

(46th episode filmed, although listed in past sources as Production #47)
Written by Art Wallace
(with Gene Coon, Gene Roddenberry, and John Meredyth Lucas, uncredited)
Directed by Ralph Senensky

Day 4 of production: Bill McGovern (bottom, center) slates a camera angle shot from the rafters of Stage 10. "Obsession" holds the record for highest body count for red-shirted crewmen (Courtesy of Gerald Gurian)

From NBC press release, issued November 15, 1967:

> Captain Kirk's career and the safety of the Enterprise are jeopardized by his compulsion to destroy a cloud-like creature which previously killed some of the crew, in "Obsession" on NBC Television Network's *Star Trek* colorcast Friday, Dec. 15.… While prospecting for a rare ore, Captain Kirk (William Shatner) recognizes an odor which reminds him of an incident 12 years before. At that time his captain and 200 crew members were killed by a gaseous mass. Kirk dispatches Ensign Rizzo (Jerry Ayres) to destroy the cloud. Rizzo lives just long enough to confirm Kirk's suspicions. Garrovick (guest star Stephen Brooks), Rizzo's replacement, is the son of the captain killed in the first accident. He too is almost killed when the cloud invades the Enterprise. Kirk then uses human bait against the creature.

Driven by guilt, Kirk delays a delivery of emergency vaccines to pursue an old nemesis, which lives on red corpuscles. The human bait: Kirk himself.

The theme to "Obsession" is identified in its title. Guilt and revenge are examined, through the actions and reactions of Kirk and Garrovick.

SOUND BITES

- *McCoy, to Kirk:* "Monsters come in many forms. And you know what's the greatest monster of them all, Jim? Guilt."

- *McCoy, to Kirk, referencing the cloud-creature, now in the ship's ventilation system:* "You didn't care what happened so long as you could hang your trophy on the wall. Well, it's not on the wall, Captain, it's *in* it!" *Spock:* "May I suggest that we no longer belabor the question of whether or not we should have gone after the creature. The matter has been rendered academic. The creature is now after *us*."

ASSESSMENT

"Obsession" is a clever spin on *Moby Dick*. It is taut and dramatic, with strong personal conflicts. Roddenberry had always seen Kirk as a futuristic Captain Horatio Hornblower. Here he becomes a 23rd Century Captain Ahab, as well.

Using *Moby Dick* as a model, the action elements of the story are intentionally kept simple. The complexities of the material rest with the characters. Kirk and Garrovick are determined to punish themselves for not living up to their own impossible expectations. And this nature of guilt and human emotion is examined by the observations of a well-meaning and intellectually curious Spock, who tells McCoy, "I require an opinion. There are many aspects of human irrationality I do not yet comprehend -- obsession for one, the persistent single-minded fixation on one idea." McCoy's delightful reaction: "*You* want advice from *me*? Then I need a drink."

Those watching may need a drink, too. Art Wallace's script, with substantial contributions by Roddenberry, Coon, and, to a lesser extent, Lucas, is a well-crafted and exciting tale … for the first three-quarters of the trek. However, both momentum and overall effectiveness falter in the final Act as some scenes become repetitive and others fail to meet *Star Trek*'s high standards.

Of the redundant beats, in a strange sequence of scenes that almost feel like script padding, Spock has deduced -- since phasers can't stop the creature -- that Kirk and Garrovick are wrong in blaming themselves for the deaths of others. His observations are ignored by both Kirk and Garrovick. Later, Kirk too realizes phasers are useless against the cloud creature. Then he explains to the younger man that they have no blood on their hands. This dramatic and sensitive moment between Kirk and Garrovick would have been more effective if the scene between Spock and Kirk, and especially the latter one between Spock and Garrovick, were eliminated.

As to the unbelievable aspects of story and character, Garrovick is immature, slow to comprehend, and prone to sulking. Yet he is the head of security?

If "Obsession" had maintained its quality and dramatic integrity throughout, it might be considered among *Star Trek*'s best, rather than merely slightly above run-of-the-mill.

THE STORY BEHIND THE STORY

Script Timeline

Art Wallace's story outline, ST #57: May 19, 1967.
Wallace's revised outline, gratis: May 23, 1967.
Wallace's 1ˢᵗ Draft teleplay: July 17, 1967.
Wallace's Revised 1ˢᵗ Draft teleplay, gratis: August 10, 1967.
Wallace's 2ⁿᵈ Draft (Mimeo Department "Yellow Cover 1ˢᵗ Draft" teleplay):
August 29, 1967.
Gene Coon's rewrite (Final Draft teleplay): September 6, 1967.
Gene Roddenberry's rewrite (Revised Final Draft): October 4, 1967.
John Meredyth Lucas' page revisions: October 5, 6, 11 & 12, 1967.

Art Wallace came to *Star Trek* with strong credentials. He wrote for Roddenberry's *The Lieutenant*, as well as Shatner's 1965 series *For the People*, and, in science fiction, for *Tom Corbett, Space Cadet* and *The Invaders*. Immediately prior to this, he spent two years working as co-creator and head writer for *Dark Shadows*. He was also a friend of Gene Roddenberry.

"Gene and I were having dinner one night," said Wallace, "and then it came to me that it wouldn't be a bad idea to do a version of *Moby Dick*, which became 'Obsession.' I just substituted the cloud for the great white whale." (179-1)

In *Moby Dick*, Herman Melville's 1851 classic, Captain Ahab, who, on a previous expedition, lost his leg to the whale known as Moby Dick, is consumed by his obsession for revenge against the beast.

On April 22, 1966, months before *Star Trek* had even premiered on NBC, Roddenberry, dictating story notes for "Space Moby Dick" to Robert Justman and John D.F. Black, said:

> It's the story of Captain Kirk becoming almost obsessed with the necessity to follow and kill the thing. This obsession, which we will strongly motivate on an emotional level, leads Kirk into diverting from his mission and normal duties as a starship commander, possibly even into risking his vessel, more men, and his career. Somewhere in the story he will, of course, realize what he is doing and pull back from it. But by that time he will be unable to do this -- the battle has been joined with the thing and he must carry out to his resolution. (GR46-1)

That's all Wallace and Roddenberry had at this point. The "thing" was undefined, as was Kirk's backstory, which would provide the reason for his obsession. But even at its embryonic stage, Roddenberry knew what he liked about the premise. His note to Justman and Black continued:

> There are several aspects to this which are good for us. Obviously we intend this to be more than a simple "monster" story. It's different from anything else we are now doing. It also shows Kirk in human error, making emotional mistakes, and we've been looking for that too. One problem inherent in this story the way Wallace sees it -- we would start on one planet, have a spaceship "chase," then end up on a second and different planet. Bobby Justman should comment on whether or not this can be done on budget. Can we redress the first planet set to look like a second planet, and so on?... We may have to hold off giving this assignment to Wallace since he leaves for Europe May 9 and will not return until the end of the month. (GR46-1)

John D.F. Black was all in favor of holding off giving out the assignment. He wrote Roddenberry:

Gene... The above mentioned piece is right flat on top of Ray Bradbury's "Moby Dick 1999" [aka "Leviathan '99"] mentioned in his letter to you, dated April 12, '66. Beware. (JDFB-46)

Sci-fi author Ray Bradbury had been invited by Roddenberry to write for *Star Trek* and had sent in his own idea for a reworking of *Moby Dick*, set in the year 1999, with the whale replaced by a comet and the sailing ship by a space ship. In 1968, *Leviathan '99* would be adapted into a 90-minute broadcast for BBC Radio 3. It starred Christopher Lee. In 2007, Bradbury published his story as a novella.

Letting this story go -- or, more so, letting a renowned science fiction writer get away -- was a great sacrifice for Roddenberry and *Star Trek*, but Roddenberry had an ethic which told him that whoever brought a story to his attention first got the assignment ... even when it meant missing an opportunity to have Ray Bradbury write a script for the series.

Like John D.F. Black, Robert Justman was also in favor of dropping the subject. His April 25 response to Roddenberry said:

Dear Crazy, the need for two separate planets defeats us both in cost and feasibility. How would we find the time necessary to change over our planet set from conception "A" to conception "B"?... A separate chase would certainly entail plenty of miniature shooting and optical special effects.... Yes, let's hold off giving out this assignment. Perhaps in our *second* or *third* season? (RJ46-1)

There was no way to predict that *Star Trek* would even survive to see a second or third season. Justman was dodging a bullet and hoping Roddenberry would forget about this whale of a tale.

By late March 1967 the bullet was fired again. NBC approved a cash advance for further story development, anticipating a second season. Roddenberry had not forgotten Wallace's idea and was somewhat obsessed himself in wanting to move forward with this Kirk-driven-by-revenge story. It had been tried before, in "The Conscience of the King," in a more stagey and action-less manner, but this new premise could be reinvigorated as a true action-adventure/science-fiction thrill ride. On April 1, 1967, he wrote Gene Coon:

Art gave us a *Moby Dick* tale of the future story last year and we've kind of reserved the general story area for him.

Wallace got his assignment and immediately changed the title from "Space Moby Dick" to "Obsession." His story outline was dated May 19, 1967.

On May 22, Roddenberry told Coon:

This is a thoroughly professional first outline and it appears Wallace has made considerable effort to study and understand our format. The story has some holes which will require imagination to fill but I'm sure Wallace can handle it. (GR46-3)

But, as all freelancers new to *Star Trek*, Wallace would need help. Roddenberry pointed out many problem areas, including:

KIRK'S MOTIVATIONS. We need greater and more pressing reasons for Kirk to risk crewmen and jeopardize his career in the way he does. I have no objection to him having an obsession about the creature but there must be more to it than presently exists.... Perhaps his captain, the man who guided his career, was killed in the incident. Or a fiancée. I suspect there must even be more than that to it. It needs almost a double whammy such as one of the men killed this time is the son of the Captain who was killed many years ago. (GR46-3)

415

These ideas -- Kirk's former captain who guided his career, and the son of that captain as a member of the Enterprise crew -- would become part of the new story.

Roddenberry continued:

THE THING. Don't we need a little more back story or scientific explanation of it? Calling it just a "gaseous cloud" and stopping there is not sufficient if we are to maintain believability we hope characterizes our series. We must at least suggest how it "eats," how it manages to travel, what level of intelligence it has, whether it is only one of a species and why, all that sort of thing.... At any rate, Art Wallace should give some thought to this area.... LIEUTENANT RIZZO. Again, I think we need better motivation for Kirk placing Rizzo under arrest. It is hard to believe that our Captain, even suffering a form of obsession, would be this unfair. Perhaps Wallace can pull it off if he motivates Kirk's obsession sufficiently but I must say I am concerned about Kirk's action here.... Don't understand how the thing could have attacked Lt. Rizzo a second time in his sealed off cabin and still have this Lt. well enough to go with Kirk down to the planet. (GR46-3)

At this stage of the story's development, Rizzo survived the first attack and remained a major character in the story. In the filmed version, Lt. Rizzo is near death after the attack and replaced as Head of Security by Ensign Garrovick, the son of Kirk's former mentor, Captain Garrovick.

One day after Roddenberry's memo, Dorothy Fontana sent her comments to Gene Coon, writing:

I find many holes in this story. Kirk seems to come off as a psychotic, not as a sound, reasonable man. Okay, if he wants to get that thing and wipe it out for the safety of the galaxy and all mankind... let's help him do it. But his behavior throughout this is highly questionable.... There is another comment about this "thing" -- it seems to have only an appetite, but no intelligence. Bob Justman has made a point on another story ["The Doomsday Machine"], since corrected, that if we must have "things" and "monsters," they should have some sort of intelligence, meaning, and purpose. In effect, they too should have character. This one does not. It just floats around and leaps out for a corpuscle feast when the author says he wants some jeopardy. (DCF46-1)

Fontana illustrated her observations about Kirk's behavior, writing:

Page 5, Paragraph 1 -- For Kirk to "literally blow his stack" at Rizzo seems to put our Captain in the class of Captain Queeg [fictional character in Herman Wouk's 1951 novel The Caine Mutiny]. At the end of the paragraph, we also hear that Kirk's mind is shut to all McCoy's arguments about his relationship with Rizzo. Why? All this paints Kirk as a real nut, unstable, unreliable in command. All right if he has his own personal reasons for keeping after this 'Thing,' and all right if he doesn't want Rizzo to make the same mistake he made with it -- but he should do it in a Kirk way -- sensible, reasonable, with some emotion but with awareness of command. (DCF46-1)

Fontana also had issues with the logic in the script, telling Coon:

Spock reports the Thing has found its way into the ship. How? There should be no openings to the outside on this ship. It's pressure sealed, probably with two hulls, all the way around. (DCF46-1)

Coon had Wallace give his outline a quick polish, *gratis*, addressing a few of the more critical notes before sending it to NBC. The extra work paid off. On June 5, Stan Robertson contacted Coon, writing:

This is an excellent and exiting story which has all the ingredients to be developed into one of those memorable *Star Trek* episodes, such as "Tomorrow Is Yesterday," which stands out not only in all our minds, but in the minds of the viewers as well. Of immeasurable importance is the characterization of Captain Kirk. We have all discussed methods by which we could add a greater dimension to the role. In this particular storyline, the writer has found such a vehicle. If the finished script comes up to the high hopes we have for this story, I would suggest that it be planned for the earliest possible production.

Coon gave Wallace the green light to proceed to teleplay so it *could* be planned for the earliest possible production. In an effort to further address Fontana's notes, Wallace was asked to make the creature a bit more cunning, and to come up with an explanation as to how it entered the ship.

The 1st Draft script arrived in mid July. Coon expressed great enthusiasm over it. Robert Justman did not. He wrote:

Dear Gene, sorry to have to disagree with you, but dislike this teleplay as much as you like it. Aside from some rather obvious technical difficulties and illogical behavior, I find that there are certain story holes and, even more important, there are certain badly developed areas of characterization. Kirk is unbelievably petulant and nasty throughout most of the script. Mr. Spock is non-existent. Dr. McCoy has a few scenes and then drops from sight.... I predicate that the odds are 1,000 to 1 for our being able to get a decent rewrite out of Art Wallace on this script. I'd say that the odds are about 50-50, if you do the rewrite yourself. (RJ46-2)

Justman suggested that Chekov play Rizzo's part, telling Coon, "It will give us someone we know and to whom we can relate." Elsewhere in Justman's massive 14-page memo, he said:

I really don't understand why Dr. McCoy goes to see Rizzo. I mean, I think we need a more plausible excuse for him to visit Rizzo. Just because we have to have someone with Rizzo when the Creature starts emanating from the ventilation shaft isn't sufficient justification. In fact, should it be Dr. McCoy who visits Rizzo? Could we possibly make use of Mr. Spock and his green blood in this sequence? If the Creature is so all-fired powerful and strong, then how would activating an emergency blower and suction from Rizzo's Cabin have any effect upon it? Perhaps if it was Mr. Spock who was in the Cabin, the Creature would by this time be giving up its attempt to get a square meal out of him and is already moving back into the ventilator. (RJ46-2)

Coon liked Justman's idea and changed the scene so that it is Spock, not McCoy, who visits the quarters belonging to Rizzo (later to be Garrovick). A better reason for the visit was given, as well, although it did detract from a scene to be played later between Kirk and Rizzo/Garrovick.

Fontana's follow-up to Coon:

I find I agree with many of RJ's comments on this script, but I am not quite as disturbed about it as he is. Well ... maybe I am ... on one point ... Kirk's obsession with getting this creature is much like Decker's in "The Doomsday Machine." ... Regarding the teaser in general, I see touches of "The Man Trap" in it ... [and] the creature, as described so far, may have a tendency to look like the creature in "Metamorphosis." Will it? It shouldn't. (DCF46-2)

In "The Man Trap," McCoy informs Kirk that crew members died from sudden depletion of body salt; here, death results from the sudden depletion of red blood corpuscles. In "Metamorphosis," Kirk and company encounter an intelligent and powerful creature that

417

appears to be a multi-colored cloud; here, the creature appears to be a white cloud.

Coon didn't share Fontana's concerns. Salt/blood; white cloud/colored cloud, who cares? And it didn't bother him that Kirk was behaving a bit like Decker. There were enough differences in Coon's mind. Kirk remained somewhat rational, after all. Decker did not.

Fontana liked Justman's idea of changing Rizzo to Chekov, but cautioned:

> Regarding the ending: We cannot of course kill Chekov. And the ending is quite contrived. We will have to figure out a way to mollify the creature, at considerable risk to our heroes, but both Kirk and Rizzo/Chekov make it back alive. (DCF46-2)

Coon wrote to Art Wallace on July 27, telling him:

> This memo probably will be quite long. Please don't let this dismay you. It is my custom, especially when the writer is in New York and I am out here, to enlarge upon every marginal comment upon a script which I am sending you. Most writers find this helpful. You may find it a pain in the ass. (GC46)

The pain in the ass went on for 13 pages, including:

> I think we are in some trouble with the ending. I keep finding it, despite our agreement in the area of the story, distasteful that the Captain ends up being saved by the ensign, who, in his turn, dies. Therefore, I would like to suggest that we make better use of one of our regular running characters, Ensign Chekov, by letting him play the part of Rizzo. To do this, of course, would mean that Chekov could not die at the ending. Because I am opposed, at this stage of the game, to the ensign dying, I see no reason we could not use Chekov, who is a character we'd like to establish much better in the series. (GC46)

Wallace turned in his freebie Revised 1st Draft script on August 10. Regarding Kirk's attempt to "mollify" the creature, baiting it with blood, Justman echoed Fontana's earlier concern and wrote to Coon:

> Perhaps you are aware of the fact that we are doing something similar in this show to what we've done in "The Man Trap." Except in "Man Trap" we attracted the creature with salt. (RJ46-3)

Beyond this, Justman was upset that, other than Rizzo being changed to Chekov, there were few significant changes made between this and the previous draft. He referenced his July 19 memo where he predicted the odds were 1,000 to 1 against them getting a worthwhile rewrite out of Wallace. His frustrated notes -- seven pages worth this time -- continued:

> You gotta be kidding with the scene description on Page 61A. You get me a "sparkling, changeable, twisting ball of light energy about 2 feet in diameter" and I will be pleased to use it in the show. Until then, forget it! (RJ46-3)

Fontana checked-in a few days later, telling Coon:

> Improved, but I still find objections in areas of logic and, to some extent, drama. (DCF46-3)

Her objections went on for five single-spaced pages.

Coon got one more rewrite out of Wallace -- the mandatory 2nd Draft. Chekov was out and Rizzo was back in. The reason for all the flip-flopping? It had now been decided that Roddenberry's idea about making the character the son of Kirk's former captain was a good one, and that Kirk would see much of himself, as a younger man, in Rizzo, better explaining his stern behavior toward the ensign.

On August 29, Justman wrote Coon:

A lot has been done to help clean up the previous version of this piece. However, I still feel that there are some tacky areas.... Although I feel that Kirk's motivation has been cleared up immensely in the area of his obsession, I do worry a little bit about his behavior near the end of Act II. He has definitely disobeyed orders from Starfleet Command and since what is sauce for the goose is also sauce for the gander, I wonder how we can justify his subordinates leaving him in control of the ship when they have already seen him relieve Ensign Rizzo from duty and confine Rizzo to quarters. Don't you feel that Captain Kirk has put his fellow officers into a rather interesting quandary? Is it necessary that we have Captain Kirk disobey orders from Starfleet Command? I realize that what Starfleet Command doesn't know, won't hurt it; but everybody else on board the ship knows what is going on. (RJ46-4)

With this suggestion, in future drafts, a scene would be added wherein Spock and McCoy confront Kirk in his quarters and ask that he explain his behavior to them, with them even suggesting they are prepared to go on record that he is unfit for command. The scene would also, for the moment, have Kirk satisfies McCoy and Spock with his answers.

Justman continued:

I am especially concerned with the fourth Act.... I humbly entreat you to find another way to handle the anti-matter routine. Covering the anti-matter with a black cloth and then later whisking off the black cloth to see a ball of light energy floating in mid-air does not exactly thrill me, or fill me with glee.... I am screaming very loudly now and I would like not to have to scream. Please let us discuss Scenes 123 and 124 as reasonable human beings with some ends in view -- those ends being the studio's bank-roll and my sanity. (RJ46-4)

In an effort to keep Justman from screaming, Coon tried his hand at a rewrite, the Final Draft, dated September 6, 1967. Then, as he prepared to step down as series producer, the problematic material was put aside ... until Coon chose John Meredyth Lucas to take over the job of reading the long and highly critical memos from Robert Justman.

When NBC ordered a pair of interim episodes, Lucas was asked to choose his two favorites from a pile of unproduced scripts Coon had left behind. The candidates, arranged by date, were:

- Gene Roddenberry's "The Omega Glory";
- Barry Trivers' "Portrait in Black and White";
- Paul Schneider's "Tomorrow the Universe";
- Norman Spinrad's "He Walked Among Us";
- Gene Coon's very different version of "He Walked Among Us";
- Margaret Armen's "The Gamesters of Triskelion";
- John T. Dugan's "Return to Tomorrow";
- Art Wallace's "Obsession";
- Jerome Bixby's "By Any Other Name";
- David Harmon's "The Expatriates" (AKA "A Piece of the Action");
- Darlene Hartman's "Shol";
- Robert Saboroff's "The Immunity Syndrome";
- and a second version of "The Omega Glory," this one by Les and Tina Pines.

All 13 teleplays were challenging to some degree. Lucas, hastily making his choice, went with what he believed to be the least problematic -- "Gamesters of Triskelion" and "Obsession."

Lucas was particularly fond of "Obsession" because Captain Kirk was portrayed as a driven and somewhat dark character. He later said, "If there was one element that I brought back to the show when I was producer, because it had been a little bit lost, it was Gene Roddenberry's inspiration for the series: Horatio Hornblower." (110-5)

Lucas sent "Obsession" to De Forest Research for coverage. Joan Pearce, after consulting with the firm's science authority, Pete Sloman, filed a report on September 29, 1967. Regarding a line in the script that read, "It moves through the rapid contraction and expansion of its unstable elements," Pearce said:

> The term "unstable elements" properly refers to those elements which undergo spontaneous change under normal conditions as radium turns to lead by radio-activity. Use of "unstable elements" here is scientific *nonsense*. Suggest delete, so line reads, "It moves through rapid contractions and expansions."

Of the line, "At that distance, the shock waves from the anti-matter explosion would severely damage the ship," Pearce told Lucas:

> Shock waves need a medium to travel through -- air, water, etc. At 25,000 kilometers, the ship will be in the vacuum of deep space. An explosion to batter the ship would have to be large enough to physically hurl huge masses of atmosphere and/or planetary debris through that distance. Shock waves will not travel in a vacuum.

Of reference to the "Starship Farragut," Pearce wrote:

> Nomenclature for Starships has hitherto indicated qualities -- e.g. Enterprise -- with names of historical personages being used for shuttlecraft. Suggest Starship Endeavor.

On October 2, Roddenberry wrote Lucas:

> I agree that this ["Obsession"] is one of our better drafts available and could be put into our schedule immediately.... I like this script, think that it can become a very exciting episode for us.

Of course, Roddenberry did have some suggestions for changes. He told Lucas:

> SPOCK'S INJURY. We've had Spock injured and hospitalized in so many recent shows, can we risk going a slightly new direction here? Instead of him being injured, they find him quite all right. The gaseous substance simply didn't work with his green blood. We can still have the same tart comment by McCoy that the creature went away with a bad taste in its mouth. (GR46-4)

Primarily, Roddenberry wanted the character of Nurse Chapel added to the story. He paid himself $2,500 to create a Revised Final Draft and wrote in a part for Majel Barrett. And the role of Security Officer Rizzo was split into two parts -- Rizzo would be killed after the first attack of the cloud monster and then replaced by Garrovick, the son of Kirk's former commander.

John Meredyth Lucas handled the page revisions to follow, on October 5, 6, 11, and 12. The script could have used one more rewrite, to remove some of the redundancy in the latter half and to strengthen the character of Garrovick, but there was no time. Filming of the episode had actually begun on October 9, at the halfway point between the four sets of page revisions by Lucas.

"Gamesters of Triskelion," planned to film first, was assigned an earlier production number. But the rewriting of "Obsession" went quicker, and the sets for this episode were less-challenging than those for "Gamesters." It also required less casting. Because of this, the two episodes flipped spots in the production schedule, even though their production numbers did not change. And this has resulted in misinformation regarding the order in which the episodes were filmed.

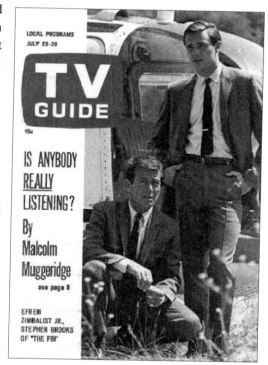

Ralph Senensky, now the third of three rotating directors (alternating with Marc Daniels and Joseph Pevney) was given the assignment. This was Senensky's fourth *Star Trek*, following his excellent work in "This Side of Paradise," "Metamorphosis," and "Bread and Circuses."

Stephen Brooks, playing the pivotal role of Ensign Garrovick, had just finished two seasons as Jim Rhodes, Efrem Zimbalist's co-star on *The F.B.I.* This was the fourteenth time Senensky gave direction to Brooks, with the

Efrem Zimbalist Jr. and Stephen Brooks
on the cover of
***TV Guide*'s July 23, 1966 issue**

director having requested him for this role. They had first met on a pair of episodes for the New York based one-hour drama, *The Nurses*, in which Brooks had a recurring role.

Regarding his decision to leave *The F.B.I.* after two seasons, Brooks said, "Acting is just playing cops and robbers -- it's basically childish.... I don't want to fall into the TV trap and go from one series to another.... [And] nowadays I seem to spend a lot of time just following Efrem through doorways or else trying to keep my hands out of my pockets like a good FBI man." (22a)

Jerry Ayres, as the doomed Ensign Rizzo, had died on *Star Trek*, earlier in "Arena." In that episode he was vaporized. He was 30 then, 31 here. Still in his future: recurring roles on *Dynasty* and the daytime soaps *General*

Jerry Ayres wore red once before ... and died ... in "Arena"
(CBS Studios, Inc.)

Hospital and *The Bold and the Beautiful*.

Eddie Paskey, William Shatner's lighting stand-in, had already appeared in 44 other episodes, usually in a red shirt, as Lt. Leslie. He later said, "I was very careful to be somewhere else when the script called for someone [in a red shirt] to die. Because I was on the set all the time [as Shatner's stand in], I knew what was in the script. I didn't want to have something happen to my character because that would have put me out of the show." (135)

For this, his 45th *Star Trek* appearance, Paskey is one of the men who *is* killed by the vampire cloud. Regardless, he continued to stand in for Shatner and returned 15 more times, often as Leslie, resurrected from the dead.

Production Diary
Filmed October 9, 10, 11, 12, 13 & 16, 1967.
(6 day production; revised budget set at $170,871)

Day 3. Camera tie-down shot on Stage 10. Shatner and Brooks stand by for the materialization effect. Note stage hand on left, using broom to smooth dirt, hiding footprints left by the actors, and two production crew members to the right, placing the bottle of plasma to be used as bait for the cloud monster
(Courtesy of Gerald Gurian)

Filming began Monday, October 9, 1967. On the night before, the majority of Americans ended their weekend with an evening of television. Six of the 25 most-watched series of the week aired on Sunday, including Stephen Brooks' old series, *The F.B.I.* on ABC, *Walt Disney's Wonderful World of Color* and *Bonanza* on NBC, and *Gentle Ben*, *The Ed Sullivan Show*, and *The Smothers Brothers Comedy Hour* on CBS. Regarding the latter two, "for the youngsters," Ed welcomed The Cowsills, singing their new record, "The Rain, the Park and Other Things," standup Lou Antonio doing a routine about violence in fairy tales and the trouble with contact lenses, and ventriloquist Señor Wences performed with his puppets. Tom and Dick Smothers followed with The Association singing the second biggest hit in the nation, "Never My Love," and comedian Pat Paulsen. Top movie at the box office was still *Bonnie and Clyde*. After 15 consecutive weeks at No. 1, *Sgt. Pepper's Lonely Hearts Club Band* by The Beatles finally yielded the summit position on Billboard's album chart to someone else -- Bobbie Gentry with *Ode to Billy Joe*. The most-played song on the radio was still "The Letter" by The Box Tops. And William Shatner had caught a cold.

The *Star Trek* company was on Desilu Stage 9, for the first of two days on the bridge. Shatner's stuffy head condition was most noticeable these two days.

Day 1, Monday, October 9, saw the filming of all the bridge scenes from Act I, Act II, and Act III, covering nearly 10 pages of the script and ending with the invasion of the creature, vanishing from space as it makes its way into the ship. Working this day: Shatner, Nimoy, Doohan, Koenig, Nichols, Stephen Brooks, and five extras, playing the parts of bridge personnel.

**Day 2. A second day on the bridge set
(Courtesy of Gerald Gurian)**

Day 2, Tuesday, October 10, took care of all of the Act IV scenes on the bridge. DeForest Kelley now joined the cast members who had worked the previous day. After filming of roughly eight pages from the script, the company made a move to the transporter room.

Day 3, Wednesday, October 11. For the first half of the day, Stage 10 was utilized as the second planet set. Jerry Finnerman used orange gels to get the inhospitable desert look. The scenes filmed here were those where Kirk and Garrovick faced the creature. Only Shatner and Brooks were on set for the morning hours. A camera tie-down was needed for a materialization effect and an explosion. Also called for on the production schedule: "puff of heavy smoke-creature."

Ralph Senensky recalled, "The creature and the smoke it gave off was a problem. Today you would do it all in post-production with opticals, but budgetary demands were that you try to do it live to save money. Trying to direct smoke to move exactly where you want it to move, and at the pace you want it to, isn't as easy as it sounds." (155-2)

Jim Rugg said, "We made clouds by having a smoke machine and having very good discipline on the stage. With no opening and closing of doors, and no fans on, you could hang smoke in the air just long enough to get a shot." (147)

Stephen Brooks, being upstaged by a large puff of smoke, said, "Acting [is] basically childish. But there is still something difficult about putting one foot in front of the other when you're on stage or before a camera." (22a)

The second half of the day was spent in Kirk's quarters, requiring a company move back to Stage 9. Only Shatner, Nimoy, and Kelley were required for this scene. Shatner's stuffy nose graduated to a full-blown fever.

Senensky spotted a marked difference in the caliber of the writing since his last visit. He said, "This was my first *Star Trek* without Gene Coon as producer -- and, of course, as writer.... I for one certainly missed him.... I cannot speak for the other directors and the other productions, but I can definitely say that there was a drop in quality from 'This Side of Paradise,' 'Metamorphosis' and 'Bread and Circuses' to the other two episodes I directed the second season [this and 'Return to Tomorrow']. And I ascribe the reason for this drop to be partly caused by the lack of Gene Coon's stewardship of the [final rewriting of the] scripts, and the rest to the impossible expectations that the episodes in this series could be filmed in five and a half days." (155-5)

Senensky used a scene from this episode as an example of how redundant dialogue suddenly appeared in the scripts. The scene is the one where Spock and McCoy confront Kirk in his quarters about his obsessive behavior -- a scene which runs for several minutes. Senensky said, "The scene starts with a strong confrontation between Dr. McCoy and Kirk but, after Spock enters, we get two and a half minutes of pure exposition. And those two and a half minutes covered the same material that had just been presented in a two minute scene between Kirk and McCoy.... There is a big difference between having your characters EXPLAIN a situation or DRAMATIZING IT." (155-5)

Regardless of some redundant dialogue, the drama caught on film is quite stirring. The performances and the blocking of the characters are uniformly excellent. Note how Shatner underplays Kirk, both while lying on his bed and sitting at his desk, and especially as DeForest Kelley delivers his "And you know what's the greatest monster of them all?" line. Shatner, as Kirk, turns off his communications monitor and swivels his chair to face his challenger, silent, cool, his eyes subtly daring McCoy to say it -- "Guilt.@ The scene plays beautifully, with director and actors in perfect harmony.

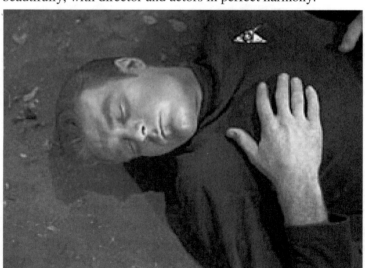

Day 4. Eddie Paskey, in whiteface, dies, even though he would continue with the series (CBS Studios, Inc.)

Day 4, Thursday, October 12, the company returned to Stage 10, redecorated with a smattering of foliage and different colored gels, giving the sky a multi-layered cool blue, blending into hot red. Filmed here were the Teaser and Act I sequences where three red-shirted security men met their deaths. On the call sheet and makeup schedule: Shatner, Nimoy, Brooks, Jerry Ayres (as Rizzo), and four extras to play red-shirted crewmen ... and soon-to-be victims. Eddie Paskey (whose character, Lt. Leslie, would return) was among them.

This episode ties the record for the highest red-shirt casualties, with four confirmed dead ... in red. "The Changeling" and "The Apple" have four red-shirts dead in each.

Day 5, Friday, October 13. While filming in the briefing room, sickbay, and McCoy's office, Shatner's cold symptoms were diminishing. However, Leonard Nimoy was showing signs of the illness. Because his cold symptoms were less noticeable this day,

Shatner recorded his Captain's log voiceovers. Also present, besides Shatner and Nimoy, were Kelley, Brooks, Doohan, Majel Barrett, Jerry Ayres (for his death scene in sickbay), and one "extra" to play a crewman in the background.

Cordrazine, the strong chemical stimulant McCoy injects into Rizzo and an invention of D.C. Fontana, was the same drug used to save Sulu in "The City on the Edge of Forever," and, when accidentally injected into McCoy, resulted in him temporarily losing his mind.

Later this night, no doubt sedated by cold medication, the two actors could watch the NBC premiere of "The Apple" and relive the explosion that resulted in long-term ringing in the ears. Shatner's ears were still ringing, and would be for decades to come. According to A.C. Nielsen, the ratings were ringing loud and clear, as well, with *Star Trek* in second place for its entire hour, losing to CBS but beating ABC.

Day 6, Monday, October 16. Filmed were scenes in McCoy's office, followed by those in the corridor outside and inside Garrovick's quarters.

Senensky said, "Gene

Day 5 Stephen Brooks in the briefing room (above, from unaired film trim; courtesy of Gerald Gurian), and Shatner with Jerry Ayres (below; CBS Studios, Inc.)

Coon had told me that he literally wrote every script; that he would hire a writer, buy a story, have the writer write it, then he would use that as the first draft and he would then rewrite it. But once Gene left, they never had a script again as good as his. An example of this is the scene where Spock talks to Stephen Brooks' character. The main reason for having this is that Spock needed to be in the room because he had to be there to meet the monster. But the script wasn't as tight as it would have been if Gene Coon had been handling the final rewriting. There would have been a better reason for him needing to be there." (155-6)

Justman, you will recall, had requested Coon find a better reason for Spock's presence. Coon, however, did not act on the request. Perhaps he would have in time, before the final shooting script was prepared. All that is known is that Lucas allowed this scene, and others like it, to go before the cameras without adjustment and proper trimming.

As for the action that followed the dialogue, Spock's behavior bordered on illogical. This part Senensky had no problem with, and rationalized, "When Spock went over to the vent, it was to shut off the valve. That I bought. Then he discovers the switch is broken, so he tries to cover the vent with his hands. I interpreted it as his half-human side acting out of desperation." (155-6)

Day 6, filming in McCoy's office; and unaired film trim of Shatner with Brooks in the ship's corridor (Courtesy of Gerald Gurian)

The only actors needed this day: Shatner, Kelley, Nimoy, Brooks, and Barrett. Extras were needed for the part of the lab technician, four security men, and four additional crewmen for the background.

Jerry Finnerman's remarkable lighting is especially noticeable during this episode. The *Star Trek* cinematographer had been experimenting with low level lighting and colored gels since the camera first rolled on "The Corbomite Maneuver" nearly a year and a half earlier. It was his idea to color the skies of the alien worlds created on Stage 10 with light rather than paint. More recently, for the dark-themed "Mirror, Mirror," he had been able to talk Marc Daniels, a former sitcom director conditioned to standard TV lighting, both bright and flat, to let him go deep into the darker hues. One of *Star Trek*'s best episodes then became one of its most visually striking. Now, with another dark-themed storyline and Ralph Senensky in the director's chair, the levels were brought down even further and more dramatic tints were painted onto the walls of the Enterprise with lighting gels. Senensky loved Finnerman's daring, and encouraged him to "trick up" the lighting as far as NBC would allow, and perhaps a bit more. Notice the somber mood created by the low level lighting and use of shadows in Kirk's quarters, then the array of varied colors splashed on the walls of the ship's corridors -- blues, reds, greens, and magentas. Note the contrasts between the coloring used for the interior of sickbay, the transporter room, and the briefing room compared to that in the hallways, as doors slide open and we see from one area into the next. The grey/blue walls of the past were few and far between. The Enterprise was staying true to the promise that opened every episode -- that the following show was being brought to us in living color ... on NBC ... even if the network was a reluctant participant with all the experimentation. For 1967, color TV had never looked so good.

Despite all its obstacles, "Obsession" was obsessively finished on schedule and within budget.

Available for editing: October 17, 1967. Rough Cut: October 26, 1967.
Final Cut: October 31.
Music Score: tracked.

Fabien Tordjmann was in charge of the editing. He and his assistant had been responsible for the editing of "Charlie X," "Miri," "Shore Leave," and "Arena," among others. No scenes were "flipped" (as Tordjmann often did, for example, in "The Enemy Within") and the cuts seem quick and purposeful ... unlike the cuts, or lack of them, made in the script.

The Westheimer Company handled the visuals. Among the new optical effects: the cloud creature and phaser beams, transporter effects, the anti-matter explosion, and numerous matte shots (images put into the view screens). The opticals showing the Enterprise orbiting planet Argus X were recycled from another episode.

Composer Sol Kaplan received the music credit for this "tracked" score. Much of his score from "The Doomsday Machine" was used to good effect.

The total cost: $170,871. This equates to $1.2 million in 2013.

Release / Reaction
Only NBC air date: 12/15/67.

Steven H. Scheuer reviewed this episode for *TV Key Previews*. Among newspapers across America to carry Scheuer's syndicated column on December 15, 1967 was *The Charleston Gazette*, serving Charleston, West Virginia. Scheuer said:

> This is another imaginative space-age mystery, handled with suspense, intuition and emotion as Captain Kirk insists on defining and destroying a vaporous cloud-like substance which has already caused the death of a number of his crewmen, despite that he already has an urgent assignment to deliver perishable vaccine to a planet in need. The reaction of Mr. Spock and Dr. McCoy to their Captain's obsession with the deadly cloud, along with the discovery of the Captain's motive, adds up to a thoroughly absorbing adventure.

Judy Crosby also reviewed the episode on December 15, 1967, for her syndicated column, *TV SCOUT*. Among the papers running the review was *The Monessen Valley Independent*, in Monessen, Pennsylvania. Crosby wrote:

> "Obsession." This episode is one of the highlights [on television] tonight. Stephen Brooks stars in his first TV role since leaving his regular role on the FBI series, playing the son of Captain Kirk's first Captain. His father was killed by a strange cloud-like creature, which also killed the entire crew of that Captain's starship -- except for Kirk. When the cloud creature shows itself again, 18 [sic] years later, Kirk becomes obsessed with the killer creature, which lives on red corpuscles and now threatens all of the lives aboard the Enterprise -- except for Mr. Spock, whose blood is green.

The positive reviews helped "Obsession" when it came time for A.C. Nielsen to do its national TV audience nose-count, especially in its second half-hour.

8:30 to 9 pm, 58.0% U.S. TVs in use.	**Share:**	**Households watching:**
NBC: *Star Trek*	28.0%	12,260,000
ABC: *Hondo*	24.3%	10,420,000
CBS: ***Gomer Pyle, U.S.M.C.***	**39.5%**	**13,940,000**
Independent stations:	8.2%	No data

9 to 9:30 pm, 58.6% U.S. TVs in use.	**Share:**	**Households watching:**
NBC: *Star Trek*	29.4%	No data
ABC: *Hondo*	25.9%	No data
CBS: ***Friday Night Movie***	**30.9%**	**No data**
Independent stations:	13.8%	No data

Star Trek was a strong second place for the entire hour, according to A.C. Nielsen's survey. The movie on CBS was the television premiere of the 1963 drama *Wall of Noise*, starring Ty Hardin and Suzanne Pleshette.

This was one of five second season episodes to be passed over for a network repeat.

Memories

Ralph Senensky said, "I liked that one. And, despite the fact that we had the tighter schedule, that one wasn't as harassing as the others had been because it was all on the soundstage. And there were just nice intimate scenes to play. And the fact that Steve Brooks was in it -- who I'd already directed in *The F.B.I.* and *The Nurses*. I asked for him in that. He was a delight. He was really a lovely, sensitive person. He was a very, very good actor, and if you really look at his scenes, he's not just saying lines -- his reactions and his line readings are really very, very nice." (155-6)

26

Episode 47: THE GAMESTERS OF TRISKELION
(47th episode filmed, listed in previous sources as Prod. #46)
Written by Margaret Armen
(with John Meredyth Lucas, uncredited)
Directed by Gene Nelson

William Shatner and Angelique Pettyjohn in NBC publicity photo (Courtesy of Gerald Gurian)

From NBC press release, issued December 12, 1967:

Captain Kirk (William Shatner), Lt. Uhura (Nichelle Nichols) and Ensign Chekov (Walter Koenig) vanish during the transporting process and find themselves prisoners of highly developed masses of brains without bodies, in "Gamesters of Triskelion" on NBC Television Network's *Star Trek* colorcast Friday, Jan. 5…. Joseph Ruskin and Angelique Pettyjohn guest star…. The three are forced down on a planet of slaves called Thralls, who exist solely for the benefit of the brain masses, called 'Providers,' whose only diversion is to watch and gamble on combat to the death among humans. Galt (Ruskin), the master Thrall, assigns drill Thralls to train the three officers for combat. Shanna [sic] (Miss Pettyjohn) is assigned to Kirk and falls in love with him. …

Kirk then challenges the Providers to a daring wager.

Spock, left in command of the Enterprise and, believing that the Landing Party was caught in a long-range transporter beam from an unexplored section of space, takes a calculated risk when he decides to send the ship halfway across the galaxy on a rescue mission.

The theme focuses on man's nature to resist any form of confinement. Even the Providers are prisoners of their own questionable evolution, demonstrating what too much time and too little mobility does to one's spirit and morality. Couch potatoes, take note.

SOUND BITES

- *Spock:* "We shall continue sensor scans. At the moment that is all we can do, except hope for some rational explanation." *McCoy:* "Hope? -- I always thought that was a human

429

failing, Mr. Spock." *Spock:* "True, doctor. Constant exposure does result in a certain degree of contamination."

- *McCoy:* "You're going to leave here without them and run off on some wild goose chase halfway across the galaxy just because you found a discrepancy in a hydrogen cloud?!" *Spock:* "Doctor, I am chasing Captain Kirk, Lieutenant Uhura, and Ensign Chekov, not some wild aquatic fowl."

- *Provider #3:* "Through eons of devoting ourselves exclusively to intellectual pursuits, we became the physically simple, mentally superior creatures you see before you." *Kirk:* "A species that enslaves other beings is hardly superior, mentally or otherwise."

- *Shahna:* "Goodbye, Jim Kirk. I will learn, and watch the lights in the sky … and remember."

ASSESSMENT

"The Gamesters of Triskelion," an imaginative and iconic science fiction tale, is fast-paced and entertaining. It is justifiably popular among fans of the series. *Entertainment Weekly*, which ranked "Gamesters" as the fourteenth best episode of the original *Star Trek*, said: "*American Gladiators* in outer space. Three brain creatures living in what looks like a big dairy case force Kirk to battle assorted opponents armed only with an enormous can opener. What's not to love?"

There is a certain degree of campiness, of course: the disembodied brains under glass and Kirk's drill-Thrall dressed in an aluminum foil Go-Go dancer outfit certainly register on the camp meter. And we've seen some of the story beats before: McCoy challenging Spock's decisions the moment the latter assumes command ("The Galileo Seven"); Kirk being punished with pain ("Charlie X"); an alien attack sending Kirk and others into a choking fit ("Metamorphosis"); and the bridge crew invited to watch the televised event of Kirk's life or death battle ("Arena"). Also, the theme, as well as the plot point of human captives kept to amuse an advanced but morally depraved race, had been explored in "The Cage."

Recycled or not, most of it works and the story ends with a stirring message of freedom.

THE STORY BEHIND THE STORY

Script Timeline
Margaret Armen's outline ST #56, "The Gamesters of Pentathlon":
April 10, 1967.
Armen's revised story outline, gratis: May 5, 1967.
Armen's 2ⁿᵈ revised story outline, gratis: May 8, 1967.
Gene Coon's revised story outline: May 12, 1967.
Armen's 1ˢᵗ Draft teleplay: June 20, 1967.
Armen's 2ⁿᵈ Draft teleplay: June 28, 1967.
Armen's script polish, gratis (Mimeo Department "Yellow Cover 1ˢᵗ Draft"):
August 1, 1967.
Armen's script polish, gratis (Final Draft teleplay): August 16, 1967.
John Meredyth Lucas's rewrite (Revised Final Draft teleplay): Sept. 28, 1967
John Meredyth Lucas's script polish (2ⁿᵈ Rev. Final Draft teleplay):
Early October 1967.
John Meredyth Lucas's staff script changes (3ʳᵈ Rev. Final Draft teleplay):
Early October 1967.

John Meredyth Lucas's further script changes (4ᵗʰ Revised Final Draft teleplay),
now "The Gamesters of Triskelion": October 13, 1967.
Additional page revisions by Lucas: October 16 & 17, 1967.

Writer Margaret Armen was the daughter of a naval officer and spent most of her childhood in Manila, Panama, Japan, and China, where she learned to speak the Mandarin language. She majored in English literature at the University of California at Berkeley, and then furthered her education at UCLA, receiving a bachelor's degree in creative writing. She married in 1945 at age 22 and started a family. While raising children, Armen worked from home, writing newspaper articles, having numerous short stories published and, finally, breaking into TV.

Armen began her career in television the same year as Dorothy Fontana, and in the same genre -- TV westerns. Armen's first script assignment was in 1959 for *Zane Grey Theater*. She also placed a script with *The Tall Men*, where Fontana worked. More westerns followed: *The Lawman*, *National Velvet*, *The Rifleman,* and *The Big Valley*. By age 45, Armen was eager to leave the westerns behind for outer space. *Star Trek*, at first, wasn't receptive.

Armen said, "There was a great deal of discrimination against women at that time, and there were only a handful of us making a living at writing for TV. During the first season, Gene Roddenberry didn't employ any women writers except for his secretary, D.C. Fontana. She wrote a script that was so good that Gene became receptive to women." (5-1)

Armen's agent had approached *Star Trek* numerous times on behalf of his client before finally getting a response in March, 1967. The order for the second season had just come through. Roddenberry took Armen's pitch while Gene Coon vacationed.

Armen had the storyline of "Gamesters of Pentathlon," as it was then called, in mind for a long while. It was originally planned as a science fiction short story about a planet where people were used as gaming animals. When *Star Trek* aired, she rethought the concept, believing it might make a good fit for the new series.

"*Star Trek* seemed the perfect vehicle," Armen said. "When I went in to Gene with it, the idea was very roughly developed, since I had never written for *Star Trek* before. But Gene saw its potential and talked it through with me until it was tailored to the *Star Trek* format." (5-1)

On April 1, 1967, Roddenberry wrote to Coon:

Margaret came in and surprised me with a truly exciting premise. And we've had a second meeting on it, clarified much of her thinking as to *Star Trek* format. She seems eager and seems to have an affinity for our type of story. (GR47-1)

Armen said, "I was so pleased when I found that I had so much rapport with Gene Roddenberry.... He's a real writer's writer. If you come in there with an idea that's a little rough, Gene can see it through a writer's eye and envision what it will become and whether or not it will work. He's marvelous that way." (5-1)

Armen turned in her story outline on April 10. Dorothy Fontana, liking both Armen and her work, wrote to Coon with one primary concern, regarding utilizing the Thralls as breeding stock. She said:

The Interfusion Interval, while nicely presented, will probably flip out NBC Broadcast Standards, if they are clever enough to realize what an Interfusion Interval is. Can we avoid the rather obvious couch and Shana lying down on it? (DCF47-1)

431

In the story, Kirk, Uhura, and Sulu are pulled off course in the shuttlecraft and forced to land on the unchartered planet Pentathlon, where they are captured and trained for combative games. During the "Interfusion Interval," Kirk is paired up with Shana (as the name was spelled at this point), "a tall beautiful Amazon," Uhura with Blail, "a gleaming Nubian," and Sulu with Taky, "a squat, furry, greenish female." Other Thralls include Lars, "a gigantic Viking," and Kloog, "a lumbering Neanderthal." The Master Thrall is Galt, who reports directly to the rulers, known as Cogitants and described as "pulsating amoeba-like creatures about the size of large jellyfish, in transparent boxes, floating in a colored fluid."

Robert Justman took note of the interfusion interval, as well, writing to Coon on April 14:

> Hopefully, we will be able to prevent Gene Roddenberry from reading about the "interfusion interval." I shudder to think what terrible ideas this quaint custom is liable to engender in his twisted and warped mind. Also, come to think of it, you'd better not let NBC hear about this either. (RJ46-1)

Overall, Justman liked Armen's story, telling Coon:

> This is a very engrossing idea and very exciting with regard to many of its sequences.... No doubt NBC will be thrilled with the effort.... However, I should caution you that I find some of the ideas contained within this story totally illogical. And I mean it! (RJ46-1)

The list of totally illogical ideas, as well as production and cost concerns, seemed endless. After all, this was a memo from Robert Justman. He continued:

> Let's not have the Nubian have pale blue eyes. He can have pale blue hair if you wish, but please -- no pale blue eyes!... Just because Blail is a Nubian, that is no reason to assign him to Uhura. Let's assign Blail to Sulu and a Greenie to Uhura [requiring a sex change for both Thralls].... Let's be careful about the number of male and female Thralls that we have screwing around and fighting and doing various things in this show. Humanoids are usually played by actors or extras and they cost a lot of money to hire and to dress and to make up. And plenty dollars is not what we have.... The life and death struggle as reputed on Page 8 and 9 between the various contestants are liable to get extremely bloody and make the Network and our viewers unhappy somehow. When you "cut a man to pieces with swords," a lot of blood tends to get spattered around and pieces of arms and limbs and other portions of the anatomy tend to go flying all over the place.... On Page 17, we establish the fact that these huge brains "enjoy physical activities through their Thralls -- on an intellectual basis." Man, if Thralls fighting Thralls is an intellectual basis of enjoyment, what would a non-intellectual basis for enjoyment be? If these "Cogitants" [Providers] are as intelligent as they claim to be, certainly they could come up with some other forms of diversions. (RJ47-1)

Armen revised her outline on May 5. The outcome was very different than the filmed version as there was no conflict on the Enterprise between Spock and McCoy and Scott. The scenes on the ship were, by and large, uneventful. All three characters were in agreement concerning how to search for their captain and the two missing officers. Halfway through the story, they find the missing shuttlecraft adrift in space. There is no explanation why the Cogitants sent it back into space or even how they accomplished this.

Fontana wrote Coon:

> Margaret has trimmed this story down considerably, and tightened it.... I believe Margaret can give us a good script with nice characterizations in it. But I also

believe we -- if the outline is an indication -- will not have enough action in it and/or enough Spock/ship material.... We find the shuttlecraft abandoned in space. We find later, in a reference, that the mental powers of the Providers put the shuttlecraft there, after it landed on the planet with Kirk, Sulu, and Uhura. Very well and good, but why? (DCF47-2)

Coon had Armen revise her outline again, *gratis*, this one dated May 8. As with the previous two drafts, the character of Galt was underused and the Providers did most of their own talking, from very nearly the outset. Of this, Roddenberry wrote Coon:

Seems to me we give away too early the fact that athletic competition is the primary diversion of the Providers. And, incidentally, we should develop in greater detail later why these rulers of the planet need diversion. The best answer that suggests itself is that, since they have lost their power of physical locomotion, since they have "evolved" too far down a blind alley, they now just provide themselves action and adventure in a vicarious way. In other words, they have "improved" their species past a point of no return, discovered too late that brains and intellectual power is not enough, that life needs movement and challenge. Having gone too far to turn back, they had to find action and excitement through other species. Just as, in today's world, many of our males find themselves prisoners of marriage, children, mortgage payments, and so on, [and] find their action and adventure vicariously through the Saturday afternoon sports programs on television. Really, the two situations are quite similar. (GR47-2)

Roddenberry's notes continued for an additional four pages, with him saying, among other things:

Suggest we look for a way to bring the shuttlecraft to this planet without getting involved in the "unknown force field," mental or otherwise. Far too many of our scripts begin this way ["Metamorphosis," along with a couple unproduced efforts]. Also, let's analyze carefully whether we want to begin this script with the shuttlecraft. Landing it always poses a problem for us.... Doubt if NBC will allow us to show brands burned into the center of the foreheads.... Like very much the fact that it is the Amazon woman who goes after Kirk to capture him. But if this is our direction, let's make the most of it -- let's not have her simply threaten him with a sword. Let's have it a man-versus-woman battle. And let's have Kirk surprised and frustrated as she whips him.... Doubt if Kellam de Forest will allow us to have "vapor trails" in space. But no doubt we can find something to take its place.... I certainly cannot believe Kirk being convinced this easily that their "only chance for escape" lies in arousing the Thralls into rebellion. That's a pretty long stretch of logic, considering he has seen precious few signs of incipient rebellion around here....
There is no reason we cannot let the "Rulers" decide that the whole thing can be decided on a contest of champions -- Kirk against Shana. And considering the fact that Kirk pulled a pretty rotten trick on her earlier, that is [he] had her drop her guard while he was feeling her up and then clubbed her from behind, she'd be pretty mad at him by now and the contest might be quite exciting. (GR47-2)

The idea of pitting Kirk against Shana (whose name was later changed to Shahna) in the climax of the story would be added. But, regarding that "pretty rotten trick," Roddenberry elaborated:

I don't really understand the sex bit between Kirk and Shana. She doesn't know what sex is? Or, more likely, she knows nothing of tender treatment between male and female.... It's going to be a little difficult to like Kirk when he "knocks her out deftly." Maybe it will work, but we'll have to be convinced it is quite necessary, since they have begun to have a quite friendly relationship just before this happens. Not that girls don't like to be knocked around a bit. My friends tell me they rather enjoy it. Is this true, Gene? Or am I being lied to by my friends? One finds so few persons one can trust nowadays. (GR47-2)

Roddenberry liked Margaret Armen, both as a writer and a person, and told Coon:

Despite the problems in Margaret Armen's revised outline, the story has qualities lacking in many we have received -- action, excitement, mounting climaxes, plus pretty sf [science fiction] basis. I would strongly recommend we find a way to get her into script as soon as possible. (GR47-2)

Roddenberry knew the only way to get Armen into script was with NBC's blessing. He therefore told Coon:

Perhaps this is one of those cases in which the best answer is for our Production Office to revise the outline, as we did in the case of Bixby. (GR47-2)

Roddenberry had been the one to revise Jerome Bixby's story outline of "Mirror, Mirror" to NBC's liking. He felt it was now Gene Coon's turn. Coon, overwhelmed with other work, instead chose to send the outline to Stan Robertson, unchanged. Contrary to Robert Justman's prediction, Stan Robertson was not "thrilled with the effort."

Robertson felt there were too many similarities between "The Gamesters of Triskelion" and "Bread and Circuses," with both stories depicting the Enterprise people being forced into gladiatorial combat. He agreed to approve the story only on the condition that Coon would revise the outline himself and distance "Gamesters" from "Circuses."

Gene Coon ran the outline through his typewriter -- now a 3rd Revised Draft -- on May 12. Bob Justman was thrilled and wrote to Coon, "Why don't you and Gene Roddenberry and D.C. Fontana write all our stories and scripts?" He continued:

I suggest that instead of a "squat, broad, immensely muscular black man," we have a "blue man" emerge to punish Uhura. I think that we can safely assume that by the time we reach *Star Trek*'s century, all "separate but equal" routines will have disappeared from the memory of men. I happened to tune in to *The Dating Game* the other day and I was horrified to see the game being played by a young Negro man and the three girls he was being tempted with were also Negroes.... No doubt, the producers and the network felt very proud of themselves, but I must be perfectly honest with you and state that I was disgusted, repulsed and angered by the antediluvian thinking that must have gone into the creation of this particular *Dating Game* presentation. That's really what I call "separate but equal." After seeing something like that, I'm kind of glad that we're on NBC after all. (RJ47-2)

NBC was the leader at this time in depicting minorities in non-stereotypical ways. On the network for this 1967-68 season, besides *Star Trek*, with TV's first interracial ensemble cast, was *I Spy*, now in its third season, and featuring the first instance on American TV of a white actor and a black actor (Robert Culp and Bill Cosby) billed equally as that series' dual leads.

Roddenberry had feedback to give, as well. Surprisingly, it was he, not Coon, who suggested adding humor to the story. Roddenberry told Coon:

We might also get some humor in this piece. For example -- Sulu has been assigned a "hairy anthropoid female" creature. Might be amusing to follow Sulu's problem here as the rulers of the planet decide he is best mated with this particular biped animal. (GR47-2)

Armen turned in her first draft script on June 20. Robert Justman was not impressed.

He told Gene Coon:

> I find this teleplay very dull. I find this teleplay very long. I find this teleplay very reminiscent of other teleplays we have done. I find we have too large a cast, too many extras, too much intricate makeup and wardrobe, and too many sets. I also find an inordinate amount of story holes. (RJ47-3)

Like Roddenberry, one area Justman found reminiscent of past episodes was the Teaser, where Kirk, Sulu, and Uhura travel in the shuttlecraft and are forced to land on a strange world. Of this, he wrote:

> We have done this Teaser before in "The Galileo Seven" and "Metamorphosis." Why do we have to have the shuttlecraft landing with our principals on the surface of a strange planet? Why is our shuttlecraft always getting banged around in some sort of space storm? Why does our shuttlecraft always have to force land on an unknown planet? Why can't we find another reason for our trio to be down on the surface of this planet? (RJ47-3)

It wasn't so much about a "reason" but in finding a *way* to get them there. The only other means Coon could think of was to have Kirk, Uhura, and Sulu simply vanish from the Enterprise and then appear on the planet Pentathlon. This popping in and popping out device had worked before, in "The Squire of Gothos," "Arena," and "Catspaw." But wouldn't using that for a fourth time be more redundant than doing the shuttlecraft-is-forced-to-land bit for a third time? Coon decided to leave the Teaser as it was.

Justman's negative memo to Coon continued. He sarcastically said:

> I am pleased to note on Page 72 that Captain Kirk finally prevails because he is a good kisser. Physical prowess, intellect, will-power -- all these are of no avail when compared with the strength of Captain Kirk's bee-stung lips. With lips such as his, one could win the universe. And lose a series. (RJ47-3)

This note too was ignored. Most TV writers will agree on one thing -- sex sells. The kiss remained.

Fontana was less critical when she read the first draft teleplay, and told Coon:

> This script seems in fairly good shape, but there is a great deal of cutting and trimming that should be done, as well as losing characters and sets.... Chekov's dialogue [on the bridge] is much too slangy and American. Margaret should be informed he plays the role with a Russian accent and usually has more formal lines of dialogue.... Act 1 is quite talky with very little action on the part of our leading characters. I wonder if it would serve us better to eliminate the man being "punished" in the gym, and instead to have Kirk, Sulu, and Uhura make one more desperate attempt at fight and escape. I don't like the idea of their just being shoved into their little cell-like rooms, knowing they are captives, with no protest at all. I suggest Kirk would try at least one physical protest [and] would try to escape. Of course it would be useless.... The story ends rather abruptly. Rather than the brain scene at the end, it might be better to have one more scene on the planet surface -- perhaps in the gym [arena] or perhaps somewhere outside -- between Kirk and Shana. It would end when Kirk and the others beam up to the ship. Or, better yet, the others could have already beamed up and Kirk has lingered behind for a moment to say goodbye to Shana. (DCF47-3)

Fontana's instincts, as usual, were spot on. Many of her ideas were inserted into the screenplay, either in the immediate draft to come or one to follow. The man being punished in the story, however, would stay, although rewritten to involve direct action with the Enterprise people.

Coon had Armen do a second draft teleplay, which arrived on June 28. More changes were needed and Coon delegated the job to Fontana of sending further notes to Armen. D.C.'s July 3rd letter to Armen began:

> We are quite pleased with the first draft [sic], but we do feel some restructuring and polish will be necessary in your revision.... This memo will be thick and specific. Please do not panic. We find such detailing is of great help to first time writers on the show.

The letter was 10 single-spaced pages long. Armen did not panic; she merely got back to writing. Years later, Fontana said, "Maggie always did a good job. She was a good solid writer and she loved this kind of stuff." (64-2)

Armen turned in a Revised 2nd Draft, *gratis*, on July 31, which was sent off to the Mimeo Department and designated as the Yellow Cover 1st Draft [from August 1].

Bob Justman wrote to Coon on August 3, fretting over the costs of filming an episode from the current script, and the impossibility of getting it all done in only six days. One area where he felt money could be saved was by eliminating the shuttlecraft, something he and Roddenberry continued to lobby against. He had other concerns. As his late night session with a Dictaphone continued, Justman told Coon:

> With respect to Shana... I am a little concerned about getting someone who can look the part and who can also "act" the part.... We are now up to the big fight in Act IV. I do not deny the fact that it is quite an interesting idea. It is liable to take another six days to stage and shoot. How would you like to have Captain Kirk volunteer to be the solitary champion? And he would be opposed to a number of Drill Thralls, which he would have to fight one at a time. (RJ47-4)

It was a change Justman had requested before. With the next draft, he would finally get his way, but it would still be a difficult and time-consuming scene to shoot.

Fontana told Coon:

> Margaret followed our suggestions closely, and in general did a nice job. [But] I find the script overlong.... Bob may have something in his suggestions to make it Kirk as a single champion, making a desperate bid to save his people.... Suggest Kirk maneuvers the Cogitants into the wager, then finds that they have choice of who will fight -- and though it's not exactly fair -- they choose to load the odds by having Kirk fight five men -- and a woman -- by himself. (DCF46-5)

Coon liked this idea, too. Armen was asked to do a fourth draft, *gratis*, now designated as the Final Draft, dated August 16. And then, after all the hard work, the script was put aside. It would not be included in NBC's initial second season order of 16 episodes.

By mid September, Gene Coon had stepped away from his production chores, handing them off to John Meredyth Lucas. With NBC's interim order for two episodes, Lucas picked "Gamesters" and "Obsession" as the best candidates. Armen's August 16 Final Draft was sent to the staff for comment. Justman wrote to Lucas on September 21, saying, "For the most part, I think Margaret Armen has done a pretty good job on her polish." "Pretty good" meant Lucas only received four pages of critical notes from Justman. Included were:

> Kirk and Shana are in an open field and running along, whilst in training. I find it difficult to buy the fact that the Cogitants or Providers, as the case may be, have decided that Kirk no longer needs any Guards. I know that it is nice to get outside and get some scope to our show. But we are going to have to do something to make me believe the sequence as presently constructed.

The solution, in time, would be the "collars of obedience." No guards were necessary once it was established that the Providers could see Kirk wherever he might be, and zap him with pain should he try to get away.

In this potentially costly scene, Armen described how a slithering vine, which she called a Delka Vine, ensnarled Shana and dragged the Amazon Drill Thrall toward a swamp, and how Kirk had to fight the tentacle vines to free her.

Justman commented:

Delka Vines are notoriously stubborn and refuse to obey commands! I have seldom seen one willingly wind itself into a noose around a pretty girl's neck. Delka Vines usually force the director and his crew to shoot a sequence in a number of Cuts. What would ordinarily take a few hours to stage with a stunt man, will take three or four times as long with a Delka Vine. Therefore, perhaps we might be able to come up with some sort of other kind of creature for Captain Kirk to fight. (RJ47-5)

In the next rewrite, that other creature would be Galt, who would appear out of thin air and confront Kirk.

Remarkably, after four drafts of a story outline (one by Coon) and four drafts of the script, the story structure and dialogue in "The Gamesters of Pentathlon" was light-years away from what would eventually be seen on the screen. Besides the collars of obedience not yet being in the story, many other elements to be seen in the filmed version were still missing, including Galt's glowing eyes and his ability to pop in and out of scenes, Shana's silver/green hair, Chekov in place of Sulu, and the conflict on the Enterprise between McCoy and Scott against Spock over the best course of action to locate Kirk and the missing officers. At least a quarter of the story structure and more than half of the dialogue in the script would still be changed.

John Meredyth Lucas was next to work on the script. His first pass -- the Revised Final Draft -- came on September 28.

This version still opened with Kirk and two crewmembers in the shuttlecraft. Uhura was one, but the other was now Chekov instead of Sulu. George Takei was trapped in his role in *The Green Berets*.

John Wayne with George Takei in *The Green Berets* ... the reason for Takei missing this plum role for Sulu (Warner Bros., 1968)

Takei later said, "There was this one particular script ... 'The Gamesters of Triskelion,' and I wanted to do it very much. Roddenberry had showed it to me before I took off for Columbus, Georgia. Well, we had some rain and that delayed the shooting of the picture and they had to change the schedule... [I]t was frustrating because I wanted to come back and do that show.... As it turned out, they rewrote it for Walter. Ensign Chekov got all of Mr. Sulu's lines. I've got to admit, though, that despite my disappointment, I was pleased that Walter was able to do it." (171-5)

Roddenberry checked in a few days after receiving the rewrite from Lucas, telling his new producer, "Dear John, a good rewrite." His memo continued:

> SHANA. Since we want a great deal of variety in our biped types found on this planet, and since Shana is a lead and we'll pay her a fair sum of money, can we use this to talk the actress into going metallic silver with her hair... so at least she is not an exact and complete Earth humanoid but still remains beautiful?...
> THRALL DISCIPLINE. Recommend we need a device, a pain implement of some sort, to be used by Galt in keeping all Thralls, including our Enterprise people, in check.... What if Galt had some sort of an "agonizer," a S.F. [sci-fi] device given him by the real rulers of the planet? All he has to do is point it at someone and press a button and the sheer pain force of it almost knocks them off their feet.... Could there be an actual physical device placed on their foreheads which this "agonize" activates?... I would certainly believe Kirk being allowed to take a run with Shana if he had this type of control exercised over him. And it would eliminate Kloog [the name for the huge Thrall] having to watch them, which is a primitive form of discipline considering the great power of the "Providers."... GENERAL. First of all, it does appear you have brought this down somewhere near a six day show. Before getting into any rewrites or polish for the above, we should meet with [Unit Production Manager] Gregg Peters and see where we are on time and budget from his point of view. (GR47-3)

All of Roddenberry's suggestions would be implemented as Lucas took charge of a 2nd and then a 3rd Revised Final Draft, both from early October. The shuttlecraft was finally removed and the much simpler, and quicker, long-distance transporter gimmick was utilized. The conflict on the Enterprise, with McCoy and Scott challenging Spock, was also finally added. And the title was changed from "The Gamesters of Pentathlon" to "The Gamesters of Triskelion."

With the new title, and a shorter script, "Gamesters" was on its way to production, planned as the first of two interim episodes ordered by NBC, to be followed by "Obsession." The price tag, however, remained a grave concern.

Another colorful memo from Robert Justman read:

> This script is quite expensive in its present state and we are going to have to do something about it. There will no doubt be a lot of screaming and crying and agonizing -- but we are going to have to do it ... without sacrificing any of the excitement, if possible. (RJ47-5)

Lucas sat down and created a 4th Revised Final Draft on October 13, scaling back some of the action called for on the planet where more actors and grander sets were required. In its place, more scenes on the bridge with McCoy and Scott continuing to badger Spock over his decision to take the Enterprise in search of the missing crew members. The dialogue in these new scenes is redundant. Lucas had a tendency to dilute the spoken lines he'd write with too much unneeded chatter, and too many repetitive "beats," and that tendency is taken to extremes here. But a day of shooting on the bridge was certainly cheaper than a day or more spent on various sets with numerous actors in wild makeup on Stage 10. And time had run out to sharpen the material further. Lucas quickly dashed off two sets of page revisions, addressing more notes from NBC Standards and Practices (AKA Broadcast Standards), on October 16 and 17, just one day before filming would commence.

Pre-Production
October 9-13 & 16, 1967 (6 days prep).

**Gene Nelson – actor and dancer turned director
(richwah.blogspot.com)**

"Obsession" was pulled forward and filmed first, allowing an extra week to try to bring expenses for "Gamesters" under control. Regardless of the delay, the challenging episode was still a rush job.

According to Gene Nelson, he was contacted when the director originally hired to handle "Gamesters" dropped out at the last minute. Production records do not give indication as to who the dropout was. Nelson, a former dancer, and director of movies featuring complex dancing sequences, was chosen because he could contribute to the choreography of the elaborate fight scenes ... and he was available on short notice.

Nelson, 47, beginning his show business career as a song and dance man, and won the Golden Globe award as Best Newcomer in 1950, for *Tea For Two*. Five years later, he played Will Parker, the rope trick cowboy in *Oklahoma!* By the early 1960s, Nelson turned to directing, handling numerous episodes of *The Rifleman, The Farmer's Daughter*, and *I Dream of Jeannie*. He also directed two Elvis Presley movies – 1963's *Kissin' Cousins* and 1965's *Harum Scarum*.

**Joseph Ruskin in a 1965 episode of *The Wild, Wild West*
(www.aveleyman.com)**

"The regular cast did all these shows before I came in, so their characters were set," Nelson said. "I thought, 'I can't change them; the only thing I can change is a reaction to something they've never done on the show before.' They would react in character, but differently than any other situation. I had more freedom with the villains." (124)

Those villains had to be booked quickly. For the important role of Galt, the Master Drill Thrall, Nelson wanted Joe Ruskin.

Ruskin was 43. He had often appeared as bad guy gangsters on *The Untouchables*; bad guy cowboys on *Gunsmoke* and *The Wild, Wild West*; bad guy spies on *The Man From U.N.C.L.E.* and *Get Smart*; and

439

bad guy Nazis on *Hogan's Heroes*. He also played a bad guy genie in *The Twilight Zone* episode "The Man in the Bottle."

Nelson said, "Joe's a good actor and an old friend of mine. My inspiration for him was Ming the Merciless from the old Buster Crabbe *Flash Gordon* serials. You'll notice when you watch the episode that you never see his feet; it's almost like he's floating. He does everything slowly, like when he electro-shocks them -- he did that just by shutting his eyes. I told him, 'Less is more.'" (124)

Ruskin remembered it as *his* idea to move less and float rather than walk. He said, "I had a gown that went from the shoulders all the way to the floor, and I had just seen the Moiseyev Dancers -- Russian folk dancers who came over -- and they had a dance in which they had robes all the way to the floor and they looked like they were on wheels ... until they opened the robes and [you saw that] they were not. And it was fascinating." (149)

For the part of Shahna, it was felt a dancer could best handle the demands of the fight scenes. Angelique Pettyjohn, when cast for this role, was 24. She had worked as an exotic dancer and made her screen debut with a low-budget sexploitation film *The Love Rebellion*. One year prior to *Star Trek*, she appeared with Elvis Presley in *Clambake*. At this time, in 1967, Pettyjohn had a recurring role in *Get Smart* as Charlie Watkins, a man disguised as a buxom blonde.

Angelique Pettyjohn in NBC publicity photo (Courtesy of Gerald Gurian)

Pettyjohn liked *Star Trek* and was excited to be called in for an audition, but had concerns about the role. She said, "I was sitting in the outer office reading the character description which said, 'A green-haired, green-eyed Amazon leaps from behind a rock, pinning [Kirk] with a spear.' ... When I went in for the interview, the first thing I said was, 'Gentlemen, before I waste my time and yours, I really don't feel I fit the description of this character... I've got the green eyes and I'm sure you can fix me up with green hair, but I'm hardly an Amazon, I'm only five foot six.' They laughed and they said, 'Look, honey, next to Shatner, you'll look like an Amazon. Go ahead and read the script.'" (140)

After auditioning, Pettyjohn was asked to pull the hair away from her forehead for a minute. She was reluctant, feeling she had a high forehead in need of bangs. But she complied and, despite her reservations, the producers liked her striking look. She was hired on the spot.

Bart LaRue, the voice of the Guardian of Forever in "The City on the Edge of Forever" and the ringside announcer in "Bread and Circuses," returned to speak for Provider #1.

Walker Edmiston provided the piercing voice of Provider #2. The kid's show host in Los Angeles had been the voice of little Balok from "The Corbomite Maneuver" and The

Keeper from "The Menagerie."

Robert Johnson, the voice of Provider #3, spoke for one of the Talosians in "The Cage" and was the voice on the self-destructing tape that gave Jim Phelps his assignments each week on *Mission: Impossible*.

Steve Sandor, Mickey Morton, and Walter Koenig, waiting for a call for "Action!"
(Unaired film trim courtesy of Gerald Gurian)

Dick Crockett, the stuntman who guided the other actors through the various fight sequences, also appeared as the Andorian Thrall. He was 52.

Steve Sandor played Lars, the Drill Thrall assigned to Uhura. He was 30 and appeared often on television between 1967 and 1998.

Mickey Morton played Kloog. The 6'7" actor was 40. He worked often in television whenever a brute or a giant was needed. From this era, he appeared on *Gilligan's Island*, *The Monkees*, *The Man from U.N.C.L.E.*, and *I Dream of Jeannie*.

Last but not least:

Jane Ross, delightful as Tamoon, the instructor Thrall smitten by Chekov, was 35, and a TV bit part player.

As for the regular supporting players:

This was Uhura's third turn as part of a landing party and she was given one of her better roles in the series.

Walter Koenig, also with an excellent role, benefitted from George Takei's

Walter Koenig and Jane Ross (as Tamoon)
(CBS Studios, Inc.)

detainment on *The Green Berets*. The writing staff was happy to make the change. Koenig told this author, "I was reading in volume one of your book that Nichelle had all this fan mail that she said she wasn't receiving. Well that happened to me! I had this enormous volume of mail filled with huge packages of things, and sack after sack of letters. And I only got them because I went to where they were [sorted]. They were not kept at the studio. They were handled by a service. Thousands and thousands of letters! Most of them were one page and were written on lined paper, so I was able to read them all. Of course, I only answered one in five hundred. Like one said, 'I am black and I hope that doesn't affect how you read this' -- something that moved me, because that person who wrote it brought up some very personal feelings. I didn't answer the ones that said I was 'groovy,' and they thought my hair was groovy." (102)

Production Diary
Filmed October 17, 18, 19, 20, 23, 24, 1967.
(6 day production; set budget: $179,844).

**Day 2: Filming of the Providers -- three brains under glass
(Unaired film trim courtesy of Gerald Gurian)**

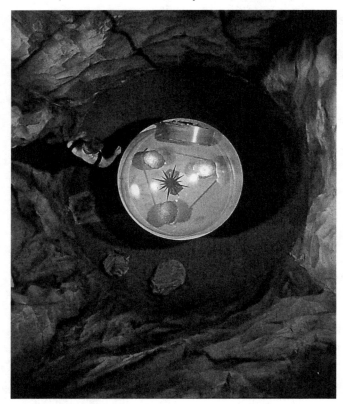

**Day 2. Camera shot taken from the rafters of the Paramount
Test Stage for a special circular, enclosed set
(Courtesy of Gerald Gurian)**

Tuesday, October 17. The rock musical *Hair* opened on Broadway. *Bonnie & Clyde* was still the biggest draw at the movie theaters. The majority of Americans spent the night before in front of their TVs, watching CBS with its Monday night block of hits: *Gunsmoke, The Lucy Show, The Andy Griffith Show*, and *Family Affair*, all in the A.C. Nielsen Top 10. At 10 p.m., the numbers were split between *The Carol Burnett Show* on CBS, *The Big Valley* on ABC, and *I Spy* on NBC. *Ode to Billy Joe* by Bobbie Gentry was still the best selling album in record stores, while U.S. radio stations had a new top song: "To Sir, With Love," by Lulu. And Johnny Carson had the cover of *TV Guide.*

And on this morning Day 1. *Star Trek* began filming "The Gamesters of Triskelion" at 8 a.m. on Desilu Stage 9. Scenes not requiring special sets were up first, on the Enterprise bridge and in the transporter room.

For Day 2, the company paid their first visit to the Paramount Test Stage, where the Provider's chambers had been built. Gene Nelson remembered, "When we were shooting that, we had designed a room like a tube. I had no way of getting a real wide shot of the room, except from overhead.... So, we climbed up the ladder onto the rigging to get the camera vise... While rear-lighting, Bill's stand-in was standing near it. The operator was getting the camera set and had to change the lens. Well, the camera was already set, so when he unscrewed the lens, it slipped out of his fingers... and hit the stand-in on the head! It knocked him out cold! We were sweating it for a little while, making sure he was O.K." (124)

Also filmed this day, the interior cell corridor scenes where Kirk, Uhura, and Chekov get a taste of the collars of obedience.

Nelson recalled, "We had a lot of fun with those collars. I said, 'People, as silly as they seem, we've got to take the collars completely seriously,' because you never saw where the shock was coming from. We also had to synchronize their reactions to the pain. We decided it should be immediate instead of gradually constricting, like in their aborted escape from the jail-house, where you think they're gonna make it until the collars stop them." (124)

This was the first day Angelique Pettyjohn was on set.

Gene Nelson said, "[Angelique Pettyjohn] was as sweet as could be. I thought she was quite good in the show... a delight.... The first time she came on the set in that costume, the crew nearly fell out of the rafters! She didn't wear a helluva lot!" (124)

Pettyjohn said, "I found Shatner to be friendly, gregarious, rather mischievous with a twinkling-eyed little smile, a really marvelous person around the set.... At first, when I came in, I was very much in awe of working with him... but he made me instantly feel very comfortable.... I thought Leonard Nimoy was marvelous, intelligent, quiet, and a very polite man. I respected him very much. I loved Nichelle Nichols. I thought she was just a doll. Walter Koenig was a really nice guy... very friendly, [but] rather quiet. He seemed to be a little on the shy side." (140)

Day 3: Filming on Paramount Test Stage for the jail cell sequences (Courtesy of Gerald Gurian)

Day 3. During the second day on the Paramount Test Stage, the scenes in Kirk's cell, Uhura's cell, and Chekov's cell were filmed. The final sequence involved Chekov and his designated mate, Tamoon.

Walter Koenig recalled, "The director was a former song and dance man who was ... just sort of tap dancing his way through this thing.... I had this big scene where this homely girl comes into the cell with me and says, 'Let me be your mate.' ... We had a very funny relationship set up, because Chekov didn't want to have anything to do with her. Because I was the junior member of the cast, my scenes were relegated to the end of the day, which is quite understandable ... but on this particular day we were pressed for time. So rather than covering me by shooting over her shoulder and covering *her* by shooting over *my* shoulder, the director only did it *one way* -- they shot it over my shoulder at her, which meant, if I were to look at her, all the audience would see would be the back of my head." (102-10)

443

Gene Nelson said, "They try desperately hard to shoot S.F. shows in the same amount of time they shoot an action-adventure.... Everybody's on edge because of the pressure. You had to make many sacrifices. I had many exciting things I planned to do, but you find that you can't and you must find another way to get it across." (124)

It was Koenig's idea to have Chekov avoid looking at the homely girl, allowing both performers to face camera. The scene worked beautifully.

Days 4, 5, and 6 were on Stage 10, where Matt Jefferies had designed the Exterior Gaming Arena. Nelson recalled, "Angelique was marvelous because she was very lithe and quick. She had enough dance training so that I could be a little more expansive with her.... Bill was very nice -- a very good actor and very energetic. He wasn't at all shy about

Day 3 (above): Filming continues on the Paramount Test Stage; Day 4 (below): The first of three on Stage 10 for the "Ext. Gaming Arena." Bill McGovern slates the arrival of Kirk, Chekov, and Uhura to the planet Triskelion (Courtesy of Gerald Gurian)

doing stunts. I remember that Bill and I talked about staging this fight, and he made it clear to me that he wanted to shoot it without a stuntman. That was fine with me; I prefer it that way, too.... As I recall, you see only one or two wide-angle shots with a difficult stunt like a real hard fall, for which I used a stuntman." (124)

For the big finale, Kirk is told he cannot step outside the triangles that match the color of his collar. Before the end of the fight, he does, yet nothing is made of it.

Defending the sloppiness, Gene Nelson said, "You get to the point where you have to build it to an ending. It just became a no-holds-barred kind of thing. Setting it up that way [with the colored sections] made it interesting but, after a while, you said, 'Screw it!'" (124)

Shatner's velour top had shrunk horribly by these final days, creeping up every time he did a stunt or took a fall. And the "midsection at mid-season" was showing through. Not knowing if there would be any more *Star Trek*s, it seemed an unnecessary expense to have a new shirt made.

It was during this time that an inside source at NBC leaked word that *Star Trek* would not receive a last minute pick-up for the balance of the season. "Gamesters" would be the last episode to film.

Bjo Trimble, a frequent visitor to the set, remembered, "The regular cast would go onto the set and do their stuff and look happy on the screen, but then, when the director called 'Cut,'

Day 4: Shatner and Koenig wait for a call to "Action!"
(Courtesy of Gerald Gurian)

they'd just look sad. And that was so unlike them, because, generally, there'd be a little banter, where they'd just joke or there'd be big smiles. So I was curious and said, 'What's going on here?' And no one would really tell us until we went over to catering. We're having a cup of coffee and I said, 'I wish I knew what was going on.' And the craft service person said, 'Oh, there's a rumor down from above that *Star Trek*'s going to be cancelled.' And we went, 'What?! Oh, my God!' And we knew, back in those days, that anything that didn't have at least three seasons was never going to be rerun." (177-8)

Angelique Pettyjohn remembered, "Three or four days after we started filming it, [John Meredyth Lucas] came in during lunch and made an announcement to the cast and crew. He was sorry to say the network had cancelled the series. Everyone was very depressed." (140)

Trimble said, "I can distinctly remember that Nichelle Nichols was so upset that, at one point, she was just sitting at her makeup mirror in tears. It was quite

Day 6: Nichelle Nichols, Steve Sandor (behind slate), Joseph Ruskin,
and unknown actor (Courtesy of Gerald Gurian)

depressing to watch people work. Actors earned their pay that day by really acting. They'd go in front of the cameras and be dramatic or comical and smile as if they meant it, then come off-camera with a sigh or a frown." (177-1)

445

Unaired film trim revealing Shatner preparing for an action sequence ... and the colored sections that director Nelson got sloppy with toward the end
(Courtesy of Gerald Gurian)

Pettyjohn added, "On my last day of shooting, I had a particular speech where I said, 'Good-bye, Jim Kirk, I will watch the lights in the sky and remember.' I had tears in my eyes and those tears were real because I was thinking that it was good-bye to *Star Trek*... I really cried, and that's how I meant it, because I knew that the series wasn't going to be shooting anymore." (140)

Within 48 hours of the dispiriting rumor, official word came from NBC -- the network had reversed its decision and was placing an order for eight more episodes.

Shatner said, "Obviously the hearsay ultimately proved to be untrue, but for a two-day period we all became convinced that *Star Trek* was a terminal case." (156-8)

After two-and-a-half days on the Gaming Area set, the cast was released, except for Shatner, Pettyjohn, and Ruskin. Still on Stage 10, the final scene took place among the ruins of the Provider's ancient city.

Ruskin said, "There was this scene with William Shatner and the girl [Shahna] where I would suddenly pop into view on a rock behind them. So, Shatner and the girl would freeze in position and the camera stopped rolling. As I stepped up onto the rock... the camera started rolling again and, in the final print, I would appear like magic on the rock. For those of us who hadn't done these kinds of special FX before, it was very exciting." (148-1)

Steve Sandor in unaired film trim sold through Lincoln Enterprises in late 1960s
(Courtesy of Jeff Szalay)

Remarkably, "Gamesters of Triskelion" finished on schedule in just six days.

Post-Production
Available for editing: October 25, 1967. Rough Cut: November 6, 1967
Final cut: November 15, 1967. Music Score: tracked.

NBC publicity photo (Courtesy of Gerald Gurian)

James Ballas, in charge of the editing, nicely handled all the action sequences. Ballas had the magic touch. He had edited "Space Seed," "This Side of Paradise," "Amok Time," "Metamorphosis," "Journey to Babel," and "The City on the Edge of Forever."

Music Editor Jim Henrikson, in a sense, provided the score. This was the first episode in the series to not list a music credit. The snippets of past scores were too evenly divided for any one composer to be singled-out. Henrikson was adept at his job, sampling music from dozens of past scores to create the soundtrack for *Star Trek*. Notice one scene, in particular, as an example of Henrikson's cleverness: when Tamoon enters Chekov's cell and brings him the news that she has been selected for him, we get a meshing of music from "I, Mudd" and "The Trouble With Tribbles," utilizing only seconds of each, but combining them together to give this scene exactly the twist it needs.

Cinema Research was responsible for putting the glow into Galt's eyes, as well as the other optical effects seen here.

Release / Reaction
Premiere air date: 1/5/68.
NBC repeat broadcast: 5/3/68.

Steven H. Scheuer reviewed the episode for *TV Key Previews*. Among newspapers across America to carry Scheuer's syndicated column on January 5, 1968 was *The News Journal*, serving Mansfield, Ohio. Scheuer said:

> "The Gamesters of Triskelion." A good entry tonight. Captain Kirk and two crew members use the transporter for a routine landing but that wonderful machine suddenly fails them and they simply disappear. While the Enterprise wanders through the galaxy looking for them, Kirk and his party are experiencing an intriguing adventure on a unknown planet where the inhabitants do nothing but fight at the bidding of their masters or "providers," who enjoy wagering on the outcome of these games.

8:30 to 9 p.m., 64.5% U.S. TVs in use.		Share:	Households watching:
NBC:	*Star Trek*	29.9%	14,060,000
ABC:	*Operation: Entertainment*	25.9%	12,540,000
CBS:	**Gomer Pyle, U.S.M.C.**	**42.0%**	**16,580,000**
Independent stations:		2.2%	No data

9 to 9:30 p.m., 65.1% U.S. TVs in use.		Share:	Households watching:
NBC:	**Star Trek**	**32.2%**	**No data**
ABC:	*Operation: Entertainment*	30.3%	No data
CBS:	*Friday Night Movie*	27.1%	No data
Independent stations:		10.4%	No data

Star Trek was at its usual second place position during the first half hour, but rose to claim the No. 1 spot at 9 p.m. It remained NBC's highest-rated Friday night show.

On ABC was *Operation: Entertainment*, the "globe-trotting variety series sending performers to entertain service men at the Nation's far-flung military bases." In other words, what some say Lucille Ball thought *Star Trek* was going to be when she gave it a green-light from Desilu. ABC sprung to buy a half-page ad for the new series in *TV Guide*, among TV newspaper sections. NBC made *Star Trek* win its time slot on its own. The movie on CBS was a repeat of the epic musical *The Music Man*, from 1962.

***

William Shatner named "The Gamesters of Triskelion" as one of his favorites of the episodes produced by John Meredyth Lucas. He regarded it to be "exciting, action-packed, and fun to shoot." (156-8)

Nichelle Nichols considered this one of her favorite episodes.

Even with the accolades, "Gamesters" was Gene Nelson's only assignment on *Star Trek*. He said, "I thought, 'If I do a good job, maybe they'll find a slot [on the show],' but it didn't happen. I would have liked to have done another couple of shows. [*Star Trek*] gave the imagination a real whirl, because there's no limit; you were able to do things you couldn't do on any other show." (124)

As for Angelique Pettyjohn, by the early 1980s, the job offers had slimmed down and she turned to "softcore porn," appearing in movies with titles like *Titillation*, *Body Talk*, and *Stalag 69*. Her stage name changed to Angel St. John, then to Heaven St. John, then merely Angelique. The opportunity to make a living through speaking engagements at numerous *Star Trek* and science fiction conventions allowed her to soon leave sexploitation films behind.

Memories

Gene Nelson said, "I never met Gene Roddenberry. I think, in terms of television, he was one of the geniuses of our time. It was a stroke of genius just getting that show on the air." (124)

Joseph Ruskin said, "As actors, we do so much junk that, occasionally, something nice comes along, and that was *Star Trek*. 'The Gamesters of Triskelion' was a well-done episode." (148-1)

27

From the Outside … Looking In

Despite NBC's reluctance to commit to a full season, *Star Trek* achieved a media frenzy during its second season, with over 150 feature articles in magazines devoted to celebrities, show business, science, and popular fashion.

Some notable examples, all from the first few months of Season Two -- September through December, 1967:

- *Castle of Frankenstein*, September 1967. Spock was on the cover. Allan Asherman, a contributor to *Spockanalia*, and later to write books on the original *Star Trek*, contributed to this first telling of "The *Star Trek* Story," condensed into six cram-filled pages, with illustrations. One picture was the face that was too horrific for network TV. The creature from "The Galileo Seven" had been given a thumbs down by NBC and all

Castle of Frankenstein, **September 1967 issue**

shots featuring the face were edited from the episode and left unseen, until printed here.

The face NBC would not allow onto the air (from "The Galileo Seven," as seen in *Castle of Frankenstein*)

For another article in the magazine, Leonard Nimoy said, "Spock is described as a 'man' with a logical turn in mind inherited from his father. Because Vulcanians regard any display of emotion as a breach of good taste, Spock rarely betrays what he is thinking or feeling, either by his speech or his facial expression. [But] he cannot mask his cat-like curiosity about everything of alien origin. He's an intriguing character, like a man with many secrets. He's perceptive, beyond normal human perception -- and yet he can be caught by surprise."

- *Screen Stories*, from September 1967, presented "Leonard Nimoy & Bill Shatner, Their Topsy-Turvy Lives." Staffer Dora Albert broke the story, writing, "The news exploded all over Hollywood, the way such sad news often does. After more than ten years of marriage, the William Shatners were having serious problems; a separation seemed to be imminent. The dark, handsome captain of the space ship which makes interplanetary voyages in *Star Trek* was having trouble steering his own matrimonial ship."

Nimoy, according to the article, was surviving the strains of a weekly television series. His 13-year marriage was on solid, if not alien, ground.

- *TV Picture Life*, for its September 1967 issue, covered the same ground, with an article called "How Leonard Nimoy Tried to Save William Shatner's Marriage!" An inside source, sounding very much like DeForest Kelley, explained, "Lately our conference table has become group therapy time with Bill airing his problems and Len giving advice. The table was Bill's idea originally. He asked that it be set up as a place where we'd meet first thing in the morning for coffee and script discussions. We rehearse there before going in front of the camera, and if there's a point of disagreement involving the script or anything to do with the show, we hash it out. It's been great and it's given us a camaraderie not usually found on a series with so many regulars. But as I said, lately Bill and Len spend a lot of time at the table with their heads close together. We all know about Bill's problems at home but he doesn't discuss them with us the way he does with Len."

- *American Cinematographer*, from October, offered "Out-of-this-world special effects for *Star Trek*," with Howard A. Anderson Company, Film Effects of Hollywood, and The Westheimer Company explaining the tricks behind their contributions to the series.

- *TV Radio Show*, in October, 1967, featured an article on Peggye Vickers, the first president of the LNNAF (Leonard Nimoy National Association of Fans). Photos were taken on the *Trek* TV set.

- *Movie Mirror*, for its October 1967 issue, ran with "My Mother Prayed God Would Forgive Me." The inside scoop: Nimoy confessed, "I was 17 when I realized for certain that I wanted to become an actor and both my parents were horrified. It simply was *not* a respectable way to make a living."

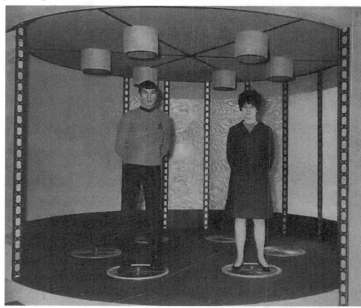

Nimoy with Peggye Vickers from October issue of *TV Radio Show* (Courtesy of Gerald Gurian)

- *Weekend Magazine*, syndicated in numerous newspapers throughout Canada, focused on Shatner, calling him "Canada's First Man in Space." According to the October 28, 1967 article, the star earned an estimated $250,000 annually from *Star Trek*.

- *The Cleveland Press*, for its *TV Showtime* magazine on November 3, featured

Nichelle Nichols' cover for *The Cleveland Press' TV Showtime* (November 3, 1967)

Nichelle Nichols as Lt. Uhura on the cover, with the caption "Enterprising Spacewoman." The article within was less uplifting. The headline proclaimed "*Trek* to Halt 5-Year Mission a Little Early." Without citing the source, the uncredited writer stated, "Unfortunately, ratings have indicated that the Enterprise's TV journey will end next summer."

- *TV Guide*, for its November 18 issue, had an artist's rendition of Kirk and Spock on its cover. This was *Star Trek*'s second turn on the jacket. For the article, which dealt with the series' rising popularity, Nimoy was quoted by Leslie Raddatz, saying, "At first I felt somewhat ill at ease. As an actor in a TV drama, I had no way of knowing what the attitude of the scientific community toward our show would be. But I don't overstate the fact when I say that the interest in the show is so intense that it would almost seem they feel we are a dramatization of the future of their space program, and they have taken us to their hearts."

According to Raddatz, "Cape Kennedy practically shuts down when *Star Trek* is on."

- *TV Star Parade,* for its November cover, proclaimed, "Psychologist Reveals Primitive Sex Appeal of Mr. Spock!"

- *Photoplay*, for its November 1967 issue, teased its readers with the headline: "Why I Go to Sex Education Classes With My Son ... A Story from an Out-of-This-World Father -- Leonard Nimoy."

- *TV Picture Life*, for November, proclaimed on its cover, "Leonard Nimoy: 'My Wife Wept When I Said I'm Through!'" Through with what, you ask? Nimoy explained, "[T]here were times when I wept out of sadness, when I was struggling to gain recognition in Hollywood and kept telling Sandy that I had to give up acting, in fairness to her and our children... Years of being rejected taught me to expect the least, to back away from something for fear of being let down. When I was worried about *Star Trek*

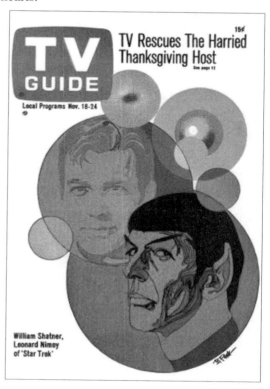

William Shatner, Leonard Nimoy of 'Star Trek'

TV Rescues The Harried Thanksgiving Host

***Star Trek*'s second turn on the cover of *TV Guide* (November 18, 1967)**

not being renewed, I held myself in rein. I didn't want to be bitterly disappointed if it wasn't renewed. At the same time, when it *was* renewed, I wasn't delirious with joy. There was no payoff, in terms of emotion, for me."

Leonard Nimoy, and wife Sandy, were everywhere in the celebrity tabloids in 1967 and '68

This time De Forest Kelley gets the girl, as *Star Trek* fan Joan Winston beams aboard

The happy ending, involving a mysterious envelope and its surprising contents: "I waited until Sandy came home. I was shaving when she arrived and I gave her the envelope, trying to be as nonchalant as possible. She began to shake, and she opened the envelope and started to read the letter. And then she and I both started to cry, me with my face still lathered for my shave!"

The reason for the happy tears? Nimoy had been nominated for an Emmy as Best Actor in a Drama.

- *TV Star Parade*, for its November issue, announced, "DeForest Kelley Is Out of the Woods." The actor said, "I guess I finally realized the popularity of *Star Trek* and the success of my role when people began stopping me on the street to comment on the show. This tremendous interest is something I hadn't been accustomed to…. I'd been fighting the heroes a long time, making a good living playing heavies. Then the series came along. It kind of shook me. It changed my image. I'm not a heavy any longer. And I'm working every day with the same people. It's interesting. A whole new thing happened to me when our space ship blasted off."

- *Movieland and TV Time*, also in November, 1967, told us "Fame Has Its Drawbacks!" Nimoy, "with a wry grin," admitted, "There is a tendency, when all this starts, to want to do everything. After all, you've been a free-lance actor for years, involved not at all in extracurricular activity. Therefore, when you start being asked, you run around trying to please everyone.

Well, you can't do it. You find you have conflicts -- and you do have a limit to your energy. So I've reached the point where I am going to have to be selective -- not go everywhere."

- *Tiger Beat* did one better for its November issue with "Leonard Nimoy Talks About Mr. Spock." That's what its young readers wanted to hear about. So Nimoy told them, "Spock had a miserable childhood. He was a child of a Vulcan father and an Earthling mother and he was raised as an outsider on Vulcan. The Vulcan kids didn't like him because he was half-Earthling and I'm sure that if he'd been raised here on Earth he would have gotten the same reaction because he was half-Vulcan. So here he was, unwanted and unloved."

What teenager couldn't relate to this story; to the ache inside over not being understood?

Nimoy continued, "But he had the intelligence to be strictly himself, no matter what that happened to be, and because he worked at being himself other people began to respect him. He learned to depend only on himself. He didn't ask other people for their opinions and he certainly didn't follow their opinion if he felt differently. He took tremendous pride in doing a good job in whatever he did.... I'm sure that there are lots of people right now who feel a little lonely or unwanted for some reason or another. I wonder if they realize that Spock felt these same things when he was growing up. But look what he did with those feelings! Instead of giving up he used them to build himself up into a person that was greater than most Vulcans and greater than most Earthlings.... I wonder how many people feel right now the way Spock did when he was a child. I wonder if Spock has made them feel any better, if they've learned some of the same things I have from him."

- Various newspapers, via a syndicated article from November 14, 1967, put the spotlight on Nimoy. The actor said, "It's an idea show, not a cartoon strip. One thing the adults enjoy is that it is scientifically conceivable. I've talked to scientists at NASA and other places, and these people tell me we're really dealing with scientific possibilities. These scientists watch the program for possible scientific stimulation."

- *TV Times*, Australia's version of *TV Guide*, had Kirk and Spock on the cover of its November 15, 1967 issue. *Star Trek* was now being beamed down under.

- *The News*, a Los Angeles based newspaper, reported on November 28, 1967 what may very well have been the first *Star Trek* event open to the public. Running for six weeks, the Art Center at Los Angeles City College presented an exhibition called "Out of this World." William Shatner was the guest of honor on the opening day. He was joined by Nimoy, Kelley, Doohan, Nichols, Takei, and Koenig. According to the article, "An atmosphere of blazing lights and eerie music set the mood for a display of humanoids, androids, aliens, and extraterrestrials created by students of three-dimensional design classes.... Ultra-modern props from the series, including robots and a model of the star ship, [are] in the display."

- *Photo TV Land*, in December 1967, tried to make something of a Shatner/Nimoy feud in the article, "Outer Space's Inside Battle." Writer Rhoda Green warned, "The public has already demanded to know more about the two stars and the press is busy supplying the stories -- include in that group the gossips and rumor mongers."

Shatner and Nimoy seemed amused by the rumors. "Len and I are great friends," said Shatner. "We respect each other and rely on one another's professional advice. We're not young kids just breaking into the business – there's no such thing as professional jealousy on our show."

Nimoy added, "What could possibly make us enemies? We all get along -- we're all working to make the show a continued success.... Sure we battle -- but it's only friendly rivalry. Oddly enough, it seems to keep us on our toes. You know that doing a show day after day for a year can get tiresome... It's hard work and long hours. But an actor can't let that physical strain show through when he's in front of the cameras. So Bill and I always find something to spark our energy.... For instance, we give each other notes on scenes we work on. I guess we're each other's critics. After he shoots a scene, I'll tell him what he did wrong or what was great about it. He does the same for me."

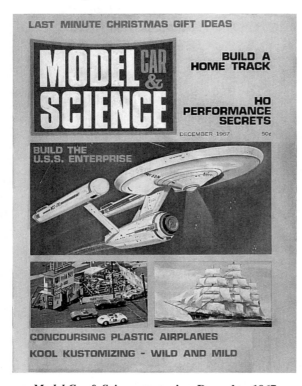

Model Car & Science **magazine, December 1967**

- *Model Car & Science* magazine featured the Enterprise on its cover for its December 1967 issue. The article was entitled, "Space Queen!" We were told:

Unless you are a retarded goat grower, living on the far slope of a forgotten mountain in Ethiopia, you have no doubt ogled the fantastic U.S.S. Enterprise, Captain James Kirk's "starship class" spaceship, on the NBC weekly television show, *Star Trek*. It's a stunning vessel, to say the least! Larger than a naval cruiser, with a crew of 430 persons (approximately one-third of them female, for those of you who dig statistics), this ship is the largest and most modern in the Starfleet Services.... AMT has duplicated this famous ship, right down to the operating "deep space" lights.... If your dealer doesn't have one left, stand by, there's more on the way! Better hustle down to your local hobby shop or department store, and get one while the getting is good! AMT has been operating around the clock, trying to keep this kit available, due to the heavy demand. This is one of the wildest shelf models that we've seen in a long time!

- *TV and Movie Play*, for December 1967, baited the teens with "Leonard Nimoy Confesses About His Emotions." Nimoy confessed, "If [Spock] didn't have any emotions, he wouldn't be interesting. Actually, Spock does have a sense of compassion though he won't allow himself to believe that. I admire his logic. It's so uncluttered. I appreciate the ability to be precise. I like to think that I am logical -- but sometimes I look back and wonder if the things I do *are* logical."

- *Movie Stars* magazine, for its December 1967 cover, had the headline: "Win Leonard Nimoy's Ears!"

- *Popular Science* devoted three pages of its December 1967 issue for "TV's *Star Trek*: How They Mix Science Fact with Fiction." James W. Wright wrote, "If you're one of the 20 odd million viewers who tune in each week to NBC-TV's highly popular *Star Trek* science fiction series, you could be getting a much closer look at the future of space exploration than you realize.... The show is the only science fiction series in history that has the cooperation and advice of the National Aeronautics and Space Administration [NASA];

that employs a research firm to go through each script with an eagle eye, weeding out things that are completely impossible or untrue; and that maintains both an extensive technical library and contacts with scientists across the U.S."

The article reported that the U.S. Navy had recently sent a group to study the layout of the Enterprise's command bridge, saying that "the functional and efficient bridge served as a model for a new communications center they were designing."

- *Mad Magazine*, in its December 1967 issue, gave *Star Trek* the dubious honor of one of its famous parodies. The five page send-up was called "Star Blecch!"

Surprise visit on *The Carol Burnett Show*, December 4, 1967

Besides his high visibility on television, promoting his record albums as well as *Star Trek*, on *The Joey Bishop Show*, *Dream Girl of '67*, *You Don't Say*, *Malibu U*, *The Pat Boone Show*, *The Hollywood Squares* (week of December 4 through December 8, 1967), and *The Today Show*, he also appeared on the December 4, 1967 episode of *The Carol Burnett Show*, as Spock, in a comedy sketch with Carol.

With all the attention from the outside looking in, few fans knew of the anxiety taking place inside of *Star Trek*.

***

After NBC's order for two interim episodes, the feeling of uncertainty in the *Star Trek* front office and on Desilu / Paramount Stages 9 and 10 continued for nearly a month. No one had any idea if they would be working beyond the filming of "The Gamesters of Triskelion." And yet, John Meredyth Lucas and his staff had to prepare more scripts just in case a request for additional episodes came through.

Much was riding on the ratings of the next few episodes.

Week Three of Season Two: the night "The Changeling" aired, the TV premiere of Alfred Hitchcock's *North by Northwest* was on CBS. *Star Trek* came in No. 2, but any good news in this placing was lost as the numbers revealed the lead over *Hondo* on ABC had decreased while the gap between NBC and CBS had widened.

Week Four: Elvis Presley and *Viva Las Vegas* gave CBS an even bigger lead. *Star Trek*'s numbers held firm with "Mirror, Mirror," as did its lock on the No. 2 slot. *Hondo* was the loser, seeing its percentages drop.

Week Five: "The Apple" delivered the same uneasy mix of good and bad news. The bad: CBS continued to dominate. The good: ABC continued to lose ground.

The renewal finally arrived late in the day on October 18 when "Gamesters" was halfway through filming. Industry interest was great enough for *Daily Variety* to place the headline "*Star Trek* Given Midseason Pickup" on its front page the following morning rather than bury it deeper in the trade paper. The order was for eight more hours, bringing the second season tally to 26. NBC reserved the option to ask for two additional episodes beyond that and scripts would have to be prepared on the outside chance that the full season order was increased to 28.

John Meredyth Lucas had dozens of story outlines and scripts to choose from that were leftover from Gene Coon's tenure as producer. He would pick a handful of what he believed to be the best, or, at least, the least expensive, or the least problematic. Many would end up going into the show files, adding to scores of stories and scripts already there, left over from Season One. These would constitute "The Voyages That Never Were, Part II."

28

The Voyages that Never Were

Gene Coon had been called the fastest typewriter in the West. For his job on *Star Trek*, he needed to be. His hands were on every draft of every story and script produced from the midpoint of the first season to very nearly the end of the second. He also put a great deal of time and energy into properties which never made it to production.

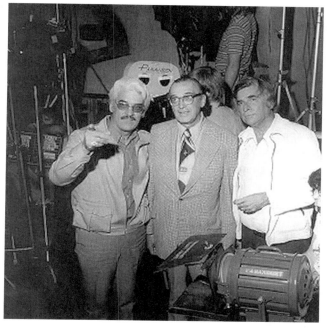

NASA aerospace engineer Jesco von Puttkamer and sci-fi author A.E. van Vogt visit Gene Roddenberry on the set of *Star Trek: The Motion Picture.* Van Vogt had tried on numerous occasions to write for *Star Trek* in the 1960s.

ST-40 (assigned Story Treatment #40), Paul Schneider's "Tomorrow the Universe," had its start at the tail end of the first season. A few months later, with the NBC pick-up, the story where Kirk encounters another Hitler was resurrected, progressing from outline to screenplay to revised screenplay.

It was an interesting and controversial subject but, like "Portrait in Black and White," from the previous year, the premise and story structure for "Tomorrow the Universe" proved to be problematic and the material was eventually abandoned. Some elements, however, did survive and appeared in "Patterns of Force," soon to be produced [see The Story Behind the Story, "Patterns of Force," for the staff notes]. Other elements, used to a better end, and played for laughs, surfaced in "A Piece of the Action."

ST-55, "The Orchid People," by John Collier and Catherine Turner, had actually come in the previous year, as an unsolicited treatment. Collier was a well-known author of fiction, including many science fiction and fantasy short stories. He had also worked in TV, providing scripts for *Alfred Hitchcock Presents* and having one of his stories adapted to *The Twilight Zone.*

On May 3, 1967, Roddenberry wrote to his staff:

Given to us at the beginning of last year.... At that time it was rejected as too soft a story and, frankly, we did not have yet enough experience for *Star Trek* to judge how to insert more action, adventure and jeopardy into this tale. At the same time, it seems to be well-written and conceived; they seemed to understand our characters, and we held onto it until now. Does it springboard any new ideas which might be added to this story to make it workable and right for us?

The story had the Enterprise answering a distress signal to an uncharted planet. Spock tries to dissuade Kirk from responding, telling him of legends about "beautiful visitors" who "decoyed those weaklings into lonely places for which they never returned." Kirk ignores the warning. He cannot disregard a call for help. On the planet, the scout team rescues two "beautiful men" and one equally appealing woman. These are the Orchid People. Once on the Enterprise, the three are immediately enchanting and seemingly irresistible to whomever they turn their charms toward. The two men seem entirely focused on the women officers, while the Orchid Woman concentrates on Kirk. Spock takes note that the strangers never seem to eat, and when they are in each another's company, they never look directly at one another. In fact, when left alone, the Orchid People face into different corners of the room. Collier wrote, "They never turn their enchanting eyes or their seductive smiles on each other." The reason for this is that they are dangerous to one another. This is how their race died off, by the people gazing into one another's eyes, with the more powerful nourishing off the weaker. These three have made a pact not to exercise their fatal powers among themselves. They have plenty of food sources among the Enterprise crew.

Fontana responded to Roddenberry later that day, saying she found similarities between this story and that of the salt-vampire in "The Man Trap." On a positive note, she thought the story had potential of being built into a Gothic horror tale and "suspense chiller." She wrote, "Collier has a knack for the chiller-type story."

It was decided to buy the story rights, but the property never progressed further. Collier and Turner had relocated to Europe and logistics, as well as time conflicts, prevented this intriguing story from being developed into a screenplay.

ST-61, "The Search for Eternity," by Roddenberry's friend, renowned science fiction author A.E. van Vogt (with 23 novels and eight collections of short stories to his credit at this time), was less intriguing, but set off a strange series of events. Van Vogt had failed to connect with his first assignment during *Star Trek* Season One -- "The Machine That Went Too Far." On March 29, 1967, having learned *Star Trek* had been renewed, van Vogt took it upon himself to revise and resubmit his previously rejected story. The new title was "Machines Are Better." He sent a note along with it, telling Roddenberry:

> I visually enjoyed doing this, which is more than I can say for last year's effort, when it all seemed complex.

In the retooled story, Kirk, Sulu, Janice Rand, and three nondescript crewmen beam down to an unexplored planet, materializing in a jungle clearing where they find an "ugly, huge, windowless" building. Inside the building is a nonfunctioning android, which Kirk beams to the Enterprise for repair by Dr. Piper (from the second *Star Trek* pilot). The android's name, he tells them, is "Number Two." We discover that he has been feuding with an android named, appropriately, "Number One." A second search leads to Number One, who is also transported to the ship. The competitiveness between the androids does not seem to pose a threat, but Kirk has little success in trying to play the part of a peacemaker since they prefer the company of Mr. Spock. Although Spock is flesh-and-blood, the androids view him as more robot-like. They especially enjoy playing chess with him. Lighthearted business soon turns to life-and-death business when Number One, who moves faster than the eye can follow, takes over the ship.

The day after receiving the outline, Robert Justman wrote to Gene Coon:

> This is a much cleaner outline than Mr. van Vogt's previous submission of last

Spring, which we had to cut off at story. In fact, it seems to be <u>exactly</u> the same story -- cleaned up a little.

On April 3, Roddenberry wrote to Coon, Justman, and Fontana:

[I] feel a bit on the hook with A.E. van Vogt, since he was a member of our "Save *Star Trek* Committee" of famous science fiction writers. Not that I intend to suggest that we should throw money away, but merely that we can do him the favor of extra careful examination and consideration. We've always felt that there might be something in this basic story.

Fontana gave it extra careful examination and consideration, and then wrote to Roddenberry:

We bought this story once. We can't re-buy it -- logically -- in a slightly revised state.... But, looking at it with a cockeyed view toward humor, we could do something with it.... Page 16-17 is a continuation of what has to be a hilarious presentation of "Life with Robot." Especially Page 17 where the robots do an Alphonse and Gaston routine about ripping out each other's wires.

"Alphonse and Gaston" was a comic strip in the early 1900s, which presented a pair of bumbling Frenchmen who never got anything of consequence accomplished because they were always insisting that the other go first. The strip was so popular that one of its catchphrases lived on for decades, often when two people caught themselves trying to go through a doorway at the same moment and thereby colliding. One would step back and graciously say, "After you, my dear Alphonse."

Fontana's memo continued:

We obviously cannot do supersonic speeds and stuff like that... [and] since "I, Mudd" also has a robot society background, we might not want to do another robot story in the same season. If we could, however, A.E. is not the man to do the revamped story or teleplay. He has NO sense of humor.... But it <u>is</u> funny, Chief.

Later that day, perhaps even before Fontana's memo hit Roddenberry's desk, van Vogt sent in a revised version of his revised outline. Two days later, to stop van Vogt from continuing to revise "Machines Are Better," Roddenberry bought the story … again. The check for $655 was written on April 6 and the story was sent to NBC for an expected second rejection.

Stan Robertson responded on May 9, citing the reason for his rejection due to this story's similarity to "I, Mudd." He was also rejecting the writer, expressing concerns over how:

Captain Kirk is portrayed as being indecisive, unmotivated, more of a "traffic cop" than a participant. Mr. Spock is shown as being illogical, even though the author keeps reminding us of his logic, and [shows] more [emotion on the] surface than we have portrayed the highly introspective Vulcan.

But much had happened in the month between buying "Machines Are Better" and Stan Robertson's reply. Within days of the purchase, a newly-enthused van Vogt sent in a batch of seven more story ideas. Roddenberry asked Gene Coon to have someone read them. Robert Justman drew the short straw. On April 10, he wrote Coon:

Page 2 of Premise #1 bears an amazing resemblance to "Who Mourns for Adonais?" -- namely that somebody grows larger and larger and larger. After that, it bears no resemblance to anything whatsoever that we would be able to depict on film.... I don't understand Premise #2, therefore I am mentally incapable of discussing it.... Premise #3 -- we approached this line of thinking to some extent in a show entitled "The City on the Edge of Forever." In that show, you will remember, we attempted to change what was necessarily destined to happen. I feel we can attempt the same thing by not pursuing this story premise. Let's leave our personal destinies alone by not attempting to make anything more out of this.... Premise #4 -- In a world gone mad, padded cells are for the sane. That's right! Where do I go to get mine?... Premise #5 -- Since this story premise results in an immediate "Mexican standoff," we would not be able even to get out of the Teaser. Therefore, we would need a commercial message of approximately 57 minutes' duration. This is against all FCC regulations.... Premise #6 -- Dear Gene: The writer himself admits that this premise is not a premise yet. Regards, Bob. Premise #7 -- Dear Gene: Regards, Bob.

Later that day, Roddenberry called van Vogt, agreeing to hear some pitches -- then picked one and designated it as ST-61. The story outline arrived the very next day, now entitled "The Search for Eternity."

ST-61, "The Search for Eternity," opens with the bridge crew waking up at their posts, having all experienced a memory lapse. In fact, the entire crew of the Enterprise has blacked out. Before being able to determine what happened, a transmission is received and Kirk is accused by a Starfleet Admiral of having destroyed planet Palada II. The Admiral calls Kirk a "rat" for having done this. The crew can't defend their captain, since all are suffering from mass amnesia and cannot remember if Kirk ordered the attack or not. Helping to incriminate their captain, one of the ship's "torpedo tubes" is empty, indicating it *had* been fired, and the enraged inhabitants of a small moon colony have pictures of the Enterprise firing on their home planet. Kirk, meanwhile, is suffering bouts of dizziness. And he hears alien voices. When he tells McCoy about this, the doctor drugs him and then announces to the crew that he has the "criminal Kirk" under control. Spock aligns himself with McCoy, accusing Kirk of being a mass murderer. Kirk is turned over to the Admiral, who has arrived in his own ship. The Admiral says, "I never did trust that man," then sentences Kirk to death by a firing squad consisting of himself, his aide, Spock, McCoy, and Sulu. They take aim on Kirk with phaser rifles. But then Spock, McCoy, and Sulu turn their guns on the Admiral and his aide. They had been only pretending to mutiny against Kirk in order to get the Admiral to beam over to the Enterprise. Trapped, the Admiral reveals himself for what he truly is, an alien called "the Rull," who is "snake-like." He hisses and tells them that the Rull have been attempting to invade the Federation, and used their power of creating illusion to make the crew of the Enterprise believe the ship's torpedoes had been fired, a planet had been destroyed, and the moon people had pictures of the attack. None of this, of course, had been true. There is then a fight and the Enterprise men defeat the Rull.

On April 13, Dorothy Fontana wrote to Gene Coon:

I find it difficult to believe a Star Fleet Admiral would under any circumstances address a starship captain as "you rat," unless, of course, said Star Fleet Admiral is portrayed by James Cagney.... I feel we have shot another $655 on a totally unusable story.... This wouldn't even qualify for *Captain Video*, and I urge cut-off on this story.... It is not worth a revision... although I anticipate another spate of unsolicited revamps from the same source. Please, please get us out of it now.

"The Search for Eternity" *was* cut-off at story. A.E. van Vogt had now been paid for three story outlines. One -- and you may wonder which -- would return, assigned to Ms.

Fontana to retool. That final chapter in the A.E. van Vogt/*Star Trek* saga to follow in Book 3.

ST-63, "Aladdin's Asteroid," was by Robert Barry, a writer with only a handful of modest TV credits but who was friendly with Roddenberry. He got the assignment off the strength of "Destination: Infection," an unsolicited story outline that Roddenberry agreed to read. It was about a spaceship disguised as an asteroid. Of this, on April 4, 1967, Fontana wrote:

> A straight lining of the actual story, rather than a back story, would make this a
> more readable and understandable submission.... However... we cannot request
> a revision without giving the writer an assignment.

> On April 5, Justman wrote:

> The writer shows definite promise. The concept is original and imaginative.
> However, talky... expensive ... difficult.

> Coon agreed, writing to Roddenberry:

> Interesting idea. Fascinating, though not worked out.... Terribly difficult to do
> from a production point of view. (But) might possibly be worth the effort.

So Roddenberry asked Coon to work with Barry and steer him in the right direction. Barry was paid to revise his story outline, with the new title of "Aladdin's Asteroid." Now that the staff could clearly see the forest through the trees, the story was immediately cut-off. *Star Trek* was not ready to take on the optical effects needed to tell a story about a world within an asteroid. That would have to wait until Season Three [see "For the World Is Hollow and I Have Touched the Sky"].

ST-64, "Shol," and its novice writer, Darlene Hartman, was a pet project of Gene Roddenberry's and Gene Coon's. Hartman, 33 at the time, and a resident of New Orleans, had sold several half-hour scripts to a local religious program produced in Mississippi. She was a fan of *Star Trek* and began submitting spec scripts through her agent. One in particular, "Shun-daki," involving the death of Spock's parents, caught the eye of Roddenberry.

> Dorothy Fontana wrote to her boss on March 23, 1967:

> My recommendation -- pass. You have Ted's script in the works ("Amok
> Time"), and my story coming up ("Journey to Babel"), and this idea infringes on
> both.

> Fontana also saw problems with encouraging Hartman to send in further material,
saying:

> New Orleans is a long way from Hollywood... and you know how lost our pro
> New York writers got when writing in a vacuum last year. I cite you two Robert
> Sheckleys and one Alvin Boretz which were cut-offs, and Don Mankiewicz's
> "Court Martial," which had to be totally overhauled start to finish and never was
> very good.

> Robert Justman agreed, writing, on March 24:

> We have a lot of talk -- we don't have enough physical conflict, or peril. And I
> feel definitely that we can do without more shows like "Errand of Mercy" and
> "Operation: Annihilate!" Those shows were loaded with talk, very static and
> slow moving, and I, for one, am not proud of them in the slightest.... So I don't
> sound negative on everything, I would like to state again that I think the
> conception of the duel between Spock and Vastik is quite exciting to me and I

think that it would be to any audience, if it is staged correctly.... (But) shy away from committing us on a purchase.... We did not solicit this manuscript.... As enthralled as I was and still am by the obvious talent displayed by the writer, the screenplay is far from workable at the present time.

After speaking with Justman, Roddenberry replied to Fontana's memo, on March 27, writing:

Have your comments on "Shun-Daki" and agree with most of them.... Rather than giving her a rewrite on any of the four scripts she sent us, I may take a $650 chance on giving her a completely new assignment and seeing how she works through the outline stage with us. Realize she is far, far away and this has rarely, if ever, been successful. But certain of her dialogue and techniques fascinate both RJ and myself and we'd hate not to risk at least that much in view of our strong feelings that she may be a potential writer for us.

Before this could happen, however, a fifth unsolicited submission arrived from the prolific and eager Miss Hartman. This time it was in the form of a story outline, called "Krail," dated May 12, 1967.

Fontana wrote to her colleagues on the May 15:

There are elements, in fact, the whole resolution, which smack strongly of "Operation: Annihilate," which was not one of our more spectacular shows.... I believe we must resolve this situation now, or we will be reading story premises all season.

Roddenberry wrote to Hartman on May 23:

Frankly, your premises do not seem to us to have the kind of potential we look for when giving a "go ahead."... They do not involve our characters deeply enough, involve their needs, strengths and weaknesses. True, the stories see our people endangered, our people then save themselves from danger, but their level of involvement is thin.

Hartman's heart was no doubt sinking, until Roddenberry wrote:

Gene Coon and I are anxious to see you get started on something and have decided to sit down together, come up with a story springboard ourselves, and send it to you. This way it will definitely be something we are interested in, assuming you like the idea and want to go ahead with it -- maybe the best way to start this first time.

Taking on the role of a mentor, Roddenberry again wrote to Hartman, on June 20. He and Coon had come up with a story premise and Roddenberry wanted to guide Hartman toward what was truly important about the story and not all the scenery and gimmicks which are inherent in most science fiction. His letter, in part, read:

Television producers examine every page of every script carefully, and from several perspectives, constantly asking themselves if the audience is sufficiently "hooked," if enough action is happening, if it is creating in the audience a positive need to stay with the show and see jeopardies resolve, mysteries answered, and so on. And as Gene Coon stated in his letter, necessary also for the very best scripts, in fact for any script we care to photograph, is the Theme -- a statement of some sort. Done subtly, never preaching; the kind of Theme which characterizes all great writing. Like Shakespeare's *Romeo & Juliet*, which makes the statement that love is really stronger and greater than death. Or in so many of Mark Train's works, which state that honesty and simplicity are in the end more effective and rewarding than deception. Or in the science fiction [sic] novel *Seven Days in May*, which warns that the military mind must constantly be subjected to civilian control if our political system is to endure. I challenge you to name a great or even a good work of fiction that is not characterized by some central, strong and meaningful Theme statement. Now, what is a story? We all know but we all tend to forget at times.... A story is a need which occurs to a person the audience cares about. We may like or hate this fictional person, but we must care about him. It may be a need for something to happen or something *not* to happen.... Stories are divided into three types -- man against nature, man against man; man against himself. Most fine stories include elements of all of these.

Hartman's outline, based on Roddenberry's and Coon's story idea, arrived July 15, 1967. Gene Coon both read and then quickly rewrote it, his version dated July 25. The following day, he wrote to Hartman, explaining the reasoning behind doing a rewrite on her treatment before sending to the network:

I loved your outline just the way you submitted it. Unfortunately, you gave us a strong Adam and Eve, Garden of Eden parallel, and just last week we finished shooting a strong Adam and Eve, Garden of Eden parallel. The resemblances were amazing. So amazing, in fact, that I anticipate a strong protest from NBC insisting that this story is still, despite my rewrite, too similar to the script we just finished shooting, which was called, incidentally, "The Apple."

The Hartman/Coon treatment of "Shol" involves the discovery of a peaceful civilization on Alpha Cygnus 12, a place reminiscent of what one might believe the Garden of Eden to have been. Kirk and his landing party arrive to observe a lovely 13-year-old girl, playfully creating art, surrounded by an audience of tame animals, attentively watching. Scattered among the peaceful woods area are numerous works of art, sculptures, tapestries and hanging mobiles. The primitive society is actually more akin to an art community. But Kirk sees indications that all is not right in this place of Nirvana. The inhabitants have little regard for themselves or their artistic creations and actually long for the end of their lives as they have known them, wishing to become one with their god, Shol. Kirk can find no elderly among them and it seems that anyone beyond the age of 40 has already been "absorbed" by Shol. And then Uhura and Chekov are accidently absorbed when they enter into an area where Shol awaits its worshippers, leaving behind only their lifeless bodies. McCoy quickly arranges to have life support units beamed down and places the bodies into them, hoping that the minds and souls of Uhura and Chekov can be recovered. Kirk brings down a detachment of security men and starts a hunt for Shol, determined to destroy it because of what it has taken from him. He comes close to doing this when Spock intervenes. Through a telepathic link with the natives, Spock has learned that the intelligence -- the souls, if you will -- of Uhura and Chekov continue to exist within Shol, and that Shol is in actuality a community of intelligences. If Kirk were to destroy it, he would also destroy his crew members. Spock wishes to allow Shol to absorb him, so he can locate the missing colleagues and, by using his mental ability to retain intellectual individuality and thereby keep from being completely absorbed, lead the others back to their bodies. Kirk allows this, catching Spock's body as it drops, then he and McCoy place it into a life-support unit. And then he waits.

Hartman and/or Coon then wrote:

The rising ethereal sound of Shol rises higher, to a frightening pitch, and it begins to be shot through with blackness. It throbs, advances, retreats ... and the Cygeans present begin to scream, to cry. The balance of Shol is obviously destroyed ... there is a great mournful sound ... and then a sound of a million sobbing voices have begun to wail all at the same time ... and Shol fades, and fades...

At this point in the outline, the bodies of Spock, Uhura, and Chekov, from within their support chambers, come back to life. Kirk is overjoyed to see his crew alive again, but they appear profoundly sad, Spock included. They believe they were more alive while inside Shol than now, having been forced to return to a lesser existence. Hartman and/or Coon continued:

> Spock is shaken, moved as he has never been moved before… His words are totally inadequate … to have dreamed, and wake with a sense of utter loss, knowing only that you had dreamed … to have been extended across the universe, limitless, without end … to realize with a sudden infallible clarity that all of the ancient beliefs had been right, and yet, in a real sense, wrong, too … "I knew, Jim," he says, trying to get it across. "I knew and I saw and I was" … but he, like the others, cannot find the words. What he does feel is intense guilt, for it was his mental discipline which threw Shol out of balance, and then destroyed the entity. He asks Kirk, "Do you know what it was you destroyed? Do you have any idea?"

At this point, the 13-year old native girl turns to Kirk. The Hartman/Coon outline says:

> Tears running down her face, staring at him, alone, sad, a tiny figure. "What will we do," she asks. "Where will we go? Why are we here now?" There is no answer, now. There never was. A sobered, strangely subdued group transport back to the ship…. And does Kirk know what he had destroyed? He nods his head, feeling the awe of it, the tragedy of it, run through him…. Paradise, Heaven, Nirvana … the eternal, the unending, the ground without beginning or end … and Man touched it, and it is gone. We carry that primal curse with us, don't we? For such a long time. Across the galaxy, never knowing what it is we are hunting for. And then we find it, and we destroy it, and continue our search. A terrible, cosmic joke, and somewhere God laughs … and it echoes down the corridors of stars, endlessly, eternally … and always unreachable.

Roddenberry, Coon, and Hartman had told a story as profound, and as vague, as the following year's *2001: A Space Odyssey*.

Trusting that his reworking of "Sohl" would do the trick, Coon closed his letter, saying:

> Stand-by for a go-ahead. Hopefully we will get it to you within four days! I think we've got a real winner here. Good luck.

Stan Robertson responded to Coon on August 1, agreeing to approve the story only on the conditions that some changes be made. He wrote:

> The supposed deaths of Uhura and Chekov are again devices which we have utilized before in our stories -- devices which have the effect of appearing on the surface to be dramatically exciting but which, when examined in the light of the broad aspect of our series, fall into the repetitious and sameness category.

Robertson also had trouble with the ending. Of this, he wrote:

> The conclusion, as written, is neither dramatically nor emotionally satisfying…. In short, what is the meaning of this story? Upon what premise is it founded? What are we saying when it's over?

Surprisingly, Robertson did not challenge Coon on the religious implications, perhaps because, with that poetic but visually vague ending, as it would be a year later when *2001* arrived in theaters, the message was open for interpretation … or misinterpretation … or bewilderment and, therefore, indifference.

And so "Shol" was approved with many strings attached. By the time this decision was reached, Darlene Hartman was already well into her 1st Draft script, which she finished and dated only three days later, on August 23. Coon remained enthusiastic after reading it, finding Hartman's writing to be "beautiful." The others disagreed.

On August 29, Robert Justman wrote:

I have just completed reading Darlene Hartman's first attempt at teleplay and, to be perfectly frank, that is what we have here. It is evident that she can write -- and write well. It is also evident that she can write science fiction better than she can write a believable teleplay. There is some poetry in her dialogue and much poetry in her scene description. Poetic pose and obscure mystery go very well in science fiction short stories -- but sometimes they don't come off so well in the medium of the spoken word and the moving picture.... Beautiful writing does not necessarily make a beautiful television drama.

Dorothy Fontana wrote to Coon:

I am sure I am going to be in the minority on this script. I am sure everyone else is going to be enchanted by the lovely descriptions and poetry and beautiful dialogue in this piece. I agree there are lovely descriptions and poetry and beautiful dialogue in this piece. I also find holes and a couple of developments that bother me a great deal. For instance, after reading the script and setting aside the poetry and esoteric themes, has anyone noticed that Captain Kirk blunders around, A) at first only receiving information, and B) making a jerk of himself in the second half? There is a built-in problem in that only Spock can be the "hero" of the resolution, be that resolution happy or sad. Not Kirk. Do you think Bill Shatner will notice this?... The basis of all this is very "Apple-like." On the other hand, there is a difference. At least in "The Apple" there was something definitely threatening our people specifically, and threatening the ship specifically. There is not that specific jeopardy here.

Coon sat down and dictated a letter to Hartman on September 5, telling her:

You are indeed a fine writer. This script is beautiful. However, beauty and fine writing are not always sufficient for our needs.

This would be one of the longer of all his many lengthy correspondences -- 23 pages in all. He had numerous suggestions as to how to sell "Shol" to its detractors and disbelievers. Perhaps the most poignant was in two lines of dialogue he suggested for the end of the script. Kirk is to say, "In God's name, what have we done?" Spock is to reply, "Yes, in God's name."

Coon closed his epic letter to Hartman, saying:

I anticipate great things out of "Shol." I think it can be one of our most exciting shows, and I am sure you will do a splendid job of it.

That splendid job -- Hartman's 2nd Draft -- was finished on October 9, 1967. Sadly, Gene Coon was no longer in a place to be of help to her … or to "Shol." Roddenberry was busy doing a rewrite of his own script, "The Omega Glory," and laying the foundation for a *Star Trek* spin-off series ("Assignment: Earth"). *Star Trek* had a new producer, and Fontana and Justman warned him away from "Shol." In an October 16 memo to John Meredyth Lucas, the new man in charge, Justman wrote:

I find D.C. Fontana's critique better written and more logical than Mrs. Hartman's script. Under no circumstances should this teleplay go back to Mrs. Hartman for repairs. We have no guarantee that we will get a revision back from

465

her in time to get it on the air this season.

The script was shelved and Darlene Hartman ended her association with *Star Trek* here, although not her association with Roddenberry. In the many phone calls she and Roddenberry exchanged, an idea for a *Star Trek* spin-off series called "Hopeship" came about. The premise involved a hospital in space, run by Dr. Mbenga (a character Roddenberry would write into "A Private Little War," and who would return for D.C. Fontana's story "That Which Survives"). The series was never realized, but Hartman did, with Roddenberry's blessing, go on to have five science fiction novels published in the 'Einai series' based on the characters and universe of *Star Trek*, under her pseudonym, Simon Lang. To prevent problems with Paramount, Kirk was retooled as Captain Paul Riker; Spock as a half-human/half-Einai science officer named Dao Marik; and the Enterprise as the U.S.S. Skipjack. Hartman's first novel was *All the Gods of Eisernon*, from 1973. It was based on her *Star Trek* story outline, "Krail." Her fifth novel in the series, *Hopeship*, brought to life the series concept she and Roddenberry had often discussed.

ST-66, "The Microbe," assigned after a pitch from John Kneubuhl and planned as his second writing assignment, following "Bread and Circuses," never even made it onto the written page. Things had gone that badly with his first script (see The Story Behind the Story for "Bread and Circuses").

ST-67, "The Joy Machine," AKA "The Root of Evil," was the third assignment given to Theodore Sturgeon. The story outline made it in on May 16, 1967. Roddenberry's word to Coon, on May 23, "Sturgeon is not up to his best form in this outline."

Coon went to work with Sturgeon, who never easily accepted constructive criticism. It was a fight, but the revised outline did arrive, hitting Coon's desk five long weeks later, on June 23. More than two months passed and by early September, 1967, the 1st Draft script had yet to materialize. Everyone at *Star Trek* wanted a third script from Theodore Sturgeon. Coon was assured by Sturgeon's agent that it was being written. The delivery was less certain (see Book 3 for more on "The Joy Machine").

ST-68, "The Lost Star," was a second assignment given to John Meredyth Lucas, writer of "The Changeling." Two drafts of a treatment were completed, from June 5 and 24, 1967. The story begins with the Enterprise hitting a force field surrounding an entire solar system, a field that has rendered the system invisible to outsiders. The ship penetrates the field into the system of the lost star but, as a result, is severely damaged. To find materials needed for repairs, a landing party beams down to a Class M planet and discovers that the world is populated by primitive people, allegedly kept as slaves by a race known as The Old Ones. The Enterprise party also spots a large modern city, unapproachable as a result of another shield. But all indications are that this city is abandoned and Kirk and Spock are told by the leaders of the primitives that the Old Ones left centuries ago and only return to punish those who break with the rules -- rules that suppress the society and cause it to degenerate.

Without the approval of the leaders, Kirk has his men begin operations to mine the ore needed to make repairs on the Enterprise, but some of these men are killed through mysterious means. Through a Vulcan mind link with Kollos, a female in training to become one of the leaders, Spock is able to ascertain that there are no Old Ones. The primitive people on this world are the descendents of the advanced civilization that once existed here. These leaders, the only ones with knowledge of the past, which is handed down to a chosen few in each new generation, have cut their people off from all outside contact. Because their ancestors came close to annihilating themselves, the leaders are fearful that outside contact will lead to self-destruction. Hidden from the people by their leaders is the truth about their heritage, that only a handful from the ancient ones survived a war and that these fearful people became the architects of all that was to follow on this world -- an isolated people with no known past and no worthwhile future. While the people live as savages, their rulers have been secretly trained in ways to tap into energy sources emitting from the ancient city and are able to use this power to not only shield their world but annihilate their enemies.

Spock, using his telepathic skills, is able to break through to Kollos and convince her that he and those from the Starfleet pose no harm, and that her people would prosper if allowed to live free and, as a race, to grow. Kollos uses her mind, and the power she is able to draw from the ancient city, to open a tunnel in space, penetrating the force shield surrounding the solar system. Once the Enterprise makes it through the tunnel, the shield closes up again. Kirk and Spock can only speculate whether Kollos will incite change on her world, or be killed by those who fear it.

Justman's comment, boiled down to two words: "Too expensive!"

On June 8, Dorothy Fontana wrote to Gene Coon:

I have a feeling this would be an all-talk show. And I foresee a dull 64 pages, no matter how sparkling the dialogue may turn out to be.

Roddenberry agreed and, on June 9, wrote to Coon:

An interesting story, intellectually stimulating, and it shows the evidence of hard work and dedication. But, as presently laid out, it is hardly the kind of action-adventure that will keep our audience with us.... Lucas works hard to give his stories believable characterizations, logic and consistency. But he is not giving us action-adventure entertainment in this. Someone should tell him that a story is defined as a "need" for something to happen or not happen -- a need which involves a jeopardy which grows greater and greater as the story progresses.... On the other hand, he probably knows all this. Maybe it's enough to simply remind him that it applies to science-fiction stories too.

On July 5, Stan Robertson, while finding Lucas's story outline to be "well written," rejected it on grounds that is was "lacking excitement, color and emotional involvement."

Lucas was asked to pitch something else that he might want to write. That something else would evolve into the episode "Patterns of Force."

ST-69, "He Walked Among Us," by Norman Spinrad, was the sci-fi author's follow-up assignment to "The Doomsday Machine." It was another man-as-a-god story, as well as another prime-directive story. The plot elements were reminiscent of the upcoming "Patterns of Force," minus all the Nazi business.

In Spinrad's story, Kirk searches for a way to reverse the interference inflicted on an alien culture by Federation scientist Dr. Theodore Bayne, or, at the least, prevent further interference. Bayne, who crash-landed on the planet Jugal, is obsessed with theories of better ways to run a developing society and has seized power to realize his concepts and goals. But Bayne is frustrated that each time he makes a change that should benefit the people of Jugal, the opposite seems to happen. Kirk would like to simply pluck Bayne from Jugal, but this is not possible since the inhabitants have come to think of him as a god and, should he vanish, the two primary power figures, King Kaneb and High Priest Lokar, will fight for control and plunge the population into a bloody war. Kaneb knows of Bayne's true origin and past. He found Bayne after his crash landing and, thinking he could use Bayne in his quest to gain power over High Priest Lokar, presented the Earthman to the people as a deity. In light of the problems now being faced on Jugal, Kaneb has come to regret doing this and Bayne's life is in danger. Kirk uses this information and also proves to Bayne that his tinkering on Jugal has done more harm than good. Bayne agrees to leave with the Enterprise, with a departing message to the people of Jugal that Kaneb and Lokar remain in their present positions, as a shared leadership.

Norman Spinrad said, "It began with Gene Roddenberry. Gene says, 'Milton Berle wants to do a show and we've got this set which we'd like to use -- it's this exterior set which is something like a semi-primitive village with overgrown weeds and shit -- so why don't you go drive down there to the Desilu backlot and take a look at it and see what you can come up with. And they had this Prime Directive -- the idea that you're not supposed to interfere with the culture of a less advanced civilization on another planet. So I came up with the idea of a guy who goes there and he's violated the Prime Directive, so they've got to get him out of there and do it in a way that they aren't violating the Directive themselves. And that was the genesis of the thing." (165-4)

The story advanced through three outlines, from May 12, 17, and 18. Fontana wrote Coon on May 18, saying:

> The story needs to be punched up -- in fact, *rewritten*.

But NBC was okay with it as presented in the third draft outline, so Coon sent Spinrad to script. The 1st Draft arrived on June 15. Justman, on June 20, wrote Coon:

> No doubt you will remember that I made a statement about Norman Spinrad evidencing definite signs of becoming a highly skilled television writer. I would like to retract this opinion. This teleplay is very sloppy.

Fontana echoed this thinking the following day, writing:

> There are too many people, not enough action, indecision and no assertiveness on the part of Kirk, and dreadful dialogue.

Coon sent Spinrad one of his notorious long letters -- 22 pages long! -- on June 26, beginning:

> We have many problems with "He Walked Among Us." In "The Doomsday Machine," wrote a story which was 90% action and 10% characterization and dialogue. In "He Walked Among Us," the situation is reversed. It is a story which depends 90% upon good, accurate, sparkling characterization delineation and dialogue. Unfortunately, we don't have these things in this version.

Spinrad tried again, sending his rewrite in on July 12. Dorothy Fontana attacked it on July 18, writing to Coon:

> What is wrong with this script is the same thing that was wrong with "The Apple," and you recall what was wrong with "The Apple." It was poorly structured, badly characterized, and had unspeakable dialogue.

And so Coon did what he had done with "The Apple," he rewrote the script himself. His 1st Draft, dated July 25, shared the writing credit with Spinrad. There were now moments of comedy where previously had been extreme seriousness.

Norman Spinrad later said, "It was quite a serious concept -- and Milton Berle, even though he was a comedian and known as 'Uncle Miltie,' had done some serious un-comedic acting -- and that's what he wanted to do. He didn't want to do a funny show. He wanted to do something serious; I understood that. But Gene Coon didn't get it. And he was the producer at this point, and he said, 'This thing needs another draft; who can I trust to do it? I know! Me!' I got really pissed off when Gene Coon said to me, 'Play ball and you'll be making a lot of money.' In other words, 'Let me steal this and we can steal some more stuff from you and you'll get half the money.' So he rewrote it into an unfunny comedy. I guess he thought that was Milton Berle, or whatever was in his head, but it was dreadful." (165-4)

Justman gave the 2nd Draft a thumbs down on July 18. On August 7, Dorothy Fontana did, as well, writing:

I'm afraid I remain somewhat unenthusiastic about this script.

Spinrad said, "It was just horrible. And I called up Roddenberry and I said, 'Gene, I've read this piece of shit and you can't shoot this! Read it!' And Gene read it and said, 'You're right; we can't do it.' So I killed my own script. It cost me a lot of money, but it was dreadful." (165-4)

"He Walked Among Us," however, was not completely dead. In fact, it came closer to getting made than any of *Star Trek*'s other unproduced scripts. It was the only one to actually be placed on the production roster. On September 22, 1967, while "Journey to Babel" was filming, and with "A Private Little War" due to start in days, Robert Justman released a schedule of the next three episodes to film. "Gamesters of Triskelion" was first, followed by "Obsession" and then "He Walked Among Us." But first it needed a rewrite to remove the comedy aspects. The job was given to Gene Coon's successor -- John Meredyth Lucas. His rewrite came in on September 28.

On October 2, Roddenberry wrote directly to Lucas, saying:

Although this draft contains many good elements and is certainly an improvement over some of the other drafts, its structure causes the story to miss. We need more jeopardies, more suspense elements, more needs -- steadily mounting all through the tale, seemingly more and more impossible to resolve until our climactic moments.... Perhaps most of all, the thing we've missed most all along every version of this script by various writers is a Theme or premise. What is this story about? What statement are we making?

No one knew, so "He Walked Among Us" was finally put aside.

ST-76 was a rebirth of ST-2, and another try at Roddenberry's "The Omega Glory," this time by Lester and Tina Pine. Les Pine had worked often for producer Blake Edwards on TV's *Peter Gunn* and *Mr. Lucky*. His wife, Tina, a former actress, had recently started writing and collaborated on a script with her husband for *I Spy*. Their version of "The Omega Glory" made it to 1st Draft script, but failed to go farther (see The Story Behind the Story for "The Omega Glory").

ST-77, "Pandora's Box," by Daniel Aubrey, who wrote for *Rat Patrol*, made it through two story drafts, dated August 8 and September 9. The story involved the discovery of rock creatures on an asteroid intended to be used as a Federation outpost. The creatures feed on plutonium and, while attempting to eat from the portable nuclear generators brought to the asteroid, they kill a couple of Enterprise crewmen. When gorged, the creatures emit surplus energy and are able to do miraculous things, such as beam themselves to the Enterprise, which one of the aliens does while in search of a new food source. Kirk, in an effort to protect his crew, devises a plan to lure the creatures to their death. Spock, however, discovers that these living rocks might prove to be useful if the surplus energy they emit can be harnessed, and if they can be communicated with.

Fontana was the first to be appalled and, on August 28, wrote to Coon:

> I do not believe asteroids have atmospheres. Our people would have to beam down with full gear *a la* "The Naked Time," which is bulky, awkward, does not look especially convincing and masks our people's expressions.... Much of the discussion about dying, and the inability of the creature to grasp such a concept has been said in much the same way in "Metamorphosis."... There are some elements of this story that are very much like "The Man Trap" from last season.

Justman wrote to Coon on September 9, saying:

> I have gotten the feeling from reading this Treatment that the creature is so goddamn hungry that it will gobble up anything that contains energy. How has it managed to keep itself alive until our landing party has come along? Can we explain it away by just saying that it has been on a terrifically long fast and that it is now gorging itself like a hungry man at a banquet table?... How come the creature gobbles up the two guys in the Transporter Room, but leaves five people alone in the Corridor? Are the five people in the Corridor the wrong flavor?... Every once in a while, as I read this material, I find myself breaking-up. The reaction means one of two things. Either the audience is going to find this effort amusing in the wrong way, or else I have a pretty weird sense of humor.... I do feel this outline bears amazing resemblances to a show we did last season called "The Devil in the Dark." The description of the monster seems to be remarkably like that of the one we had in last year's effort.

By calling "The Devil in the Dark" an "effort," Justman was letting Coon know that he did not consider the episode to have been successful. And this was an episode Coon had written. Roddenberry, in fact, did not care for "The Devil in the Dark" until the fans started referring to it as a classic.

Regarding "The Devil in the Dark," Justman told this author, "I appreciated the story. I appreciated the point of the story. I may have appreciated the teleplay, at various stages of its development. I did not feel we pulled that one off. Not entirely. Now many people believe it to be one of our best. And I appreciate that." (94-1)

Justman's memo to Coon continued:

> It seems to digest its victims in the same way, also. Of course, last year's creature [the Horta] did not have the ability to dematerialize at will, but it did have the ability to lay an awful lot of eggs. If we go ahead with this project, I hope that the creature does not lay another kind of egg.... Perhaps by this time you have received a vague impression that I am dissatisfied with this story. Well, don't jump to conclusions. It is quite impossible for a person to be dissatisfied with a story if there is no story to be dissatisfied with.... By this time in the season, I am not interested in conducting written seminars on the art of constructing believable dramatic fare. I'm going to leave you with one question. Would you, as a writer, be able to turn in something like this to a producer and honestly expect to be paid for your effort?

These stories, in all, cost the producers of *Star Trek* a great deal of money, effort, and time. Regardless, the toll was not as great as it had been during Season One. The reason there were fewer casualties was that Hollywood's TV writers now knew what *Star Trek* looked like. The toll on Gene Coon, however, had been high. He had put much hope, and work, in Darlene Hartman's "Shol," and less hope, but just as much work, in Paul Schneider's "Tomorrow the World" and Norman Spinrad's "He Walked Among Us." Coupled with all the blood, sweat, and tears that went into the 23 second season scripts he worked on that did make the cut, Coon had lost his will to keep up the fight.

Now it was up to John Meredyth Lucas to continue on. Despite these rejects, there were several more scripts handled off from Coon to Lucas to make it before the camera. The first of those was "The Immunity Syndrome."

29

Episode 48: THE IMMUNITY SYNDROME

Written by Robert Sabaroff
(with John Meredyth Lucas, uncredited)
Directed by Joseph Pevney

Spock "feels" the death of 400 Vulcans
(Unaired film trim courtesy of Gerald Gurian)

From NBC press release, issued December 28, 1967:

Captain Kirk (William Shatner) and his crew must destroy a virus which has annihilated three solar systems and another starship or suffer the same fate, in "The Immunity Syndrome" on NBC Television Network's *Star Trek* colorcast Friday, Jan. 10…. The Enterprise is en route for rest and recreation when Star Fleet Command orders Kirk to investigate the disappearance of Starship Intrepid. Simultaneously, Mr. Spock (Leonard Nimoy) suffers a spasm. Upon recovering he announces that he "felt" the death of the Intrepid and 400 Vulcans who were aboard. When the Enterprise gets close enough to probe a black mass which threatens the very existence of the known universe, Kirk has no alternative but to pierce it with his own ship and attack from within.

TV Guide didn't limit itself to the NBC press releases when seeking programming information for its magazine. Its editors would often solicit material directly from the *Star Trek* offices. While the synopsis were much shorter in *TV Guide*, as required by the magazine's format (unless meant to accompany a CLOSE-UP listing), they were often more succinct than the press releases circulated by the network, as the listing from the magazine's January 13, 1968 issue demonstrated:

In "The Immunity Syndrome," the Enterprise assumes the role of an antibody as it penetrates a one-celled organism 11,000 miles long. The energy-draining invader has already annihilated an entire star system -- and is about to reproduce. This episode features psychedelic special effects created by Frank Van der Veer.

As the Enterprise loses power, and is pulled closer to certain destruction, the crew becomes weaker and Dr. McCoy deduces they are dying. Aided by chemical stimulants, Kirk and his bridge personnel struggle to stay at their posts. Time is quickly running out. To escape the pull and appetite of the giant "amoeba," more information is needed than an unmanned probe can supply. Spock and McCoy each volunteer to pilot a shuttlecraft into the center of the space phenomenon, clearly a suicide mission. Kirk must decide which of his friends will die.

By design, at the center of this story is the age-old question, "Who am I?" The intent of the writer was to propose one possible answer: In order to form a balance in the universe, we are collectively interconnected elements in a greater design. For the rest of us, "The Immunity Syndrome" will more likely fall into the less esoteric category of "Man against Nature."

SOUND BITES

- *Kirk:* "This thing's 11,000 miles long - and it's just one cell. When it divides into millions, we'll be the virus invading its body!" *McCoy:* "Now, isn't that a thought ... here we are, antibodies of our own galaxy, attacking an invading germ. It would be ironic indeed if that were our sole destiny, wouldn't it?"
- *McCoy, to Spock:* "Vulcan dignity? How can I grant you what I don't understand?" *Spock:* "Then employ one of your own superstitions. Wish me luck."
- *McCoy, interrupting a conversation between Kirk and Spock:* "Shut up, Spock, we're rescuing you." *Spock's voice, from speaker:* "Why, thank you, Captain McCoy."

ASSESSMENT

No one had ever seen anything like it, and anyone with a color television set in January 1968 was in for a treat. The optical effects, for their time, were stunning.

The direction, too, is top notch. Joseph Pevney was able to deliver a fascinating concept, rich with personal jeopardy and conflict, from a script somewhat stagnant and in need of maybe just one more polish.

With the written material needing a bit more sharpening, and a proper Tag scene, which this episode badly lacks, "The Immunity Syndrome" is not *Star Trek* at its best, but it isn't far off. The concept is intriguing, the drama taut, and the visuals are dazzling. Do we really need better than this?

THE STORY BEHIND THE STORY

Script Timeline:
Robert Sabaroff's story outline, ST #74: August 7, 1967.
Sabaroff's revised story outline, gratis: August 14, 1967.
Sabaroff's 1ˢᵗ Draft script: September 8, 1967.
Sabaroff's 2ⁿᵈ Draft script: October 9, 1967.
John Meredyth Lucas' rewrite (Final Draft): October 17, 1967.
Additional page revisions by Lucas: October 20, 23 & 24.

Robert Sabaroff wrote short stories before breaking into television. One of these,

473

"Ding Dong Ghoul," published in the June 1960 issue of *Playboy*, indicated his interest in horror and science fiction, even though his first TV credits were mostly westerns. He provided scripts for *Death Valley Days*, *The Deputy*, and Jeffrey Hunter's western series, *Temple Houston*, as well as multiple episodes of *The Virginian* and *Bonanza*. Sabaroff got his chance at filmed science fiction with two episodes of *The Invaders*, written just before coming to *Star Trek*. For the big screen, he had recently finished the screenplay for 1968's *The Split*, starring Jim Brown, Diahann Carroll, and Ernest Borgnine. Also in the cast, Gene Hackman and Donald Sutherland. An example of Sabaroff's catchy writing in this story of robbers who squabble over $85,000 in hot loot comes when Sutherland's character tells Jim Brown, "Listen, Marty, the last man I killed I did it for $5,000. For $85,000 I'd kill you 17 times."

Sabaroff had been keeping an eye on *Star Trek*. He said, "You had to watch a lot of episodes of *Star Trek* to write for it. You had to know how those characters talked and reacted." (150)

Once Sabaroff felt familiar with the show, he requested a meeting with Gene Coon. He said, "Gene explained that they had run out of guest star money but they still had a special FX budget. He asked me to write a story that wouldn't require a guest star." (150)

For his inspiration, Sabaroff turned to the inner depths of biology and envisioned a monster that would be a single-celled organism. The structure of the story, at this stage, was very different from what was eventually filmed.

In Sabaroff's first stab at an outline, it is medical staff member Dr. Loretta Meyers, not McCoy, who competes with Spock for the assignment to take the shuttlecraft into the heart of the amoeba. Sabaroff's treatment tells us:

> Loretta believes that the alien body is a giant virus, spawned by spontaneous generation in a force field and a sea of hydrogen atoms. But a virus can only function inside a living cell. Kirk is stunned by the concept that the Universe itself is a cell -- the solar system, star clusters, even galaxies being only bundles of greater matter arranged toward the construction of a super-organism.... They [Kirk and Loretta] reflect that it would be indeed ironic if the ultimate function and historical purpose of Man's evolution were to serve the function of antibodies to the universe -- a line of defense against viral bodies seeking to make the Universe sneeze -- an ignominious *raison d'etre* indeed, by Kirk's standards. The most noble one, by Loretta's. She wonders who the Universe is.

NBC preferred that theoretical notions of this type *not* be bantered about in their prime time entertainment broadcasts. The part about the irony if "the ultimate function and historical purpose of Man's evolution were to serve [as] the function of antibodies to the universe" was stricken.

Something else to do with Sabaroff's story which was not clearly communicated in the final shooting script, but clear as a bell in the first outline, was articulated by Sabaroff writing:

> The chemical corrosion taking place on the [shuttle] craft is unparalleled in

design anticipation, and she [Loretta] soon realizes that the orgasm is attempting to DIGEST the craft.

The idea of life being drained out of the crew had not yet been added to the story. But there was a "surge of power" which affected the crew. Sabaroff wrote:

Every man aboard somehow feeling he has seen the face of death -- death within his being -- not the exterior death whose reality has long been such a close part of their lives.

Prouder Gene Coon liked the intellectual aspects present in the story outline for "The Immunity Syndrome." Associate Producer Robert Justman, as usual, was less impressed. On August 7, Justman wrote Coon:

It is a very interesting "sci-fi" short story, [but] I do not see how one can make a *Star Trek* out of this submission. I anticipate a very talky screenplay and a general lack of action and conflict. I cannot see a story that is evidently quite clear to you. You are the Producer and you make more money than I do -- therefore, you must be right. But I still have the bathroom! (RJ48-1)

Justman's office came with a private toilet and sink. Coon's did not.

Story consultant Dorothy Fontana followed one day later, writing Coon:

It is esoteric, but not *Star Trek* adventure. There is too much talk and discussion delineated and hardly any action.... There is no human involvement of our people. No head-on conflicts between them. There is, in fact, very little they can fight. Therefore, they must have discussions on it. This is dull. NBC will say it's too cerebral, too eternal, and not what they bought as a series. They will be right. (DCF48-1)

But Coon liked this *Fantastic Voyage*-type idea for *Star Trek* and appreciated the subtle elements hidden within the story. He was determined he could work the bugs out of Sabaroff's intriguing premise. For the revised outline, Coon wanted Kirk's emotional stakes increased and had Sabaroff drop the character of Dr. Loretta Meyers.

Sabaroff said, "When you don't have a guest star or an antagonist that can be characterized, you must construct conflict within your ensemble. I got that with the rivalry between Spock and McCoy for the 'privilege' of entering this creature. Kirk has to choose between his two friends, which gives him an emotional dilemma -- another obligatory element." (150)

More tension was created by having the crew slowly dying, as Kirk and his bridge personnel, pumped full of stimulants, hang on by a thin thread.

Sabaroff credited Coon with helping steer his story toward the conflict that would keep it interesting despite the economy being used in sets and cast. Coon, he said, was "a very under-remembered man who was one of the major creative forces of *Star Trek*." (150)

Ironically, by the time the 1st Draft script arrived, on September 8, Coon was transferring the script development duties for episodes outside of the initial NBC order for 16 to John Meredyth Lucas -- and "The Immunity Syndrome" became one of those passed into Lucas's care.

On September 14, Dorothy Fontana directed a memo to Lucas, writing:

475

In general, I have mixed feelings regarding this script. I think it can be very exciting, [but] I feel a distinct lack of complete characterization of our leads and poor usage of them.... In all, I feel Bob [Sabaroff] has missed in many areas of character development.... We must be more visual and go more with the people involved, not with their voices. And there must be a wrap that has a bit more action... we should see it, not hear about it in voice over. (DCF48-2)

Justman told Lucas:

At the beginning of Act III, Kirk prevents McCoy from going with Spock in the Shuttlecraft because McCoy is very indispensible "on board the Enterprise." If he is so indispensible, then why was he allowed to inject himself with a universal anti-toxin in Act I? (RJ48-2)

The universal anti-toxin would be stricken.

Sabaroff turned in his 2nd Draft teleplay on October 9. The ending remained dark, and very cerebral. Kirk asks the computer, "Assessment -- probability of recurrence of current phenomenon?" The computer answers, "The period of the human existence may expect to encounter the occurrence of new life three times. You who built me evolved from the first such occurrence. You who built me have just ended the hope of the second. Your comprehension and my program are insufficient to conceive the third." At this point, Spock, who is listening, slowly closes his eyes. FADE OUT.

Lucas remained busy producing the two interim episodes, handling the final rewrites of "Gamesters of Triskelion," from the last days of September through October 12, and then "Obsession," from October 13 through 17. It was on October 17, while "Gamesters" -- the second of those two episodes to film -- was in its first day of production that Lucas finally turned his attention to the script for the next episode ... without even knowing if there would be a next episode. During that painful 48-hours period, as rumors circulated throughout the production offices and onto the soundstage about *Star Trek* being finished, Lucas rewrote "The Immunity Syndrome."

"The show was in constant trouble for scripts and lead time to prepare and make air dates," Lucas said. "Networks did little to contribute to the welfare of their series. They would wait until the last second to announce pickups ... but by then it was almost too late." (110-6)

In Lucas's mind, "The Immunity Syndrome" was the logical choice for episode 19 of Season Two. It was a ship-bound bottle show requiring no new sets, and only the main cast, including regular bit players Eddie Paskey, William Blackburn, and Frank da Vinci, were required. "The Immunity Syndrome" could easily be rushed into production with little preparation. The greater challenge for an episode such as this would be on the back end with the photographic effects.

It was late in the day on October 18 before NBC gave *Star Trek* its mid season pickup. Lucas had roughed out a revised draft of the script one day before and now had only seven days before the episode was set to start filming. His first decision was to not waste any time reading memos.

"When I arrived, everybody had a dictating machine and would write long communications, critiques and suggestions on the script in work," Lucas later said. "These

476

were sometimes helpful but the time consumed in the practice of gathering everybody's opinion was considerable. Everybody dictated, secretaries were tied up in the typing of these memos and everybody read everybody else's comments, using up still more time. I would have preferred a call to say, 'This isn't good.' Or 'We can't afford this.' I discontinued the use of my machine and, of course, so did everyone else." (110-6)

Lucas took his notes from Fontana and Justman over the phone, making it possible for him to spend every possible minute writing toward his deadline, but making it impossible for us to know who contributed further ideas to the script as it was developed. While considering the various suggestions from his creative staff, Lucas rushed through three more rewrites, on October 20, 23, and 24.

De Forest Research continued to send in notes to help guide Lucas through his rewrites. Peter Sloman, who read all the scripts with Joan Pearce and wrote the memos advising the producers what was possible and what was not, said, "At the point that *Star Trek* came along, it was the best of what there was. And there were times when it was great. I mean, there were episodes that were really brilliantly done. But, at the same time, it could have been better if they had gone for a smaller audience of geeks. But then they wouldn't even have gotten past the first season. So, I think that *Star Trek* did a very good job of treading that line. It did look real. And it did feel real. You get the feeling that it could look like that. It could be like that. It might not be but it could be. It was plausible. Not probable but plausible." (158a)

Filming began on October 25 without the loss of a single day for the production company. Lucas was then free to turn his attention toward "A Piece of the Action," the next script slated to film.

Pre-Production
October 17–20 & 23-24, 1967; (6 prep days; budget set at $171,391).

Joseph Pevney returned after several weeks away from *Star Trek* to resume his duties as one of the series' three rotating directors. However, this would be Pevney's final *Trek* (see "Production Diary").

Along with all the last minute rewrites, another down-to-the-wire decision concerned the casting of the helmsman. Due to bad weather, George Takei was still on the set of *The Green Berets*. John Winston's character, Lt. Kyle, always in the transporter room, was brought forward to man the helm in place of Sulu.

John Wayne with George Takei on location for *The Green Berets*, **way over its shooting schedule (Warner Bros., 1968)**

"I was usually stuck down in the transporter room," Winston said. "So, when the scenes were shot, I'd say my few lines and let them move on to do the rest of the show. But they did put me on the bridge once or twice and I got a good look at how they managed the madness of that short six day schedule. That was Shatner, again. I have great admiration for him, because he could pick up a page of dialogue and that was it -- it got done. He'd look at it and he'd do it. And do it right. And then on to the next page. Very excellent." (189a)

Production Diary
Filmed October 25, 26, 27, 30, 31 and November 1, 1967.
(6 day production)

Director Joseph Pevney (left) takes his final trek,
with Nichols, Kelley, Shatner, and Koenig
(Courtesy of Gerald Gurian)

Wednesday, October 25, 1967. *The Jungle Book* was brand new in the movie houses and already box office champ. *The Red Skelton Hour* had attracted more TV viewers than any other show the night before. "To Sir, With Love," by Lulu, continued to get the most airplay on U.S. radio stations. The top seller in record stores was *Diana Ross & The Supremes Greatest Hits*, followed by The Beatles' *Sgt. Pepper's Lonely Hearts Club Band*. New on the newsstands was the first issue of *Rolling Stone Magazine*, with John Lennon on its cover. And it only cost 25 cents. A pack of cigarettes was 30 cents. A McDonald's Big Mac, introduced this year, was 45 cents. And *Star Trek* began production of "The Immunity Syndrome" on Desilu/Paramount Stage 9 and the bridge set.

Day 1. The Teaser and first half of Act I were filmed in sequential order.

478

Day 2, Thursday. On the same set, director Pevney filmed the balance of the Act I bridge scenes, followed by all of those in Act II and most of Act III.

Day 3. John Winston dons a gold top to take over for George Takei at the helm (Courtesy of Gerald Gurian)

Day 3, Friday. Another full day was spent on the bridge set, finishing the scenes needed there for Act III and all of Act IV.

William Shatner and Joseph Pevney added a near-perfect ending to the episode. The script, as a result of all the rushed rewriting, ended abruptly with Lt. Kyle reporting that Spock's shuttlecraft was back on the hangar deck. With the story's intense drama having concluded only seconds before, all John Meredyth Lucas could think of was to have Kirk tell Chekov to lay in course for Star Base Six, warp factor Five. Feeling a need for more punch, Pevney and Shatner conspired to sneak in a little naughty business. Kirk repeated his line from the beginning of the story -- creating a dialogue bookend -- about looking forward to resting on some "lovely planet," during which Pevney aimed a pretty short-skirted yeoman at the Captain, with a report for him to sign. Shatner said "I'm looking forward to a nice period of rest and relaxation on some lovely …," and then paused as he looked at and admired the Yeoman. Only after she smiled and turned away did he finish with the word "planet," at which point he exchanged mischievous looks with McCoy.

Later this night, NBC premiered "Catspaw." *Star Trek* placed second in the Nielsens for its entire hour.

Day 4, Monday. During the morning hours, filming took place in Kirk's quarters, followed by the briefing room. A Sulu double appears in the briefing room scene and, in a small way, Sulu's continued presence as a member of the Enterprise crew is conveyed.

During the afternoon, the company filmed in engineering.

Day 5, Tuesday. Work began on Stage 10 for the scenes inside the shuttlecraft. Only Leonard Nimoy was needed. He had his usual 6:30 a.m. makeup call, and reported to the set at 8 a.m. to begin filming. DeForest Kelley had a 9:15 a.m. makeup call. He was on the set at 10 a.m. to work with Nimoy in the corridor outside the hangar deck, also built onto Stage 10. Majel Barrett had a 9:30 a.m. makeup call, and was on set at 11 a.m. for the medical lab scene, with the crew now back on Stage 9. William Shatner arrived for makeup at 12 noon. He was on the set at 1 p.m. (following the lunch break) for his scenes with Spock and McCoy in the examination room and sickbay. Five extras were also booked for this day.

Visiting the set was Peggye Vickers, from Garland, Texas. Ms. Vickers was 27 and had written to Nimoy asking permission to start a fan club for him in her home town. It began in February 1967 and, in eight months, had grown to 1,197 members. As a thank you, Nimoy paid to bring Vickers to Los Angeles for a visit to his home and the *Star Trek* sets. *TV Radio Show* covered the promotional event for its October 1967 issue (to be printed again in the January 1968 issue of sister magazine *TV Radio Mirror*), with pictures of Vickers posing with Nimoy and director Joe Pevney, then with Spock on the transporter platform, on the bridge, and by the shuttlecraft on the hangar deck. She said, "When Leonard was in a scene, I sat on the sidelines watching. I got to talk to everyone. Nichelle Nichols was especially nice -- she showed me some new photographs that had been taken of her -- and I was really impressed

Day 5. Peggye Vickers visits Nimoy on Stage 10
(*TV Radio Mirror*, **January 1968**)

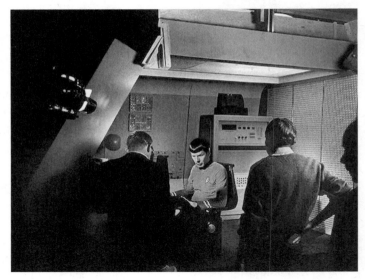

Day 5. Nimoy blocks his scene with director Pevney (on left) for the interior shuttlecraft, on Stage 10 (Courtesy of Gerald Gurian)

with the authenticity of the set. The spaceship looked so real. The biggest thrill of the day for me was lunch. I just had a tuna sandwich and a Coke, but I stood in line with Leonard and the other cast members at the lunch truck parked outside the stage. This really made me feel like one of them."

Day 6, Wednesday, November 1, 1967. Pevney filmed in sickbay and the exam room, finishing on schedule.

This was Joseph Pevney's fourteenth and final episode of *Star Trek*. He explained, "When Gene Coon left the show, much of the discipline had gone. From the time I made 'Arena' to the time I did my last show, there was a hell of a difference.... The actors were already ingrained in behavior patterns which didn't permit new inventiveness which was, as they felt, opposed to their character.... That was the beginning of the problem. Bill wouldn't do certain scenes because 'Kirk wouldn't do that.' Leonard certainly felt that way, and very strongly, because his character was so deeply ingrained that he knew precisely how Spock would behave in a setting.... This attitude on their part was right in certain respects, with the actor protecting himself, but wrong in the fact that their minds were closed to new inventiveness.... Now, I don't bend with that kind of stuff. The director *is* the director. You want to be a director? Go. Be a director. But when *I* am the director and you're the actor, you make the greatest contribution you can, and *I* make the choices.... I couldn't enjoy working on *Star Trek* anymore. The show's whole character had changed for me." (141-1)

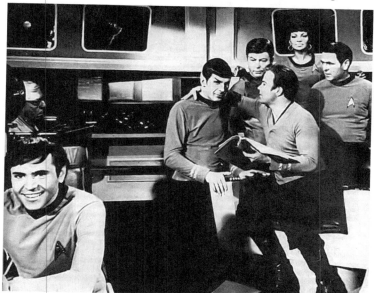

Director Pevney said, "When Gene Coon left the show, much of the discipline had gone." (Photo courtesy of Gerald Gurian)

Nimoy, disagreeing with Pevney's thinking, said, "I've always felt very strongly that the actor is the protector of the character. The character is stuck with the actor who plays him. It is sort of a father/son relationship. The actor is the keeper of the character, in terms of developing the character and in terms of the continuity and credibility of the character. The writers come and go, the producers come and go and the directors come and go. Those are revolving door jobs. It's up to the actor to keep the character protected." (128-9)

Defending his right to know what Kirk would and would not do, Shatner said, "I think there's a great deal of my own personality in the character, if only because, with 79 shows, day after day, week after week, year after year, the fatigue is such that you can only try to be as honest about yourself as possible. Fatigue wipes away any subterfuge that you might be able to use as an actor in character roles, or trying to delineate something that might not be entirely you.... You're so tired that it can only be you, so I think that in Kirk there's a great deal of me." (156-7)

Robert Sabaroff saw no problem in the performances, and said, "It was a pleasure to write for good actors. I wrote stuff that I wouldn't have dared without the fore-knowledge that they were able to execute it. Many actors are lost without an antagonist to play off of. This episode had to be totally internal to the ensemble cast and it took good acting to pull it off. William Shatner was quite a character. He was able to play his role with force and command, but at the same time with a sense of humor and irony, which was necessary to make it work. Leonard Nimoy was absolutely brilliant." (150)

Post-Production
Available for editing: November 2, 1967. Rough Cut: November 9. Final Cut: November 20.
Music Score: tracked.

Donald R. Rode and Edit Team 4 handled the cutting. As it had happened with "The Corbomite Maneuver," the tension on the bridge, where most of the action takes place, was kept interesting and gripping through meticulous editing, heavily favoring reaction shots.

A reject from the post-production sessions -- a composition shot of the Enterprise (filmed against a green screen) and colored oils pressed between two glass slides (Courtesy of Bob Olsen)

Some not-so-sleight-of-hand work in the editing room was meant to cover up an oversight made during production. When Spock and McCoy are standing outside the hangar deck, McCoy is wearing his short-sleeved top, but the insert shot of him operating the door controls shows a man's arm in a long-sleeved blue uniform. While editing, Rode decided he needed a close-up shot of a control panel, which Joseph Pevney had not provided. Jerry Finnerman was asked to get the shot, using a hand double for Kelley. Wardrobe, knowing only that a blue uniform was needed, sent the long-sleeved top that McCoy most often wore.

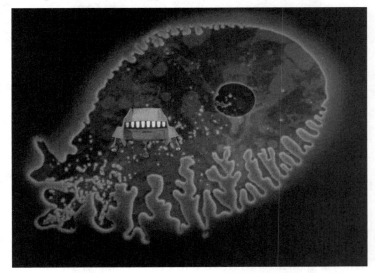

Unaired film trim from "The Immunity Syndrome" (Courtesy of Gerald Gurian)

The picture used in the end title sequence of the shiny-skinned, bald man, was from a

482

makeup test for the upcoming "Return to Tomorrow." The model was William Blackburn.

The challenge of "The Immunity Syndrome" was not so much with the production, but with the post-production. Optical effects never before imagined were needed for this episode. The process used to create the amoeba in space involved using colored oils and water, mixed together and pressed between glass slides, then photographed with a microscopic lens. And, as we all know, oil and water do not mix, allowing for the different shapes and even how some shapes would swell and then contract, as the glass slides were manipulated. After two months, Frank Van der Veer and his team did not disappoint. For their time, these effects were truly mind-boggling.

The impressive shots of the Enterprise, seen here and in the previous episode ("Gamesters of Triskelion"), however, were contributed by Howard Anderson Company and Film Effects of Hollywood, uncredited.

Working at De Forest Research, Pete Sloman's job was to read every story outline and each draft of the scripts, looking for things that were scientifically possible ... or impossible. He said, "I don't like watching the shows I work on. For one thing, knowing what was coming is sort of annoying. And after a while you get to know how an actor is going to deliver a line. I knew exactly how a certain actor was going to deliver his line, and it was actually kind of unsettling. So I usually don't watch the shows I work on but I *did* watch *Star Trek* because I liked to see what they did with the production design. The photographic effects were state of the art for their time. And the thing was, you had guys like Matt Jefferies and Irving Feinberg, who were just masters of their craft. And that bridge set was wonderful. As a visual, as something that seemed plausible, it really worked. I've rarely seen star ships that looked as good on the interior. And I found most of that believable." (158a)

Specifically regarding the photographic effects, and how the shots of the 11-foot, 2-inch Enterprise compared to the computer generated images to come in future spin-offs from *Star Trek*, Sloman said, "There is something about CGI that just doesn't have the weight. I look at really good CGI and then you look at the work that they did with that large Enterprise miniature, for instance, or the work from *2001*, or the folks on the original *Star Wars*, when the Imperial cruiser comes overhead -- and that's one of the great visual moments in the history of movies -- and there really is very little that can stand up to what they were able to accomplish with those miniatures." (158a)

This is the first episode funded and controlled by the new studio, with the Paramount Television logo replacing that of Desilu. Being a bottle show with no guest stars, the first Paramount episode was brought in close to its $171,391 budget.

Release / Reaction:
Premiere air date: 1/19/68. NBC repeat broadcast: 6/7/68.

Steven H. Scheuer reviewed the episode for *TV Key Previews*. Among newspapers across America to carry Scheuer's syndicated column on June 7, 1968 (for the encore broadcast of "The Immunity Syndrome") was *The Evening News*, serving Daytona Beach, Florida. Scheuer said:

There is a combination of excellent special effects, an imaginative story and first-rate action tonight on *Star Trek*, again making this series a good bet.

Captain Kirk and the Enterprise penetrate a giant cell, 11,000 miles long. In reality, it is a virus germ which has already destroyed three solar systems and is on the verge of reproduction. The entire program rests on this story with none but the regular cast involved.

RATINGS / Nielsen National report for Friday, February 19, 1968:

8:30 to 9 pm, 63.0% U.S. TVs in use.	Share:	Households watching:
NBC: *Star Trek*	26.2%	12,380,000
ABC: *Operation: Entertainment*	25.0%	12,150,000
CBS: **Gomer Pyle, U.S.M.C.**	**43.8%**	**17,190,000**
Independent stations:	5.0%	No data

9 to 9:30 pm, 65.1% U.S. TVs in use.	Share:	Households watching:
NBC: *Star Trek*	26.3%	No data
ABC: *Operation: Entertainment*	27.4%	No data
CBS: **Friday Night Movie**	**32.0%**	**No data**
Independent stations:	14.3%	No data

It was an eye-opening episode of *Star Trek*. The ratings, per Nielsen, said it did about the same as all the episodes for this season -- in second place. During the second half, however, it slipped under *Operation: Entertainment* by about 1% of the households watching TV at this time. The ABC series had the popular Dick Cavett as host for this segment, with a show from Fort Hood, Texas, featuring performances by Louis Armstrong, Joanie Sommers, and Richard Pryor. The movie on CBS was the television premiere of *633 Squadron*, a 1964 World War II thriller starring Cliff Robertson.

Memories

Gene Roddenberry said, "Getting that episode on the network was a small miracle because of NBC not wanting to challenge anyone's ideas concerning the origin of life or the purpose of Man. Some things were lost from the story as a result." (145)

Robert Justman said, "It was always a difficult task in deciding which episodes would not repeat. There was no question this episode would make the cut, due to the photographic effects if for no other reason. In fact, there may have been no other reason. That reason was reason enough." (94-1)

30

Episode 49: A PIECE OF THE ACTION

Written by Gene L. Coon and David Harmon
Directed by James Komack

Nimoy and Shatner making a fashion statement … circa 1920s (NBC publicity photo courtesy of Gerald Gurian)

From NBC press release, issued December 21, 1967:

The superior technology of the Enterprise crew is temporarily unable to cope with the gangster tactics of the Planet Iotia II, in "A Piece of the Action," a drama on NBC Television Network's *Star Trek* colorcast Friday, Jan. 12…. Anthony Caruso, Victor Tayback and Lee Delano guest-star…. Captain Kirk (William Shatner), Mr. Spock (Leonard Nimoy) and Dr. McCoy (DeForest Kelley) beam down to Iotia to check rumors that the development of the planet was halted by moral decay a hundred years before. They learn the source of the problem is a book on "Chicago Mobs of the Twenties," which the Iotians have adopted as their bible. The bosses, among whom [Bela Oxmyx] (Caruso), Krage [*sic*] (Tayback) and Kalo (Delano) are the most powerful, have their hoods and henchmen, and the populace pays for protection. Kirk employs gangster tactics against them.

The contamination was left on Sigma Iotia a century earlier when the Federation ship U.S.S. Horizon visited. Now Kirk and company, in an attempt to live up to the Federation's mandate of "non-interference," must find a way to put things right on this world divided by warring mobster gangs. But Bela Oxmyx, the Top Dog gang leader, is determined to use the Enterprise's weapons to make some "hits" and take over the other "territories."

The hook: *The Untouchables* in outerspace. The theme: how imitation can be dangerous flattery.

SOUND BITES

- *Oxmyx:* "Nobody helps nobody but himself." *Spock:* "Sir, you are employing a double negative."

- *Oxmyx, to Spock:* "The most co-operative man in this world is a dead man. And if

485

you don't keep your mouth shut, you're going to be co-operating."

- *Krako:* "What do you think, we're stupid?" *Kirk:* "No, I don't think you're stupid, Mr. Krako. I just think your behavior is arrested." *Krako:* "I ain't never been arrested in my whole life!"

- *Krako:* "I got rights!" *Scotty:* "You got nothin'! Now you mind your place, mister, or you'll be wearin' concrete galoshes." *Krako:* "You mean cement overshoes?" *Scotty:* "Uh ... aye."

- *Kirk:* "Are you afraid of cars?" *Spock:* "Not at all, Captain. It's your driving that alarms me."

- *Kirk:* "Listen -- da Federation's movin' in.... You play ball, and we'll cut ya in for a piece of da pie." *Krako:* "But ... I thought you guys had some kind of law. No interference?" *Kirk:* "Who's interfering? We're just taking over."

ASSESSMENT

"A Piece of the Action," very popular with fans of the series, and considered by some to be *Star Trek*'s funniest episode, has snappy dialogue, clever direction, and delightful performances. There is a subtle purpose to all this madness, as well. People throughout history have been heavily influenced by fashion, trends, pop icons, and characters of modern literature, including ultra cool tough guys seen in motion pictures and television. This story is rich in social satire, even though we may be too distracted while laughing at these inept wannabe gangsters to see the parallels to our own lives. Substitute tattoos and iPods for felt hats and submachine guns; replace old gangster lingo with modern-day slang; texting and tweeting instead of getting on the "blower," and then ask yourself, aren't all of us, and our children, just as silly as Bela Oxmyx, Jojo Krako, and the rest of the gang?

THE STORY BEHIND THE STORY

Script Timeline
David Harmon's story outline, ST-75, "The Expatriates": August 8, 1967.
Harmon's 1st Draft teleplay, same title: August 16, 1967.
Harmon's 2nd Draft teleplay: September 5, 1967.
Gene Coon's rewrite, new 1st Draft teleplay, now called "Mission into Chaos":
September 28, 1967.
Coon's revised draft (first three Acts), now called "A Piece of the Action": early
October 1967.
Coon's revised draft (Act 4), "A Piece of the Action": October 25, 1967.
Staff rewrite under John Meredyth Lucas (Final Draft teleplay): Oct. 30, 1967.
Additional staff generated revisions: Oct. 31 and Nov. 2 & 7, 1967.

Gene Roddenberry came up with an idea very much like this story -- in one sentence -- from his 1964 *Star Trek* series proposal. "President Capone" was summed up, simply, "A parallel world, Chicago ten years after Al Capone won and imposed gangland statutes upon a nation." Roddenberry tried to take the concept further with writer George Clayton Johnson, who submitted a story outline in 1966 called "Chicago II." But it was abandoned.

David Harmon, who had written "The Deadly Years," had a similar idea with "The Expatriates," where the Enterprise chases an old-styled ship which is manned by descendents of former residents of Earth. Having been away from Earth for a long time, they adapted the language, attitudes, and ethics of old Chicago mobsters, influenced by a book about 1920s gangsters.

Harmon said, "I felt that Western civilization is based on a Judeo-Christian ethic. So what I did was say ... 'Suppose the people salvaged a book called *The Life of Al Capone*, which they treated as their version of The Bible, and from which they built their own society.'" (79-2)

Producer Gene Coon liked how the story made comment on the imitative influences of literature, television, and film on social development in an absurdist way.

Associate Producer Robert Justman's first impression of "The Expatriates" was negative. On August 9, 1967, he wrote to Coon:

At the present time, [this] has elements of a good story, but it also has elements of a bad story. I am not certain what kind of a story this is at the present time. I know it isn't a drama. I know it isn't a comedy. I don't think this is a drama-comedy or a comedy-drama. I certainly think that its comedic aspects are too broad and heavy-handed. After a while, I got pretty tired of the not-so-subtle parallels that the author draws. (RJ49-1)

Tired as he was, Justman mustered up the energy to give Coon five pages of notes, including:

Since we establish the fact that these Mafiosos have left Earth some time well after the present day, and since we also establish the fact that they dress like 1920 hoodlums and bear strong resemblance to Elliot Ness and his friends, how do we explain the basic discrepancy in technology? Why is it that these criminals have regressed, technologically speaking, from the high degree of sophistication inherent even in the 1990s [when their ship left Earth] to the low degree of sophistication inherent in the 1920s to 1930s? Witness the use of submachine guns and pinstriped suits and touring cars and other devises no doubt too numerous to mention. (RJ49-1)

As Justman read Harmon's outline further, he became more confused, telling Coon:

I am not against mini-skirts, however I feel that there is a dichotomy inherent when we have a "mini-skirted secretary" in an Elliot-Ness-type milieu. What about the inconsistency between operating like John Dillinger on one hand and having spaceships probing out into various areas on the other hand? Even more puzzling to me is the fact that we establish that these people, uncomplicated as they are, have devised a laser beam "strong enough to cut through the hull of the Enterprise," and are keeping the Enterprise at bay with it. Really, Gene, I fail to believe this in any way.... Who would you like to be your next Associate Producer? (RJ49-1)

Script Consultant Dorothy Fontana's memo to Coon bluntly stated:

As I mentioned to you the other day, I do not like this story. RJ has pointed out a number of inconsistencies in logic in it. One of the grossest is why the Mafia-types had gone back to the Al Capone dress, atmosphere, etc., when their ancestors departed from a world that will undoubtedly be as changed from our current times as our times are changed from the '20s and '30s.... NBC will undoubtedly love this story [but] I find there is nothing of value in it... no Theme of importance. As Bob says, this is not a tragic comedy, or a comedy drama. It is a waste of time. (DCF49-1)

Coon, amused by this bizarre tale, disagreed with the criticism and sent Harmon to work on a screenplay. When the 1st Draft arrived, more anguished memos hit Coon's desk. On August 22, Justman wrote:

Most of the objections I raised with respect to this property in the story outline

487

are still unresolved. Most of the defects in logic are still present. I still don't know whether this is a comedy or drama. I think it is not very good in either respect. However, from what I have seen of David Harmon's work previously ["The Deadly Years"], he should be able to effect great improvements in his revisions. (RJ49-2)

After nine pages of dense and highly critical notes, Justman told Coon:

As you know very well, I do not believe that the civilization of this planet should have originally come from Earth. I much prefer the idea of a civilization which has developed fairly consistently like our own civilization, but which has other precepts -- precepts which teach the exact opposite of our own so-called morality. (RJ49-2)

Justman's idea would finally click in Coon's head, along with a back-story element where the contamination was caused by a visiting Federation ship's crew member who left behind a book on the Chicago mobs of old Earth. For the moment, however, Coon was not open to such alterations.

Fontana was one day behind Justman with her memo, and just as harsh. She wrote:

I started out taking your word for it that the script was not all that bad, but I soon found I had comments on nearly every page. I agree with Bob that, as of this writing, David Harmon has failed us badly. He has presented us with a script neither drama nor comedy, tremendous sets and cast, no particular theme or importance, and totally impotent lead characters.... What is the Theme of this story? If it is the point that a society is constructed and running on what we consider immorality, then this is not sufficiently well drawn. What type story is it? It is neither fish nor fowl -- not comedy or drama. Nothing is terribly imperative. There is no feeling of real danger to our people or our ship. All the so-called heavies are inept and one-dimensional characters -- and our regulars are cursed with lethargy, disinterest, and a certain amount of ineptitude themselves. I feel David has done badly by us, and that major surgery is absolutely imperative. (DCF49-2)

Fontana's memo went on for 11 pages. Coon was getting no encouragement on this one. The premise struck him as funny and he knew that he could easily sprinkle in the necessary laughs, as long as Harmon's story structure conveyed the necessary jeopardy situations as well. It seemed child's play to Coon, so he sent Harmon to work on a second draft teleplay, with very few pertinent design changes requested.

Harmon's revised draft, dated September 5, 1967, did little to change Fontana's opinion, prompting another bitter memo to Coon, stating:

I think David Harmon has not delivered a script satisfying in any way. We cannot shoot this piece of drek as it is and, unless it receives one hell of an overhaul, to shoot it at all would be a vast detriment to *Star Trek*.... In case you think I'm angry, you're quite right.

Fontana also cried foul regarding the "cast and sets of millions," saying:

This, of course, we can cut down. But why didn't the author make the effort after we have said from the beginning that it must be cut down? (DCF49-3)

After 10 pages of notes, she told Coon:

The script, as it stands, will have to be restructured and rewritten from Teaser to Fade Out. It lacks Theme, importance, action, jeopardy, character and drama. It goes nowhere, it does nothing. It doesn't even say anything. This has been what has been wrong with it from the beginning story outline, and it has never been rectified. I stress we must begin from the beginning and lay out a new story, strengthen all characters, and give the story Theme and purpose as well as action and drama. (DCF49-3)

Learning that Coon had decided to step down as producer and, therefore, stop working on scripts that, if produced at all, would come after the term of his contract ended with second season Episode 16, Justman held off on responding to Harmon's 2nd Draft ... until Coon's replacement was chosen.

On September 13, 1967, his sarcasm in check, "R.J." wrote to the new series new producer, John Meredyth Lucas:

As I mentioned in conversation the other day, I don't feel that the writer has been able to achieve the sort of quality in this re-write that we were looking for. Finally, I don't know whether this is a comedy or a tragedy. I have a sincere fear that it is going to end up a tragedy, if we don't find a way to solve some of the problems.... The original idea that he had for this story was to contrast a completely amoral society with our own. To contrast what we consider to be right and fair with what another civilization with an entirely opposite viewpoint would consider to be right and fair. That is the "science-fiction" flavor which we have tended to overlook so far in this teleplay. That is the whole ball of wax and that is the reason why we went ahead with this project in the first place. That is what we have to discover at the beginning of the show and that is what we have to be able to reconcile ourselves with at the end of the show.

Justman's memo took the script apart, piece by piece, for seven more pages, including:

Although the generic names of the characters on the surface of the planet have been changed to protect ourselves from the adherents of the "Italian-American Protection League", the characterizations are rather two-dimensional to say the least. To me, Bela and his hoods and Krako and his hoods are straight out of "The Untouchables."

Gene Coon contacted Lucas on September 18, writing:

Despite the fact that this is the second draft, there remains a great deal of work to be done. I suggest that, as D.C. Fontana says, a major restructuring and rewrite is in the offing.... Boy oh boy, have we got too many characters.... If one were to ask me what I would do about the dialogue, and indeed the structure, I should say "What dialogue and what structure?" I dare say the fault for much of this is mine, for buying the story in the form in which I bought it. I cop-out on this only by saying that I could have written an extremely good and exciting and well-written *Star Trek* episode using that story outline as a rough guide. My problem would seem to be that I anticipate that the rest of the world will react to a given situation exactly as I do. It seldom happens. (GC49)

After 11 pages of apologetic notes, Coon told Lucas:

Well, sir, I hate to do this to you at this stage of the game. We have a great many problems with this script. In all probability you will want to sit down and devise a new story structure. I hate to see a script, when rewritten, come in in this shape, but we certainly have one here. If, during the several weeks I have left, I am able to help you somewhat with this, I will, of course, be glad to. (GC49)

Coon's offer was accepted. And, since the former producer was being invited to write one last *Star Trek* script, it was going to be a full-blown comedy. Lucas, at Roddenberry's insistence, could throw it away, but Coon was not about to try to get serious, especially with this particular concept. His screenplay, from September, was called "Mission

489

into Chaos." The title fit not only the material, but the evolution of the script itself. Justman's idea that these people did not come from Earth was added, augmented by Coon's idea of a visiting space ship from Earth, and a book brought aboard that ship that had influenced the evolution of this alien society.

In early October, before anyone could respond, and before Coon's departure from the *Star Trek* offices, a partial revised draft, three-quarters finished, was turned in. The new title: "A Piece of the Action."

On October 18, the day NBC's order for eight additional second season episodes came in, Robert Justman wrote to Gene Roddenberry:

> I have read Gene Coon's Three-Act revision... I find "A Piece of the Action" charming and amusing and do wish that we had a Fourth Act to go along with it. Do you think that we have any chance at all of getting a Fourth Act out of Gene Coon? Do you think you might want to call him in New York and see if he couldn't devote a day to turning out a Fourth Act for us?... The reason why I am so eager is that Gene has a certain style and flare for comedy and I would like to see that same style and flare continued on into the Fourth Act. More importantly, I would hope that this would be the show that we would give to James Komack to direct. If so, we have to get cracking on this property right away.

Roddenberry agreed the series needed usable scripts, quickly, to fulfill the sudden eight episode pick-up. And "A Piece of the Action," although sillier than Roddenberry envisioned *Star Trek* being, was indeed a perfect fit for the talents of James Komack. John Meredyth Lucas agreed and Coon typed up a fourth Act on October 25. Lucas tidied it up a bit for the Final Draft five days later, with page revisions to follow, based on suggestions from Fontana, Justman, and the comedy-director James Komack, on October 31 and, as the cameras rolled, on November 2 and 7.

Pre-Production
October 25–27 & 30-31 & November 1, 1967 (6 days prep)

Bill Bixby, James Komack, Brandon Cruz, and Miyoshi Umeki in *The Courtship of Eddie's Father* (ABC promo photo, 1969)

James Komack, 43, was a former stand-up comic who became an actor, writer, director, and producer on television. At this time, Komack was primarily known for episodic comedy, having written and directed for *My Favorite Martian* and *Get Smart*. But he also had experience at directing action shows, like *Tarzan* and *Combat!*

Komack said, "I was a natural contender because I had done long forms and was [also] a comedy director. I had really enjoyed the show, read the script, made some adjustments

490

and said, 'I would love to do this,' and I found myself on the starship Enterprise. This was fun because it was a comedy, and Bill Shatner loves to do comedy.... Something that was fun for me was having Spock and Kirk come down with this great intellect and intelligence that they possess, and having them deal with monkeys. These guys had an I.Q. of about room temperature." (103-1)

Regarding those monkeys:

Anthony Caruso, playing Bela Oxmyx, was 51, and a long-time veteran of television and films. His career spanned 1940 through 1990, with hundreds of roles. A reliable performer, Caruso often played American Indians and gangsters. He made such a good "heavy" that he plated 14 different roles in 14 different episodes of *Gunsmoke*, almost always as a "heavy."

Anthony Caruso in an episode of *Get Smart* (www.aveleyman.com)

Vic Tayback, as Krako, was 37 and nine years into a career spanning five decades. Prior to this, he had appeared in *Get Smart*, *The Monkees*, and *Gunsmoke*, but never in prominent roles.

"That may have been the thing that got his TV career going," Joe D'Agosta said of casting Tayback. "He was a pal. We knew each other from when I was acting in the theater. We'd help each other. Vic got all the old man parts. He looked 40 years old at 20. And a powerful actor. I supported his career; I'd bring Vic in to auditions for a lot of roles, because he was *right* for a lot of roles. But then he'd lose to bigger names. This *Star Trek* may have been the thing that changed all that; a very memorable role for him." (43-4)

The most memorable role was still several years away, as Mel, the short-order cook, in both the film *Alice Doesn't Live Here Anymore* and its television counterpart, *Alice*.

Vic Tayback in his most famous role, as Mel, in *Alice* (Warner Bros., 1976)

Steven Marlo, as Zabo, was 40. His acting career, spanning 1956 through 1990, brought over 100 roles. Shortly before his appearance here, Marlo showed up more than once each in *Ben Casey* (as Ben's brother Jack), *Combat!*, and *Star Trek*'s Friday night competitor, *Hondo*.

Lee Delano, as Kalo, was 36. He stayed busy on the big and small screens, usually in small roles, between 1963 and 1997. Prior to this, he was a guest player on *Voyage to the Bottom of the Sea*.

491

Jay Jones, as Mirt, was both actor and stunt man. He had appeared before on *Star Trek*. As Crewman Jackson, he died in the Teaser for "Catspaw." As Ensign Mallory, he died from an exploding rock in "The Apple." And now, as Mirt, he died from a barrage of machine gun bullets. Jones would return to *Star Trek* to die again.

Day 3: Filming on the exterior sets of Paramount with Lee Delano and Jay Jones (Courtesy of Gerald Gurian)

John Harmon, playing Tepo, was 62. He had appeared in *Star Trek* once before, as Rodent, in "The City on the Edge of Forever."

Sheldon Collins, "Tough Kid," was active as a child actor during this time. He had just played Pete Whittaker, the son of Carl Reiner's character in *The Russians Are Coming, the Russians Are Coming*, as well as Arnold Bailey, a friend of Opie's in numerous episodes of *The Andy Griffith Show*. He was twelve when he did this *Star Trek*.

John Harmon was last seen on *Star Trek* in "The City on the Edge of Forever" (CBS Studios, Inc.)

William Blackburn returned as Lt. Hadley, stationed at the helm. For this episode, the character was finally given his name.

James Doohan had a field day with "A Piece of the Action." Not only was there a plum comedy role for Scotty but Doohan also provided the voice of the radio announcer ("That was the Jailbreakers with their latest recording, on *Request Time*, brought to you by Bang, Bang, the makers of the sweetest little automatic in the world!").

Due to the nature of this material,

Sheldon Collins in *The Russians Are Coming, the Russians Are Coming* (1966, United Artists)

James Komack didn't face the problems that prompted Joe Pevney to abruptly leave *Star Trek* only days before. In an interview for *Trek Classic*, Komack said, "Usually when you're a director working on episodic television, the actors mostly know their parts, who they are and what they do, and all you're doing is trying to find new ways for them to move around. That's where they formulate their own characters ... they say, 'I've been doing this show for three years, I would never say that.' You can't argue with the guy. But in this episode I could say, 'Hold it. You're down in the 20th Century, pal. You're dealing with morons. You've never done this before, so therefore you *could* say this.' And they would buy it that way. But not in the spaceship. In the Enterprise, they had it down." (103-2)

Production Diary
Filmed November 2, 3, 6, 7, 8 & 9, 1967 (6 day production, budget set at $176,171).

Thursday, November 2, 1967. *Cool Hand Luke*, starring Paul Newman, was box office champ at the movie houses with Walt Disney's *The Jungle Book* close on its tail. *Diana Ross and the Supremes' Greatest Hits* still was the top-selling album in record shops. The Beatles were hanging in after nearly six months, with *Sgt. Pepper's Lonely Hearts Club Band*, at No. 2. Lulu's "To Sir, With Love," from the Sidney Poitier movie of the same title, held strong as the most-played song on U.S. radio stations, for the third of five weeks at the summit. The TV shows with the largest audiences from the night before, all in the Nielsen Top 20: *The Beverly Hillbillies*, *Green Acres*, and *The Virginian*. Stuart Whitman, star of *Cimarron Strip*, had the cover of *TV Guide*. Joe Namath had the cover of *Sports Illustrated*. Twiggy had the cover of *Vogue*. Skinny was "in." And laughter rang out from Desilu/Paramount Stage 8 as *Star Trek* commenced production on "A Piece of the Action."

Day 1, with Anthony Caruso, Leonard Nimoy, and Bill McGovern in Bela's office
(Courtesy of Gerald Gurian)

Day 1, Thursday. Filming took place in the interior of Bela's office. Because Matt Jefferies had provided the production design for Desilu's *The Untouchables*, a series set in gangster-plagued Chicago of the 1920s and '30s, the sets seen in this episode came easy. The merger with Paramount also helped, allowing for additional stages beyond *Star Trek*'s Stage 9 and 10, and a second 1920s era city street with building facades.

Day 2, Friday.

Nichelle Nichols, as Lt. Uhura, was on the cover of *TV Showtime*, a newspaper supplement, with the caption "Enterprising Spacewoman." Nichols would have been pleased to receive her copy if it hadn't been for the headline of the article on Page 5 -- "*Trek* to Halt 5-Year Mission a Little Early." Without indicating its source, or the name of its writer, *TV Showtime* stated, "Unfortunately, ratings have indicated that the Enterprise's TV journey will end next summer."

With this disappointing news circulating among the cast and crew, the company did further filming in Bela's office, then on to the scene in the warehouse room where Kirk played the game of Fizzbin.

Day 2. Front row, left to right: Anthony Caruso , William Shatner, Vic Tayback, Leonard Nimoy, and DeForest Kelley (Unaired film trim courtesy of Gerald Gurian)

Komack said, "Like most good comedy, a great deal of 'A Piece of the Action' was improvised, particularly the Fizzbin card game played by Captain Kirk and a group of dim-witted gangsters. They just sat down and did it.... Shatner really thought of this idea, and I embellished it." (103-1)

Komack was willing to stray from the written word, something TV directors rarely do, because he wasn't expecting to be hired again. His friends at *Star Trek* had been waiting for the right episode -- a comedy -- to assign to him as a one-time job. Besides, it was now looking as though there wouldn't be many more *Star Trek*s and, with Coon in New York, certainly no more comedies.

After filming wrapped for this day, with one of *Star Trek*'s three comic episodes, NBC premiered one of the others -- "I, Mudd." *Star Trek* came in a strong second place this night, with 25.9% of the viewing audience compared to ABC's take of 20.1%. CBS, of course, had the lead.

Day 3, Monday, November 6. The company moved to Paramount's outdoor set of McFadden Street for "Exterior City Square" and "Exterior Bela's Office." Here, the climactic shoot-out, as well as the machine-gun hit from the Teaser, was filmed.

"The gangster scenes in the room were all fine," said Komack. "The exterior stuff with the cars going by, bullets going off and them hitting the ground, and

Day 5. Shatner enjoying the chance to play comedy (Courtesy of Gerald Gurian)

making some kind of reality out of a backlot, was a little more difficult. [The *Star Trek* company] wasn't really prepared for it. They weren't used to it, and so it was a little slower for me." (103-1)

Day 4, Tuesday. The company moved to Boston Street on the Paramount lot for more exteriors, including the scene with young Sheldon Collins, then into Gower Street Stage 11 to film the scenes in the interior Radio Room.

Day 5, Wednesday. More filming on Stage 11, including interior corridors and the interior of Krako's office.

Day 6, Thursday, November 9. Komack moved onto Stage 9 and filmed the Enterprise bridge scenes, as well as the interior turbo-lift and interior transporter room. This first-time director of *Star Trek* finished on schedule.

Day 5. Shatner, Tayback, and Nimoy
(CBS Studios, Inc).

"A Piece of the Action" began with a flawed concept and a problematic script, one which Robert Justman feared would go from comedy to a tragedy for *Star Trek*. The writing process truly was a mission into chaos. But with the comedic talents of Gene Coon, James Komack, William Shatner, Leonard Nimoy, James Doohan, and a bright and inspired cast of guest players, this became a standout episode ... and arguably the series' funniest hour.

Gene Coon had the last laugh.

Post-Production
Available for editing: November 10, 1967.
Rough Cut: November 16. Final Cut: November 27. Music Score: tracked.

Fabien Tordjmann and Edit Team #3 did the cutting. Tordjmann had always been designated the darker episodes, such as "The Enemy Within," "Miri," "Arena," "The Devil in the Dark," and "Operation: Annihilate!" This was a pleasant change for Tordjmann, and he said, "One of the only comedies they ever had, directed by Jimmy Komack. I had a lot of fun working with Jimmy." (176)

As with all the show's directors, Komack worked closely with the editors preparing the "rough cut" this episode, Also know as the "director's cut." After this, the producers (Roddenberry, Lucas, and Justman) would screen the film and ask for further changes, creating the "final cut."

The Westheimer Company provided the optical effects, including transporter, phasers, and matte shots (images inserted into the view screens). Note that the phaser beams are a different color here than usual, being that Westheimer was not the post production house which normally added in this animation.

Release / Reaction
Premiere air date: 1/12/68. NBC repeat broadcast: 8/30/68.

Steven H. Scheuer reviewed the episode for *TV Key Previews*. Among newspapers across America to carry Scheuer's syndicated column on January 12, 1968 was *The*

495

Robesonian, serving Lumberton, North Carolina. Scheuer, normally having only praise for *Star Trek*, wrote:

> This is a fair show but only for *Star Trek* regulars. It is an idea which must have looked sensational as an outline but somehow it does not quite come across in its finished form. The Enterprise visits a planet on the edge of the galaxy where its last contact with the Federation left its inhabitants believing in the "Good Book," which was left behind. The book is actually a history of Chicago gangs of the prohibition era. This is why Captain Kirk and his men find them living in that era, complete with machine guns, slang and suits.

Judy Crosby also reviewed the episode on January 12, 1968, for her syndicated column, *TV SCOUT*. Among the papers running the review was *The Monessen Valley Independent*, in Monessen, Pennsylvania. Crosby said:

> This show pulls off another imaginative wrinkle from *Star Trek*'s bag of tricks by having the Enterprise set down on a planet that is straight out of prohibition times. Kirk, Spock and McCoy, after beaming down, find its inhabitants are paying protection money to a pair of gang bosses who are fully equipped with hoods, molls and machine guns. With all of their superior skills, our spacemen are still stymied by all of the knuckles, bullets and bomb tactics. That is, until Kirk finally remembers what to do when in Rome.

RATINGS / Nielsen National report for Friday, February 12, 1968:

8:30 to 9 p.m., 65.4% U.S. TVs in use.		**Share:**	**Households watching:**
NBC:	*Star Trek* (first half)	26.6%	12,940,000
ABC:	*Operation: Entertainment*	24.5%	12,880,000
CBS:	***Gomer Pyle, U.S.M.C.***	**43.8%**	**17,470,000**
Independent stations:		5.1%	No data
9 to 9:30 p.m., 67.6% U.S. TVs in use.		**Share:**	**Households watching:**
NBC:	*Star Trek* (second half)	25.8%	No Data
ABC:	*Operation: Entertainment*	26.0%	No Data
CBS:	***Friday Night Movie***	**36.6%**	**No Data**
Independent stations:		11.6%	No data

Gomer Pyle had an excellent partner on this night. The movie at 9 p.m. was the television premiere of Blake Edwards' 1964 comedy *A Shot in the Dark*, the sequel to *The Pink Panther*, marking Peter Sellers' return as fumbling French detective Clouseau. But it was just another day at the races, and *Star Trek* performed well, winning the first half-hour against *Operation: Entertainment*, with the latter half going down as a near tie. George Carlin was guest host on *Entertainment*, this time beaming out of Lackland Air Force Base in San Antonio, Texas. Stand-up Bill Dana was there, playing his popular José Jiménez character, and Roy Clark was one of three musical performers.

Star Trek had new back-end support beginning with the broadcast of this episode. *Accidental Family* had been removed from the schedule and replaced by a nighttime version of *The Hollywood Squares*, a runaway daytime hit for the network. It was of little help. The 12,940,000 households *Star Trek* brought in dwindled to 8,060,000 for *Squares*, followed by an under-performing NBC news special, "Projection '68."

When NBC repeated "A Piece of the Action" on August 30, 1968, Kirk, Spock, and McCoy appeared on the cover of *TV Guide*. This was the third time *Star Trek* graced the top-selling magazine's front cover, and this helped with the ratings, especially during the second half-hour.

RATINGS / Nielsen National report for Friday, August 30, 1968:

8:30 to 9 p.m., 47.5% U.S. TVs in use.

		Share:	Households watching:
NBC:	*Star Trek* (first half)	25.9%	6,660,000
ABC:	*Man in a Suitcase* (first half)	16.2%	9,800,000
CBS:	**Gomer Pyle, U.S.M.C.**	**40.4%**	**12,210,000**
Local independent stations:		17.5%	No data

9 to 9:30 p.m., 51.1% U.S. TVs in use.

		Share:	Households watching:
NBC:	*Star Trek* (second half)	26.7%	No data
ABC:	*Man in a Suitcase* (second half)	17.0%	No data
CBS:	**Friday Night Movie**	**29.6%**	**No data**
Local independent stations:		26.7%	No data

It was summer. Families were on vacation; fewer were home watching television then when the episode first aired. Nonetheless, *Star Trek* did well with the percentages of those who were sitting in front of their TV sets. As it had often been, *Star Trek* was NBC's highest-rated Friday night show. After the numbers increased when handed-off to *Tarzan*, they dropped down by nearly three million households for the nighttime version of *The Hollywood Squares*, then down again, by another three million, for the NBC "Actuality Special" entitled *New America*.

From the Mailbag

Received the week after "A Piece of the Action" aired on NBC:

Dear Mr. Justman... Last week, as usual, *Star Trek* was extremely well done. And it was partly due to "A Piece of the Action" that I am writing this letter. I was wondering if I could have a picture of Spock in the suit from the '20s. I also wanted to know if I could have some pictures from "Journey to Babel," especially one of the operations on Spock, and a picture of the duel between Kirk and the Thralls from "The Gamesters of Triskelion." ... This may sound like a strange question, but how do you help a teacher who wants to write to *Star Trek* to tell everyone how much she likes the show, but won't because she's afraid someone will laugh at her because she's acting like a teenager? She told me to tell you that she loves the show and recommends it for everyone, young and old. Live long and prosper. Karla S.

Memories

Robert Justman said, "I fought against that one perhaps more so than any other episode we did. I could not understand why Gene Coon wanted that story. But I must admit he pulled it off with the humor he added. And Gene [Roddenberry] allowed him to do so. I will not try to explain that. It will have to remain a mystery, for for you as well as for me." (94-1)

497

31

Episode 50: BY ANY OTHER NAME

Written by D.C. Fontana and Jerome Bixby
Story by Jerome Bixby
Directed by Marc Daniels

From NBC press release:

Warren Stevens and William Shatner
(CBS Studios, Inc.)

Captain Kirk (William Shatner) answers a distress call which turns out to be a ruse by a superior race to capture the Enterprise and its crew in "By Any Other Name" on NBC Television Network's *Star Trek* colorcast Friday, Feb 23.... A crew from an unknown galaxy, which is disintegrating, was sent out centuries before to conquer a new galaxy for its inhabitants. The current descendants, under leadership of Rojan (guest star Warren Stevens), feel that they have found this new galaxy in the Federation, but their own ship crashes and they need the Enterprise to make the return [trip]. Captain Kirk employs a simple but powerful method to prevent a takeover by Rojan. Barbara Bouchet portrays Kelinda and Stewart Moss is cast as Hanar, two of Rojan's allies.

The real point of the story -- that simple method employed by Kirk -- involves the Kelvans' unfamiliarity with the human form they have assumed. Kirk's only hope: to find each of the Kelvans' Achilles' heel, including an attempt to exploit the repressed affections between Rojan and Kelinda.

The theme: a study in being human, and the weaknesses and temptations we must all learn to live with.

SOUND BITES

- *Spock:* "Immense beings ... a hundred limbs that resemble tentacles, but are not... Minds of such control and capacity that each limb could do a different job.... The Kelvans have superior intellectual capacity. But to gain it, they apparently sacrificed anything that would tend to distract them. Perceptive senses such as smell or taste ... and, of course, emotions."

- *Kelinda:* "This business of love. You have devoted much literature to it. Why do you build such a mystique around a simple biological function?"

- Tomar: "What is it?" *Scotty:* "Well, it's … uh …" (looks at liquor bottle; takes a sniff) "… It's green."

ASSESSMENT

We've seen the Enterprise taken over before, by Khan in "Space Seed" and Norman in "I, Mudd." What sets "By Any Other Name" apart is the means of the takeover and the unique circumstances regarding the invaders assuming our form. By experiencing human feelings and desires, the aliens become less alien. This story was therefore different enough, and interesting enough, to be filmed ... but the end results are mixed.

"By Any Other Name" suffers from an overused science fiction premise -- alien invaders want to conquer Earth. *Star Trek* had always avoided this *War of the Worlds*-type cliché ... until now. And the set-up required more exposition than normally necessary for us to understand the intent and capabilities of the antagonists. The who, what, and where results in too much talk. Also, because NBC wanted planet shows, a great deal of time is spent on Stage 10. To pacify the network, the cameras stay on the planet while we are told about the Enterprise being taken over. Again, the dialogue is pure exposition.

The equally-tired and overused "crew held captive" bit -- this time in a cave -- gives the landing party little to do except look for a means to escape. In "A Taste of Armageddon," Spock used mental suggestion to have a guard think he and his fellow prisoners had gotten away. He tries again here. When this fails to gain them freedom, another old trick is used -- one of the captives will fake an illness. We saw it in "I, Mudd" and "Bread and Circuses" and countless other episodes of other series from this era.

The first act is further hampered by wooden performances, and a planet set that cannot escape the quick-to-spot trappings of a stage, despite great effort and expense by Matt Jefferies to create a small lake and groupings of colorful flora ... and that cave.

Once the story moves to the ship, things improve and, fortunately, that is where the majority of the episode takes place. Effective conflicts begin, as do the theme and visual elements which set this story apart. By Act III, comedy kicks in, too, courtesy of Dorothy Fontana.

Despite a so-so start, "By Any Other Name" ends up an entertaining and memorable *Star Trek* adventure.

THE STORY BEHIND THE STORY

Script Timeline

Jerome Bixby's story outline, ST -71: April 27, 1967.
Bixby's Revised Story Outline, gratis: June 7, 1967.
Bixby's 2ⁿᵈ Revised Story Outline, gratis: June 26, 1967.
Bixby's 1ˢᵗ Draft teleplay: July 31, 1967.
Bixby's 2ⁿᵈ Draft teleplay: September 9, 1967.
Bixby's script polish, gratis (Mimeo Dept. "Yellow Cover 1ˢᵗ Draft" teleplay):
October 9, 1967.
D.C. Fontana's rewrite (Final Draft teleplay): October 31, 1967.
Fontana's polish (Revised Final Draft teleplay): November 7, 1967.
Staff page revisions, under John Meredyth Lucas: Nov. 8, 9, 10 & 13, 1967.

Jerome Bixby so dazzled the *Star Trek* staffers with his original story for "Mirror, Mirror" that he was given a second assignment before even beginning a screenplay for the first. He had written two drafts of his story outline for "Mirror, Mirror" when NBC rejected the property, citing it too hard to follow. While Roddenberry wrote a third draft of the treatment, Bixby began thinking of other possible stories he could submit. Roddenberry's treatment of "Mirror, Mirror" got NBC's Stan Robertson to reverse his rejection and Bixby was asked in for a meeting to discuss how to proceed with the script. Before leaving the studio that day in early April 1967, Bixby pitched his idea for "By Any Other Name." He went home not only with a go-ahead to write the script for "Mirror, Mirror," but a contract to begin work on the story outline for his second assignment. For the next five months, he divided his time between the two projects.

Surprisingly, Bixby turned in his treatment for "By Any Other Name" before his 1st Draft script for "Mirror, Mirror," the property producer Gene Coon was more anxious to receive.

The title of the new story came from Shakespeare. A line from *Romeo and Juliet* reads, "What's in a name? That which we call a rose, by any other name, would smell as sweet." The expression is often used to convey the idea that, although you can change the name of something, the nature of a person or thing will remain the same. In this story, the Dvenyens (later to be renamed Kelvans) take on human form, yet are anything but human.

Second Season Script Consultant Dorothy Fontana said, "The thing that may have sold that story was the idea of 'These are aliens, [but] what do they feel? What can we make them feel as human beings? What can we do to them [to] make them understand who we are?'" (64-2)

Bixby's story outline from April 27, 1967 had more than that to it. Knowing the journey home will take nearly 300 years, and needing the crew to serve them on the Enterprise, the Dvenyens order the humans to reproduce so they may "provide future generations of crew-slaves." In the end, without any intentional prompting from the humans, the Dvenyens succumb to the needs of their newfound flesh and the weaknesses of the human condition, prompting them to become less efficient, dropping their guard and allowing Kirk and his crew to regain control of the ship.

On May 8, Gene Roddenberry wrote Gene Coon:

> Agree with your comments on Bixby's new story -- not bad. Interesting ... [but] too little story to sustain four Acts. Needs subplot. (GR50-1)

Roddenberry had written a story somewhat like this in 1956. "The Secret Weapon of 117," an episode from a 30-minute anthology series, starred Ricardo Montalban and Susan Morrow as a couple from outer space, sent to spy on Earth defenses. The pair, transformed from their original state into a human male and female, soon discovered that their newfound human biology interfered with the mission. In the end, after just 30 minutes of screen time, they fell in love and abandoned their duties in order to live as humans. The story was structured in the style of a half-hour episode of *The Twilight Zone* -- a quick set up, 20 minutes or so of character conflict, followed by a twist ending and a last word from the sponsor.

Roddenberry's memo to Coon continued:

> The basic story is a fairly simple and short one which might not carry us for the four full Acts of a one-hour show. Basically, it is capture [of the Enterprise] -- which might happen fairly fast if we are to grab our audience and set up jeopardies -- [then] life aboard while [the crew is] plotting sabotage and mutiny to get the Enterprise back into their control, and finally recapturing the ship and solving the problem. If we want our *Star Trek* pace, avoiding the long

philosophical dialogue which can hurt a tale like this, then it appears to me we will need considerable more interwoven sub-story. I think there is a potential here for such -- the fact that they are required to pair off and mate. A la last year's tale "The Naked Time," we might have an opportunity here to probe quite deeply into our main running characters under such a situation. If they are absolutely forced to do this -- must do it or they will die or others will die -- then who would they pick? What is Kirk's idea of an ideal woman? And Spock's? And McCoy's? Would there be disappointments as a chosen mate prefers someone else? Obviously we can't put our running characters in a situation where they would be saying to the audience, 'I'd rather die than fuck?' That's pretty unbelievable. Equally obvious they can't drag women to their cabins with a glad cry. Perhaps the answer is that they believe they ultimately will be able to recapture this vessel and although they may pretend to be involved in liaisons in order to save lives, they can hardly actually let themselves become so involved because this would create situations which would make normal command and discipline impossible from then on. At any rate, this does introduce possibilities of very dramatic sub-stories. (GR50-1)

Associate Producer Robert Justman also felt the story, as written, might not sustain an audience's interest for 60 minutes. In a May 26 memo -- written the same day Bixby's 1st Draft script for "Mirror, Mirror" arrived -- Justman told Coon:

> If the trip back to the galaxy from which the invaders have come is going to take 300 years, shouldn't our captain and crew lay in a large supply of razor blades? It is quite possible that they may die of boredom a few months prior to the expiration of the 300-year trip.... How many of these aliens do we have on board? Can we afford it? How do these aliens keep control of our 430-man crew? (RJ50-1)

In time, after a few more drafts, the aliens would have a device enabling them to paralyze their enemies and, in even later drafts, a second device used to change their enemies' form into a small block of freeze-dried chemicals. But no one had any of these problem-solving ideas yet. Everyone's attention was far more focused on the first draft script for "Mirror, Mirror" and all the other time-urgent properties to arrive during this four-week period, including the final staff rewriting for "Catspaw," "Metamorphosis," "Friday's Child," and "Who Mourns for Adonais?," the first staff rewrite for "Amok Time," Norman Spinrad's 2nd Draft script of "The Doomsday Machine," Robert Bloch's 1st Draft script for "Wolf in the Fold," John Meredyth Lucas's 2nd Draft script and D.C. Fontana's subsequent rewrite of "The Changeling," various story outline drafts plus a 1st Draft script for Max Ehrlich's "The Apple," two drafts of the story outline for Art Wallace's "Obsession," three drafts of the story outline for Margaret Armen's "Gamesters of Pentathlon" (as it was called at this time), a story outline by John T. Dugan for the upcoming "Return to Tomorrow," and numerous other properties that would be developed but never see the light of a TV screen.

With all this overlapping work going on, and with Bixby's treatment for "By Any Other Name" sitting at the top of a pile on his desk, Justman continued dictating his memo to Coon, saying:

> I feel that we should spend a lot more of the story on the surface of the planet prior to getting under way to head away from our own galaxy. (RJ50-1)

NBC, of course, would want it that way. Justman wanted it that way, too, in order to keep the episode from becoming stagnant.

Justman pointed out to Coon:

> There is a very weak point in this story; and that is the fact that the aliens reach a

state of subconscious yearning to return to the planet colony they have just left without the benefit of having been worked on by Captain Kirk. As it is right now, Captain Kirk is rather passive in this regard. The aliens are wiping themselves out emotionally without any help from our heroes. Don't you think that it should be Captain Kirk who takes a positive course of action as a result of some clues he has been able to accumulate and who personally goes to work on the leaders of these invaders? And once the realization is brought out into the open and the leader of the aliens is engaged in a losing psychic battle, certainly Mr. Spock and Dr. McCoy and all the other regulars would join with Captain Kirk in ganging up on these beings. (RJ50-1)

Therefore, it was Justman who had the germ of an idea that would lead to the best scenes in the episode, although D.C. Fontana would be the one to visualize and write those scenes -- Kirk romancing Kelinda and arousing homicidal jealousy in Rojan; McCoy shooting Hanar full of vitamins (stimulants, actually), thusly making him edgy and driving him to challenge Rojan; and Scotty introducing Tomar to the joys of alcohol, and attempting to drink the alien under the table. At this stage of development, it was just a vague idea, with Justman closing his memo to Coon:

> If I were to be asked whether we should proceed ahead and commission a screenplay from this story treatment, I would have to answer, "Don't ask me." (RJ50-1)

Many of Justman's concerns were addressed in Bixby's revised story outline, *gratis*, on June 7, while the staff was anxiously waiting for the writer to revise his script for "Mirror, Mirror." Some of Roddenberry's ideas were added in as well, including more drama concerning the crew-slaves being forced to mate. Kirk is specifically instructed to have sex with a female crew member named Lt. Leslie Thompson.

Two days after receiving the revised outline, Roddenberry wrote Coon:

> I believe it has the makings of an excellent *Star Trek* episode.... The idea of our entire ship company being prisoners and slaves would work well. Strangely, though, considering the type of story it is, we need more science fiction in it. The jeopardies should seem greater, certainly stranger, and should frighten us more than they do. And, finally, we need an ending which will come as a surprise.... The Dvenyens, at present, come off as pretty nice guys and gals, not too dissimilar to our own people. A number of times they threaten to punish, then change their minds because they are intrinsically decent. Seems to me these aliens from another galaxy will have to be pointed [toward] bolder stakes, given strange customs which have first frightened or even repelled us. They simply won't be very interesting, won't create sufficient jeopardy for us if Bixby goes the way of his description "hard but not harsh, military but not savage." Am much afraid they'll come off wishy-washy and we'll never realize the full science fiction potential that could be in this strange race from another galaxy. Why not have them punish our people, increasing punishments as Kirk keeps trying to devise ways of escape -- punishments that are strange, almost horrible, ways that seem wanton, illogical, unnecessary. Then, as our show develops and we begin to move toward Act Four, we can begin to see why they are that way and what the inner logic of all their ways is. (GR50-2)

Coon instructed Bixby to add more science fiction, more sexual tension, and more torture. Also, per Roddenberry's previous request, to use this story as a means of stripping the lead *Star Trek* characters to their basic impulses and revealing their hidden sides, as had been accomplished in "The Naked Time." The torturing of Kirk, then, would result in the near mental collapse of the Captain.

502

Before these changes could be made, Dorothy Fontana contacted Coon, on June 12, writing:

> The question of mating Enterprise people has come up in other scripts. We did it last year in Pilot #1, "The Menagerie," and are doing it this year in "Gamesters of Pentathlon" ... I question if we need it again. Agreed, we're all big boys and girls, but, frankly, Kirk's image starts to trouble me a lot when we have him, ah, succumbing to "nervous needs" midway through the story and then walking away from the girl at the end. It makes him seem like a bastard to me, and I don't care if he HAS "elevated a shy girl to woman." That kind of line is a large pile of bologna. (DC50-2)

Coon gave Bixby additional instructions to cut back on the bologna, but the mating gimmick would stay ... for the time being. One change would have Kirk not succumbing to "nervous needs" and thereby refusing to make love to Lt. Thompson (his chosen mate). She is resistant, as well, admitting to him that she loves another. Per Roddenberry's request, Kirk's decision to turn the ship over to the Dvenyens is weighing heavy on his shoulders and the thought of making love to a pretty crew woman is the farthest thing from his mind.

Fontana continued:

> In general, I like the story. But I want to know exactly what Bixby is going to deliver in terms of straight-line story that NBC will buy. I don't think they would accept the generalities and assurances of plot development this present submission contains. (DC50-2)

On June 16, Coon wrote to Bixby, "Generally speaking, we are very enthusiastic about your story." Then came six pages of "buts," including:

> The Enterprise and our crew has been through too many situations similar to this to let any race make them evacuate the ship, or turn it over to the aliens.... I would suggest to you the possibility that the Dvenyens, where science is rather more advanced than ours, have a transporter device which can work from the surface of the planet, and beam up to the Enterprise, throughout the ship, a number of armed men, who could suddenly take control, would have our crew covered, and thus would take the ship. This device would be beyond our own technical abilities, would seem to work for us, and would get over the big problem of how do the aliens capture the ship.

As we know, this would be added. Coon continued:

> I think we must establish the power and the inhumanity of the Dvenyens... in which we can predict the horrible type of life it would be for humans if the Dvenyens come back and were successful in their takeover attempt.

This too would be added, although not to NBC's liking.

There was also a problem in Bixby's use of Mr. Spock for the mating scenes and a back-story provided by the writer regarding the Vulcan's sexual orientation. Coon told Bixby:

> Mr. Spock does not come into heat only when Saturn is in cancer. We have done a complete show about Mr. Spock's breeding habits, which originally were those similar to the salmon on Earth. That is, he had to essentially swim up stream and spawn. But due to the experience he went through in an episode called "Amok Time," Mr. Spock's human side won out and he can screw like anyone else.... We will, of course, unfortunately need a rewrite on the story with these points incorporated before we can turn it over to NBC. The sooner you can do it, the better. Thank you very kindly, and hurry up with the rewrite on "Mirror, Mirror" so that we can shoot it.

The rewrite on "Mirror, Mirror" arrived a week later, followed by Bixby's 2nd Revised Outline for "By Any Other Name," *gratis*, on June 26. This third draft of the treatment was forwarded to NBC.

On July 5, the network's Stan Robertson wrote to Coon:

> Because this story deals with planet life and those beings which inhabit this planet, we believe that right off the bat we have something going for us which will result in a "plus" with the viewers. As our research, public response, and our own creative inclination indicate, our viewers are more receptive to stories of this nature.

Justman had been right here -- the first quarter of the story took place on a planet rather than the Enterprise, and NBC was expectantly happy. But NBC also wanted changes. One concern had to do with Bixby honoring Roddenberry's request that the aliens be more frightening. Now in the story, to punish Kirk for trying to escape, the Dvenyens subject him to a "memory-amplifier gadget." In the outline, Bixby wrote:

> The device can be dialed, as it were, to boost any emotion. Kirk is dialed to "Guilt" -- and is in Hellish torture -- for even the best man feels lousy about crappy things he has done. Kirk moans -- he weeps -- he craves suicide, as magnified emotions wallop him. The way he failed to save a crewman in a certain tight spot -- the way he accidentally killed an innocent, during another -- the way he treated that girl on Rigel 4.

Jerome Bixby was thinking like a science fiction author, not a television writer. Stan Robertson's reaction, to Coon:

> In Act II, when Captain Kirk is subjected to the "memory-amplifier" and his hidden "guilt" feelings are exposed, we believe it would be a catastrophic mistake to have him, as the writer indicates, "crave suicide," feel remorse over the "innocent" crewmen he accidentally killed, or to infer that he was less than a gentleman with "that girl on Rigel 4." These may all be human and understandable emotions and feelings but we believe that they are not in keeping with the heroic proportions we have attempted to establish in the viewer's mind of our series star. The references should be deleted and in their places something less damaging to the character of Kirk should be inserted.... The Tag scene in Act II, as currently written, is unacceptable from a standpoint of good taste. We think it would be very offensive to the viewer to see "Ten Enterprise crewmen executed before our eyes, fading in agony, one by one, as Kirk flinches." ... The scenes as described in Act III in which "Kirk, McCoy, and even Spock, find themselves with mates, with whom they cohabit or else" are unacceptable from standpoint of good taste and to the damage such could do to the public acceptance of our continuing stars.... As currently written, Rusjan [later Rojan] appears in the conclusion of our story to be portrayed as a sympathetic character. If, indeed, this is the writer's intention, we believe that we must lay strong ground work earlier that what he has done, the evilness which surrounds him, is the only way of life that he knows and that he was acting only in the best tradition of his culture. (SR50)

Bixby was given further notes -- a bigger list of areas not to tread -- then sent off to write his screenplay for "By Any Other Name," as Dorothy Fontana took charge of the "Mirror, Mirror" rewrite. The 1st Draft script of the former was delivered July 31. Still present, despite NBC's strong objection, was Kirk being picked to mate with Lt. Leslie Thompson. Also still present, the execution of dozens of the Enterprise crew while a pained Kirk is forced to watch, and news that more crew members have been gathered on the shuttlecraft hangar deck and, with the opening of the bay doors, sucked out into the vacuum of space.

The tone of the script, as with the next two drafts to come, was relentlessly dark. And Roddenberry and Coon were clearly not opposed to dark.

Of this first draft, Bob Justman sent a mixed review to Coon, saying:

> I think there is a helluva idea contained here and I only wish that it had been realized correctly.... Perhaps this idea is marvelous, but it is unmemorable insofar as a believable teleplay goes. Perhaps what we have is an interesting science fiction concept and an impossible commercial television property. (RJ50-2)

Justman knew this television property was not going to be abandoned, so, despite being in the middle of a weekend getaway with his wife, Jackie, he rolled up his sleeves and went through the script line by line. Among many notes to Coon, "R.J." wrote:

> For the benefit of the viewers at home who do not read every *Star Trek* script, I suggest that Rusjan, or one of his henchmen, does something visually to freeze our landing party into "action-stances, unable to move." We can then use the newly invented device of a Sound Effect in conjunction with this visual movement to help sell to those viewers who have forgotten to read the scene description exactly what is happening.... You may have been able to determine from the tone of this memo thus far that I am still in my expensive rented home on Lido Isle -- and not enjoying what I am paying a lot of money for. I can predict to you that this slight irritability is going to continue throughout the rest of this memo and any other memos that I dictate this weekend. (RJ50-2)

In time, Justman would get his sound effect. At this moment, however, with his vacation interrupted, his irritability continued -- for eight more pages. Among his complaints:

> From time to time throughout this script -- in fact, in just about every major sequence -- one can detect rather puzzling story holes or gaps in logic. Also, events are discussed by Principal Characters, which should have been seen by the audience. I get the feeling at times that this is a radio script, rather than a television script. (RJ50-2)

Two days later, Dorothy Fontana, who had just finished her rewrite on "Mirror, Mirror" and was in better spirits than Justman, wrote Coon:

> I do think Bixby will work out very well for us, if we can keep him to the hard line of action-sf-adventure and a lot less talk. This is a script in which he has gone somewhat astray, but I believe he can pull it together for us and make as interesting a story as "Mirror, Mirror."

Fontana, however, agreed with many of Justman's criticisms, and added seven pages of her own critical assessment.

Gene Coon digested the memos from Justman and Fontana, and then sent Jerome Bixby 17 pages of notes. He wrote:

> Let me say that I think that we have here the story we want to tell, and it is quite well done. However, there are certain areas which will need work, certain areas of logic and certain crew that do not jibe with prior established *modus operandi* of the Enterprise and its personnel.... The major story structure is fine, the major points are all there. We need to cut down at least ten pages out of the show. We must be sure the Dvenyens aren't so sloppy in guarding our people and we must show our people being clever and intelligent and outwitting them.

Coon ended his long memo to Bixby, saying, "Get it done, and maybe we can do another one." (GC50-2)

The other one Coon referred to was yet another story Bixby had submitted, while awaiting feedback on his script for "By Any Other Name." That story, "Magic Stone," was received and given coverage notes by Dorothy Fontana during the second week of August (more on this in "The Story Behind the Story" for "Day of the Dove"). It took Bixby nearly six weeks to "get it down.' By then, Gene Coon, while still working in the *Star Trek* offices, had surrendered the producer's chair to John Meredyth Lucas.

Fontana and Justman were not enthusiastic over Bixby's rewrite. On September 12, Justman made this clear to new producer Lucas, writing, "I don't feel we have the sort of re-write we expected from Jerome Bixby." (RJ50-3)

Coon, still at the studio, assisting with the transition of responsibilities and monitoring the negative comments, sent a memo of his own to Lucas, dated September 15, 1967. The eight pages began:

> Despite some of the comments from other contributors, to your peace of mind, I think that this is a good script. I only wish all our second drafts were this good. To be sure, there is work to be done, but compared to most of the work we do around here, this is a snap. I think it will make one hell of a show. I think, for the future, you should treat Jerome Bixby very nice. He is going to come in very handy if we get picked up for next year. (GC50-3)

The new producer, however, felt "By Any Other Name" had more going *against* it than for it. Jerome Bixby later said, "I wrote a story, they liked it, then I did a [script] and they didn't like it, and, looking back, I can see why. I did the one thing that Roddenberry was most against: 'Don't become obsessed with the immensity of it all.' And I did.... I dealt extensively with all this subjective stuff produced in man's loneliness, disorientation, grief... and I gave them 45 pages [out of 60 pages] of the immensity of it all. And so Dorothy Fontana, without my knowledge, darn it, started to do a rewrite." (16-2)

Bixby tidied the script up a bit before it was sent off to the Mimeo Department to be reformatted as the Yellow Cover 1st Draft from October 9, which was then distributed to the production staff, De Forest Research and NBC. A more detailed reworking was soon to come.

Fontana said, "'By Any Other Name' was a major, major rewrite. Bixby was a good writer, but it wasn't working for *Star Trek*. We had no right to ask for more than a light polish after the second draft was in, [but it needed] a rewrite. That's what they were paying us to do. That's what Gene Coon and I did a lot of." (64-1)

With this one, Fontana and Coon struggled to find a solution to the mechanical problems of the storyline while John Meredyth Lucas stayed busy rewriting other scripts.

Fontana said, "The biggest problem we had was how half a dozen people take over a starship with a crew of 400. How do we do this? And Gene Coon and I wrestled with it, and we booted it around, and we tried and we tried, but we couldn't figure it out. How the heck do you get half a dozen people to overcome 400 people and put them in thrall except for the essential bridge crew that we needed? And we walked into Roddenberry's office and we explained the problem. He had on his desk a kind of octagonal Mexican onyx that I had brought him back one time from a trip, that he used as a paper weight, and he started pushing it around on his desk and saying, 'Well, what if they had a machine that turned people into a shape that was something like this?' And it works for me. So, once we got that licked, everything else was fine, because all you had to deal with was the immediate characters... and, once we had that gimmick in place, then it all worked. We didn't even have to have the extras around for very much. Actually, that's where we really saved money. It was primarily a 'bottle show' except for the one bit down on the planet. Didn't have a whole lot of special effects in it, except for the barrier, which was reused [from 'Where No Man Has Gone Before'], [and then] normal flybys and stuff like that. And those were stock shots. So it was a reasonably inexpensive show to do." (64-1)

The Dvenyens were now called the Kelvans (much easier to pronounce). And now that the Kelvans had a means of controlling the Enterprise people, there was no longer a need for the cruel instances of intimidation that NBC was so set against. And, with the crew members reduced to crystallized blocks -- a form of suspended animation -- there was no need for them to be forced to breed in order to assure future generations of slaves to run the ship. NBC's other objection -- and one Fontana had, due to the similarities between that aspect of this property and "Gamesters of Triskelion" -- had also been resolved.

Fontana's rewrite, designated as the Final Draft, was delivered October 31, with her Revised Final Draft arriving on November 7. Joan Pearce of De Forest Research, knowing this was a rush job in order to keep the cameras rolling on Stages 9 and 10 without interruption, hurried her notes back to John Meredyth Lucas later the same day.

As for the Kelvans' ability to freeze the landing party members, Pearce (after confirming with the firm's science authority, Peter Sloman) wrote:

> If all nerve impulses are paralyzed, the organism will die because the automatic as well as the voluntary muscles will be affected. Suggest … a selective field that neutralizes nerve-impulses to voluntary muscles. (KDF51)

Regarding dialogue in the script stating that the journey would take 300 years, Pearce wrote:

> If Warp 14 equates 8,192 times light speed, then the precise figure announced by Mr. Scott of 280 years will enable time to travel at Warp 14 a total distance of 2,293,760 light years, slightly farther than the actual distance to the Nebula in Andromeda, M-31…. M-31 is 2,200,000 light years distance, the furthest object visible to the naked eye. (KDF51)

No other produced science fiction series bothered to put their scripts through this type of scrutiny, but Gene Roddenberry had insisted on it and the creative staff understood the importance of complying.

Regarding the line of dialogue, "There is a strange energy barrier at the rim of your galaxy," Pearce wrote:

> There is no scientific justification for this element in the story that our galaxy, or any other, has a defined rim, also without astronomical support. Present thinking is that the stellar population gradually diminishes. The "edge of the galaxy" concept was the major scientific criticism made with reference to Star Trek [episode "Where No Man Has Gone Before'] by Isaac Asimov in the TV Guide article on television science fiction. (KDF51)

Asimov, later to become a fan of the series, had blasted Star Trek on this plot device. Despite this, the barrier at the edge of the galaxy had already been established, and the use of stock footage from the second pilot would save the series substantial expense.

Joan Pearce's notes were received on the morning of Wednesday, November 8. There was no time for a complete rewrite -- the episode was due to begin production on Friday, bright and early. Lucas hurried the script through a series of page revisions, to address some of Pearce's comments, and ignore others, with pages dated from later that Wednesday, then again on Thursday, then again on Friday, November 10, as cameras began rolling, and, finally, on Monday, November 13, the second day of production. Fontana's re-imagined script, both clever and entertaining, was filmed with no major changes.

Fontana had turned down writing credit on "Catspaw," "Wolf in the Fold," and "The Changeling," even though her producer bosses believed she did enough rewriting to warrant acknowledgment. This time, however, with the substantial retooling, she was given co-writing credit with Bixby.

Three things stood out about the final script in Fontana's mind. First was the contribution by Roddenberry, the idea to turn the crew into little blocks of a condensed substance. The second came from Coon, of which Fontana said, "This is Gene Coon's suggestion: at the beginning, where you see these two people, the woman and the man, science and security people, boiled down to their essence, and one of them is crushed, and you figure 'It's got to be the security guy, right?,' but it isn't, it's the woman ... and she dies." (64-1)

The third thing that tickled Fontana was of her own design. She said, "The idea of using the growing humanity on them -- because they were not familiar with the sensation. That one turned out to be a fun one because we got to play with those guys." (64-2)

Pre-Production
November 2-3 & 6-9, 1967 (6 prep days)

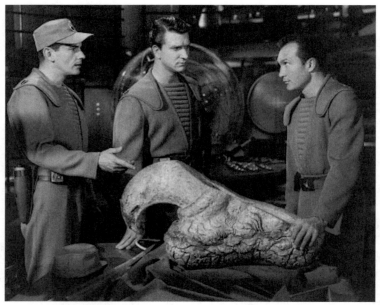

Jack Kelly, Leslie Nielsen, and Warren Stevens in *Forbidden Planet* (MGM, 1956)

Warren Stevens, cast as Rojan, was 48. He worked often in films and television, beginning his career in 1949. He played the ship's doctor in the sci-fi classic *Forbidden Planet*, and appeared on TV in *The Outer Limits*, *The Twilight Zone*, and *Voyage to the Bottom of the Sea*. Stevens was so well respected and popular during this time that, for several years running, he averaged one prominent guest star appearance per month.

Stevens said, "I was doing a *Bonanza* for Marc Daniels, who was directing. And, at one point, during the last days on *Bonanza*, I asked, 'Where are you going next, Marc?' He said, 'I have to go to Paramount and do one of those *Star Trek* things.' I said, 'They owe me one over there' -- and it's true, I forget why, but they owed me a show at Paramount. Well, we finished the *Bonanza* and about a week later I got a call from Paramount; Marc was gonna do this thing, and that's how I did the *Star Trek*, because he remembered that they 'owed' me one." (169)

Barbara Bouchet, cast as Kelinda, Kirk's romantic assignment, was 24. A former beauty contest winner, Bouchet broke into show business as a model in TV commercials. She was also a one-time girlfriend of James Darren, who was co-star of *The Time Tunnel*. Bouchet's career was catching fire at the time she did this *Star Trek*. In 1969, she was the female lead in *Stoney*, and again in 1970 for *Red Hot Shot*. Shortly after that, fed up with the sexpot roles she was being offered in Hollywood, Bouchet moved to Italy where she became a major star of the Italian cinema.

Stewart Moss, 29, as Hanar, the Kelvan who becomes unglued with the help of McCoy's stimulants, was making his second appearance on *Star Trek*. As Joe Tormolen, he had died (by falling on a butter knife) in "The Naked Time." Very busy in television, Moss appeared in eight episodes of *Hogan's Heroes*, along with guest spots during this time on *The Fugitive*, *Rawhide*, *12 O'Clock High*, *Bonanza*, *Perry Mason*, and *The Invaders*. Regarding his return to *Star Trek*, Moss said, "I was a big Sci-Fi fan before *ST*. I literally had

Barbara Bouchet with David Niven in *Casino Royale* (Columbia Pictures, 1967)

read most if not all of Heinlein, Bradbury, Sturgeon, Asimov, etc., so I saw most, if not all, of first year episodes [of *Star Trek*].... [T]he writing was first class and groundbreaking." (122-4)

Stewart Moss early 1960s casting photo (Courtesy of Stewart Moss)

Moss had been impressed with the script for "The Naked Time." Regarding "By Any Other Name," he said, "It was good but not noteworthy." (122-4)

Leslie (AKA Lezlie) Dalton, playing Drea, the Kelvan at the helm, was 24. Her agent, Angela Loo Levy, daughter of famed Hollywood talent agent Bessie Loo, had an in with Marc Daniels and was able to arrange an audition. Dalton recalled, "I had seen *Star Trek* and really loved the show. I remember being asked in the office with Gene Roddenberry and somebody else, and Marc was there. At the end, very dramatically on my part, I said, 'I think *Star Trek* is the grandest program on television.' There was a moment of silence, and then Gene Roddenberry looked at me, very serious, and he said, 'Thank you, thank you very much.' And I knew he meant it. Here I was, this little girl, barely out of drama school, and he was beyond gracious; he was totally sincere." (43a)

As he often did, Roddenberry left the final casting decisions up to his director. Daniels wanted to continue looking.

**Dean Martin's Golddiggers, circa 1969.
Dalton is on the left in the front
(NBC promotional picture)**

"That first time I showed up for the audition, I came in with a very nice outfit, almost East Coast in style," Dalton remembered. "It was orange and it was a very classy outfit, and I wore orange heels. And when I came back from the audition, Angela said, 'You didn't get it. Marc thinks you're not sexy enough.' And she said, 'I'm going to talk him into letting you go back. Wear something really sexy this time.' So I thought, 'I'll fix them,' and I put on fishnet stockings, spiked heels, a mini-skirt that was a good six inches above the knee, and a little tank top that showed cleavage down to the middle of the chest. Marc was expecting me, but not the way I looked. I walked into the room and it was like Marc actually reeled back. He took a step backward, like a wind had hit him. It was the funniest reaction, and he looked at me and said, 'Okay! Okay, thank you very much.' I left and called Angela and she said, 'You got it!'" (43a)

Within a year, Dalton joined Dean Martin's Golddiggers. The 1970s brought numerous appearances on series such as *S.W.A.T.* and *Switch*, before she joined the cast of *The Guiding Light* in the 1980s.

Robert Fortier was Tomar. At 41, he had appeared in three episodes of *The Outer Limits*, including the classic "Demon with a Glass Hand," as an alien named Budge. During his successful career in television, Fortier made multiple appearances on *The Loretta Young Show*, *Gunsmoke*, and *Combat!* He had a recurring role in the western, *The Gallant Men*, as Major Jergens, and, prior to *Star Trek*, he worked with William Shatner in the unsold pilot for "Alexander the Great."

Julie Cobb, as Leslie Thompson, was the only crew woman in red to ever be killed on *Star Trek*. She was making her dramatic TV debut here. She said, "I had done a TV commercial a couple years before, for Heinz ketchup, but *Star Trek* was my

**Robert Fortier (on right, with Barry Morse),
about to be shot in "Controlled Experiment,"
a 1964 comic episode of *The Outer Limits*,
which co-starred *Star Trek*'s Grace Lee Whitney**

510

Julie Cobb, launched by *Star Trek* into a successful TV career, is seen here in a 1971 episode of *The Brady Bunch* (verybradyblog.blogspot.com)

first SAG [Screen Actors of America] television job. It was a big deal to get that job. My parents [film and TV star Lee J. Cobb and stage actress Helen Beverley] were both okay with me wanting to act, but I didn't get that role because of my dad. I was just going on auditions in those days, reading for things, and I met with Joe D'Agosta and Marc Daniels. And I got the part! So my first real job in TV became a classic!" (32-1)

A hundred more jobs followed in television, including recurring roles on *Growing Pains*, *Magnum, P.I.* (as Magnum's cousin Karen), and 22 episodes of *Charles in Charge*. One of her proudest moments was when she was able to act with her famous father. Cobb said, "Two years before he passed away, my dad and I did a classic episode of *Gunsmoke* together called 'The Colonel,' and it's a killer. He was heartbreaking in it." (32-1)

Carl Byrd played Lt. Shea (the red shirt who survives on the planet while Julie Cobb's character does not). His acting career spanned 1967 through 1984, and included appearances from this period on *I Dream of Jeannie*, *The Flying Nun*, *Gomer Pyle, U.S.M.C.*, *Daktari*, and *Julia*.

NBC COLOR TELEVISION

Carl Byrd with Diahann Carroll, in 1968 episode of *Julia* (NBC promotional photo)

Production Diary
Filmed Nov. 10, 13, 14, 15, 16 & 17, 1967 (6 day production, budget set at $178,428).

The six day production began Friday, November 10, under the time-efficient control of Marc Daniels. This was the week that Carl B. Stokes was sworn in as mayor of Cleveland, Ohio, making him the first black man to serve as mayor of a major U.S. city (and putting him on the November 17, 1967 cover of *Time* magazine). Another first: Surveyor 6 was the first man-made object to lift off from the moon for a return trip to Earth. "To Sir, With Love" was still getting the most spins on radio station turntables, and the Sidney Poitier movie of the same name was doing brisk business in the movie houses. Walt Disney's *The Jungle Book* was king of the box office.

Day 1 began on Stage 10, for the planet set, and, for the first time in the series, the script called for a lake. Set Designer Matt Jefferies and Set Decorator John Dywer worked together to create one.

Dwyer recalled, "We had plastic sheets under the water, of course, surrounded by all that dirt and sand that had been hauled in. Underneath that was the concrete floor of the stage. But there were storage areas under that --

Unaired film trim showing the body of water on Stage 10 that would soon spring a leak (Photo courtesy of Gerald Gurian)

and, after we filled that little lake up, and maybe several hours of filming, it started leaking through, so we had water raining down into the storage area below. And we had to hurry down and get a lot of things out of there, and cover others. Fortunately, they only needed that set for one day, so we were able to drain it before damage was done, or we may have had a swimming pool down underneath." (57-4)

In charge of the camera crew was cinematographer Keith C. Smith, who stepped in at the last minute to replace an ailing Jerry Finnerman. Working hard to maintain the visual integrity of *Star Trek*, Smith received the ultimate compliment when no one watching could tell that the series' regular Director of Photography was absent. Smith was 46 and had led the camera units for episodes of *Burke's Law*, *My Favorite Martian*, and *Honey West*.

Day 2 was spent finishing up on Stage 10, starting with the crushing of the polyhedron (Courtesy of Gerald Gurian)

From this day's filming, take notice of Kirk's eyes when he is frozen. They move. This was William Shatner's choice. He believed that, since Kirk could still hear Rojan speak, it stood to reason he could still see. He moved his eyes to convey this. And doing so also let the television audience in on the idea that Kirk was frozen but very much aware of what was happening. Nimoy and Kelley did the opposite. They reasoned that total paralysis meant *total* paralysis. No one was necessarily wrong here, except perhaps for director Daniels, who failed to get his actors onto the same page.

Regarding her one-day's job on *Star Trek*, Julie Cobb told *Starlog* magazine, "I was *terrified* doing that show. I was 19 years old and it was my first professional acting job on television. I was *very* nervous... William Shatner had worked with my father before [in *The Brothers Karamazov*] and he knew it was my first job. He was very kind and supportive." (32)

In an interview with this author, she added, "The whole thing I remember the most about that experience was, in those days, because of the nature of film, and its development, that you had to wear a great deal of pancake makeup. You were so caked with orange pancake makeup that when you looked in the mirror you literally wanted to die. It looked so awful. But, of course, the way the film was processed in those days, it looked normal by the time it was screened." (32-1)

Helping Cobb through her case of the jitters, besides the support of Shatner, was the presence of Nimoy and Daniels. Cobb said, "I was more than nervous; I was scared. I was in that little mini-skirt, and that orange pancake, and Shatner was wonderful. He was very serious about the work, but otherwise funny, and sweet and caring. And Leonard Nimoy had been an acting teacher of mine when I was about 16. He was a popular acting teacher in L.A., and I was in his class ... for about a minute. Marc Daniels was a great old friend of my parents. He was a terrific man; very reassuring. So I felt very well taken care of on that show." (32-1)

"Metamorphosis" had its premiere on NBC this night.

Day 2, Monday, November 13. The company was still on Stage 10, taking a few last shots on the planet set, then moving into the Cave/Jail set.

Day 3, filming on the bridge with Walter Koenig and Lezlie Dalton at the helm
(Courtesy of Gerald Gurian)

Day 3, Tuesday. The company moved to Stage 9 and remained there until the end of production. On this day, the bridge scenes were filmed, as well as one scene from Interior Life Support.

Lezlie Dalton said, "I thought the sets were quite ingenious. It was very, very creative, really. And it was interesting because there was no front wall on the bridge when we were filming. So, when you're looking at that screen -- where they take a shot of the screen and that's what you're supposed to be looking at from the console -- what you're seeing is Marc Daniels and the rest of the crew and the lights on the soundstage." (43a)

Dalton wasn't as taken by her costume. She said, "I wore a form-fitting jumpsuit, and I'll tell you frankly, not to detract from the talent of the wardrobe people, which was considerable, but I despised it, and I despised it for one reason only -- the way I looked in it. I was not a fat girl, but ever since I'd taken home economics in high school and learned to bake pies, which I would of course eat, my hips were larger than they should have been. I felt fine from the waist up; everything looked great, but from the waist down I was very self-conscious. I was sitting at the helm a lot, but they took one shot of me going up the steps to

513

the upper level of the bridge, and I remember one of the guys saying, 'Let's get this,' and they put the camera right beneath my butt and tracked me going up those steps, and I was so humiliated. And I'll tell you what, I had those extra inches off in the next six months and I've never had them back. That humiliated me so badly that it fixed me for life." (43a)

Regarding director and star, and the relationship between them, Dalton said, "Marc Daniels wasn't a huggy kissy guy; he was just forthright and spoke the truth. There was something very nice about Marc and I quite liked him. But William Shatner was trying Marc's patience. I found Bill to be like a high school kid; he was just having too much fun. I didn't find him at all obnoxious; he wasn't rude or abusive in any way, he was actually rather endearing, but he was just kind of boyish; he was very playful and young for his years. And there was this guy who was visiting the set who Bill liked, and he'd go over to talk to him.

Day 5. McGovern slates a shot as Shatner, who Lezlie Dalton called "very playful," Kelley and Nimoy in stitches … and even gets a smile out of Doohan (Courtesy of Gerald Gurian).

And Marc would call for a break. But, finally, after about half a day of this happening, Marc just blew and he started to scream. After that, Shatner calmed down … for a day. The next day he was back at it a bit, but he was a little more responsive to Marc." (43a)

Day 4, Wednesday. Filming took place in the exam room, the medical lab, and Kelinda's quarters.

Warren Stevens said, "We were rehearsing one of the kiss scenes, where [Kelinda] was explaining to me how humans apologize. In the rehearsal, we kissed, and Marc Daniels yelled, 'Close your mouth!' And I remember saying, 'Hey, it's only a rehearsal!'" (169)

Bouchet said, "Being a Hollywood beauty was a mixed blessing. Men are men, with all that testosterone, and when a pretty girl comes in front of them

Robert Fortier and DeForest Kelley in unaired film trim shot on Day 5 of production (Courtesy of Gerald Gurian)

what can you expect?" (19-1)

Day 5, Thursday. Scenes shot this day included those in engineering, the corridor, the elevator, and then work began in the rec room, for the scene where Kirk, Spock, McCoy, and Scotty discuss their delemma ... and notice that Tomar has developed quite a fondness for bulk fuel – also known as food.

Day 6, Friday. More work in the rec room, including the fight between Kirk and Rojan. For this, the wardrobe department had come up with a temporary solution concerning Kirk's ever-shrinking uniform top. During his fight sequences in "Gamesters of Triskelion," a lot of waistline skin was showing each time he'd swing an arm, do a kick or fall to the stage floor. For the fight here, Wardrobe outfitted him with a black t-shirt, securely tucked into his black pants, under his uniform top. The velour top rose up, as expected, but, this time, no skin showed through.

Day 6. Robert Fortier and the famous drinking scene in Scotty's quarters, saved for the end of the production (Courtesy of Gerald Gurian)

Also, note the makeup used on Warren Stevens in this scene and, in the next scene to film for Robert Fortier. While on the planet, as seen in the teaser and Act 1, and even their first scenes on the ship in Act II and III, the Kelvans are pale in appearance. As they become more emotional -- *more human* -- flesh tones were gradually used.

For the latter part of the afternoon, James Doohan and Robert Fortier did their drinking routine in Mr. Scott's cabin. This is the only time we visited Scotty's quarters. Decorations include drafting tools, a tartan kilt, bagpipes and medieval armor ... and more than a few bottles of booze.

Dorothy Fontana said, "The most fun of that [episode] was the Jimmy Doohan drinking scene ... and Jimmy made it even funnier. And, you know, the other guy [Robert Fortier] was playing right along with him. They were having a great time." (64-2)

The ever-reliable Marc Daniels finished on schedule, allowing cast and crew to make it home in time to see the NBC premiere of "Journey to Babel," one no one wanted to miss.

Post-Production
Available for editing: Nov. 20, 1967. Rough Cut: December 1, 1967.
Final Cut: December 11, 1967. Music Score recorded on December 22, 1967.

James Ballas and his team handled the editing. The pacing is effectively brisk. This was the eleventh and final *Star Trek* episode for Ballas, who went on to work for Rod Serling's *Night Gallery*. His legacy at *Star Trek* lived on in such classics as "Space Seed," "Amok Time," "Journey to Babel," and "The City on the Edge of Forever."

The Howard A. Anderson Company provided new opticals, including transporter effects and the glow around the victims of the Kelvan neural paralyzer. All shots of the

Enterprise had been seen before. The barrier at the edge of the galaxy, of course, was from "Where No Man Has Gone Before."

Composer Fred Steiner provided a partial score, combining new compositions with tracked music from past episodes. The reason for creating new music at this point in the season was because nothing in the library worked well when Scotty was getting Tomar drunk. The music Steiner provided mixed as nicely as an aged oak scotch. Also recorded at this session, from December 22, and courtesy of Mr. Steiner, was the "flag music" for the upcoming episode, "The Omega Glory."

Release / Reaction
Premiere air date: 2/23/68. NBC repeat broadcast: 5/31/68.

Steven H. Scheuer reviewed this episode for *TV Key Previews*. Among newspapers across America to carry Scheuer's syndicated column on February 23, 1968 was *The News Journal*, serving Mansfield, Ohio. Scheuer, wrote:

> A good and interesting show. In the first half, the Enterprise faces another seriously hopeless situation in space as a group of superior beings from another planet conquer the spaceship. The situation turns around in the end, with an amusing and delightful solution.

Judy Crosby also reviewed the episode on February 23, 1968, for her syndicated column, *TV SCOUT*. Among the papers running the review was *The Monessen Valley Independent*, in Monessen, Pennsylvania. Crosby, less impressed than Scheuer, said:

> Well, once again, the Captain and crew of the Enterprise are taken prisoner and once again, the situation looks pretty grim. Warren Stevens guest stars as the leader of a space exploration party -- beings with superior intelligence who capture the starship with the intent of it taking the place of their own crashed space vehicle for their trip home. Kirk uses a human strategy to overcome his superior adversaries.

Lezlie Dalton recalled the first airing of "By Any Other Name" vividly. She said, "I remember sitting with a friend, named Victor, and analyzing it. And I remember sitting there watching and saying, 'Oh, Vic, look at that, oh my God.' And I was making notes about how 'this had to be changed' and 'that had to be changed.' And at the top of the list, of course, was to take some inches off the hips. It's funny, because I thought, 'Don't worry, the whole world won't see it. But, eventually, the whole world did." (43a)

Julie Cobb was also in front of her TV, and said, "I believe I was watching with my mother, and my boyfriend at the time. I thought it was very well-done and entertaining. And thought-provoking. But I was of course critical of myself, of the way I looked in the mini-skirt. I was scared to death, and I suppose that worked out, being that the character I was playing had good reason to be scared, too." (32-1)

RATINGS / Nielsen National report for Friday, February 23, 1968:

8:30 to 9 p.m., 61.4% U.S. TVs in use.	Share:	Households watching:
NBC: *Star Trek* (first half)	25.2%	11,540,000
ABC: *Operation: Entertainment*	27.6%	13,330,000
CBS: **Gomer Pyle, U.S.M.C.**	**40.4%**	**15,400,000**
Independent stations:	6.8%	No data

9 to 9:30 pm, 62.8% U.S. TVs in use.		Share:	Households watching:
NBC:	*Star Trek* (second half)	25.2%	No data
ABC:	*Operation: Entertainment*	30.2%	No data
CBS:	**Friday Night Movie**	**33.9%**	**No data**
Independent stations:		10.7%	No data

It was a bad night for *Star Trek*, in third place from start to finish. CBS had a lock on the No. 1 slot with *Gomer Pyle* and a second airing of the epic all-star WWII movie *The Great Escape*. The Steve McQueen action picture had gone up against "Amok Time" at the beginning of the season and done severe damage then. Now it knocked *Star Trek* to the mat a second time. On ABC, the variety series *Operation: Entertainment* was beaming out of Lackland Air Force Base in San Antonio, Texas with country singer (and future pork sausage mogul) Jimmy Dean hosting and singing. Comedy was provided by Shelley Berman, with additional music by the Righteous Brothers, singing their No. 1 hit "You've Lost That Loving Feeling," and Dusty Springfield, singing her Top 10 hit, "You Don't Have to Say You Love Me." The competition for *Star Trek* was formidable.

Another part of the problem in the ratings was lack of promotion. CBS bought a full page ad for *Gomer Pyle* and *The Great Escape* in *TV Guide* as well as in other TV magazines and newspapers. ABC, with the music hit makers appearing on *Operation: Entertainment*, wisely booked ad spots on pop and country radio stations, as well as paying for print ads. NBC, as usual, did no promotion for *Star Trek*.

And then there was NBC's Friday night schedule, beginning with *Star Trek*'s lead-in show, *Tarzan* (destined to be cancelled by the end of the season). The back-end "support" was the low-rated nighttime version of *The Hollywood Squares* (prompting many of *Star Trek*'s 11,540,000 households to change channels, bringing the number down to 7,500,000) and a news report on over-population in viewership, which was under-populated, depleting the numbers further to 6,660,000.

Memories

Lezlie Dalton said, "Warren Stevens was a very, very nice person. He was a doll; he was a lovely guy. I was just impressed generally with the kind of people on that show. Bill was charming and fun. Nimoy was a marvelous gentleman. So was DeForest Kelley. Lovely people." (43a)

Barbara Bouchet said, "I remember thinking of *Star Trek* as being a successful show. I suppose that's why I tried out for the part.... William Shatner is my only memory. I had a big crush on him and we went out a few times.@ (19)

Stewart Moss said, A[Playing] Hanar was a good time.... My only frustration on that show was striking out with Barbara Bouchet. After a delightful week in her company, I asked her out to dinner. She just stared at me for a moment, smiled, and answered, 'But for what purpose? You're an attractive man, but what can you do for me?'" (122-2)

Julie Cobb said, "I wasn't a Trekkie, and I don't think there were Trekkies yet; it was too new. But it was a great show, and it was history-making, ultimately. We had a family connection to *Star Trek*. I did the original series, my daughter -- who is no longer acting, she's now an attorney -- had her first TV job on *Star Trek: Voyager*, and then my ex-husband, James Cromwell, was in the film, *Star Trek: First Contact*. He played Zefram Cochrane. So it was a real family affair." (32-1)

Lezlie Dalton adds, "It's quite a phenomenon. I've have had day jobs now and then -- meaning jobs outside of the industry -- and when I do that type of work, I don't talk about my being an actress. Number One, you don't want them thinking you're going to run off and do acting, which, of course, you are. So I'll keep it to myself. But every now and then it will come out. Someone will know me from a show like *The Guiding Light* and they'll say, 'Oh, you did that! What was that like? What else have you done?' And the minute I say *Star Trek*, all the people who were not very interested in what you were talking about are up and over and talking to you. The effect is amazing." (43a)

"By Any Other Name" began with Jerome Bixby. Therefore, his is the last word: "It came out kind of a lightweight episode. The drinking contest with Robert Fortier was a funny, funny bit. When he collapsed, I thought it was the best part of the story." (16-2)

32

Episode 51: RETURN TO TOMORROW

Written by Gene Roddenberry (uncredited)
Story by John T. Dugan (as John Kingsbridge)
Directed by Ralph Senensky

From NBC press release, issued January 10, 1968:

Captain Kirk (William Shatner), Mr. Spock (Leonard Nimoy) and Lieutenant Commander Anne [sic] Mulhall (guest-star Diana Muldaur) risk death when they lend their bodies to two-billion-year-old brains in 'Return to Tomorrow' on NBC Television Network's *Star Trek* colorcast Friday, Feb. 9....

**Shatner invents a new dance craze – "Do the Shat"
(CBS Studios, Inc.)**

When the Enterprise answers a distress call from a remote planet and beams down to investigate, the crew confronts the preserved brains. Dr. McCoy (DeForest Kelley) plans to study the phenomenon and the other three consent to having the brains inhabit their bodies while the brains devise robot-type housings for themselves so they can become mobile. The plan progresses as proposed until the brain inhabiting Spock's body decides it wants to keep the human form.

The aliens, Sargon, Thalassa, and Henoch, are the sole survivors of their race. They believe that Earthlings and Vulcans alike may be among their descendants. The people who once populated their world evolved to the point where they dared to consider themselves gods, resulting in war which brought an end to their civilization. Sargon and his wife, Thalassa, are from one side of the dispute. Henoch, the alien who is using Spock's body, is from the other.

In a recurring *Star Trek* theme, "Return to Tomorrow" explores the plight of highly-advanced aliens who, despite their accomplishments and their wisdom, are wrongly tempted by the pleasures of the flesh. Further explored -- the pitfalls of a superiority complex.

SOUND BITES

- *McCoy, addressing the flickering receptacles containing Kirk and Spock's conscious minds:* "You and your blasted rent-a-body agreement, Kirk! The only half-way pleasant thing about this is you, Spock. Must be embarrassing for a logical superior Vulcan not to have a larger flicker than that."

- *McCoy:* "Neither Jim nor I can trade a body we don't own. It belongs to a young woman who ..." *Thalassa:* A<u>Who</u> you hardly know, almost a stranger to you." *McCoy:* <u>AI will not peddle flesh!</u>"

- *Kirk, to McCoy, and the others in the briefing room:* "They used to say if man could fly, he'd have wings ... but he <u>did</u> fly. He discovered he had to. Do you wish that the first Apollo mission hadn't reached the moon, or that we hadn't gone to Mars or the nearest star? That's like saying you wish that you still operated with scalpels and sewed your patients up with catgut like your great-great-great-grandfather used to. I'm in command. I could order this. But I'm not ... because ... Dr. McCoy is right in pointing out the enormous danger potential in any contact with life and intelligence as fantastically advanced as this. But I must point out that the possibilities, the potential for knowledge and advancement is equally great. Risk ... risk is our business! That's what this starship is all about ... that's why we're aboard her!"

ASSESSMENT

"Return to Tomorrow" has a powerful opening. We are led to believe the booming masculine voice which penetrates the bridge and refers to Earth people as his "children" could be God. Despite its similarities to "Who Mourns For Adonais?," this plot device works well to catch our attention.

There are other moments of déjà vu in this episode. As in "Charlie X" and "The Gamesters of Triskelion," Kirk is again afflicted with pain. It seems the level of pain increases with each occurrence ... or, at least, the level of acting does. And a member of the Enterprise crew appears to have died, only to be resurrected. As it had happened in "Amok Time," it's Kirk. But we know he really isn't dead. We've seen this before and know it's a trick. And then we see it yet again, as it appears that Spock dies ... only to live again.

If the pompous and humorless tone of Sargon, with his constant referral to the Enterprise crew as "my children," and to Kirk as "my son," and to Thalassa, in the body of Dr. Ann Mulhall, as "my beloved," is heavy-handed, blame Roddenberry, who wrote the script, uncredited.

Shatner's acting borders on hammy. In particular, the briefing room speech about "risk" is over-the-top. It is preachy and taken to the limit as the camera pushes in on Kirk, with too much music building to too much of a crescendo.

The entire feel for "Return to Tomorrow" is out of synch with *Star Trek*'s second season. The writing, coming from Roddenberry, not Coon, is one reason. The characters are overly formal, lacking in humor, and making speeches in place of honest communication. Also, the music, provided by George Duning, serves as an audio blueprint for most of the scores to come in the third year. "Return to Tomorrow" is, in fact, a glimpse of *Star Trek*'s tomorrow. If you like this, then you may also enjoy "Spock's Brain" and "Turnabout Intruder."

Regardless, the concept behind the episode is original, intriguing and, best of all, Nimoy is allowed an opportunity to grin from ear to pointed ear and play a dastardly rascal. Nimoy, as Henoch, is an absolute delight and his performance brings an element of humor to a script which otherwise is so lacking in that area. These things alone make this inconsistent trek worth taking.

THE STORY BEHIND THE STORY

Script Timeline
John T. Dugan's story outline, ST-58: Early May, 1967.
Gene Coon's revised outline: May 9, 1967.
Dugan's 1ˢᵗ Draft teleplay: received June 29, 1967.
Dugan's 2ⁿᵈ Draft teleplay: October 11, 1967 (rec'd 10/13).
Gene Roddenberry's rewrite: early November, 1967.
Page revisions by Roddenberry and Lucas: November 18, 20, 21, 22 & 24, 1967.

Contrary to information given in many past books about *Star Trek*, John Kingsbridge was not a pseudonym for Gene Roddenberry, but for writer John T. Dugan. The confusion came from the writing credits on the final shooting script -- "Teleplay by Gene Roddenberry, Story by John T. Dugan" -- compared to the screen credit, telling us "Return to Tomorrow" was written by John Kingsbridge. Many believed Roddenberry opted for a pseudonym after watching the rough edit because he wasn't happy with the results. This is not so. Roddenberry was very proud of his script and very pleased with the end product. John T. Dugan was the one who was unhappy, and remained so for nearly four decades. Much of the bad blood had to do with religious beliefs.

Dugan was a graduate of Fordham University in New York, where his first play, "Martyr Without Tears," was presented in 1942 while its playwright was serving overseas as a Lieutenant in the Army. After the end of World War II, Dugan resumed his academic pursuit, earning his Master of Fine Arts degree from the Catholic University of America, then his doctorate in theater from the University of Minnesota. He returned to the Catholic University to begin his first career, as a teacher, a 15-year pursuit which took him to the University of California at Berkeley and, in Los Angeles, UCLA. Dugan retired from teaching in 1960 when he began selling scripts to television. His first job seemed an obvious step -- writing for the Catholic series *Insight*, a half-hour anthology. Dugan soon shifted to westerns, medical dramas, and war stories, with writing assignments on *Bonanza*, *Ben Casey*, and *Twelve O'Clock High*, among other series.

Dugan had met both Gene Roddenberry and Gene Coon at various Writers Guild functions and casual friendliness led to an invitation to seek out writing assignments, both at *The Lieutenant* in 1963 and, now, at *Star Trek*. *The Lieutenant* job, for Roddenberry, didn't pan out, with Dugan's assignment being cut off at story. Now Dugan had a shot with producer Gene Coon, who took his pitch on April 5, 1967, and then, impressed by the unique concept as well as the strong central theme, ordered a treatment, delivered in the first few days of May.

The title was explained in a line of dialogue -- later to be dropped - where Henoch, while "sexually molesting" Ann Mullhall, says, "A return to a tomorrow ... that might have been." Then, as he "kisses her brutally," he adds, "And <u>will</u> be."

Gene Roddenberry didn't mind all the brutal kissing and, on May 8, wrote to Coon:

I am delighted you put Dugan to work on a story. He shows great inventiveness and ingenuity. I think his outline may have to be simplified a bit, but it is a pleasure to read a story in which science fiction and inventiveness will not have to be added. And a pleasure to read a story in which there are basic urgencies [and] growing jeopardies ... I like the ingenuity and imagination displayed in this story. Once we straight line it, simplify it, guaranteeing we have the mass

521

audience with us all the time, it should be a delight for all involved. (GR51-1)

The science fiction and inventiveness may have already been in place, but the outline was otherwise overly-intellectual in its presentation, not something kids watching TV at 8:30 on a Friday night, or the average 1967 American, for that matter, were likely to connect with. Roddenberry continued:

> [But] we have got to have the heart of this -- what will seem to the mass audience to be a straight line action-adventure tale -- fairly understandable. It must be put in terms and language they can understand. We should discuss with Dugan our theory that we "can have our cake and eat it too" by doing action-adventure in a way that will attract and hold both our mass audience and our intellectuals. If we have to risk losing either audience, then the risk has to be that of losing the intellectual audience. Frankly, I think this story is interesting enough to hold both if we sit down with Dugan and talk it out very carefully. (GR51-1)

Roddenberry dictated four additional pages of notes, with both questions and suggestions. He asked Coon:

> Why is Henoch such a villain? Isn't he of the same high-minded intellectually brilliant race as Sargon? We must be certain that this is strongly motivated. (GR51-1)

In Dugan's outline, Henoch is not just a hedonist, but a tactless cad. He leers after women, uses crude language to get their attention and grossly overeats. He delights in all pleasures of the flesh, so Kirk uses a non-pleasure to get him to abandon Spock's body -- unrelenting intolerable pain. Of this, Roddenberry said:

> I cannot quite believe that the physical pain or abuse would send a brilliantly advanced intellectual like Henoch running frightened back into his own brain. It will have to be explained a little better for me. (GR51-1)

With this memo, it was Roddenberry's idea not to use other actor's voices when the aliens inhabit the bodies of Kirk, Spock, and Yeoman Ann Mulhall (she wouldn't be made an astrobiologist until later drafts). He felt it would be easier, and more effective, to put reverb on the voices of Shatner, Nimoy, and whichever actress was to play Thalassa.

Coon wasn't interested in having that sit-down talk with Dugan that Roddenberry had asked for. Coon was buried in work and needed to get the outline to NBC. So he tidied it up himself the next day, trying to connect the dots in a way that Stan Robertson at the network could comprehend.

Robertson wasn't as impressed as Roddenberry over the concept. He dropped by to discuss the matter with Coon, who, in order to keep the story from being "cut off," used Roddenberry's memo to demonstrate the further changes that could be made. On May 15, Robertson sent Coon a letter, insisting the "highly cerebral portions of the story" be eliminated and the "complex nature of the plot" be simplified. He wrote:

> We agreed that those elements which are contained in Gene Roddenberry's lengthy memo to the writer, John T. Dugan, which I read in your office, would be incorporated into the storyline and into the finished script. (SR51-1)

Regarding the same story outline, Associate Producer Robert Justman wrote Coon on May 26, saying:

> I think I like this Treatment, but then again I'm not sure because, although the writing is very fine, half the time I don't understand it.... I think that there is

much intellect displayed here. But I think that too often it is too esoteric and confusing. I would not be surprised to hear that the Network has requested us to simplify this Treatment before going to screenplay. And I wouldn't blame them. (RJ51-1)

Dugan was asked to straight-line his story. It took a month for the first draft script to arrive. On June 29, in a letter accompanying the script, Dugan wrote to Coon and Roddenberry:

Yes, gentlemen, there really is a John Dugan. And to prove it, herewith three copies of "Return to Tomorrow." The date on the cover is not a lie, but the date I sincerely thought I'd deliver the script; and I would have -- except for the earthquake that opened the earth and devoured the original ms [manuscript]. And the changes I wanted to make. (JTD51-1)

The earthquake had been a minor one. Saying it swallowed the script was akin to a kid telling his teacher, "I did the homework but my dog ate it." It was a strange message for a professional writer to send with a script submission, even if he had liked the two Genes on the couple of occasions they had met in the past. And it got stranger.

Dugan's letter continued:

You will note, one hopes, that I followed each and every suggestion of both Gene C. & Gene R. -- and, despite this, the script seems to work very well.... I think you will find that I have simplified the technical aspects -- which should warm your cockles. Of your heart, that is.... Also, I think all your running characters are used sufficiently for them to earn their paychecks, and to keep them in the mind's eye of the audience. Please note that our leads, when playing the Arretans, speak in their own voices. This was my original intention, Gene R. -- which I apparently did not make clear in the story. Of course this is better for us in many ways -- including the obviating of dubbing.... Finally: Please like it. You know how $#%*! sensitive I am.... Writer & Fan, John. (JTD51-1)

In this script, unlike the finalized episode, the receptacles which contain the intellects of Sargon, Thalassa, and Henoch are not glowing balls. Sargon's receptacle -- the first to be encountered -- is described as "about 20 inches square, a speaker-grid set in its façade, its cover off and set to one side.... Under a clear plastic covering lies a large, glowing brain floating in a clear fluid."

On July 3, Script Consultant Dorothy Fontana wrote to Coon:

Overall, I like this script very much. Although there is not much action, I believe the script is interesting and the relationships of the characters will work very well. The roles delineated will provide a challenge to our actors' abilities, which should heighten their interest in the piece and their subsequent performances. (DCF51-1)

Two days later, Justman, taking the counter-point, wrote to Coon:

I think we have in this script a perfect example of how to take an interesting idea and completely screw it up. If you are looking for a way to force our most rabid fans to transfer loyalties, I suggest that you have found it.... If we have a stupid Captain and an illogical Mr. Spock, we are going to start out with a confused audience. Captain Kirk is stupid because he allows himself to be bamboozled by these brains and makes a willing pawn in their attempt to rejuvenate themselves. I can't in any way believe that Captain Kirk would allow himself or his crew to be used in this manner.... He seems to be almost too naive and trusting to be a starship Captain.... Mr. Spock is totally illogical. For him to champion Sargon's cause is not Spockian in the least. There is not sufficient information for him to

523

go on, nor is there sufficient cause for him to put such blinding faith and trust in the intentions of Sargon.... It's tough enough to sell the fact that some outside agency has taken over the bodies and minds of our Principals while we continue to use our Principal Voices in only slightly altered form. But then to continue on with the idea and put Principal's Voice in a brain box machine is even more confusing.... Please remember the situation we had in a show entitled "The Alternative Factor." It must be apparent at all times who is who and what is what. If we confuse the audience, we will confuse the whole story.... I suggest that you get John Dugan to re-structure and re-characterize the show as best he can and then let's all of us go to work on it and clean it up, before we ever submit it to the network. I greatly fear that the Network will love the show in its present form. (RJ51-2)

After various rewrites, an effort was made to address Justman's concerns. In time, Kirk was given better motivation for going along with Sargon's wishes. "Does that frighten you, James Kirk," Sargon dares him. A man like Kirk is not going to allow anyone to suggest he is afraid. Plus, he tells us, after being touched by Sargon's mind that he is convinced the alien is sincere. It is insinuated that Spock gains trust for Sargon through use of his Vulcan psychic ability. These explanations help slightly. And then, later still in the writing process, Roddenberry wrote Kirk's impassioned and somewhat preachy speech about the Enterprise's mission, and the greatness of men who, for the sake of scientific and spiritual enlightenment, were not afraid to encounter the unknown.

But, as of June 13, Dugan was still the man at the typewriter keys and all of these things had yet to be reasoned out. Coon, trying to inspire and influence the tone and direction of the script, and to convey that playtime was over and it was now work time, wrote to Dugan:

Dear John, granted, you are a most sensitive writer. I am a most sensitive producer. Now the cop-outs are out of the way. Let us turn to the script. (GC51-1)

Sixteen single-spaced pages of very frank, even somewhat harsh notes followed. Coon wrote:

I take here, and thereafter, violent exception with your choice of dialogue for Henoch [when in] Spock. "Alright girlie, lead the way," and other 1919 devices you have Mr. Henoch saying. Even could Henoch read minds, I fail to see where he would come up with this sort of jazz. I have no objections to Henoch making a verbal slap on the ass... and other such characteristics, but I do not like to have him talking like an adolescent Joe Penner [1930s-era vaudeville, radio and film comedian]. Please, let's not make him so flip, dated and corny.... Thalassa's line is not only a little corny, but it would seem to me that her line and Henoch's line would be a little dirty. This may be because I have a dirty mind. If so, I am not the only man in this country who has a dirty mind.... Henoch keeps coming off like the jolly good fellow who is a traveling salesman in ladies underwear.... Kirk's first speech [is] a most unlikely speech for our Captain to make. Have you ever heard anyone say, "The pleasant titillations of the flesh"? If you have, watch him.... All of this is highly mystical, theological, religious, and non-*Star Trek*. I feel the urge for prayer.... See what happens when a sensitive writer submits a sensitive script to a sensitive producer? Yours sensitively, Gene L. Coon. (GC51-1)

At the bottom of a copy of this memo -- the copy that was only sent to Roddenberry -- Coon added, "Dear Gene, I quit." (GC51-1)

It was a joke. But most humor is rooted in truth. Coon was not only growing tired, but becoming fed up.

It took Dugan nearly a month to respond, not with a revised script but with a letter. On July 21, he wrote Coon:

> Frankly, your memo sent me into a prolonged and profound state of shock. Recovering somewhat, I have been thinking about it, and wondering how to respond without seeming argumentative and/or peevish.... Although it isn't the primary cause of my shock, I might point out that it strikes me as unfair to the writer to wait until after the first draft to ask for changes in the basic concepts & elements which were clearly spelled out in the original story [outline], and/or the revised story, and/or discussed & modified in the conference preceding the go ahead on the teleplay.... I merely suggest that we'd be a helluva lot further ahead if objections in re [reference] the above had been voiced <u>before</u> I started writing the teleplay. (JTD51-2)

Dugan countered Coon's critical notes with seven pages of his own, dissecting many things that were in Coon's letter. He wrote:

> Now I come to the real crotch of the matter: The questions & comments in the memo that seem to imply that my ms [manuscript] was written with half a head -- and that in the clouds -- and my preserves since, I submit, my script was read with <u>half an eye</u> -- written with a lot more attention & devotion to detail than was granted in the reading. This it is that you're not going to get any arguments from me when you say you threw me some substantial curves; I might also add: a few low balls, too. Particularly shocking when they weren't even called for.... Page 23. The word is spelled "gramm<u>a</u>r," not "gramm<u>e</u>r." If you take the "secretary" cop-out, we'll be even. (JTD51-2)

If Coon didn't know it before, he certainly did now -- he wasn't just dealing with a proud writer, but a former teacher.

Continuing, Dugan responded to Coon's note regarding the script calling for three different underground chambers on the planet. Dugan wrote:

> Why three chambers? Not because I am, like all writers, a lovable, impractical child, with no mind for costs, etc. But because it is necessitated by the exigencies of plot creditability. (JTD51-2)

Coon had told Dugan some portions of his script -- mostly scenes with Henoch -- were too sex-driven. Dugan retorted:

> What's wrong with sex? Propagation & perpetuation? I understand it to be the strongest drive of man. I even think the audience has heard about it. And there's nothing dirty about it. And let's all grow up.... So enough of memos. <u>Please</u> don't anybody there respond with a memo to me.... I will, accordingly, await your phone call. NOT your memo. (JTD51-2)

Coon waited a few weeks before calling Dugan. Between mounting creative differences with Roddenberry, particularly concerning comedy elements in the series, and dealing with argumentative writers like John T. Dugan, Coon wanted out. Shortly after making the call to Dugan, Coon resigned.

It took three months to get a 2nd Draft from Dugan, received on October 13. By then, John Meredyth Lucas was sitting in the producer's chair.

Fontana still liked the story and felt a good show could come from it, provided they got busy with some rewriting. She told Lucas:

> Instead of a Yeoman, which is a rather nondescript occupation, I would prefer to

see Anne [correct spelling at this time] as a Lieutenant/Scientist -- maybe even a Lieutenant Commander. I would prefer to see the actress who plays the role as a mature woman, and not a cutesie-pie little chick.

As she read about the three brains and a proposed fight between Sargon and Henoch, while in the bodies of Kirk and Spock, Fontana was struck by a sense of déjà vu. She told Lucas:

> We are now doing "Gamesters," in which we have exposed brains -- three in number -- doing a lot of tricks. And we have done the Kirk beats up on Spock -- or Spock beats up on Kirk -- several times this year also [in the early drafts of "Bread and Circuses" and all drafts for "Amok Time"]. I think we must apply ourselves to getting around the Kirk-Spock fight at the end if at all humanly possible. (DC51-2)

Justman believed the amount of work required was more than time, budget and patience could accommodate. He told Lucas:

> The second draft is in much better shape than Mr. Dugan's previous submission, but I feel it needs quite a bit of work to get it into shooting shape. There are still certain grey areas in this script which "beg explanation," as our good friend Kellam de Forest [might] say. (RJ51-3)

By this time, their good friend Kellam de Forest had turned his attention away from *Star Trek* and instead focused on series that did not require the reader to have a science background. The coverage notes sent to *Star Trek* never identified the writer. Throughout much of the first season, it was Pete Sloman, who then passed the job on to Joan Pearce, although continuing to advise her on the scientific validity. It was actually Pearce who wrote the sometimes caustic-sounding reports, and often used the phrase, "This begs explanation."

Justman continued:

> We should not allow our audience to become confused.... We do not have Phaser rifles. Phaser rifles are expensive to design and construct. Now that the studio is owned by Gulf-Western, I do not foresee any possibilities of our being able to obtain Phaser rifles. Fact is, I overheard someone discussing the possibility of *Star Trek* using Phaser sling-shots.... On this page, Christine reads the following speech: "Somehow I always sleep better knowing their power is shut off for the night." I wish I could say the same thing about President Johnson.... The supposedly straight dialogue in this script can be cleaned up and made believable without too much difficulty, I think. However, the comic-relief dialogue liberally scattered throughout the pages of this teleplay boggles the imagination. I knew a writer who became wealthy while delivering material like this to various shows. His rich aunt in Duluth [Minnesota] died and left him a million dollars. (RJ51-3)

Stan Robertson agreed with Justman over the questionable humor. Beyond this, the NBC man found the material from this former Catholic University teacher to be "sacrilegious."

In Dugan's script, Sargon tells the Enterprise landing party how, after his world became uninhabitable, two of its people -- a man and a woman -- left the dead world in the last space ship for an *uninhabited* planet very much like their own. The planet was Earth. "Yes, Captain," Sargon says. "The man and woman from this planet were your 'Adam' and 'Eve.'"

Kirk does not even react to this. He merely, and immediately, asks more questions about the other receptacles -- the other potential survivors. And away the story goes.

Robertson wrote to Lucas on November 9, saying:

> The basis of this story is a philosophical premise which seems to us to be faulty and not solidly founded. It has been our experience that the most successful *Star Trek* episodes have been those stories which were based on action-adventure ideas to which a philosophical point of view or moral were added as underlying or secondary themes to the telling of our stories. Conversely, those episodes in our series ("Wolf in the Fold," "Conscience of the King," etc.) which have been below our usual standard of excellence have been just the reverse.... The plot point, which is important to our story as now written, that Adam and Eve were the original implanters of the "floating brains," is one which, in our opinion, is not well founded logically, dramatically, or taste-wise. If, for instance, we "buy" the writer's premise about Adam and Eve, then, without carrying the position through to an objective conclusion -- as the writer has not done -- we are openly and without benefit of "reasonable reasoning" being sacrilegious. This, as you understand, could and would offend a large segment of our audience. On the other hand, if we do not utilize the Adam and Eve device, then the important plot point is meaningless.... In conclusion, it would be our recommendation at this juncture and in the script's present form that we postpone its production indefinitely. (SR51-2)

But *Star Trek*, with its last-minute back-end order of eight episodes, needed scripts. And so Roddenberry took over. He had always liked Dugan's story and felt confident that he could salvage it. To counter Robertson's concerns, Roddenberry made it clear very early on in the script that Sargon only speculated that Adam and Eve were descendants of the Arretans (from the planet Arret, which is Terra -- also known as Earth -- spelled backwards). Even with this point softened, Roddenberry had Dr. Ann Mulhall quickly counter, "It is our belief that we evolved independently." And then Roddenberry had Sargon back-pedaling by saying that perhaps his seeds were planted on Vulcan, and not Earth.

It seemed to do the trick, even with all the "my children," "my son," and "my beloved" lines that found their way into Roddenberry's rewrites. His Final Draft was delivered in early November, with page revisions arriving on November 18, 20, 21, 22 and 24.

Following the rewrites closely were "first reader" Joan Pearce and "second reader" Peter Sloman at De Forest Research. Sloman said, "We realized that they were occasionally getting writers who didn't know what they were talking about. And we had a certain level of contempt for the writers who blew it, but not for the show, because Gene was too good a guy to come up with something that was totally worthless. Gene Roddenberry was a wonderful fellow. He was a thoughtful man and you don't get that too often in Hollywood. Most of the time you get the concept that we're dealing in a product and that's all we do, we crank out sausages which are then stuck into your television and they show up on the screen. But Gene cared not only about the quality of the production values, but he cared about the quality of the thinking that went into the scripts. And that is very rare nowadays." (158a)

It is hard today to appreciate, or even understand, the limitations present in 1967 regarding the average television writer's exposure to science fiction. The ways in which science fiction was handled in the movies or, worse, in television, was almost always aimed exclusively toward a juvenile audience. For a researcher such as Pete Sloman, who prided himself in his knowledge of science fact, and how to best use it in science fiction, it was very painful to witness the mishandling of the genre on TV.

527

Sloman said, "Back in the days when there were just the three networks, there was nowhere else to go, so you had to learn to deal with the lowest denominator product, because what else are you going to do -- read a book? But when it came to the science fiction shows of that day [which included *Lost in Space*, *Voyage to the Bottom of the Sea*, *Time Tunnel*, and *Land of the Giants* -- all from producer Irwin Allen], you did have a chance at seeing at least one thing that was worthwhile. And that was *Star Trek*." (158a)

While undertaking the rewriting, Roddenberry added his name to the title page, taking the "teleplay by" credit. Dugan was downgraded to "story by." Roddenberry was justified in doing this. The premise, the character's names, and approximately 50 percent of the plotting were all he retained from Dugan's script, but every line of dialogue had been changed. Therefore, while it was still mostly Dugan's story, it was now all Roddenberry's writing.

Comparing the two scripts, Roddenberry's is certainly the better. Dugan, while doing an exceptionally good job capturing the voices and attitudes of the series' regular characters, delivered a script redundant in its plotting and, insofar as its characterization elements, not believable. For instance, it is made obvious almost from the moment we meet him that Henoch is up to no good. There is no subtlety. He has absolutely no empathy for others, is impatient, often angry and bullying, with obvious intentions of rebelling against Sargon and Thalassa and keeping Spock's body for himself. He is remarkably flirtatious with Thalassa, arrogantly suggesting she would have a better time with him than Sargon. He is also cartoonishly hedonistic, shoveling plateful after plateful of food into Spock's body, even when Spock's consciousness attempts to be heard, groaning about all the gluttony, begging that no more food be consumed. Henoch tells Spock to "shut up" and gobbles down more food. Roddenberry wisely eliminated this business.

One of the most successful elements of Roddenberry's script, barely present in Dugan's, is the amusement Henoch conveys while in Spock's body, allowing the normally non-smiling Spock to grin, and even flirt. Also, in Roddenberry's version, Sargon and Thalassa, while over-serious and somewhat pompous, are at least portrayed as less ignorant when it comes to Henoch's intentions.

"John never thought the script was problematic," said Dorothy Fontana. "He was really kind of bitter about that rewrite. As I recall, the script wasn't that bad, but it did need some work. And Roddenberry did it." (64-1)

Roddenberry knew this would go to the Writers Guild Arbitration Board. He was confident they would see things his way, especially in light of it being a 100% dialogue rewrite. Dugan was equally confident the Board would rule in his favor, and was convinced Roddenberry was trying to "steal" his credit. He said, "I was staggered at this development, and when the script went into arbitration by a jury of my peers, it came back as 'Written by John T. Dugan.' So Gene had tried to claim a credit that he was not entitled to." (54)

Nearly four-and-a-half decades later, Roddenberry's son Rod said, "My father was not a perfect man. I watched him rewrite scripts, and he would rewrite *everything*. So I can feel empathy for the writers who he rewrote. But it was his prerogative. It was his show. They have a right to complain about that, of course. The only stories that do bother me are where it becomes 'stealing credit,' and whether my father deserved it or not and all those sorts of things. I don't think my father was evil where he went out to steal credit from people. But when he made his contributions, he decided to put his name where he felt it should be." (145a)

Despite the WGA decision, Dugan did not want his name associated with the material. In his rewrite, Roddenberry, a man who rebelled against organized religion, had Sargon tell his wife that they could not allow themselves to exist in a human world and should therefore depart into oblivion.

"That line totally went against my philosophy and cosmology," Dugan said. "I didn't want to be associated with it. This oblivion idea is Roddenberry's philosophy, not mine. My philosophy was that these entities would exist as spirits for eternity, but they wouldn't have their bodies. That might be a small thing, but I have a reputation and a philosophy, and everybody who knows me knows what I stand for; I certainly don't stand for oblivion in the afterlife. So I used my pseudonym [John Kingsbridge]. When you write a script, you don't expect to have your 'world view' changed by a producer. The rest of Roddenberry's changes were all trivial, as I said in my letter to the arbiters; the big thing was the change in the episode's philosophy." (54)

Pre-Production
November 13-17, 1967 (5 prep days)

Diana Muldaur

Given little notice, Ralph Senensky was hired to direct. This episode was intended for Joseph Pevney, but Pevney had had enough. Senensky said, "I did that episode after I received a last-minute request for me to do it. I originally said, 'I can't,' because there was a conflict; a Jewish holiday fell in there. There was only one day that was a conflict. [Herb] Solow and [John] Lucas put their heads together, and they worked it out so I could do the show and go home at four o'clock on that day, and John Meredyth Lucas would come down and finish the day's work for me. He worked it out... and, for years, when I saw Johnny, he would always call himself the Yom Kippur director -- *my* Yom Kippur replacement." (155-3)

This was Senensky's fifth *Star Trek*. Due to the last-minute change of directors, the normal six days for preparation had to be squeezed to five. This meant the casting process had to go faster than usual. Fortunately, only one guest performer was needed, although the demands on this actress would be immense.

Dorothy Fontana said, "The biggest problem on that [episode] came down to the acting, and partly some of the writing, in that we had to have these people *in* our characters' bodies. Now, how do they talk? How do they express themselves? What are the feelings?... How do we make that work and sell it?" (64-2)

The burden, then, with mixed results, fell on Senensky, Shatner, Nimoy, and guest player Diana Muldaur, cast as Dr. Ann Mulhall.

Muldaur was 29. This was only her third year performing before the camera, but she had quickly become an in-demand actress and had been featured prominently in episodes of *Dr. Kildare, I Spy, Run for Your Life*, and *Gunsmoke*.

"I had done about five or six shows with [Diana] and suggested her for 'Return to Tomorrow,'" said Senensky. "And, of course, they loved her. She's a beautiful lady; such a good and solid actress." (155-3)

As for the regulars, *The Green Berets* had finally wrapped and George Takei was back. He later recalled, "I returned to Los Angeles heartsick and resentful. The scripts I had taken with me to Georgia had all been filmed. The lines I had so anxiously committed to memory had already been spoken by someone else.... The show that I returned to was titled 'Return to Tomorrow.' Tomorrow indeed! It was like returning to the dinner table after briefly excusing myself only to find my meal cold and half eaten by someone else." (171-4)

While Takei was underwhelmed by his role, Nimoy struck gold. His part was one of the best he was given in the entire series, and he turned in a spectacular performance. Majel Barrett was also given one of her better roles, and does flawless work. Nichelle Nichols, as Uhura, has a good moment -- and a tortured, blood curdling scream. Along with being Scotty, James Doohan provided Sargon's voice when not in the body of Kirk.

Doohan said, "They can do practically anything with your voice, stretch it, compact it, take out the highs or lows. *They* mostly manage that; you can't give yourself credit for that sort of stuff. Sargon was much lower than I normally speak, but they did that all electronically." (52-1)

And then there was poor Bill Blackburn. He was introduced to claustrophobia when sewn into the rabbit costume for "Shore Leave." Later he was one of three men to wear the Gorn suit in "Arena." And now he was to play the "android housing" that Henoch was building for Thalassa to live out her time in (see "Production Diary").

Production Diary
Filmed November 20, 21, 22, 24, 27 & 28, 1967.
(6 day production; revised set budget: $175,586)

Filming began Monday, November 20 and continued for two days before the Thanksgiving Thursday holiday on November 23. During this week, General William Westmoreland, in charge of U.S. forces in Vietnam, told the press, "I am absolutely certain that whereas in 1965 the enemy was winning, today he is certainly losing." 11,153 American soldiers died in Vietnam this year alone. But, according to Westmoreland's calculations, over 100,000 North Vietnamese had died in the same period. Back in the U.S.A., Walt Disney's *The Jungle Book* remained champ at the box office, again leading Paul Newman's *Cool Hand Luke*. "Incense and Peppermint," by The Strawberry Alarm Clock, was the song getting the most airplay on Top 40 radio stations. Diana Ross and The Supremes still had hold of the top-selling album, according to *Billboard* magazine, with their first Greatest Hits collection. The Beatles were close behind in record store sales with *Sgt. Pepper's Lonely Hearts Club Band*, now in one of the top two positions in the charts for nearly five months. And *Strange Days*, the second album by The Doors, had just risen to third place. You could buy any of them for about four bucks ($6 list).

Bill Blackburn recalled arriving to work one day and being told, "'You're going to wear a skull cap, and we're going to paint you to make it look like you're plastic.'" (17a)

Blackburn later said, "Apparently there was something they weren't sure about. They shaved my chest, and they put the makeup on my face and body. Then they brought out a big pot of acetate -- and that's what they used to paint that stuff on my body. They kept watching, and I thought, 'What's going on?' They weren't sure how my skin was going to react. Of course, it burned for a few seconds, especially on my chest where I'd been shaved. Once the burning stopped,

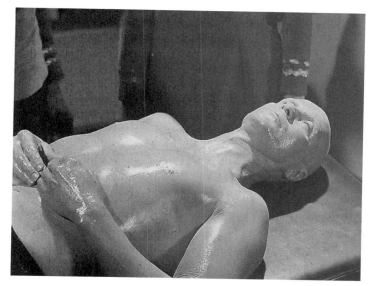

Bill Blackburn painted to look like plastic
(Unaired film trim courtesy of Gerald Gurian)

they put more of the acetate on me. They left a space on my back open, because they were worried about my skin being oxygen-starved." (17a)

The process of application was grueling. The duration of wearing the coating became unbearable.

Blackburn continued: "So I'm standing there with this stuff all over me, and, all of a sudden, they decided to do the scene later. This was about 9 a.m., and 'later' meant *really* later. At the end of the day, I'm finally doing the damn thing. I had this stuff on all day long; I couldn't even move my face because it would have cracked. So, finally, they said, 'Lie down now; Spock's going to make this speech. Can you hold your breath?' Well, I'm a swimmer, and I can hold my breath for two minutes. But I didn't realize how long the speech was, and I'm lying there and lying there, and I'm holding my breath, and Leonard is droning on and on. And, finally, the scene ended and Ralph Senensky said, 'Good job.' I started to pull my face and make-up off, and [Assistant Director] 'Tiger' Shapiro is in the back saying, 'Well, you wanted to be in show business, God dammit, you got it!'" (17a)

The moment was filmed and became a well-circulated *Star Trek* blooper.

After having one day off for Thanksgiving, cast and crew were back on the job on Friday, November 24. Shatner's weight gain appeared to have peaked with this episode. Note when Sargon, in Kirk's body, collapses onto the briefing room floor. Wardrobe again had Shatner wear a black t-shirt under his velour top, which prevented the white skin from showing, but, with him flat on his back, there was no hiding the gut that had been building since before mid-season. Like many Americans, Shatner began dieting *after* Turkey Day. A slight weight loss would begin to be detectable in the next episode to film, more so in work spanning the weeks to follow.

Star Trek was pre-empted on this night by NBC for a Tijuana Brass special.

The company resumed work on Monday, and wrapped, on schedule, Tuesday, November 28.

The production itself was rushed. Director Senensky was normally given seven days to film a 60-minute television episode on most other series. The rule at *Star Trek* had always been six days, although this goal was rarely achieved during the first season. Of the 21 episodes shot so far for Season Two, 10 had gone over their planned six day schedule, including two of the three directed by Senensky. With two-to-one against him, the director fully understood the importance of making the score even and bringing assignment No. 4 in on time. He later said, "Gulf-Western, owner of Paramount right next door, had purchased Desilu. The wall separating the two studios had been torn down and it was now just one big unhappy family. When I first came to *Star Trek*, Gene Coon told me that although the shows were supposed to be scheduled for a six day shoot, actually it was averaging out to six and a half days per episode. The edict from the new owners was that ALL SHOWS MUST BE COMPLETED IN SIX DAYS. But there was more. A normal shooting day had a crew call of 7:30 a.m. for an 8 a.m. shoot. The day ended at 7 p.m. Another order from the new management was that filming must end at 6:12 p.m. That was 48 minutes less per day. Forty-eight minutes times six [days] is 288 minutes. 288 minutes divided by 60 [minutes] is 4.8 hours, just 12 minutes less than 5 hours, which is a half a day's shooting time. In other words, it was now being demanded that *Star Trek* be filmed in five-and-a-half days." (155-5)

Unaired film trim with Muldaur and Nimoy in the underground chamber Matt Jefferies built onto Stage 10
(Courtesy of Gerald Gurian)

"Return to Tomorrow" was Senensky's least favorite episode of those he directed for *Star Trek*. In an interview for this book he said, "Bill Shatner was always competent, except in 'Return to Tomorrow.' I thought that it was so badly acted. It was just a strange show and, in retrospect, I think it was one of those shows that you would read as science fiction, but you couldn't really act it. Leonard is okay, because he approached the role with a little more depth than Shatner did. And Diana Muldaur, who I had of course worked with before, is so much better (and exciting) in 'Is There in Truth No Beauty?' The material was almost self-defeating. It wasn't Roddenberry's best work and, I'll say this, too, if Gene Coon were still there that show might have been able to work. Coon wrote better dialogue than Roddenberry. The aliens really weren't characters, they were just types." (155-6)

Senensky felt the rushed schedule was the most damaging factor. He said, "There wasn't the time to work with the performances more. You get a take where all the lines make sense and you just have to go with it. I never really had to say much to Shatner -- to any of them. They knew their characters better than I did. And they were always so right on. The main thing for the director was just to stage it and photograph it and to get it in before the time ran out. But at that time, in that episode, anyway, Shatner struck me as being like Bob Culp, who I'd just directed on *I Spy*. Both talented guys, but their approach to acting was not always as sincere as it could have been. They were more into being stars than being actors." (155-6)

Not all the acting was off the mark. Regarding Nimoy, Senensky said, "What I appreciated so much in Leonard's performance of this totally evil man was the way he charmingly played against the evil. That is something in which I so strongly believe. Charming evil is so much more effective." (155-5)

Regardless of the rush, a script that needed a little more work, and one particularly heavy-handed performance, Senensky remained impressed by the themes presented on *Star Trek*. He said, "By the latter 1960s, television -- a voice delivering any sort of message -- had pretty much been muted. Action had replaced the thoughtful dramas of TV's Golden Age. That was why *Star Trek* was so unique. It could comment on current issues using them as adventures of the future. But *Star Trek*

Shatner, ready for his close-up ... for Day 4 of the production (Courtesy of Gerald Gurian)

many times went a step further, becoming prescient in presenting our dreams for the future. Kirk's speech [in this episode] about space is an example. It was written and filmed two years *before* Neil Armstrong walked on the moon." (155-5)

And Senensky remained a fan of *Star Trek*'s cinematographer, adding, "In spite of Paramount Studio's cutting almost a half-day from the shooting schedule, Jerry Finnerman's photography remained exemplary. His lighting as always continued not only to light the bodies, but it illuminated the inner drama." (155-5)

Note the brilliant blues, greens, and Finnerman's favorite shade of purple -- magenta -- used on the walls of

There was rarely a bad moment between Kelley and Shatner on *Star Trek* (Courtesy of Gerald Gurian)

the transporter room, the briefing room, and sickbay, every bit as vibrant as in the last Senensky-directed episode, "Obsession." The other rotating directors, Marc Daniels and

Joseph Pevney, had not allowed Finnerman to go quite this far with the coloring on the ship's walls. It was the combination of Senensky and Finnerman which made for the most striking onboard visuals.

Despite the apparent impossible goal, Senensky finished his assignment in what equated to five-and-a-half days of production. The results, for the most part, are good. Even quite good. But there are moments, performances which certainly should have been done over, if time had only permitted.

Post-Production
Available for editing: November 29, 1967. Rough Cut: December 5, 1967.
Final Cut: December 1, 1967. Music Score recorded on December 29.

Donald Rode handled the editing. Ralph Senensky stayed closely involved, since voiceover work was needed to complete the episode. And this is when he became certain that "Return to Tomorrow" would be his least favorite of the *Star Trek*s he had directed. He recalled, "When we filmed the scene where Sargon inhabits Kirk's body, I recognized Bill's performance had taken it to the limits, but I still found it acceptable. When viewing the scene in the completed film, I have always been uncomfortable with [it]." (155-5)

During post production, Senensky recorded James Doohan doing the voice of Sargon from whenever we didn't hear it emitting from Kirk's mouth. It was both stilted and bombastic, but not due to lack of skill or judgment on the part of Doohan. Senensky explained that Doohan patterned his approach to match that as delivered during the production by Shatner. And then, of course, there was that pompous dialogue in the script assigned to the character of Sargon. Senensky said, "During Doohan's early acting career he had appeared on some 4,000 radio programs, a medium where the voice was the only means an actor had to express his performance, and Doohan became a master. What ideally could have been done in post production was to have taken Doohan onto the looping stage and recorded him doing Sargon's speeches in the scenes when Sargon occupied Kirk's body and replaced Shatner's voice with HIS voice…. Doohan's voice should have been overlaid on ALL of the scenes in the film when Kirk's body was the receptacle for Sargon…. But the added time plus the added expense it would have taken to complete the film would have been prohibitive." (155-5)

Van der Veer Photo Effects gave us the new visuals (everything excluding the Enterprise flybys). They chose to put the planet in the corner of the viewing screen, always a plus, and added in the transporter effects. Less effective are the flames around McCoy, a manifestation of Thalassa's rage. These are

DeForest Kelley acts as if flames are burning him from either side. The effect had yet to be added in (Courtesy of Gerald Gurian)

534

among the crudest opticals seen in the series.

Composer George Duning returned from his successful work on "Metamorphosis" to create the score for this and, at the same time, a partial score for the next episode on the roster – "Patterns of Force."

"I've been a [*Star Trek*] fan for years," Duning said for *The Star Trek Interview Book*, "I still watch the shows occasionally … 'cause I was a space buff when I was a 15-year-old kid. I was interested in space and that sort of thing, so I've always been a science fiction fan."

Release / Reaction
Premiere air date: 2/9/68. NBC repeat broadcast: 8/2/68.

Steven H. Scheuer reviewed this episode for *TV Key Previews*. Among newspapers across America to carry Scheuer's syndicated column on February 9, 1968 was *The Bridgeport Post*, serving Bridgeport, Connecticut. Scheuer, wrote:

> A weird and far-out plot, even for this series but it's quite an interesting one. Summoned to a planet much like Earth, the Enterprise finds a highly advanced civilization that destroyed itself two billion years ago. However, a few of its brains survived and now they want to borrow a few human bodies to launch an extremely worthwhile project. Kirk makes the initial and risky body loan and naturally, complications ensue. Although it is all a bit confusing, you'll want to stay with it and watch both Captain Kirk and Mr. Spock die.

Judy Crosby also reviewed the episode on February 9, 1968, for her syndicated column, *TV SCOUT*. Among the papers running the review was *The Monessen Valley Independent*, in Monessen, Pennsylvania. Crosby, less impressed than Scheuer, said:

> This show is almost comedic, with an episode title that might have been, "The Bible According to *Star Trek*." It concerns formless humans discovered on a planet destroyed by radiation two billion years ago, and they take over the bodies of Kirk and Spock. These last two humans now want to head back to a planet called Earth. If you don't guess their names as Adam and Eve, then you aren't trying.

The episode was also reviewed on February 9, 1968 for *TV TODAY*, a syndicated column that ran in numerous newspapers, including *The Milwaukee Sentinel*, in Milwaukee, Wisconsin. The critic, who clearly did not pay close attention to the plot points involving Dr. McCoy, wrote:

> This episode smacks of the old fright films seen on the late, late show. Alien brain forms enter the bodies of Captain Kirk, Mr. Spock and Lt. Cdr. Anne [sic] Mulhall as part of an experiment that is being conducted by Dr. McCoy, who is studying the brains on the distant planet that these creatures inhabit. Now, with the three alien brains and not the three Enterprise officers in control of things, it becomes a very dangerous situation.

RATINGS / Nielsen National report for Friday, February 9, 1968:

8:30 to 9 p.m., 60.6% U.S. TVs in use.	**Share:**	**Households watching:**
NBC: *Star Trek* (first half)	28.1%	14,000,000
ABC: *Winter Olympics*	22.4%	11,420,000
CBS: ***Gomer Pyle, U.S.M.C.***	**45.1%**	**17,750,000**
Independent stations:	4.4%	No data

9 to 9:30 p.m., 61.5% U.S. TVs in use.	Share:	Households watching:
NBC: *Star Trek* (second half)	**30.3%**	**No data**
ABC: *Winter Olympics*	24.5%	No data
CBS: *Friday Night Movie*	30.1%	No data
Independent stations:	15.0%	No data

For its first half-hour, *Star Trek* locked in the No. 2 position, ahead of the Winter Olympics broadcast on ABC. From 9 to 9:30, it won its time slot, although just slightly ahead of the CBS movie -- the television premiere of the 1964 World War II drama *The Secret Invasion*, starring Stewart Granger and Mickey Rooney. The Olympics came in third.

Star Trek remained NBC's highest-rated Friday night show. *Tarzan* managed 12,940,000 households, raised to 14,000,000 by *Star Trek*, then dropped to 9,070,000 for the primetime version of *The Hollywood Squares*, improving to 11,590,000 at 10 p.m. for the country music special, "Music from the Land."

***

Roddenberry was so pleased by his own work with the script for "Return to Tomorrow" that he chose it to represent *Star Trek* for consideration in that year's Writers Guild Awards -- above the scripts for "Amok Time," "Metamorphosis" and "Journey to Babel." The Guild, wanting to acknowledge the excellent writing being done at *Star Trek*, as it had the previous year with "The City on the Edge of Forever," gave the script an awards nomination in the category of Best-Written Dramatic Episode, even though it was clearly not the best from Season Two. But Roddenberry's attempt to pay tribute to himself backfired. With the decision coming from the Arbitration Board giving full credit for the script to Dugan, the prestigious nomination went to an unknown named John Kingsbridge. Regardless, "Return to Tomorrow" did not win.

The battle over credit, and the ensuing bad blood continued.

The WGA decision that John T. Dugan, using the pseudonym John Kingsbridge, receive sole writing credit, was honored only on the episode itself. In 1973 for *Star Trek 9*, a Bantam Book adaptation by James Blish, Dugan shared the credit with Roddenberry ... and Dugan's actual name was used on this occasion, not his pseudonym.

Dugan wrote to the WGA and complained. An investigation was conducted. The findings: Blish, who lived in England, used the scripts as a guide for his novelizations -- and the Final Draft for "Return to Tomorrow," as typed in November 1967 prior to the WGA action, listed Roddenberry as having written the teleplay and "Dugan" as having provided the story.

Nineteen years later, "Return to Tomorrow" was released to Home Video by Paramount Pictures. Again there was a discrepancy over the credit.

Dugan complained, "I was livid. I mean, to be an original *Star Trek* writer is quite a thing. Then, to have your credit stolen by the god of *Star Trek* is a cheap shot. I put the tape in and saw that the credit is fine on the show itself, but what pissed me off was that it's not correct on the jacket.... I don't even know if I've gotten my royalties correct, or if I've been splitting them with Roddenberry all these years!" (54)

Dugan was preparing a lawsuit against Paramount Pictures and Gene Roddenberry in

1992 when he was diagnosed with cancer. His last word on the subject: "In light of the fact that I have a limited period of time left ... I agreed to settle. So Paramount sent me a nice big check." (54)

Memories

Diana Muldaur talked with *Starlog* in 1989, saying, "The qualities that I admired in [Gene Roddenberry] were his creativity.... In Hollywood, they buy you because you're creative and then try to take it all out of you, to make you commercial. And he never gave in."

John T. Dugan said, "You have no control as a writer; you do your job and then step back and hope for the best. All in all, I was pleased, and I had no objections to the actors' performances." (54)

Ralph Senensky disagreed about the performances. He said, "It's funny, but when we get into 'Obsession,' 'Bread and Circuses,' and 'Return to Tomorrow,' which were all shot on that crazy, fast schedule, it's like I shot them on fast-forward and my primary memory of them is just trying to get them done.... The pressure was there to try and give the actor the chance to give a performance, which wasn't always easy." (155-2)

33

Episode 52: PATTERNS OF FORCE

Written by John Meredyth Lucas
Directed by Vincent McEveety

Nazis in space (Unaired film trim courtesy of Gerald Gurian)

From NBC press release, issued January 19, 1968:

Captain Kirk (William Shatner) and Mr. Spock (Leonard Nimoy) are captured on a warlike planet with a Nazi-type regime while searching for a cultural observer from whom nothing had been heard for five years, in "Patterns of Force" on NBC Television Network's *Star Trek* colorcast of Friday, Feb 16.... Kirk and Spock are imprisoned and tortured by the regime which rules the planet Ekos and learn that their captors are bent on eliminating immigrants from the planet Zeon. Isak (Richard Evans), also a prisoner, helps them escape to the Zeon underground. Assisted by Daras (Valora Noland) and later by Eneg (Patrick Horgan), they find John Gill (David Brian), the missing observer, who is being used by Deputy Fuhrer Melakon (Skip Homeier) as a front for wholesale extermination of a peaceful people.

It is discovered that Gill, a teacher from Kirk's Academy days, sent to Ekos to secretly observe the planetary development, had ignored the Federation mandate of non-interference in order to become the Ekosians' leader. Now, Kirk must undo the damage, which includes aborting an attack Ekos is preparing to launch on its sister planet Zeon.

The theme: power corrupts even those who think they know better. If great care is not taken, the history of man will repeat ... in other countries ... and even on other worlds.

SOUND BITES

- *Spock, to Kirk:* "You should make a very convincing Nazi."
- *Kirk, with Spock kneeling on his back:* "I don't care if you hit the broad side of a barn. Just hurry, please." *Spock:* "Captain, why should I aim at such a structure?"
- *Melakon, regarding Spock:* "Note the sinister eyes and malformed ears. Definitely an inferior race; the low forehead denoting stupidity; the dull look of a trapped animal."
- *Kirk:* "But why Nazi Germany? You studied history; you knew what the Nazis were!" *John Gill:* "Most efficient state Earth ever knew." *Spock:* "Quite true, Captain. A tiny country -- beaten, bankrupt, defeated -- rose in just a few short years to stand one step away from global domination."

- Isak: "If we adopt the ways of the Nazis, we're as bad as the Nazis."

- John Gill: "Even historians fail to learn from history. They repeat the same mistakes."

ASSESSMENT

While lacking in subtlety, "Patterns of Force" nonetheless entertains. The Teaser, portraying a missile attack on the Enterprise from a planet that should not have the technology to instigate such hostility is intriguing. The first few minutes of Act I continue to entice, as Kirk and Spock watch government propaganda on a giant video screen in the middle of an outdoor square, and then watch in astonishment as storm troopers chase down and kick a helpless "Zeon pig." Then the heavy-handedness begins as the camera pans up from the man being brutalized to the swastika arm bands on his tormentors.

What follows is not all bad. The comedy certainly works, as a long-suffering Kirk gives Spock a boost onto his freshly flogged back; or Melakon, to Spock's deadpan response, deduces that Vulcans are an inferior race, and even somewhat stupid looking; or McCoy, materializing in a closet, struggles with his ill-fitting vintage World War II boots; or Kirk, putting a German Officer's cap onto his head, is told by Spock that he will make a convincing Nazi. Director Vincent McEveety gets good results from the guest actors playing members of the resistance. As contrived as the story may be, the sincerity of their performances helps to disguise a premise that is for the most part absurd. And Lucas's story delivers a statement concerning the inherent flaws and dangers of the "leader principle."

However, the characterizations seen here are one-dimensional stereotypes with little more than cartoon treatment of a menace that could otherwise be truly villainous. Likewise, the dialogue is often forced and melodramatic; and the writer's obvious goal, to examine and explain how people like the Nazis could seduce a nation and gain unconditional power, then become perverted by that power, is never achieved. Other problematic areas: an expert historian thinks it's a good idea to emulate Nazi Germany's fascist policies; the closing idea that the removal of one bad guy will cause these imitative people to immediately become "a fine addition to the Federation"; and, of course, the unmentioned fact that everybody on two nearby planets seems to speak English.

"Patterns of Force" is certainly not a disaster. Its entertainment value supersedes its story holes and hamfistedness. And, as Spock says, Kirk does make a convincing Nazi.

THE STORY BEHIND THE STORY

Script Timeline

Paul Schneider's story outline, ST-40, "Tomorrow the Universe": December 13, 1966.
Schneider's 1ˢᵗ Draft teleplay: January 20, 1967.
Schneider's 2ⁿᵈ Draft teleplay: March 3, 1967.
Schneider's Rev. 2ⁿᵈ Draft teleplay, gratis: June 1, 1967.
John Meredyth Lucas's story outline, "Patterns of Force," ST -73: June 7, 1967.
Lucas's revised story outline, gratis: June 19, 1967.
Lucas's 2ⁿᵈ revised story outline, gratis: June 26, 1967.
Lucas's 1ˢᵗ Draft teleplay: late October, 1967.
Lucas's 2ⁿᵈ Draft teleplay: November, 1967.
Lucas's script revisions, as producer: November 24, 27, 28 & 30, 1967.

After impressing Producer Gene Coon with his script for "The Changeling," despite heavy rewriting by Script Consultant D.C. Fontana, and not being blamed -- by Coon, anyway -- for what kept his story outline for "The Lost Star" from progressing to screenplay, John Meredyth Lucas returned for a third assignment. He wanted to do a story about a parallel planet that falls under the control of the biggest, baddest heavies Hollywood had ever known -- the Nazis.

Lucas later said, "The totalitarian society, particularly the Nazis, has always intrigued me. How could something like that have come about? Of course, I know the history, but how, in the minds of people, could this have possibly happened? I started off with the premise that I would try to explain it... that Nazism created an efficient society for accomplishing specific ends, and this is what the guy from the Federation attempted to utilize. But then, like in the past, an entire nation got swept up in it." (110-3)

Coon was way ahead of Lucas and had already bought a Nazi-themed story from Paul Schneider. "Tomorrow the Universe," in fact, opened very much like "Patterns of Force." The Teasers in both scripts were almost identical. And both stories had a member of the Federation interfering with an alien society and introducing a Nazi-like system, right down to the swastikas and goose-stepping.

On December 16, 1966, regarding the story outline for "Tomorrow the Universe," NBC production manager Stan Robertson wrote to Gene Coon:

> Instruct the writer to please avoid the obvious temptation one can understand he would possess to make this an overly philosophical and talky script.

Schneider was given notes, warned of NBC's concerns, and then sent off to write a screenplay. The script arrived on January 20, 1967. Dorothy Fontana responded first, writing Coon:

> We have here a talk piece with an unbelievable development and resolution.... I urgently recommend a complete structural overhaul from Act II on....
> Alternatively, to fix up the story that now exists boggles the mind. (DCF52-1)

Associate Producer Robert Justman wrote to Coon on the same day, equally as boggled. Among his notes:

> I like the idea of the script very much [but] I don't think the writer has realized the full potential of what could be accomplished here. However, he *has* realized too much potential in the area of spending money. (RJ52-1)

Paul Schneider was called in for a meeting, then sent home to improve his script. Of his rewrite, Fontana wrote Coon:

> Change the title, please. This is a heart-rending plea from the depths of my soul. Every time I see the current title I have visions of a 1930's Republic serial. (DCF52-2)

Days later, Justman told Coon:

> This is undoubtedly a new low for professional writers. I would also characterize it as amateur night in Dixie.... I fail to see why we continue to go back for further punishment from people with whom we have had sad experiences in the past.... This present screenplay is badly constructed; the characterizations are well nigh unbelievably vapid; the dialogue is nauseating; most of the action is unstageable; the opticals are unbelievable and incredibly expensive. (RJ52-2)

The sad experiences Justman alluded to were the rewriting of "Balance of Terror" and "The Squire of Gothos." Others on staff, such as first season associate producer and script consultant John D.F. Black felt Schneider had done well by *Star Trek* with those scripts. But now, with "Tomorrow the Universe," Justman predicted Fontana would have to do a complete rewrite if the script were to be salvaged.

Gene Roddenberry had a meeting with Schneider while Gene Coon vacationed, bringing Coon up to speed in a memo dated April 1, 1967. Roddenberry wrote:

> [I] told him his rewrite is completely unacceptable as a *Star Trek* episode. [I] spent time with him explaining why, point for point, used fairly strong language in pointing out all the totally illogical and unbelievable items. In short, hoping to intrigue him into something which might possibly save the script and the investment, challenge him to omit all the clichés, stereotyped characters, illogical plot turns, and so on. Got his attention finally when I suggested that maybe a fascist civilization might be right for a certain kind of planet and certain kind of biped humanoid. What if this was the point of the story? Hitler did make the trains run on time and gave the German people a sense of purpose and suppose he had accomplished this, along with a few small ugly things, but without the hate hysteria and mass murder? (GR52-1)

Coon had Schneider do a script polish, constituting a Revised 2nd Draft teleplay. Of this, Fontana wrote that she believed it was "much improved" but there were "still things about it that are troublesome and should be fixed." (DCF52-3)

Of the same draft, Justman told Coon:

> I must take issue with you. It was my impression that you were not entirely satisfied with Paul's latest version of this story. I personally think you are a very kind man. I think D.C. Fontana also is much too kind when she says that she finds the script "much improved." I find the script much changed, but not improved in the slightest. I feel we have hit a new low. However, I have not yet read "The Apple," so I may be mistaken, in degree if not in kind. (RJ52-3)

And we all know now what Robert Justman thought of "The Apple."

Even as the staff was responding so negatively to the third draft of "Tomorrow the Universe," the story outline for "Patterns of Force" was being distributed. No one knew what Coon was up to and all were caught off guard in finding two "Nazis in Space" stories being developed simultaneously.

Dorothy Fontana, in her next memo to Coon, was firmly planted on the fence with the new material. Worrying about the scope, and the cost in realizing this, she wrote:

> Page 11 will bust our piggy bank. The only suggestion, outside of hiring Nuremberg Stadium and resurrecting the Third Reich, might be to take advantage of the fact that these people are advanced enough to have television. President Johnson does not appear in front of hordes to make his policy statements. He appears on NBC, CBS and ABC and a multitude of radio pick-ups. Let us have Gill and the others appearing on Telosian TV, and perhaps we can limit this sequence to a couple important characters, sound stage and TV crew. I don't know if that's any less expensive, but it beats an outdoor amphitheater crowded by cheering mobs.... [And] we might change the name of one planet from Telos to something else. Talos IV was the planet in "The Menagerie" and we referred to it many times. (DCF52-3)

Robert Justman, one day later, sent his thoughts to Coon, writing:

> On the last page of this story treatment, we again have Captain Kirk deciding to hide information from Starfleet Command. He determines that he should not mention the mistake that John Gill made. As usual, Captain Kirk goes blithely on his way, changing history and hiding information from his immediate

superiors. This sort of action is, as you are no doubt well aware, a general Court Martial offense. It also indicates that Captain Kirk likes to play God. (RJ52-4)

Justman had a bigger concern over the not-so-new story. He told Coon:

No doubt you are aware that this story bears great similarities to the property that Paul Schneider is working on and has been working on for these many months. I should like to suggest that we do not use Nazi Germany as our source material for this story.

The other solution, of course, would be to junk the Schneider script and keep the Nazis in "Patterns of Force." Reaction to this new story, although not overwhelmingly positive, was better than staff opinions of "Tomorrow the Universe." Work on the latter was abruptly stopped and the script shelved. Coon then ordered a revised draft of the story outline for "Patterns of Force." Lucas completed this on July 19 and mailed it off to the *Star Trek* production offices.

Five days later, Dorothy Fontana wrote Coon:

Concerning our intrepid heroes and their escape from the cell: despite their star age technology, I seriously question whether they could make a laser with an electric wire and no tools of any kind. How about something really crude -- like the old 'my buddy is sick' gag? Something that Spock would consider totally illogical -- but which works, much to his dismay. (DCF52-5)

The solution for enabling a jail break was yet to be decided, but the "my buddy is sick" gag would not be used here and instead saved for "I, Mudd" … and "Bread and Circuses" … and "By Any Other Name."

Justman wrote Coon the next day, saying:

As far as I am concerned, this revision in the story is as much a bore as the previous version. For any definitive comments, I fear you will have to depend upon D.C. Fontana, as I find myself overcome with an immense lethargy in reading this submission. Since the story bears such marked resemblance to Paul Schneider's piece, I suggest that we do the same with it as we have done with the other story. (RJ52-5)

Perhaps it would have been junked, if not for a letter that arrived from NBC a few weeks later. On August 4, Stan Robertson wrote to Coon:

One of the contingencies upon which this outline was approved was your statement that our previous considered story dealing with a Nazi type theme has been abandoned. We would add that it is our suggestion that we not dwell too heavily on the speeches, philosophy, etc., of the Nazi-like group, but concentrate more on the visual excitement which is obviously inherent in this well plotted storyline. (SR52-2)

Finally, a positive word. Robertson found the storyline to be "well plotted." It had been a long hard road, but Gene Coon would have his Nazis in space ... except for one small problem -- the journey had taken so long that *Star Trek* now had no further need for scripts, at least, not until the mid season pick-up came in.

By the time the script for this episode was written, Gene Coon was gone, and the writer of "Patterns of Force" was also the producer of "Patterns of Force." And who was going to tell the new producer of *Star Trek* that his latest script was not up to par?

Lucas said, "Thankfully, there was very little problem in terms of covering such dramatic material. Gene [Roddenberry] tended to do no censorship on that basis. He would come in and, if anything, would encourage wilder statements. He was a very adventurous guy, so there was no opposition in terms of 'My God, what are you writing about?'" (110-5)

Roddenberry, in fact, was busy with his latest rewrite of "The Omega Glory" and preparing "Assignment: Earth." "Patterns of Force" was the least of his concerns.

Lucas enjoyed this freedom and wrote the script as he saw best. And he had fun with the names. "Eneg" is an inside joke. It is "Gene" spelled backwards. The name "Zeon" is taken from "Zion." "Abraham" became "Abrom," "David" switched to "Davod." And "Isaac" was adjusted to "Isak."

Stan Robertson wrote to Lucas:

Kirk and Spock's escape from the prison cell seems to be a little too contrived to be believable. Cannot we possibly utilize something which calls upon Spock to display some of his Vulcan logic or physical prowess -- or some device which Kirk has secreted on himself which the society in which they are held captive has no conception? (SR52-2)

This "device" grew into the concept of the "transponder," a small unit implanted under a crewmember's skin as a security measure for planet survey teams. The 1960s version of GPS tracking proved awfully useful for this episode when series leads found themselves unexpectedly captured by a pack of Nazi lookalikes.

Fontana wrote producer Lucas a tactful memo concerning writer Lucas's script. Among her notes:

Why are the government buildings so far away from the beam-down point? Our people always transport down at some idiot place where they have to walk for miles to get where they are going.... [Can't] have Kirk and Spock standing around in open daylight with their silly uniforms on. They should beam down in some sort of costume, supposedly of the planet's civilization.... Overall I believe there should be a faster move into the heart of the story, cut out much of the expository sequence where everyone stands around giving Kirk information, and retain Zeon Isak through the story. (DCF52-6)

Lucas, whose early drafts for "The Changeling" and future scripts, such as "Elaan of Troyius" and "That Which Survives," were big on "expository sequences where everyone stands around" and talks. Fontana had done the trimming on his script for "The Changeling," as others would for the latter titles. But, with this outing, the only editing would be done by Lucas himself. To his credit, he acted on D.C.'s suggestion and pruned the script greatly.

Another suggestion from Fontana helped to add some humor into the otherwise dark screenplay. She told Lucas:

I foresee a great deal of laughing as everyone pictures the frantic sewing and cobbling to make up a Gestapo uniform for McCoy in the space of time we have here -- also McCoy leaping down to the Transporter Room, and changing en route. I just don't believe the time sequence as put down here. (DCF52-6)

After discussing the problem it was decided *not* to change the time sequence. Instead, the scene was intentionally written to be funny, as McCoy beams into the broom closet, struggling to pull on his military boots. Fontana was instrumental in making suggestions as to how to have scenes such as this work. She was, after all, the only one of the three staff writers left -- with Roddenberry and Lucas being the others -- who had a talent for crafting funny scenes.

Fontana later said, "After Gene Coon decided to leave, John was not a bad choice to replace him. He did know the show. He was an experienced writer/producer. He and I had a good relationship in regard to scripts and stories. He didn't have the sense of humor Gene

Coon had, but he had a sound understanding of how a series worked and knew how to exercise it. On 'Patterns of Force,' John took notes and implemented them. He was a thorough professional." (64-4a)

Pre-Production
November 21-22 & 24 & 28, 1967 (4 prep days).

"Skippy" Homeier, playing a Nazi youth in
***Tomorrow the World*, with Betty Field**
(United Artists, 1944)

Director Vincent McEveety was back for the first time in the second season. During Season One he handled "Miri," "Balance of Terror," and "Dagger of the Mind." Now that Joseph Pevney was out, McEveety was slated to alternate episodes with Marc Daniels, Ralph Senensky, and John Meredyth Lucas. Due to the Thanksgiving holiday, McEveety was allotted only four prep days instead of the usual six.

Skip Homeier, as Melakon, was 37. He began his career at 14 as "Skippy" Homeier. Coincidentally, his first film role, in 1944, had him cast as a callous German youth for *Tomorrow the World*. Homeier also had a successful career as a TV guest player. He visited hundreds of series, appearing frequently on *The Virginian*, *Voyage to the Bottom of the Sea*, *Combat!*, and *Alfred Hitchcock Presents*. He was given his own NBC series in 1960, as *Dan Raven*, a cop whose beat was the Hollywood division -- a show that sounded surprisingly like Roddenberry's Screen Gems pilot of one year earlier, *Night Stick*. Homeier also showed up on *The Outer Limits*, with James Doohan, in the episode "Expanding Human."

Homeier returned to *Star Trek* as the guest star in one of its most notorious episodes: "The Way to Eden."

Richard Evans, as Isak, was 32. His career in front of the camera kicked off in 1958. He made multiple appearances on *Gunsmoke*, *The Rifleman*, and *Bonanza*. He had a guest spot in Jeffrey Hunter's series, *Temple Houston*, and on Roddenberry's series, *The Lieutenant*. Prior to working here, Evans had a recurring role in the prime time soap *Peyton Place*.

Valora Noland, as Daras, began

Richard Evans in *The Rifleman*

acting for the camera in 1961. Prior to *Star Trek*, she had the female lead in *A Hot Summer Game* and *Passionate Strangers*, and was featured prominently in exploitation fare, such as *Sex and the College Girl*. She had most recently worked with John Wayne in *The War Wagon*.

William Wintersole, as Abrom, was 36. Before "Patterns of Force," Wintersole appeared in *The Outer Limits*, *The Wild, Wild West*, and *The Invaders*. Later, the soaps kept him gainfully employed. Joe D'Agosta, who before becoming *Star Trek*'s casting director had been an actor from the stage, knew

Valora Noland

Wintersole's work, but not from TV or films.

Wintersole said, "I had done a play, which was a very, very successful production in Los Angeles, and D'Agosta knew me from that. And he was very good to me, booking me for that *Star Trek* and also for five *Mission: Impossible* episodes." (189b)

Patrick Horgan, as Chairman Eneg, was 38. His TV career, with some film work, began in 1956. Born in Nottingham, England, Horgan was a Sherlock Holmes enthusiast. He appeared in plays about Holmes and performed in numerous Sherlock Holmes audio novels. He was also the author of *The Detection of Sherlock Holmes*. In television, he primarily kept active in the soaps, including recurring roles over the years on *The Guiding Light*, *One Life to Live*, *The Doctors*, and *Ryan's Hope*.

William Wintersole in *Mission: Impossible*

Horgan said, "I watched *Star Trek* religiously; every week in fact. I've always been a science fiction fan, so was forever concerned as to whether those shows were getting it right or not. And, of course, they

Patrick Horgan in *Mission: Impossible*

can't possibly get it right, because how do you know what right is going to be? But *Star Trek* had the good actors, and a good team, and I just loved it." (84a)

The script Horgan was sent was atypical of *Star Trek*. He said, "I was fascinated with it; I thought it was great stuff. And when I first read that script, I wondered where those names had come from. My name was Eneg. Could that not be Gene backwards? It's a learned chap who seems to be from the wrong planet. I suppose you could say that about Gene Roddenberry." (84a)

David Brian, casting photo, circa 1950

David Brian, 53, played John Gill. Roddenberry knew Brian, having written several scripts for the actor's mid-1950's series, *Mr. District Attorney*, a low cost ZIV production. Brian was somewhat of a star then, having begun his career on a high note, nominated for a Golden Globe award in 1949 as Best Supporting Actor for *Intruder in the Dust*.

Gilbert Green, 53, playing the S.S. Major, was often cast as Germans and Nazi-types on TV, for series such as *Hogan's Heroes* and *Get Smart*. He had also appeared in Roddenberry's *The Lieutenant*.

Ed McCready, as the S.S. Trooper, made his third appearance on *Star Trek*. He was previously seen as Boy Creature in "Miri" and, less noticeably, as an inmate in "Dagger of the Mind." He returned twice more, for parts in "The Omega Glory" and "Spectre of the Gun."

Ralph Maurer, who appeared in "Return of the Archons" under the name of Lev Mailer, was cast as an S.S. Lieutenant. In "Archons," he played Bilar, the reveler who called out "Festival, festival!" Of this second *Trek*, Maurer said, "The next year when I came to do the Nazi thing, that's how they greeted me. When they saw me, everybody [yelled] 'Festival!' ... You could feel the harmony on the set. It was very easy to work with them." (112)

Bart La Rue, the famed voice for the Guardian of Forever, played the Newscaster.

William Blackburn played two silent roles this time, seen again at the helm, as Lt. Hadley, and on the planet, as a German Trooper. One of those roles -- the one at the helm -- should have gone to George Takei whose Sulu, after all, had been missing from the series for such a long period just returned for the previous episode. But the cost of hiring Takei for such a small part in this episode could not be justified.

Production Diary
Filmed November 29, 30, December 1, 4, 5 & 6, 1967.
(6 day production; budget set at $179,780)

Filming began Wednesday, November 29, 1967. Actor Theo Marcuse, who played Korob in "Catspaw," was killed in a car crash. British forces withdrew from Yemen as the country declared its independence and became The People's Democratic Republic of Yemen. Julie Nixon and David Eisenhower announced their engagement. Senator Eugene McCarthy began his run for the Presidency of the United States. *The CBS Evening News with Walter Cronkite* was the most watched news show and where most Americans learned of these events. The night before, *The Red Skelton Show*, also on CBS, attracted the most-television viewers. On the show: Arthur Godfrey doing comedy bits with Red, and the vocal group The Harper's Bizarre performing "Chattanooga Choo Choo" and "Anything Goes." Disney's *The Jungle Book* was still selling more tickets than any other film in American movie houses. The top-selling album in record stores was the new one by The Monkees – their fourth – *Pisces, Aquarius, Capricorn & Jones, Ltd.* Their new single, "Daydream Believer," was getting more airplay on U.S. radio stations than any other song. "The Rain, the Park & Other Things" by The Cowsills settled in at No. 2.

Day 1. Production began with outdoor shooting on the Paramount backlot, including "Exterior City Street," "Side Entrance to Chancellery," "Exterior Street Corner," "Exterior Alley," and "Exterior Chancellery."

Day 1. Bill McGovern slating a shot on the Paramount backlot (Courtesy of Gerald Gurian)

John Meredyth Lucas, who liked being on set and was sticking close to director McEveety, recalled, "[We were] using some of the office buildings on the Paramount lot as backgrounds. Between set-ups I ran up to say hello to Hal Wallis, with whom I started as a feature writer … [and] as I rushed back to the set, I was intercepted by a man who introduced himself, wondering if we might be relatives -- *his* name was Lucas. He was very friendly and obviously wanted to talk but I had spent more time than I had planned with Hal. My assistant told me the crew was ready for the next shot and I was skirting the outer edge of my schedule. I quickly brushed the visitor off and [we] shot the scene. When I looked up again, he was gone. George Lucas went on to do his unforgettable *Star Wars* trilogies and now has an empire north of San Francisco doing most of the elaborate special effects for all companies. My timing has never been very good." (110-6)

To the contrary, and as discussed earlier, Lucas's timing was almost always very good. It was good timing that landed him the job on *Star Trek*.

Day 2, Thursday. Work took place on Stage 9 with most of the Enterprise sets collapsed to make room for additional building. The transporter room was shot, then on to new temporary sets for "Underground Room" and "Newscaster Room."

William Wintersole worked this day, as Abrom, the senior member of the underground movement who seems to be shot dead, but is only testing Kirk and Spock. He recalled, "It was a brief sequence, shot maybe twice. In and out. And we did do it that way. With those schedules, there was no other approach. You hit your mark, you say your lines. But that isn't the thing they are truly paying you for. They are paying you to never lose your character and always perform at the top of your ability to bring that character to life in the circumstances that have been explained. Doing television is, in many ways, like performing on the stage. If you make a mistake in a stage production, you can't stop and do it again. You know your character and you do what that character would do to move forward, despite a prop breaking or another actor forgetting a line. You think, in that moment, what would my character do, and you continue. And that allows a sequence of scenes such as these to be shot quickly." (189b)

Day 2. Much of the Enterprise was collapsed to make room on Stage 9 for a special set -- "Underground Room."
(Unaired film trim courtesy of Bill Krewson and Gerald Gurian)

"In-and-Out-Burger Acting" (referencing a U.S. fast food chain) is what Wintersole called it. But his performance, like the others playing the underground resistance members in this episode, brings a level of authenticity and passion to their otherwise small roles that is stirring. Wintersole explained, "On stage we play to the audience. In a situation such as this, you do what you must to bring that character to life, but you don't play for the camera crew and you don't play for anybody but the other actors and your director and, indirectly, you play for that magic light that is inside that camera. You know that it opens the world, like a portal, to what you're doing right at that moment. And it will forever open that world, like it is now, with the fans that stay involved with this series and these episodes." (189b)

And that is magic.

Day 2, Shatner and Nimoy having a ball with the jail cell scene
(Courtesy of Fred Walder)

Day 3, Friday, December 1. The entire day was spent filming the Nazi jail cell on Stage 11 (normally reserved for *Mission: Impossible*), where we see green stripes of blood on Spock's back after he is flogged.

It seemed like a promotable episode -- Nazis in space -- and, in particular, a promotable scene -- Kirk and Spock in jail being flogged by the Nazi menace, with Spock seen for the first time stripped to the waist.

So, the press was paraded through on this day, including reporters for a couple of teen magazines. Nimoy didn't mind being photographed bare-chested with that green blood smeared over his wounds, but he preferred not to be photographed for the scene where he and

Kirk put on the Nazi uniforms. Army Archerd, for *Daily Variety*, reported on December 8, 1967:

> Leonard Nimoy, Nazi-uniform-disguised for a *Star Trek* seg, nixed posing for still pix while swastika'd, with the American Breed group on their first studio trek.... Nimoy was understandably doubly sensitive about such publicity pix -- he'll guest at the Wilshire Blvd. Temple children's Chanukah services Dec. 29.

Day 2: A good day for the press
(Courtesy of Gerald Gurian)

Next, fan Kim Larson was ushered in, followed by a photographer for *FaVE* magazine, for a photo-exposé on her visit to Hollywood and the *Star Trek* set.

Larson told *FaVE* feature writer Kam Lytton, "When we got to the *Star Trek* studios on Gower Street I was really surprised. I thought the Monkee set had been hard to get onto, and the Columbia Ranch, too, but this was ridiculous! They checked us out like we were spies or something even though they already knew we were coming!"

Security had become that much of a problem wherever *Star Trek* filmed, even more so, as Larson noted, than on *The Monkees'* filming locations at the height of Monkeemania.

Larson continued, "As we walked in the Stage 11 door this buzzer went off and some man yelled, 'Quiet!' from over in the corner. We tiptoed up to where they were filming. Picture this: Leonard Nimoy (Mr. Spock), in *jail*, stripped to the waist, with *green* blood all over him! That was my first sight of the *Star Trek* stars and you can believe I won't forget it for a long time!... They finished with that particular scene and started to film another when someone yells out, 'Makeup!', and this man comes running over. He brushed some more green stuff all over Mr. Spock's back to make it look like he'd been whipped and then they started with the next scene.... Well, I'd been so involved with seeing Leonard Nimoy covered in green blood in that jail that I hadn't noticed the other things around, that is until some Nazi soldier comes over and starts to get in front of the cameras. Nazi? Yep. You see, the story is that the 'Enterprise' crash lands [sic] on a foreign planet that has made itself like

Nimoy opts not to submit to the razor as Roddenbery had Shatner do
(Courtesy of Gerald Gurian)

Nazi Germany. So I look around and there are Nazis all over the place! With machine guns! It really gave me a creepy feeling!

"Well, they got through with the next scene and Kam took me over to where Leonard was sitting and introduced us. He's really sharp and his pointed ears look as real as you could imagine -- close up, too! I thought they would look hard but they don't!... We took some pictures over on another part of the set and he did something that I really feel honored about. I found out later that he *never* smiles when his pointed ears are on because it's not in character with Mr. Spock, but for the picture with me – he smiled! Kam [Lytton] and Roland, *FaVE*'s photographer, were really surprised too!"

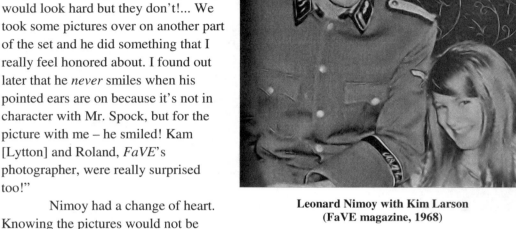
Leonard Nimoy with Kim Larson
(FaVE magazine, 1968)

Nimoy had a change of heart. Knowing the pictures would not be printed until the February 1968 (to coincide with the broadcast of the episode), he posed with Larson, in German military uniform.

Larson was likely sitting in front of a TV set at 8:30 that night. "Friday's Child" had its only NBC airing. *Star Trek* was ranked as a solid second place for its entire hour. After *Star Trek* ended this night, the NBC audience dropped from 10,860,000 households to 6,440,000 for *Accidental Family*.

Day 4, on Stage 10 for "Interior Broadcast Room" set
(Courtesy of Gerald Gurian)

Day 4, Monday. Stage 10 was used for many of the sets within the Nazi headquarters, including "Interior Lower Corridor," "Interior S.S. Lab," and "Interior Broadcast Room."

Patrick Horgan, on his second day of filming, said, "I do remember one rather charming incident. I was coming in one morning and Bill Shatner [who'd put on weight] was struggling to squeeze into his costume, and he says to me, 'Have you noticed that these uniforms seem to be shrinking?' I said, 'Oh … Well, no, I don't seem to be having any trouble with mine.' He had a good sense of humor about it. He was a very affable fellow; a real joy to work with." (84a)

Day 5, Tuesday. Another day on Stage 10, this time filming in "Interior Corridor," "Interior Main Room," and "Exterior Decoration Area."

Horgan recalled, "As a director, Vincent [McEveety] was very good. You never got into a situation where they were going to wiggle around for another take and another take and another take. He knew exactly what he wanted." (84a)

Day 6. Work ends on home ground and Stage 9
(Courtesy of Gerald Gurian)

Or McEveety knew exactly how little a six-day production schedule would allow for. He was discovering, as Ralph Senensky had before this, that the new management at Paramount was not going to allow for overtime, or added days. Even gifted directors like Senensky and McEveety, whose productions were always a notch above the average *Star Trek*, were now under far greater scrutiny … and the threat of termination.

Day 6, Wednesday, December 6, 1967. Production wrapped, on schedule, with filming in the cloakroom on Stage 10, as McCoy struggles to pull on his undersized boots, then a move back to Stage 9 for all the scenes on the bridge.

Post-Production
Available for editing December 7, 1967. Rough Cut: December 18, 1967.
Final Cut: January 2, 1968. Music Score recorded on December 29, 1967.

Fabien Tordjmann did the cutting. V-2 rocket footage from World War II Germany was used in the newscast showing Ekosian missiles.

The Westheimer Company provided the animated nuclear blast seen in this episode. However, the attacking V-2 rocket on the bridge viewing screen is reused footage of the Orion ship from "Journey to Babel."

Composer George Duning provided this partial score, which was recorded in conjunction with the music for "Return to Tomorrow." Duning's primary contribution here was the goose-stepping Nazi march ("Military Mite"), very much *overused* and about as subtle as getting kicked in the gut by a storm trooper.

Release / Reaction
Only NBC air date: 2/16/68.

NBC chose the "Nazis in space" (with an attractive blonde-haired woman) approach to promoting this episode with the publicity photos sent to newspapers across America. The teen and celebrity magazines took a different approach, instead choosing to run pictures from the jail room scene of Kirk and Spock being flogged, revealing the green marks on the Vulcan's back,

Syndicated critic Judy Crosby covered this episode for her column, *TV SCOUT*. Among the papers running the review on February 16, 1968, was *The Pittsburgh Press*, serving Pittsburgh, Pennsylvania. Crosby selected "Patterns of Force" as worth watching but, despite the endorsement, hardly raved. She wrote:

Valora Noland with Shatner in NBC publicity photo
(Courtesy of Bob Olsen)

> There is a blending of the past and future when the Enterprise crew stumble into a recreation of Nazi Germany. It is a planet called Ekos with a militaristic government and political philosophy akin to the regime of the Third Reich, including a plan for extermination of all immigrants from the planet Zeon. Valora Noland and William Shatner are embroiled in this Nazi-type plot. Skip Homeier and David Brian are also featured.

RATINGS / Nielsen report for Friday, February 16, 1968:

8:30 to 9 p.m., 60.6% U.S. TVs in use.	Share:	Households watching:
NBC: *Star Trek* (first half)	24.3%	11,420,000
ABC: *Operation: Entertainment*	24.1%	11,320,000
CBS: *Gomer Pyle, U.S.M.C.*	**43.8%**	**16,630,000**
Independent stations:	7.8%	No data

9 to 9:30 p.m., 61.5% U.S. TVs in use.	Share:	Households watching:
NBC: *Star Trek* (second half)	25.4%	No data
ABC: *Operation: Entertainment*	25.6%	No data
CBS: *Friday Night Movie*	**34.1%**	**No data**
Independent stations:	14.9%	No data

CBS was boss, with *Gomer Pyle* followed by the 1964 comedy *The World of Henry Orient*, starring Peter Sellers and Paula Prentiss. The fight for second place was a close one. Tim Conway was this week's funnyman host of *Operation: Entertainment*, entertaining the troops at George Air Force Base, Victorville, California. Guests included comedian Paul Lynde, singer Florence Henderson, and musical groups Sergio Mendes & Brazil '66 and

Martha and the Vandellas. During its first half-hour, *Star Trek* led by 100,000 households. From 9 to 9:30 p.m., *Operation: Entertainment* took the lead by an equal amount of homes (a 0.2% audience share above *Star Trek*'s take).

As always, there was no media promotion by NBC for *Star Trek*, and no back-end support to lure audience members away from the CBS movie. *Trek*'s 11,420,000 households dropped to 7,670,000 for *Hollywood Squares*, and then fell again to 5,320,000 for *Bell Telephone Hour*'s presentation of "The Sounds and Sights of Chicago," exploring "the Windy City's cultural blend of American inspirations and immigrant influences."

***

The director of this episode agreed that there was little subtlety in "Patterns of Force." Vincent McEveety said, "I didn't like it. To me, it was manufactured. There was nothing real about it. If you don't have something to hang on to, something to where, as a human being, you could say, 'That could have been me.' If you don't have that value in a show, it's hardly worth the effort. It doesn't matter if it's science fiction or a western, you have to believe the character. And then you're touched. But I was a little bit embarrassed by that one -- not specifically of what I did or what I didn't do, but this show I just felt didn't have it; there was nothing there to grab on to. I liked John [Meredyth Lucas], but I never felt John was a particularly good writer. He may have been a good producer -- although outside of a few outstanding producers, Gene Roddenberry being one of them, I never really figured out what a producer does. I know what he pretends to do. I mean, John Mantley [*Gunsmoke*] was a great producer, and Gene Roddenberry, and I was really blessed to have those two guys. Gene Roddenberry always had a purpose in whatever he was doing. John Mantley was the same kind of producer. Now, to me, that's what a producer should be -- that's his primary function, to make sure there's something to say, then helping with the cast, the director, and all of that. But so many of the people who put the cloak on and go through all the motions, with all the smoke screens and all the dialogue they have, don't come up with anything." (117-4)

One person who did find the episode had something to say was Paul Schneider. Feeling he had been plagiarized, Schneider filed an arbitration action with the Writers Guild of America.

On February 28, 1968, Roddenberry wrote to Gary Ellingsworth at the WGA:

I double checked with both John Lucas and Gene Coon and they assure me that John never read Paul Schneider's story or script, and, in fact, John Lucas was only lately aware that Schneider had written a Nazi script.... Gene Coon informed me that having paid Paul Schneider full price for the script, he presumed we owned the "Nazi idea," but felt that, since he was not using Schneider's story, he had no obligation to clear Lucas's assignment.

On May 23, 1968, Paul Schneider tried to bury the hatchet. His brief letter to Roddenberry read:

Dear Gene, a note I've been meaning to write, because I believe it's due.... I've been told about the Guild arbitration judgment that the "Patterns of Force" script for *Star Trek* was strictly by John Meredyth Lucas. Obviously I was wrong -- I misread the situation -- and I owe apologies to you and Mr. Lucas... which I now tender.... My sincere apologies.

Schneider, who did receive sole credit for the scripts "Balance of Terror" and "The

Squire of Gothos," did not write again for the original *Star Trek*. He would, however, return in 1973 to write "The Terratin Incident" for *Star Trek: The Animated Series*.

Both the makers of *Star Trek* and NBC agreed that this episode missed the mark. It was not given a repeat airing on the network.

Because of its subject matter, "Patterns of Force" was withheld from broadcast in Germany for over three decades. A translated version was finally aired there in 1999, but only late at night on pay-TV.

Memories

Vincent McEveety said, "That was my least favorite show that they gave me to do. It was just pretentious. It was forced. I didn't care for anything in it." (117-4)

James Doohan, who fought against the Axis armies in World War II, said, "During this episode, all I could think about was how gullible the German people were. They were suckered into Hitler -- and some of them loved it. There will always be those who appeal to the worst instincts in humanity." (52-1)

On the opposite side of the coin, *Star Trek*, according to William Wintersole, the leader of the underground movement in this episode, appealed to the best instincts in humanity. He said, "The fans saw in it -- and felt in it -- what was happening in the world. And it being put in science fiction form, put somewhere in the future so it wasn't like watching a newscast, gave them the room to think about what it was that was being said. TV, with its entertainment shows, wouldn't do political statements at that time, but this unique concept made it possible to make those statements. And that took root in the fans." (189b)

34

Episode 53: THE ULTIMATE COMPUTER

Written by D.C. Fontana
Story by Laurence N. Wolfe
Directed by John Meredyth Lucas

**Composite shot of 11-foot, 2-inch Enterprise with Space Station K-7 miniature
built for "The Trouble with Tribbles"
(CBS Studios, Inc.)**

From NBC press release, issued February 7, 1968:

> Captain Kirk (William Shatner) has no choice but to participate in an exercise
> which replaces him as commanding officer of the Enterprise, in "The Ultimate
> Computer" on NBC Television Network's *Star Trek* colorcast Friday, March
> 8.... Dr. Richard Daystrom (guest-star William Marshall) has developed the last
> word in computers, which the fleet command orders installed on the Enterprise,
> replacing all but 20 of the crew. War games are scheduled with the Enterprise as
> target and Star Fleet, under Commodore Wesley (Barry Russo), in pursuit. The
> computer performs perfectly until a single distraction upsets the responses and it
> goes berserk.

TV Guide, for its March 2, 1968 issue, was zeroing in on the episode's theme:

> "The Ultimate Computer" probes the problem of man vs. machine. The question
> is more than academic for Captain Kirk, who's temporarily replaced by a
> computer. The machine can think -- and will ensure its own survival at any cost.

Dr. Richard Daystrom, using his own mental patterns to program the M-5 Multitronic system, was a "boy wonder" who gained fame by revolutionizing computer design 25 years earlier. It is his "Duotronic systems" that currently serve the Enterprise. But Daystrom has secretly struggled to live up to the expectations of his peers and his own tortured ego. His growing paranoia has been imprinted into the M-5, which is now running the Enterprise.

The theme deals with ambition, and how it can push one to madness, be it man or machine made by man.

SOUND BITES

- *McCoy:* "Did you see the love light in Spock's eyes? The right computer finally came along." … *Spock:* "The most unfortunate lack in current computer programming is that there is nothing available to immediately replace the starship surgeon."

- *McCoy:* "Please, Spock, do me a favor and don't say it's fascinating." Spock: "No. But it is ... interesting."

- *McCoy:* "We're all sorry for the other guy when he loses his job to a machine. When it comes to your job, that's different. And it always will be different."

- *Spock:* "Computers make excellent and efficient servants, but I have no wish to serve under them. Captain, a starship also runs on loyalty to one man. And nothing can replace it ... or him."

- *McCoy:* "Fantastic machine, the M-5. No off switch." *Daystrom:* "You don't shut a child off when it makes a mistake. M-5 is growing, learning." *McCoy:* "Learning to kill." *Daystrom:* "To defend itself. It's quite a different thing."

ASSESSMENT

"The Ultimate Computer" is as relevant now as in 1968 when people were beginning to lose their jobs to computers and automated systems. There is, and was, great satisfaction in watching the dynamic James Kirk fight and defeat his would-be mechanical replacement of people.

Kirk has reason to distrust computers. He was nearly brought down by one in "Court Martial." He pulled the plug on a computer used to wage war in "A Taste of Armageddon," and two others that enslaved the people who worshiped them, in "Return of the Archons" and "The Apple." This episode was the fourth and final time Kirk used logic to short-circuit a mechanical mind. The first was in "The Return of the Archons," followed by "The Changeling" and then, played strictly for laughs, in "I, Mudd." The new wrinkle here: this machine's failing resulted in being very much like a human, handicapped with both ambition and a confused sense of morality.

An effective episode in all regards, "The Ultimate Computer" is perhaps the most successful of those produced by John Meredyth Lucas (taking into account that the superior "Journey to Babel," despite the screen credit, was actually produced by Gene Coon). Since Lucas also served as director, it is a double victory.

THE STORY BEHIND THE STORY

Script Timeline:
Laurence N. Wolfe's "spec" script: September/October, 1967 (Rec'd 10/13/67).
Wolfe's Revised 1ˢᵗ Draft teleplay, ST #79: November 9, 1967.
D.C. Fontana's 1ˢᵗ Draft (Teaser and Act I): December 1, 1967.
D.C. Fontana's 1ˢᵗ Draft (Act II): December 2, 1967.
D.C. Fontana's 1ˢᵗ Draft (Act III): December 3, 1967.
D.C. Fontana's 1ˢᵗ Draft (Act IV): December 4, 1967.
D.C. Fontana's rewrite: December 5, 1967.
Fontana's second revised draft: December 6, 1967.
Additional page revisions by John Meredyth Lucas: December 11 & 13, 1967.

Laurence N. Wolfe had never sold a screenplay. He was a mathematician with an interest in computers. He was also a fan of *Star Trek*. When Wolfe wrote his script for "The Ultimate Computer," the release of *2001: A Space Odyssey*, considered the great sci-fi man-versus-machine story of the 1960s, was still more than six months away. With its broadcast in early March, 1968, "Ultimate" beat both the film and the book versions of *2001* to the marketplace by a full month. History can sometimes be proven wrong. Laurence N. Wolfe, a one-hit wonder, aided by D.C. Fontana and John Meredyth Lucas, was first to depict a computer-run spaceship turning to murder to preserve its existence, not Arthur C. Clarke and Stanley Kubrick.

Another great science fiction writer helped this page of history be written. Wolfe knew Ray Bradbury, who, in turn, was friendly with Gene Roddenberry. As a favor to Wolfe, Bradbury passed the script on to *Star Trek*. As a favor to Bradbury, Roddenberry read it.

On October 13, 1967, Roddenberry handed the script to his new producer, John Meredyth Lucas. His note read:

> It looks pretty good to me, a better than average first draft. Not only an inexpensive shipboard story which can be done for fair budget, but also potentially very entertaining and exciting.... Certainly I like it better than some of the disasters we have had on hand. (GR53-1)

The "disasters" Roddenberry referenced were the scripts left over from Gene Coon's tenure, that had to be rescued, such as "Return to Tomorrow," which Roddenberry himself felt he rescued; "The Omega Glory," which Roddenberry had just taken away from Les and Tina Pine; "A Piece of the Action," which Coon was called back to fix; "By Any Other Name," which Fontana had salvaged; and two that were not coming together: "He Walked Among Us," which its own writer, Norman Spinrad, asked to have killed; and "Shol," by TV novice Darlene Hartman. In his memo to Lucas, Roddenberry made suggestions for changes to be made to "The Ultimate Computer" before the new producers even had a chance to read the script, including:

> We have a wonderful thing in Captain Kirk being ordered by Starfleet Command to have his ship taken over by a computer and I think we can make a bit more of Kirk's quandary and personal feelings. Also, the regular characters we do see, such as Spock, have not enough point of view of their own on all this. It might be interesting, for example, if Spock was, at first, fascinated by this whole possibility since he is himself rather a "computer man." ... Not enough action, of course. Too much talking about the threat that "Tensor Five" [the name of the computer at this point] is, not enough action-adventure sequences of our people being threatened by it, having to escape, possibly such things as

doors suddenly closing and almost crushing them if they hadn't seen it and jumped in time, or whatever. (GR53-1)

Roddenberry, so distracted by the writing of a Robin Hood pilot script when "Wolf in the Fold" went through its final script polishing and filming, had forgotten that the device of a computer causing doors to shut on crew members had already been used. His note to Lucas continued:

> Climax should involve last split-second hair breadth destruction of other vessels, or of the Enterprise, not simply a fight against the computer itself. We need a stronger build toward climax, more elements involved, more jeopardy, all ascending to the point where everyone and everything hangs on the brink of disaster. And, of course, we need our people, principally Spock and Kirk, resolving it in some clever way.... Daner [later to be renamed Daystrom] should be better motivated and let's consider the possibility of the fact that the fantastic new computer has "seduced" him or tricked him or whatever, in addition to whatever personal and professional reasons Daner has for his actions. (GR53-1)

Star Trek had recently purchased a treatment written on spec, later to be known as "The Trouble with Tribbles," but never a full script. Prior to this, Jerome Bixby ("Mirror, Mirror" and "By Any Other Name") made his introduction to the series by way of an unsolicited manuscript, as did Darlene Hartman (later to write the unproduced "Shol"). While neither of these initial submissions were purchased, both writers received assignments to develop new and different stories, working within the system. But John Meredyth Lucas was in a hurry to find something worth shooting. Robert Justman needed something that could be produced easily. And Roddenberry was still hoping to convince Ray Bradbury to try his hand at writing for *Star Trek*. Wolfe happened to be in the right place at the right time with the right material.

Lucas later said, "In the case of 'The Ultimate Computer,' I suppose I liked the M-5 because it was another 'technology is power' story, which have always fascinated me." (110-3)

Lucas, of course, had written a "technology is power" story of his own with "The Changeling."

Justman agreed with Roddenberry that the script was "a better-than-average first draft," but, on October 18, 1967, sent a word of caution to Lucas that there was "too much talk and not enough action throughout" and that the "characterizations seem to have gone awry." (RJ53-1)

Justman wrote:

> The story itself is clever and very "sci-fi" in concept. The author does have a tendency to be very weak in the areas of characterization and logical behavior.... I am not just talking about our regulars. I find that Mr. Daner [later to be named Daystrom] is particularly "Mickey Mouse" in his characterization and rather unbelievable as a human being. (RJ53-1)

Justman was already looking for ways to save money and told Lucas:

> Instead of having this story begin at "Starfleet Headquarters," I suggest that we do a little re-writing and have the Enterprise parked in space near a space station. Perhaps you are unaware of it, but we have just had some space station footage composed [for "The Trouble with Tribbles"].... Since I feel that the script ends rather abruptly, I suggest that we have some sort of an action sequence near the end, which involves the Enterprise and other vessels engaged in these particular "war games." Perhaps we might take the

liberty of introducing a Romulan Vessel, which has slipped into this sector of the quadrant and has stealthily entered into these war games with the end of wreaking havoc and sowing the seeds of confusion amongst Starfleet ranks. (RJ53-1)

Dorothy Fontana wrote to Lucas the next day, her primary contention over the new material was with the ending -- Kirk talking the computer to death. She told Lucas:

> I believe we have a similarity problem going for us -- conflict with two shows we have already shot this season. One is, of course, "The Changeling." Another is the last Act of "Wolf in the Fold," which involves an alien entity entering the Enterprise computer and taking over the ship, trying to kill the personnel by slamming doors on them and what-have-you. I do not think that the computer "Tensor Five" is visual enough to draw a great deal of excitement from. "The Changeling" was a nice little critter we could use and play with -- he had a voice and even, in a way, a personality. Tensor Five does not. Tensor Five does, however, develop in much the same way "The Changeling" -- as a machine -- did.... I am not happy about the prospect of doing another show much like the two we are already programming for this year. Your decision. (DCF53-1)

Fontana had done rewrites for both "The Changeling" and 'Wolf in the Fold." And, since Lucas was the original writer of "The Changeling," both had good reason not to want to see their work repeated. But "The Ultimate Computer" would be a bottle show, augmented by stock optical effects, and therefore would be relatively easy, quick, and inexpensive to produce, without losing too much quality.

A decision was made to go forward. Wolfe was brought in for a brainstorming session with Lucas and Fontana and given very specific notes as to how to modify the material. On November 9, he turned in his second draft screenplay. Three days later, Dorothy Fontana wrote to Lucas, bemoaning:

> We wasted several hours in meeting with Mr. Wolfe and lining out the story we wanted. We have received same script with a few pages inserted and some names changed.... I recall Mr. Wolfe taking copious notes as we defined the direction and specific plot points the story should take. He may have taken them in "cuneiform" because I see damn few of them in the script I have in front of me.... We have been short-changed here. Another eager writer has come into our midst, listened to our comments and specific instructions for changes and merely gone his own way -- giving us only nominal revision. This script lies there, rarely gets up and moves, has no clear-cut characterizations either on the part of our regulars or the guest Daner [Daystrom]. We have spent another large batch of money for a script we are going to have to largely rewrite ourselves.... This is "Changeling" stuff. We should not repeat it. (DCF53-2)

One week later, Robert Justman wrote to Lucas:

> If only the teleplay were as brilliant and incisive as D.C. Fontana's analysis, we would have a winner!... This teleplay needs a rewrite, if it is to be shootable. Mr. Wolfe is not the one to do it. (RJ53-2)

D.C., however, *was*. She said, "'The Ultimate Computer' was a major, major rewrite. Laurence Wolfe wasn't that experienced in the business.... [He] had a good idea but he refused to make changes that Gene Roddenberry and the producer [John Meredyth Lucas] asked him to do. They gave him notes upon notes upon notes from the first draft script, and he wrote it the way he wanted to. He brought back a script where, in essence, he moved a few commas around. It was the same script, and [John Meredyth Lucas] handed it to me and said, 'Fix it.' So I made it more *Star Trek*, because, before, it was mostly about the computer and

Dr. Daystrom. Well, he's our guest star, but where are Kirk and Spock in all this? Where is McCoy? Where are the people we care about? We are only going to see Daystrom once. It was really that, making it more *Star Trek*; making it more *our* series. What we had to do was inject more Kirk than anything else. You know, what does this mean to him? He had to prove that he was still needed. Man versus machine." (64-1 & 64-2)

Due to its similarities to "The Changeling," Fontana wanted to change the way Kirk defeated the M-5 computer. But the battle of wits between the man and the mad machine simply served the story too well to be discarded.

"The nice thing -- that was always in the Wolfe script -- was that the machine wound up having a moral attitude," said Fontana. "'I've killed all those people, I murdered them, therefore I am a criminal, I'm wrong and I must die.'" (64-1)

Fontana proved herself to be a good stand-in for the departed Gene Coon when it came to keeping the intrinsic humor in place in *Star Trek*, especially in respect to the teasing between McCoy and Spock. One example is when Spock tells McCoy, "It would be most interesting to impress your memory engrams on a computer, Doctor. The resulting torrential flood of illogic would be most entertaining." That the final episodes of Season Two, which had not passed through Gene Coon's typewriter at any time, should still have the distinctive vocal sparring between these two characters can be attributed to Dorothy Fontana.

Also in the script by Wolfe, and retained by Fontana, Commodore Wesley's insensitive remark to Kirk, calling him "Captain Dunsel," a way of telling Kirk that he no longer serves a useful purpose. This was Wolfe's invention.

In order to jettison the problematic scripts for "Shol" and "He Walked Among Us," dropping them off the production schedule to be replaced by something better, Roddenberry turned his attention to shaping up his script for "The Omega Glory" while Lucas had Fontana begin her "page one rewrite" of "The Ultimate Computer" during the final days of November, with production slated to begin in little more than a week. The Teaser and Act I for the script were turned in on Friday, December 1st, with an additional Act written each day over the weekend and finishing on Monday. NBC received the Teaser and Act I on Friday, then Acts II and III on Monday, followed by Act IV on Tuesday, December 5. Fontana had already begun her script polish that same day. The network, however, was not happy.

Lucas said, "In the rush to get it before the cameras, I neglected to inform NBC and get official approval. Stan Robertson took exception. He had previously written me about a script Roddenberry had tried to revive without his approval [see the upcoming "The Omega Glory"] and threatened to take 'an arbitrary position' should it happen again. It had happened." (110-6)

On December 6, a very upset Stan Robertson wrote to Lucas:

This will confirm... our displeasure over having received, piece meal fashion between December 1 and December 5, the above titled script, which you have scheduled for production without our approval on December 7.... Your filming of the teleplay is at your own risk. This is to inform you that at the time of our viewing of the rough cut we will exercise our option as to the acceptability or non-acceptability of this property.

It was a small gamble. Lucas was confident he had a winner in "The Ultimate Computer," which he planned to safeguard by directing himself.

Stan Robertson was not the only one who was unhappy over the manner in which the rushed rewriting of "The Ultimate Computer" had been handled. During its third day of production, on December 11, a wounded Laurence Wolfe wrote to Gene Roddenberry:

This letter is in reference to my script.... After it was purchased, I was asked to make several changes, which I did over a period of six days. I was then led to believe it was satisfactory. Now I find that Dorothy Fontana re-worked it, and she is to be given sole teleplay credit. I feel that I should have been notified if any other writer was at work on the script; at least it would have been good form to do so. Further, even though her changes are substantial, I feel I deserve to share teleplay credit with her.

On December 13, as "Computer" continued to film, Roddenberry responded to Laurence Wolfe, with a copy of his letter sent to their mutual friend, Ray Bradbury. Roddenberry cordially began:

Dear Mr. Wolfe, thank you for your letter regarding your script, "The Ultimate Computer." I am sure you understand that when any script is purchased by a production company, any further changes deemed necessary by the production staff can be made at their discretion. Miss Fontana's job as Script Consultant included making whatever revisions are requested by our producer and director, John Meredyth Lucas, or by last minute network or production requirements.... By sending you all copies of all revised scripts, we automatically informed you of the revisions made in your teleplay. The placing of Miss Fontana's name on the [title page] credits is also the standard way of informing the Writers Guild of America that she is <u>requesting</u> credit for her work on the script. The WGA will now automatically arbitrate the credits since there is a member of a production staff involved, thus protecting you as a freelance writer from anyone in a production office arbitrarily taking credit from you. They will notify you by mail of the arbitration, and three Guild members will read <u>all</u> material written on the script to determine the final screen credit. In other words, the producers do not decide what the credit will be. It is not final until three writers divorced from *Star Trek* determine it.... I hope this calms your fears. As a longtime freelancer myself, I have felt well protected for years by WGA in this manner.... Meanwhile, we have received your second story outline, and we are looking forward to meeting with you on it.

The Writers Guild Arbitration Board decided against giving Laurence Wolfe a joint teleplay credit. Perhaps as a consolation prize, or to protect his friendship with Ray Bradbury, Roddenberry purchased the second story Wolfe sent in, called "Galatea of Polydor." *Star Trek* had no need for further story ideas at this time. The Second Season was wrapping and there was no guarantee, and very little belief, that there would be a third season. Wolfe was paid, but the story was left unused.

Pre-Production
November 28-30 and December 1 & 4-6, 1967 (7 prep days)

There were only two guest players in "The Ultimate Computer," and no new sets required. This allowed the episode to sail through pre-production even as the script was being finalized. Seven days were available, yet less than six were used.

William Marshall, booked to play Dr. Richard Daystrom, was 43. He was classically-trained with experience on the stage, as well as films and television. Marshall had been cast as doctors, judges, military officers, Harlem detectives, African kings, African prime ministers, and oddball intellectuals. His greatest claim to fame came after *Star Trek*, during the era of "blaxploitation" films. In 1972, he played the title character in *Blacula* and, again, in 1973, for the sequel, *Scream, Blacula, Scream*. Marshall's true love, however, was Shakespeare, and he finally had a chance to play it before the cameras, as *Othello*, for a 1981 Direct to Video release.

William Marshall in *Blacula*
(American International Pictures, 1972)

Marshall was immediately struck by the material. For a 1998 interview with *Starlog* he said, "It was an extremely thought-provoking story and an extremely challenging role. Daystrom is a man of science and also a man of great morality. But he's unaware that he is also a man of great arrogance…. The concept of reasoning with a machine structured to one's *own* cerebral engrams is haunting." (115)

Marshall knew the role being offered was a rare part for a black man on 1967 American TV. He said, "Roddenberry and company are to be lauded for welcoming the breakthrough." (115)

John Meredyth Lucas said, "We were able to use a number of black actors in important parts at a time when the television screens were glaringly white. Roddenberry had already started this and was completely in favor of the practice. The Starship Enterprise was crewed by people of all races. Gene and NBC both urged minority involvement in the show and this, after all, was the future where such racial acceptance was natural." (110-6)

But Marshall had been given the script only days before the start of production. He said, "It felt like I only had minutes to prepare for this role. I had a lot of lines to learn. It was a last minute job, but I liked the role and the challenge it presented.... *Star Trek* was a relatively rich experience." (115)

Barry Russo, here as Commodore Wesley, was featured in "The Devil in the Dark" as Lt. Commander Giotto, head of security. He worked often on *The Untouchables*, *77 Sunset Strip*, and *The F.B.I.* From 1964 through 1966, he was a regular on the soap *The Young Marrieds*.

Sean Morgan, this time as Ensign Harper, the crewman who is zapped out of existence by M-5, also played Lt. O'Neil in "The Return of the Archons" and, again, for the upcoming "The Tholian Web."

Nimoy with Barry Russo
(Unaired film trim courtesy of Gerald Gurian)

Production Diary
Filmed December 7, 8, 11, 12, 13 & 14, 1967.
(6 day production; revised set budget: $176,451)

Regardless of the threat from NBC, filming, like the sneak attack 26 years before on Pearl Harbor, began bright and early on the morning of December 7. This was the week in 1967 when the other famous person named Spock -- Dr. Benjamin Spock -- was arrested for protesting the Vietnam War. The Doors' Jim Morrison was also arrested, while performing on stage, for getting the youthful audience so riled-up that the police found him accountable for disturbing the peace. Bert Lahr, the cowardly lion in *The Wizard of Oz,* and who had been the pitchman for Lay's Potato Chips throughout 1967, died. *Hell's Angels on Wheels*, starring Adam Roarke, Jack Nicholson, and Sabrina Scharf (later to guest star in the *Star Trek* episode "The Paradise Syndrome") was new in the movie houses and an immediate box office champ. "Daydream Believer," by the Monkees, was still getting the most spins on U.S. radio stations, and the group's *Pisces, Aquarius, Capricorn & Jones, Ltd.* remained the top-selling album in record stores. Marlo Thomas, of *That Girl*, hugged her producer dad, Danny Thomas, on the cover of *TV Guide*. And *Star Trek* tied with *The Monkees* TV series for drawing the most fan letters at NBC.

Day 1, Thursday. First up, and for three full days of production, filming on the Stage 9 bridge set.

John Meredyth Lucas was able to wear two hats, serving as both producer and director, because his work as *Star Trek*'s show-runner was winding down. The next two episodes, based on scripts by Roddenberry, were already in pre-production, with Roddenberry in charge of the latter of the two, also handling the rewrites.

The direction for this episode was fluid and extremely energized. Many of the angles used to cover the action on the bridge are fresh, and the blocking throughout is often distinctive.

Day 2 of filming, with Takei back in the cast
(Courtesy of Gerald Gurian)

Day 2, Friday, December 8. The second of three days on the bridge. William Marshall said, "Shatner was a man whose head was way out to here [stretches his hands apart], and yet all my scenes were with him…. Leonard Nimoy playing Spock was appropriate casting. He was in some of my scenes, but he had little to say; he was quiet on and off camera. Unfortunately, Shatner was the talkative one. Everyone else was fine: Cooperative, inventive and inviting the best from each other and the guest stars. You sensed they were creative family and that you had been invited into that family." (115)

Three pictures taken on the same day on the bridge set
(Unaired film trim courtesy of Gerald Gurian)

"The Deadly Years" had its network premiere this night. A.C. Nielsen showed *Star Trek* in second place for its entire hour.

Day 3, Monday. A final day on the Enterprise bridge.

We've been told before, in Fontana's "Tomorrow Is Yesterday," that there were twelve ships like the Enterprise in the fleet. One, destroyed in "The Doomsday Machine," was the U.S.S. Constellation. We encounter the Lexington, the Hood, the Potemkin, and the Excalibur here. Still to come: the Exeter in "The Omega Glory" the Defiant in "The Tholian Web." Mentioned but not seen in the series, the starships Farragut ("Obsession") and the Intrepid ("Court Martial" and "The Immunity Syndrome").

Day 4, Tuesday. Work began on the bridge set again, but this time redressed to appear as that of the

Starship Lexington. The Captain's chair was modified, giving it the high back used in the

"Mirror" Enterprise from "Mirror, Mirror." Barry Russo was needed for this scene, as well as the next, in the Enterprise transporter room. The afternoon was spent filming in the briefing room.

Day 5, Wednesday. Production took place in sickbay, the corridor, the turbolift, another corridor, the Jefferies tube, and a third corridor, in that order.

One example of the fluid camerawork Lucas

accomplished with Jerry Finnerman is when Kirk, Spock, and McCoy step from the turbo-lift, in mid-conference, and continue to talk as they briskly walk down a long section of corridor, and then enter engineering. This was done in the days before the Steadicam. To get this shot, Lucas had Finnerman remove one side of the corridor wall to make room for dolly tracks. The camera, with its operators, mounted on the dolly being pushed along the well-oiled track, allowed Lucas to get coverage on more than one page of dialogue in a single, fluid take.

Bill McGovern slates a shot during Day 6 of filming
(Courtesy of Gerald Gurian)

The return trip with Kirk and McCoy, sans Spock, was a bit trickier. Due to time constraints, the lights set for the earlier sequence could not be readjusted, so the two men walked in the opposite direction, their backs to camera. Lucas blocked the shot so Kirk and McCoy could pause during key moments of the two pages of dialogue, turn and look back in the direction of the engineering room where the subject of their conversation, Daystrom, was hooking up his M-5 unit. Again, the entire scene was staged in a single shot, with no alternate camera angles and no cutting. It was a flawless take, squeezed into a brisk six-day shooting schedule.

Day 6, Thursday, December 14. The company spent the entire day in the engineering room. John Meredyth Lucas's secretary, Ande Richardson, was there to see some of the action. She recalled, "Bill was working with a black actor, Bill Marshall, who was very tall. And Shatner went for the apple crate. He'd stand on it when they had to do a 'two shot.' And then they'd shoot it. Or Bill [Shatner] would want the scene staged so Bill Marshall was sort of kneeling on the

Unaired film trim of the M-5 (Courtesy of Gerald Gurian)

floor working on something, so you couldn't see how tall he was in comparison. Bill was very protective of his character and his screen image in that way. And, of course, Bill Marshall didn't think too highly of it." (144a)

"William Shatner was a bit of a bother," Marshall said. "There was an ego there that

I would rather not have had an experience with." (115)

Marshall was not saying that Shatner was unpleasant. To the contrary, he recalled, "He seemed to be admiring me, which is okay, but you get a little worried about that. All I care about is, 'Will my exchange with this man be believable in the show?' For the most part, it worked." (115)

The last shots were taken in Kirk's cabin. The 20th Century Earth poem Kirk quotes to McCoy is "Sea Fever" by John Masefield. The poet had died on May 12, 1967, seven months before this episode was filmed. The same verse would be quoted again in *Star Trek V: The Final Frontier*.

Production wrapped at 7:40 p.m., one hour and twenty minutes into overtime. No one was going to tell the director of the episode to stop shooting at 6:20 p.m. when he was also the producer of the series.

Post-Production
Available for editing: December 15, 1967. Rough Cut: December 28. Final Cut: January 9, 1968.
Music Score: tracked.

John Hanley, a member of one of the editing teams, was bumped up to serve as Lead Editor for the only time in his career. He also worked as a Sound Editor, for which he shared in an Emmy Award for the TV movie *The Night That Panicked America*.

The Howard Anderson Company provided the optical effects. New here: a transporter effect (which, for unknown reasons, looks a bit different than usual); the energy beam that disintegrates crewman Harper; a series of composite shots, combining stock images of the Enterprise with Deep Space Station K-7 from "The Trouble with Tribbles"; and placing four Enterprise images into one shot to create an "attack force" of starships. Recycled from past episodes, along with K-7, is the Botany Bay, from "Space Seed," and the crippled Constellation, from "The Doomsday Machine."

Release / Reaction
Premiere air date: 3/8/68. NBC repeat broadcast: 6/28/68.

Steven H. Scheuer reviewed this episode for *TV Key Previews*. Among newspapers across America to carry Scheuer's syndicated column on March 8, 1968 was *The Robesonian*, serving Lumberton, North Carolina. Scheuer wrote:

> "Ultimate Computer." Using as its focal point that the debate today, about man being replaced by computers, will still be a pertinent issue in the time of the Enterprise, this drama illustrates what happens when a machine, purported to be perfect, is given absolute control of the spaceship. As usual in *Star Trek*, the problem posed here is more exciting than its conclusion. In this case, the computer has been programmed by an embittered genius. But the attitude of the regulars toward the machine's potential remains fascinating and the actions of the starship under the computer's command will sustain your interest throughout this story.

Judy Crosby reviewed the episode on March 8, 1968 for her syndicated column, *TV SCOUT*. Among the newspapers running the review was *The St. Petersburg Times*, serving Tampa Bay and St. Petersburg, Florida. Crosby said:

> Anyone who has ever experienced the bloodiness of political in-fighting will really appreciate the predicament of Captain Kirk tonight. It is man vs. machine

when the Captain is replaced by a computer during an exercise. The problem is the machine's perfect performance, compounded by its determination to keep its job.

RATINGS / Nielsen National report for Friday, March 8, 1968:

8:30 to 9 p.m., 57.9% U.S. TVs in use.   **Audience Share:**

NBC:	*Star Trek* (first half)	26.4
ABC:	*Operation: Entertainment*	25.5
CBS:	**Gomer Pyle, U.S.M.C.**	**37.9**

9 to 9:30 p.m., 59.5% U.S. TVs in use.   **Audience share:**

NBC:	*Star Trek* (second half)	26.5%
ABC:	*Operation: Entertainment*	27.5%
CBS:	**Friday Night Movie**	**28.4%**
Independent stations:		17.6%

Based on audience share, *Star Trek* was in second place during the first half-hour, a nose ahead of *Operation: Entertainment* on ABC, transmitting out of Fort Hood, Texas, with country star Roger Miller hosting and singing his hits "King of the Road," "Chug-A-Lug," and "Engine, Engine No. 9." After 9 p.m., *Entertainment* snuck ahead, taking the No. 2 slot. The CBS movie had the lead by a couple of percentage points with an encore airing of *The Sins of Rachel Cade*, starring Angie Dickinson, Peter Finch, and Roger Moore. The movie had a leg up -- CBS paid for ad space in *TV Guide* and elsewhere. NBC chose not to promote. The split between the three networks, however, had all staying within one ratings point of each other.

***

The fast and cheap "Ultimate Computer" is a well-regarded and popular episode. In 1998, William Marshall said, "I've seen 'The Ultimate Computer' three times over the years. It holds up extremely well, in my judgment." (115)

NBC agreed, and did not have to follow through with Stan Robertson's threat to reject this episode which was rushed through the writing process without network approval. In fact, it was liked enough to be given a repeat broadcast in June 1968, just three months after it first aired.

Episode 54: THE OMEGA GLORY

Written by Gene Roddenberry
Directed by Vincent McEveety

Morgan Woodward returns to *Star Trek* as a renegade starship commander (Unaired film trim courtesy of Gerald Gurian)

From NBC press release, issued February 6, 1968:

Captain Kirk (William Shatner) and part of his crew are exposed to a deadly disease when they board the Starship Exeter, whose crew died under mysterious circumstances, in "The Omega Glory" on NBC Television Network's *Star Trek* colorcast Friday, March 1.... The Exeter's log reveals its crew died of a virus picked up on the planet Omega. The only surviving member is Captain Tracey (Morgan Woodward), who remained behind and became immunized. Traveling to Omega, Kirk ascertains Tracey's real motive for remaining. He then realizes there is no alternative but to convince Cloud William (Roy Jenson), leader of Omega's freedom loving faction, that Tracey is their enemy.

Tracey, stranded on the planet, has sided with the more civilized of the two warring factions. He is seemingly unaffected by the loss of his command, and is obsessed with his belief that something in the atmosphere of Omega IV can induce near immortality in humans.

The theme examines how a worthwhile cause helps nobody if its original intent is forgotten. In addition to the theme, there is a message: Liberty and justice are for all -- including our enemies.

SOUND BITES

- *Medical Officer Carter, on the Exeter's tape log:* "If you've come aboard this ship, you're dead men."

- *Tracey:* "They sacrificed <u>hundreds</u> just to draw us out in the open. And then they came, and they came! We drained four of our phasers, and they still came! We killed thousands and they still came!"

- *McCoy:* "Leave medicine to medical men, Captain Tracey; you found no Fountain of Youth here. People here live longer now because it's *natural* for them to!"

- *McCoy:* "Spock, I've found that evil usually triumphs unless good is very, very

568

careful."

- Cloud William: "Ay plegli ianectu flaggen, tupep like for stahn -" *Kirk, interrupting:* "And to the republic for which it stands, one nation under God, indivisible, with liberty and justice for all…. Liberty and freedom have to be more than just words. They must apply to everyone or they mean nothing!"

ASSESSMENT

"The Omega Glory" has spent more than four decades at the center of a debate: Was it one of *Star Trek*'s best or worst?

"Glory" is a paradox. It is marred by a few awkward moments, seeming to dominate one's overall opinion of the material. Yet this is a better-than-average production. It benefits from inspired direction, energized and passionate performances, especially from William Shatner and Morgan Woodward, vigorous and realistic fight sequences (between Kirk and Cloud William, and then, even more intense and gritty, between Kirk and Tracey), and some fascinating concepts: a virus that reduces a human being to a few pounds of crystallized remains; Tracey's belief that he has found the Fountain of Youth; an accusation that Spock is Satan; and, finally, the fantastic -- both good and bad -- concept that there could be another United States on an alien world with another Thomas Jefferson penning another Declaration of Independence. But, with all these pluses, one can't help but squirm a bit when the tattered flag of the United States is paraded across our television screens to the accompaniment of "The Star-Spangled Banner." For many, it all seemed rather self-glorifying for this U.S. made show. And, for the detractors, because of this, the whole point to the episode is lost.

One of *Star Trek*'s most controversial and -- according to Gene Roddenberry, Dorothy Fontana, and Vincent McEveety -- misunderstood moments
(CBS Studios, Inc.)

Dorothy Fontana recalled, "Somebody got nasty about it one time and said, 'Oh, but he was saying that the United States was the greatest kind of political body.' And I said, 'No, no, no, it's the *Declaration of Independence.* It's 'We the People'; it's [the] words and [they're] *beautiful words*; it's [the] expression of ideas and ideals that he was really talking about… because Gene had great reverence for both the Constitution and the Declaration. He really did. I guess as an old cop and old Air Corps guy, he had that reverence for the flag; for the institution. [But he] acknowledged they could be wrong. Like, he opposed Vietnam. [Yet] he had reverence for the words [in the Declaration of Independence] and he really, really revered Thomas Jefferson, as a thinker and a writer." (64-2)

569

And there lies the blemish on this old "Glory" -- a misunderstanding of intent; a failure on the part of the writer -- and the producer and director -- to better communicate the intent of the material.

Political agendas aside, lack of subtlety notwithstanding, miscommunication forgiven, "Glory" deserves reassessment by those who have damned it over the years. This is most certainly a quality endeavor in nearly every regard.

THE STORY BEHIND THE STORY

Script Timeline

Gene Roddenberry's story outline, ST #3: April 20, 1965.
Roddenberry's revised outline: April 23, 1965.
Roddenberry's 2nd revised outline: April 25, 1965.
Roddenberry's 1st Draft teleplay: April 28, 1965.
Roddenberry's Revised 1st Draft teleplay: May 21, 1965.
Roddenberry's 2nd Draft teleplay: March 1966.
Les & Tina Pine's 1st Draft teleplay: September 19, 1967.
Roddenberry's revised teleplay (Mimeo Dept. "Yellow Cover 1st Draft"):
Late November 1967.
Roddenberry's script polish (Final Draft teleplay): December 11, 1967.
Roddenberry's further polish (Revised Final Draft teleplay): Dec. 15, 1967.
Additional page revisions by John Meredyth Lucas: Dec. 18, 19 & 20, 1967.

Gene Roddenberry's story outline and 1st Draft script for "The Omega Glory" were written in 1965 as one of three candidates for *Star Trek*'s second pilot. "Mudd's Women" and "Where No Man Has Gone Before" were also in the competition. "Glory" was passed over. It was the first of many rejections for this tale.

"Gene Roddenberry's script wasn't very good," said Herb Solow in his and Robert Justman's book, *Inside Star Trek: The Real Story.* "It was unnecessary to point it out to him; he was the first to recognize it."

Roddenberry would have disagreed. He liked his concept of a parallel world where the United States and Communist China actually fought the war that he hoped would be avoided at all costs on our planet; he liked the idea of a modern day search for the Fountain of Youth; and he liked the science fiction flavoring -- the idea of a disease, a leftover curse of the war that could rob the human body of water and reduce a person to a few pounds of crystals.

Roddenberry's script had a lot going for it, but no one at Desilu or NBC seemed excited.

Gene Coon was handed the script before the end of *Star Trek*'s first season. He, too, was reluctant to take it on and chose to write a couple scripts of his own ("The Devil in the Dark" and "Errand of Mercy") to fill the slots needed on the production roster when "Glory" and another script ("Portrait in Black and White") did not meet network approval.

When the second season arrived, Roddenberry pushed to get "The Omega Glory" back into development and agreed to hand it off to Lester and Tina Pine, a husband and wife freelancing team. Les, 49, was a frequent writer for many series, including *Peter Gunn* and *Ben Casey*. In 1965, he began collaborating with wife Tina, who previously worked as an actress. She was 43. The Pines had recently collaborated on scripts for *The Big Valley* and *I Spy*.

Of the Pines' version, Dorothy Fontana, on October 4, 1967, writing to Coon's replacement, John Meredyth Lucas, stated:

> As I have already said to both you and GR, this so-called script is a catastrophe beyond any we have ever had before (and Gene, I include "Portrait in Black and White"). (DCF54)

The notorious "Portrait in Black and White" was, in many ways, another "Omega Glory." It, too, was a Gene Roddenberry story, although the actual script was written by Barry Trivers, fresh off of writing "The Conscience of the King." And it, too, was an Earth parallel story, but, instead of giving commentary on the issues of West versus East, with Democracy fighting Communism, "Black and White" focused on the clash between the U.S. Civil War era North and the South, racial bigotry, and slavery.

The message-heavy "Black and White" failed to win supporters -- at the *Star Trek* production offices, at Desilu, at NBC. Stan Robertson, in particular, disapproved of the premise, writing to Roddenberry on August 26, 1966 that the story was "unacceptable" and didn't "fit into the *Star Trek* concept."

Both Herb Solow and Robert Justman stated that Roddenberry was "angered by the rejection" and the turning down of the racially-charged script "helped to sour his ensuing relationship with the NBC program executive." (94-8)

And now Dorothy Fontana was telling Roddenberry, via a message to Lucas, that the Pines' version of "The Omega Glory" was as worthless as his beloved "Portrait in Black and White."

Fontana's criticism continued:

> Rather than devote 25 pages of memo to what is wrong with it, since <u>everything</u> is wrong with it, I officially recommend here that we immediately pay off the Pines and do not ask them to do any revision on what is already unsavable. (DCF54)

The Pines were dismissed. Roddenberry buckled down to work on a new version of his script for "The Omega Glory." John Meredyth Lucas, looking out for *Star Trek*, stayed in the office and wrote to Mary Dorfman at the Writers Guild of America. He told her:

> "The Omega Glory" was written by Gene Roddenberry in 1965 but shelved because of the high production costs involved. This year it was assigned to Tina and Les Pine for a rewrite which they delivered on September 19, 1967. The rewritten script did not in any way meet our needs and was immediately shelved. Gene Roddenberry then returned to his original script and rewrote it for our final shooting script. (JML54)

As the fruits of Roddenberry's labors were distributed to Lucas, Justman, and Fontana, the staff was uncharacteristically silent. The barrage of memos normally prompted by the arrival of a new screenplay at the *Star Trek* offices did not come. The writer of this latest script, after all, was the boss.

It took Robert Justman 30 years to break the silence, finally saying, "I wrote a memo in which my comments were devastating. However, not wanting to hurt his feelings, I tore up the memo and made a few suggestions orally. He took the advice but, as anyone who has seen the episode knows, it didn't do much good." (94-8)

NBC's Stan Robertson had no reason to be silent. After reading Roddenberry's latest draft, he wrote to Lucas:

> On March 25, 1966, prior to the production of the first season of *Star Trek* films,

571

agreement was reached in writing with Gene Roddenberry that "The Omega Glory" would be placed in "inventory" and, at his discretion, reworked and again submitted to us at a future date for our re-evaluation. Except for a few minor changes, we cannot distinguish enough differences in the 1966 script and the script received last Wednesday, November 28, to warrant an approval. Our basic objections, as discussed at great length with Mr. Roddenberry in 1966, are still, we feel, valid. However, in view of the fact that, as you advised me, you scheduled this script for production without gaining NBC approval, our position has to be either arbitrary or academic. We prefer neither. We will, however, on the basis of my telephone conversations with Gene Roddenberry on Monday morning, in which he promised to "personally re-write Omega Glory to our satisfaction" prior to its being produced, grant you an approval based on those conditions. I must remind you again, John, that we, in the future, will take an arbitrary position, regardless of production schedules, that no story for *Star Trek* will be approved unless you and your staff adhere to the clearly spelled out contractual requirements. (SR54)

Robertson had created a loophole for Roddenberry. The changes he promised the NBC production manager were not made until the day the episode started filming. Among them, Roddenberry appeared to have borrowed from a story treatment credited to William Shatner, and dated, April 29, 1966. "Web of Death" began:

The Enterprise is on a mission to find out the whereabouts of a sister ship, the U.S.S. Momentous, which has disappeared under mysterious circumstances. In the vicinity of Urus III, the sister ship is sighted.... CAPTAIN KIRK and crew slowly approach the ship that is the duplicate of the Enterprise. There is something strange about her. The ship is hanging motionless above the planet and does not answer any of the signals sent to it by the Enterprise.... A boarding party is sent to the ship -- Kirk, SPOCK and the DOCTOR. They are materialized into the Momentous, and they search the ship. No one is aboard.... And to compound the mystery, there are piles of clothes – uniforms, underwear, shoes -- lying in disarray at all the key positions. Even the Captain's clothes in the Captain's chair.

The similarities between the two stories end here. But all indications are that Roddenberry had gotten one hell of an opening for his script from Shatner.

On the morning production began, a memo addressed to "Director & Cast" was included with a new draft of the script -- the Revised Final Draft. It read:

I am including in here some revisions which do not necessarily shoot [today] -- Friday -- but I am sure you want to get the flavor and nature of the changes in mind. The McCoy lab sequences for [today's] shooting have been polished and should be shot as they are except for any revisions which Vince McEveety and I mutually agree upon. The reason -- I'm setting up another scene based upon what is said and done in [today's] work. [I] know you are deliriously happy to get this hours ahead of time rather than on our usual late season schedule of minutes ahead of time. (GR54-1)

To help with sagging morale, Roddenberry included some good news:

Our [Nielsen] rating bounded up to 30% and there seems to be every hope that our fan campaign may help it to go higher. Best ... Glorious Rewriter -- formerly Glorious Leader. (GR54-1)

Each day, as the production continued, a few more minor changes were sent to the set by the Glorious Rewriter. Roddenberry, after all, despite what anyone else had to say, liked his script.

Pre-Production
December 7-8 & 11-14, 1967 (6 prep days).

Morgan Woodward as Boss Godfrey in
Cool Hand Luke (Warner Bros., 1967)

Roy Jenson as Bloodworth in
The Duchess and the Dirtwater Fox
(Twentieth Century Fox, 1975)

Vincent McEveety was hired to direct his fifth *Star Trek*.

Morgan Woodward, prematurely grey at age 42, played Captain Ron Tracey. Woodward said, "'Omega Glory' was simply a good man gone bad, perhaps because of some ego-induced insanity. Captain Tracey didn't become a starship captain by being a jerk or a bad guy. It was just a good man gone bad. That's the way I tried to play him." (192-2)

Director McEveety said, "Morgan Woodward was the one that I used mostly [in various shows], because he was such an interesting character, I thought. He gave such dimension to a character. He could play crazy and he could play very nice. And, by saying dimension, I'm saying you could get elements of both at the same time. Good and bad. Real." (117-4)

Woodward had previously appeared on *Star Trek* as Simon Van Gelder in "Dagger of the Mind," which was also directed by McEveety. The two men knew one another from *Gunsmoke*. By the time the western left the air in 1975, Woodward held the record for the most guest appearances on the series, with 19. While this episode was being filmed, Woodward was being seen on the big screen in one of 1967's biggest hits, *Cool Hand Luke*, starring Paul Newman.

Roy Jenson, as Cloud William, was 40. He began his career as a stunt double for Robert Mitchum, and then landed over 200 jobs as an actor between 1951 and 1999, usually as the bad guy. In a 1987 interview, Jenson said, "I really like playing the nasty heavies." He was identified as "bully" in an episode of *Wagon Train*, "Bruiser" on *The Untouchables*, "gunman" on *The Outer Limits*, "strangler" and "Man starting the bar fight" on two separate episodes of *The Fugitive*, "assassin" on *The Man From*

573

U.N.C.L.E., "thug" on *Get Smart*, "Bloody Bob Agnew" on *Cimarron Strip*, "Sledge" on *Bonanza*, and "brawler" on *Laredo*, to name a few. He was the first man to be beat up by Cain on *Kung Fu*, and was the henchman who slit open the nose of private eye J.J. Gites (Jack

Nicholson) with a knife in *Chinatown*. Jenson said, "It was kind of a thrill to do [*Star Trek*] because I hadn't done any of those; I had done mostly westerns. I think I got the part because I looked good in a bearskin... and I could mumble the lines out." (92)

Irene Kelly played Sirah. She was fairly new to TV and appeared mostly in minor roles. Next to this *Star Trek*, her most notable role was as the female lead in a little known but well-regarded 1972 satanic exploitation film, *Enter the Devil*.

Irene Kelly with Roy Jenson in unaired film trim (Courtesy of Gerald Gurian)

Art work created for "The Omega Glory" (Courtesy of Gerald Gurian)

"The Return of the Archons."

Ed McCready played the doomed Dr. Carter on the Exeter. He had previously been seen as the mutant boy creature in "Miri" and a Nazi in "Patterns of Force."

David L. Ross returned as Lt. Galloway, after being prominently featured in "Miri," "Return of the Archons," "A Taste of Armageddon," and "The City on the Edge of Forever." He had his biggest part here, with dialogue, and a death scene. But it was not the end of the road for Ross or the character of Galloway. Both would be back for "Turnabout Intruder." In "Day of the Dove," Ross would play yet another crew member, named Lt. Johnson.

Morgan Farley, 69, played the Yang Scholar seen in the final Act. Under the shaggy grey wig and beard, it is hard to recognize him as the actor who also played the humorless Hacom in

Production began on Friday, December 15. During this week, the Silver Bay Bridge in West Virginia collapsed in the middle of evening rush hour, spilling 31 cars into the Ohio River and killing 46 people. The Federal minimum wage was raised to $1.40 per hour. In most parts of the country you could rent a medium-sized house for $125 per month. Or buy a new medium-sized car for $2,750, and then fill it up for 33 cents per gallon. The Monkees' "Daydream Believer" was still the song playing most on U.S. Top 40 radio stations, with Gladys Knight and the Pips' "I Heard It Through the Grapevine," close behind at No. 2. The Monkees also continued to have a lock on the top-selling album slot in record stores with *Pisces, Aquarius, Capricorn & Jones, Ltd.*, in its third of five weeks at the summit. *Guess Who's Coming to Dinner* with Sidney Poitier, Spencer Tracy, and Katharine Hepburn, had just been released and was taking the lead at the box office away

Shatner studies his dialogue for the scenes filmed in the "Interior Jail Cell Block"
(Courtesy of Gerald Gurian)

from *The Jungle Book* and *Hell's Angels on Wheels*. The most-watched series from the night before was *The Dean Martin Show*, where Bob Newhart performed his classic sketch "Defusing a Bomb," and Dom Deluise appeared as a Superman wannabe. Warren Beatty and Faye Donaway, of *Bonnie & Clyde* (with the headline, "The New Cinema … Violence … Sex … Art"), had the cover of

Day 1, "Int. Village Lab" set on Stage 11
(Unaired film trim courtesy of Gerald Gurian)

Time magazine. Sebastian Cabot, of *Family Affair*, had the cover of *TV Guide*. And *Star Trek* rolled film on "The Omega Glory."

Day 1, Friday. Stage 11 was being loaned to *Star Trek* while *Mission: Impossible* was on break. For the first day here, many of the scenes written for the "Interior Village Lab" were filmed, including the disintegration of Lt. Galloway.

Day 2, Monday. Work continued in the "Village Lab," with McCoy's research and Tracey being given the news that it was the normal evolution on this planet that allowed people to live past 1,000. After the lunch break, the company filmed on a second set built here -- the "Interior Jail Cell Block," including all the wider shots and those featuring Spock and Tracey.

Day 3: Paramount "B" Tank, used for the village streets (Unaired film trim from the Matt Jefferies Collection courtesy of Gerald Gurian)

Day 3, Tuesday. While the set designers and decorators worked on Stage 11, replacing the "Int. Village Lab" set with the "Int. Men's House" set, the company filmed on the Paramount "B" Tank, where they had previously shot the village sequences needed in "A Private Little War." That village, with new dressing, now served as the home of the Kohms. Among the scenes shot;

Day 3, filming the fight between Kirk and Cloud William (Unaired film trims courtesy of Gerald Gurian)

the beam down of Kirk and his landing team; interrupting the beheading of Cloud William; and then Kirk's outdoor fight with Tracey.

Day 4, Wednesday. Back on Stage 11, with more work taking place on the Jail set during the morning hours, this time focusing on tighter coverage for the fight between Kirk and Cloud William, and then the latter ripping the bars from the window for his escape. McEveety fell behind, delaying the company's move to the new set prepared here the day before (the "Int. Men's House"), until mid afternoon. Numerous extras were needed for this scene where the Yangs celebrate their victory and bring Kirk, Spock, McCoy, and Tracey in for their moment of reckoning.

Day 5, Thursday. The entire day was spent filming more pages of dialogue on the "Int. Men's House" set built on Stage 11. This was planned to be the last day spent here, but the big finale fight between Kirk and Tracey, beautifully choreographed and photographed, took longer than expected, resulting in the schedule for the next day having to be revised.

Day 5 (above), on the "Int. Men's Room" set built onto Stage 11; and (below) as Kirk fights Tracey (Unaired film trims courtesy of Gerald Gurian)

For the fight sequences with Kirk, Shatner accepted the help of stunt man Paul Baxley. Woodward, however, worked without a double.

Day 6, Friday, December 22. Shatner's impassioned speech to the Kohms, including his reciting the Declaration of Independence, was filmed. This sequence, originally planned for the previous day, had been bumped to was supposed to be the last

day of the shoot. After Day 6, the company would have gotten a week off, bookended by two weekends, as an extended break before the commencement of the next episode, "Assignment: Earth." But there were scenes remaining to be filmed for the Enterprise and its sister ship, the Exeter. Knowing these still remained, McEveety was allowed to slow his pace and shoot extra

577

coverage for the sequences set in the "Int. Men's House."

At the end of the day, the company pre-lit Stage 9, ensuring an early start on the seventh day of production. Later this night, "Wolf in the Fold" had its only network airing.

Day 7, Tuesday, December 26. All the scenes taking place on the Enterprise and the Exeter were filmed.

Director McEveety remembered that, although cast and crew remained professional and

Day 7, with the production ending on familiar ground –
Stage 9 Enterprise sets (also redressed to pass for the U.S.S. Exeter)
(Unaired film trim courtesy of Gerald Gurian)

dedicated in all ways, the mood on the set was colored by the rumors in the air. He said, "Everybody felt that *Star Trek* was on its last legs. Nobody wanted it to be, but they felt it wasn't going to be picked up." (117-4)

But no one held back a fraction of a single percent. William Shatner, in particular, had quite a workout in "The Omega Glory," including numerous wrestling matches with two very large men, Morgan Woodward, standing 6'3", and Roy Jenson, a hefty 6'2". Under McEveety's excellent direction, the fights are superb. In addition, and adding to the overall gritty feel of "Omega Glory," the set design, lighting, and photography are all above average.

McEveety said, "I thought it was Bill's best performance, at least in the episodes that I had, particularly when he read the Constitution. That was an incredible reading. And I felt that [episode] was very, very exceptional, with the writing and the whole thing." (117-4)

Refusing to compromise on quality, McEveety ran one day over.

Post-Production
Available for editing on December 27, 1967. Rough Cut: January 5, 1968.
Final Cut: February 1.
Partial Music Score recorded on December 22, 1967.

The mixed impressions that dogged "Glory" from its inception did not end with the filming.

As told by Robert Justman and Herbert Solow, in *Inside Star Trek: the Real Story*, James Ballas, the editor who had been assigned this episode, was standing at the bar next to William Shatner during the *Star Trek* Christmas party of 1967. As both men waited for their drinks -- and it appeared Ballas had already had a few -- the editor volunteered his opinion of "Glory," as well as Shatner's acting technique.

Witnesses remember Ballas telling Shatner that "Glory" was a "real turkey," adding that Shatner's choices as an actor did not help the editors. "You always telegraph your reactions, and, in this episode, it's more of a problem than ever," Ballas allegedly said, then added, "It doesn't make my job any easier, because they're so damned hard to cut around. The camera doesn't lie, you know." (94-8)

An argument followed. Shatner later shared with Roddenberry that the editor assigned to "Glory" thought the material, written by Roddenberry, lacked quality. Ballas did not finish the episode. Nor would he cut for *Star Trek* again.

Bill Brame was promoted to Head Editor, abruptly taking over for James D. Ballas, who had abruptly taken over for Robert Swanson after the cutting of "The Menagerie." Brame was 39 and had worked as an assistant editor on the 1964 Cold War thriller *Seven Days in May*. Brame's work here was good. He would continue to lead Edit Team #1 in the third year.

Cinema Research provided the optical effects, including the impressive image of two starships as the Enterprise stays a safe distance from the Exeter and the planet it orbits. This was a composite shot, utilizing two different views of the 11-foot, 2-inch Enterprise model.

Composer Fred Steiner arranged the "Star-Spangled Banner" motifs for this episode, with a score that was, otherwise, made up from far superior tracked music.

This was the last of nine episodes to be produced by John Meredyth Lucas. His association with *Star Trek*, however, was not over. Lucas would return to the series as a writer and a director.

When the episode cleared post production, Robert Justman sent a letter to Morgan Woodward, telling the actor:

> Thought you might be interested in knowing how the looping on "The Omega Glory" turned out. Relax -- all is well! What you did turned out to be exactly what Gene Roddenberry and I were after. I don't know how you did it, but you hit just the exactly correct balance point. There are subtle nuances present now that really enhance your characterization. So, thank you and we hope that you will enjoy the results on Friday night, March 1, 1968. (RJ54)

Some things to take note of:

- Roy Jenson's voice was electronically altered and slowed down for the role of Cloud William. In the preview "trailer," his voice is unaltered. The line of dialogue, "The fight is done when one is dead," sounds very flat without the modulation.

- NBC Broadcast Standards was against showing women's navels in the 1960s. Sirah, the Yang woman who shared a jail cell with Cloud William, was not supposed to bare her entire midriff. But, for a moment, when she was rendered unconscious by a FSNP (Famous Spock Neck Pinch), her navel became visible. When we see her again, Sirah, still out cold, has somehow covered her belly button with a limp hand.

- We learn that it may be possible to teach the Vulcan neck pinch to a human when Kirk says, "You should teach me that some time." Spock replies, with taxed patience, "I have tried."

- Harvey Lynn and Kellam de Forest usually made sure that the scientific information on *Star Trek* was accurate. But one wrong piece of information slipped by. McCoy says that a human being is 96% water. The actual figure is closer to 60%.

This was the last episode to credit Herb Solow as Executive in Charge of Production. Solow's next employer would be MGM, where he served as Vice President in charge of Television Production. Among the series he oversaw in 1969: *Medical Center*, *The Courtship of Eddie's Father*, and, with Robert H. Justman in the producer's chair, *Then Came Bronson*.

Release / Reaction
Premiere air date: 3/1/68.
NBC repeat broadcast: 7/26/68.

Roddenberry was very proud of his script for "The Omega Glory." He also believed director, editor and cast had excelled at their jobs and the episode was something special. On February 20, 1968, he wrote Jack Reynolds at Paramount, suggesting "The Omega Glory" get a full page ad

Herb Solow at his going away party, with Leonard Nimoy (Courtesy of Gerald Gurian)

in the trades a few days before its March 1 broadcast premiere. He wanted Paramount to push the episode for Emmy award consideration. Reynolds said "No."

Undaunted, Roddenberry wrote Stan Robertson, suggesting "Glory" was too good to waste as a late season installment. He wanted it held back for the launch of *Star Trek*'s third year, provided there was a third year. In an effort to get NBC to agree to a renewal commitment, he wrote:

> One of the great problems of all shows is to have a smasheroo opening episode, and we've really got one here!

Robertson said "No."

On February 26, Roddenberry again wrote to Robertson, stating that Robert Justman agreed that the episode was "deserving of a bit of promotion" -- the same Robert Justman who later said he didn't think much of "The Omega Glory." Roddenberry pushed further, requesting that, if NBC wasn't ready to commit to a third season, at least Robertson could use his influence at the network to arrange for some on-air promo spots. But, after the first season, NBC never did on-air promo spots for *Star Trek*, and, again, the answer was "No."

That same day, Roddenberry sent a letter to Hank Grant at the *Hollywood Reporter*. "Many think ['The Omega Glory'] is a rather unique piece," he told the entertainment columnist, in hopes of getting some free press. Grant's silence said "No."

Determined to shine a spotlight on what he felt was one of *Star Trek*'s best, Roddenberry struck a deal with GAF Corporation to release "The Omega Glory" as a View-Master 3-D disc set. This was the first of five *Star Trek* programs (and the only one from the original series) to be adapted onto View-Master reels. For this, the three-foot model of the Enterprise was lent to Don Jim, a Los Angeles photographer. Jim had also visited the set during filming to snap pictures of the action in 3-D.

Judy Crosby put another spotlight on "The Omega Glory" when she selected it for review for the March 1, 1968 edition of her syndicated column, *TV SCOUT*. Among the newspapers carrying her column was *The Syracuse Herald Journal,* serving Syracuse, New York. Crosby said:

> Tonight's episode is loaded with people, fancy settings and a lot of good action in a plot that pits two starship captains against each other. Kirk and company find a starship floundering around in space and with all of its crew turned into crystal by a mysterious disease. The Captain (Morgan Woodward) of the doomed ship is the only survivor since he had stayed behind on the planet, where his crew had contracted the disease, in order to learn the secret of the planet's immunization process -- something like Ponce de Leon's fountain of youth.

RATINGS / Nielsen report for Friday, March 1, 1968:

8:30 to 9 p.m., 60.0% U.S. TVs in use.

		Households watching:	Share:
NBC:	*Star Trek*	11,140,000	No data
ABC:	*Operation: Entertainment*	12,660,000	No data
CBS:	**Gomer Pyle, U.S.M.C.**	**16,020,000**	**No data**

9 to 9:30 p.m., 61.5% U.S. TVs in use.

		Households watching:	Share:
NBC:	*Star Trek*	No data	26.2%
ABC:	*Operation: Entertainment*	No data	27.7%
CBS:	**Friday Night Movie**	**No data**	**32.4%**
Independent stations:			13.7%

"The Omega Glory" could have used the promotion Roddenberry was asking for. Without on-air plugs, or newspaper ads, or radio spots (and *Star Trek* had none of these), the series slipped into third place, just under *Operation: Entertainment*, with Tim Conway as the comedy guest host, making the troops laugh at George Air Force Base in Victorville, California, supported by impressionist David Frye and music acts with the Mills Brothers and Jackie Wilson. Both shows were badly out-distanced in the Nielsen's by *Gomer Pyle* and the CBS movie -- the television premiere of 1963's *Flight from Ashiya*, starring Yul Brynner and Richard Widmark as members of the Air-Sea Rescue Service searching for survivors of a sunken vessel.

For those who were watching "The Omega Glory," this story of East-versus-West struck a chord due to its unintentional timing. This patriotic but thoughtful piece of propaganda aired immediately following the month-long February Tet Offensive, the most bloody period for American servicemen in the Vietnam war, where over 80,000 communist troops struck more than 100 towns and cities in the largest military operation yet conducted by either side.

From the Mailbag

Following the broadcast of "The Omega Glory":

> Please Mr. Roddenberry... don't let *Star Trek* become another run-of-the-grade-B type of science-fiction show. There have been some unhappy signs of this,

and we're worried.... Why must we be bombarded by planets identical with Earth "except for one little thing." This was handled very cleverly in "A Piece of the Action," but elsewhere it has varied between disappointment and utterly poor.... We both nearly turned off "The Omega Glory" in the middle!... Please, bring back your original standards. Write us another "Menagerie" and let the "Omega" be past. If we fans have any voice in the creation of *Star Trek*, then we say, "Keep it the way it was. That is what we want." - Sherna C., Parsippany, New Jersey, and Devra L., Brooklyn, New York.

Memories

Herb Solow called this "a less-than-mediocre episode." (161-3)

William Shatner said, "'The Omega Glory' [screenplay] had a history of rejection... but there was no keeping a mediocre script down. It does have some fascinating political commentaries for its time... and some excellent action sequences." (156-2)

Dorothy Fontana said, "That was Roddenberry all the way. I didn't think it was our best episode. However, I always did like the speech that Kirk says about the 'words,' about the Declaration of Independence. 'We the People' was really a great speech and Bill delivered it well." (64-2)

Vincent McEveety said, "I loved that show. I thought that was something very special." (117-4)

Roy Jenson said, "'The Omega Glory' ... was a pleasure to do.... Bill Shatner was a real gentleman and a profound pro.... And, of course, at that time, *Star Trek* was one of the best shows on the air." (92)

Gene Roddenberry said, "Next to the first pilot and the two-part envelope ['The Menagerie'], I suppose that may have been the one I was most pleased with where I had taken a writing credit. Of course, there had been others where I did most of the writing but did not list my name. And there may have been episodes I thought turned out better, such as the first Romulan one. But 'The Omega Glory,' I was pleased with, even if others don't see it that way." (145)

36

Episode 55: ASSIGNMENT: EARTH

Written by Art Wallace and Gene Roddenberry
Directed by Marc Daniels

From NBC press release, issued February 27, 1968:

The Enterprise crew returns to the 20th century to learn how the Earth survived 1968 and nearly witnesses the destruction of the world, in "Assignment: Earth" on the NBC Television Network's *Star Trek* colorcast Friday, March 29.... A 20th-century man, Gary Seven (guest-star Robert Lansing), who has been living on another planet, appears aboard the Enterprise and informs Captain Kirk (William Shatner)

Robert Lansing and his favorite of the seven cats
(NBC publicity photo courtesy of Gerald Gurian)

that Seven's mission is to prevent world holocaust by stopping the United States from launching the first warhead. Kirk and Spock (Leonard Nimoy) aren't sure if Seven is a friend or enemy and attempt to stop him. Roberta Lincoln (Teri Garr), a 1968 secretary, is trapped between factions and becomes an unwitting threat to each.

Divine intervention is the theme. The guiding hand does not come from a God, however, but from alien beings and the human they have trained. And, well-needed in 1968 (and beyond), the story delivers a warning against rushing into conflict -- especially a conflict that could end civilization.

SOUND BITES

- *Spock, regarding 1968:* "Current Earth crises would fill a tape bank, Captain."
- *Scotty:* "It's impossible to hide a whole planet." *Gary Seven:* "Impossible for you, not for them."
- *Roberta Lincoln:* "I know this world needs help. That's why some of my generation are kind of crazy and rebels, you know? We wonder if we're going to be alive when we're thirty."

ASSESSMENT

In 1968, there were no H-bombs in orbit around the Earth. This was a pretend situation invented to create an entertaining hour of TV ... and to deliver a warning. There was good reason to be concerned.

In the early 1960s, H-bombs were being flown around the planet on board long-range, high altitude jets. Some had been lost. In one case, an Air Force jet experiencing mechanical problems had been forced to jettison its payload of nuclear weapons into the sea. Roddenberry, a former war pilot and now a pacifist, feared it was only a matter of time before a true disaster occurred. And, thus, *Star Trek* made its most direct anti-armaments statement. This story does not take place on an alien world. Nor does it take place in the future. The "what if" was intentionally kept closer to home. 1968 was chosen to force the audience into realizing that this danger -- *this madness* -- was already knocking at their front door.

To the credit of NBC, the storyline was approved. There was no resistance over "Assignment: Earth" having only one villain -- the men in charge, the faceless enemy of the U.S. military machine.

The structure of the story is unique. The two opposing characters -- Kirk and Seven -- have a common goal, but differ in how to reach it.

THE STORY BEHIND THE STORY

Script Timeline
Gene Roddenberry's story outline, "Seven": April 20, 1965.
Roddenberry's revised outlines: April 23 & 25, 1965.
Roddenberry's "rough draft" pilot script: November 14, 1966.
Roddenberry's revised teleplay: November 16, 1966.
Art Wallace's pilot spec script, "Space Cop": Early 1967.
Roddenberry and Wallace collaboration, "Assignment: Earth" story outline,
ST #78: October 21, 1967.
Wallace's revised story outline, gratis: Nov. 13, 1966.
Wallace's 1ˢᵗ Draft teleplay: November 21, 1967.
Wallace's Revised 1ˢᵗ Draft teleplay, gratis: December 11, 1967.
Wallace's 2ⁿᵈ Draft teleplay: December 14, 1967.
Wallace's rewrite, gratis (now credited as "Teleplay by Wallace, Story by
Roddenberry & Wallace): December 18, 1967.
Roddenberry's light script polish (Mimeo Department "Yellow Cover"
1ˢᵗ Draft): December 20, 1967.
Roddenberry's rewrite (Final Draft teleplay): January 1, 1968.
Additional page revisions by Roddenberry: January 3, 5 & 9, 1968.

"Assignment: Earth" was designed as a pilot for a new series. Each week Gary Seven, assisted by Roberta Lincoln, would be on a mission to save Earth from itself.

Robert Lansing, for a 1989 interview with *Starlog*, said, "What Gene had done was go to futurists and scientists and ask them what advanced societies out in space might do toward more primitive societies like ours. One of the futurists said that they would probably kidnap children from various planets, take them to their superior civilizations, raise them, teach and enlighten them, and then put them back as adults to lead their worlds in more peaceful ways. That was the idea behind Gary Seven."

Roddenberry toyed around with his concept of a man taken and then returned to Earth in order to save humankind from itself in a series of story outlines, from April 20, 23, and 25, 1965. A "rough script" called "Seven," with a note reading, "Not for NBC's eyes," was distributed to a select few on November 14, 1966 for the purpose of setting a budget and attracting a star. Nowhere in the script were the *Star Trek* series' characters mentioned.

On November 16, Roddenberry polished his teleplay, then, on November 20, wrote to Lloyd Bridges, of *Sea Hunt* fame, whom he affectionately called "Bud." He wrote:

> Dear Bud: Just completed a pilot script, unusual half-hour of drama and comedy, which kind of excites me. Per the chat we had about such things, am immediately air mailing you a copy, unofficially and personally. (GR55-1)

Roddenberry wanted to attach a star before approaching the network with the concept and was hoping the man who said "no" to playing Captain of the Enterprise would agree to be Gary Seven. Bridges, however, was still uninterested in anything that might be perceived as juvenile and politely declined after reading Roddenberry's sketchy 45-page script.

Roddenberry next took a pitch meeting with the programming development executives at Desilu. The studio liked the concept well enough to take it to NBC Burbank. A short while later, Roddenberry learned that his friend and veteran *Star Trek* writer Art Wallace had taken a pitch meeting with Bill Storke, Program Development at NBC, East Coast. Wallace's idea was called "Space Cop."

Interviewed for *Starlog* in 1986, Art Wallace said, "They had said that Gene Roddenberry had come up with a very similar idea… which was about a man from tomorrow who takes care of Earth's present."

In a June 14, 1967 memo to Herb Solow, Roddenberry said:

> He [Art Wallace] reports that they are quite interested in this idea and wants to know whether we want to pursue a joint development or whether we prefer to go it alone. I think we owe Wallace an answer on this. (GR55-2)

Wallace later said, "So, I saw Gene and we decided to pool the idea." (179-1)

On August 16, Roddenberry wrote Solow that he and Wallace had talked earlier in the day and would get together to rough out a story during a trip Roddenberry was planning to New York on the 30th of the month.

On October 12, after the meeting in New York, before commencing their collaboration, Roddenberry wrote to Wallace:

> I wanted to let you know that our Friday night spot, with a failing show after us [*Accidental Family*] and the CBS Movie having been a blockbuster, has seen *Star Trek* in the Number Two position and our ratings not rising as fast or as high as we had hoped. In my talks with the Network, they seem optimistic that this should pose no problem and *Star Trek* will be picked up for a final eight episodes this year, one of which would be the spin off. But networks being networks, they give no guarantees. I am presently agitating strongly with them for a shift of evening, pointing out to them that our *Tarzan* lead-in is working mainly as [a] lead in for *Gomer Pyle* [on CBS], since same type of audience watches the two shows and then a great bulk of the audience stays with CBS for the movies. We should be at least in the Top Twenty by now and although we have been the high-rated show on NBC for Friday night, our share of the audience has fluctuated between 25 and 30%, and the Nielsen rating has not gotten into the generally accepted "safe" 17's [ratings points]. Next Wednesday is the deadline on which NBC informs us of pickup, so we'll know very shortly. (GR55-3)

That pickup came on October 18. On October 21, Roddenberry and Wallace finished their pilot spin-off outline which now included the characters of *Star Trek*.

The spin-off was still a new concept. Steve McQueen's *Wanted: Dead or Alive* was the first, in 1958, spinning from Robert Culp's western, *Trackdown*. In 1960, *Pete and Gladys* spun out of *December Bride*, and *The Andy Griffith Show* got its start as an episode on *The Danny Thomas Show*. In 1964, *Gomer Pyle, U.S.M.C.* was recruited from *The Andy Griffith Show*. One year later, *Green Acres* came out of *Petticoat Junction*, while *The Girl from U.N.C.L.E.* started as an episode of its male equivalent, *The Man from U.N.C.L.E.*, and *Burke's Law* birthed *Honey West*. One year later, as "Assignment: Earth" was being planned, Patrick McGoohan, having already moved his John Drake character from the half-hour *Danger Man* to the 60-minute *Secret Agent*, had taken on a similar spy-with-a-conscience role in *The Prisoner*, TV's first miniseries. TV's biggest spin-offs were yet to come, but the formula was now in place.

On November 8, 1967, Roddenberry received the go-ahead from NBC and Paramount to proceed with his plan to shoot the final *Star Trek* episode of the season as a back door pilot film.

On November 13, Robert Justman, choosing his words carefully, sent a memo to Roddenberry, saying:

> You are probably right when you say that this is a very fine, exciting story and will be a real good piece of entertainment. As for myself, I have ambivalent feelings about it. I am not sure that it will <u>not</u> be an exciting property, but I do not feel confident that it will be exciting as a spin-off in its present form. However, let us assume that this series premise is valuable, in which case I should like to go through the Treatment and point out certain areas that I feel need some careful examination. (RJ55-1)

Justman presented nine pages of things he felt that required careful examination. He then expressed his greatest concern, about Art Wallace and the work he had previously done on his only other *Star Trek* assignment -- "Obsession." Justman warned:

> From what I can remember of that episode, the original story was full of holes and badly constructed. His first draft teleplay and subsequent polish did not do very much to improve the situation. We had to work our butts off to get that episode into shootable shape and it did not come easily or quickly. Please don't let the fact that the concept of this show is extremely intriguing blind us to any inherent weaknesses in the construction of this story and the characterizations contained within it. (RJ55-1)

On November 14, Roddenberry informed his staff, including producer John Meredyth Lucas, that it was still unknown if NBC would have them make a 27th or a 28th episode. Emmet G. Lavery, Jr., a Desilu executive serving as a liaison between the studio and the network, wrote to Ed Perlstein, Desilu Legal Aid, saying:

> I think that December 15 we should get a response from NBC, although the inquiry should be made before that because we want notification of additional programming by that date so as to avoid any… lay-offs… and to continue production until completion of all programming for this season. (EGL55)

If the network didn't exercise its option for an additional one or two episodes, then production was planned to wrap for the season on January 3, 1968, with show number 26. But two additional scripts had to be on hand, nonetheless, just in case NBC wanted a full season of 28. The two scripts held in reserve: Darlene Hartman's "Shol" and Norman Spinrad's "He

Walked Among Us."

As for "Assignment: Earth," the final episode to be produced for the season, be it episode 26, 27, or 28, Paramount had yet to decide if it would allocate additional money beyond the normal per-episode amount due *Star Trek*, even though pilots are always budgeted higher than regular episodes.

On December 12, 1967, regarding the Revised 1st Draft by Wallace, Dorothy Fontana wrote to Roddenberry, telling her boss:

> I find the story material very timely, due to the recent headlines regarding the Soviet capability to orbit a warhead. And I believe the audience will also identify with the plot and theme because of this. (DCF55-1)

However, Fontana was "personally disturbed and disappointed" to see many ideas from previous *Star Trek* episodes recycled into the script. Citing "exact scene lifting" from "The City on the Edge of Forever" and her own "Tomorrow Is Yesterday," Fontana pleaded, "Please, *please* consider changes." (DCF55-1)

Robert Justman's concerns had more to do with budget. He wrote:

> On page 19, we establish just how the book-lined wall separates to disclose the computer panel. As presently constitutes, we would have to platform this set to accomplish the action indicated. I would prefer that we come up with something equally clever and less expensive. (RJ55-2)

Lansing and Garr on the special elevated office set built by Matt Jefferies. The platform allowed for the wall concealing the computer to be supported by wheels below the floor of the set and slide open and closed (Unaired film trim from the Matt Jefferies Collection; courtesy of Gerald Gurian)

This was one budget-cutting suggestion from Justman which was ignored. Roddenberry would have his sliding bookcase, platform and all.

Roddenberry stayed in close contact with Wallace and, on December 2, sent his collaborator nine pages of script notes. The next day, nine more. The day after that, Roddenberry sent a memo to Stan Robertson requesting permission for the Enterprise to dial in a signal from Earth -- a television transmission showing a scene from NBC's hit western *Bonanza*.

David Freeman of NBC wrote to Roddenberry on December 15 saying that everyone at the network, and at *Bonanza*, loved the idea of having the western play on the view screen of the Enterprise, but if even a few seconds of the *Bonanza* clip were used on *Star Trek*, according to SAG rules, WGA rules, and DGA rules, all the "*Bonanza* people" would have to be paid for an appearance, plus releases would be needed from the writer(s), director, and producer(s) of the episode featured. The red tape and potential expense killed an otherwise great idea that would have *Star Trek* and *Bonanza* fans talking to this day.

On December 20, Roddenberry did a light polish on Wallace's latest draft and sent the material to the Mimeo Department to be formatted as a Yellow Cover 1st Draft script. This was then forwarded to De Forest Research for coverage.

Joan Pearce, speaking on behalf of De Forest, wrote back on December 22, picking a bone over the story element having the United States firing nuclear warheads into space. She said:

> This would constitute a deliberate violation by the United States of the newly signed -- January 1967 -- Treaty for the Peaceful Exploration of Outer Space which contains a specific prohibition against nuclear weapons in space. To dramatize such an event could bring serious repercussions from the United States government and might lead to discontinuation of NASA cooperation. (FDF55)

To change it, however, would completely gut the script, with too little time left to devise and write a new one. Roddenberry, in a rare occurrence of going against the advice of De Forest Research, stuck with the story he had, thereby risking alienation from the U.S. government and NASA for *Star Trek*, should it continue, and "Assignment: Earth," should it make it to series. Under no obligation to share notes from De Forest Research with the network, Roddenberry chose to keep NBC in the dark as to the risk he was taking. He had a reason for being so secretive.

Roddenberry had been down this road before, and to tragic results. He lost a series because of his determination to tell a story that the Pentagon objected to. "To Set It Right" was an episode of *The Lieutenant* that dealt with racial prejudice in the military. The Marine Corps, who allowed *The Lieutenant* to film at Camp Pendleton in California, had issues with the controversial material. Roddenberry put it into production anyway, thereby jeopardizing the endorsement of the Marines, and risking losing Camp Pendleton and all it offered -- troops, uniforms, buildings, vehicles, and armaments – as a filming location. NBC, in an effort to appease the military, decided against airing "To Set It Right" and refused to pay a licensing fee to MGM, the makers the series. Roddenberry, determined not to be censored, brought in the NAACP (National Association for the Advancement of Colored People) to put pressure on the network to reverse its decision and allow "To Set It Right" to be seen. He later boasted, "They lowered the boom on NBC." (145-11)

There are discrepancies in the records as to what happened next. Most sources say that NBC buckled and aired the episode on February 22, 1964. Others state that "To Set It Right" was not aired. What is known is that the Marine Corps withdrew its endorsement of the series and Camp Pendleton was closed for filming. Despite satisfactory ratings, after losing the stamp of approval from the Marines, NBC cancelled *The Lieutenant*, leaving MGM with 29 hour-long episodes, too few to allow for a syndicated package. As a result, the studio disassociated itself from its maverick writer/producer, forcing Roddenberry to take his next creative property, *Star Trek*, elsewhere.

Remarkably, having been burned once, Roddenberry was playing with fire again.

On Tuesday, December 26, "The Omega Glory" wrapped production. For six days, the *Star Trek* stages were dark. During this time, Art Wallace was out of town for the holidays and Roddenberry rewrote the script for "Assignment: Earth."

On Saturday, January 6, 1968, at the halfway mark of the production, as cast and crew rested, Wallace wrote to Roddenberry:

> I have no quarrel with your version [of the script]. I think it's fine. My only quarrel is that it's not _my_ version ... and I suppose the only logical answer you can give me is that I wasn't there when the shit hit the fan.... Too bad all had to be done in such a rush. (AW55)

On Monday morning, January 8, as filming resumed, Roddenberry wrote back:

> Am pleased you understand. It's been a grind to produce, particularly with NBC withholding the extra money, then, unknown to you, Paramount insisting we do it _strictly_ on episode budget.... I'm sorry it had to be in such a rush, too. But the production staff, actors, director and crew have really knocked themselves out to give us the best possible [pilot] and it may work out very well. Let's both cross our fingers.

The following day, Roddenberry sent a letter to Tony Ford, Art Wallace's New York based literary agent. He wrote:

> I know Art is a bit unhappy about the changes or at least out of the fact that he was not in on them. And I am sure I would feel similar if the positions were reversed. But I think you can see from the number of colored pages here that we kept changing and revising right up to the last moment in order to get it finished on time and on budget. Or almost on time and on budget. Not only did NBC deny us extra money but Paramount suddenly tightened up at the last moment and began leaning all over me to do it on regular episode schedule and cost. But I think we got a good show.

On January 11, Tony Ford wrote back:

> I like what you did, especially considering the number of rugs you had pulled out from under you.... Yes, Art was a bit unhappy, and you size it up accurately, I am sure, when you say you would have probably felt the same way had positions been reversed. And I want you to know that in personal conversations with Art, he really understood and in most cases agreed with what you did.

Art Wallace was paid well for his work on the script. Since this was a pilot, he earned $14,000, plus residuals, instead of the going rate of $4,500. Even with this fat paycheck, Wallace ended his association with _Star Trek_ here. The man who created _Dark Shadows_ returned to the world of daytime serials as story consultant for _All My Children_. He also continued to freelance for prime time television, including two science fiction series: _Space: 1999_ and _Planet of the Apes_.

Wallace later said, "I must admit that I've been a very busy writer throughout the years, and I didn't know _Star Trek_ was going to be rerun 20 times. If I had known that, I would have written more." (179-1)

Pre-Production
December 18-22 & 26-29, 1967 (9 prep days).

On November 15, although still hoping to persuade Lloyd Bridges to take the role of Gary Seven, Roddenberry was also considering Patrick McGoohan, Patrick O'Neal, Tony Franciosa, Burt Reynolds, and Robert Lansing for the lead.

On December 3, Roddenberry received word from NASA that footage of rocket launchings and general Cape Kennedy stock footage would be provided to _Star Trek_. This footage is more historic than most watching could know, as it documents the preparation and launching of the first Saturn V multi-stage rocket, which was used for all the Apollo missions

589

to come. The unmanned capsule at the top is, in fact, Apollo 4. This was the first to make it into space. Apollo 1 through 3 never got off the ground. The images of the rocket separating and discarding its stages, with the shrinking Earth behind it, are, to this day, breathtaking.

The storage buildings at the rocket base were actually studio buildings on the Paramount lot, with NASA footage of Apollo rockets matted in above them. In a commendable example of attention to detail, Launch Director Cromwell's car appears to be an exact match to the car seen in one of the stock footage sequences taken at Cape Kennedy. There was also new footage shot at the Cape specifically for this episode.

Matte shot, blending footage shot at Cape Kennedy with a scene filmed on the Paramount lot. The building to the right is actually a soundstage (Unaired film trim from the Matt Jefferies Collection; Courtesy of Gerald Gurian)

It was during this period that Roddenberry zeroed in on his Gary Seven. Robert Lansing said, "At the time, Gene was a good friend, but I was a New York snob actor, come out to Hollywood. Many folks in my self-perceived position didn't do *Star Trek* because it was considered a kid's show, or a young show at any rate." (105-1)

But Roddenberry was persistent and finally Lansing relented. Just six days before the episode was set to film, on December 28, Lansing signed a contract with a pay rate of $3,000. If "Assignment: Earth" sold as a series, he would get a bonus of $7,000 for the pilot, with a guarantee of $7,500 for each new episode. This was top dollar in 1967 and 1968.

Robert Lansing, at 39, truly carried the status of a "guest star." He had been a gainfully-employed actor on the stage in New York in the early 1960s, then had worked steadily on television and in films since 1956. He had already starred in three series: *87th Precinct* in 1961, *Twelve O'Clock High* in 1965, and *The Man Who Never Was* in 1966. Roddenberry knew

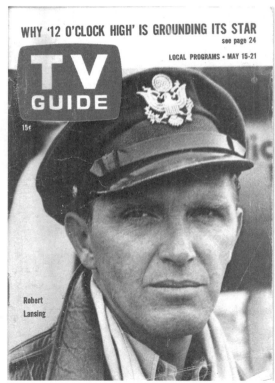

Robert Lansing's second cover of *TV Guide*, for *12 O'Clock High*, following an earlier one for his 1961-62 series, *87th Precinct*

Lansing from the unsold 1965 pilot film *The Long Hunt of April Savage*, which Roddenberry produced.

Teri Garr won the role of Roberta Lincoln. She later said that *Star Trek* was her "first big break as an actress." Her father, Eddie Garr, was an actor on the stage in New York, with some film work; her mother, Phyllis Garr, was a dancer who later became a costumer in TV. Starting in 1963, young Teri was a bit player and a dancer in Elvis Presley movies. Thanks to an introduction made by her mother, she had also appeared in a 1965 episode of *That Girl*. But she was still struggling.

"A friend in my acting class told me that they were casting a guest role on *Star Trek*, which was in its second season and already a huge hit," Garr recalled for her memoir. "This role was supposed to spin off into its own series.... It was going to be tough to get an audition -- all the big agents were clamoring to get their clients seen, and my agent wasn't in that league.

Quirky Teri Garr under water

She was great at making calls, but not so likely to have them returned. Luckily, my friend from acting class had an in and helped me get through the door."

Even with this "in," Garr had little hope. She shared, "I never thought I would get the part because I was still really just a dancer. Commercials and *That Girl* were small potatoes as far as *Star Trek* was concerned; they practically didn't count.... Then I read the script and saw that in the first scene my character was flustered because she was late. I thought: 'Well, I'm always late. I can do late.' After I did the reading they asked me to come in for a screen test. I'd never had a screen test before!" (71-2)

The two candidates for playing Roberta Lincoln at this point were Dawn Wells, famous for her role as Mary Ann from *Gilligan's Island*, which had just been cancelled, and this relatively unknown named Teri Garr. Of Wells' audition, Roddenberry's notes from the time reveal his thinking: "Good actress, but nothing really special in looks." Fans of *Gilligan's Island*, and all those millions of teenage boys who had a crush on Mary Ann, would disagree. Of Teri Garr, Roddenberry wrote, "Very interesting -- a good quality all of her own."

Garr said, "They cut my hair short and put me in front of a camera. They had me turn in a circle very slowly. Then they asked me easy questions, like, 'What's your name?' and 'Where were you born?' I was overjoyed to be having a screen test. I didn't dare hope I'd get any further, but the next thing I knew, they were calling me to appear on set. I was dizzy with joy -- and that dizziness helped me get into character." (71-2)

The day after Lansing was signed, just five days before the start of filming, Garr inked her contract for $750. She was promised $550 per episode, should "Assignment: Earth" go to series.

Lansing remembered, "She hadn't had much experience then, but she had this kooky personality that certainly worked. Gene saw that very early on and dressed her for it, used her for it, and worked her with it." (105-1)

"Gene got into everything," said Robert Justman about Roddenberry's hands-on approach to producing this episode. "Sets, props, special effects, casting of actors, casting of a black pussycat, and costumes -- *especially costumes*. The clothes worn by guest star and potential new series lead Robert Lansing were not a problem. He wore what any self-respecting alien visitor would wear: a Brooks Brothers suit and a sincere tie. But owing to Gene's odd taste in ladies' ready-to-wear, Lansing's co-star, Teri Garr, made a fashion statement that set back 'haute couture' at least several hundred light-years. I watched resignedly as Gene, up to his old tricks, kept costume designer Bill Theiss busy, taking a tuck here and a trim there.... Teri understood the machinations of show business, having come from a performing family, so she didn't object when, just before her first scene on stage, Gene went to work on her costume again. He kneeled down, gathered up her already scant skirt, and told Bill Theiss, 'It's too long, Bill.' Teri rolled her eyes." (94-8)

Also in the cast:

Lincoln Demyan, as "Sergeant," whom Gary Seven puts to sleep, was 42. His familiar face was often seen on camera from 1961 through 1974, mostly in westerns.

Morgan Jones played Colonel Nesvig. He appeared in over 100 films and television programs, beginning in 1952 and including *Forbidden Planet*.

Don Keefer played Cromwell, the Mission Control security supervisor. Without the mustache, he can be seen as Don Hollis in "It's a Good Life," the famous *Twilight Zone* episode in which young Billy Mumy sends people he dislikes into the "corn field." Keefer was the party guest who got turned into a jack-in-the-box.

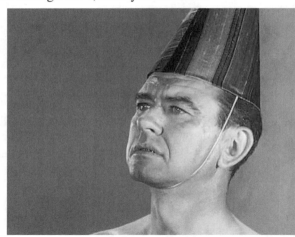

Don Keefer, as a jack-in-the-box on *The Twilight Zone* (CBS promotional photo); and Bruce Mars in a cameo as a befuddled New York City police officer (CBS Studios, Inc)

Bruce Mars, who appeared as the rascally Finnegan in "Shore Leave," returned for a smaller role, but one that is nonetheless a delight. He is Charlie, one of the two Policemen who accidentally get beamed onto the Enterprise.

Mars said, "I had known Marc Daniels from before, from out in New York. He wasn't a good friend, but I had known him. I got a call from the casting guy [Joe D'Agosta] and he said, 'Bruce, you doing anything right now?' I said, 'No.' And he said, 'Would you like to make a few bucks to feed your dog and pay your rent?' And I said, 'Yes!' Because, man, I was broke. I was working in construction and digging ditches trying to make ends meet. So I went in there

for one day and made a few hundred bucks. And it paid the rent and my dog Butch ate wonderfully for at least two weeks." (113a)

Ted Gehring played the other cop. He was 38 and early in a career that brought him more than 150 roles for TV and film, including a turn on William Shatner's cop show *T.J. Hooker*.

Victoria Vetri, seen far too briefly as Isis in human form, was 23. She worked steadily in television from 1962 through 1975 under the stage name of Angela Dorian. After appearing in a photo spread in *Playboy* magazine, as Miss September 1967, Dorian changed her performing name to Victoria Vetri. She was hot off that issue of *Playboy* when "Assignment: Earth" filmed. By the time the episode first aired, Vetri had been named Playmate of the Year. Sex sells, and top-billing in films such as *When Dinosaurs Ruled the Earth* (1970) and *Invasion of the Bee Girls* (1973) followed.

William Blackburn, seen often sitting at the helm as Lt. Hadley, makes a rare appearance out of his Starfleet uniform, as a rocket control room technician.

Victoria Vetri, as a blonde this time, for the lead in *When Dinosaurs Ruled the Earth* **(Warner Bros., 1970)**

Barbara Babcock, previously seen in "A Taste of Armageddon," and featured as the voice of Trelane's mother in "The Squire of Gothos," provided two separate voices for this episode -- the Beta 5 computer ... and Isis the cat. She said, "They didn't want to use a real cat's voice because there was such a range of emotion that this cat went through. It was almost human. So that's why they picked a human being to do her -- and that was lots of fun.... To be hired to play an animal was one of the most exciting things of all." (7)

Bartell La Rue, often heard in *Star Trek* episodes, is back, this time as the voice of Mission Control. He was the studio announcer in "Bread and Circuses," and the broadcast announcer in "Patterns of Force," and provided the voice for the Guardian of Forever in "The City on the Edge of Forever."

Giving direction to all these performers, Marc Daniels excelled with his 13th *Star Trek* assignment.

Production Diary
Filmed January 2, 3, 4, 5, 8, 9 & 10, 1968.
(Planned as 6 day production; ran one day over for total of 7; revised budget set at $193,495)

After the filming of "The Omega Glory," the *Star Trek* stages went dark, from December 25, 1967 through January 3, 1968, while Roddenberry prepared his backdoor pilot -- "Assignment: Earth." NBC had an option for two additional episodes, which would have brought the Second Season order to 28, but chose to hold at 26. John Meredyth Lucas remained in the offices overseeing the editing of "The Omega Glory," while Robert Justman and his production personnel stayed busy working with Roddenberry. No one knew if "Assignment: Earth" would close out the series. Anxiety was high; morale was expectantly low.

Production began Tuesday, January 2, 1968. "The Trouble with Tribbles" had its network premiere the previous Friday. It was NBC's top-rated show of the evening and came in second during its time period.

On New Year's Day, Evel Knievel failed to make a motorcycle jump of the fountain at Caesar's Palace. On this day, Dr. Christiaan Barnard performed the second heart transplant. The first attempt on December 3, 1967, had been a failure. For the second attempt, the patient survived for 14 months. *The Graduate*, introducing Dustin Hoffman, and with a soundtrack by Simon and Garfunkel, was the biggest draw at the movie houses. The Beatles had the song getting the most spins on U.S. radio stations with "Hello, Goodbye," and their album, *Magical Mystery Tour*, was the new top seller in record stores. Right behind it, The Rolling Stones with *Their Satanic Majesties Request*.

Work started on Stage 9. This was the Enterprise day with filming taking place in engineering, sickbay, the bridge, and the transporter room. Work finished with the production one-quarter of a day behind. This rarely happened with Marc Daniels, but this was, after all, a pilot.

Day 2, Wednesday, was spent on the Paramount Marathon Stage 5, a new location for *Star Trek*. The sets were for Gary Seven's office, the apartment building hallway, and Seven's "library."

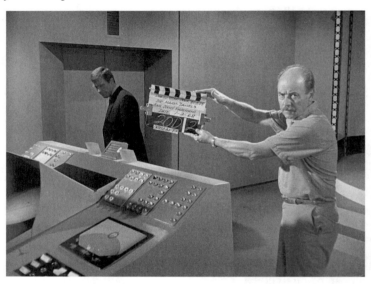

Day 1 of filming, on the second day of 1968, with Bill McGovern slating a shot featuring Robert Lansing (Courtesy of Gerald Gurian)

Bjo Trimble, visiting the set with her husband John, recalled, "Robert Lansing was playing with the little servo mechanism that he carried in his lapel, going 'Click, click, click.' And [prop master] Irving Feinberg walked up and said, 'Don't play with that.' And he took it away!' Robert Lansing was the big guest star, and he looked over and said, 'Can he do that?' And everyone said, 'Uh huh.' Here's the thing, though, extras and even maybe some of the guest stars made a little extra money by taking the stuff. Especially the extras. They were adding a little to their income by stealing everything in sight. *Star Trek* fans visiting the set were blamed for it. But it was mostly extras." (177-8)

Enjoying getting the star treatment, Teri Garr said, "*Star Trek* was the first job where I had a fairly big (for me) speaking part. Up until then, as a dancer, I'd been treated like an extra. But suddenly everything was focused on me. As I read over my lines, one person was tugging my dress, someone else was combing my hair, and a third person was doing my makeup. I realized that I wouldn't have a moment of solitude to get into character, that dealing with those distractions was part of the job." (71-2)

Lansing recalled, "She had a terrible time with this bit where she had to hit me with a box and knock me out. She was so nervous that finally I said, 'Teri, *hit* me.' And she gave me such a clobber that she nearly *did* knock me out. Gene said it didn't look right and we had to do it again." (105-1)

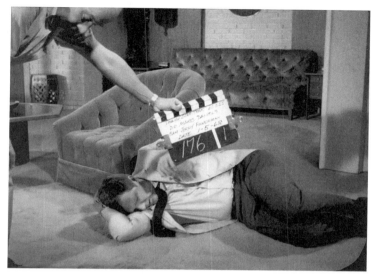

Day 4: Lansing said Teri Garr had a "terrible time" hitting him (above); Teri Garr and *Playboy* centerfold model Angela Dorian (aka Victoria Vetri) (Courtesy of Gerald Gurian)

Production for this day ended three-eighths of a day behind.

Days 3 and 4, Thursday and Friday, were also spent on the sets for Seven's library and office. At the end of this, the company was one-half day behind. Later in the night on Friday, "The Gamesters of Triskelion" first aired on NBC. Fans watching "Gamesters" had no idea that the cast of their favorite show was in the midst of filming what everyone at *Star Trek* feared would be the very last episode. Again, *Star Trek* came in second in its time period

and was NBC's highest-rated show of the night.

The production resumed for Day 5, Monday, with outdoor filming at Windsor Street on the Gower lot. Among the shots taken, Kirk and Spock, in civilian Twentieth Century Earth attire, walking the streets of New York.

Day 6, Tuesday, which was planned as the last day, brought the production to Stage 10 for the set described as "Int. Blockhouse." This was the Mission Control room.

Dorothy Fontana said, "I think the greatest accomplishment we did on that was create Mission Control. That was a tough job, because we had to bring in a lot of stuff. Normally, we tried to keep things manageable, because we couldn't afford to bring in a lot or build a lot. But, for that one, they were able to do a little bit more with the sets." (64-2)

Marc Daniels was not as impressed, saying, "We were simulating Mission Control, which, on our budget, was not easy. You had to make do with very abbreviated sets." (44-2)

Later on Day 6, the company moved back to Stage 9 for scenes in the briefing room, then additional filming in the transporter room, this time with a different cat.

Lansing said, "The fun with that show was working with the cats. We had three black cats. [The] cats would have a certain propensity... one would like somebody, would want to follow them around, so that day, you would release the cat that would probably do what you wanted it to do." (105-1)

Bjo Trimble remembered more cats than Lansing did, saying, "They had *seven* black cats there, all of which knew one trick. Each one did a separate thing. And one was friendly enough to where you could pick it up and hold it, where the others would resist, or lashing their tails, which shows they are not happy. They had one cat that could walk across the high beams that Gary Seven was out on. And one that could be planted on the couch. Believe it or not, that was his trick! The one that Spock held had a cold -- the *cat* had a cold, not Leonard

Day 5: Nimoy and Shatner on outdoor Windsor Street set on the Gower lot, with boom microphone above their heads
(Courtesy of Kipp Teague)

Nimoy and a cat about to sneeze on his shirt, in a scene from Day 6
(Unaired film trim courtesy of Gerald Gurian)

Nimoy. And they were ready to shoot and the poor cat turned his nose into Nimoy's chest and sneezed. And Nimoy sat there for a minute or so and then said, 'I have cat sneeze on the front of my shirt.' It was just so funny because here is Spock saying something like 'cat sneeze.' We're very animal friendly, so we talked to the cat wrangler and he was very proud of his cats because all exactly matched in stature. You wouldn't have been able to tell a bit of difference between most of them." (177-8)

Lansing said, "One of the cats took a great liking to me. It was always loose on the set when I was working, so it happened that the stuff on the rocket gantry was all ad lib. I would say something like, 'Isis, come on, you're getting in the way. You know, there is a bit of a hurry. This is not the time to be jealous.' We added meows in later." (105-1)

Trimble said, "Cats, of course, no matter how well you train them, are easily distracted. They are far more nervous of lights and so on than a dog. And if a light is moved or anything like that, they want to know what it is and will turn their heads. So it did take a little longer, but, frankly, with working with that many animals, it went rather smoothly." (177-8)

Marc Daniels' only comment on the reasons for falling behind, "We had a cat featured in it, which is always a problem." (44-2)

More trouble because of the cats. A grim-faced Bill McGovern, back in the transporter room for pickup shots on Day 6 (Courtesy of Gerald Gurian)

Day 7, Wednesday, January 10. With costs running over, and more problems with the cats, the company returned to Stage 9, for the bridge, the briefing room and, yet again, the transporter room. And then, back to Stage 10 for another try at the rocket gantry sequence, with Lansing ad-libbing to his cat-of-the-day.

Principal photography wrapped one day over schedule. The *Star Trek* cast was dismissed, perhaps for the last time. "A Piece of the Action" had its premiere broadcast two evenings later, on Friday, January 12. For the cast and crew of *Star Trek*, watching the comedy was surely a bittersweet affair.

Post-Production

Available for editing on January 11, 1968. Rough Cut: January 19, 1968.
Final Cut: February 16. Revised Final Cut: February 23, 1968.
Music Score: tracked.

Donald R. Rode and Edit Team 2 took over. Their work was so good that, in June, 1969, Rode received his second Emmy nomination for an episode of *Star Trek*. The reason it took so long, happening in 1969 instead of 1968, was that "Assignment: Earth," although from the 1967-68 TV season, aired too late to be included in that year's awards competition. Rode didn't mind waiting. He had another nomination in June of 1968 -- for "The Doomsday Machine."

Van der Veer Photo Effects was the main contributor of the matte shots and other photographic and post effects.

This was the only episode of *Star Trek* to not credit a studio executive as being in charge of the production. Herbert F. Solow had just left Paramount Television, and Douglas S. Cramer, who would supervise all future episodes, had yet to take charge.

Even as the making of "Assignment: Earth" was winding down, the battles were not yet over. Roddenberry had to fight for his sole producing credit, even though it was acknowledged he had been more involved than normal, and had in fact provided "substantial services." It was assumed by the studio, and maybe even John Meredyth Lucas, that Lucas would share in the credit.

On January 15, 1968, Roddenberry wrote to Emmet Lavery, at Paramount legal affairs:

> I produced "Assignment: Earth." My services were not "substantial," they were total, and I think if you will check with John Reynolds [President of Paramount Television Division] you will find I worked closely with him and Leo Pepin [Paramount TV Production Supervisor] in actively and totally producing the show, services which are continuing on at this date and necessarily will continue until a final print is ready for delivery to the network. Insofar as John Meredyth Lucas goes, he was necessarily retained on staff until last week since he had produced up through [episode] Number 25.

Roddenberry got his credit, his pilot, and Robert Lansing. But he didn't get a series.

When the final post-production bills were paid, the total cost of "Assignment: Earth" reached $193,495. A larger than usual part of the budget went to the writers.

Release / Reaction
Premiere air date: 3/29/68. NBC repeat broadcast: 8/9/68.

For its premiere broadcast on March 29, 1968, "Assignment: Earth" was the fifth episode of *Star Trek* to receive a *TV Guide* half page CLOSE-UP listing. "Metamorphosis," which was produced and aired first, was the sixth episode to be so acknowledged when it was repeated by NBC on July 19, 1968.

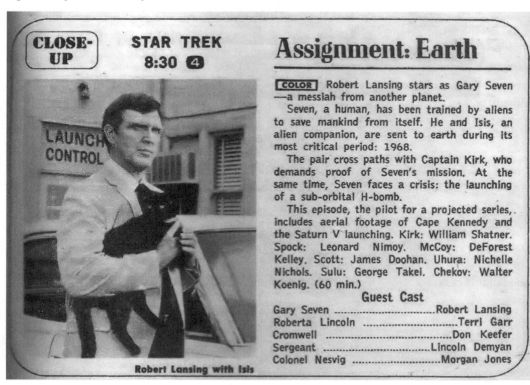

CLOSE-UP STAR TREK 8:30 ④ **Assignment: Earth**

[COLOR] Robert Lansing stars as Gary Seven —a messiah from another planet.

Seven, a human, has been trained by aliens to save mankind from itself. He and Isis, an alien companion, are sent to earth during its most critical period: 1968.

The pair cross paths with Captain Kirk, who demands proof of Seven's mission. At the same time, Seven faces a crisis: the launching of a sub-orbital H-bomb.

This episode, the pilot for a projected series, includes aerial footage of Cape Kennedy and the Saturn V launching. Kirk: William Shatner. Spock: Leonard Nimoy. McCoy: DeForest Kelley. Scott: James Doohan. Uhura: Nichelle Nichols. Sulu: George Takei. Chekov: Walter Koenig. (60 min.)

Guest Cast

Gary Seven ....Robert Lansing
Roberta Lincoln ....Terri Garr
Cromwell ....Don Keefer
Sergeant ....Lincoln Demyan
Colonel Nesvig ....Morgan Jones

Robert Lansing with Isis

From *TV Guide* CLOSE-UP listing, March 23, 1968 issue

Steven H. Scheuer reviewed this episode for *TV Key Previews*. Among newspapers across America to carry Scheuer's syndicated column on March 29, 1968 was *The Meridien Journal*, serving Meridien, Ohio. Scheuer hadn't seen the episode, but instead based his review on the Final Draft script, which still included the scene where the bridge crew of the Enterprise tune in *Bonanza*. He wrote:

> The most intriguing aspect of this complicated episode is the Enterprise's tangle with an event in history, way back in the year of 1968, while ostensibly on a mission to determine how Earth managed to "survive the desperate problems faced during that critical year." Captain Kirk's crew enjoy watching an episode of *Bonanza* until they come face to face with a 20th Century being whose identity and mission to save Earth from nuclear destruction is something they question and pursue. Ordinary mortals will find this one confusing but science fiction fans might have a ball.

Robert Lansing in NBC publicity photo (geared more to launch a new series than promote an episode of *Star Trek*) (Courtesy of Gerald Gurian)

RATINGS / Nielsen National report for Friday, March 29, 1968:

8:30 to 9 p.m., 59.3% U.S. TVs in use.	Share:	Households watching:
NBC: *Star Trek*	26.1%	11,540,000
ABC: *Operation: Entertainment*	23.3%	10,980,000
CBS: **Gomer Pyle, U.S.M.C.**	**45.1%**	**16,520,000**
Independent stations:	5.5%	No data

9 to 9:30 p.m., 60.5% U.S. TVs in use.	Share:	Households watching:
NBC: *Star Trek*	27.7%	No data
ABC: *Operation: Entertainment*	25.7%	No data
CBS: **Friday Night Movie**	**33.4%**	**No data**
Independent stations:	No data	No data

The CLOSE-UP listing in *TV Guide* helped *Star Trek* get back into second place, where it had been for most of the season. Singer Ed Ames hosted *Operation: Entertainment*, put on for the Seabees at Port Hueneme, California. Michelle Lee was a singing guest and Pete Barbutti handled the funny stuff. On CBS, following *Gomer*, was the television premiere of 1961's *The Hellions*, a western-type drama set in South Africa as a lone lawman, played by Richard Todd, stands up to a group terrorizing his town.

Again, *Star Trek* was NBC's best bet on Fridays. *Tarzan* attracted 10,140,000 households, improved upon by *Star Trek* to 11,540,000, then down to 10,250,000 for a *Hallmark Hall of Fame* special, "Give Us Barabbas."

***

No one knew if "Assignment: Earth" would be given a repeat airing on NBC. This, after all, was not a standard episode.

On March 8, 1968, Robert Justman wrote to Roddenberry:

> As you know, we have a list of 21 repeats made up for this coming season. Not included among these is "Assignment: Earth." If it sells as a series, it will replace "The Deadly Years" on September 6, 1968. Should NBC not want "Assignment: Earth" and should you be successful in selling it to some other network, then I envision serious difficulties in being able to get it on the Re-run Schedule. There might be some small objection from the National Biscuit Company, should such a situation arise.

Many things changed in the next few months. "Assignment: Earth" did not go to series. The airdate Justman reserved for it, to bump a repeat of "The Deadly Years" on September 6, 1968, became unavailable when the network decided to air a football game in prime time -- the Cincinnati Bengals versus the San Diego Chargers. Justman shuffled the rerun schedule and fitted "Assignment: Earth" in on August 9 instead, followed by "The Deadly Years" on August 16. The second season episodes to miss out on getting an encore network airing were "Friday's Child," "Obsession," "Wolf in the Fold," "Patterns of Force" and the satirical and entertaining "Bread and Circuses."

Despite "Assignment: Earth" failing to launch a series, it did launch a star.

Teri Garr said, "When I landed the coveted *Star Trek* part, I finally got real representation." (71-2)

Her new agent was at William Morris, the biggest talent agency in Hollywood. By the 1970s, as "Assignment: Earth" repeated over and over on hundreds of stations across America, Garr was becoming a familiar face -- that unknown actress on a *Star Trek* episode with the quirky way about her. One day Garr went with her mother to an army surplus store to shop for jeans. She recalled how the dressing rooms were full, so she half hid behind the stacks of jeans and was about to "shimmy" into a pair when she was startled by a man who introduced himself as Chris Bearde, a writer/producer for a TV variety series. Garr remembered, "While I stood there in my underwear, trying to play it cool, he said, 'I saw you on *Star Trek*. You're a very good actress." (71-2)

Suddenly Garr had a career, hired by Bearde to be part of the recurring ensemble cast on *The Sonny and Cher Comedy Hour*. Within a few years of regular TV employment, winning standout roles in big screen hits followed, such as *Young Frankenstein*, *Oh, God!*, *Close Encounters of the Third Kind*, and *The Black Stallion*. The 1980s brought *Mr. Mom* and *Tootsie*, for which she was nominated for an Academy Award.

Robert Lansing would never get another series as star, but he did play a supporting character in three more series: *Automan*, from 1983-84, *The Equalizer*, from its 1988-89 season, and *Kung Fu: The Legend Continues*, from 1993-94.

Bruce Mars, who had a small role here as one of the two New York City police officers whisked to the Enterprise, is best remembered by fans of *Star Trek* for playing Finnegan in the previous season's "Shore Leave." He was winding down his career as an actor at this time. He said, "Shortly after doing that, in 1969, I became a monk. I had been meditating and was spiritually inclined for all those years while doing plays in New York and television in Los Angeles. And I decided that I wanted to give my life over to serving people, and seeking God and just being as good as I could be." (113a)

From the Mailbag

Following the NBC broadcast:

> To Whom It May Concern, How did the Enterprise get back to the 20th century in "Assignment: Earth"? Cass F.L.T., Jr.

The response:

> An experiment in duplicating the accidental time travel in "Tomorrow is Yesterday" -- the experiment apparently worked, since the Enterprise made it to the 20th century and back to their own time. But, presumably, further experiments in time travel will be made only with great caution because of the danger of changing history (as happened in "City on the Edge of Forever"). Ruth Berman, for the 1968 newsletter *Inside Star Trek*.

Memories

Dorothy Fontana said, "It wasn't the most successful *Star Trek* episode simply because it was geared to be a possible spin-off. You always have to sacrifice something when you do that. But it worked all right. I didn't have anything to do with it, except for greatly admiring Robert Lansing as I had. Teri Garr was new to me, but I thought she was charming. But Lansing I had liked from *87th Precinct*. I had always admired his work, so I went down to the set a couple of times to watch him work. Gary Seven was an interesting character." (64-2)

Robert Lansing said, "It was a damned good script and a lot of fun." (105-1)

Art Wallace said, "It was a very good pilot, and it's a shame because, I think, if they had done it as a series with just Gary Seven, it would have been a very successful show." (179-1)

Teri Garr said, "I played Roberta Lincoln, a dippy secretary in a pink and orange costume with a very short skirt. Had the spin-off succeeded, I would have continued on as an Earthling agent, working to preserve humanity. In a very short skirt." (71-2)

On a different day, Garr said, "Thank God [it didn't sell]. Otherwise, all I would get would be *Star Trek* questions for the rest of my natural life -- and probably my unnatural life." (71-1)

Bruce Mars said, "It's been 45 years ago and I still get 5-to-10 fan letters every single month from people who were born only 20 to 30 years ago. Just the other day I got an envelope in the mail with a couple photos of Finnegan, and the fellow asked me to sign them. And get this, he's 17! He says he and his friends watch the show on DVD and he says, 'We say the lines along with you.' But everything is connected. When something is meaningful, it just stays alive." (113a)

37

For the Record

As 1968 began, media attention on *Star Trek* was greater than ever before.

- *TV Star Parade* gave Nimoy a piece of its January 1968 cover, promising that "Leonard Nimoy Speaks Out on LSD, Religion and Dirty Movies." A second cover story: "Bill Shatner's Month At-A-Time Marriage." When explaining about the greatest threat to his marriage – the thing that almost caused a divorce -- Shatner said, "The femme fatale actually is *Star Trek*.... It is a tireless schedule. It is known to be a marriage hazard."

- *TV Radio Mirror*, for the same month, gave us "The 'Other Girl' in Leonard Nimoy's Life." It was Peggye Vickers, who started the first Leonard Nimoy fan club and reported from the *Star Trek* set. We first read about her in

TV Weekly, January 26, 1968

Shatner giving cooking tips in the January 19, 1968 issue of
The Chicago Tribune

the October 1967 issue of *TV Radio Show*.

- *TV Star Parade*, for January, presented "*Star Trek* DesignBCostume Contest." All you had to do:

Design a costume for any one of the *Star Trek* stars or even something you'd like to see a guest star wear. Use the weirdest designs you can think of! Note exactly what fabric is being used and the colors.

The judge: Bill Theiss.

The prize: a *Star Trek* shirt, your choice, green (which photographed as gold due to the velour material used), blue, or red, or a Yeoman's uniform, in any of the three *Star Trek* colors.

- *The Chicago Tribune*, on January 19, printed a filler piece called "Commander on TV's *Star Trek* whips up fruit combination." Shatner shared cooking tips.

- *TV Weekly*, on January 26, had Nimoy/Spock on its cover. For the article, writer/critic Jim McPherson examined the four current science fiction series on television. *Star Trek* got the best score. Irwin Allen got the lowest grades, with McPherson writing, "If you want to rot your brains out, watch *Lost in Space*."

- *16 Magazine* had its eye – and a pictorial feature called "Meet Walter Koenig (*Star Trek*'s Chekov)" for its February 1968 issue. The article began:

> EVERY FRIDAY NIGHT the international star ship Enterprise casts off for another wild ride through the boundless universe on NBC-TV's *Star Trek*. One of the newest members of the star ship's crew is a handsome young actor named Walter Koenig (pronounced Kay-nig), who plays the part of 'Chekov'. Here, for the first time, is the inside story of Walter 'Chekov' Koenig.

Koenig had something far greater going for him than Shatner's recipes -- youth. The teen magazine promised, "You'll be reading more about him soon -- right here in the pages of *16*.

- *TV Picture Life* kept its focus on the Nimoy family for its February issue, in an article with the heading, "Now That Success Has Finally Come, Leonard Nimoy Faces Every Star's Heartbreak ... 'Is My Wife's Love Enough For Me?'"

February 1968 issue of *TV Star Parade*

- *Analog*, "the science fiction and science *fact* magazine," printed a 16-page article in its February issue called "To Make a *Star Trek*," by G. Harry Stine.

Stine wrote:

Star Trek is, of course, the first really adult, consistently high-level science-fiction show that's appeared on TV. And as all good science-fiction must, it has an extensive, carefully worked out background of detail that never directly appears on the screen -- yet is the reason *Star Trek* has the internal integrity it has. Did you know that the Enterprise is 947 feet long? Built in orbit, and incapable of landing?

- *TV Star Parade*, for its February 1968 issue, devoted its cover to the stars of *Star Trek*. DeForest Kelley and Nichelle

Nichols had the most space, making room for smaller images of "Leonard Nimoy & children" and "William Shatner & children." The bold headline: "What the Stars Predict for *Star Trek*'s Children." Melanie Shatner, we were told, "has the greatest opportunity to be a leader with the Jupiterian rays that bless her" but:

> … it's probably a good thing that she is not the oldest, for her stars point to the fact that she would enter into any new venture that enticed her, dragging along whomever she could.

Regarding sister Leslie, we were told:

> [Leslie], though much quieter and inclined to seem withdrawn, is the thinker…. She is in a position to understand particular situations that others are unable to and because of this come out the winner.

Good news for Lisabeth. The prediction:

> She will have more lucrative notions this year for all concerned in her young life. She is a self-starter. All this year she will put into action many of the things she only thought about in the past. She will skip over the tedious attitudes of others and go into an exploratory phase. She may decide to write or paint. The first part of the year may find her restless because she will want more privacy of thought and find it difficult to achieve because of her sisters.

Mostly, she would find it difficult to have more privacy because Hollywood celebrity magazines were making her and her siblings celebrities in their own right … and all because their dad was captain of a starship.

- *Screen Stars*, for its February cover, ran the headline, "How Leonard Nimoy Helps Addicts Live Again." The answer: He was making visits to Hollywood's House of Synanon, a rehab center, and using his celebrity to try to make a positive impression.

- *TV Picture Life* announced on its February cover, "*Star Trek* Drops Nimoy!" "The Startling Story" regarding Nimoy's near replacement prior to the start of Season Two was a year old, but this was the first time it had been leaked to the public. The breaking news:

> Leonard Nimoy was suspended! Off the show! The *Star Trek* producers were looking around for someone else to take over his role. A man who had played another Vulcan with pointed ears was considered the most likely actor to become the new Spock. How had it happened? How could the producer's of television's number one science-fiction show let their most popular hero get away? What could Nimoy possibly have done to make the brass angry enough to call his agent and inform him that his client would no longer be working on *Star Trek*?

Of course, the actor earmarked to replace Nimoy -- Lawrence Montaigne -- had not played a Vulcan, but a Romulan, in "Balance of Terror." His turn at playing a Vulcan would come after the fact. And Nimoy was not suspended but ordered to return to work with his current contract or face suspension and firing. And his agent was not notified that Nimoy was off the show, but would be prevented from working elsewhere for the duration of the term of his contract if he did not return to the show. Worse, from a reporting point of view, after calling Nimoy for comment, the magazine went with the prepared statement -- it was all a misunderstanding started by Nimoy's desire to offer notes on a script. Nimoy recalled the incident when he and John D.F. Black had a disagreement over the script for "The Naked Time." He allegedly told the "reporter," "I should have known I had come at a bad time when I opened his door and he barked, 'Now what do you want?' We all have bad days and this was obviously one of his. What was worse, and what I didn't know, was that he had written the script I was complaining about." Black, identified only as the series' "associate producer," was portrayed as the stereotypical Hollywood executive -- stubborn, impatient, ego-driven, bullying ... and wrong.

Interviewed for this book, John D.F. Black could not recall ever having any problems with Leonard Nimoy. Nor could wife Mary Black.

When interviewed, John D.F. said, "We were always open to input from the actors. The only person I had problems with at *Star Trek* was Gene Roddenberry. And Leonard can certainly relate to that." (17)

- *Young Catholic Messenger* (Teacher's Edition), from February 23, presented a commentary by William Kuhns, who wrote:

> The imagination behind the [*Star Trek*] scripts and the tremendous uniqueness in each adventure give the stories a range of vitality rare in a series program. And its scientific basis is as authentic as expert advisers can make it.

- *16 Magazine*, for March 1968, had a back cover pinup of Walter Koenig, in Nehru jacket. Inside this issue, the scoop: "My Hates & Loves," by Walter Koenig, in which "STAR TREK's Chekov confides the things that BUG him -- and the things that he DIGS!" Among the hates: "People with closed minds," "to see girls wearing pedal pushers," "Bermuda shorts on men," and "even the thought of eating snails, eels or squid." The loves:

Magazines like *FaVE* and *16* were making Walter Koenig into a reluctant teen heartthrob

"Pete Seeger, The Beatles and The Mamas and the Papas," "writing scripts," his Hungarian sheepdog, "Pan," and "my wife Judy."

- *FaVE!* magazine, of its March issue, sent fan Kim Larson to the *Star Trek* set for a day to watch the filming of "Patterns of Force." Feature writer Kam Lytton was along to write down Larson's observations. Larson said:

> I'd thought of the "Enterprise" as being a big spaceship that they move around in to film. We walked in the Stage 10 [sic] door and – it was nowhere to be seen! I thought maybe the "Enterprise" was over on the other side of the set somewhere and started to look for it when Kam stopped me and asked me where I was going. Then she pointed out this little set in the corner, all dark and everything, and I recognized the corridor of the "Enterprise"! The "Enterprise" is a conglomeration of different sets all over that gigantic sound stage that they somehow turn into something glamorous when they put lights on them.... We

went over to the bridge and that was the most exciting. The flashing control panels are really groovy! I sat in all the chairs on the bridge so that now when I see *Star Trek* I'll be able to say -- I sat in that very chair!

- *Motion Picture* magazine, for its March issue, presented, "Leonard Nimoy: 'The Names They Call Me Back Home.'"

- *United Press International* circulated an article by Vernon Scott to numerous newspapers on March 31. Under the title of "Is There a Doctor in the House," DeForest Kelley talked about how he had remained married to his wife, Carolyn, since 1945; how they lived in a two bedroom, two bathroom house in the quiet San Fernando Valley community of Sherman Oaks, and it was all they needed. "Small birds need small nests," Kelley said.

- *TV Star Parade* had the Shatner family on its cover in April 1968 to go along with the story: "Bill Shatner: 'I've Been Betrayed Emotionally!'"

- *16 Magazine* had Walter Koenig sharing the cover of its April issue with Davy Jones and Micky Dolenz of The Monkees.

- *TV Radio Movie Guide* had Spock on its April cover and the tease, "Leonard Nimoy: The Girls Who Beg for His Love!!"

- *Movie & TV Time* had a feature article on Shatner for its April issue, with the heading, "The Fan Letters I Answer First!" Shatner said, "I reply first to the person who guesses that I'm really trying to do my best. When I find this kind of awareness in a letter, I can't put it aside. Imagining I don't care a lot about what a fan thinks of

TV Star Parade, **April 1968**

my efforts is so wrong. Believe me, I do! I always remember I must please someone I can't see to really succeed as I want to."

- *Photoplay* magazine bought a full page ad in the April 1, 1968 issue of *Variety* to announce its 46th Annual Gold Medal Award winners. Paul Newman was the magazines pick for Favorite Male Star. Barbara Stanwyck, thanks to her TV series *The Big Valley*, was Favorite Female Star. Carol Burnett was Favorite Comedy Star. *The Dirty Dozen* was Movie of the Year. And *Star Trek* was voted Most Popular Television Series.

- *The Chronicle-Telegram*, serving Lorain County, Ohio, had an article by Gary Bainbridge, on April 9. The headline read, "Nimoy Can 'Hardly Believe' His Popularity With Teens." The actor was in Cleveland plugging his new album, *Two Sides of Leonard Nimoy*.

When asked if stars of TV series eventually go stale and give less than their all, he answered, "Perhaps in some series, but not in *Star Trek*. The plots are so varied and the characters so complicated we are constantly on our toes just keeping in character."

- *Columbia Features*, a news service, distributed a syndicated article on April 11 giving the spotlight to Shatner. Interviewed by Kurt Lassen, the headline read "Shatner Thrilled with Space Show." He boasted, "Several of the programs we have done on *Star Trek* were based on story lines I dreamed up. I enjoy writing, but with the series I don't get the time to actually write the scripts."

Indeed, "The Omega Glory" had sampled the Teaser and the start of Act I an unproduced story outline credited to Shatner, called "Web in Space."

- *Teen* magazine, for May of 1968, ran the article, "The Ears Have It! -- Pointedly."

- *16 Magazine*, for May, had Walter Koenig on its cover, again sharing space with Davy and Micky of The Monkees and, this time, also with teenage heartthrob Sajid Khan of NBC's *Maya*.

- *TV Star Parade* presented three separate *Star Trek* related features in its June 1968 issue. Shatner had "The Lesson He Never Forgot." James Doohan was featured in "His Rocky Road to Happiness." And, to round things off, several pages of pictures went along with "Shopping with the Leonard Nimoys."

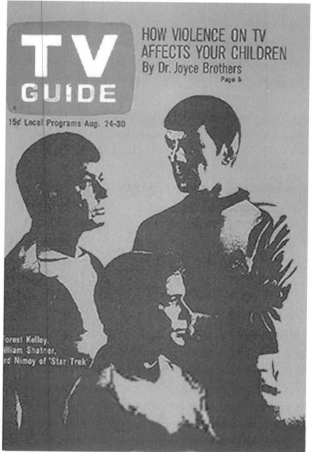

Star Trek's on the cover of top-selling magazine
TV Guide, it's third time in two years (August, 1968)

- *The Chicago Tribune*, on July 8, 1968, ran the headline: "Acting in Series Has Its Drawbacks." DeForest Kelley was quoted by writer Clay Gowran, "It doesn't happen anymore, but it used to be that people could phone the studio, ask for the *Star Trek* set, and be connected, just like that. You'd be shooting a scene, maybe on some distant and hostile planet, and the phone on the sound stage would ring, and it'd be a fan calling up to talk a little and to tell us how much he liked the show."

- *TV Guide*, on August 24, 1968, had *Star Trek* on its cover for the third time in as many years. Kirk, Spock, and McCoy were pictured. The article focused on Kelley and his struggle to establish himself in show business. Kelley said, "There was a time when I was ready to change my name to DeForest Lawn."

With his co-star status on *Star Trek*, Kelley's fortunes had finally changed. When his name ran for the first time in *TV Guide* for a

1968 crossword puzzle, wife Carolyn Kelley clipped the page and framed it to hang on the wall. "It's not an Oscar or an Emmy," said Kelley, "but to an actor it's something."

Star Trek was immensely popular while it aired on NBC. And everyone knew it -- even NBC.

***

On March 8, 1968, while still awaiting word if there would be a third season, Robert Justman didn't even know if there would be a second rerun season. His letter to Paramount President Emmet Lavery, Jr. read:

> As of tonight, March 8th, there only remain three weeks until we are finished with virgin showings of *Star Trek* episodes. Commencing on April 5th, we are into our Repeat Season. If there is any way you can find to needle the National Biscuit Company into giving us at least a partial order on Repeats, it would be much appreciated by everyone concerned.... We are starting to get damaged again with respect to publicity on Repeat Telecasts, due to the fact that we cannot release a schedule. We're really not asking NBC to bargain away its collective soul in giving us an order for, say, 12 or 13 Repeats. The Network knows damn well it's not going to play an hour of organ music every Friday night until the Republican and Democrat Conventions late this Summer.

Justman was actually already compiling his unofficial list. Draft One went out days before to producers Roddenberry and Lucas, and Stan Robertson at the network. Then, one day before writing to Lavery, and after Lucas had moved out of his office, Justman wrote again to Robertson, removing Lucas' "Patterns of Force" from the list and opting instead for "The Apple." He told Robertson:

> I have also revised the Release Order of the first six Re-runs, due to the fact that I want to have a shot at getting a "Spotlight" from *TV Guide* on either "Amok Time" or "Who Mourns for Adonais?" Therefore, I have moved those shows back and substituted "I, Mudd" and "Mirror, Mirror" in their stead.

Moving his favorite episode back would give *TV Guide* more time to consider their merits. All the swapping around did little good. As it turned out, neither "Amok Time" nor "Who Mourns for Adonais?," a pair of episodes the creative staff were most proud of, garnered *TV Guide* CLOSE-UP listings. The two that did were the final first-run episode of the season, "Assignment: Earth," and the repeat of "Metamorphosis."

Justman's choices of episodes to exclude from repeating included, surprisingly, the highly entertaining "Friday's Child," which boasted Klingons, location filming, and a notable guest star (Catwoman herself -- Julie Newmar). And it had been written by D.C. Fontana, with rewrite by Gene Roddenberry. Also passed over was "Bread and Circuses," an episode that seemed to have something for everyone -- action, conflict, humor, satire, location production, and the wallop of a twist ending. And it was a Gene Roddenberry / Gene Coon script. Justman later stated the omission for this one was made to appease a certain executive at the network who rightfully believed the target of the script's satire was NBC itself.

Three other omissions from Justman's latest summer repeat list were "Return to Tomorrow," an episode marred by some heavy-handed Roddenberry speeches and a hammy performance from Shatner; "A Private Little War," again a victim of heavy-handed writing and acting; and "The Omega Glory," based on a script that Justman particularly loathed. But Roddenberry had written the final shooting scripts for all three and overrode Justman to make

608

sure they saw a second airing. And this meant other episodes had to be dropped from the list to make room.

"Wolf in the Fold," an episode Stan Robertson at NBC felt was weak, was given the boot. The subtle-as-a-kick-in-the-head-by-the-boot-of-a-Nazi-Storm-Trooper "Patterns of Force" remained a no show from the list, and no one was complaining about this omission. Regarding "Assignment: Earth," another one written by Roddenberry (with Art Wallace), Justman told Roddenberry that should NBC pass on buying the series, having the pilot air on the network just as Ashley-Famous was trying to peddle the series to ABC and CBS would not be advantageous. Roddenberry reluctantly agreed. Four months later it was not only clear NBC didn't want the spin-off series but neither did the network's competitors. At that point, Roddenberry insisted it be added in for a repeat broadcast. By this time, there were only four nights of repeats left open, with "Obsession," "The Deadly Years," "A Private Little War," and "A Piece of the Action," respectively. Something had to give way, and, although well-liked by staff and the network, "Obsession" was considered the least likely to be missed.

***

March 9, 1968. The 15th Annual Motion Picture Sound Editors Awards dinner was held at the Century-Plaza Hotel. *Bonnie and Clyde* and *Dr. Doolittle* shared the award in the motion picture category. *Star Trek* took the award for the television category, beating out *Mission: Impossible*, *Garrison's Gorillas*, and *Run for Your Life*. Gene Roddenberry was on hand to see Barbara Anderson (past guest star on the first season episode "The Conscience of the King") hand out awards to the *Star Trek* team -- supervising re-recording mixer Elden Ruberg, supervising sound editor Douglas H. Grindstaff, and sound editors Joseph Kavigan, Gilbert Marchant, and Richard Raderman.

March 15, 1968. Paramount anted up for a full page in *Variety*, congratulating *Star Trek* for winning the Golden Reel Award.

March 22, 1968. *Star Trek* had two scripts nominated at the Writers Guild Awards for the Best Dramatic-Episodic -- "The Return of the Archons," Final Draft, by Boris Sobelman, with story by Gene Roddenberry, and "The City on the Edge of Forever," First Draft, by Harlan Ellison. Roddenberry sent in "Archons" as *Star Trek*'s official submission for award consideration. Ellison, the maverick writer at odds with *Star Trek*, sent in his First Draft as a means of protesting all the rewriting by the staff. Ellison got the award … and decades of bragging rights.

Ellison told this author in 2013, "When I went to the awards, Gene Coon nearly choked on his dinner. He was sitting right down in front of me when I said what I said about the rewriting ['Never let them rewrite you!']. There's nothing I've ever done in my 79 years that has not in some way impaired my progress, but I'm one of those people whom the maxim was invented -- 'A man who knows you can be frightened knows you're a man that can be bought.' So whether I was working for Aaron Spelling, Darryl Zanuck, or Gene Roddenberry, I just have a very, very, very, very, very high fear threshold, [meaning] I'm not afraid of anything, and that is a great flaw. It doesn't mean you're brave necessarily, it means you don't know when to turn and run when the snake is rattling." (58)

March 26, 1968. Shatner, Nimoy, and Roddenberry appeared on the *Merv Griffin Show* to accept the Photoplay Award, presented to *Star Trek* for Top Television Show of the Year.

609

April 17, 1968. Nominations for the 1967-68 Emmy awards were released to the press. In the strange category of Special Classification of Outstanding Individual Achievement, the Westheimer Company was acknowledged for Special Photographic Effects as seen in "Metamorphosis." It was a crowded category, with *Star Trek*'s photo effects competing against Sound Editing for *Mission: Impossible*; Best Writing for a Children's Special and Best Direction for a Children's Special, both for "You're In Love, Charlie Brown"; Best Choreographer for "Movin' With Nancy [Sinatra]"; and a pair of Best Performer noms, for Pat Paulsen on *The Smothers Brothers Comedy Hour* and Art Carney on *The Jackie Gleason Show*. The Academy was serious. Photographic Effects versus Sound Editing versus Writing versus Direction versus Acting.

For Outstanding Achievement in Film Editing, Donald R. Rode was nominated for "The Doomsday Machine," and pitted against editors for *Mission: Impossible*, an NBC news program called "Four Days in Omaha," a Bob Hope special, and an episode of the *Bell Telephone Hour*.

Leonard Nimoy was again nominated for Outstanding Performance by an Actor in a Supporting Role in a Drama. His opponents on this occasion: Milburn Stone for *Gunsmoke*; Joseph Campanella for *Mannix*, and Lawrence Dobkin -- the same Lawrence Dobkin who directed *Star Trek* episode "Charlie X" -- for a *CBS Playhouse* special.

And *Star Trek* was again up for Outstanding Dramatic Series. With the exception of one new entry, *NET Playhouse*, the competition was the same as the previous year -- *Mission: Impossible*, *The Avengers*, *I Spy*, and *Run for Your Life*.

May 19, 1968. At the Emmys, *Star Trek* lost in all four categories. The Westheimer Company's photo effects for "Metamorphosis" couldn't match the appeal of Pat Paulsen and Art Carney, a pair of flesh-and-blood popular celebrities, who tied and, therefore, both received Emmys. Peter Johnson, who cut "Sights and Sounds" for the *Bell Telephone Hour*, beat Donald Rode, editor of "The Doomsday Machine." *Gunsmoke*'s Doc Adams was better liked by the

Pat Paulsen (with Barbara Bain of *Mission: Impossible*) holds one of the Emmys *Star Trek* gave up

Academy than *Star Trek*'s Mr. Spock. And the Best Drama Emmy was again handed to *Mission: Impossible* instead of *Star Trek*.

***

1968 Aladdin *Star Trek* dome top lunch box and Thermos

Regarding the merchandising:

Ray Plastics put out the *Star Trek* Tracer Gun ... and, also, the Tracer Gun Rifle ... with Kirk and Spock on the packaging.

Remco had the *Star Trek* Astro Walkie-Talkie. It was their usual Astro Walkie-Talkie, with the name *Star Trek* on the package, along with the images of Kirk and Spock.

Hasbro manufactured a triple-threat: the *Star Trek* Target Game, the *Star Trek* Double Action Bagatelle Pinball Game, and the *Star Trek* Marble Maze Game. The likeness of Kirk and Spock were present to ensure brisk business on all three.

Of better quality, Aladdin Industries issued the *Star Trek* Dome Top Lunch Box, with thermos. Pictured: cartoon drawings of Kirk, Spock, Uhura, and the Enterprise.

The most anticipated tie-in was music to the ears of many fans -- Leonard Nimoy's follow up to the highly successful Dot Records release, *Mr. Spock's Music from Outer Space*. With this new LP, however, there would be half as much Spock and twice as much Nimoy.

"I don't make personal appearances as Spock," Nimoy told Ruth Berman in 1968, for *Inside Star Trek*. "I go as myself. And you remember my first record from Dot [had] emphasis on *Spock*. But [this] second one [is] *Two Sides of Leonard Nimoy*."

The album cover

Nimoy's second album ... half-Vulcan (Side 1) ... and half-human (Side 2)

featured the two Nimoys, one with pointed ears, the other with rounded ear tops, each facing the other. Side One was devoted to the Vulcan, while Side Two focused on the human.

611

Charles Grean was back in the producer's chair, and wrote or co-wrote six of the 13 selections.

Featured on Spock's side, "Highly Illogical," a bit of self-parody set to 1967 Adult Contemporary pop by Charles Grean, followed by "The Difference Between Us" and "Once I Smiled," the latter being a collaboration between Grean and Nimoy, giving Nimoy his second songwriting credit on record. "Spock Thoughts" was a work of thievery. It was a reciting of Max Ehrmann's 1927 poem "Desiderata," set to a lush score. The prose, best described as preachy, appealed to Roddenberry, who changed one word and was given a co-writing credit, along with Grean, who composed the backing music. Roddenberry almost got away with it. He and others believed Ehrmann's 1927 copyright had long since expired and the poem was in the public domain. The copyright hadn't, and the poem wasn't. As for Nimoy and Grean's recording, it, like Ehrmann's poem, is somewhat historic and Roddenberry's instincts for what could make an oddball pop hit were not far off the mark. In 1971, four years after Nimoy's take on "Desiderata," radio DJ Les Crane had a Top Ten national hit with the "song," clearly inspired by the Nimoy/Grean approach. One year after that, National Lampoon charted with a parody of Crane's recording. Their send-up was called "Deteriorata."

Filling out the Spock side: "By Myself," "Follow Your Star," and "Amphibious Assault," a collaboration between Grean and Mason Williams. Williams was a folk guitarist/songwriter/TV-comedy-writer who worked on *The Smothers Brothers Comedy Hour*, and just a few months shy of stardom with his instrumental hit "Classical Gas."

Side Two opened with the infamous "The Ballad of Bilbo Baggins," which had previously been released as a non-charting single. "Cotton Candy," a song written by Cliff Ralke, a member of the *Star Trek* camera crew, and previously issued as the B-side of the "Bilbo Baggins" single, came next. After that, "Gentle on My Mind," by folker John Harford, and a recent hit for Glen Campbell. It helped to establish who Nimoy wanted to be -- a folk singer. Band 4, "Miranda," is the album's best moment. Written by Bart Howard, better known for "Fly Me to the Moon," this lovely classic-folk song suited Nimoy's baritone voice well. Band 5, "If I Were a Carpenter," by folker Tim Hardin, was, if nothing else, curious. Band 6, "Love of the Common People," brought the record to an end. Nimoy did it first, but the song would resurface in a year as a minor hit for the singing group The Winstons.

The music critic from *Variety* gave *Two Sides* a thumbs up on March 27, writing:

Leonard Nimoy, the Mr. Spock of the *Star Trek* TV series, has developed a neat groove for himself with his talk-sing disk performances. In this outing, he has some sharply written material in "Highly Illogical," "Once I Smiled," "Follow Your Star," "The Ballad of Bilbo Baggins," "Love of the Common People," among some contemporary hits.

The album did well, with 13 weeks in the Billboard album charts, starting on February 24, 1968. It did half the business as the first Nimoy LP, but Dot wasn't complaining.

"Let's face it," Nimoy said at the time, "I'm an actor who records. I'd be terribly surprised, not unhappy mind you, if this singing career turned into anything big. I'm not passing judgment on my capabilities, but I'm 37 and have been an actor for 17 years. I'm just off the ground as a singer.... I'm not Sinatra."

Comic book king Western Publishing delivered its second Gold Key Comic's *Star Trek* issue, entitled "The Devil's Isle of Space," concerning a prison planet. The first issue, "Planet of No Return," had been published in early 1967.

**Second collection of *Star Trek* short stories based on first season TV scripts
(Bantam Books, 1968)
and second Gold Key *Star Trek* comic book
(Western Publishing, 1968)**

Also in February, the paperback *Star Trek 2* hit the book racks, after being delayed a couple of months while author James Blish made changes to his manuscript at the insistence of the *Star Trek* creative staff. This was the second Bantam short story collection of past *Star Trek* episodes, all from the series' first season.

In March, 1968, after numerous delays, came *Mission to Horatius*, a Whitman hardback novelette, by Mack Reynolds, with illustrations by Sparky Moore.

Reynolds, a science fiction author with numerous books, including the Joe Mauser series, beginning with 1962's *Mercenary from Tomorrow*, and the "United Planets" series, launched by 1965's *Planetary Agent X*, seemed a perfect fit for *Star Trek*. His storyline covered some familiar ground, duplicating elements from "Bread and Circuses" and "Patterns of Force," both of which had not yet aired at the time of the writing of his book.

After reading the soon-to-be published manuscript, John Meredyth Lucas, on November 3, 1967, wrote to Desilu Legal Head Ed Perlstein, saying:

> Mack Reynolds' novelization of *Star Trek* is not technically in bad taste, but it is extremely dull and, even considering the juvenile market, badly written. If anything, one should write better for juveniles.

On November 14, Roddenberry wrote Perlstein:

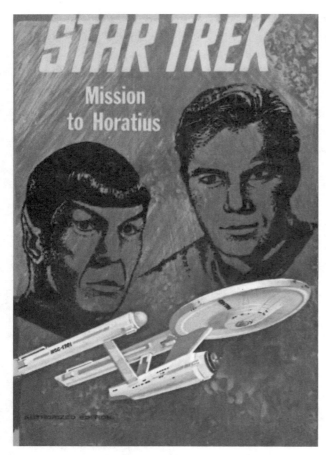

Whitman hardback from 1968

I agree completely with JML on Mack Reynolds' novelization of *Star Trek*. I am particularly upset and made nervous by some of the bad taste in it -- Uhura as a "Negress" who breaks into a spiritual, etc.... I think we must go on the assumption that *Star Trek* will continue on television for many years and is a valuable property worth protecting and I personally would rather blow a deal like this than see the property harmed.... I recommend strongly that in this deal and in all future book, magazine, or comic book deals that we insist on enough advanced time for copy so that it can be checked over carefully.

On February 20, 1968, Roddenberry sent five pages of notes to Perlstein concerning the *Mission to Horatius* book, along with one compliment:

Incidentally, I should say at this point that I like many things that Reynolds has done in this story and I trust he will forgive me emphasizing the negative rather than the positive in these comments.

A revision of Reynolds' manuscript was quickly made and sent to the printers.

For those of us old enough to have been there, all of this comes as little surprise -- *Star Trek* was immensely popular, in 1966, 1967, and 1968. Only historical revisionists, with four decades of gullible press, have created the folklore that says otherwise. May the record now be corrected.

38

Stand and Be Counted

March on NBC Burbank (January 1968)

TV Week's Second Annual Poll, listing the prime-time series of 1967, based on "Favorites by Age Group," found *Star Trek* to be No. 1 in two important groups -- 20 to 30 year olds, as well as those from 30 to 40. *Mission: Impossible*, the darling at the Emmy awards, came in second.

Variety reported that the University of Chicago conducted a poll of high schools in its area, ranking all network shows in the order of the most frequently watched. The Top 10, in the order of their preference, were, *I Spy*, *Mission: Impossible*, *The Man from U.N.C.L.E.*, *Star Trek*, *Get Smart*, *Time Tunnel*, *The Monkees*, *Hawk*, *The Fugitive*, and *Hogan's Heroes*.

A.C. Nielsen also supported the belief by many that *Star Trek* was a popular series, even though NBC said otherwise. According to Nielsen, *Star Trek* placed within the overall Top 10 during the summer of 1967. To publicize the news, KNBC, the network-owned station in Los Angeles, had a picture taken of the Enterprise bridge where a giant sign read:

Blast off! *Star Trek* premiere, 1967-1968 season -- Sept. 15, 1967, 8:30 p.m., NBC Channel 4. *In First Ten in Nielsen Rating*.

Within the first five weeks of the new season, NBC realized it had made a mistake in moving *Star Trek* from Thursday to Friday nights. While remaining the network's most-watched show on the night it aired, several million of *Star Trek*'s viewers from the previous season did not make the move to Fridays. A worse mistake involved *The Man from U.N.C.L.E.*, which the network, in hopes of cashing in on the success of the ultra-campy *Batman*, allowed MGM to convert from an espionage show to a parody of an espionage show. This had alienated its audience and *U.N.C.L.E.*, a hit just a few months earlier, was now dying in its Monday 8 to 9 p.m. slot, despite a strong lead-in from *The Monkees*. On October 25, 1967, *Variety* reported:

Promotional sign placed on the bridge of the Enterprise for a press party thrown by NBC-owned Los Angeles station KNBC 4 (Author's collection)

Per present thinking at the web, *Star Trek* would be shifted out of 8:30 on Friday to replace *UNCLE* and that move has the network mulling a possible restructuring of Friday. That would include the bumping of *Accidental Family*, giving NBC 90 minutes to reprogram between *Tarzan* at 7:30 and *Bell Tel Hour*/News Actualities at 10.

Star Trek's gain, however, would have been the network's loss -- at least in regard to Friday nights. With *Star Trek* gone, the entire night's lineup would collapse. So when NBC pulled *U.N.C.L.E.* from the schedule in early January, it was replaced with a new experimental show -- *Rowan and Martin's Laugh-In* -- instead of *Star Trek*. Meanwhile, *Star Trek* remained the network's cornerstone for Fridays.

A Nielsen poll for demographic testing, covering October 23 to December 3, 1967 (of the new season), ranked *Star Trek* at No. 4 with teenagers.

On December 21, 1967, Robert Justman sent a memo to "All Concerned," telling them:

Since the Canadian Network which airs *Star Trek* has chosen not to take the NBC Pre-empt entitled "Flesh & Blood," in January, our first episode of the season, which was entitled "Amok Time," will be aired in Canada instead.... Canada will have one more repeat than NBC in U.S.... By the way, I think everyone can take pride in the knowledge that *Star Trek* is Number Two in that country and the Network up there would rather rerun *Star Trek* than a new NBC Special.

Arbitron Ratings Service in the U.S. also reported good news. A national survey taken in 61 markets from Spring 1968 showed *Star Trek* had over a 30 share -- that make-it-or-break-it number the networks and their sponsors were so taken with. In fact, according to the survey, the average share for *Star Trek* in these 61 prime markets was 39.5%.

Another measuring tool was the number of Enterprise model kits sold. Prior to 1967, the top-seller associated with a television series was the *Munsters* model car. It moved one million units over a two-year period. The Enterprise model had sold as many in less than one year.

Still another yardstick came with the response Leonard Nimoy received during his personal appearances across the country. In a 1973 interview for David Gerrold's book *The World of Star Trek*, Nimoy said, "I remember that the fan reaction was tremendous. I would go out on personal appearances and the fans would just come running. Sometimes there was a danger of them being crushed. It happened at Macy's in New York once. It was very scary. And another time in South Carolina. I had just flown in from New York. It was late at night -- about midnight -- and I got off this commuter airplane... and I couldn't see because there were so many lights [pointed at] it. I didn't know what they were, and suddenly I realized there was a crowd of hundreds and hundreds of people and that all of those searchlights were for me. It was absolutely astonishing. They had signs saying 'Up *Star Trek*!' … It was a tremendous turnout for a small town at this airport, giving it the aura of a grand opening."

For his book, *I Am Spock*, Nimoy recalled how he once signed over 8,000 autographs in one sitting during a record tour. And he was receiving over 2,000 fan letters a week, a situation that got out of hand when *16 Magazine* reported his home address in its April 1967 issue.

"I hadn't seen the article, but realized what had happened after a flood of mail started coming to the house," Nimoy wrote. "After a few days, the postman refused to deliver the mail because there was so much of it. The post office finally hauled it to us by truck, and for weeks we lived with a literal mountain of mail in the living room, sometimes so high that it was taller than I was." (128-3)

Walter Koenig, in *The World of Star Trek*, told that, as a result of being "pushed" by *16 Magazine*, he was receiving about 650 letters a week, which, at that time, was considered an "enormous" amount.

The entire cast was buried in fan mail.

"The greatest fan letter I ever received," said Kelley, "I opened it up and there was cardboard inside and pasted on it was a marijuana cigarette. And it said, 'Dear DeForest, you have turned me on so many times, I would like to repay the favor. [Signed] One of your female fans.'" (98-8)

Nimoy's fan mail became so immense that he hired Teresa Victor, a personal assistant whose primary job was to be a buffer between him and his more overenthusiastic fans. And there were many.

One wrote:

617

Dear *Star Trek*... Spock is beautiful -- his beautiful body and hairy chest are terrif!... I just got his new album, and, when he sang "I'd Love Making Love to You," I wanted to go out and howl at the moon! Sometimes, oh, I'll say it, catty or not, sometimes when I feel jealous of his wife, I'm glad in a way that he does have a tiring long work day and might be too tired for her when he gets home!

Another began:

Dear Mr. Spock... I don't feel it's wrong to take my life, but since I've watched you, Mr. Spock, I now feel it's illogical to waste life, even mine. I don't expect you to understand that, not even my parents understand me. But that's the way I feel.

Fans identified with *Star Trek* and talked to the series as if it were a person. One such letter read:

Dear *Star Trek*... The program has changed my life! It was after the episode "The City on the Edge of Forever" by Harlan Ellison that the characters became real to me. I began to live in a fantasy that occupied almost every waking moment. I went through a great emotional upheaval, my thinking has been altered, and I feel like a new and better person.

Another said:

Dear *Star Trek*... I would appreciate the addresses of Mr. and Mrs. Gene Roddenberry, William Shatner, Leonard Nimoy, DeForest Kelley, James Doohan, Nichelle Nichols, George Takei, Walter Koenig, D.C. Fontana, and Matt Jefferies. Please do not disappoint me.

And then the people writing the letters began gathering.

At Worldcon '67, during the Labor Day weekend, a contingent of Canadian fans showed up wearing Spock ears. Later, for the Masquerade Ball, nine people arrived dressed as Spock. It was a curiosity ... and an indication of things to come.

And then they started writing fanzines.

Vulcanalia, by Dana Friese (President) and Elyse Pines (treasurer) is believed to be the first *Star Trek* fanzine, with volume 1 from January 1967. Friese wrote for that issue:

Anyone wishing to have the tapes of past "Star Trek" shows, contact the Treas., Elyse Pines. She has tapes of all shows from "Miri" onward.

Those tapes, of course, were audio, not video.

Spockanalia, compiled by Sherna Comerford and Devra Langsam, was also launched in 1967.

ST-Phile, by Juanita Coulson and Kay Anderson, was circulated in early 1968.

By summer, because of her association with *Spockanalia*, Ruth Berman was tapped by Roddenberry to edit *Inside Star Trek*, an official newsletter for the series. Its first issue went out in July 1968 to fans who wrote in to the show. *Inside Star Trek* was given the full support of those who worked on the series and, throughout its dozen issues over the next twelve months, it featured interviews with the cast and crew and articles by many *Star Trek* insiders. It also established the mail order business which would quickly evolve into Lincoln

Enterprises (AKA *Star Trek* Enterprises).

    Anti-Matter, a fanzine by Carol Lee, came in 1968.

    Galileo 7, by Kathryn Bushman, also from 1968, featured poetry and art. Prior to this, Bushman had been providing much of the artwork for *Spockanalia*.

April 1968 issue of fanzine *Plak Tow* (artist unknown)

Plak Tow, by Shirley Meech, who had served as assistant editor for *Spockanalia*, also came in 1968 and included news about the "Save *Star Trek*" campaign.

And *Triskelion*, by D.E. Dabbs and Russell Bradley, from 1968, contained cartoons, artwork and stories.

The legions of fans were growing.

Nimoy recalled how the throngs at his public appearances sometimes resembled the adulation aimed toward the Beatles, which would then require the orchestration of Beatle-like escapes. During one record promotion tour, at an autograph signing in a Long Island department store, the crowd pushed forward to such a degree that the "protective gates" began collapsing. The store manager hurried Nimoy away to a back office, where both were trapped by the crowd. The only way out was up to the roof. A call was placed to the fire department, so Nimoy and the store manager could be rescued by hook-and-ladder.

    The fan reaction came as a complete shock to DeForest Kelley who had no idea of the popularity *Star Trek* had generated. During the Spring break of 1968, Kelley and his wife, Carolyn, traveled to New York where they took in an afternoon performance of the Broadway stage production of *Cabaret*. In the lobby, the two separated when Carolyn went to the restroom. As Kelley waited for his wife, he spotted a couple of women looking his way. He said, "They came over and handed me their programs to sign, and I signed them, and a couple more came over and handed me their programs to sign, and I started to sign them. And after about ten minutes, there was a whole mob. I looked up, looking for Carolyn, and I couldn't see her. I was in the middle of a seething -- *actually a seething* -- mob. And finally, I saw Carolyn -- just her head -- coming up the steps from the ladies' room. I literally was surrounded and I couldn't get away, and Carolyn waved at me, and I waved to her, and she pointed like this, 'I'm going to the seats.' They finally had to call the ushers and a security man.

"The women in the theater were getting up out of their seats, mind you, and coming into the aisle to get to me.... This was a complete shock to me. And they were all standing up in the balconies and yelling '*Star Trek*' and '*McCoy*.' It was wild. Finally, they got me down to my seat and, when I sat down, we were in the middle of a row of nuns -- sisters on each side of us. So, people are in the aisles and they're passing programs over, and the nuns are handing me these programs, and I'm signing them. It was such a mess that they were holding the curtain of the show, there was so much noise. This nun that was sitting next to me, she said, 'This must be a terrible annoyance for you wherever you go.' ... It was equally as bad getting out of there. I wanted to go backstage and say hello to Joel Grey, but I couldn't. The ushers came and got me, surrounded me, got me to the side of the theater and put me in a cab like a mechanical doll or something. That was the first time I was ever mobbed, and it was completely shocking." (98-8)

Trying to explain all the *Star Trek*-mania, William Shatner said, "It has action-adventure, with lots of fights and villains, so the kids like it. On another level we deal with a philosophical concept - - that what's alien isn't necessarily evil - - so we reach their parents. Many of our episodes deal with scientific concepts, so our program entertains the technicians and space scientists. And with the hippies we have a far-out show. They think we're psychedelic." (166-20)

And the legions of fans continued to grow. Regardless, nearly all involved with the series believed the second season would be their last.

Tuesday, January 9, 1968. The cast and crew of *Star Trek* finished filming "Assignment: Earth." Advertising writer Stephen Poe was there, taking notes for a later book, *The Making of Star Trek*. The book would be credited to both Gene Roddenberry and Stephen E. Whitfield, Poe's pseudonym. His observation of the wrap party was "a strange affair -- a mixture of party atmosphere and half-voiced despair." (181)

Those gathered shared recollections and humorous speeches, but the mood on Stage 9 was dampened by the possibility that this would be the last such gathering. NBC had dragged their feet ordering the final episodes for the second season until the last possible moment. And then the network's option to make it a 28-episode season instead of a 26-episode season was not exercised. Not a positive sign for a third year commitment.

No one talked of their worries. Nothing was to be accomplished by it. The celebrating came to an end. The crowd dwindled. By midnight, only one person was left.

Poe said, "I remember standing there, alone in the middle of the darkened stage, after everyone had gone. It was an incongruous sight -- paper cups, plates, and napkins scattered about -- the make-shift bar standing beside the engineering room -- the remnants of a 20th century party mixed in with the interior of a 23rd century starship. A starship that might never again go a-voyaging through the uncharted reaches of space. I experienced the sadness then -- I knew how the others felt -- and understood."

***

620

In early 1968, history was made on television. It didn't have to do with the first televised presidential debate, which changed the course of an election, or when a teary-eyed Walter Cronkite told us President Kennedy had died, or when the Beatles appeared on *The Ed Sullivan* show to the largest TV audience ever assembled, or when man first walked on the moon and the event was seen around the world. This moment had to do with the "Save *Star Trek* Campaign." This moment in history had its beginning five months earlier.

October 17, 1967. Gene Roddenberry sent a memo to his staff.

> NBC informs us that *Star Trek* has now passed *The Monkees* and is the Number One show in all the nation in Fan Mail received! Not only this, but every report is that *Star Trek*'s fan response is by far the most devoted and enthusiastic by all measurements.

Many of the letters pleaded with the network to move the series back to Thursday nights, or to any night other than Friday. One letter, typical of so many, came from a college administrator at the University of Wisconsin. It read:

> Last year my students told me about *Star Trek*, and I have been a faithful watcher ever since. I really enjoy the maturity of the plot line on most of the programs in the series, and the occasional shows which utilize humor are very entertaining.... In my position I receive quite a bit of feedback from the student body and both their and my only complaint is the scheduling of the show. Friday night is usually "night out" on the campus and we are all having to decide between *Star Trek* and the local beer emporium. We all love *Star Trek*, but could you please schedule it on another night?

The college administrator was one of tens of thousands who took the time to write in, and one of millions who shared these feelings. Two others were John and Bjo Trimble, the science fiction enthusiasts Roddenberry had met at the convention he visited on Labor Day weekend of 1966. They had since become V.I.P.s on the *Star Trek* set, and were visiting in October when rumors were circulating that the series would soon be cancelled.

Bjo Trimble said, "We were talking about that while driving back to Oakland. My husband started all of this. He said, 'You know, that was very sad. There ought to be something we can do about this.' Now, that's a dangerous thing to say to me. So, the rest of the way home we talked about a way to get a hold of the fans and let them know what was happening, because the networks would not let anyone know. They'd just say 'This has been cancelled,' when it was too late to do anything about it." (177-8)

The time needed to drive from Los Angeles to Oakland is roughly six hours. The Trimbles took that time to come up with a battle plan to save *Star Trek*.

So we kind of worked out a way to reach the fans -- and, remember, this is way before computers. It would involve an extensive mailing campaign, but we thought we could pull it off because we knew science fiction fans, and we figured we could get some mailing lists from people and so on. As we got home, I said, 'We'd better call Gene and find out if he wants us to do this, because, if he's thrown in the towel, this could be a wasted effort on our part. So we phoned Gene, and he had just come out of a meeting where he had said, 'If there was only some way we could reach the fans.' It was an amazing coincidence. I said, 'We would like access to *Star Trek*'s fan mail, if possible, and get addresses from that. We're also writing and phoning to see if we can get TriCon's mailing list, and also from a dealer or two that we knew who had extensive mailing lists.' Of course, Gene wanted to get his hands in there, and we said, '<u>No</u>, you cannot be involved, because that's the first thing NBC's going to accuse you of.' They'll say, 'You manipulated this; you paid for this, and all of that.' We said, 'You cannot do this, otherwise it undermines the whole fan effort.' So he reluctantly didn't pay for any of our costs, except toward the end when we had one more push to make and were out of money." (177-8)

The Trimbles contacted friends at the World Science Fiction Convention, asking for their mailing lists. A bookseller the Trimbles knew provided them with a list of people who had special-ordered science fiction books. Roddenberry helped by raiding the Paramount mailroom, confiscating several sacks of *Star Trek* fan mail.

December 1, 1967. Bjo Trimble drafted a letter that she and her husband mimeographed and mailed to hundreds of *Star Trek* fans and dozens of science fiction fanzines. The announcement read:

> Action <u>NOW</u> is of the essence.... I just got a call from Gene Roddenberry... it is highly likely that *Star Trek* will die if something isn't done.... [W]e don't have much time to work.... Morton Werner, head of programming for NBC-TV, Rockefeller Center, New York, is one of the main people who will decide whether or not *Star Trek* lives. Letters should be personally addressed to him.... We want to combat the good ol' traditional American attitude of 'well, my one vote won't count much...' because your one tiny letter just may be <u>the</u> letter that topples the scales in the right direction. If thousands of fans just sit around moaning about the death of *Star Trek*, they will get exactly what they deserve: *Gomer Pyle*!... But if thousands of fans get off their big fat typers and W*R*I*T*E letters, and do it soon (like, <u>NOW</u>), it could happen that the man in charge of this sort of thing will be more impressed with our letters than with the damned Nielsen ratings.... So pass the word, and write some letters, people; it's up to us fans to keep *Star Trek* on TV. Our own inaction will assure that it never sees a third season!

December 6, 1967. Mixed signals were coming from the network. Stephen (Poe) Whitfield, who had been meeting with NBC executives in New York, shared the results of one of those meetings in a letter to Roddenberry. He wrote:

> During the course of the conversation, Norman [Lunenfeld] admitted that, at one point in the past, concerns had been expressed as to whether *Star Trek* could stay on the air. Now, however, all concerned seem to feel that the show has gotten so strong, and is getting stronger, that it is settling down for a nice, long run.

Roddenberry didn't believe it. He had no trust in the network, so he encouraged Bjo Trimble to proceed with the "Save *Star Trek* Campaign." Interviewed for this book, she said, "When the idea hit us to do this, it was right about the time we were moving from Oakland down to Los Angeles. We moved into a funky old house off Wilshire that we got for a good price; and we weren't far from the studio. And we had some fans around us that we talked to and corresponded with. So our weekend mailing party had about three dozen people. A couple of them stayed overnight -- just slept on the floor. And John went out to the Post Office and learned that brand new coding system -- zip code. It had just been introduced, and we were told the only way to send bulk mail was if we sorted it by zip code. So we had boxes all over the house and we tossed all the stuff to be sorted into that, and then John bundled it and took it down to the Post Office. We burned up three little home folding machines before we said, 'Oh the heck with that,' and got people to fold. We had a mimeograph machine in our basement and one weekend we had a full couple days of printing, labeling, stamping, folding, and getting mail ready, and Gene did send over a catering truck with a couple of cases of soft drinks and a giant tray of lunch stuff. I called him and said, 'Gene, I accept this because we're rather low on food funds. This is lovely, but don't do it again.' Because we really didn't want any touch of Gene being part of this. Everyone learned to either love or hate spaghetti and chili because it was all we could afford. But we were all working toward a major common goal. The letters went out and said, 'To continue this campaign, we need help.' We would get dollar bills, and we'd get rolls of stamps; we would open an envelope and it would have a $50 bill; and then reams of paper left on our doorstep. The fans really caught on to it and they responded. Oh my God, they responded.." (177-8)

NBC admitted to receiving about 6,000 letters a week. Trimble believed the numbers were much higher. Interviewed by David Gerrold in *The World of Star Trek*, she said, "We mailed out these flyers listing all this information to about 800 people -- the mailing list of the last big science fiction convention, so we were reaching right away much of science fiction fandom. My main point in the cover letter was, 'See how many other people you can reach.' And people would then write back and say, 'Send me more flyers, I can run them through my local company paper.' ... One man Xeroxed his letter and sent it through all the departments of the largest Polaroid division. And Polaroid turned out to be one of the holding companies that owned NBC corporation. Employees above a certain level owned stock in the company, so that provided a little irony because they were writing in to NBC as stockholders.... Several college newspapers either duplicated the letter or told people where to write.... *The Kansas City Star Tribune* phoned us and we gave them an hour-and-a-half interview... and got hundreds of letters in response because they reprinted our address in the article.... High school kids would write in for more letters and pass them out to friends.... Several high school newspapers repeated the information.... One employee from NASA wrote us from Texas.... And a SAC officer, out of the main SAC base, wherever that is, wrote and asked for 50 copies.... Mensa, which is a social club for geniuses, copied our letter entirely in their official newspaper, and that went out to about 6,000 members of the organization.... This kind of thing went on for weeks.... We found we had created a monster."

A future member of Mensa, Thomas West, was 13 in 1968. He recalled, "Having been interested in science since the ripe old age of as far back as I can remember, *Star Trek* felt [like it was] written for me. I had seen every *Trek* episode as it premiered [and] I learned much about who I am and how to think of the world around me from Kirk, Bones, Spock, and Scotty. When I heard it was being cancelled, it felt as I would be losing family members… and the food for thought in so many areas of existence. I don't remember where or how I heard of the letter writing campaign. I only remember something about 'Trekkers Unite' and writing a letter to the address I had." (180aa)

With the influx of mail growing on a daily basis, NBC started an investigation to find the culprit behind the organized protest. As Trimble had predicted, the network immediately focused on Roddenberry, but could uncover nothing to tie him with the letter writing campaign.

Trimble said, "There were a great many people around Gene who had no idea what we were doing. When we came to visit, Gene was always very careful to keep it 'fan visiting set.' We kept it that way, too.... NBC kept accusing Gene and looking around Paramount to find out who was doing this, but no one really knew. Only Majel [Barrett] and one or two other people who were close to Gene knew." (177-5)

The domino effect had begun. Trimble said, "We'd get letters from people from all over the country, telling us what they were doing to help; like we got a letter from some kid who said, 'I went around town and collected 50 names.' Their efforts were just wonderful. We were so touched and so amazed. And this was all before computers. Unfortunately, we later found out that NBC counted each petition as just one letter. And they did this with all the petitions. Even though you collected 50 signatures, it just counted as one." (177-8)

Learning as she went along, Bjo Trimble revised her letter from the "Committee to Save STAR TREK" to read, in part:

A. Petitions seem to be a waste of time. One thousand letters seem to have much more effect than a single petition signed with even ten thousand names. It's that bulging mailbag that really impresses them.

B. Never mention STAR TREK on the envelope of your letter to a network or TV station, as this only results in it being forwarded unopened to Gene Roddenberry. If possible, use a typewriter to address the envelope or use business or school letterhead envelopes if they are available. Sloppy letters which appear to come from minors are often shunted aside without being opened.

C. In addition to sending letters to NBC, good targets are home town newspaper TV columnists, home town TV stations carrying NBC shows, Paramount studios, Inc., in Hollywood, California, and TV GUIDE. Of course, the inventiveness of STAR TREK fans has taken the campaign into weird and wonderful directions too. Examples are "Bring Back STAR TREK" bumper strips on every taxi cab in a home town, friendly pressure on government officials for help, "Mister Spock for Mayor" write-in campaigns during election years, and so on. Actually anything will work that results in news publicity.

D. Avoid the situation where fans use the same words or phrases in their letters or telegrams. When everyone is saying almost exactly the same thing, it appears to be an organized campaign, and they refuse to believe it's us but instead suspect the whole thing is merely Gene Roddenberry stirring up discontent in the hinterlands.

Letters were soon arriving at NBC by the tens of thousands. Trimble said, "By now the news media had gotten wind of all this, and NBC was steadfastly denying that they were receiving any amount of mail that would affect their decision. We learned about how many letters NBC really received in a roundabout way.... one of the people who worked at the company NBC used [to correlate mail].... NBC was lying to everyone." (177-5)

December, 1967. NBC was learning exactly how devoted *Star Trek*'s fan base was. As a result, and as reported by *Variety* in the last days of 1967, the network decided to move *Star Trek* to a better night... although a later time slot.

Science Fiction Times reported in its January 1968 issue:

Beginning this month *Star Trek* will be seen at 10 p.m. on Monday, replacing *I*

624

Spy. According to *Variety*, the move was made to get *I Spy* to an earlier hour because it was losing viewers. *Star Trek* was put in the 10:00 slot because it was felt that it had an audience who would devotedly follow it to the new hour.

The fanzine newsletter also covered the "New Campaign to Save *Star Trek*" and printed the latest letter from Bjo Trimble, calling on fans to write NBC.

The new time slot never materialized. *I Spy* remained at 10 p.m. on Monday, locking horns with *The Carol Burnett Show*. *Star Trek* remained at 8:30 p.m. Friday, battling *Gomer Pyle* and the start of *The CBS Friday Night Movie*. The NBC Friday night schedule depended on it.

Encouraged by indications that NBC was taking a bashing, Roddenberry personally paid for the printing of several thousand bumper stickers. One said "I Grok Spock," and another read, "*Star Trek* Lives!" And, oh yes, "Spock for President."

Roddenberry wanted to hit NBC close to home. He put a bug in the Trimbles' ears that if stickers were given to local fans, these *Star Trek* enthusiasts could sneak onto the NBC parking lot and target cars belonging to the network executives. Bjo Trimble telephoned a group of especially radical Cal Tech fans who had already offered to storm the halls of the network. They agreed to handle the West Coast offices.

Trimble wrote about this in one of her communications to the fans, saying:

> Keep in mind that a good sense of humor will secure far more publicity than single-minded zealousness. For example, we have always had a secret place in our hearts for the Cal Tech students who got into the exclusive executive men's room at NBC and put "Save STAR TREK" stickers on all the washbowl mirrors. Even one NBC vice-president laughed at that. (He's the grey-haired fellow there who starts the elevators now.)

Another obsessively-driven fan, Wanda Kendall, met with Roddenberry and volunteered to fly to New York and single-handedly assault Rockefeller Center. He paid the $350 to get her to New York and back. Bjo Trimble said, "Wanda Kendall was not part of our group. She worked over at Universal and lived out at the far end of the San Fernando Valley. When she finished her workday, she would go around in the Universal building and try to drum-up support, until she was asked to stop. Gene picked her for several reasons -- one was that she was a good belly dancer; she came to one of their parties and danced. And she was a remarkably pretty girl. She looked like what everybody thought Wonder Woman should look like. And, remember, those were the days of short dresses." (177-8)

Kendall told David Alexander, author of *Star Trek Creator*, "I was handing out bumper stickers on the street, [and] was interviewed by some newspapers while I was there. But [I] thought I should be able to put these bumper stickers on cars that count, NBC executives. Of course, they weren't going to let me into the NBC parking lot, so I watched to see what was going on. I saw that the limousine drivers would frequently stop, get out and talk to the guard at the gate before they went in and picked up their passenger.... I waited until one of them did that and, when the limo was empty, I climbed into the back with all my bumper stickers and hid until he drove in. When the driver got out, I jumped out and began plastering bumper stickers everywhere I could.... I spent a good amount of time in the executive parking area and probably decorated between 200 and 300 bumpers, almost all of them Lincolns and Cadillacs.... Later, I managed to find a couple of *Star Trek* fans who got me into the executive offices. I was ushered into private offices where I left 'Mr. Spock for President' bumper stickers on desks. I laid them on desks, I didn't stick them on any desks. I also pinned them to office bulletin boards everywhere I could."

Bjo Trimble said, "Wanda Kendall wandered through the NBC offices back East. And, probably because she was a very, very pretty girl, nobody stopped her. And she was handing out 'I Grok Spock' bumper stickers and information about *Star Trek* to the secretaries. She went to lunch with one, and this secretary told her that one of the [network's key] efforts was going to be to kill off *Star Trek*. And it was because Gene Roddenberry was such a loose cannon." (177-8)

January 6, 1968. On Saturday night, when "Assignment: Earth" was being filmed, approximately 1,000 protestors [the numbers vary depending on the source] marched on NBC Burbank. The network had been tipped-off about the demonstration. Cal Tech students had been granted a permit from the city to parade in front of the network building.

KRLA, the number one Top 40 radio station in Los Angeles, helped promote the event. The day of the march, between turntable spins of The Beatles' "Hello Goodbye" and The Monkees' "Daydream Believer," listeners heard the stirring announcement over *Star Trek* theme music:

> KRLA proudly joins the courageous scientists at the California Institute of Technology in their fight to save *Star Trek* from cancellation. Shoulder to shoulder we shall blend our many voices in a mighty chorus of protest to General Bob Sarnoff [Chairman of the Board and President of NBC]. Save *Star Trek* from cancellation! Join the "Save *Star Trek* Committee" in a torchlight parade and march on the NBC Studios in Burbank this Saturday night. Armed with picket signs and torches, we shall overcome! Beginning our march at Verdugo Park at 8 p.m., save *Star Trek* tonight!

A meeting of network executives was quickly arranged. Present were NBC Vice President Herb Schlosser; another V.P., Henry "Hank" Rieger; Director of Current Programs Jerry Stanley; Facilities Vice President Dick Welsh; and Legal Vice President Richard Harper Graham. Two would be chosen to stay late and meet the protestors. None wanted the job. Rieger and Stanley were drafted.

"Save *Star Trek*" rally, January 1968

The marchers were reportedly spearheaded by 300 students from Cal Tech. The second largest contingent was from USC. Other participants came from the University of Arizona and the University of Nevada. They carried signs that read, "It is totally illogical to cancel *Star Trek*," "Make logic, not cancellation," and "Pointed Ears Forever."

Hank Rieger and Jerry Stanley met the protestors with a prepared statement. "NBC appreciates your interest in *Star Trek*. We, here on the West Coast, support a renewal. Your views will definitely be considered by our management in New York."

It wasn't just a line to placate the crowd. New York was not only watching, they were actually worried.

Hank Rieger told *Inside Star Trek: The Real Story*, "In all my years in the business, I've never heard of anything like this happening."

January 8, 1969. In his column for *Daily Variety*, Jack Hellman wrote:

> You have Hank Rieger's word for it that NBC has no intention at this time of yanking *Star Trek*. He has the support of Nielsen's 16.5 rating and 28% share. We know of a dozen shows that would settle for that.

Star Trek began the second season in the Bottom 20. Out of 85 prime time series, with a 16.5 rating, it was now fluctuating between Number #55 and #65. No other Friday night show was doing better ... except for *Gomer Pyle* and *The CBS Friday Night Movie*. But no official word of renewal had come. No time slot had been offered. Was the statement from Hank Reiger just a ploy to head-off further protests?

January 9, 1968. Roddenberry wrote a letter to Isaac Asimov, saying:

> Although we knew it was going to happen, it was the students' idea to do it and we very carefully stayed out of the picture. I did ride my motorcycle up, disguised by the hard hat and plastic face shield, [and] watched from a distance. I was pretty safe since I looked rather like a member of 'Hells Angels' and this is hardly the image NBC executives have of its executive producers. [I] almost froze to death during it since the march happened at 8:00 p.m. and it was getting down to freezing in Burbank at that time.... Rather exciting. They marched from a nearby park and they could be heard coming several blocks away as they chanted various slogans. It was a torchlight parade, extremely well ordered and mannerly. They had a parade permit from the Burbank Police Department, who stopped traffic at the intersections for the kids. In fact, the Police were very complimentary.

January 20, 1968. *TV Guide* announced that the magazine had been inundated by a "surprising" amount of letters "protesting against possible cancellation of *Star Trek*." Yet the official word from NBC, according to the editor, was that "there are no plans to cancel the popular show."

January 20, 1968. *San Mateo Times* (California) conducted a television ratings poll of its own, in which 2,533 readers were asked what their favorite current network shows were. The Top 10 were as follows: 1) *Star Trek*, 2) *Mission: Impossible*, 3) *Ironside*, 4) *The FBI*, 5) *The Monkees*, 6) *Garrison's Gorillas*, 7) *The Avengers*, 8) *The Invaders*, 9) *I Spy*, 10) *The Flying Nun*.

627

Polling 2,533 people constituted such an in-depth survey for a single market that, when the results were sent to NBC-Burbank, an impressed network official commented, "That's a bigger audience sample than the [one we get from] A.C. Nielsen or Arbitron!"

January 27, 1968. *TV Guide* followed up when Richard K. Doan, for "The Doan Report," wrote:

> Again, as it was last year, NBC is being hammered by an organized "Save *Star Trek*" campaign, allegedly instigated by a sci-fi magazine. Some of the letters, coming in at a rate of 1,000 a week, threaten to blow up the network if the series is canceled. NBC officials vow no decision has been reached, saying none is likely, on any show, until close to Valentine's Day [February 14]. Rating-wise, *Star Trek* is a borderline case.

January 29, 1968. *Newsweek*, with "End of Trek?," reported on the march, which they tallied as having 500 protestors. The story alleged that NBC had recently received 16,000 letters, including a petition signed by 1,764 students in Ohio, and a letter from an Oregon Rocket Society. It went on to say Canadian fans took out newspaper ads to unite other fans to save the show. Despite the outpouring of fan enthusiasm, 20% of the NBC network's affiliates preferred placing *The Grand Ole Opry* in *Star Trek*'s Friday night time slot [although nearly all carried *Star Trek*, showing better sense than their network and scheduling it to air on a different night of the week]. Roddenberry, quoted for the article, said, "What frightens me is that what we see on TV depends only on whether it will sell deodorant."

The dig did not help Roddenberry's already-strained relationship with the network ... and TV sponsors. But comments in the press such as this did help fuel the flames behind the letter writing campaign.

"Our campaign kept building and building as word of it got around," Trimble said. "This was early 1968 already, and there had been protest marches against NBC in Los Angeles, New York, and San Francisco. All in all, I'd say we sent out about 4,000 flyers to people all over the country.... At last, Gene Roddenberry's secretary, Penny Unger, heard that the mail to NBC had topped one million pieces, and we were all pretty jubilant about that." (177-7)

One such letter, dated January 31, 1968, read:

> Just a few lines to let you know we loyal *Star Trek* fans here in Georgia are rebelling against NBC. We just heard that they're threatening to take it off next season, and [we] have banded together for a fight to the finish. *Star Trek* has more fans than you can imagine, but television is about to find out just how many. We've sent the hue and cry all over the cotton-pickin' country, and even as I write this, letters of protest are pouring into Mr. Mort Werner's office in New York.... We are sincerely hoping our support will halt this idiotic talk of cancellation and keep our favorite show on the air for many long seasons.... At any rate, we're very appreciative of having had even one season of rare literary genius in a weekly series. Mr. Spock is so uniquely original that he brings tears of envy from the eyes of any writer who ever cursed a typewriter. I couldn't love the Enterprise's crew any more if they were my own creation.... As a fellow writer, I salute you! May your literary superiority inspire other writers as it has inspired me. *Star Trek* will live forever in the hearts of its fans. Sincerely Yours, Susan E. Spaeth. Cornelia, Georgia.

Spaeth was 20 when she wrote this letter. She went on to be a successful writer, under the name of Diana Palmer, and by 2013 she had published nearly one hundred books.

January 31, 1968. *Variety* reported that, because of "whacking mail," NBC was leaning toward renewing *Star Trek*, with it on the first rough draft of the fall schedule, as the network's "leadoff hour" on Friday nights at 7:30 p.m.

The fans weren't buying it.

Doug Drexler, who was an avid *Star Trek* fan, living in his family's home on Long Island, New York, recalled, "The first I'd heard of it was a letter from Bjo. And I remember it as being a cold hand closing over my heart, because back then when you cancelled a show, it was just like killing everybody on the show. You couldn't buy a video tape. And, if you were lucky, maybe it would be syndicated later on. So I got this thing from Bjo and I snapped right away into being very militant. She had guidelines of who to write to and how to address people and things like that. And I literally went on a campaign at school and was stopping everybody. And I made flyers that I would pass out. I organized the Centereach Committee to save *Star Trek*. And I organized a core group of people who were writing letters every single day. I think it was Julian Goodman, the President of NBC at the time. We were writing to him. And, of course, I was writing to all the local newspapers. And I wrote the *Long Island Press*, and I wrote *Newsday* and *The Daily News*. And the *Press* responded with an article and mentioned us in it. But *Newsday* really came through. I was in class and I got called to the principal's office and I didn't know why. I got there and there was Bobby Erikson, who apparently was like a cousin of Isaac Asimov. And he called the school and asked for me, and I was interviewed and it appeared in the newspaper in a day or two." (52a)

February 1, 1968. Bobby Erikson's interview with Doug Drexler appeared in Harvey Aronson column for *Newsday* with the headline, "This Group Isn't Way Out, But Its Cause Is." Aronson wrote:

> One of the great qualities about young people today is their willingness to commit themselves to causes. They're out there fighting for what matters. They are willing to put their ideals on the line. They are willing to be ... well, political. There is the new left and the new right, and then there is the Centereach Committee to Save *Star Trek*. That's right, the Centereach Committee to Save *Star Trek*. The committee is a 20-man action group from Dawnwood Junior High School headed by Douglas Drexler, a 14-year-old idealist. Or, as Douglas explains his role, "I'm the instigator. I make the other kids write to NBC. We're writing every day." ... The letters, as every intellectual in the country well knows, are part of a national movement to save television's *Star Trek*, a first-rate show about a spaceship's crew traveling through the universe.... Obviously, and I should admit this at the outset. I'm prejudiced. I think it's right up there with *The Avengers*.... Anyway, people started writing letters after it was announced that NBC had filled *Star Trek*'s current time slot with a new show for next season [*The Name of the Game*]. To date, the network has received more than 20,000 letters, and the program is being given a 50-50 chance of survival. A key point here is whether the letters will help. Normally, they don't. Or as an NBC spokesman laid it on the line, "They might help, and they might not." But the important thing is that Douglas Drexler and the other members of the Centereach Committee to Save *Star Trek* care. They're taking an interest in their community;

629

they're trying to save a shaky culture from the ravages of situation comedies and Jerry Lewis. They're out there in the mails trying to hold off the Philistines. Or as Douglas tells it like it is: "I don't think television can afford to lose such a show -- a show that so boldly predicts man's future." ... The show's producer says he has received fan letters from such persons as science fiction writer Isaac Asimov and Gov. Rockefeller. Asimov confirmed this yesterday. "I'm a bug on *Star Trek*," he said. "It's the only program that makes a serious and solemn attempt to present adult science fiction to a mass adult audience." What's more, he said, the fight to save *Star Trek* is the cause *célèbre* of science fiction fans these days.... When I was a kid, we were wasting our time sending away for Lone Ranger rings and playing cards behind the candy store. We were grown kids playing with bottle caps, and flipping bubble gun cards. That's why today's kids have it all over us. At least, they care about what matters. They ask for values, and we give them phoniness. Pap. That's what we give them. *Gilligan's Island* and *Peyton Place* -- that's how we sell them out. And now we want to take away *Star Trek*, which has to be an oasis of meaning in a desert of inanity. I'm glad these young people are getting involved, and I think it's healthy that *Star Trek* pickets have appeared at Radio City in New York and the Burbank studios in Los Angeles. And I agree with Douglas Drexler, who's not afraid to speak his mind. Or as he throws down the gauntlet: "I pity NBC if *Star Trek* goes off the air."

Drexler said, "All of a sudden I was like a celebrity in school. I had been the kid who wasn't hip and kind of weird, and kinky, like the man from Mars, and all of a sudden this weird guy was cool. In every class I went to that day, the teacher read the article to the whole class. It not only changed things for me at school, but it made me realize that a kid could have some kind of an impact that a newspaper would write an article." (52a)

February 1, 1968. Isaac Asimov wrote to Roddenberry:

I am told *Star Trek* has been cancelled, but apparently the fight goes on. Two newspapers have already called me for an estimate of its worth and I gave them an earful.

February 1, 1968. Roddenberry dashed off a letter to Herb Schlosser, NBC's Vice President of Programming. He pointed out that the fan mail being received at Paramount each week was exceeding 6,000 letters. Local polls across the nation showed *Star Trek* to be an audience favorite. One sample, from the previous week, rated the series as "first with youth" *and* "first with adults."

In addition, the stars of *Star Trek* rated exceptionally high. Dean Martin was found to be the "favorite screen personality," but Leonard Nimoy came in second on that popularity list, and William Shatner came in third. Roddenberry also informed the network that AMT's Enterprise "is now [the] top selling model kit in toy history."

Roddenberry continued:

Literally dozens of top TV newspaper writers, in only the last few weeks, have begun to equate *Star Trek* with TV's all time finest programs.... Whether first season on Thursday or second season on Friday, *Star Trek* has moved steadily upward, finally reaching top NBC show for the evening. Friday was an honest scheduling mistake and no one argues now that *Tarzan* was the ideal lead in not for *Star Trek* but for *Gomer Pyle*. And analysis of Friday ratings must take into account *Star Trek* was followed [on NBC] by one and one half hours of disaster programs (*Accidental Family* and *Bell Telephone Hour*). It also had the dubious distinction of coming up against more blockbuster movies than any other NBC show, including *The Great Escape, Music Man, A Shot in the Dark*, and *The Apartment*.

In conclusion, Roddenberry promised, if the network were to renew *Star Trek* for a third year, he would buy scripts only from established *Star Trek* writers. Gene Coon was committed to provide six, with the same number from D.C. Fontana, and they could count on eight scripts from Roddenberry himself.

February 9, 1968. An unnamed NBC spokesman admitted to syndicated columnist Ernie Kreiling that "It's probably the greatest letter writing campaign in NBC history." The network man credited, or blamed, three science fiction magazines, *Galaxy, If*, and *Analog*, with sparking the campaign to save *Star Trek*. On this day, the network was estimating the odds 60-40 that *Star Trek* would continue. NBC had blinked.

February 10, 1968. *TV Guide*'s Richard K. Doan reported, for the "Nervous Nellie days in network telly, the programmers are sweating out what CBS's Mike Dann characterizes as 'the huge annual chess game' of scheduling next season's shows." At the top of the list: "NBC was still weighing what to do about *Star Trek*."

From the letters section in the same issue, R. Osborne of Paterson, New Jersey, wrote:

NBC shouldn't even think of canceling *Star Trek*, the most literate, original, and thought-provoking series. TV's image is already badly tarnished; should *Star Trek* be canceled, its image will be shattered beyond repair.

February 11, 1968. A wire news story picked up by numerous newspapers reported:

NBC and television columnists all over the country have been bombarded for the past several months with letters from *Star Trek* fans expressing alarm over a report that the science fiction series would be cancelled... Within the next few days, a decision will be made whether to give *Star Trek* a third network season or drop it at the end of summer reruns... The program actually has an excellent chance for survival. In the three-cornered network fight for audiences, it usually comes in second -- and the tough competition is CBS's *Gomer Pyle* and feature movies... NBC, too, is happy that the series has a special appeal to what the researchers call a "quality audience." ... Networks make their program decisions with the help of information gathered by research outfits. And most sponsors who scatter their messages over programs are concerned with the cost of reaching potential customers. The cost of reaching 1,000 homes now averages $4.30 in prime evening time. NBC's [*Bell*] *Telephone Hour* [following *Star Trek* on Friday nights], for instance, has a cost per thousand of $13, since the smaller the audience, the higher the cost. *Star Trek* costs $4.70 per thousand, but as one research man observed, "The sponsors get that quality audience."

February 12, 1968. *Broadcasting* magazine reported that NBC "network and agency sources" still had an "iffy" list, which included *Star Trek*'s lead-in series, *Tarzan*. Of the ten series originally on the list, three were now definitely cancelled, and two were leaning toward being saved. Of those two, and supporting the report in *Variety* from a week and a half earlier, *Broadcasting* wrote:

> *The Jerry Lewis Show* may return but in an earlier time period and *Star Trek* probably will also be scheduled in a new time period.

February 16, 1968. Headline on the front page of *Daily Variety* read, "Hint Renewal of *Star Trek* on NBC." The trade paper reported:

> A strong indication of possible renewal for Paramount TV's *Star Trek* series for next season came yesterday when NBC okayed $10,000 for preparation of scripts for term. Exec producer Gene Roddenberry received the greenlight for expenditure of coin, just as he neared the deadline for readying the sci-fi series. In another week, it would have been too late to rev up stories and plans for next fall, exec said.... *Trek* has been regarded as iffy for next season, but the NBC-TV move makes series a solid likelihood for the web's 1968-69 lineup.

February 17, 1968. More letters in *TV Guide*. N.H. Zimmer, from Metairie, Louisiana, wrote, "If NBC kills *Star Trek*, my 132 seventh-grade boys vow to use a phaser on our NBC affiliate." D. Hillman, of Burbank, California, wrote, "Dear Peacock: If the Enterprise leaves its Hollywood orbit, I'll pluck out your feathers -- one by one."

More letters appeared in *TV Guide* during the following weeks. From Tecumseh, Michigan:

> Greetings! We, the inhabitants of the Omicron Delta system, salute you. In *Star Trek*, you have finally created a television program worthy of intergalactic recognition. Should you discontinue it, we will have no alternative but to destroy your planet.

February 17, 1968. *TV Week*, a syndicated *TV Guide*-like magazine, featured Kirk, Spock, McCoy, and Uhura on the cover. The article within, by Marian Dern, reported:

> The fate of the U.S.S. Enterprise's trek lives not in the stars but in the offices of the NBC network in New York where the decision on cancellation or renewal of *Star Trek* will be made at any moment.... According to *TV Week*'s recent annual poll of readers, the show is Number One favorite of both adults and children. Other newspaper polls have also shown it to be a top choice.

February 18, 1968. *The New York Times* reported that *Star Trek* had been "suspended" by NBC.

February 19, 1968. *Broadcasting* reported that NBC was contemplating "retention" of *Star Trek* and might put it into its Monday night schedule with a 7:30 or 8 p.m. start time.

February 19, 1968. Roddenberry again wrote to Asimov, saying:

> Toward the end of last week we received $10,000 advance story money for a third season of *Star Trek*. While this does not mean we are definitely on the schedule, it does make things look very much better. NBC is notoriously cheap and I can't believe they'd spend $10,000 without a pretty fair intention of going a third season.... Latest rumors on this is that we are definitely back on the schedule [after having been firmly off it seven or eight weeks ago] and that our new time will probably be eight o'clock Monday, or seven-thirty Friday. The Monday time seems to be winning at the present moment.

Another correspondence from Roddenberry, also sent on February 19, this time to a writer friend, said:

> We heard from a New York source that letters to the Network passed the one million mark! It's hard to believe that figure and I'm trying to check up on it, but whatever the final tally, we do know the letters to NBC began to peak a couple of months ago and, at one time, I heard they received over 2,000 a day. Whatever the final tally, it's obvious now it was the all-time-high fan response to any show.... We were off the schedule, wiped out, finished, about six to eight weeks ago. But the letters kept coming, increasing in volume rather than leveling off. It upset them enough that a committee was formed of six Network Vice Presidents to investigate the matter. Shortly afterward, we began to reappear on the schedule again.

February 20, 1968. *Daily Variety* gives front page coverage with the headline "NBC High On *Trek*." The trade paper reported:

> While NBC has officially withheld any decision on the renewal of shows for next season, it was said by a spokesman for the network in Burbank that *Star Trek* is a certain holdover.

That was the word from the West Coast, anyway. As for the East, the article continued:

> NBC in N.Y. was quoted as saying that not until the entire schedule has been drafted will there be any definitive word on any single show.

Regardless, the network was hinting at *Star Trek* having Mondays at 7:30, replacing *The Monkees* and the first half of *Rowan & Martin's Laugh-In*, "likely" to be moved. The most recent episode of *The Monkees* had pulled a 17.5 rating. *Laugh-In* had an 18.8. *Star Trek*'s most recent episode garnered a 17.0 rating. The article discussed how, "In past seasons the cutoff was pegged at 20 rating and 30 audience share," but that "many other elements figure into the final decision of the network and sponsors, such as mail."

Beyond the mail, any show on a Friday night with damning competition that was only one-half to one-and-a-quarter ratings points under a pair of Monday shows with light competition certainly deserved to be a contender. That Monday night competition was the one-year-old and already cancelled *Cowboy in Africa* on ABC and *Gunsmoke*, in a thirteenth season and attracting an older audience demographic, on CBS.

February 21, 1968: In a letter to *Spockanalia*, Walter Koenig wrote:

> Mr. Roddenberry will again personally produce the show if the series is picked up for a third season, and he has assured me that Mr. Chekov will be developed in depth.... However, *Star Trek* has not been picked up officially at this writing and it would be premature for me to conjecture on the direction Mr. Chekov's character will go. Also, I'm a little superstitious and I'm queasy about jumping the gun.

February 21, 1968. *The Associated Press* carried a story titled "*Star Trek* is saved from cancellation ax." In the article, Cynthia Lowry wrote:

> *Star Trek* fans, who have been writing letters and picketing network headquarters to keep the show from being cancelled, may now relax. The program has

633

definitely been included in NBC's 1968-69 schedule and, provided sponsors can be found, will be among the survivors next September.

The loophole for NBC: "provided sponsors can be found."

February 21, 1968. *Weekly Variety* printed the "1st Draft" of the "TV Nets' 1968-69 Schedule." *Star Trek* was planned for Monday, 7:30 p.m., against *Gunsmoke* and a new series on ABC, *The Mod Squad*. Making room -- the cancellation of *The Monkees* and the shifting of *Rowan & Martin's Laugh-In* to Fridays at 10 p.m.

A separate report in the same issue ran with the headline, "*Star Trek* Saved from Death Row by Write-In Vote." There was no mention in this announcement that a sponsor was needed. The trade said:

> Most shows are saved by sponsors or by ratings. *Star Trek* has the distinction of being a series saved by postage stamps.... [T]he mail pull on the show has been terrific -- one of the greatest for a series in NBC's experience, according to those responsible for writing replies -- and, satisfied that the write-in has been spontaneous, the web is to give it another go in a different berth. In fact, the web is eager to circulate word that *Star Trek* is definitely back for next fall to reassure the agitated letter-writers. Most of the letters, a source says, are from highly literate people, many of them in the professional fields, including educators at college level. NBC has penciled it in for Mondays at 7:30 p.m., with word that it may not remain there but that its renewal is assured. The series might be assigned the Saturday 7:30 p.m. period instead.

February 27, 1968. Walter E. Whitaker of the National Aeronautics and Space Administration sent a letter to Edward Milkis, finalizing the permission needed for *Star Trek* to use NASA footage in the episode "Assignment: Earth." He added a personal note, telling Milkis:

> Good luck with this possible new series. We understand that *Star Trek* will continue next season and should have a better time slot. If this rumor is true, we offer congratulations to Gene Roddenberry and all of you.

Some of *Star Trek*'s most loyal viewers were those who worked at NASA.

March 1, 1968. Friday at 9:28 p.m. Following the first run airing of "The Omega Glory," NBC and *Star Trek* made history ... again. For the second year in a row, the network surrendered on-the-air. The voice of NBC said:

> And now an announcement of interest to all viewers of *Star Trek*. We are pleased to tell you that *Star Trek* will continue to be seen on NBC television. We know you will be looking forward to seeing the weekly adventures in space on *Star Trek*.

"We had no clue the show had been renewed," Bjo Trimble said. "And so when it hit, when they made the announcement, we were all watching, and over the credits came this voice. It was one of those -- 'Uh... did he really say that?' -- Because it was so unprecedented for any station to do that. And the phone just rang off the wall, with people calling in saying, 'Oh my God, did you hear that?!'" (177-8)

March 4, 1968. On Monday, NBC put it in writing -- with a press release. The network was anxious to get the word out through all avenues. The release read:

In response to unprecedented viewer reaction in support of the continuing of the NBC Television Network's *Star Trek* series, plans for continuing the series in the Fall were announced on NBC-TV immediately following last Friday night's episode of the space adventure series. The announcement will be repeated following next Friday's program [March 8].... From early December to date, NBC has received 114,667 pieces of mail in support of *Star Trek*, and 52,151 in the month of February alone.

Trimble said, "A few weeks later, NBC told *TV Guide* that they had gotten 200,000 pieces of mail. And, in subsequent years, that number has steadily dropped." (177-7)

The exact number of letters received by the network can never be known. As for the higher estimate, Trimble explained, "Gene got the 'million letters to NBC' thing from the young man who worked for the computer company that had processed all the letters. In those days, not even big businesses had much in the way of computers, so when they had some major stuff to be done, they'd send it out to one of the big mainframe computer houses. And this guy told Gene that they had processed a million letters." (177-8)

March 4, 1968. *Broadcasting* magazine printed the second draft of the network's 1968-69 schedule. *Star Trek* remained at 7:30 Monday night, with NBC asking $36,000 for one-minute of commercial time.

March 7, 1968. Roddenberry sent a memo to Shatner and Nimoy, saying:

Received a call from NBC today asking us to please ask the fans to "stop already!" It seems that in the last six days, since the announcement was made that *Star Trek* would stay on the air, they have already received over 70,000 letters thanking the network.

Trimble recalled, "Eventually, we had an NBC man from Burbank come out and talk to us on the *Star Trek* set one night, and he asked us if we would tell him how we had done it. How had we reached so many people so fast? And how had we gotten the information to them about who to write and how to address the envelope and how to phrase the letter politely? Of course, we didn't tell him. We might have to do it again someday." (177-7)

Trimble was clearly planning a fight for the next year. And so was NBC.

March 12, 1968. Knowing Paramount wouldn't share the information with NBC, Roddenberry billed the studio for his out-of-pocket expenses in the "Save *Star Trek* Campaign." The invoice included $303 for 5,000 bumper stickers, $263 for 54 *Star Trek* drinking glasses [given away to public relations people, the press, and some fans], $350 for sending Wanda Kendall to New York, and $60 for *Star Trek* t-shirts. The total bill: $977.

According to Herb Solow, NBC executives reacted angrily to all the manipulation.

March 16, 1968. *TV Guide* printed a letter from the top man at NBC. It read:

As most of your readers probably already know, NBC has renewed *Star Trek* for the 1968-69 season. While we were formulating next season's schedule, more than 100,000 viewers -- one of the largest totals in our history -- wrote or wired their support for *Star Trek*. Obviously, it is not possible to answer such a large volume of mail individually, so I, therefore, extend a general thanks on behalf of NBC management to your readers who took the time and trouble to communicate with us. The response was gratifying. Mort Werner, Vice

President, NBC Television Network, New York.

March 31, 1968. *Today's TV Tab* wrote:

> If you have watched *Star Trek* recently, you have heard the announcement at the end of the show saying the series will return next season. The joke around the studio where the series is filmed is that NBC made the announcement to stop the flood of mail that has been pouring in since the word got around that the series might be cancelled. But it didn't work. After the first announcement was made, over 77,000 letters saying "Thank you" came in within two days.

April 19, 1968. *Spockanalia* #2 was printed and put into the mail. Co-editors Sherna Comerford and Devra Langsam printed a missive from Dorothy Fontana. In part, Fontana said:

> We were off the NBC schedule -- dropped -- cancelled. The letters, marches, and all the rest of it were immeasurable help in getting us put back on the schedule.... The renewal was due to many factors -- over a million letters and petitions, the student protests, Gene Roddenberry's literate, reasonable and persuasive assault in personal trips to New York to speak to the decision-makers there. We had definitely been off the schedule -- and then the mail began to pour in. It cost NBC a great deal in hiring extra staff to answer it ... because much of it was from people of some standing in industry, professions and so on. These could not be answered by a routine form letter. So, we cost NBC some money -- and all of you kept us on the air.

June 15, 1968. Richard K. Doan, for *TV Guide*, in an attempt to explain network thinking, wrote:

> One way to look at it, suggests NBC's astute Paul Klein -- vice president, believe it or not, in charge of audience measurement -- is to think of TV as a colossal theater seating about twenty-three million people. Now, everything is relative, Klein points out. For example, the number of people it would take to fill a Broadway theater to overflowing would look like a mere handful in Yankee Stadium. So, in TV's theater, ten million doesn't look like very much. Fifteen, sixteen million isn't enough! Twenty million? Well, that'll do.... Klein is a big demographics man and he also sometimes thinks of the TV audience as a huge "people pie." He explains: "Nielsen ratings are home ratings. That's the wrong kind of pie. The right kind is people pie. For instance, we're dropping *Tarzan*, which was getting an acceptable home rating but hasn't been delivering the right kind of people. Too many kids and old ladies. *Tarzan* people are worth less to the advertiser than, say, *Star Trek* people. We're renewing *Star Trek* partly because we got 115,000 letters asking us to, but also because it delivers a quality, salable audience. It has as many upper-income, better-educated males watching as CBS has watching NFL football, which sells for about $65,000 a minute, while *Star Trek* costs the advertiser only about $40,000 a minute.

In the same issue, Roddenberry was quoted, saying, "The greatest single depressing quality in TV is how many viewers per dollar will determine what stays on the air. We are all prisoners of our commerce-dominated system. Television is getting worse and worse and worse, and I think it's got to get even worse before it gets better."

July 7, 1967. *The Los Angeles Times* printed pictures from "Journey to Babel" along

636

with the headline "All Systems 'Go' For *Star Trek*." The top newspaper in the show business capital of the world told us:

> To the delight of *Star Trek* partisans, all systems are "go" again on the U.S.S. Enterprise and the space craft will be visiting exotic galaxies for another season on NBC…. Toward the end of the season there were disturbing rumors circulating that NBC was canceling the series. Almost immediately, NBC was inundated with thousands of protests. Students from scientifically-oriented universities literally marched on NBC -- even delegations from MIT and Caltech. In a rare showing of candor, NBC admitted this had an "influence" on saving the series. The turn of events was so startling that it began to sound like a far-fetched science-fiction story. But *Star Trek* will return.

July 28, 1968. Uhura had the cover of *TV Magazine*, a Sunday television supplement carried by numerous newspapers in the U.S. The headline on the cover: "Startling Support for *Star Trek*." For the cover story, Frank Judge wrote:

> NBC did far more than threaten the fatal crash of a fictional spaceship when it planned the cancellation of *Star Trek*. It also set off the greatest save-the-show deluge of fan mail in television history.

And we're still talking about it today.

***

By the time Dorothy Fontana's statement about the remarkable accomplishment achieved by the fans appeared in the April 19, 1968 issue of *Spockanalia #2* … or Richard K. Doan explained NBC's thinking regarding the renewal in the June 18 issue of *TV Guide* … or Frank Judge wrote about how the letter writing campaign had made television history for the July 28 issue of *TV Magazine* … the sweet taste of victory had turned bitter for *Star Trek*. The fans, jubilant over the news that there would be a third season, didn't know it yet but decisions at NBC and Paramount, and subsequent reactive decisions by Gene Roddenberry, had pre-destined the third season of their favorite series to be the last. And the challenge to maintain the quality would be greater than ever.

Popular opinion tells us that the third season of the original *Star Trek* was the weakest. Few fans will debate that. Yet there are many good episodes that were produced for the third year, even some which would be fair to judge as excellent. And no one involved with the production was trying any less. No one had lost their talent. No one had stopped caring. So why was there a decline? The answers are many. And many of those are surprising.

The simple fact is … *Star Trek*'s most difficult battles were about to begin.

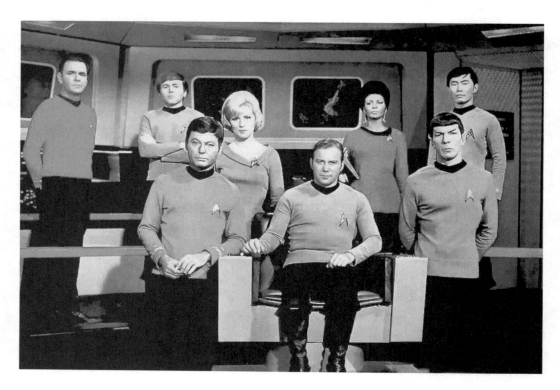

Preparing to do battle, May 1968
(Courtesy of Gerald Gurian)

APPENDIX / SEASON TWO QUICK REFERENCE:

STAR TREK first and second season story assignments (in order given):

ST #	Title:	Writer:
ST-1.	The Cage	Gene Roddenberry
2.	Where No Man Has Gone Before	Samuel A. Peeples
3.	The Omega Glory	Gene Roddenberry
4.	Warrior World	Stephen Kandel
4a.	Mudd's Women	Stephen Kandel; Roddenberry's story
5.	Dagger of the Mind	Shimon Wincelberg
6.	The Corbomite Maneuver	Jerry Sohl
7.	The City on the Edge of Forever	Harlan Ellison
8.	What Are Little Girls Made Of?	Robert Bloch
9.	The Naked Time	John D.F. Black
10.	The Machine That Went Too Far	A.E. van Vogt
11.	Chicago II	George C. Johnson; Roddenberry's idea
12.	Miri	Adrian Spies
13.	The Man Trap	Lee Erwin; reassigned to George C. Johnson
14.	The Enemy Within	Richard Matheson
15.	Alien Spirit	Norman Katkov
16.	The Galileo Seven	Oliver Crawford
17.	The Conscience of the King	Barry Trivers
18.	Balance of Terror	Paul Schneider
19.	Untitled	Jack Guss
20.	Journey to Reolite	Alfred Brenner
21.	Charlie X	D.C. Fontana; Gene Roddenberry's story
22.	Return to Eden	Alvin Boretz
23.	Court Martial	Don Mankiewicz
24.	Shore Leave	Theodore Sturgeon; Roddenberry's idea
25.	Rites of Fertility	Robert Sheckley
ST-1a.	From the First Day to the Last	John D.F. Black *
ST-1b.	The Menagerie	Gene Roddenberry *
26.	This Side of Paradise	Jerry Soul
27.	Sisters in Space	Robert Sheckley
28.	Portrait in Black & White	Barry Trivers; Roddenberry's concept
29.	Rock-A-Bye Baby or Die!	George Clayton Johnson
30.	The Squire of Gothos	Paul Schneider
31.	The Squaw	Shimon Wincelberg
32.	Accident of Love	Allen Balter & William Woodfield
33.	The Return of the Archons	Boris Sobelman; Gene Roddenberry's idea
34.	The Alternative Factor	Don Ingalls
35.	Space Seed (aka Botany Bay)	Carey Wilbur
36.	A Taste of Armageddon	Robert Hammer
37.	Dreadnought	Alf Harris & Jeeli Jacobs
38.	Tomorrow Is Yesterday	D.C. Fontana
39.	Arena	Gene L. Coon
40.	Tomorrow the Universe (aka World of Warriors)	Paul Schneider
41.	Amok Time	Theodore Sturgeon; Roddenberry's idea
42.	Operation: Annihilate! (aka Operation: Destroy)	Steven Carabatsos; Roddenberry's idea
43.	Friday's Child	D.C. Fontana
44.	The Devil in the Dark	Gene L. Coon
45.	Errand of Mercy	Gene L. Coon
46.	The Doomsday Machine	Norman Spinrad

47.	Mirror, Mirror	James Bixby
48.	Bread and Circuses	John Kneubuhl
49.	A Private Little War	Don Ingalls
50.	Who Mourns For Adonais?	Gilbert Ralston
51.	Catspaw	Robert Bloch
52.	The Wizard of Odd	Lewis Reed
53.	The Changeling	John Meredyth Lucas
54.	I, Mudd	Stephen Kandel
55.	The Orchid People	John Collie and Catherine Turney
56.	The Gamesters of Pentathalon (Triskelion)	Margaret Armen
57.	Space Moby Dick / Obsession	Art Wallace
58.	Return to Tomorrow	John Dugan
59.	Metamorphosis	Gene L. Coon
60.	The Apple	Max Ehrlich
61.	The Search for Eternity	A.E. van Vogt
62.	Wolf in the Fold	Robert Bloch
63.	Aladdin=s Asteroid	Robert Barry
64.	Shol	Darlene Hartman
65.	Journey to Babel	D.C. Fontana
66.	The Microbe	John Kneubuhl
67.	The Root of Evil (aka The Joy Machine)	Theodore Sturgeon
68.	The Lost Star	John Meredyth Lucas
69.	He Walked Among Us	Norman Spinrad
70.	The Deadly Years	David P. Harmon
71.	By Any Other Name	Jerome Bixby
72.	The Trouble with Tribbles	David Gerrold
73.	Patterns of Force	John Meredyth Lucas
74.	The Immunity Syndrome	Robert Sabaroff
75.	A Piece of the Action (aka Mission Into Chaos)	David P. Harmon
76.	The Omega Glory (version 2)	Les & Tina Pine; Gene Roddenberry's story
77.	Pandora=s Box	Daniel Aubrey
78.	Assignment: Earth	Art Wallace & Gene Roddenberry
79.	The Ultimate Computer	Laurence N. Wolfe
80.	Galatea of Polydor	Laurence N. Wolfe

* ST-1, "The Cage," was the first *Star Trek* story assignment. "From the First Day to the Last," catalogued as ST-1a, was John D.F. Black's envelope script designed to turn "The Cage" into a two-part episode. "The Menagerie," catalogued as ST-1b, was Gene Roddenberry's version of the envelope script.

STAR TREK second season episodes (in order filmed):

Prod #:	Title:	Director:	Days:
30.	Catspaw	Joseph Pevney	7 ¼
31.	Metamorphosis	Ralph Senensky	6 ½
32.	Friday's Child	D.C. Fontana	6 ¼
33.	Who Mourns For Adonais?	Marc Daniels	7
34.	Amok Time	Joseph Pevney	7
35.	The Doomsday Machine	Marc Daniels	5
36.	Wolf in the Fold	Joseph Pevney	6
37.	The Changeling	Marc Daniels	6 ¼
38.	The Apple	Joseph Pevney	6 ¾
39.	Mirror, Mirror	Marc Daniels	7 ½
40.	The Deadly Years	Joseph Pevney	6 ½
41.	I, Mudd	Marc Daniels	6
42.	The Trouble with Tribbles	Joseph Pevney	6
43.	Bread and Circuses	Ralph Senensky	7
44.	Journey to Babel	Joseph Pevney	6
45.	A Private Little War	Marc Daniels	6
46.	Obsession	Ralph Senensky	6
47.	The Gamesters of Triskelion	Gene Nelson	6
48.	The Immunity Syndrome	Joseph Pevney	6
49.	A Piece of the Action	James Komack	6
50.	By Any Other Name	Marc Daniels	6
51.	Return to Tomorrow	Ralph Senensky	6
52.	Patterns of Force	Vincent McEveety	6
53.	The Ultimate Computer	John Meredyth Lucas	6
54.	The Omega Glory	Vincent McEveety	7
55.	Assignment: Earth	Marc Daniels	7

STAR TREK second season broadcast schedule:

Air Date:	Title:
09/15/67	Amok Time
09/22/67	Who Mourns for Adonais?
09/29/67	The Changeling
10/06/67	Mirror, Mirror
10/13/67	The Apple
10/20/67	The Doomsday Machine
10/27/67	Catspaw
11/03/67	I, Mudd
11/10/67	Metamorphosis
11/17/67	Journey to Babel
11/24/67	(pre-emption) – Tijuana Brass Special
12/01/67	Friday's Child
12/08/67	The Deadly Years
12/15/67	Obsession
12/22/67	Wolf in the Fold
12/29/67	The Trouble with Tribbles
01/05/68	The Gamesters of Triskelion
01/12/68	A Piece of the Action
01/19/68	The Immunity Syndrome
01/26/68	(pre-emption) – Drama special "Flesh and Blood"
02/02/68	A Private Little War
02/09/68	Return to Tomorrow
02/16/68	Patterns of Force
02/23/68	By Any Other Name
03/01/68	The Omega Glory
03/08/68	The Ultimate Computer
03/15/68	Bread and Circuses
03/22/68	(pre-emption) – Ringling Brothers Circus Special
03/29/68	Assignment: Earth (*TV Guide* CLOSE-UP listing)
04/05/68	(repeat) – I, Mudd
04/12/68	(repeat) – Mirror, Mirror
04/19/68	(repeat) – The Doomsday Machine
04/26/68	(repeat) – Amok Time
05/03/68	(repeat) – The Gamesters of Triskelion
05/10/68	(repeat) – Who Mourns for Adonais?
05/17/68	(repeat) – The Changeling
05/24/68	(repeat) – Catspaw
05/31/68	(repeat) – By Any Other Name
06/07/68	(repeat) – The Immunity Syndrome
06/14/68	(pre-emption) – News special "The Art Game"
06/21/68	(repeat) – The Trouble with Tribbles
06/28/68	(repeat) – The Ultimate Computer
07/05/68	(repeat) – Journey to Babel
07/12/68	(repeat) – The Apple
07/19/68	(repeat) – Metamorphosis (*TV Guide* CLOSE-UP listing)
07/26/68	(repeat) – The Omega Glory
08/02/68	(repeat) – Return to Tomorrow
08/09/68	(repeat) – Assignment: Earth
08/16/68	(repeat) – The Deadly Years
08/23/68	(repeat) – A Private Little War
08/30/68	(repeat) – A Piece of the Action
09/06/68	(pre-emption) – Cincinnati Bengals vs. San Diego Chargers
09/13/68	(pre-emption) – News special "Ordeal in the City"

BIBLIOGRAPHY

WEBSITES:

www.startrekpropauthority.com
www.memory-alpha.org
www.startrek.com
www.startrekhistory.com
www.trekcore.com
www.retroweb.com/startrek.html
www.mystartrekscrapbook.blogspot.com
www.orionpress.com/unseenelements

BOOKS:

Beam Me Up, Scotty, by James Doohan with Peter David (Pocket Books, December 1996).
Beyond Uhura: Star Trek and Other Memories, by Nichelle Nichols (G.P. Putnam's Sons, 1994).
Best of Enterprise Incidents, The, edited by James Van Hise (Pioneer Books, 1990).
Best of Trek, The, edited by Walter Irwin and G.B. Love (Signet Books, April 1978).
Best of Trek #2, The, edited by Walter Irwin and G.B. Love (Signet Books, March 1980).
Boarding the Enterprise, by David Gerrold and Robert J. Sawyer (Benbella Books, 2006).
Boldly Writing: A Trekker Fan and Zine History, 1967-1987, by Joan Marie Verba (FTL Publications, 1996).
Captains' Logs, by Edward Gross and Mark A. Altman (Little, Brown and Company, 1995).
City on the Edge of Forever, The, by Harlan Ellison (White Wolf Publishing, September 1996).
Desilu: The Story of Lucille Ball and Desi Arnaz, by Coyne Steven Sanders and Tom Gilbert (Quill / William Morris, 1993).
Eighty Odd Years in Hollywood, by John Meredyth Lucas (McFarland & Company, 2004).
Encyclopedia of Trekkie Memorabilia, by Chris Gentry & Sally Gibson-Downs (Books Americana, 1988).
From Sawdust to Stardust: The Biography of DeForest Kelley, by Terry Lee Rioux (Pocket Books, February 2005).
Gene Roddenberry: The Last Conversation, by Yvonne Fern (University of California Press, 1994).
Gene Roddenberry: The Myth and the Man Behind Star Trek, by Joel Engel (Hyperion, 1994).
Great Birds of the Galaxy, by Edward Gross and Mark A. Altman (BoxTree Limited, 1994).
Greenberg's Guide to Star Trek Collectibles, by Christine Gentry and Sally Gibson-Downs (Greenberg Publishing, 1991).
I Am Not Spock, by Leonard Nimoy (Celestial Arts, November 1975).
I Am Spock, by Leonard Nimoy (Hyperion, 1996).
Inside Star Trek: The Real Story, by Herbert F. Solow and Robert H. Justman (Pocket Books, June 1996).
Longest Trek: My Tour of the Galaxy, The, by Grace Lee Whitney with Jim Denney (Quill Driver Books / World Dancer Press, 1998).
Making of Star Trek, The, by Stephen E. Whitfield and Gene Roddenberry (Ballantine Books, September 1968).
Making of the Trek Conventions, The, by Joan Winston (Playboy Press, November 1979).
Music of Star Trek, The, by Jeff Bond (Lone Eagle Publishing, 1999).
On the Good Ship Enterprise: My 15 Years with Star Trek, by Bjo Trimble (The Donning Company / Publishers, 1983).
Science Fiction Television Series: Episode Guides, Histories, and Casts and Credits for 62 Prime Time Shows, 1959 through 1989, by Mark Phillips and Frank Garcia (McFarland & Co., 1996)
Shatner: Where No Man ..., by William Shatner, Sondra Marshak and Myrna Culbreath (Temp Star Books, 1979).
Speedbumps: Flooring it through Hollywood, by Teri Garr with Henriette Mantel (Plume Book / Penguin Group, November 2006).
Starlog: Star Trek's Greatest Guest Stars, edited by David McDonnell (HarperCollins, January 1997).
Star Trek, adapted by James Blish (Bantam Books, January 1967).
Star Trek 2, adapted by James Blish (Bantam Books, February 1968).
Star Trek 3, adapted by James Blish (Bantam Books, April 1969).
Star Trek 4, adapted by James Blish (Bantam Books, July 1971).
Star Trek 5, adapted by James Blish (Bantam Books, February 1972).
Star Trek 6, adapted by James Blish (Bantam Books, April 1972).
Star Trek 7, adapted by James Blish (Bantam Books, July 1972).
Star Trek 8, adapted by James Blish (Bantam Books, November 1972).

Star Trek 9, adapted by James Blish (Bantam Books, August 1973).
Star Trek 10, adapted by James Blish (Bantam Books, February 1974).
Star Trek 11, adapted by James Blish (Bantam Books, April 1975).
Star Trek 12, adapted by James Blish with J.A. Lawrence (Bantam Books, November 1977).
Star Trek 13: Mudd's Angels, adapted by J.A. Lawrence (Bantam Books, May 1978).
Star Trek, No. 1: "K-G, Planet of Death," aka "The Planet of No Return" (Western Printing, 1967)
Star Trek, No. 2: "The Devil's Isle of Space" (Western Printing, 1968)
Star Trek, No. 3: "Invasion of the City Builders" (Western Printing, 1968)
Star Trek, No. 4: "The Peril of Planet Quick Change" (Western Printing, June 1969)
Star Trek, No. 5: "The Ghost Planet" (Western Printing, September 1969)
Star Trek, No. 6: "When Planets Collide" (Western Printing, December 1969)
Star Trek, No. 7: "The Voodoo Planet" (Western Printing, March 1970)
Star Trek, No. 8: "The Youth Trap" (Western Printing, September 1970)
Star Trek, No. 9: "The Legacy of Lazarus" (Western Printing, February 1971)
Star Trek: An Annotated Guide to Recourses on the Development, the Phenomenon, the People, the Television Series, the Films, the Novels and the Recordings, by Susan R. Gibberman (McFarland & Company, 1991).
Star Trek Compendium, The, by Allan Asherman (Pocket Books, 1986)
Star Trek Creator, by David Alexander (Roc Books / Penguin Group, June 1994).
Star Trek Fotonovel #1, City on the Edge of Forever, "Encounter with an Ellison," by Sandra Cawson (Bantam Books, November 1977).
Star Trek Fotonovel #5, Metamorphosis, "Interview with Elinor Donahue," by Caryle Eagle (Bantam Books, February 1978).
Star Trek Fotonovel #6, All Our Yesterdays, "Conversation with Zarabeth," by Lesa Kite (Bantam Books, March 1978).
Star Trek Fotonovel #10, Day of the Dove, "Interview with Michael Ansara," by Lesa Kite (Bantam Books, August 1978).
Star Trek Interview Book, The, by Allan Asherman (Pocket Books, July 1988).
Star Trek Lives!, by Jaqueline Lichtenberg, Sondra Marshak and Joan Winston (Bantam Books, July 1975).
Star Trek Memories, by William Shatner with Chris Kreski (HarperCollins, July 1994).
Star Trek: Mission to Horatius, by Mack Reynolds (Western Publishing Company, 1968).
The Complete Directory to Prime Time Network TV Shows, by Tim Brooks and Earle Marsh (Ballantine Books, May 1979).
To the Stars: The Autobiography of George Takei, by George Takei (Pocket Books, October 1994).
Trek Classic, by Edward Gross (Image Publishing of New York, 1991).
Trouble with Tribbles, The, by David Gerrold (Ballantine Books, May 1973).
TV69, "Star Trek," by Dave Kaufman (Signet Books, 1968).
Unauthorized History of Trek, The, by James Van Hise (HarperCollins, November 1995).
World of Star Trek, The, by David Gerrold (Ballantine Books, May 1973).

NEWSPAPER & MAGAZINE ARTICLES:

Weekly Variety, September 30, 1942, "Radio Reviews: *The Shadow*," written by Max Ehrlich.
Weekly Variety, March 6, 1946, "Studio Contracts" -- Marc Daniels and DeForest Kelley.
Weekly Variety, March 27, 1946, "Radio Reviews: A*merican Portrait*," written by Max Ehrlich.
Daily Variety, April 18, 1946, "35th P-T Feature" -- *Fear in the Night* starring DeForest Kelley.
Daily Variety, December 23, 1946, "*Variety Girl* Halts Until Friday" -- co-starring DeForest Kelley.
Daily Variety, December 26, 1946, "New Contracts" -- DeForest Kelley renewed by Paramount.
Weekly Variety, February 19, 1947, "Film Reviews: Fear in the Night," starring DeForest Kelley.
Variety, June 16, 1947; full page ad and sampling of reviews for *Fear in the Night*, starring DeForest Kelley.
Weekly Variety, July 16, 1947, "Film Reviews: *Variety Girl*, co-starring DeForest Kelley.
Daily Variety, July 25, 1947, "Kelley Portrays Pastor" – DeForest Kelley on loan out from Paramount to Apex Film Corp.
Daily Variety, September 3, 1947, "Chatter" -- DeForest Kelley back from P.R. tour for Paramount.
Weekly Variety, October 20, 1947, Full page ad for *Variety Girl*, co-starring DeForest Kelley.
Daily Variety, June 22, 1948, "Film Reviews: *Canon City*," co-starring DeForest Kelley.
Weekly Variety, February 9, 1949, "From the Production Centres," update on radio and book work for Max Ehrlich.
Weekly Variety, February 1, 1950, "Radio Reviews: *Mark Trail*," written by Max Ehrlich.
Weekly Variety, September 13, 1950, "Television Review: *Sure as Fate*: 'Nightfall,'" written by Max Ehrlich.
Weekly Variety, April 11, 1951, "Television Reviews: *Treasury Men in Action*: 'Case of the Careless Junkman,'" written by Max Ehrlich.

Daily Variety, April 17, 1952, "Film Preview: *Kid Monk Baroni*," co-starring Leonard Nimoy.

Daily Variety, June 17, 1953, "Film Reviews: *The Beast from 20,000 Fathoms*," co-written by Fred Freiberger.

Daily Variety, June 19, 1953, "Television Reviews: *Favorite Story*: 'The Man Who Sold His Shadow,'" starring DeForest Kelley.

Daily Variety, July 17, 1953, "Ass't Directors to Air Their Prod'n Problems at Roundtable Parleys" -- Robert Justman.

Weekly Variety, September 2, 1953, "Television Reviews: *The Big Story*," written by Max Ehrlich.

Daily Variety, December 1, 1953, "Telepix Reviews: *Pepsi-Cola Playhouse*: 'Frozen Escape,'" co-starring DeForest Kelley.

Weekly Variety, April 7, 1954, "New Telepix Show: *Mr. District Attorney*."

Daily Variety, June 7, 1954, "Telepix Reviews: *Schlitz Playhouse of Stars*: 'Whale on the Beach,'" teleplay by Carey Wilbur.

Daily Variety, November 8, 1954, Telepix Reviews: *Inside Out*" -- DeForest Kelley.

Dailey Variety, December 2, 1954, "Telpix Reviews: *Storm Signal*" -- DeForest Kelley.

Daily Variety, May 19, 1955, "Telepix Reviews: *Science Fiction Theatre*: 'Y.O.R.D.,'" with DeForest Kelley.

Weekly Variety, July 13, 1955, "Film Reviews: *The Big Bluff*," screenplay by Fred Freidberger.

Daily Variety, September 26, 1955, "Telepix Reviews: *I Led Three Lives*."

Daily Variety, October 5, 1955, "Telepix Reviews: *Highway Patrol*."

Dailey Variety, February 2, 1956, "*Fox* at Bay" -- Robert Justman.

Daily Variety, March 6, 1956, "Kelley to Recreate OK Role for Hal Wallis."

Daily Variety, March 9, 1956, "Telepix Reviews: *Chevron Hall of Stars*: 'Secret Weapon of 117,'" teleplay by Robert Wesley (AKA Gene Roddenberry).

Daily Variety, May 18, 1956, "*Gunfight* Wounds Force Kelley from *Oklahoman*."

Daily Variety, June 31, 1956, "Film Review: *Magnificent Roughnecks*," screenplay by Stephen Kandel.

Weekly Variety, August 15, 1956, "Kidney Trouble Kayos Plummer, Shatner Subs."

Daily Variety, October 4, 1956, "Telepix Reviews: *Dr. Christian*."

Weekly Variety, October 10, 1956, "Television Reviews: *West Point*."

Daily Variety, November 23, 1956, "Telepix Reviews: *Stage for Tucson*."

Daily Variety, February 27, 1957, "Television Reviews: *Studio One*: 'The Defender'"; co-starring William Shatner.

Daily Variety, April 2, 1957, "'Eye' for Shatner," appearing on *Alfred Hitchcock*.

Weekly Variety, April 24, 1957, "Film Reviews: *The Girl in the Kremlin*"; screenplay by Gene L. Coon and Robert Hill.

Weekly Variety, May 1, 1957, "Legit Bits," William and Gloria Shatner quit Ontario play.

Daily Variety, May 7, 1957, "MGM Pacts Shatner."

Daily Variety, May 17, 1957, production date set for *The Brothers Karamazov*, co-staring Shatner.

Daily Variety, June 27, 1957, "Revue Pacts Coon."

Daily Variety, August 12, 1957, "Telepix Review: *Hands of the Enemy*" -- DeForest Kelley.

Daily Variety, August 13, 1957, "Telepix Reviews: *Kill and Run*" -- DeForest Kelley.

Weekly Variety, August 14, 1957, production continuing on *Brothers Karamazov* -- Shatner.

Daily Variety, September 16, 1957, "Telepix Reviews: *Have Gun, Will Travel*."

Daily Variety, September 23, 1957, "Telepix Reviews: *Schlitz Playhouse*: 'One Way Out'"; teleplay by Gene Coon.

Daily Variety, September 26, 1957, "Telepix Reviews: *Boots and Saddles*: 'The Gatling Gun'"; teleplay by Gene Roddenberry.

Weekly Variety, October 2, 1957, "Television Reviews: *Harbourmaster*: 'The Thievingest Dog,'" writer Carey Wilbur; and "Tele Follow-Up Comment: *Studio One*: Mutiny on the Shark, Parts 1 & 2," written by Max Ehrlich.

Daily Variety, October 3, 1957, "Telepix Reviews: *Assignment Foreign Legion*: 'The Outcast,' teleplay by Max Ehrlich.

Daily Variety, October 4, 1957, "Telepix Reviews: *The Walter Winchell File*: 'Country Boy'"; teleplay by Adrian Spies.

Daily Variety, October 7, 1957, "Telepix Reviews: *Harbor Command*" and, with John Meredyth Lucas directing, review for *The Court of the Last Resort*.

Daily Variety, November 26, 1957, "Film Review: *Man in the Shadow*"; screenplay by Gene Coon.

Daily Variety, November 27, 1957, "Telepix Reviews: *Suspicion*: 'The Flight'"; teleplay by Halsted Welles and Gene Coon.

Daily Variety, December 16, 1957, "Telepix Reviews: *Jane Wyman Theatre*: 'The Perfect Alibi,'" teleplay by Roddenberry.

Daily Variety, January 9, 1958, "Light and Airy," by Jack Hellman, about "Sam Houston" pilot.

Daily Variety, January 13, 1958, "Telepix Reviews: *Schlitz Playhouse*: 'Guys Like O'Malley'"; teleplay by Gene Coon.

Daily Variety, January 29, 1958, "Tele Review: *Studio One in Hollywood*: 'Balance of Terror,'" teleplay by Max Ehrlich.

Weekly Variety, February 5, 1958, "Film Reviews: *Crash Landing*," screenplay by Fred Freiberger.

Daily Variety, February 6, 1958, "Light and Airy," by Jack Hellman, update Screen Gems' "Sam Houston" project.

Weekly Variety, February 19, 1958, "Film Reviews: *Brothers Karamazov*"; with William Shatner.

Daily Variety, February 19, 1958, "Froug on *Natche*."

Daily Variety, April 14, 1958, "Telepix Reviews: *Shadow of a Dead Man*" -- DeForest Kelley.

Daily Variety, April 24, 1958, "Film Reviews: *Blood Arrow*," screenplay by Fred Freiberger.

Weekly Variety, June 4, 1958, "Film Reviews" -- *The Law and Jake Wade*, with DeForest Kelley.

Daily Variety, June 18, 1958, "Telepix Reviews: *Johnny Risk*" -- teleplay by Fred Freiberger, starring DeForest Kelley.

Daily Variety, June 23, 1958, "Television Reviews: *Playhouse 90:* 'A Town Has Turned to Dust'"; with Shatner.

Daily Variety, August 27, 1958, "15 Writers Set to do *Bat Masterson* Segs," including Roddenberry.

Daily Variety, September 12, 1958, "Legit Tryout: *The World of Suzie Wong*"; review for Shatner play.

Daily Variety, September 29, 1958, "Telepix Reviews: *Jefferson Drum*."

Weekly Variety, October 1, 1958, "Television Reviews: *The Californians*: 'Dishonor for Matt Wayne,'" teleplay by Carey Wilbur.

Daily Variety, October 9, 1958, "Telepix Reviews: *Rescue 8*: 'The Ferris Wheel'"; teleplay by Gene Coon and Loren Dayle.

Daily Variety, October 13, 1958, "Telepix Reviews: *Cimarron City*: 'I, the People'" - teleplay by Gene Coon.

Weekly Variety, October 22, 1958, "Shows on Broadway: *The World of Suzie Wong*"; starring Shatner.

Daily Variety, November 11, 1958, "21 Teleplays Named for WGA Awards from Shows Since Axed"; includes nomination for Roddenberry.

Daily Variety, November 21, 1958, "West Downs East in Radio-TV Competition of Writers Guild" -- Gene Roddenberry wins for "Helen of Abajinian."

Daily Variety, March 3, 1959, "Short Shorts" -- son born to Robert Justman.

Weekly Variety, March 18, 1959, "ABC-TVs Complete Fall Lineup," includes "Big Walk," created by Roddenberry.

Weekly Variety, April 1, 1959, "Film Reviews: *Warlock*" – with DeForest Kelley.

Daily Variety, April 27, 1959, "Light and Airy," by Jack Hellman; update on Roddenberry's "Big Walk."

Weekly Variety, May 6, 1959, "$7,000,000 in Pilots Down Drain; 200 Made But Only 35 Sold"; with update on "The Big Walk," by Roddenberry.

Daily Variety, May 25, 1959, "Capra Named Prez at Anni SDG Meet" – Robert Justman voted V.P.

Daily Variety, June 2, 1959, "Sound and Picture," by Bob Chandler; status on Roddenberry deal with Screen Gems.

Weekly Variety, June 17, 1959, "Baptists' AM-TV Awards"; honoring Roddenberry.

Daily Variety, June 19, 1959, "Just for Variety," by Army Archerd, "TV 'heavy' DeForest Kelley." by Fred Freiberger and co-starring DeForest Kelley.

Weekly Variety, July 29, 1959, "British Com'l TV in Quest of Some Patterns; Ehrlich Series"; Max Ehrlich is script editor for *No Hiding Place*.

Daily Variety, August 4, 1959, "Geraghty to Rein Wrather Whiplash Skein in Australia"; Don Ingalls head writer and script supervisor.

Daily Variety, October 5, 1959, "Telepix Review: Hotel de Paree."

Weekly Variety, October 7, 1959, "Syndication Reviews: *Lock Up*"; teleplay by Gene Coon.

Daily Variety, October 20, 1959, "Telepix Reviews: *General Electric Theater*: 'The Tallest Marine'"; teleplay by Gene Coon.

Daily Variety, October 30, 1959, Telepix Review: *The Four Just Men*: 'The Battle of the Bridge'"; teleplay by Gene Coon.

Daily Variety, November 2, 1959, "Telepix Review: *Desilu Playhouse*: 'So Tender, So Profane'"; teleplay by Adrian Spies.

Daily Variety, December 11, 1959, "Scribe Trio Joins Hal Hudson in New *Weapon* TV Oater"; Roddenberry deal.

Daily Variety, December 15, 1959, "Television Reviews: *Sunday Showcase*: 'The Indestructible Mr. Gore'"; starring Shatner.

Weekly Variety, December 16, 1959, "Screen Gems Loaded with Projects but Dozier Limits Pilots to 8 or 10"; includes update on Roddenberry's "The Big Walk."

Daily Variety, December 31, 1959, "Nimoy in Genet Legiter."

Daily Variety, January 15, 1960, "Gene Roddenberry Signs Exclusive Pact at SG."

Daily Variety, January 25, 1960, "Telepix Review: *Westinghouse Desilu Playhouse*: 'Meeting at Apalachin'"; teleplay by Adrian Spies.

Weekly Variety, January 27, 1960, "Tele Follow-Up comment: *Desilu Playhouse*."

Daily Variety, February 9, 1960, "Just for Variety," by Army Archerd"; update on "333 Montgomery Street."

Weekly Variety, March 23, 1960, "Film Reviews: *Thirteen Fighting Men*," co-screenplay by Robert Hamner.

Daily Variety, April 8, 1960, *Deathwatch* ad with reviews -- Leonard Nimoy.

Daily Variety, May 16, 1960, "Television Reviews: *Westinghouse Desilu Playhouse*: 'City in Bondage'"; teleplay by Adrian Spies.

Weekly Variety, May 18, 1960, "Par TV in 2-Ply Sale; *Wrangler*, *Garland* All Set"; Roddenberry as writer and apprentice producer.

Daily Variety, June 15, 1960, "Television Reviews: *Alcoa Theatre*: '333 Montgomery'"; writer/producer Gene Roddenberry; co-starring DeForest Kelley.

Daily Variety, June 22, 1960, "Film Review: *House of Usher*," screenplay by Richard Matheson.

Weekly Variety, June 29, 1960. "*Wrangler*, *Diagnosis* Summer TV Entries Incept Pioneer Techniques," by Bob Chandler; concerning show involving Roddenberry.

Weekly Variety; June 30, 1960; review samplings for Shimon Wincelberg's *Kataki*.

Weekly Variety, July 6, 1960, "Par-TV *Wrangler* in Sponsor Jam"; series involving Roddenberry.

Weekly Variety, July 27, 1960, "*Wrangler* Gets Timid Go-Ahead"; Roddenberry involved in series.

Daily Variety, August 8, 1960, "Tele Review: *Wrangler*"; writer/producer Roddenberry.

Weekly Variety, August 10, 1960, Television Reviews: *Wrangler*"; writer/producer Roddenberry.

Daily Variety, September 6, 1960, "WGA 'Scabbing' Probe Still On"; Barry Trivers is WGA disciplinary committee chairman.

Daily Variety, September 12, 1960, "Telepix Reviews: The Tall Man," creator/writer/producer Samuel Peeples.

Weekly Variety, September 21, 1960, "Foreign Television Reviews: *Whiplash*"; teleplay by Roddenberry.

Variety, November 9, 1960, "Jeffrey Hunter Sees Playing Savior Start, Not End of Big Acting Roles."

Daily Variety, November 21, 1961, "150 Pilots Toe Prod'n Mark" -- Roddenberry's *Defiance County*.

Weekly Variety, November 22, 1961, "SG Gets TV Rights to *Farmer's Daughter*" - Roddenberry's *APO 923*.

Daily Variety, November 28, 1960, "*Tomorrow* for Culp," pilot written by Richard Matheson.

Daily Variety, December 15, 1960, "Justman TV Liaison" -- Robert Justman at MGM.

Weekly Variety, January 18, 1961, "Syndication Review: *Tallahassee 7000*: 'Man Bait,'" teleplay by Max Ehrlich.

Daily Variety, February 3, 1961, "Film Review: *The Long Rope*," screenplay by Robert Hamner.

Daily Variety, March 22, 1961, "Shatner's 2-Bagger."

Daily Variety, April 26, 1961, "Film Reviews: *Master of the World*," screenplay by Richard Matheson.

Daily Variety, May 5, 1961, "Wind *Nuremberg* Shooting at Revue"; with Shatner.

Daily Variety, May 22, 1961, "Schnee Elected WGA-West Prez"; Barry Trivers is second V.P.

Daily Variety, June 8, 1961, "Television on Trial"; with Roddenberry as moderator.

Daily Variety, June 12, 1961, "Reveal New Crop of Sponsor Taboos as Writers Guild Puts 'TV on Trial,'" by Larry Tubelle; quoting Roddenberry.

Daily Variety, June 29, 1961, "Light and Airy," by Jack Hellman; quoting Gene Coon.

Daily Variety, July 3, 1961, "Film Review: *The Naked Edge*," based on Max Ehrlich novel *First Train to Babylon*.

Daily Variety, July 28, 1961, *Meanwhile Back at the Front* ad with review samplings; book by Gene Coon.

Daily Variety, August 4, 1961, "Sam Peeples Preps New Revue Series."

Weekly Variety, August 9, 1961, "Film Reviews: *The Pit and the Pendulum*," screenplay by Richard Matheson.

Daily Variety, August 18, 1961, "Room for Shatner with Julie Harris"; Shatner into play.

Daily Variety, September 14, 1961, "Groucho Marx Set as Dramatic Lead in GE's *Hold Out*" – teleplay by Max Ehrlich.

Daily Variety, September 19, 1961, "Film Review: *Explosive Generation*," starring William Shatner.

Daily Variety, October 4, 1961, "Telepix Reviews: *Shannon*: 'The Embezzler's Daughter'"; teleplay by Roddenberry.

Weekly Variety, October 4, 1961, "Television Reviews: *Wagon Train*: 'The Captain Dan Brady Story'"; teleplay by Gene Coon; and "Shows Out of Town: *A Shot in the Dark*," starring Shatner.

Weekly Variety, October 11, 1961, "Film Reviews: *King of Kings*," starring Jeffrey Hunter.

Weekly Variety, October 18, 1961, "Film Reviews: *Judgment in Nuremberg*"; featuring Shatner.

Weekly Variety, October 25, 1961, "Shows on Broadway: *A Shot in the Dark*"; starring Shatner.

Daily Variety, November 21, 1961, "On All Channels," by Dave Kaufman; concerning *Wrangler*, series Roddenberry worked on; "150 Pilots Toe Prod'n Mark," announcing "Defiance County" and "Douglass Selby."

Weekly Variety, November 22, 1961, "SG Gets TV Rights to Farmer's Daughter," plus update on Roddenberry's "APO 923."

Daily Variety, December 19, 1961, "CBS-TV Financing 2 More SG Pilots" -- Roddenberry's "APO 923" and "Defiance County"; also "On All channels," by Dave Kaufman, with update on "Douglass Selby."

Weekly Variety, December 20, 1961, "CBS-TV Practically All Set with '62-'63 Shows," including Roddenberry's "APO 923" and "Defiance County."

Daily Variety, December 27, 1961, "Four Screen Gems Pilots Will Roll Early Next Month," including Roddenberry's "APO 923" and "Defiance County."

Daily Variety, January 4, 1962, "ABC-TV Partnering Kovacs' New Series with Screen Gems"; status on "Defiance County" and "APO 923," both created by Roddenberry.

Daily Variety, January 5, 1962, "Bronson in Empire," with news that Roddenberry's "Defiance County" begins filming on January 8.

Daily Variety, February 2, 1967, "No CBS Shotgun on Shows," with Oscar Katz's word on Roddenberry's "APO 923."

Daily Variety, February 7, 1962, "Duning Tunes 'Defiance'"; update on Roddenberry pilot.

Daily Variety, February 26, 1962, "CBS-TV Adds Heft to Sat. Sked; Slots Jackie Gleason," bumping Roddenberry's "APO 923."

Daily Variety, March 1, 1962, "Light and Airy," by Jack Hellman, update on Roddenberry's "APO 923."

Daily Variety, April 27, 1962, "Light and Airy," by Jack Hellman; quoting Don Ingalls about *Have Gun, Will Travel*.

Daily Variety, May 9, 1962, "Shatner Exiting *Shot*."

Daily Variety, May 18, 1962, "7 Winners in Writers Guild B'casting Script Scramble" -- Christopher Knopf, Barry Trivers, Shimon Wincelberg, Alvin Boretz.

Weekly Variety, May 23, 1962, "Film Reviews: *The Intruder*"; starring Shatner.

Weekly Variety, May 30, 1962, "Film Reviews: *Tales of Terror*," screenplay by Richard Matheson.

Daily Variety, August 9, 1962, "Light and Airy," by Jack Hellman; update on "Doug Selby" pilot.

Daily Variety, August 14, 1962, "On All Channels," by Dave Kaufman; update on "Doug Selby" pilot.

Daily Variety, August 27, 1962, "Light and Airy," by Jack Hellman" -- Don Ingalls on *Have Gun, Will Travel*.

Weekly Variety, October 3, 1962, "'4 Window Girl' as MGM Series," with news on Roddenberry's *The Lieutenant*.

Daily Variety, October 15, 1962, "Telepix Reviews: *McHale's Navy*: 'An Ensign for McHale'"; teleplay by Gene Coon.

Daily Variety, October 25, 1962, "Telepix Followup: *The Lloyd Bridges Show*: 'The Testing Ground,'" co-teleplay by Barry Trivers.

Daily Variety, November 23, 1962, "Telepix Folo-Ups: *The Eleventh Hour*: 'Hooray, Hooray, the Circus Is Coming to Town'"; teleplay by Gene Coon.

Daily Variety, December 11, 1962, "Roddenberry Reining Seg of *Virginian*."

Daily Variety, January 2, 1963, "Lockwood to Play Leatherneck *Lieutenant* for MGM-TV."

Daily Variety, January 9, 1963, "Legit Bits"; report on Leonard Nimoy Theater.

Daily Variety, January 21, 1963, "Susan Silo Harvests *Lieutenant* Role."

Daily Variety, January 31, 1963, "Film Reviews: *The Raven*," screenplay by Richard Matheson.

Daily Variety, February 1, 1963, "Vee's 1962 Gig Net Whee $194,000"; Bobby Vee training under Nimoy.

Daily Variety, February 7, 1963, "MGM's *Lieutenant* to NBC Next Fall"; Roddenberry creator/writer/producer.

Daily Variety, April 3, 1963, "MGM *Lieutenant* Musters 5 Scribes, Three Directors."

Daily Variety, April 24, 1963, "Record 64 Scribes Plotting MGM-TV Series for Fall" -- Art Wallace, Lee Erwin, Shimon Wincelberg.

Weekly Variety, July 24, 1963, "New York Sound Track," Jeffrey Hunter forced out of *The Long Flight*.

Daily Variety, June 26, 1963, "On All Channels: Marines Balk at *Lt.* Script," by Dave Kaufman; quoting Roddenberry.

Daily Variety, August 13, 1963, "On All Channels," by Dave Kaufman; quoting Roddenberry.

Daily Variety, September 16, 1963, "Telepix Reviews: *The Lieutenant*"; Roddenberry series.

Daily Variety, September 18, 1963, "Telepix Reviews: *Wagon Train*: 'The Molly Kincaid Story'"; teleplay by Gene Coon.

Weekly Variety, September 18, 1963, "Television Reviews: *The Lieutenant*," created and produced by Roddenberry.

Weekly Variety, September 25, 1963, "Television Reviews: *Temple Houston*," starring Jeffrey Hunter.

Daily Variety, October 7, 1963, "No Network Can Dictate Artistic Policy to Ingalls; Quits *McPheeters*."

Daily Variety, October 17, 1963, "Henley for *Queens*"; production for Leonard Nimoy Theatre.

Weekly Variety, October 23, 1963, "30 City Nielsen: ABC Swingin'" – *The Lieutenant*.

Daily Variety, October 24, 1963, "*Great* Roles for 4 More;" Shatner pilot project.

Daily Variety, October 25, 1963, "Telepix Follow-Up Reviews: *Channing*"; with Shatner.
Daily Variety, November 5, 1963, "Telepix Followup: *Arrest and Trial*: 'The Witnesses," teleplay by Max Ehrlich.
Daily Variety, November 6, 1963, "Don Ingalls Joins Revue Today as Staff Producer."
Daily Variety, November 8, 1963, "Ingalls on Revue's *Virginian* Series."
Daily Variety, November 12, 1963, "Not Enough Slices in TV Pie"; quoting Roddenberry; "*Temple Houston*'s Format Change Is Planned by Bluel"; series starring Jeffrey Hunter.
Daily Variety, November 26, 1963, "Shatner in *Sun*."
Daily Variety, December 11, 1963, "Chatter"; Vic Morrow to direct Nimoy in *Deathwatch* pic.
Daily Variety, December 16, 1963, "Telepix Follow-Up Reviews: *Temple Houston*," staring Jeffrey Hunter, teleplay by Carey Wilbur.
Daily Variety, December 18, 1963, "On All Channels," by Dave Kaufman; Don Ingalls creates fantasy pilot "Lucifer's Folly."
Weekly Variety, January 15, 1964, "Film Reviews: *The Man from Galveston*," starring Jeffrey Hunter.
Daily Variety, January 22, 1964, "Film Reviews: *The Comedy of Terror*," screenplay by Richard Matheson.
Daily Variety, February 3, 1964, "Janet Blair Cast as 'Lady' for *Destry*"; produced by Gene Coon.
Daily Variety, February 24, 1964, "Telepix Followup: *The Lieutenant*, 'To Set It Right'"; Roddenberry production; Lee Erwin script.
Daily Variety, February 26, 1964, "Screen Gems, Four Star Tie in WGA Nominations Tally" -- noms for Norman Katkov.
Weekly Variety, March 4, 1964, "Film Reviews: *Gunfight at Comanche Creek*," co-starring DeForest Kelley.
Daily Variety, March 10, 1964, "On All Channels: 'Point' Is Broken," by Dave Kaufman; quoting Roddenberry.
Daily Variety, March 17, 1964, "Name Fred Freiberger Exec on *Lawmaker*."
Daily Variety, March 20, 1964, "MGM-TV's *Lieutenant* at Ease After 'Kill'."
Daily Variety, May 6, 1964, "Freiberger Switches from *Casey* to *People*."
Daily Variety, May 13, 1964, "Roddenberry Reins Pilots for Desilu."
Weekly Variety, May 27, 1964: "Film Reviews: *The Killers*"; screenplay by Gene Coon.
Daily Variety, July 28, 1964, "On All Channels," by Dave Kaufman; D.C. Fontana script work.
Daily Variety, August 3, 1964, "Legit Reviews: *The Bald Soprano*," directed by Joseph Sargent.
Weekly Variety, August 12, 1964, "NBC-TV Yens Indie Product"; Roddenberry created pilot "Assignment 100." And "Desilu and NBC-TV Setting Co-Prod'n *Assignment* Deal"; announcing *Star Trek* pilot.
Daily Variety, August 19, 1964, "Stockholders Given Roseate Desilu Report"; *Star Trek* plans.
Daily Variety, September 8, 1964, "Kandel, Avedon Plot Pilots at SG."
Daily Variety, September 21, 1964, "Telepix Reviews: *Kentucky Jones*," directed by Joseph Sargent.
Weekly Variety, September 30, 1964, "Shatner 'Project'-ed"; ; Shatner back at MGM; "Film Reviews: *The Outrage*"; featuring Shatner.
Daily Variety, October 6, 1964, "On All Channels," by Dave Kaufman; "Blood of the A.E.F." project for Roddenberry, as well as *Star Trek*, for Desilu.
Weekly Variety, October 14, 1964, "Film Reviews: Where Love Has Gone" -- with DeForest Kelley.
Daily Variety, October 19, 1964, "Television Reviews: *Bob Hope Chrysler Theatre*, 'Have Girls – Will Travel,' co-teleplay by Robert Hamner.
Daily Variety, November 11, 1964, "Len Nimoy Takes *Trek*"; first actor signed.
Daily Variety, November 19, 1964, "*Star Trek* Pilot for Jeff Hunter"; second actor signed.
Daily Variety, December 1, 1964, "Just for Variety," by Army Archerd; Susan Oliver third signed, called "Greenfinger" and "Bulgarian Pic Wins Peace Fest; Shatner ('Intruders') Best Actor."
Daily Variety, December 4, 1964, "John Hoyt Joins *Trek*"; fourth actor signed.
Daily Variety, December 16, 1964, "Desilu's 26-Week Net 424G, Un 6%" and "Telepic Followup: Voyage to the Bottom of the Sea: 'The Ghost of Moby Dick,'" teleplay by Robert Hamner.
Daily Variety, February 2, 1965, "Television Reviews: *For the People*"; Shatner series.
Weekly Variety, February 3, 1965, "Television Reviews: *For the People*"; 2nd review for Shatner series.
Daily Variety, February 24, 1965, "Congratulations on *For the People*"; review samplings.
Daily Variety, March 22, 1965, "Freiberger Producer of TV *Shenandoah*."
Daily Variety, April 27, 1965, "Film Reviews: *Die! Die! My Darling!*," screenplay by Richard Matheson.
Daily Variety, May 4, 1965, "NBC-TV Taking 2nd Look at Desilu Pilot."
Weekly Variety, May 12, 1965, "'Definite Maybe' for Two Unsold Desilu Pilots."
TV Guide, May 29, 1965, "TV Teletype: Neil Hickey Reports."
Daily Variety, June 1, 1965, "All the Channels: Allen's 1997 Space Shot 1st Primetime Cliffhanger," by Dave Kaufman; quoting Irwin Allen.
Weekly Variety, June 23, 1965, "Desilu Plots 17 Series for '66."
The Milwaukee Journal, July 4, 1965, "Happy in Hollywood," by J.D. Spiro.
Daily Variety, July 9, 1965, "Ihnat Joins *Police*"; first actor signed.

Daily Variety, July 13, 1965, "Fennelly Picks Up *Shenandoah* Producership Freiberger Relinquished."

Daily Variety, August 12, 1965, "NBC-TV to Decide Fate of 70 Future Projects Next Week."

Weekly Variety, August 18, 1965, "NBC-TV Sifting its Projects for '66-'67."

Daily Variety, September 9, 1965, "Desilu in ABC-TV Deal for *Savage*."

Daily Variety, September 14, 1965, "Telepix Reviews: *A Man Called Shenandoah*: 'The Onslaught,'" produced by Freiberger.

Daily Variety, September 15, 1965, "Another *Savage* TV Role for Bob Lansing."

The New York Times, September 16, 1965, review of *Lost in Space*, by Jack Gould.

Daily Variety, September 17, 1965, "Telepix Reviews: *Lost in Space*."

Daily Variety, September 20, 1965, "Telepix Reviews: *The Wild, Wild West*," teleplay by Gilbert Ralston.

Daily Variety, September 21, 1965, "Telepix Reviews: *Voyage to the Bottom of the Sea*: 'Jonah and the Whale.'"

Weekly Variety, September 22, 1965, "Television Reviews: *The Wild, Wild West*," teleplay by Gilbert Ralston, and "Television Reviews: *Mr. Roberts*," produced by James Komack, and "Television Reviews: *Lost in Space*," written by S. Bar-David, and "Television Reviews: *Ben Casey*," produced by John Meredyth Lucas.

Weekly Variety, September 29, 1965, "Television Review: *The Fugitive*" -- written by Robert Hamner.

Weekly Variety, November 10, 1965, "*Gunsmoke* in CBS' *Wild West*: Freiberger & Garrison Ambushed as Freshman Oater Gets 6th Producer, Leacock."

Daily Variety, November 24, 1965, "Film Reviews: *Die, Monster, Die*," screenplay by Jerry Sohl.

Weekly Variety, December 1, 1965, ABC's 'Them Dogfaces,'" with update on "The Long Hunt for April Savage."

Daily Variety, December 24, 1965, "Majors Talk Young Blood but Don't Tap Any: Shatner."

Weekly Variety, September 29, 1965, "Television Reviews: *The Fugitive*: 'Middle of a Heat Wave,'" teleplay by Robert Hamner.

Daily Variety, "January 12, 1966, "On All Channels: Bob Conrad Wants the Job of His *Wild* Exec Producer," by Dave Kaufman.

Daily Variety, February 9, 1966, "On All Channels: Argues There's Space for Her Show, Tho Batman Winged It," by Dave Kaufman.

Daily Variety, February 21, 1966, "Film Review: *Monster of Terror*," screenplay by Jerry Sohl.

Weekly Variety, February 23, 1966, "New Season at first Blush," with *Star Trek* and "April Savage" on schedules.

Daily Variety, March 1, 1966, "NBC Buys *Star Trek*, Desilu Sci-Fi Series."

Weekly Variety, March 2, 1966, "Next Season's Three Net Schedule -- First Round."

TV Guide, March 5, 1966, "For the Record," by Henry Harding.

Weekly Variety, March 9, 1966, "Oscar Katz Calls Quits at Desilu."

Weekly Variety, March 16, 1966, "Next Season's 3 Net Schedule -- 14th Round," with *Star Trek* and "April Savage" on slate.

Daily Variety, March 17, 1966, "Coon Scripts WB's *First to Fight*."

Daily Variety, "May 12, 1966, "Nine Directors on *Trek*."

Daily Variety, March 21, 1966, "Film Review: *Deathwatch*," starring Leonard Nimoy.

Daily Variety, March 24, 1966, "Lennart Wins WGA's Laurel" -- nom for Harlan Ellison.

Daily Variety, March 25, 1966, "Kandel *Iron* Producer."

Daily Variety, April 12, 1966, "Television Reviews: *Scalplock*," produced by Stephen Kandel, directed by James Goldstone, written by Kandel and Goldstone.

Daily Variety, May 23, 1966, "Two *Star* Aides Named."

Daily Variety, May 26, 1966, "Ingalls *High* Aide."

TV Guide, May 28, 1966, "TV Teletype: Joseph Finnigan Reports."

Daily Variety, June 7, 1966, "On All Channels: *Trek* into Future," by Dave Kaufman.

Daily Variety, June 9, 1966, "Just for *Variety*," by Army Archerd.

Oakland Tribune, June 19, 1966, "TV Enters the Space Race," by Bob MacKenzie.

Weekly Variety, July 13, 1966, "Desilu Posts a $15,000,000 Prod. Budget for '67-'68."

Daily Variety, July 13, 1966, "Film Review: *Frankenstein Conquers the World*," with screenplay by Jerry Sohl.

Daily Variety, July 15, 1966, "Just for *Variety*," by Army Archerd.

Indiana Evening Gazette, August 9, 1966, "Televisionese Tough Language," by Cynthia Lowary.

Daily Variety, August 9, 1966, "Coons [sic] *Trek* Producer."

TV Guide, August 13, 1966, "For the Record," by Henry Harding.

Weekly Variety, August 31, 1966, "Film Reviews: *Chamber of Horrors*," screenplay by Stephen Kandel.

The Indianapolis Star, TV Week, August 28, 1966, Grace Lee Whitney as Yeoman Janice Rand on cover, syndicated article, "*Star Trek* Resembles Space *Twilight Zone*," no author credited.

Daily Variety, September 1, 1966, article: "Roddenberry Talking Trek at Convention," no author credited.

TV Guide, September 3, 1966, program listing for "The Man Trap," Thursday, September 8, plus "Sneak a Peak at NBC Week" ad.

The Buffalo Evening News, September 3, 1966, "*Star Trek*: New Series Pits 400-Man Craft Against Space," by Charles Witbeck."

St. Louis Post-Dispatch TV Magazine, September 4, 1966, William Shatner as Captain Kirk on cover, plus NBC "Sneak Previews" ad.

Daily Variety, September 7, 1966, "On All Channels: Shatner's Heroic Switch," by Dave Kaufman.

Daily Variety, September 8, 1966, "Telepix Review: *Star Trek*," by Helm.

Indiana Evening Gazette, September 8, 1966, "TV Tonight."

The Times Recorder, September 8, 1966, "What's on the Air," by Naomi.

TV Guide, September 10, 1966, editor's preview of *Star Trek*, "Thursday on NBC" ad, "NBC Week Is Here" ad, and program listing for "Charlie X," Thursday, September 15.

Daily Variety, September 12, 1966, "Telepix Reviews: *The Time Tunnel*: 'Rendezvous with Yesterday.'"

Daily Variety, September 13, 1966, "Telepix Reviews: *The Iron Horse*: 'The Rails Run West,'" written and produced by Stephen Kandel, directed by James Goldstone.

Weekly Variety, September 14, 1966, "Television Reviews: *Star Trek*" and "Television Off to the Races: Previews Reveal the Racial Mix," by Les Brown; "The Overnight Scores: Trendex & Arbitrons"; and *Star Trek* review by Trau, and *Time Tunnel* review.

The New York Times, September 16, 1966, "TV: Spies, Space and the Stagestruck," review of "Charlie X," by Jack Gould.

Daily Variety, September 16, 1966, "Telepix Reviews: *Lost in Space*."

TV Guide, September 17, 1966, NBC "The Blockbusters" ad, and program listing for "Where No Man Has Gone Before," Thursday, September 22 listing.

Broadcasting, September 19, 1966, "Critics' Views of Hits, Misses," sampling *Star Trek* reviews in *The Los Angeles Times*, by Hal Humphrey, *The Boston Globe*, by Percy Shain, *The New York Post*, by Bob Wilson, *The Philadelphia Inquirer*, by Harry Harris, *The Chicago American*, by Bill Irvin, and *The Washington Post*, by Lawrence Laurent.

Weekly Variety, September 21, 1966, "Television Reviews: *Voyage to the Bottom of the Sea*: 'Monster from the Inferno.'"

Daily Variety, September 23, 1966, "Telepix Folo-Up Reviews: *Bob Hope Chrysler Theatre*: 'Time of Flight,'" teleplay by Richard Matheson.

TV Guide, September 24, 1966, NBC "The Blockbusters!" ad, and program listing for "The Naked Time," Thursday, September 29.

Broadcasting, September 26, 1966, Trendix ratings for September 18 and 22.

Weekly Variety, September 28, 1966, "Television Reviews: *Lost in Space*."

TV Guide, October 1, 1966, program listing for "The Enemy Within," Thursday, October 6.

Broadcasting, October 3, 1966, "Trendex Top-40 Programs."

TV Guide, October 8, 1966, NBC "*Star Trek / The Hero*" ad, and program listing for "Mudd's Women," Thursday, October 13.

Broadcasting, October 10, 1966, *Star Trek* to be sponsored by Brown & Williamson.

Daily Variety, October 11, 1966, Nielsen Ratings, *Star Trek* at No. 33; "Eight New Shows in TvQ's Top 20," "*Star Trek* in Top 20."

Weekly Variety, October 12, 1966, "TV's New Top 40," *Star Trek* at No. 31, and "Eight New shows in TvQ's Top 20," which includes *Star Trek*.

TV Guide, October 15, 1966, "No One Ever Upsets the Star," by Michael Fessier, Jr., viewer letter by Judy Pugh, Seattle, program listing for "What Are Little Girls Made Of?," Thursday, October 20.

Syracuse Herald-American, October 16, 1966, "Shatner, Star of a Series, 'Hooked' on UFO Phenomenon," by J.E.V.

The New York Times, October 16, 1966, "How Does Your Favorite Rate? Maybe Higher Than You Think," by Jack Gould.

Broadcasting, October 17, 1966, "The Ratings: A Photo Finish," *Star Trek* at No. 33.

TV Guide, October 22, 1966, program listing for "Miri," Thursday, October 27.

Boston Sunday Herald TV Magazine, October 23, 1966, Leonard Nimoy as Mr. Spock on cover, plus article "How TV Science Fiction Tries to Outshine Cape Kennedy," by Frank Judge.

Weekly Variety, October 26, 1966, "New Shows Have Male Appeal: TvQ," *Star Trek* at No. 2.

TV Guide, October 29, 1966, program listing for "Dagger of the Mind," Thursday, November 3.

Broadcasting, October 31, 1966, "NBC Leads Second Nielsen" and "Movies Are Viewer Favorites," TvQ placing *Star Trek* as favorite new show and No. 2 of 90 prime timers.

Weekly Variety, November 2, 1966, "Frisco Festival Reviews: *Incubus*"; starring Shatner.

TV Guide, November 5, 1966, viewer letter from Andrew Porter, and program listing for "The Corbomite Maneuver," Thursday, November 10, 1966.

TV Guide, November 12, 1966, NBC "Color Us Total" *Star Trek* ad, and program listing for "The Menagerie, Part 1," Thursday, November 17.

Broadcasting, November 14, 1966, "Two More Shows Axed," *Star Trek* in "Top Half" of ratings.

TV Guide, November 19, 1966, program listing for "The Menagerie, Part 2," Thursday, November 24.

TV Guide, November 26, 1966, "What Are a Few Galaxies Among Friends?," by Isaac Asimov, and program listing for "Jack Benny Special," Thursday, December 1, pre-empting *Star Trek*.

Broadcasting, November 28, 1966, "Agency Radio-TV Bill Soars Upward."

TV Guide, December 3, 1966, program listings for "The Conscience of the King," Thursday, December 8.

Broadcasting, December 5, 1966, "TvQ's Top-10 Programs by Age," *Star Trek* No. 5 out of 90 prime timers, all ages.

Daily Variety, December 9, 1966, "*Star Trek* Given Another Hitch."

TV Guide, December 10, 1966, program listing for "Balance of Terror," Thursday, December 15.

TV Guide, December 17, 1966, "Is This the Worst Season?," and program listing for repeat of "What Are Little Girls Made Of?," Thursday, December 22.

Boston Sunday Herald, December 18, 1966, "Shatner Catches a Big Wave," syndicated article from Hollywood, no author credited.

TV Guide, December 24, 1966, "Letters" by Samuel A. Peeples and response by Isaac Asimov, plus program listing for "Shore Leave," Thursday, December 29.

TV Guide, December 31, 1966, program listing for "The Galileo Seven," Thursday, January 6.

Ebony, January 1967, Nichelle Nichols as Lt. Uhura on cover, plus "A New Star in the TV Heavens" picture article, no author credited.

The Cleveland Press TV Showtime, January 6, 1967, with Leonard Nimoy as Mr. Spock on cover, plus article "New Breed of TV Hero," by Tom Weigel.

TV Guide, January 7, 1967, "The Doan Report: Happy NBC Plans Few Changes," plus "TV Teletype: Hollywood," by Joseph Finnigan, and program listing for "The Squire of Gothos," Thursday, January 7, 1967.

Jet, January 12, 1967, "Launch Write-In Drive to Save TV Series *Star Trek*," no author credited.

Syracuse Herald-Journal, January 12, 1967, "Dum De Dum Dum of *Dragnet* Returns," along with spot pick of "Squire of Gothos."

Valley Times TV Week, January 14, 1967, William Shatner as Captain Kirk on cover.

TV Guide, January 14, 1967, program listing for "Arena," Thursday, January 19.

Daily Variety, January 16, 1967, "John Drew Barrymore Reprimanded by SAG for Balking at *Star* Role," no author credited.

Daily Variety, January 19, 1967, "Who's Where."

TV Guide, January 21, 1967, "Letters," by Alice Richards, and program listing for "Tomorrow Is Yesterday," Thursday, January 26.

Broadcasting. January 23, 1967, Polaroid buys sponsorship of *Star Trek*; "Second Season Loses to Movies," with Arbitron and Trendex ratings for "The Squire of Gothos."

Daily Variety, January 25, 1967, report on Roddenberry in hospital.

Weekly Variety, January 25, 1967, "Film Reviews: *First to Fight*," screenplay by Gene L. Coon.

TV Guide, January 28, 1967, program listing for "Court Martial," Thursday, February 2.

Chronicle-Telegram, February 2, 1967, "Television in Review," Thursday, February 2 planned airing of "The Alternative Factor."

TV Guide, February 4, 1967, program listing for "The Return of the Archons," Thursday, February 9.

Broadcasting, February 6, 1967, "A Profusion of Price Tags on Network Minutes."

Daily Variety, February 8, 1967, "Desilu *Mission* Complete Sellout in Latin America."

Daily Variety, February 9, 1967, "Seek 'Star' Femme Regular to Do *Trek* at Desilu."

Oakland Tribune, February 10, 1967, "Bob MacKenzie on Television."

TV Guide, February 11, 1967, program listing for "Space Seed," Thursday, February 16.

Broadcasting, February 13, 1967, "No Deal Yet on Desilu."

Daily Variety, February 16, 1967, "Light and Airy," by Jack Hellman.

TV Guide, February 18, 1967, "Letters," by Mrs. Glen Tortorich, and program listing for "A Taste of Armageddon," Thursday, February 23.

Broadcasting, February 20, 1967, "Desilu, Famous Players to G & W" and "Annual Chess Game Stars: Networks Getting Set for Fall Season."

TV Guide, February 25, 1967, program listing for "This Side of Paradise," Thursday, March 2.

Broadcasting, February 27, 1967, "National Nielsens Give CBS Three in a Row."

Daily Variety, February 27, 1967, "How NBC and ABC Programs Shape Up (As of Now) for '68."

TV Guide, March 4, 1967, William Shatner as Captain Kirk and Leonard Nimoy as Mr. Spock on cover, with article "Product of Two Worlds," by Leslie Raddatz, plus program listing for "The Devil in the Dark," Thursday, March 4.

Daily Variety, March 7, 1967, "NBC-TV Renewal for *Star Trek*."

TV Guide, March 16, 1967, program listing for "Circus," Thursday, March 16, pre-empting *Star Trek*.
TV Guide, March 18, 1967, program listing for "Errand of Mercy," Thursday, March 23.
Syracuse Herald-Journal, March 23, 1967, "TV Tonight" spot pick for "Errand of Mercy."
TV Guide, March 25, 1967, "Review: *Star Trek*," by Cleveland Amory, and program listing for "The Alternative Factor," Thursday, March 30.
Daily Variety, March 28, 1967, "On All Channels: Herb Solow's Crystal Ball," by Dave Kaufman.
Weekly Variety, March 29, 1967, "Desilu's Budget Soars to Record $21-Mil for '67-'68."
TV Radio Mirror, April 1967, "Leonard Nimoy: Success Has Turned My Marriage Upside Down," by William Tusher.
Photo Screen, April 1968, "Leonard Nimoy: I Was a Teen-Age Wallflower."
TV Picture Life, April 1967, "William Shatner, Leonard Nimoy, DeForest Kelley: How Life Can Be Stranger Than Fiction."
16 Magazine, April 1967, "The Real Nimoy!"
TV Guide, April 1, 1967, CLOSE–UP listing for "The City on the Edge of Forever," Thursday, April 6.
Syracuse Herald-Tribune, April 6, 1967, "TV Tonight" spot pick for "The City on the Edge of Forever."
TV Guide, April 8, 1967, program listing for "Operation – Annihilate!," Thursday, April 13.
Los Angeles Herald-Examiner TV Weekly, April 16, 1967, "Spock, the Mysterious," by Charles Witbeck.
Weekly Variety, April 17, 1967, full-page ad for *Star Trek* from Desilu.
Weekly Variety, April 19, 1967, "Record Reviews: *Leonard Nimoy: Mr. Spock's Music from Outer Space*."
Daily Variety, April 24, 1967, "Oscarcast Runaway Leader of Latest 30-City Nielsen."
Daily Variety, April 26, 1967, "On All Channels: Seek a Filly for *Horse*," by Dave Kaufman.
Daily Variety, April 26, 1967, "Just for *Variety*," by Army Archerd.
Syracuse Herald-Journal, April 27, 1967, "TV Tonight" spot pick for repeat of "The Naked Time."
TV Guide, April 29, 1967, "Mr. Spock Is Dreamy," by Isaac Asimov.
Daily Variety, May 2, 1967, "CBS Wins Emmy Nominee Race" and "Barrier on *Trek*."
Daily Variety, May 12, 1967, full page "Thank You" from Howard A. Anderson Co. concerning Emmy nomination.
TV Guide, May 13, 1967, "Who Said TV Has to Make Sense?," by Stanley Frank, and "He Sees Beyond the Cameras."
Chronicle-Telegram, May 20, 1967, "Most Viewer Suggestions Go into TV Wastebaskets.," by Gene Handsaker.
TV Guide, May 20, 1967, "Review by Cleveland Amory: Second Thoughts."
Weekly Variety, May 24, 1967, "TvQ Does Some Share-Cropping on New Season, and It Comes Up NBC," by Bill Greenley.
Daily Variety, May 31, 1967, "On All Channels," by Dave Kaufman.
TV Guide, June 3, 1967, CLOSE-UP listing for repeat of "Shore Leave," Thursday, June 8.
Daily Variety, June 9, 1967, Joseph D'Agosta casting for Desilu's *Star Trek*, *The Lucy Show*, *Mission: Impossible* and *Mannix*.
Weekly Variety, June 14, 1967, "Negro Employment in Network TV Extends to Seven Nights Next Fall," by Murray Horowitz.
Daily Variety, June 21, 1967, "On All Channels," by Dave Kaufman.
Daily Variety, June 28, 1967, "On All Channels," by Dave Kaufman.
Star Trek: K-G, Planet of Death, July 1967, Western Publishing.
TV Star Parade, July 1967, "Dressing Room Secrets of *Star Trek*."
16 Magazine, July 1967, "My Other Life," by Leonard Nimoy.
Silver Screen, July 1967, "Why Leonard Nimoy Hides His Two Children."
TV Guide, July 15, 1967, "Let Me Off at the Next Planet," no author credited.
TV Guide, July 22, 1967, Dot Records ad for "Leonard Nimoy Presents Mr. Spock's Music from Outer Space."
TV Week, July 23, 1967, "Jackrabbit Hunt on Motorcycle."
Daily Variety, July 28, 1967, "Just for *Variety*," by Army Archerd, *Star Trek* wins NAACP Image Award.
TV Guide, July 29, 1967, CLOSE-UP listing for repeat of "Balance of Terror," Thursday, August 3.
Modern Screen, August 1967, "How Leonard Nimoy Conquers His Earthly Problems."
TV Star Parade, August 1967, William Shatner as Captain Kirk and Leonard Nimoy as Mr. Spock on cover, plus articles "Leonard Nimoy's Deathwatch," by Susan Dennis, and "Bill Shatner's Triple Threat," by Lilyan Jones.
TV Radio Mirror, August 1967, Leonard Nimoy as Mr. Spock on cover, plus article "How a Man with Pointed Ears Feels -- Deep Down -- When the Makeup is Off," by Louise Almond.
Star Trek Mail Call, August 1967, from NBC.
TV Guide, August 5, 1967, CLOSE-UP listing for repeat of "This Side of Paradise," Thursday, August 10.
TV Guide, August 12, 1967, program listing for "An Evening at Tanglewood," pre-empting *Star Trek*.
Daily Variety, August 14, 1967, "NAACP Hands Out First Image Awards."

653

Daily Variety, August 30, 1967, "With *Trek* on Hiatus, Stars on Promo Prowl."

Daily Variety, August 31, 1967, "Gene Coon Quits; Lucas Reins *Trek*."

TV Star Annual, No. 23, Early Fall 1967, William Shatner as Captain Kirk and Leonard Nimoy as Mr. Spock on cover.

Screen Stories, September 1967, "Leonard Nimoy and Bill Shatner: Their Topsy-Turvy Lives," by Dora Albert.

Castle of Frankenstein, No. 11, September 1967, Leonard Nimoy as Mr. Spock on cover, plus articles "The Star Trek Story," by Allan Asherman, and "Saucers Do Exist."

TV Picture Life, September 1967, "How Leonard Nimoy Tried to Save William Shatner's Marriage!"

TV Guide, September 2, 1967, program listing for "Police Story," Friday, September 7.

TV Guide, September 9, 1967, "NBC Week" ad, and program listing for "Amok Time," Friday, September 15.

The Times Recorder, September 24, 1967, UPI article "*Star Trek*'s Nichelle Nichols Lives in Integrated Wilshire.," by Vernon Scott.

Broadcasting, September 25, 1967, "Few of TV's Virgin Shows Look like Hits"; ratings for "Amok Time."

The News, September 28, 1967, "*Star Trek* Creator Wins Hugo Award."

The Times Recorder, September 29, 1967, "What's on the Air," by Naomi, spot pick for "The Changeling."

Movie Mirror, October 1967, "Leonard Nimoy: My Mother Prayed God Would Forgive Me," by Judy Merlin.

Broadcasting, October 2, 1967, "New Shows Get No Brass Ring."

TV Guide, October 14, 1967, "4 X 4 Twins = 2000 Androids" picture article for upcoming "I. Mudd."

Daily Variety, October 19, 1967, "*Star Trek* Given Midseason Pickup."

Victoria Daily Times, October 28, 1967, "Canada's First Man in Space," by Walter Roessing.

Movieland, November 1967, Leonard Nimoy: Fame Has its Drawbacks!"

Photoplay, November 1967, "Leonard Nimoy: Why I Go to Sex Education Classes with My Son."

TV Picture Life, November 1967, "Leonard Nimoy: My Wife Wept When I Said I'm Through."

Tiger Beat, November 1967, Leonard Nimoy as Mr. Spock on cover, plus articles "Leonard Nimoy's Confessions about His Emotions" and "Bill Shatner: Restless Man Looking for a Challenge."

TV Star Parade, November 1967, with articles "DeForest Kelley Is Out of This World" and "Psychologists Reveals the Primitive Sex Appeal of Dr. [*sic*] Spock," by Jane Harrol.

The Cleveland Press: TV Showtime, November 3, 1967, Nichelle Nichols as Lt. Uhura on cover; "*Trek* to Halt 5-Year Mission a Little Early."

Chronicle-Telegraph, November 11, 1967, "*Star Trek*'s Spock Speechless in Name Only."

Daily Variety, November 14, 1967, "On All Channels: Art Wallace *Earth* Producer," by Dave Kaufman.

TV TIMES, November 15, 1967, William Shatner as Captain Kirk and Leonard Nimoy as Mr. Spock on cover.

TV Guide, November 18, 1967, William Shatner as Captain Kirk and Leonard Nimoy as Mr. Spock on cover, with article "*Star Trek* Wins the Ricky Schwartz Award," by Leslie Raddatz, and full-page RCA Victor color TV ad featuring Kirk and Spock.

Syracuse Herald-American, November 26, 1967, spot pick for "Friday's Child."

The News, November 28, 1967, "Dimensional Design Art on Exhibit."

The Times Recorder, November 29, 1967, "What's on the Air," by Naomi, spot pick for "The Trouble with Tribbles."

Model Car & Science, December 1967, U.S.S. Enterprise on cover, plus "Space Queen!" article, no author credited.

Popular Science, December 1967, "TV's *Star Trek*: How They Mix Science Fact with Fiction," by James W. Wright.

Photo TV Land, December 1967, "Outer Space's Inside Battle," by Rhonda Green.

Mad Magazine, December 1967, "Star Blecch," by Dick de Bartolo and Mort Drucker.

Castle of Frankenstein, No. 12, December 1967, with Leonard Nimoy as Mr. Spock on cover, and article, "STAR TREK Star Spock Speaks."

TV Star Parade, December 1967, "Space Age Crew Enjoys Old Fashioned Barbecue."

TV and Movie Play, December 1967, "Leonard Nimoy's Confessions About His Emotions."

Daily Variety, December 8, 1967, "Just for Variety," by Army Archerd -- Nimoy in Nazi uniform.

Save *Star Trek* letter, December 11, 1967, by John & Bjo Trimble.

TV Radio Mirror, January 1968, "The 'Other Girl' in Leonard Nimoy's Life," a pictorial article as fan club head Peggye Vickers visits the set.

TV Star Parade, January 1968, "Leonard Nimoy Speaks Out on LSD, Religion and Dirty Movies!"

TV Radio Mirror, January 1968, "The Other Girl in Leonard Nimoy's Life," by Gary Denton.

Screen and TV Album, January 1968, "Leonard Nimoy: He's Filled with Emotion."

The Times Recorder, January 5, 1968, "What's on the Air," by Naomi, spot pick for "The Gamesters of Triskelion."

Daily Variety, January 8, 1968, "Light and Airy," by Jack Hellman.
Broadcasting, January 8, 1968, Carnation to sponsor *Star Trek*.
TV TIMES, January 10, 1968, Leonard Nimoy as Mr. Spock on cover.
Daily Variety, January 16, 1968, "Coon Takes Reins on *Takes a Thief*" – Gene Coon, producing.
Daily Variety, January 23, 1967, "On All Channels: Roddenberry Joins Ranks of Disenchanted TV Creators," by Dave Kaufman.
Daily Variety, January 24, 1968, "On All Channels: Creators Who Would Do a TV Fadeout," by Dave Kaufman -- Roddenberry on the TV business.
The Telegram TV Weekly, January 26, 1968, Leonard Nimoy as Mr. Spock on cover, plus article "That Undiscovered Country Where Things Go Bleep in the Night," by Jim McPherson.
Daily Variety, January 30, 1968, "On All Channels," by Dave Kaufman -- *Gene Coon* on taking producing *It Takes a Thief*.
Weekly Variety, January 31, 1968, "September Mourn Dropsheet: Agonizing Over Marginal Series," by Les Brown.
Analog Science Fiction / Science Fact, February 1968, "To Make a *Star Trek*."
Inside Star Trek, issue 8, February 1968, George Takei interviewed by Ruth Berman.
TV Star Parade, February 1968, "What the Stars Predict for *Star Trek*'s Children."
TV Picture Life, February 1968, "Leonard Nimoy Dropped!"
Screen Stars, February, 1968, "How Leonard Nimoy Helps Addicts Live Again," by Katherine Devino.
TV Picture Life, February 1968, "Now That Success Has Finally Come, Leonard Nimoy Faces Every Star's Heartbreak."
The News, February 2, 1968, "A Closer Look at Television," by Ernie Kreiling.
Weekly Variety, February 7, 1968, "Film Sound Editors' Picks."
Broadcasting. February 12, 1968, NBC "iffy" list.
Daily Variety, February 16, 1968, "Hint Renewal of *Star Trek* on NBC."
Broadcasting, February 19, 1968, *Star Trek* may move to Monday.
Daily Variety, February 20, 1968, "NBC High on *Trek*."
Weekly Variety, February 21, 1968, "*Star Trek* Saved from Death Row by Write-In Vote" -- planned for Monday at 7:30 p.m.
The Valley Independent, February 23, 1968, "Television Tonight," spot pick for "By Any Other Name."
Broadcasting, February 26, 1968, *Star Trek* scheduled for Mondays at 7:30 p.m.
TV Picture Life, March 1968, "I'll Never Forgive Nimoy and Shatner!"
Motion Picture, March 1968, "Leonard Nimoy: The Names They Call Him Back Home."
Broadcasting, March 4, 1968, sponsorship needed to keep *Star Trek* on Mondays at 7:30; letters protesting rumors of cancellation arriving at NBC.
Daily Variety, March 4, 1968, "U Expands Videal for Gene Coon."
TV TIMES, March 13, 1968, William Shatner as Captain Kirk on cover.
Weekly Variety, March 13, 1968, "TV Nets' 1968-69 Schedule (2nd Draft)" with *Star Trek* on Mondays, plus "Writers Guild Nominates 13 Shows," with Harlan Ellison for "The City on the Edge of Forever" pitted against Boris Sobelman for "The Return of the Archons."
Variety, March 15, 1968, full-page ad congratulating Glen Glenn Sound for Golden Reel Award for *Star Trek*, plus full-page ad from Paramount for same award.
Broadcasting, March 18, 1968, "*Laugh-In* Staying Put" -- *Star Trek* goes to Fridays instead of Mondays.
Daily Variety, March 18, 1968, "*Trek* May Be off NBC's Track in Fall."
Daily Variety, March 19, 1968, "The Return of the Archons" nominated for 1967 WGA award.
Weekly Variety, March 20, 1968, "Re-Recording Mixers Now Recognized: Editor's Golden Reel Trophy Goes to *Bonnie, Doolittle* and *Star Trek*."
Daily Variety, March 25, 1968, "Writers Guild Laurels Casey Robinson; Seaton Wins Davies Award; Show Dull" -- Harlan Ellison wins for "The City on the Edge of Forever."
Daily Variety, March 27, 1968, "Bitter at NBC, So Roddenberry Moves Upstairs" and review for *Two Sides of Leonard Nimoy*.
TV Guide, March 29, 1968, CLOSE-UP listing for "Assignment: Earth."
Daily Variety, March 29, 1968, "'Man in Middle' U's Next 2-Hour Film for CBS-TV" assignment for Coon.
Sunday Herald Traveler, March 31, 1968, "Is There a Doctor in the House?," by Vernon Scott.
Teen Screen, April 1968, William Shatner as Captain Kirk on cover, with article concerning torchlight parades in front of NBC.
TV Radio Movie Guide, April 1968, "Leonard Nimoy: The Girls That Beg for His Love."
Variety, April 1, 1968, *Photoplay* awards *Star Trek* as "Most Popular Television Show" and "Fred Freiberger *Trek* Coproducer."
Broadcasting, April 8, 1968, "TV Program Outlook," TvQ predicts *Star Trek* to fail at Fridays at 10 p.m.
Chronicle-Telegram, April 9, 1968, "Nimoy Can Hardly Believe His Popularity with Teens," by Gary Bainbridge.

The Valley Independent, April 11, 1968, "Shatner Thrilled with Space Show," by Kurt Lassen.

Daily Variety, April 17, 1968, Emmy nominations.

Broadcasting, April 22, 1968, Pepsico sponsors *Star Trek*.

Daily Variety, April 26, 1968, "13 *Star Trek* Scribes," includes David Gerrold, Jerry Sohl, Theodore Sturgeon, Marc Daniels and David Harmon.

16 Magazine, May 1968, "The Many Faces of the *Star Trek*kers."

Teen, May 1968, "The Ears Have It! -- Pointedly!"

Weekly Variety, May 1, 1968, "U *Middle* for CBS-TV" -- written by Gene Coon.

Los Angeles Times, "Negro Family in Place," by Hal Humphrey.

Weekly Variety, May 15, 1968, "Film Reviews: *Journey to Shiloh*" – written by Gene Coon, plus full-page Desilu ad congratulating Roddenberry, Coon, Nimoy, Jim Rugg, Howard Anderson, Film Effects of Hollywood and Westheimer on their Emmy nominations..

Variety, May 16, 1968, full-page congratulations from Roddenberry to Joseph Westheimer for Emmy nomination.

Daily Variety, May 21, 1968, "Nimoy Turns Thrush on Phyllis Diller Show."

Daily Variety, June 4, 1968, "2 Trek Promotions" – Gregg Peters and Edward Milkis.

Daily Variety, June 5, 1968, "Roddenberry Starts Feature Filming in 2-Pic NGC Deal" plus "Network News Makes Noise for 1st Time in Chi School Poll."

Daily Variety, June 12, 1968, "General TV Crackdown on Violence" – Gene Coon rewriting violence out of scripts.

TV Guide, June 22, 1968, "The Intergalactic Golden Boy," by Robert Higgins.

L.A. Times West Magazine, June 23, 1968, "Although Leonard Nimoy Is a Star He's Still His Mama's Boy," by Caryl Rivers.

Gene Roddenberry letter to fans announcing mail order company, July 1968, in first Lincoln enterprises catalogue.

Daily Variety, July 1, 1968, "Nine *Star Trek* Scribes."

Daily Variety, July 9, 1968, "7 *Star* Directors," including Michael O'Herlihy and Paul Stanley.

Weekly Variety, July 10, 1968, "New NBC Scatter Biz."

TV Guide, July 19, 1968, CLOSE-UP listing for repeat of "Metamorphosis," Friday, July 25, 1967.

TV Guide, July 27, 1968, "Who's Watching What?," by Dick Hobson.

Sunday Herald Telegram TV Magazine, July 28, 1968, Nichelle Nichols as Lt. Uhura on cover, with "How Cast Alone Kept Show on Air," by Frank Judge.

TV TIMES, July 31, 1968, William Shatner as Captain Kirk and Leonard Nimoy as Mr. Spock on cover.

TV Radio Mirror, August 1968, "The Terrible Price Leonard Nimoy Paid to Be True to His God."

TV Radio Movie Guide, August 1968, Leonard Nimoy as Mr. Spock on cover with articles "Nimoy: He Flew the Plane Himself," "Shatner: I Can't Control My Temper" and "Kelley: Wants to Put Nimoy in a Time Capsule!"

Who's Who in TV, Late Summer 1968, with William Shatner as Captain Kirk and Leonard Nimoy as Mr. Spock on cover.

Daily Variety, August 8, 1968, "Light and Airy," by Jack Hellman. Interview with Fred Freiberger.

Daily Variety, August 9, 1968, "Trek Slow, So Par Changes Directors" – about Ralph Senensky being replaced on "The Tholian Web."

Daily Variety, August 15, 1968, "Shari Lewis and Mate Plot *Trek* chapter."

The Edwardsville Intelligencer, August 16, 1968, "TV Scout," spot pick for repeat of "The Deadly Years."

Daily Variety, August 21, 1968, "On All Channels: Harlan Ellison on TV's *Sins*," interviewed by Dave Kaufman, plus review of Leonard Nimoy album *The Way I Feel*.

TV Guide, August 24, 1968, William Shatner as Captain Kirk, Leonard Nimoy as Mr. Spock and DeForest Kelley as Dr. McCoy on cover; "Where Is the Welcome Mat?" article.

The New York Times, August 25, 1968, "Girls All Want to Touch the Ears," by Digby Diehl.

Inside Star Trek, issue 2, August 1968, by D.C. Fontana; Fred Phillips interview,

Inside Star Trek, issue 3, September 1968, Dorothy C. Fontana interviewed by Ruth Berman; DeForest Kelley interviewed by Ruth Berman.

TV Star Parade, September 1968, "Leonard Nimoy's Family Reunion."

Daily Variety, September 4, 1968, "On All Channels: The Lonely *Trek*," by Dave Kaufman.

The Times Recorder, September 20, 1968, "What's on the Air," by Naomi, spot pick on "Spock's Brain."

Daily Variety, September 23, 1968, "Spock's Brain" review, by Murf, and *Land of the Giants* review.

Daily Variety, September 24, 1968, Nielsen ratings for New York.

Broadcasting, September 30, 1968, First Showdown at the Ratings Coral" -- for "Spock's Brain."

Inside Star Trek, issue 4, Oct. 1968, by Irving Feinberg; Walter Matt Jefferies interviewed by Dorothy Fontana.

Inside TV, October 1968, "DeForest Kelley: His Stardom Trek Was Filled with Heartbreak," by Bea Barr.

Screen and TV Album, October 1968, "Up Up Up and Away."

13-1.	Belli, Caesar	*Starlog #121*, interviewed by Eric Niderost, August 1987.
13-2.	Belli, Caesar	*Star Trek Communicator*, interviewed by Kevin Dilmore, December 1998.
14.	Belli, Melvin	*Starlog #121*, interviewed by Eric Niderost, Aug. 1987.
15.	Bergere, Lee	*Starlog #112*, interviewed by Frank Garcia & Mark Phillips, November 1986.
16-1.	Bixby, Jerome	*Cinefantastique*, July 1996.
16-2.	Bixby, Jerome	*Star Trek Interview Book*, interviewed by Allan Asherman (Pocket Books, 1988).
16-3.	Bixby, Jerome	*Trek Classic*, interviewed by Edward Gross (Image Publishing of New York, 1991).
16-4.	Bixby, Jerome	*Captain's Logs*, interviewed by Edward Gross & Mark Altman (Little, Brown, 1995)
17.	**Black, John D.F.**	**Author interview, 2013.**
17-1.	Black, John D.F.	*Gene Roddenberry: The Myth and the Man Behind Star Trek*, interviewed by Joel Engel (Hyperion, 1994).
17-2.	Black, John D.F.	*Star Trek: TOS Box Set*, Season 1.
17-3.	Black, John D.F.	StarTrek.com interview, date unknown.
17-4.	Black, John D.F.	*Trek Classic*, interviewed by Edward Gross (Image Publishing of New York, 1991).
17-5.	Black, John D.F.	*Starlog* Star Trek 25th Anniversary Special, 1991.
17a.	**Black, Mary Stilwell**	**Author interview, April 2013.**
17b.	**Blackburn, Bill**	**Author interview, May 2008.**
18-1.	Bloch, Robert	*Cinefantastique*, interviewed by Ben Herndon, March 1987.
18-2.	Bloch, Robert	*Cinefantastique*, July 1996.
18-3.	Bloch, Robert	*Enterprise Incidents*, November 1979.
18-4.	Bloch, Robert	*Starlog #113*, interviewed by Randy & Jean-Marc Lofficier, December 1986.
19.	Bouchet, Barbara	*Starlog #141*, interviewed by Mark Phillips, April 1989.
19-1.	Bouchet, Barbara	imdb.com
19a.	**Bower, Antoinette**	**Letter to author, 2013.**
20.	Bradshaw, Booker T.	*Starlog #206*, interviewed by Mark Phillips, Sept. 1994.
21.	Brill, Charlie	Sci Fi Channel, 1997.
21-1.	**Brill, Charlie**	**Author's interview, 2013.**
22-1.	Brooks, Rolland	*Cinefantastique*, interviewed by Ben Herndon, March 1987.
22-2.	Brooks, Rolland	*Cinefantastique*, July 1996.
22a.	Brooks, Stephen	*TV Guide*, July 23, 1965, interviewed by Leslie Raddatz.
23-1.	Brown, Mark Robert	*Star Trek Communicator*, interviewed by Kevin Dilmore, December 1998.
23-2.	Brown, Mark Robert	startrek.com staff interview, September 9, 2010.
24.	Brown, Robert	*Starlog #163*, interviewed by Duanne S. Arnott, Feb. 1991.
24-1.	**Brown, Robert**	**Author interview, 2013.**
26-1.	Butler, Robert	*Starlog #117*, interviewed by Edward Gross, April 1987.
26-2.	Butler, Robert	*Star Trek Interview Book*, interviewed by Allan Asherman (Pocket Books, 1988).
26-3.	Butler, Robert	Archive of American Television, interviewed by Stephen Abramson, January 2004.

27-1.	Campbell, William	*From Sawdust to Stardust*, interviewed by Lee Rioux (Pocket Books, February 2005)
27-2.	Campbell, William	Sci Fi Channel, 1997.
27-3.	Campbell, William	*Starlog #138*, interviewed by Steven H. Wilson, Jan. 1989.
27-4.	Campbell, William	*Star Trek: TOS* Box Set, Season 1.
27-5.	Campbell, William	*Star Trek Greatest Guest Stars*, interviewed by Robert Greenberger & Ian Spelling (HarperPaperbacks, 1997)
27-6.	Campbell, William	*Star Trek Memories*, interviewed by William Shatner (1994, HarperPrism)
27-7.	Campbell, William	*The World of Star Trek*, interviewed by David Gerrold (Ballantine Books, 1973)
27-8.	Campbell, William	*Captains' Logs*, interviewed by Edward Gross & Mark A. Altman (Little, Brown, 1995)
28-1.	Carabatsos, Steven	*Starlog #168*, interviewed by Edward Gross, July 1991.
28-2.	Carabatsos, Steven	*Trek Classic*, interviewed by Edward Gross (Image Publishing of New York, 1991)
29	**Carmel, Roger C.**	**Author's interview, 1982.**
29-1.	Carmel, Roger C.	*Trek Classic*, interviewed by Edward Gross (Image Publishing of New York, 1991)
29-2.	Carmel, Roger C.	*Starlog #127*, interviewed by Dan Madsen, Feb. 1988.
29-3.	Carmel, Roger C.	*Star Trek's Greatest Guest Stars*, interviewed by Dan Madsen (HarperCollins, 1997)
30.	Carr, Paul	*Starlog #155*, interviewed by Bill & Jennifer Florence, June 1990.
31.	Cassidy, Ted	*Starlog #115*, interviewed Joel Eisner, February 1987.
31-1	Chambers, John	*Questar*, interviewed by Elaine Santangelo, December 1980.
31a.	Chapnick, Morris	*The Making of Star Trek*, interviewed by Stephen E. Whitfield (Ballantine Books, 1968)
31b.	**Chomsky, Marvin**	**Author interview, 2011.**
31c.	Clarke, Arthur C.	*TV Guide: Star Trek: Four Generations*, 1995.
31d.	Clark, Bobby	Roddenberry.com, interviewed by John and Ken, 2013.
31e.	**Clark, Bobby**	**Author interview, 2013.**
32.	Cobb, Julie	*Starlog #133*, interviewed by Mark Phillips & Frank Garcia, August 1988.
32-1.	**Cobb, Julie**	**Author's interview, 2013.**
33-1.	Colicos, John	*Starlog #138*, interviewed by Peter Bloch-Hansen, January 1989.
33-2	Colicos, John	*Star Trek Communicator*, interviewed by Chris Roe, October 1995.
33-3.	Colicos, John	*Star Trek's Greatest Guest Stars*, interviewed by Peter Bloch-Hansen (HarperCollins, 1997).
33a.	Collins, Joan	*TV Guide, Star Trek 30 Year Special Magazine*, 1996.
34.	Colodny, Lester	*Great Birds of the Galaxy*, by Edward Gross & Mark A. Altman (Boxtree Limited, 1994).
35.	Comi, Paul	*Starlog #157*, interviewed by Mark Phillips, Aug. 1990.
35-1.	**Comi, Paul**	**Author interview, 2013.**

36.	Cook, Elisha	*Starlog #119*, interviewed by Bill Warren, June 1987.
36aa.	Cook, Elisha	*Science Fiction Television Series: Episode Guides, Histories, and Cast s and Credits for 62 Prime-Time Shows, 1959 through 1989*, interviewed by Mark Phillips and Frank Garcia (McFarland & Co., 2006)
35a.	Cookerly, Jack	*The Quarterly Journal of the Library of Congress*, 1982, "Keeping Score of the Scores: Music for *Star Trek*," interviewed by Fred Steiner.
36a.	Coon, Gene	*The Making of Star Trek*, interviewed by Stephen E. Whitfield (Ballantine Books, 1968).
36b.	Coon, Gene	*The Trouble with Tribbles*, memos included in book by David Gerrold (Ballantine Books, 1973).
36c.	Coon, Gene	*The Trouble with Tribbles*, as told to David Gerrold (Ballantine Books, 1973).
36d.	Coon, Gene	*TV Guide*, July 15, 1967, "Let Me Off at the Next Planet."
37-1.	Courage, Alexander	*The Music of Star Trek*, interviewed by Jeff Bond (Lone Eagle Publishing, 1999).
37-2.	Courage, Alexander	*Starlog #107*, interviewed by Randy & Jean-Marc Lofficier, June 1986.
37-3.	Courage, Alexander	*Cinefantastique*, interviewed by Hans Siden, March 1987.
37-4.	Courage, Alexander	*The Quarterly Journal of the Library of Congress*, 1982, "Keeping Score of the Scores: Music for *Star Trek*, interviewed by Fred Steiner.
38.	Cory, Jeff	*Starlog #149*, interviewed by Kathryn M. Drennan, December 1989.
39-1.	Craig, Yvonne	*Starlog #149*, interviewed by Kyle Counts, Dec. 1989.
39-2.	Craig, Yvonne	startrekpeople.com, February 1997.
39-3.	Craig, Yvonne	*From Ballet to the Batcave and Beyond*, by Yvonne Craig (Kudu Press, 2000)
40.	Cramer, Douglass	*Gene Roddenberry: The Myth and the Man Behind Star Trek*, interviewed by Joel Engle (Hyperion, 1994).
41.	Crawford, John	*Starlog #223*, interviewed by Joel Eisner, Feb. 1996.
42-1.	Crawford, Oliver	*Great Birds of the Galaxy*, interviewed by Edward Gross (Boxtree Limited, 1994)
42-2.	Crawford, Oliver	*Starlog #140*, interviewed by Edward Gross, March 1989.
42-3.	Crawford, Oliver	*Trek Classic*, interviewed by Edward Gross, (Image Publishing of New York, 1991)
42-4.	Crawford, Oliver	imdb.com
43.	**D'Agosta, Joe**	**Author interview, 2010.**
43-1.	D'Agosta, Joe	*Cinefantastique*, July 1996.
43-2.	D'Agosta, Joe	*Star Trek Memories*, interviewed by William Shatner (HarperCollins, 1984)
43-3.	D'Agosta, Joe	*Inside Star Trek issue #7*, by Joe D'Agosta, 1968.
43a.	**Dalton, Lezlie**	**Author interview, March 2012.**
44-1.	Daniels, Marc	*Great Birds of the Galaxy*, interviewed by Edward Gross (Boxtree Limited, 1994).
44-2.	Daniels, Marc	*Starlog #114*, interviewed by Edward Gross, Jan. 1987.
44-3.	Daniels, Marc	*The Star Trek Interview Book*, interviewed by Allan Asherman (Pocket Books, 1988).
44-4.	Daniels, Marc	*Trek Classic*, interviewed by Edward Gross (Image Publishing of New York, 1991).
44-5.	Daniels, Marc	*Variety*, July 27, 1949, "Light Up the Drama," by Marc Daniels.

44-6.	Daniels, Marc	*Variety*, November 12, 1958, "TNT's Marc Daniels Believes TVs Closed-Circuit Show Biz Is Dynamite," interviewed by Jo Ranson.
44-7.	Daniels, Marc	*New York Times*, April 29, 1989.
45.	Dante, Michael	*Starlog #174*, interviewed by Mark Phillips, Jan. 1992.
45-1.	**Dante, Michael**	**Author interview, 2013.**
45a.	Darby, Kim	popcultureaddict.com, "Truth and Grit," interviewed by Sam Tweedle, September 2010.
46.	Datin, Richard C.	*Cinefantastique*, July 1996.
47.	**De Lugo, Win**	**Author interview, 2010.**
48.	Ditmars, Ivan	*The Music of Star Trek*, interviewed by Jeff Bond (Lone Eagle, 1998)
49.	Dobkin, Lawrence	*The Star Trek Interview Book*, interviewed by Allan Asherman (Pocket Books, 1988).
50.	**Donahue, Elinor**	**Author interview, 2013**
50-1.	Donahue, Elinor	*Starlog #130*, interviewed by Frank Garcia, May 1988.
50-2.	Donahue, Elinor	Archive of American Television, interviewed by Jennifer Howard, April 25, 2006.
50-3.	Donahue, Elinor	*Star Trek Fotonovel #5*, interviewed by Caryle Eagle (Bantam Books, February 1978).
51.	**Donner, Jack**	**Author interview, 2012.**
51a.	Donner, Jack	Sci Fi Channel, 1997.
52.	**Doohan, James**	**Author interview, 1992.**
52-1.	Doohan, James	*Beam Me Up, Scotty*, interviewed by Peter David (Pocket Books, 1996).
52-2.	Doohan, James	*The Best of Trek*, interviewed by Walter Irwin & G.B. Love (Signet Books, 1978).
52-3.	Doohan, James	*Cinefantastique*, July 1996.
52-4.	Doohan, James	Sci Fi Channel, 1997.
52-5.	Doohan, James	*Shatner: Where No Man …*, interviewed by Sondra Marshak & Myrna Culbreath (Tempo Books, 1979).
52-6.	Doohan, James	*Star Trek Communicator*, interviewed by Dan Madsen, August 1999.
52-7.	Doohan, James	*The World of Star Trek*, interviewed by David Gerrold (Ballantine Books, 1973).
52-8a.	Doohan, James	*TV Star Parade*, June 1968, interviewed by Roger Elwood.
52-8.	Doohan, James	*Inside Star Trek issue #5*, interviewed by Ruth Berman, Nov. 1968.
52a.	**Drexler, Doug**	**Arthur's interview, 2013.**
53.	Dromm, Andrea	*Starlog Yearbook*, interviewed by Mark Phillips, Aug. 1998.
54.	Dugan, John T.	*Starlog #194*, interviewed by Bill Florence, Sept. 1993.
55-1.	Duning, George	*The Music of Star Trek*, interviewed by Jeff Bong (Lone Eagle, 1999).
55-2.	Duning, George	*The Star Trek Interview Book*, interviewed by Allan Asherman (Pocket Books, 1988).
56.	Dunn, Linwood	*Cinefantastique*, July 1996.
57-1.	Dwyer, John	*Cinefantastique*, July 1996.
57-2.	Dwyer, John	*Star Trek* Box Set, Season #2.
57-3.	Dwyer, John	*Inside Star Trek issue #1*, interviewed by Dorothy C. Fontana, July 1968.
57-4.	**Dwyer, John**	**Author interview, 2010.**

57a.	Ehrlich, Jake	Telegram from Ehrlich, January 29, 1960, in the Kelley Home Archives, CA, Jake Ehrlich collection, cited in *From Sawdust to Stardust*, by Terry Lee Rioux (Pocket Books, February 2005)
57b.	Eitner, Don	*Science Fiction Television Series: Episode Guides, Histories, and Cast s and Credits for 62 Prime-Time Shows, 1959 through 1989*, interviewed by Mark Phillips and Frank Garcia (McFarland & Co., 2006)
58.	**Ellison, Harlan**	**Author interview, 2013.**
58-1.	Ellison, Harlan	*Cinefantastique, Volume 17, No. 2*, interviewed by Ben Hernson, March 1987.
58-2.	Ellison, Harlan	*The City on the Edge of Forever*, by Harlan Ellison (White Wolf Publishing, 1996).
58-3.	Ellison, Harlan	Sci Fi Channel, 1997.
58-4.	Ellison, Harlan	*Trek Classic*, interviewed by Edward Gross (Image Publishing of New York, 1991).
58-5.	Ellison, Harlan	*The Trouble with Tribbles*, interviewed by David Gerrold (Ballantine Books, 1973).
58-6.	Ellison, Harlan	*Star Trek Fotonovel #1*, interviewed by Sandra Cawson (Bantam Books, November 1977).
58a.	Felton, Norman	*Gene Roddenberry: The Myth and the Man Behind StarTrek*, interviewed by Joel Engel (Hyperion, 1994).
58b.	Feinberg, Irving	*Inside Star Trek, issue 4*, by Irving Feinberg, Oct. 1968.
58bb.	Felton, Norman	*Gene Roddenberry: The Myth and the Man Behind StarTrek*, by Joel Engel (Hyperion, 1994).
58c.	**Erman, John**	**Author interview, 2011.**
59.	Ferdin, Pamelyn	*Star Trek Communicator*, interviewed by Kevin Dilmore, Dec. 1998.
60.	Fernandez, Jackie	*Great Birds of the Galaxy*, interviewed by Edward Gross (Boxtree Limited, 1994).
62.	Finley, Jack	*The Star Trek Interview Book*, interviewed by Allan Asherman (Pocket, 1988).
63-1.	Finnerman, Gerald Perry	*Cinefantastique Vol. 17, No. 2*, interviewed by Dennis Fischer, March 1987.
63-2.	Finnerman, Gerald Perry	*Television: Companion to the PBS Series*, interviewed by Michael Winship, 1988.
63-3.	Finnerman, Gerald Perry	Archive of Television, interviewed by Karen Herman, Oct. 8, 2002.
64-1.	**Fontana, Dorothy C.**	**Author interview, 1994.**
64-2.	**Fontana, Dorothy C.**	**Author interview, 2007.**
64-3.	**Fontana, Dorothy C.**	**Author interview, 2007.**
64-4.	**Fontana, Dorothy C.**	**Author interview, 2007.**
64-4a.	**Fontana, Dorothy C.**	**Author's email interview, 2012.**
64-4b.	**Fontana, Dorothy C.**	**Notes sent to Author, 2013.**
64-5.	Fontana, Dorothy C.	*Cinefantastique, Vol. 17, No. 2*, interviewed by Ben Herndon, March 1987.
64-6.	Fontana, Dorothy C.	*Cinefantastique*, July 1996.
64-7.	Fontana, Dorothy C.	*The City on the Edge of Forever*, interviewed by Harlan Ellison (White Wolf Publishing, 1996).
64-8.	Fontana, Dorothy C.	*Enterprise Incidents #7*, interviewed by Dennis Fischer, Nov. 1979.
64-9.	Fontana, Dorothy C.	*From Sawdust to Stardust*, interviewed by Terry Lee Rioux (Pocket Books, 2005)

64-10.	Fontana, Dorothy C.	*Gene Roddenberry: The Myth and the Man Behind StarTrek*, from Foreword by D.C. Fontana and interview by Joel Engel (Hyperion, 1994).
64-11.	Fontana, Dorothy C.	*Great Birds of the Galaxy*, interviewed by Edward Gross (Boxtree Limited, 1994).
64-12.	Fontana, Dorothy C.	*Starlog #41*, letter from Dorothy Fontana, Dec. 1980.
64-13.	Fontana, Dorothy C.	*Starlog #118*, interviewed by Edward Gross, May 1987.
64-14.	Fontana, Dorothy C.	*Star Trek: TOS* Box Set, Season 2.
64-15.	Fontana, Dorothy C.	*Star Trek Lives!*, by Jacqueline Lichtenberg, Sondra Marshak & Joan Winston (Bantam Books, 1973).
64-16.	Fontana, Dorothy C.	*Star Trek Memories*, interviewed by William Shatner (HarperCollins, 1994).
64-17.	Fontana, Dorothy C.	*Trek Classic*, interviewed by Edward Gross (Image Publishing of New York, 1991).
64-18.	Fontana, Dorothy C.	*The World of Star Trek*, interviewed by David Gerrold (Ballantine Books, 1973).
64-19.	Fontana, Dorothy C.	*Captain's Logs*, interviewed by Edward Gross (Little, Brown, 1995).
64-20.	Fontana, Dorothy C.	*Inside Star Trek, issue 2*, by D.C. Fontana, August 1968.
64-21.	Fontana, Dorothy C.	*Inside Star Trek, issue 3*, interviewed by Ruth Berman, Sept. 1968.
64-22.	Fontana, Dorothy C.	*Star Trek Monthly*, issue 26, April 1997.
65.	**Forest, Michael**	**Author interview, 2011.**
66-1.	Francis, Al	*The Star Trek Interview Book*, interviewed by Allan Asherman (Pocket Books, 1988).
66-2.	Francis, Al	*Star Trek Memories*, interviewed by William Shatner (HarperCollins, 1994)
67-1.	Frankham, David	*Starlog #153*, interviewed by Jimmie Hollifield II, April 1990.
67-2.	**Frankham, David**	**Author interview, 2011.**
67a.	**Freiberger, Ben**	**Author interview, 2011.**
68-1.	Freiberger, Fred	*Starlog #39*, interviewed by Mike Clark & Bill Cotter, October 1980.
68-2.	Freiberger, Fred	*Star Trek Memories*, interviewed by William Shatner (HarperCollins, 1994)
68-3.	Freiberger, Fred	*The Star Trek Interview Book*, interviewed by Allan Asherman (Pocket Books, 1988).
68-4.	Freiberger, Fred	*Trek Classic*, interviewed by Edward Gross (Image Publishing of New York, 1991).
68-5.	Freiberger, Fred	*Great Birds of the Galaxy*, interviewed by Edward Gross (BoxTree Limited, 1994).
68-6.	Freiberger, Fred	Sci Fi Channel, 1997.
68-7.	Freiberger, Fred	*Star Trek: The Magazine*, December 1999.
68-8.	Freiberger, Fred	*Captain's Logs*, interviewed by Edward Gross (Little, Brown, 1995).
68a.	**Freiberger, Lisa**	**Author interview, 2011.**
69-1.	Fried, Gerald	*The Music of Star Trek*, by Jeff Bond (Lone Eagle, 1999).
69-2.	Fried, Gerald	*Starlog #169*, interviewed by David Hirsch, Aug. 1991.
69-3.	Fried, Gerald	*The Star Trek Interview Book*, interviewed by Allan Asherman (Pocket Books, 1988).
64-4.	Fried, Gerald	Archive of American Television.
69-5.	**Fried, Gerald**	**Author interview, 2011.**
69a.	Friedman, Mal	*Starlog* #283, interviewed by Mark Phillips, Feb. 2001.
70.	Furia, Jr., John	*Great Birds of the Galaxy*, interviewed by Edward Gross (BoxTree Limited, 1994).
70a.	Gardner, Erle Stanley	*Star Trek Creator*, by David Alexander, letters from the Estate of Erle Stanley Gardner (Penguin Books, 1994).

71-1.	Garr, Teri	*Star Trek's Greatest Gust Stars*, interviewed by Bill Warren (HarperCollins, 1997).
72-2.	Garr, Teri	*Speedbumps: Flooring It Through Hollywood*, by Teri Garr (Plume Printing, 2006).
72-1.	George, Tanya Lemani	*Starlog Yearbook*, interviewed by Pat Jankiewicz, August 1998.
72-2.	**George, Tanya Lemani**	**Author interview, May 2011.**
73-1.	**Gerrold, David**	**Author interview, 2007.**
73-2.	Gerrold, David	BBC interview, unknown date.
73-3.	Gerrold, David	*Gene Roddenberry: The Myth and the Man Behind Star Trek*, interviewed by Joel Engel (Hyperion, 1994).
73-4.	Gerrold, David	*Great Birds of the Galaxy*, interviewed by Edward Gross (BoxTree Limited, 1994).
73-5.	Gerrold, David	*Starlog #41*, by David Gerrold, December 1980.
73-6.	Gerrold, David	*The Trouble with Tribbles*, by David Gerrold (Ballantine 1973).
73-7.	Gerrold, David	*The World of Star Trek*, by David Gerrold (Ballantine, 1973).
73-8.	Gerrold, David	*Cinefantastique*, July 1996.
73-9.	Gerrold, David	*Captain's Logs*, interviewed by Edward Gross (Little, Brown, 1995).
73-10.	Gerrold, David	*Sensor Readings*, interviewed by Don Hardin, April 1, 1984.
73a.	Gillis, Jackson	*Star Trek Creator*, by David Alexander (Penguin Books, 1994).
74.	Goldberg, Whoopi	*Star Trek's Greatest Guest Stars*, interviews by Marc Shapiro & Ian Spelling (HarperCollins, 1997).
75-1.	Goldstone, James	*Cinefantastique*, July 1996.
75-2.	Goldstone, James	*The Star Trek Interview Book*, interviewed by Allan Asherman (Pocket Books, 1988).
75-3.	Goldstone, James	*Trek Classic*, interviewed by Edward Gross (Image Publishing of New York, 1991).
76-1.	Grindstaff, Douglass	*Cinefantastique*, July 1996.
76-2.	Grindstaff, Douglass	*The Star Trek Interview Book*, interviewed by Allan Asherman (Pocket Books, 1988).
77.	Halsey, Dorris	*Great Birds of the Galaxy*, interviewed by Edward Gross (BoxTree Limited, 1994).
78.	Hamner, Robert	*Starlog #199*, interviewed by Mark Phillips, Feb. 1994.
78a.	Held, Karl	*Science Fiction Television Series: Episode Guides, Histories, and Casts and Credits for 62 Prime-Time Shows, 1959 through 1989*, interviewed by Mark Phillips and Frank Garcia (McFarland & Co., 2006)
79-1.	Harmon, David P.	*Great Birds of the Galaxy*, interviewed by Edward Gross (BoxTree Limited, 1994).
79-2.	Harmon, David P.	*Starlog #117*, interviewed by Edward Gross, April 1987.
79-3.	Harmon, David P.	*Trek Classic*, interviewed by Edward Gross (Image Publishing of New York, 1991).
80-1.	Hartley, Mariette	*Starlog #180*, interviewed by Lee Goldberg, July 1992.
80-2.	Hartley, Mariette	Sci Fi Channel, 1997.
80-3.	Hartley, Mariette	*Star Trek Fotonovel #6*, interviewed by Lesa Kite (Bantam Books, March 1978).
81.	Hays, Kathryn	*Star Trek Communicator*, interviewed by Brass Mclean, Dec. 1998.

82-1.	Heinemann, Arthur	*Starlog #147*, interviewed by Edward Gross, Oct. 1989.
82-2.	Heinemann, Arthur	*Trek Classic*, interviewed by Edward Gross (Image Publishing of New York, 1991).
82-3.	Heinemann, Arthur	*Captain's Logs*, interviewed by Edward Gross (Little, Brown, 1995).
83.	Holman, Rex	*Starlog #152*, interviewed by Bill Warren, March 1990.
84.	Holly, Ed	*Desilu*, by Coyne Steven Sanders & Tom Gilbert (William Morrow and Company, 1993).
84a.	**Horgan, Patrick**	**Author's interview, 2013.**
85.	**Howard, Clint**	**Author interview, 2010.**
86.	Hoyt, John	*Starlog #113*, interviewed by Anthony Timpone, Dec. 1986.
86a.	Hunter, Jeffrey	*Milwaukee Journal*, July 4, 1965, "Happy in Hollywood," interviewed by J.D. Spiro.
86b.	Hunter, Jeffrey	*Los Angeles Citizen News*, January 30, 1965, interviewed by Joan Schmitt.
87-1.	Huxley, Craig	*Starlog #112*, November 1986.
87-2.	Huxley, Craig	*Star Trek Communicator*, interviewed by Kevin Dilmore, Dec. 1998.
87-3.	Huxley, Craig	*Science Fiction Television Series: Episode Guides, Histories, and Casts and Credits for 62 Prime-Time Shows, 1959 through 1989*, interviewed by Mark Phillips and Frank Garcia (McFarland & Co., 2006)
88-1.	Hyde, Bruce	*Entertainment Weekly*, January 18, 1995.
88-2.	Hyde, Bruce	*Starlog #112*, by interviewed Frank Garcia, Nov. 1986.
88-3.	Hyde, Bruce	ww.StarTrekHistory.com
88-4	**Hyde, Bruce**	**Author interview, December 9, 2010.**
89.	Ingalls, Don	*Starlog #179*, interviewed by Lee Goldberg, June 1992.
90.	Jackson, Sherry	Sci Fi Channel, 1997.
90-1.	**Jackson, Sherry**	**Author's interview, 2013.**
91-1.	Jefferies, Walter Matt	BBC interview, date unknown.
91-2.	Jefferies, Walter Matt	*Cinefantastique*, interviewed by Ben Hernson, March 1987.
91-3.	Jefferies, Walter Matt	*Gene Roddenberry: The Myth and the Man Behind Star Trek*, interviewed by Joel Engel (Hyperion, 1994).
91-4.	Jefferies, Walter Matt	*The Making of Star Trek*, interviewed by Stephen E. Whitfield (Ballantine, 1968).
91-5.	Jefferies, Walter Matt	*Star Trek: TOS* Box Set, Season 2.
91-6.	Jefferies, Walter Matt	www.startrek.com
91-7.	Jefferies, Walter Matt	*The Star Trek Interview Book*, interviewed by Allan Asherman (Pocket Books, 1988).
91-8.	Jefferies, Walter Matt	*Star Trek Memories*, interviewed by William Shatner (HarperCollins 1994).
91-9.	Jefferies, Walter Matt	*Inside Star Trek, issue 4*, interviewed by Dorothy Fontana, Oct. 1968.
91-10.	Jefferies, Walter Matt	*Inside Star Trek, issue 12*, by Matt Jefferies.
91-11.	Jefferies, Walter Matt	*Star Trek The Magazine*, May 2001.
92.	Jenson, Roy	Sci Fi Channel, 1997.
92a.	**Jewell, Lois**	**Author's interview, August 2013.**

93-1.	**Johnson, George Clayton**	**Author interview, 2007.**
93-2.	Johnson, George Clayton	*Cinefantastique*, July 1996.
93-3	Johnson, George Clayton	*Starlog #174*, interviewed by Bill Warren, January 1992.
93-4.	Johnson, George Clayton	*The Star Trek Interview Book*, interviewed by Allan Asherman (Pocket Books, 1988).
93-5.	Johnson, George Clayton	*Trek Classic*, interviewed by Allan Asherman (Image Publishing of New York, 1991).
93a.	Jones, Jay "Jimmy"	*Starlog #283*, interviewed by Mark Phillips, Feb. 2001.
93b.	Jones, Jay "Jimmy"	*Science Fiction Television Series*, by Mark Phillips and Frank Garcia (McFarland & Company, 1996)
94-1.	**Justman, Robert H.**	**Author interview, 2007.**
94-2.	Justman, Robert H.	BBC interview, date unknown.
94-3.	Justman, Robert H.	*From Sawdust to Stardust*, interviewed by Terry Lee Rioux (Pocket Books, 2005).
94-4.	Justman, Robert H.	*Star Trek Memories*, interviewed by William Shatner (HarperCollins, 1994).
94-5.	Justman, Robert H.	*Gene Roddenberry: The Man and the Myth Behind StarTrek*, interviewed by Joel Engel (Hyperion, 1994).
94-6.	Justman, Robert H.	*Gene Roddenberry: The Last Conversation*, interviewed by Yvonne Fern (University of California Press, 1994).
94-7.	Justman, Robert H.	*Great Birds of the Galaxy*, interviewed by Edward Gross (BoxTree Limited, 1994).
94-8.	Justman, Robert H.	*Inside Star Trek: The Real Story*, specific text written by Robert Justman (Pocket Books, 1996).
94-9.	Justman, Robert H.	*The Music of Star Trek*, interviewed by Jeff Bond (Lone Eagle, 1999).
94-10.	Justman, Robert H.	Sci Fi Channel, 1997.
94-11.	Justman, Robert H.	*Star Trek: TOS* Box Set, Season 1.
94-12.	Justman, Robert H.	*Star Trek: TOS* Box Set, Season 2.
94-13.	Justman, Robert H.	*Star Trek: TOS* Box Set, Season 3.
94-14.	Justman, Robert H.	*Trek Classic*, interviewed by Edward Gross (Image Publishing of New York, 1991).
94-15.	Justman, Robert H.	*The World of Star Trek*, interviewed by David Gerrold (Ballantine Books, 1973).
94-16.	Justman, Robert H.	*Captain's Logs*, interviewed by Edward Gross (Little, Brown, 1995).
94-17.	Justman, Robert H.	*The Star Trek Interview Book*, interviewed by Allan Asherman (Pocket Books, 1988).
94-18.	Justman, Robert	*The Quarterly Journal of the Library of Congress*, 1982, "Keeping Score of the Scores: Music for *Star Trek*," interviewed by Fred Steiner.
94-19.	Justman, Robert	*Star Trek: The Original Series – Soundtrack Collection*, 2012, by Jeff Bond.
94-20.	Justman, Robert H.	Letter written, December 12, 2001.
95-1.	**Kandel, Stephen**	**Author interview, 2007.**
95-2.	Kandel, Stephen	*Starlog #117*, interviewed by Edward Gross, April 1987.
95-3.	Kandel, Stephen	*The Star Trek Interview Book*, interviewed by Allan Asherman (Pocket Books, 1988).
95-4.	Kandel, Stephen	*Trek Classic*, interviewed by Edward Gross (Image Publishing of New York, 1991).
95-5	**Kandel, Stephen**	**Author interview, 2010.**
95a.	Kaplan, Sol	*The Music of Star Trek*, interviewed by Jeff Bond (Lone Eagle, 1999).
96-1.	Katz, Oscar	*Star Trek Creator*, interviewed by David Alexander (Penguin Books, 1994).
96-2.	Katz, Oscar	*Captain's Logs*, by Edward Gross and Mark A. Altman (Little, Brown.1995).

97-1.	Kellerman, Sally	Sci Fi Channel, 1997.
97-2.	Kellerman, Sally	www.startrek.com, staff interview, September 16, 2010.
98-1.	Kelley, DeForest	*From Sawdust to Stardust*, interviewed by Terry Lee Rioux (Pocket Books, 2005).
98-1a.	Kelley, DeForest	*A Harvest of Memories*, working ms. by Kristine Smith, Kelly Home Archives, CA, cited in *From Sawdust to Stardust*, by Terry Lee Rioux (Pocket Books, 2005).
98-1b.	Kelley, DeForest	Correspondence from Denver Kelley, as printed in *From Sawdust to Stardust*, by Terry Lee Rioux (Pocket Books, 2005).
98-1c.	Kelley, DeForest	Speech given at St. Petersburg, Florida, November 1991 by Kelley; cited in *From Sawdust to Stardust*, by Terry Lee Rioux (Pocket Books, 2005).
98-2.	Kelley, DeForest	*History of Trek* compilation, interviewed by Joseph Gulick (Pioneer Books, 1991).
98-3.	Kelley, DeForest	Sci Fi Channel, 1997
98-4.	Kelley, DeForest	*Shatner: Where No Man …,* William Shatner, Sondra Marshak and Myrna Culbreath (Tempo Books, 1979).
98-5	Kelley, DeForest	*Starlog #38*, interviewed by Karen E. Wilson, Sept. 1980.
98-6.	Kelley, DeForest	*The Star Trek Interview Book*, interviewed by Allan Asherman (Pocket Books, 1988).
98-7.	Kelley, DeForest	*Star Trek Memories*, interviewed by William Shatner (HarperCollins, 1994).
98-8.	Kelley, DeForest	*The World of Star Trek*, interviewed by David Gerrold (Ballantine Books, 1973).
98-9.	Kelley, DeForest	*Inside Star Trek, issue 3*, interviewed by Ruth Berman, Sept. 1968.
98-10.	Kelley, DeForest	*Sunday Herald Traveler*, March 31, 1968, "Is There a Doctor in the House?," interviewed by Vernon Scott.
98-11.	Kelley, DeForest	*TV Star Parade*, November 1967, "DeForest Kelley Is Out of This World," interviewed by Jane Harrol.
98-12.	Kelley, DeForest	www.imdb.com.
98-13.	Kelley, DeForest	*TV Picture Life*, March 1968, "I'll Never Forgive Nimoy and Shatner," interviewed by Seli Groves.
98-14.	Kelley, DeForest	DeForest Kelley file, Academy of Motion Pictures Arts and Sciences, Los Angeles California, as told to Paramount Publicist A.C. Lyles.
98-15.	Kelley, DeForest	*TV Guide*, August 24, 1968, "Where Is the Welcome Mat?" interviewed by staff writer.
99.	Kendall, Wanda	*Star Trek Creator*, interviewed by David Alexander (Penguin Books, 1994).
100-1.	Kenney, Sean	*Starlog #113*, interviewed by Frank Garcis, Dec. 1986.
100-2.	**Kenney, Sean**	**Author interview, 2010.**
100-3	Kenney, Sean	*Captain Pike Found Alive!* by Sean Kenney (2013 Outskirts Press)
101.	Kenwith, Herb	*Starlog #179*, interviewed by Pat Jankiewicz, June 1992.
101a.	Knopf, Christopher	*Gene Roddenberry: The Myth and the Man Behind StarTrek*, interviewed by Joel Engel (Hyperion, 1994).
102.	**Koenig, Walter**	**Author's interview, July 2013**
102-1.	Koenig, Walter	BBC interview, date unknown.
102-2.	Koenig, Walter	*The Best of Trek*, edited by Love & Erwin; section by Walter Koenig (Signet Books, 1978).
102-3.	Koenig, Walter	*Cinefantastique*, July 1996.
102-4.	Koenig, Walter	Sci Fi Channel, 1997.
102-5.	Koenig, Walter	*Star Trek* Box Set, Season 2.
102-6.	Keonig, Walter	*Star Trek* Box Set, Season 3.
102-7.	Koenig, Walter	*The Star Trek Interview Book*, interviewed by Allan Asherman (Pocket Books, 1988).
102-8.	Koenig, Walter	*Star Trek Memories*, interviewed by William Shatner (HarperCollins, 1994).

102-9.	Koenig, Walter	*Star Trek: The Official Fan Club Magazine #75*, interviewed by Dan Madsen, August 1990.
102-10.	Keonig, Walter	*The World of Star Trek*, interviewed by David Gerrold (Ballantine, 1973).
102-11.	Koenig, Walter	*TV Guide: Star Trek 25th Anniversary Special*.
102-12.	Koenig, Walter	*Captain's Logs*, interviewed by Edward Gross (Little, Brown, 1995).
102-13.	Koenig, Walter	*Warped Factor: The Neurotic's Guide to the Universe*, by Walter Koenig (Taylor Publishing, 1998).
103-1.	Komack, James	*Starlog #140*, interviewed by Edward Gross, March 1989.
103-2.	Komack, James	*Trek Classic*, interviewed by Edward Gross (Image Publishing of New York, 1991).
103a.	**Kovack, Nancy**	**Author's interview, 2013**
104.	Kovack, Nancy	*Starlog #151*, interviewed by Tom Weaver, Feb. 1990.
103b.	**Kranzler, Bryna**	**Letter to Author, 2013.**
104a.	**Landau, Martin**	**Author interview, 2006.**
104c.	Landers, Harry	classicTVhistory.wordpress.org
105-1.	Lansing, Robert	*Starlog #149*, interviewed by Peter Bloch-Hansen, December 1989.
105-2.	Lansing, Robert	*Star Trek's Greatest Guest Stars*, interviewed by Peter Bloch-Hansen (HarperCollins, 1997).
106.	Larson, Glen	*Great Birds of the Galaxy*, by Edward Gross and Mark A. Altman (BoxTree Limited, 1994).
107-1.	Lenard, Mark	*Cinefantastique*, July 1996.
107-2.	Lenard, Mark	*Starlog #42*, interviewed by Alan Brender, Jan. 1981.
107-3.	Lenard, Mark	*Star Trek's Greatest Guest Stars*, by Robert Greenberger and David McDonnell (HarperCollins, 1997).
108-1.	Lewis, Shari	*Starlog #172*, interviewed by Pat Jankiewicz, Nov. 1991.
108-2.	Lewis, Shari	*People*, February 2, 1976.
108a.	**Lewis, Trelaine**	**Author's interview, 2013.**
109.	**Lockwood, Gary**	**Author interview, March 2011.**
109-1	Lockwood, Gary	*Starlog #124*, interviewed by Edward Gross, Nov. 1987.
109-2.	Lockwood, Gary	*Trek Classic*, interviewed by Edward Gross (Image Publishing of New York, 1991).
109a.	Lundin, Vic	*Science Fiction Television Series: Episode Guides, Histories, and Casts and Credits for 62 Prime-Time Shows, 1959 through 1989*, interviewed by Mark Phillips and Frank Garcia (McFarland & Co., 2006)
110-1.	Lucas, John Meredyth	*Great Birds of the Galaxy*, interviewed by Edward Gross (BoxTree Limited, 1994).
110-2.	Lucas, John Meredyth	*Inside Star Trek: The Real Story*, interviewed by Robert Justman and Herb Solow (Pocket Books, 1996).
110-3.	Lucas, John Meredyth	*Starlog #112*, interviewed by Edward Gross, Nov. 1986.
110-4.	Lucas, John Meredyth	*Star Trek Memories*, interviewed by William Shatner and/or Chris Kreski (HarperCillins, 1994).
110-5.	Lucas, John Meredyth	*Trek Classic*, interviewed by Edward Gross (Image Publishing of New York, 1991).
110-6.	Lucas, John Meredyth	*Eight Odd Years in Hollywood*, by John Meredyth Lucas (McFarland & Co., 2004).

111-1	Luna, Barbra	Sci Fi channel, 1997.
111-2	Luna, Barbra	*Starlog #235*, interviewed by Pat Jankiewicz, Feb. 1997.
111-3.	**Luna, Barbra**	**Author interview, 2011.**
112.	Mailer, Lev	www.StarTrekHistory.com
113-1	Mankiewicz, Don	*Starlog #177*, interviewed by Bill Florence, April 1992.
113-2.	Mankiewicz, Don	www.classictvhistory.com, interviewed by Steven W. Bowie, 2007.
113-3	**Mankiewicz, Don**	**Author interview, 2011.**
113a	**Mars, Bruce**	**Author interview, 2013.**
113b.	**Marshall, Don**	**Author interview, 2011.**
114.	Marshall, Sarah	*Star Trek: The Official Fan Club Magazine #80*, Interviewed by John S. Davis, June 1991.
115.	Marshall, William	*Starlog #255*, interviewed by Pat Jankiewicz & Mark Phillips, October 1998.
116.	**Martell, Tasha "Arlene"**	**Author interview, May 2011.**
116a.	Matheson, Richard	Archive of American Television, interviewed by Karen Haman, April 16, 2006.
116b.	**Matheson, Richard**	**Author interview, May 2011.**
117-1.	McEveety, Vincent	*Starlog #144*, interviewed by Edward Gross, July 1989.
117-2.	McEveety, Vincent	*Trek Classic*, interviewed by Edward Gross (Image Publishing of New York, 1991).
117-3.	McEveety, Vincent	*Captain's Logs*, interviewed by Edward Gross (Little, Brown, 1995).
117-4.	**McEveety, Vincent**	**Author interview, 2011.**
117a.	Menhoff, George	*Inside Star Trek, issue 12*, by George Menhoff, 1969.
118-1.	Meriwether, Lee	Sci Fi Channel, 1987.
118-2.	Meriwether, Lee	*Starlog #153*, interviewed by Kyle Counts, April 1990.
118-3.	**Meriwether, Lee**	**Author interview, July 2011.**
119-1.	Milkis, Eddie	*Cinefantastique*, July 1996.
119-2.	Milkis, Eddie	*Star Trek Memories*, interviewed by William Shatner and/or Chris Kreski (HarperCollins, 1994).
119aa.	Mines, Stephen	*Starlog #283*, interviewed by Mark Phillips, February 2001.
119a.	**Montaigne, Lawrence**	**Author interview, 2011.**
120-1	Montalban, Ricardo	*Starlog #62*, interviewed by Robert Greenberger, September 1982.
120-2.	Montalban, Ricardo	*Star Trek: TOS Box Set, Season 1.*
120-3.	Montalban, Ricardo	*Star Trek's Greatest Guest Stars*, interviewed by Robert Greenberger (HarperCollins, 1997).
120a.	Moore, Ronald D.	Memory Alpha internet interview, June 24, 1997.
120b.	**Morgan, Sean**	**Author interview, 2010.**
121.	Moss, Arnold	*Starlog #130*, interviewed by Diane Butler, May 1988.
122-1.	Moss, Stewart	Sci Fi Channel, 1997.
122-2.	Moss, Stewart	*Starlog #133*, interviewed by Mark Phillips, Aug. 1988.
122-3.	**Moss, Stewart**	**Author interview, March 2011.**
122-4.	**Moss, Stewart**	**Author email interview, 2013.**

| 123. | Muldaur, Diana | *Starlog #141*, interviewed by Bill Warren, April 1989. |

| 123b. | Mullendore, Joseph | "The Music of *Star Trek*: Profiles in Styles," interviewed by Fred Steiner, 1982. |

| **123a.** | **Muskat, Joyce** | **Author interview, June 2011.** |

| 124. | Nelson, Gene | *Starlog #180*, interviewed by Pat Jankiewicz, July 1992. |

| 125-1. | Newland, John | *Starlog #130*, interviewed by John McCarty, May 1988. |
| 125-2. | Newland, John | Blog interview by John Kenneth Muir, 1999. |

| **126.** | **Newmar, Julie** | **Author interview, November 2010.** |

127-1.	Nichols, Nichelle	BBC interview, date unknown.
127-2.	Nichols, Nichelle	*Beyond Uhura*, by Nichelle Nichols (G.P. Putnam's Sons, 1994).
127-3.	Nichols, Nichelle	*Cinefantastique*, July 1996.
127-4.	Nichols, Nichelle	Sci Fi Channel, 1997.
127-5.	Nichols, Nichelle	*Shatner: Where No Man ...* , by William Shatner, Sondra Marshak and Myrna Culbreath (Tempo Books, 1979).
127-6.	Nichols, Nichelle	*Star Trek: TOS* Box Set, Season 2.
127-7.	Nichols, Nichelle	*Star Trek: TOS* Box Set, Season 3.
127-8.	Nichols, Nichelle	*The Star Trek Interview Book*, interviewed by Allan Asherman (Pocket Books, 1988).
127-9.	Nichols, Nichelle	*Star Trek Memories*, interviewed by William Shatner and/or Chris Kreski (HarperCollins, 1994).
127-10.	Nichols, Nichelle	*The World of Star Trek*, interviewed by David Gerrold (Ballantine Books, 1973).
127-11.	Nichols, Nichelle	www.*StarTrek*.com, staff interview, October 19, 2010.
127-12.	Nichols, Nichelle	*TV Guide*, July 15, 1967, "Let Me Off at the Next Planet."

128.	**Nimoy, Leonard**	**Author interview, 2013.**
128-1.	Nimoy, Leonard	*Gene Roddenberry: The Myth and the Man Behind Star Trek*, interviewed by Joel Engel (Hyperion, 1994).
128-2.	Nimoy, Leonard	*Great Birds of the Galaxy*, interviewed by Edward Gross and/or Mark A. Altman (BoxTree Limited, 1994).
128-3.	Nimoy, Leonard	*I Am Spock*, by Leonard Nimoy (Hyperion, 1996).
128-3a.	Nimoy, Leonard	*I Am Not Spock*, by Leonard Nimoy (Celestial Arts, November 1975)
128-4.	Nimoy, Leonard	Sci Fi Channel, 1997.
128-5.	Nimoy, Leonard	*Shatner: Where No Man ...* , byWilliam Shatner, Sondra Marshak and Myrna Culbreath (Tempo Books, 1979).
128-6.	Nimoy, Leonard	*Star Trek: TOS* Box Set, Season 1.
128-7.	Nimoy, Leonard	*Star Trek: TOS* Box Set, Season 2.
128-8.	Nimoy, Leonard	*Star Trek: TOS* Box Set, Season 3.
128-9.	Nimoy, Leonard	*Star Trek Communicator*, interviewed by Chris Roe, June 1996.
128-10.	Nimoy, Leonard	*Star Trek Communicator*, August 1999.
128-11.	Nimoy, Leonard	*The Star Trek Interview Book*, interviewed by Allan Asherman (Pocket Books, 1988).
128-12.	Nimoy, Leonard	*Star Trek Lives!*, by Jacqueline Lichtenberg, Sondra Marshak and Joan Winston (Bantam Books, 1975).
128-13.	Nimoy, Leonard	*Star Trek Memories*, interviewed by William Shatner and/or Chris Kreski (HarperCollins, 1994).
128-14.	Nimoy, Leonard	*Trek Classic*, by Edward Gross (Image Publishing of New York,1991).
128-15.	Nimoy, Leonard	*The World of Star Trek*, interviewed by David Gerrold (Ballantine, 1973).
128-16.	Nimoy, Leonard	*Inside Star Trek, issue 6*, interviewed by Ruth Berman, Dec. 1968.
128-17.	Nimoy, Leonard	*New York Times*, "Girls All Want to Touch the Ears," interviewed by Digby Diehl, August 25, 1968.
128-18.	Nimoy, Leonard	*Archive of American Television*, interviewed by Karen Herman, November 2, 2002.

128-19.	Nimoy, Leonard	*Photo TV Land*, December 1967, "Outer Space's Inside Battle," interviewed by Rhonda Green.
128-20.	Nimoy, Leonard	*Screen Stories*, September 1967, "Leonard Nimoy and Bill Shatner: Their Topsy-Turvy Lives," interviewed by Dora Albert.
128-21.	Nimoy, Leonard	*TV Guide*, March 4, 1967, "Product of Two Worlds," interviewed by Leslie Raddatz.
128-22.	Nimoy, Leonard	*Los Angeles Herald-Examiner TV Weekly*, "Spock, the Mysterious," interviewed by Charles Witbeck.
128-23.	Nimoy, Leonard	*TV Star Parade*, August 1967, "Leonard Nimoy's *Deathwatch*," interviewed by Susan Dennis.
128-24.	Nimoy, Leonard	www.ontd-startrek.livejournal.com, "Company of Angels Turns 50 (And Celebrates with Its First Director, Leonard Nimoy)," interviewed by Steven Leigh Morris.
128-25.	Nimoy, Leonard	*Monsters of the Movies*, August 1975. Interviewed by Mike Harrison and Jeff Gelb.
128-26.	Nimoy, Leonard	BBC 1, 1971. Interviewed by Michael Aspel.
128a.	Nimoy, Sandra	*TV Guide*, March 4, 1967, "Product of Two Worlds," interviewed by Leslie Raddatz.
129-1.	**Nuyen, France**	**Author interview, April 12, 2012.**
129-2.	Nuyen, France	*Star Trek: The Official Fan Club Magazine #76*, interviewed by John S. Davis, October 1990.
130	**O'Connell, William**	**Author's interview, 2013.**
130-1.	O'Connell, William	*Science Fiction Television Series* by Mark Phillips and Frank Garcia (McFarland & Company, 2006)
131.	O'Herlihy, Michael	*Starlog #131*, interviewed by Edward Gross, June 1988.
132,	Oliver, Susan	*Starlog #135*, interviewed by Frank Garcia, Oct. 1988.
133.	Opatoshu, David	*Starlog #236*, interviewed by K.M. Drennan, June 1997.
134.	Oswald, Gerd	*Cinefantastique*, July 1996.
134a.	**Parrish, Leslie**	**Author interview, 2011.**
135-1.	Paskey, Eddie	*Starlog #132*, interviewed by Kathleen M. Gooch, July 1988.
135-2.	**Paskey, Eddie**	**Author interview, 2011.**
136-1.	Peeples, Samuel	*Gene Roddenberry: The Myth and the Man Behind Star Trek*, by Joel Engel (Hyperion, 1994).
136-2.	Peeples, Samuel	*Starlog #122*, interviewed by Edward Gross, Sept. 1987.
136-3.	Peeples, Samuel	*The Star Trek Interview Book*, interviewed by Allan Asherman (Pocket, 1988).
137.	Penn, Leo	*Starlog #179*, interviewed by Pat Jankiewicz, June 1992.
138.	Perrin, Vic	*Starlog #155*, interviewed by Mike Clark & Mark Phillips, June 1990.
139.	Perry, Roger	*Starlog #117*, interviewed by Mark Phillips, April 1987.
139-1.	**Perry, Roger**	**Author interview, 2013.**
140.	Pettyjohn, Angelique	*The Best of Enterprise Incidents*, interviewed by James Van Hise (Pioneer Books, 1990).
141-1.	Pevney, Joseph	*Starlog #126*, interviewed by Edward Gross, Jan. 1988.
141-2.	Pevney, Joseph	*The Star Trek Interview Book*, interviewed by Allan Asherman (Pocket Books, 1988).

141-3.	Pevney, Joseph	*Trek Classic*, by Edward Gross (Image Publishing of New York, 1991).
142-1.	Phillips, Fred	*Cinefantastique*, interviewed by Ben Hernson, March 1987.
142-2.	Phillips, Fred	*The Making of Star Trek*, interviewed by Stephen E. Whitfield (Ballantine, 1968).
143-4.	Phillips, Fred	*Inside Star Trek, issue 2*.
143-4.	Phillips, Fred	*Inside Star Trek, issue 3*, interviewed by Fred Phillips, August 1968.
143a.	**Pillsbury, Garth**	**Author's interview, 2013.**
143.	Pine, Phillip	*Starlog #130*, interviewed by Mark Phillips, May 1988.
141a.	Raff, Robert	*The Star Trek Interview Book*, interviewed by Allan Asherman (Pocket Books, 1988).
141b.	Raff, Robert	*The Quarterly Journal of the Library of Congress*, 1982, "Keeping Score of the Scores: *Music for Star Trek*, interviewed by Fred Steiner.
141-1.	Ralston, Gilbert	*Great Birds of the Galaxies*, interviewed by Edward Gross (BoxTree Limited, 1994)
144-2.	Ralston, Gilbert	*Starlog #112*, interviewed by Edward Gross, Nov. 1986.
144-3.	Ralston, Gilbert	*Trek Classic*, interviewed by Edward Gross (Image Publishing of New York, 1991).
144b.	**Richardson, Andre**	**Author's interview, 2013 (aka Andre Richardson-Kinryd).**
144a.	Riegler, Hank	*Inside Star Trek: The Real Story*, interviewed by Robert Justman and/or Herb Solow (Pocket Books, 1996).
145.	**Roddenberry, Gene**	**Author interview, 1982 and 1990.**
145-1.	Roddenberry, Gene	*Cinefantastique*, interviewed by Ben Hernson, March 1987.
145-2.	Roddenberry, Gene	*Gene Roddenberry: The Last Conversation*, interviewed by Yvonne Fern (University of California Press, 1994).
145-3.	Roddenberry, Gene	*Great Birds of the Galaxy*, by Edward Gross and Mark Altman (BoxTree Limited, 1994).
145-4.	Roddenberry, Gene	*The Making of Star Trek*, interviewed by Stephen E. Whitfield (Ballantine, 1968).
145-5.	Roddenberry, Gene	*Shatner: Where No Man … *, byWilliam Shatner, Sondra Marshak and Myrna Culbreath (Tempo Books, 1979).
145-6.	Roddenberry, Gene	*Star Trek: TOS* Box Set, Season 1.
145-7.	Roddenberry, Gene	*Star Trek Creator*, by David Alexander (Penguin, 1994).
145-8.	Roddenberry, Gene	*Star Trek Lives!*, by Jacqueline Lichtenberg, Sondra Marshak and Joan Winston (Bantam Books, 1975).
145-9.	Roddenberry, Gene	*The Star Trek Interview Book*, interviewed by Allan Asherman (Pocket Books, 1988).
145-10.	Roddenberry, Gene	*The World of Star Trek*, by David Gerrold (Ballantine, 1973).
145-11.	Roddenberry, Gene	*Trek Classic*, by Edward Gross (Image Publishing of New York, 1991).
145-12.	**Roddenberry, Gene**	**Author interview, 1990.**
145-13.	Roddenberry, Gene	*Inside Star Trek, issue 1*, by Gene Roddenberry, 1968.
145-14.	Roddenberry, Gene	*Daily Variety*, June 7, 1966, interviewed by Dave Kaufman.
145-15.	Roddenberry, Gene	*Daily Variety*, July 15, 1966, "Just for Variety," interviewed by Army Archerd.
145-16.	Roddenberry, Gene	*Daily Variety*, January 16, 1967, "John Drew Barrymore Reprimanded by SAG for Balking at *Star* Role."
145-17.	Roddenberry, Gene	*Daily Variety*, February 9, 1967, "Seek 'Star' Femme Regular to do *Trek* at Desilu."
145-18.	Roddenberry, Gene	*Daily Variety*, February 16, 1967, "Light and Airy," interviewed by Jack Hellman.
145-19.	Roddenberry, Gene	*Daily Variety*, June 21, 1967, "On All Channels," interviewed by Dave Kaufman.

145-20.	Roddenberry, Gene	*Daily Variety*, June 28, 1967, "On All Channels," interviewed by Dave Kaufman.
145-21.	Roddenberry, Gene	*TV Guide*, July 15, 1967, "Let Me Off at the Next Planet."
145-22.	Roddenberry, Gene	*TV Guide*, March 4, 1967, "Product of Two Worlds," interviewed by Leslie Raddatz.
145-23.	Roddenberry, Gene	*The Humanist*, March/April 1991, interviewed by David Alexander.
145-24.	Roddenberry, Gene	*Gene Roddenberry: The Myth and the Man Behind StarTrek*, by Joel Engel.
145-25.	Roddenberry, Gene	*The Quarterly Journal of the Library of Congress*, 1982, "Keeping Score of the Scores: Music for *Star Trek*," interviewed by Fred Steiner.
145-26.	Roddenberry, Gene	*Starlog*, interviewed by Jeff Szalay, October 1981.
145a.	**Rod Roddenberry**	**Author interview, 2012.**
145b.	Rogers, Elizabeth	*Science Fiction Television Series*, by Mark Phillips and Frank Garcia (McFarland & Company, 1996)
145c.	Rogers, Elizabeth	Previously unpublished interview conducted by Mark Phillips, January 3, 1996.
146.	Rolfe, Sam	*Gene Roddenberry: The Myth and the Man Behind Star Trek*, interviewed by Joel Engel (Hyperion, 1994).
147.	Rugg, Jim	*Cinefantastique*, interviewed by Ben Hernson, March 1987.
148.	Ruskin, Joseph	*Starlog #188*, interviewed by Mark Phillips, March 1993.
149.	Ruskin, Joseph	Sci Fi Channel, 1997.
150.	Sabaroff, Robert	*Starlog #203*, interviewed by Mark Phillips, June 1994.
151.	**Sargent, Joseph**	**Author interview, 2010.**
153.	Schlessinger, Dr. Laura	*Star Trek Communicator*, by Dr. Laura Schlessinger, June 1998.
153a.	Schlosser, Herbert	*Inside Star Trek: The Real Story*, interviewed by Robert Justman and/or Herb Solow (Pocket Books, 1996)
154.	Schneider, Paul	*Trek Classic*, interviewed by Edward Gross (Image Publishing of New York, 1991).
155-1	Senensky, Ralph	*Great Birds of the Galaxy*, interviewed by Edward Gross (BoxTree Limited, 1994).
155-2.	Senensky, Ralph	*Starlog #172*, interviewed by Edward Gross, Nov. 1991.
155-3.	Senensky, Ralph	*The Star Trek Interview Book*, interviewed by Allan Asherman (Pocket Books, 1988).
155-4.	Senensky, Ralph	*Trek Classic*, interviewed by Edward Gross (Image Publishing of New York, 1991).
155-5.	Senensky, Ralph	www.senesnsky.com, webpage blog, 2010.
155-6.	**Senensky, Ralph**	**Author interview, 2011.**
155a-1.	Shatner, Lisabeth	*Captain's Log: William Shatner's Personal Account of the Making of Star Trek V: The Final Frontier*, by William Shatner (*Star Trek* Publishing, 1989).
155a-2.	Shatner, Lisabeth	Personal blog.
166-1.	Shatner, William	*Great Birds of the Galaxy*, by Edward Gross and Mark Altman (BoxTree Limited, 1994).
166-2.	Shatner, William	Sci Fi Channel, 1997.
166-3.	Shatner, William	*Shatner: Where No Man ...* , byWilliam Shatner, Sondra Marshak and Myrna Culbreath (Tempo Books, 1979).
166-4.	Shatner, William	*Star Trek: TOS* Box Set, Season 1.

166-5.	Shatner, William	*Star Trek: TOS* Box Set, Season 2.
166-6.	Shatner, William	*Star Trek Communicator*, August 1999.
166-7.	Shatner, William	*The Star Trek Interview Book*, interviewed by Allan Asherman (Pocket Books, 1988).
166-8.	Shatner, William	*Star Trek Memories*, by William Shatner and Chris Kreski (HarperCollins, 1994).
166-9.	Shatner, William	*The World of Star Trek*, interviewed by David Gerrold (Ballantine, 1973).
166-10.	Shatner, William	*Trek Classic*, by Edward Gross (Image Publishing of New York, 1991).
166-11.	Shatner, William	*TV Week*, August 28, 1966, "*Star Trek* Resembles Space *Twilight Zone.*"
166-12.	Shatner, William	*Daily Variety*, September 7, 1966, "Shatner's Heroic Shift," interviewed by Dave Kaufman.
166-13.	Shatner, William	*Daily Variety*, July 15, 1966, "Just for Variety," interviewed by Army Archerd.
166-14.	Shatner, William	*TV Guide*, October 15, 1966, "No One Ever Upsets the STAR," interviewed by Michael Fessier, Jr.
166-15.	Shatner, William	*Syracuse Herald-American*, October 16, 1966, "Shatner, Star of TV Series, 'Hooked' on UFO Phenomenon."
166-16.	Shatner, William	*Boston Sunday Herald*, December 18, 1966, "Shatner Catches a Big Wave."
166-17.	Shatner, William	*Victoria Daily Times*, October 28, 1967, "Canada's First Man in Space," interviewed by Walter Roessing.
166-18.	Shatner, William	*Photo TV Land*, December 1967, "Outer Space's Inside Battle," interviewed by Rhonda Green.
166-19.	Shatner, William	*Screen Stories*, Sept. 1967, "Leonard Nimoy and Bill Shatner: Their Topsy-Turvy Lives," interviewed by Dora Albert.
166-20.	Shatner, William	www.imdb.com, cited as from 1966.
157.	Shutan, Jan	*Starlog #199*, interviewed by Pat Jankiewicz, Feb. 1994.
158.	Slavin, George F.	*Starlog #171*, interviewed by Bill Florence, Oct. 1991.
158a.	**Sloman, Peter**	**Author's interview, 2013.**
159-1.	Soble, Ron	*Starlog #152*, interviewed by Mark Phillips, March 1990.
159-2.	Soble, Ron	Sci Fi Channel, 1997.
159-3.	Soble, Ron	www.imdb.com
160-1.	Sohl, Jerry	*Gene Roddenberry: The Myth and the Man Behind Star Trek*, interviewed by Joel Engel (Hyperion, 1994).
160-2.	Sohl, Jerry	*Starlog #135*, interviewed by Edward Gross, October 1988.
160-3.	Sohl, Jerry	*Starlog #136*, interviewed by Edward Gross, November 1988.
160-4.	Sohl, Jerry	*Trek Classic*, interviewed by Edward Gross (Image Publishing of New York, 1991).
161-1.	Solow, Herbert F.	CJAD AM, interviewed by Peter Anthony Holder, Sept. 1996.
162-2.	Solow, Herbert F.	*Gene Roddenberry: The Myth and the Man Behind Star Trek*, interviewed by Joel Engel (Hyperion, 1994).
162-3.	Solow, Herbert F.	*Inside Star Trek: The Real Story*, by Herb Solow and Robert Justman (Pocket Books, 1996).
162-4.	Solow, Herbert F.	Sci Fi Channel, 1997.
161-5.	Solow, Herbert F.	*Starlog #241*, interviewed by Ian Spelling, August 1997.
161-6.	Solow, Herbert F.	*Star Trek Communicator, issue #107*, interviewed by Dan Madsen, June 1996.
161-7.	Solow, Herbert F.	*Daily Variety*, March 28, 1967, "On All Channels: Herb Solow's Crystal Ball," interviewed by Dave Kaufman.
162.	Sorokin, Joseph	*The Star Trek Interview Book*, interviewed by Allan Asherman (Pocket Books, 1988).

163-1.	Sorel, Louise	*Starlog #249*, interviewed by Mark Phillips, April 1998.
163-2.	Sorel, Louise	*Star Trek: The Official Fan Club Magazine #74*, interviewed by John S. Davis, June 1990.
163-3.	**Sorel, Louise**	**Author interview, 2011.**
164-1.	Spies, Adrian	*Starlog #130*, interviewed by Edward Gross, May 1988.
164-2.	Spies, Adrian	*Trek Classic*, interviewed by Edward Gross (Image Publishing of New York, 1991).
165-1.	**Spinrad, Norman**	**Author interview, 2011.**
165-2.	Spinrad, Norman	*The Star Trek Interview Book*, interviewed by Allan Asherman (Pocket Books, 1988).
165-3.	Spinrad, Norman	*Trek Classic*, by Edward Gross (Image Publishing of New York, 1991).
166.	Stanley, Jerry	*Gene Roddenberry: The Myth and the Man Behind StarTrek*, interviewed by Joel Engel (Hyperion, 1994).
167.	Unnamed Series Insider	*Great Birds of the Galaxy*, by Edward Gross and Mark Altman (BoxTree Limited, 1994).
168.	Steiner, Fred	*The Music of Star Trek*, interviewed by Jeff Bond (Lone Eagle, 1999).
168-1	Steiner, Fred	*The Quarterly Journal of the Library of Congress*, 1982, "Keeping Score of the Scores: Music for *Star Trek*," by Fred Steiner.
169.	Stevens, Warren	*Star Trek Communicator*, interviewed by Kevin Dilmore, Dec. 1998.
169a.	Stilwell-Black, Mary	*Gene Roddenberry: The Myth and the Man Behind StarTrek*, interviewed by Joel Engel (Hyperion, 1994).
169b.	Sturgeon, Theodore	*Fangoria #10*, January 1981.
170.	Sullivan, Liam	*Starlog #162*, interviewed by Mark Phillips, Jan. 1991.
171-1.	Takei, George	*Cinefantastique*, July 1996.
171-2.	Takei, George	Sci Fi Channel, 1997.
171-3.	Takei, George	*Star Trek: TOS* Box Set, Season 2.
171-4.	Takei, George	*To the Stars*, by George Takei (Pocket Books, 1994).
171-5.	Takei, George	*The World of Star Trek*, interviewed by David Gerrold (Ballantine, 1973).
171-6.	Takei, George	*Inside Star Trek, issue 8*, interviewed by Ruth Berman, 1968.
171-7.	Takei, George	*TV Guide Star Trek 25th Anniversary Special*, 1991.
171b.	Tarcher, Jeremy	*People*, February 2, 1976.
172-1.	Theiss, William	*Cinefantastique*, July 1996.
172-2.	Theiss, William	startrekpropauthority.com, interviewed by James Magna, 1988.
172-3.	Theiss, William	*Inside Star Trek, issue 6*, interviewed by D.C. Fontana, Dec. 1968.
172-4.	Theiss, William	*Inside Star Trek, issue 7*, interviewed by D.C. Fontana, 1968.
173-1.	Throne, Malachi	*Starlog #190*, interviewed by Joel Eisner, May 1993.
173-2.	**Throne, Malachi**	**Author interview, 2011.**
174.	Tinker, Grant	*Gene Roddenberry: The Myth and the Man Behind Star Trek*, interviewed by Joel Engel (Hyperion, 1994).
176.	Tordjmann, Fabien	*The Star Trek Interview Book*, interviewed by Allan Asherman (Pocket Books, 1988).

37. THE CHANGELING

Gene Roddenberry	GR37-1	to Coon	4/1/67
	GR37-2	to Coon	4/12/67
	GR37-3	to Coon	5/8/67
Robert Justman	RJ37-1	to Roddenberry	3/20/67
	RJ37-2	to Coon	4/17/67
	RJ37-3	to Coon	5/22/67
	RJ37-4	to Coon	6/1/67
Gene Coon	GC37	to Lucas	4/14/67
D.C. Fontana	DC37-1	to Coon	4/13/67
	DC37-2	to Coon	5/3/67
Stan Robertson	SR37	to Roddenberry	4/3/67
Broadcast Standards	BS37	-	3/27/67

38. THE APPLE

Gene Roddenberry	GR38	to Coon	5/9/67
Robert Justman	RJ38-1	to Coon	4/10/67
	RJ38-2	to Coon	6/27/67
	RJ38-3	to Coon	6/30/67
Gene Coon	GC38-1	to Max Ehrlich	4/21/67
	GC38-2	to Ehrlich	5/9/67
	GC38-3	to Ehrlich	6/2/67
D.C. Fontana	DC38-1	to Coon	4/11/67
	DC38-2	to Coon	5/31/67
	DC38-3	to Coon	7/3/67
	DC38-4	to Coon	7/11/67
Stan Robertson	SR38	to Coon	5/9/67
De Forest Research	DFR38	-	7/10/67

39. MIRROR, MIRROR

Gene Roddenberry	GR39-1	to Coon	4/1/67
	GR39-2	to Coon	5/29/67
Robert Justman	RJ39	to Coon	2/28/67
D.C. Fontana	DC39-1	to Coon	3/4/67
	DC39-2	to Coon	5/29/67
Stan Robertson	SR39-1	to Roddenberry	3/16/67
	SR39-2	to Roddenberry	4/6/67

40. THE DEADLY YEARS

Gene Roddenberry	GR40	to Coon	5/22/67
Robert Justman	RJ40-1	to Coon	7/7/67
	RJ40-2	to Coon	7/23/67
	RJ40-3	to Coon	Date unknown
D.C. Fontana	DC40-1	to Coon	3/4/67
	DC40-2	to Coon	5/19/67
	DC40-3	to Coon	6/21/67
Leonard Nimoy	LM40	to Roddenberry	7/24/67
Stan Robertson	SR40	to Coon	6/8/67

41. I, MUDD

Gene Roddenberry	GR41-1	to Stephen Kandel	3/27/67
	GR41-2	to Coon	4/1/67
	GR41-3	to Coon	6/8/66
Robert Justman	RJ41-1	to Roddenberry	3/23/67
	RJ41-2	to Coon	4/21/67
	RJ41-3	to Coon	6/6/67
	RJ41-4	to Coon	7/5/67
Gene Coon	GC41	to Kandel	6/9/67
D.C. Fontana	DC41-1	to Coon	6/7/67
	DC41-2	to Coon	7/5/67
Stan Robertson	SR41	to Roddenberry	3/31/67

42. THE TROUBLE WITH TRIBBLES

Robert Justman	RJ42	to Coon	7/5/67
D.C. Fontana	DC42-1	to Coon	6/20/67
	DC42-2	to Coon	6/26/67
De Forest Research	DFR42	-	8/11/67

43. BREAD AND CIRCUSES

John Kneubuhl	JK43	to Roddenberry	3/17/67
Gene Roddenberry	GR43-1	to John Kneubuhl	3/14/67
	GR43-2	to Coon	4/17/67
	GR43-3	to Coon	5/9/67
	GR43-4	to Greg Peters	9/12/67
	GR43-5	to Ralph Senensky	9/15/67
	GR43-6	to Reilly	10/2/67
	GR43-7	after	Date unknown
Robert Justman	RJ43-1	to Roddenberry	3/20/67
	RJ43-2	to Coon	4/14/67
	RJ43-3	to Coon	8/28/67
Gene Coon	GC43-1	-	9/19/67
	GC43-2	to WGA	9/19/67

D.C. Fontana	DC43-1	to Coon	4/14/67
	DC43-2	to Coon	5/2/67
	DC43-3	to Coon	8/11/67
Stan Robertson	SR43-1	to Roddenberry	3/23/67
	SR43-2	to Coon	5/23/67
De Forest Research	DFR43	to staff	9/15/67
Broadcast Standards	BS43	to staff	7/5/67

44. JOURNEY TO BABEL

Robert Justman	RJ44-1	to Coon	8/15/67
	RJ44-2	to Coon	8/24/67
Stan Robertson	SR44	to Coon	7/7/67

45. A PRIVATE LITTLE WAR

Gene Roddenberry	GR45-1	to Coon	4/1/67
	GR45-2	to Coon	5/8/67
	GR45-3	to Coon	6/9/67
Robert Justman	RJ45-1	to Coon	5/26/67
	RJ45-2	to Coon	Date unknown
	RJ45-3	to Coon	8/11/67
	RJ45-4	to Coon	9/5/67
Gene Coon	GC45	to Don Ingalls	8/21/67
D.C. Fontana	DC45-1	to Coon	6/8/67
	DC45-2	to Coon	8/11/67
Stan Robertson	SR45	to Lucas	11/2/67
Broadcast Standards	BS45	-	9/25/67

46. OBSESSION

Gene Roddenberry	GR46-1	to staff	4/22/66
	GR46-2	to Coon	4/1/67
	GR46-3	to Lucas	10/2/67
Robert Justman	RJ46-1	to Roddenberry	4/25/66
	RJ46-2	to Coon	7/19/67
	RJ46-3	to Coon	8/16/67
	RJ46-4	to Coon	8/29/67
John D.F. Black	JDFB46	to Roddenberry	4/26/66
Gene Coon	GC46	to Wallace	7/27/67
D.C. Fontana	DC46-1	to Coon	5/23/67
	DC46-2	to Coon	7/24/67
	DC46-3	to Coon	8/16/67
Stan Robertson	SR46	to Coon	6/5/67

47. THE GAMESTERS OF TRISKELION

Gene Roddenberry	GR47-1	to Coon	4/1/67
	GR47-2	to Coon	5/9/67
	GR47-3	to Lucas	10/2/67

Robert Justman	RJ47-1	to Coon	4/14/67
	RJ47-2	to Coon	5/29/67
	RJ47-3	to Coon	6/26/67
	RJ47-4	to Coon	8/3/67
	RJ47-5	to Lucas	9/21/67

| D.C. Fontana | DC47-1 | to Coon | 4/13/67 |
| | DC47-2 | to Margaret Armen | 7/3/67 |

| Stan Robertson | SR47 | to Coon | 5/15/67 |

48. THE IMMUNITY SYNDROME

| Robert Justman | RJ48 | to Coon | 8/9/67 |

| D.C. Fontana | DC48-1 | to Coon | 8/10/67 |
| | DC48-2 | to Lucas | 9/14/67 |

49. A PIECE OF THE ACTION

Robert Justman	RJ49-1	to Coon	8/9/67
	RJ49-2	to Coon	8/22/67
	RJ49-3	to Lucas	9/13/67
	RJ49-4	to Roddenberry	10/18/67

| Gene Coon | GC49 | to Lucas | 9/18/67 |

D.C. Fontana	DC49-1	to Coon	8/10/67
	DC49-2	to Coon	8/23/67
	DC49-3	to Coon	9/11/67

50. BY ANY OTHER NAME

| Gene Roddenberry | GR50-1 | to Coon | 5/8/67 |
| | GR50-2 | to Coon | 6/9/67 |

Robert Justman	RJ50-1	to Coon	5/26/67
	RJ50-2	to Coon	8/7/67
	RJ50-3	to Lucas	9/12/67

Gene Coon	GC50-1	to Jerome Bixby	6/16/67
	GC50-2	to Bixby	8/11/67
	GC50-3	to Lucas	9/15/67

D.C. Fontana	DC50-1	to Coon	6/12/67
	DC50-2	to Coon	8/9/67
	DC50-3	to Coon	9/9/67

| Stan Robertson | SR50 | to Coon | 7/5/67 |

| De Forest Research | DFR50 | - | 11/7/67 |

51. RETURN TO TOMORROW

John T. Dugan	JD51-1	to GR & GC	6/29/67
	JD51-2	to Coon	7/21/67
Gene Roddenberry	GR51	to Coon	5/8/67
Robert Justman	RJ51-1	to Coon	5/26/67
	RJ51-2	to Coon	7/5/67
	RJ51-3	to Lucas	10/20/67
Gene Coon	GC51	to John T. Dugan	7/13/67
D.C. Fontana	DC51-1	to Coon	7/3/67
	DC51-2	to Lucas	10/19/67
Stan Robertson	SR51-1	to Coon	5/15/67
	SR51-2	to Lucas	11/9/67

52. PATTERNS OF FORCE

Gene Roddenberry	GR52-1	to WGA	2/28/68
	GR52-2	to Coon	4/1/67
Robert Justman	RJ52-1	to Coon	7/11/67
	RJ52-2	to Coon	7/25/67
D.C. Fontana	DC52-1	to Coon	7/10/67
	DC52-2	to Coon	7/24/67
	DC52-3	to Lucas	11/12/67
Stan Robertson	SR52	to Coon	8/4/67
Paul Schneider	PS52	to Roddenberry	5/23/68

53. THE OMEGA GLORY

Gene Roddenberry	GR53-1	to all	12/14/67
	GR53-2	to Reynolds	2/20/68
	GR53-3	to Stan Robertson	2/20/67
	GR53-4	to Robertson	2/26/67
Robert Justman	RJ53	to M. Woodward	2/9/67
D.C. Fontana	DC53	to Lucas	10/4/67
John M. Lucas	JML53	to WGA	12/22/67
Stan Robertson	SR53	to Lucas	12/6/67

54. THE ULTIMATE COMPUTER

Laurence Wolfe	LW54	to Roddenberry	12/11/67
Gene Roddenberry	GR54-1	to Lucas	10/13/67
	GR54-2	to Laurence Wolfe	12/13/67

Robert Justman	RJ54-1	to Roddenberry	10/18/67
	RJ54-2	to Lucas	11/20/67
D.C. Fontana	DC54-1	to Lucas	10/19/67
	DC54-2	to Lucas	11/12/67
Stan Robertson	SR54	to Lucas	12/6/67

55. ASSIGNMENT: EARTH

Art Wallace	AW55	to Roddenberry	1/6/68
Tony Ford	TF55-1	to Roddenberry	1/11/68
	TF55-2	to Roddenberry	4/5/68
Gene Roddenberry	GR55-1	to Lloyd Bridges	11/30/66
	GR55-2	to Herb Solow	6/14/67
	GR55-3	to Solow	8/16/67
	GR55-4	to Wallace	10/12/67
	GR55-5	to Wallace	1/8/68
	GR55-6	to Tony Ford	1/9/68
	GR55-7	to Ernest Lavery	1/15/68
Robert Justman	RJ55-1	to Roddenberry	11/13/67
	RJ55-2	to Roddenberry	3/8/68
D.C. Fontana	DC55-1	to Roddenberry	11/12/67
	DC55-2	to Roddenberry	12/12/67
De Forest Research	DFR55	to staff	12/22/67
Ernest G. Lavery	EGL55	to Ed Pearlstein	11/14/67
Walter E. Whitaker	WEW55	to Eddie Milkis	2/27/68